PACIFIC MEXICO

BRUCE WHIPPERMAN

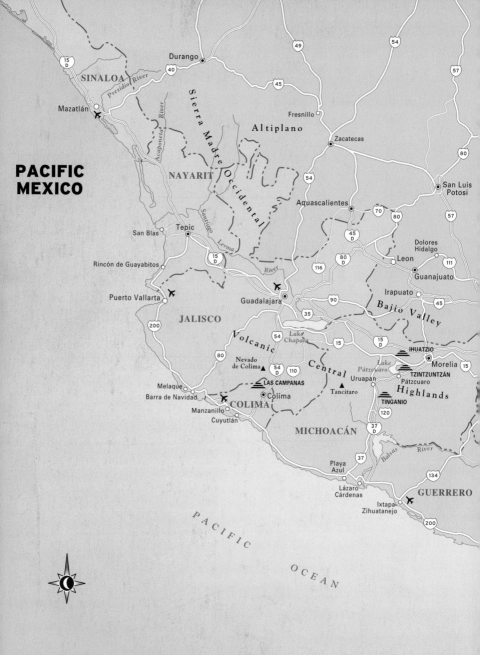

PACIFIC MEXICO

SINALOA

Durango

Mazatlán

Presidio River

Acaponeta River

Sierra Madre Occidental

Altiplano

Fresnillo

Zacatecas

NAYARIT

Santiago River

Lerma

River

San Luis Potosi

Aquascalientes

Tepic

San Blas

Rincón de Guayabitos

Dolores Hidalgo

Leon

Guanajuato

Irapuato

Puerto Vallarta

Guadalajara

Bajío Valley

JALISCO

Volcanic

Lake Chapala

Central

Nevado de Colima

LAS CAMPANAS

Colíma

Tancitaro

IHUATZIO

TZINTZUNTZÁN

Pátzcuaro

Morelia

Lake Pátzcuaro

Uruapan

Highlands

TINGANIO

Melaque

Barra de Navidad

Manzanillo

Cuyutlán

COLIMA

MICHOACÁN

Balsas

River

Playa Azul

Lázaro Cárdenas

Ixtapa Zihuatanejo

GUERRERO

PACIFIC OCEAN

0   50 mi

0   50 km

DISCOVER PACIFIC MEXICO

Pacific Mexico, that long, palm-tufted western seashore, is truly a land of perpetual summer, a place where gentle billows wash seemingly endless miles of golden beaches, and where frigate birds, lifted by balmy onshore breezes, seem to be always soaring overhead.

Although Pacific Mexico is a world away from the bustle of San Francisco, Denver, or Chicago, it's really not very far. It begins at Mazatlán, just three hours by plane or 24 hours by bus south of the border. Scarcely a generation ago, most of Pacific Mexico was dotted with a few sleepy, isolated towns and fishing villages, reachable only by sea or rugged mountain roads from the interior. That gradually began to change, until, in 1984, the last link of Mexico's Pacific Coast Highway 200 was completed, opening a plumy, thousand-mile path for exploring Mexico and the new tourist region of Pacific Mexico.

The choices seem endless. Visitors now can explore a necklace of beach resorts, some glittering and fashionable, such as Mazatlán,

Mitla, Valley of Oaxaca

Puerto Vallarta, Ixtapa, Zihuatanejo, and Acapulco, and others drowsy and downscale, such as San Blas, Melaque, Cuyutlán, Playa Azul, Pie de la Cuesta, and Puerto Ángel. In between the resorts rise forested headlands, interspersed with palm-shaded, pearly strands where the fishing is good and the living easy.

When weary of lazing in the sun, visitors can enjoy a trove of ocean sports. Pacific Mexico's water is always balmy and fine to fish, swim, surf, sailboard, kayak, water-ski, snorkel, and scuba dive in. For nature enthusiasts, dozens of lush jungle-fringed coastal lagoons are ripe for wildlife viewing and photography.

The coastal strip would be enough, but Pacific Mexico offers much more: within an hour's flight or a day's drive of the tropical shoreline rise the temperate oak- and pine-tufted highland valleys. Here, colonial cities — Guadalajara, Tepic, Colima, Pátzcuaro, Taxco, and Oaxaca — offer irresistible handicrafts, colorful festivals, baroque monuments, and barely explored ruins of long-forgotten empires.

Coffee beans are an important cash crop in Nayarit, Guerrero, and Oaxaca.

The people of Pacific Mexico, mostly of mixed Spanish and native descent, love a party and have arranged their calendar with plenty of them. Nationally, the entire month of December is filled with fiestas, from the grand Virgin of Guadalupe celebration to the posada processions and midnight masses around December 25 to the Day of the Kings on January 6. The revelry picks up again during Carnaval (Mardi Gras), usually in February, and climaxes several weeks later in a week-long Semana Santa (Holy Week) celebration, when everyone in Mexico seems to be at the beach. Dozens of big local celebrations add to the fun, such as the Guelaguetza dance festival in Oaxaca and the Day of the Dead festivals in the states of Michoacán, Guerrero, and Oaxaca.

Part and parcel of Pacific Mexico's fiestas are its vibrant world-class cuisine, such as quesadillas, enchiladas, *sopes*, *tlayudas*, *guisado*, unique mole sauces, and the habanero, jalapeño, and poblano chiles used in dozens of flavorful dishes. A growing new cadre of Mexican chefs are returning to the basics and experimenting with traditional ingredients, such as *venado* (wild game venison),

the smoking Volcán de Fuego (on the left) and the dormant Nevado de Colima, in Colima

conejo (rabbit), *cuitlacoche* (black-corn mushroom fungus), and *chapulines* (small fried grasshoppers).

Beneath Pacific Mexico's modern veneer is an ancient, traditional land. Millions of indigenous peoples – the Cora and Huichol in Nayarit and Jalisco, the Purépecha in Michoacán, and the Amusgos, Mixtecs, and Zapotecs, and many others, in Guerrero and Oaxaca – speak a score of linguistically separate tongues. The people go about their lives, tending their *milpas* (cornfields), walking to their weekly *tianguis* (market), and getting tipsy and dancing the whole day and half the night in their patronal festivals as they have for untold generations.

The noble monuments of Pacific Mexico's native peoples remain for all to see today: regal Tzintzuntzán (Place of the Hummingbirds), the Michoacán capital of the Purépecha emperors; storied Xochicalco, the birthplace of the living god-king Quetzalcoatl, near Taxco; and, in Oaxaca, splendid Monte Albán, Latin America's first true metropolis, and gem-like Mitla, whose pure Zapotec-speaking residents preserve their ancient heritage to the present day.

Piedra Tlacoyunque is a worthwhile Costa Grande stop.

Besides the native influence, Spanish traditions and history loom large in Pacific Mexico. For it was in Pacific Mexico, generations before the pilgrims landed at Plymouth Rock, that Spanish explorers finally realized Christopher Columbus's old dream of trade with the Orient via a western sea route. The Spanish influence remains visible and vibrant, in the people themselves, and also in the Spanish language and the richly embellished monumental old churches, houses, and public buildings, especially in Guadalajara, Acapulco, Taxco, Pátzcuaro, and Oaxaca.

In short, Pacific Mexico is easy to visit, enjoy, and appreciate, whether you prefer glamorous luxury, backcountry adventure, or a little bit of both.

Oxen are still used for plowing and pulling carts in rural Pacific Mexico.

Contents

The Lay of the Land 16
Planning Your Trip... 22
Explore Pacific Mexico 24
The 28-Day Best of Pacific Mexico............................... 24
Best Beaches... 26
Outdoor Adventures... 27
Treasures of Old Mexico.. 29
One Day In 30

Mazatlán and Southern Sinaloa...................... 32
Sights 36
Beaches 47
Accommodations... 49
Food... 59
Entertainment and Events....................................... 62
Sports and Recreation 65
Shopping.. 69
Information... 72

Services 73
Getting There and Away. 75
Southern Sinaloa. 77

The Nayarit Coast. 83
Road to San Blas 87
San Blas and Vicinity 93
Tepic 111
Playa Chacala. 123
Rincón de Guayabitos and La Peñita 127
South of Guayabitos 137

Guadalajara. 149
Sights 154
Accommodations. 163
Food. 168
Entertainment and Events. 171
Sports and Recreation 174
Shopping. 175
Information and Services. 180
Getting Around 182
Getting There and Away. 183

Puerto Vallarta 189
Sights 195
Beaches 201
Accommodations. 205
Food. 221
Entertainment and Events. 226
Sports and Recreation 235
Shopping. 239

Information. 244
Services 247
Getting Around 249
Getting There and Away. 250
Around the Bay of Banderas 253

The Jalisco Coast 263
Road to Barra de Navidad 266
Barra de Navidad and Melaque. 288

Manzanillo and Colima. 310
Sights 314
Accommodations. 321
Food. 327
Entertainment and Events. 330
Sports and Recreation 332
Shopping. 335
Information and Services. 336
Getting There and Away. 338
Excursions from Manzanillo. 341
Colima and Vicinity 343
South Colima Beaches 356

The Michoacán Coast and Pátzcuaro. 365
Northwestern Michoacán Beaches. 370
Playa Azul. 377
Pátzcuaro. 382
Uruapan 412
West of Uruapan 424
Lázaro Cárdenas. 428
Road to Troncones, Ixtapa, and Zihuatanejo 431

Ixtapa, Zihuatanejo, and the Costa Grande....... 436
Ixtapa and Zihuatanejo 440
The Costa Grande 476

Acapulco and Taxco.................................. 488
Sights 493
Accommodations.. 501
Food.. 511
Entertainment 515
Sports and Recreation 517
Shopping... 520
Information... 522
Services 523
Getting There and Away.. 525
Taxco... 527

The Costa Chica.................................... 548
Road to Puerto Escondido...................................... 552
Puerto Escondido 568
Puerto Ángel and Vicinity 588
Bays of Huatulco and Vicinity.................................. 604

Oaxaca City and Valley.............................. 626
Sights 634
Accommodations.. 640
Food.. 647
Entertainment and Events..................................... 650
Sports and Recreation 652
Shopping... 653
Information... 656
Services 657

Getting There and Away.. 659
Around the Valley of Oaxaca...................................... 662

Background... 679
Land and Sea.. 679
Flora and Fauna.. 681
History 688
Economy and Government....................................... 704
People and Culture.. 708
Arts and Crafts 716

Essentials.. 724
Getting There... 724
Getting Around 736
Visas and Officialdom... 741
Sports and Recreation.. 745
Accommodations... 750
Food and Drink.. 756
Shopping... 761
Conduct and Customs... 762
Tips for Travelers 765
Health and Safety 768
Information and Services.. 772

Resources... 775
Glossary 775
Spanish Phrasebook.. 777
Suggested Reading... 783
Internet Resources... 789

Index.. 794

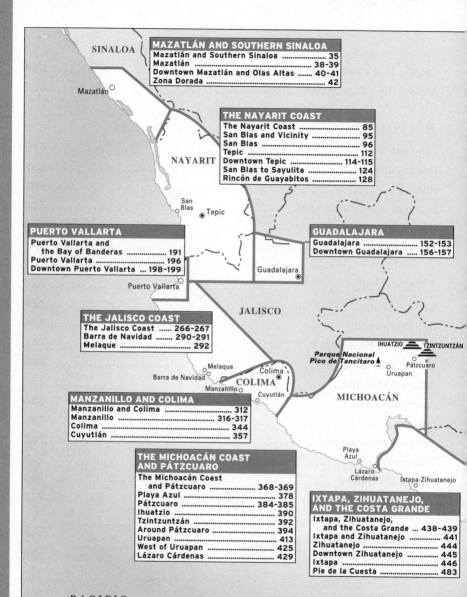

SINALOA

Mazatlán

MAZATLÁN AND SOUTHERN SINALOA
Mazatlán and Southern Sinaloa 35
Mazatlán 38-39
Downtown Mazatlán and Olas Altas 40-41
Zona Dorada 42

THE NAYARIT COAST
The Nayarit Coast 85
San Blas and Vicinity 95
San Blas 96
Tepic 112
Downtown Tepic 114-115
San Blas to Sayulita 124
Rincón de Guayabitos 128

NAYARIT

San
Blas

Tepic

PUERTO VALLARTA
Puerto Vallarta and
   the Bay of Banderas 191
Puerto Vallarta 196
Downtown Puerto Vallarta ... 198-199

Puerto Vallarta

Guadalajara

GUADALAJARA
Guadalajara 152-153
Downtown Guadalajara 156-157

JALISCO

THE JALISCO COAST
The Jalisco Coast 266-267
Barra de Navidad 290-291
Melaque 292

IHUATZIO   TZINTZUNTZÁN

Parque Nacional
Pico de Tancítaro

Pátzcuaro

Uruapan

Melaque

Colima

COLIMA

Barra de Navidad

Manzanillo

Cuyutlán

MICHOACÁN

MANZANILLO AND COLIMA
Manzanillo and Colima 312
Manzanillo 316-317
Colima 344
Cuyutlán 357

THE MICHOACÁN COAST
AND PÁTZCUARO
The Michoacán Coast
   and Pátzcuaro 368-369
Playa Azul 378
Pátzcuaro 384-385
Ihuatzio 390
Tzintzuntzán 392
Around Pátzcuaro 394
Uruapan 413
West of Uruapan 425
Lázaro Cárdenas 429

Playa
Azul

Lázaro
Cárdenas

Ixtapa-Zihuatanejo

IXTAPA, ZIHUATANEJO,
AND THE COSTA GRANDE
Ixtapa, Zihuatanejo,
   and the Costa Grande ... 438-439
Ixtapa and Zihuatanejo 441
Zihuatanejo 444
Downtown Zihuatanejo 445
Ixtapa 446
Pie de la Cuesta 483

PACIFIC

OCEAN

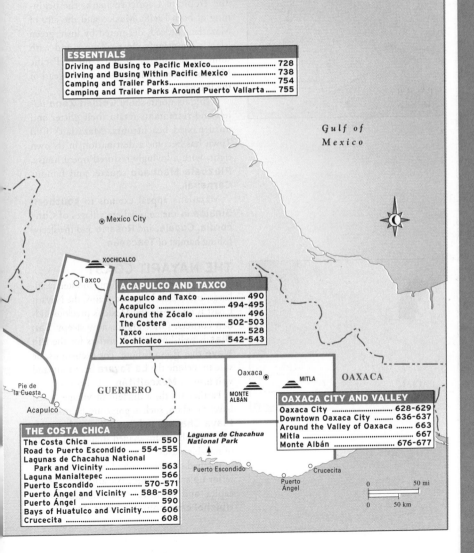

MAP CONTENTS

ESSENTIALS
Driving and Busing to Pacific Mexico 728
Driving and Busing Within Pacific Mexico 738
Camping and Trailer Parks 754
Camping and Trailer Parks Around Puerto Vallarta 755

Gulf of
Mexico

⊛ Mexico City

XOCHICALCO

Taxco

ACAPULCO AND TAXCO
Acapulco and Taxco 490
Acapulco 494–495
Around the Zócalo 496
The Costera 502–503
Taxco 528
Xochicalco 542–543

Oaxaca ◉   MITLA   OAXACA

GUERRERO   MONTE
                  ALBÁN

OAXACA CITY AND VALLEY
Oaxaca City 628–629
Downtown Oaxaca City 636–637
Around the Valley of Oaxaca 663
Mitla 667
Monte Albán 676–677

Pie de
la Cuesta

Acapulco

THE COSTA CHICA
The Costa Chica 550
Road to Puerto Escondido 554–555
Lagunas de Chacahua National
  Park and Vicinity 563
Laguna Manialtepec 566
Puerto Escondido 570–571
Puerto Ángel and Vicinity 588–589
Puerto Ángel 590
Bays of Huatulco and Vicinity 606
Crucecita 608

*Lagunas de Chacahua
National Park*

Puerto Escondido   Crucecita

Puerto
Ángel

0   50 mi

0   50 km

The Lay of the Land

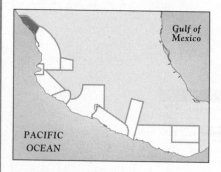

MAZATLÁN AND SOUTHERN SINALOA

The Tropic of Capricorn marks the beginning of both Pacific Mexico and the city of Mazatlán. Indeed, decorated by lush, green islands temptingly close offshore and with some of the silkiest beach sand in Pacific Mexico, Mazatlán deserves its label "Pearl of the Pacific."

While its north-shore **Golden Zone** hotels and restaurants retain their glitter and unsurpassed beachfronts, Mazatlán's Old Town has become a destination in its own right, with a lovingly restored opera house, **Plazuela Machado** square, and famous **Carnaval.**

Mazatlán's appeal extends to **southern Sinaloa** in the colonial-era villages of **Concordia, Copala,** and **Rosario** and the sleepy fishing hamlet of **Teacapán.**

THE NAYARIT COAST

With its creamy beaches, plumy forested headlands, and orchard-swathed plains, the Nayarit Coast is one of Pacific Mexico's precious hidden corners. Once grand, now sleepy **San Blas** is well-known with surfers for the **Big Wave** that rises offshore. For excursions, be sure to include the **La Tovara** boat tour, and visit historic **Mexcaltitán** island-town.

Farther south, a diadem of village beach havens beckon, such as gorgeous, palm-tufted **Playa Chacala** and **Sayulita,** with a long, very strollable palm-shaded strand and plenty of surfable waves.

Perched on the cane-and-corn volcanic interior upland is **Tepic,** Nayarit's petite state capital and bountiful shopping ground for **Huichol ceremonial handicrafts.**

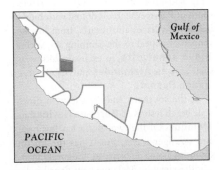

GUADALAJARA

Just three hours inland by bus or car spreads the grand, mountain-rimmed metropolis of Guadalajara, that historic "Most Mexican of Cities," brimming with a treasury of art, handicrafts, fine food, world-class music and theater, and traditional Mexico delights.

Although Guadalajara is sprawling, the heart of old Guadalajara is easily explorable on foot. Highlights include the cathedral, Guadalajara home of the Virgin of Zapopan, the Teatro Degollado, with its timeless classical facade, and finally majestic Hospicio Cabañas museum, replete with the art of the renowned Guadalajara master José Clemente Orozco.

Guadalajara is heaven for handicrafts shoppers. For the best at the lowest prices, go to suburban Tlaquepaque and Tonalá home-workshop villages.

PUERTO VALLARTA

Puerto Vallarta's good fortune is in large part due to its uniquely lovely setting, on the sheltered inner edge of the broad, blue Bay of Banderas. Puerto Vallarta is additionally blessed with the Isla Río Cuale, an island that basks in the petite River Cuale right in the heart of old Puerto Vallarta. Here, folks stroll under the shade of great tropical trees, past stalls filled with fetching handicrafts, and relax at riverside cafés.

Puerto Vallarta's balmy nights bring out the crowds to enjoy the street artists at work, clowns, and performances in the plaza-front Los Arcos amphitheater and later stroll the row of shops, restaurants, and nightclubs along the shorefront *malecón* walkway.

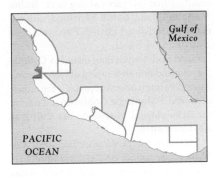

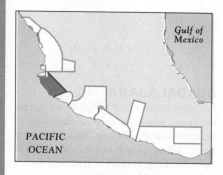

THE JALISCO COAST

The long, curving southern Jalisco coastline, the "Costa Alegre," or "Happy Coast," is for travelers who hanker for roads less traveled. This 150-mile (242-km) shoreline stretch south of Puerto Vallarta is dotted with hidden beachside villages and resorts, from low-key spots that appeal to the camping set, such as **Playa Tenacatita,** to exclusive hideaways such as **Las Alamandas** and **El Careyes Beach Resort.**

At the southern end are the twin down-scale beach resorts of **Barra de Navidad** and **Melaque.** Of the two, Barra has less beach and stronger waves, but it has the mirror-smooth Laguna de Navidad, for kayaking and wildlife viewing. Melaque next door has lots of good budget-to-moderately priced hotels on a lovely beachfront.

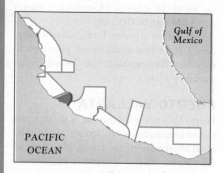

MANZANILLO AND COLIMA

Manzanillo, the midsized port city that rocketed to fame on the heels of the 1970s movie *10,* retains its glamorous popularity. The metropolitan zone spreads along a plumy coastline that includes two big bays, **Bahía Manzanillo** and **Bahía Santiago,** with the mansion and hotel-dotted **Península de Santiago** in between.

Good roads lead an hour inland to **Colima,** the refined diminutive capital of Colima state. Around its intimate central *jardín* is the mural-decorated **Palacio de Gobierno** and nearby the archaeological **Museo de las Culturas del Occidente.**

Excursions from Colima include idyllic **Comala** village and its **Hacienda Noguera** art museum to the north, and delightful **Agua Fria** natural spring and **El Salto** waterfall to the west.

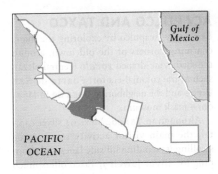

THE MICHOACÁN COAST AND PÁTZCUARO

Highway 200 heads into a Michoacán few outsiders know, where drowsy beach mini-paradises bask, tucked between lushly forested headland ramparts.

Inland from the coast, the road leads to upland **Pátzcuaro,** the blue-sky lakeshore realm of the proud Purépecha people. Besides its cultural treasures and uniquely attractive handicrafts, Pátzcuaro is a base for the unmissable excursions to **Isla Janitzio** and the monumental ruined imperial cities of **Ihuatzio** and **Tzintzuntzán.**

Nearby is balmy semi-tropical **Uruapan,** Michoacán's second city, with its fern-festooned **Parque Nacional Lic. Eduardo Ruiz** in the lush canyon of the Río Cupatitzio. An hour by road farther is the contrastingly stark **Volcán Paracutín.**

IXTAPA, ZIHUATANEJO, AND THE COSTA GRANDE

Zihuatanejo, once a small fishing village on a moon-shaped blue bay, retains a bit of its relaxed country ambience despite the winter visitor influx. In contrast, **Ixtapa,** Zihuatanejo's highrise cousin-resort five miles to the northwest, appeals to those who prefer something fashionably up-to-date.

Nevertheless, both resorts offer plenty of sun, sea, sand, and water sports, plus local excursions, such as to pristine **Isla Ixtapa** and **Playa las Gatas.**

Extending southeast along the 150-mile (242-km) Highway 200 stretch to Acapulco is the **Costa Grande** (Big Coast). Just before Acapulco is the charmingly downscale resort village of **Pie de la Cuesta,** with the double attraction of a breezy wild beach on one side, and glassy freshwater **Laguna Coyuca** on the other.

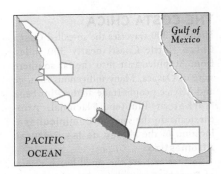

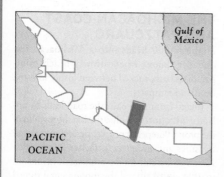

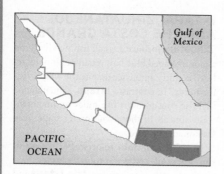

ACAPULCO AND TAXCO

Best enjoy Acapulco by exploring the many charming corners of the old town, around the shady vine-draped *zócalo* (central plaza), such as the colonial-era fort **Fuerte de San Diego** and the neighboring **Casa de la Máscara** mask museum.

Although in **Taxco,** Mexico's silver capital, the main visitor activity seems to be strolling its winding hillside lanes and shopping for **silver jewelry,** Taxco offers much more, notably the grand **Santa Prisca** church and a naturally gorgeous mountain setting, especially as viewed from the **cableway** to the top of Monte Taxco. Out of town is the unmissable monumental duo, the grand **Grutas de Cacahuamilpa** limestone caverns and the legendary **Xochicalco** archaeological site.

THE COSTA CHICA

Highway 200 traverses the so-called **Costa Chica** (Little Coast) nearly 300 miles, from Acapulco east into the far southern state of Oaxaca. Many indigenous Amusgo and Mixtec people trade at the **Pinotepa Market** at Pinotepa Nacional; Afro-Mexicans do the same at **Cuajinicuilapa,** location of the **Museo de las Culturas Afromestizo.**

Farther east are the small beach resorts of **Puerto Escondido, Puerto Ángel,** and **Bays of Huatulco.** Puerto Escondido hosts spectacular surfing challenges at **Playa Zicatela.** Nearby hidden beaches and bird-watching haven **Laguna Manialtepec** add to the attractions. **Puerto Ángel** retains its drowsy bayside village ambience, while the lovely blue **Bays of Huatulco** project, Oaxaca's plan for a luxury resort, is developing steadily but slowly.

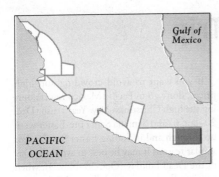

Gulf of Mexico

PACIFIC OCEAN

OAXACA CITY AND VALLEY

North from the Oaxaca Coast is the mountain-rimmed state capital **Oaxaca,** arguably Mexico's most enjoyable colonial city. Its downtown is blessed with a tranquil central plaza, a historic **cathedral,** the **Templo y Ex-Convento de Santo Domingo,** and adjacent world-class **Museo Regional de las Culturas de Oaxaca.** Added plusses are its colorful markets and many excellent handicrafts shops.

The surrounding **Valley of Oaxaca** offers even more. Not far east is **Teotitlán del Valle,** a weavers village, the **Tlacolula Sunday market,** and renowned **Mitla** archaeological site. Go southwest to the **Zaachila** Thursday market and archaeological zone, and finally to the west, the unmissable ancient mountaintop **Monte Albán** complex of grand plazas, regal pyramids, and mysterious tombs.

Planning Your Trip

Clearly it would take a year to thoroughly explore Pacific Mexico. Even to uncover most of the highlights, it would take at least two busy months. But unless you like living out of a suitcase, that might get wearing.

Instead, you might plan something more leisurely, perhaps a three- or four-week adventure to explore the best of Pacific Mexico's interesting and beautiful places. Another, shorter strategy would be to explore Pacific Mexico in a number of separate 10-day to two-week trips, from regional gateways such as Puerto Vallarta, Acapulco, or Oaxaca.

WHEN TO GO

Although temperatures and rainfall are crucial in deciding when to go to Pacific Mexico, they don't tell the whole story. Crowds, high-priced high seasons, and low-priced low seasons are also factors. The first thing to know is that Pacific Mexico has two sharply defined seasons: wet summer-fall and dry winter-spring.

Pacific Mexico is too hot in the summer, some people say. This, however, isn't always the case. In fact, increased summer cloud cover and showers can actually push average daily July, August, and September temperatures lower than bright and clear April, May, and June. The other summer plus is the vegetation. If you like lush, green landscapes, the summer-fall may be your season, especially in the highlands.

By contrast, during the admittedly sunnier and more temperate winter, it usually hasn't rained for months. In natural areas, trees are bare of leaves, grass is brown, and cactuses sometimes seem to be the only green plants. The landscape continues dry and dusty Feb.–Apr., turning hot in May, until the cooling rains arrive and green breaks out again by late June.

If you want to avoid crowding and high prices, don't go to Pacific Mexico resorts during the high Christmas–New Year's rush (Dec. 20–Jan. 6) and Semana Santa pre-Easter week up through and including Easter Sunday. For similar reasons it may be best to avoid the Day of the Dead holiday (Oct. 30–Nov. 3), when tourists flock in, especially in Michoacán, Guerrero, and Oaxaca. On the other hand, if you want to join in the fiesta merrymaking, be sure to get your hotel reservations six months early.

Well, then when should you go? If you shun crowds, but like the sunny, temperate winter, January, a low-occupancy miniseason, is a good bet, especially on the beach. The landscape still retains some green, and hotels often offer discounts.

September through mid-December are also good months to go. Hotel prices are cheapest, the landscape is lush and green, and the weather is cooler and not so rainy. However, in September, some beach resorts, especially Ixtapa, Zihuatanejo, Troncones, Manzanillo, and to a lesser extent, Puerto Vallarta, are too empty for folks who enjoy lots of company. Although beaches are beautifully uncrowded, your favorite restaurants and entertainments may be closed until mid-October. The pace picks up, however, October–mid-December, when moderate temperatures, blue skies, lush landscape, low prices, and just enough company create the best of all possible Pacific Mexico worlds.

HOW TO GET THERE

Most Pacific Mexico–bound travelers go by air (3–5 hours flying time) from the North American gateways on both scheduled and charter flights.

For cost-conscious travelers, express buses provide a safe and sure route to Pacific Mexico.

Hundreds of buses head south daily from central bus stations *(camioneras centrales)* in the south-of-the-border towns of Tijuana, Mexicali, Nogales, Ciudad Juárez, Nuevo Laredo, Reynosa, and Matamoros. By all means, for comfort and speed, go luxury-class (about $80–100, 20–30 hours).

Although it isn't a route for everyone, many travelers drive their cars or RVs to Pacific Mexico. Driving time runs 2–4 south-of-the-border days at the wheel, and costs around $40–80 in (very worthwhile) expressway tolls for passenger cars and light trucks (about triple that for motor homes).

WHAT TO TAKE

"Men wear pants, ladies be beautiful" was once the dress code of one of Pacific Mexico's classiest hotels. Men in casual Pacific Mexico can get by easily without a jacket, women with simple skirts and blouses.

Loose-fitting, hand-washable, easy-to-dry clothes make for trouble-free tropical vacationing. Synthetic or cotton-synthetic-blend shirts, blouses, pants, socks, and underwear will fit the bill everywhere in the coastal Pacific Mexico region. For breezy nights, bring a lightweight windbreaker. If you're going to the highlands (Guadalajara, Pátzcuaro, Taxco, Oaxaca), add a medium-weight jacket.

In all cases, leave showy, expensive clothes and jewelry at home. Stow items that you cannot lose in your hotel safe or carry them with you in a sturdy zipped purse or a waist pouch on your front side.

What you pack depends on how mobile you want to be. If you're staying the whole time at a self-contained resort, you can take the two suitcases and one carry-on allowed by airlines. If, on the other hand, you're going to be moving around a lot, you'd do better to condense everything to one easily carried bag with wheels that doubles as luggage and soft backpack. Experienced travelers accomplish this by packing prudently and tightly, choosing items that will do double or triple duty.

Campers will have to be super-careful to accomplish one-bag packing. Fortunately, camping along the tropical coast requires no sleeping bag. Simply use a hammock (buy it in Mexico) or a sleeping pad and a sheet for cover. In the winter, you may, at most, need a light blanket. A compact tent that you and your companion can share is a must against bugs, as is mosquito repellent. A first-aid kit is absolutely necessary.

Explore Pacific Mexico

THE 28-DAY BEST OF PACIFIC MEXICO

Here's a step-by-step example for a four-week adventure to explore some of Pacific Mexico's fascinating, charming, and simply beautiful places. Although this itinerary begins and ends in Puerto Vallarta, it's a circle tour and could begin and end anywhere along the route. It could be done by either car or local bus.

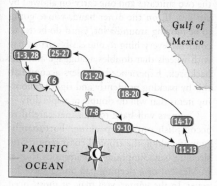

Days 1-3

Arrive in **Puerto Vallarta,** rest, and enjoy dinner out at Cafe la Olla or Restaurant Trio. Spend the next day strolling around **old town:** Isla Río Cuale, Gringo Gulch, Plaza de Armas, and the *malecón*. Also browse the **arts and handicrafts** downtown. On day 3, take a day cruise that includes snorkeling at **Los Arcos** and a walk around **Yelapa.**

Days 4-5

Travel to **Melaque** (four hours). Taxi over to **Barra de Navidad** to explore the town and get dinner. Relax the next day: Stroll Melaque's downtown and beach, or go for a Barra lagoon tour and dinner at **La Colimilla** restaurant.

Day 6

Travel to **Colima** (three hours). Check into your downtown hotel and walk around the plaza. Visit the folk-art **Museo de Culturas Populares** and the archaeological **Museo de Culturas del Occidente.** Have dinner at El Charco de la Higuera restaurant.

Days 7-8

Travel to **Zihuatanejo** (seven hours). Check out downtown, browse for handicrafts, and have dinner at Tamales y Atoles "Ány" or, for a splurge, at Restaurant Il Mare. The next morning, ride a launch to **Playa las Gatas** for breakfast, sunning, and snorkeling. Return in the afternoon, and taxi over to the **Playa la Ropa** for a beach stroll and a sunset dinner.

Days 9-10

Travel to **Acapulco** (three hours), spend the afternoon around the old-town plaza, the museum at the old **Fuerte de San Diego** and the nearby **Casa de la Máscara.** Enjoy sunset cocktails at the Hotel los Flamingos *mirador*. In the morning, taxi uphill to **Palma Sola** archaeological site and park. In the afternoon, ride a boat from Playa Caleta to offshore **Isla Roqueta** for lunch, hiking the island trail (two hours), and exploring hidden beaches. That evening, join the crowd viewing the cliff divers at **La Quebrada.**

Days 11-13

Travel to **Puerto Ángel** (six hours). Stroll (via the beachfront *andador*) to **Playa Panteón** for snorkeling, sun, and dinner at Cordelia's or Alquimista restaurant. On day 12, spend the morning on the beach at **Zipolite**, continue to Mazunte for the **Centro Mexicano de la Tortuga.** Have dinner at the oceanview Alta Mira Bungalows. Day 13 would be well spent out of town, at **Laguna Manialtepec** on a lagoon tour and bird-watching; at **Río Copalita** for river rafting, horseback riding, or waterfall exploring; or in the foothills above the **Bays of Huatulco**

Days 14-17

Drive or bus (seven hours) or hop over by plane (one hour) from the Huatulco airport to **Oaxaca**. Stroll the Oaxaca *zócalo*, then relax for dinner at a *zócalo*-front café. Browse some of the many nearby **galleries** and **handicrafts stores.** Day 15, do some serious in-town sightseeing, including the downtown **cathedral, Juárez Market,** the church and ex-convent of **Santo Domingo,** the adjacent **Museo Regional de las Culturas de Oaxaca,** the **Museo Arte Prehispánico de Rufino Tamayo,** and the museum and **Basílica de Nuestra Señora de la Soledad.** Day 16, spend in the **Valley of Oaxaca** west of town, visiting El Tule, Teotitlán del Valle weaving village, and the Mitla archaeological site. Day 17, explore **Monte Albán** in the morning, and continue to nearby **Arrazola** village for *alebrijes* (fantastic wooden animals) and **Atzompa** pottery village.

Days 18-20

Travel to **Taxco** (7–10 hours). On the arrival evening, stroll the *zócalo* and browse the silver shops. Take the next day to see the sights, such as **Santa Prisca church, Museo Guillermo Spratling,** and the **Museo Platería.** On day 20, visit **Grutas de Cacahuamilpa** limestone cave national park. If you book a tour, or start early enough with your own wheels, you'll have time to also visit legendary **Xochicalco** archaeological site 25 miles (40 km) farther.

Days 21-24

Travel to **Pátzcuaro** (10–12 hours—all of day 21). On day 22, explore Pátzcuaro's plazas, ex-convent **Casa de Once Patios** handicrafts center, **Ex-Colegio San Nicolás** museum, and **Ex-Templo San Agustín.** Spend day 23 on a boat excursion to **Janitzio and Yuñuen islands.** On day 24, take a trip to **Santa Clara de Cobre** copper village and **Laguna Zirahuén** for lunch. Return through Pátzcuaro, continuing to **Tzintzuntzán** archaeological site and town.

Days 25-28

Travel to **Guadalajara** (five hours). Check into your downtown hotel and go out sightseeing around the cathedral. Day 26, continue sightseeing downtown; in the morning, be sure to view the murals and the **Museo José Clemente Orozco** in the **Hospicio Cabañas,** and go to the **Mercado Libertad.** In the afternoon, taxi to **Zapopan** to visit the **Basílica of the Virgin of Zapopan** and the adjoining **Museo Huichol Wirrarica.** On day 27, transfer to a **Tlaquepaque** hotel, and do some serious handicrafts browsing on main streets Independencia and Juárez. Spend the evening at El Parián entertainment center for dinner, the mariachis, and folkloric dance show. Return to **Puerto Vallarta** on day 28 (one hour by air, five hours by bus or car).

BEST BEACHES

These are many of Pacific Mexico's loveliest stretches of sand. Nearly all are good for most beach delights, such as surf fishing, camping, beachcombing, swimming, snorkeling, and surfing. Beaches, however, are often good for particular reasons. Here are some of the very best, in each region.

Mazatlán and Southern Sinaloa

Most Beautiful: Rock-studded islets, a trove of shells, and sheltered tidepools add to the beauty of Playa Cerritos.

Silkiest Sand: The hands-down winner is Playa Sábalo; the sand feels like a soft, silken carpet.

Best Sunsets: With its silhouetted offshore islands, Playa Gaviotas has the best sunset view in Pacific Mexico.

The Nayarit Coast

Most Beautiful: Playa Chacala, on its intimate, half-moon bay, is picture-perfect.

Most Pristine: Near Rincón de Guayabitos, Playa Punta Raza is an isolated strand, with crystalline water and few visitors.

Most Child-Friendly: Playa Guayabitos has a shallow cove and many beachfront *palapa* restaurants.

Best Surfing: Playa Matanchén, at San Blas, is one of the four best surfing beaches in Pacific Mexico.

Most Wildly Spectacular: With its powerful close-in waves and host of seabirds overhead, Playa San Francisco, south of Guayabitos, is the only beach in Pacific Mexico to get this title.

Puerto Vallarta

Best for Everything: Playa los Muertos, with gentle waves and fishing, is a good all-around choice.

Most Beautiful: Playa Boca de Tomatlán is picturesquely tucked on the shore of a petite, blue bay.

The Jalisco Coast

Most Beautiful: Rugged sea stacks shelter the north end of Playa Melaque, by Barra de Navidad, making for a striking scene.

Most Pristine: Playa Maito is a haven of clear waters and has only a few visitors.

Most Child-Friendly: Playa Perula, on Chamela Bay, curves behind the headland, making for safe waterplay.

Most Intimate: Small Playa Tehualmixtle is an idyllic blue nook on the way to Barra de Navidad.

Manzanillo

Best for Everything: Playa Audiencia offers golden-black sands for sunning and picnicking, as well as kayak and boogie board rentals.

Best Surf Fishing: The surf fishing is excellent in Playa de Oro's untamed setting.

The Michoacán Coast

Best Surfing: Playa la Ticla and Barra de Nexpa are two famous surfing beaches.

Ixtapa, Zihuatanejo, and the Costa Grande

Best Sunsets: Mile-long Playa la Ropa, in Zihuatanejo, offers a striking setting for its unobstructed sunset views.

Best Surf Fishing: Turbulent, close-in surf and super-clean water produce ideal fishing conditions at Playa Las Pozas, south of Zihuatanejo.

Most Intimate: Located on Isla Ixtapa, Playa Coral lies next to an intimate, rocky bay.

Best Snorkeling: Calm, clear waters and beachside outfitters make Playa las Gatas in Zihuatanejo a snorkeling haven.

Acapulco

Most Child-Friendly: The waves at Playa Caleta are blue ripples, gentle and safe for the little ones.

Best Surf Fishing: With its powerful

waves, Playa Pie de la Cuesta is another good spot for fishing.

Most Intimate: Playa las Palmitas, on Isla Roqueta, is small and hidden, so you can spend as much time here as you want.

The Costa Chica

Best for Everything: Playa Zipolite, in Oaxaca, has it all: palm groves, sea cliffs, surfing, and a string of restaurants.

Most Pristine: Bahía Cacaluta, at the Bays of Huatulco, offers an isolated beach at the end of an unpaved, sandy road.

Most Child-Friendly: Playa Principal, at Puerto Escondido, draws families with its calm, wade-able waters.

Best Surfing: Puerto Escondido's Playa Zicatela is the best of Pacific Mexico's top surfing beaches.

Most Intimate: Playa Carrizalillo, at Puerto Escondido, and the beach at Bahía el Organo, at Huatulco, are precious little headland-enfolded dabs of sand.

Best Snorkeling: Puerto Ángel's Playa Estacahuite is the best for snorkeling and scuba diving right off the beach. Also good is Playa Carrizalillo, at Puerto Escondido.

OUTDOOR ADVENTURES

Pacific Mexico abounds with mountains and hills for hiking and climbing; jungle canopies for touring; waterfalls, cascades, and springs for swimming and bathing; rivers for rafting; caves for exploring; coasts and offshore islands for kayaking; mangrove lagoons for boating and bird-watching; and a wildlife treasury, from iguanas and crocodiles to whales, seals, and dolphins, for watching and photographing. Here are Pacific Mexico's best of all of the above, by type.

Hiking

A couple of short climbs are conveniently in towns: In Mazatlán, climb the **Cerro Creston** (500 feet, 150 meters) to El Faro, the world's highest lighthouse; in Manzanillo, climb to the breezy summit of **Cerro Cruz** (1,000 feet, 300 meters). Much more challenging is the climb to the giant dormant volcano **Nevado de Colima** (14,220 feet, 4,334 meters) near Colima—a rough road goes to about 11,500 feet, and you hike the rest of the way. In Michoacán, near Uruapan, climb dormant 1,700-foot (500-meter) **Paricutin** volcano, or also-dormant **Pico de Tancítaro** volcano (11,420 feet, 3,843 meters). In the Bays of Huatulco (Oaxaca), do some hiking along forest trails to the remote bays of **El Organo** (0.5 mile, 0.3 km), **Cacaluta** (2 miles, 3.2 km), or **Chacacual** (5 miles, 8 km).

Surfing

Pacific Mexico's recognized four best surfing beaches are, in order, **Playa Zicatela,** at Puerto Escondido (Oaxaca); **Playa Matanchén,** at San Blas (Nayarit Coast); and **Playa la Ticla** and **Barra de Nexpa,** on the Michoacán Coast.

Snorkeling

Few beaches afford good snorkeling and scuba diving opportunities right off the beach. These do, however: **Playa Estacahuite,** at Puerto Ángel (Oaxaca), is the best; **Playa Mora** near Playa Tenacatita (Jalisco) and **Playas las Gatas** at Zihuatanejo are also excellent. Others that are especially good and scenic are **Playa Cuachalatate** on Isla Ixtapa (Zihuatanejo), **Playa Roqueta** on Isla Roqueta (Acapulco), and **Playa Entrega** and **Bahía el Maguey** in Huatulco (Oaxaca).

Jungle Canopy Ride

At **Las Juntas** village on the Jalisco Coast, ride suspended from a cable down through the tropical forest canopy.

Natural Springs, Lakes, and Waterfalls

Pacific Mexico abounds with lakes, waterfalls, and natural springs that bubble up, crystal clear, in both the wet season and dry, and make great destinations for swimming, picnicking, and camping. Some are warm, for soaking in, like a hot tub.

Easily accessible examples are **La Tovara** spring and **Tecuitata** and **El Cora** waterfalls near San Blas on the Nayarit Coast; **Laguna Santa María** near Tepic (Nayarit); *balnearios* (bathing parks) **Los Camachos** and **El Paraíso** on the north edge of Guadalajara; **Chino's Paradise** waterfalls near Puerto Vallarta; and **El Salto** waterfall and **Agua Fria** spring in the mountains, north of Manzanillo.

Others are the warm spring at **Tlalpuyeque**, near Tehualmixtle on the Jalisco Coast, and the very hot spring **Atotonilco**, at San José Manialtepec, near Puerto Escondido (Oaxaca).

River Rafting and Kayaking

Although many of Pacific Mexico's rivers, such as the Río Ameca in Jalisco, the Ríos Balsas and Papagayo in Guerrero, and the Río Verde in Oaxaca, are kayakable or raftable with your own equipment, one—the **Río Copalita**, near the Bays of Huatulco (Oaxaca)—adds the convenience of guided rafting tours.

Bring your own kayak, and you can put it in the water in many dozens of choice Pacific Mexico locations. **Laguna Manialtepec** is a pristine, mangrove-decorated lagoon, near Puerto Escondido (Oaxaca), rich in wildlife, and accessible to camping, *palapa* restaurants, and open ocean beaches. More or less the same is true of **Laguna Barra de Potosí**, near Zihuatanejo, except it's also close to charming bed-and-breakfast hotels. Excellent sheltered ocean kayaking is easy right from the beaches at **Isla Ixtapa**, near Ixtapa and Zihuatanejo, and **Isla Roqueta** near Acapulco. Other excellent kayaking spots are in the Bays of Huatulco (Oaxaca), especially **Playa Entrega** (in Bahía Santa Cruz), **Bahía el Maguey**, and **Bahía Tangolunda**. All three are accessible to beach camping spots, *palapa* restaurants, and hotels.

Cave Exploring

Pacific Mexico abounds with limestone caves, especially in the southern states of Guerrero and Oaxaca. Most are remote, except the best of all: the great **Grutas de Cacahuamilpa**, near Taxco.

Bird-Watching and Wildlife Viewing

Although you can do this on any Pacific Mexico beach at any time, some places are crowded with birds and wildlife. Best of the best are the tropical forests and mangrove lagoons around **San Blas** on the Nayarit Coast. As a starter, go on the **La Tovara Jungle River Trip.** If you want more, hire a guide to take you to eco-sanctuary **Isla Isabel** for an overnight, or do an extended tour in the grand San Blas mangrove hinterland. Other wildlife-rich mangrove lagoons with tours and excursion boats available are at **Cuyutlán**, near Manzanillo; **Laguna Tres Palos**, at Barra Vieja, near Acapulco; **Laguna Barra de Potosí**, near Zihuatanejo; and **Lagunas de Chacahua National Park** and **Laguna Manialtepec** near Puerto Escondido on the Costa Chica.

RVing and Camping

Although there are fewer RV parks in Pacific Mexico than there once were, about three or four dozen RV parks are mostly concentrated around resort towns in Pacific Mexico's northern half. They vary, but most supply electricity, sewer drainage, and water for $12–25 per night. The best overall are right at scenic beach or lake locations, provide all facilities, and have competent and friendly management. These are **Koala Bungalows and Trailer Park** at Laguna Santa María near Tepic (Nayarit), **La Peñita Trailer Park** at La Peñita, **Trailer Park Oasis** at Lo de Marco (Nayarit), **Sayulita Trailer Park** at Sayulita (Nayarit), and **Trailer Park Playa Luces** at Pie de la Cuesta, near Acapulco.

All formal campgrounds in Pacific Mexico are privately owned. By and large, the best tenting opportunities are at the trailer parks. Nevertheless, besides the trailer parks, many informal but customary spots welcome campers. These are usually on the beach, at or near *palapa* restaurants, which allow you to set up beneath their *ramada* in exchange for selling you a meal or two. The best spots are **Laguna Santa María, Playa Tenacatita, Playa Boca de Iguanas, Playa la Brisa, Faro de Bucerías, Barra de Nexpa, Playa Ventura,** and **Bahía San Agustín.** For all of these, the locations are pristine and lovely, the local people are welcoming, the locations are secure, and nearby groceries and *palapa* restaurants are available for food and supplies.

TREASURES OF OLD MEXICO

Pacific Mexico preserves a wealth of tradition in its museums, galleries, cathedrals, basilicas and pilgrimage sites, theaters and opera houses, and archaeological sites. Nearly all of these are in or near large towns and state capitals.

Mazatlán

The restored **Teatro Ángela Peralta** opera house mounts a full roster of drama, ballet, folkloric dance, and symphony performances, and the **Museo Arqueología** is a fascinating trove of early Mazatlán artifacts, from petroglyphs to ceramics. The **Museo de Arte** displays the works of noted local and nationally recognized painters, sculptors, and graphic artists.

Tepic, Mexcaltitán, and San Blas

The offerings in this trio of towns in the Nayarit Coast region include Tepic's **Museo Regional de Antropología y Historía; Museo Amado Nervo,** which showcases the poet's life and works; the **Templo y Ex-Convento de la Cruz de Zacate;** Mexcaltitán's **museum of the Mexicans;** and San Blas's 18th-century **Nuestra Señora del Rosario** church and the *contaduría* atop breezy hilltop Cerro San Basilio.

Guadalajara

For museums, there's the **Museo Regional de Guadalajara,** which illustrates local history, and the **Museo José Clemente Orozco** (in the Hospicio Cabañas), where the muralist's work appears on the walls. **Teatro Degollado** opera house is worth a look, if only for the classic facade and sumptuous interior. The **cathedral** and the **Basílica de la Virgen de Zapopan** are two noteworthy religious sights. Don't miss **Museo Huichol Wirrarica** shop and museum of Huichol ceremonial crafts.

Colima

The **Museo de Culturas Populares** features folk art, and the **Museo de Culturas del Occidente** exhibits delightful pre-Columbian pottery collections. **La Campana Archaeological Zone** is a monumental reconstruction of Colima's former capital. At **Hacienda Noguera,** examine the works of artist Alejandro Rangel.

Pátzcuaro

This town is a colonial treasure with the 16th-century **Ex-Colegio San Nicolás** museum, the pilgrimage spot **Basílica María Inmaculada de la Salud** (Mary Immaculate of Health), and the mural by Juan O'Gorman at **Ex-Templo San Agustín**. For archaeology, the out-of-town sites of **Ihuatzio** and **Tzintzuntzán** archaeological zones uncover ruined imperial cities.

Acapulco

In Acapulco's old town, visit world-class **Fuerte de San Diego** for a lesson of Acapulco's rich history of galleons, Chinese treasure, and pirates. Its neighbor, **Casa de la Máscara**, is a fascinating museum of masks. On a hilltop overlooking the city's west side, the leafy hillside park of **Palma Sola** archaeological site is dotted with a trove of fascinating petroglyphs.

Taxco

Taxco has a fascinating history, and in-town highlights are the spectacularly baroque **Santa Prisca church**, the **Museo Guillermo Spratling** for archaeology, and the **Casa de Humboldt** colonial museum. The legendary **Xochicalco** archaeological site lies out of town, but history enthusiasts might enjoy an excursion to **Ixcateopan** village nearby to view the remains and museum honoring the Aztec's gritty last emperor, Cuauhtémoc.

Oaxaca

In addition to numerous in-town sights like the **cathedral, Teatro Alcalá** opera house, **Casa de Cortés** contemporary art museum, **Ex-Convento de Santa Catalina, Museo Regional de las Culturas de Oaxaca,** and **Casa de Juárez** museum, Oaxaca is a base for archaeological excursions to the **Yagul, Mitla, Zaachila,** and **Monte Albán** sites.

ONE DAY IN . . .

If you're arriving on a cruise ship, or hurrying through, and all you have is a day, you could still enjoy it strolling and taxi-ing around some of Pacific Mexico's prime destinations. In Mazatlán, you can spend a whole very leisurely day around Old Town. You can easily enjoy your day in Puerto Vallarta along the Río Cuale and the old town south of the river. Most of your time in Acapulco would be best spent enjoying the old-Mexico delights around the shady *zócalo*.

MAZATLÁN
Morning

Start early for breakfast at **Pastelería Panamá** near the Mazatlán main downtown plaza. Browse the handicraft-filled lanes of the **town market,** then visit the plaza-front **basílica**. Afterward, take a stroll around **Plazuela Machado;** on the west side, there's the venerable family-home-museum **Casa Machado,** and on the opposite side, the **Teatro Ángela Peralta** is worth a look if you can get inside. Browse through some of

the nearby **art and handicrafts galleries,** such as Nidart, Viejo Mazatlán, and Regalos Indio. Continue west along Sixto Osuna, and take a half-hour each for the **Museo Arqueología** and the **Museo de Arte.** By then it should be time for lunch at **Restaurant Bahía** or nearby **El Shrimp Bucket.**

Afternoon

After lunch, hail a taxi to uphill **Cerro Vigía** to see the antique cannon and enjoy the airy view, and continue by taxi downhill to the sportfishing fleet (*flotas deportivas*) dock. If you're in the mood for it, continue to the dock's west end and the cul-de-sac that marks the trail to **Cerro Creston**. Best reserve this uphill hike for the cooler part of the afternoon. When you arrive on top, you can enjoy sunset and maybe later (bring a flashlight for the descent) the wheeling beacons of the great lighthouse, the world's highest, atop the summit.

PUERTO VALLARTA
Morning
Start in old town; stroll upstream along the **Isla Río Cuale,** and be sure to stop by the **Municipal Handicrafts Market** at the upstream Avenida Insurgentes Bridge. Have lunch upstairs at one of the riverview food stalls or at the showplace **Le Bistro.**

Afternoon
Continue uphill and wander the lanes of **Gringo Gulch** and tour **Casa Kimberly,** former home of Elizabeth Taylor and Richard Burton. Return downhill and have a look inside the town **church,** dedicated to the Virgin of Guadalupe. Make a loop around to the downtown **Plaza de Armas** central square and the seafront **Los Arcos** amphitheater. Walk north along the airy seafront *malecón.* Spend the rest of your time browsing the **galleries** and **handicrafts stores** on Calle Corona and Avenida Juárez. If you have time, enjoy a light dinner at **Restaurant Las Palomas** on the *malecón,* or perhaps **Restaurant Xitomates** on Avenida Juárez.

ACAPULCO
Morning
Start out early with breakfast on the *zócalo,* at homey **Café los Amigos.** Take a turn around the *zócalo,* have a look inside the art deco plaza-front church, and cross over to the sportfishing dock to see what the catch has been so far. Next, stroll east, past the cruise ship dock, to **Fuerte de San Diego** and spend at least an hour exploring the 18th-century fort. Afterward, spend a half-hour at the nearby **Casa de la Máscara** (House of Masks). Have lunch at **Sanborn's** or at **Restaurant la Flor de Acapulco** back at the *zócalo.* If it's early enough, taxi five minutes to the Hotel Mirador at **La Quebrada** for lunch before the cliff diver show at 1 P.M.

Afternoon
After seeing the cliff diver show, hire a taxi to take you to the **Palma Sola** archaeological site and its shady hillside park on the city's eastern mountain flank. Taxi back downhill to the **Hotel los Flamingos,** and enjoy sunset cocktails at the panoramic viewpoint gazebo.

MAZATLÁN AND SOUTHERN SINALOA

Mazatlán (pop. 750,000) spreads for 15 sun-splashed miles along a thumb of land that extends southward into the Pacific just below the Tropic of Cancer. Mazatlán, 800 highway miles (1,300 km) south of Tucson, Arizona, marks the beginning of the Mexican tropics: a palmy land of perpetual summer and a refuge from winter cold for growing numbers of international vacationers.

Mazatlán's beauty is renowned. Its shoreline, sprinkled with beckoning islands and miles of golden beaches and blue lagoons, aptly deserves its title "Pearl of the Pacific."

Despite its popularity as a tourist destination, Mazatlán owes its existence to local industry. As well as being the leading manufacturing center in the state of Sinaloa, Mazatlán is home port for a huge commercial and sportfishing

fleet, whose annual catch of shrimp, tuna, and swordfish amounts to thousands of tons.

Mazatlán, consequently, lives independently of tourism. The vacationers come and frolic on the beach beside their "Golden Zone" hotels, while in the Old Town at the southern tip of the Mazatlán peninsula, life goes on in old-Mexico style, in the markets, the churches, and the shady plazas scattered throughout the traditional neighborhoods.

Although the Zona Dorada (Golden Zone) resort hotel neighborhood, which developed on the north end of town beginning in the 1960s, retains its popularity, Old Mazatlán, a once-crumbling neighborhood of the 19th-century mansions of Mazatlán's well-to-do, has been gradually restored, beginning with the original opera house, Teatro Ángela Peralta,

HIGHLIGHTS

Plazuela Machado: This unmissable heart of Old Mazatlán brims with a treasury of good cafés and restaurants, handicrafts, museums, and entertainment. In your stroll around, be sure to stop by the beautifully restored Teatro Ángela Peralta and take a look inside the Casa Machado former mansion, now a museum of Old Mazatlán (page 37).

Museo Arqueología: Here, a host of intriguing petroglyphs, human and animal figurines, and sophisticated multicolored ceramics yield fascinating glimpses into the lives and minds of Mazatlán's early inhabitants (page 43).

Cerro Vigía: Taxi to the summit, where colonial soldiers kept a 200-year vigil for pirates and where you can enjoy the offshore breeze and take in the airy panorama that stretches from Cerro Creston and El Faro (Mazatlán's lighthouse, the highest natural lighthouse in the world), past the busy harbor and the trio of offshore islands, all the way to the sculpted domes of the Sierra Madre on the far western horizon (page 45).

Boat Tours: Ride a tour boat, such as the Yate *Fiesta*, for close-up views of Mazatlán's fishing fleet, inner harbor, offshore sea lion islets Dos Hermanos (Two Brothers), the islands Chivos (Goats), Venados (Deer), and Lobos (Wolves), dolphins, and maybe even a humpback whale or two along the way (page 45).

Aquarium: Arrive early at Latin America's largest aquarium, and see it all, including sea lion shows, shoals of colorful tropical fish, and a botanical garden, with a pair of mammoth crocodiles (page 46).

Playa Sábalo: With palms drowsing in the breeze, frigate birds soaring overhead, and the silkiest sand of Pacific Mexico, this beach cannot be missed (page 48).

Playa Cerritos: The most beautiful beach in Mazatlán, which features rock-studded islets and sheltered tidepools, is also the best spot for fishing (page 49).

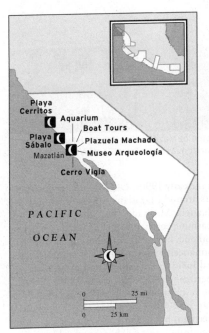

LOOK FOR **(** TO FIND RECOMMENDED SIGHTS, ACTIVITIES, DINING, AND LODGING.

some of Mazatlán's offshore islands on the horizon, as seen from Cerro Vigía

in the early 1990s. Old Mazatlán, which centers around Mazatlán's original main square, Plazuela Machado, has blossomed into a charming entertainment and restaurant neighborhood, blooming with music and dance performances, museums, arts and crafts galleries, and inviting hotels, bed-and-breakfasts, and apartments. A few blocks west of the Plazuela, the restoration of the 1940s-era Hotel Freeman in 2002 (now called the Hotel Posada Freeman) has added vitality to the Olas Altas shorefront resort neighborhood, which is likewise resurging, with new businesses, shops, restaurants, and cafés.

The Old Town hills have always been important in Mazatlán's history. Cerro Vigía, a quarter mile south of Olas Altas, was, for hundreds of years, the lookout point for soldiers watching for pirates and marauders on the horizon. A half mile south of that rises 514-foot Cerro Creston, where El Faro, the world's highest natural lighthouse, still sends its reassuring, wheeling beams of light far out to ships at sea.

Although the Old Town has the old-Mexico charm, the Golden Zone has the beaches and the spectacular sunset horizons. The beaches, after all, are the best places to appreciate the tropical beauty of Mazatlán. To truly enjoy Mazatlán, you must get off the busy boulevard, go to the beach, and look west, especially around the close of day. There, the radiant sunsets are made even lovelier by the dark contrasting silhouettes of Mazatlán's offshore Islas Pájaros, Venados, and Chivos.

PLANNING YOUR TIME

One of the best ways to visit Mazatlán is to spend time in both the Golden Zone and the Old Town. One strategy would be to lodge in the Golden Zone, and visit the Old Town at least a couple of days by public bus ($1) or taxi (four miles, 6 km, $5–10). Alternatively, during one Mazatlán week, you could spend four days in a Golden Zone hotel, where you could get your fill of sunning by the pool, strolling the beach, and splashing in the ocean. With kids in tow, take them to Mazatlán's world-class aquarium and/or the Mazagua water park. Then switch to an Old Town lodging for three days of relaxing in the sidewalk cafés, promenading the plaza, browsing the Friday–Saturday bazaar, visiting the cathedral and the market, and exploring the shops, museums, and sights. Sometime in between, take a boat tour, either around the harbor and coastal islands or to Stone Island. In both the Golden Zone and the Old Town, neighborhoods, restaurants, shopping, and entertainment are equally good, so you can enjoy plenty of those things in both places.

With a day or two more, you might head out for an overnight excursion to the southern Sinaloa foothill village of Concordia for handicrafts and continue to the colonial gold-mining village of Copala. With another day, head south to Rosario, home of *ranchera* singer Lola Beltrán, and the south-seas beach and mangrove village of Teacapán for fishing, wildlife viewing, maybe surfing or boogie-boarding, and perhaps beach camping.

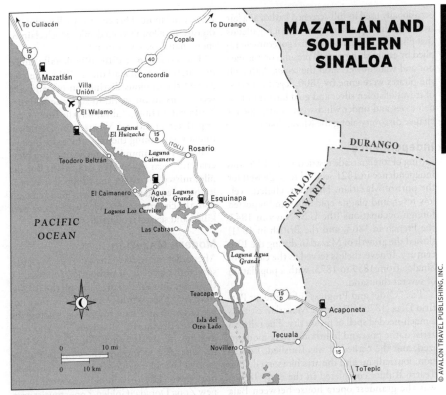

MAZATLÁN AND SOUTHERN SINALOA

HISTORY
Before Columbus

For Mexico, Mazatlán is not an old city. Most of its public buildings have stood for less than 100 years. Evidence of local human settlement dates back before recorded history, however. Scientists reckon petroglyphs found on offshore islands may be as much as 10,000 years old.

During the 1930s, archaeologists began uncovering exquisite polychrome pottery, with elaborate black and red designs, indicative of a high culture. Unlike their renowned Tarascan, Aztec, and Toltec highland neighbors, these ancient potters, known as the Totorames, built no pyramids and left no inscriptions. They had been gone a dozen generations before conquistador Nuño de Guzmán burned his way through Sinaloa in 1531.

Colonial Times

The rapacious Guzmán may have been responsible for the name "Mazatlán," which, curiously, is a name of Nahuatl (Aztec language) rather than local origin. Since Aztecs rarely ventured anywhere near present-day Mazatlán, the name Mazatlán (Place of the Deer) presents an intriguing mystery. Historians speculate that a Nahuatl-speaking interpreter working for Guzmán may have translated the name from the local language.

Mazatlán was first mentioned in 1602 as the name of a small village, San Juan Bautista de Mazatlán (now called Villa Union), 30 miles south of present-day Mazatlán, which was not yet colonized.

English and French pirates, however, soon discovered Mazatlán's benefits. They occasionally used its hill-screened harbor as a lair from which to pounce upon the rich galleons that plied the coast. The colonial government replied by establishing a small presidio on the harbor and watchtowers atop the *cerros*. Although the pirates were gone by 1800, legends persist of troves of stolen silver and gold buried in hidden caves and under windswept sands, ripe for chance discovery along the Mazatlán coast.

Independence

Lifting of foreign trade restrictions in 1820 and independence in 1821 seemed to bode well for the port of Mazatlán. However, cholera, yellow fever, and plague epidemics and repeated foreign occupations (the U.S. Navy in 1847, the French in 1864, and the British in 1871) slowed the growth of Mazatlán during the 19th century. It nevertheless served as the capital of Sinaloa from 1859 to 1873, with a population of several thousand.

The "Order and Progress" of President Porfirio Díaz (1876–1910) gave Mazatlán citizens a much-needed spell of prosperity. The railroad arrived, the port and lighthouse were modernized, and the cathedral was finished. Education, journalism, and the arts blossomed. The Teatro Rubio, completed in the early 1890s, was the grandest opera house between Baja California and Tepic.

The opera company of the renowned diva Ángela Peralta, the "Mexican Nightingale," arrived and gave a number of enthusiastically received recitals in Mazatlán in August 1883. Tragically, Peralta and most of her company fell victim to a disastrous yellow fever epidemic, which claimed more than 2,500 Mazatlán lives.

The revolution of 1910–1917 literally rained destruction on Mazatlán. In 1914, the city gained the dubious distinction of being the second city in the world to suffer aerial bombardment. (Tripoli, Libya, was the first.) General (later president) Venustiano Carranza, intent upon taking the city, ordered a biplane to bomb the ammunition magazine atop Nevería Hill, near downtown Mazatlán. But the pilot missed the target and dropped the crude leather-wrapped package of dynamite and nails onto the city streets instead. Two citizens were killed and several wounded.

Modern Mazatlán

After order was restored in the 1920s, Mazatlán soared to a decade of prosperity, followed by the deflation and depression of the 1930s. Recovery after World War II led to port improvements and new highways, setting the stage for the tourist "discovery" of Mazatlán during the 1960s and 1970s. The city limits expanded to include the strand of white sand (Playa Norte) north of the original old port town. High-rise hotels sprouted in the new Zona Dorada (Golden Zone) tourist area, which, coupled with Mazatlán's traditional fishing industry, provided thousands of new jobs for an increasingly affluentpopulation that, by the 21st century, had reached three-quarters of a million.

Sights

Mazatlán owes its life to the sea. The city's main artery, which changes its name five times as it winds northward, never strays far from the shore. From beneath the rugged perch of El Faro (Lighthouse) at the tip of the Mazatlán peninsula, the *malecón* (seawall) boulevard curves northward past the venerable hotels and sidewalk cafés of the Olas Altas (High Waves) neighborhood. From there it snakes along a succession of rocky points and sandy beaches, continuing through the glitzy lineup of Golden Zone beach hotels and restaurants. Next the boulevard loops inland for a spell, curving around a marina and back to the beach. The hotels thin out as it continues past condo complexes, groves of trees and, finally, grassy dunes and a sheltered cove beneath Punta Cerritos hill, 15 miles from where it started.

A welter of local buses run to and fro along identical main-artery routes. From the downtown central plaza they head along the *malecón,* continuing north through the Zona Dorada to various north-end destinations, which are marked on the windshields. Fares should run about half a dollar.

Small, open-air taxis, called **pulmonías,** seating two or three passengers, provide quicker and more convenient service. The average *pulmonía* ("pneumonia," directly translated) ride should total no more than $3–4, longer rides no more than $6. Agree on the price before you get in, and if you think it's too high, hail another *pulmonía* and your driver will usually come to his senses. The same rules apply to taxi rides, which run about double the price of *pulmonías.*

You can also get around Mazatlán by joining a tour. Hotel travel desks or travel agencies can set you up with one. Boat tours offer yet more options.

A WALK AROUND DOWNTOWN MAZATLÁN

Let the towering double spire of the **Catedral Basílica de la Purísima Concepción** (6 A.M.– 1 P.M. and 4–8 P.M. daily) guide you to the very center of Old Mazatlán. Begun by the Bishop Pedro Loza y Pardave in 1856, the cathedral was built on the site of an ancient native temple, atop a filled lagoon. Mazatlán's turbulent history delayed its completion until 1899 and final elevation in 1937 to the status of a basilica.

Inside, the image of the city's patron saint, the Virgen de la Purísima Concepción (Virgin of the Immaculate Conception) stands over the gilded, baroque main altar, while overhead soar rounded Renaissance domes and pious, pointed gothic arches. On the left, as you exit, pause and notice the shrine to the popular Virgin of Guadalupe.

In front of the cathedral, the verdant tropical foliage of the central **Plaza de la**

Moorish-style arches and tile decorate the facade of Mazatlán's plaza-front Catedral Basílica de la Purísima Concepción.

© BRUCE WHIPPERMAN

República encloses the traditional wrought-iron Porfirian bandstand. ("Porfirian," after turn-of-the-20th-century President Porfirio Díaz, is roughly equal to "Victorian.") To the right is the **Palacio Municipal** (City Hall), where on the eve before Independence Day, Sept. 16, the *presidente municipal* (township president) shouts from the balcony the traditional Grito de Dolores above a patriotic and tipsy crowd.

◖ PLAZUELA MACHADO

After enjoying the sights and aromas of the colorful **Mercado Central** (Central Market) two blocks behind the cathedral, reverse your path and head south on Juárez, the main street that borders the market's west side. Two blocks after the plaza, turn right at Constitución, and go one block to Plazuela Machado, Mazatlán's original central plaza, especially colorful during the Friday–Saturday handicrafts fair. The *plazuela* was named in honor of Juan Nepomuceno Machado,

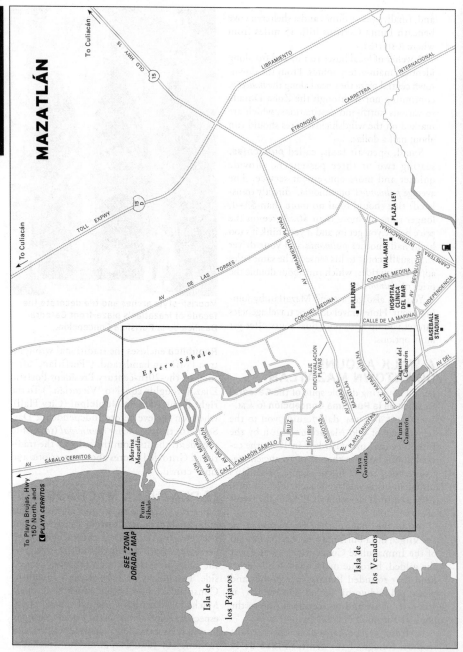

MAZATLÁN

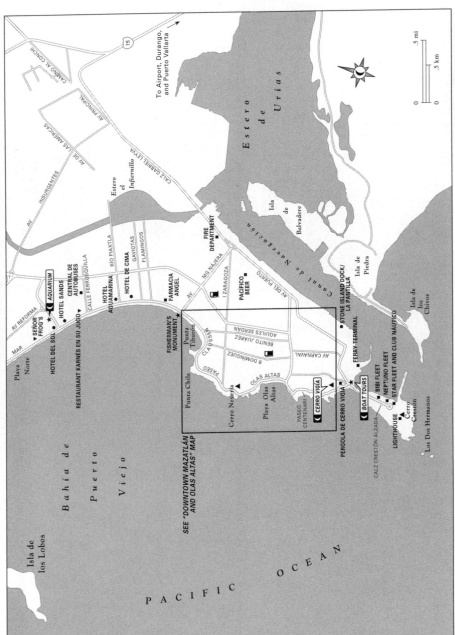

© AVALON TRAVEL PUBLISHING, INC.

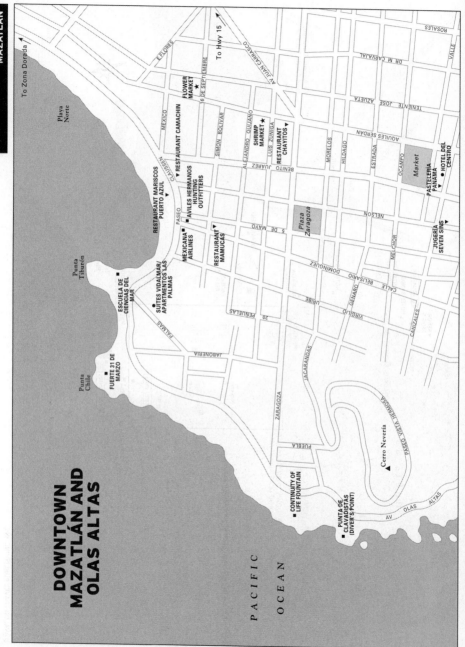

DOWNTOWN MAZATLÁN AND OLAS ALTAS

PACIFIC OCEAN

To Zona Dorada

Playa Norte

Punta Tiburón

Punta Chile

FUERTE 31 DE MARZO

ESCUELA DE CIENCIAS DEL MAR

SUITES VIDALMAR/ APARTMENTOS LAS PALMAS

CONTINUITY OF LIFE FOUNTAIN

PUNTA DE CLAVADISTAS (DIVER'S POINT)

Cerro Nevería

AV OLAS ALTAS

PASEO VISTA HERMOSA

PUEBLA

ZARAGOZA

JABONERÍA

JACARANDAS

PALMAS

20

PEÑUELAS

URIBE

VIRGILIO

GENARO

CALLE BEUSARIO DOMÍNGUEZ

CANIZALES

5 DE MAYO

MELCHOR

NELSON

Plaza Zaragoza

RESTAURANT MANUCAS

MEXICANA AIRLINES

AVILES HERMANOS HUNTING OUTFITTERS

RESTAURANT MARISCOS PUERTO AZUL

PASEO

CLAUSSEN

MEXICO

RESTAURANT CAMACHIN

E. FLORES

16 DE SEPTIEMBRE

FLOWER MARKET ★

AV JUAN CARRASCO

To Hwy 15

SIMON BOLIVAR

ALEJANDRO QUIJANO

BENITO JUAREZ

LUIS ZUÑIGA

SHRIMP MARKET ★

RESTAURANT CHAYITOS

MORELOS

HILDAGO

ESTRADA

AQUILES SERDÁN

TENIENTE JOSÉ AZUETA

DR M CARVAJAL

VALLE

ROSALES

OCAMPO

Market

PASTELERÍA PANAMÁ

HOTEL DEL CENTRO

JUGERÍA SEVEN SINS

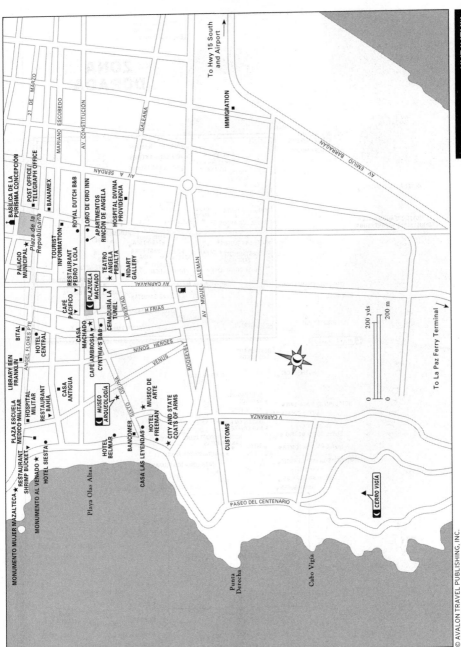

To Hwy 15 South and Airport →

IMMIGRATION ■

AV. EMILIO BARRAGÁN

21 DE MARZO

MARIANO ESCOBEDO

GALEANA

AV. A SERDÁN

AV. CONSTITUCIÓN

BASÍLICA DE LA PURÍSIMA CONCEPCIÓN
POST OFFICE/TELEGRAPH OFFICE ■
BANAMEX ■
ROYAL DUTCH B&B ●
LORO DE ORO INN ●
APARTMENTOS RINCÓN DE ANGELA ●
HOSPITAL DIVINA PROVIDENCIA ■

PALACIO MUNICIPAL ★
Plaza de la Republicana
TOURIST INFORMATION ■
RESTAURANT PEDRO Y LOLA ●
TEATRO ÁNGELA PERALTA ★
NIDART GALLERY ■

CAFÉ PACIFICO ●
PLAZUELA MACHADO
CENADURIA LA TÚNEL ●
LIBERTAD
H FRIAS

AV CARNAVAL
AV MIGUEL ALEMAN

CASA MACHADO ▼ ★
CAFÉ AMBROSIA ●
CYNTHIA'S B&B ●
NIÑOS HEROES
VENUS
ROOSEVELT
SIXTO OSUNA

HOTEL CENTRAL ■
BITAL ■
LIBRARY BEN FRANKLIN ■
ANGEL FLORES PTE
HOSPITAL MILITAR ▼
CASA ANTIGUA ■
MUSEO ARQUEOLOGÍA
MUSEO DE ARTE ■

PLAZA ESCUELA MÉDICO MILITAR ■
RESTAURANT BAHIA ▼
BANCOMER ●
HOTEL BELMAR ●
HOTEL FREEMAN ●
CITY AND STATE COATS OF ARMS ★
CASA LAS LEYENDAS ●

MONUMENTO MUJER MAZALTECA ★
RESTAURANT SHRIMP BUCKET ▼
MONUMENTO AL VENADO ●
HOTEL SIESTA ●

Playa Olas Altas

V CARRANZA

CUSTOMS ■

200 yds
200 m
0

To La Paz Ferry Terminal →

PASEO DEL CENTENARIO

CERRO VIGÍA ▲

Punta Derecha

Cabo Vigía

© AVALON TRAVEL PUBLISHING, INC.

MAZATLÁN

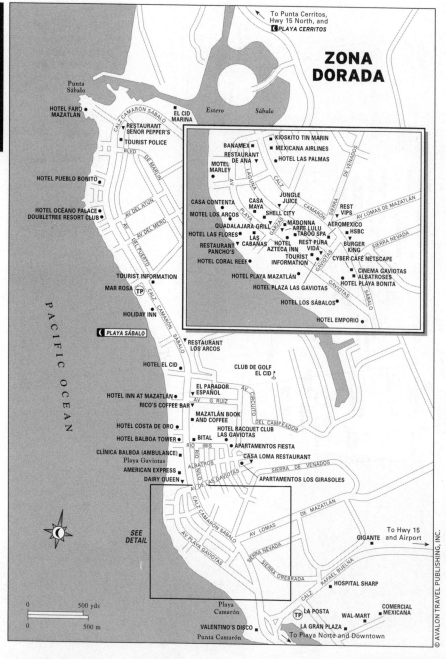

To Punta Cerritos,
Hwy 15 North, and
PLAYA CERRITOS

ZONA
DORADA

Punta
Sábalo

HOTEL FARO
MAZATLÁN

CALZ CAMARÓN SÁBALO   Estero   Sábalo

EL CID
MARINA

RESTAURANT
SEÑOR PEPPER'S

TOURIST POLICE

BLVD

DE MARLIN

HOTEL PUEBLO BONITO

KIOSKITO TIN MARIN

BANAMEX   MEXICANA AIRLINES
RESTAURANT
DE ANA   HOTEL LAS PALMAS
MOTEL
MARLEY

AV DEL ATÚN

HOTEL OCÉANO PALACE
DOUBLETREE RESORT CLUB

AV DEL MERO

AV DEL PUERTO

CASA CONTENTA   CASA   JUNGLE
                 MAYA   JUICE
MOTEL LOS ARCOS   SHELL CITY
GUADALAJARA GRILL   MADONNA
HOTEL LAS FLORES   LAS   ARRE LULU
                 CABAÑAS   TABOO SPA
RESTAURANT   HOTEL   REST PURA
PANCHO'S   AZTECA INN   VIDA
HOTEL CORAL REEF   TOURIST
            INFORMATION

DE VENADOS

AV LOMAS DE MAZATLÁN

REST
VIPS
AEROMEXICO
        HSBC
BURGER
KING

CYBER CAFÉ NETSCAPE

SIERRA NEVADA

CINEMA GAVIOTAS
    ALBATROSES
HOTEL PLAYA BONITA

GAVIOTAS

SÁBALO

HOTEL PLAYA MAZATLÁN

HOTEL PLAZA LAS GAVIOTAS

HOTEL LOS SÁBALOS

TOURIST INFORMATION

MAR ROSA TP

HOLIDAY INN

PLAYA SÁBALO

P A C I F I C   O C E A N

HOTEL EMPORIO

RESTAURANT
LOS ARCOS

HOTEL EL CID

CLUB DE GOLF
EL CID

EL PARADOR
ESPAÑOL

AV CIRCUITO

HOTEL INN AT MAZATLÁN
RICO'S COFFEE BAR

AV G RUIZ

MAZATLÁN BOOK
AND COFFEE

DEL CAMPEADOR

HOTEL COSTA DE ORO

HOTEL RACQUET CLUB
LAS GAVIOTAS

HOTEL BALBOA TOWER   BITAL

RÍO IBIS

APARTAMENTOS FIESTA

CLÍNICA BALBOA (AMBULANCE)
Playa Gaviotas
AMERICAN EXPRESS
DAIRY QUEEN

RÍO NILO

ALBATROS

CASA LOMA RESTAURANT

SIERRA DE VENADOS

AV DE LAS GAVIOTAS

APARTAMENTOS LOS GIRASOLES

CALZ CAMARÓN SÁBALO

SEE
DETAIL

AV PLAYA GAVIOTAS

DE MAZATLÁN

AV LOMAS

SIERRA NEVADA

To Hwy 15
and Airport

GIGANTE

SIERRA OREBRADA

RAFAEL BUELNA

HOSPITAL SHARP

0   500 yds
0   500 m

Playa
Camarón

TP LA POSTA

CALZ

WAL-MART

COMERCIAL
MEXICANA

VALENTINO'S DISCO
Punta Camarón

LA GRAN PLAZA
To Playa Norte and Downtown

© BRUCE WHIPPERMAN

The Plazuela Machado, Mazatlán's original main plaza, is the heart of Mazatlán's up-and-coming Old Town.

a founding father of Filipino descent who donated the land. The venerable Porfirian buildings and monuments clustered along the surrounding streets include the **Teatro Ángela Peralta,** completed around 1890 and recently restored and dedicated to diva Ángela Peralta.

At the west end of the Plazuela, along Calle Heriberto Frías, walk beneath the **Portales de Cannobio,** the arcade of the 1846 estate house of apple grower Luis Cannobio, a 19th-century Italian-born resident. The Cannobio family occupied the upper floor while operating a pharmacy at street level beneath the portals.

In those days, Plazuela Machado was the hub of Mazatlán life. The activity that buzzed around a lineup of mining and assay offices on adjacent **Calle de Oro** (now Calle Sixto Osuna) bubbled over with merrymaking (and still does) during the yearly Lenten celebration at Carnaval.

The present owners of the old Cannobio house, now renamed **Casa Machado** (Consti-tución 79, tel. 669/982-1440, 10 A.M.–6 P.M. daily), have reopened it as a museum. They invite visitors to "find their way to the inner memories" of Mazatlán in the upper-floor rooms, decorated with antique reminders—polished provincial French furniture, bright Carnaval costumes, and lacy four-poster beds—of Old Mazatlán.

For a shady break, take a seat at one of the **sidewalk cafés** on the plaza's north side (or the refined **Café Memorial** across from the Teatro Ángela Peralta); or go inside and sample the menu at restaurant **Lola and Pedro** at the plaza's northeast corner, Carnaval and Constitución.

◖ MUSEO ARQUEOLOGÍA

Continue west a few blocks toward the ocean from Plazuela Machado along Calle Sixto Osuna and step into the small Museo Arqueología (Sixto de Osuna 76, tel. 669/981-1455, 10 A.M.–2 P.M. and 4–6 P.M. Mon.–Sat., 10 A.M.–3 P.M. Sun.) and peruse its well-organized exhibits outlining Sinaloan

ÁNGELA PERALTA

Diva Ángela Peralta (1845-1883) was thrilling audiences in Europe's great opera houses by the age of 16, when a Spanish journalist dubbed her the "Mexican Nightingale." On May 13, 1863, she brought down the house at La Scala in Milan with an angelic performance of *Lucia de Lammermoor*.

During Ángela's second European tour she charmed maestro Guiseppi Verdi into bringing his entire company across the Atlantic so she could sing *Aida* in Mexico City. With Verdi conducting, Ángela inaugurated the 1873 Mexico City season on a pinnacle of fame.

Legends abound of the fiercely nationalistic Peralta. She once got the last word in a téte-á-téte with Europe's most famous Italian soprano of the time. In an unforgettable joint recital, Ángela courteously extended first bows to the haughty Italian diva, who remarked of her own performance, "That is the way we sing in Italy." Ángela Peralta rejoined, "Mine was the way we sing in heaven."

Not content with mere performance, Ángela Peralta went on to excel as a composer, librettist, and impresario, organizing her own opera companies. Her success and outspoken ways earned her enemies in high places, however. In 1873, Mexico City bluebloods were shocked to find out Ángela was having an affair with her lawyer, Julian Montiel y Duarte. (It didn't seem to matter that Peralta was widowed and Montiel single at the time.) Much of Mexico City's high society boycotted her performances; when that didn't work, they sent hecklers to harass her. Liberals, however, defended her, and Peralta finally regained her audience in the early 1880s with a heartrending performance of *Linda de Chamounix*. She kept her vow, however, to never sing again in Mexico City.

Her star-crossed life came to an early end on August 30, 1883. Touring with her company in western Mexico, a Mazatlán yellow fever epidemic claimed her life and the lives of 76 of her 80-member company. On her deathbed, she married Montiel y Duarte, the only man she ever loved. Later, her remains were removed to Mexico City, where they now lie enshrined at the Rotunda de Hombres Ilustres (Rotunda of Illustrious Men).

prehistory and culture. The displays include case after case of petroglyphs, human and animal figurines, and the distinctive red-and black-glazed ancient polychrome pottery of Sinaloa.

MUSEO DE ARTE

Half a block farther west and south around the corner of V. Carranza, take a look inside the Museo de Arte (entrance on west side of V. Carranza, half a block south of Sixto Osuna, tel. 669/985-3502, 10 A.M.–2 P.M. and 4–7 P.M. Mon.–Sat., 10 A.M.–2 P.M. Sun.), which displays the works of noted local and nationally recognized painters, sculptors, and graphic artists.

OLAS ALTAS

Continue west one short block to the *malecón* (seawall) **Avenida Olas Altas**. This airy, café-lined stretch of boulevard and adjacent beach was at one time *the* tourist zone of Mazatlán. It extends from the **Monumento al Venado** (Monument to the Deer) at its north end, at Avenida Ángel Flores, south a few blocks past the restored Hotel Freeman to the **Escudos de Sinaloa y Mazatlán** (State and City Coats of Arms of Sinaloa and Mazatlán). There, Avenida Olas Altas changes names, in front of the distinguished 1889 school building at the foot of steep Cerro Vigía, where the boulevard, now **Paseo del Centenario,** climbs to its breezy south-end summit viewpoint.

Step inside the lobby of the restored 1940s-era **Hotel Posada Freeman.** Perhaps more than any event, the Freeman's return to life in late 2002 signaled the resurgence of Old Mazatlán. The Freeman's shiny five-star reincarnation offers an impressive array of amenities, including an 11th-floor open-air swimming pool, a lavishly equipped gym, Internet access in each room, a business center, convention facilities, and much more. (For Hotel Posada Freeman lodging details, see the *Accommodations* section.)

Outside, nearby, you might pause a while and soak up the flavor of Old Mazatlán. Take a seat at one of the sidewalk cafés; later look around the lobby of the old Hotel Belmar. Notice the wall map a few steps inside the entrance door, dated 1948, when the entire state of Sinaloa had a population of less than half of present-day Mazatlán, and the whole country had a population equal to Mexico City's today.

⬤ CERRO VIGÍA

Now, unless you're in the mood for a steep hike, bargain for a *pulmonía* to take you up Paseo Centenario, the southern extension of Avenida Olas Altas, to the **Pergola de Cerro Vigía** viewpoint at the top of the hill. There, next to the old cannon (stamped by its proud London maker "Vavaseur no. 830, 1875"), you get the sweep of the whole city.

Cerro Vigía is the spot where, according to tradition, the colonial soldiers of the old Mazatlán presidio maintained their 200-year vigil, scanning the horizon for pirates. Step across the little hilltop plaza and down to the **Café el Mirador** (open noon–9 P.M. daily) and enjoy lunch, a drink, and the view.

CERRO CRESTON AND EL FARO

To the south rises Mazatlán's tallest hill, Cerro Creston, topped by the El Faro lighthouse, whose 515-foot (157-meter) elevation qualifies it as the world's highest natural lighthouse. Along the jetty/landfill that connects Cerro Creston to the mainland lie the docks and anchored boats of the *flotas deportivas* (sportfishing fleets). Every morning, in season, they take loads of anglers out in search of big fighting marlin and sailfish.

⬤ BOAT TOURS

Taking a boat tour is one of the best ways to experience close-up views of sea life without

© BRUCE WHIPPERMAN

An antique cannon perches atop the summit of Cerro Vigía.

getting in the water. Harbor tour boats also depart from the same docks as the sportfishing fleets. The yacht **Fiesta** (tel. 669/981-7154 or 669/982-3130) leaves regularly at 11 A.M. for a harbor and island cruise, passing the inner harbor shrimp fleet, circling past the lighthouse, sea lion island (winter only), and Mazatlán's offshore islands, Islas Chivos, Pájaros, and Venados. Tickets cost about $15 per person for the three-hour trip. For information and reservations, call or go to the Zona Dorada office across from the Hotel Las Palmas on Camarón Sábalo.

Trimaran **Kolonahe** offers a pair of tours from the north-end Marina el Cid: a 9:30 A.M. island tour that includes part of the harbor tour as described above, as well as a landing at Isla Venados for swimming, tidepooling, strolling, lunch, and sunning on the beach, returning in early afternoon. Later, at 2:30 P.M., the *Kolonahe* heads seaward again for an open-bar sunset cruise (about $35). For more information and reservations, contact a travel agent or call the El Cid Marina (tel. 669/916-3468).

Across the south-side deep-water harbor entrance looms the bulk of **Isla de Piedra** (Stone Island), actually a peninsula. Its southern beach stretches to the horizon in a narrowing white thread, beneath the dark green plumes of Mexico's third-largest coconut grove. If you've a hankering to explore, ride the tour boat catamaran **Sábalo** to Stone Island. For details, contact a travel agent or dial the catamaran dock, tel. 669/986-4930.

CERRO NEVERÍA

The rounded profile of Cerro Nevería (Icehouse Hill) rises above the patchwork of city streets, south of the Olas Altas neighborhood. Its unique label originated during the mid-1800s, when the tunnels that pock the hill served for storage of ice imported from San Francisco, California. Now the hilltop holds a number of radio and microwave beacons. The northerly view from atop Cerro Nevería reveals a spectacular panorama of city, beach, and offshore islands. Get there via Calle Puebla, which

climbs uphill, from the west end of downtown Calle Zaragoza. Keep going uphill at every fork. Before the summit, follow the cobbled driveway to the summit, where you'll see the long, graceful sweep of wave-tossed Playa Norte, and the three offshore islands basking in the blue Pacific.

◖ AQUARIUM

Mazatlán boasts Latin America's largest aquarium (Av. de los Deportes 111, tel. 669/981-7816 or 669/981-7817, 9:30 A.M.–6 P.M. daily, admission about $6 adults, $4 kids), with many big, well-maintained tanks of flinty-eyed sharks, clownish wide-bodied box fish, and shoals of luminescent damselfish. Outside, don't miss the tropical botanical garden, where you'll find a pair of monstrously large crocodiles. Time your arrival to take in one of the four daily sea lion and bird shows at around 10:30 A.M., noon, and 3 and 4:30 P.M. The aquarium is just off Avenida del Mar about a mile south of Valentino's (watch for the Acuario sign on the beach boulevard).

PUNTA CAMARÓN AND OFFSHORE ISLANDS

The curving white ribbon of sand north of the downtown area traces the *malecón* northward to Punta Camarón and the Golden Zone, marked by the cluster of shoreline high-rise hotels. Offshore from Punta Camarón, Mazatlán's three islands—**Chivos** (Rams) and **Venados** (Deer), nearest, and **Pájaros** (Birds) on the horizon—seem to float offshore like a trio of sleeping whales.

ALONG PASEO CLAUSSEN

Return back downhill to Avenida Olas Altas. Moving south from the Hotel Posada Freeman, pass the Statue of the Deer in the middle of the intersection where the *malecón* becomes Paseo Claussen. Named for the rich German immigrant who financed the blasting of the scenic drive, Paseo Claussen continues around the wave-tossed foot of Cerro Nevería. First, you will pass a striking bronze sculpture, the **Monumento Mujer Mazalteca**.

Nearby, a yawning cave (plugged by heavy bars) pierces the hill. Known by local people as the **Caverna del Diablo** (Devil's Cave), it served as an escape route for soldiers guarding the ammunition stored in caves farther up the hill.

Not far ahead, a four-story platform at the **Punta de Clavadistas** (Divers' Point) towers above the wave-swept tidepools. The divers—professionals who take their work very seriously, especially at low tide, when their dives must coincide with the arrival of a big swell—perform a number of times daily, more frequently on Sundays and holidays.

Moving north, you'll pass the big **Continuidad de la Vida** (Flow of Life) sculpture, popular with crowds of local folks who arrive evenings to watch its colored fountains. Continue another block to the 1892 fort turned maritime office, **Fuerte 31 de Marzo,** named in honor of the heroic stand of the local garrison, which repelled a French invasion on March 31, 1864.

© BRUCE WHIPPERMAN

watching the divers at Punta de Clavadistas

Beaches

OLAS ALTAS TO PUNTA CAMARÓN

Exploration of Mazatlán's beaches can start at Avenida Olas Altas, where narrow **Playa Olas Altas** offers some water sports opportunities. The strip is wide and clean enough for wading, sunning, bodysurfing, and boogie boarding. Swimmers take care: The waves often break suddenly and recede strongly. Locally popular intermediate surfing breaks angle shoreward along both north and south ends. Bring your own equipment, since there's rarely any for rent on this largely locals-only beach.

For fly- and bait-casting (although the beach surf is too murky to catch much), casts from the rocks on either end may yield rewards worth the effort.

Continuing north around Paseo Claussen, past the fort, you'll come to the wave-tossed **Pinos** cove next to the modern Ciencias del Mar (Marine Sciences) college. Although the narrow strand here is

suitable for no more than wading, the rocks provide good casting spots, and the left-breaking swells challenge beginning and intermediate surfers.

Next comes the small boat cove where **Playa Norte** begins. Unfortunately, the first one-mile stretch is too polluted for much more than strolling, because of the waste from the fleet of fishing *lanchas.*

A mile farther north, beginning around the oafish **Monumento al Pescador** (Fisherman's Monument), known popularly as the *monos bichis* ("naked monkeys") monument, where Paseo Claussen becomes Avenida del Mar, a relatively wide, clean white strand extends for three miles. This stretch is popular with local families and is uncrowded except during holidays. On calm days the waves break gently and gradually; other times they can be rough. If so, stick by a lifeguard if you see one.

Beginning and intermediate surfers congregate

at the north end of this beach, on both flanks of **Punta Camarón** (marked by the needle spires of Valentino's disco), where the swells break gradually left. For fisherfolk, the rocks on the point are good spots for casting.

ZONA DORADA

At Punta Camarón (marked by the white spires of Valentino's disco) beachfront Avenida del Mar becomes Calz. Camarón Sábalo, which winds northward through the clutter of Zona Dorada streetside eateries, crafts shops, travel agencies, and banks.

The way to enjoy and understand the Zona Dorada is not on the boulevard, but on the beach a few blocks away. The lineup of hotels immediately north of Punta Camarón testifies to the beauty of Playa Camarón and Playa Gaviotas. These shining strands—with oft-gentle rolling waves, crystal sand, and glowing, island-silhouetted sunsets—give meaning to the label "Golden Zone": golden memories for visitors and gold in the pockets of the Mazatlán folks lucky enough to own or work in the Zona Dorada. (Sometimes it seems as if half the town *is* trying to work there. During the low-season months of September and October, beachfront crafts and food vendors often outnumber the sunbathers.)

Although the **Playas Camarón** and **Gaviotas** are often lumped together, the beaches themselves contrast sharply. The more southerly Playa Camarón is oft-narrow and steep, with coarse, yellow sand. Its waves often break suddenly and recede strongly. At such times, bodysurfing on Playa Camarón is a thrilling but potentially hazardous pastime.

Despite the popularity of this strip, small shells, such as mother-of-pearl and lovely rust-brown-mottled little clams, are sometimes plentiful.

About 500 yards north of the point, near the Las Flores Hotel, Playa Camarón becomes Playa Gaviotas. There, the beach changes to Playa Gaviotas's silky smooth sand and lazy slope. Waves usually roll in gently and always for a long distance. They are not good for surfing, since they head straight into the beach and tend to break all at once along a long front, rather than angling left or right.

Playa Sábalo is known for its gentle surf and soft sand.

© BRUCE WHIPPERMAN

◖ PLAYA SÁBALO

Another quarter mile north in the Zona Dorada, around Hotel el Cid, Playa Gaviotas becomes its identically lovely northward extension, Playa Sábalo, which stretches another mile to Punta Sábalo at the Hotel Playa Real (formerly Camino Real). The soft sand here is the silkiest of all the beaches in Pacific Mexico.

Past the rocks of Punta Sábalo, the waters of the **Estero Sábalo** tidal lagoon (now the Marina Mazatlán's outer harbor) ebb through a boat channel. The beach boulevard loops a mile inland, past the El Cid Marina, then Marina Mazatlán, curving north, then west, back to the beach, where it becomes Calz. Sábalo Cerritos.

PLAYA BRUJAS

The strand north of Punta Sábalo, called Playa Brujas, in places begins to resemble a wild beach along undeveloped stretches of its northern reaches. Grass sways atop the dunes, flocks of sandpipers probe the wave-washed sand, pelicans and frigate birds glide overhead, and shells and driftwood accumulate. Gentle waves, fine for beginning surfing or boogie boarding, roll in from about 100 yards out.

Playa Brujas is named for the *brujas,* female witch doctors, who used to perform their rituals there. If you're thirsty or hungry by that time, a seafood restaurant at the end of the beach before the hill will gladly accommodate you. Also, a sign advertises "Bilingual Horses" for beachfront rides.

PLAYA CERRITOS

On the north side of the hill that marks Punta Cerritos nestles intimate Playa Cerritos, where more seafood *palapa* restaurants perch at the very end of the beach boulevard. On the left, a rocky tidepool shelf juts into the waves, forming a protected cove. This, some say, is the best fishing spot in Mazatlán. It appears so; half a dozen *lanchas* are usually pulled up on the rocky beach, while offshore, one or two divers hunt for oysters in the clear, calm morning waters. At water's edge a trove of pretty shells—small clams, limpets, oysters, and, who knows, maybe even a petite pearl or two—litters the sand.

HIKES

The best hike in Mazatlán leads right along the beach. Just walk any of your favorite stretches. You could do the whole thing (or part of it) starting anywhere—Olas Altas, Playa Norte, Playa Gaviotas—and walking as far north (to avoid having the sun in your eyes) as you want. Other than a hat and sunscreen, you won't have to carry anything along; beach restaurants and stores along the way will provide the goodies. Neither will you have to walk back; just grab the bus or a *pulmonía* back to town whenever you decide you've walked enough.

Another good hike leads to the summit of **Cerro Creston** and provides a close, interesting look at **El Faro.** The trail begins at the foot of the hill, at the end of the pavement past the *flotas deportivas* (sportfishing fleets) docks. Wear a hat, and take some insect repellent, water, and maybe food for a breezy summit picnic.

Follow the initially wide track as it zigzags up the hill. Sometimes overhung by vines, leafy trees, and gnarled cacti, the trail narrows to a rocky path about halfway to the summit. Nearing the top, you wind your way beside rocky outcroppings until you come to the fence around the lighthouse. If your group is small, the keeper may let you in for a look around and to sign his book. He claims the lighthouse is 400 years old.

If you arrive around dusk (bring a flashlight), you will see the beacon in action. The dazzling 1.5-million-watt beacon rotates gradually, like the spokes of a heavenly chariot, with a trio of brilliant, wheeling pencils of light focused by the great antique Fresnel lens atop the tower.

At least one local agency offers a city and **hiking tour** that includes a guided climb to the lighthouse summit. It customarily begins at 3 P.M., ending with a sunset view from the hilltop. The $19 tariff includes drinks on the bus and free hotel pickup. Call a travel agent, such as Vista Tours (tel. 669/986-8610, www.vistatours.com.mx).

Accommodations

You can nearly predict the room price of a hotel by its position on a Mazatlán map. The farther north away from the old downtown, the newer and more expensive it's likely to be.

DOWNTOWN

At one time, all Mazatlán hotels were downtown. But during the 1980s and 1990s the plush new hotels and condos on the Playa Norte-Zona Dorada resort beach strip drew away most of the high-ticket vacationers, leaving the old Olas Altas tourist zone to the sprinkling of travelers who seek the charms of traditional Mexico and Mexican families on Sunday outings. The exception to this is the week after Christmas, the week before Easter, and, most of all, Carnaval (Mardi Gras, usually in late February or March), when Olas Altas is awash with merrymakers.

Hotels

UNDER $50

Budget travelers hankering to be near the center of colorful downtown bustle often stay at the no-frills **Hotel del Centro** (Canizales 717, Mazatlán, Sinaloa 82000, tel. 669/981-2673, $20 d, $30 during fiestas), within sight of the cathedral, right around the corner from the market. (The hotel's streetfront, although busy, is too narrow for buses and is consequently not overly noisy.) The 24 rooms have a/c and TV. There's not much in the clean rooms but the basics. No matter; the attraction of this part of town is what's outside the door.

For a little more luxury in the downtown district, walk about four blocks to the quieter, west side of the cathedral, to **Hotel Central** (Calle Belisario Domínguez 2 Sur, corner of Calle Ángel Flores, Mazatlán, Sinaloa 82000, tel./fax 669/982-1866 or 669/982-1955, hotel. central@yahoo.com.mx, $15 s or d in one bed, $3 extra person, $40 d during fiestas). Past the upstairs lobby you'll find a small restaurant, a friendly place for meeting other travelers, and three floors of cool, modern-style rooms. Rates for the 40 rooms, with a/c, TV, and phone, go up during Carnaval, Easter, and Christmas holidays.

Four blocks farther west, on scenic shorefront Avenida Olas Altas, stands the venerable six-story oceanfront ❰ **Hotel Belmar** (Av. Olas Altas 166, Mazatlán, Sinaloa 82000, tel. 669/985-1112, fax 669/981-3428, U.S. and Canada toll-free tel. 877/BELMAR-1, info@ hotelbelmar.com.mx, www.hotelbelmar.com .mx, $28 d, $33 with view, higher during fiestas). Although now faded, the hotel still welcomes the longtimers who remember when it was *the* hotel in Mazatlán. Belmar offers 200 rooms, with a/c, phone, and parking. Rates run as much as 50 percent higher during holidays. Its old amenities remain: pool, nearby sidewalk restaurants, parking, and many ocean-view rooms, some carpeted and modern and some so old and makeshift they're quaint.

A block farther south, the popular ❰ **Hotel La Siesta** (Av. Olas Altas 11, Mazatlán, Sinaloa 82000, tel. 669/981-2640 or 669/981-2334, toll-free Mex. tel. 800/711-5229, fax 669/982-2633, info@lasiesta.com.mx, www .lasiesta.com.mx, $45 d, $55 ocean view, up to $150 d during fiestas) provides a solid, moderately priced option for enjoying the flavor of the Olas Altas neighborhood. The 57 rooms have TV, a/c, phones, and lobby Internet access. (Some, however, are showing wear. Look at more than one before choosing.) For balcony views of Carnaval or lovely sunsets any time of the year, reserve one of the several oceanfront rooms. Another extra is the charming old inner patio, decorated by the colorful umbrellas of El Shrimp Bucket restaurant and shaded by towering, leafy trees festooned with hanging air-roots. Rates can run up to $150 d during Carnaval, Christmas, and Easter.

$50-100

The owners of the ❰ **Hotel Posada Freeman** (or, lately, the Best Western Hotel Posada Freeman Express, at Av. Olas Altas 79 Sur, corner of Sixto Osuna, Mazatlán, Sinaloa 82000, 669/985-6060, fax 669/985-6064, toll-free Mex. tel. 01-800/614-1652, Best Western reservations U.S. and Canada toll-free tel. 800/528-1234, info@freemanhotel.com, www .bestwestern.com, $95), formerly the Hotel Freeman, have taken a giant step toward reenergizing Old Mazatlán, with their two-year restoration of this 1940s-era hostelry. Reopened as the Hotel Posada Freeman in November 2002, the place now gleams with a host of five-star amenities, including an 11th-floor open-air swimming pool, a lavishly equipped gym, Internet access in each room, and a business center and convention facilities. The 100 or so deluxe rooms ordinarily rent from about $95.

Bed-and-Breakfasts and Apartments

UNDER $50

Old Mazatlán's revival has attracted a sprinkling of bed-and-breakfast inns and apartments in the city lanes just inland from Avenida Olas

The 1960s-era Hotel Posada Freeman, restored in 2002, now anchors a re-energized Olas Altas resort area.

Altas and around Plazuela Machado. Start half a block east of the Plazuela Machado, at **Apartmentos Rincón de Angela** (Constitución 610, Mazatlán, Sinaloa 82000, tel. 669/981-1551, cellular tel. 044-669/929-4833, angelaapartments@hotmail.com, www.pacific pearl.com/directconnect/directrent.htm, $270/week, $500/month), adjacent and behind the Teatro Ángela Peralta. The owners have created an inviting cluster of three attractively decorated rustic-chic kitchenette studio apartments, tucked around a quiet, inviting interior patio. All are fully furnished with a queen-sized beds, up-to-date appliances, cable TV, and a/c.

Next door, welcoming California expatriate Tony Feuer invites visitors to stay at his 🌙 **Loro de Oro Inn** (Golden Parrot; Constitución 622, tel./fax 669/982-8996, U.S. tel. 714/369-8205, ldo@mazinfo.com, www.mazinfo.com/LDO, $49 studio, $99 suite). He offers four comfortable, attractively decorated kitchenette studio apartments, and two large and luxurious suites, all built around a lovely designer pool-patio.

All rentals have modern baths, tiled floors, and wireless Internet. There's a 10 percent discount to rent by the week, 40 percent off for monthly rental. Adults only, no pets.

$50-100

Cross the street to **Royal Dutch Bed and Breakfast** (Constitución 610, Mazatlán, Sinaloa 82000, tel. 669/981-4396, roydutch@ mzt.megared.net.mx, www.royaldutchcasade santamaria.com, $75 d). Here, the Dutch expatriate owner and his Mexican wife offer three clean, comfortable homey rooms with bath; the price includes breakfast, afternoon tea, fans, and cable TV. One day is free with a one-week rental; monthly discounts are negotiable.

About a half mile north, where Paseo Claussen bends east around Cerro Nevería, a big sign on the hill above the Ciencias del Mar (Marine Sciences) college marks **Suites Vidalmar** (Calle Las Palmas 15, Mazatlán, Sinaloa 82000, tel. 669/981-2190 or 669/981-2197, suitesvidalmar@yahoo.com, credit cards not accepted, $43 for two persons, $60 for four, $130 suite, higher during fiestas). The modern stucco apartment complex clusters artfully above a blue designer swimming pool with a sweeping view of the nearby rocky bay and northward-curving shoreline. Ten immaculate one-bedroom suites, all spacious, tastefully furnished, with kitchenettes, can accommodate four in two double beds. One airy, two-story suite accommodates five adults. Amenities include a/c, phones, parking, pool, and kitchenettes; rates go up about 50 percent during holidays. This is a place for those who want a restful vacation while enjoying quiet pursuits: cooking, basking in the sun, reading, and watching sunsets from the comfort of their own home in Mazatlán. For holidays, the winter season, and weekends, be sure to reserve early.

The same management operates **Apartmentos Las Palmas** (Calle Las Palmas 15, Mazatlán, Sinaloa 82000, tel. 669/981-2190 or 669/981-2197, suitesvidalmar@yahoo.com, credit cards not accepted, $35 d, $65 during fiestas), a stack of apartments and a penthouse across the street. Although plainer than the Suites Vidalmar, the kitchenette apartments are large, very clean, modern, and spartan but thoughtfully furnished and sleep up to four. Residents have access to the pool across the street. Same address and phone as Suites Vidalmar; the 11 one-bedroom apartments have a/c and parking.

Back south, in the Olas Altas district, in late 2005 enterprising owner Cynthia Romero renovated an old family house tucked on a quiet corner of Plazuela Machado and christened it **El Meson de Cynthia Bed and Breakfast** (Sixto Osuna 408, corner of Heriberto Frías, tel. 669/136-0284, U.S. tel. 310/633-8739, cynthia@mesondecynthia.com, www.elmesonde cynthia.com, $60–$85 d). Rooms, on three floors, are simply, comfortably (but not very thoughtfully) furnished, with beige ceramic tile floors, high ceilings, and kitchenettes. They vary from simply large to two huge suites, big enough for family of four. Plusses here are a rooftop Plazuela Machado-view patio and proximity to the restaurants, cafés and colorful ambience right outside the door. Prices are right, and include a/c, shiny, modern standard bathrooms, and Continental breakfast.

OVER $100

Two blocks west of Plazuela Machado, the distinguished **Melville Boutique Hotel** (Constitución 99, Mazatlán, Sinaloa 82000, tel./fax 669/982-8474 or 669/981-4519, U.S.-Canada toll-free tel. 866/395-2881, info@the melville.com, www.themelville.com, $95–$140, higher during fiestas), sits at the corner of Niños Héroes. Originally renovated to be a retirement residence, the Melville now rents to mostly senior overnight guests. Little has been spared to restore the beauty of this 19th-century former convent. The entrance leads to a lovely, tranquil inner fountain-patio, enfolded by a graceful arched portico. Stroll around the portico, past the graceful lobby, dining room-restaurant, and salon and library. The 18 one- and two-bedroom apartments, mostly upstairs, are comfortably furnished with modern-style, handcrafted wooden furniture, attractive wall

art, soft beds, and microwave-equipped kitchenettes. Low-season rates are about $95 for one bedroom, $140 for two bedrooms, including full breakfast. Winter high-season tariffs run about 20 percent more.

Location (just a block from breezy Avenida Olas Altas), space, and simple elegance make (**Casa de Leyendas** (Venustiano Carranza 4, Centro Histórico, Mazatlán, Sinaloa 82000, tel. 669/981-6180, U.S. tel. 602/445-6192, info@casadeleyendas.com, www.casade leyendas.com, $95–$135) an irresistible choice for a few days or a week or more in the lovely heart of Mazatlán Old Town. Owners Sharon and Glen Sorrie accommodate guests with six spacious rooms, artfully tucked upstairs and down in their newly renovated historic family home. Guest rooms are handsomely furnished with hand-hewn wood furniture, tasteful wall art, and king- and queen-sized beds with wrought-iron bedsteads. Airy hidden patios, ocean views, a small blue pool with hot tub, and a baronial dining room complete the lovely picture. Tariffs include modern-standard tiled bathrooms, full breakfast, and wireless Internet.

PLAYA NORTE

During the 1960s, Mazatlán burst its old city limits at the end of Paseo Claussen and spilled northward along the long sand crescent called Playa Norte. Now, a three-mile string of 1960s-style hotels and motels lines the breezy beachfront of Avenida del Mar, an extension of Paseo Claussen.

Hotels
UNDER $50

Just past the Pizza Hut appears the smallish facade of the motel-style, family-friendly **Hotel del Sol** (Av. del Mar s/n, P.O. Box 400, Mazatlán, Sinaloa 82000, tel./fax 669/985-1103, hoteldelsol@mzt.megared.net.mx, $32 d, $45 d with kitchenette). A few steps from the streetfront reception, you will find that the Motel del Sol is roomier than it looks. Its dozen-odd rooms cluster around an inviting pool and patio where, on one corner, a clownish plaster duck squirts water from his beak. Inside, tasteful wood furniture, white walls, and spotless tile floors decorate the spacious rooms. Rates include a/c, phones, TV, and parking, and there's a discount for monthly rentals.

A few blocks south, next to the popular Restaurant Señor Frog's, comes the **Hotel Sands** (Av. del Mar 1910, P.O. Box 309, Mazatlán, Sinaloa 82000, tel. 669/982-0000, 669/982-0800, or 669/982-0600, fax 669/982-1025, hotelsandsarenas@red2000.com.mx, www.hotelsandsarenas.com, $50 d, $60 ocean view, $75–$90 d during fiestas). If you don't mind a bit of traffic noise from the avenue, here you have the ingredients for a pleasant beach vacation: 50 clean, sea-view rooms with balconies overlooking an inviting pool patio, with a/c, phones, cable TV, restaurant, and parking.

$50-100

Still farther south, find the elegantly modern **Hotel Aguamarina** (Av. del Mar 110, P.O. Box 345, Mazatlán, Sinaloa 82000, tel. 669/981-7080, toll-free Mex. tel. 01-800/716-9580, fax 669/982-4624, info@aguamarina.com, www.aguamarina.com, $85 d, $100 d high season). With a low-rise stucco motel facade, built around an inviting pool and patio, its rooms (either ocean- or garden-view) are large and gracefully decorated with native-style handmade wood furniture. The wall art hangs tastefully on colonial-style textured white interiors. The 101 rooms offer a/c, cable TV, phones, parking, pool, and an airy, high-ceilinged restaurant.

ZONA DORADA

Along a six-mile strip of golden sand rise Mazatlán's newest, plushest hotels. But unlike in some other world-class resorts, the Zona Dorada is not wall-to-wall high-rises. In the breezy, palm-fringed spaces between the big hotels, there are many excellent moderately priced hotels and apartment complexes.

Hotels
UNDER $50

Prime beachfront location boosts the desirability of the tattered **Hotel el Coral Reef** (Av. Playa Gaviotas 4, Mazatlán, Sinaloa 82110, tel. 669/913-2941, hotelcoralreef@hotmail.com, $45 d, $110 d during fiestas). Tucked just north of the landmark Hotel Playa Mazatlán, the Coral Reef's guests enjoy a stunning view of the green slopes of offshore Isla los Venados, a modest sometimes-open restaurant, and oceanfront pool-patio. If you can put up with very tired management and the mostly run-down (but sea-view) rooms, the prices are certainly right, especially between September–December 15 and January–February. Prices more than double when Mexican families crowd in during Carnaval, Easter, July, August, and Christmas–New Year's.

$50-100

The **Hotel Playa Bonita** (Av. Playa Gaviotas 27, P.O. Box 501, Mazatlán, Sinaloa 82110, tel. 669/983-8000, toll-free Mex. tel. 01-800/696-0000, fax 669/983-5361, $40 s or d, $65 s or d during fiestas), formerly Hotel Tropicana and now partly a time-share, shares virtually everything—beach, shopping, restaurants, and nightlife—with Zona Dorada luxury hotels except prices. For many savvy vacationers, the hotel's other big pluses—spacious rooms, private ocean-view balconies, big marble baths—far outweigh the half-block walk to the beach. To assure yourself of the best room (top floor, beachside), reserve early. Amenities include a/c, phones, a small lobby-front pool, beach club, restaurant/bar, and full wheelchair access.

The owner of the Hotel Siesta downtown brings similar good management to the **Hotel Azteca Inn** (Av. Playa Gaviotas 307, P.O. Box 841, Mazatlán, Sinaloa 82110, tel. 669/913-4477 or 669/913-4655, toll-free Mex. tel. 800/716-9770, fax 669/913-7476, info@aztecainn.com.mx, www.aztecainn.com.mx, $68 s or d high season, $45 s or d low), right in the middle of the Zona Dorada bustle and one short block from the beach. Here, guests enjoy about 70 comfortably furnished, immaculate semideluxe rooms, arranged motel-style, in two floors around an inviting inner pool patio. Rentals include a/c, TV, restaurant, wireless Internet access, and parking.

A block farther south, the low-rise **Hotel Plaza Las Gaviotas** (Bugambilias 100, P.O. Box 970, Mazatlán, Sinaloa 82110, tel. 669/913-4496 or 669/913-4433, fax 669/913-6685, plazagaviotas@mzt.megared.net.mx, www.hotelplazagaviotas.com, $45 d, $68 d during fiestas), tucked just off Avenida Playa Gaviotas, is easy to miss. The petite but attractive lobby leads to a leafy inner patio with a small pool, a favorite of the Mexican families that fill the hotel during holidays. The surrounding rooms are clean, tiled, and decorated in light pastels. (Maintenance, however, remains a weakness; look at more than one room before choosing.) Management will bargain on room rates, especially weekdays or long-term. There's cable TV, a/c, and lower-floor wheelchair access, but no restaurant.

The mostly young guests at the **Hotel Emporio Mazatlán** (Camarón Sábalo 51, P.O. Box 795, Mazatlán, Sinaloa 82110, tel. 669/983-4822, toll-free Mex. tel. 800/716-9555, toll-free U.S. tel. 800/782-4298, toll-free Canada tel. 866/210-0928, fax 669/984-4532, reservaciones@hoteles emporio.com, www.hotelesemporio.com, $90 d, $180 d during fiestas) enjoy luxurious beachfront amenities at reasonable rates. The hotel's design makes the most of its already enviable location. The rooms, in a pair of sunny, breeze-swept tiers, enclose a spacious two-pool patio that looks out on a gorgeous beach, sea, and sunset vista. Upstairs, most guest rooms have private sea-view balconies and are tiled, clean, and simply but thoughtfully decorated in blues and whites. Amenities include nightly pop music in the patio (be prepared with earplugs), TV, a/c, parking, and full wheelchair access.

A few blocks north towers the beachfront semideluxe **Hotel Las Flores** (Playa Gaviotas 212, P.O. Box 583, Mazatlán, Sinaloa 82110, tel. 669/913-5100 or 669/913-5788, toll-free U.S. tel. 800/452-0627, toll-free Canada tel. 877/756-7529, fax 669/914-3400 and 669/914-3422, h.flores@mazatlan.com.mx, www.las flores.com.mx, $160 d), very popular with North American winter package vacationers. Most of the rooms and suites feature soothing blue and white decor. Many units have kitchenettes, while all enjoy expansive ocean views. Downstairs, the lobby spreads to an attractive restaurant, pool-bar, and tables beneath thatched-roof beachside *palapas*. During holiday seasons, the 119 accommodations rent for about $160 d for standard studio ($175 w/ kitchenette), $270 for deluxe suite with kitchenette; during low season, they offer three nights for the price of two. Rentals include a/c, TV, phones, and parking.

OVER $100

Smack in the middle of Avenida Playa Gaviotas stands the landmark of the Zona Dorada, ◖ **Hotel Playa Mazatlán** (Av. Playa Gaviotas 202, P.O. Box 207, Mazatlán, Sinaloa 82110, tel. 669/989-0555, toll-free Mex. tel. 01-800/716-9567, toll-free U.S.-Canada tel. 800/762-5816, fax 669/914-0366, info@ hotelplayamazatlan.com.mx, www.hotel playamazatlan.com.mx, $125 d), the first hotel built (despite many doubters) on what was once an isolated sand strip far from the city center. Even during the September and October low-occupancy months (when many Zona Dorada hotels and restaurants are virtually empty), everyone—Mexicans and foreigners alike—still flocks to Hotel Playa Mazatlán. The band plays every night, the Fiesta Mexicana buffet show goes on every Saturday, and the fireworks boom and flash above the beach Sunday nights during high season. To enjoy the Playa Mazatlán, you don't have to stay there; evenings, just order something at the beachside *palapa* terrace restaurant and enjoy the music, the breeze, and the same ocean view shared by its luxurious rooms. The 408 rooms go for about $125 d for "standard" grade (but nevertheless deluxe) with ocean view, $110 with garden view. The larger "deluxe" rooms, all with ocean view, go for about $140. Christmas-New Year and Easter season prices are higher. All with a/c, cable TV, phones, pool, hot tub, parking, and full wheelchair access. Low-season packages and promotional discounts are sometimes available.

For another classy tropical retreat, walk or taxi northward about a mile to the **(Hotel Inn at Mazatlán** (Camarón Sábalo 6291, P.O. Box 1292, Mazatlán, Sinaloa 82110, tel. 669/913-5900 or 669/913-5354, toll-free U.S. tel. 866/826-5454, fax 669/913-4782, info@inatmaz.com, www.innatmaz.com, $135 studio), right on silky Playa Camarón. Although mostly a time-share (guests buy a room for a specified week or two each year), it rents out the vacant units hotel-style. All guests, whether owners or one-time renters, receive the same tender loving service. Every lovely feature of the Hotel Inn at Mazatlán shines with care and planning, from the excellent inside-outside beach-view restaurant and the artistically curved pool to the palms' sunset silhouettes and the spacious, luxuriously appointed housekeeping accommodations, ranging from studios ($135) through one-and two-bedroom units ($200, $250), all the way up to multi-bedroom penthouses for around $500. All rentals enjoy a/c, phones, TV, tennis, and parking. Reservations are generally necessary.

No discussion of Mazatlán hotels would be complete without mention of the megaresort **Hotel el Cid** (Camarón Sábalo s/n, P.O. Box 813, Mazatlán, Sinaloa 82110, tel. 669/913-3333, toll-free Mex.tel. 01-800/716-9800, toll-free U.S./Can. tel. 800/525-1925, fax 669/914-1311, reservat@elcid.com, www.elcid.com, $100 d, $120 during fiestas), the hotel that tries to be everything. The huge complex, which spreads over the north end of Avenida Camarón Sábalo, claims to be the biggest in Mexico—with 1,200 rooms in four separate hotels, more than a dozen bars and restaurants, health club and spa, kids' club, giant glittering disco, country club subdivision, marina development, a world-class 18-hole golf course, and 17 tennis courts. Size, however, lends El Cid a definite institutional feeling, as if everyone, the 2,000 employees and 3,000 guests alike, were anonymous. The El Cid's saving grace (besides its lovely beachfront) may be its huge pool. It meanders among the three hotels, a palm-fringed blue lagoon complete with an artificial (albeit very clever artificial) rock water slide, waterfall, and diving platform straight from an old Tarzan movie. The poolside crowd of guests, from ages 4–90, enjoy watching each other slipping, sliding, and jumping into the cool water. Room rates start at about $100 d, $120 holidays, and come with everything, including complete wheelchair access. El Cid often offers cheaper promotions, and there's an all-inclusive option that can run as low as $60 per person per night, double occupancy, obtainable through travel agents or the reservations office.

Apartments
UNDER $50
For just about the most charming budget accommodation in Mazatlán, check out **(Fiesta Apartmentos** (Calle Ibis 502, Mazatlán, Sinaloa 82110, tel. 669/913-5355 or 669/913-1764, hudsontmaz@yahoo.com, www.hudsontours.com, $30–$45 d), at the corner of Río de la Plata, three blocks directly inland from beachside landmark Balboa Tower. This complex of studios and one- and two-bedroom apartments lies within a jungle-garden blooming with bushy mangos, hanging vines, snoozing dogs, and chirping birds. Hardworking owner-manager Yolanda Olivera and her carpenter spouse built the place from the ground up while raising a family during the 1970s and 1980s. The tile-decorated units are all uniquely furnished with husband-made wooden chairs and tables, folk art, toilet, hot shower, and double beds. Larger units have an additional bed, a sofa or two, and a kitchenette. Moreover, the prices are certainly right: The 10 studios and one-bedroom apartments, all with kitchenettes, rent from about $30/day ($500/month) for two; larger two-bedroom units go for about $45/day ($650/month). Add $10 per extra person. All apartments come with a/c, fans, and parking; reservations are necessary during the winter.

Right next door is the less personal but equally unique **Racquet Club Las Gaviotas**

(Calle Ibis at Bravo, P.O. Box 173, Mazatlán, Sinaloa 82000, tel. 669/913-5939 or 669/916-0225, gaviotas@mzt.megared.net.mx, www .pacificpearl.com/Racquet_Club_Gaviotas/ apartments.htm, $600–$850/month). Step inside the gate and find an inviting village of bungalow-style apartments and condominiums spread around a spacious palm-shaded swimming pool and garden. While a comfortable, moderately priced vacation lodging for anyone, this is a paradise for tennis buffs on a budget, with its row of seven well-maintained (three clay and four hard) courts. The bungalows themselves are spacious, spartan semideluxe, one- and two-bedroom units with a living room/dining room furnished in Spanish-style tile and wood and equipped with modern kitchenettes. The 20 units rent from about $600/month for a one-bedroom bungalow and $850/month for two bedrooms (with higher daily and weekly rates, fans and daily cleaning service included). Lower units are wheelchair-accessible. Reservations are mandatory year-round.

$50-100

Just as lovely (but minus the tennis courts) is the nearby **Los Girasoles** (Av. Gaviotas 709, Mazatlán, Sinaloa 82110, tel./fax 669/913-5288, $50–$75 d, higher during fiestas), a stucco apartment complex built around an inviting pool patio and garden five blocks from the beach at the end of Gaviotas, next to Restaurant Casa Loma. When ripe, the fruit of the banana trees that fringe the garden can be picked by guests. Inside, the airy Mexican-style wood and tile kitchenette apartments are sparely but comfortably furnished and spotless. The 20 units (both one- and two-bedroom) run $50/day or $800/month for the one-bedroom units, $75 and $950 for two bedrooms. Holiday prices are about 20 percent higher. Rental includes a/c, TV, parking in front, and daily cleaning service. (Los Girasoles owner Eleanora Aguilar also rents Villa Tranquila, a beachfront two-bedroom, three-bath house, $140 for two, $180 for four, or about $2,400/month.)

Right on Mazatlán's loveliest beachfront stand a number of small, moderately priced lodgings along Avenida Playa Gaviotas, which, about a block north of Valentino's, loops left, one way, away from noisy Calz. Camarón Sábalo.

Guests at the two-story **Hotel Marley** (Av. Playa Gaviotas 226, P.O. Box 214, Mazatlán, Sinaloa 82000, tel./fax 669/913-5533, motmarley@mzt.megared.net.mx, www.travel bymexico.com/sina/marley, $80–$135 d) can choose between upper- or ground-level one- or two-bedroom units, all with living rooms and fully furnished kitchenettes, with daily maid service and air-conditioned bedrooms. Extras include parking and attractive garden grounds that spread from an inviting pool patio. A few of the apartments are right on the beach. For the most privacy and best views, reserve one of the beachfront upper units early. Rates run, year-round, about $80 d for one bedroom (with two double beds), $135 for two bedrooms (four double beds) for four people. One-month rentals receive an approximate 10 percent discount; add about $9 per additional person.

Accommodations at **Motel los Arcos** (Playa Gaviotas 214, P.O. Box 132, tel./fax 669/913-5066, mlarcos@mzt.megared.net .mx, $100–$110 d), a block south next to Hotel Las Flores, are similar to those at the Motel Marley. A new pool is bound to please many of the guests who return yearly to enjoy the sparkling sun, sea, and sand, right from their front doorsteps. The 16 clean, brightly furnished kitchenette view apartments rent, year-round, for about $100 d for one bedroom, $110 d for two bedrooms for four people. Add about $10 per additional person.

Right between the Marley and the los Arcos is the charming ⦗**C**⦘ **Casa Contenta** (Av. Playa Gaviotas 224, tel. 669/913-4976, fax 669/913-9986, reservaciones@casacontenta .com.mx, www.casacontenta.com.mx, $95 d, $70 d low season), a comfortable two-story complex that lives up to its name. Step past the off-street parking and you will find seven roomy, tastefully furnished one-bedroom kitchenette apartments tucked behind a luxurious family house, all within a manicured garden. Besides the creamy beach and small pool in the backyard, Casa Contenta residents can enjoy good restaurants and the entertainment of plush hotels within a few minutes' walk. Reserve early: prices run about $95 a day high season, $70 low for an apartment, $200 high season, $150 low for the house. The apartments rent for about $1,700 monthly, about $4,000 for the house. All include daily cleaning service, a/c, cable TV, and parking. Lower-level units have limited wheelchair access.

BEYOND THE ZONA DORADA
Bungalows
UNDER $50

Vacationers who hanker for a more rustic atmosphere and who are willing to put up with rough accommodations in exchange for a gorgeous beach may enjoy the **Bungalows Playa Escondida** (Calz. Sábalo Cerritos 999, P.O. Boxes 682 and 202, Mazatlán, Sinaloa 82110, tel./fax 669/988-0077, $30–50 for one bedroom) on palmy Playa Cerritos, about five miles north of the Zona Dorada. Administered by the trailer park office across the boulevard, the 20 (six of them not usable at this writing) whitewashed bungalows laze beneath a swaying coconut palm grove.

The spartan kitchenette units stand in parallel rows facing the ocean. The more heavily used (and oft-storm-damaged) beachfront row enjoys sweeping ocean views, while the others lie sheltered beneath the palms behind the dune. During the winter season you can enjoy plenty of company at the trailer park pool across the street. Stores and restaurants are within a short drive. The bungalows rent from about $30 for the smaller one-bedroom units, sleeping four, and $50 for the larger, sleeping 6–8, with a/c. One-month rentals customarily have run about $900 and $1,100 per month, for the smaller and larger units, respectively.

HOMESTAY PROGRAM

Besides offering Spanish classes, the privately owned downtown **Centro de Idiomas** (Language Center; Callejon Aurora 203, tel. 669/985-5606, fax 669/982-2053, info@spanishlink.org, www.spanishlink.org) runs a homestay program. Participants live with a Mexican family (about $200/week, including three meals). The center also offers person-to-person contacts, in which such visiting professionals as teachers, nurses, and doctors meet with and learn from their local counterparts.

LONG-TERM RENTALS

One of the better sources of rentals is the classified (print or online) section of the tourist newspaper *Pacific Pearl* (tel. 669/913-4411, fax 669/913-0117, www.pacificpearl.com).

A number of real estate agents offer long-term apartment, condominium, and house rentals. One of the most useful is **Gonzalez-Henderson Real Estate** (tel. 669/913-8925 or 669/913-9913, rikkigh@hotmail.com, or www.pacificpearl.com/gh/); local real estate agent Rikki Gonzales lists dozens of rental properties all over Mazatlán.

Also very experienced is English-speaking real estate agent **Lupita Bernal** (tel. 669/914-1753, fax 669/914-5082, local cell 044/669/925-7145, lupitabernal@prodigy.net.mx, www.pacificpearl.com/bernalre).

For the more luxurious condominium and beachfront rental houses, you might contact Kim and Mike Peters of Sinaloa Sun Properties (tel. 669/916-7794, fax 669/914-0456, mkpeters@mazinfo.com, www.sinaloasun.com).

Yet another potentially fruitful source is the worldwide website **Vacation Rentals by Owner** (www.vrbo.com), listing dozens of Mazatlán rentals, mostly beachfront condominiums.

RV AND TRAILER PARKS

Mazatlán's beachfront trailer space is an increasingly scarce commodity, victim to rising land values. If you're planning on a Christmas stay, phone or mail in your reservation and deposit by September or you may be out of luck, especially for the choice spaces.

One trailer park owner determined never to sell out is Gabriela C. Aguilar van Duyn, of **Mar Rosa Trailer Park** (Calz. Camarón Sábalo 702, P.O. Box 435, Mazatlán, Sinaloa 82000, tel./fax 669/913-6187), mar_rosarv@ mzt.megared.net.mx, g_banduyn@yahoo .com, g_duyn@yahoo.com, $14–28 RV site winter, $13–21 low season) just north of the Hotel Holiday Inn. Besides being the on-the-spot manager, Gabriela is Mazatlán's informal one-woman welcoming committee and information source. "I will never sell," she says. "The people who come here are my friends, like my family." If you ask if she has a pool, she will probably point to the beach a few feet away and say, "One big pool." During high season, Gabriela offers about 55 spaces, some shaded, with all hookups, for $14–28/ day winter, $13–21 low (about $400/month, $3,100 for four months) depending on location. With toilets, hot showers, a/c power, and cable TV; it's near stores and restaurants; leashed dogs are okay.

Alternatively (on Calz. R. Buelna, two blocks inland from Valentino's Disco), the **Trailer Park La Posta** (Rafael Buelna 7, P.O. Box 362, Mazatlán, Sinaloa 82000, tel./fax 669/983-5310, lapostarvpark@hotmail.com, $15–20 RV site) spreads beneath the shade of a banana, mango, and avocado grove (all-you-can-eat in season). Residents enjoy a plethora of facilities, including all hookups, showers and toilets, a big pool and sundeck, shaded picnic area, shady *palapas,* a small store, wireless Internet, 30-amps for a/c, and the beach two blocks away. The 180 spaces rent for about $15–20/day or about $120/week or $400/month. Early winter reservations are generally necessary.

In the quieter beach country a block from north-end Playa Cerritos, the **Playa Escondida Trailer Park** (Calz. Sábalo Cerritos 999, P.O. Box 682 or 202, Mazatlán, Sinaloa 82110, tel./fax 669/988-0077, $18 RV site) spreads for acres beneath a lazy old co-

conut grove. Residents enjoy direct access to the long, uncrowded beach across the road and to nearby minimarkets and restaurants. They can also stay in the trailer park's rough Bungalows Playa Escondida across the street. The 200 spaces run about $18/day or $380/ month, with all hookups, a big saltwater pool, rec room, hot showers, and toilets; leashed dogs are okay.

In the same north-end neigborhood, try the beachfront **Trailer Park Mar-a-Villas** (just north of the big Quinta del Mar development, tel. 669/984-0400, $14 RV site), with about 25 functioning spaces with all hookups, concrete pads, and showers and toilets, all tucked into a big, palm-shaded beachfront lot. The owner, Alfredo, who lives in the adjacent house by the beach, charges about $14/day, tents $10, with discounts for long-term stays.

CAMPING

Although there is no established public campground in Mazatlán, camping is allowed for a fee in all the trailer parks noted above except Mar Rosa—notably Playa Escondida with its beachfront palm grove and quiet, palmy Mar-a-Villas.

If, however, you prefer solitary beach camping, there are empty grassy dunes at far northerly **Playa Cerritos** and **Playa Brujas** that appear ripe for tenting. If you are uncertain about the safety or propriety of a likely-looking spot, inquire at a local business, such as the beachside restaurant at Playa Bruja.

Other, more isolated spots (be sure to bring water) lie along the long curve of sand on the south shore of **Stone Island;** catch a ride on the launch across from the Stone Island dock, at the foot of Avenida Gutiérrez Najera on Playa Sur.

Camping is also permitted on **Isla Venados,** a mile off Playa Sábalo. Ride the boat from the El Cid beachfront. On Isla Venados, don't set up your tent on the narrow beach; it's under water at high tide. Carry out all of your trash.

Food

Mazatlán abounds in good food. The competition is so fierce that bad eateries don't survive. The best are easy to spot because they have customers even during the quiet September–November low season.

SNACKS, BAKERIES, MARKETS, AND COFFEE HOUSES

With care, you can do quite well right on the street downtown. An afternoon cluster of folks around a streetside cart piled with oyster shells and shrimp is your clue that the fare is fresh, tasty, and reasonably priced. These carts usually occupy the same place every day and, for most of them, the quality of their food is a matter of honor. One of the best is **Santos el Burro Feliz** (which usually occupies a spot at 61 Calle Sixto Osuna, three blocks west of the Plazuela Machado, outside the family house across from the Archaeological Museum). Try the dozen-oyster cocktail, enough for two, for $10.

In the same neighborhood, sometime, you must take a seat at one of the **sidewalk cafés** around the Plazuela Machado. For example, at the café beneath the Portal de Cenobbio on the west side, try simply a cappuccino ($1.50) or maybe a cream of mushroom soup ($4) or perhaps a light lunch of shrimp stroganoff ($9).

If you're cooking your own meals or simply hanker for some fresh fruit and vegetables, the best place to find the crispest of everything is the **Central Market** (corner of Calles Benito Juárez and Melchor Ocampo, 6 A.M.–6 P.M. daily), two short blocks behind the cathedral.

After an hour of hard market bargaining, you may be in the mood for a cool, restful lunch. If so, step upstairs inside the market to the leafy balcony *fonda* over the corner of Juárez and Valle and enjoy the scene.

You can also try the petite juice shop **Jugería Siete Pecados Naturales** (Seven Natural Sins; 1710 Guillermo Nelson, 8 A.M.–6 P.M. Mon.–Sat., 8:30 A.M.–2 P.M. Sun.) for a sandwich, salad, or fruit drink; it's a block behind the cathedral.

Alternatively, just south of the market, enter the cool, air-conditioned interior of **Pastelería Panamá** (Av. Juárez, corner of Canizales, tel. 669/985-1853, 8 A.M.–10 P.M. daily). Enjoy one of the tasty lunch specials ($4–6) or treat yourself to the excellent *helado chocolate* (chocolate ice cream, $2).

Afterward, just outside the door, you may see the *churro* cart that always seems to be parked at that corner. Try three of these uniquely Mexican, foot-long, thin sugar doughnuts for $1.

For fabulous pastries, visit the Pastelería Panamá's **bakery** branch, a block west of Plazuela Machado, corner of Sixto Osuna and B. Domínguez.

Get the richest coffee in town at (**Café Rico's** (in the Zona Dorada, on Cámaron Sábalo, corner of Gabriel Ruiz, across from the Inn at Mazatlán, tel. 669/913-1444, 7 A.M.–11 P.M. daily). Unusually thoughtful indoor and outdoor seating and luxurious touches—a gorgeous wall mural, soft stuffed chairs and couches—only enhance Rico's rich cappucino, latte, and fine pastry (don't miss the banana pie) offerings.

RESTAURANTS
Downtown and Olas Altas

The better downtown restaurants are concentrated around Plazuela Machado and the Olas Altas *malecón*.

On Plazuela Machado, you can have it all at (**Café Pacífico** (corner of Constitución and Heriberto Frías, tel. 669/985-2060, 10 A.M.–midnight daily, dinner around $15 plus wine). For starters, try the chilled Spanish *gazpacho*, continue with olive and goat cheese-stuffed artichokes or two-color soup with corn and *cuitlacoche*, and climax with Tenochtitlán beef tenderloin, smothered in chipotle sauce.

Three stars for food and ambience go to **Restaurant Pedro and Lola** (corner of Constitución and Carnaval, tel. 669/982-2589,

6 P.M.–2 A.M. daily, entrées $9–17), named after the celebrated Mexican singers Pedro Infante and Lola Beltrán. Here, step into a cool, casual-chic bohemian atmosphere, take a table, and choose from a menu long on salads ($4–7) and seafood ($9–17) and short on meat. It offers live jazz and nouvelle classical music with supper Friday and Saturday.

For a local-style treat, in the same neighborhood and tucked just off the southeast corner of Plazuela Machado, enjoy the popular supper fare of the **Cenaduría el Tunel** (Carnaval 1207, 6–10 P.M., daily, entrées about $4). El Tunel's entry leads you through to a narrow corridor where customers are enjoying the craft of a squad of grandmotherly chefs who carry out their mission at stoves in the interior dining room. The delectable enchiladas, crunchy tacos, rich *pozole* (pork or chicken with hominy stew) (all about $4), and creamy refried beans ($2) are bound to please all devotees of true Mexican food.

Walk a block west of Plazuela Machado, to refined **(Café Ambrosia** (Sixto Osuna 26, corner of B. Domínguez, tel. 669/985-0333, 11 A.M.–11 P.M. daily, sandwiches $3–6) for both healthy and fine vegetarian cuisine. Besides a fresh daily appetizer menu (check out the *setas,* hearty, meatlike mushrooms, $4), Café Ambrosia offers a gourmet menu of wholesome salads (avocado and mixed vegetables, $4), soups (cream of beet, $4), enchiladas, pastas, and veggie sandwiches ($3–6).

Continue west two blocks and north one block to **(Restaurant Bahía** (M. Escobedo 203, tel. 669/981-2645, noon–8 P.M. Mon.–Sat., except Oct. 1–15, when the shrimp fleet is gone fishing; credit cards not accepted, entrées $8–10), a block from Avenida Olas Altas, behind the Hotel Siesta. What is arguably the best seafood cooking in town has earned the title "La Catedral de Ceviche" for the owner-chef and her family, who continue a tradition begun by her parents in 1950. Make up a party to share a maximum of their home-style regional specialties, such as *pescado zarondeado, pescado relleno de camarón* (both about $10), and *filete de pescado al mojo* ($8).

If you're in a party mood, head to **El Shrimp Bucket** (Av. Olas Altas 11, bottom floor of Hotel La Siesta, tel. 669/981-6350, 6 A.M.–11 P.M. daily, bucket of shrimp $20). The restaurant, hung with a riot of taffeta flowers and balloons inside, with the marimba combo humming away by dinnertime in the tropical patio outside, is a fiesta waiting to happen. This is especially true when you call for the bounteous bucket of shrimp ($20, enough for two or three), which the kitchen will fix exactly as you wish—breaded, grilled, steamed, or barbecued. Breakfasts are also very popular here.

For local-style "real" Mexican food, all roads seem to lead to **(Cenaduría Chayito,** on the northwest side of downtown (corner of Calle Teniente Azueta and Avenida Juan Carrasco, 2–11 P.M. daily, entrées $6–9). Here, in a cool, genteel family atmosphere, choose from a long menu of tacos ($1.50), tostada (actually a salad, $3), enchiladas *gorditas*(made with thick tortillas, $2) *pozole* (savory hominy soup with all the fixin's, $3), plus many meat plates ($6–9, with salad and baked potato), including beef brochette, *arrachera* steak, and *costilla* (pork ribs).

Playa Norte

It's hard to imagine a restaurant closer to the source than the rough-and-ready family-style **Restaurant el Camachín** (97 Paseo Claussen and 5 de Mayo, tel. 669/985-0197, 9 A.M.–10 P.M. daily, entrées $6–12), situated where the boats bring the fish in every morning. In true Mexican tradition, the restaurant augments many of its dishes with flavorful sauces, which vary from a mild salsa Oriental (onions, celery, and a bit of soy) to a peppery salsa ranchero. Pick your favorite and have it served with the recommended catch of the day.

Another good seafood bet is **Mamucas** (404 Bolivar Poniente/West, tel. 669/981-3490, 10:30 A.M.–9:30 P.M. daily, entrées $7–14), Mazatlán's "King of Seafood" for more than a generation, two blocks from the Paseo Claussen *malecón.* The specialties are *parillada de mariscos*—grilled seafood, you pick which—and *pescado zarandeado en brasero*—fish, toss-broiled in a wood-fired brazier.

Farther north, in the middle of the Playa Norte *malecón*, a bright sign marks **Karnes en Su Jugo** (Av. del Mar 550, tel. 669/982-1322, 1 P.M.–1 A.M. daily; credit cards not accepted, entrées $6–15), just south of the Hotel Sands. If personable owner Jorge Pérez (who, with his red hair, looks more like a Swede than most Swedes do) is there, let him place your order: you'll find a bounteous table, likely set with a plate of savory roast beef in juice, hot melted Chihuahua white cheese, refried beans, and enough salsa and hot corn tortillas for a dozen yummy tacos or tostadas.

A stay in Mazatlán wouldn't be complete without a trip to **Señor Frog's** (Calz. Camarón Sábalo s/n, tel. 669/982-1925, noon–past midnight daily, entrées around $12), the second (El Shrimp Bucket was the first), and perhaps the best, creation of late owner Carlos Anderson's worldwide chain. Many extreme adjectives—brash, bold, loud, risqué, funny, far-out—have been used to describe the waiters, patrons, and the music at Señor Frog's. Most everyone agrees the ribs ($12) are the best and the margaritas ($4) the most potent in town.

Zona Dorada

Despite their Golden Zone locations, Zona Dorada restaurants aren't necessarily expensive. When you're in a sweat from shopping, sunburn, and street vendors, and you're ready to escape from Mexico, try Mexico's first **Dairy Queen** (Camarón Sábalo 500, corner of Playa Gaviotas, tel. 669/916-1522, 10 A.M.–11 P.M. daily). The hot dogs ($1–3) and soft ice cream goodies ($1–3) will taste as good here as at home.

At the same corner, across the street, soak in the atmosphere of old Spain in the cool, dark wood-and-brick *bodega* ambience of **◖ Restaurant Rioja** (tel. 669/916-6180 or 669/913-0203, 11:30 A.M.–11 P.M. daily, entrées $10–12). Welcoming owner-chef Meliton Osuna Escalera invites his customers to start out with *tapas* (such as Manchego cheese, steamed clams, or *gazpacho*, $3–5). The entrée menu, although short, offers tasty choices, including Bilbaina fish fillet, black pepper beef

fillet, and the star of the show, the *paella* heaping with savory rice, pan-fried with a heap of clams, shrimp, fish, and much more, enough for two.

For a fine place to start out the day, go two blocks south from the Dairy Queen corner to the Zona Dorada branch of the **Pastelería Panamá** (on Camarón Sábalo at Garzas, tel. 669/914-0612, 7 A.M.–11 P.M. daily). Here, folks flock for everything from ham and eggs and hamburgers ($3–5) to *enchiladas suizas* ($5) and chocolate malts ($3).

Much of the same is available at the refined coffee-shop-style **Restaurant VIPs** (a few blocks farther south on Camarón Sábalo, across from Cinemas Gaviotas y Albatroses, tel. 669/914-0754, 7 A.M.–midnight daily, entrées $4–8). Here you'll find Denny's-modeled food and cool a/c, along with crisp salads, hot entrées, and luscious desserts. Moreover, the restaurant features a bookstore, where you can browse till midnight over one of Mazatlán's biggest assortment of English-language magazines.

Mexican-food fanciers will enjoy the tostada, taco, ceviche, and shrimp offerings of snack shop **Arre Lulu** (on side street Las Garzas, across from the high-profile Guadalajara Grill, 8 A.M.–11 P.M. daily, $3–8).

For good Mexican-style macrobiotic fare, step across to the beach side of Calz. Camarón Sábalo to side street Gaviotas (across from Hotel Playa Mazatlán) and the restaurant **Pura Vida** (tel. 669/916-5815, 8 A.M.–10 P.M. daily, menu items $2–6). Here, in an airy air-conditioned space, a bustling cadre of youthful waiters serves from a long list of fresh fruit drinks, light veggie sandwiches, whole-wheat pizza, vegetable and fruit salads, yogurt, granola, omelettes, and much more.

In a relaxed outdoor resort setting, enjoy breakfast or lunch at the airy beach-view restaurant **Terraza Playa** (at Hotel Playa Mazatlán, R.T. Av. Playa Gaviotas 202, tel. 669/913-4455, 7 A.M.–11 P.M. daily; entrées $5–10), so popular that tables are sometimes hard to get. This is especially true some Sunday nights when families begin to arrive two hours early for the free 8 P.M. fireworks show.

The Terraza Playa offers excellent entrées, such as *pescado Veracruzana,* for $5–10.

A spectacular beachfront view, cool breezes, snappy service, and fresh salads, sandwiches, and seafood keep patrons coming year-round to restaurant (] **Pancho's** (at the beach end of the small complex across from Shell City, tel. 669/914-0911, 7 A.M.–11 P.M. daily, $4–10). During the winter season, when vacationers crowd in, come early. The dozen tables can fill by noon.

Find one of the Zona Dorada's hidden culinary gems, **La Cocina de Ana** (Laguna 49, near the Dairy Queen corner behind Banamex, tel. 669/916-3119, noon–8 P.M. Mon.–Sat., noon–4 P.M. only July–Oct., entrées $3–7). Cooking is a labor of love of the friendly owner, and it shows, in her hearty, healthy daily buffet of chili, paella, Chinese food, soup, and fish.

For impeccable service and gorgeous, palm-framed sunsets, try the restaurant **Papagayo** (at the Hotel Inn at Mazatlán, Camarón Sábalo 6291, between Hotels el Cid and Costa de Oro, tel. 669/913-5500, 7 A.M.–10 P.M. daily; entrées around $12). The menu caters to the tastes of the mostly middle-aged North American clientele, with salad bar ($5) and reasonably priced complete dinner specials, notably a mouthwatering chicken-rib combo.

One of the most successfully exclusive restaurants in town is **Casa Loma** (Gaviotas 104, tel. 669/913-5398, 1:30–10 P.M. daily; credit cards accepted, entrées $18–20), which, besides tucking itself behind a wall on a quiet dead-end street, often manages to close July–October. (Call ahead to check.) The Casa Loma secret: A secluded location, subdued tropical atmosphere, excellent service, and a selection of tasty international specialties continue to attract a clubby list of affluent patrons. Some of the dishes include longtime favorites such as French onion soup, osso buco (veal shank), and shrimp *a la diabla.* Reservations are mandatory.

The low-key facade of **Señor Pepper's** (Camarón Sábalo, far north end, across from the Hotel Playa Real, tel. 669/914-0101, 5–11 P.M. daily; entrées $35–50) gives little hint of what's inside: a flight of fancy away from Mexico to some Victorian polished brass, mirror, and wood-paneled miniplanet, more San Francisco than San Francisco ever was. When you sit down at a table and ask for a menu, the tuxedo-attired waiter will probably do a double take, scurry away, and return with a small tray of a few thick steaks, a pork chop huge enough for two, and a big lobster. You choose one of these as the basis for your dinner. The meal proceeds from there like a Mozart symphony, through each delectable course, until dessert ($15), invariably served with a flourish. Reservations are recommended.

Entertainment and Events

SIDEWALK CAFÉS

Take a seat at one of the several shady Plazuela Machado sidewalk cafés and watch the passing parade. Later, you can enjoy the same by strolling a few blocks west to shorefront **Avenida Olas Altas** and take in the scene from a table at one of the cafés clustered around the old Hotel Belmar. If it's summer and you're lucky, you may get a chance to enjoy a Pacific Mexico rainstorm. It usually starts with a few warm drops on the side-walk. Then the wind starts the palms swaying. Pretty soon the lightning is crackling and the rain is pouring as if from a million celestial faucets. But no matter; you're comfortably seated, and even if you happen to get a little wet it's so warm you'll dry off right away.

Late afternoons on Olas Altas yield a feast of quiet people-watching delights. Perch yourself on the old *malecón* and watch the sunset, the surfers tackling the high waves *(olas altas)* offshore, and the kids, old folks, and loving couples strolling along the sidewalk.

After dark, stroll a few blocks south along the oceanfront, past the divers' point, and join the crowd at streetside enjoying the rainbow flutter and flash of the lights on the *Flow of Life* fountain.

Later, if you're in the mood for livelier entertainment, return to the sidewalk coffeehouse and restaurant **Copa de Leche** (Av. Olas Altas, next to the Hotel Belmar), where a live trio entertains patrons Thursday, Friday, and Saturday evenings.

NIGHTLIFE
Dancing and Discos

Dance music is plentiful in Mazatlán. You can start out by enjoying drinks or dinner with the medium-volume bands that play from around 8 P.M. at the more popular Golden Zone hotels, especially the **Playa Mazatlán,** tel. 669/989-0555, and others, such as **El Cid,** tel. 669/913-3333, and **Los Sábalos,** tel. 669/983-5333 or 669/983-5409. During the high season in late fall-winter, restaurant El Parador Español, tel. 669/913-0767, offers **flamenco** entertainment Friday and Saturday nights.

Then, after around 11 P.M., while the Mazatlán night is still young, go out and jump at one of several local discos. **Valentino's,** tel. 669/984-1666, with its jumble of white spires and turrets, perches on Punta Camarón, inspiring intense curiosity, if not wonder, among newcomers. Its three separate dance floors have the requisite flashing lights and speakers varying from loud and louder to loudest (with a booming bass audible for a couple of miles up and down the beach).

On the other hand, what **El Caracol,** at El Cid (tel. 669/913-3333, open seasonally Tues.–Sat.) lacks on the outside, it makes up on the inside. Here, one huge dance floor is split beneath two upper levels; patrons can navigate to the lower by sliding down a chute or slithering down a brass firehouse pole.

The discos, which charge a cover of about $20 and expect you to dress casually but decently (slacks and shirts, dresses or skirts and

blouses, and shoes), open around 10 P.M. and go on until 4 or 5 in the morning.

Bars and Hangouts

Mazatlán has a few romantic, softly lighted piano bars. Besides the suave **Mikonos** piano bar (at Camarón Sábalo and Rafael Buelna, on the left side of Valentino's disco), you can sample the elegant sophistication of **Señor Pepper's,** tel. 669/914-1101, a piano bar across from the Hotel Playa Real at the north end of Camarón Sábalo.

For high-volume 1970s rock and beer-and-popcorn camaraderie, **Jungle Juice** restaurant's upstairs bar on side street Garzas, corner of Laguna (one block north and one block inland from Hotel Playa Mazatlán), tel. 669/913-3315, is literally wall-to-wall customers during the high season. The same is true for the seasonally raucus **Guadalajara Grill,** diagonally across the street, and the open-air cantina **Shrimp Factory** around the corner (except at the Shrimp Factory there's more air). If all these bore you, walk south three blocks and rock to the high-volume salsa at **Tony's,** at the corner of Avenida Playa Gaviotas and Calz. Camarón Sábalo.

THEATER AND CINEMA

Mazatlán's busy menu of performances—drama, classical ballet, folkloric dance, symphony—centers around the **Teatro Ángela Peralta** at the Plazuela Machado's southwest corner. The schedule is fullest around the October–November **Sinaloa Fiesta de los Artes.**

For programs and more information, see the cultural calendar in either the *Viejo Mazatlán* or *Pacific Pearl* tourist newspapers. Also, you can drop by or call the Teatro Ángela Peralta box office (tel. 669/987-4447, in Spanish).

A number of Mazatlán cinemas screen first-run Hollywood movies, from about 4 P.M. ($3) daily. Try the six-screen **Cinemas Gaviotas** (Camarón Sábalo 218, tel. 669/983-7545), a few blocks north of Valentino's disco.

Tourist Shows

While a number of hotels present folkloric song and dance shows, the Hotel Playa Mazatlán's **Fiesta Mexicana** remains the hands-down favorite. The entire three-hour extravaganza, including a sumptuous buffet, begins at 7 P.M. sharp Tuesday and Saturday during high season (Saturday only during low). Call either the hotel (tel. 669/989-0555 or 669/913-5320) or a travel agent for confirmation and tickets, which run about $30 per adult, kids half price. There's a gratis beach fireworks show Sunday (high season only) at 8 P.M. It's popular, so arrive an hour early to ensure a good seat. Call the hotel to confirm.

Others are trying harder. Wednesday nights at 7:30 P.M., Hotel el Cid succeeds in capturing the flavor of Mexico with a folkloric fiesta, including a bountiful buffet, followed by a succession of colorful extravaganzas, varying from choruses of whirling señoritas and their *charro* partners to rope-flinging *vaqueros*. Call the Hotel el Cid (tel. 669/913-3333) for information and reservations (about $32, half price for kids).

FIESTAS

Mazatlán's century-old **Carnaval** is among Mexico's liveliest Mardi Gras celebrations. The merrymaking begins the week before Ash Wednesday (46 days before Easter Sunday, usually late February or early March), when the faithful ceremoniously receive ash marks on their foreheads, beginning the period of fasting called Lent. Mazatlán Carnaval anticipates all this in a weeklong festival of folk dances, balls, ballets, literature readings, beauty contests, and flower games. The celebration peaks on Shrove Tuesday (the day before the beginning of Lent) with a parade of floats and riotous revelers, which by this time includes everyone in town, culminating along Avenida Olas Altas. If you'd like to join in, reserve your hotel room (streetfront rooms at

the Hotels Posada Freeman, Siesta, and Belmar are best for Carnaval) at least six months in advance.

Fall visitors can enjoy events of the **Sinaloa Fiesta de los Artes,** which lately has begun around October 20 and continued through the first week in November. Find the list of programs, which include classical music and ballet and folkloric dance, in the tourist newspapers, *Pacific Pearl,* tel. 669/913-0117, or *Viejo Mazatlán,* tel./fax 669/985-3781.

Mazatlán heats up again for the December 8 patronal **Fiesta de la Inmaculada** (Feast of the Immaculate Conception), which kicks off two solid weeks of merrymaking, first with the **Fiesta de la Virgen de Guadalupe** (Virgin of Guadalupe) on December 12 and later with traditional Christmas Eve *posada* processions and midnight and early-morning Masses (*mañanitas*) through December 25.

KID-FRIENDLY ATTRACTIONS

When your kids get tired of digging in the sand and splashing in the pool, take them to the **aquarium.**

For a different kind of frolic, take the kids to **Mazagua** water park (Playa Cerritos s/n, tel./fax 669/988-0041, 10 A.M.–6 P.M. daily, around $10 for everyone over 3 years old), where they can slip down the 100-foot-long Kamikaze slide, swish along on the toboggan, loll in the wave pool, or simply splash in the regular pool. Follow the right fork toward Highway 15 near the north end of Calz. Camarón Sábalo and you'll immediately see the water park on the left. The park has a restaurant and snack bar.

During the adult fun and games of Carnaval, there's no reason your kids have to feel left out if you take them to the **"Carnival."** You'll find it by looking for the Ferris wheel (customarily near the bus terminal on Calle Tamazula and the Highway 15 downtown ingress boulevard, behind the Hotel Sands.

Sports and Recreation

A good morning place to start wandering around is the little beach at the beginning of Playa Norte, at the north end of Avenida 5 de Mayo, where the fishers sell their daily catches. As the cluster of buyers busily bid for the choicest tuna, shrimp, *dorado* (mahimahi), and mackerel, pelicans and seagulls scurry after the leftovers.

Come back later, around supper time, to enjoy the end product: fresh-cooked seafood (try Restaurant Camachín), accompanied by the tunes of one of many strolling mariachi bands, perhaps even one of the famous Sinaloan-style brass bands. If someone else is paying, just sit back and enjoy, especially the tuba solo. If you are paying, make sure that you agree upon the price, usually around $2 per selection, before the performance begins.

Around noon, the area around the central plaza downtown (Juárez and Ángel Flores) is equally entertaining. Take a seat beneath the shade of the big trees and get your shoes polished for about $1.

SHADY PLAZAS AND LIVELY MARKETS

Downtown Mazatlán has a number of neighborhood squares and colorful small markets (best in the morning or early afternoon) within strolling distance of the central plaza. Six blocks north along Calle Guillermo Nelson, take a turn around **Plaza Zaragoza.** Then, from the plaza's northeast corner, head two blocks east and a block north to the **shrimp market** at the corner of Aquiles Serdán and Luis Zuñiga, where a platoon of vendors offer buckets of plump, fresh-off-the-boat shrimp. Continue two blocks north along Zuñiga to the **flower market,** at the corner of 16 de Septiembre, stuffed with lovely bouquets of roses, lilies, marigolds, and much more.

West of the central plaza, two short blocks

© BRUCE WHIPPERMAN

Mornings are especially colorful at Mazatlán's flower market.

behind the Palacio Municipal, find the **Plazuela de los Leones** (corner of Calles Ángel Flores and Niños Héroes), marked by a pair of brass lions guarding the city library. Upstairs, you can browse the venerable collection of the all-English **Benjamin Franklin Library.**

In a southerly direction from the cathedral, stroll along Juárez three blocks; at Constitución, turn right one block to **Plazuela Machado,** the gem of old Mazatlán. Depending upon the time, you may want to stop for a soda or juice at a sidewalk café or *refresquería* on the north side of plaza, or a light lunch and a round of billiards at the friendly, elegantly Victorian-style (or Porfirian) Café Pacífico at the adjacent corner. Across the square, in the midafternoons on school days, you can take a park bench seat and listen to the sounds of violin lessons that sometimes waft down from the upstairs chambers of the Academia Ángela Peralta.

If you're in the mood for a little browsing, take in the Plazuela Machado **bazaar** Fridays and Saturdays beginning around noon. Booths of local artists, artisans, and entrepreneurs line the square, offering everything from fine handmade jewelry and art-to-wear, to antiques, books, and bric-a-brac.

WALKING, JOGGING, AND HORSEBACK RIDING

The Mazatlán heat keeps walkers and joggers near the shoreline. On the beaches themselves, the long, flat strands of Playa Norte (along Avenida del Mar), Playa Gaviotas (north from about the Hotel los Flores), and the adjoining Playa Sábalo (north from about El Cid) provide firm stretches for walking and jogging. If you prefer an even firmer surface, the best uncluttered stretch of the *malecón* seaside sidewalk is along Avenida del Mar from Valentino's disco south about three miles to the Fisherman's Monument.

Let the horse take you beach-walking from Ginger's Bilingual Horses (north end of Playa Bruja, tel. 669/988-1254 or 669/922-2026, www.mazinfo.com/gingershorses/index.htm, 10 A.M.–4 P.M. Mon.–Sat., $25/hr. To reach the Bilingual Horses, take a taxi, about $8, or

ride the Cerritos bus all the way north, to the end of the line.

WATER SPORTS

During days of calm water, you can safely swim beyond the gentle breakers, about 50 yards off **Playa Gaviotas** and **Playa Sábalo.** Heed the usual precautions.

On rough-water days, you'll have to do your laps in a hotel pool, since there is no public pool in Mazatlán. Some of the big hotels, especially El Cid, tel. 669/913-3333 in the Zona Dorada, allow free day-use of their pool by nonguests.

There are several challenging intermediate **surfing** spots along the Mazatlán shoreline, mostly adjacent to rocky points, such as **Pinos** (next to Ciencias del Mar off Paseo Claussen), **Punta Camarón** (at Valentino's disco), and **Punta Cerritos** at the far north end of the *malecón.* Mazatlán's best rock-free surfing beach is uncrowded north-end **Playa Brujas,** with consistent 3–6-foot swells.

Bodysurfing and boogie boarding are popular on Mazatlán's beaches. Boogie boards rent for about $3 an hour on the beachfronts of some Zona Dorada hotels, such as Los Sábalos, Playa Mazatlán, El Cid, and Hotel Playa Real.

Sailboarding is possible nearly anywhere along Mazatlán's beaches. An especially good, smooth spot is the protected inlet at the north end of Avenida Sábalo Cerritos. Bring your own equipment, as there's little sailboarding rental gear available in Mazatlán.

Aqua Sports Center at El Cid, tel. 669/913-3333, ext. 3341, and beach shops at other hotels rent kayaks ($25 per hour) and Hobie Cats, small catamaran sailboats ($30 per hour, three-person limit) to paddle or sail from the beach.

Snorkeling and Scuba Diving

The water near Mazatlán's beaches is often too churned up for good visibility. Serious snorkelers and divers head offshore to the outer shoals of Isla Venados and Isla Chivos. A number of shops along the Zona Dorada beaches arrange such trips. The best-equipped is **El Cid's Aqua**

Sports Center, tel. 669/913-3333, ext. 3341, marked by the clutter of equipment on the beach by Hotel el Cid. A three-hour scuba excursion, including equipment and instructor, runs $100 per person ($30 for pool instruction, $70 for a one-tank dive), while snorkelers can go along for about $30, including mask and fins.

Personal Watercraft and Parasailing

The highly maneuverable snowmobile-like personal watercraft have completely replaced water-skiing at Mazatlán. Three or four of them can usually be seen tearing up the water, hotdogging over big waves, gyrating between the swells, and racing each other far offshore. For a not-so-cheap thrill, rent one of them at **Aqua Sports Center** at El Cid, tel. 669/913-3333, ext. 3341, which has the best and most equipment, for about $50 per half-hour for one, $70 for two people.

Parasailing chutes are continually ballooning high over Zona Dorada beaches. For about $30 for a 10-minute ride, you can fly like a bird; arrangements can be made at any of the following hotels: El Cid, Playa Mazatlán, or Playa Real.

Boat Launching

If you have your own boat, you can launch it at one of several public ramps in Mazatlán. One ramp is at the **Ciencias del Mar** college (on the point just past the boat cove on Paseo Claussen). The school office inside sells tickets for about $20 to use the ramp for one day 7 A.M.–6 P.M. The tariff for a one-month permit is only about triple that. That entitles you to anchor your boat, among a dozen neighbors, in the sheltered Playa Norte cove for a month. No facilities are available except the ramp, however.

Another boat ramp is at **Club Náutico** (Explanada del Faro s/n, Mazatlán, Sinaloa 82000, tel./fax 669/981-5195), at the far end of the line of sportfishing docks, below the lighthouse hill. A one-day launching permit runs about $20, plus $6 per day docking fee. The club has a first-class yacht harbor with hoists, a repair shop, and gasoline, but unfortunately little or no room for outsiders to store boats, either in or out of the water. You may, however, be able to get permission to park your boat and trailer on the road outside the gate.

You may also launch and dock your boat at the **El Cid Marina** (at the north end of Calz. Camarón Sábalo, just after the Hotel Faro Mazatlán, el. 669/916-3468 or 669/913-3333, ext. 6598, fax 669/916-6294, gcecevallos @elcid.com.mx, www.elcid.com) for about $35 per day (three-day minimum), $350 per month.

SPORTFISHING

Competent captains and years of experience have placed Mazatlán among the world's leading billfish (marlin, swordfish, and sailfish) ports. The several licensed *flotas deportivas* (sports fleets) line up along the jetty road beneath the south-end El Faro point. They vary, mostly in size of fleet; some have two or three boats, others have a dozen. Boats generally return with about three big fish—one of them a whopping marlin or sailfish—per day.

The biggest is the **Bill Heimpel Star Fleet,** owned and operated by personable Bill Heimpel, a descendant of a German immigrant family. During the high season he organizes groups so you can fish without having to rent a whole boat. One day's fishing runs about $100 per person (add $20 for a nonfishing guest), including tackle and drinks. Entire boats for about eight passengers (five of whom can fish at a time) rent for around $350 per day, complete. During the May–October low season, reservations only a few days in advance are all that is necessary; winter high-season reservations are highly recommended at least a month in advance. For more information, contact the fleet, P.O. Box 129B, Camionera Central, Mazatlán, Sinaloa 82000, tel./fax 669/982-2665 or 669/982-3878, toll-free U.S. tel. 888/882-9614, starfleet@mazatlan.com.mx, www.starfleet.com.mx.

A bit farther down the scale, you can check out some of the local boats right at the dock, such as **Bibi Fleet** (tel. 669/981-3649, fax

669/982-5155, gogetem@bibifleet.com, www .bibifleet.com) and **Flota Anna Mar** (tel. 669/982-3830). Both Bibi and Anna Mar customarily rent out a big 42-foot, six-person boat with skipper, bait, and poles for billfish for about $250 low season, $300 high. Ask and they may also be able to furnish a group of four with a well-equipped *super-panga* (super-launch), with shade cover and skipper, for half a day to catch medium-sized fry, such as 30-pound tuna, or *sierra,* for around $200.

On the other hand, if price is not a big factor, go to the **El Cid Marina** (tel. 669/916-3468 or 669/913-3333, ext. 6598, fax 669/916-6294, gcecevallos@elcid.com.mx, www.elcid.com) at the north end of Calz. Camarón Sábalo, where the boulevard bends right around the lagoon, just after the Hotel Faro Mazatlán. There **Aries Fleet,** which "proudly supports the Catch and Release program of the Billfish Foundation," offers either individual reservations in season at about $100 per person, or five elaborately equipped boats to rent. Complete charters run from about $375 (28 feet, five lines) to $450 (35 feet, six passengers, five lines) and up. For more information and reservations, call a travel agent or contact Aries Fleet directly.

If you're on a tight fishing budget, try negotiating with one of the fishermen on **Playa Norte** (at the foot of 5 de Mayo at Paseo Claussen) to take you and a few friends out in his *panga* for half a day. He can supply lines and bait enough to bring in several big mahimahi and red snapper for a total price of maybe $75, depending on the season.

ECOADVENTURING

The very professional and green **Sendero Mexico** (tel./fax 669/940-8687 or 669/940-6688, info@senderomexico.com, www.sendero mexico.com), affiliated with the American Birding Association, guides a number of low- and medium-difficulty nature adventure tours. Choose from kayaking offshore islands, bird-watching in mangrove wetlands and upland forest, foothill woodland hiking and over-

night camping, mountain biking, snorkeling, and more.

Onca Explorations (Av. del Mar 1022, on the Playa Norte *malecón,* tel. 669/990-1632, local cell 044-669/116-0301, oscarguzon@oncaexplorations.com, www .oncaexplorations.com), run by professional biologist and nature lover Oscar Guzón, offers an intriguing trio of local excursions: an offshore humpback whale and Pacific bottlenose dolphin-watching expedition (5 hours, usually December–March); an exploration of the fascinatingly ancient Las Labradas hidden beach petroglyph site (6 hours, year-round); and an offshore-island hiking-snorkeling adventure tour, with harbor seals, dolphins, and flocks of sea birds to see along the way (4 hours, year-round).

Alternatively, check out **Hudson Tours** (tel. 669/913-5355, local cell 044-669/994-5730, hudsonmaz@yahoo.com, www.hudsontours .com), operated by very experienced surf instructor, guide, and nature enthusiast Robert Hudson. He offers a wide range of small-group tours and activities, from city tours and country hikes to surfing lessons and spearfishing.

Pronatours (in the El Cid hotel complex at Plaza Dorada, tel. 669/916-7720 or 669/913-3333, ext. 3490 or 6581, pronatours@elcid .com.mx, www.elcid.com), besides leading Mazatlan city tours and regional excursions, also guides a number of easy outdoor tours. These include a turtle hatchery, offshore Deer Island, Stone Island jungle tour, and kayaking, snorkeling, scuba diving, and deep-sea fishing.

TENNIS AND GOLF

If you're planning on playing lots of tennis in Mazatlán, check into one of the several hotels, such as Playa Mazatlán, Inn at Mazatlán, or El Cid, that have courts. The El Cid tennis courts (tel. 669/913-3333, ext. 3261) charge $16/hour even for guests. You can rent a court at the moderately priced **Racquet Club Las Gaviotas,** tel. 669/913-5939 (three clay, four hard courts, some lighted), for about $10/hour. Tennis lessons, about $20/hour, are also available. They're popular and likely to be crowded during the winter season, however.

In-town Mazatlán golf is rather exclusive. The 18-hole course at **El Cid,** tel. 669/913-3333, ext. 3261, is the only one within the city limits, and during the high winter-spring season it may allow only its guests (and those of a few other deluxe hotels) to play. On the other hand, during low season, outsiders may play for a $75 greens and a $20 caddy fee. Two-person carts rent for about $50.

Mazatlán's other golf course is the **Golf Club Estrella del Mar,** accessible by taxi or car off the airport entrance road. About a quarter mile before the airport terminal, turn right at the signed side road; continue nine miles until you get to the boat landing, where a launch will take you across to the golf course. Fees run about $110 ($75 May–Oct.), cart included. The club runs early-morning shuttles from its Zona Dorada office, next to Banamex, near the Dairy Queen, corner of Gaviotas and Camarón Sábalo; call the golf course at tel. 669/982-3300, ext. 3019, or its Zona Dorada office, tel. 669/914-0362, or toll-free Mexico tel. 01-800/727-4653, for information and schedule.

SPECTATOR SPORTS

Every Sunday from mid-December through Easter, bullfights (not really "fights"), called *corridas de toros,* are held at the big bullring, Plaza Monumental (Av. R. Buelna at Av. de la Marina), about a mile from the beach. The ritual begins at 4 P.M. sharp. Get your tickets through a travel agency or at the bullring.

A few times a year, the Mazatlán professional association of *charros* (gentleman cowboys) holds a rodeolike *charreada.* Some events (such as jumping from one racing, unbroken horse to another, or trying to flatten an angry steer by twisting its tail!) make the garden-variety North American rodeo appear tame. For more information, consult a travel agency or Mazatlán Tourist Information, tel. 669/981-8883 to -8887, near the Plazuela Machado.

Los Venados (The Deer), Mazatlán's entry in the Mexican Pacific Coast Baseball (Béisbol) League (AAA), begins its schedule in early October and continues into the spring. Get your tickets at the stadium (Estadio Teodoro Mariscal), whose night lights are so bright that when the team is home you can't help but see a quarter mile inland from beachfront Avenida del Mar. Baseball fever in Mazatlán heats up to epidemic proportions when Culiacán, Los Venados's archrival, is in town.

Shopping

Judging from the platoons of racks in the Zona Dorada and the Mercado Central, T-shirts would seem to be the chief export of Mazatlán. Behind the racks, however, Mazatlán's curio shops stock an amazing bounty of handicrafts from all over the country. The best route to quality purchases at reasonable prices is first to look downtown for the lowest prices, next search the Zona Dorada for the best quality, and then make your choice.

CENTRAL MARKET

The town *mercado* occupies one square block near the cathedral, between Calles Juárez, Ocampo, Serdan, and Valle. Here, bargaining is both expected and essential unless you don't mind paying $20 for a $5 item.

Although the colorful mélange of meat and vegetable stalls occupies most of the floor space, several small handicrafts shops are tucked inside on the Juárez and Valle sides (west and south) and along all four outside sidewalks. For example, nothing typifies Mexico more than huaraches. One of Mazatlán's best selections is the family-owned **Huarachería Internacional,** on the outside market sidewalk at the corner of Ocampo and Juárez. Its goods, much from the highlands of

Michoacán, are all authentic and, with bargaining, very reasonably priced.

OLD TOWN SHOPS AND THE PLAZUELA MACHADO BAZAAR

The restored Olas Altas (Old Town) district has attracted a number of worthy galleries and silver, handicrafts, and antique shops. The original is **Casa Antigua,** two blocks east of Olas Altas (Mariano Escobedo 206 Poniente, tel. 669/982-5236, 9 A.M.–5 P.M. Mon.–Sat.). Browse its eclectic all-Mexico assortment—shiny papier-mâché, glittering jewelry, Tlaquepaque stoneware, exquisite Talavera ware, and much more.

Walk a few blocks east, near the Plazuela Machado and the Teatro Ángela Peralta, and visit **Nidart** gallery and workshop (Libertad 45, half a block south of the theater, at the corner of Carnaval, tel. 669/985-5991, www.nidart .com, 10 A.M.–3 P.M. Mon.–Sat.). A labor of love of artist-founders Rak and Loa, Nidart showcases a museum of unique art for sale. Items vary from whimsical ceramic figurines and silver kaleidoscopes to indigenous pottery curios and fanciful leather sculptures. An absolute must-see; it's very hard to visit without buying something.

Additional Old Town shops and galleries that are also worth a look include **Regalos Indio** (Ángel Flores 206 Poniente, tel. 669/981-3753, Mon.–Sat. 9 A.M.–6 P.M.); **Viejo Mazatlán** (Sixto Osuna 309, tel. 669/982-2798); and **Arte Activo** (Heriberto Frías 1502, by the Plazuela Machado, west side, tel. 669/982-5608), which offers paintings and sculpture.

Community leaders have lately promoted the arts and crafts **bazaar** Friday and Saturday afternoons and evenings, beginning around noon. Booths of local artists, artisans, and entrepreneurs offer a wide range, from fine handmade jewelry and art to wear, to antiques and used books.

ZONA DORADA

The Zona Dorada presents a grand variety of shops, in small shopping centers, hotel malls, and streetside along Avenida Camarón Sábalo. Nearly everything you're looking for, however, probably can be found in the concentration of many good and unusual shops along the side street Avenida Playa Gaviotas, which forks left, one-way, off Avenida Camarón Sábalo a block north of Valentino's disco. The following are a few highlights, as you move north on Avenida Playa Gaviotas.

One of your first stops should be at a pair of shops in the Hotel Playa Mazatlán shopping center on the beach side of Avenida Playa Gaviotas.

First, let the attractive selection of **Mexico, Mexico** (tel. 669/989-0555, ext. 1000, 9 A.M.– 8 P.M. Mon.–Sat., 10 A.M.–4 P.M. Sun.) lead you on, past its racks of colorful women's cotton resortwear, mysterious Huichol *cuadras* (yarn paintings), eerie Jalisco masks, and shining Oaxaca tinware.

Continue one door uphill to admire the glistening collection of the **Playa** silver store (tel. 669/989-0555, ext. 222). Virtually all Mexican silver jewelry is crafted far away, in Taxco,

selecting costume jewelry at the Plazuela Machado Bazaar

© BRUCE WHIPPERMAN

Guerrero. Without bargaining, Mazatlán silver prices may be a bit steep. You can compare prices against other shops or ask the staff to weigh the piece. Many shops sell silver jewelry from one U.S. dollar per gram for simple pieces. If your choice costs significantly more than that, you'd better bargain.

Back on the street, head north half a block to the big **Mister Indio** all-Mexico crafts store next to the Azteca Inn (tel. 669/913-4923, 9 A.M.–7:30 P.M., Mon.–Sat.). Here, owners display an out-of-the-ordinary selection, including bronze and ceramic sculpture and attractive classical fresco reproduction fragments.

Continue half a block north to the corner of side-street Garzas (marked by the Shrimp Factory restaurant-bar). Turn the corner and continue one block east, to the corner of Laguna, and find **Madonna** (tel. 669/914-2389, 9 A.M.–8 P.M. Mon.–Sat.). Inside, enjoy the artfully selected all-Mexico jewelry and crafts assortment, including much reasonably priced (from $.80 per gram) silver from Taxco, a fetching collection of indigenous Huichol beaded artifacts, iridescent opals, and intriguing wood and stone masks.

Back on Avenida Playa Gaviotas, a block north, step into **Shell City** (Av. Playa Gaviotas 407, tel. 669/913-1301, 9 A.M.–8 P.M. daily), a de facto museum of shells (and perhaps the reason they've become so scarce on Mazatlán's beaches). Constellations of pearly curios—swirling conches, iridescent abalones, bushy corals, and, in one single deviation, whimsical coconut faces—fill Shell City's seeming acres of displays.

After Shell City, move next door, north, to **Centro Comercial Pancho's** and look over the welter of goods—silver, *huipiles,* ceramics, onyx—for sale. Best here are probably **Rossana's Curios,** with its minimuseum of huaraches and, across the aisle, **El Buho** (tel. 669/916-5486), with a treasury of Huichol art—bead masks, ceremonial cups, yarn paintings—and miniatures, wooden skeletons, and papier-mâché *alebrijes* (fanciful animals).

Cross the street, to the beach side, and continue your browsing in the intimate beachfront **Las Cabañas** mall. Some shops stand out:

Garcia's (tel. 669/913-8246), with a trove of fine ceramics; **Mr. Patrick** (tel. 669/914-0400), with fine pewter, across the aisle; **Melissa and Mike** (tel. 669/913-097), with handsome Taxco silver; and farther back, where the ocean breeze blows through, **Yama Mara,** with a treasury of hand-embroidered *traje* and *ropa típica huipiles* and dresses from Oaxaca, Chiapas, Puebla, and Yucatán. Beyond that, take a break at a breezy, sea-view table at **Restaurant Pancho's.**

Return across the street a few doors north to **Pardo Jewelry** (411 Av. Playa Gaviotas, tel./fax 669/914-3354, tel. 669/914-1000, 9:30 A.M.–8 P.M. Mon.–Sat.), which specializes in fine gems. The glittering silver- and gold-set diamonds, rubies, emeralds, lapis, opals, and amethysts are worth appreciating whether you're buying or not.

SUPERMARKETS AND WAREHOUSE STORES

For a big, air-conditioned selection of everything, from hardware and cosmetics to film and groceries, local people and tourists flock to Mexico's Kmart look-alikes, **Gigante** on Rafael Buelna, about a mile inland from Valentino's disco, tel. 669/986-7298, 9 A.M.–9 P.M. daily), and **Comercial Mexicana** (at the **Gran Plaza** mall, tel. 669/984-3090). Get to the Gran Plaza by following Rafael Buelna inland from Valentino's, turn right just past the La Posta trailer park, and continue for a quarter mile to Comercial Mexicana's big orange pelican emblem.

Both **Wal-Mart** and **Sam's Club** have arrived in Mazatlán. The former is also at the Gran Plaza off Avenida Reforma (go west from Valentino's disco along Rafael Buelna a few blocks; after the La Posta Trailer Park, turn right on Reforma and continue to the Gran Plaza on the left.) Find Sam's Club on the downtown ingress boulevard, old Highway 15, about a quarter mile south of its intersection with Avenida Rafael Buelna, near the corner of Calle Lucio Blanco.

PHOTOGRAPHY

Although many big hotel shops develop and sell film, their services are limited and expensive.

Competition lowers the prices on "photo row," Calle Ángel Flores downtown, just west of the central plaza. Try **Photo Arauz** (Ángel Flores 607, tel. 669/982-2015, 8 A.M.–8 P.M. Mon.– Sat., 8 A.M.–2 P.M. Sun.) for both digital and film supplies, including reasonable one-hour developing and jumbo printing ($12) and several point-and-shoot cameras.

Information

TOURIST INFORMATION OFFICE

Lots of help and literature are available at Mazatlán government tourism headquarters, in the Old Town at the corner of Carnaval and Mariano Escobedo, a block north from the northeast corner of Plazuela Machado, 9 A.M.–5 P.M. Mon.–Fri. Alternatively, contact them via tel. 669/981-8883 through - 8887, fax 669/981-8890 or 669/981-8891, email tursina@prodigy.net.mx or informacion .turismo@sinaloa.gob.mx, or visit www .sinaloa-travel.com.

PUBLICATIONS

Several stores in the Zona Dorado slake visitors' thirst for English-language books, newspapers, and magazines. Perhaps the most bountiful selection is at **Mazatlán Book and Coffee Company** (across from Hotel Costa de Oro, behind Banco Santander Serfin, tel. 669/916-7899, 10 A.M.–3 P.M. Wed.–Sat. low season, 10 A.M.–9 P.M. high). Select from a small library of novels, magazines, maps, and dictionaries (and there's a certified masseuse next door).

Half a block north, corner of Camarón Sábalo and G. Ruiz, drop into **Rico's Coffee Bar** (tel. 669/913-1444, 8 A.M.–11 P.M. daily) for the latest American, Canadian, and British newspapers and magazines.

You can sample the big magazine rack at **Restaurant VIPs** (across Camarón Sábalo from the Cinemas Gaviotas, tel. 669/914-0754 or 669/913-4016, 7 A.M.–midnight daily). It stocks several dozen titles, mostly popular novels and many U.S. magazines.

During the November–Easter high season, you will often find the *Los Angeles Times, USA Today,* and the daily English-language Miami *Herald* at **Kioskito Tin Marin** (at Gaviotas, diagonally across Camarón Sábalo from the Dairy Queen, 10 A.M.–8 P.M. daily).

Old Mazatlán's revival now includes an English-language **rental library** (Sixto Osuna 115, 9 A.M.–2 P.M. Mon.–Sat.)

For announcements of local cultural events, tours, restaurants, and interesting feature articles, pick up a copies of *Pacific Pearl* and *Viejo Mazatlán,* Mazatlán's visitors' monthlies, widely available at tourist shops, restaurants, and hotels. If you can't find copies, call or drop into their respective offices: *Pacific Pearl* in shopping Plaza San Jorge, across the street, south, behind the pharmacy, from the Dairy Queen corner (tel./fax 669/913-0117, tel. 669/913-4411, webmaster@pacificpearl.com, www .pacificpearl.com, 9 A.M.–5 P.M. Mon.–Fri., 9 A.M.–2 P.M. Sat.), or subscribe online for $13; *Viejo Mazatlán* downtown, at Belasario Domínguez 1401A (tel. 669/985-3781, tel/fax 669/982-2798, editor@viejo-mazatlan .com, www.viejo-mazatlan.com).

PUBLIC LIBRARY

Mazatlán's respectable public library is downtown, at **Plazuela de los Leones,** on Ángel Flores a few short blocks behind the Palacio Municipal (8 A.M.–8 P.M. Mon.–Fri., 9 A.M.–noon Sat.). Of special interest is the upper-floor **Benjamin Franklin Library,** row upon row of venerable volumes of classic American literature.

Services

MONEY EXCHANGE

All banks compensate for short hours by 24-hour ATMs, which have become the peso source of choice in Mazatlán. During bank hours, obtain the most pesos for cash and traveler's checks at **Banamex** (Camarón Sábalo 424, tel. 669/914-0000 or 669/914-0001, or 669/914-0002), in the Zona Dorada across the corner, south, from Dairy Queen. Banamex has both an ATM and a special longer-hours cashier outside and to the right of the regular bank, which may be open 9 A.M. to as late as 4 P.M. Mon.–Fri., 10 A.M.–2 P.M. Sat. during the high winter season. The downtown main branch, also with ATM at the central plaza, corner of Juárez and Ángel Flores, tel. 669/982-7733, changes both Canadian and U.S. dollars and traveler's checks 9 A.M.–4 P.M. Mon.–Fri., closed weekends.

On the other hand, **HSBC** (Hong Kong Shanghai Banking Corporation) offers both ATM and much longer money-changing hours: 8 A.M.–7 P.M. Mon.–Fri., 8 A.M.–3 P.M. Sat., at two branches, on Camarón Sábalo, about three blocks north of Dairy Queen, tel. 669/916-3425, and downtown, corner of Belisario Domínguez and Ángel Flores, four short blocks west of the main plaza downtown, tel. 669/982-5579.

Furthermore, after a long absence, there's a bank doing business on Avenida Olas Altas: **Bancomer** (corner of Sixto Osuna tel. 669/981-2090 or 669/985-0386, 8:30 A.M.–4 P.M. Mon.–Fri.).

After bank hours, change cash and traveler's checks at one of the many **casas de cambio** by the banks along Calz. Camarón Sábalo (such as the counter at the north end of Avenida Playa Gaviotas, across from Dairy Queen, open 9:30 A.M.–6:30 P.M. Mon.–Sat., 10 A.M.–4 P.M. Sun., tel. 669/913-9209).

American Express maintains a Zona Dorada money counter and travel agency on Camarón Sábalo (half a block north of the Dairy Queen, 9 A.M.–6 P.M. Mon.–Fri., 9 A.M.–1 P.M. Sat., tel. 669/913-0600, fax 669/916-5908). It gives bank rates for American Express U.S. dollar traveler's checks; no other traveler's checks are accepted, however.

COMMUNICATIONS

For routine mail, use the mailboxes *(buzones)* at the big hotels, such as Los Sábalos, Playa Mazatlán, El Cid, and others.

Otherwise, go to one of the branch **post offices.** The main branch *(correo)* is next to the central plaza downtown (corner of Juárez and Ángel Flores, tel. 669/981-2121, 8 A.M.–6:30 P.M. Mon.–Fri., 9 A.M.–1 P.M. Sat., philatelic services in the morning only). Alternatively, go to the central bus station branch (four blocks inland from Playa Norte, behind the Hotel Sands, 8 A.M.–3 P.M. Mon.–Fri.).

Telecomunicaciones, which offers public telephone, fax, Internet, and money orders, has two Mazatlán branches, both open 8 A.M.–7:30 P.M. Mon.–Fri., 8 A.M.–noon Sat.–Sun. Choose either the downtown branch, in the post office building, tel. 669/981-2220, or the central bus station branch, tel./fax 669/982-0354.

Post@Ship (on Calz. Camarón Sábalo, across from VIPs restaurant a few blocks south of Dairy Queen, tel. 669/916-4010, fax 669/916-4011, 9 A.M.–6:30 P.M. Mon.–Fri., 9 A.M.–2 P.M. Sat.) provides many postal services and more, including stamps, mailboxes, Mexpost express mail, P.O. boxes with a Laredo, Texas, address, fax, Internet access, and word processing.

It's much cheaper and usually quicker to use Ladatel calling cards in sidewalk public telephones. The cards are widely available in denominations of about $3, $5, and $10 at streetfront liquor stores, pharmacies, and mini-markets. For street-phone calls to the United States and Canada, simply dial 001, then the area code and local number.

HOSPITALS AND PHARMACIES

If you get sick, it's probably best to let your hotel get you a physician. Otherwise, go to one of

Mazatlán's several good hospitals. A 24-hour on-duty staff of specialists earns the **Hospital Militar** high recommendations. Despite its exclusive-sounding title, anyone can receive for-fee treatment at the Hospital Militar, in the Olas Altas district (Malpica and Venus, one block from the Hotel Siesta, tel. 669/981-2079).

Another good place to be sick is the shiny, big **Hospital Sharp** (Rafael Buelna and Calz. Jesus Kumate, about a quarter mile along Buelna from Valentino's disco, tel. 669/986-5676). One of Mexico's newest and best, Hospital Sharp has a cadre of highly trained specialists using its mountain of high-tech equipment to set new Mexican diagnostic and care standards. Prices, however, are generally much higher than in other Mexican hospitals.

The **Cruz Roja** (private Red Cross; tel. 669/981-3690) operates ambulances and is usually called to auto accidents when the victims are incapacitated. The Cruz Roja hospital is not highly recommended, however. Tell the ambulance to take you to Hospital Militar or Sharp, if you can manage it.

If you must have a bona fide American-trained doctor, try surgeon Dr. Gilberto Robles Guevara's **Clínica Mazatlán** (Zaragoza 609, corner 5 de Mayo, office tel. 669/981-2917, home tel. 669/985-1923) on the downtown "doctors' row." Dr. Robles Guevara is the local affiliate of IAMAT, the International Association for Medical Assistance to Travelers.

Farmacias in Mexico are allowed wide latitude to diagnose illnesses and dispense medicines. For a physician and pharmacy all in one, and right on the *malecón,* try **Farmacia Ángel,** run by friendly Dr. Ángel Avila Tirado, who examines, diagnoses, prescribes, and rings up the sale on the spot. Find him on Avenida del Mar, one block north of the Fisherman's Monument, tel. 669/982-4746 or 669/981-6831, 9 A.M.–9 P.M. daily.

Another good pharmacy is **Farmacia Moderna,** with many Mazatlán branches, all open 8 A.M.–9 P.M. Mon.–Sat.: downtown, at the corner of 5 de Mayo and 21 Marzo, behind the Palacio Municipal, tel. 669/981-0202 or 669/981-6266; in the Zona Dorada, next

to Banamex, just south of Dairy Queen, tel. 669/913-4277 or 669/913-4333; also in the Zona Dorada, at Plaza Pueblito, across from the Inn at Mazatlán, tel. 669/914-0044 (this one is also open on Sundays). After hours, call the 24-hour prescription number, tel. 669/916-5233.

POLICE AND FIRE EMERGENCIES

For police emergencies in the Zona Dorada, the special **Policía Turística,** which patrols the Zona Dorada exclusively, can respond quickly. Have a taxi whisk you to the Golden Zone sub-station, or dial emergency number 080.

For downtown police emergencies, contact the *preventiva* police, in the Palacio Municipal on the central plaza, or dial emergency number 066.

In case of fire, call the *bomberos* (firefighters), emergency number 068.

IMMIGRATION AND CUSTOMS

If you lose your tourist card, be prepared by having made a copy beforehand; next best is your airline ticket itinerary or receipt, indicating your arrival date in Mexico. Take one or both of these to **Migración** at the airport (tel. 669/981-6611, 10 A.M.–4 P.M. daily); or to Aquiles Serdán and Playas Gemelas, on the south side of downtown, two blocks north of the ferry dock (tel. 669/981-3813, 8 A.M.–2 P.M. Mon.–Fri., closed weekends). This downtown office is also the place to extend your visa (up to 180 days total).

For customs matters, contact the **Aduana** (customs) at the airport, tel. 669/982-2461; or in the old historic building at V. Carranza 107, corner of Cruz, in the Olas Altas district, tel. 669/981-6109 or 669/981-1570; both are open 8:30 A.M.–6 P.M. Mon.–Fri.

CONSULATES

The **United States Consular Agent** helps U.S. citizens with legal and other urgent matters at the Golden Zone office on Avenida Playa Gaviotas, directly across from the Hotel Playa Mazatlán (tel./fax 669/916-5889, mazagent@mzt.megared.net, 10 A.M.–2 P.M. Mon.–Fri.). In true emergencies, call local Mazatlán cell tel.

044-669/918-0303, or call the closest U.S. consulate, in Hermosillo, tel. 01-662/289-3500, or in Mexico City, tel. 01-55/5080-2000.

The **Canadian Consular Office** on Avenida Playa Gaviotas, just adjacent to the Hotel Playa Mazatlán, tel. 669/913-7320, fax 669/914-6655, is open 9 A.M.–1 P.M. Mon.–Fri. In an emergency, contact the embassy in Mexico City, toll-free tel. 01-800/706-2900.

Belgium, Finland, Italy, Germany, and France customarily maintain Mazatlán consular officers. See the local telephone Yellow Pages, under *Embajadas, Legaciones, y Consulados,* for contact telephone numbers, or ask the U.S. or Canadian agents above.

LANGUAGE COURSES AND LESSONS

The downtown **Centro de Idiomas** (Language Center; Callejon Aurora 203, a block or two west of Plazuela Machado, tel. 669/985-5606, fax 669/982-2053, info@spanishlink .org, www.spanishlink.org), owned and operated by very knowledgeable American resident Dixie Davis, offers good beginning and advanced Spanish courses. Registration and all materials run about $100; tuition is about $130/week for small, two-hour daily classes. The center also arranges homestay and person-to-person programs.

Alternatively, you could check out the Spanish schools and teachers who regularly advertise in the *Viejo Mazatlán* and *Pacific Pearl* tourist newspapers. These include **Martha Armenta,** director of the English/Spanish for All language school (tel./fax 669/986-2471, www .mexonline.com/efa.htm), or experienced translator and teacher **Sean Hennesy** (669/913-2484, email sinaloaverdesticky@ yahoo.com).

Getting There and Away

BY AIR

A number of reliable U.S. and Mexican airlines connect Mazatlán with many destinations in Mexico and the United States.

Alaska Airlines flights connect daily with Los Angeles, San Francisco, Portland, Seattle-Tacoma, and Spokane (seasonally). The local flight information office is at the airport, tel. 669/985-2730. For reservations and tickets, call a travel agent, such as American Express, tel. 669/913-0600, or the local Alaska Airlines agent at 669/981-4813.

Mexicana Airlines flights connect daily with Los Angeles, Denver (via affiliate Frontier Airlines), Mexico City, and Los Cabos. The local reservations office is in the Zona Dorada, tel. 669/913-0772. For flight information and reservations, call toll-free Mex. tel. 800/502-2000.

Aeroméxico and affiliated **Aerolitoral** flights connect daily with San Diego (high season only), Phoenix, Tijuana, Mexico City, Durango, Hermosillo, La Paz, Guadalajara, Torreón, and Monterrey. The local reservations/information offices are in the Zona Dorada, at Calz. Camarón Sábalo 310, tel. 669/914-1111 or 669/914-1609, and at the airport, tel. 669/982-3444, 669/982-4894, or 669/914-1621. For flight information and reservations, dial toll-free tel 01-800/021-4000.

Aerocalifornia Airlines flights connect with Los Angeles, Mexico City, La Paz, Tijuana, Los Cabos, and Torreón. For reservations, call a travel agent or the airline office at Hotel el Cid, tel. 669/913-2042. For flight information, call the airport office at tel. 669/985-2557.

U.S. Airways (formerly America West Airlines) flights connect with Phoenix. For reservations and flight information, call tel. 669/981-1184, or toll-free U.S. tel. 001-800/235-9292.

Continental Airlines Express connects daily once a week with Houston. Call toll-free

Mex. tel. 01-800/900-5000 for information and reservations.

Mazatlán Airport Arrival and Departure

For arrivees, the Mazatlán Airport (code-designated MZT, officially the General Rafael Buelna Airport) offers a modicum of services. At this writing, two HSBC ATMs and a Banamex ATM are functioning, a money exchange booth operates 9 A.M.–5 P.M. daily, and car rental agents meet flights. A newsstand sells American newspapers (seasonally Nov.–Apr.) and English-language paperbacks and magazines.

However, tourist information and hotel booking services are lacking. You should arrive with first-night hotel reservations and guidebook in hand. Otherwise, you'll be at the mercy of the taxi driver, who will most likely collect a commission from the hotel where he deposits you.

Local airport **car rental** agency booths include: AGA, tel. 669/914-4405 or 669/981-3580, reserva@agarentacar.com.mx; Budget, tel. 669/913-2000, fax 669/914-3611, budget_aeropuerto_mzt@hotmail.com; National, tel. 669/913-6000, fax 669/913-9087; Hertz, tel. 669/913-6060 or 669/913-4955, fax 669/914-2523; and Alamo, tel. 669/981-2266 or 669/913-1010, reservaciones@alamorentacar.com.mx.

Taxi and *colectivo* transportation for the 15-mile (25-km) ride into town is well organized. Booths (in the arrival hall, across from the car rentals) sell both kinds of tickets: *colectivo* about $6 per person, taxi about $25 per car. No public bus runs from town to the airport.

For departure, *colectivos* are harder to find around hotels than are departing tourists. Share a regular taxi and save on your return to the airport.

The **international airport departure tax** runs about $15. If your ticket price doesn't cover it, be prepared to pay up. If you've lost your tourist card and haven't had time to get a duplicate at immigration, you may be able to avoid the $20 departure fine by presenting a photocopy of your original tourist card.

BY CAR OR RV

Three main highway routes reach Mazatlán: from the United States through Nogales and Culiacán; from the northeast, through Durango; and from the southeast, from Guadalajara or Puerto Vallarta through Tepic.

The quickest and safest way to drive to Mazatlán from the U.S. western border is by Mexico National Highway 15, which connects with U.S. I-19 from Tucson, at Nogales, Mexico. A four-lane superhighway for nearly all the 743-mile (1,195-km) route, Highway 15 allows a safe, steady 55 mph (90 kph) pace. Although the tolls total about $60 for a car (more for trailers and big RVs), the safety and decreased wear and tear are well worth it. Take it easy and allow yourself at least two full days' travel to or from Nogales.

Heading to Mazatlán from the northeast, the winding (but spectacular) two-lane National Highway 40 crosses the Sierra Madre Occidental from Durango. Steep grades over the 7,350-foot (2,235-meter) pass will stretch the trip into a better part of a day, even though it totals only 198 miles (318 km). During the winter, snow can (but rarely does) block the summit for a few hours.

Heading southeast, heavy traffic slows progress along the mostly two-lane narrow northern section of National Highway 15, which connects with Tepic (182 miles, 293 km, four hours). At Tepic, toll *(cuota)* expressway Highway 15 D smooths the way to Guadalajara (141 miles, 227 km, three hours). Allow a full day for this trip.

About the same is required for the Mazatlán–Puerto Vallarta highway connection. Both legs, first the two-lane National Highway 15 (182 miles, 293 km, four hours) connecting at Tepic with the second leg, two-lane Highway 200 (104 miles, 167 km, three hours) to Puerto Vallarta, are subject to slowing by heavy traffic, and the trip requires a full day.

BY BUS

It's best to hire a taxi to take you (and your luggage) to the **central de autobúses** (central bus terminal), at the corner of Highway 15 ingress boulevard and Calle Chachalulas, about two miles north of downtown and four blocks from Playa Norte beach, behind the Sands Hotel.

Although the terminal is divided into *primera clase* (first class) and *segunda clase* (second class), counters on both sides sell both tickets. First class (with an air-conditioned waiting room) is on the far right, around the inside terminal corridor corner. Facilities include a kept-luggage section (*guarda de equipaje,* about $7/day), a post office, public phone and fax office, many public Ladatel card–operated long-distance telephones (buy Ladatel cards in the Elite air-conditioned first-class waiting room snack counter), and a few lunch stands and stores where travelers can buy food, pure water, and drinks. Stock up before you leave.

Several well-equipped bus lines provide frequent local departures. Go first- or luxury-class whenever possible. The service, speed, and reserved seats (*asientos reservados)* of first-class buses far outweigh their small additional cost. Parent company **Estrella Blanca** (which includes Elite, Futura, Transportes Chihuahuenses, and luxury-class Turistar) provides the most departures and the widest range, connecting the entire Pacific corridor, all the way to Acapulco, with border points from California to the Gulf of Mexico. Independent line **Transportes del Pacífico** successfully competes in the northwest, offering both first- and luxury-class departures, connecting Puerto Vallarta with California and Arizona border crossings. All connections listed below are first class and depart locally (*salidas locales)* unless otherwise noted.

First-class **Elite** buses, tel. 669/981-5308, connect with southeast destinations of Tepic, Guadalajara, Morelia, Aguascalientes, Querétaro, and Mexico City and intermediate points. At least one daily *salida de paso* (bus passing through) connects en route south with Tepic, Puerto Vallarta, Manzanillo, Zihuatanejo, and Acapulco; in the opposite direction many buses connect with northwest destinations of Culiacán, Los Mochis, Nogales, Mexicali, and Tijuana, including many intermediate points.

Transportes Chihuahuenses buses, tel. 669/981-5308, connect north via Durango, Chihuahua, Ciudad Juárez, and intermediate points.

Luxury-class **Futura** (FU) departures, tel. 669/981-2335, connect northeast with Monterrey, via Durango, Torreón, and Saltillo.

Independent **Transportes del Pacífico,** tel. 669/982-0577, *salidas de paso* connect hourly en route northwest to Tijuana and southeast to Tepic, Guadalajara, Mexico City, and intermediate points. You can change buses at Tepic, however, and continue to Puerto Vallarta.

In the second-class section, to the left as you enter the terminal, many daily **Transportes Norte de Sonora** (TNS) buses, tel. 669/981-5308, connect with all points along the northwest Pacific route (including Culiacán, Agua Prieta, and Tijuana), southeast with Guadalajara, Querétaro, and Mexico City, and south with Tepic, San Blas, Puerto Vallarta, and intermediate points.

Southern Sinaloa

National Highway 15 winds southward from Mazatlán through a lush, palm-dotted patchwork of pasture, fields, and jungle-clad hills. To the east rise the sculpted domes of the Sierra Madre Occidental, while on the west, a grand, island-studded marshland stretches to a virtually unbroken barrier of ocean sand.

A number of interesting side trips await visitors willing to stray an hour or two from Highway 200. In the Sierra foothills lie the tradition-rich village towns of **Concordia, Copala,** and **Rosario,** with their baroque colonial-era monuments, attractive handicrafts, and tasty regional food.

On the ocean side, kayakers, surfers, beachcombers, and folks who like to fish might enjoy

Shops at the roadside near Concordia offer traditional wooden furniture.

a stay at the beach and mangrove lagoon village of **Teacapán.** Those who linger have their choice of accommodations, from a sprinkling of comfortable hotels and trailer parks to dozens of miles of pristine golden sand beaches, ripe for RV or tent camping.

CONCORDIA, COPALA, AND ROSARIO

These easily accessible colonial-era towns offer charming off-the-beaten-track glimpses of country Mexico. You can go by tour (contact either Vista Tours in the Zona Dorada, on Camarón Sábalo, tel. 669/986-8610, www .vistatours.com.mx, or Pronatur, 669/916-7720 or 669/913-3333, ext. 3490 or 6581, email pronatours@elcid.com, www.elcid.com), or long-distance bus (take a Durango-westbound bus for Concordia and Copala, a Tepic-south-bound for Rosario), or car. If driving, mark your odometer at the Highway 15-Highway 40 fork, where you head for Concordia and Copala, east along Highway 40, toward the mountains. After winding through lush, sum-mer and fall wildflower–decorated foothills, you'll notice that roadside pottery factories begin appearing around Mile 10 (Km 16). Their offerings, all made in local family work-shops, fashioned in a treasury of fetching floral, animal, and human (some erotic) designs from local pre-Columbian tradition.

Concordia

Near the pair of bridges at Mile 12 (Km 19) that mark the entrance to Concordia (pop. 5,000), shops make and sell a wealth of sturdy, chestnut-varnished, colonial-style furniture.

For an interesting side excursion, fork sharply right onto a dirt road at the west end of the first bridge. After about 100 yards, bear left and continue another 100 yards, then bear left again, off the road, to a tree-shaded warm spring (*manantial;* mah-NAHN-tee-ahl), where women wash clothes in big collecting basins. Ask respectfully if bathing is permitted (say *¿Es permitido bañar?*). If so, you can bathe as the local folks do, with bathing suit or with your clothes on, usually in the

© BRUCE WHIPPERMAN

last, coolest basin that is generally reserved for bathing.

For a hearty lunch or dinner, head left after the bridge to the center of town and Concordia's distinguished, hacienda-style **Restaurant el Granero** (Morelos 21, tel. 694/968-0763 or 694/968-0666, open daily for breakfast, lunch and early dinner, $3–11), serving lots of good home-cooked regional food, from crisp vegetable salad to tender steak (*menudo* is a specialty), since 1881.

As for services, Concordia has pharmacies, doctors, a 24-hour Centro de Salud, tel. 694/968-0101, and a Banamex, open 9 A.M.– 4 P.M. Mon.–Fri., with 24-hour ATM.

Copala

After continuing through Concordia, pass through a creek (or over it if the bridge is finished), inviting for picnicking and perhaps swimming during the clear-water winter-spring dry season, at Mile 20 (Km 32). A riverbank mini-super grocery offers food and drink.

Eight miles farther (at Km 45 km), turn right at the signed Copala side road. Copala, an old gold-mining town founded by conquistador Francisco Ibarra in 1565, continues in the present as a picture-perfect stop for the trickle of tourists who venture out from Mazatlán. Hillside lanes wind to a petite plaza and old colonial church.

When the last tour bus departs, at around 3 P.M., you'll have the place nearly to yourself, save for a few local bench-warmers, a scattering of kids and dogs, and the obligatory chickens scratching around the plaza. The "new" plaza-front church, built in 1624 and dedicated to San José, replaced the original. It presides over the few festivities (Easter, Virgin of Guadalupe on December 12, and Christmas, especially March 16, the day of San José, when Copala livens up.

For food, bring a picnic lunch, or try the streetside *taquerías* or one of the pair of relaxing tourist spots, either ◖ **Daniel's Hotel and Restaurant,** on the right, just as you enter town, or the **Copala Butter Company** on the east side of the town plaza.

In recent years, Daniel, the friendly expatriate American owner-manager of Daniel's, and his wife have leased their restaurant to other managers. Nevertheless, they still offer lodging in comfortable hacienda-style rooms for about $20 d. For a room reservation, recommended on weekends and holidays, leave a message, in Spanish, with the Copala long-distance phone operator, tel. 200/124-4873.

Although Daniel's Restaurant (tel. 694/951-8386, 8 A.M.–5 P.M. daily, $3–10) probably has the best food, offering hearty country Mexican specialties, the Copala Butter Company (Copala local tel. 669/922-9391, cell tel. 01-669/149-9420 from Mazatlán, 044-669/149-9420 locally, Mazatlán local tel. 669/981-3224) on the town plaza, has the most personality. Friendly owner Jesús Morales and his wife have gathered a minimuseum of artifacts from the local mine diggings, which closed operations in 1980. Besides meals beneath their antique hacienda roof, they also offer five genuinely rustic rooms that open onto a long town- and valley-view porch. Step back 150 years and stay overnight for only about $20 d.

Rosario

Back on Highway 15, continue south to Rosario (pop. 10,000), about 56 miles (90 km) south of Mazatlán. Like many Mexican towns, Rosario got its boom-town start by virtue of a local gold and silver bonanza, discovered in 1655. Mining continued until 1945, leaving a honeycomb of 45 miles (70 km) of unstable tunnels beneath the present town. Now and then they cave in, most famously around 1800, destroying the orginal town church, which was later carried, stone by stone, and rebuilt at its present, secure location.

Besides its gilded past, Rosario has at least two claims to fame: its rebuilt colonial-era church, the **Misión de Nuestra Señora del Rosario** (Mission of Our Lady of the Rosary), and its favorite daughter, world-renowned *ranchera*-style singer Lola Beltrán (1935–1996).

Find the church (watch for the tall, steepled bell-tower) just after the town's entrance arch, visible southbound, off the right (west) side of Highway 15. Inside rises the lofty, renowned baroque gold altarpiece *(retablo)* known as the "Million Dollar Altar," finished in 1759, a gilded-foliage abode for a choir of angels and cherubs.

Afterwards follow the signs south about half a mile to the **Museo Lola Beltrán** (Calle Borrego, 7 A.M.–9 P.M. daily), across the street from the original, half-ruined 1731 **Church of the Rosary.**

In one room, the museum displays a lovely photo portrait and several stunning costumes of Lola Beltrán. Other rooms exhibit a fascinating collection (tools, wheels, photos of miners and their families, and ancient pottery and stone sculptures) from Rosario's past.

Near the museum, you might enjoy a half-hour stroll, exploring the idyllic, blue-green **Laguna Iguanero** pond nearby and the ruins of the old Church of the Rosary. Exit the museum, turn right, then after half a block, head left past a house, and continue about 100 feet to a hanging bridge *(puenta colgante)* that

leads to an island, with picture-perfect views of Laguna Iguanero. Shady tables provide a lovely setting for a picnic (provided you can ignore, or maybe even pick up, a possible bit of trash).

On your way back, at the end of the bridge, you'll see the mossy old church that began collapsing after the subterranean mines caved in and left yawning chasms that filled with water, forming the lake.

Finally, you might make your way back a few blocks north to Calle Lola Beltrán #19, former home of Lola Beltrán. Now, the front part of the family house has been dressed up for a party and operated as **Restaurant Tiro Antonio** (tel. 694/952-1255, 9 A.M.–10 P.M. daily) by Lola's sister. It's a colorful but unpretentious (like Lola herself) spot, with a long menu of all-Mexican country-style goodies, from tacos ($3) to savory garlic shrimp ($7).

For a restful poolside *comida* and/or overnight lodging in Rosario, try the **Hotel Yuaco** (on the highway, east side, tel./fax 694/952-1222, about $30 d), a couple of blocks south of the entrance arch.

TEACAPÁN

The downscale little beach resorts of Teacapán and Novillero (across the astuary in the state of Nayarit) have not yet been "discovered." They remain quiet retreats for lovers of sun, sand, simple lodgings, and superfresh seafood. Trucks travel from all over Sinaloa and Nayarit to buy shrimp and fish here.

Although Teacapán and Novillero are only a few miles apart, the Río San Pedro estuary that divides Sinaloa from Nayarit also divides Teacapán from Novillero. Novillero's south-side peninsula is identified by Teacapán residents as simply Isla del Otro Lado (Island on the Other Side).

The small town of Teacapán (pop. 3,000) lies along the sandy northeast edge of the estuary, which most residents know only as *la boca,* the river "mouth." Tambora, Teacapán's broad beach, borders a stately old palm grove on the open ocean a couple of miles north of the town.

© BRUCE WHIPPERMAN

Church of the Rosary

The most scenic sights are just west of the village center, on the estuary, a lazy place, where people walk very slowly. Here, a crumbling old dinghy returns to the sand; there, native-style *canoas* lie casually beneath the palms.

Beach Activities

Despite depletion of the Teacapán lagoon, ocean fishing remains good off Tambora beach. Watch for the sign on the right about two miles before town. You can rent a *lancha* or shove off in your own boat right on the beach.

Tambora is a very broad silky sand beach where the waves normally roll in gently from about 100 yards out, breaking gradually both left and right for surfing. Sailboarding would also be good here; the water is too sandy for snorkeling. Various clam, cowrie, and cockle shells turn up at seasonal times. Permanent beachside *palapa* restaurants serve fresh seafood and drinks. Other food and supplies are available in stores back in town.

Laguna Agua Grande

As it approaches the sea, the Río San Pedro, which forms the Sinaloa-Nayarit border, curves and broadens into a broad brackish lake, Laguna Agua Grande. Fisherfolk traditionally have made their living from the bounty of its waters, as have a host of waterbirds and myriad other creatures that inhabit its mangrove reaches. Overfishing has unfortunately forced the government to severely limit fish, shrimp, and shellfish catches. The government has had to enforce its rules with roadside inspections and military presence.

Consequently, an increasing number of boats have begun plying the waters hauling not fish but ecotourists and bird-watchers. If you have your own boat, you can do the same, or hire an angler to take you. A convenient site for either boat launching or hiring is at the end of Avenida Niños Héroes, just one block north of the Teacapán plaza. Follow the gravel road east for about 1.5 miles to the small fishing camp and improvised boat ramp.

Accommodations and Food

Teacapán visitors enjoy at least two reliable accommodations. About 22 miles (35 km) from Esquinapa on Highway 15 you pass a sign advertising the **Hotel Rancho los Angeles** (tel./fax 695/953-1344, rivera@hotmail.com, www.teacapan.com, $40–55 d, $15 RV site). If you continue along the side road to the beach, you will find a restaurant (open until around 6 P.M.), bar, beautiful big pool, and an adjacent trailer park. Upstairs is a luxurious three-room suite that opens to a big deck overlooking a breezy, palm-fringed ocean vista. As the manager says, "The music we have here is the music of the waves." No TV, but plenty of sun, sand, and solitude; the upstairs rents for about $55 per day. Other smaller but equally luxurious rooms downstairs rent for about $40 per day. A three-bedroom cottage beneath the palm grove a short walk away goes for about $150 per day. The approximately 60 unshaded trailer spaces go for about $15 per day, $100 per week, $300 per month, including all hookups, toilets, showers, and use of the pool. For reservations, contact the hotel directly in Teacapán. (During the high winter season, hotel residents enjoy lots of company in the restaurant, especially from the trailer park people. Summers, by contrast, are for those who prefer solitude.)

Rancho los Angeles's personable owner, Ernesto Rivera, M.D., and his son Jorge offer to guide small groups of guests to a unique nearby **archaeological site,** which they describe as a former pyramid, 100 feet high, made completely of sea shells. They say that an archaeologist, Dr. Stuart Scott of the University of Buffalo, New York, investigated the site, as yet undeveloped, in the 1970s. The trip, which they say takes a full day, leads through savannah and mangrove wetlands, habitat to a trove of wildlife, including crocodiles, dolphins, turtles, fish, and dozens of bird species. Bring your repellent, water, a hat, binoculars, and your bird identification book.

Development has arrived at Teacapán in the form of **C Hotel Villas Coral** (tel. 695/954-5477, Spanish only, $75 villa, $10 RV or tent site) in the lovely green park beneath the estuary-front palm grove just before entering town. As an anchor to what appears to be a budding second-home development, owners have built and furnished four lovely rustic-chic tile and stucco minivillas around an inviting pool-patio. Rentals run about $75 for four, with a/c and kitchenette; there's a beach club restaurant and tennis court. Tent camping is also allowed, beneath the palms by the estuary beach. Figure about $10 per tent or RV (self-contained only, no hookups). Call for reservations (probably not necessary except for Christmas and Easter).

RVers and trailer folks are welcome at the palm-shadowed 40-space beachfront **trailer park** (adjacent to the north-end Tambora beach restaurant, tel./fax 695/953-1609 or tel./fax 695/953-1344, rivera@hotmail.com, www.teacapan.com, $15 RV site), owned by Rancho los Angeles. Amenities include showers and hammocks beneath a shady beachfront *palapa*. Get there along the signed road from the highway; turn right into the driveway just after the big white house on the right.

Camping is customary most anywhere, either on the sand or beneath the big palm grove that edges the shoreline, curving south back to the estuary. To the north, the beach stretches, wild and breeze-swept, for several miles.

For food, Teacapán has two or three small grocery stores and a sprinkling of taco stands and *loncherías* along its one main street. Of the **restaurants** that line the west-side estuary beach, most established is seafood **Restaurant Mr. Wayne** (from the name of an American friend of the Mexican owner). He employs his own fisherman to bring the best *pargo, robalo,* and *mero* to the barbecue every afternoon.

Services

Along the main street back in Teacapán town, residents enjoy the services of a doctor, a pharmacy, a fairly well-stocked grocery, and a long-distance telephone office.

An estuary-front **boat ramp** is available for public use at the beachfront park back in town. Find it by turning right (heading south) at the official blue boat sign in the middle of town.

Getting There

Teacapán is accessible from Highway 15 by Sinaloa Highway 5–23 from Esquinapa. Ride either the local *urbano* or the red- and blue-striped Transportes Esquinapa buses from in front of the little park adjacent to the plaza cathedral or the bus station at the Teacapán turnoff at the north edge of town.

Southbound drivers, just before you enter downtown Esquinapa, a diversion funnels through traffic one-way to the right, then left within a block or two. Instead of following left, continue straight ahead for several blocks until you arrive at the asphalt westbound highway out of town, where you continue straight ahead for Teacapán. The all-paved 24 miles (38 km) passes quickly, through bushy thorn forest and past shallow lagoons dotted with waterbirds and rafts of wild lotus. Palm groves and broad fields of *chiles,* which make Sinaloa one of Mexico's top *chile*-producing states, line the roadside.

Esquinapa (pop. 40,000), a busy farm town, has a recommendable overnight hotel, the **IQ de Esquinapa** (Gabriel Leyva 7 Sur, tel./fax 695/953-0471, 695/953-0782, or 695/953-0396, $30 d), with restaurant, a block from the downtown plaza. The 30 semideluxe (but worn) rooms around an enclosed courtyard have TV, a/c, phones, and parking.

THE NAYARIT COAST

Nayarit's long, tufted coastline is one of the hidden, untouristed gems of Pacific Mexico. It blooms with verdant mountain and shoreline forests, orchard-swathed plains, great reaches of wildlife-rich mangrove wetlands, and seemingly limitless strands of golden sand.

Moreover, a sprinkling of amenities—restaurants, comfortable hotels, trailer parks, and camping spots—make life easy and relaxed in the Nayarit Coast's necklace of petite beachside resorts. Moving from north to south, little places with diminutive-sounding names such as Novillero, Las Islitas, Los Cocos, Chacala, Guayabitos, Lo de Marcos, San Pancho, and Sayulita offer an exceptional mix of south-seas delights. These include plenty of beach sunning, strolling, swimming, surfing, fishing, kayaking, and

bird-, dolphin- and whale-watching, all readily accessible to those willing to follow the road south.

Along the way, just past San Blas, by bus or car, you can trace the sand-decorated curve of broad Bay of Matanchén, with its world-class surfing breaks at picturesque Las Islitas beach at its north end, and a pair of petite beachfront hotels and a trailer park at Playa los Cocos at the bay's south end.

Also popular is jewel-like Playa Chacala, with its creamy half-moon beach, regal palm grove, homey local lodgings, and a pair of rustic-chic hotel-spas. Farther south is Rincón de Guayabitos, a favorite of both Mexican families and a large contingent of Canadian and American RVers, who flee the winter frost for a few easy months in Guayabitos's beachfront

HIGHLIGHTS

◖ Mexcaltitán: Its virtually certain identity as the Aztlán of legend makes this sleepy island village, known as the Venice of Mexico, an unmissable stop (page 89).

◖ Cerro de San Basilio: Make this airy hilltop your first stop in San Blas: You can enjoy a panorama of the colonial town and the surrounding mangrove wetland (page 95).

◖ La Tovara Jungle River Trip: A trove of wildlife, from cormorants and herons to turtles and crocodiles, is just the beginning of this uniquely lovely excursion into San Blas's mangrove hinterland (page 99).

◖ Crater Lake Santa María de Oro: This ancient volcanic bowl, now brimming with cool, clear water, green-forested slopes, and a scattering of lodgings both luxurious (Santa María Resort) and moderate (Koala Bungalows), including a trailer park and campground, make a perfect place to wind down for a few days (page 117).

◖ Shopping for Huichol Ceremonial Handicrafts: Right at the source, at least four stores (three near the Plaza Principal–Casa Aguet, Tienda de Artesanías Wereme, and Casa Aguiar–and Artesanías Cicurl near the south-side Plaza Constituyentes) offer very reasonably priced, authentic Huichol handicrafts. A fifth good source is the line-up of Huichol native-owned stalls in the front portico of City Hall, at the west end of the main Plaza Principal (page 121).

◖ Sayulita: Although this petite beach paradise has been "discovered" by a cadre of international, mostly youngish winter visitors, its palm-decorated, very snoozable and surfable beach, picture-perfect south end cove, and good restaurants, hotels, a campground and a trailer park, make it a fine spot to enjoy the local action for a day or a week (page 143).

LOOK FOR ◖ TO FIND RECOMMENDED SIGHTS, ACTIVITIES, DINING, AND LODGING.

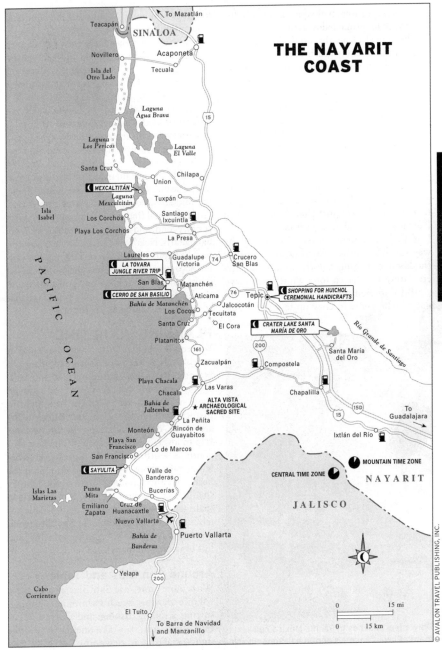

THE NAYARIT COAST

To Mazatlán

Teacapán

SINALOA

Novillero

Acaponeta

Tecuala

Isla del
Otro Lado

Laguna
Agua Brava

15

Laguna
Los Pericos

Laguna
El Valle

Santa Cruz

Chilapa

Union

MEXCALTITÁN

Tuxpán

Laguna
Mexcaltitán

Isla
Isabel

Los Corchos

Santiago
Ixcuintla

Playa Los Corchos

La Presa

Laureles

Guadalupe
Victoria

74

Crucero
San Blas

LA TOVARA
JUNGLE RIVER TRIP

P
A
C
I
F
I
C

San Blas

Matanchén

CERRO DE SAN BASILIO

Aticama

76

Tepic

SHOPPING FOR HUICHOL
CEREMONIAL HANDICRAFTS

Bahía de Matanchén

Jalcocotán

Los Cocos

Tecuitata

Santa Cruz

El Cora

CRATER LAKE SANTA
MARÍA DE ORO

Río Grande de Santiago

Platanitos

O
C
E
A
N

161

200

Santa María
del Oro

Zacualpán

Compostela

Playa Chacala

Chacala

Las Varas

Chapalilla

Bahía de
Jaltemba

ALTA VISTA
ARCHAEOLOGICAL
SACRED SITE

15

150D

To
Guadalajara

La Peñita

Monteón

Rincón de
Guayabitos

Ixtlán del Río

Playa San
Francisco

San Francisco

Lo de Marcos

SAYULITA

Valle de
Banderas

MOUNTAIN TIME ZONE

Islas Las
Marietas

Punta
Mita

Bucerías

CENTRAL TIME ZONE

NAYARIT

Emiliano
Zapata

Cruz de
Huanacaxtle

JALISCO

Nuevo Vallarta

Bahía de
Banderas

Puerto Vallarta

Yelapa

200

Cabo
Corrientes

El Tuito

To Barra de Navidad
and Manzanillo

0   15 mi

0   15 km

trailer parks, fishing, barbequeing, and playing cards with longtime fellow returnees.

The appeal of nearby Lo de Marcos is its wide, family-friendly beach, sheltered by headlands on both sides and bordered by a sprinkling of beach bungalows and palm-shaded RV parks and campgrounds.

The unmissable Playa San Francisco (known locally as San Pancho) still retains its sleepy beach village ambience, but is also home to a growing community of North American vacationers and retirees. They come mainly for San Pancho's abundant natural tranquility, taking long strolls along palm-shaded forest trails or gazing at the brilliant night sky and the spectacularly turbulent surf that dashes up San Pancho's long, golden beachfront.

Your last (but not least) stop along the way south should be Sayulita, once mostly the home of fishing families and oyster divers. Now, it's a haven for a winter platoon of youthful foreign sunbathers and surfer wannabes, who come to cozy up in comfortable lodgings and enjoy Sayulita's good food and colorful village life.

The Nayarit Coast, however, offers even more. Lovers of history and indigenous tradition should visit Mexcaltitán, the car-free "Venice of Mexico" island town and probable homeland of the Aztecs.

Farther south lies the once-renowned San Blas, sprinkled with reminders of its notable past and now the center for birdwatching and ecotouring in its vast mangrove jungle and forest hinterland.

A little further inland, atop the lush corn-and-cane Nayarit upland plateau, nestles Tepic, the mid-sized colonial-era Nayarit state capital. Here you'll find fascinating museums, tasty country food, and a trove of intriguing Huichol handicrafts. Nearby you can visit the sylvan crater lake Laguna Santa María. This area has various accommodation options, including a trailer park, campground, lakefront bungalows, and the luxurious, yet moderately priced, chalet-style lakeshore Santa María Resort.

PLANNING YOUR TIME

You could spend as little as two days and as much as two weeks or more exploring the Nayarit Coast, depending on your interests. If you have only two days, it's best to spend them near the beach, with the first night in history- and wildlife-rich **San Blas.** In the afternoon, don't miss taking the **jungle river trip** to lovely La Tovara spring. The next day, continue south, via **Tepic,** for some Huichol handicrafts shopping and an overnight at the beach, at either **Chacala** (good seafood, lovely small beach, country village), **San Francisco** (palm-shadowed forest trails, comfortable hotels, spectacular wild beach), or **Sayulita** (good hotels and restaurants, beginning surfing, and lots of winter company).

Around San Blas and Tepic

With more time, use San Blas as a base for wildlife-viewing, beach swimming, sunning, surfing, strolling, fishing, and adventures farther afield. You can take one day to see the sights, starting at viewpoint **Cerro de San**

© BRUCE WHIPPERMAN

Only a few beaches in Pacific Mexico can match Playa Chacala's gentle half-moon curve.

Basilio, then back in town around the plaza, the restored *aduana* (customs house) and museum, the Hotel Bucanero, the restored Hotel Hacienda Flamingos, and the El Pozo estuaryfront. Hire a boat to take you across the estuary to Isla del Rey for a bird-watching stroll to the open-ocean beach and back.

Another day could be spent on the jungle river trip to **La Tovara** spring, for swimming and lunch, reserving the afternoon for resting by your hotel pool or at Playa Borrego. On another day, you might take an excursion north by bus or car through Santiago Ixcuintla, continuing to **Mexcaltitán** for perhaps an overnight. With more time, do a **waterfall hike** and/or a tour offshore to marine wildlife sanctuary **Isla Isabel,** for snorkeling, scuba diving, and plenty of bird-, whale-, and dolphin-watching.

Heading south, travel to the lush, green summit plateau of Nayarit's coastal mountains, for an overnight in **Tepic,** the Nayarit state capital, nestled in its fertile volcano-rimmed valley. Tepic is both the rich source of a trove of colorful and uniquely enigmatic Huichol ritual handicrafts and jumping-off point for an overnight or two at the blue, forest-rimmed volcanic crater lake **Laguna Santa María de Oro.**

Along the Road to Puerto Vallarta

Unmissable along your way south is incompa-rably lovely **Playa Chacala,** with its half-moon beach, regal palm grove, good beachfront seafood restaurants, and homey local lodgings. For a splurge, stay a night or two at **Mar de Jade** rustic-chic hotel-spa.

You might enjoy a few days at **Rincón de Guayabitos,** the Mexican family favorite resort of the entire Nayarit Coast, largely for its many moderately priced but comfortable housekeeping bungalows and tranquil waves. If you're driving an RV, you might enjoy a few days (or an entire winter) staying at one of Guayabitos's several beachfront trailer parks, enjoying the company of a crowd of (mostly Canadian and American) fellow RVers, lots of freshly caught barbequed fish, and plenty of shady hammock time.

Half an hour farther south, spend at least an afternoon (or with more time, a few days) at **Playa San Francisco** (locally, San Pancho), a still-sleepy beach village, now home to a community of North American vacationers and retirees.

Finally at least spend an afternoon at **Sayulita,** strolling the beach, taking a surfing lesson, and enjoying a meal at one of the good local restaurants. With more time, you could stretch your visit to as much as a week, hiking shady forest trails, refining your surfing skills, soaking up the sun, or doing plenty of good reading on the palm-shadowed beachfront.

Road to San Blas

Although a few scattered fishing villages edge this 150-mile (250-km) coastline, it remains mostly wild, the domain of shorebirds and waterfowl, and, in the most remote mangrove reaches, jaguars and crocodiles. Its driftwood-strewn beaches invite adventurous trekkers, RV campers, and travelers who enjoy Pacific Mexico beaches at their untouristed best.

NOVILLERO

Little Novillero (pop. about 1,000) enjoys one of the longest (55 miles, 90 km), smoothest stretches of sand in Mexico. The waves roll in gently from 100 yards out and swish lazily along a velvety, nearly level beach. Here, all of the ingredients for a perfectly tranquil country beach stay come together: *palapa* seafood restaurants, rustic hotels, a big palm grove for RV or tent camping, ocean fishing, and a broad creamy strand for beachcombers and wilderness campers stretching for dozens of miles south of town.

Novillero's mangrove hinterland, about a mile inland from the beach, is a yet-to-be-discovered wildlife-viewing wonderland. You might be able to enjoy such an opportunity by hiring a local boatman (expect to pay about $15 an hour after bargaining) to take your party on an excursion along the mangrove-laced jungle waterways. Ask at the hotel, around town, or in the fishing village beneath the estuary bridge (about two miles before town).

Accommodations and Food

New and only a block from the beach is the eight-unit, semi-deluxe **Suites Playa Novilleros** (tel. 389/253-2580 or 389/253-2594, $45 d). Amenities include eight, large and comfortable tile-floored rooms, with kitchenettes, an ocean-view terrace, and a blue swimming pool; rentals include hot-water baths and fans.

Second place goes to (slightly worn at this writing) beachfront **Hotel Pacifico** (Playa Novillero, Nayarit, tel. 323/729-239-4648 or 323/729-2770, Canadian info tel. 664/999-7298, info@hotelpacifico.net, www.hotel pacifico.net, $32 d, $45 for a/c). Here, Canadian owners offer about 20 beach-view rooms, in two motel-style stories, with modern-standard baths, with TV, fans, big blue pool, parking, and restaurant.

In the unlikely eventuality that the above hotels are full, try the downscale, very basic, family-run **Hotel Miramar** (about $15 d) on the beach across the street from Hotel Pacifico, or **Hotel and Restaurant Puerto Azul,** back three blocks from the beach.

For food, Novillero offers a sprinkling of choices: a well-stocked country grocery (here called the "minisuper") and half a dozen *palapa* restaurants accustomed to serving a generation of vacationers. Best choices are probably **Beto's El Marinero,** on the beach next to the Hotel Miramar, offering eggs and pancakes for breakfast ($3) and smoked fish *sarandeado* ($14, enough for two or three), and lots of shrimp choices for lunch or early dinner. Open 8 A.M.–6 P.M. daily.

Another good choice would be to walk three blocks south on the road closest to the beach to **Rikki's** all-round Mexican open-air restaurant, with breakfasts ($3), lots of chicken and pork tacos, enchiladas, spaghetti, and more ($3–5), open 8 A.M.–10 P.M. daily. Other choices include the **Hotel Pacifico bar and grill,** and the **Hotel Miramar** beachfront seafood *palapa*.

Getting There

Novillero is about halfway between Tepic and Mazatlán, a two-hour ride either way, plus another half hour (22 miles, 35 km) by paved side road from Highway 15. Get there by bus via Transportes Victoria local bus from the highway to Tecuala, where you continue by minibus or *colectivo* van.

For drivers heading south on Highway 15, turn west (right) only a few hundred yards south of the Pemex station (and junction to Acaponeta), 92 miles (158 km) south of Mazatlán, at the paved side road signed Tecuala. Continue about 8 miles (13 km) and, as you're entering Tecuala, turn right just after the Pemex station. Continue another half mile and turn right at the paved highway, which continues west another 14 miles (22 km) west to Novillero.

© BRUCE WHIPPERMAN

An enshrined Jesus watches over the lagoon at Novillero.

© BRUCE WHIPPERMAN

Shrimp, crabs, and lobster, caught by *lanchas* (motorized fishing boats) are Mexcaltitán's main sources of income.

◖ MEXCALTITÁN

Mexcaltitán (pop. 2,000), the "House of the Mexicans," represents much more than just a scenic little island town. Archaeological evidence indicates Mexcaltitán may actually be the legendary Aztlán (Place of the Herons) where, in A.D. 1091, the Aztecs, who called themselves the México (may-SHEE-kah), began their generations-long migration to the Valley of Mexico.

Each year on June 28 and 29, the feast days of St. Peter and St. Paul, residents of Mexcaltitán and surrounding villages dress up in feathered headdresses and jaguar robes and breathe life into their tradition. They celebrate the opening of the shrimp season by staging a grand regatta, driven by friendly competition between decorated boats carrying rival images of saints Peter and Paul.

Sights

From either of the Mexcaltitán road's-end embarcaderos, boat workers ferry you across (about $1 per person for *colectivo*, $5 for private boat,

each way) to Mexcaltitán island-village, some of whose inhabitants have never crossed the channel to the mainland. The town itself is not unlike many Mexican small towns, except more tranquil, thanks to absence of motor vehicles.

Mexcaltitán is prepared for visitors, however. Instituto Nacional de Arqueología y Historia (INAH) has put together an excellent **museum** (across the central plaza from the town church, 10 A.M.–2 P.M. and 4–7 P.M. Tues.–Sun.) with several rooms of artifacts, photos, paintings, and maps describing the cultural regions of pre-Columbian Mexico. The displays climax at the museum's centerpiece exhibit, which tells the story of the Aztecs' epic migration to the Valley of Mexico from legendary Aztlán, now believed by experts to be present-day Mexcaltitán.

Outside, the proud village **church** (step inside and admire the heroic St. Peter above the altar) and City Hall preside over the central plaza, from which the town streets radiate to the broad lagoon that surrounds the town.

At the watery lagoon-ends of the streets,

AZTLÁN

During their first meeting in imperial Tenochtitlán, the Aztec Emperor Moctezuma informed Hernán Cortés that "from the records which we have long possessed and which are handed down from our ancestors, it is known that no one, neither I nor the others who inhabit this land of Anahuac, are native to it. We are strangers and we came from far outer parts."

Although the Aztecs had forgotten exactly where it was, they agreed on the name and nature of the place from which they came: Aztlán, a magical island with seven allegorical caves, each representing an Aztec subtribe – of which the México, last to complete the migration, had clawed its way to dominion. Aztlán, the Aztecs also knew, lay somewhere vaguely to the northwest, and their migration to Anahuac, the present-day Valley of Mexico, had taken many generations.

For centuries, historians puzzled and argued over the precise location of Aztlán, placing it as far away as Alaska and as near as Lake Chapala. This is curious, for there was an actual Aztlán – a chiefdom well known at the time of the Spanish conquest. Renegade conquistador Nuño de Guzmán immediately determined its location, and three days before Christmas in 1529, headed out with a small army of followers, driven by dreams of a new Aztec empire in western Mexico. However, when Guzmán arrived at Aztlán – present-day San Felipe Aztatlán village, near Tuxpan in Nayarit – he found no golden city. Others who followed, such as Vásquez de Coronado and Francisco de Ibarra, vainly continued to scour northwestern Mexico, seeking the mythical "Seven Cities of Cíbola," which they confused with the legend of Aztlán's seven caves.

Guzmán probably came closest to the original site. Scarcely a dozen miles due west of his trail through San Felipe Aztatlán is the small island-town of Mexcaltitán, which a number of experts now believe to be the original Aztlán. Many circumstances uphold their argument. The spelling common to Mexcaltitán and México is no coincidence, they say. The name Aztlán, furthermore, is probably a contraction of Aztatlán, which translates as Place of the Herons – the birds flock in abundance around Mexcaltitán. Moreover, a 1579 map of New Spain by renowned cartographer Ortelius shows an Aztlán exactly where Mexcaltitán is today.

The argument goes on: The Codex Boturini, a 16th-century reconstruction of previous Aztec records, reveals a pictogram of Aztecs leaving Aztlán, punting a canoe with an oar. Both the peculiar shape of the canoe and the manner of punting are common to both old Tenochtitlán and present-day Mexcaltitán.

Most compelling, perhaps, is the layout of Mexcaltitán itself. As in a pocket-sized Tenochtitlán, north-south and east-west avenues radiate from a central plaza, dividing the island into four quadrants. A single circular, plaza-centered street arcs through the avenues, joining the neighborhoods.

If you visit Mexcaltitán, you'll find it's easy to imagine Aztec life as it must have been in Tenochtitlán of old, where many people depended on fishing, rarely left their island, and, especially during the rainy season, navigated their city streets in canoes.

---

village fisherfolk set out in the late afternoon in canoes and boats for the open-ocean fishing grounds where, as night falls, they use kerosene lanterns to attract shrimp into their nets. Occasionally during the rainy season, water floods the town, and folks must navigate the streets as Venice-style canals.

Accommodations and Food

At the view-edge of the lagoon behind the museum stands Mexcaltitán's first official tourist lodging, the **Hotel Ruta Azteca** (Mexcaltitán, Nayarit, tel. 323/235-6020, or leave a message at the town telephone operator, tel. 323/235-6077, $25 d). More like a guesthouse than a hotel, it has four plain, tiled rooms with bath, some with a/c, with hot-water baths. A relaxing extra is the hotel's airy lagoon-vista veranda downstairs. Except for the Saints Peter and Paul festival and regatta during the last week in June, reservations are usually not necessary.

On the town plaza opposite the church stands airy **El Camarón** seafood restaurant; there's also a sometimes-noisy restaurant/bar at the south-side dock that has more and better food. A third option is the good **Mariscos Kika** (tel. 327/235-6054, noon–dusk daily) seafood restaurant, visible across the lagoon from the south-side dock. Reach it by hired (or the restaurant's) boat. Its kid-friendly facilities include a pair of kiddie pools and a water slide.

Getting There

By car, southbound from Mazatlán, Mexcaltitán is accessible from Highway 15, 136 miles (219 km) south of Mazatlán, at a signed turnoff with gas station, four miles south of Chilapa village. Initially paved, the access road changes to rough gravel for its last half through the bushy wetland, decorated by rafts of Mexican lotus lilies and flocks of preening, stalking, and fluttering egrets, herons, and cormorants, finally arriving at Embarcadero la Ticha after 28 miles (45 km).

By car, northbound from Tepic and Puerto Vallarta via Highway 15, follow the signed Santiago Ixcuintla turnoff, 38 miles (60 km) north of Tepic; continue five miles (eight km) past Santiago Ixcuintla to the signed and paved Mexcaltitán side road, which continues another 15 miles (25 miles, 40 km, total from Highway 15) to the La Batanga embarcadero (boat landing).

By bus, southbound, ask your bus driver to let you off at the Santiago Ixcuintla (pronounced eeks-KOOEEN-tlah) turnoff from Highway 15, where you can catch a local bus into town. If it's early, continue (about an hour) by local bus or *colectivo* to Mexcaltitán Embarcadero la Batanga.

Northbound, go from Tepic or San Blas bus stations by Transportes Noreste de Nayarit blue buses direct to Santiago Ixcuintla. Continue as described above.

SANTIAGO IXCUINTLA

If you take the southern approach to Mexcaltitán, you get the bonus of Santiago Ixcuintla (pop. 20,000) on the north bank of the Río Grande de Santiago, Mexico's longest river. Get there via the signed turnoff from Highway 15, 38 miles (60 km) north of Tepic; continue five miles to the town.

Just past the solitary hill that marks the town, turn right at the first opportunity, onto the one-way main street 20 de Noviembre, which in a couple of blocks runs past the picturesque main plaza. Linger a bit to admire the voluptuous Porfirian nymphs who decorate the restored bandstand and the pretty colonial church. Stroll beneath the shaded porticos and visit the colorful market two blocks north of the plaza.

Although the town's scenic appeal is considerable, the Huichol people are the best reason to come to Santiago Ixcuintla. Hundreds of Huichol families migrate seasonally (late winter and early spring, especially) from their Sierra Madre high-country homeland to work for a few dollars a day in the local tobacco fields. For many Huichol, their migration in search of money includes a serious hidden cost. In the mountains, they have their homes, their friends and relatives around them, and the familiar rituals and ceremonies they have tenaciously preserved in their centuries-long struggle against Mexicanization. But when the Huichol come to lowland towns and cities, they often encounter the mocking laughter and hostile stares of townspeople, whose Spanish language they do not understand, and whose city ways seem alien. As strangers in a strange land, the pressure for the migrant Huichol to give up their old costumes, language, and ceremonies to become like everyone else is powerful indeed.

Centro Cultural Huichol

Be sure to reserve part of your time in Santiago Ixcuintla to stop by the Centro Cultural Huichol (20 de Noviembre 452, Santiago Ixcuintla, Nayarit 63300, cehuichol@hotmail .com). The immediate mission of founders Mariano and Susana Valadez—he a Huichol artist and community leader, and she a U.S.-born anthropologist—is to ensure that the

THE HUICHOL

Because the Huichol have retained more of their traditional religion than perhaps any other group of indigenous Mexicans, they offer a glimpse into the lives and beliefs of dozens of now-vanished Mesoamerican peoples.

The Huichols' collective wariness, plus their isolation in rugged mountain canyons and valleys, has saved them from the ravages of modern Mexico. Despite increased tourist, government, and mestizo contact, prosperity and better health swelled the Huichol population to around 20,000 by the late 1990s.

Although many have migrated to coastal farming towns and cities such as Tepic and Guadalajara, several thousand Huichol remain in their ancestral heartland roughly 50 miles (80 km) northeast of Tepic as the crow flies. They cultivate corn and raise cattle on 400 *rancherías* in five municipalities not far from the winding Altengo River valley: Guadalupe Ocotán in Nayarit and Tuxpán de Bolanos, San Sebastián Teponahuaxtlán, Santa Catarina, and San Andrés Cohamiata in Jalisco.

Although studied by a procession of researchers since Carl Lumholtz's seminal work in the 1890s, the remote Huichol and their religion remain enigmatic. As Lumholtz said, "Religion to them is a personal matter, not an institution and therefore their life is religion – from the cradle to the grave, wrapped up in symbolism."

Hints of what it means to be Huichol can be gleaned from their art. Huichol art contains representations of the prototype deities – Grandfather Sun, Grandmother Earth, Brother Deer, Mother Maize – that once guided the destinies of many North American peoples. It blooms with tangible mystical symbols, from green-faced Mother Earth (Tatei Urianaka) and the dripping Rain Goddess (Tatei Matiniera), to the ray-festooned Father Sun (Tayau) and the antlered folk hero Brother Kauyumari, forever battling the evil sorcerer Kieri.

The Huichol are famous for their use of the hallucinogen peyote, their bridge to the divine. The humble cactus – from which the peyote "buttons" are gathered and eaten – grows in the Huichols' Elysian land of Wirikuta, in the San Luis Potosí desert 300 miles east of their homeland, around the old gold-mining town of Real de Catorce.

To the Huichol, a journey to Wirikuta is a dangerous trip to heaven. Preparations go on for weeks and include innumerable prayers and ceremonies, as well as the crafting of feathered arrows, bowls, gourds, and paintings for the gods who live along the way. Only the chosen – village shamans, temple elders, those fulfilling vows or seeking visions – may make the journey. Each participant in effect becomes a god whose identity and very life are divined and protected by the shaman en route to Wirikuta.

Huichol people endure, with their traditions intact and growing. Their instrument is the Centro Cultural Huichol, a clinic, dining hall, dormitory, library, craftsmaking shop, sale gallery, and interpretive center that provides crucial focus and support for local migratory Huichol people.

Lately, Susana has moved on to open another center, high in the mountains at Huejuquilla El Alto, Jalisco. Mariano continues the original mission in Santiago Ixquintla. As well as filling vital human needs, both of their centers actively nurture the vital elements of an endangered heritage. This heritage belongs not only to the Huichol, but to the lost generations of indigenous peoples—Aleut, Yahi, Lacandones, and myriad others—who succumbed to European diseases and were massacred in innumerable fields, from Wounded Knee and the Valley of Mexico all the way to Tierra del Fuego.

Although they concentrate on the immediate needs of people, Mariano and Susana and their respective staffs also reach out to local, national, and international communities. The Santiago Ixcuintla center's entry corridor is decorated with illustrated Huichol legends in Spanish, especially for Mexican visitors. An adjacent gallery exhibits a treasury of Huichol art for sale—yarn paintings, masks, jewelry, gourds, God's eyes—adorned with the colorful deities and animated heavenly motifs of the Huichol pantheon.

The two centers invite volunteers, especially those with secretarial, computer, language, and other skills, to help with projects. If you don't have the time, they also solicit donations of money and equipment.

They also sell their handicrafts on their website, www.beadsofbeauty.net, and through stores, such as La Hamaca Gallery in Sayulita, on the southern Nayarit Coast, tel. 322/227-5817, www.sayulitalife.com.

Get to the Santiago Ixcuintla Centro Cultural Huichol by heading away from the river, along 20 de Noviembre, the main street that borders the central plaza. Within a mile, you'll see the Centro Cultural Huichol, No. 452, on the right.

For more information about Susana's other center and about Huichol culture in general, contact Susana at huicholcenter@juno.com or visit www.beadsofbeauty.net, or telephone her office in Santa Fe, New Mexico, tel. 505/983-7182. You can also travel to Susana's mountain center either by charter airplane from Tepic, or by Hwy. 54 north from Guadalajara through Zacatecas, thence Fresnillo, then west via Hwy. 44 to Huejuquilla El Alto), a good day's trip from Tepic. Give Susana at least a week's notice, at Mex. tel. 457/983-7054 at her Centro Indígena

Huichol (Calle Victoria 24, Huejuqilla El Alto, Jalisco 46000).

Accommodations and Food

If you decide on a Santiago Ixcuintla overnight, stay at the **Hotel Casino Plaza** (Arteaga and Ocampo, Santiago Ixcuintla, Nayarit, tel./fax 323/235-0850, 323/235-0851, or 323/235-0852, $27 d), near the plaza downtown. It has a good downstairs restaurant/bar and about 35 basic rooms around an inner parking patio, with TV, a/c, hot shower baths, and parking.

Services

Santiago Ixcuintla is an important regional business center with a number of services. Banks, all with 24-hour ATMs, include long-hours HSBC bank on the south side of the plaza, at Hidalgo and Zaragoza, 8 A.M.–7 P.M. Mon.–Fri., 8 A.M.–3 P.M. Sat.; Banamex at 20 de Noviembre and Hidalgo, tel. 323/235-0053, 9 A.M.–4 P.M. Mon.–Fri.; and Bancomer, at 20 de Noviembre and Morelos, 8:30 A.M.–4 P.M. Mon.–Fri., 10 A.M.–2 P.M. Sat.

Find the *correo* (post office) at Allende 23, east side of the plaza, tel. 323/235-0214, 8:30 A.M.–3 P.M. Mon.–Fri. *Telecomunicaciones* (Zaragoza Ote. 200, tel./fax 323/235-0989, 8 A.M.–8 P.M. Mon.–Sat.) provides long-distance phone, public fax and telegraph service.

Two grades of unleaded gasoline should be available at the Pemex station on the east-side highway (toward Highway 15) as you head out of town.

San Blas and Vicinity

San Blas (pop. about 15,000) is a small town slumbering beneath a big coconut grove. Life goes on in the plaza as if San Blas has always been an ordinary Mexican village. But once San Blas was anything but ordinary. During its latter 18th-century glory days, San Blas was Mexico's burgeoning Pacific military headquarters and port, with a population of 30,000. Ships from Spain's Pacific Rim colonies crowded its harbor, silks and gold filled its counting houses, and noble Spanish officers and their mantilla-graced ladies strolled the plaza on Sunday afternoons.

Times change, however. Politics and San Blas's pesky *jejenes* (hey-HEY-nays, invisible "no-see-um" biting gnats) have always conspired to deflate any temporary fortunes the town may enjoy. The *jejenes'* breeding ground,

© BRUCE WHIPPERMAN

A plazafront banner in San Blas exhorts local folks to donate for needy children in San Blas.

a vast hinterland of mangrove marshes, may paradoxically give rise to a new, more prosperous San Blas. These thousands of acres of waterlogged mangrove jungle and savanna are a nursery-home for dozens of Mexico's endangered species. This rich trove is now protected by ecologically aware governments and communities, and admired (not unlike the game parks of Africa) by increasing numbers of ecotourists.

HISTORY
Conquest and Colonization

San Blas and the neighboring, southward-curving Bay of Matanchén were reconnoitered by gold-hungry conquistador Nuño de Guzmán in May 1530. His expedition noted the protected anchorages in the bay and the Estero el Pozo adjacent to the present town. Occasionally during the 16th and 17th centuries, Spanish traders in their galleons and the pirates lying in wait for them would drop anchor in the *estero* or the adjacent Bay

of Matanchén for rendezvous, resupply, or cargo transfer.

By the latter third of the 18th century, New Spain, reacting to the Russian and English threats in the North Pacific, launched plans for the colonization of California through a new port called San Blas.

The town was officially founded atop the hill of San Basilio in 1768. Streets were surveyed; docks were built. Old documents record that more than 100 pioneer families received a plot of land and "a pick, an adze, an axe, a machete, a plow...a pair of oxen, a cow, a mule, four she-goats and a billy, four sheep, a sow, four hens and a rooster."

People and animals multiplied, and soon San Blas became the seat of Spain's eastern Pacific naval command. Meanwhile, simultaneously with the founding of the town, the celebrated Father Junípero Serra set out for California with 14 missionary brothers on *La Concepción*, a sailing vessel built on Matanchén beach just south of San Blas.

Independence

New Spain's colonial grandeur, however, crumbled in the bloody 1810–1821 war for independence, taking San Blas with it. In December 1810, the *insurgente* commander captured the Spanish fort atop San Basilio hill and sent 43 of its cannons to fellow rebel-priest Miguel Hidalgo to use against the Spanish loyalists around Guadalajara.

After independence, fewer and fewer ships called at San Blas; the docks fell into disrepair, and the town slipped into somnolence, then complete slumber when President Lerdo de Tejada closed San Blas to foreign commerce in 1872.

SIGHTS AND ACTIVITIES
C Cerro de San Basilio

The overlook atop the Cerro de San Basilio is the best spot to orient yourself to San Blas.

From this breezy point, the palm-shaded grid of streets stretches to the sunset side of **El Pozo** estuary and the lighthouse-hill beyond it. Behind you, on the east, the mangrove-lined **San Cristóbal** river estuary meanders south to the Bay of Matanchén. Along the south shore, the crystalline white line of San Blas's main beach, **Playa el Borrego** (Sheep Beach), stretches between the two estuary mouths.

While you're atop the hill, take a look around the old ***contaduría*** counting house and fort (built in 1770), where riches were tallied and stored en route to Mexico City or to the Philippines and China. Several of the original great cannons still stand guard at the viewpoint like aging sentinels waiting for long-dead adversaries.

Behind and a bit downhill from the weathered stone arches of the *contaduría* stand the

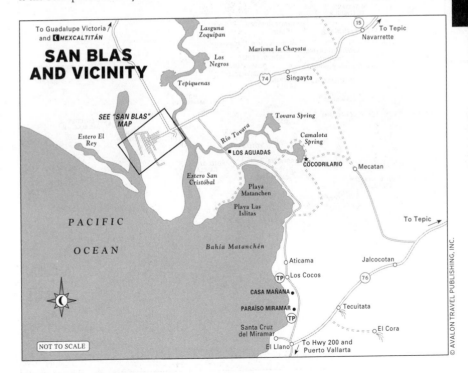

THE NAYARIT COAST

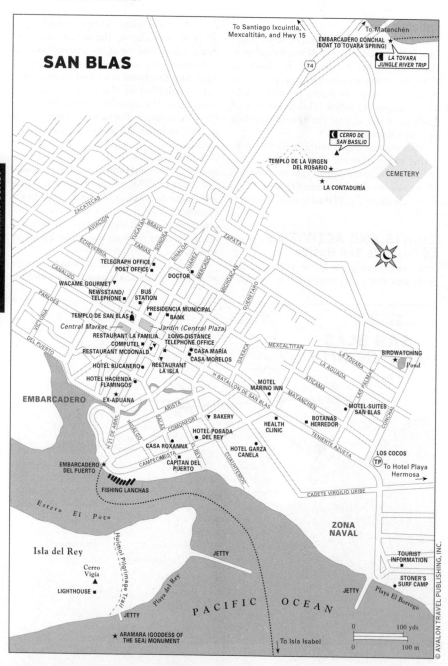

SAN BLAS

To Santiago Ixcuintla, Mexcaltitán, and Hwy 15

To Matanchén

EMBARCADERO CONCHAL
(BOAT TO TOVARA SPRING)

LA TOVARA
JUNGLE RIVER TRIP

74

CERRO DE
SAN BASILIO

TEMPLO DE LA VIRGEN
DEL ROSARIO

CEMETERY

LA CONTADURÍA

ZACATECAS

AVIACION

ECHEVERRIA

YUCATAN

BRAVO

SONORA

FARIAS

SINALOA

JUAREZ

MERCADO

ZAPATA

MICHOACAN

QUERETARO

CANALIZO

TELEGRAPH OFFICE
POST OFFICE

DOCTOR

PAREDES

WACAME GOURMET

NEWSSTAND/
TELEPHONE

BUS
STATION

PRESIDENCIA MUNICIPAL

VICTORIA

TEMPLO DE SAN BLAS

BANK

Central Market

Jardín (Central Plaza)

DEL PUERTO

RESTAURANT LA FAMILIA
COMPUTEL

LONG-DISTANCE
TELEPHONE OFFICE

MEXCALTITAN

BIRDWATCHING

RESTAURANT MCDONALD

CASA MARÍA

LA TOVARA

Pond

CASA MORELOS

LA AGUADA

HOTEL BUCANERO

RESTAURANT
LA ISLA

LAS PALMAS

HOTEL HACIENDA
FLAMINGOS

H BATALLON DE SAN BLAS

ATICAMA

EMBARCADERO

EX-ADUANA

MOTEL
MARINO INN

MAYANCHEN

MOTEL-SUITES
SAN BLAS

ARISTA

H 21 DE ABRIL

HIDALGO

SALAS

COMONFORT

BAKERY

HEALTH
CLINIC

BOTANAS
HERREDOR

CONCHAL

TENIENTE AZUETA

HOTEL POSADA
DEL REY

CASA ROXANNA

EL REY

CAMPECHE

ARISTA

CAPITAN DEL
PUERTO

CUAUHTEMOC

HOTEL GARZA
CANELA

LOS COCOS

TP

To Hotel Playa
Hermosa

EMBARCADERO
DEL PUERTO

FISHING LANCHAS

CADETE VIRGILIO URIBE

Estero El Pozo

ZONA
NAVAL

Isla del Rey

Cerro
Vigía

Huichol Pilgrimage Trail

JETTY

TOURIST
INFORMATION

LIGHTHOUSE

STONER'S
SURF CAMP

Playa del Rey

JETTY

Playa El Borrego

JETTY

PACIFIC OCEAN

To Isla Isabel

ARAMARA (GODDESS OF
THE SEA) MONUMENT

0   100 yds

0   100 m

© AVALON TRAVEL PUBLISHING, INC.

interior of Nuestra Señora del Rosario

the top of Cerro Vigía, the southern hill-tip of Isla del Rey (actually a peninsula). Here, the first beacon shone during the latter third of the 18th century.

Although only a few town folks ever bother to cross over to the island, it is an important Easter pilgrimage and wedding site for Huichol people from the remote Nayarit and Jalisco mountains. Huichol have been gathering on the Isla del Rey for centuries to make offerings to Aramara, their goddess of the sea. A not-so-coincidental shrine to a Catholic virgin-saint stands on an offshore sea rock, visible from the beach-endpoint of the Huichol pilgrimage a few hundred yards beyond the lighthouse.

Sadly, a large cave sacred to the Huichol at the foot of Cerro Vigía was demolished by the government during the early 1970s to provide rock for a breakwater. Fortunately, President Salinas de Gortari partly compensated for the insult by deeding the sacred site to the Huichols during the early 1990s.

Two weeks before Easter, Huichol people begin arriving by the dozens, the men decked out in flamboyant feathered hats. On the ocean beach, 10 minutes' walk straight across the island, anyone can respectfully watch them perform their rituals: elaborate marriages, feasts, and offerings of little boats laden with arrows and food, consecrated to the sea goddess to ensure good hunting and crops and many healthy children.

Playa Borrego

San Blas's most convenient beach is Playa Borrego, at the south end of Calle Cuauhtémoc about a mile south of town. With a lineup of *palapas* for food and drinks, the mile-long, broad, fine-sand beach is ripe for all beach activities except snorkeling (because of the murky water). Shoals of shells—clams, cockles, mother-of-pearl—wash up on Borrego Beach during storms. Fishing is often good, especially when casting from the jetty and rocks at the north and south ends.

Hotel Playa Hermosa

For a glimpse of a relic from San Blas's recent

gaping portals and towering, moss-stained belfry of the old church of **Nuestra Señora del Rosario,** built in 1769. Undamaged by war, it remained an active church until at least 1872, around the time when poet Henry W. Longfellow was inspired by the silencing and removal of its aging bells.

Downhill, historic houses and ruins dot San Blas town. The old hotels Bucanero and Hacienda Flamingos on the main street, Juárez, leading past the central plaza, preserve much of their old-world charm. Just across the street from the Hacienda Flamingos, you can admire the restored, monumental brick colonnade of the 19th-century former **Aduana,** now a cultural center. Continue west along Juárez to the El Pozo estuary. At that shoreline spot, gaze across the El Pozo channel. This was both the jumping-off point for colonization of the Californias and the anchorage of the silk- and porcelain-laden Manila galleons and the bullion ships from the northern mines.

Cerro Vigía

El Faro (lighthouse) across the estuary marks

THE BELLS OF SAN BLAS

Renowned Romantic poet Henry Wadsworth Longfellow (1807-1882) most likely read about San Blas during the early 1870s, just after the town's port was closed to foreign trade. With the ships gone, and not even the trickle of tourists it now enjoys, the San Blas of Longfellow's time was perhaps even dustier and quieter than it is today.

San Blas must have meant quite a lot to him.Ten years later, ill and dying, Longfellow hastened to complete "The Bells of San Blas," his very last poem, finished nine days before he died on March 24, 1882. Longfellow wrote of the silent bells of the old Nuestro Señora del Rosario (Our Lady of the Rosary) church, whose arches, albeit mossy and frail, still rise proudly atop the summit of Cerro San Basilio.

What say the Bells of San Blas
To the ships that southward pass
From the harbor of Mazatlán?
To them it is nothing more
Than the sound of surf on the shore, –
Nothing more to master or man.

But to me, a dreamer of dreams,
To whom what is and what seems
Are often one and the same, –
The Bells of San Blas to me
Have a strange, wild melody,
And are something more than a name

For bells are the voice of the church;
They have tones that touch and search
The hearts of young and old;
One sound to all, yet each
Lends a meaning to their speech,
And the meaning is manifold.

They are a voice of the Past,
Of an age that is fading fast,
Of a power austere and grand;
When the flag of Spain unfurled
Its folds o'er this western world,
And the Priest was lord of the land.

The chapel that once looked down
On the little seaport town
Has crumbled into the dust
And on oaken beams below
The bells swing to and fro,
And are green with mould and rust.

"Is then, the old faith dead,"
They say, "and in its stead
Is some new faith proclaimed,

That we are forced to remain
Naked to sun and rain,
Unsheltered and ashamed?

"Once in our tower aloof
We rang over wall and roof
Our warnings and our complaints;
And round about us there
The white doves filled the air,
Like the white souls of the saints.

"The saints! Ah, have they grown
Forgetful of their own?
Are they asleep, or dead,
That open to the sky
Their ruined Missions lie,
No longer tenanted?

"Oh, bring us back once more
The vanished days of yore,
When the world with faith was filled;
Bring back the fervid zeal,
The hearts of fire and steel,
The hands that believe and build.

"Then from our tower again
We will send over land and main
Our voices of command,
Like exiled kings who return
To their thrones, and the people learn
That the Priest is lord of the land!"

O Bells of San Blas, in vain
Ye call back the Past again!
The Past is deaf to your prayer;
Out of the shadows of night
The world rolls into light;
It is daybreak everywhere.

past, head across town to the crumbling Hotel Playa Hermosa. Here, one evening in 1951, President Miguel Alemán came to dedicate San Blas's first luxury hotel. As the story goes, the *jejenes* descended and bit the president so fiercely the entire entourage cleared out before he even finished his speech. Rumors have circulated around town for years that someone's going to reopen the Playa Hermosa, but judging from the vines creeping up the walls and the orchids blossoming on the balconies, they'd better hurry or the jungle is going to get the old place first. To get there, follow H. Batallón toward the beach, turn left just after the Los Cocos Trailer Park, and continue along the jungle road for about half a mile.

【 La Tovara Jungle River Trip

On the downstream side of the bridge over Estero San Cristóbal, launches-for-hire will take you up the Río Tovara, a side channel that winds about a mile downstream into the jungle.

The channel quickly narrows into a dark tree-tunnel, edged by great curtainlike swaths of mangrove roots. Big snowy *garza* (egrets) peer out from leafy branches; startled turtles slip off their soggy perches into the river, while big submerged roots, like gigantic pythons, bulge out of the inky water. Riots of luxuriant plants—white lilies, green ferns, red *romelia* orchids—hang from the trees and line the banks.

Finally you reach Tovara Springs, which well from the base of a verdant cliff. On one side, a bamboo-sheltered *palapa* restaurant serves refreshments; on the other, families picnic in a hillside pavilion. In the middle, everyone jumps in and paddles in the clear, cool water.

You can enjoy this trip in two ways: the longer, three-hour excursion as described ($40 per boatload of 6–8) from El Conchal landing on the estuary, or the shorter version (two hours, $30 per boatload) beginning upriver at road-accessible Las Aguadas near Matanchén village. Either drive, taxi, or ride the *blanco* (white) bus or the navy-blue Transportes Noreste bus.

The more leisurely three-hour trip allows more chances (especially in the early morning) to spot an ocelot or crocodile, or a giant boa

constrictor hanging from a limb (no kidding). Many of the boatmen are very professional; if you want to view wildlife, tell them, and they'll go more slowly and keep a sharp lookout.

Some boatmen offer more extensive trips to less-disturbed sites deeper in the jungle. These include the Camalota spring, a branch of the Río Tovara (where a local *ejido* maintains a crocodile breeding station) and the even more remote and pristine Tepiqueñas, Los Negros, and Zoquipan lagoons in the San Cristóbal Estero's upper reaches.

In light of the possible wildlife-watching rewards, trip prices are very reasonable. For example, the very knowledgeable bird specialist Oscar Partida Hernández (Comonfort 134 Pte., San Blas, Nayarit 63740, tel. 323/285-0324) will guide a four-person boatload to La Tovara for about $50. If Oscar is busy, call "Chencho" Banuelos (tel. 323/285-0716) for a comparably excellent trip. More extensive options include a combined Camalota-La Tovara trip (allow 4–5 hours) for about $40 for four or Tepiqueñas and Los Negros (six hours, 7 A.M. departure) for about $60.

Isla Isabel

Isla Isabel is a two-mile-square offshore wildlife study area 40 miles (65 km) and three hours north by boat. The cone of an extinct volcano, Isla Isabel is now home to a small government station of ecoscientists and a host of nesting boobies, frigate birds, and white-tailed tropic birds. Fish and sea mammals, especially dolphins and sometimes whales, abound in the surrounding clear waters. Although it's not a recreational area, local authorities allow serious visitors, accompanied by authorized guides, for a few days of camping, snorkeling, scuba diving, and wildlife-watching. A primitive dormitory can accommodate several people. Bring everything, including food and bedding.

Contact experienced and licensed boat captain Ricardo (Pato) Murillo (tel. 323/285-1281) or equally well-qualified captain Santos Villafuente (at the Hotel Brisas del Mar, tel. 323/285-0870, cell local tel. 044-311/109-1993) for arrangements and prices. Tariffs

© BRUCE WHIPPERMAN

Great white herons and the smaller cattle egrets are among the many dozens of bird species commonly spotted around San Blas.

typically run $250 per day for parties of up to four people. Stormy summer and fall weather limits most Isla Isabel trips to the sunnier, calmer winter-spring season. For additional information and advice, check with manager Josefina Vasquéz, at the Hotel Garza Canela front desk (Mexico or U.S. toll-free 800/713-2313, local tel. 323/285-0112, 323/285-0307, or 323/285-0480, fax 323/285-0308, hotel@garzacanela.com, www.garzacanela.com).

Whale-Watching

Alternatively, a number of San Blas captains take visitors on less extensive, but nevertheless potentially rewarding wildlife-viewing excursions November–April. Sightings might include humpback, gray, and sperm whales, dolphins, seals, sea lions, turtles, manta rays, and flocks of birds, including gulls, frigate birds, cormorants, boobies, terns, and much more. Contact either the captains Pato Murillo or Santos Villafuente or super-experienced, English-speaking Tony Aguayo, at home (tel.

323/285-0364) or at his "office," the little palapa to the left of the small floating boat dock at the El Pozo estuary end of Juárez. A typical five-hour excursion runs about $150 for up to six passengers.

Bird-watching

Although San Blas's extensive mangrove and mountain jungle hinterlands are renowned for their birds and wildlife, rewarding bird-watching can start in the early morning right at the edge of town. Follow Calle Conchal right (southeast) one block from Suites San Blas, then left (northeast) to a small pond. With binoculars, you might get some good views of local species of cormorants, flycatchers, grebes, herons, jacanas, and motmots. A copy of Chalif and Petersen's *Field Guide to Mexican Birds* or Steve Howell's *Bird-Finding Guide to Mexico* will assist in further identification.

Rewarding bird-watching is also possible on **Isla del Rey.** Bargain for a launch (from the foot of Juárez, about $4 round-trip) across to the opposite shore. Watch for wood, clapper, and Virginia rails, and boat-billed herons near the estuary shore. Then follow the track across the island (looking for warblers and a number of species of sparrows) to the beach, where you might enjoy good views of plovers, terns, Heerman's gulls, and rafts of pelicans.

Alternatively, look around the hillside cemetery and the ruins atop **Cerro de San Basilio** for good early-morning views of hummingbirds, falcons, owls, and American redstarts.

You can include serious bird-watching with your boat trip through the mangrove channels branching from the **Estero San Cristóbal** and the **Río Tovara.** This is especially true if you obtain the services of a wildlife-sensitive guide, such as Oscar Partida (tel. 323/285-0324), "Chencho" Banuelos (tel. 323/285-0716), or Armando Santiago (tel. 323/285-0859, dolpacarm@yahoo.com). Expect to pay about $60 for a half-day trip for four persons.

Besides the above, **Armando Navarette** (Sonora 179, San Blas, no phone) offers bird-watching hikes, especially around Singayta in the foothills, where birders routinely identify 30–40 species in a two-hour adventure. Such an excursion might also include a coffee plantation visit, hiking along the old royal road to Tepic, and plenty of tropical fauna and flora, including butterflies, wildflowers, and giant vines and trees, such as *ceiba, arbolde,* and the peeling, red *papillo* tree. Armando's fee for such a trip, lasting around five hours, runs about $20 per person, plus your own or rented transportation.

Others suggest bird-watching tours and packages. One of the best organized, known simply as **San Blas Birds** (sanblasbirds@aol.com, www.sanblasbirds.com), lists tours varying from one to seven days. The longer tours include lodging; for example, three days including lodging at Hotel Posada del Rey runs around $400 per person; the same out of Hotel Garza Canela, about $600 per person.

For more details on bird-watching and hiking around San Blas, look for a copy of the now-out-of-print booklet *Where to Find Birds in San Blas, Nayarit* ($4) by Rosalind Novick

and Lan Sing Wu, at the shop at Garza Canela Hotel. The hotel shop also usually sells the *Checklist of Birds Found in San Blas, Nayarit* or the new *Birder's Guide to San Blas,* published by San Blas Birds.

Waterfall Hikes and Ecotours

A number of waterfalls decorate the lush jungle foothills above the Bay of Matanchén. Two of these, near Tecuitata and El Cora villages, respectively, are accessible from the Santa Cruz-Tepic Highway 76 about 10 miles (16 km) south of San Blas. The local *autobús blanco* will take you most of the way. It runs south to Santa Cruz every two hours 8:30 A.M.–4:30 P.M. from the downtown corner of Juárez and Paredes.

While rugged adventurers may guide themselves to the waterfalls, others rely upon guides **Armando Navarette,** local ecoleader **Juan "Bananas" Garcia,** or **Lucio Rodríguez** (inquire at Tourist Information on Mercado southeast of the plaza, or with Josefina Vasquéz at the Hotel Garza Canela).

During the December–April clear-weather season, veteran scuba diver and instructor Douglas Storms offers hiking, bird-watching, kayaking, snorkel and scuba adventures, and more, out of his **Adventure Center** headquarters (Juárez 187 B, 246, San Blas, tel. 323/285-1418, doug@divingbeyond.com, www.divingbeyond.com). Off season, contact him in Sausalito, California (tel. 415/331-7925 or 415/325-3789), at 700 Waldo Point, Sausalito, CA 94965.

Alternatively, you might look into the services of Canadian photographer-guide John Stewart, founder of **Seven Sunset Tours** (www.sevensunsets.com), who works out of Casa Mañana on Playa los Cocos several miles south of San Blas. John and his staff like to lead their clients on eco-friendly tours to local villages, hidden beaches, waterfalls, bird-watching and much more.

Ecotouring in Singayta

The latter-day local growth of shrimp-pond aquaculture and the associated wildlife habitat destruction has prompted action by eco-activists in San Blas and neighboring communities, such as Singayta, five miles east of San Blas.

Singayta villagers began taking positive action around 2000. Since then, they have established a nursery for reintroduction of threatened native plants, a crocodile breeding farm, and an **environmental awareness center** to educate visitors and residents about the destructive reality of shrimp-pond aquaculture.

To back all this up, Singayta offers a menu of **guided ecotours** (www.singayta.com and www.elmanglar.com). These include canoe trips into the mangrove wetland, walking tours, mountain bike rentals, donkey cart and horseback tours, and more. A restaurant offers meals and refreshments. You might also find out more about Singayta from knowledgeable ecoleader and guide Juan "Bananas" Garcia.

Get to Singayta by car along Tepic Hwy. 74, about five miles (8 km) straight east of the San Blas plaza; or, by bus, from the San Blas plaza-front bus station, by one of the hourly Tepic-bound buses.

ACCOMMODATIONS

San Blas has several hotels, none of them huge, but all with personality. They are not likely to be full even during the high winter season (unless the surf off Mantanchén Beach runs high for an unusually long spell).

Under $50

Soak in the full natural beach experience at one of San Blas's most economical accommodations, **Stoner's Surf Camp** (Playa Borrego, San Blas, Nayarit 63740, stoners@stonerssurfcamp.com, www.stonerssurfcamp.com, $20 s, $15 d high season, $10 and $15 low, $3pp tent site). Rustically snug bamboo and thatch cabañitas come complete with fan, mosquito net, towels and sheets; guests share the toilets and showers. Amenities include restaurant, use of kitchen, use of surfboard ($3 for all day) and bikes for cabaña guests. Camping, with use of kitchen, runs $3 per person; tent rentals are available.

Slightly up the economic scale, the family-run *casa de huéspedes* (guesthouse) **Casa María** (corner of Canalizo and Michoacán, tel.

323/285-1057, $18 s, $23 d) makes a reality of the old Spanish saying *"Mi casa es su casa."* There are about 12 rooms around a homey, cluttered patio, and María offers to do everything for the guests except give them baths. Not spic and span, but very friendly and with kitchen privileges, fans, hot-water showers, and washing machine included.

You can also get a comfortable room at María's adjacent original guesthouse, **Casa Morelos** (108 Heróico Batallón, tel. 323/285-1345, $14 s, $18 d), operated by her daughter, Magdalena, who rents by drop-in only.

A few blocks away, a block west of the plaza, the **Hotel Bucanero** (Calle Juárez 75, San Blas, Nayarit 63740, tel. 323/285-0101, $15 s, $20 d) appears to be living up to its name. A stanza from the *Song of the Pirate* emblazons one wall, a big stuffed crocodile bares its teeth beside the other, and a crusty sunken anchor and cannons decorate the shady patio. Despite peeling paint, the 32 rooms (with ceiling fans and hot water) retain a bit of spacious, old-world charm, with high-beamed ceilings under the ruddy roof tile. (High, circular vent windows in some rooms cannot be closed, however. Use repellent or your mosquito net.) Outside, the big pool and leafy old patio/courtyard provide plenty of nooks for daytime snoozing and socializing. A noisy nighttime (winter-spring seasonal) bar, however, keeps most guests without earplugs jumping until about midnight.

Although the facilities of the four-star **Motel Marino Inn** (Av. H. Batallón s/n, San Blas, Nayarit 63740, tel. 323/285-0303, $45 s or d) look fine on paper, the place is bare of most usual hotel amenities. The 60 rooms are comfortable enough for a night or two, with air-conditioning, a pool (if it's working), and private balconies. You'll find it on the north-end edge of town, few blocks before the beach. Credit cards are accepted.

In the same, palm-shadowed, country fringe of town not far from Playa Borrego is the **Motel-Suites San Blas** (Calles Aticama and Las Palmas, San Blas, Nayarit 63740, tel. 323/285- 0505, vimais66@hotmail.com, $27 d, $50 for four), left off H. Batallón a few blocks after the Motel Marino. Its pool, patio, playground, game room, and spacious but somewhat worn suites with kitchenettes (dishes and utensils *not* included) are nicely suited for active families. Another plus here are the several rooms with private view verandas overlooking the neighboring lush, wildlife-rich forest. The 23 fan-only suites include 16 one-bedrooms for two adults and kids ($27) and seven two-bedrooms accommodating four adults with kids ($50); credit cards are accepted.

The lively, family-operated **Hotel Posada del Rey** (Calle Campeche 10, San Blas, Nayarit 63740, tel. 323/285-0123, posadadelrey@ sanblasmail.com, www.sanblasmexico.com/ posadadelrey, $32 s or d) seems to be trying hardest. It encloses a small but inviting pool and patio beneath a top-floor viewpoint bar (and high-season-only restaurant) that bubbles with continuous soft rock and salsa tunes. The 13 rooms have a/c, and you can bargain for a low-season discount; credit cards are not accepted.

$50-100

Tucked on a quiet San Blas back street, half a block from the sleepy El Pozo Estuary, **Casa Roxanna Bungalows** (Callejon El Rey 1, San Blas, Nayarit 63740, tel. 323/285-0573, casaroxanna@yahoo.com, www.casaroxanna .sanblasmexico.com, $65 d) is a hidden gem among San Blas lodgings. Its manicured green lawn, blue double-laned lap pool, and regal fan palms make its refinement immediately apparent upon entering its tranquil garden compound. The four comfortable, spacious bungalows ($65 d, add $5 each additional adult), with two double beds, furnished kitchenettes, and cool air-conditioning confirm the initial impression. One large deluxe room and a studio bungalow with kitchenette rent for about $55; all with air-conditioning, satellite TV, and parking.

Back in the middle of town, three blocks west along Juárez from the plaza, newly renovated ◖ **Hotel Hacienda Flamingos** (Juárez 105, San Blas, Nayarit 63740, local tel. 323/285-0930, fax 323/285-0485, Mazatlán tel./fax 669/985-2727 or 669/985-5252, reservaciones @sanblas.com.mx, www.sanblas.com.mx, $90

d) lives on as a splendid reminder of old San Blas. Owners have spared little in restoring this 1863 German consulate and trading house to its original graceful condition. Now, the fountain flows once more in the tranquil, tropical inner patio, furnished with period chairs and tables and a gallery of old San Blas photos on the walls. A side door leads outside to a luxuriously elegant swimming pool and spacious garden, sprinkled with recliners, a grass-carpeted badminton court, and a croquet set ready for service. Inside, the rooms are no less than you'd expect: luxuriously airy and high-ceilinged, with elegantly simple decor, replete with Porfirian-era touches and wall art; and with baths, gleaming with polished traditional-style fixtures. Rates for the 10 rooms may rise around Christmas and Easter holidays.

Another of San Blas's jewels is the refined, resort-style ◖ **Hotel Garza Canela** (Paredes 106 Sur, San Blas, Nayarit 63740, Mexico U.S. toll-free 800/713-2313, local tel. 323/285-0112, 323/285-0307, or 323/285-0480, fax 323/285-0308, hotel@garzacanela .com, www.garzacanela.com, $90 s, $115 d high season, $70 and $90 low), tucked away at the south end of town, two blocks off H. Batallón. The careful management of its Vásquez family owners (Señorita Josefina Vásquez in charge) glows everywhere: manicured garden grounds, crystal-blue pool, immaculate sundeck, and centerpiece restaurant. The 60 cool, air-conditioned rooms are tiled, tastefully furnished, and squeaky clean. Rates include a hearty breakfast, cable TV, and much more. Credit cards are accepted. The family also runs a travel agency and an outstanding crafts and gift shop on the premises.

San Blas folks offer several other worthy hotel, bungalow, and apartment lodging choices. For more information, visit the excellent **www.sanblasdirectory.com** website.

Trailer Parks and Campgrounds

San Blas's only trailer park, **Los Cocos** (Calle Teniente Azueta, San Blas, Nayarit 63740, tel. 323/285-0055, loscocos@sanblasmexico.com, $13 RV site), is a two-minute walk from the wide, yellow sands of Playa el Borrego. Friendly management, spacious, palm-shaded grassy grounds, pull-throughs, unusually clean showers and toilet facilities, a laundry next door, fishing, and a good, air-conditioned bar with satellite TV all make this place a magnet for RVers and tenters from Mazatlán to Puerto Vallarta. The biting *jejenes* require the use of strong repellent for residents to enjoy the balmy evenings. The 100 spaces rent for about $13 per day for two people, $2 for each additional person, with all hookups, one day free per week for longer stays. Amenities include a bar, out front, open 10 A.M.–2 P.M. daily.

The *jejenes* and occasional local toughs and peeping Toms make **camping** on close-in Borrego Beach a less-than-ideal possibility (although some adventurers set up tents beside the beachfront palapa restaurants). A better option is to camp on Playa Borrego at **Stoner's Surf Camp,** for $3 per person, with kitchen privileges.

Isla del Rey (across Estero El Pozo, accessible by *lancha* from the foot of Calle Juárez) presents possibilities for prepared trekker-tenters. Pack in everything, including water. For intensely dedicated adventurers, the same is true for ecosanctuary **Isla Isabel,** three hours by hired boat from San Blas.

For those less equipped, the palm-lined strands of **Playa las Islitas, Playa Matanchén,** and **Playa Cocos** on the Bay of Matanchén also might afford camping possibilities as long as you bring plenty of good insect repellent.

FOOD
Snacks, Stalls, and Markets
During the mornings and early afternoons, try the fruit stands, groceries (such as **Abarrotes Flavia,** tel. 323/285-1214, 6 A.M.–9 P.M. daily), *fondas,* and *jugerías* in and around the **Central Market** (which, incidentally, is the coolest non-air-conditioned daytime spot in town). For example, refresh yourself at **Jugos Mimi** juice stand. During the summer look for the exotic Asian jackfruit relative *yaca:* green, round, and as large as a football. Enjoy a *liquado* whipped from its deliciously mild pulp.

Late afternoons and evenings, many semi-permanent streetside stands around the plaza, such as the **Taquería Las Cuatas,** at the northwest corner, by the City Hall, offers tasty *antojitos* and drinks.

For sit-down snacks every day until midnight, drop in to the **Lonchería Ledmar** (facing the plaza near the Canalizo-Juárez corner) for a hot *torta,* hamburger, quesadilla, tostada, or fresh-squeezed *jugo* (juice). For a change of venue, you can enjoy about the same at the **Terraza** café on the opposite side of the plaza.

Get your fresh cupcakes, cookies, and crispy *bolillos* at the **panadería** (at Comonfort and Cuauhtémoc, closed Sun.), around the uptown corner from Hotel Posada del Rey. You can get similar (but not quite so fresh) goodies at the small bakery outlet across from the plaza (corner of Juárez and Canalizo).

Restaurants
Family-managed **Restaurant McDonald** (36 Juárez, tel. 323/285-0432, 7 A.M.–10 P.M. daily, $3–7), half a block west of the plaza, is one of the gathering places of San Blas. Its bit-of-everything menu features soups, meat, and seafood, plus a hamburger that beats no-relation U.S. McDonald's by a mile.

As an option, step across the street to the **Wala** restaurant (tel. 323/285-0863, 8 A.M.–10 P.M. Mon.–Sat., $3–7) for breakfast, lunch, or dinner. Its long menu of offerings—tasty salads, pastas, seafood, and fish fillets, crisply prepared and served in a simple but clean and inviting setting—will never go out of style. Everything is good; simply pick out your favorite.

Another good sit-down option is the airy plaza-front **Cha Cha's** (tel. 323/285-0041, 8 A.M.–10 P.M. daily, $3–8). Here, you can choose from a sandwich or full dinner, such as a professionally prepared and served fresh fish filet or spaghetti á la Bolognese.

For TV with dinner, the **Restaurant la Familia** (H. Batallón, half a block south of plaza, lunch and dinner Mon.–Sat., $6–8) is just the place. American movies, Mexican curio-hung walls, and leafy garden patio supply the ambience, while a reasonably priced seafood and meat menu furnishes the food.

The Tijuana-trained owner/chef of **Wacame Gourmet** (at Yucatán 18, two blocks north of the plaza, to Canalizo, then turn right, cell 044-311/105-5382, noon–10 P.M. Thurs.–Tues., $4–6) puts out delicious soups (try the hot-and-sour), chicken chop suey, pork chow mein, stir-fried broccoli, and much more. He named his establishment Wacame (wah-KAH-may) in honor of the home town in Japan of his Tijuana employer/mentors.

Cross to the adjacent corner and enter the refined marine atmosphere of **Restaurant la Isla** (on Mercado, tel. 323/285-0407, 2–10 P.M. Tues.–Sun., $6–10). As ceiling fans whir overhead and a guitarist strums softly in the background, the net-draped walls display a museum-load of nautical curiosities, from antique Japanese floats and Tahitian shells to New England ship models. Davy Jones notwithstanding, both local folks and visitors choose this place mainly for its good fish and shrimp entrées.

San Blas's class-act restaurant is **El Delfín** (at Hotel Garza Canela, Cuauhtémoc 106, tel. 323/285-0112, 8–10 A.M. and 1–9 P.M. daily, $4–14). Potted tropical plants and leafy planter-dividers enhance the genteel atmosphere of this air-conditioned dining room-in-the-round. Meticulous preparation and service, bountiful breakfasts, savory dinner soups, and fresh salad, seafood, and meat entrées keep customers returning year after year; credit cards accepted.

ENTERTAINMENT

Sleepy San Blas's entertainment is of the local, informal variety. Visitors content themselves with strolling the beach or riding the waves by day, and reading, watching TV, listening to mariachis, or dancing at a handful of clubs by night.

Nightlife

Owner/manager Mike McDonald works hard to keep **Mike's Place** (Juárez 36), on the second floor of his family's restaurant, the classiest club in town. He keeps the lights flashing and the small dance floor thumping with blues, Latin, and 1960s rock tunes from his own

guitar, accompanied by his equally excellent drum and electronic-piano partners. Listen to live music Saturday nights 9 P.M.–midnight during the summer low season, and Tuesday–Saturday during the fall-winter high season. He usually charges a small cover; drinks are reasonably priced.

Another good option (and a good spot to meet people) is the **San Blas Social Club** bar, which sometimes offers jazz in season. Check it out at the northeast plaza corner, across the street from Cha Cha's restaurant.

A few other places require nothing more than your ears to find. During high season, music booms out of low-life **Botanas Herredor** (down H. Batallón, a block past the Marino Inn). The same is true seasonally at the bar at the **Hotel Bucanero** (Calle Juárez 75, tel. 323/285-0101).

SPORTS AND RECREATION
Surfing

Playa Borrego has one of the surf breaks that has made San Blas a surfing mecca. Surfers begin arriving in San Blas in May when the waves begin to grow, and as long as the surf's up, they'll stay around until at least October. Veterans recognize at least five breaks, sprinkled, in succession, from the Borrego break (beginning, intermediate, advanced), at Playa Borrego, to the Las Islitas (intermediate, advanced) break at Playa Las Islitas. These breaks, depending on seasonal conditions, can challenge all surfers, from beginners to advanced.

To find out about all of this, visit **Stoner's Surf Camp** on Playa Borrego, beach side of the entrance parking lot. Here, welcoming owner-operator Nikki Kath, besides renting boogie boards ($2/hr.) and surfboards ($3/hr.) offers surf lessons ($15/hr.), and also runs a restaurant, a hotel, and a small campground on the premises.

If you want to learn to surf, or are already a surfer wanting to improve your skills, Stoner's is ready for you, with champion instructor Jose "Pompi" Manuel Cano, who owns a long list of awards that he began winning in 1980, at the age of eight. For much more surfing information, visit the Stoner's Surf Camp website, www.stonerssurfcamp.com.

Although some intermediate- and beginner-level surf rolls in at Borrego Beach, nearly all of San Blas's board action goes on at world-class surfing mecca Matanchén Beach. The mild offshore currents and gentle, undertow-free slope of Borrego Beach are nearly always safe for good swimming, bodysurfing, sailboarding, and boogie boarding. In town, Juan "Bananas" Garcia (H. Battallón 219, tel. 323/285-0462) rents surfboards and boogie boards at his café.

Snorkeling and Scuba Diving

Snorkeling and scuba diving are possible during the clear-water December–April season. That's when California-based scuba instructor **Douglas Storms** (tel. 323/285-1418, doug@divingbeyond.com, www.divingbeyond.com), offers snorkel and scuba lessons and excursions out of his Adventure Center headquarters, at 187B Juárez, a block from the estero El Pozo dock. Off-season, you can contact him in Sausalito, California (415/331-7925, or 415/325-3789).

Sportfishing

Tony Aguayo (tel. 323/285-0364) and Ricardo "Pato" Murillo (tel. 323/285-1281) are highly recommended to lead big-game deep-sea fishing excursions. Tony's "office" is the *palapa* shelter to the left of the little dock at the El Pozo estuary, at the foot of Calle Juárez. Both Tony and Ricardo regularly captain big-boat excursions for tough-fighting marlin, dorado, and sailfish. Their fee will run about $300 for a seven-hour expedition for up to three people, including big boat, tackle, and bait.

On the other hand, a number of other good-eating fish are not so difficult to catch. Check with Tony or other captains, such as Antonio Palmas at the Hotel Garza Canela, or one of the owners of the many craft docked by the estuary shoreline at the foot of Juárez. For perhaps $150, they'll take three or four of you for a *lancha* outing, which most likely will result in four or five hefty 10-pound snapper, mackerel,

tuna, or yellowtail; afterward you can ask your favorite restaurant to cook them for a feast.

During the last few days in May, San Blas hosts its long-running (30-plus years) **International Fishing Tournament.** The entrance fee runs around $600; prizes vary from automobiles to Mercury outboards and Penn International fishing rods. For more information, contact Tony Aguayo or Pato Murillo, or ask at the local tourist information office, downtown at the Presidencia Municipal.

Walking and Jogging

The cooling late-afternoon sea breeze and the soft but firm sand of **Playa Borrego** (south end of H. Batallón) make it the best place around town for a walk or jog. Arm yourself against *jejenes* with repellent and long pants, especially around sunset.

SHOPPING

San Blas visitors ordinarily spend little of their time shopping. For basics, the stalls at the **Central Market** (6 A.M.–2 P.M. daily) offer good tropical fruits, meats, and staples. For used clothes and a little bit of everything else, a **flea market** (known in Mexico as a *tianguis*) operates on Calle Canalizo a block past the bus station (away from the *jardín*) Saturday morning and early afternoon.

Up-to-date photography services and supplies have arrived in San Blas, at **Foto Studio America** (Juárez 91, next to Restaurant McDonald, 8 A.M.–2 P.M. and 4–9 P.M. daily, tel. 323/285-1209). Here, find many cameras, films, and both color and black-and-white film and digital developing service.

Handicrafts

Although San Blas has relatively few handicrafts sources, the shop at the **Hotel Garza Canela** has arguably the finest for-sale handicrafts collections in Nayarit state. Lovingly selected pieces from the famous Pacific Coast crafts centers—Guadalajara, Tlaquepaque, Tonalá, Pátzcuaro, Olinalá, Taxco, Oaxaca, and elsewhere—decorate the shop's cabinets, counters, and shelves.

You'll find many common but nevertheless attractive handicrafts in the **crafts stalls** that occupy the San Blas main plaza daily.

INFORMATION AND SERVICES
Tourist Information Office

San Blas has two tourist information offices. The main one (9 A.M.–3 P.M. and 4–6 P.M. Mon.–Fri., 10 A.M.–2 P.M. Sat., tel. 323/285-0221) is inside the Presidencia Municipal, at the interior patio's southeast corner. The other office, staffed by personable Cari Luz Aguilar, is at Playa Borrego (9 A.M.–3 P.M. daily; if she's out of the office on business, contact her via local cell tel. 044-311/134-3356, long distance 01-311/134-3356, email kariluz2@hotmail.com).

Alternatively, for information, tickets, and tours, see very well-informed **Josefina Vásquez,** both the desk manager and travel agent at the Hotel Garza Canela.

Bank

Banamex (Juárez 36 Ote., tel. 323/285-0031, 9 A.M.–4 P.M. Mon.–Fri.), one block east of the plaza, with a 24-hour ATM, exchanges U.S. traveler's checks and cash.

Communications

The *correo* (tel. 323/285-0295, 8 A.M.–3 P.M. Mon.–Fri., 9 A.M.–noon Sat.), and *telégrafo* (tel. 323/285-0115, 8 A.M.–2 P.M. Mon.–Fri.) stand side by side at Sonora and Echeverría (one block behind, one block east of the plaza church).

In addition to the long-distance public phone stands that sprinkle the town, there are a number of old-fashioned *larga distancia* stores. Most prominent is the **Computel** (on Juárez, just west of the plaza, across from Restaurant McDonald, 8 A.M.–9 P.M. daily).

Internet access has arrived at a number of spots; for example, try **Café Net San Blas** (on H. Batallón, tel. 323/285-1082, 9 A.M.–10 P.M. daily), the hole-in-the wall store near the plaza's southwest corner.

Health and Emergencies

For routine remedies and non-prescription drugs, go to **Farmacia Mas Por Menos** (More for Less), at Juáez 66, across from Restaurant McDonald (no telephone, though you can call Restaurant McDonald, tel. 323/285-0432, 8:30 A.M.–1 P.M. and 4–9 P.M. daily).

Alternatively, go to **Farmacia Económica** (H. Batallón and Mercado, tel. 323/285-0111, 8:30 A.M.–1 P.M. and 4:30–9 P.M. Mon.–Sat., 8:30 A.M.–2 P.M. Sun.)

For medical consultations, visit very highly recommended Dr. Alejandro Davalos, available at his office, tel. 323/285-0331, on Juárez, corner of Farias, three blocks east of the plaza. If he's too busy, you could consult with general practitioner **Dr. Rene Diaz Elias,** at his Farmacia Mas Por Menos (8:30 A.M.–1 P.M. Mon.–Sat.)

Moreover, you can go to San Blas's respectable local small hospital, the government 24-hour **Centro de Salud** (Yucatán and H. Batallón, across from the Motel Marino Inn, tel. 323/285-1207).

For **police** (on Canalizo, tel. 323/285-0221) emergencies, contact the headquarters, on the left side of and behind the Presidencia Municipal.

Immigration and Customs

San Blas no longer has either Migración or Aduana offices. If you lose your tourist card, you'll have to go to the Secretaría de Gobernación in Tepic (Oaxaca no. 220 Sur) or, better, to Migración at the airport in Puerto Vallarta a day before you're scheduled to fly home. For customs matters, go to the Aduana in Puerto Vallarta for the necessary paperwork.

GETTING THERE AND AWAY
By Car or RV

To and from the north and east, paved roads connect San Blas to main-route National Highway 15. From the northeast, National Highway 74 winds 19 miles (31 km) downhill from its junction about 160 miles (260 km) south of Mazatlán and 22 miles (35 km) north of Tepic. From its Highway 15 turnoff (marked by a Pemex gas station), Highway 74 winds through a forest of vine-draped trees and tall palms. Go slowly; the road lacks a shoulder, and cattle or people may appear unexpectedly around any blind, grass-shrouded bend.

From the east, Nayarit Highway 76 leaves Highway 15 at its signed "Miramar" turnoff at the northern edge of Tepic. The road winds downhill about 3,000 feet (1,000 m) through a jungly mountain forest to the shoreline Santa Cruz and Miramar villages. It continues along the Bahía de Matanchén shoreline to San Blas, a total of 43 miles (70 km) from Tepic. Although this route generally has more shoulder than Highway 74, frequent pedestrians and occasional unexpected cattle necessitate caution.

To and from Puerto Vallarta, the highway coastal cutoff at Las Varas bypasses the slow climb up the mountain to Tepic, shortening the San Blas-Puerto Vallarta connection to about 94 miles (151 km), or about 2.5 hours.

By Bus

The **San Blas bus terminal** stands adjacent to the new plaza-front church, corner of Calles Sinaloa and Canalizo. From **Mazatlán**, and points north, ride an early Tepic-bound Estrella Blanca affiliate bus (first-class Elite or second-class Transportes Norte de Sonora) or a first-class Transportes Norte del Pacifico. Either ride all the way to Tepic, where you can catch one of many connections to San Blas, or, if it's still daytime, ask the bus driver to drop you at the San Blas junction of Highways 15 and 74 (marked by a Pemex station on the right) about 160 miles (260 km) south of Mazatlán, where you can catch a taxi, or *colectivo* van, or blue and white Transportes Noroeste de Nayarit bus to San Blas.

To and from **Puerto Vallarta,** bus travelers have two ways to connect to San Blas. Quickest is via one of the **Transportes Norte de Sonora** (Puerto Vallarta tel. 323/285-0043) departures, which connect daily with San Blas. They depart from the new Puerto Vallarta bus station north of the airport; get your ticket at the Elite-Estrella Blanca desk (tel. 322/290-1001).

If you're too late for the Transportes Norte de Sonora connection, go via Transportes Pacifico from Puerto Vallarta (tel. 322/290-

1008) to the Tepic bus station, where you might be early enough to catch the last of several daily local buses that connect with San Blas, run by Transportes Norte de Sonora (Tepic tel. 311/213-2315) or **Transportes Noroeste de Nayarit** (Tepic tel. 311/212-2325, connect by taxi from their Tepic city-center station to the Tepic central bus station on the outskirts of town).

Several daily second-class navy blue and white Transportes Noroeste de Nayarit departures (about 8 and 10 A.M.) connect south from Tepic with the Bay of Matanchén points of Matanchén, Los Cocos, and Santa Cruz de Miramar. Other departures connect east with Tepic, and north with Santiago Ixcuintla, via intermediate points of Guadalupe Victoria and Villa Hidalgo.

A local *autobús blanco* connects San Blas south with the Bay of Matanchén points of Las Aguadas, Matanchén, Aticama, Los Cocos, and Santa Cruz. It departs from the downtown corner of Paredes and Sinaloa (a block west of the old church) four times daily, approximately every two hours between 8:30 A.M.–4:30 P.M.

AROUND THE BAY OF MATANCHÉN

The shoreline of the Bahía de Matanchén sweeps southward from San Blas, lined with an easily accessible, pearly crescent of sand, ripe for beachcombers and tent campers. In the luxuriant foothill forest above the bay, trails lead to bubbling waterfalls and idyllic jungle pools, fine for picnicking or wilderness camping. The villages of Matanchén, Aticama, Los Cocos, and Santa Cruz del Miramar dot this strand with *palapa* restaurants and stores offering food and basic supplies. A pair of trailer parks and two good small hotels provide accommodations.

Beaches and Activities

The beaches of **Matanchén** and **Las Islitas** make an inseparable pair. Las Islitas (if heading south, turn right at the Matanchén village junction) is dotted by little outcroppings topped by miniature jungles of swaying palms

© BRUCE WHIPPERMAN

The rocky islets of Las Islitas provide perfect perches for watching for the Big Wave.

and spreading trees. One of these is home for a colony of surfers waiting for the Big Wave, the Holy Grail of surfing. The Big Wave is one of the occasional gigantic 20-foot breakers that rise off Playa Las Islitas and carry surfers as much as a mile and a quarter—an official Guinness world record—to the soft sand of Playa Matanchén.

About three miles (5 km) south of Matanchén village, a sign marks a side road to a *cocodrilario* (crocodile farm). At the end of the two-mile track (negotiable only when dry), you'll arrive at El Tanque, a spring-fed pond, home of the **Ejido de la Palma crocodile farm.** About 50 toothy crocs, large and small, snooze in the sun within several enclosures. Half the fun is the adjacent spring-fed freshwater lagoon, so crystal clear you can see half a dozen big fish wriggling beneath the surface. Nearby, ancient trees swathed in vines and orchids tower overhead, butterflies flutter past, and turtles sun themselves on mossy logs. Bring a picnic lunch, your binoculars and bird book, insect repellent, and bathing suit.

Accommodations and Food

For camping, the intimate, protected curves of sand around Playa Islitas are ideal. Although few facilities exist (save for a few winter-season food *palapas*), the beach-combing, swimming, fishing from the rocks, shell-collecting, and surfing are usually good even without the Big Wave. The water, however, isn't clear enough for good snorkeling. Campers, be prepared with plenty of good insect repellent.

In surfing season (Aug.–Feb.), the Team Banana and other *palapa*-shops open up at Matanchén and Las Islitas to rent surfboards and sell what each of them claims to be the "world's original banana bread."

Getting Around

Drive, taxi, or ride the local *autobús blanco* Santa Cruz del Miramar–bound bus, which departs several times a day from the corner of Paredes and Sinaloa, a block west of the San Blas church. Also, you can ride a Puerto Vallarta-bound second-class Transportes Norte de Sonora; or alternatively the second-class navy blue and white Noroeste de Nayarit bus, which leave the San Blas bus station about three times daily and goes around the bay, past Santa Cruz, all the way to Highway 200 at Las Varas.

South from Matanchén

Bending south from Playa Islitas past a growing lineup of beachfront *palapa* restaurants, the superwide and shallow (like a giant kiddie pool) Playa Matanchén stretches to a palm-fringed ribbon of sand, washed by gentle rollers and dotted with a few weekend homes and *palapa* restarants where you can set up a tent for a small fee.

As you continue down the road a mile farther, past the crocodile farm and a marine sciences school, the beach sand gives way to rocky shoals beneath a jungle headland. The road curves and climbs to the shoreline village of **Aticama** (small stores and restaurants) and continues along a beachside coconut grove, name-source of the bordering Playa los Cocos. Unfortunately, the ocean is eroding the beach, leaving a crumbling, 10-foot embankment along a mostly rocky shore.

The place is, nevertheless, balmy and beautiful enough to attract a winter RV colony to **Trailer Park Playa Amor** (c/o gerente Javier López, Playa los Cocos, San Blas, Nayarit 63740, tel. 323/231-2200, $12–18 RV site), overlooking the waves, right in the middle of Playa los Cocos. The park offers about 30 grassy spaces for very reasonable prices. Rentals run $12, and $13 ($18 for a/c power), for small and large RVs, respectively, with all hookups, showers, and toilets; pets are welcome. You can expect plenty of friendly company during the winter, when prior reservations, especially on weekends, are recommended.

Casa Mañana

About eight miles (13 km) south of San Blas (or 2.5 miles north of Paraíso Miramar), the diminutive shoreline retreat Casa Mañana (P.O. Box 49, San Blas, Nayarit 63740, tel./fax 323/254-9080 or 323/254-9090, toll-free Mex. tel. 01-800/202-2079, reinhard@ prodigy.net.mx, www.casa-manana.com, $37 –53 d) perches at the south end of breezy Los Cocos beach. Owned and managed by an Austrian man, Reinhardt, and his Mexican wife, Lourdes, Casa Mañana's two double-storied tiers of rooms rise over a homey, spic-and-span, beach-view restaurant and pool deck and garden. Very popular with Europeans and North Americans seeking south-seas tranquility on a budget, Casa Mañana offers fishing, beachcombing, hiking, and swimming right from its palm-adorned front yard. The 26 rooms rent for about $53 d, with a/c and ocean view, or $37 d, with a/c but no view. Add about 40 percent during Christmas–New Year and Easter holidays. All rentals customarily get one day free per week stay. Longer-stay discounts may be negotiable, and winter and holiday reservations are very strongly recommended.

If you're staying at Casa Mañana, you might look into the services of **Seven Sunsets Tours** (www.sevensunsets.com, click on guides) of photographer-guide John Stewart, who operates out of Casa Mañana. His mission is to guide his clients to experience the "real" Mexico, via nature-friendly strolls, hikes, and horseback rides to off-the-beaten-track local sites.

Waterfall Hikes

A number of pristine creeks tumble down boulder-strewn beds and foam over cliffs as waterfalls *(cataratas)* in the jungle above the Bay of Matanchén. Some of these are easily accessible and perfect for a day of hiking, picnicking, and swimming. Don't hesitate to ask for directions: *"¿Dónde está el camino a la catarata, por favor?"* ("Where is the path to the waterfall, please?") If you would like a guide, ask, *"¿Hay guía, por favor?"* One (or all) of the local crowd of kids may immediately volunteer.

You can get to within walking distance of the waterfall near **Tecuitata** village either by car, taxi, or the Tepic-bound bus; it's about five miles (eight km) uphill out of Santa Cruz along Nayarit Highway 76. A half mile uphill past Tecuitata, a sign reading "Balneario Nuevo Chapultepec" marks a dirt road heading downhill a half mile to a creek and a bridge. Cross over to the other side ($3 entrance fee), where you'll find a *palapa* restaurant, a hillside water slide, and a small swimming pool.

Continue upstream along the right-hand bank of the creek for a much rarer treat. Half the fun are the sylvan jungle delights—flashing butterflies, pendulous leafy vines, gurgling little cascades—along the meandering path. The other half is at the end, where the creek spurts through a verdure-framed fissure and splashes into a cool, broad pool festooned with green, giant-leafed *chalata* (taro in Hawaii, tapioca in Africa). Both the pool area and the trail have several possible campsites. Bring everything, especially your water-purification kit and insect repellent. Known locally as Arroyo Campsite, it is popular with kids and women who bring their washing.

Another waterfall, the highest in the area, near the village of **El Cora,** is harder to get to but the reward is even more spectacular. Again, on the west-east Santa Cruz-Tepic Highway 76, a good gravel road to El Cora branches south just before Tecuitata. At road's end, after about eight kilometers, you can park by a banana-loading platform. From here, the walk (less than an hour) climaxes with a steep, rugged descent to the rippling, crystal pool at the bottom of the waterfall.

While rugged adventurers may find their own way to the waterfalls, others rely upon guides John Stewart (see *Casa Mañana*), Armando S. Navarrete (at home, Sonora 179, San Blas, Nayarit 63740), and the founder of Grupo Ecologio in San Blas, Juan "Bananas" Garcia (at his café, La Tumba de Yaco, H. Batallón 173, tel. 323/285-0462.

Shortcut South to Puerto Vallarta

The all-paved Nayarit Highway 161 allows Puerto Vallarta–bound drivers to bypass the old route—the slow, roundabout climb and descent—via Tepic. Instead, Highway 161 forks right, south, from Tepic-bound Highway 76 (about 11 miles, 18 km, south of San Blas), a mile past Santa Cruz village. It continues through lush foothill farms and tropical forest, joining Highway 200 at Las Varas, about 53 miles (85 km) north of Puerto Vallarta.

Travelers who wish to explore Tepic, Nayarit's colonial state capital, and its lush, volcano-rimmed valley, should continue uphill along Highway 76.

Tepic

Tepic (elev. 3,001 feet, 915 meters) basks in a lush highland valley beneath a trio of giant, slumbering volcanoes: 7,600-foot Sanganguey and 6,630-foot Tepetiltic in the east and south, and the brooding Volcán San Juan (7,350 feet, 2,240 meters) in the west. The waters that trickle from their cool green slopes have nurtured verdant valley fields and gardens for millennia. The city's name reflects its fertile surroundings; it's from the Náhuatl *tepictli,* meaning "land of corn."

Resembling a prosperous U.S. county seat, Tepic (pop. 200,000) is the state capital and the service, manufacturing, and governmental center for the entire state. Local people flock to deposit in its banks, shop in its stores, and visit its diminutive main-street state legislature.

The **Huichol** people are among the many who come to trade in Tepic. The Huichol fly in from their remote mountain villages, loaded with crafts—yarn paintings, beaded masks, ceremonial gourds, god's eyes—which they sell at local handicrafts stores. Tepic has thus accumulated troves of intriguing Huichol ceremonial art, whose animal and human forms symbolize the Huichol's animistic world view.

You can very easily meet the Huichol people most any day in downtown Tepic. They welcome visitors to view the handicrafts that they offer for sale in a **mini-market,** beneath the sheltering

THE NAYARIT COAST

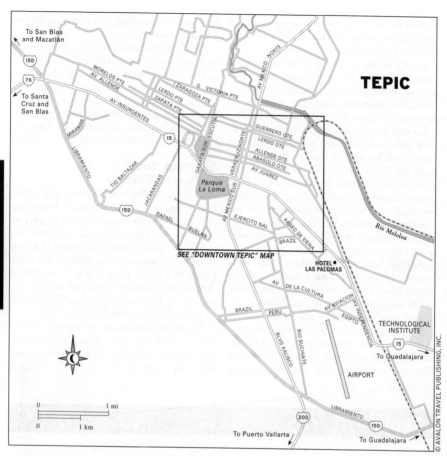

portal of the Tepic Presidencia Municipal (City Hall), at the west side of the Tepic city center plaza.

Beyond the city limits, the Tepic valley offers an unusual bonus for lovers of the outdoors. About 45 minutes southeast of town by car, sylvan mountain-rimmed lake Santa María de Oro offers comfortable bungalow lodgings and a modest RV park and campground, fine for a relaxing day or week of camping, hiking, swimming, kayaking, rowboating, and wildlife viewing.

HISTORY

Scholars believe that, around A.D. 1160, the valley of Tepic may have been a stopping place for a generation of the México (Aztecs) on their way to the Valley of Mexico. By the eve of the conquest, however, Tepic was ruled by the kingdom of Xalisco (whose capital occupied the same ground as the present-day city of Jalisco on Highway 200, a few miles south of Tepic).

In 1524, the expedition headed by the great conquistador's nephew, Francisco Cortés de San Buenaventura, explored the valley in peaceful contrast to those who followed. The renegade conquistador Nuño de Guzmán, bent on accumulating gold and *indígena* slaves, arrived in May 1530 and seized the valley in the name of King Charles V. After building a lodging house for hoped-for future immigrants, Guzmán hurried north, burning a pathway to Sinaloa. He returned a year later and founded a settlement near Tepic, which he named, pretentiously, Espíritu Santo de la Mayor España. In 1532 the king ordered his settlement's name changed to Santiago de Compostela. Today it remains Nayarit's oldest municipality, 23 miles (37 km) south of present-day Tepic.

Immigrants soon began colonizing the countryside of the sprawling new dominion of Nueva Galicia, which today includes the modern states of Jalisco, Nayarit, and Sinaloa. Guzmán managed to remain as governor until 1536, when the new viceroy, Antonio Mendoza, finally had him arrested and sent back to Spain in chains.

With Guzmán gone, Nueva Galicia began to thrive. The colonists settled down to raising cattle, wheat, and fruit; the padres founded churches, schools, and hospitals. Explorers set out for new lands: Coronado to New Mexico in 1539, Legazpi and Urdaneta across the Pacific in 1563, Vizcaíno to California and Oregon in 1602, and Father Kino to Arizona in 1687. Father Junípero Serra stayed in Tepic for several months en route to the Californias in 1767. Excitement rose in Tepic when a column of 200 Spanish dragoons came through on their way to establishing the port of San Blas in 1768.

San Blas's glory days were numbered, as were Spain's. Insurgents captured its fort cannons and sent them to defend Guadalajara in 1810, and finally President Lerdo de Tejada closed the port to foreign commerce in 1872.

Now, however, trains, jet airplanes, and a seemingly interminable flow of giant diesel trucks carry mountains of produce and manufactured products through Tepic to the Mexican Pacific and the United States. Commerce hums in suburban factories and in banks, stores, and shops around the plaza, where the aging colonial cathedral rises, a brooding reminder of the old days that few have time to remember.

SIGHTS

Tepic has two main plazas and two main highways. If you're only passing through, stay

on the *libramiento* Highway 15 throughway, which efficiently conducts traffic around the city-center congestion. An interchange at the south edge of town distributes Highway 200 traffic approaching from Puerto Vallarta three ways: east (to *libramiento* Highway 15 toward Guadalajara); north (to *libramiento* Highway 15 toward San Blas, Mazatlán, and the United States), or downtown along Boulevard Xalisco. Just past the *libramiento*'s north end, an overpass directs traffic either west to Miramar-Santa Cruz and San Blas via Nayarit Highway 76 or north along Highway 15.

Avenida México, Tepic's main north-south downtown street, angles from Boulevard Xalisco just south of big **Parque la Loma.** A few blocks farther north, it crosses Avenida Insurgentes and continues downtown past the two main plazas: first Plaza Constituyentes, and then Plaza Principal, about a half mile farther north.

A Walk Around Downtown

The **cathedral,** adjacent to Avenida México, at

Tepic's towering downtown cathedral

the east side of the Plaza Principal, marks the center of town. Dating from 1750, the cathedral was dedicated to the Purísima Concepción (Immaculate Conception). Its twin neogothic bell towers rise somberly over everything else in town, while inside, cheerier white walls and neoclassic gilded arches lead toward the main altar. There, the pious, all-forgiving Virgen de la Asunción appears to soar to heaven, borne by a choir of adoring cherubs.

The workaday **Presidencia Municipal** (City-County Hall) stands on the plaza opposite the cathedral, while the **municipal tourist information office,** with many good brochures, is just north of it, at the corner of Puebla and Amado Nervo. Back across the plaza, behind the cathedral and a half block to the north at 284 Zacatecas Nte., the **Museo Amado Nervo** (tel. 311/212-2916, 9 A.M.–2 P.M. and 4–7 P.M. Mon.–Fri., 10 A.M.–2 P.M. Sat.) occupies the house where the renowned poet was born on August 27, 1870. The four-room permanent exhibition displays photos, original works, a bust of Nervo, and paintings donated by artists J. L. Soto, Sofía Bassi, and Erlinda T. Fuentes.

Return to the plaza and join the shoppers beneath the arches in front of the Hotel Fray Junípero Serra on the plaza's south side, where a platoon of shoe shiners ply their trade.

Head around the corner, south, along Avenida México. After about two blocks you will reach the venerable 18th-century former mansion that houses the **Museo Regional de Antropología y Historia de Tepic** (Av. México 91 Nte., tel. 311/212-1900, 9 A.M.–7 P.M. Mon.–Fri., 9 A.M.–3 P.M. Sat. and Sun.). The palatial residence was built in 1762 with profits from sugarcane, cattle, and wheat. Since then, the mansion's spacious, high-ceilinged chambers have echoed with the voices of generations of occupants, including the German consul, Maximiliano Delius, during the 1880s. Now, its downstairs rooms house a changing exhibition of charming, earthy, pre-Columbian pottery artifacts from the museum's collection. These have included dancing dogs, a man scaling a fish, a boy riding a turtle, a dog with a

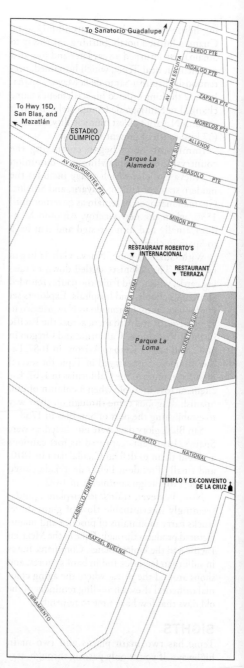

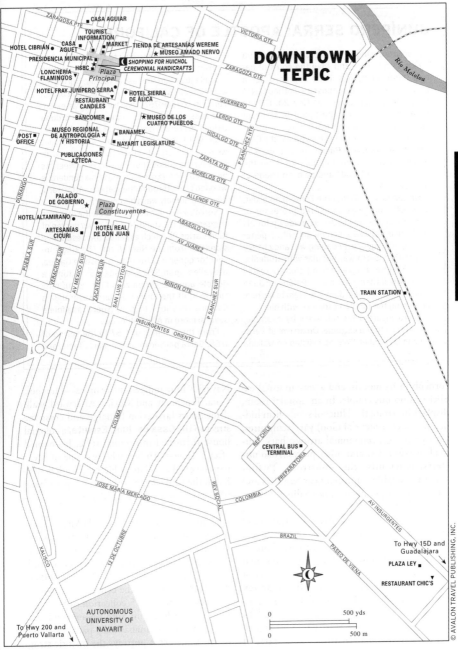

THE NAYARIT COAST

© AVALON TRAVEL PUBLISHING, INC.

JUNÍPERO SERRA: APOSTLE OF CALIFORNIA

His untiring, single-minded drive to found a string of missions and save the souls of native Californians has lifted Junípero Serra to prominence and proposed sainthood. Not long after he was born – on Nov. 24, 1713, to illiterate parents on the Spanish island of Mallorca – he showed a fascination for books and learning. After taking his vows at the Convent of St. Francis in Palma on Sept. 15, 1731, he changed his name to Junípero, after the "merry jester of God" and beloved friend of St. Francis Assisi.

Ordained in 1738 into the Franciscan order, Junípero soon was appointed professor of theology at the age of 30. He made up for his slight five foot, two inch height with a penetrating intelligence, engaging wit, and cheery disposition. Serra was popular with students, and when he received the missionary call in 1748, two of them – Francisco Palóu and Juan Bautista Crespi – accompanied him to Mexico, beginning his lifelong sojourn with him.

Serra inspired his followers by example, sometimes to the extreme. On arrival at Veracruz in December 1749, he insisted on walking the rough road all the way to Mexico City. The injuries he suffered led to a serious infection that plagued him the rest of his life. During his association with the Mexico City College of San Fernando (1750-1767), which included an extensive mission among the Pames Indians around Jalpan, in present-day Querétaro state, he practiced self-flagellation and wore an undercoat woven with sharp bits of wire. Often he would inspire his indigenous flock during Holy Week, as he played the role of Jesus, lugging a ponderous wooden cross through the stations. Afterward, he would humbly wash his converts' feet.

Serra's later mission to the Californias was triggered by the June 24, 1767, royal decree of King Carlos III, which expelled the Jesuit missionaries from the New World. The king's inspector general of the Indies, José de Galvez, prevailed upon Serra, at age 55, to fulfill a double agenda: organize a Franciscan mission to staff the former Jesuits' several Baja California missions, then push north and found several more in Alta California.

From the summer of 1767 to the spring of 1768, Serra paused in Guadalajara, Tepic, and

---

corncob in its mouth, and a very unusual explicitly amorous couple. In an upstairs room, displays illustrate the Huichol symbolism hidden in the *cicuri* (eye of God) yarn sculptures, yarn paintings, ceremonial arrows, hats, musical instruments, and other pieces. Also upstairs, don't miss the monstrous, 15-foot stuffed crocodile, captured near San Blas and donated by ex-president Carlos Salinas de Gortari in 1989.

If you have time, cross Avenida México and continue one block along Hidalgo to take a peek inside a pair of other historic homes, now serving as museums. Within the restored colonial-era house at the southwest corner of Hidalgo and Zacatecas is the **Museo de los Cuatro Pueblos** (Museum of the Four Peoples; tel. 311/212-1705, 9 A.M.–2 P.M. and 4–7 P.M. Mon.–Fri., 10 A.M.–2 P.M. Sat.), which exhibits traditional costumes and crafts of

Nayarit's four indigenous peoples—Huichol, Cora, Tepehuan, and México. Afterward, walk three doors farther on Hidalgo and cross the street to the **Casa de Juan Escuita,** a colonial house furnished in original style. It's named after a Tepic-born boy who was one of Mexico's beloved six "Niños Héroes," cadets who fell in the futile defense of Chapultepec Castle (the "Halls of Montezuma") against U.S. Marines in 1846.

Continue south along Avenida México; pass the state legislature across the street on the left and, two blocks farther, on your right, along the west side of the plaza, spreads the Spanish classical facade of the State of Nayarit **Palacio de Gobierno.** Inside the center rises a cupola decorated with a 1975 collection of fiery murals by artist José Luis Soto. In a second, rear building, a long, unabashedly patriotic mural by the same artist portrays the historic strug-

San Blas with his fellow missionaries en route to the Californias. They sailed north from San Blas on March 12, 1768.

They found the Baja California missions in disarray. The soldiers, left in custody of the missions, were running amok – raping native women, murdering their husbands, and squandering supplies. With the cooperation of military commander and governor Gaspar de Portolá, Serra managed to set things straight within a year and continue northward. On March 25, 1769, Serra, weak with fever, had two men lift him onto his mule, beginning the 1,000-mile desert trek from Loreto to San Diego. On May 17 Serra's leg became so infected that Portolá insisted he return to Loreto. Serra refused. "I shall not turn back.... I would gladly be left among the pagans if such be the will of God."

Serra, however, was always practical. He asked the mule driver's advice: "Imagine I am one of your mules with a sore on his leg. Give me the same treatment." The mule driver applied the ordinary remedy, a soothing ointment of herbs mixed with lard. Serra resumed

the trip and reached San Diego, where, on July 16, 1769, he founded San Diego Mission.

The following years would see Serra laboring on, trekking by muleback up and down California, founding eight more missions, encouraging the padres whom he assigned, and teaching and caring for the welfare of the Native Americans in his charge. Given the few padres (only two per mission) and the few stores brought by the occasional supply ship from San Blas, it was a monumental, backbreaking task.

In the end, Serra's sacrifices probably shortened his life. On August 18, 1784, at his beloved headquarters mission in Carmel, Serra spent his last days with Palóu, his companion of 40 years. Palóu gave the last sacrament, and two days afterward, Serra, in pain, retraced the stations of the cross with his congregation for the last time. He died peacefully in his cell eight days later.

Whatever one believes about Spain's colonial role, the fate of the indigenous inhabitants, and sainthood, it is hard not to be awed by this compassionate, gritty little man who would not turn back.

gles of the Mexican people against despotism, corruption, and foreign domination.

Continuing about a mile south of Plaza Constituyentes past Insurgentes, where Avenida México crosses Ejército Nacional, you will find the **Templo y Ex-Convento de la Cruz de Zacate** (Church and Ex-Convent of the Cross of Grass). This venerable and lately restored monument has two claims to fame: the rooms where Father Junípero Serra stayed for several months in 1767 en route to California, and the miraculous cross that you can see in the open-air enclosure adjacent to the sanctuary. According to chroniclers, the cross-shaped patch of grass has grown for centuries (from either 1540 or 1619, depending upon the account), needing neither water nor cultivation. While you're there, pick up some of the excellent brochures at the **Nayarit State Tourism** desk at the building's front entrance.

❰ Crater Lake Santa María de Oro
Easily accessible by car and about 45 minutes south of town, by either old Highway 15 or the new toll *autopista,* Laguna Santa María, tucked into an ancient volcanic caldera, offers near-perfect opportunities for outdoor relaxation and camping. The lake itself, reachable via a good paved road, is big, blue, and rimmed by forested, wildlife-rich hills. You can hike trails through shady woods to ridgetop panoramic viewpoints. Afterward, cool off with a swim in the lake. On another day, row a rental boat across the lake and explore hidden, tree-shaded inlets and sunny, secluded beaches, and sit in a palm-fringed grassy park enjoying the lake view and the orange blossom-scented evening air.

The driving force behind this seemingly too-good-to-be-true scene is Chris French, the personable owner/operator of lakeshore Koala Bungalows and Trailer Park. He's dedicated to preserving the beauty of the lake and its surroundings. It seems a miracle that, lacking any visible government protection, the lake and its forest hinterland remain lovely and pristine. The answer may lie partly in its isolation, the relatively sparse local population, and the enlightened conservation efforts of Chris and his neighbors.

ACCOMMODATIONS
Under $50

Starting in the north, near the Plaza Principal, **Hotel Cibrián,** a block and a half behind the Presidencia Municipal (Amado Nervo 163 Pte., Tepic, Nayarit 63000, tel. 311/212-8698, fax 311/216-1461, $19 s, $23 d, $28 t; credit cards not accepted), offers 46 clean, no-frills rooms with bath, ceiling fans, telephones, parking, and local restaurant. The Cibrián's small drawback is the noise that might filter into your room through louvered windows facing the tile (and therefore sound-reflective) hallways. Nevertheless, for the price, it's a Tepic best buy.

On Avenida México, half a block south of the cathedral, the **Hotel Sierra de Álica** (AH-lee-kah; Av. México 180 Nte., Tepic, Nayarit 63000, tel. 311/212-0325, h_sierradealica@hotmail.com, $27 s, $40 d) remains a longtime favorite of Tepic business travelers. Plain but comfortable rooms upstairs and a very good restaurant downstairs reflect the Sierra de Álica's solid unpretentiousness. The 60 rooms all have air-conditioning, satellite TV, phones, and parking; credit cards are accepted.

Several blocks north, on Mina, west of Plaza Constituyentes, half a block from the Avenida México plaza corner, **Hotel Altamirano** (Mina 19 Pte., Tepic, Nayarit 63000, tel. 311/212-7131, $18 s or d in one bed, $28 d in two beds) offers 31 clean but basic bare-bulb rooms with bath at budget rates.

$50-100

Right on the Plaza Principal stands the five-story tower of Tepic's **Hotel Fray Junípero Serra** (Lerdo 23 Pte., Tepic, Nayarit 63000, tel. 311/212-2525, fax 311/212-0251, www.frayjunipero.com.mx, frayjunipero@tepic

.megared.net.mx, $75 s $83 d). Although there is no pool at this site, the hotel offers spacious, tastefully furnished view rooms with deluxe amenities, efficient service, convenient parking, and a cool and tranquil plaza-front restaurant. The 90 rooms have air-conditioning, satellite TV, and phones. There is limited wheelchair access and credit cards are accepted. **Hotel Real de Don Juan** (Av. México 105 Sur, Tepic, Nayarit 63000, tel. 311/216-1880 or 311/216-1828, realdedonjuan@hotmail.com, $84 s or d) on Plaza Constituyentes appears to be succeeding in its efforts to become Tepic's class-act hotel. A plush, tranquil lobby and adjoining restaurant/bar matches the luxury of the king-sized beds, thick carpets, marble baths, and soft pastels of the rooms. The 48 rooms have air-conditioning, TV, parking, and limited wheelchair access; credit cards are accepted.

If you prefer to stay out of the busy downtown, you have at least two good options. On the north end, three miles from the city center, try the graceful, 50-room **Hotel Bugam Villas** (Insurgentes and Libramiento Pte., Tepic, Nayarit 63000, tel. 311/218-0225, 311/215-4600, fax 311/215-4601, bugamvillashotel@hotmail.com, bugamvillas@prodigy.net.mx, $76 s or d). From the lobby, the grounds extend past lovely, spreading *higuera* (native wild fig) trees to the two-story stucco and red-tile-roofed units. Inside, the rooms are clean with high ceilings, huge beds, marble shower baths, air-conditioning, TV, and phone. The elegant, cool, and serene restaurant leads outside to an airy dining veranda that overlooks a manicured shady garden. The food is appealing, professionally presented (but slowly served), and moderately priced. The only blot on this near-perfect picture is the noise (which choice of room can moderate considerably) from the trucks on the expressway nearby. Parking available; credit cards are accepted.

On the opposite, east, side of town, another good choice is the motel-style **Hotel Las Palomas** (Av. Insurgentes 2100 Ote., Tepic, Nayarit 63000, toll-free Mex. tel. 01-800/713-8500, tel./fax 311/214-0239, tel. 311/214-0948, reservaciones@laspalomashotel.com.mx, www.laspalomashotel.com.mx, $83 s or d), about two miles southeast of the city center. The two stories of double rooms and suites surround a colonial-chic pool and parking patio. The reception opens into an airy solarium restaurant, especially inviting for breakfast. The 67 clean and comfortable Spanish-style, tile-floored rooms have air-conditioning, satellite TV, and phones; credit cards are accepted.

Resorts

For a luxuriously rustic lakeside option, in the mountains an hour's drive south of Tepic, consider the (**Santa María Resort** on the lush, semi-tropical Crater Lake Santa María shoreline (reserve in Tepic, at Roble 210, Colonia San Juan, Tepic, Nayarit 63130, toll-free Mex. tel. 01-800/786-2742, tel./fax 311/214-6834, or directly at the hotel, tel. 311/213-2654, www .santamariaresort.com, $100–140 d, $220–380 cabin). Here, you can experience complete relaxation on the sylvan north side of the lake, in a simple chalet-style low-rise hotel that blends gracefully into its semi-tropical woodland park, shaded by a spreading green grove of palm, pochotle, and jacaranda trees. You could while away a day or a week here, hiking in the surrounding hillside forest, swimming, kayaking, or fishing on the lake, and savoring evening sunset dinners in the lakeview restaurant.

The 20 accommodations are all lovingly designed, in natural wood and stone, rising to airy beamed ceilings, and opening to private lake-view patios. Select from either luxuriously spacious room suites in the hotel section ($140 d Fri.–Sun., $100 Mon.–Thurs.) to even more roomy one- and two-bedroom housekeeping cabins, sleeping four and six, respectively ($300 and $380 Fri.–Sun., $220 and $270 Mon.–Thurs.), all with ceiling fans, a/c, and large bathrooms. Rates customarily rise by about 20 percent during Christmas–New Year, Easter, and July–August holidays.

Trailer Parks and Campgrounds

Although Tepic has lost its former trailer parks to development, RV and tent camping and comfortable rooms and bungalows are available outside of town at the (**Koala Bungalows and Trailer Park** (P.O. Box 14, Santa María de Oro, Nayarit 63830, Tepic local cell tel. 044-311/264-3698, long-distance tel. 01-311/264-3698, koala@nayarit.com, www.geocities .com/cfrenchkoala, $30–71 rooms, $10 RV site, $4 pp tent site) at the semitropical mountain lake Santa María, about 45 minutes southeast of Tepic. Owner Chris French maintains a tranquil, palm-studded lakeside park, with bungalow-style rooms, houses, RV and tent sites, a snack bar, kiddie pool, and rowboat and kayak rentals. Chris's accommodations vary; they include five simply decorated but comfortable double garden rooms with bath, for $30 for up to four; four kitchenette apartment-bungalows ($43) for up to four; and a small two-bedroom house with kitchen ($57) for four and a larger house with kitchen ($71) for up to seven. About 20 well-maintained shady RV sites rent for $10 daily, $60 weekly, with all hookups, toilets, and showers. Add $2 per day for air-conditioning power. Campsites go for about $4 per adult, $3 per child, per night. Weekends at Koala Bungalows tend to bustle with local families; weekdays, when the few guests are traveling couples, are more tranquil.

Get to Crater Lake Santa María by bus or by car, either along Highway 15 *libre* (non-toll) or the new toll Highway 15D *(cuota autopista)* to Guadalajara, which begins at Tepic's far southeast suburb. From *libre* Highway 15, about 16 miles (26 km) southeast of Tepic, between roadside kilometer markers 194 and 195, follow the signed turnoff left (north) toward Santa María del Oro town. Keep on five more miles (eight km) to the town (pop. 3,000). Continue another five miles (eight km), winding downhill to the lake. For a breathtaking lake view, stop at the roadside viewpoint about a mile past the town. At the lakeshore intersection, either head left a few hundred yards to Koala Bungalows and Trailer Park; or, for the Santa María Resort, turn right and continue about three miles (five km) to the signed driveway on the lake's north shore. From the 15D toll *autopista* follow the signed "Santa María del Oro" exit.

THE NAYARIT COAST

Proceed to the town and continue, winding downhill to the lake, as described above.

Laguna Santa María is accessible by bus as well, starting from the second-class bus terminal in downtown Tepic (from the cathedral, walk four blocks north along Avenida Mexico; at Victoria, turn east a few steps to #9, at the station driveway). The relevant ticket booth (the *taquilla* of Transportes Noroeste de Nayarit, tel. 311/212-2325) is inside at the back. Buses leave for Santa María de Oro town several times daily. At Santa María del Oro, catch a taxi or *colectivo* van or truck (about $1) to the lakeshore downhill, where a left turn gets you to Koala Bungalows within a five-minute walk, and a right turn leads to the Santa María Resort on the north side of the lake within another three miles.

You can also ride a long-distance second-class Guadalajara-bound bus from the Central Camionera (Central Bus Station, on Insurgentes, southeast of the Tepic town center) to Santa María del Oro town, where you can catch a taxi, local bus, or collective van the remaining five miles downhill to the lake.

FOOD

Traffic noise and exhaust smoke sometimes sully the atmosphere in downtown restaurants. The **Hotel Fray Junípero Serra** restaurant (Lerdo 23 Pte., tel. 311/212-2525, 7 A.M.– 10 P.M. daily, entrees $5–10) does not suffer such a drawback, however, in air-conditioned serenity behind its plate glass, plaza-front windows. Choose from a very recognizable menu of soups, salads, and sandwiches ($3–6), and pasta, meat, and fish entrees ($5–10); credit cards are accepted.

A much humbler but colorful and relatively quiet lunch or supper spot is the downtown favorite **Lonchería Flamingos** (tel. 311/212-1560, 10 A.M.–10:30 P.M., Thurs.,–Tues., entrées $2–5) on Puebla Nte., half a block north behind the Presidencia Municipal, where a cadre of spirited female chefs put out a continuous supply of steaming *tortas,* tostadas, tacos, *hamburguesas,* and *chocomiles.* The *tortas,* although tasty, are small. Best try the tostadas,

which are served on a huge, yummy, crunchy corn tortilla.

Discover a hidden gem in the homey but refined and *tranquilo* ⟨ **Restaurant la Sierra** (tel. 323/212-0322, 7:30 A.M.–9 P.M. daily), tucked to one side downstairs at the Hotel Sierra de Alica. Although the hard-working family owners start the day off with a number of good breakfasts with all the Mexican trimmings ($2–5), their hearty four-course *comida corrid* set lunch (soup, choice of entrée, dessert and natural fruit *agua,* $5) served 1:30–6 P.M., is the day's main event.

Another fancier, but nevertheless popular downtown restaurant choice is the **Restaurant Altamirano** (Av. México 109 Sur, 8 A.M.– 8 P.M. Mon.–Sat., 8 A.M.–4 P.M. Sun., entrées $3–6) in the big Hotel Real de Don Juan at the southeast corner of Plaza Constituyentes. Here, in a clean rustic-chic atmosphere, businesspeople lunch in the daytime, and middle- and upper-class Tepic families stop for snacks after the movies. The appetizing menu includes a host of Mexican entrées plus a number of international favorites, including spaghetti, hamburgers, omelettes, and pancakes.

About a mile south of downtown, across Insurgentes from Parque la Loma, a loyal cadre of middle- and upper-class patrons keep the coffee shop-style **Restaurant Terraza** (tel. 311/213-2180, 7 A.M.–11 P.M. daily, entrées $3–6) bustling morning till night. A major attraction, besides the food, is the racks of books and magazines that patrons enjoy reading, along with the good omelettes, spaghetti, and sandwiches.

Tepic people enjoy a number of good suburban restaurants. On the north side of town, one of the best is the refined **Restaurant Higuera** at the Hotel Bugam Villas (entrées $5–10). In the southeast suburb, **Chic's** (tel. 311/214-2810, 7 A.M.–10:30 P.M. daily, entrées $4–8), a Mexican version of Denny's, on Avenida Insurgentes by the big Plaza Ley shopping center, about 1.5 miles from downtown, offers a bit of everything for the travel-weary: tasty American-style specialties, air-conditioned ambience, and a miniplayground for kids around back.

If Chic's is not to your liking, go into Plaza Ley nearby for about half a dozen more alternative pizzerias, *jugerías, taquerías,* and *loncherías.*

For a deluxe treat, go to **Restaurant Roberto's Internacional** (Paseo de la Loma 472, at the corner of Avenida Insurgentes, west side of La Loma park, tel. 311/213-2085, 1–11 P.M., Mon.–Sat., entrees $8–20). Here, attentive waiters, subdued 1960s-style decor, crisp service, and good international specialties set a luxurious but relaxing tone.

🄲 SHOPPING FOR HUICHOL CEREMONIAL HANDICRAFTS

Its for-sale collections of Huichol art provide an excellent reason for stopping in Tepic. While at the downtown main plaza, be sure to make a shopping stop beneath the portal in front of the Tepic Presidencia Municipal (City Hall). Here a small village of Huichol vendors in their bright native dress offer a trove of both traditional

Huichol craftspeople sell handicrafts beneath the Presidencia Municipal portal in Tepic.

ceremonial and latter-day for-tourist (but nevertheless both fetching and handmade) crafts.

Afterwards you can continue to several downtown shops that specialize in Huichol goods. These shop owners have been involved with the Huichol for years, helping them preserve their religion and traditional skills in the face of ever-insistent modernization and development.

Starting near the Plaza Principal, the **Casa Aguet** (132 Amado Nervo, tel. 311/212-4130; 9 A.M.–2 P.M. and 4–8 P.M. Mon.–Sat., 10 A.M.–1:30 P.M. Sun.), a block behind the Presidencia Municipal (look for the second-story black-and-white "Artesanías Huichol" sign) has an upstairs attic-museum of Huichol art. The founder's son, personable Miguel Aguet, knows the Huichol well. Moreover, he guarantees the "lowest prices in town." His copy of *Art of the Huichol Indians* furnishes authoritative explanations of the intriguing animal and human painting motifs. He sells wholesale to dealers.

The small government handicrafts store, **Tienda de Artesanías Wereme** (corner of Amado Nervo and Mérida, next to the Presidencia Municipal, 9 A.M.–2 P.M. and 4–7 P.M. Mon.–Fri., 9 A.M.–2 P.M. Sat.), stocks some Huichol and other handicrafts. The staff, however, does not appear as knowledgeable as the private merchants.

If you can manage only one stop in Tepic, make it one block north of the plaza at **Casa Aguiar** (Zaragoza 100 Pte., corner of Mérida, tel. 311/212-0694, 10 A.M.–2 P.M. and 4–7:30 P.M. Mon.–Sat.), where elderly Alicia and Carmela Aguiar carry on their family tradition of Huichol crafts. In the parlor of their graceful old ancestral home, they offer a colorful galaxy of artifacts, both antique and new. Eerie beaded masks, venerable ceremonial hats, votive arrows, god's eyes, and huge yarn *cuadras,* blooming like Buddhist *tankas,* fill the cabinets and line the walls.

Several blocks south on Avenida México, **Artesanías Cicuri** (140 Sur, just past Plaza Constituyentes and across from the Hotel Real de Don Juan, tel. 311/212-3714 or 311/212-1466, 9 A.M.–8 P.M. Mon.–Sat.) names itself after the renowned *cicuri,* the "eye of God" of the Huichol. Its collection is both extensive and particularly fine, especially the beaded masks.

INFORMATION

Tepic's **municipal tourist information office** (tel. 311/212-8036, 9 A.M.–8 P.M. daily) is at the Plaza Principal's northwest corner, just north of the Presidencia Municipal (City Hall), at the corner of Amado Nervo and Puebla. It dispenses information and a tableful of excellent brochures, many in English.

Nayarit State Tourism offices (tel. 311/214-8074, 311/214-8075, 311/214-8076, Mexico toll-free 01-800/523-0160, www.visit nayarit.com, infotur@visitnayarit.com, 8 A.M.–8 P.M. daily) are in the Convento de la Cruz at Avenida México and Calzada Ejercito, about a mile south of the cathedral. Stop by the information booth, which stocks excellent brochures.

English-language books and magazines are scarce in Tepic. **Newsstands** beneath the plaza portals just west of the Hotel Fray Junípero Serra might have the Miami *Herald* in the afternoon. The **Restaurant Terraza** on Insurgentes, across from Parque la Loma, between Querétaro and Oaxaca (tel. 311/213-2180, 7 A.M.–11 P.M. daily), also may have the Miami *Herald* (telephone first) and a couple of dozen popular American magazines, such as *Time, Newsweek,* and *National Geographic.*

SERVICES

For the best exchange rates, go to a bank (all with ATMs), such as the main **Banamex** branch on Avendia México at Zapata (9 A.M.–4 P.M. Mon.–Fri., 10 A.M.–2 P.M. Sat.). If the lines at Banamex are too long, go to **Bancomer** (tel. 311/212-0260, 9 A.M.–4 P.M. Mon.–Fri., 10 A.M.–2 P.M. Sat.) across the street, or longhours **HSBC** bank on the main square next to the Presidencia Municipal (Mérida 184 Nte., tel. 311/212-4238 or 311/212-5130, open for U.S. dollar money exchange 8:30 A.M.–7 P.M. Mon.–Sat.). After hours, use a bank ATM.

Tepic's **post office** is downtown about two blocks west and three blocks south of the Plaza Principal (Durango Nte. 27, tel. 311/212-0130,

corner of Morelos Pte., 8 A.M.–5:30 P.M. Mon.–Fri., 8:30 A.M.–noon Sat.).

Telecomunicaciones (Av. México, corner of Morelos, tel. 311/212-9655, 8 A.M.–7 P.M. Mon.–Fri., 8 A.M.–4 P.M. Sat., 9 A.M.–1 P.M. Sun.), which provides telegraph, telephone, and public fax, has both a downtown branch and a Central de Autobuses branch (tel. 311/213-2327, 8 A.M.–1 P.M. Mon.–Fri.).

If you need a doctor, contact the **Sanatorio Guadalupe** (Juan Escuita 68 Nte., tel. 311/212-9401 or 311/212-2713), seven blocks west of the Plaza Principal. It has a 24-hour emergency room and a group of specialists on call. A fire-department paramedic squad is also available by calling 311/213-1809.

For **police** call the emergency number 066; for **fire** emergencies, call the *bomberos* (firefighters), tel. 311/213-1607.

GETTING THERE AND AWAY
By Car or RV

Main highways connect Tepic with Puerto Vallarta in the south, San Blas in the west, Guadalajara in the east, and Mazatlán in the north.

Two-lane Highway 200 from Puerto Vallarta is in good-to-fair condition for its 104-mile (167-km) length. Curves, traffic, and the 3,000-foot Tepic grade, however, usually slow the northbound trip to about three hours, a bit less southbound.

A pair of routes (both about 43 miles, 70 km) connect Tepic with **San Blas.** The more scenic of the two takes about an hour and a half, heading south from San Blas along the Bay of Matanchén to Santa Cruz village, then climbing 3,000 feet west to Tepic via Nayarit Highway 76. The quicker (one-hour) route leads east from San Blas first along National Highway 74, climbing through the tropical forest to Highway 15 D, where four lanes guide traffic rapidly to Tepic.

To and from **Mazatlán,** traffic, towns, and rough spots slow progress along the 182-mile (293-km), two-lane stretch of National Highway 15. Expect four or five hours of driving time under good conditions.

The same is true of the winding, 141-mile

(227-km) continuation of Highway 15 eastward over the Sierra Madre Occidental to **Guadalajara.** Fortunately, a *cuota autopista* (toll superhighway 15D), which begins at Tepic's southeastern edge, eliminates two hours of driving time, in exchange for about $30 in auto tolls, $60 for motorhomes. Allow about three hours by *autopista* and at least five hours without.

By Bus

The shiny, modern **Central Camionera** on Insurgentes Sur about a mile southeast of downtown has many services, including a tourist information office, left-luggage lockers, a cafeteria, a post office, long-distance telephone, and public fax. Booths *(taquillas)* offering higher-class bus service are generally on the station's left (east) side; the lower class is on the right (west) side as you enter.

Transportes Pacífico (tel. 311/213-2313) has many first- and second-class local departures, connecting south with Puerto Vallarta, east with Guadalajara and Mexico City, and north with Mazatlán, and the U.S. border at Tijuana and Nogales.

Estrella Blanca (tel. 311/213-2315), operating through its subsidiaries, provides many second-class, first-class, and super-first-class direct connections north, east, and south. First-class Elite departures connect north with the U.S. border (Nogales and Tijuana) via Mazatlán, and south with Acapulco via Puerto Vallarta, Barra de Navidad, Manzanillo, and Zihuatanejo. First-class Transportes Norte departures connect, through Guadalajara, north with Saltillo and Monterrey. Super-first-class Futura connects, through Guadalajara, with Mexico City. First-class Transportes Chihuahuenses connects north with the U.S. border (Ciudad Juárez) via Aguascalientes, Zacatecas, and Torreón. Second-class Transportes Norte de Sonora departures connect north, through Mazatlán and Nogales, Mexicali, and Tijuana, at the U.S. border.

Transportes Norte de Sonora (tel. 311/213-2315) sells tickets for hourly daytime second-class connections with San Blas and with Santiago Ixcuintla, where you can continue by local bus to the Mexcaltitán embarcadero.

Besides providing many first-class connections with Guadalajara, independent **Ómnibus de Mexico** (tel. 311/213-1323), provides a few departures that connect, via Guadalajara, north with Fresnillo, Torreón, and the U.S. border at Ciudad Juárez, and northeast with Aguascalientes, Zacatecas, Saltillo, Monterrey, and the U.S. border, at Matamoros.

By Train

The now-privatized Mexican Pacific Railway no longer offers passenger service. Until further notice, passenger trains, which clickety-clacked along the rails for generations, connecting Guadalajara, Tepic, and the U.S. border at Nogales and Mexicali, are mere fading memories.

Playa Chacala

The lush, 100-mile stretch between Tepic and Puerto Vallarta is a Pacific Eden of flowery tropical forest and pearly palm-shaded beaches, largely unknown to the outside world. The gateway Mexican National Highway 200 is still relatively new and development has barely begun. Only a few towns and a scattering of villages, with their pastures, tobacco fields, and tropical fruit orchards, encroach upon the vine-strewn jungle.

Side roads off Highway 200 provide exotic, close-up glimpses of Nayarit's tangled, tropical woodland, but rarely will they lead to such a delightful surprise as the green-tufted golden crescent of Playa Chacala and its diminutive neighbor, Playa Chacalilla

Nineteen miles (31 km) north of Rincón de Guayabitos, follow the six-mile, newly paved road to the great old palm grove at Chacala. Beyond the line of rustic *palapa* seafood

THE NAYARIT COAST

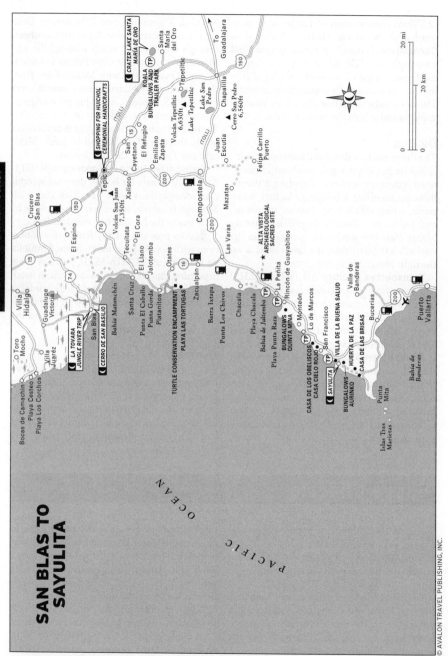

SAN BLAS TO SAYULITA

CRATER LAKE SANTA MARÍA DE ORO (TP)

Santa María del Oro

KOALA BUNGALOWS AND TRAILER PARK

SHOPPING FOR HUICHOL CEREMONIAL HANDICRAFTS

Volcán Tepetiltic 6,630ft
Lake Tepetiltic
Tepetiltic

Lake San Pedro

Chapalilla

Cerro San Pedro 6,560ft

To Guadalajara

15D

San Cayetano
El Refugio
Emiliano Zapata

Juan Escutia

Felipe Carrillo Puerto

Tepic (TP)

San Juan
Xalisco
El Cora

Mazatán

Compostela

ALTA VISTA ARCHAEOLOGICAL SACRED SITE

Crucero San Blas

15D

El Espino

Volcán San Juan 7,350ft

Tecuitata
El Llano
Jalotemba
Otates

Santa Cruz

Punta El Caballo
Punta Gorda
Platanitos

Zacualpán

Las Varas

La Peñita

Rincón de Guayabitos

Villa Hidalgo

15

Guadalupe Victoria

Villa Juárez

74

LA TOVARA JUNGLE RIVER TRIP

CERRO DE SAN BASILIO

San Blas

Bahía Matanchén

Barra Ixtapa

Punta Los Chivos

Chacala

Playa Chacala

Bahía de Jaltemba

Playa Punta Raza

BUNGALOWS QUINTA MINA (TP)

Lo de Marcos

Monteón

San Francisco

CASA DE LOS OBELISCOS
CASA CIELO ROJO

SAYULITA (TP)

BUNGALOWS AURINKO

VILLA DE LA BUENA SALUD

HUERTA DE LA PAZ
CASA DE LAS BRISAS

Valle de Banderas

Bucerías

200

Puerto Vallarta

Bahía de Banderas

Punta Mita

Islas Tres Marietas

Toro Mocho

Bocas de Camachín
Playa Cesteo
Playa Los Corchos

TURTLE CONSERVATION ENCAMPMENT PLAYA LAS TORTUGAS

PACIFIC OCEAN

20 mi
20 km

Playa Chacala's gently curving strand, majestic palm grove, and forested headlands make it one of Pacific Mexico's loveliest beaches.

restaurants lies a heavenly curve of sand, enfolded on both sides by palm-tipped headlands.

A mile farther north, past Chacala village on the headland, the road ends at Playa Chacalilla, Playa Chacala's miniature twin. (The status of public access to Playa Chacalilla is in doubt at this writing because of condo construction on the site.)

BEACHSIDE ACTIVITIES

Playa Chacala's oft-gentle surf is good for close-in bodysurfing, boogie boarding, swimming, and beginning-to-intermediate surfing. The water is generally clear enough for snorkeling off the rocks on either side of the beach. If you bring your equipment, kayaking, sailboarding, and sailing are possible. The sheltered north end cove is nearly always tranquil and safe, even for tiny tots. Fishing is so good, many local people make their living at it. Chacala Bay is so rich and clean that tourists sometimes eat oysters right off the rocks.

Supplied by the beachside restaurants (especially recommended: **Restaurant Las** **Brisas,** for good breaded shrimp; **Restaurant El Amigo,** for special *El Tlaxtihuille* shrimp broth soup) and **Restaurant Acela** and the stores in the village, Playa Chacala is ideal for tent or self-contained RV camping. Now that the road is paved, motor homes and trailers should be able to get there painlessly.

Boatmen on the beach, or at the dock at the bay's far north end, offer excursions (figure about $20 per hour) to nearby secluded beaches, such as **Playa la Caleta** for surfing and **Playa Las Cuevas** (the Caves) for picnicking, swimming, and snorkeling. Be prepared with your own food, drinks, and equipment.

Horseback rides along local jungle trails are available from providers at the beach. Concha, owner of Casa Concha (tel. 327/219-4019), offers bird- and wildlife-watching hikes.

ACCOMMODATIONS
Mar de Jade

Mar de Jade (U.S. toll-free 800/257-0532, or in Puerto Vallarta tel. 322/222-1171 or 327/219-4060, or in Chacala tel. 327/209-4060 or 327/209-4070, fax 327/209-4080, info@ mardejade.com, www.mardejade.com, $140–175 pp), the holistic-style living center at the south end of Playa Chacala, offers some unique alternatives. Laura del Valle, Mar de Jade's personable and dynamic physician/founder, has worked steadily since the early 1980s building living facilities and a learning center while simultaneously establishing a local health clinic. Now, Mar de Jade offers Spanish-language and volunteer programs for people who enjoy the tropics but want to do more than laze in the sun. A major thrust is interaction with local people. Spanish, for example, is the preferred language at the dinner table.

Previous visitors will notice, however, that Mar de Jade has headed upscale. Once, its lodgings were thatched adobe and brick or spartan apartments. Now, semideluxe and deluxe lodgings are nestled into a flowery, jungle-like hillside garden complex. The approximately 30 rooms and spacious suites are simply but elegantly decorated with designer rustic tile, pastel-toned drapes and bedspreads, and interior touches of wood and stucco. Stone pathways lead to the beachside main center, which consists of a dining room, kitchen, offices, library, and classroom overlooking the sea.

While Mar de Jade's purpose is serious, it has nothing against visitors who *do* want to laze in the sun, beachcomb, and soak in the beachfront pool and whirlpool tub. Mar de Jade invites travelers to make reservations and stay as long as they like, for about $140 per person, double occupancy (for the simplest accommodations) to about $175 (for the deluxe master suites), November–April, including three meals, tax and gratuity. Children with parents stay for about $30 each. Low season May–October rates run about 25 percent less. Discounts may be negotiable for stays of three weeks or longer.

The core educational program is a three-week Spanish course (about $300 for three weeks), although it does offer one- and two-week options for those who can't stay the full three weeks. Volunteer work-study programs, such as organic gardening, kitchen assistance, carpentry, maintenance, arts and crafts instruction, and teaching English might be arranged. Sometimes participants volunteer to join staff in local work, such as at the medical clinic or on construction projects.

Majahua Spa Bed and Breakfast

Civil engineer and builder José Enrique del Valle, who owns the jungle forest parcel above Mar de Jade, has worked hard to put his land to good use. His dream-come-true, Majahua (tel. 327/219-4053, 327/219-4054, or 327/219-4055, reservations@majahua.com, www.majahua.com, $135–350 d), now regularly receives guests. José and his staff offer four luxuriously rustic and private accommodations, an open-air restaurant, and a sprinkling of spa services. The lodgings, which blend artfully into the verdant tropical-forested hillside, are all lovingly designed and hand-built of stucco and tile, with various sleeping options (that include double, king-sized, and kid-sized beds), modern standard baths, and luxurious thatched *palapa* roofs.

Accommodations vary from the La Puerta honeymoon suite just above the restaurant, moving upward, through mid-sized double suites A and B, to the airy top-level view "penthouse" palapa suite C, big enough for five. In the middle, a small spa section offers massage, facials, and aromatherapy. High-season (Dec. 1–May 30) rates begin at about $130 for two, and run upward to about $350 for the big "penthouse" palapa suite. All lodging prices include breakfast.

For his more active guests, José offers to lead (or get a guide to lead) all-day wildlife viewing and hiking excursions, including a nearby extinct volcano crater lake (elev. 750 feet).

Techos de Mexico

José, along with the help of many others, notably Susana Escobido, have led Chacala's transition from a drowsy subsistence fishing village to a growing tourist destination. Now, with the help of many U.S. and Canadian volunteers, Chacala people, under the umbrella of the national **Techos de Mexico** (Roofs of Mexico) program, have built modern-standard tourist accommodations into their homes. They invite travelers to come and stay at very reasonable rates, around $20–40 for two, sometimes including breakfast.

All the following home-grown budget lodgings, unless otherwise noted, can be reserved either by telephone or by email. The growing list includes: **Casa Gracia** (tel. 327/219-4021 or 327/219-4067, sescobido@aol.com); **Casa Aurora** (tel. 327/219-4027 or 327/219-4067, sescobido@aol.com, $35–45), which has four rooms, fan, sea view, and parking; **Casa Beatriz** (327/219-4005), which has two rooms, fan, sea view, and parking; **Casa Doña Lupe** (alatawah@gmail.com), which has one lovely room, fan, sea view, and parking; and **Casa Concha** (327/219-4019, email conchaguanahani_234@hotmail.com, $25–35), which has three rooms with fan, sea view, and parking.

Chacala is a small village; all of the above are within three blocks of the beach and excellent fresh seafood *palapa* restaurants. For much more Chacala information, visit www.playachacala.com, or www.casapacificachacala, or http://chacalabudgetrentals.blogspot.com/.

Although not part of the Techos de Mexico, the **Hotel las Brisas** (reservaciones@lasbrisaschacala.com, www.lasbrisaschacala.com, tel.

327/219-4015, $45 nightly, $35 monthly rate) is locally owned and operated. The rooms (sheltered beneath the rustic *palapa* of a good beachfront restaurant) could be heaven for beach-lovers, smack on the lovely Chacala beachfront. The nine smallish accommodations, mostly all upstairs, are conveniently removed from restaurant hubbub below. They are attractively decorated in pastels, with private baths, a/c, cable TV, and in-house wireless Internet. Get your winter reservations early.

Casa Pacifica

Besides helping lead the Chacala community, sparkplug Susana Escobido offers her own lodging, the lovely sea-view ◖ **Casa Pacifica** (in Mexico, tel. 327/219-4067, in U.S. 760/300-3908, local Chacala cell tel. 044-327/102-0861, sescobido@aol.com, www.casapacificachacala.com, $50–70 d). Choose from three invitingly comfortable modern-standard rooms with fan, hot-water shower bath, and breakfast. Rentals run $60–70 d high season, $50 low, with no breakfast low season. Extras include Susana's airy Mauna Kea Restaurant (busy, especially for the great breakfasts, in high season, closed low) on a breezy sunset-view hillside above petite Chacalilla Bay.

THE NAYARIT COAST

Rincón de Guayabitos and La Peñita

Rincón de Guayabitos (pop. about 3,000 permanent, maybe 8,000 in winter) lies an hour's drive north of Puerto Vallarta, at the tiny south-end *rincón* (wrinkle) of the broad, mountain-rimmed Bay of Jaltemba. The full name of Rincón de Guayabitos's sister town, La Peñita (Little Rock) de Jaltemba, comes from its perch on the sandy edge of the bay.

Once upon a time, Rincón de Guayabitos (or simply Guayabitos, meaning Little Guavas) lived up to its diminutive name. During the 1970s, however, the government decided Rincón de Guayabitos would become both a resort and one of three places in the Puerto

Vallarta region where foreigners could own property. Today Rincón de Guayabitos is a summer, Christmas, and Easter haven for Mexicans, and a winter retreat for U.S. and Canadian citizens weary of glitzy, pricey resorts.

SIGHTS

Guayabitos and La Peñita (pop. around 10,000) represent practically a single town. Guayabitos has the hotels and the scenic beach village ambience, while two miles north La Peñita's main street, **Emiliano Zapata,** bustles with stores, restaurants, a bank, and a bus station.

THE NAYARIT COAST

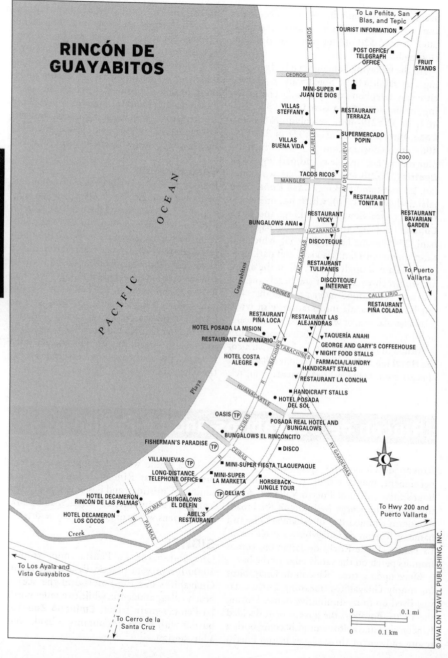

RINCÓN DE GUAYABITOS

To La Peñita, San Blas, and Tepic

TOURIST INFORMATION

POST OFFICE/ TELEGRAPH OFFICE

FRUIT STANDS

CEDROS

R. CEDROS

MINI-SUPER JUAN DE DIOS

VILLAS STEFFANY

RESTAURANT TERRAZA

SUPERMERCADO POPIN

VILLAS BUENA VIDA

R. LAURELES

AV DEL SOL NUEVO

200

TACOS RICOS

MANGLES

RESTAURANT TONITA II

RESTAURANT BAVARIAN GARDEN

RESTAURANT VICKY

BUNGALOWS ANAI

JACARANDAS

To Puerto Vallarta

R. JACARANDAS

DISCOTEQUE

OCEAN

RESTAURANT TULIPANES

COLORINES

DISCOTEQUE/ INTERNET

CALLE LIRIO

RESTAURANT PIÑA COLADA

Guayabitos

RESTAURANT PIÑA LOCA

RESTAURANT LAS ALEJANDRAS

HOTEL POSADA LA MISION

TAQUERÍA ANAHI

RESTAURANT CAMPANARIO

GEORGE AND GARY'S COFFEEHOUSE

NIGHT FOOD STALLS

HOTEL COSTA ALEGRE

R. TABACHINES

FARMACIA/LAUNDRY

HANDICRAFT STALLS

PACIFIC

RESTAURANT LA CONCHA

HUANACAXTLE

HANDICRAFT STALLS

HOTEL POSADA DEL SOL

Playa

OASIS TP

R. CEIBAS

POSADA REAL HOTEL AND BUNGALOWS

BUNGALOWS EL RINCONCITO

FISHERMAN'S PARADISE TP

DISCO

VILLANUEVAS TP

MINI-SUPER FIESTA TLAQUEPAQUE

AV GARDENIAS

LONG-DISTANCE TELEPHONE OFFICE

MINI-SUPER LA MARKETA

HORSEBACK JUNGLE TOUR

TP DELIA'S

HOTEL DECAMERON RINCON DE LAS PALMAS

BUNGALOWS EL DELFIN

R. PALMAS

HOTEL DECAMERON LOS COCOS

ABEL'S RESTAURANT

To Hwy 200 and Puerto Vallarta

R. PALMAS

Creek

To Los Ayala and Vista Guayabitos

To Cerro de la Santa Cruz

0   0.1 mi

0   0.1 km

© AVALON TRAVEL PUBLISHING, INC.

© BRUCE WHIPPERMAN

Rincón de Guayabitos drowses beside its petite, calm bay.

Guayabitos's main street, **Avenida del Sol Nuevo,** curves lazily for about a mile parallel to the beach. From the Avenida, several short streets and *andandos* (walkways) lead to a line of *retornos* (cul-de-sacs). The choicest of Guayabitos's community of small hotels, bungalow complexes, and trailer parks lie here within a block of the beach. You will also find several good restaurants nearby.

Isla Islote

Only a few miles offshore, the rock-studded humpback of Isla Islote may be seen from every spot along the bay. A flotilla of wooden glass-bottomed launches plies the Guayabitos shoreline, ready to whisk visitors across to the island. For about $20 per hour, parties of up to eight can view fish through the boat bottom and see the colonies of nesting terns, frigate birds, and boobies on Islote's guano-plastered far side. You might see dolphins playing in your boat's wake, or perhaps a pod of whales spouting and diving nearby.

BEACHES AND ACTIVITIES

The main beach, **Playa Guayabitos-La Peñita,** curves two miles north from the rocky Guayabitos headland and point, growing wider and steeper at La Peñita. The shallow south-end Guayabitos cove, lined by *palapa* restaurants and dotted with boats, is a favorite of Mexican families on Sundays and holidays. They play in the one-foot surf, ride the boats, and eat barbecued fish. During the busy Christmas and Easter holidays, the beach can get a bit crowded and messy from the people, boats, and fishing.

Farther along toward La Peñita, the beach broadens and becomes much cleaner, with surf good for swimming, bodysurfing, and boogie boarding. Afternoon winds are often brisk enough for sailing and sailboarding, though you must bring your own equipment. Scuba and snorkeling are good, especially during the November–May dry season, near offshore Isla Islote, accessible via rental boat from Guayabitos. Local stores sell inexpensive but serviceable masks, snorkels, and fins.

A mile north of La Peñita, just past the palm-dotted headland, another long, inviting beach begins, offering good chances for surf fishing and beginning and intermediate surfing.

Aquatic sports concentrate around the south end of Guayabitos beach, where launches ply the waters, offering banana (towed-tube) rides and **snorkeling** at offshore Isla Islote. Rent a **sportfishing** launch along the beach. If you want to launch your own boat, ask at the Fisherman's Paradise Trailer Park if you can use their ramp for a fee.

Cerro de la Santa Cruz

Some breezy afternoon, you might enjoy following the 225-step pilgrimage (May 3 and Easter) path to the summit of Cerro de la Santa Cruz (Hill of the Holy Cross). From the top of La Cruz, as it's locally known, appreciate the ocean, beach, and cloud-tipped mountain panorama of the Bay of Jaltemba. Find the trail at the south end of Guayabitos's main street, Avenida del Sol Nuevo. Turn left at the crossroads and look for the path heading uphill.

Playa los Muertos

Also at the south end of Avenida Sol Nuevo, follow the crossroad to the right, toward Los Ayala. Just as the road reaches its summit, curving left around the Guayabitos headland, notice a dirt road forking right, downhill. It continues through a cemetery to Playa los Muertos (Beach of the Dead), where the graves come right down to the beach.

Ghosts notwithstanding, this is a scenic little sandy cove. On fair days, get your fill of safe swimming, sunning on the beach, or tidepooling among the clustered oysters and mussels and the skittering crabs. (Recently, the owners of houses above the beach have placed a gate across the private entrance road to discourage cars. They cannot legally bar people from the beach, so even if you have to hire a launch to drop you off and pick you up there, Playa los Muertos is worth it.)

ACCOMMODATIONS
Guayabitos Hotels

Rincón de Guayabitos has far more hotels than any other town in Nayarit, including the state capital, Tepic. Competition keeps standards high and prices, for the most part, moderate. During the low season (Sept.–Dec. 15), most places are more than half empty and ready to bargain. During the winter season, the livelier part of town is at the south end, where the foreigners, mostly Canadian and American RV folks, congregate.

Guayabitos has many lodgings that call themselves "bungalows." This generally implies a motel-type suite with kitchenette and less service, but sleeping more people than most hotel rooms. For long stays or if you want to save money by cooking your own meals, bungalows can be an attractive option.

Note: Virtually all of the following lodgings have a web page in the Guayabitos general website, www.guayabitos.com.

UNDER $50

Start right in the middle of the town, on the south end of Andando Huanacaxtle, where the kindly owner of ◖ **Hotel Posada del Sol** (tel. 327/274-0043, fax 327/273-1319, from $45 d), half a block from the beach, offers 30 tastefully furnished kitchenette bungalows around a palmy garden-pool-patio. Best are the upper-level units, on the north side, with a/c and garden-view patio-balconies. Economical long-term discounts are negotiable. This charming place, as you would expect, is very popular and full in winter with a crowd of retired, long-time returnees. Get your reservations in early.

A good beachfront choice is the neocolonial-style **Hotel Posada la Misión** (Retorno Tabachines 6, Rincón de Guayabitos, Nayarit 63727, tel./fax 327/274-0357, 327/274-0895, or 327/274-1000, posadamision@prodigy .net.mx, $40 d), whose centerpiece is a beach-view restaurant/bar. Extras include an inviting azure pool and patio, thoughtfully screened off from the parking. Its rooms are high-ceilinged and comfortable, except for the unimaginative bare-bulb lighting; bring your favorite bulb-clip lampshades. Rents range from the smaller, but comfortable, economy double-bed rooms for about $40, to larger kitchenette suites sleeping six for about $65, all the way up to a pair of big kitchenette bungalows for about $80, all higher during Christmas and Easter holidays. Amenities include the good El Campanario restaurant out in front, ocean-view restaurant-bar, air-conditioning, ceiling fans, and parking; credit cards are accepted.

$50-100

Right-on-the-beach **Bungalows El Rinconcito** (Retorno Ceibas s/n and Calle Ceibas, P.O. Box 19, Rincón de Guayabitos, Nayarit 63727, tel./fax 327/274-0229, bws_elrinconcito@hotmail .com, $50–60 high season) remains one of the best lodging buys in Guayabitos. The smallish whitewashed complex set back from the street offers large, tastefully furnished units with yellow and blue tile kitchens and solid, Spanish-style dark-wood chairs and beds. Its ocean-side patio opens to a grassy garden overlooking the surf. The seven one-bedroom bungalows rent for about $50 high season, $40 low, with fans and parking. Three two-bedroom bungalows rent for about $60 high season, $50 low. Discounts are generally negotiable for longer-term stays.

One of the most family-friendly off-beach Guayabitos lodgings is **Bungalows El Delfín** (Retorno Ceibas and Andando Cocoteros, Rincón de Guayabitos, P.O. Box 12, Nayarit 63727, tel./fax 327/274-0385, beldefin@yahoo .com, www.bungalowseldelfin.com, $50 d), managed by friendly owners Francisco and Delia Orozco. Amenities include an intimate banana- and palm-fringed pool and patio, including recliners and umbrellas for resting and reading. Chairs on the shaded porch/walkways in front of the three room-tiers invite quiet relaxation and conversation with neighbors. The spacious four-person suites are large and plainly furnished, with basic stove, refrigerator, and utensils, rear laundry porches, and big, tiled toilet-showers. The 23 bungalows with kitchenette sleep four and rent for about $50 d high season, $40 low, $28/day for one-month rental, with ceiling fans, pool, and parking; small dogs and cats are allowed.

Just as deluxe but bigger is the beachfront family-oriented **Hotel Costa Alegre** (Retorno Tabachines s/n at Calle Tabachines, Rincón de

The Hotel Costa Alegre has one of Guayabitos's most inviting pool patios.

© BRUCE WHIPPERMAN

THE NAYARIT COAST

Guayabitos, Nayarit 63727, tel./fax 327/274-0241, 327/274-0242, or 327/274-0243, Mex. toll-free tel. 01-800/710-5683, costa alegre_4@hotmail.com, www.costaalegre suites.com, $75–90 d), where the Guayabitos beach broadens. Its plusses include a big blue pool and patio on the street side and a broad, grassy, ocean-view garden on the beach side. Although the rooms are adequate, most of the regiment of kitchenette bungalows are set away from the beach with no view but the back of neighboring rooms. The most scenic choices are the several upper-tier oceanfront rooms, all with sliding glass doors leading to private sea-view balconies. Some rooms are in better repair than others; look at more than one before paying. The 30 view rooms run about $75 d ($370/week); the 80 kitchenette bungalows $90 ($440/week). Amenities include air-conditioning, pool, parking, and restaurant/bar; credit cards are accepted.

Travelers who like lots of ready-made entertainment and an all-inclusive option, with all drinks, entertainment, and food included, should consider the compact, pool-and-patio ambience of the **Hotel Decameron Rincón de las Palmas** (Retorno Palmas, corner of Calle Palmas, Rincón de Guayabitos, Nayarit 63727, tel. 327/274-0190, fax 327/274-0138, $75 pp). On the south end of the beach, with an airy beach-view restaurant and bar for sitting and socializing, this is a lodging for those who want company. Guests may often have a hard time *not* getting acquainted. The smallish rooms are packed in two double parallel breezeway tiers around a pool and patio above the beach. Right outside your room during the high season, you will probably have your pick of around 50 sunbathing bodies to gaze at and meet. This hotel, once independent, is owned and operated by its big neighbor **Hotel Decameron los Cocos,** which handles reservations (in a Bucerías office, tel. 329/298-1104, 329/298-1107, reservas .mx@decameron.com, www.decameron.com), mandatory in winter. Specify the Hotel Rincón de las Palmas (or Cocos II, as it's now known), or you might be put in the oversize Los Cocos. The 40 rooms rent, high season, all-inclusive,

for $75 per person, double occupancy, with all drinks, food, and in-house entertainment included, with air-conditioning, pool, TV, tennis court, breezy sea-view restaurant and bar, and parking; credit cards are accepted.

For lots of peace and quiet in a deluxe tropical setting, the **Bungalows Anai** (Calle Jacarandas and Retorno Jacarandas, P.O. Box 44, Rincón de Guayabitos, Nayarit 63727, tel./fax 327/274-0245, anaisuitesan@prodigy.net.mx, www.suitesanai.com, $72 d) is just about the best on the beach. The 12 apartments, each with private ocean-view balcony, in three separate four-unit sections, stand graciously to one side. They overlook a spacious, plant-bedecked garden, shaded by a magnificent grove of drowsy coconut palms. The garden leads to an ocean-view pool-patio and whirlpool tub, where a few guests read, socialize, and take in the beachside scene below. Inside, the two-bedroom apartments are simply but thoughtfully furnished in natural wood, bamboo, and tile and come with bath, three double beds, furnished kitchen, fans, air-conditioning, and TV. Rentals run about $72 for two, add about $12 for each additional person, one-week minimum stay.

A couple of blocks farther north, **◀ Villas Stefany** (Retorno Laureles 12 Poniente, Rincón de Guayabitos, Nayarit 63727, tel./fax 327/274-0536, 327/274-0537 or 327/274-0963, operoma@hotmail.com, www.steffanyvillas .com.mx, $85 suite) offers a contrasting deluxe alternative. Guests in the 32 suites enjoy private balconies overlooking a lush pool, patio, and garden and ocean vista. The accommodations, simply but comfortably furnished in pastels, wood, and tile, have a living room with two sofa beds, a furnished kitchenette and one bedroom with one double bed and a bath; other extras include cable TV, telephone, and air-conditioning. Rentals run about $85 ($70 daily rate for one week, $60/day for one month) except holidays and July–August summer vacations; stay three nights and you often get the fourth night free. Amenities include a good restaurant, pool, lobby bar and credit cards accepted; street parking only, however.

Guayabitos Trailer Parks

All Guayabitos trailer parks are customarily wall-to-wall RVs most of the winter. Some old-timers have painted and marked out their spaces for years of future occupancy. The best spaces of the bunch are all booked by mid-October. And although the longtime residents are polite enough, some of them are clannish and don't go out of their way to welcome new kids on the block.

This is fortunately not true at **Delia's** (Retorno Ceibas 4, Rincón de Guayabitos, Nayarit 63727, tel. 327/274-0226, tel. 327/274-0397, tel. 327/274-0398, or tel. 327/274-0399, $14 RV site, $7 tent site), Guayabitos's homiest trailer park. Friendly owner Delia Bond Valdez and her daughter Rosa Delia have 12 spaces ($14/night, $350/month all year), some often unfilled even during the high season. Their place, alas, is not right on the beach, nor is it as tidy as some folks would like. On the other hand, Delia offers a little store and a long-distance phone service right next to the premises. She also rents three bungalows for about $500 a month. Spaces have all hookups (but insufficient power for a/c), showers, toilets, and room for big rigs; pets are okay, extra person $5. Space for camper vans costs $250/mo. with all hookups, tent spaces go for $7/day, $225/mo.

The rest of Guayabitos's trailer parks line up along the beach. The single one among them that celebrates a traditional Christmas Eve *posada* procession is the **Bungalows and Trailer Park Villanuevas** (Retorno Ceibas s/n, P.O. Box 25, Rincón de Guayabitos, Nayarit 63727, tel. 327/274-0391, $22 RV site, $35 bungalow), managed by friendly Lydia Villanuevas. Allowing for 30 spaces, including three drive-throughs, the park can still stuff in some big rigs, although room is at a premium. The sea-view *palapa* restaurant is very popular with Guayabitos longtimers. Spaces go for about $22/daily (or $19/day monthly), with all hookups. There's a restaurant, showers, toilets, and a boat ramp, and pets are allowed. Bungalows (tel. 327/274-0606), in a big building on one side rent for about $35, with kitchenette.

Next door to the north comes **Fisherman's**

Paradise Trailer Park (Retorno Ceibas s/n, Rincón de Guayabitos, Nayarit 63727, tel. 327/274-0014, fax 327/274-0525, paraiso-delpescador@hotmail.com, $20 RV site), which is also popular as a mango-lover's paradise. Several spreading mango trees shade the park's 33 concrete pads, and during the late spring and summer when the mangos are ripe, you might be able to park under your own tree. Winter-season spaces rent for about $20/day for two people, minimum 15-day rental (or $18 for a three-month rental), with all hookups, showers, toilets, and lovely pool and patio; pets are okay, and add $4.75 per extra person.

Neighboring **Trailer Park Oasis** (Retorno Ceibas s/n, Apdo. 52, Rincón de Guayabitos, Nayarit 63727, tel. 327/274-0361, $24 RV site) is among Guayabitos's most deluxe and spacious trailer parks. Its 19 all-concrete, partly palm-shaded spaces are wide and long enough for 40-foot rigs. Pluses include green grassy oceanview grounds, beautiful blue pool, a designer restaurant, and a luxury ocean-view *palapa* overlooking the beach. Spaces rent for about $24/day, with all hookups, showers, toilets, fish-cleaning facility, beautiful beachfront pool, and boat ramp; pets okay.

La Peñita Motel and Trailer Park

It will be good news to many longtime Mexico vacationers that **Motel Russell** (Calle Ruben C. Jaramillo no. 24, La Peñita de Jaltemba, Nayarit, tel. 327/274-0959, $15 1br, $20 2br) remains open and ready for guests. The scene is vintage tropical Mexico—peeling paint, snoozing cats, lazy palms, and a beautiful beach with boats casually pulled onto the sand a few steps from your door 00 all for rock-bottom prices. Come and populate the place while octogenarian owner Mary Cárdenas Nichols is still around to tell stories about "the way things used to be." There are about 15 clean, spartan apartments (most in need of repair) with one bedroom ($15) or two bedrooms ($20), all with fans, kitchenette, and refrigerator; discounts negotiable for one-month rental. Great fishing from the front yard, and it's two blocks from practically everything else in La Peñita.

THE NAYARIT COAST

For a fee, Mary may let you set up your tent or park your self-contained RV on one of the old beachfront trailer spaces. Get there by driving to the beach end of La Peñita's main street, Emiliano Zapata. Turn right and parallel the beach for about two blocks.

Residents at the big **La Peñita RV Park** (P.O. Box 22, La Peñita, Nayarit 63727, tel. 327/274-0996, reserve Nov.–April tel. 327/274-1593, June–Oct. U.S. 250/286-1803; U.S. fax toll-free 800/858-0604, carole@lapenita rvpark.com or lapenitarpark@hotmail.com, www.lapenitarvpark.com, $18 RV site, $16 tent site) enjoy a breezy ocean-view location one mile north of La Peñita; watch for the big highway sign. Its 128 grassy spaces ($18/day, $450/month) are sprinkled over a shady hillside park, overlooking a golden beach and bay, with all hookups; closed May–October. The many amenities include a pool, hilltop terrace club, wireless Internet, taco Tuesdays with free margaritas, hamburger night, laundry, showers and toilets, and surfing, boogie boarding, and surf fishing. Tenters are welcome for $16 per tent for two. Get your winter reservations to the owners.

FOOD
Fruit Stands and Minimarkets

The orchard country along Highway 200 north of Puerto Vallarta offers a feast of tropical fruits. Roadside stands at Guayabitos, La Peñita, and especially at Las Varas, half an hour north, offer mounds of papayas, mangos, melons, and pineapples in season. Watch out also for more exotic species, such as the *guanábana,* which looks like a spiny mango, but whose pulpy interior looks and smells much like its Asian cousin, the jackfruit.

A number of Guayabitos mini-supers supply a little bit of everything. Try **Mini-super La Marketa** (Retorno Ceibas across from Trailer Park Villanueva, tel. 327/274-0399, 7 A.M.–8 P.M. Mon–Sat., 7 A.M.–2:30 P.M. Sun.) for vegetables, a small deli, and general groceries. Competing next door is **Mini-Super Fiesta Tlaquepaque Fiesta** (tel. 327/274-0434, 8 A.M.–8 P.M. Mon–Sat.). On the north end

Ceviche is commonly sold on Playa Rincón de Guayabitos.

of Avenida del Sol Nuevo, **Mini-super Juan de Dios** and **Supermercado Popin** (both open 8 A.M.–9 P.M. daily) opposite the church and Hotel Peñamar, respectively, stock more, including fresh baked goods.

For larger, fresher selections of everything, go to one of the big main-street *fruterías* or supermarkets in La Peñita, such as **Supermercado Lorena** on main street E. Zapata, in the middle of town (tel. 327/274-0255, 8 A.M.–10 P.M. daily).

Cafés and Restaurants

Several Guayabitos cafés and restaurants offer good food and service during the busy winter, spring, and July–August seasons. Some, however, either close or restrict their hours during the midsummer and September–November low seasons.

By location, moving from the Guayabitos south end, first find tidy, budget **Abel's Restaurant** *palapa* (south end of Avenida del Sol Nuevo, behind Bungalows Delfín, 7 A.M.–

9 P.M. daily, dinner $3–7). Start off your day right with a home-cooked North American-style breakfast ($2–3), such as French toast, pancakes, or eggs any style. Return for lunch or dinner ($3–7) with one of Abel's hearty *burrita* or *azteca* soups, followed by a tasty meat, fish, or chicken plate.

For supper, you can't enjoy a tastier option than the family-run 【 **Taquería Anahi** (middle of Avenida Sol Nuevo, east side, corner of Tabachines, early morning–10 P.M. daily year round, $1–3). Here, dedicated cooks put out hearty tacos, enchiladas, spicy *pozole* (shredded pork roast and hominy vegetable stew), and much more.

Right across the street, don't miss **George and Gary's Coffee House** (tel. 327/274-0400, 7 A.M.–9 P.M. daily), for the best morning coffee in town. Later, drop by for a cool-down afternoon treat, such as George's **mocha frappe.** Master of the show is personable, knowledgeable civic leader and former professor of veterinary medicine, **Jorge Castuera.** If there's something you want to know about Guayabitos, Jorge is the person to ask.

A few doors north, the clean, local-style **Restaurant Las Alejandras** (tel. 327/274-0488, 8 A.M.–9 P.M. daily in season, $3–7) offers good breakfasts and a general Mexican-style menu.

From Avenida Sol Nuevo, walk a block toward the beach to one of Guayabitos's best, the moderately priced restaurant **Campanario** (Retorno Tabachines 6 at Calle Tabachines, tel. 327/274-0357, 8 A.M.–9 P.M. daily high season, 8 A.M.–5 P.M. low, $5–12), in front of the Hotel Posada la Misión. The menu, a longtime favorite of the North American RV colony, features bountiful fresh seafood, meat, and Mexican plates; credit cards are accepted. (For a variation on a similar comfort food theme, try equally popular **Restaurant la Piña Loca** across the street.)

A good place to start your day is in a comfortable booth at coffee shop-style, air-conditioned 【 **Restaurant Tulipanes** (Av. Sol Nuevo, south corner of Jacarandas, tel. 327/274-0575, 8 A.M.–10 P.M. daily, $3–7).

Pick from a long list of hearty breakfast combos ($4–5), including eggs, bacon and hash browns, hot cakes, and French toast. Return for lunch and dinner ($3–7), for guacamole ($3), soups and salads ($3), and pasta, chicken, and fish.

Finally, be sure not to miss Guayabitos's hands-down best restaurant, the 【 **Bavarian Garden** (on Hwy. 200, at the south-end signal and entrance to town, tel. 327/274-2136, open Nov.–Easter 5 A.M.–9 P.M. Mon.–Sat., 8 A.M.–9 P.M. Sun. with sumptuous morning brunch, entrees $9–$10) Here, you and probably at least a dozen winter-season (reservations recommended) diners will enjoy a feast, with entrees such as *kassler ripchen* (smoked pork chops, $10) or savory Hungarian goulash (substitute German potato pancakes for rice, $9), topped off with home-made *apfel strudel* ($3) and rich espresso. Wunderbar! Note: May–October low-season hours are 5–9 P.M. Mon.–Wed. and Fri.–Sat., 8 A.M.–2 P.M. Sun. for brunch.)

Also on Highway 200, a quarter mile south of Bavarian Garden at the Los Ayala crossing, satisfy your need for good Italian food at the highly recommended new **Restaurant Ricardo** (noon–9 P.M. daily, $5–10) Select from a menu that includes plenty of good salads ($5), pastas ($6–9), pizza ($5–10), and lasagna ($8).

ENTERTAINMENT

Guayabitos's spot for romantics is **Vista Guayabitos** restaurant (noon–10 P.M. daily) on the south edge of town. Little has been spared to afford a perfect spot to enjoy a refreshment and the airy panoramic view of Guayabitos's curving, cloud-tipped shoreline. Follow the south road to Los Ayala; at the big hilltop curve, follow the driveway on the right, steeply uphill.

Although Guayabitos is a resort for those who mostly love peace and quiet, a few nightspots, findable by the noise they emanate, operate along Avenida del Sol Nuevo. One of the liveliest and longest-lasting is Charley's live music cabaret, at the corner of Tabachines and the big, booming discoteque at the corner of Avenida Sol Nuevo and Jacarandas (from around 9 P.M. most nights, especially Fridays and Saturdays).

If oldies but goodies are your thing, the Bavarian Garden restaurant offers live '40s through '70s tunes and country music for dancing, 7–9 P.M. Wednesdays. and Fridays during the Nov.–May high season.

INFORMATION AND SERVICES

Nayarit State Turismo maintains an **information office** (tel. 327/274-0693, 9 A.M.– 7 P.M. Fri.–Wed.) at the north end of Avenida del Sol Nuevo, by the highway.

If you can't find out what you want at the *turismo,* an excellent alternative source is **Jorge Castuera,** the well-informed, personable, English-speaking owner of George and Gary's Coffee House (Av. del Sol Nuevo, corner of Tabachines). Jorge also runs a launderette and a book exchange: Bring one in, get one back.

Communications

The *correo* (tel. 327/274-0717, 8 A.M.–2 P.M. Mon.–Fri.) and the *telecom* (8 A.M.–2 P.M. Mon.–Fri.) stand side by side in the park, just north of the town church.

Long-distance telephoning is most conveniently and economically done on public street telephones with Ladatel phone cards, widely available in stores along Avenida del Sol Nuevo. A $5 Ladatel card will get you about 10 minutes of time to the United States or Canada (dial 001, then the area code and local number) on a street telephone. Lacking a phone card, go to George and Gary's Coffee House, where owner Jorge Castuera offers long-distance telephone service.

Money Exchange

Although Guayabitos has no exchange agency as such, some of the minimarkets may exchange U.S. or Canadian dollars or traveler's checks. More pesos for your U.S. and Canadian cash or traveler's checks are available at the **Bancomer** branch (with ATM) in La Peñita (on the highway, about three doors south

of main Av. E. Zapata crossing, tel. 327/274-0237, 9 A.M.–4 P.M. Mon.–Fri.).

Health and Emergencies

Guayabitos has a **paramedic ambulance** (tel. 327/274-1561), operated by the firefighters *(bomberos).* If necessary, they can take you in a hurry 14 miles (22 km) south to the small general hospital in San Francisco, tel. 311/258-4077, that offers X-ray, laboratory, gynecological, pediatric, and internal medicine consultations and services, both at regular hours (10:30 A.M.–noon and 4–6 P.M.) and on 24-hour emergency call.

Alternatively, for local medical consultations in La Peñita, go to the highly recommended small, private 24-hour **Clínica Rentería** (Calle Valle de Acapulco, tel. 327/274-0140). A surgeon, a gynecologist, and a general practitioner (Raul Rentería, M.D.) are on call there. For medical consultations and simple remedies in Guayabitos, see Dr. Alfredo Rentería, M.D., at his pharmacy (Av. del Sol Nuevo a few doors north of Tabachines, tel. 327/274-0747).

Tours and Guides

A few local guides lead tours into the lush, wildlife-rich Guayabitos hinterland. Most accessible is **Indalesio Muñoz,** who leads horseback nature trail rides directly from his corral on the south end of Avenida del Sol Nuevo, across from the Hotel Bugambilias. Tariff is about $20 per person for a two-hour ride.

Highly recommended English-speaking guide **Esteban Valdivia** (home tel. 327/274-0805, Restaurant Pina Colada tel. 327/274-1211) offers more extensive tours to unusual, untouristed local sites. His itinerary can include such intriguing destinations as hidden Las Miñitas bay and beach near Lo de Marcos, Jamurca hot mineral pools, and the Alta Vista Archaeological Sacred Site near Las Varas, and the jungle river boat tour to La Tovara spring in San Blas and the sylvan volcanic Crater Lake Laguna Santa María, in the Sierra southeast of Tepic.

For more guide recommendations, check with knowledgable Jorge Castuera at George and Gary's Coffee House, tel. 327/274-0400, or the Guayabitos tourist information office, tel. 327/274-0693.

GETTING THERE AND AWAY

Transportes Pacífico first- and second-class buses (southbound for Puerto Vallarta, and northbound for Tepic, Guadalajara, and Mazatlán) routinely stop (about twice every daylight hour, each direction) both at the main highway entrance to Guayabitos's Avenida del Sol Nuevo and at La Peñita's main Hwy. 200 crossing. The same is true of Estrella Blanca buses (Transporte Norte de Sonora, southbound to Puerto Vallarta and northbound to San Blas; and Elite, southbound to Puerto Vallarta, Manzanillo, Ixtapa, Zihuatanejo, and Acapulco, and northbound to Tepic, Guadalajara, Mazatlan and the U.S. border.)

At La Peñita, Transportes Pacifico and Estrella Blanca cooperate, sharing a pair of stations (and tel. 327/274-0001), on opposite sides of the main highway crossing corner.

Also at La Peñita, a third line, **Primera Plus** luxury buses en route between Puerto Vallarta and Guadalajara, also stop at a separate small station next to the Transportes Pacífico-Estrella Blanca station.

The Guayabitos coast is easily accessible by **taxi** (about $60 for four) from the Puerto Vallarta International Airport, the busy terminal for flight connections with U.S. and Mexican destinations. Buses (which you must board at the Puerto Vallarta bus station, north of the airport) and taxis cover the 39-mile (62 km) distance to Guayabitos in around an hour.

South of Guayabitos

PLAYA LOS AYALA

Continue along the road about another mile to the once sleepy but now up-and-coming settlement and one-mile yellow strand of Playa los Ayala. Although local-style beachside *palapa* restaurants and bungalow accommodations are blossoming, the long, lovely Playa los Ayalas retains its Sunday popularity among local families. All of the beach sports possible at Guayabitos are possible here, with the added advantage of a much cleaner beach.

Like Guayabitos, Los Ayala has its secluded south-end cove. Follow the path up the beach-end headland. Ten minutes' walk along a tropical forest trail leads you to the romantic little jungle-enfolded sand crescent called **Playa del Beso** (Beach of the Kiss). Except during holidays, for hours on end few if any people come here.

Among the best of Los Ayala's accommodations is **Bungalows Quinta Mina** (Los Ayala, Nayarit 63727, tel./fax 327/274-1141 or 327/274-1321, $50 1 br low season). This three-story stack of modern kitchenette apartments enfolds an inviting beachfront pool and patio. Here, adults lounge around the small pool, while their kids frolic in a beachside kiddie pool. Upstairs, the dozen or so one-bedroom units, sleeping four, are simply but attractively furnished, with large rustic floor tiles, soft couches, white stucco walls, and shiny shower bathrooms. Low-season rentals run about $50 for up to four, except holidays and *puentes* (long weekends).

If the Quinta Mina is full, check out the Los Ayala branch of the popular Rincón de Guayabitos lodging **Bungalows el Delfín** (Av. Estero 228, Los Ayala, Nayara 63727, tel. 327/274-0971, www.bungalowseldelfin.com), with 11 lodgings on the beach and a pool in the backyard.

PLAYA PUNTA RAZA

The road to Playa Punta Raza, while only about three miles long, requires a maneuverable high-clearance vehicle and dry weather. The reward is a long, wild beach perfect for beachcombing and camping. Bring everything, including water.

Three miles south of Guayabitos along Highway 200, turn off west at El Monteón; pass through the village, and turn right at Calle Punta Raza just before the pavement ends. Continue along the rough road through the creek and over the ridge north of town. At the summit, stop and feast your eyes on the valley view below, then continue down through the near-virgin jungle, barely scratched by a few poor cornfields. About a mile downhill from the summit, stop to see if the seasonal hillside Hotel and Restaurant Rincón del Cielo on the right is open.

At the bottom of the steep grade, the track parallels the beach beneath big trees; sandy trails run through the brush to the beach. This drive should be attempted by four-wheel-drive and experienced sand drivers only—it's very easy to get stuck. You will probably have two straight miles of pristine, jungle-backed sand virtually to yourself.

The beach itself slopes steeply, with the resulting close-in crashing waves and undertow. The water would be fine for splashing, but swimmers be careful. Because of the jungle hinterland, birds and other wildlife are plentiful here. Bring your insect repellent, binoculars, and identification books.

Turtles arrive seasonally to lay eggs here, mostly in late summer and fall. Look for their obvious tracks in the sand. The turtles attract predators: cats, iguanas, birds, and human poachers. If you find an egg nest, either report it to the local volunteers or keep watch over it; your reward may be to witness the emergence and return to the ocean of dozens of baby turtles.

If the **Hotel and Restaurant Rincón del Cielo** is open, it affords the opportunity of enjoying an overnight at Playa Punta Raza without the effort of camping. Pioneering owners María Zavala and Juan Bernal offer five immaculate, simply but lovingly decorated rooms. Two are at the jungle's edge ($45 d), one is at the ground level in their whimsical, medieval-style stone tower ($55 d), the two others enjoy airy view perches above the surf ($65). Without electricity, María and Juan and their nighttime guests manage well using gas for light and refrigeration in their restaurant (seafood, salads, and pasta) and candle- and hurricane-lantern-light in the rooms. Make reservations (not usually necessary) by leaving a message with the telephone operator in Monteón (tel. 327/274-7070).

PLAYA LO DE MARCOS

Follow the signed Lo de Marcos turnoff 31 miles (49 km) north of the Puerto Vallarta airport (or 8 miles/13 km south of Rincón de Guayabitos). Continue about a mile through the town to the long, sandy beach, dotted with a baker's dozen seafood *palapa* restaurants. Playa Lo de Marcos is popular with Mexican families; on Sunday and holidays they dig into the fine golden sand and frolic in the gentle, rolling waves. The surf of the nearly level, very wide Playa Lo de Marcos is good for all aquatic sports except surfing. The south end has a rocky tidepool shelf, fine for bait-casting. During the clear-water late fall–winter season,

© BRUCE WHIPPERMAN

Playa Lo de Marcos, with golden sand and gentle billows, is usually quiet on weekdays.

scuba divers and snorkelers rent boats and head to pristine offshore Isla Islote.

Accommodations

The constant flow of vacationing Mexican families supports a pair of moderately priced hotels on the main street, on the right, about a quarter-mile from the highway. Best by far is **Hotel Bungalows Las Tortugas** (Luis Echevarría 28, Lo de Marcos, Nayarit, tel./fax 327/275-0092, $35 d). The major attraction is the layout of about 18 kitchenette apartments in two stories around a broad, invitingly tropical, designer pool and patio, with kiddie pool and hot tub. Inside, the units, all with kitchenettes, TV, dishes and utensils, and fans, are bare-bulb (bring your own lampshade), sparely but comfortably furnished, spacious, and clean. The second-floor apartments, with king-sized beds, are more inviting than some others. Look at more than one before deciding. Asking rates run high, but, except during holidays and some weekends, discounts may be negotiable, so be sure to ask for a *descuento* (days-koo-AYN-toh).

If Las Tortugas is full, take a look at the plainer but recommendable **Bungalows Padre Nuestro** (tel. 327/275-0025, fax 327/275-0055, $33 except Christmas and Easter holidays), a few doors back toward the highway, with pool and a big family-friendly grassy picnic *palapa* and patio in back. Although the approximately 20 kitchenette apartments are plain, they're clean and the prices are right.

For something fancier, consider the big **Villas and Bungalows Tlaquepaque** (Pie de Avenida Luís Echeverría, Lo de Marcos, Nayarit, tel./fax 327/275-0080, villastlaquepaque@prodigy.net.mx, www.villastlaquepaque.com, $45 d studio low season). Past the imposing neocolonial front gate and reception spreads a manicured, grassy park, with luxurious blue-pool patio, basketball court, soccer field, and kiddie playground, interspersed among handsome accommodations tiers. Lodgings vary from one-bedroom studios to big three-bedroom, three-bath extended-family suites.

The lodgings themselves are immaculate and handsomely decorated in white stucco, bright Spanish tiles, and traditional handcrafted wooden furniture. A number of the studios are cozy and comfortable, with bright garden views and two double beds. Considering all the family-friendly facilities, the lower-end prices are moderate, beginning at about $45 d for the studios during the low season (Sept.–Dec. 15 and Jan.–March), with breakfast sometimes included, and ranging up to $150 for two-bedroom family suites. Look at several options before choosing. With plenty of space to run around and only a block from the beach, this is a great place for kids. Reservations generally not necessary, except July–August and Christmas and Easter holidays and maybe some weekends.

If you prefer to stay closer to the sand and waves, a sprinkling of newish family-friendly beachfront lodgings appears promising: Check out **Bungalows Arco Iris** (Camino a las Minitas 22, Lo de Marcos, Nayarit, tel. 327/275-0321, $32 d low season). Here in a big apartment-style complex, you have your choice of seven simply furnished rooms ($32 d, $40 holidays) with hot-water showers, or seven one-bedroom bungalows ($55 d, $70 holidays) with kitchenette. All have TV, fans, and a beachside pool/patio. Get there by turning left from the main town highway entrance street, at the last road before the beach.

Also on the beachfront, a block farther south, get a bit more for your money at welcoming **Bungalows El Coral** (Camino a las Minitas 39, tel. 327/275-0008, elcoraldelodemarcos@hotmail.com, $32 d), with a big beautiful pool-patio. Here, rooms run about $32 d, kitchenette bungalows about $40 d, with cable and fans (or a/c for an additional $10).

Trailer Parks and Campgrounds

Lo de Marcos has a number of beachfront trailer parks, popular during the winter with American and Canadian RV retirees. Best of the bunch is the **El Caracol** trailer park and bungalow complex (P.O. Box 89, La Peñita de Jaltemba, Nayarit 63726, tel./fax 327/275-0050, elcaracol_mx@tripod.com or elcaracol_mx@hotmail.com, www.elcaracol_mx.tripod.com, $19 d RV site, $55 d bungalow). The trailer park section offers about 15 concrete-pad spaces in a palm- and banana-shaded grassy park right on the beach. There's a small beachfront kiddie pool-patio, all hookups, and immaculate hot-shower and toilet facilities. The spaces rent for about $19 d/day, $18 d monthly, $16 d for a 95-day stay, add $4/day for a/c power. Add $5/day per extra person. Dogs are not generally welcome. It's popular, so make winter reservations July or August.

Caracol's bungalows are also well-appointed. They are available with one bedroom (for up to three) or two bedrooms (for up to five), comfortably furnished with all the comforts of Hamburg (the owner is German), including fans, optional air-conditioning, and kitchenettes. Daily rates run from $55 for two people in a one-bedroom bungalow, up to about $85 for five people in a two-bedroom bungalow, add $5 for a/c in the one-bedroom, $10 for a/c in the two-bedroom. Long term-rates, for a three-month rental, can sometimes be negotiated to as low as $25 daily for a one-bedroom and $35 daily for a two-bedroom. Get your reservations in early.

Tent, RV camping, and bungalow lodgings are available at the trailer park **Pequeña Paraíso** (Carretera a Las Miñitas no.1938, Lo de Marcos, Nayarit, tel. 327/275-0089, $200/week apartment, $17 RV site, $5 tent site), beside the jungle headland at the south end of the beach. Here, the manager welcomes visitors to the spacious, palm-shaded beachside grove. Basic but clean apartments rent for about $200 per week, with kitchenette, hot-water showers and fans. RV spaces ($17/day, $120/week, $450/month) have all hookups, with showers and toilets. Dozens of grass-carpeted, palm-shaded tent spaces rent for about $5 per person per day. Stores in town nearby can furnish basic supplies. Reserve, especially during the winter.

Get to the beachfront bungalows and trailer parks by turning left just before the beach, at the foot-of-the-town main street (which leads straight from the highway). Continue about

another mile to El Caracol, on the right, and El Pequeño Paraíso, a hundred yards farther.

If those two are full, a few other trailer parks are recommendable. Best appears to be beachfront trailer park **Pretty Sunset** (tel./fax 327/275-0024 or 327/275-0055, $20 RV site, with about 18 complete hookup sites ($20/day, $450/mo.) in a mostly unshaded but spacious beachfront park. Another similarly equipped, but smaller, option along the same beachfront is **Trailer Park and Bungalows Huerta de Iguanas** (tel. 327/275-0089).

If they're all full, you're most likely to get a tent or RV space at the huge, overflow-style RV park of the Villas y Bungalows Tlaquepaque, **Trailer Park and Campground El Refugio** (Pie de Avenida Luís Echeverría, Lo de Marcos, Nayarit, tel./fax 327/275-0080, villastlaquepaque@prodigy.net.mx, www.villastlaquepaque.com, $20 per day, $500 per month) on the north end of the beach.

PLAYA LAS MIÑITAS AND PLAYA EL VENADO

Continuing south along the Lo de Marcos beach road past the trailer parks, you will soon come to two small sandy beaches, Playa Las Miñitas and Playa el Venado. Both of these pretty, rock-enfolded strands, especially El Venado, are likely to be crowded on weekends, but mostly empty midweek, with lots of empty *palapas*, ripe for a tent. Even if for a day, bring your swimsuit, picnic lunch, and snorkeling gear.

PLAYA SAN FRANCISCO

The idyllic beach and drowsy country ambience of the former mango-processing village of San Francisco (San Pancho, locals call it, pop. about 1,000) offers yet another bundle of pleasant surprises. Exit Highway 200 at the road sign 25 miles (40 km) north of the Puerto Vallarta airport and continue straight through the town to the beach.

The broad, golden-white sand enclosed by palm-tipped green headlands extends for a half-mile on both sides of the town. Big, open ocean waves (take care; there's often strong undertow) frequently pound the beach for nearly its entire length. Beach *palapa* restaurants provide food and drinks. If you're enticed into staying, a sprinkling of good restaurants, hotels, and bed-and-breakfasts offer food and accommodations.

Offshore, flocks of pelicans dive for fish while frigate birds sail overhead. At night during the rainy months, sea turtles come ashore to lay their egg clutches, which a determined group of volunteers tries to protect from poachers.

Founded in 1992, the **Grupo Ecológico de la Costa Verde,** headquartered in Puerto Vallarta, has been instrumental in rescuing the Puerto Vallarta region's sea turtle populations from the brink of extinction. Spurred on by a dedicated cadre of volunteers, the organization's San Pancho chapter has led the effort, by working to increase the San Pancho Olive Ridley nesting turtle population tenfold, from about 70 to 700 active yearly nests in five years. The San Pancho chapter (Calle America Latina 102, tel. 311/258-4100, grupo-eco@project-tortuga.org, www .project-tortuga.org) welcomes volunteers.

Sights and Shopping

San Francisco has aquired a history museum that tells stories of the local past, from the days of the old *haciendas* to President Luis Echeverría, who came, fell in love with San Pancho, and gave the town its first big boost. Find the museum on Avenida Tercer Mundo, corner of Calle Latina America. Hours vary, depending upon the availability of volunteers.

A few arts and crafts gallery-shops sprinkle main street Avenida Tercer Mundo. In the middle of town, the **Oasis** gift shop sells crafts and T-shirts, profits from which go to the local turtle protection project. **Galería Corazón** (9 A.M.–5 P.M. Mon.–Sat., closed July through Sept.), across Avenida Tercer Mundo from the Calandria Realty, features an eclectic assortment of locally crafted candles, ceramics, woodcrafts, textiles, and more.

Accommodations

$50-100

On a quiet, flowery San Pancho side street, American owners rebuilt a venerable house, thus creating the stylish **Hotel Cielo Rojo** (Red Sky) bed-and-breakfast (Calle Asia 6, San Francisco, Nayarit 63732, tel./fax 311/258-4155, hotelcielorojo@yahoo.com, www.hotel cielorojo.com, $45 d low season, $55 d high). A tiled entrance walkway guides visitors indoors through an artfully decorated small lobby to an airy breakfast garden patio, partially sheltered by a *palapa* roof. A hot tub is tucked on one side.

Stairs lead to three upper-room stories, of six spacious rooms and a larger suite, all tucked beneath a handsomely rustic top-floor, *palapa*-roofed two bedroom suite. The accommodations themselves are simply but elegantly furnished with handcrafted wood furniture, arts and crafts, designer lamps, and colorful native-style handcrafted bedspreads. The exquisitely tiled bathrooms are fitted with gleaming modern-standard wash basins, toilets, and showers. The six rooms (with either queen-sized beds or two twins) rent for about $45 d low season, $55 high; the larger suite (with one queen, one twin) goes for about $70 low season, $80 high. The top-floor two-bedroom suite goes for about $100 high season, $80 low; all with ceiling fans and continental breakfast included.

Lovers of nature and solitude should head north of town (past the Costa Azul Adventure Resort) and continue a mile and a fraction (about 2 km) along the gravel coastal road to a signed driveway leading through the palm-tufted tropical forest. At road's end, find **Bungalows Lydia** (San Francisco, Km 111, Carretera Puerto Vallarta-Tepic, Nayarit 63732, tel. 311/258-4337 or 311/258-4338, bungalowslydia @hotmail.com, www.bungalowslydia.com, and www.vrbo.com/8853, $80–160 high season), the mini-Eden and life dream-made-true of sprightly and welcoming Lydia Cisneros Mora. Her (and her sister's) offering consists of four smallish but clean kitchenette studios ($70 low season, $80 high) and two larger one-bedroom bungalow suites (one for $90 low season, $110 high, the other for $140 low, $160 high, for up to six), with hot-water shower baths, all simply but thoughtfully decorated in whites and pastels. They're set in a charming oceanfront garden on a spectacularly rocky point buffeted by wild, foaming surf—the place is kept nearly bug-free by the ocean breeze. Discounts are negotiable for longer-term rentals; no phones or TV, but plenty of fresh air, sunsets, and animal friends: coatis, raccoons, armadillos, and squirrels (ardillas) in the neighboring vine-hung tropical forest. Paths lead down to a pair of secluded beaches, separated by a rocky outcropping, naturally equipped with an oceanfront tidepool whirlpool bath.

Nature notwithstanding, Lydia is part and parcel of the charm of her place. She bustles around, followed by her dog-companions, watering the plants, adjusting the generator, bringing in the laundry, and generally being helpful for her guests. When asked why she and her sister are out in this isolated spot, Lydia says (in Spanish, of course): "I started renting out rooms. Every time I made enough money, I would build another bungalow. The money I make allows me to help people in town and gives me time to read my Bible."

If on the other hand, you prefer to stay in the village, consider **(Palapas Las Iguanas** (Calle Tercer Mundo, San Francisco, Nayarit 63732, $80–$115 high season) at the edge of a shady palm grove, only half a block from the beach. Realtors Geno Lamphiear and his partner Elvia Garcia (Av. Tercer Mundo 50, tel. 311/258-4285, genolamphiear@hotmail.com, www.calandriarealty.com) manage the rentals, divided between a thatched open-air *palapa* complex and a more conventional, but nevertheless attractive, enclosed apartment section. The *palapa* section is made for romantics: two cozy open-air studios and a larger suite beneath a luxurious palm-thatch *palapa* fit for an Aztec king, with luxuries—gleaming designer baths, soft queen-sized beds, designer tile floors, up-to-date kitchenettes—that an Aztec king never dreamed of. Being open, however, mosquito nets (above each bed) must be used, especially during the summer and fall. The studios go for $80 d high season, $60 low; the suite, for $90 high, $75 low. For their more practical guests, Geno and Elvia also offer two comfortably enclosed, fan-equipped kitchenette apartments

next door. The smaller, Casita Tamarindo, is a petite, one-bedroom studio with small kitchenette (for $72 d low season, $75 d high); the larger, Casa Tamarindo, is a spacious two-bedroom, two-bath apartment with full kitchen ($104 low season, $115 high).

OVER $100
Back on the town main street, a sign on the right marks the good gravel road to the **Costa Azul Adventure Resort** (224 Av. del Mar, Suite D, San Clemente, CA 92672, local Mexico tel. 311/258-4120, fax 311/258-4099; U.S./Can. 949/498-3223 or toll-free 800/365-7613, fax 949/498-6300; getaway@costaazul .com, www.costaazul.com, $120 d high season). In-hotel activity centers around the beach and the palm-shaded pool-patio and adjacent restaurant-bar. Farther afield, hotel guides lead guests (at extra cost) on kayaking, biking, surfing, and snorkeling trips and naturalist-guided horseback rides along nearby coves, beaches, and jungle trails.

The main hotel building, at the foot of a hillside of magnificent Colima palms, offers 20 large, comfortable suites. Uphill, sheltered beneath the palms, stand eight villas (six one-bedroom and a pair of two-bedroom). Suites in the main hotel building rent, high season, for about $120 d; the one-bedroom villas go for about $160 d, and the two-bedroom villas, about $300, for up to six. Up to two children under 12 stay free. Reservations are strongly recommended, especially in the winter.

Past Costa Azul north a block or two, turn downhill toward the beach and continue another block north to lovely, secluded **(Casa de los Obeliscos** (reservations@casaobelisco .com, www.casaobelisco.com, $225 suite high season). Here, welcoming American owners have created their version of paradise for their guests to enjoy. They offer four super-comfortable airy, art-and-tile-decorated suites, two of them with private ocean-view patios, all overlooking a luscious, hibiscus-decorated pool-patio garden. Rates run $180 low season, $225 high season ($275 Christmas-New Year holiday) including a big breakfast. Sorry, no children under 16 or pets; closed August and September. Get your reservations in early, by email only. (In emergencies only, but not for reservations, call U.S. tel. 415/233-4252, or local Mexico tel. 311/258-4315.)

RENTAL AGENTS

For the many other San Francisco villa, house, or apartment rentals, consult friendly real estate agents Geno Lamphiear and Elvia Garcia, at Calandria Realty (Av. Tercer Mundo 50, tel. 311/258-4285, genolamphiear@hotmail.com, www.calandriarealty.com) in front of Restaurant Ola Rica on the main street. You might also consult **Feibel Real Estate** (Av. Tercer Mundo 91, tel./fax 311/258-4041, fred@flffeibel.com, www.flffeibel.com), with more listings of vacation rentals and for-sale homes.

Food

The growing local community of middle-class Americans, Canadians, and Mexicans and the trickle of Puerto Vallarta visitors support a number of recommendable in-town eateries.

For Mexican supper, start at **Cenaduría Delfín** (on the main street, after 5 P.M.), about a block from the beach. The house specialty is yummy *pozole* on Saturday and Sunday nights. On another night, head straight to Eva's **Red Chairs** taco stand, past the hospital, at the foot of the hill, on the way to Restaurant del Mar.

On the same main street in the middle of town, nearly everyone in San Pancho recommends **◖ La Ola Rica Restaurant and Bar** (6–11 P.M. Tues.–Sun., $5–12). Welcoming owners Triny and Gloria offer fresh seafood and Mexican supper specialties. For good Italian pasta and pizza, go to *palapa* **Restaurant Pizzeria Galloly** (tel. 311/258-4135, $6–12), on the south side of the main street about four blocks from the beach.

European-tropical fusion cuisine has arrived in San Pancho, at **◖ Cafe del Mar** (5–11 P.M. Thurs.–Tues, $10–15, closed June–Sept.) on the hill northeast above the village. Local expatriates rave about the sauces, succulent fish, homemade pasta, exotic drinks ($4), and yummy chocolate cake ($3) that Belgian-born chef

Almandine produces daily. Get there by following the street past the hospital (about a quarter mile from the highway), pass Eva's Red Chairs taco stand, and follow the signs uphill.

Geno Lamphiear of Calandria Realty recommends a pair of home-grown sources of fine food: Home-cooked seafood abounds at country-style fish market and restaurant **La Chalupa** (noon–6 or 7 P.M. daily, $5–10) on the beach. Here, get everything—fish, oysters, clams, octopus, shrimp—super-fresh, either for lunch or early dinner beneath the *palapa*, or for takeout dinner at home. Geno also recommends the new **Bottega de Sapori** Italian bakery, for fresh breads, pizza, lasagna, and desserts. Find it on Calle Latina America, about a block from main street Avenida Tercer Mundo.

Health and Emergencies

San Francisco residents benefit from a modest local general hospital (tel. 311/258-4077), with ambulance, emergency room, and doctors on call 24 hours. Find it off the main street, to the right (north), about a quarter-mile from the highway.

◖ SAYULITA

Little Sayulita (pop. 3,000), 22 miles (35 km) north of the Puerto Vallarta airport, was once the kind of spot that romantics hankered for: a drowsy village on a palmy arc of sand, a hidden retreat for those who enjoy the quiet pleasures and local color of Mexico. And while Sayulita during low season still resembles that former description, it's become much busier during the fall-winter vacation season.

Once only a destination for Puerto Vallarta day-trippers, Sayulita now is host to a yearly influx of RV retirees and youthful Americans, Canadians, Europeans, and Japanese who have made the village their fall-winter destination of choice. (If, howevever, you hanker for the tranquility of old Sayulita, simply come during the uncrowded Aug.–Nov. season, when Sayulita reverts to its former sleepy village self.)

Nevertheless, any time of the year, Sayulita's amenities remain: clean waters for swimming, bodysurfing, and beginning-to-intermediate

THE NAYARIT COAST

The oft-gentle surfing breaks at Playa Sayulita are popular with a winter cadre of beginning surfers.

© BRUCE WHIPPERMAN

surfing; fishing; colorful country ambience; and plenty of warm sun during the day and cool offshore breezes at night.

Accommodations
UNDER $50

Sayulita's perennial favorite budget accommodations are the economical, clean and comfortable rooms at (**Sayulita Trailer Park,** on the north-end beachfront. Besides the clean and comfortable budget rooms ($30/day d, one day free per week), you could opt for one of about a dozen simply but thoughtfully furnished kitchenette bungalows ($75/day d, one day free per week), four of them smack on the lovely, palm-shaded beachfront ($475 d/week). (Add about $50/week per extra person.) During the two weeks before Easter and December 15–31, rates rise about 20 percent, and reservations must include a minimum seven-day stay and a 50 percent deposit. Get reservations (for winter, best six months in advance) through the owners, Thies and Cristina Rohlfs, either in Mex-

ico City (Mexico city office tel. 55/5390-2750, home 55/5572-1335, sayupark@prodigy.net.mx, www.pacificbungalow.com) or in Sayulita directly (tel./fax 329/291-3126, Nov.–May).

Right in the center of town find the 1950s-vintage, auto court-style **Bungalows Las Gaviotas** (Calle Gaviotas 12, Sayulita, Nayarit 63727, tel. 329/291-3218, $35 d high season). Here, you can choose between three fan-only rooms ($25 low season, $35 high), sleeping in one double bed, or five bungalows ($55), with two beds and kitchenette, sleeping at least four. All units are clean, with a reading lamp, and bright blue and white tile floors. Other plusses include its quiet side-street location, one block from the beautiful beach on one side, and half a block from good restaurants and the colorful village square on the other. One negative is that you'll probably have to put up with noise from the cars coming and going from the parking lot outside your door. Best reserve ahead, especially on weekends, and the very busy Christmas and Easter holidays.

The lodging most likely to have a room when everything else is filled is the downscale, emergency-only **Hotel Sayulita,** on the beach. Although the owner, at the hardware store next door, asks about $27 d, $36 t, for 33 very basic rooms around a cavernous interior courtyard, you might be able to bargain for a better price. He accepts no reservations; during the crowded winter season, arrive early enough to assure yourself a room.

$50-100

Longtime expatriate resident Adrienne "Tía Adriana" Adams, the owner, and son Greg Adams, the on-site manager, of the bed-and-breakfast **Villa de la Buena Salud** (tel./fax 329/291-3029, Mex. toll-free tel. 888/793-3673, stayinsayu@yahoo.com, www.tiaadrianas .com, $50–120 d high season, $30–60 low season) rent about a dozen comfortable, thoughtfully decorated rooms and suites with bath, including breakfast high season for two, minimum three nights. Her airy, art-draped, three-story house is a short block from the main Sayulita beachfront. Although her upper-floor rooms are for adults only, families with children are welcome in two downstairs apartments ($55 low season and $110 high), with kitchen, VCR, and TV. Adriana also offers five comfortable lodgings in a hilltop view "Hideaway" designer villa ($40–120 high season). Adrienne enjoys dozens of repeat customers; get your winter reservations in early. She receives reservations (stayinsayu@yahoo.com, www.tiaadrianas.com) July–Oct. in California (1495 San Elijo, Cardiff, CA 92007, 760/632-7716, fax 760/632-8585) and Nov.–June in Sayulita.

On the north side of town, find luxuriously lovely **C** **Villas Sayulita** (tel./fax 329/291-3063, tel. 329/291-3065, villasayulita@ hotmail.com, www.villassayulita.com, $65 low season, $75 d high) on a quiet street about two long blocks uphill from the beach. Owners offer about a dozen spacious kitchenette suites on lower and upper floors, adjacent to an invitingly intimate tropical pool patio with picnic *palapa*. The suites themselves are lov-

ingly designed and immaculately maintained, with TV, air-conditioning, attractive rustic tile floors, deluxe modern baths, and soaring arched ceilings. Some beds are king-sized, with pullout for kids, others with two double beds.

Back near the town center, the gorgeous *palapa*-chic **C** **Bungalows Aurinko** (Calle Marlin, Sayulita, Nayarit 63727, tel. 329/291-3150, info@sayulita-vacations.com, www .sayulita-vacations.com, $80 d high season) offers an excellent alternative. Labor of love of its friendly owner/builder Nazario Carranza, Aurinko (Sun in the Finnish language) glows with his handiwork: hand-crafted natural wood bedstands and dressers, rustically luxurious whitewashed walls, adorned with native arts and crafts, all beneath a handsome, towering *palapa* roof, only a block from the beach. The five one-bedroom units rent from about $80 d in high season, $65 low. A pair of two-bedroom units go for about $125 each in high season, $97 low, and a gorgeous penthouse suite goes for about $105 high season, $95 low; all with modern bathrooms, airy patio kitchens, and ceiling fans.

At the end of the south-side beach road, the designer cabañas of hotel **Villa Amor** (U.S. tel. 619/291-3010, local tel. 329/291-3010, fax 329/291-3018, info@villaamor.com, www .villaamor.com, $85–370) dot the leafy headland. Villa Amor offers about 35 owner-designed architecture-as-art rustic *palapa*-chic view dwellings ($85–370, higher Christmas-New Year and Easter seasons). Accommodations, many open-air, vary from two-bedroom, 2.5-bath house-sized full kitchen suites, down to modest but still deluxe refrigerator-and-sink studios, all enjoying vistas of Sayulita's petite bay, with fans only, no phones, and no TV. Most beds are king- or queen-sized, and colors range from soft pastels to white. Credit cards are not accepted. (The only possible drawback to all this luxury might be the open-air *palapa* architecture of some, but not all, of the accommodations, which although inviting, might be a bit buggy and damp during summer rainy spells or chilly during mid-winter cool snaps.)

THE NAYARIT COAST

THE NAYARIT COAST

TRAILER PARK AND CAMPGROUND

RV folks love the north-side **⟨ Sayulita Trailer Park** (year-round fax 55/5390-2750, Dec.–May tel./fax 329/291-3126, sayupark@ prodigy.net.mx, www.pacificbungalow.com, $17 RV site) in a big, sandy, palm-shaded lot, with about 36 hookups (some for rigs up to 40 feet) and some room for tents, right on the beach. Guests enjoy just about everything— good clean showers and toilets, electricity, drinking water, a used-book shelf, concrete pads, dump station, pets okay—for about $17/day for two people, one day free per week, discounts possible for extended stays. Add about $4 per extra person. Get reservations (for winter, best six months in advance) through the owners, Thies and Cristina Rohlfs, email sayupark@prodigy.net.mx.

Trying just as hard is Sayulita's downscale campground, gated and enclosed **Palmar del Camarón,** in a big palm grove, on the gorgeous, palm-shadowed, north-side beachfront. The environmentally conscious owner (tel. 329/291-3373, no reservations accepted, always room for one more, $30 d cabaña, $5 pp tent site), who looks exactly like actor Harrison Ford, known locally as "Camarón," offers plenty of grassy spots for tents and smaller self-contained vans needing no hookups. Tent spaces ($5 pp) are first-come, first-served, with showers, toilets, and *palapas* for shelter against sun and rain. Camarón also rents rustic *palapa* cabañas ($30 d), with mosquito nets and private toilet and shower. Other extras include a beachfront *palapa* restaurant, and security lockers. Find it as you enter town from Highway 200, by going right at the lane that borders the baseball field. After a block and a half, turn right into the campground gate.

RENTAL AGENTS

Drawn by the quiet pleasures of country Mexico, a number of prosperous American, Canadian, and Mexican folks have built comfortable vacation homes in and around Sayulita and are renting them out. **Avalos Real Estate** (tel./fax 329/291-3122, www.move2sayulita .com), Sayulita's original real estate agent, lists such properties for rental or sale. For more information and listings, you may also contact the U.S. agent (805/481-7260 or toll-free fax 800/899-4167).

Also check out **Garcia Realty** (Revolución 41, tel./fax 329/291-3058, garciarealty@msn .com, www.sayulita-garciarealty.com, www .sayulita-realestate.com) on the main street, a few doors north of the town plaza. Besides rentals, they list homes and villas for sale.

Food

Vegetables, groceries, and baked goods are available at a pair of stores by the town plaza, or at Abarrotes Doria, just south of the bridge, on Revolución, the main ingress street from the highway. Local-syle food is supplied by a lineup of plaza taco stands at night, and some beachfront *palapa* restaurants. Bountiful breakfasts, lunches, and early dinners are the main event at **Choco Banana,** on the town plaza (6 A.M.–6 P.M. daily) with lots of hearty American-style breakfasts ($3–5), veggie and meat burgers ($4), fish fillets ($6), carrot cake ($2), and espresso ($1).

A bit higher up the scale, a number of recommendable restaurants dot Sayulita's streets and beachfront. One of the best established is **Pedro's** once humble, now elegant, seafood *palapa,* on the south-end beachfront, tel. 329/291-3090. Here, the main events are the freshest catches of the day, cooked with European flair, such as mahi mahi (dorado) Portofino style, and local oysters, octopus, fish, and shrimp cooked up as bouillabaisse seafood stew ($10–15)

You can get just as fresh Mexican-style seafood (fish and shrimp any style, fish tacos and tortas, $4–8) at neighboring **El Costeño** restaurant, also on the Sayulita main beachfront.

In town, on the main street Revolución, family-owned **La Fiesta** restaurant is a party ready to happen, especially on weekends. The whole family including the waiters and the audience usually get into the act. The sparkplug is the father, Miguel, who both emcees and plays the keyboard, often accompanied by his daughter, who sings like a songbird. Besides all this, their lovingly prepared Mexican specialties ($5–10), with bottomless hot, handmade tortillas, are among the best on the Nayarit Coast.

For refined, south-seas ambience (soft music, candles, and dreamy Paul Gaugin prints), go to **Restaurant Sayulita** (Revolución, corner of Gaviotas, tel. 329/291-3511, 5–11:30 P.M. daily, entrees $5–12), just off the main street. Here, pick from a varied Mexican-international menu (moles, soups, chiles rellenos, steak, dorado fillet).

Chinese food has arrived in Sayulita, at the **Dragon Rojo** (on Gaviotas, a block from the beach, corner of Navarrete, 3 P.M.–midnight daily, $3–10), the Sayulita branch of the well-known Puerto Vallarta restaurant. The gang's all there: wonton soup, egg foo yung, chow mein, and plenty of curries, seafood, meat, and vegetable specialties.

Return another day, across Revolución, to restaurant-pizzeria **"Si Hay Olitas"** ("Yes, there are some little waves," 7 A.M.–9 P.M. daily, entrees $4–12) for your choice of ribs, hamburgers, chicken, or Mexican specialties, such as *molcajete* (nopal cactus leaves, leeks, with chicken or beef strips), flaming fajitas, and good in-house pizza.

Owner-chef Miguel Muro of **Casa de Chile Rellenos** (on Revolucion, a block south of the plaza, tel. 329/291-3511, 1–11 P.M. daily, entrees $8–$12) has raised the *chile relleno* (stuffed chile) to a high art. He offers a quartet of delicious variations: cheese, vegetarian, tuna, or chicken ($8) Alternative options include bountiful salads ($5), barbequed ribs ($9), and T-bone steak with baked potato ($12), all served in a tranquil candle-lit atmosphere, enhanced by low-volume melodies and whirring ceiling fans.

Shopping

Among the best of the handicrafts galleries that dot Sayulita's main street is **La Hamaca Gallery** (9 A.M.–8 P.M. daily, tel. 322/227-5817). Offerings include much fine and decorative ceramics, Day of the Dead curios, and a selection of Huichol art, sales of which benefit the nonprofit Huichol Center for Cultural Survival.

Surfing and Touring

Veteral surfer-hotelier **Mario Rubio** rents beach chairs, umbrellas, boogie boards, snorkel gear, surfboards, kayaks, and offers surfing lessons, right on the main beach. He also arranges jungle tours, horseback rides, guided foot hikes, and hotel-surfing packages. Contact him at his "Duende Surf Dawgs" beach rental stall.

Surfboard rentals and surfing lessons are also the main business of very professional **Luna Azul** surf shop (on the beach, foot of Calle Marlin, by Pedro's restaurant, a block south and a block downhill from the town plaza, tel. 329/291-2009, www.lunazul.com).

For fishing, surfing, and snorkeling excursions, contact local **captain Fidel Ponci** and his wife, Leticia (leticiasayulita@hotmail.com, tel. 329/291-3563, www.sayulitalife.com/business/fidel.htm). Sayulita is Fidel's hometown, so he knows the best local spots.

Local Rancho Manuel (tel. 322/132-7683) offers **horseback tours** along shady paths through the Sayulita tropical forest. Get tickets at the Restaurant Costeó on the beach, or at the Ranch itself, about four blocks up Calle Gaviotas, east, past the town plaza and the church.

Greg Adams, manager of La Casa de Buen Salud (tel. 329/291-3029) arranges local day tours to waterfalls, a hot spring, Alta Vista sacred site, La Tovara spring in San Blas, Mexcaltitán, and much more.

Information and Services

A number of businesses keep busy serving Sayulita's visitors. For general information, fax, and Internet connection, go to **Garcia Realty** (Revolución 41, tel./fax 329/291-3058, garcia realty@msn.com) on the main street, a few doors north of the town plaza. They also list vacation rentals and homes and villas for sale.

Change your dollars to pesos at **Casa de Cambio Sayulita,** on the south side of the Sayulita town plaza. Find it open 10 A.M.–2 P.M. and 4–8 P.M. Mon.–Sat.

Books, newspapers, and magazines are available at **Librería Sayulita** (Miramar 17A, two short blocks north of the bridge to

Miramar and left half a block, tel. 329/291-3382, libreriasayulita@yahoo.com.mx, 10 A.M.–8 P.M. daily). Besides a respectable new and used book collection, the personable owners stock newspapers such as *USA Today,* the *New York Times,* and the Miami *Herald,* and a number of popular U.S. magazines, during the October–May high season. They also offer Spanish, French, and guitar lessons, and coffee.

Spanish-language classes and lessons are also offered by **Total Immersion Language School,** of instructor-owners Steve and Maiira Poole. For more information call tel. 329/291-3573 or U.S. tel. 562/716-6044, email info@sayulita-villas.com.

Sayulita Life, a website (www.sayulitalife .com) that amounts to a good community newspaper, offers a load of informative advertisements from hotels and surf shops, to doctors and horseback rides, plus public service announcements, maps, local news, and an events calendar.

As for laundry, get yours done at the *lavandería* (Revolución 9, 8 A.M.–8 P.M. Mon.–Sat.) a block north of the river bridge.

For remedies and medical consultations, you have at least two choices: **Doctora Rosa Flores Alegria,** who consults 3–9 P.M. Mon.–Sat., 9 A.M.–4 P.M. Sun., at her Farmacia America (Revolución 14, half a block south of the bridge, 9 A.M.–2 P.M. and 4–8 P.M. daily); or **Doctor Miguel de Dios Arroyo** 9 A.M.–2 P.M. and 4:30–9:30 P.M. at his pharmacy (Revolución 41, half a block south of the town plaza, tel. 329/291-3555).

GUADALAJARA

Pacific Mexico residents often go to Guadalajara (pop. three million, elev. 5,214 feet, 1,589 meters), the capital of Jalisco, for the same reason Californians frequently go to Los Angeles: to shop. Guadalajara offers Mexico's richest treasury of decorative art and handicrafts. These include a small mountain of fine stoneware, brilliant glass, supple leather, rich papier-mâché, rustic furniture, and much more, available in the most attractive profusion in the suburban cottage-factory villages of Tlaquepaque and Tonalá.

But that's only part of the fascination. Although Guadalajarans like to think of themselves as different (calling themselves, uniquely, "Tapatíos"), their city is renowned as the "most Mexican" of cities. Crowds flock to Guadalajara to bask in its mild, springlike sunshine,

savor its music, and admire its grand plazas, distinguished monuments, arresting murals, fascinating museums, and fine cuisine.

Also known as the "City of Roses," Guadalajara is replete with old-Mexico delights. From the simplest experience, such as the deliciously unmistakable aroma of hot corn tortillas to the most dazzling, such as the whirl of the folkloric dancers' skirts and insistent rap of their heels, dreams of Mexico often come true here.

And no Mexican metropolis is easier to get to than Guadalajara. It is only three hours inland from the Pacific Coast by car and less than an hour from Puerto Vallarta or Mexico City by air.

PLANNING YOUR TIME

Although you could spend at least a week savoring the manifold museums, murals,

HIGHLIGHTS

◖ **Catedral de Guadalajara:** A double steeple of glistening yellow tiles and the remains of the martyred, 3rd-century Virgin of Innocence and the beloved Virgin of Zapopan are the inside must-sees (page 155).

◖ **Teatro Degollado:** A classic facade and a glittering interior, said to be comparable to Milan's La Scala, make this an essential stop on your downtown Guadalajara stroll (page 158).

◖ **Plaza Tapatía:** This visionary-sized plaza is downtown Guadalajara's great open space, decorated by grand fountains, distinguished sculptures, the Centro Joyero (jewelry shopping center), the grand Mercado Libertad, and the Hospicio Cabañas at the far eastern end (page 158).

◖ **Hospicio Cabañas:** Inside Latin American's largest colonial building, the Museo José Clemente Orozco houses the collected works of the renowned muralist and his grand masterpiece, the *Man of Fire* on the overhead cupola (page 159).

◖ **Zapopan:** Go to Zapopan, northwest of downtown Guadalajara, to visit the Virgin of Zapopan in her basilica. Afterward, stop by the Huichol museum/crafts shop, just outside the front of the basilica (page 160).

◖ **Tlaquepaque:** Although fine handicrafts are Tlaquepaque's original claim to fame, this village-within-a-town is also a worthy

destination on its own, with a trove of good restaurants, hotels, and charming old-Mexico diversions (page 176).

LOOK FOR ◖ TO FIND RECOMMENDED SIGHTS, ACTIVITIES, DINING, AND LODGING.

markets, shrines, and shopping of Guadalajara, you can budget your time to visit most of the highlights in two or three fairly leisurely days. (Hint: If you can, try to avoid Monday for downtown Guadalajara sightseeing, since most museums are closed Mondays. Instead, visit Tlaquepaque-Tonalá and continue with downtown Guadalajara on Tuesday. Also, be aware that, on Sundays, some sights are open shorter hours.)

Start your downtown Guadalajara sightseeing at the city-center **Catedral de Guadalajara** (Guadalajara Cathedral). Continue to the visionary-

scale **Plaza Tapatía** and the adjacent giant **Mercado Libertad.** Spend the rest of your day admiring the grand murals and other works of José Clemente Orozco in the historic **Hospicio Cabañas** (Instituto Cultural Cabañas), Latin America's largest colonial-era building.

On your second day, go by tour or taxi to **Tlaquepaque** and stroll the main shopping streets of Independencia and Juárez, admiring and selecting from the stunning array of handicrafts offered by the many attractive shops. Along the way, be sure to visit the **Museo Regional de Cerámica y Arte Popular.**

If you have enough time, continue to **Tonalá,** where, besides exploring some of the excellent handicrafts stores, be sure also to visit some of the several **factory stores** that welcome visitors. Optionally, spend an overnight at one of Tlaquepaque's excellent bed-and-breakfasts, such as the **Quinta Don José.**

On a successive day, spend at least a morning or afternoon in **Zapopan.** At the **Basílica de la Virgen de Zapopan** (Basilica of the Virgin of Zapopan), visit the Virgin inside the nave, and, just out the front door, the fascinating **Museo Huichol** (Huichol Museum) and the adjacent **Museo de la Virgen** (Museum of the Virgin). Enjoy lunch or early dinner downhill from the basilica, at the Greek sidewalk **Restaurant Zorba Agios.**

HISTORY
Before Columbus
The broad Atemajac Valley, where the Guadalajara metropolis now spreads, has nurtured humans for hundreds of generations. Discovered remains date back at least 10,000 years. The Río Lerma-Santiago, Mexico's longest river, which meanders across five states, has nourished Atemajac Valley cornfields for at least three millennia.

Peace and plenty led to prosperity. By A.D. 300, high cultures were occupying western Mexico. They built grand pyramids and ceremonial plazas and left sophisticated animal- and human-motif pottery in unique bottle-shaped underground tombs all over the present-day states of Jalisco, Nayarit, and Colima. Intriguingly, similar tombs are also found in Colombia and Ecuador.

During the next 1,000 years, waves of migrants swept across the Valley of Atemajac: Toltecs from the northeast, the Aztecs much later from the west. As Toltec power declined during the 13th century, the Tarascan civilization took root in Michoacán to the south and filled the power vacuum left by the Toltecs. On the eve of the Spanish conquest, semiautonomous local chiefdoms, tributaries of the Tarascan Emperor, shared the Atemajac valley.

Conquest and Colonization
The fall of the Aztecs in 1521 and the Tarascans a few years later made the Valley of Atemajac a plum ripe for the picking. In the late 1520s, while Cortés was absent in Spain, the opportunistic Nuño de Guzmán vaulted himself to power in Mexico City on the backs of the native peoples and at the expense of Cortés's friends and relatives. Suspecting correctly that his glory days in Mexico City were numbered, Guzmán cleared out three days before Christmas 1529, at the head of a small army of adventurers seeking new conquests in western Mexico. They raped, ravaged, and burned for half a dozen years, inciting dozens of previously pacified tribes to rebellion.

Hostile Mexican attacks repeatedly foiled Guzmán's attempts to establish his western Mexico capital, which he wanted to name after his Spanish hometown, Guadalajara (from the Arabic *wad al hadjarah,* or river of stones). Ironically, it wasn't until the year of Guzmán's death in Spain, in 1542, six years after his arrest by royal authorities, that the present Guadalajara was founded. At the downtown Plaza de Los Fundadores, a panoramic bronze frieze shows cofounders Doña Beátriz de Hernández and governor Cristóbal de Oñate christening the soon-to-become-capital of the "Kingdom of Nueva Galicia."

The city grew; its now-venerable public buildings rose at the edges of sweeping plazas, from which expeditions set out to explore other lands. In 1563, Legazpi and Urdaneta sailed west to conquer the Philippines; the year 1602 saw Vizcaíno sail for the Californias and the Pacific Northwest. In 1687 Father Kino left for 27 years of mission-building in Sonora and what would be Arizona and New Mexico; finally, during the 1760s, Father Junípero Serra and Captain Gaspar de Portola began their arduous trek to discover San Francisco Bay and found a string of California missions.

During Spain's Mexican twilight, Guadalajara was a virtual imperial city, ruling all of northwest Mexico, a domain twice the size of Britain's 13 American colonies.

GUADALAJARA

GUADALAJARA

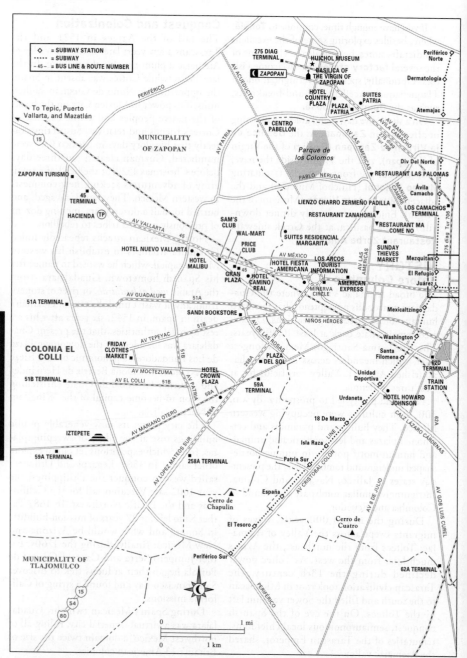

- ◇ = SUBWAY STATION
- ⋯⋯ = SUBWAY
- – 45 – = BUS LINE & ROUTE NUMBER

To Tepic, Puerto
Vallarta, and Mazatlán

15

ZAPOPAN TURISMO

45
TERMINAL

HACIENDA **TP**

AV VALLARTA

HOTEL NUEVO VALLARTA

HOTEL
MALIBU

GRAN
PLAZA

AV GUADALUPE

51A

51A TERMINAL

SANDI BOOKSTORE

51B

**COLONIA EL
COLLI**

FRIDAY
CLOTHES
MARKET

AV TEPEYAC

51B

AV MOCTEZUMA

51B TERMINAL

AV EL COLLI

51B

HOTEL
CROWN
PLAZA

59A

**59A
TERMINAL**

AV MARIANO OTERO

258A

IZTEPETE

AV LOPEZ MATEOS SUR

59A TERMINAL

258A TERMINAL

**MUNICIPALITY OF
TLAJOMULCO**

15

54

80

PERIFÉRICO

PERIFÉRICO

MUNICIPALITY
OF ZAPOPAN

PABLO NERUDA

Parque de
los Colomos

AV ACUEDUCTO

AV PATRIA

**275 DIAG
TERMINAL**

HUICHOL MUSEUM
BASILICA OF
THE VIRGIN OF
ZAPOPAN

ZAPOPAN

HOTEL
COUNTRY
PLAZA

PLAZA
PATRIA

SUITES
PATRIA

CENTRO
PABELLÓN

AV ZAPOPAN

AV LAS AMERICAS

Periférico
Norte

Dermatología

Atemajac

**275 diag
Tur 706**

AV MANUEL ÁVILA CAMACHO

Div Del Norte

RESTAURANT LAS PALOMAS

Ávila
Camacho

MANUEL
CARRERE

LOS CAMACHOS
TERMINAL

275 diag Tur 706

LIENZO CHARRO ZERMEÑO PADILLA

RESTAURANT ZANAHORIA

SAM'S
CLUB

WAL-MART

PRICE
CLUB

SUITES RESIDENCIAL
MARGARITA

AV MÉXICO

HOTEL FIESTA
AMERICANA

HOTEL
CAMINO
REAL

LOS ARCOS
TOURIST
INFORMATION

MINERVA
CIRCLE

▼RESTAURANT MA
COME NO

SUNDAY
THIEVES
MARKET

AMERICAN
EXPRESS

AV LAS
AMERICAS

Mezquitan

El Refugio

Juárez

AV DE LAS ROSAS

NIÑOS HÉROES

Mexicaltzingo

Washington

Santa
Filomena

258A

PLAZA
DEL SOL

Unidad
Deportiva

**62D
TERMINAL**

TRAIN
STATION

Urdaneta

HOTEL HOWARD
JOHNSON

AV PATRIA

59A

18 De Marzo

Isla Raza

Patria Sur

AV CRISTOBAL COLON

LINE 1

CALZ LÁZARO CÁRDENAS

62A

AV 8 DE JULIO

AV GOB LUIS CUREL

Cerro de
Chapulin

España

El Tesoro

Cerro de
Cuatro

Periférico Sur

PERIFÉRICO

62A TERMINAL

N

0   1 mi

0   1 km

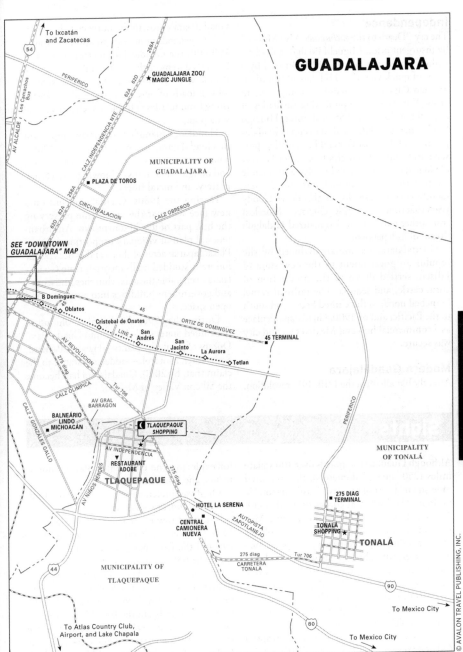

GUADALAJARA

To Ixcatán
and Zacatecas

54

PERIFÉRICO

Av Alcalde / Los Camachos Bus

CALZ INDEPENDENCIA NTE

258A

62D

62A

GUADALAJARA ZOO/
★ MAGIC JUNGLE

MUNICIPALITY OF
GUADALAJARA

■ PLAZA DE TOROS

CIRCUNVALACION

CALZ OBREROS

258A

62A

62D

SEE "DOWNTOWN
GUADALAJARA" MAP

B Dominguez
45
Oblatos
Cristobal de Onates
45
ORTIZ DE DOMINGUEZ
45 TERMINAL ■
LINE 2
San
Andrés
San
Jacinto
La Aurora
Tetlan

AV REVOLUCION

275 diag

CALZ J GONZALES GALLO

CALZ OLIMPICA

AV GRAL
BARRAGON

Tur 706

BALNEÁRIO
LINDO
MICHOACÁN

Tlaquepaque
Shopping

AV INDEPENDENCIA

▼
RESTAURANT
ADOBE

TLAQUEPAQUE

AV NIÑOS HEROES

275 diag

PERIFÉRICO

MUNICIPALITY
OF TONALÁ

275 DIAG
TERMINAL ■

HOTEL LA SERENA

CENTRAL
CAMIONERA
NUEVA

AUTOPISTA
ZAPOTLANEJO

TONALÁ
SHOPPING ★

TONALÁ

44

MUNICIPALITY OF

TLAQUEPAQUE

275 diag
CARRETERA
TONALA

Tur 706

90

To Mexico City

To Atlas Country Club,
Airport, and Lake Chapala

80

To Mexico City

GUADALAJARA

Independence

The cry, "Death to the *gachupines,* Viva México" by insurgent priest Miguel Hidalgo ignited rebellion on September 16, 1810. Buoyed by a series of quick victories, Hidalgo advanced on Mexico City in command of a huge ragtag army. But, facing the punishing fusillades of a small but disciplined Spanish force, Hidalgo lost his nerve and decided to occupy Guadalajara instead. Loyalist General Felix Calleja pursued and routed Hidalgo's forces, not far east of Guadalajara. Although Hidalgo and Allende escaped, they were captured in the north a few months later. It wasn't for another dozen bloody years that others (Iturbide, Guerrero, Morelos) from other parts of Mexico realized Hidalgo's dream of independence.

Guadalajara, its domain reduced by the republican government to the new state of Jalisco, settled down to the production of corn, cattle, and tequila. The railroad came, branched north to the United States and south to the Pacific, and by 1900, Guadalajara's place as a commercial hub and Mexico's second city was secure.

Modern Guadalajara

After the bloodbath of the 1910–1917 revolution, Guadalajara's growth far outpaced the country's in general. From a population of around 100,000, the Guadalajara metropolitan area ballooned to more than three million by 2005. People were drawn from the countryside by jobs in loads of new factories, making everything from textiles and shoes to chemicals and soda pop.

Handicraft manufacture, always important in Guadalajara, zoomed during the 1960s, when waves of jet-riding tourists came, saw, and bought mountains of blown glass, leather, pottery, and metal finery.

During the 1980s, Guadalajara put on a new face while at the same time preserving the best part of its old downtown. An urban-renewal plan of visionary proportions created Plaza Tapatía: acres of shops and offices beside fountain-studded malls incorporating Guadalajara's venerable theaters, churches, museums, and government buildings into a single grand open space.

During the 1990s the digital revolution in the United States spilled over into Guadalajara. Dozens of giant new plants—Hewlett-Packard, Sony, Intel, Motorola—added substance to the claim that, by 2000, Guadalajara had become the Silicon Valley of Mexico.

Sights

Although Guadalajara sprawls over 100 square miles (250 square kilometers), the treasured mile-square heart of the city is easily explorable on foot. The cathedral corner of north-south Avenida 16 de Septiembre and Avenida Morelos marks the center of town. A few blocks south, another important artery, east-west Avenida Juárez, runs above the new metro subway line through the central business district, while a few blocks east, Avenida Independencia runs north-south, beneath Plaza Tapatía and past the main Mercado Libertad to the railway station a couple of miles south.

The twin steeples of the **Guadalajara Cathedral** serve as an excellent starting point for exploring the city-center plazas, monuments, and museums.

Or, if you prefer, any time of the day, climb into a *calandria* (horse-drawn carriage) for a ride around town; carriages are available on Liceo between the Rotunda de Hombres Ilustres and the Regional Museum, just north of the cathedral, for about $15/hour.

Afternoons any day, and Sunday in particular, are good for people-watching around Guadalajara's many downtown plazas. Favorite strolling grounds are the broad Plaza Tapatía west of the cathedral and, especially in the evening, the pedestrian mall-streets, such as Colón, Galeana, Morelos, and Moreno, which meander south and west from cathedral-front Plaza Guadalajara.

The former villages of Zapopan, Tlaquepaque, and Tonalá, although now suburbs of the greater Guadalajara metropolis, are nevertheless distinct and important municipalities, with about two-thirds of the land area and about half the population of the Guadalajara metropolitan zone. They enjoy their own plaza-centers, governments, and large country hinterlands. They have become destinations in their own right and make rewarding day trips and overnight excursions outside the city-center.

THE CATHEDRAL AND CENTRAL PLAZAS
◖ Catedral de Guadalajara

The cathedral, dedicated to the Virgin of the Assumption when it was begun in 1561, was finished about 30 years later. A potpourri of styles—Moorish, Gothic, Renaissance, and Classic—make up its spires, arches, and facades. Although an earthquake demolished its steeples in 1818, they were rebuilt and resurfaced with cheery canary-yellow tiles in 1854.

Inside, side altars and white facades lead up to the principal altar, built over a tomb containing the remains of several former clergy, including the mummified heart of renowned Bishop Cabañas. One of the main attractions is the **Virgin of Innocence,** in the small chapel just to the left of the entrance. The glass-enclosed figure contains the bones of a 12-year-old girl who was martyred in the 3rd century, forgotten, then rediscovered in the Vatican catacombs in 1786 and shipped to Guadalajara in 1788. The legend claims she died protecting her virginity; it is equally likely that she was martyred for refusing to recant her Christian faith.

Somewhere near the main altar you'll find either a copy of or the authentic **Virgin of Zapopan.** Between June and October 12, the tiny, adored figure will be the authentic "La Generala," as she's affectionately known; on October 12, a tumultuous crowd of worshippers escorts her to the basilica in Zapopan, where she remains until brought back to Guadalajara the next June.

Outside, broad plazas surround the cathedral:

© BRUCE WHIPPERMAN

The Catedral de Guadalajara (background), beyond the Plaza de Armas, is the summer home of Guadalajara's beloved Virgin of Zapopan.

the **Plaza Guadalajara,** in front (west) of the cathedral, then as you move counterclockwise, the **Plaza de Armas** to the south, **Plaza Liberación** to the east (behind), and the plaza known as **Rotonda de los Hombres Ilustres** (or just La Rotonda) to the north of the cathedral.

Rotonda de los Hombres Ilustres

Across Avenida Morelos, the block-square Rotonda de los Hombres Ilustres plaza is bordered by 16 sculptures of Jalisco's eminent citizens. Their remains lie beneath the monumental stone rotunda in the center; their bronze statues line the sidewalk. Right at the corner you'll find the figure of revered Jalisco Governor Ignacio Vallarta; a few steps farther north stands the statue of José Clemente Orozco, legally blind when he executed his great works of art. Continue around the plaza, and you will be rewarded a view of a recent addition to the Hombres Ilustres statues: the celebrated humanist and teacher Irene Robledo Garcia.

GUADALAJARA

Map legend:
- ◇ = SUBWAY STATION
- ••••• = SUBWAY
- – 45 – = BUS LINE & ROUTE NUMBER

Streets and labels (as shown on map):

GARIBALDI

◇ Mezquitan

REFORMA

ZARAGOZA

SANTA MONICA

PEDRO LOZA

275 diag

AV ALCADE

LICEO

CALZ DEL FEDERALISMO

LINE 1

MEZQUITAN

BARCENAS

CONTRERAS MEDELLIN

GONZALEZ ORTEGA

TEMPLO DE SANTA MONICA

CASA DE LOS PERROS ★

258A

SAN FELIPE

258A

JUAN MANUEL

258A

MUSEO DE LA CIUDAD ★

HOTEL LA ROTONDA ●

SANDY'S ●

INDEPENDENCIA – Par Vial –

Plaza de los Hombres Ilustres

ROTONDA ■

MUSEO REGIONAL DE GUADALAJARA ★

HIDALGO – Par Vial –

Par Vial

El Refugio ◇

Par Vial

Plaza Guadalajara

CATEDRAL DE GUADALAJARA ☾

MORELOS

GALERÍAS EL CONVENTO ■

RESTAURANT SAN MIGUEL ▼

HOTEL INTERNACIONAL ●

INTERNET ACCESS ■

FARMACIA ABC

COLON

Tur 706

Plaza de Armas ■

TOURIST INFORMATION ●

PEDRO MORENO

EX-CONVENTO DEL CARMEN ●

RESTAURANT LA GRAN CHINA ▼

▼ MADOKA

RESTAURANT CHONG WAH ▼

Plaza Universidad ◇

Juárez ◇ •••• LINE 2 ••••

AV JUAREZ

275 diag

GIGANTE ■

MCDONALD'S ▼

SANBORN'S ●

▼ SANBORN'S

BANCOMER ■

LÓPEZ COTILLA

HOTEL FÉNIX ●

POSADA SAN RAFAEL ●

HOTEL POSADA REGIS ●

45

FCO IMADERO

HOTEL CERVANTES ●

● HOTEL APOSENTO

● HOTEL HAMILTON

RESTAURANT MÁLAGA ▼

45

PRISCILIANO SANCHEZ

CALZ DEL FEDERALISMO

LINE 1

PAVO

8 JULIO

ENRIQUE GONZALEZ MARTINEZ

DONATO GUERRA

CAPILLA DE ARANZAZU ♠

Parque San Francisco

MIGUEL BLANCO

OCAMPO

GALEANA

MOLOZ

TEMPLO DE SAN FRANCISCO DE ASIS ♠

AV 16 DE SEPTIEMBRE

CORONA

275 diag

LIBERTAD – – 51A 51B

LEANDRO VALLE

51B, 51A ■ TERMINAL

51A 51B

GUADALAJARA

DOWNTOWN GUADALAJARA

Parque

Morelos

258A SAN DIEGO

PINO SUAREZ

BELEN

HUMBOLDT

258A

BAEZA ALZAGA

VENUSTIANO CARRANZA

FEDERACIÓN

INDUSTRIA

REPÚBLICA

HIDALGO

CALZ INDEPENDENCIA

62D 62A

POST OFFICE

HOTEL DE MENDOZA

CONGRESO DEL ESTADO

PALACIO DE JUSTICIA

TEMPLO DE SANTA MARÍA DE GRACIAS

FRISA DE LOS FUNDADORES

Plaza de los Fundadores

IMOLACIÓN DE QUETZALCOATL

OROZCO MURALS (INSTITUTO CULTURAL CABAÑAS)

TOURIST INFORMATION

HOSPICIO CABAÑAS

Plaza de la Liberación

TEATRO DEGOLLADO

TOURIST INFORMATION

LA RINCONADA

PLAZA TAPATÍA

MORELOS MALL

DEGOLLADO

CENTRO JOYERO

Pedestrian Overpass

RODRIGUEZ

HOTEL FRANCÉS

PALACIO DE GOBIERNO

MERCADO LIBERTAD

HOTEL ROMA

San Juan de Dios

LINE 2

HUERTO

AV JAVIER MINA

MERCADO

BANAMEX

HOLIDAY INN HOTEL & SUITES

Plaza de los Mariachis

MONEY CHANGERS

MOLINA

AV ALVARO OBREGÓN

CALZ INDEPENDENCIA

ANTONIO TORRES

HOTEL UNIVERSO

TELECOMUNICACIONES

45

45

GIGANTES

J. LUIS VERDIA

NIGHTCLUB

NIGHTCLUB

HOTEL LATINO

MAESTRANZA

62D 62A

45

GÓMEZ FARÍAS

CABAÑAS

HOTEL SAN FRANCISCO PLAZA

62D 62A

28 DE ENERO

INSURGENTES

ALDAMA

AV REVOLUCIÓN

MEDRANO

To Tlaquepaque, Tonalá, Hwy 90, and Hwy 80

Tur 708

275 diag

0   100 yds

0   100 m

GUADALAJARA

© AVALON TRAVEL PUBLISHING, INC.

Museo Regional de Guadalajara

Adjacent to and east of the Rotondo de los Hombres Ilustres, the colonial building behind the lineup of horse-drawn *calandrias* housed the Seminario de San José for six generations after its construction in 1696. During the 1800s it served variously as a barracks and a public lecture hall, and, since 1918, it has housed the Museo Regional de Guadalajara (60 Liceo, tel. 33/3614-2227, 9 A.M.–6:30 P.M. Tues.–Sat., 9 A.M.–5 P.M. Sun.).

Inside, tiers of rooms surrounding a tree-shaded interior patio illustrate local history. Exhibits depict scenes from as early as the Big Bang and continue with a hulking mastodon skeleton and whimsical animal and human figurines recovered from the bottle-shaped tombs of Jalisco, Nayarit, and Colima. Upstairs rooms contain life-sized displays of traditional fishing methods at nearby Lake Chapala, and costumes and culture of the regional Cora, Huichol, Tepehuan, and México peoples.

Plaza Liberación

Back outside, head east two blocks down Avenida Hidalgo, paralleling the expansive Plaza Liberación directly behind the cathedral. On your left you will pass the baroque facades of the *Congreso del Estado* (state legislature) and the *Palacio de Justicia* (state supreme court) buildings. Ahead at the east end of Plaza Liberación rises the timeless silhouette of the Teatro Degollado.

(Teatro Degollado

The theater's classic, columned facade rises to an epic marble frieze depicting Apollo and the nine muses. Inside, the Degollado's resplendent grand salon rivals the gilded refinement of Milan's renowned La Scala. Overhead, its ceiling glows with Gerardo Suárez's panorama of canto IV of Dante's *Divine Comedy,* complete with its immortal cast—Julius Caesar, Homer, Virgil, Saladin—and the robed and wreathed author himself in the middle. Named for the millionaire Governor Degollado, who financed its construction, the theater opened with appropriate fanfare on September 13, 1866, with a production of *Lucia de Lammermoor,* starring Ángela Pe-

ralta, the renowned "Mexican Nightingale." An ever-changing menu of artists still graces the Degollado's stage. These include an excellent local folkloric ballet troupe every Sunday morning.

Frisa de los Fundadores

Walk behind the Degollado theater, to the **Plaza de los Fundadores** where a modern bronze frieze, the *Frisa de los Fundadores,* decorates its back side. Appropriately, a mere two blocks from the spot where the city was founded, the 68-foot sculpture shows Guadalajara's cofounders facing each other on opposite sides of a big tree. Governor Cristóbal de Oñate strikes the tree with his sword, while Doña Beátriz de Hernández holds a fighting cock, symbolizing her gritty determination (and that of dozens of fellow settlers) that Guadalajara's location should remain put.

EAST OF THE CATHEDRAL
(Plaza Tapatía

East of the cathedral, 17 broad acres of the Plaza Tapatía complex extend ahead for several blocks across subplazas, fountains, and malls. Initially wide in the foreground of Plaza de los Fundadores, the Tapatía narrows between a double row of shops and offices, then widens into a broad esplanade and continues beside a long pool/fountain that leads to the monumental, domed **Hospicio Cabañas** a third of a mile away. Along the Tapatía's lateral flanks, a pair of long malls—continuations of Avs. Hidalgo and Morelos—parallel the central Paseo Degollado mall for two blocks.

The eastern end of the Morelos mall, on the right (the south side facing east), is highlighted by the striking bronze *escudo* (coat of arms) of Guadalajara. Embodying the essence of the original 16th-century coat of arms authorized by Emperor Charles V, the *escudo* shows a pair of lions protecting a pine tree (with leaves, rather than needles). The lions represent the warrior's determination and discipline, and the solitary pine symbolizes noble ideals.

Continue east, to where the Plaza Tapatía widens, giving room for the sculpture-fountain *Imolación de Quetzalcoatl,* designed and executed by Víctor Manuel Contreras in 1982. Four bronze serpent-birds, representing knowledge and the spirit of humankind, stretch toward heaven at the ends of a giant cross. In the center, a towering bronze spiral represents the unquenchable flame of Quetzalcoatl, transforming all that it touches. Locals call the sculpture the "big corkscrew," however.

Mercado Libertad

At this point, Avenida Independencia runs directly beneath Plaza Tapatía, past the adjacent sprawling Mercado Libertad, built in 1958 on the site of the traditional Guadalajara *tianguis* (open-air market), known since pre-Columbian times. Follow the elevated pedestrian walkway to explore the Libertad's produce, meat, fish, herbs, food, and handicrafts stalls.

◖ Hospicio Cabañas

Behind the long pool/fountain at the east end of Plaza Tapatía stands the domed neoclas-

The Hospicio Cabañas is named after Bishop Cabañas, who had it built as a hospice for the sick, poor, and homeless.

sic Hospicio Cabañas, the largest and one of the most remarkable colonial buildings in the Americas, designed and financed by Bishop Juan Ruiz de Cabañas; construction was complete in 1810. The purpose of the "Guadalajara House of Charity and Mercy," as the good bishop originally named it, a home for the sick, helpless, and homeless, was fulfilled for 170 years. Although still successfully serving as an orphanage during the 1970s, time had taken its toll on the Hospicio Cabañas. The city and state governments built a new orphanage in the suburbs, restored the old building, and changed its purpose. It now houses a center for the arts, the **Instituto Cultural Cabañas** (Cabañas 8, tel. 33/3618-2800, ext. 31009, 10:15 A.M.–5:45 P.M. Tues.–Sat., 10:15 A.M.–3 P.M. Sun.). Public programs include classes and films, and instrumental, chorale, and dance concerts. While you're there, pick up a copy of the event schedule *(horario de eventos)*.

Inside, seemingly endless ranks of corridors pass a host of sculpture-decorated patios. Practice rooms resound with the clatter of dancing feet and the halting strains of apprentice violins, horns, and pianos. Exhibition halls and studios of the **Museo José Clemente Orozco** (José Clemente Orozco Museum) occupy a large fraction of the rooms, while the great muralist's brooding work spreads over a corresponding fraction of the walls. Words such as dark, fiery, nihilistic, even apocalyptic would not be too strong to describe the panoramas that Orozco executed (1938–1939) in the soaring chapel beneath the central dome. On one wall, an Aztec goddess wears a necklace of human hearts; on another, armored automaton-soldiers menace Indian captives; while in the cupola overhead, Orozco's *Man of Fire,* wreathed in flame, appears to soar into a hellishly red-hot sky.

Plaza de los Mariachis

On Independencia, just south of the Mercado Libertad, musicians at the Plaza de los Mariachis continue the second century of a tradition born when mariachi (cowboy troubadour) groups first appeared during the 1860s in Guadalajara. The musical hubbub peaks

GUADALAJARA

Saturday nights and Sunday afternoons as musicians gather, singing while they wait to be hired for serenades and parties.

Parque Agua Azul

Some sunny afternoon, hire a taxi (about $2 from the city center) and find out why Guadalajara families love Parque Agua Azul. The entrance is on Independencia, about a mile south of Plaza Tapatía. It's a green, shaded place where you can walk, roll, sleep, or lie on the grass. When weary of that, head for the bird park, admire the banana-beaked toucans and squawking macaws, and continue into the aviary where free-flying birds flutter overhead. Nearby, duck into the *mariposario* (butterfly farm) and enjoy the flickering rainbow hues of a host of *mariposas.* Continue to the orchids in a towering hothouse, festooned with growing blossoms and misted continuously by a rainbow of spray from the center. Before other temptations draw you away, stop for a while at the open-air band or symphony concert in the amphitheater. The park is open 10 A.M.–6 P.M. Tues.–Sun., entrance $1.

SOUTH OF THE CATHEDRAL
Palacio de Gobierno

Just a block east and half a block south of the cathedral front, let the Palacio de Gobierno (on Armas's east side, open 9:30 A.M.–8:30 P.M. daily) be the first stop of your south-side walking tour. At the **city tourism information booth** or *módulo de información* (open 9 A.M.–3 P.M. and 4–7 P.M. Mon.–Fri., 10 A.M.–12:30 P.M. Sat. and Sun.), just inside the entrance, ask for a copy of the superb all-color *Points of Interest* bilingual foldout map and guide. The sidewalk in front of the Palacio de Gobierno is a good spot to find a highly recommended local guide, **Mr. Xiao Lin** (tel. 33/3607-6786), who explains the murals inside and accepts only donations.

The Palacio de Gobierno's main attraction is the epic 1937 **Orozco mural** in the stairwell, right side of the inner patio. Father Miguel Hidalgo, with torch in hand, like an avenging angel, leads Mexico's struggle against the evil stooges of Communism, Capitalism, Fascism, and Catholicism. Don't miss the villains, such as General Porfirio

Díaz and the idiotic Benito Mussolini (middle right panel), or the heroes, such as mustachioed Emiliano Zapata (in campesino white cotton).

◖ ZAPOPAN

Zapopan (sah-POH-pahn) town center, about six miles northwest of downtown Guadalajara, is the capital of the sprawling municipalty of the same name. Once a country province seemingly far removed from downtown Guadalajara, westward development—shiny electronics factories, green golf courses, broad highrise-lined boulevards, and wealthy neighborhoods—have spilled over into once-sleepy Zapopan until its municipality, in aggregate, now rivals the wealth and population (about a million and a half) of the Guadalajara municipality next door.

The Basílica de Nuestra Señora de Zapopan

Zapopan is famous for its soaring baroque (1730) **basilica,** home of the renowned Vir-

The Basílica de Nuestra Señora de Zapopan is the focus of a continual flow of pilgrims who arrive to ask for the Virgin's blessing.

gin of Zapopan. The legendary image, one of the beloved "three sisters" virgins of Mexico, has enjoyed generations of popularity so enormous that it must be seen to be believed. Local folks, whenever they happen by, often stop to say a prayer (or at least make the sign of the cross as they pass) in front of the basilica gate. Inside, the faithful crawl the length of the sanctuary to pay their respects to the diminutive blue-and-white figure. The adoration comes to a head on October 12, when a rollicking crowd of hundreds of thousands accompanies the Virgin of Zapopan from her downtown Guadalajara cathedral summer home to Zapopan, where she stays from October 13 until June.

Museo Huichol Wirrarica

Be sure to look over the displays of Huichol indigenous handicrafts in the **Museo Tienda Artesanías Huichol Wirrarica** (on your left as you exit the basilica, tel. 33/3636-4430, 9:30 A.M.–1:30 P.M. Mon.–Sat., 10 A.M.–2 P.M. Sun.), commonly known as Museo Huichol (Huichol Museum). Sale items include eerie beaded masks, intriguing yarn paintings, and *ojos de dios* (God's eyes) yarn sculptures. Later, browse for bargains among the handicrafts stalls in front of the basilica and in the municipal market in the adjacent plaza on the corner of Avenida Hidalgo and Calle Eva Briseño.

Museo de la Virgen

Also don't miss the very interesting Museo de la Virgen (Museum of the Virgin) next to the Huichol Museum, open approximately the same hours. You'll find a treasury of mementos and excellent detailed exhibits of the Virgin of Zapopan's history.

Getting There

From downtown Guadalajara, local Zapopan-marked buses (275 Diagonal or air-conditioned Tur 706) pass north through the downtown center, stopping every few blocks along main thoroughfare Avenida 16 de Septiembre. By car, follow Avenida Manuel Avila Camacho,

which diagonals northwest from Avenida Alcalde about four miles north of the city center, continuing to Zapopan, marked by the big baroque arch on the left. After one block, turn left onto Avenida Hidalgo, the double main street of Zapopan. Within four blocks you'll see the plaza and the double-steepled basilica on the left.

For more information about Zapopan sights, stop by the **Zapopan tourist information office** (Av. Vallarta 6503, tels. 33/3100-0754, 33/3100-0755, 33/3100-0756, 33/3100-0757, 33/3100-0758 and 33/3100-0759, turismo@zapopan.gob.mx, www.zapopan.gob.mx, 8 A.M.–8 P.M. Mon.–Fri.), at Plaza Concentro, upstairs offices 13G and 14G, just a block inside the west-side *periférico* (peripheral boulevard). It's best to telephone or email before you arrive.

TLAQUEPAQUE AND TONALÁ

Tlaquepaque and Tonalá, in Guadalajara's southeast suburb, are among Mexico's most

Tonalá's Queen Cihualpilli fiercely resisted Spanish domination.

© BRUCE WHIPPERMAN

GUADALAJARA

THE THREE SISTERS OF MEXICO

In all of Mexico, only the Virgin of Guadalupe exceeds in adoration the all-Jalisco trio – the "Three Sister" Virgins of Talpa, Zapopan, and San Juan de los Lagos. Yearly they draw millions of humble Mexican pilgrims who bus, walk, hitchhike, or even crawl to festivals honoring the virgins. Each Virgin's popularity springs from some persistent, endearing legend. The Virgin of Talpa defied a haughty bishop's efforts to cage her; the Virgin of Zapopan rescued Guadalajara from war and disaster; the Virgin of San Juan de los Lagos restored a dead child to life.

Talpa, Zapopan, and San Juan de los Lagos townsfolk have built towering basilicas to shelter and honor each Virgin. Each small and fragile figurine is draped in fine silk and jewels and worshipped by a continuous stream of pilgrims. During a Virgin festival the image is lifted aloft by a platoon of richly costumed bearers and paraded to the clamor, tumult, and cheers of sometimes a million or more of the faithful.

Even if you choose to avoid the crowds and visit Talpa, Zapopan, or San Juan de los Lagos on a nonfestival day, you'll soon see that the hubbub continues nevertheless. Pilgrims come and go, bands and mariachis play, and curio stands stuffed with gilded devotional goods crowd the basilica square.

Get to Talpa and San Juan de los Lagos best by tour or bus. If driving, for Talpa, go via the left fork signed Tala or Ameca off Highway 15 west, about 15 miles past the west periférico edge of Guadalajara. Continue another three hours, via Tala and Ameca, to Talpa. For San Juan de los Lagos, from the southeast edge of Guadalajara follow Highway 90 Mexico City direction, 15 miles out of town, to its big cloverleaf intersection with expressway Highway 80, north, about another hour and a half to San Juan de Los Lagos. Both Talpa and San Juan de los Lagos have restaurants and comfortable lodgings.

---

renowned handicrafts villages and are worth at least a day visit (better an overnight) for handicrafts alone. Tlaquepaque (tlah-kay-PAH-kay), about five miles southeast from the city center, besides being a folkloric dance and mariachi entertainment center, is renowned for regal baroque furniture reproductions, blown and stained glass, fine ceramics, leather, designer lamps, pewter, and much more.

Tonalá, another five miles farther, retains plenty of its colorful country ambience. Shops abound, offering treasuries of Tonalá's celebrated high-fired stoneware, home furnishings, ceramics, paper flowers, and its famous ceramic, brass, and papier-mâché animal figurines. The most exciting, but crowded, time to visit Tonalá is during the Thursday and Sunday markets.

In addition to their must-see shopping opportunities, both Tonalá and Tlaquepaque are destinations in themselves, offering many good restaurants and hotels.

Start out with a late afternoon or early evening stroll around Tlaquepaque's central *jardín* and sample the bounty of old-Mexico food, such as loads of tacos, sweet corn, home-style potato chips, sweet fruit *aguas,* and chilled coconut juice.

For light exercise, bat an *aeroglobo* (big, plastic, sausage-shaped balloon) around to your heart's content. Cool down with a stroll along the rows of handicrafts and trinket stalls. Bargain for good deals, especially in leather wallets, belts, purses, and $3 silver diamond rings.

For restful, sit-down café entertainment, take a seat inside the adjacent block-square, porticoed **El Parián** entertainment garden. Order your favorite *antojitos* (such as tamales, tacos, and enchiladas) and enjoy the evening mariachi and folkloric dance show (usually beginning around 9 P.M., earlier Sundays).

Accommodations

Good, reasonably priced accommodations are plentiful in downtown Guadalajara, within easy strolling distance of the city's broad plazas and historic monuments.

AROUND THE CATHEDRAL

Several good hotels, mostly in the moderate price range, sprinkle the bustling blocks north and south of the city center cathedral.

Under $50

One of Guadalajara's best-buy budget hotels is **Hotel Latino** (Prisciliano Sánchez 74, Guadalajara, Jalisco 44100, tel. 33/3614-4484 or 33/3614-6214, $21 s, $22 d, $24 d king-sized, $25 t). Although a plain, small-lobby hotel, the Latino nevertheless offers its guest a modicum of amenities. The 57 rooms in four stories (no elevator) are clean, carpeted, and thoughtfully furnished, albeit a bit worn around the edges. Baths are modern-standard, with shiny tile showers and marble sinks. Rates include water-cooled fan, cable TV, phones, and parking.

The second-floor **(Hotel Posada Regis** (Corona 171, Guadalajara, Jalisco 44100, tel. 33/3614-8633 or tel./fax 33/3613-3026, posadaregis@usa.net, http://posadaregis.tripod.com, credit cards accepted, $26 s, $33 d, $45 t) offers both economy and a bit of old-world charm, right smack in the middle of the city-center action. Its clean and comfortable high-ceilinged rooms enclose a gracious Porfirian-era indoor lobby/atrium. Evening videos, friendly atmosphere, and a good breakfast/lunch café provide opportunities for relaxed exchanges with other travelers. The 19 rooms have TV, phones, and fans, but no parking. (Note: When heading to the Posada Regis website, be sure to type in the "http://" prefix instead of "www."; a blogger has unfortunately blocked the latter.)

Central location, comfortable rooms, and modest prices explain the popularity of the nearby **Hotel Universo** (López Cotilla 161, Guadalajara, Jalisco 44100, tel./fax 33/3613-2815, credit cards accepted, $42 s, $43 d, suites from about $50), corner of Cotilla and Degollado, just three blocks south of the Teatro Degollado. Guests enjoy renovated, carpeted, and draped air-conditioned rooms with wood furniture and ceiling-to-floor tiled bathrooms. The 137 rooms and suites have a/c, cable TV, phones, reliable restaurant, travel agent, and parking.

Just two blocks south, the competent owners of the Hotel Universo also run the authentically colonial **(Hotel San Francisco Plaza** (Degollado 267, Guadalajara, Jalisco 44100, tel. 33/3613-8954, fax 33/3613-3257, credit cards accepted, $46 s, $49 d). The reception area opens to an airy, charming, and tranquil inner patio, where big soft chairs invite relaxation amid a leafy garden of potted plants. In the evenings, the venerable arched stone corridors gleam with cut-crystal lanterns. Upstairs, the rooms are high-ceilinged, with wooden handmade furniture, bedside reading lamps, and sentimental old-Mexico paintings on the walls. Each room has a phone, water-cooled fan, cable TV, and a large, modern-standard bathroom with marble sink. Parking is included. Downstairs, guests enjoy an airy, reliable restaurant and an adjacent outside patio. (Hint: Choose a room on the hotel's south side, away from the bus noise and vibration on busy Prisciliano Sánchez.)

$50-100

A choice location, on a tranquil side street just a block north of the cathedral, explains part of the success of the 33-room **Hotel la Rotonda** (Liceo 130, Guadalajara, Jalisco 44100; tel./fax 33/3614-1017, toll-free Mex. tel. 01-800/964-8700, larotonda@hoteleselectos.com, www.hoteleselectos.com, credit cards accepted, $50 s, $60 d). Past the small reception of this former mansion, you enter a bright courtyard, decorated by old-world stone arches, where guests linger over breakfast. Farther on, corridors lead past intimate rear patios. Most rooms open onto the upstairs courtyard-view balcony, bordered by potted plants and a gilded iron railing. Inside, rooms vary in size, but all are floored with attractively rustic tiles and appointed with immaculate, up-to-date bathrooms and solid, polished hardwood furniture. Asking rates include phones, cable TV, and fans. There's a restaurant, bar, small events salon, and parking.

The three-story, authentically baroque **(Hotel Frances** (Maestranza 35, Guadalajara, Jalisco 44100, tel. 33/3613-0936, fax 33/3658-2831, fax 33/3613-1190, reserva@ hotelfrances.com, www.hotelfrances.com, credit cards accepted, $66 s or d) rises among its fellow monuments on a quiet side street just a block south of the Teatro Degollado. The Frances, Guadalajara's first fancy hotel, built in 1610, has been restored to its original splendor. The 40-odd rooms, all with bath, glow with polished wood, bright tile, and fancy frosted cut-glass windows. Downstairs, an elegant chandelier illuminates the dignified, plant-decorated interior patio and adjacent restaurant. However, to increase business, owners have installed medium volume **live mariachi music** downstairs until 11:30 P.M., Friday, which for some may not fit with the hotel's otherwise refined ambience. Rates, however, run a very reasonable $66 (s or d) with fans and parking.

Guests at close-in **Hotel Roma** (Av. Juárez 170, Guadalajara, Jalisco 44100, tel. 33/3614-8650, fax 33/3614-2629, reservashtlroma@ hotmail.com, credit cards accepted, $72 s or d), two blocks south, three blocks east of the cathedral, enjoy amenities—plush lobby, shiny restaurant/bar, rooftop rose garden, and (unheated outdoor) pool—usually available only at pricier hostelries. Although asking rates run a reasonable $72 s or d, you may be able to get a discount if you ask. All rooms come with continental breakfast, TV, phones, a/c, parking, and limited wheelchair access. Some rooms, although clean and comfortable, are small. Look before moving in.

Over $100

The midsized colonial-facade **(Hotel de Mendoza** (V. Carranza 16, Guadalajara, Jalisco 44100, tel. 33/3613-4646, fax 33/3613-7310,

hotel@demendoza.com.mx, www.demendoza .com.mx, credit cards accepted, $100 s or d, $130 suite), only a couple of blocks north of the Teatro Degollado, is a longtime favorite of Guadalajara repeat visitors. Refined traditional embellishments—neo-Renaissance murals and wall portraits, rich dark paneling, glittering candelabra—grace the lobby, while upstairs, carpeted halls lead to spacious, comfortable rooms furnished with tasteful dark decor, including large baths, thick towels, and many other extras. The 100 rooms and suites come with cable TV, phones, a/c, a small indoor pool, refined restaurant, gym, whirlpool bath, parking, and some wheelchair access; third night (by reservation only) sometimes free.

Back south a few blocks, the **Holiday Inn Hotel and Suites** (211 Juárez, tel./fax 33/3560-1200, tel. 33/3613-1763, U.S.-Canada toll-free 800/315-2621, U.S. toll-free 888/465-4329, holidaycentro@prodigy.net.mx, www.holiday inn.com, credit cards accepted, $85 s, $105 d) offers a host of deluxe amenities. Upstairs, rooms are luxuriously appointed in soothing pastels, marble baths, plush carpets, and large beds, and come with cable TV, phones, a/c, parking, classy restaurant, gym, but no pool.

WEST OF THE CATHEDRAL

A number of budget and moderately priced hotels dot the west-side blocks on or around Calle Madero, within walking distance of the cathedral.

Under $50

The very plain but very economical **Hotel Hamilton** (Madero 381, Guadalajara, Jalisco 44100, tel. 33/3614-6726, $12 s or d, $19 t) offers a superbudget option. Although the 32 bare-bulb rooms with hot-water showers are plain and could use a good scrubbing, their steel doors, although drab, do enhance security. For maximum quiet and light, get a room in back, away from the street. Rooms include fans and hotel safe, but no parking.

A block south and half a block west, on Prisciliano Sánchez between Ocampo and Donato Guerra, the venerable standby **(Hotel Sevilla**

(Prisciliano Sánchez 413, Guadalajara, Jalisco 44100, tel./fax 33/3614-9354 or 33/3614-9037, fax 33/3614-9172, $25 s, $29 d, $38 t) offers basic accommodations at budget prices. Its 80 plain but comfortable rooms are furnished in dark brown wood and rugs to match. For more light and quiet, get an upper-story room away from the street. Amenities include a lobby with TV, private shower baths, parking, a hotel safe for storing valuables, fans, and phone; a good restaurant is open Monday–Saturday.

The homey, backpacker-friendly **Posada San Rafael** (López Cotilla 619, Guadalajara, Jalisco 44100, tel. 33/3614-9146, posadasanrafael @usa.net, sanrafael@avantel.net, or www .sanrafael1.tripod.com, credit cards accepted, $26 s or d in one bed, $37 d in two beds, $40 t), one block off Juárez, near the corner of Calle 8 Julio, is about 10 blocks from the cathedral. Its 12 simply but gaily decorated rooms with bath and fans are spread around a light, colorfully restored central patio. Tightly managed by the friendly on-site owner, the San Rafael's prices are certainly right. Try for a room in the back, away from the noisy street.

$50-100

Two blocks east and one block south, at the northeast corner of Prisciliano Sánchez and Donato Guerra, step up from the sidewalk and enter the cool, contemporary-classic interior of the ◖ **Hotel Cervantes** (442 Prisciliano Sánchez, tel./fax 33/3613-6686 or 33/3613-6846, reservaciones@hotelcervantes.com.mx, www.hotelcervantes.com.mx, credit cards accepted, $56 s, $62 d). Here everything, from the marble-and-brass lobby, the modern-chic restaurant, and bar, pool, and exercise room downstairs to the big beds, plush carpets, and shiny marble baths of the rooms upstairs, seems perfect for the enjoyment of its predominantly business clientele. Rates include TV, phones, parking, and a/c.

TLAQUEPAQUE

Tlaquepaque offers comfortable lodging choices, by virtue of some savvy Tlaquepaque innkeepers who have merged the North American bed-and-breakfast tradition with the Mexican *posada* style of accommodation for those visitors who appreciate the best of both worlds.

Under $50

Budget travelers will appreciate the **Posada de la Media Luna** (Inn of the Half Moon; Juárez 36, San Pedro Tlaquepaque 45500, tel. 33/3657-7631 or 33/3124-6522, fax 33/3635-6054, pinaluna@hotmail.com.mx, pinaluna@prodigy.net.mx, www.hotellamedia luna.com, credit cards accepted, $27 s, $33 d, $46 t or q), centrally situated just a block east of El Parián entertainment center and the plaza. The owners, with bright paint and lots of savvy, have turned something potentially humdrum into an attractive lodging, elevated away from the noise and bustle on busy Calle Juárez downstairs. About 20 rooms line both sides of a long, sunny upstairs patio, invitingly decorated with potted plants and umbrella-shaded tables for breakfast and relaxation. The rooms themselves are clean, and simply but comfortably furnished with pastel bedspreads, rustic wooden furniture, and some reading lamps. Baths are likewise clean and well-maintained, with hot-water showers. Prices include fans, TV, and continental breakfast, but no parking.

Over $50

Also situated close in, just two blocks south of the town plaza, is the ◖ **Hotel Quinta Don José** (Reforma 139, San Pedro Tlaquepaque, Jalisco 45500, tel. 33/3635-7522, toll-free Mex. tel. 01-800/700-2223, toll-free U.S./Can. tel. 866/629-3753, fax 33/3659-9315, info@ quintadonjose.com, www.quintadonjose.com, credit cards accepted, $75–90 d, $115–140 suite). Personable American-Mexican owner-spouses Arturo Magaña and Estela Cortez have converted a spreading, architect-designed family house compound into a tranquil garden lodging with 14 comfortable rooms and suites (some with kitchenettes), and a two-bedroom apartment, all tucked around a beautiful summer-warm (but unheated) blue lap swimming pool. They have added a comfortable bar and sitting area where guests enjoy socializing after a hard day seeing the sights.

The suites are all lovingly decorated with plenty of gorgeous tile, fetching handicrafts, heirloom-quality hand-sewn bedspreads, and polished rustic wooden furniture. Alternatively, guests can choose from eight comfortable, invitingly furnished rooms at reasonable rates. The rooms, very invitingly decorated and comfortable, rent from about $75 d for one double bed, upward to about $90 for two double beds or one king-sized. The suites, four of which open on to the pool-patio, run about $115, with either a single king-sized or a pair of double beds. The similarly attractive two-bedroom loft suite goes for about $140. All lodgings include a generous full breakfast buffet and a load of extras, including cable TV, fans and a/c, free laundry service, in-house wireless Internet connection, parking, and bus and airport transfer for about $20 per person

Other good Tlaquepaque accommodations that you might check out include the **Casa del Retono** (Matomoros 102, San Pedro Tlaquepaque, Jalisco 45500, tel./fax 33/3587-3989, info@lacasadelretono.com.mx, www.lacasadelretono.com.mx, $50 s, $60 d, $75 t) and **Villa del Ensueño** (Florida 305, San Pedro Tlaquepaque, Jalisco 45500, tel. 33/3635-8792, fax 33/3659-6152, U.S. toll-free tel. 800/220-8689, U.S. fax 818/597-0637, ensueno1@prodigy.net.mx, www.villadelensueno.com, rooms and suites $100–130).

TONALÁ

Tonalá's several recommendable hotels were built to accommodate the platoons of professional buyers that visit Tonalá year-round. Make reservations, especially for the Saturday and Wednesday nights before the big Sunday and Thursday outdoor *tianguis* (markets).

Under $50

On the southwest side of town, the **Hotel Casa de las Palomas** (Anesagasti 125, Tonalá, Jalisco 45400, tel./fax 33/3683-5542

or 33/3683-5542, reserve@casdelaspalomas.com, www.casadelaspalomas.com, $30 s, $33 d, $35 t), at the corner of Cinco de Mayo, caters mostly to business clientele. Past the small front lobby area, the hotel's two upper floors of 22 rooms overlook an inner parking courtyard. Little has been spared to make the rooms attractive and comfortable, including creamy pastel bedspreads, rustic-chic tile floors, designer reading lamps, and modern-standard shower bathrooms, plus satellite TV, fans, Internet access, and parking. The hotel's only apparent drawback is the noise and exhaust from the cars in the parking courtyard. Alleviate this problem by getting a third-floor room.

On the south side, four blocks along Madero south of the plaza, find **Hotel Hacienda del Sol** (Cruz Blanca 44, Tonalá, Jalisco 45400, tel./fax 33/3683-0275, 33/3683-5141, 33/3683-5142, reserve@hotelhaciendadelsol.com, www.hotelhaciendadelsol.com, credit cards accepted, $28 s, $35 d, $35 d or t in two beds, and $40 for four). Inside, guests enjoy a spacious courtyard, leading upstairs to about 30 new, clean, comfortable rooms, furnished with either one king-sized or two single or two double beds and attractively tiled, modern-standard shower baths, plus fans, telephone, and cable TV. Extras include handcrafted furniture, designer bed lamps, rustic wall art, fax and Internet access, and a truck to move merchandise.

A pair of recommendable Tonalá budget hotel options that you might consider are **Hotel Tonalá** (Madero 22, Tonalá, Jalisco 45400, tel./fax 33/3683-0595, 33/3683-4892, reservaciones@hoteltonala@hotmail.com, www.hoteltonala.com, $20 s or d in one bed, or $25 d in two beds) in the middle of the downtown shopping action, and **Mi Hotelito** (E. Zapata 76, Tonalá, Jalisco 45400, hotelito@tonala.com.mx, www.tonala.com.mx/mihotelito/, $32 t and q; suites $37 for up to four).

BUS STATION AND AIRPORT HOTELS

Two hotels on the edge of town offer interesting bus- and air travel options, respectively.

Bus travelers might enjoy a soft-bed overnight at the long-distance bus station, at Guadalajara's far southeast edge, about 20 minutes (figure $8, by taxi), or 30 minutes ($1, by TUR 706 a/c bus) from downtown. They can have it all at the two-pool, one-restaurant, moderately priced modern **Hotel la Serena Central** (Carretera Zapotlanejo 1500, Guadalajara, Jalisco 45625, tel. 33/3600-0910, fax 33/3600-1974, reservas@aranzazu.com.mx, www.arazazu.com.mx $38 s or d). Bus and truck noise may be a problem. Ask for a quiet *(tranquilo)* room. The 600 tidy and comfortable rooms, all with bath, do vary; look at more than one before moving in.

For air travelers, the luxuriously spacious and airy **Hotel Aeropuerto Casa Grande** (Calle Interior, Aeropuerto Internacional Miguel Hidalgo s/n, Guadalajara, Jalisco 45640, tel. 33/3678-9000, toll-free Mex tel. 01-800/366-4200, fax 33/3678-9002, reserva@casagrande .com.mx, ventas@casagrande.com.mx, www .casagrande.com.mx, credit cards accepted, $115 d), is just outside the airport terminal exit door. Comfortable rooms have with TV, phone, big bed, and a/c, and there's a pool, restaurant, and bar downstairs.

TRAILER PARKS

Although Guadalajara no longer has any in-town trailer parks, good, out-of-town alternatives exist. Check out the southwest-side **San José del Tajo Trailer Park** (Av. López Mateos Sur, P.O. Box 31-242, Guadalajara, Jalisco 45051, tel. 33/3686-1738, www.ontheroadin .com/interior/sanjosedeltajo.htm, $18 RV site), about a mile north of the Santa Anita Country Club and Golf Course. Its very adequate facilities include about 150 shady spaces

with all hookups, toilets, showers, pool, clubroom, and tennis court. RV spaces run about $18/day, $140/week, $400/month, or $13/day (for a three-month stay). Find it on the southern extension of Avenida López Mateos Sur (Highways 15, 54, and 80; watch for the sign on the right) about three miles (five km) south of the *periférico.* Northbound, it's about half a mile (one km) north of the Santa Anita village exit.

For a relaxing resort option, consider family-friendly **Chimulco** water park (tel. 387/778-0014 or 387/778-0209, Guadalajara tel. 33/3616-9696 or 33/3616-9393, fax 387/778-0161, chimulco2000@hotmail.com, www.chimulco .com.mx, $18 RV site), a warm spring resort, bungalows ($60 for a family), and trailer park at Villa Corona, about 38 miles (60 km), an hour's drive southwest of downtown. Besides a wealth of aquatic delights, from an elaborate water park to half a dozen pools of naturally healing mineral water, trailer and RV guests enjoy plenty of room, including about 50 concrete pads with all hookups, for about $18 nightly, about $400/month, with 20-amp hookups, many pull-through spaces, shade, laundry, barbecue grills, minimart, and much more.

Get to Chimulco via Avenida López Mateos Sur. about 16 miles (26 km) south of the *periférico* (peripheral boulevard), where you turn off the expressway right, onto Highway 80 (Melaque–Barra de Navidad direction) west. Continue approximately another seven miles (11 km) to Villa Corona, where you turn left, westbound, at the "Chimulco" sign. Agua Caliente is another quarter mile west, past Chimulco.

Food

Downtown Guadalajara is not overloaded with eateries, and many of them close early. Nevertheless, an adequate sprinkling of restaurants, cafés, taco shops, and bakeries serve the daily host of workers, shoppers, and sightseeing visitors that frequent the historic and bustling city center.

AROUND THE CATHEDRAL
Coffee Shops and Light Fare

For breakfast, lunch, or supper right in the middle of town, you can always rely on **Sanborn's** (corner of Juárez and 16 de Septiembre, tel. 33/3613-6283, 6 A.M.–1 A.M. Sun.–Thurs., 24 hours Fri.–Sat., entrees $5–12), which retains the 1950s ambience of its former Denny's owners. Entrées are midrange, from breakfasts at around $5 to salads and sandwiches ($3–6) and dinner plates ($5–12). For a similar, local-style budget coffee shop, go directly upstairs, to **Restaurant la Esquina** (7 A.M.–midnight daily). Or cross the street to the adjacent north corner, to the original **Sanborn's** (tel. 33/3613-6267, 33/3613-6264, 7:30 A.M.–11 P.M. daily). Besides being a tranquil, refined North American–style coffee shop, this Sanborn's branch has a big gift shop at ground level and a bookstore, with English-language paperbacks and magazines, downstairs.

At **◖ Sandy's** (at mezzanine level on the corner a block north of the cathedral front, tel. 33/3345-4636, 7 A.M.–10:30 P.M. Mon.–Thurs., Fri. and Sat. 7 A.M.–midnight) a choice plaza and cathedral view, service with a flourish, and weekend evening live music make the typical, but tasty, coffee shop menu of soups, salads, sandwiches ($2–7), meat, pasta, and Mexican plates ($4–10) seem like an occasion.

For a light breakfast or a break during a hard afternoon of sightseeing, you have at least two options. Stop in at **Croissants Alfredo** bakery (north side of Plaza Liberación (in front and east of the Teatro Degollado, tel. 33/3613-2694, 7:30 A.M.–9 P.M. daily). Luscious goodies—flaky croissants, crisp cookies, tasty tarts, and good coffee ($1–3)—can keep you going for hours.

If you need a real break from Mexican cuisine, go to **McDonald's** (at Juárez and Colón, one short block west of Sanborn's, tel. 33/3613-7307, 8 A.M.–10 P.M. daily) for breakfast. An Egg McMuffin, served until noon daily, with ham, hash browns, and coffee, runs about $5.

At the no-nonsense but worthy **Restaurant Málaga** (16 de Septiembre 210, tel. 33/3614-3815, 7 A.M.–10 P.M. daily), the hard-working owner really does come from Málaga, Spain. The food shows it: an eclectic list of hearty breakfasts ($3–7), which include hand-squeezed orange juice and good coffee. The menu offers many salads and sandwiches ($3–7), desserts, and savory espresso. Credit cards are accepted.

The Restaurant Málaga's prices seem to have risen lately. You can get similar fare and good service at the **Cafe Madrid** a few blocks north (on Juárez, between Corona and 16 de Septiembre, tel. 33/3614-9504, 8 A.M.–10:30 P.M. daily).

Mexican

The masterfully restored Porfirian **La Rinconada** restaurant (86 Morelos on the Morelos strolling mall, behind the Teatro Degollado, tel. 33/3613-9914, noon–10 P.M. Mon.–Sat., entrees $4–8) offers Mexican-style fare. The mostly tourist and middle-class local customers enjoy La Rinconada for its good tacos, tortas, and enchiladas ($2–4), plus meat, fish, and fowl entrées ($4–8). Entertainment arrives in the form of mariachis who wander in from the Plaza de los Mariachis nearby. By 4 P.M. many afternoons, two or three groups are filling the place with their melodies.

Nearby, a pair of places for good local food stand out. Try **◖ La Chata** (Corona 126, between Cotilla and Juárez, next to Bancomer, tel. 33/3617-2853, 1 P.M.–1 A.M. daily, entrees $4–10). Although plenty good for lunch ($4–8), *cena* (supper) ($4–10) is when the cadre of female cooks come into their own. Here you can have it all: tacos, *chiles rellenos*, tostadas, enchiladas, *pozole, moles,* and a dozen other delights you've probably never heard of, all cooked the way *mamacita* used to do it. Recent renovations and acceptance of credit cards have attracted a gentrified clientele and have consequently led to higher prices.

If La Chata's jump upscale has put it beyond your budget, go instead to **La Playita** (half a block north, on Juárez, near Corona, tel. 33/3614-5747, 9–12:30 A.M. daily, $3–6), with a similarly Mexican but more economical menu.

WEST OF THE CATHEDRAL
Coffee Shops and Light Fare
Local coffee-and-conversation café-hangout **Madoka** (Medillin, between Juárez and Moreno, 8 A.M.–11 P.M. daily), five blocks west and a block south of the Catedral, is as much a cultural experience as it is an eatery. Devotees enjoy many coffees ($1–2) plus a broad menu, from omelets and hamburgers to *carne asada* ($3–6).

If you're in the mood for a restful lunch or dinner, head west a few blocks to the airy interior patio of **Restaurant San Miguel** (enter from the west side of Donato Guerra, between Morelos and Pedro Moreno, tel. 33/3613-0809 8:30 A.M.–midnight Tues.–Sat., 8:30 A.M.–9 P.M. Sun., and 8:30 A.M.–6 P.M. Mon., entrees $6–12). Enjoy salad, soup, or a sandwich ($4–6), or a full meal ($6–12), while you take in the tranquil, traditional ambience. Around you rise the venerable arches and walls of Guadalajara's oldest convent for women, founded by the sisters of Santa Teresa de Jesús, in 1694. The old institution's topsy-turvy history mirrors that of Mexico itself. After its founding, it became the home for the Virgin of Zapopan until her present sanctuary was built decades later. In the 1860s, the nuns were expelled by the liberal forces during the War of the Reforms. They were allowed to return by President Díaz in 1895, only to be pushed out by revolutionary general Venustiano Carranza in 1914. The sisters bounced back, returning after the

revolution subsided in 1919, but were again expelled by President Calles during the *cristero* rebellion in 1925. Liberal but conciliatory President Lázaro Cárdenas allowed their return in 1939. Finally, the mostly aged sisters vacated their old home, this time voluntarily and for the last time, in 1977.

Chinese
Continue a few blocks west along Juárez to **Restaurant la Gran China** (Juárez 590, between Martinez and 8 Julio, tel. 33/3613-1447, noon–9 P.M. daily, entrees $5–8), where the Cantonese owner/chef puts out an authentic and tasty array of dishes. Despite the reality of La Gran China's crisp bok choy, succulent spareribs, and smooth savory noodles ($5–8), they nevertheless seem a small miracle here, half a world away from Hong Kong.

For a variation, try Gran China's plainer, more economical, but equally authentic neighboring **Restaurant Chong Wah** (Juárez 558, half a block east, at the corner of E.G. Martinez, tel. 33/3613-9950; 11 A.M.–10 P.M. daily).

EAST OF THE CATHEDRAL
For budget meals, local folks flock to the acres of *fondas* (permanent food stalls) on the second floor of the **Mercado Libertad** (at the east end of Plaza Tapatía, 7 A.M.–6 P.M. daily). Hearty homestyle fare, including Guadalajara's specialty, *birria*—pork, goat, or lamb in savory, spiced tomato-chicken broth—is at its safest and best here. It's hard to go wrong if you make sure your choices are hot and steaming ($2–5). Market stalls, furthermore, depend on repeat customers and are generally very careful that their offerings are wholesome. Be sure to douse fresh vegetables with plenty of lime *(limón)* juice, however.

SOUTH OF THE CATHEDRAL
For local-style food, dining prospects are good around the Parque San Francisco, about five blocks south of the cathedral.

Mexican
The prime south-side spot is the **Plaza Nueve Esquinas,** on Colón, just two blocks south of

the Parque San Francisco. Guadalajara families flock here afternoons and early evenings to feast on traditional Jalisco *birria* barbequed sheep and goat, served up by half a dozen surrounding restaurants. Among the best is restaurant **(Birrias Nueve Esquinas** (tel. 33/3613-6260, 9 A.M.–10 P.M. Mon.–Sat., 9 A.M.–6:30 P.M. Sun.). Specialties include *birria de chivo tatemada a fuego lento* (*birria* of goat roasted over a low fire, $8) and *barbacoa de borrego en pencos de maguey* (barbecued lamb in maguey leaf, $8). Alternatively, they offer plenty of more familiar goodies, such as lamb in vegetable and chicken consommé, cheeseburgers with french fries, guacamole *con totopos* (with chips), salad, tacos, and quesadillas ($4–8).

At Corona 250, corner of Prisciliano Sánchez, north side of Parque San Francisco, stands another local favorite, **Taquería las Faroles.** Mexican traditional food lovers can have it all: six kinds of tacos, plus quesadillas, *gringas, torta ahogada* (Mexican dipped sandwich), and much more ($2–6).

TLAQUEPAQUE AND TONALÁ

A sprinkling of good restaurants dot Tlaquepaque's main shopping street, Independencia. Starting on the west side and moving east, first find **Restaurant Casa Fuerte** (Independencia 224, tel. 33/3639-6481, noon–8 P.M. daily, credit cards accepted, $5–12), just past the corner of Cruz Verde. Step inside to an airy inner patio where, afternoons, a trio plays, and waiters serve a menu of hearty, innovative specialties, including soups, salads, Mexican plates, seafood, poultry, and meat ($5–12), which completes the attractive picture.

Enter the class-act **(Restaurant el Adobe** (just past the next east corner, tel. 33/3657-2792, open 12:30–7 P.M. daily, credit cards accepted, entrees $10–13). Here, Mexican nouveau cuisine reigns. For starters, try Mexican stuffed wontons ($5), continue with mushroom soup or passion salad ($5–7), then macaroni in mescal sauce or cheese-stuffed chicken breast ($10–13). Finish with an espresso ($3). A flute, guitar, and bass trio performs 2:30–6 P.M.

In **Tonalá,** some recommendable Mexican country-style restaurants provide relaxing respites for visitors.

Moving across town from south to north, first find **Restaurant el Rincón del Sol** (16 de Septiembre 61, tel. 33/3683-1989, 33/3683-1940, 7 A.M.–10 P.M. Mon.–Sat., 3–6 P.M. Sun., credit cards accepted, entrees $4–10), on the southwest corner of Madero, two blocks south of the main plaza. In a relaxing hacienda-style patio, kick back and savor Tonalá food at its most typical. House specialties include a number of styles of beef fillets, fondue with chorizo sausage, quesadillas with *cuitlacoche* (cooked black corn mushroom), cream of carrot soup, and salad (green or chef) ($4–10).

Three blocks north, step inside refined **Restaurant Los Geranios** (Hidalgo 69, tel. 33/3383-0486, 11 A.M.–5 P.M. daily Sun.–Fri., credit cards accepted, entrees around $6), half a block north of the plaza. Operated by the artisan-proprietors of Bazar Sermel next door, Los Geranios specializes in light, innovative, Mexican-style lunch and early supper specialties. For example, start with onion soup or green salad ($4), continue with a plate of enchiladas or maybe chicken *en mole* ($6), and finish with flan custard ($2) for dessert.

ZAPOPAN

For a refreshing sightseeing break, visit Zapopan's best, the Greek-owned and -operated **Restaurant Zorba Agios Aggelos** (at the Zapopan entrance arch, four blocks directly downhill from the basilica, tel. 33/3833-1131, 8 A.M.–11 P.M. daily, credit cards accepted, $4–15), the popular *taverna* meeting ground of Guadalajara's Greek community. Take a seat beneath one of the shady umbrellas out front and let the impression grow that you've been transported to some Greek island halfway around the world. The menu—gyros and falafel, moussaka, kabobs, dolmas (stuffed grape leaves) ($4–15), and retsina wine ($20)—completes the fantasy. Join in the fun with guitar music Wednesday evenings, jazz Thursdays, and sometimes with Greek circle and line dancing on Friday and Saturday evenings, around 7 P.M.–1 A.M.

Entertainment and Events

To find current entertainment options and events, pick up the events schedule at the Instituto Cultural Cabañas, behind the long pool/fountain at the east end of Plaza Tapatía, or the tourist information office, in the Plaza Tapatía, on Paseo Morelos, the mall-extension of Avenida Morelos, behind the Teatro Degollado at Morelos 102, or the Teatro Degollado box office.

Still another good source of events is the weekly English-language Guadalajara **Reporter.** If you can't find a newsstand copy, call the office, at Duque de Rivas 254, Guadalajara, tel. 33/3615-2177. For more information, visit www.guadalajarareporter.com.

THEATER AND CONCERTS

If you time it right, you can enjoy the concert that **Jalisco State Band** has provided since

The Jalisco State Band performs weekly beneath the ornate roof of the Plaza de Armas kiosk.

© BRUCE WHIPPERMAN

1898, in the Plaza de Armas adjacent to the cathedral (Thurs. at 6 p.m., Sun. at 6:30 p.m.). Mariachis perform in the same bandstand Wednesdays at 6:30 p.m.

The **Teatro Degollado** is host to world-class opera, symphony, and ballet events. While you're in the Plaza Liberación, drop by the theater box office *taquilla* (tah-KEE-yah, open 10 a.m.–8 p.m.a.m. daily) and ask for a *lista de eventos.* You can also call (or ask your hotel desk clerk to call) the theater box office at tel. 33/3614-4773, for reservations and information. For a very typical Mexican treat, attend one of the Teatro Degollado's regular 10 a.m. Sunday University of Guadalajara folkloric ballet performances. They're immensely popular; get tickets in advance.

You can also sample the offerings of the **Instituto Cultural Cabañas** (tel. 33/3818-2800, ext. 31016, 10:15 a.m.–5:45 p.m. Tues.–Sat.; 10:15 a.m.–3 p.m. Sun.). It sponsors many films, music, dance and dramatic events, both experimental and traditional. For more information, ask at the Hospicio Cabañas admission desk, tel. 33/3618-2800, ext. 31009.

In your wanderings, don't forget to stop by the **Plaza de Los Mariachis,** just east of the Plaza Tapatía, adjacent to the Mercado Libertad and the big boulevard, Independencia, that runs beneath the Plaza Tapatía. Take a sidewalk table, have a drink or snack and listen to the mariachis' sometimes soulful, sometimes bright, but always enjoyable, offerings.

NIGHTLIFE

A few clubs accommodate folks who want to unwind downtown. The **Hotel Fénix** lobby bar (Corona 160, tel. 33/3614-5714), just two blocks south of the cathedral, often offers evening music until about midnight. Call to confirm.

Many also enjoy the lively mariachi music at the **Hotel Frances** (Maestranza 35, tel. 33/3613-1190 or 33/3613-0936), Friday nights until 11:30 p.m.

GUADALAJARA

Tlaquepaque folks dress their town up for the National Ceramics Fair from mid-June through mid-July.

Devotees of disco might like visiting the pair of clubs (customarily crowded with 20- and 30-somethings most Friday and Saturday nights), on Maestranza, between Sánchez and Madero. The **Meridiana 60** (tel. 33/3613-8489; 10 A.M.–2 A.M. Wed.–Sat.), the more genteel of the two, is decorated inside with colored lights flashing on jungly vine-hung walls and offers no-cover live salsa-rock music beginning around 9 P.M.

A few doors south and across the street, **Bar-Discoteca Maskaras** (tel. 33/3614-8103, 7 P.M.–3 A.M. daily) operates a downstairs bar and a no-cover upstairs discoteque (with the door shut so neighbors can sleep and customers can hear each other talk downstairs).

FIESTAS

Although Guadalajarans always seem to be celebrating, the town really heats up during its three major annual festivals. Starting the second week in June, the southeast neighborhood, formerly the separate village of Tlaquepaque, is host to the **National Ceramics Fair.** Besides its celebrated stoneware, Tlaquepaque shops and stalls are stuffed with a riot of ceramics and folk crafts from all over Mexico, while cockfights, regional food, folk dances, fireworks, and mariachis fill its streets.

A few months later, the entire city, Mexican states, and foreign countries get into the **Festival of October.** For a month, everyone contributes something, from ballet performances, plays, and soccer games to selling papier-mâché parrots and sweet corn in the plazas. Concurrently, Guadalajarans celebrate the traditional **Festival of the Virgin of Zapopan.** Church plazas are awash with merrymakers enjoying food, mariachis, dances (don't miss the Dance of the Conquest), and fireworks. The merrymaking peaks on October 12, when a huge crowd conducts the Virgin from the downtown cathedral to Zapopan. The merrymakers' numbers often swell to a million faithful who escort the Virgin, accompanied by ranks of costumed saints, devils, Spanish conquistadores, and Aztec chiefs.

(For a list of national fiestas, all celebrated in Guadalajara, see *Festivals and Events* in the *People* section of the *Background* chapter.)

BULLFIGHTS AND RODEOS

Winter is the main season for *corridas de toros*, or bullfights. The bulls charge and the crowds roar *"Olé"* (oh-LAY) Sunday afternoons at the Guadalajara Plaza de Toros (bullring), on Calz. Independencia about two miles north of the Mercado Libertad.

Local associations of *charros* (gentleman cowboys) often stage rodeolike *charreadas* weekends at nearby *lienzos charro* (rodeo rings). The most frequently staged *charreadas* begin most Sundays at noon, at the **Lienzo Charro de Jalisco,** at 577 Dr. Michel, just beyond the southeast side of Parque Agua Azul. Call tel. 33/3619-0315 to confirm.

You can also watch out for posters, or ask at your hotel desk or the tourist information office, tel. 33/3688-1600, for *corrida de toros* and *charreada* details and dates.

THE TEQUILA EXPRESS

Ride the very popular tourist train (usually Sat. and Sun. around 10 A.M.) to the town of **Amatitán,** an hour west of Guadalajara, for a tour of the Herradura tequila liquor factory in the historic **ex-Hacienda San José.** Included are viewing of the blue *agave* harvesting process, a Mexican buffet, and a folkloric show, including dances, mariachis, a roping exhibition, and handicrafts.

Tequila Express tickets, including all transportation, drinks, entertainment, and food, run about $70 per adult, kids (6–11 years) $41, children under 6 free. Tickets are available at the Chamber of Commerce downtown branch (at Morelos 395, on the south side of the plaza across 16 de Septiembre from the cathedral front, tel. 33/3614-3145, 9 A.M.–2:30 P.M. and 3:30–6 P.M.

MARIACHIS

Mariachis, those thoroughly Mexican troubador bands, have spread from their birthplace in Jalisco throughout Mexico and into much of the United States. The name itself reveals their origin. "Mariachi" originated with the French *mariage* (marriage). When French influence peaked during the 1864-1867 reign of Maximilian, Jaliscans transposed *mariage* to "mariachi," a label they began to identify with the five-piece folk bands that played for weddings.

The original ensembles, consisting of a pair of violins, *vihuela* (large eight-stringed guitar), *jarana* (small guitar), and harp, played exclusively traditional melodies. Song titles such as "Las Moscas" (The Flies), "El Venado" (The Stag), and "La Papaya" thinly disguised their universal themes, mostly concerning love.

Although such all-string folk bands still play in Jalisco, notably in Tecatitlán and other rural areas, they've largely been replaced by droves of trumpet-driven commercial mariachis. The man who sparked the shift was probably Emilio Azcárraga Vidaurreta, the director of radio station XEW, which began broadcasting in Mexico City in 1930. In those low-fidelity days, the subdued sound of the harp didn't broadcast well, so Azcárraga suggested the trumpet as a replacement. It was so successful that the trumpet has become the signature sound of present-day mariachis.

Still, mariachis mostly do what they've always done – serenade sweethearts, play for weddings and parties, even accompany church Masses. They seem to be forever strolling around town plazas on Saturday nights and Sunday afternoons, looking for jobs. Their fees, which should be agreed upon before they start, often depend on union scale per song, per serenade, or per hour.

Sometimes mariachis serve as a kind of live jukebox which, for a coin, will play your old favorite. And even if it's a slightly tired but sentimental "Mañanitas" or "Cielito Lindo," you can't help but be moved by the singing violins, bright trumpets, and soothing guitars.

Mon.–Fri). Ticketmaster (tel. 33/3818-3800) also sells Tequila Express tickets, for an added fee, by telephone, with a credit card. (If you're not fluent in Spanish, ask someone fluent in Spanish, such as your hotel desk clerk, to call for you.)

The Tequila Express departs from the main Guadalajara rail station, at the south end of downtown (on Calz. Independencia, two blocks south of Parque Agua Azul). For loads of more information, visit www.tequilaexpress.com.mx.

Sports and Recreation

WALKING, JOGGING, AND EXERCISE GYMS

Walkers and joggers enjoy several spots around Guadalajara. Close in, the **Plaza Liberación** behind the cathedral provides a traffic-free (although concrete) jogging and walking space. Avoid the crowds with morning workouts. If you prefer grass underfoot, try **Parque Agua Azul** (10 A.M.–6 P.M. Tues.–Sat., entrance $1) on Calz. Independencia about a mile south of the Libertad Market.

An even better jogging-walking space is the **Parque de los Colomos**—hundreds of acres of greenery, laced by jogging trails, four miles northwest from the city center, before Zapopan; open daily 7 A.M.–7 P.M., tel. 33/3641-7633. Get there by taxi or bus 51C, which begins at the old bus terminal, near Parque Agua Azul, and continues north along Avenida 16 de Septiembre, through downtown Guadalajara.

Workout gyms are relatively plentiful in Guadalajara's affluent west-side neighborhoods. In Minerva-Chapultepec, you have your choice of at least two **Gold's Gyms,** one of them at Av. Vallarta 1791, south side of the street, three blocks west of Chapultepec, tel. 33/3630-2221 and 33/3616-0419; and another several blocks south, at Niños Héroes 2851, tel. 33/3647-4960.

For a gym with a **swimming pool** take a bus (Par Vial from downtown) west, to the **World Gym** (Jesús Garcia 804, corner of Manuel Ángel de Quevedo, tel. 33/3640-0704, 33/3640-0576, 6:30 A.M.–10 P.M. Mon.–Fri., 5:30 A.M.–5 P.M. Sat.). Find it off Avenida López Mateos about a mile north of the Los Arcos Arch and the

CHARREADAS

The many Jalisco lovers of *charrera*, the sport of horsemanship, enjoy a long-venerated tradition. Boys and girls, coached by their parents, practice riding skills from the time they learn to mount a horse. Privileged young people become noble *charros* or *charras* or *coronelas* – gentleman cowboys and cowgirls – whose equestrian habits follow old aristocratic Spanish fashion, complete with broad sombrero, brocaded suit or dress, and silver spurs.

The years of long preparation culminate in the *charreada*, which entire communities anticipate with relish. Although superficially similar to an Arizona rodeo, a Jalisco *charreada* differs substantially. The festivities take place in a *lienzo charro*, literally, the passageway through which the bulls, horses, and other animals run from the corral to the ring. First comes the *cala de caballo*, a test of the horse and rider. The *charros* or *charras* must gallop full speed across the ring and make the horse stop on a dime. Next is the *piales de lienzo*, a roping exhibition during which an untamed horse must be halted and held by having its feet roped. Other bold performances include *jineteo de toro* (bull riding and throwing) and the super-hazardous *paso de la muerte*, in which a rider tries to jump upon an untamed bronco from his or her own galloping mount. *Charreadas* often end in a flourish with the *escaramuza charra*, a spectacular show of riding skill by *charras* in full, colorful dress.

GUADALAJARA

Minerva Circle. Turn left at Garcia, and continue two blocks to the corner of Quevedo.

TENNIS, GOLF, AND SWIMMING

Although Guadalajara has virtually no public tennis courts, the west-side **Hotel Camino Real** (Av. Vallarta 5005, tel. 33/3134-2424) rents its tennis courts to the public, by appointment, for about $10 per hour. The Hotels Fiesta Americana (Aurelio Aceves 225, Glorieta Minerva, tel. 33/3818-1400) and the Hotel Crowne Plaza (Av. López Mateos Sur 2500, tel. 33/3634-1034) have courts for guests only.

The 18-hole **Atlas Country Club Golf Course** (tel. 33/3689-2620, dawn to dusk Tues.–Sun.) welcomes nonmembers for both tennis and golf for a fee. Tennis courts run about $13 per hour; golf greens fees runs about $90 Mon.–Fri. and $110 Saturday and Sunday. Clubs and carts rent for about $30 and $35; a caddy will cost about $14. Get there via Chapala Highway 44, the south-of-town extension of Calz. J. Gonzales Gallo. The golf course is 1.1 miles (1.8 km) south of the *periférico* on the east side of the expressway, behind the big SCI electronics plant.

Nearly all the luxury hotels have swimming pools. Two of the prettiest (but unheated) pools perch atop moderately priced hotels downtown: the **Roma** (corner Juárez and Degollado, tel. 33/3614-8650) in the heart of downtown, and the **Cervantes** (442 Prisciliano Sáchez, tel. 33/3613-6686), a few blocks west of the cathedral.

If your hotel doesn't have a pool, go to the very popular public pool and picnic ground at Balneario Lindo Michoacán (Rio Barco 1614, corner Calz. J. Gonzalez Gallo, tel. 33/3635-9399, 8 A.M.–6 P.M. daily, $6 adults, $3 kids). Find it about two miles along Gallo southeast of Parque Agua Azul.

Shopping

Shopping for handicrafts is a prime motivation for visiting Guadalajara. The biggest source of the more common handicrafts under one roof is the downtown **Mercado Libertad**, adjacent to the Plaza Tapatía. For finer goods and wider selections, however, serious handicrafts shoppers go to suburban **Tlaquepaque** and **Tonalá** villages, which rank at the top among Mexico's premier handicrafts sources.

DOWNTOWN

The **Mercado Libertad** market, sprawling at the east end of Plaza Tapatía, has several specialty areas distributed through two main sections. Most of the handicrafts are on the bottom, downstairs floor. While selection varies, from guitars, jewelry, and trinkets, to piñatas, sweets, baskets, and sombreros, leather predominates, in jackets, belts, saddles, and the most huaraches you'll ever see under one roof. Also downstairs, don't miss browsing intriguing spice and *yerba* (herb) stalls, which

Guadalajara's Mercado Libertad

feature mounds of curious dried plants, gathered from the wild, often by village *curanderos* (traditional healers). Before you leave, be sure to look over the piñatas, which make colorful, lightweight gifts.

When you get hungry and weary of shopping, sample some of the many excellent hearty offerings of the acre of *fondas* (food stalls) in the market upstairs.

Two other promising downtown handicrafts sources in the Plaza Tapatía vicinity are at the **tourist information office** at Morelos 102, and the indigenous Huichol vendors in the adjacent alley, called Rincón del Diablo.

You might also find what you're looking for at the government **Casa de Artesanías Agua Azul** (Calz. Gonzales Gallo 20, corner of Independencia and Gonzales Gallo, tel./fax 33/3619-4664 or 33/3619-5179, 10 A.M.–6 P.M. Mon.–Fri., 10 A.M.–5 P.M. Sat., 10 A.M.–2 P.M. Sun.), about a mile south of downtown, adjacent to Parque Agua Azul (best go by taxi, $2). Here, you can choose from brilliant stoneware, handsome gold and silver jewelry, and endearing ceramic, brass, and papier-mâché animals.

Magno Centro Joyero

For **jewelry,** the Magno Centro Joyero (Magno Jewelry Center; next to the Mercado Libertad, tel. 33/3562-2011, most stores open 9 A.M.–6 or 7 P.M. daily) that towers over the south edge of the Plaza Tapatía is worth a visit. A battalion of shops in a pair of airy, modern (ground and basement) floors display mostly moderately priced (10- and 14-karat gold) necklaces, rings, amulets, bracelets, chains, and more. The styles and prices reflect the modest incomes of the shoppers. Stones, while plentiful and sparkling, are usually glass or zircon imitations, although some authentic rubies *(rubis),* diamonds *(diamantes),* and emeralds *(esmeraldas)* are available in certain stores if you ask. Cultured pearls, however, are common and quite reasonably priced.

◖ TLAQUEPAQUE

Tlaquepaque was once a sleepy village of potters separated by miles of countryside from Gua-

dalajara. Attracted by the quiet of the country, rich families built palatial homes during the 19th century. Now, entrepreneurs have moved in and converted them into upscale restaurants, art galleries, and showrooms, decorated with fine Tonalá and Tlaquepaque ceramics, glass, metalwork, and papier-mâché.

In spite of having been swallowed by the Guadalajara metropolis, Tlaquepaque still has the feel and look of a small colonial town, with its cathedral and central square leading westward onto the mansion-decorated main street, now mall, **Avenida Independencia.** A second major shopping street, **Avenida Juárez,** runs parallel to and one block south of Independencia.

Museo Regional de Cerámica y Arte Popular

Although generally pricier than Tonalá, Tlaquepaque still has plenty of bargains. For fine examples of traditional Tlaquepaque and Tonalá crafts, make your first stop in the Museo Regional de Cerámica y Arte Popular (237 Independencia, tel. 33/3635-5404, 10 A.M.–6 P.M. Tues.–Sun.). Then, price the showier, upscale merchandise in the galleries along Avenida Independencia, making sure that you save some time to visit **Avenida Juárez,** one block south, downhill.

Avenida Independencia

Start half a block west of the museum, at the intersection of Independencia and Alfarareros (Potters), at a regally restored former mansion, now gallery **Antigua de México** (Independencia 255, tel. 33/3635-3402, antiguademexico@infosel.net.mx, 10 A.M.– 2 P.M. and 3–7 P.M. Mon.–Fri., 10 A.M.–6 P.M. Sat.). One of the few studios in Mexico to manufacture fine 17th-century-style furniture, Antigua de Mexico's displays offer handsome troves of baroque gilt-wood reproductions.

East half a block and across the street, find the **Sergio Bustamante** gallery (tel. 33/3639-5519, www.sergiobustamante.com.mx, 10 A.M.–7 P.M. Mon.– Sat., noon–4 P.M. Sun.), an upscale outlet for the famous sculptor's arresting, whimsical studies in juxtaposition. Bustamante supervises an entire Guadalajara studio-factory of artists who put out hundreds of one-of-a-kind variations on a few human, animal, and vegetable themes. Prices seem to depend mainly on size; rings and bracelets may go for as little as $200, while a two-foot humanoid chicken may run $2,000. Don't miss the restroom.

Half a block farther, leather is seemingly sacred at **San Piel** (Saint Leather; Independencia 225A, tel. 33/3659-6582, 10 A.M.–7 P.M. Mon.–Sat., 10:30 A.M.–6:30 P.M. Sun.). Items, all made at the owner's Guadalajara factory, include supple jackets, stylish purses, luggage large and small, bags and briefcases, belts, and more. Combat the high asking prices by offering half the marked price.

A block farther east, find Guadalajara's king of baroque reproductions, **Agustín Parra** (Independencia 154 and 158, on the north side of the street, near the corner of P. Sánchez, tel. 33/3657-8530, tel./fax 33/3657-0316, www.agustinparra.com.mx, 10 A.M.–7 P.M. Mon.–Sat., 10 A.M.–4 P.M. Sun.). Inside, find a treasury of new baroque-style art, including rococo-framed religious paintings and scroll-like gilded chairs and tables, or a magnificent 15-foot $500,000 *retablo* (altarpiece) for your family chapel. (Delivery is extra.)

While you're there, be sure to visit the small museum inside that exhibits the papal chair that Parra built for the visit of Pope John Paul II in 2002.

Avenida Juárez

Although few, if any, of the Avenida Juárez shops are as spectacularly upscale as some of the shops on Independencia, many excellent handicrafts, bargainable to very reasonable prices, can be the reward of concentrated effort here. Begin half a block east of Avenida Matamoros and work your way west.

Start on the south side of the street, about a block south and a block east of Agustín Parra, at **Rikatti Arte Mexicano** (at Juárez 131A, tel. 33/3343-7233, fax 3343-7234, ventas@rikatti .com, www.rikatti.com, 10 A.M.–3 P.M. and 4–7:30 P.M. Mon.–Sat.), for a lovingly selected and displayed small museum of decorative art. Although the glassware (gleaming goblets, stat-

uesque vases, bright mirrors) first catches your eye, the entire collection (elegant lamps, fetching animal motif purses, one-of-a-kind tables and chairs, and much more) is worth a look.

For more leather goods, return half a block west, to **Jiménez Hermanos Piel** (Juárez 145, near the corner of Matamoros, tel. 33/3635-1821, 10 A.M.–8 P.M. Mon.–Sat., 10:30 A.M.–3:30 P.M. Sun.). Here, you can admire a supple selection of jackets, purses, wallets, belts, backpacks, and much more. What's even better is that the staff are experts in made-to-order goods. Be prepared with a sample (or at least a drawing) of what you want. With 30 years in the business behind it, Jiménez Hermanos Piel backs up its goods with a lifetime guarantee.

Continue west, to the southwest corner of Miranda, and treat yourself to **Fábricas Mona's** big fabric shop (Juárez 205, tel. 33/3635-6681, 33/3659-1715, fax 33/3659-3112, monas@ prodigy.net.mx, 10 A.M.–6:30 P.M. Mon.–Sat., 11 A.M.–2:30 P.M. Sun.). Wander through this wonderland of textiles, mostly handwoven and hand-embroidered, from all over Mexico, with much from Oaxaca. You'll find shelf after shelf of tablecloths, napkins (*servilletas*), throw rugs (*tapetes*), serapes, vests, *huipiles*, skirts (*faldas*), shirts (*camisas*), blouses (*blusas*), pillowcases (*fundas*), curtains (*cortinas*), and a miniwarehouse of fabric by the roll.

Getting There

Most conveniently, hire a taxi (about $12 round-trip and well worth it) or ride the usually crowded city bus 275 (look for "Tlaquepaque" scrawled on the front window) or the air-conditioned "Turquesa" TUR bus along downtown Avenida 16 de Septiembre. By car, from the center of town, drive Avenida Revolución southeast about four miles to the Niños Héroes traffic circle. From Avenida Niños Héroes, the first right off the traffic circle, continue about a mile to the west end of Avenida Independencia, on the left.

TONALÁ

About five miles past Tlaquepaque, Tonalá perches at Guadalajara's country edge. When the Spanish arrived in the 1520s, Tonalá was dominant among the small kingdoms of the Atemajac Valley. Tonalá's widow-queen and her royal court were adorned by the glittering handiwork of an honored class of silver and gold crafters. Although the Spaniards carted off the valuables, the tradition of Tonalá craftsmanship remains today. To the visitor, everyone in Tonalá seems to be making something. Tonalá family patios are piled with their specialties, whether they be low-fired pottery, high-fired ceramic stoneware, brass, papier-mâché or wood furnishings.

Moreover, right at the source, bargains couldn't be better. Dozens of shops dot the few blocks around Tonalá's central plaza corner of north-south Avenida Hidalgo (north of the plaza; but called Avenida Madero south of it) and east-west Avenida Juárez. For super bargaining opportunities and *mucho* holiday excitement and color, visit the Thursday and Sunday *tianguis* (market), which spreads along the tree-lined *periférico* highway about four blocks west of the Tonalá plaza.

Museo Regional Tonallán

Make the petite Museo Regional Tonallán your first stop (Ramón Corona 75, near the corner of Constitución, tel. 33/3683-2519, 9 A.M.–2 P.M. Mon.–Fri.), about two blocks east and two blocks north of the town plaza.

Permanent exhibits trace local crafts in a historical context, through the early goldsmithing and pottery tradition, to Tonalá's diversified modern treasury of ceramics, papier-mâché, metals and iron, woodcrafts, and glass.

Tonalá Shopping Tour

After the museum, go back west along Constitución to Hidalgo, where several shops stand out. Among the most outstanding is factory shop **Galería Bernabe** (Hidalgo 83, tel./fax 33/3683-0877 or 33/3683-0040, 9 A.M.– 6 P.M. Mon.–Fri., 8 A.M.–3 P.M. Sat.–Sun.). Celebrated founders of the 200-year-old *petatillo* (little petal) double-fired technique, Bernabe specializes in intricate, fetching animal and plant designs in black, green, and

white. Some of the best pieces are reminiscent of fine ancient Chinese ceramics. Offerings vary, from glistening vases, pitchers, and bowls, to gorgeous table settings for a dozen or more. If you can't find exactly what you want, Bernabe will execute your own design to order.

Half a block farther south, don't miss **El Bazar de Sermel** (Hidalgo 67, tel. 33/3683-0010, fax 33/3683-0160, 9 A.M.–6:30 P.M. Mon.–Fri., 9 A.M.–2 P.M. Sat., 10 A.M.–3 P.M. Sun.). Here, master craftspeople have refined the Tonalá papier-mâché tradition to a fine art. Stop in and pick out the life-sized flamingo, pony, giraffe, or zebra you've always wanted for your living room.

Walk south two blocks to to **La Mexicanía** (13 Hidalgo, at the northwest plaza corner of Juáez, tel. 33/3683-0152, 11 A.M.–7 P.M. Mon.–Sat., 11 A.M.–3 P.M. Sun.). In the 14 years that I've been coming to Tonalá, La Mexicanía has prospered and expanded by virtue of its diverse, all-Mexico collection. This is heaven for Mexico handicrafts lovers. If you've wanted a particular item—a weaving or a *huipil* from Oaxaca, a jaguar mask from Guerrero, a guitar from Michoacán, an ironwood sailfish from Sonora, a Huichol yarn painting, or a Guanajuato papier-mâché clown—it's here.

Many interesting shops dot Avenida Madero, south of the plaza. Be sure to stop in at **Antiguas Santiago** (Madero 42, tel. 33/3683-0641, 9 A.M.–6:30 P.M. Mon.–Sat., 10 A.M.–3 P.M. Sun.) for a museum of designer glass—lamps, vases, bowls—in a myriad of fantastic colors, shapes, and sizes, too lovely to resist.

More pleasant surprises are in store a few steps farther south, at **Vidrio Soplado** (Blown Glass; Madero 42, tel. 33/3683-0641, 10 A.M.–6 P.M. Mon.–Sat., 10 A.M.–4 P.M. Sun.). Here, admire all the lovely *esferas* (colored glass balls), vases, tumblers, and goblets you'll ever need.

Half a block farther south, step into **Artesanías Alba** (Madero 85B, tel. 33/3683-1414, 10 A.M.–7 P.M. Mon.–Sat., 10 A.M.–

5 P.M. Sun.) for a trove of fetching high-fired Guanajuato-made Talavera-lookalike pottery (with prices much more reasonable than the genuine Puebla Talavera ware). Choose among a large selection of lovely urns, vases, bowls, and bathroom sinks.

Tonalá Factory Stores

Several renowned Tonalá factories (especially ceramic and glass) welcome visitors into their showroom and adjacent workshops. With your handicrafts appetite whetted by the excellent Galería Bernabe, continue north half a block, turn left, then right at Morelos to **Los Caporales**' big factory store (Morelos 161, tel./fax 33/3683-0312, info@ceramicacaporales .com, www.ceramicacaporales.com, 9 A.M.– 6 P.M. Mon.–Fri., 10 A.M.–2 P.M. Sat.). Los Caporales specializes in glistening, high-fired *corcho*-technique ware, from decorative animal figurines to utilitarian plates, bowls, and vases. Past the rear of the showroom, tour the factory, where workers begin with humble clay that they mix, mold, smooth, paint, glaze, and finally fire into handsome works of art.

Continue a block north, turn left on López Cotilla, and continue half a block to celebrated **Artesanías Erandi** (López Cotilla 118, tel. 33/3683-0253, fax 33/3683-0871, ventas@ erandi.com, www.erandi.com, 9 A.M.–6 P.M. Mon.–Fri., 9 A.M.–2 P.M. Sat.). Here, you're at the source of the much-imitated high-fired Erandi style, well-known all over Mexico and much of the world. Step into the rear factory and view craftspeople putting life into the fetching motifs: curled-up cats, preening ducks, bearded men-in-the-moon.

An extended Tonalá shopping tour wouldn't be complete without a visit to at least one of Tonalá's glass factories. The most interesting is **Vidrios Jimón,** on the south side of town (best take a taxi) to Calle Santos Degollado, near the corner of Avenida Tonalá (8 A.M.–5 P.M. Mon.–Fri., 8 A.M.– 2 P.M. Sat., 10 A.M.–2 P.M. Sun. store only). Out front, the factory sounds like a volcano from the roar of the gas-fired ovens inside. Enter through the store, which displays a

© BRUCE WHIPPERMAN

A number of Tonalá factory stores welcome visitors into their workrooms.

shiny, multicolored array of mirrored glass balls, yellow, blue, silver, red. Continue inside to view the fascinating technique of twisting, stretching, blowing, and cutting red-hot molten glass into lovely shapes.

Getting There

From downtown Guadalajara, by far the best option is to go by taxi (about $20 round-trip) or air-conditioned TUR 706 bus, or alternatively, the cheaper but oft-crowded city bus 275 (look for "Tonalá" scrawled on the windshield) from the stops on downtown Avenida 16 de Septiembre. By car, drive Avenida Revolución about six miles southeast of the city center to the big Plaza Camachines (New Bus Station/Camionera Central Nueva). Follow the Highway 90 Carretera Zapotlanejo expressway (Mexico City direction, east). After about two miles, exit right at the signed Tonalá off-ramp (then turn left and cross over the Carretera), then right at the first street; three blocks farther, turn left and within a few blocks you'll be at the Tonalá central plaza.

GUADALAJARA

Information and Services

TOURIST INFORMATION

The main state of Jalisco tourist information office is near the Plaza Tapatía, on Paseo Morelos, the mall extension of Avenida Morelos, behind the Teatro Degollado (Morelos 102, tel. 33/3668-1600 or 33/3668-1601, fax 33/3668-1686, hgonzale@jalisco.gob.mx, www.visita.jalisco.gob.mx, 9 A.M.–8 P.M. Mon.–Fri., 10 A.M.–2 P.M. Sat. and Sun.).

The City of Guadalajara Convention and Visitors Bureau (tel./fax 33/3122-7544, tel. 33/3616-9150, ofvc@gdlmidestino.com.mx, www.guadlajaramidestino.com), maintains at least three **tourist information booths** (*módulos de información*). One is in the foyer of the Palacio de Gobierno, on Corona, adjacent to the Plaza de Armas, a block east and half a block south from the cathedral front. Ask for a copy of city tourism's superb all-color *Points of Interest* bilingual foldout map and guide. Open 9:30 A.M.–2:30 P.M. and 5–7 P.M. Mon.–Fri., 10 A.M.–12:30 P.M. Sat. and Sun.

Another such booth is often open in the Plaza Tapatía, east side, where the plaza broadens out, by the Imolación de Quetzalcoatl fountain; a third is in the monumental Los Arcos arch, near the Minerva Circle, on Avenida Vallarta, about two miles west of downtown. The tourist information booth is at street level, the administrative offices upstairs. Open 9 A.M.–6 P.M. Mon.–Sat., 9 A.M.–4 P.M. Sun.

Guides

A good guide can provide an easy route to exploring Guadalajara. One of the best people to ask about Guadalajara guides is experienced guide **Lynn Mendez,** who staffs the state of Jalisco tourist information office (Paseo Morelos 102, tel. 33/3668-1600, 33/3668-1601) on Plaza Tapatóa. She recommends professional tour guides **Roberto Arellano,** tel. 33/3657-8376, former president of the Guadalajara Guides Association; **Fernando Mediana,** tel. 33/3654-5957; and **Octavio Estrada,** 33/3632-7306.

Another very well prepared and personable guide is American-Mexican inkeeper Arturo Magaña, co-owner of Quinta Don José in Tlaquepaque (U.S.-Canada toll-free tel. 866/629-3753, Guadalajara tel. 33/3635-7522, fax 33/3659-9315, info@quintadonjose.com, www.quintadonjose.com).

If Arturo's very popular tours are booked up, he recommends a pair of excellent guides: Four stars go to both **Ramiro Roma** (tel./fax 33/3631-4242, or cell tel. 044-33/3661-6202 in Guadalajara, or long-distance 33/3661-6202 outside Guadalajara); and **Lino Gabriel González Nuño** (tel. 33/3152-0324, fax 33/3635-4049, linogabriel@hotmail.com, www.mexonline.com/guadalajaratours.htm), who specializes in customized Guadalajara tours (downtown, shopping in Tlaquepaque and Tonalá, archaeological sites, and more).

MONEY EXCHANGE

Change more types of money (U.S., Canadian, German, Japanese, French, Italian, and Swiss) for the best rates at the downtown street-front **Banamex** office and ATM (Juárez 237, corner of Corona, tel. 33/3252-1226, 9 A.M.–4 P.M. Mon.–Fri.).

If Banamex is closed or its lines are too long, opt for a more convenient bank. Downtown Guadalajara has a squad of bank branches, all with ATMs. Prominent among them is **HSBC,** with the longest hours, and a pair of downtown branches: one at Libertad 410, tel. 33/3658-0869, 33/3658-1125, 8 A.M.–7 P.M. Mon.–Fri., 8 A.M.–3 P.M. Sat.); the other is across the street from the cathedral front, at the northwest corner of Alcalde and Molina (tel. 33/3613-2501 or 3614-7515, open the same hours). Another is **BBV-Bancomer** (around the corner from Banamex, on Corona between Cotilla and Juárez).

After bank hours, go to one of the several *casas de cambio* (money changers) nearby, a block east of Banamex, on Cotilla between Maestranza and Corona.

Guadalajara's only **American Express** branch is on the west side of town (Plaza Los

Arcos, Av. Vallarta 2440, tel. 33/3818-2323, fax 33/3616-7665, 9 A.M.–6 P.M. Mon.–Fri., 9 A.M.–1 P.M. Sat.), about three miles west of the city center. It provides both travel-agency and member financial services, including personal-check and traveler's-check cashing.

CONSULATES

Many countries maintain Guadalajara consular offices. The **U.S. consulate** is about a mile and a half west of the city center (Progreso 175, between Cotilla and Libertad, tel. 33/3628-2100 and 33/3268-2200). Service hours for American citizens are 8 A.M.–11 P.M. Mon.–Fri.

The **Canadian consulate** is in the Hotel Fiesta Americana, about three miles west of the city center (Aurelio Aceves 225, local 31, near the intersection of Avenidas López Mateos and Vallarta, tel. 33/3615-6215, fax 3615-8665, 8:30 A.M.–2 P.M. and 3–5 P.M. Mon.–Fri.). In emergencies after business hours, call the Canadian embassy in Mexico City, toll-free tel. 01-800/706-2900.

Consular agents from a number of other countries customarily hold Guadalajara office hours and/or might be reachable through the **Consular Association of Guadalajara,** tel. 33/3616-0629.

Contact the **British consulate** by either calling tel. 33/3343-9505 or the Canadian consulate contact number. Contact the **German consulate** downtown at Madero 215, tel. 33/3613-9623; the **French consulate** at López Mateos 484, tel. 33/3616-5516, 9:30 A.M.–2 P.M. Mon.–Fri.; the **Italian consulate** at López Mateos 790, corner E. Parra, tel. 33/3616-1700 or 33/3616-8688, fax 33/3616-2092, 11 A.M.–2 P.M. Tues.–Fri.; and the **Spanish Consulate,** tel. 33/3630-0450, 33/3630-0822, 8:30 A.M.–1 P.M. Mon.–Fri.

If all else fails, consult the local Yellow Pages under *"Embajadas, Legaciones y Consulados."*

HEALTH AND EMERGENCIES

If you need a doctor or hospital, ask your hotel desk or, in an emergency, go to the **Hospital Americas** (Av. Americas 932, Guadalajara 44620, tel. 33/3817-3141 and for emergencies, tel. 33/3817-3004), with many specialists on call. The hospital accepts the coverage of many American HMOs; all staff is U.S.-trained and all hospitalization is in private rooms, with TV, phone, and private bathroom. Alternatively, call the highly recommended **Hospital del Carmen** (tel. 33/3813-0042; in emergency, tel. 33/3813-1224).

For routine medications, one of the best sources is the Guadalajara chain **Farmacia Guadalajara,** with many branches; there's one at the southwest-side Plaza del Sol, call tel. 33/3121-2887 or 33/3121-6515. For after-hours prescriptions, Farmacia Guadalajara offers a **24-hour prescription delivery service,** tel. 33/3818-1818. Another good pharmacy option is **Farmacia ABC,** with likewise many branches; there's one downtown, at 518 P. Moreno between M. Ocampo and D. Guerra, tel. 33/3614-2950, 7:30 A.M.–10 P.M. daily.

For **police** and **fire emergencies,** dial the emergency numbers 066 or 080, or hail a taxi to take you to the nearest police or fire station.

COMMUNICATIONS
Mail

The downtown **Guadalajara post office** is two blocks north of the Teatro Degollado, just past the Hotel Mendoza, corner of Independencia and V. Carranza, tel. 33/3614-2482, open 8 A.M.–7 P.M. Mon.–Fri., 9 A.M.–1 P.M. Sat.

Telephone and Internet Access

Telecom offers public telephone and fax in the city center, at Degollado and Madero, below the city *juzgado* (jail) (tel. 33/3613-8584, 8 A.M.–6 P.M. Mon.–Fri., 9 A.M.–noon Sat.)

Connect with the Internet downtown at **CYBER@Z** store, on the east side of the Plaza de los Fundadores, behind the Teatro Degollado (tel. 33/3658-1162, 8 A.M.–midnight daily).

PUBLICATIONS

Among the best Guadalajara sources of English-language magazines is **Sanborn's,** the gift, book,

GUADALAJARA

and coffee shop chain. Find one downtown at the corner of Juárez and 16 de Septiembre, tel. 33/3613-6267, 33/3613-6264, 7:30 A.M.–11 P.M. daily. Two others are at **Plaza Vallarta** (Av. Vallarta 1600, tel. 33/3615-5894, 7–1 A.M. daily) and **Plaza del Sol** (2718 López Mateos Sur, tel. 33/3647-2510 or 3647-2514, 7–1 A.M. daily).

You can usually get an English-language newspaper, such as *USA Today* or the *Miami Herald* Mexico edition, at one of the newsstands edging the Plaza Guadalajara (formerly Plaza Laureles), across from the cathedral.

While you're downtown, if you see a copy of the informative local weekly, the *Guadalajara Colony Reporter,* buy it. Its pages will be stuffed with valuable items for visitors, including local events calendars, restaurant and performance reviews, meaty feature articles on local customs and excursions, and entertainment, restaurant, hotel, and rental listings. (If you can't find one, contact the *Reporter,* tel. 33/3615-2177, fax 33/3615-2177, reporter@megared.net.mx, www.guadalajarareporter.com, and ask where you can get a copy.)

Additionally, suburban southwest-side **Librería Sandi** (Find Sandi at Tepeyac 718, Colonia Chapalita, Guadalajara, tel. 33/3121-0863, 9:30 A.M.–7 P.M. Mon.–Fri., 9:30 A.M.–2 P.M. Sat.) always has the *Reporter* plus the best selection of English-language books in the Guadalajara region.

LANGUAGE AND CULTURAL COURSES

The University of Guadalajara's **Centro de Estudios Para Extranjeros** (Study Center for Foreigners) conducts an ongoing program of cultural studies for visitors. Besides formal language, history, and art instruction, students may also opt for accommodations with local families. Write or visit the center (off Av. Alcalde about 10 blocks north of the cathedral) at Tomás S. V. Gómez 125, P.O. Box 1-2130, Guadalajara, Jalisco 44100, tel. 33/3616-4399, fax 33/3616-4013, cepe@corp.udg.mx, www.cepe.udg.mx.You can also visit the **west-side center,** three blocks north of the Los Arcos monumental arch, on Gómez between Avenidas Mexico and Justo Sierra; telephone first for a *cita* (appointment).

PHOTOGRAPHY

The several branches of the **Laboratorios Julio** chain offer quick photofinishing and a big stock of photo supplies both digital and film. There's a big downtown branch (Colón 125 between Juárez and Cotilla, tel. 33/3614-2850, 10 A.M.–8 P.M. Mon.–Sat., 11 A.M.–7 P.M. Sun.), or visit the west side (Av. Americas 425, corner of Manuel Acuña, tel. 33/3344-5470, 9 A.M.–7:30 P.M. Mon.–Fri., 9–2:30 P.M. Sat.).

Getting Around

BY TAXI OR CITY BUS

Guadalajara's host of taxis, metered and reasonably priced, are by far the quickest and most convenient way to get around Guadalajara and its suburbs. One-way fares run $2–3 anywhere downtown, and $4–10 to the suburbs: Minerva-Chapultepec district 10 minutes west; and the *central camionera nueva* (new long-distance bus station) 15–25 minutes southeast, and Zapopan 20 minutes northeast.

City buses offer much cheaper ($1 or less), but slower and oft-crowded options. Figure about double the taxi time. Some routes are especially crowded; be prepared to stand and make sure your valuable are safely zipped away in a waistband, purse, or pocket. (One notable exception is the air-conditioned TUR buses, especially the **TUR 706,** that runs diagonally north-south through the city center, past the Cathedral, connecting Tlaquepaque and Tonalá in the southeast suburbs with Zapopan in the northwest.) For bus routes, see the maps *Guadalajara* and *Downtown Guadalajara* or visit the handy website www.rutasjalisco.com.

SUBWAY, GUADALAJARA STYLE

Since the early 1990s, Guadalajarans have enjoyed a new underground train system, which they call simply the **Tren Ligero** (Light Train). It's nothing fancy, a kind of Motel 6 of subway lines – inexpensive, efficient, and reliable. A pair of intersecting lines, Linea 1 and Linea 2, carry passengers in approximately north-south and east-west directions, along a total of 15 miles (25 km) of track. The station most visitors see first is the Plaza Universidad (on line 2), accessible by staircases that descend near the city-center corner of Juárez and Colón, across Juárez, from Sanborn's restaurant.

Downstairs, if you want to take a ride, deposit the specified number of pesos in machines, which will give you in exchange a brass *ficha* token, good for one ride and one transfer. If you opt to transfer, you have to do it at Juárez station, the next stop west of Plaza Universidad, where lines 1 and 2 intersect. (Hint: It's best to begin your Guadalajara subway adventure before 9 P.M.; the Tren Ligero goes to sleep by about 11 P.M.)

BY CAR, TOUR, OR GUIDE

Traffic congestion, impatient drivers, and potholes make a **rental or personal car** a generally undesirable option, especially in the city center, where drivers should stow their cars in a public garage (about $.50 per hour) and do their sightseeing on foot.

The good news is, however, that Guadalajara drivers enjoy exceptionally large numbers of helpful over-the-street green traffic direction signs. So, if you're good at coping with traffic and asking for directions in Spanish when you get lost, a car would be useful for excursions to the suburbs and surrounding countryside. Any member of the platoon of car rental agencies at the airport will gladly fill your need a shiny subcompact might run $50/day, $200/week, while an SUV might cost $100/$500.

If, on the other hand, a hassle-free guided tour appeals to you, consult your hotel travel desk, a travel agent, or a well-equipped agency such as **Panoramex** (Federalismo Sur 944, tel. 33/3810-5005, 33/3810-5057, 33/3810-5160, or 33/3810-5109, www.panoramex.com.mx). Or alternatively, hop on to one of the red double-decker tour buses that the Jalisco Tourism Secretariat runs hourly every day from the street that runs along the north side of the downtown cathedral. Get your ticket at the bus. For more information, call Jalisco state tourism, at tel. 33/3688-1601, or drop by their information desk, at Morelos 102 behind the Teatro Degollado.

GUADALAJARA

Getting There and Away

Guadalajara is a major transportation hub, with several four-lane expressways heading in all directions, 150 international and domestic flight arrivals daily, and hundreds of shiny buses heading heading out every day for everywhere in Mexico.

BY AIR

Several air carriers connect the **Guadalajara Airport** (officially, the Miguel Hidalgo International Airport, code-designated GDL) with many U.S. and Mexican destinations.

Major Carriers

Mexicana Airlines flights (Mexico toll-free tel. 01-800/502-2000, or in Guadalajara, tel. 33/3837-7000, arrivals and departures tel. 33/3688-5775), connect with U.S. destinations of Los Angeles, San Francisco, San Jose, Oakland, Sacramento, Portland, Las Vegas, and Chicago, and Mexican destinations of

Minerva, Guadalajara's patron deity, guards the city's western gate.

© BRUCE WHIPPERMAN

Los Cabos, Puerto Vallarta, Tijuana, Mexicali, and Mexico City.

Aeroméxico and partner line **Aerolitoral** flights (reservations, arrivals and departures Mexico toll-free tel. 01-800/021-4000) connect with U.S. destinations of Los Angeles, Ontario (California), Las Vegas and Phoenix; and Mexican destinations of Ciudad Juárez, Hermosillo, Chihuahua, Veracruz, Torreón, Puerto Vallarta, Acapulco, Culiacán, Monterrey, Tijuana, and Mexico City.

Aerocalifornia (reservations toll-free Mexico tel. 01-800/237-6225, tel. 33/3616-9393, airport flight information, tel. 33/3688-5514) connects with U.S. destinations of Los Angeles and Tucson and Mexican destinations of Tijuana, Mazatlán, La Paz, Los Cabos, Culiacán, Los Mochis, Tepic, Durango, Monterrey, Hermosillo, Torreón, and Mexico City.

Aviacsa Airlines (reservations toll-free Mexico tel. 01-800/006-2200, flight information 33/3123-1751, 33/3688-6033) connects with Mexican destinations of Monterrey, Tijuana, Mexicali, and Mexico City.

International Carriers

U.S.-flagged carriers that connect with United States gateways include: **American Airlines,** reservations toll-free in Mexico, tel. 01-800/904-6000, which connects daily with Dallas and Chicago; **Delta Air Lines,** toll-free Mex. tel. 800/123-4710, which connects daily with Atlanta and Los Angeles; **Continental Airlines,** toll-free Mex. tel. 01-800/900-5000, which connects daily with Houston; and **U.S. Airways,** formerly America West (from Mexico, dial the airline's toll-free U.S. numbers direct: tel. 001-800/235-9292), which connects seasonally with Phoenix. **Alaska Airlines** (toll-free U.S. tel. 001-800/426-0333), connects daily with Los Angeles; and **ATA** (America Trans Air; U.S. toll-free dial direct 001-800/435-9282, airport flight arrival information 33/3688-5929, 33/3688-6531) connects daily with Chicago.

Minor Mexican Carriers

Other Mexican carriers include **Azteca Airlines** (reservations in Mexico toll-free tel. 01-800/229-8322, flight information 33/3630-4616) which connects with the U.S. destination of Ontario, California, and Mexican destinations of Tijuana, Cancùn, and Mexico City; **Avolar Airlines** (reservations in Mexico toll free tel. 01-800/212-8652, airport flight arrivals tel. 33/3688-8064), which connects with Tijuana, La Paz, Los Mochis, Culiacan, Durango, and Cuernavaca; and **Volaris Airlines** (reservations in Mexico toll-free tel. 01-800/122-8000, airport flight arrivals tel.33/3688-8029), which connects with Tijuana, Toluca, and Monterrey.

For information and reservations for all of the above, you may also contact a travel agent, such as American Express, tel. 33/3818-2323, fax 33/3616-7665.

Airport Arrival and Departure

As you exit the terminal door, to your right you'll see money exchange counters and an HSBC bank (tel. 33/3688-5689, 8 A.M.–7 P.M. Mon.–Fri., 8 A.M.–3 P.M. Sat.) with 24-hour ATM to ease your Guadalajara airport arrival.

Right next to the HSBC bank, find a friendly **travel agent,** Agencia del Lago (tel. 33/3688-5100 or 33/3688-5105, 9 A.M.–7 P.M. Mon.–Sat.), who arranges hotel and air reservations, car rentals, tours, and more.

Many **car-rental agencies** maintain arrival hall booths: **Avis,** tel. 33/3688-5656 or 33/3688-5784; **Alamo,** tel. 33/3613-5551 or 33/3613-5560, alamogdl@prodigy.net.mx; **Aries,** tel. 33/3688-5400 or 33/3688-5272, fax 33/3345-8050; **Arrasa,** tel. 33/3615-0522; **Budget,** tel. 33/3613-0027 or 33/3613-0286, fax 33/3688-5400 or 33/3688-5531; **Dollar,** 33/3688-5956 or 33/3688-5958, dollar@megared.net.mx; **Hertz,** tel. 33/3688-5633 or 33/3688-6080, fax 33/3688-6070; **National,** tel. 33/3614-7175 or 33/3614-7994, fax 33/3688-5645; **Optima,** tel. 33/3688-5532 or 33/3812-0437.

Ground transportation is likewise well organized for shuttling arrivees the 12 miles (19 kilometers) along Chapala Highway 44 into town. *Colectivos* vans at the departure curb take passengers downtown for about $2 per person. **Private taxis** (*taxis especiales*) do the same for both Guadalajara downtown ($18 for 1–4 people), and Lake Chapala ($25) to northshore destinations. Get taxi tickets at booths (*taquillas*) at both departure and arrival ends of the terminal.

Travelers on a tight budget can save more money by riding the red and white **Autotransportes Guadalajara-Chapala** bus (ridden by mostly local people, but usable by everyone), which stops outside the terminal (on the right side, after you exit, in front of airport Hotel Casa Grande) and continues either downtown to the old bus station (Camionera Central Vieja) or to nearby Zapote village—where, on the highway, you can catch another similar bus, bound for Lake Chapala.

Many simple and economical card-operated public telephones are also available; buy telephone cards ($3, $5, or $10) at the snack bar by the far right-hand terminal exit. Also here you'll find a newsstand (lobby floor), bookstore (upstairs), and many crafts and gift shops.

Airport departure is equally simple, as long as you save enough cash for your international departure tax of $19 ($12 federal tax, $7 local), unless it's already included in your ticket.

If you have time before your departure, spend it comfortably at one of the two good Wings restaurants, downstairs and upstairs.

Don't lose your tourist card. If you do, be prepared with a copy or some evidence (such as a ticket stub to verify your Mexico arrival date) to present to airport **Migración** (get to the terminal as early as possible) to avoid a fine and red tape.

BY CAR OR RV

Four major routes connect the Guadalajara region to the rest of Mexico. To or from **Tepic-Compostela-Puerto Vallarta,** federal Highway 15 winds about 141 miles (227 kilometers) over the Sierra Madre Occidental crest. Highway 15D, the *cuota* (toll) expressway, although expensive ($30 for a car, RVs more), greatly increases safety, decreases wear and tear, and cuts the Guadalajara–Tepic driving time from five to three hours. The *libre* (free) route, by contrast, has two oft-congested lanes that twist steeply up and down the high pass and bump through towns. For safety, allow around five hours via the *libre* route to and from Tepic.

To and from Puerto Vallarta, bypass Tepic via the toll *corta* (cutoff) that connects Highways 15 and 15D (at Chapalilla) with Highway 200 (at Compostela). Figure on 4.5 hours total if you use the entire toll expressway (about $20), 6.5 hours if you don't.

To and from Barra de Navidad in the southwest, traffic winds smoothly (but sometimes slowly) along two-lane Highway 80 for the 190 miles (306 kilometers) to and from Guadalajara. Allow around four hours.

An easier road connection to and from Barra de Navidad runs through Manzanillo and Colima along *autopistas* (superhighways) 200, 110, and 54D. Easy grades allow a leisurely 55 mph (90 kph) most of the way for this 192-mile (311-kilometer) trip. Allow about four hours to or from Manzanillo; add another hour for the additional smooth 38 miles (61 kilometers) of Highway 200 to or from Barra de Navidad (follow the Manzanillo town toll bypass).

To or from Lake Chapala in the south, the four level, straight lanes of Highway 44 whisk traffic safely the 33 miles (53 kilometers) to or from Guadalajara in about 45 minutes.

BY REGIONAL BUS

Guadalajara has two bus terminals, one new, one old. The new terminal in the southeast suburb offers mostly first- and luxury-class long-distance direct connections to outlying Jalisco destinations and other parts of Mexico.

The old terminal, **Camionera Central Vieja,** offers many dozens of mostly second-class bus departures to hundreds of Guadalajara regional towns, villages, and crossroads, mostly west, south, and east of the city. The old terminal occupies about two square city blocks on the southeast edge of downtown, two blocks east of Calzada Independencia and a block north of Parque Agua Azul.

The buses occupy a large interior lot sandwiched between ticketing halls: *sala A* on the north side (Calle Los Angeles) and *sala B* on the south side (Calle 5 de Febrero).

Sala B, which services west and southwest destinations, handles most of the traffic. It has a modicum of services, including lots of phone booths operable with economical Ladatel phone cards, luggage lockers (east end), and food counters. The following partial list runs from eastern to western destinations:

Transportes Ceocuitatlán (tel. 33/3619-3989, 33/3619-8891) serves west and northwest destinations, including the *periférico* (end of Avenida Vallarta) west, La Venta and the Bosque de Primavera, Amatitán, Tequila, and Tala.

"Azul" (blue) **Autobuses Guadalajara-Talpa-Mascota** (tel. 33/3619-7079, 33/3124-1902) connects, via Highway 70 and Ameca, with far southwestern destinations of Talpa and Mascota.

"Servicios Coordinados" **Flecha Amarilla** (tel. 33/3619-4533) connects with southwestern destinations of Ameca, Cocula, Villa Corona (*balnearios* Chimulco and Aguascalientes), Navajas, La Villita, and Cruz Vieja.

Transportes Guadalajara Bella Vista (tel. 33/3619-2619) connects with southwest destinations past the *periférico* (end of López Mateos), Acatlán, and Villa Corona (*balnearios* Chimulco and Aguascalientes).

Transportes Guadalajara-La Vega-Cocula (tel. 33/3650-3033) connects via Highway 15 with southwest destinations of Etzatlán, La Vega (reservoir fishing), Teuchtitlan (monumental pyramids) and Cocula.

Autocamiones del Pacífico (tel. 33/3619-9654) connects via Highway 80 with the far southwest villages of El Limón, Tolimán, La Villa, Los Guajes, Chiquilistán, and Tuxcacuesco.

Omnibus de la Ribera (tel. 33/3650-0605) connects south via Avenida López Mateos Sur with the Lake Chapala northwest shore towns of Zapotitán, Las Cuatas, Buena Vista, Jocotepec, and warm-spring resort San Juan Cosala.

Sala A, on the opposite, north side of the bus lot, services **southern to eastern destinations.** Moving from the building's east to west end:

Autotransportes Guadalajara-Chapala (tel. 33/3619-5675), the major Lake Chapala line, connects with north-shore destinations of Chapala, Ajijic, and Jocotepec. Luxury- and first-class tickets are available.

"Servicios Coordinados" **Flecha Amarilla** (tel. 33/3619-4533) connects with southeast destinations of El Salto (the monumental falls of the Río Lerma-Santiago), El Verde, IBM, El Muey, La Alameda, and the Highway 44 Corredor Industrial.

ADO (Autobuses del Occidente, tel. 33/3679-0453) connects with southern and eastern destinations of La Laja, La Punta, La Jauja, and Zapotlanejo.

BY LONG-DISTANCE BUS

The long-distance Guadalajara **Camionera Central Nueva** (New Central Bus Terminal) is at least 20 minutes by taxi (about $8) from the city center. The huge modern complex sprawls past the southeast-sector intersection of the old Tonalá Highway (Carretera Antigua

Tonalá) and the Zapotlanejo Autopista (Freeway) Highway 90. Tell your taxi driver which bus line you want or where you want to go, and you'll be dropped at one of the terminal's seven big *módulos* (buildings). For arrival and departure convenience, you might consider staying at the adjacent moderately priced Hotel La Serena.

Each of the seven *módulos* is self-contained, with restrooms, cafeteria or snack bar, stores offering snack foods (but few fruits or veggies), bottled drinks, common medicines and drugs, and handicrafts. Additionally, *módulos* 1, 3, and 7 have public long-distance telephone and fax service. *Módulos* 2 and 3 have left-luggage service, and *módulo* 3 has hotel reservations agent Sendetur ($70 and up, Guadalajara, Mazatlán, Acapulco, Puerto Vallarta, and Mexico City).

Dozens of competing bus lines offer departures. The current king of the heap is **Estrella Blanca,** which operates a host of subsidiaries, notably Elite, Turistar, Futura, Transportes del Norte, Transportes Norte de Sonora, and Transportes Chihuahuenses. Second-largest and trying harder is **Flecha Amarilla,** which offers "Servicios Coordinados" through several subsidiaries. Trying even harder are the biggest independents: Omnibus de Mexico, Enlaces Terrestres Nacionals ("National Ground Network"), Transportes Pacífico, and Autobuses del Occidente, all of which would very much like to be your bus company.

To northwest **Pacific Coast** destinations, go to *módulo* 3. Take first-class **Elite,** tel. 33/3679-0485, via Tepic and Mazatlán, to the U.S. border at Nogales, Mexicali, or Tijuana. Alternatively, ride first-class Transportes Pacífico, tel. 33/3600-0211, for the same northwest Pacific destinations as Elite. For southwest Pacific Coast destinations, go by **Transportes Pacífico,** tel. 33/3600-0211, in *módulo* 3 or *módulo* 4, for small southwest Nayarit coastal towns and villages such as Las Varas, La Peñita, and Rincón de Guayabitos, en route to Puerto Vallarta. You can ride second-class **Transportes Norte de Sonora** west and northwest, tel. 33/3679-0463, *módulo*

4, to smaller northern Nayarit and Sinaloa towns, such as Tepic, San Blas, Santiago Ixcuintla-Mexcaltitán, Acaponeta-Novillero, and Escuinapa-Teacapán.

For far southern Pacific destinations of **Zihuatanejo, Acapulco, and the Oaxaca coast** you can go one of two ways: Direct to Acapulco by **Futura** (*módulo* 7) east to Toluca and Cuernavaca, then south, all in one day, bypassing Mexico City (one or two buses per day). Alternatively, go less directly via Elite (*módulo* 3) west to Tepic or Puerto Vallarta (or by a **Flecha Amarilla** affiliate, tel. 33/3600-0770, *módulo* 1, south to Tecomán), where you must transfer to a Zihuatanejo-Acapulco southbound Elite bus. This may necessitate an overnight in either Tepic, Puerto Vallarta, Barra de Navidad, Manzanillo, or Tecomán and at least two days traveling (along the splendidly scenic coastal Pacific route, however), depending upon connections. Finally, in Acapulco, connections will be available southeast to the Oaxaca coast.

If you're bound southeast directly to the city of **Oaxaca,** go conveniently by Futura (*módulo* 7) to Mexico City Norte (North) station, where you transfer, via ADO (Autobuses del Oriente), Omnibus de Mexico, or Cristóbal Colón southeast direct to Oaxaca City.

At *módulo* 4, allied lines Autocamiones del Pacífico and Transportes Cihuatlán, tel. 33/3600-0076 (second-class) or tel. 33/3600-0598 (first class), together offer service south along scenic mountain Highway 80 to the Pacific via Autlán to **Melaque, Barra de Navidad,** and **Manzanillo.**

For eastern to southern destinations in **Jalisco, Guanajuato, Aguascalientes, Michoacán,** and **Colima,** go to either *módulo* 1 or 2. In *módulo* 2, ride first-class **ETN,** tel. 33/3600-0501, east to Celaya, León, and Aguascalientes, or west and southwest to Uruapan, Morelia, Colima, Manzanillo, and Puerto Vallarta. In *módulo* 1, Flecha Amarilla subsidiary lines, tel. 33/3600-0398, offer service to a swarm of northeast destinations, including León, Guanajuato, and San Miguel de la Allende, and southeast and south to Uruapan, Morelia, Puerto Vallarta, Manzanillo, Barra de

GUADALAJARA

Navidad, and untouristed villages (such as El Super, Careyes, La Manzanilla, Tomatlán, and El Tuito) on the Jalisco Coast. From *módulo* 2, **La Linea and La Linea Plus,** tel. 33/3600-0055, offer departures southeast to Michoacán destinations of Zamora, Zitácuaro, Quiroga, Pátzcuaro, Uruapan, and Morelia. Also in *módulo* 2, **Autotransportes Sur de Jalisco** second-class buses offer southern departures, via old Highway 54 or *autopista* 54D, via Sayula, Ciudad Guzmán, Colima, to Tecomán, thence southeast via the Michoacán Coast to Lázaro Cárdenas, or northwest via Cuyutlán to Manzanillo.

Omnibus de Mexico, tel. 33/3600-0085 or 33/3600-0718, dominates *módulo* 6, offering broad service in all directions. To the north and northeast, buses connect to the U.S. border at Juárez via Zacatecas, Saltillo, Durango, Torreón, Fresnillo, and Chihuahua; to Monterrey via Saltillo; and northeast, via Tampico, to the U.S. border at Reynosa and Matamoros. Buses also connect east, with Mexico City, and west, with Tepic.

Additionally, Omnibus de Mexico offers first-class connections south, with Ciudad Guzmán and Colima, and north with regional destinations of Nochistlán and Colotlán.

In *módulo* 7, Estrella Blanca subsidiary lines mostly offer connections north. For example, ride first-class Transportes Chihuahuenses, tel. 33/3679-0404, north via San Juan de los Lagos, Zacatecas, Durango, Torreón, Chihuahua, all the way to the border at Ciudad Juárez. You may also ride luxury-class Turistar, tel. 33/3679-0404, either along the same routes as Transportes Chihuahuenses or northeasterly via San Juan de los Lagos, Zacatecas, Saltillo, and Monterrey to Matamoros, at the U.S. border.

BY TRAIN

Passenger rail service to and from Guadalajara has been stopped by the privatization of Mexican Railways' Pacific route. Unless future government subsidies offset private losses, Pacific passenger trains will have gone the way of buggy whips and Stanley Steamers.

PUERTO VALLARTA

The town of Puerto Vallarta (pop. 350,000) perches at the most tranquil recess of one of the Pacific Ocean's largest, deepest bays, the Bay of Banderas. The bay's many blessings—golden beaches, sparkling sunshine, blue waters, and the seafood that they nurture—are magnets for a steady stream of seekers of paradise on earth.

Visitors find that Puerto Vallarta is really two towns in one: a new town strung along the hotel strip on its northern beaches, and an old town nestled beneath jungly hills on both sides of a small river, the Río Cuale. Travelers arriving from the north, whether by plane, bus, or car, see the modern Puerto Vallarta first, a parade of luxury hotels, condominiums, apartments, and shopping centers. Visitors can stay for a month in a shiny new Vallarta hotel, sun on the beach every day, disco every night, and return home, never having experienced the old Puerto Vallarta.

And that would be a pity, for old Puerto Vallarta offers a trove of delights that long-time fans flock south of the border to enjoy. The lovely heart of old Puerto Vallarta is the verdant, tree-shaded island *(isla)* that basks in the middle of the Río Cuale. Upstream, on the hill above the river, spreads Gringo Gulch, a delightfully confusing maze of cobbled lanes that wind among the picturesque homes of Puerto Vallarta's well-to-do. Back downhill, north of the river, stretches the breezy *malecón* oceanfront walkway, with its feast of handicrafts shops, art galleries, restaurants—both trendy-chic and traditional Mexican—and night party spots.

HIGHLIGHTS

€ **A Walk Along Isla Río Cuale:** Start your Puerto Vallarta adventure on exactly the right foot, with a stroll along this tree-shadowed, vine-hung islet in the middle of old Puerto Vallarta. Along the way peruse the sprinkling of handicrafts and art stalls, enjoy the cooling breeze from one of the hanging bridges over the river, and stop for a refreshment at one of the downstream riverside restaurants (page 196).

€ **Gringo Gulch:** Wander the cobbled lanes directly uphill from Puerto Vallarta's town church, where the picturesque homes of Puerto Vallarta's well-to-do (don't miss Casa Kimberley, former home of actors Richard Burton and Elizabeth Taylor) seem to offer pleasant surprises beyond each charming corner (page 197).

€ **Plaza de Armas:** Early evening offers a host of surprises, from musical performances and clowns to spray-can art and *elote* (steaming corn on the cob) around Puerto Vallarta's main plaza and the adjoining *malecón*, the oceanfront walkway (page 200).

€ **Mismaloya and Los Arcos:** Stroll down the beach at Mismaloya and look around the set of the movie *Night of the Iguana*. North, offshore beyond the Mismaloya cove, Los Arcos, a federal underwater park and ecopreserve offers some of the best snorkeling around Puerto Vallarta (page 202).

€ **Day Cruises:** A prime Puerto Vallarta diversion is a relaxing boat tour that begins with snorkeling at *Los Arcos* sea rocks marine sanctuary and continues south along the shore, finally stopping for a few hours at care-free south-seas *Yelapa* village for

refreshment on the beach and splashing at a nearby waterfall and swimming hole (page 205).

€ **Playa Anclote:** This coral-strewn strand of beach features shallow waters that are perfect for beginning surfers. Enjoy a relaxing lunch at one of the beachside *palapa* restaurants (page 260).

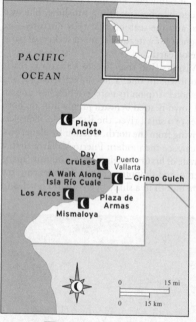

LOOK FOR € TO FIND RECOMMENDED SIGHTS, ACTIVITIES, DINING, AND LODGING.

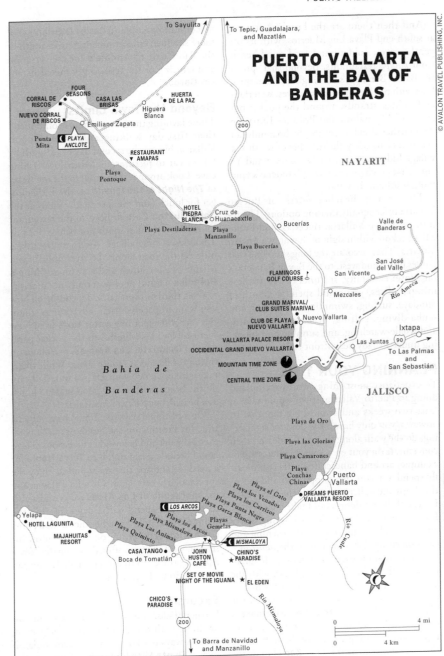

© AVALON TRAVEL PUBLISHING, INC.

PUERTO VALLARTA AND THE BAY OF BANDERAS

To Sayulita

To Tepic, Guadalajara, and Mazatlán

FOUR SEASONS

CORRAL DE RISCOS
CASA LAS BRISAS
NUEVO CORRAL DE RISCOS
Emiliano Zapata

HUERTA DE LA PAZ
Higuera Blanca

Punta Mita
PLAYA ANCLOTE

RESTAURANT AMAPAS

NAYARIT

Playa Pontoque

HOTEL PIEDRA BLANCA
Cruz de Huanacaxtle

Valle de Banderas

Playa Destiladeras
Playa Manzanillo
Bucerías

Playa Bucerías

San José del Valle

FLAMINGOS GOLF COURSE
San Vicente

Mezcales
Río Ameca

GRAND MARIVAL/ CLUB SUITES MARIVAL
CLUB DE PLAYA NUEVO VALLARTA
Nuevo Vallarta

Bahía de Banderas

VALLARTA PALACE RESORT
OCCIDENTAL GRAND NUEVO VALLARTA

Las Juntas
Ixtapa
90
To Las Palmas and San Sebastián

MOUNTAIN TIME ZONE

CENTRAL TIME ZONE

JALISCO

Playa de Oro

Playa las Glorias

Playa Camarones

Playa Conchas Chinas
Puerto Vallarta

Playa el Gato
Playa los Venados
Playa los Carrizos
Playa Punta Negra
Playa Garza Blanca
DREAMS PUERTO VALLARTA RESORT

Yelapa
HOTEL LAGUNITA

LOS ARCOS
Playa los Arcos
Playa Mismaloya
Playa Las Ánimas
Playa Quimixto

Playas Gemelas

Río Cuale

MAJAHUITAS RESORT

CASA TANGO
Boca de Tomatlán
JOHN HUSTON CAFÉ
MISMALOYA
CHINO'S PARADISE

SET OF MOVIE NIGHT OF THE IGUANA
EL EDEN

CHICO'S PARADISE
200
Río Mismaloya

To Barra de Navidad and Manzanillo

0   4 mi
0   4 km

And then there are the beaches, starting at south-end Playa Los Muertos, with its oft-gentle waves, golden sand, and good beach-front *palapa* restaurants. Beyond that spreads the Bay of Banderas's curving shoreline, sprinkled with picturesque fishing coves, waterfalls, and hidden strands, around the pocket paradises of Mismaloya and Boca de Tomatlán. And farther afield, accessible by boat only, adventurers can enjoy the delights of south-seas village hideaways, such as Quimixto and Yelapa, that perch on the Bay of Banderas's vine-hung southern shoreline.

The creamy beaches north of Puerto Vallarta offer equally inviting options. The resorts of Nuevo Vallarta, Bucerías, and Punta Mita beckon within sight of downtown Puerto Vallarta. They decorate the long shoreline that curves north and west, to the Bay of Banderas's far sunset extremity, at Punta Mita. At these miniparadises, you could spend a month of Sundays, surfing, swimming, snorkeling and scuba diving, golfing, beachcombing, bird- and whale-watching, and sunning and snoozing under a shady beachfront *palapa*.

PLANNING YOUR TIME

To experience most things worth seeing and doing in Puerto Vallarta Town would take at least two weeks and at most six months. If, however, you only have a few days for sightseeing, do the walk along the Isla Cuale and then concentrate on your own favorite interests. For example, art and handicrafts buffs could easily spend a day or two popping in and out of the shops and galleries south of the Río Cuale. Lovers of the outdoors could take a day cruise for snorkeling and waterfall swimming. Party animals could spend most of the evening and early morning club-hopping on the *malecón*.

Idle away some evenings strolling the main plaza north of the Río Cuale, laugh with the clowns, or take in a concert or performance at Los Arcos amphitheater (shore side of the plaza), have dinner at **Trio, Los Xitomates,** or the very hot **De Santos.** Finally, you might top off your evening at some of the clubs along the *malecón*, such as the zany **Zoo** club or the

raucous (bring earplugs) **Carlos O'Brian's.** For more subdued entertainment, return south of the Río Cuale to **Andale's** for conversation and dancing or the refined gay-mixed piano-bar **Garbo.**

Beyond the Town Limits

Those favoring the great outdoors could spend their first day walking around old Puerto Vallarta, but on the second day head south by bus or car to picturesque Mismaloya fishing cove. Look around, then stroll to the movie set of *The Night of the Iguana* nearby. Either linger for lunch (and the spectacular view) at the **John Huston Cafe** or head to the restaurant **Le Kliff** a few miles south just before Boca de Tomatlán fishing village. Alternatively, hike a mile up the road along the river uphill from Mismaloya for lunch and a swim at **Chino's Paradise** natural pool-waterfalls-restaurant.

On a third or fourth day, depending on how you want to pace yourself, adventurers might ride one of the morning **water taxis** from New Pier on Playa los Muertos to the pocket paradises of **Quimixto, Las Animas,** or **Yelapa** on the Bay of Banderas's south shore. While there, take a hike, drench yourself in a waterfall, sun on the beach, and enjoy a good seafood lunch at a beachfront *palapa* restaurant.

On additional days, be sure to reserve some time for sunning on the beach or at the pool, then sally out and enjoy other diversions. These could include a trip uphill to **Terra Noble** for a massage and spa treatment and to enjoy the spectacularly airy view. Or take a day cruise for **snorkeling at Los Arcos** rocks and a visit to Yelapa; or spend half a day exploring the **Gringo Gulch** uphill neighborhood (don't miss **Casa Kimberly**) either on your own or, in-season, with the tour offered (seasonally Nov.–April) by the Club Internacional de la Amistad (International Friendship Club).

Excursions

Farther afield, you could spend a day (or two or three, with overnights) busing or driving to hideaways not far north of Puerto Vallarta, such as **Punta Mita** for lunch, sunning, swim-

© BRUCE WHIPPERMAN

Puerto Vallarta's offshore sea rocks, now called Los Arcos, were first recorded in the log of Spanish explorer Pedro de Alvarado in 1541.

ming, and maybe surfing, or **Sayulita** or **Playa San Franscisco** for the same.

Consider heading farther north and spending two or three more days enjoying the delights of pocket paradises such as **Chacala** or sleepy surfing-and-wildlife haven **San Blas.**

You can do the same in the southern direction, heading to idyllic downscale **Tehualmixtle** or rustically upscale **Hotelito Desconocido.** Or visit the incomparably lovely hotel and spa **El Careyes** or the petite beach resort towns of **Melaque** and **Barra de Navidad.**

For seekers of fine art, fascinating museums, grand plazas, historic monuments, exciting theater and dance performances, and fine dining, consider a two- to four-day side trip to **Guadalajara.** Stay either in the city center or in the handicrafts wonderland of **Tlaqapaque** (tlah-kah-PAH-kay) and simply enjoy yourself, shopping, dining, sightseeing, and afterwards resting in the balmy shade or sun next to your hotel pool.

HISTORY
Before Columbus

For centuries before the arrival of the Spanish, the coastal region that includes present-day Puerto Vallarta was subject to the kingdom of Xalisco, centered near the modern Nayarit city of Xalisco. Founded around A.D. 600, the Xalisco civilization was ruled by chiefs who worshipped a trinity of gods: foremost, Naye, a legendary former chief elevated to a fierce god of war; the more benign Teopiltzin, god of rain and fertility; and wise Heri, the god of knowledge.

Recent archaeological evidence indicates another influence: the Aztecs. It seems they left Náhuatl-speaking colonies along the southern Nayarit coastal valleys during their centuries-long migration to the Valley of Mexico.

Conquest and Colonization

Some of those Aztec villages still remained when the Spanish conquistador Francisco Cortés de Buenaventura, nephew of Hernán Cortés, arrived on the Jalisco-Nayarit Coast in 1524.

NIGHT OF THE IGUANA: THE MAKING OF PUERTO VALLARTA

The idea to film Tennessee Williams's play *The Night of the Iguana* in Puerto Vallarta was born in the bar of the Beverly Hills Hotel. In mid-1963, director John Huston, whose movies had earned a raft of Academy Awards, met with Guillermo Wulff, a Mexican architect and engineer. For the film's location, Wulff proposed Mismaloya, an isolated cove south of Puerto Vallarta. On leased land, Wulff would build the movie set and cottages for staff housing, which he, Huston, and producer Ray Stark would later sell for a profit as tourist accommodations.

Most directors would have been scared away by the Mismaloya jungle, where they would find no roads, phones, or electricity. But, according to Alex Masden, one of Huston's biographers, Huston loved Mismaloya: "To me, *Night of the Iguana* was a picnic, a gathering of friends, a real vacation."

A "gathering of friends," indeed. The script required most of the cast to be dissolute, mentally ill, or both: a blonde nymphet tries to seduce an alcoholic defrocked minister while his dead friend's love-starved, hard-drinking widow keeps a clutch of vulturous biddies from destroying his last bit of self-respect – all while an iguana roped to a post passively awaits its slaughter.

Huston's casting was perfect. The actors simply played themselves. Richard Burton (the minister) came supplied with plenty of booze. Burton's lover, Elizabeth Taylor, who was not part of the cast and still married to singer Eddie Fisher, accompanied him. Sue Lyon (the nymphet) came with her lovesick boyfriend, whose wife was rooming with Sue's mother; Ava Gardner (the widow) became the toast of Puerto Vallarta while romping with her local beach paramour; Tennessee Williams, who was advising the director, came with his lover Freddy; while Deborah Kerr, who acted the only prim lead role, jokingly complained that she was the only one not having an affair.

With so many mercurial personalities isolated together in Mismaloya, the international press flew to Puerto Vallarta in droves to record the expected fireworks. Huston gave each of the six stars, as well as Elizabeth Taylor, a velvet-lined case containing a gold Derringer with five bullets, each engraved with the names of the others. Unexpectedly, and partly because of Huston's considerable charm, none of the bullets were used. Bored by the lack of major explosions, the press corps discovered Puerto Vallarta instead.

As Huston explained later to writer Lawrence Grobel: "That was the beginning of its popularity, which was a mixed blessing." Huston nevertheless returned to the area and built a home on the Bay of Banderas, where he lived the last 11 years of his life. Burton and Taylor bought Puerto Vallarta houses, got married, and also stayed for years. Although his Mismaloya tourist accommodations scheme never panned out, Guillermo Wulff became wealthy building for the rich and famous many of the houses and condominiums that now dot Puerto Vallarta's jungly hillsides and golden beaches.

In a broad, mountain-rimmed valley, an army of 20,000 warriors, their bows decorated with colored cotton banners, temporarily blocked the conquistador's path. The assemblage was so impressive that Cortés called the fertile vale of the Ameca River north of present Puerto Vallarta the Valle de las Banderas (Valley of the Banners). Thus the great bay later became known as the Bahía de Banderas.

The first certain record of the Bay of Banderas itself is in the log of conquistador Don Pedro de Alvarado, who sailed into the bay in 1541 and disembarked (probably at Mismaloya) near some massive sea rocks. He named these Las Peñas, and they're undoubtedly the same as the present Los Arcos rocks that draw boatloads of snorkelers and divers.

For 300 years the Bay of Banderas slept under the sun. Galleons occasionally watered there; a few pirates hid in its jungle-fringed coves waiting for them.

Independence

The rebellion of 1810–1821 freed Mexico, and a generation later, as with many of Mexico's cities, the lure of gold and silver led to the settlement of Puerto Vallarta. Enterprising merchant Don Guadalupe Sanchez made a fortune here—ironically, not from gold, but from salt for ore processing, which he hauled from the beach to the mines above the headwaters of the Río Cuale. In 1851 Don Guadalupe built a hut and brought his wife and children. Their tiny trading station grew into a little town, Puerto de las Peñas, at the mouth of the river.

Later, the local government founded the present municipality, which, on May 31, 1918, officially became Puerto Vallarta, in honor of the celebrated jurist and former governor of Jalisco, Ignacio L. Vallarta (1830–1893).

However, the Cuale mines eventually petered out, and Puerto Vallarta, isolated, with no road to the outside world, slumbered again.

Modern Puerto Vallarta

But it didn't slumber for long. Passenger planes began arriving sporadically from Tepic and Guadalajara in the 1950s, and a gravel road was pushed through from Tepic in the 1960s. The international airport was built, the coast road was paved, and tourist hotels sprouted on the beaches. Perhaps most notably, in 1963, director John Huston, at the peak of his creative genius, arrived with Richard Burton, Elizabeth Taylor, Ava Gardner, and Deborah Kerr to film *The Night of the Iguana*. Huston, Burton, and Taylor stayed on for years, waking Puerto Vallarta from its long doze. It hasn't slept since.

Sights

A place as gorgeous as Puerto Vallarta is full of memorable sights, from its grand hilltop bayview vistas and tropical forest cascades, to the charmingly intimate hidden corners of Gringo Gulch, and the close-up views of the squadrons of multicolored fish that festoon the foot of the great Los Arcos offshore sea rocks.

Puerto Vallarta is a long beach town, stretching about five miles from the Riviera-like Conchas Chinas condo headland at the south end. Heading north, you'll encounter the popular Playa los Muertos and the intimate old Río Cuale neighborhood, joined across the river by the busy (but beachless) central *malecón* shopping and restaurant bayfront. North of there, the beaches resume again at Playa Camarones and continue past the Zona Hotelera (Hotel Zone) string of big resorts to the Marina complex, where tour boats and cruise liners depart from the Terminal Maritima dock. In the Marina's northern basin lie the Peines (pay-EE-nays) sportfishing and Club de Yates docks. A mile farther north, the city ends at the bustling international airport.

One basic thoroughfare serves the entire beachfront. Officially Búlevar Francisco Medina Ascencio, it's commonly called the **Carretera Aeropuerto** (Airport Highway), though it changes names three times as it conducts express traffic south past the Zona Hotelera. Narrowing, it first becomes the cobbled Avenida México, then Paseo Díaz Ordaz along the seafront *malecón* with tourist restaurants, clubs, and shops, changing finally to Avenida Morelos before it passes the Presidencia Municipal (City Hall) and central plaza.

When southbound traffic reaches Isla Río Cuale, the tree-shaded, midstream island where the city's pioneers built their huts, it slows to a crawl and finally dissipates in the colorful old neighborhood on the south side of the river.

There being little traffic south of the Cuale, people walk everywhere—and slowly, because of the heat. Mornings, men in sombreros lead burros down to the mouth of the river to gather sand. Little *papelerías, misceláneas,* and streetside *taquerías* serve the local folks, while small restaurants, hotels, and clubs serve the visitors.

◖ A WALK ALONG ISLA RÍO CUALE

Start at the **Museo Río Cuale,** a joint government-volunteer effort near the downstream tip of Isla Río Cuale. Inside is a fine three-room collection of pre-Columbian ceramics excavated in Jalisco, Nayarit, and Colima, including some especially attractive female sculptures and some charming representations of Colima's famously fetching dogs. The museum's website, www.tiendadelmuseo.com.mx, illustrates a number of for-sale examples. Find the museum open 9 A.M.–2 P.M. and 4–7 P.M. daily.

Head upstream beneath the bridge and enjoy the shady *paseo* of shops and restaurants. For fun, stroll out on one of the two quaint suspension bridges over the river. Evenings, these are the coolest spots in Puerto Vallarta, as night air often funnels down the Cuale valley, creating a refreshing breeze along the length of the clear, tree-draped river.

The **Río Cuale** was not always so clean. Once upon a time, a few dozen foreign residents, tired of looking down upon the littered riverbank, came out one Sunday and began hauling trash from the riverbed. Embarrassed by the example, a neighborhood crowd pitched in. The river has been much cleaner ever since.

Farther upstream, on the adjacent riverbank, stands the

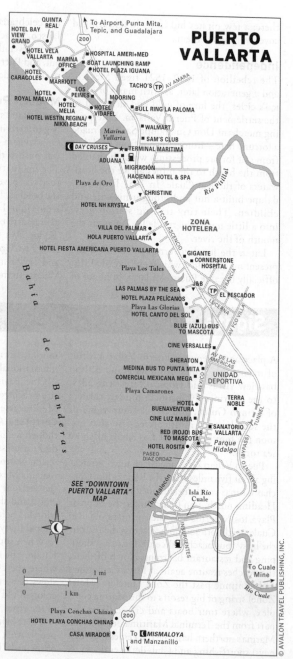

PUERTO VALLARTA

© AVALON TRAVEL PUBLISHING, INC.

a burro passing through Gringo Gulch

Mercado Municipal Río Cuale, a honeycomb of stalls stuffed with crafts from all over Mexico. Continue past the upriver bridge (Av. Insurgentes) to **Plaza John Huston,** marked by a pensive bronze likeness of the renowned Hollywood director who helped put Puerto Vallarta on the map with his filming of Tennessee Williams's *The Night of the Iguana* in 1963.

About 100 yards farther on, stop in at the small gallery of the **Centro Cultural Vallartense,** a volunteer organization that conducts art classes, sponsors shows of promising artists, and sometimes invites local artists to meet the public and interested amateurs for informal instruction and idea exchange. Ask the volunteer on duty for more information or see the community events listings in *Vallarta Today* or the *Vallarta Tribune,* the local English-language newspapers.

A few more steps upstream, at a small plaza, stands the new headquarters and auditorium of the city-sponsored **Centro Cultural Cuale.** On the left side of the courtyard are the Centro Cultural's graphic and fine arts courses. (A schedule of courses open to the general public is posted by the Centro Cultural's office by the auditorium, 10 A.M.–2 P.M. and 4–7 P.M. Mon.–Sat.)

Walk a few steps farther upstream to the boulder-strewn far point of the island, where you can enjoy the airy river panorama: clear (in dry season) rushing water, framed by great riverbank trees, verdant canyon ramparts, and distant, cloud-capped mountains.

◖ GRINGO GULCH

The steep, villa-dotted hillside that rises above the Isla Río Cuale's upstream end is called Gringo Gulch for the colony of rich *norteamericanos* who own big homes there. It's an interesting place for a stroll.

Gringo Gulch is best accessible by climbing the east-side hill above and behind the town church. Get there most directly either by following the stone pathway uphill (past the HSBC bank) north of the upstream Río Cuale bridge, or by walking east along Calle Zaragoza, the

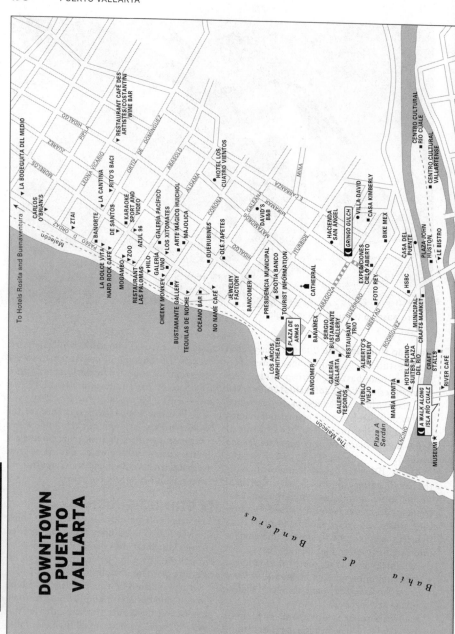

DOWNTOWN PUERTO VALLARTA

To Hotels Rosita and Buenaventura

LA BODEGUITA DEL MEDIO
CARLOS O'BRIAN'S
MORELOS
JUAREZ
PIPILA
HIDALGO
LEONA VICARIO
PASEO D ORDAZ
Malecón

ZTAI
BANORTE
LA CANTINA
RITO'S BACI
DE SANTOS
ORTIZ DE DOMÍNGUEZ
RESTAURANT CAFÉ DES ARTISTES/COSTANTINI WINE BAR
KARAOKÉ SPORT AND VIDEO
AZUL 96
ABASOLO
ALDAMA
HOTEL LOS CUATRO VIENTOS
MINA
CENTRO CULTURAL RIO CUALE
CENTRO CULTURAL VALLARTENSE

LA DOLCE VITA
HARD ROCK CAFÉ
MOGAMBO
ZOO
HILO
GALERÍA PACÍFICO
GALERÍA UNO
LOS XITOMATES
ARTE MÁGICO HUICHOL
CORONA
GALEANA
MATAMOROS
E. CARRANZA

RESTAURANT LAS PALOMAS
CHEEKY MONKEY
MAJOLICA
QUERUBINES
HIDALGO
DAVID'S B&B
HACIENDA SAN ANGEL
GRINGO GULCH
VILLA DAVID
CASA KIMBERLY
BIKE MEX

BUSTAMANTE GALLERY
TEQUILAS DE NOCHE
OCEANO BAR
NO NAME CAFÉ
OLÉ TAPETES
JEWELRY FACTORY
ITURBIDE
EXPEDICIONES CIELO ABIERTO
FOTO REY
CASA DEL PUENTE
PLAZA JOHN HUSTON
LE BISTRO

BANCOMER
PRESIDENCIA MUNICIPAL
SCOTIA BANCO
TOURIST INFORMATION
CATHEDRAL
HSBC

LOS ARCOS AMPHITHEATER
PLAZA DE ARMAS
SÉRGIO BUSTAMANTE GALLERY
RESTAURANT TRÍO
GUERRERO
LIBERTAD
MUNICIPAL CRAFTS MARKET

BANCOMER
GALERÍA VALLARTA
ALBERTO'S JEWELRY
RODRIGUEZ

GALERÍA TESOROS
PUEBLO VIEJO
HOTEL ENCINO-SUITES PLAZA DEL RÍO
CRAFT STALLS

MARÍA BONITA
ENCINO
A WALK ALONG ISLA RÍO CUALE
RIVER CAFÉ

Plaza A Serdán
The Malecón
MUSEUM

Bahía de Banderas

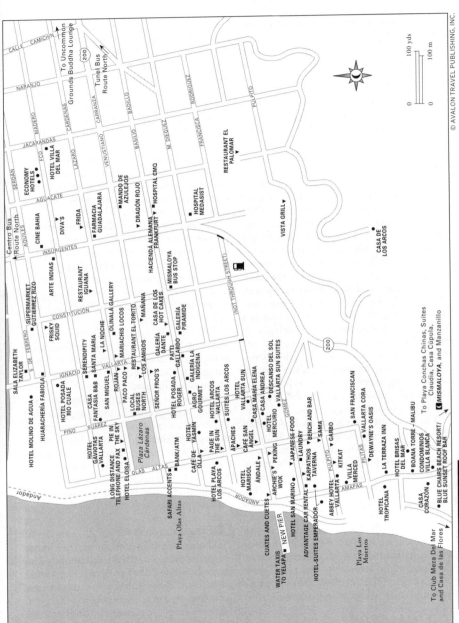

© AVALON TRAVEL PUBLISHING, INC.

PUERTO VALLARTA

100 yds
0
100 m
0

To Uncommon
Grounds Buddha Lounge

CALLE CAMICHIN
NARANJO
JACARANDAS
SERDAN
AGUACATE
INSURGENTES
CONSTITUCIÓN
IGNACIO
PINO SUAREZ
OLAS ALTAS
AMADOR
Playa Olas Altas

FCO
MADERO
CARDENAS
CARRANZA
LAZARO
BADILLO
BASILIO
RODRIGUEZ
PULPITO
FRANCISCA
M. DIEGUEZ
VENUSTIANO
5 DE FEBRERO
VALLARTA
GOMEZ
PULPITO
PILITAS
AMAPAS

Centro Bus Route North
Tunel Bus Route North
(200)

To Uncommon Grounds Buddha Lounge

HOTEL VILLA DEL MAR
ECONOMY HOTELS
CINE BAHIA
DIVA'S
FRIDA
FARMACIA GUADALAJARA
MANDO DE AZULEJOS
DRAGÓN ROJO
HACIENDA ALEMANA FRANKFURT
HOSPITAL CMQ
HOSPITAL MEDASIST
RESTAURANT EL PALOMAR
VISTA GRILL

SALA ELIZABETH TAYLOR
SUPERMARKET GUTIERREZ RIZO
ARTE INDIAS
FRISKY SQUID
RESTAURANT IGUANA
SERENDIPITY
OLINALÁ GALLERY
CASA FANTASÍA B&B
SANTA MARIA
LA NOCHE
MARIACHIS LOCOS
ROJAN
MAÑANA
RESTAURANT EL-TORITO
CASA DE LOS HOT CAKES
GALERÍA PIRAMIDE
PACO PACO
LOS AMIGOS
GALERÍA DANTE
PATTI GALLARDO
GALERÍA LA INDIGENA

MISMALOYA BUS STOP

CASA DE LOS ARCOS

HUARACHERIA FABIOLA
HOTEL POSADA RÍO CUALE
SAN MIGUEL

HOTEL MOLINO DE AGUA
HOTEL GAVIOTAS VALLARTA
PIE IN THE SKY
HOTEL ELOISA
LONG DISTANCE TELEPHONE AND FAX
Plaza Lázaro Cárdenas
BANK/ATM
CAFE DE OLLA
PAGE IN THE SUN
ANDALE
SEÑOR FROG'S
HOTEL POSADA ROGER
AGRO GOURMET
HOTEL ARCOS VALLARTA
SUITES LOS ARCOS
HOTEL ARCOS
SUITES LOS ARCOS
HOTEL VALLARTA SUN
DESCANSO DEL SOL
VALLARTA SUN SUITES
SAN FRANCISCAN

HOTEL PLAYA LOS ARCOS
HOTEL MARISOL
APACHES
CAFE SAN ANGEL
HOTEL MERCURIO
CASA ANDREA
CASA MARIA ELENA

SAFARI ACCENTS
ARCHIE'S
PEKING
JAPANESE FOOD
KARPATHOS
BENCH AND BAR
SAMA
GARBO
VILLA MERCED
KITKAT
VALLARTA CORA
SAN FRANCISCAN
DEWAYNE'S OASIS
LA TERRAZA INN

CUATES AND CUETES
NEW PIER
HOTEL SAN MARINO
LAUNDRY
ADVANTAGE CAR RENTAL
TAVERNA
ABBEY HOTEL VALLARTA
HOTEL BRISAS DEL MAR

WATER TAXIS TO YELAPA
HOTEL-SUITES EMPERADOR
HOTEL TROPICANA
CASA CORAZÓN
CONDOMINIOS VILLA BLANCA
BOANA TORRE / MALIBU
BLUE CHAIRS BEACH RESORT/
BLUE SUNSET ROOF BAR

Playa Los Muertos

To Club Meza Del Mar and Casa de las Flores

To Playa Conchas Chinas, Suites Claudia, Casa Cupula, MISMALOYA, and Manzanillo

NOT THROUGH STREET

street that runs along the main downtown plaza's south side. In each case, follow the steep staircases that will bring you to the corner of Zaragoza and Miramar, where you are at the gateway to Gringo Gulch. Wander the winding lanes and enjoy the picturesque scenes that appear around each rickety-chic corner. For example, note the luxurious *palapas* perched atop the tall villa on Miramar, half a block above Zaragoza.

During your meanderings, don't miss the Gringo Gulch centerpiece mansion at Zaragoza 446, once owned by Elizabeth Taylor. (You'll scarcely be able to miss it, for it has a pink passageway arching over the street.) The house was a gift to Taylor from Richard Burton. After they were married, they also bought the house on the other side of Zaragoza, renovated it, and built a pool; thus the passageway became necessary. The house across the street, no. 446, is now the **Casa Kimberley,** a private Elizabeth Taylor-Richard Burton museum, which offers public tours for about $8 per person (and also bed-and-breakfast lodging, with pool, $75 d low season, $110 high). Call (tel. 322/222-1336) or visit www.casakimberley .com for details. Although Casa Kimberley is still accepting reservations on its website, at the time of publication the museum and bed-and-breakfast was closed to the public.

The **Club Internacional de la Amistad** (International Friendship Club; tel. 322/222-5466, www.ifcvallarta.com) conducts very popular weekly seasonal tours of some of Puerto Vallarta's showplace homes, seasonally between Thanksgiving and Easter. The club asks about $30 per person as a contribution to its charitable activities.

Another worthwhile Puerto Vallarta guided stroll is the regular **Art Walk** tour of noted local galleries. For more information, contact Barbara Peters, personable owner of Galería Vallarta (tel. 322/222-0290, webart@galeria vallarta.com, www.galeriavallarta.com).

THE *MALECÓN*

Several of Puerto Vallarta's other memorable sights lie downhill, on or near the *malecón*

seafront walkway. First, let the much-photographed belfry of the main town church be your guide. Named **La Parroquia de Nuestra Señora de Guadalupe,** for the city's patron saint, the church is relatively new (1951) and undistinguished except for the very unusual huge crown atop the tower. Curiously, it was modeled after the crown of the tragic 19th-century Empress Carlota, who went insane after her husband was executed. On the church steps, a native woman sometimes sells textiles, which she weaves on the spot with a traditional backstrap loom (in Mexican Spanish, *tela de otate,* loom of bamboo, from the Náhuatl *otlatl,* bamboo).

The *malecón* marks the Bay of Banderas's innermost point. From there the shoreline curves westerly many miles on both sides, adorned by dozens of sandy beaches. On a clear day, look toward the bay's wave-washed far western extremities, where you can see Punta Mita on the distant northwest horizon and Punta La Iglesia to the far southwest.

A number of far-out modernistic sculptures highlight the *malecón;* so many of them seem to depict extraterrestial beings that it's interesting to try and puzzle out what the various sculptors had in mind.

The *malecón* action regularly climaxes in the evening, and especially Saturday nights around 10 P.M. when everyone in town seems be on the *malecón* either strolling the sidewalk or riding a car. Kids chase each other, octogenarians hobble along, lovers embrace, souped-up cars blow hot, flaring exhausts from their tailpipes, and the sand sculptors build their fantasies on the beach below.

(Plaza de Armas

Head across the main town square, the Plaza de Armas, flanked by the Presidencia Municipal on its north side, and the Los Arcos (The Arches) amphiteater, marked by the arches picturesquely set at the seafront, at the beginning of *malecón*. Although interesting enough by day, Los Arcos frequently forms a backdrop for a colorful flurry of evening: snack stalls, sidewalk arts and crafts, playful clowns, and free evening music and dance performances. From there, the *malecón* walkway stretches north along the seafront about a mile, toward the Zona Hotelera, which you can see along the curving beachfront.

TERRA NOBLE

The dreamchild of owner-artist Jorge Rubio, Terra Noble (9 A.M.–4 P.M. Mon.–Sat., admission about $5), on a vista hilltop above the middle of town, is at least unique and at best exhilarating. It's a New Age-style retreat, spreading downhill through a breathtakingly scenic tropical deciduous forest at the western edge of the big Agua Azul Nature Reserve hinterland. The headquarters building is a latter-day interpretation of a traditional Mexican mud-and-wattle house. The inside, with curved ceilings and passageways dotted with round window-holes, leaves the impression of the interior of a huge hunk of swiss cheese.

Besides its singular building and parklike grounds, Terra Noble is a serious healing center, featuring massage ($75 per hour) or an all-day treatment ($160) that includes massage, a saunalike *temascal* sweat bath and shamanistic ceremony, tarot reading, and more. It also offers day sculpture and painting workshops.

Regardless of whether you get the full treatment, Terra Noble is worth a visit, if for nothing more than a look around and a picnic (pack a lunch). Contact Terra Noble ahead of time to verify hours (tel. 322/223-3530, fax 322/222-5400, info@terranoble.com, www.terranoble.com). Get there by car, taxi, or any local bus that follows the *libramiento* through the hills east of town. Follow the side road, signed Par Vial Zona Centro, about 100 yards south of the summit tunnel (not the short tunnel at the south end), on the west (ocean) side of the *libramiento*. After about a half mile curving uphill, you'll see the Terra Noble entrance sign on the view side of the road.

Beaches

Beaches along the Puerto Vallarta coast are ephemeral things. During the June–September rainy season, waves, often stormy and rough, can wash sand out to sea, leaving clay and isolated rocks where your favorite beach used to be. But then, the calm, dry winter months arrive and the sand returns, transforming your favorite beach back to the warm, broad, golden strand that you remember.

PLAYA LOS MUERTOS

Generations ago, when Puerto Vallarta was a small, isolated town, there was only one beach, Playa los Muertos, the strand of yellow sand that stretches for a mile south of the Río Cuale. Old-timers still remember the Sundays and holidays when it seemed as if half the families in Puerto Vallarta had come south of the Río Cuale, to Los Muertos especially, to play in the surf and sand.

This is still largely true, although now droves of winter-season North American vacationers and residents have joined them. Fortunately, Playa los Muertos is now much cleaner than during the polluted 1980s. The fish are coming back, as evidenced by the flocks of diving pelicans and the crowd of folks who drop lines every day from the **New Pier** (foot of Francisca Rodriguez).

Fishing is even better off the rocks on the south end of the beach. *Lisa* (mullet), *sierra* (mackerel), *pargo* (snapper), and *torito* are commonly caught anywhere along close-in beaches. On certain unpredictable occasions, fish (and one memorable time even giant 30-pound squids) swarm offshore in such abundance that anyone can pick them out of the water barehanded.

Gentle waves and lack of undertow make Playa los Muertos generally safe for wading and good for swimming beyond the close-in breakers. The same breakers, however, eliminate Los

starting the day with breakfast on Playa los Muertos

© BRUCE WHIPPERMAN

Muertos for bodysurfing, boogie boarding, or surfing (except occasionally at the far south end).

PLAYA CONCHAS CHINAS

Playa Conchas Chinas (Chinese, or "Curly," Shells Beach) is not one beach but a series of small sandy coves dotted by rocky outcroppings beneath the condo-clogged hillside that extends for about a mile south of Playa los Muertos. A number of streets and driveways lead to the beach from the Manzanillo Highway 200 (the extension of Insurgentes) south of town. Drive, take a taxi, or ride one of the many minibuses marked Mismaloya or Boca that leave from the corner of Constitución and Calle Basilio Badillo, just below Insurgentes, or hike along the tidepools from Los Muertos.

Fishing off the rocks is good here; the water is even clear enough for some snorkeling. Bring your own gear, however, as there's none for rent. The usually gentle waves make any kind of surfing very doubtful.

BEACHES SOUTH OF TOWN

Beach lovers can spend a month of Sundays poking around the many little beaches south of town. Drive, take a taxi, or hop a Mismaloya or Boca minibus from the corner of Badillo and Constitución.

Just watch out the window, and when you see a likely spot, ask the driver to stop. Say "*Pare* (PAH-ray) *por favor.*" The location will most likely be one of several lovely *playas:* **El Gato** (Cat), **Los Venados** (Deer), **Los Carrizos** (Reeds), **Punta Negra** (Black Point), **Garza Blanca** (White Heron), or **Gemelas** (Twins).

Although many of these little sand crescents have big hotels and condos, it doesn't matter because beaches are public in Mexico up to the high-tide line. There is always some path to the beach used by local folks. Just ask "*¿Dónde está el camino* (road, path) *a la playa?*" and someone will probably point the way.

◖ MISMALOYA AND LOS ARCOS

If you ride all the way to Playa Mismaloya, you will not be disappointed, despite the oversized Hotel Jolla de Mismaloya crowding the beach. Follow the dirt road just past the hotel to the intimate little curve of sand and lagoon where the cool, clear Mismaloya stream meets the sea. A rainbow of fishing *lanchas* (boats) lie beached around the lagoon's edges, in front of a line of beachside *palapa* restaurants.

Continue a few hundred yards past the *palapas* to the ruins of the movie set of *The Night of the Iguana*. Besides being built for the actual filming, the rooms behind those now-crumbling stucco walls served as lodging, dining, and working quarters for the dozens of crew members who camped here for those eight busy months in 1963.

Stop for food (big fish fillet plate, any style, with all the trimmings, $8, or breakfast eggs from the restaurant's own hens) or a drink at the **Restaurant las Gaviotas** *palapas* across the river.

Alternatively, for food and nostalgia, go to the viewpoint **John Huston Cafe** off the ocean side of the highway, on Mismaloya Bay's south headland. If the John Huston Cafe is closed, visit the similarly spectacular view at **Le Kliff** restaurant (by the highway, about three miles south of Mismaloya, tel. 322/228-0666, 10 A.M.–10 P.M. daily).

For still another Mismaloya treat, visit nearby **Chino's Paradise** (11 A.M.–5 P.M. daily). Follow the riverside lower road that forks upstream at the north end of the bridge across the road from the hotel. Arrive in the mid-morning (around 10) or late afternoon (around 3) to avoid the tour-bus rush. Chino's streamside *palapas* nestle like big mushrooms on a jungle hillside above a cool, cascading creek. Adventurous guests enjoy sliding down the cascades (be careful—some have injured themselves seriously), while others content themselves with lying in the sun or lolling in sandy-bottomed, clear pools. Beneath the *palapas*, Chino's serves respectable but uninspired seafood and steak plates and Mexican *antojitos*.

For a more rustic alternative, follow the road another mile uphill to **El Edén** (daily until about 5 P.M.), a jungle swimming hole, complete with

From Los Arcos (The Arches) in Puerto Vallarta, the blue Bay of Banderas stretches to the western horizon.

© BRUCE WHIPPERMAN

food, *palapas*, a natural pool, a Tarzan-style rope swing, and a forest canopy ride.

Fishing, especially casting from the rocks beneath the movie set, and every other kind of beach activity are good at Mismaloya, except surfing and boogie boarding, for which the waves are generally too gentle.

Snorkeling at Los Arcos

North, offshore beyond the Mismaloya cove, rise the green-brushed Los Arcos sea rocks, a federal underwater park and ecopreserve. The name comes from the arching grottoes that channel completely through the bases of the largest sea rocks. Los Arcos is one of the best snorkeling grounds around Puerto Vallarta. Get there by hiring a glass-bottomed boat in the lagoon.

Snorkeling near the wave-washed Los Arcos is a Puerto Vallarta "must do." Swirling bunches of green algae and branching ruddy corals attract schools of grazing parrot, angel, butterfly, and goat fish. Curious pencil-thin

PUERTO VALLARTA

cornet fish may sniff you as they pass, while big croakers and sturgeon will slowly drift, scavenging along the coral-littered depths.

BOCA DE TOMATLÁN

Three miles south of Mismaloya is Boca de Tomatlán, a tranquil country village overlooking a broad strip of yellow sand bordering a petite blue bay. *Palapa* restaurants supply enough food and shade for days of easy relaxation.

If you decide to linger, contact **Agustín Bas,** a personable, English-speaking Argentinian expatriate. He and his partner, Marjorie Torrance, offer lodging in their gorgeous two-bedroom, three-bath jungle bayfront **Casa Tango** (tel. 322/224-7398 or 322/228-1019, U.S. tel. 310/494-9970, vallarta@casatango.com, www .casatango.com). Low-season (May–Sept.) tariffs run about $80 per day, $550 weekly ($120 and $790 high season Oct.–April) for up to six, including airport pickup. (Agustín and Marjorie also offer many other vacation rentals and personalized guided snorkeling, fishing, horseback, and other tours, specializing in the verdant Bay of Banderas southern shoreline; for more info visit www.tangorentals.com.)

You can continue by *colectivo* water taxi (about $4 per person) to the pristine paradises of Las Ánimas, Quimixto, and Yelapa farther south. **Las Ánimas** has seafood, *palapas,* an idyllic beach, and snorkeling; the same is true for **Quimixto,** which also has a waterfall nearby for splashing.

Yelapa, a settlement nestled below lush palm-crowned hills beside an aquamarine cove, is home for perhaps a hundred local families and a small colony of expatriates. For visitors, it offers a glimpse of South Seas life as it was before the automobile. Accessible only by sea, Yelapa's residents get around on foot or horseback. A waterfall cascades through the tropical forest above the village, and a string of *palapa* restaurants lines the beach. Lodging is available in the *palapa*-roofed cabanas of the rustic **Hotel Lagunita** (tel. 322/209-5055 or 322/209-5056, info@hotel-lagunita.com, www.hotel-lagunita.com; $70 d low season, $95 high). Reservations are especially recommended during the winter high season.

NORTH-END (ZONA HOTELERA) BEACHES

These are Puerto Vallarta's cleanest, least-crowded in-town beaches, despite the many hotels that line them. Beginning at the Hotel Rosita at the north end of the *malecón*, **Playas Camarones, Las Glorias, Los Tules,** and **Playa de Oro** form a continuous three-mile strand to the Marina. Stubby rock jetties about every quarter-mile have succeeded in retaining a 50-yard-wide strip of golden sand most of the way.

The sand is grainy, midway between coarse and fine. The waves are usually gentle, breaking right at the water's edge, and the ocean past the breakers is fairly clear (10- or 20-ft. visibility) and blue. Stormy weather occasionally dredges up clam, cockle, limpet, oyster, and other shells from the offshore depths.

Fishing by pole, net, or simply line is common along here. Surfing, bodysurfing, and boogie boarding, however, are not. All other beach sports, especially the high-powered variety, are available at nearly every hotel along the strand.

Farther north, along the shore past the Maritime Terminal-Marina Harbor entrance, the beach narrows to a seasonally rocky strip at the oceanfronts of a row of big resort hotels.

BEACH HIKES

A pair of good close-in hikes are possible. For either of them, don't forget a sun hat, sunscreen, bug repellent, a shirt, and some light shoes. On the south side, walk from Playa los Muertos about a mile and a half (two and a half kilometers) along the little beaches and tidepools to Playa Conchas Chinas. Start at either end and take half a day to swim, snorkel, sun, and poke among the rocks.

The more ambitious can hike the entire three-mile beach strip from the northern end of the *malecón* to the Marina. If you start by 9 A.M. you'll enjoy the cool of the morning with the sun at your back. Stop along the way at the showplace pools and beach restaurants of hotels such as the Sheraton, the Canto del Sol, the Fiesta Americana Vallarta, and NH

Krystal. Walk back, or opt for a return by taxi or city bus.

WATER TAXIS

Puerto Vallarta visitors can also reach the little southern beaches of Quimixto, Las Animas, and Yelapa from Puerto Vallarta itself. You have two options: fast water taxis or one of several all-day tourist cruises. The water taxis (about $20 round-trip), which allow you more time at your destination, customarily leave the Playa los Muertos New Pier three times in the morning, at about 10:30, 11, and 11:30 A.M. high season (11 and 11:30 A.M. low season). In the afternoon, they return twice, at around 4 and 4:30 P.M. high season (but once only, at around 4 P.M. low season). The morning departures allow about three hours for lunch and swimming at either the Quimixto or Yelapa waterfalls. For more information and tickets, call the New Pier water taxi office, tel. 322/222-0680, or contact water taxi manager Lucas Donahue by email: businessyelapa@hotmail.com.

The more leisurely tourist cruises leave around 9 A.M. (returning by mid-to-late afternoon) from the Terminal Maritima (cruise ship dock) on the north-side marina harbor complex.

◖ Day Cruises

The most reliable of the tourist cruises are offered by Princess Cruises. They operate four boats, which each follow separate routes. Itineraries do vary from time to time; call tel. 322/224-4777 and/or visit www.crucerosprincesa.com.mx for updated details and reservations. The package for all daytime cruises includes light breakfast, fish or chicken lunch, open beer-and-soft-drink bar, on-board live music show and dancing for about $50 per person.

The roomiest boat is the big **Princess Yelapa,** a tripled-decked steel tub with space for hundreds. The route follows the south coastline, passing for a view of Los Arcos sea rocks, continuing to idyllic Majahuitas for an hour of snorkeling. Later, at Yelapa, passengers disembark for about two hours to sun on the beach or hike to the waterfall (by horseback, if desired).

Princess Cruises also runs the **Sarape,** a smaller motor cruiser accommodating around 60 people, for snorkeling at Los Arcos, continuing to Las Animas and Quimixto for a hike (or horseback ride) and swimming at a waterfall.

Other variations are offered by the midsize cruiser **Vagabundo** (snorkeling at Los Arcos and sunning and snorkeling at Las Animas), and the larger **Princess Vallarta,** a scaled-down version of the *Princess Yelapa,* for snorkeling and wildlife-viewing at the Islas Caletas and sunning on creamy Playa Blanca on the Bay of Banderas' north shore.

For romantics, the **Princess Vallarta** also offers a 6–9 P.M. sunset cruise, with snacks, open bar, and live music for dancing, also for about $50 per person.

If you tend toward seasickness, fortify yourself with Dramamine before these cruises. Destination disembarkation at Las Animas, Quimixto, and Yelapa is by motor launch and can be difficult for travelers with disabilities.

Accommodations

In Puerto Vallarta you can usually get any type of lodging you want, for a reasonable rate. The location sets the tone, however. The relaxed, relatively tranquil but charming neighborhood south of the Río Cuale (especially around Avenida Olas Altas) has many moderately priced hotels, apartments, and condos within easy walking distance of restaurants, shopping, and services. Many of the best-buy small and medium-sized hotels are close to, if not right on, lively Playa los Muertos. While no strict dividing line separates the types of lodgings, hotels generally offer rooms with maximum service (desk, daily cleaning, restaurant, pool) but no kitchens for shorter-term guests, while apartments and condos virtually always offer

PUERTO VALLARTA

SPLENDID ISOLATION

A sprinkling of luxuriously secluded upscale miniresorts, perfect for a few days of quiet tropical relaxation, have opened in some remote corners of the Puerto Vallarta region. Being hideaways, they are not always easily accessible. But for those willing to make an extra effort, the rewards are rustically luxurious accommodations in lovely natural settings.

In order of proximity to Puerto Vallarta, first comes the minihaven **Majahuitas Resort** (tel. 322/293-4506 or U.S. tel. 831/336-5036, www.mexicanbeachresort.com; or contact Mexico Boutique Hotels, U.S./Can. toll-free 800/728-9098, www.mexicoboutiquehotels .com, $250 for two, low season, meals included; $375 high), tucked into a diminutive palm-shaded golden strand on the bay between Quimixto and Yelapa. Here, guests have their choice of seven uniquely decorated cabanas, including a honeymoon suite. Solar panels supply electricity, and a luxuriously appointed central house serves as dining room and common area. A spring-fed pool, sunning, snorkeling, and horseback and hiking excursions into the surrounding tropical forest provide diversions for guests. Get to Majahuitas by water taxi, from the beach at Boca de Tomatlán, acces-

sible by car or the Boca-marked buses, from the south-of-Cuale corner of Basilio Badillo, one block downhill from Insurgentes.

The following three splendidly isolated small resorts are tucked along the Jalisco Coast south of Puerto Vallarta and are road-accessible from Highway 200. (They are also described in the *Jalisco Coast* chapter, which you should consult for more detailed contact and access information.)

Find **Hotelito Desconocido** (toll-free U.S./ Can. tel. 800/851-1143 or toll-free Mex. tel. 01-800/013-1313, hotelito@hotelito.com, www .hotelito.com, $340 d April 15–Dec. 20 low season, $450 d high season, includes breakfast and all activities) basking on a pristine lagoon and beach two hours south of Puerto Vallarta. Here, builders have created a colony of thatched designer houses on stilts. From a distance, it looks like a native fishing village. However, inside the houses (called *palafitos* by their Italian creator), elegantly simple furnishings – antiques, plush bath towels, and artfully draped mosquito nets – set the tone. Lighting is by candle and oil lantern only. Roof solar panels power ceiling fans and warm showers. Outside, nature blooms, from squadrons of

---

multiple-room furnished kitchen units at daily rates, which can be greatly reduced for longer stays. If you're staying more than two weeks, you'll save money and also enjoy more of the comforts of home in a good apartment or condo rental.

RÍO CUALE AND SOUTH
Under $50

On Avenida Francisco I. Madero, just downhill from the corner of Jacarandas, stand Puerto Vallarta's most recommendable economy hotels. These bare-bulb, but respectable and clean, one-star hostelries have tiers of interior rooms with few amenities other than four walls, a shower bath (check for hot water), and a double bed. The prices, however, are certainly right. The best of the bunch are probably **Hotel**

Analiz (Madero 429, Puerto Vallarta, Jalisco 48300, tel. 322/222-1757, $16 s, $20 d) and **Hotel Bernal** (tel. 322/222-3605, $18 s, $23 d), next door. Also, you might check out **Hotel Cartagena** (Madero 426, tel. 322/222-6914, $21 s, $25 d), across the street.

Even more worthy is the slightly pricier **Hotel Villa del Mar** (Madero 440, Puerto Vallarta, Jalisco 48300, tel. 322/222-0785, h_villadelmar@hotmail.com, $25–30 d), whose longtime loyal patrons swear by it as the one remnant of Puerto Vallarta "like it used to be." The austere dark-wood lobby on the corner of Madero and Jacarandas leads to a double warren of clean upstairs rooms, arranged in interior and exterior sections. (Above that is a top-floor cluster of attractive budget-priced studio kitchenette apartments.) The 30

pelicans wheeling above the waves by day to a brilliant overhead carpet of southern stars by night. In the morning, roll over in bed and pull a rope that raises a flag, and your morning coffee soon arrives. For the active, a full menu, including volleyball, billiards, bird-watching, kayaking, and mountain biking, can fill the day. Reservations are strongly recommended.

About 30 miles farther south, the small sign at Km 83 gives no hint of the pleasant surprises that **Las Alamandas** (toll-free U.S./Can. tel. 888/882-9616, www.alamandas.com, $425 low season, $520 high, and up) conceals behind its guarded gate. Solitude and elegant simplicity seem to have been the driving concepts in the mind of Isabel Goldsmith, daughter of the late British tycoon Sir James Goldsmith, when she acquired control of the property in the latter 1980s. Although born into wealth, Isabel has not been idle. She converted her dream of paradise – a small, luxuriously isolated resort on an idyllic beach in Puerto Vallarta's sylvan coastal hinterland – into reality. Now, her guests (22 maximum) enjoy accommodations that vary from luxuriously simple studios ($425 low season, $520 high) to villas that sleep six ($1,600, low season, $2,200

high), all with full breakfast. Activities include a health club, tennis, horseback riding, bicycling, fishing, and lagoon and river excursions.

Alternatively, you can enjoy isolation at more moderate rates at **Hotel Punta Serena** (reservations through Blue Bay Club los Angeles Locos, tel. 315/351-5020 ext. 4013, or ext. 4011, fax 315/351-5412, www.puntaserena .com, $170 d low season, $200 high), perching on a high headland overlooking the blue Bay of Tenacatita. From the hotel lobby, walkways meander to the tile-roofed lodging units, spread over a palmy park-like garden. The lodging units themselves (all with a/c) are designer spartan, in white and blue, with modern baths, luxuriously high ceilings, and broad ocean vistas from view balconies.

Here you can enjoy it all: an adults-only romantic retreat, with all meals and in-house activites – a big blue ocean-view pool/patio, sauna, sea-vista hot tub, gym, clothing-optional settings – included. Added-cost amenities include native Mexican *temazcal,* hot room, and massage and spa services. Additionally, at no extra cost, you can also enjoy all of the lively sports, discoing, and beach action at the Blue Bay Club los Angeles Locos on the beach downhill.

or so exterior-facing rooms (about $25 s, $30 d year-round) are generally the best, with non-deluxe but comfortable amenities, including queen-sized beds, tradional dark-wood décor, more light and quiet, and in some cases even private street-view balconies. The less desirable interior-wing rooms (about $20 s, $25 d year-round), by contrast, have windows that line walkways around a sound-reflective, and therefore often noisy, interior tiled atrium, and guests must draw curtains for quiet and privacy. Rooms vary, so inspect a few before you decide. No TV, phones, or pool, and credit cards are not accepted.

The **Hotel Yasmín** (Basilio Badillo 168, Puerto Vallarta, Jalisco 48380, tel. 322/222-0087, about $35 s, $40 d with fan, add $5 for a/c, year-round), downhill at Pino Suárez, a

block from the beach, offers another budget choice. The Yasmín's plusses are its plant-festooned inner patio, and Café de Olla, a good restaurant next door. Its minus (whenever I've been there) is a glum management. Although the three stories of plain rooms are clean, many are small. You can compensate by renting one of the lighter, more secluded sunny-side upper rooms.

$50-100

Just across the Avenida Vallarta (downstream) bridge stands the renovated **Hotel Encino-Suites Plaza del Río** (Av. Juárez 122, Puerto Vallarta, Jalisco 48300, tel. 322/222-0051 or 322/222-0280, in Mexico tel. 01-800/326-3600, fax 322/222-2573, info@hotelencino .com, www.hotelencino.com, $56 s, $62 d,

$110 suite, high season). The lobby opens into a pleasant, tropical fountain-patio, enfolded by three levels of about 75 rooms total. They go for about $56 s, $62 d high season; ask for a low-season *paquete* (discount package). Inside, rooms are tastefully decorated in blue and white, many with ocean or city-hill views. Many large, similarly appointed one- and two-bedroom kitchenette suites (about $82 low season, $110 high) are available in an adjoining building. From the rooftop pool and sundeck, guests enjoy a panoramic view of the surrounding jungly hills above the white-stucco-and-tile old town, spreading to the blue, mountain-rimmed bay. Monthly rental discounts can run as much as 50 percent, and amenities include air-conditioning in rooms (no a/c in suites) phones, security boxes, and restaurant/bar.

Back just south of the river, at the downhill corner of Avenida Vallarta and Avenida Serdán, the diminutive **Hotel Posada Río Cuale** (Av. Aquiles Serdán 242, P.O. Box 146, Puerto Vallarta 48300, tel./fax 322/222-0450 or 322/222-0914, riocuale@prodigy.net .mx, $47 d low season, $65 d high) packs a lot of hotel into a small space. Good management is the key to this picturesque warren of 20 rooms that clusters beside its good restaurant/bar and a small but pleasant pool and patio. Tasteful brown and brick decor makes the rooms somewhat dark, especially on the ground floor. Artful lighting, however, improves this. There's a/c, and credit cards are accepted. Unless you like diesel-bus noise, try to avoid getting a room on the busy Avenida Vallarta side of the hotel.

A few blocks farther south on Playa los Muertos, the seven-story apartment-style **Hotel-Suites Emperador** (Amapas 114, Puerto Vallarta, Jalisco 48380, tel. 322/222-5143, fax 322/222-1767, info@hotelemperadorpv .com, www.hotelemperadorpv.com, $65–95 d high season) offers ocean-view lodgings at moderate prices. Although the hotel fronts the beach, it has no beach entrance nor beach facilities. It does, however, offer a small but inviting pool and patio for guests half a block away. The hotel, in two sections (formerly Hotel Las

Glorias and Suites Emperador, respectively) on opposite sides of Amapas, offers either hill views ($50 d low season, $65 d high) or ocean views ($65 d low season, $95 d high), with a/c, phones, TV, and credit cards accepted.

Also south of the river, the seven-story, high-rise, moderately priced **Hotel Gaviotas Vallarta** (Madero 176, Puerto Vallarta, Jalisco 48300, tel. 322/222-1500 or 322/222-5518, fax 322/222-5516, info@hotelgaviota.com, www .hotelgaviota.com, $50 s, $55 d with fan, $75 and $83 with a/c) is curiously hidden, though just half a block from the Playa los Muertos. Clean, well managed, and recently renovated, the hotel rises in eight tile-and-brick stories around an inviting, plant-decorated interior pool/patio. A small Internet snack bar serves guests downstairs, while upstairs, guests enjoy ocean vistas directly from their rooms or from arch-framed breezeways just outside their doorways. There are 84 clean and comfortable semideluxe rooms; add $7 to the room rate for TV.

Upstream from the Avenida Insurgentes bridge, you'll find **Casa del Puente** (Av. Insurgentes, Puerto Vallarta, Jalisco 48380, tel. 322/222-0749, or call Molly Stokes at U.S. toll-free tel. 888/666-9540 or 415/513-5313, casadelpuente@yahoo.com, www.casa delpuente.com, $40 d low season, $60 high) tucked on the north riverbank upstream from a bridge-front sidewalk restaurant. The elegant villa-home of Molly Stokes, grandniece of celebrated naturalist John Muir, Casa del Puente is a lovely home-away-from-home. Antiques and art adorn the spacious, high-beamed-ceiling rooms, while outside its windows and around the decks, great trees spread, tropical birds flit and chatter, jungle hills rise, and the river gurgles, hidden from the city hubbub nearby. Molly offers three lodging options: an upstairs river-view room with big bath and double bed ($40 low season, $60 high), a spacious one-bedroom/one-bath apartment ($50 d low season, $90 d high), and a two-bedroom/two-bath apartment ($60 low, $95 high), with wireless internet access. Discounts may be negotiated, depending upon season and length of stay. Reserve early for the winter season.

Casa María Elena (Francisca Rodríguez 163, Puerto Vallarta, Jalisco 48380, tel. 322/222-0113, fax 322/223-1380, mariazs@prodigy.net.mx, $35 low season, $50 high) has eight attractive fan-only brick-and-tile units stand in a four-story stack on a quiet, cobbled side street just a block and a half from the beach. The immaculate, light, and spacious units have living room with TV, bedroom, and modern kitchenettes (toaster oven and coffeemaker). A one-week rental gets a 10 percent discount; longer-term discounts are negotiable. Guests also enjoy the option of in-house Internet access and three weekly hours of free Spanish language or cooking lessons taught by the owner, María Elena Zermeño.

Recent renovations have boosted the venerable **C Hotel Eloisa** (Calle Lázaro Cárdenas 170, Puerto Vallarta, Jalisco 48300, tel./fax 322/222-6465, 322/222-0286, or 322/223-3650, info@hotel-eloisa.com, www.hotel eloisa.com, $55 d low season, $65 high; studios and suites $75–85) from ho-hum to invitingly attractive. Find it two blocks south of the river, on the quiet, bus-free north (cul-de-sac) side of Plaza Lázaro Cárdenas. The hotel's five floors of approximately 75 rooms ($55 d low season, $65 high) and kitchenette studios and suites ($20 more) enclose an appealingly light and airy inner atrium. Downstairs, past the small lobby, guests enjoy a modest restaurant/bar and a small but inviting pool/patio. Upstairs, standard-grade rooms are decorated with white tile floors, bright pastel bedspreads, king-sized (or a pair of double) beds, shiny, modern shower baths, and pleasingly traditional wood furniture and doors. Many rooms open to sunny, plaza-view balconies. Studios and suites are similarly decorated but larger, with kitchenettes, one or two bedrooms, and a living/dining room. A breezy rooftop sundeck with a view completes the attractive picture. All rooms have satellite TV and air-conditioning or fans (or both), and it's only a block from the beach. Discounts for long-term rentals are negotiable.

Another good choice, two blocks uphill from the beach in the heart of the Olas Altas neighborhood, is the **Hotel Vallarta Sun** (Francisca Rodríguez 169, tel./fax 322/223-1523, vallarta sun@usa.net, $65 d, $1,200/month year-round). Here, about 20 spacious rooms with balconies overlook a sunny pool patio. Inside, rooms are clean, attractive, and comfortable, with modern-standard bathrooms and queen-sized beds.

The **Hotel Arcos Vallarta** (M. Dieguez 171, Puerto Vallarta, Jalisco 48380, tel. 322/222-0712, $62 d low season, $80 d high) is on a quiet cul-de-sac. Its amenities include a rooftop pool/patio with a city and hill view. The Arcos Vallarta (formerly Hotel Fontana) is a sister property of (and is reservable through) the Hotel Playa Los Arcos, with 42 thoughtfully furnished pastel rooms built around a soaring interior atrium; credit cards are accepted.

Vacationers who need beachfront ambience often pick the **Hotel San Marino** (Rudolfo Gómez 111, Puerto Vallarta, Jalisco 48380, tel. 322/222-1555, or 322/222-3050, reservations@hotelsanmarino.com, www.hotelsan marino.com, $90 d low season, $100 high; $110 d suites low season, $125 high) right in the middle of the Playa los Muerto action. The San Marino's soaring *palapa* restaurant patio opens to an oceanfront pool and courtyard with a sundeck. Occupants of all 160 renovated, marble-floored, pastel-and-white rooms enjoy city, mountain, or ocean views, with air-conditioning, cable TV, phones, and access to the bar and two restaurants.

A major Olas Altas neighborhood activity hub is the **Hotel Playa los Arcos** (middle of the block between Calles Basilio Badillo and M. Dieguez), a favorite of a generation of savvy American and Canadian winter vacationers. The Playa los Arcos (Olas Altas 380, Puerto Vallarta, Jalisco 48380, tel. 322/222-0583 or 322/222-7100, toll-free U.S. 800/648-2403 or Can. 888/729-9590, fax 322/222-7104, hoteles@playalosarcos.com, www.playalosarcos.com, $90 d economy low season, $100 d high; $117 d superior low season, $125 high) is the flagship of a triad that includes the nearby Hotel Arcos Vallarta and

PUERTO VALLARTA

the apartments Suites Los Arcos; it handles bookings for all three, and guests are welcome to enjoy all of the Playa los Arcos's leisurely beachfront facilities.

All three of these lodgings have swimming pools and many comfortable, tastefully decorated, air-conditioned rooms with TV, phones, and small refrigerators in many rooms. The mecca, however, is the bustling Playa los Arcos, with its compact palm- and vine-decorated inner pool/patio sundeck, restaurant with salad bar, live music every night, and beach chairs in the sand beneath shady palms or golden sun. The Hotel Playa los Arcos's 175 rooms come in two grades, economy and superior; superior-grade rooms sometimes have with ocean views. Many guests pay much less by prebooking bargain air-hotel packages through travel agents or the Internet; credit cards are accepted. During low season (May–mid-July, September, October, and sometimes November and even January), all three hotels often offer promotions, such as a 20 percent senior discount, two kids under 12 free when sharing a room with parents, long-term discounts, or third night free.

The family-friendly **(Hotel Tropicana** (Amapas 214, Puerto Vallarta, Jalisco 48380, tel. 322/222-0912, fax 322/222-6737, email tropicana@prodigy.net.mx, www.htropicana pv.com, standard room $85 d low season, superior $105, with breakfast; add about 15 percent high season) is one of the plushest hotels on Playa los Muertos. Guests benefit both from spacious rooms in a brand-new wing and an airy pool/patio and a flock of beachfront amenities—sundeck, restaurant, volleyball, and shady *palapas*—that spread all the way to the surf. Upstairs, virtually all of the comfortable, older semi-deluxe standard-grade rooms and the newer superior-grade deluxe rooms enjoy private balconies and ocean vistas. All rooms have air-conditioning and cable TV, and credit cards are accepted. It won't hurt to ask for a promotional price *("promoción")*, especially weekdays and low season.

The all-inclusive family-friendly **Club Meza del Mar** (Amapas 380, Puerto Vallarta 48300, tel. 322/222-4888, fax 322/222-2308, info@ clubmeza.com, www.clubmeza.com, minimum three-night stay, $100 budget room, $140 holidays; $140 standard room, $170 holidays; $240 suite, $280 holidays; $280 two-bedroom suite, $340 holidays) stairsteps uphill from Playa los Muertos beach. A host of longtime returnees swear by the hotel's food, service, and friendly company of fellow guests, who, during the winter, seem to be divided equally between Americans and English- and French-speaking Canadians. The Meza del Mar's 127 rooms and suites are distributed among two adjacent buildings: the Main Tower, a high-rise with view overlooking the pool deck, and the Ocean Building, a three-story tier with views right over the beach. Guests in the preferred rooms, most of which are in the Ocean Building, enjoy private balconies and the sound of the waves outside their window. Other guests are quite happy with the expansive ocean view from the top floors of the Main Tower.

The rooms themselves, while not super-deluxe, are clean and comfortably furnished, many in the Mexican *equipal* style of hand-crafted leather furniture. All rooms have air-conditioning, but no TV or phones, and only limited wheelchair access. Rooms vary, so ask to see others if your assigned room isn't satisfactory. Rates vary according to season and grade of room and include all food (not gourmet, but wholesome), drinks, and entertainment in the hotel's restaurants, bars, pools, and beachfront club. Kids under 17 with adults stay free. Ask about promotions, such as "free" nights and "half-price" rates that are often available any time other than holidays. (Note: Although the hotel will accept walk-in guests at approximately the above rates, reservations from outside Mexico must be made through the Denver, Colorado, agent, via toll-free U.S. tel. 888/694-0010, or local tel. 303/321-7779, fax 303/322-1939, and rates will differ, principally because they must include air transportation to Puerto Vallarta.)

Over $100

Back near Avenida Olas Altas, find the apartment-style **Suites Los Arcos** (on M. Dieguez, book through Hotel Playa Los Arcos,

$103 d low season, $125 d high), with a long blue pool/patio and an airy sitting area to one side of the lobby. Upstairs are 15 studio apartments, simply but attractively furnished in tile, wood furniture, and pastel-blue sofas and bedspreads. All have baths (some with shower bath), king-sized beds, furnished kitchenette, air-conditioning, TV, and private balcony.

Although the **(Hotel Molino de Agua** (corner of Ignacio Vallarta and Aquiles Serdán, Puerto Vallarta 48380, tel. 322/222-1907, fax 322/222-6056, info@molinodeagua.com, www.molinodeagua.com, $80 d cabana low season, $105 high; $120 d beachside room low season, $165 high) occupies two Río Cuale riverfront blocks right on the beach, many visitors miss it completely. Its tranquil colony of rustic-chic cabañas hides in a jungle garden of cackling parrots, giant-leafed vines, and monumental, spreading *hule* (rubber) trees. Most of the 40 cabanas are at ground level and unfortunately don't feel completely private inside unless you close the shutters, which seems a shame in a tropical garden. The very popular beachside upstairs rooms remedy this problem. Amenities include two pools, restaurant, air-conditioning, parking, and massage services, and credit cards are accepted. (Note: At this writing, the Hotel Molino de Agua was closed for renovations. Hopefully this lovely showplace lodging will be open for guests by the time you read this.)

SOUTH OF TOWN
$50-100
Take a bus or drive the Manzanillo Highway 200 (the southward extension of Insurgentes) about a mile south of town and your reward will be the **Hotel Playa Conchas Chinas** (P.O. Box 346, Puerto Vallarta, Jalisco 48390, tel./fax 322/221-5770 or 322/221-5763, info@conchaschinas.com or hconchas@pvnet.com.mx, www.conchaschinas.com, $90 d "studio superior" room low season, $110 high; $115 "studio deluxe" one-bedroom low, $130 high), which offers a bit of charm and luscious seaside ambience at moderate rates. The stucco-and-brick complex rambles several levels down

a palm-shaded hillside (with dozens of stairs to climb) to a petite pool/patio overlooking an intimate cove on Conchas Chinas beach. Here, gulls soar, pelicans dive, palm trees sway, and sandy crescents nestle between tide pool-dotted sandstone outcroppings. The 19 lodgings themselves come in two grades. "Studio superior" rooms are spacious, decorated in Mexican traditional tile-brick and furnished in brown wood with kitchenette and tub bath; most have an ocean view. "Studio deluxe" grade adds a bedroom, ocean-view patio/balcony, and a whirlpool tub. Amenities include air-conditioning, phones, and the romantic El Set sunset restaurant above and a beachfront breakfast café below; there is no elevator or wheelchair access; credit cards are accepted. Low-season discounts, such as one day free for a four-day stay or two days free for a one-week stay, are sometimes offered.

$100-150
Another mile south, you can enjoy the extravagant isolation of the **Dreams Puerto Vallarta Resort and Spa** (reserve at Playa de las Estacas, Puerto Vallarta, Jalisco 48300, tel. 322/226-5000, U.S./Can. toll-free tel. 866/2-DREAMS, fax 322/221-6000, reservations@dreamspuertovallarta.com.mx, www.dreamsresorts.com, $170 pp main tower low season, $250 high; $240 pp Club tower low, $320 high) at correspondingly extravagant prices. The region's first world-class hotel, the Dreams Puerto Vallarta (formerly the Hotel Camino Real) has aged gracefully. It's luxuriously set in a lush tropical valley, with polished wooden walkways that wind along a beachside garden intermingled with blue swimming pools. The totally self-contained resort on a secluded, seasonally narrow strip of golden-white sand offers a host of vacation delights: luxury view rooms in the main tower or the Royal Beach Club tower, all in-house food and drinks, water sports, restaurants, bars, live music, shows, and supervised children's activities for one all-inclusive price. Rooms in the Royal Beach Club tower have hot tubs and wheelchair access.

NORTH OF RÍO CUALE

Hotels generally get more luxurious and expensive the farther north of the Río Cuale you look. The far northern section, on the Marina's ocean side, with a line-up of several big international chain hotels, is isolated several miles from downtown and has only a narrow beach, often with more rocks than sand. Most of the central part of downtown, which begins at the Río Cuale and stretches for about a mile north along the *malecón,* has no good beach except at the far north end and is generally too noisy and congested for comfortable lodgings, with some exceptions.

$50-100

One of the sprinkling of good downtown hotel options is the longtime **Hotel Los Cuatro Vientos** (Matamoros 520, P.O. Box 83, Puerto Vallarta, Jalisco 48300, tel./fax 322/222-0161 or 322/222-2831, fourwinds@pvnet.com.mx, www.chezelena.com, $35 s or d, $50 suite low season; $68 s or d, $78 suite high), perched in the quiet, picturesque hillside neighborhood above and a few blocks north of main town church. The 16 rooms and suites are tucked in tiers above a flowery patio and restaurant Chez Elena, and beneath a rooftop panoramic view sundeck. The fan-only units are simply but attractively decorated in colonial style, with tile, brick, and traditional furniture and crafts. Rates go up Dec. 15–Jan. 6,and include with continental breakfast (during Oct.–June high season only) and a small pool; credit cards are accepted. Rooms vary, so check more than one before paying your money.

At the north end of the *malecón* stands one of Puerto Vallarta's popular old mainstays, the beachfront **Hotel Rosita** (Díaz Ordaz 901, corner of 31 de Octubre; P.O. Box 32, Puerto Vallarta, Jalisco 48300, tel./fax 322/223-2185, 322/223-2000, or 322/223-2151, sales@hotel rosita.com, www.hotelrosita.com, $66–95 d low season, $95–140 high). It's centered around a grassy, palm-shadowed, ocean-view pool, patio, and restaurant, with plenty of space for relaxing and socializing. Most of the spacious rooms, of *típica* Mexican tile, white stucco, and wood, either look out to the ocean, or down upon the tranquil patio scene, while some, to be avoided if possible, border the noisy, smoggy main street. An unfortunate, but probably necessary, wire security fence mars the ocean view from the patio. Egress to the beach, Playa Camarón, is through a south-side gate. The Rosita's 115 rooms include fans or air-conditioning, security boxes, and a bar; credit cards are accepted.

$100-150

The **Hotel Buenaventura** (Av. México 1301, P.O. Box 8B, Puerto Vallarta, Jalisco 48350, tel. 322/226-7000, fax 322/222-3546, toll-free reservations in Mex. tel. 800/713-2888 or in U.S. 888/859-9439, ventas@buenaventura online.com, www.hotelbuenaventura.com.mx, $130 d low season, $180 high), on the beach several blocks farther north, where the airport boulevard narrows as it enters the old town, is one of Puerto Vallarta's few north-side close-in deluxe hotels. The lobby rises to an airy wood-beamed atrium and then opens toward the beach through a jungle walkway festooned with giant hanging leafy philodendrons and exotic palms. At the beachfront Los Tucanes Beach Club, a wide, palm-silhouetted pool/patio borders a line of shade *palapas* along the creamy yellow-gray sand beach. Most of the smallish rooms, decorated in wood, tile, and earth-tone drapes and bedspreads, open to petite, private, ocean-facing balconies. The 236 rooms include air-conditioning, phones, buffet breakfast, restaurant, bar, and live music in season; credit cards are accepted.

Over $150

Only superlatives can possibly describe the **C Hacienda San Ángel** (reserve at Miramar 336, Puerto Vallarta, Jalisco 48300, direct by U.S. tel. 415/738-8220, or local tel. 322/222-2692 or 322/221-2277, fax 322/223-1941, info@haciendasanangel.com, www .haciendasanangel.com, $250–480 d low season, $325–700 high), life project of personable owner-manager Janice Chatterton. She invites her guests to enjoy her hacienda, once the house of celebrated actor Richard Burton, as their home-away-from-home in Puerto Vallarta. Beginning in the early 1990s, Janice bought the three adjacent houses, which, with consummate design and decorative skill, she integrated into her present grand mansion.

Janice has spared little to adorn her abode with a heavenly choir of cherubs, saints, adored Madonnas, and a veritable museum of handsome old-world antique furnishings. She and her four-dog family invite visitors to enjoy any one of 14 uniquely designed and decorated suites, many with airy town and ocean vistas. She also offers a cluster of four of her rooms as Villa La Luna, for a group of up to 10 people, for $1,700 low season, $2,130 high. All accommodations come with fans, air-conditioning, cable TV, DVD player, phone, continental breakfast, wireless in-house Internet, and a load of luxurious extras, including a full-service gourmet restaurant and two lovely heated pools. No children under 16. (You may also reserve her accommodations through Mexico Boutique Hotels, toll-free in U.S. and Can. 800/728-9098, or in Mex. 01-800/508-7923, info@mexicoboutiquehotels.com, www.mexicoboutiquehotels.com).

ZONA HOTELERA

Near the north end of the downtown *malecón*, where the good beach resumes at Playa Camarones, so do the beachfront hotels. They continue, dotting the tranquil, golden strands of Playa las Glorias, Playa los Tules, and Playa de Oro. On these beaches are the plush hotels (actually self-contained resorts) from which you must have wheels to escape to the shopping, restaurants, and piquant sights and sounds of old Puerto Vallarta.

Puerto Vallarta's plush hostelries vary widely, and higher tariffs do not guarantee quality. Nevertheless, some of Pacific Mexico's best-buy luxury gems glitter among the 20-odd hotels lining Puerto Vallarta's north-end Zona Hotelera beaches. The prices listed are "rack rates": the highest prices paid by walk-in customers. Much cheaper—as much as a 50 percent discount—airfare-lodging packages are often available, especially during low seasons (Jan.,

May and June, and Sept.–Nov.). Get yourself a good buy by shopping around among hotels, the Internet, and travel agents several weeks before departure.

$50-100

At the far north end, just before the cruise ship Terminal Maritima, stands the neocolonial **⟨ Hacienda Hotel and Spa** (Paseo de la Marina, P.O. Box 95B, Puerto Vallarta, Jalisco 48310, tel. 322/226-6667, fax 322/226-6672, info@haciendaonline.com.mx, www.haciendaonline.com.mx, $80 d low season, $95 d high; all-inclusive, $70 pp low season, $100 high). One of the Zona Hotelera's best-buy options, the hacienda offers a load of amenities at moderate rates. Its 155 rooms, arranged in low-rise tiers, enfold a leafy-green patio/garden, graced by a blue free-form pool and a slender, rustic shade *palapa*. On one side, water gurgles from a neo-antique aqueduct, while guests linger at the adjacent airy restaurant. The rooms are spacious, with high, hand-hewn-beam ceilings, marble floors, and rustic-chic tile and brick baths, and include air-conditioning, phones, cable TV, some wheelchair access, and credit cards accepted. The only slight drawback to all this is guests must walk a couple of short blocks to the beach. Spa services, such as a *temescal* sauna, facials, many massage options, reflexology, and aromatherapy, are abundant but cost extra.

Another worthy option about a mile south is the hotel **Las Palmas by the Sea** (Km 2.5 Bulevar Francisco Medina Ascencio, Puerto Vallarta, Jalisco 48300, tel. 322/226-1220, fax 322/226-1268, reservaciones@laspalmasresort.com, www.laspalmasresort.com, all-inclusive $75 pp low season, $100 high; kids under 12 $15 low season, $30 high; kids 13 and above, $20 low season, $35 high). Past the reception, an airy, rustic *palapa* rises over the lobby, which opens to a palmy beachside pool/patio. Here, on the wide, sparkling Playa las Glorias, opportunities for aquatic sports are at their best, with the hotel's sport shop (snorkeling, fishing, Hobie Cat sailboats, parasailing) right on the beachfront. The 225 rooms come with all food, drinks, and in-house entertainment. Guests in most rooms enjoy private ocean-view balconies, and comfortable, semi-deluxe furnishings, with air-conditioning, phones, TV, restaurant, snack bar, bars, pool, and parking; credit cards are accepted. Check the website for promotional packages, such as kids under 9 free, or third night free during times of low occupancy (Sept.–Nov. and May–June).

$100-150

A few blocks farther south, the **Hotel Plaza Pelícanos** (Km 2.5 Bulevar Francisco Medina Ascencio, Puerto Vallarta, Jalisco 48300, tel. 322/224-1010, fax 322/224-3618; toll-free in Mex. 01-800/713-2152, reservapelicanos@hotelesgdlplaza.com.mx, www.hotelesgdlplaza.com.mx, all-inclusive $145 s, $130 d pp low season; $170 and $155 pp high), a Mexican-owned hotel, caters mostly to North American clientele during the winter, and Mexicans during national holidays, before Easter week, and in August. The Hotel Plaza Pelícanos is divided perfunctorily into sections I and section II. Although tariffs are the same in both, the preferred section is II (the graceful former Hotel Plaza las Glorias), where a blue swimming pool meanders beneath a manicured patio/grove of rustling palms. Behind the Spanish-style stucco, brick, and tile facade, the luxurious rooms overlook the patio and ocean from small view balconies, and are tile-floored, with decor in dark wood, white stucco, and blue and pastels. All 237 rooms include air-conditioning, cable TV, two pools, bars, beachfront jogging track, restaurants, and parking.

Next door to the south, find the **Hotel Canto del Sol** (Km 2.5 Bulevar Francisco Ascencio, Plaza las Glorias, Puerto Vallarta, Jalisco 48300, tel. 322/226-0123 exts. 4142, 4143, 4144; fax 322/224-4437 and 322/224-5236, info@cantodelsol.com, www.cantodelsol.com, $100 s or d low season, $130 high; all-inclusive $110 pp low season, $130 high, kids 5–12 $30 low season, $35 high; 13–17 $35 low $65 high). During the high winter season, Hotel Canto del Sol (formerly Hotel Continental Plaza) bustles all day with tennis in

the eight-court John Newcombe Tennis Club next door, and aerobics, water polo, and volleyball in the big central pool, and parasailing, jetboating, and sailboarding from the golden Playa las Glorias beach. The luxurious but smallish rooms, decorated in soothing pastels, open to balconies overlooking the broad, palm-decorated patio. All-inclusive packages cover all in-house food, drinks, and entertainment. Third night is often gratis, especially during May–June and Sept.–Oct. low seasons. Amenities include air-conditioning, shows, water aerobics, tennis, kid's club, restaurants, bars, sauna, hot tub, exercise room, wheelchair access, and parking.

For another bountiful option, return a mile north to the **Hotel NH Krystal** (Av. de las Garzas s/n, Puerto Vallarta, Jalisco 48300, tel. 322/224-0202 or toll-free in Mex. 800/903-3300 in U.S. toll-free 888/726-0528, Canada, 866/299-7096, fax 322/226-0738, www.nh-hoteles.com, $87 d low season, $140 high, two kids under 12 free). Stay here and you get more than a mere hotel: This palmy, low-rise, roomy resort-village (one of the few Puerto Vallarta luxury resorts designed by and for Mexicans) is exactly what a Mexican Walt Disney would have built. Don't be put off by the rather gloomy lobby (the new European owners are trying to save electricity), just feast your eyes on the amenities spread over its 34 beachside acres: a flock of deluxe garden bungalows that open onto private pool/patios, a Porfirian bandstand that stands proudly at the center, while nearby a colonial-style aqueduct gushes water into a pool at the edge of a serene, spacious, palm-shaded park. Guests who prefer a livelier environment can have it. Dancing, in season, goes on in the lobby or beside the huge, meandering beachside pool, where the music is anything but serene. The NH Krystal's 460 deluxe rooms and suites include air-conditioning, phones, cable TV, 44 pools (no joke!), multiple restaurants, and all sports.

Over $150

Right in the middle of the hotel zone, the ◖ **Hotel Fiesta Americana Puerto Vallarta**

(P.O. Box 270, Puerto Vallarta, Jalisco 48300, tel. 322/226-2100 or toll-free in U.S./Can. 800/FIESTA-1 or 800/343-7821, fax 322/224-2108, conciergefapv@posadas.com.mx, www .fiestaamericana.com, $120 d low season, $240 d high, two kids under 12 free) is for many the best hotel in town. The lobby *palapa,* the world's largest, is an attraction unto itself. Its 10-story palm-thatch chimney draws air upward, creating a continuously cool breeze through the open-air reception. Outside, the high-rise rampart of ocean-view rooms overlooks a pool and garden of earthly delights, complete with a gushing pool fountain, water volleyball, swim-up bar, and in-pool recliners. Beyond spreads a 150-foot-wide strip of wave-washed yellow sand. Amenities include air-conditioning, TV, phones, all sports, aerobics, three restaurants, huge pool, three bars, wheelchair access, and parking.

Next door to the north, the all-inclusive **Hola Puerto Vallarta** (Km 2.5, Av. de las Palmas s/n, Puerto Vallarta, Jalisco 48300, tel. 322/224-4446, toll-free in Mex. 01-800/327-0000, fax 322/224-4447, reservas@holapuerto vallarta.com, www.holapuertovallarta.com, all-inclusive $110 pp low season, $150 high, kids 7–11 $30, 12–17 $50), formerly the Qualton Club, offers an attractive all-inclusive option for vacationers who enjoy lots of food, fun, and company. On a typical winter-season day, hundreds of fellow sunbathing guests line the rather cramped poolside, while a few steps away dozens more relax beneath shady beachfront *palapas.* Nights glow with beach buffet theme dinners—Italian, Mexican, Chinese, and more—for hundreds, followed by shows where guests often become part of the entertainment. The list goes on—constant food, open bars, complete gym and spa, tennis by night or day, scuba lessons, volleyball, water sports, free disco, golf privileges, stress therapy, yoga, aerobics galore—all included. If you want relief from the hubbub, you can always escape to the greener, more spacious Fiesta Americana poolside next door. The hotel's 320 rooms, all with private view balconies, are luxuriously decorated in pastels and include

air-conditioning, cable TV, phone, and wheelchair access; credit cards are accepted.

APARTMENT, CONDO, AND HOUSE RENTALS
Puerto Vallarta abounds with apartments and condominiums, mostly available for one week or more. Many of the best-buy Puerto Vallarta apartments and condos are concentrated in the colorful Olas Altas–Conchas Chinas southside district and high-season rates run from about $500 per month for modest studios to $1,000 and more for three-bedroom houses.

One of the most recommendable local apartment and condo rental agents is friendly **Bayside Properties** (F. Rodríguez 160, tel. 322/223-0898 or 322/223-4418, fax 322/223-0898, dosgatos@pvnet.com.mx, www.bayside propertiespv.com), a few doors uphill from Avenida Olas Altas in the heart of the Olas Altas district.

Other well-established south-of-Cuale rental agencies that you may find useful are **Tropicasa Realty** (Pulpito 45A, corner of Olas Altas, tel. 322/222-6505, fax 322/222-2555, rentals@tropicasa.com or patricia@tropicasa .com, www.tropicasa.com) and **Tango Rentals** of personable Agustín Bas and his partner Marjorie Torrance (tel. 322/224-7398 or 322/228-1019, U.S. tel. 310/494-9970, email marjorie@ tangorentals.com, or visit www.tangorentals .com). They offer a wide range of vacation rentals, from modest condos to luxurious villas, especially in the intimate south-of-Cuale neighborhood.

A number of U.S.-based agencies specialize in the more luxurious rentals scattered all over the city.

Other apartments are rentable directly through local managers. The following includes a brief listing of some of the best-buy Olas Altas apartments. Some managers declined to state specific weekly or monthly rates, preferring to leave specific prices negotiable with prospective tenants.

Under $500 per Month
Among the most economical best-buy apartments

Due to Puerto Vallarta's steep hills, a mechanical boost is needed in front of this condominium.

© BRUCE WHIPPERMAN

are the top-floor (no elevator) studio apartments at the **Hotel Villa del Mar** (Francisco I. Madero 440, Puerto Vallarta, Jalisco 48300, tel. 322/222-0785, h_villadelmar@hotmail .com, $40/day, $400/month low season; $45/day, $450/month high), a block south of the Río Cuale and four blocks uphill from Avenida Insurgentes. The several apartments are attractively decorated in rustic brick, dark wood, and tile, with furnished kitchenette, double bed in one corner, and most with city- and hill-view private balconies.

$500-1,000 per Month

Above Playa Los Muertos, a steep path winds uphill to the 59-unit condo-style **Hotel Brisas del Mar** (Privada Abedul 10, Puerto Vallarta, Jalisco 48300, tel. 322/222-1821, fax 322/222-1800, $65/night, $600/month low season; $80/night, $800 high), whose big white main building is perched a short block below the highway. Rooms are comfortable, featuring one-bedroom kitchenette suites with private view balconies, air-conditioning, and big

view pool deck (check to see if it's being maintained). Get there either by car or taxi from the highway (via cul de sac Privada Abedul, about 0.3 mi. south of the gas station) or by climbing the stairs from Amapas through the doorway at no. 307, labeled Casa del Tigre.

Back downhill, the **Casa María Elena** (Francisca Rodríguez 163, Puerto Vallarta, Jalisco 48380, tel. 322/222-0113, fax 322/223-1380, mariazs@prodigy.net.mx, $40/day studio low season, $55/day high; ($50/day 1br low season, $75/day high) is owned and operated by English-speaking María Elena Zermeño Santana. She offers eight attractive fan-only studio and one-bedroom apartments, 10 percent discount for a one-week rental; longer-term discounts are negotiable. Guests enjoy the option of either free Spanish-language or cooking lessons taught by María Elena.

Also very recommendable in the same price range is the **Hotel Encino-Suites Plaza del Río** (Av. Juárez 122, Puerto Vallarta, Jalisco 48300, tel. 322/222-0051 or 322/222-0280), at the north foot of the Av. Vallarta Río Cuale bridge.

Over $1,000 per Month

Alternatively, check out lovely ⚓ **Casa Andrea** (Francisca Rodríguez 174, Puerto Vallarta, Jalisco 48380, tel./fax 322/222-1213, casaandrea@aol.com, www.casaandrea.com, $350/week 1br low season, $500 high; $700/week 2br low season, $900 high). Friendly and helpful on-site owner Andrea offers 10 attractively decorated and comfortable and one- and two-bedroom balcony apartments and a view penthouse, overlooking an invitingly tropical pool/patio. Apartments include big beds, kitchens, fans, and a library, small exercise room, and a community TV down by the pool. For the winter, get reservations in by June.

A few doors uphill, consider **Vallarta Sun Suites** (Gómez 169, Puerto Vallarta, Jalisco 48380, tel. 322/222-6200, fax 322/222-4836, $65/day, $1,300/month low season; $90/day and $1,500/month high). Perched on a quiet side street, four stories of comfortably furnished new one-bedroom kitchenette apartments overlook a sunny pool patio just two blocks from the beach. Make your reservations at Hotel Vallarta Sun (Francisca Rodríguez 169, tel./fax 322/223-1523, vallartasun@usa.net), one block south.

GAY-FRIENDLY ACCOMMODATIONS

Puerto Vallarta offers a wide variety of gay-friendly hotels, villas, and bed-and-breakfasts. All of the properties listed below advertise in the local gay media, and the majority, if not all, are gay-owned.

$50-100

With their popular rooftop sunset bar, **Descanso del Sol** (Pino Suárez 583, Zona Romántica, 322/222-5229, www.descansodelsol .com, $59–74 d low, $84–99 d high, junior suites low $89 d, junior suites high $123 d, suites low $118 d, suites high $150 d) attracts the young, buff gay crowd even if it's just for cocktails. Guests vary from the gym-built to the gym-phobic, but Descanso is a friendly three-floor 24-room place that makes everyone feel at home. While rooms could use an upgrade, the comfortable, well-located property has an eclectic feel with colorful tiles, kitschy accents, and plastic terrace chairs.

Climb the hill to find your private apartment-like room at **La Terraza Inn** (Amapas 299, Amapas, 322/223-5431, www.terrazainn .com, $52–57 d low, $82–87 d high), a friendly gay-owned inn just a block up from Playa los Muertos on Amapas. Upper terrace rooms have a bit of a view beyond the high-rise in front, but each of the 10 rooms, renovated in the summer of 2006, is spacious and comfortable and has a terrace. Some rooms with kitchenettes allow you to eat at home. Guests also have access to the inn's laundry, WiFi, cafeteria, and on-call massage service. Pets are allowed and, in fact, if you leave your window open, neighborhood cats may just pop in for a peek.

When a carefree vacation is on the horizon, the young and restless choose the men-only **Vallarta Cora** (Pilitas 174, Zona Romántica, 322/223-2815, www.vallartacora.com, $95 d, other rates by email), where it seems the parents are always away while leaving you the keys to the main house. The four-story white stucco tower houses 14 clean tiled rooms with basic amenities, living room, dining room, kitchenette, air-conditioning, balcony, and oval-shaped bathtub. The happening pool area is open to the public for weekly pool parties, while the Bola Bar features a hot tub that can accommodate up to 60 people, all clothing-optional. Two-for-one happy hours and the new behind-the-bar steam room keep this place hopping.

Back downhill in the Olas Altas neighborhood, on a quiet uphill side street, stands the modest but well-managed **Hotel Mercurio** (Francisca Rodríguez 168, tel./fax 322/222-4793, www.hotel-mercurio.com, $59 s or d low season, $83 s or d high, studio with kitchenette $82 s or d low, $100 s or d high). The small lobby leads to an intimate leafy pool patio, enclosed by three tiers of rooms simply decorated in rustic wood, tile, and stucco, with TV, air-conditioning, and shower bath; credit cards are accepted. During times of low occupancy, the Mercurio sometimes offers promotions, such as kids free with parents or fourth day free. Ask before you reserve.

Directly above the Playa los Muertos south shoreline, the breezy plant-decorated room tiers of ◖ **Casa Corazón** (Amapas 326, tel./fax 322/222-6364 or 322/222-2738, U.S./Can. tel. 866/648-6893, www.casacorazonvallarta .com, small rooms $30 s, $45 d low season, $60 s, $75 d high; large rooms with kitchenette $50 s, $60 d low season, $65 s or $95 d high) stairstep down its beachfront hillside. The 24 rooms, while not deluxe, are comfortably decorated with tile, brick, and arts and crafts. Guests in some of the most popular rooms enjoy spacious, sunny oceanview patios.

$100-150

The modern nine-floor tower of **Boana Torre-Malibu** (Amapas 325, Zona Romántica, 322/222-6695, www.boana.net, $40–70 d low, $80–125 d high) offers special rates for longer stays, giving you the option of experiencing condo living right in the Zona Romántica just across from the gay beach at Playa los Muertos. All apartments have one or two bedrooms with a separate kitchen and living area with balcony, and guests have access to what is called "the largest gay pool in the city." The on-site travel agency will book tours and day cruises for you, although finding something to do shouldn't be a problem here—the location puts you within easy walking distance of the best restaurants, coffee shops, and bars.

Casa de las Flores (Calle Santa Barbara 359, Zona Romántica, 322/120-5242 or U.S. tel. 510/763-3913, www.casadelasflorespv.com, $100–125 d low, $100–170 d high, $125–250 d holiday) is a much-photographed quirky bed-and-breakfast that allows pets and children. This property has a rambling, homey atmosphere with some air-conditioned rooms, Internet access, fully equipped kitchen and bar, dipping pool for the main house, maid service, and cable TV. Located within walking distance of Playa los Muertos, the casa offers impressive views of the bay from its terraces. While

not focused solely on the gay community, Las Flores is gay-owned. Long-term rates are available May–October, and the minimum stay is seven nights.

The interior-focused **Casa Fantasia B&B** (Pino Suárez 203 at Francisco Madero, Zona Romántica, 322/223-2444, www.mexonline .com/casafantasia.htm, $60–80 d low, $120–150 d high) offers a haven from the busy streets and beaches of the Zona Romántica. While unregistered guests are not allowed into the rooms, all other needs will be met with friendly, attentive service. The champagne happy hour and full breakfast at the sunny poolside are de rigueur. Only a block from the beach, this gay-owned guest house is decorated like a hacienda, with antiques and priceless works of art in all five suites and two rooms.

In a personalized condo atmosphere, **Suites Claudia** (Abedul 630, Carr. Mismaloya Km 1.5, South Shore, 322/222-4223, www .suites-claudia.com, $90–100 d low, $110–130 d high, suites $150 d low, $250 d high) takes care of all your needs from the minute you arrive. Five floors up with pool area, this property offers views of the ocean, a location that's easy walking distance into town, and comfortable contemporary Mexican-style handcrafted furniture that's colorful and homey. Fully equipped kitchens allow you to stay at home and sit on your private terrace to drink in the view. Help with reservations at local restaurants is yours for the asking.

The deluxe men-only, clothing-optional **Villa David** (Galeana 348, Gringo Gulch, 322/223-0315, from the U.S. 877/832-3315, www .villadavidpv.com, $70 d low season, $108 high; $92 d suites low, $151 d high) offers comfortable neighborhood living in a homey and elegant setting at moderate rates. Villa David's ten rooms enfold an intimate, leafy tropical pool patio overlooking panoramic vistas of Puerto Vallarta, bay, and mountains. The rooms, decorated with 19th century–style traditional hardwood furniture, embellished with reading lamps and hand-sewn bedspreads, likewise all enjoy bay views. Rooms come with private baths, fans, and hearty buffet breakfast. Other amenities include a common kitchen and living room with TV and DVD, in-house wireless Internet, roof-top viewing deck, and a hot-tub deck with bar. Guests enjoy easy walking access to both Río Cuale and *malecón* sights, galleries, shops, and restaurants.

Over $150

Forty-two rooms and 12 suites make up **Abbey Hotel Vallarta** (Púlpito 138, Zona Romántica, 322/222-4488, www.abbeyhotelvallarta.com, $150–190 d high), a modern tower-style hotel right on the gay beach in the Zona Romántica. All rooms are invitingly furnished, with immaculate tile floors, modern hardwood furniture, and private town- or oceanview balconies. Amenities include an in-room safety deposit box, air-conditioning, telephone, cable TV, and high-speed Internet access. Suites include kitchenettes and a large living room with dining area. Other on-site offerings include a reserved beach area, swimming pool, and Jacuzzi as well as restaurant and bar. For an additional charge, VIP airport pickup, in-room massage, and your choice of local tours and outings are also available.

When you need to feel the comfort and services of the international gay community, head to the **Blue Chairs Beach Resort,** perched on the south side of breezy Playa los Muertos (Malecón 4, 322/222-5040, U.S./Can. tel. 866/514-7969, www.bluechairs.com, $60 s or d low season, $100 high; $110 s or d suite low season, $150 high; $119 s or d villa low, $230 high; $20 per additional person). Gay-owned for six years, the hotel, which advertises itself as the world's largest gay-and-lesbian beachfront resort, is a six-story stack of about forty comfortably furnished rooms and suites. The most economical rooms offer a partial ocean view; ocean views are standard in the kitchenette junior suites and one-bedroom villas. During the busy winter season, you can join the hotel's buzz of activity, starting with a friendly crowd that congregates in the hotel's famous beachfront blue chairs, and continuing with anything from bingo and karaoke to laughing with the crowd at drag shows and theme parties. All lodgings come with private baths, fans,

air-conditioning, and cable TV, as well as use of the rooftop restaurant and pool.

The constantly improving **Casa Cúpula** (129 Callejon de la Igualdad, Zona Romántica, 322/223-2484, www.casacupula.com, $160–279 d regular, $195–310 d high, suites $275–375) has recently added a gym to its services. The gay-owned and -managed bed-and-breakfast promises you personal service, and you will not only feel cared for but pampered while staying in one of the 10 rooms. Located above the highway in a quiet area surrounded by the peaceful jungle, it's the sort of place where you'll see hummingbirds flitting around the relaxing lounge area and pool. Chef Jim Jardine comes from San Francisco and serves up relaxed home-style gourmet cuisine.

Casa de Los Arcos (Hortensias 168, Alta Vista, 322/222-5990, www.casadelosarcos.com, $100–200 d low, $150–275 d high, weekly rates), a four-casita hillside villa, allows the option of renting the entire place for groups of family or friends, or, when available, renting a separate casita. Each casita features its own living room, dining area, kitchen, and private terrace with air-conditioning in the closed areas. The house is fully staffed Monday through Saturday; the cook is available Sunday for an extra charge. What's great about this residence is that you and a group of friends can all stay in one place, but you'll have your privacy when you need it, as well as large common living areas. The atmosphere has a very Mexican flavor, and the open-air *palapa* roof and private terraces will help you relax.

A boutique condo-hotel located right in the Romantic Zone, the **San Franciscan** (Pilitas 213, Zona Romántica, 322/222-6473, www.san-franciscan.com; $66–100 d low, $130–189 d high, 4 bdrms $179 d low, $360 d high) offers a protected haven with 20 rooms and easy access to any of the services outside the gates. The five floors host a variety of room types, including large suites that can accommodate groups of up to six or eight. Amenities and services include free long-distance calls to the United States and Canada, free Internet access, no rate increase for regular registered customers for ten years, air-conditioning, kitchens with microwaves, cookware, silverware, and china, and just about anything else to make your stay comfortable. Adults only, no pets.

Real Estate Brokers

Bayside Properties (Francisca Rodríguez 160, 322/222-8148, www.baysidepropertiespv .com), a gay-friendly rental and real estate sales operation owned by two women, handles many of the downtown and south-side apartments and condominiums.

Another woman-owned gay-friendly establishment, **Cochran Real Estate** (Leona Vicario 230-D, Zona Romántica, 322/221-6146, www.vallartaliving.com) focuses on service both in rentals and real estate sales.

Home mortgages are not the norm in Mexico, but now that they are possible, gay-owned **Mexlend** (322/222-7377, www.mexlend.com) is one of the leading lenders.

One of the partners of **Paradise Properties** (Atún 118, Las Gaviotas, 322/224-5416, www .paradisepropertiespv.com) is gay; this more recently founded agency focuses on personal service in sales and rentals.

The founder and many of the staff of **Puerto Vallarta Rentals Premier Vacations** (Francisca Rodríguez 152, Zona Romántica, 322/222-0638, www.pvrpv.com) are gay. This successful rental operation handles villas as well as tours and other services.

The gay-owned **Rainbow Realty** (Calle Malecón 2, Playa los Muertos, Zona Romántica, 322/223-3005, www.rainbowrealtyvallarta .com) focuses on service, sales, and rentals for the gay community.

Gay-owned **Timothy Fuller & Associates** (Rodolfo Gómez 122, Zona Romántica, 322/222-1535, www.timothyfuller.com) is a partnership of well-trained rental and real estate professionals.

The founding partner of extremely successful **Tropicasa** (Púlpito 145-A, Zona Romántica, 322/222-6505, www.tropicasa.com) is an active member of the gay community as well as the president of the local real estate association and the local Make a Wish foundation.

Boca de Tomatlán's water taxis to Yelapa are handy for those who are camping outside Puerto Vallarta's city limits.

Venegas World Start Realty (Olas Altas 463, Zona Romántica, 322/222-2111, www.venegasrealty.com) is one of the active members of the gay community, involved in fundraising in addition to real estate sales, rentals, and services.

TRAILER PARKS AND CAMPING

Puerto Vallarta visitors enjoy two good trailer parks. The smallish, palm-shaded **Trailer Park El Pescador** (Francia 143, P.O. Box 141, Puerto Vallarta, Jalisco 48300, tel. 322/224-2828, $21 RV site) is two blocks off the highway on Francia at the corner of Lucerna, a few blocks north of the *libramiento* downtown bypass fork. The 65 spaces (four blocks from the Playa las Glorias) have all hookups, including showers, toilets, long-distance phone access, and launderette. One free day per week, one free week per month; pets are okay. Luxury hotel pools and good restaurants are nearby.

Farther out, but much more spacious, is **Tacho's Trailer Park** (P.O. Box 315, Puerto Vallarta, Jalisco 48300, tel. 322/224-2163, $22 RV site), half a mile from Highway 200 on Avenida Aramara, the road that branches inland across the airport highway from the cruise ship dock. Tacho's offers a large grassy yard with some palms, bananas, and other trees for shade. The 100 spaces include all hookups and use of showers, toilets, laundry room, pool and *palapa*, and shuffleboard courts. Pads are paved, and pets are okay. One free week on monthly rental.

Other than the trailer parks, Puerto Vallarta has precious few campsites within the city limits. Plenty of camping possibilities exist outside the city, however. Especially inviting are the pearly little beaches, such as Las Animas, Quimixto, Caballo, and others, that dot the wild coastline between Boca de Tomatlán and Yelapa. *Colectivo* water taxis regularly head for these beaches for about $5 per person from Boca de Tomatlán. Local stores at Quimixto, Las Animas, and Boca de Tomatlán can provide water (bring water purification tablets or filter) and basic supplies.

Food

Puerto Vallarta is brimming with good food. In the winter, when the sun-hungry vacationers crowd in, a table at even an average restaurant may require a reservation. During the low season, however, Puerto Vallarta's best eateries are easy to spot. They are the ones with the customers.

Good Puerto Vallarta eating is not limited to sit-down restaurants. Many food stalls offer wholesome, inexpensive meals and snacks to hosts of loyal repeat customers. It's hard to go wrong with hot, prepared-on-the-spot food. Each stand specializes in one type of fare—seafood, *tortas,* tacos, hot dogs—and occupies the same location daily, beginning around noon.

STALLS, SNACKS, AND BREAKFAST
South of Río Cuale

A number of food stalls concentrate along Avenida Constitución, Francisco Madero, and Pino Suárez just south of the Río Cuale; several others cluster on the side-street corners of Avenida Olas Altas a few blocks away.

One of the stalls, the **Calamar Aventurero** (The Frisky Squid; tel. 322/222-6479, Mon.–Sat. 9 A.M.–7 P.M., $2–6), has become a very popular open-air seafood restaurant, at the corner of Aquiles Serdán and Constitución. Choose from smoked marlin tacos, ceviche, fish burritos, and much more.

Some of the most colorful, untouristed places to eat in town are, paradoxically, at the tourist mecca Mercado Municipal on the Río Cuale, at the Avenida Insurgentes bridge. The *fondas* (7 A.M.–6 P.M. daily) tucked on the upstairs floor (climb the streetside staircase) specialize in steaming, home-style soups, fish, meat, tacos, *moles,* and *chiles rellenos* ($2–4).

Point out your order to the cook and take a seat at the cool, river-view seating area.

For breakfast, **La Casa de los Hot Cakes** (Basilio Badillo 289, btwn. I. Vallarta and Constitución, tel. 322/222-6272, 8 A.M.–2 P.M. Tues.–Sun., $4–6), skillfully orchestrated by personable travel writer-turned-restaurateur Memo Barroso, has become a Puerto Vallarta institution. Memo's only meal is breakfast. Besides bountiful Mexican and North American breakfasts—orange juice or fruit, eggs, toast, and hash browns for about $5—Memo offers an indulgent list of pancakes. Try his nut-topped, peanut butter-filled O. Henry chocolate pancakes, for example. For lighter eaters, vegetarian and less indulgent options are available. Memo's latest love is coffee. If you're lucky enough to be near Casa de los Hot Cakes at the right time, simply follow your nose to the source of the heavenly aroma of his roasting beans—premium estate-grown only, from Oaxaca, Chiapas, and Veracruz.

Another good spot for breakfast is the airy beachfront terrace of the **Hotel Playa Los Arcos** restaurant (380 Olas Altas, 7–11:30 A.M. daily, $4–7). Here the ambience—tour boats arriving and leaving, the passing sidewalk scene, the swishing waves, the swaying palms—is half the fun. The other half is the food, either a hearty $7 buffet or a briskly served à la carte choice of your heart's desire, from fruit and oatmeal to eggs, bacon, and hash browns.

Shorter on scenery but longer on food and service is **Café Tizoc** (on Olas Altas, btwn. Rodríguez and Gómez, tel. 322/223-2554, 8 A.M.–11 P.M. daily, $3–5). Here the main event is great hash browns and "slam" breakfasts, introduced by the friendly, semiretired headwaiter, who worked for a dozen years at Denny's in Las Vegas, Nevada. Food and service are so good that you'll most likely return to try lunch and supper.

North of Río Cuale

Although food stalls are less numerous north of the Río Cuale, you can fill up quite well with the sprinkling of evening taco, hot dog, and sweet corn *(elote)* stands around the downtown plaza.

The tourist favorite **No Name Café** (on the *malecón* btwn. Galeana and Mina, tel. 322/223-2508, 9 A.M.–midnight daily), two blocks north of the main plaza, is a fine place to start out your north-of-Cuale morning. Choose from many breakfasts ($3–5), including hotcakes, eggs, potatoes, toast, and fruit. Come back for a dinner ($4–12) of soup, salad, ribs, chicken, or fish.

Folks who prefer a more refined traditional Mexican setting go to the longtime **Restaurant Las Palomas** (at the *malecón* corner of Aldama, from 8 A.M. daily, tel. 322/222-3675) three blocks farther north, with plenty of good breakfasts ($4–7).

Alternatively, try **Tuti Fruti** *lonchería* (corner of Morelos and Corona, tel. 322/222-9621, 8 A.M.–11 P.M. Mon.–Sat., $3–4), an inviting nook (bus noise notwithstanding) for a refreshing snack, especially while sightseeing or shopping around the *malecón*. You could even eat breakfast, lunch, and dinner there, starting with juice and granola or eggs in the morning, a *torta* and a *liquado* during the afternoon, and an *hamburguesa* for an evening snack.

COFFEEHOUSES

Good coffee is plentiful in Puerto Vallarta, where many cafés roast from their own private sources of beans. The best coffeehouses are sprinkled along Avenida Olas Altas, just a block from Playa los Muertos. Here, coffee-and book-lovers get the best of both worlds at **C Page in the Sun** (corner Olas Altas and M. Dieguez, 7 A.M.–midnight daily, tel. 322/1273), diagonally across from Hotel Playa Olas Altas. Longtimers sip coffee and play chess while others enjoy their pick of lattes, cappuccinos, ice cream, muffins, and walls of used paperbacks and magazines.

Exactly one block farther up Olas Altas, take a table at the **Café San Ángel** (corner of Rodríguez, 8 A.M.–10 P.M. daily, $3–5) and soak up the sidewalk scene. Here, you can enjoy breakfast or a sandwich or dessert and good coffee in a dozen varieties.

For fancier offerings and refined ambience, go to the old-Europe-style **Café Maximilian** (380 Olas Altas, tel. 322/222-5058, 8 A.M.–midnight daily, closed Sun. in low season) on the sidewalk in front of Hotel Playa los Arcos.

On the north side of town, coffee lovers can also get their fill, especially at one of the sprinkling of coffeehouses that have recently started up on handicrafts-rich Calle Corona, just a block and a half inland from the *malecón*.

RESTAURANTS
Río Cuale and South
Note: If you're coming to Puerto Vallarta mainly for its gourmet offerings, avoid, if possible, September and October, when some of the best restaurants are closed.

Archie's Wok (Francisca Rodríguez 130, btwn. Avenida Olas Altas and the beach, tel. 322/222-0411, 2–11 P.M. Mon.–Sat., entrées $8–15) is the founding member of a miniature "gourmet ghetto" that is flourishing in the Olas Altas neighborhood. The founder, now deceased, was John Huston's longtime friend and personal chef. However, Archie's widow, Cindy Alpenia, carries on the culinary mission. A large local following swears by her menu of vegetables, fish, meat, and noodles. Favorites include Thai coconut fish, barbecued ribs Hoi Sin, and spicy fried Thai noodles. Make up a party of three or four, and each can order a favorite. Arrive early—there's usually a line by 7:30 P.M. for dinner; Visa accepted.

Next door to Archie's Wok, **Restaurant Peking** (F. Rodríguez 136, tel. 322/222-2264, noon–10 P.M. daily, entrees $6–8) adds a new, refined version of Chinese cooking to Puerto Vallarta's already rich gastronomic treasury. Perhaps the promise of "the only Chinese-born chef in Puerto Vallarta" is its secret to success, but whatever, the food, whether a light lunch of spring rolls and wonton soup or a dinner of stir-fried scallops, kung pao chicken, and a whole fish, is bound to please.

One block due north, across from the Hotel Plaza San Marino, **Karpathos Taverna** (R. Gomez 110, tel. 322/223-1562, 4–11 P.M. Mon.–Sat., entrees $3–12) has acquired a considerable local following by creating a little corner of Greece here in Puerto Vallarta. Although the ambience comes, in part, from very correct service and the Greek folk melodies emanating from the sound system, the food—genuine Greek olives, feta cheese, rolled grape leaves, savory moussaka (layered eggplant), piquant roast lamb, garlic-rubbed fish with olive oil—seems a small miracle here, half a world from the source.

Head back down Olas Altas to **Restaurant Kaiser Maximilian** (Olas Altas 380B, tel. 322/222-5058, reservations tel. 322/223-0760, 4–11 P.M. daily, entrees $12–13), at the Hotel Playa los Arcos, a prominent member of the growing roll of Olas Altos gourmet gems. Here, the Austrian expatriate owner skillfully orchestrates a cadre of chefs and waiters to produce a little bit of Vienna with a hint of California cuisine. From his long list of appetizers, consider starting off with prune-stuffed mountain quail in nine-spice sauce with polenta ($13) continue with organic salad greens in vinaigrette ($5), and finish with scalloped *rahm-schnitzel* with noodles in a cream mushroom sauce ($12) accompanied by a Monte Xanic Baja California chenin blanc ($20). If you have room, top everything off with Viennese apple strudel ($5). Alas, the only thing missing at the Maximilian is zither music playing softly in the background. Reservations strongly recommended.

Mexican food is well represented south of Cuale by a duo of good restaurants, Los Arbolitos and **The Café de Olla** (Basilio Badillo 168, tel. 322/223-1626, 9 A.M.–11 P.M. daily except Tuesday, entrees $6–10), a few doors uphill from the Olas Altas corner. During high season it will be recognizable by the flock of evening customers waiting by the door. Café de Olla serves Mexican food the way it's supposed to be, starting with enough salsa and *totopos* (chips) to make appetizers irrelevant. Your choice comes next: either chicken, ribs, and steaks from the streetfront grill, or the savory *antojitos* platters piled with tacos, tostadas, *chiles rellenos,* or enchiladas by themselves or all together in its unbeatable *plato mexicano*. Prepare by skipping lunch and arriving for an early dinner to give your tummy time to digest it all before bed.

As Archie's Wok did in the Olas Altas neighborhood, Memo Barroso's Casa de los hot Cakes has sparked a small restaurant and café renaissance on Basilio Badillo, now so popular it's becoming known as the "Calle de Cafes."

Another good place to feast is **Hacienda Alemana Frankfurt** (Basilio Badillo 378, one-half block uphill from Insurgentes, tel. 322/2071, 11 A.M.–10 P.M. daily, $8–13), the closest thing to a German *Biergarten* south of New Braunfels, Texas. Brainchild of master chef Michael Pohl, who started out with a budget hotel in 1995 (which still operates) and expanded to a garden restaurant a few years later, works his miracle with aplomb. Besides all of the German favorites, such as smoked pork chops with sauerkraut, Wiener schnitzel, bratwurst, and melt-in-your-mouth *apfel strudel*, Michael also offers popular French, Italian, and vegetarian specialties. If you can manage to skip lunch, go for Michael's all-out effort: a genuine Bavarian buffet (about $18, served Nov. through April, 6–10 P.M. Mon., Wed., and Sat., call to confirm).

If, on the other hand, you're hungry for Chinese food, go to **Dragón Rojo** (Insurgentes 323, btwn. V. Carranza and B. Badillo, tel. 322/222-0175, 1–11 P.M. daily, $5–10). Here, competent chefs put out a respectable line of the usual San Francisco-style Cantonese specialties.

A number of good restaurants offer both leisurely ambience and good food right on the bank of the Río Cuale. Moving upstream, start at the **(River Café,** beneath the downstream Avenida Vallarta bridge (tel. 322/223-0788, 9 A.M.–10 P.M. daily, entrees $8–14). Owners have earned a solid reputation, with a gorgeously tranquil streambank location, tasty international-style cuisine, and attentive service. Here, breakfast (omelettes $6–8), lunch (River Café Salad, $8) and sandwiches (vegetarian, $9), and supper (ribs, fish, and Mexican specialties, $8–14) are equally enjoyable.

Relaxing instrumental music afternoons and subdued evening jazz evenings completes the River Café's attractive picture.

For indulgently rich but good food and luxuriously leafy atmosphere, the showplace **Le Bistro** (Isla Río Cuale 16A, tel. 322/222-0283, 9 A.M.–11:30 P.M. Mon.–Sat., $10–20) is tops, just upstream from the Avenida Insurgentes bridge. Renovations with lots of marble and tile have replaced some of the former bohemian-chic décor with European-elegant. Nevertheless the relaxed, exotic ambience still remains: The river gurgles past outdoor tables, and giant-leafed plants festoon a glass ceiling, while jazz CDs play so realistically that you look in vain for the combo. It's first come, first served—reservations not accepted.

For good Mexican food, **Los Arbolitos** (Camino Rivera 184, tel. 322/223-1050, 8 A.M.–11 P.M. daily, $6–12) remains very popular with longtime Puerto Vallarta visitors, despite its out-of-the-way location (bear right at the upper end of Avenida Lázaro Cárdenas, way upstream along the Río Cuale). Here, homestyle Mexican specialties reign supreme. The house pride and joy is the Mexican plate ($12), although it serves dozens of other Mexican and international favorites. Colorful decor, second-floor river-view location, and attentive service spell plenty of satisfied customers.

Your stay in Puerto Vallarta would not be complete without sunset cocktails and dinner beneath the stars at one of Puerto Vallarta's south-of-Cuale hillside view restaurants. Of these, the **Vista Grill** (formerly Señor Chico's, at Púlpito 377, tel. 322/222-3570, 5–11 P.M. daily; reservations recommended, $10–25) continues as a visitor favorite, for its romantic atmosphere and airy town and bay view. Soft guitar solos, flickering candlelight, pastel-pink tablecloths, balmy night air, and the twinkling lights of the city below are virtually certain to make your Puerto Vallarta visit even more memorable. (Best get there by taxi. If not, turn left at Púlpito, the first left turn possible uphill past the gasoline station as you head south on Highway 200 out of town. After about two winding blocks, you'll see the Vista Grill on the left as the street tops a rise.) Winter nights, bring a sweater or jacket. The offshore breeze by 9 P.M. may be a bit cool.

North of Río Cuale

The success of the **◖ Restaurant Trio** (264 Guerrero, btwn. Hidalgo and Matamoros, tel. 322/222-2196, noon–3:30 P.M. and 6 P.M.–midnight, reservations recommended, entrees $10–16), two short blocks north of the Río Cuale, flows from an innovative Mediterranean menu and its cool, elegant candlelit atmosphere. Imaginative combinations of traditional ingredients, attentive service, and satisfying desserts topped off with savory espresso have kept customers coming back for years.

Within the bustle of the *malecón* restaurant row stands the longtime favorite **Las Palomas** (*malecón* at Aldama, tel. 322/222-3675, 8 A.M.–10 P.M. Mon.–Sat., 9 A.M.–5 P.M. Sun., entrees $5–12). Soothing suppertime live marimba music and graceful colonial decor, all beneath a towering big beamed ceiling, afford a restful contrast from the sidewalk hubbub just outside the door. Both the breakfasts and the lunch and dinner entrées (nearly all Mexican style) are tasty and bountiful.

If, however, you hanker for home-cooked Italian food, stop by **Rito's Baci** (corner of Juárez and Ortíz de Dominguez, tel. 322/222-6448, 3–11 P.M. daily, $6–12), the labor of love of the sometimes taciturn but warmhearted owner-chef, who stays open seven days a week because his "customers would be disappointed if I closed." His establishment, as plain as Kansas in July, requires no atmosphere other than Rito himself, a member of the Mexican football league hall of fame. All of his hearty specialties, from the pestos through the pastas and the eggplant Parmesan, are handmade from his family's traditional recipes.

A pair of once up-and-coming restaurants, De Santos and Los Xitomates (hee-toh-MAH-tays), on Morelos, have achieved solid success. Both rely on the current popularity of innovative Mexican cuisine. At **Los Xitomates** (570 Morelos, btwn. Aldama and Corona, tel. 322/222-1695, 6 P.M.–midnight daily,

$10–18), soft music and flickering candles set the stage, while good wine and Continental-North American-Mexican fusion cuisine provide the performance. You might start off with romaine-avocado salad dressed with Roquefort, accompanied by a glass of Chilean Calixa chardonnay ($5), followed by either barbequed breast of chicken, grilled rib-eye steak, or rice with wild mushrooms and chiles serranos; or try the steak, cut thin, accompanied by a glass of good red Chilean Concordia shiraz ($4). Reservations recommended, especially weekends.

At **◖ Restaurant de Santos** (Morelos 771, tel. 322/223-3052 or 322/223-3053, 5 P.M.–2 A.M. daily, $6–23; reservations strongly recommended), a couple of blocks farther north and across the street, the atmosphere is young, lively, and often crowded. You may have to settle for a seat at the bar, but the food is delicious and imaginative no matter where you sit. You might start with grilled asparagus in olive oil and balsamic vinaigrette, and continue with a truly delectable salmon fillet, wrapped and baked in mashed potatoes. Or take your pick from dozens more: salads, pizzas, pastas, seafood, and meats. Good for pairing are the Chilean Santa Digna sauvignon blanc and cabernet, both $5.

Good macrobiotic and vegan cuisine is getting a foothold at a number of Puerto Vallarta locations. Refined but relaxed **◖ Planeta Vegetariana** (270 Iturbide, near corner of Hidalgo, close to the church, tel. 322/222-3073, 8 A.M.–10 P.M., entrees aound $6) has achieved renown with a healthy and delicious offering for Puerto Vallarta's growing cadre of health-conscious visitors and locals. It's easy to imagine some visitor-devotees eating all their meals there. For breakfast, you could indulge in the buffet ($7) with lots of juices, fruit, pancakes, muffins, and cereals. Come back for lunch for savory-spicy black bean salad ($4) and maybe some soy enchiladas ($5). Top the day off with a supper of eggplant-banana lasagna ($6), and follow it with fruit salad ($3) for dessert.

A trio of romantic hillside restaurants concludes this selection of north-of-Cuale dining options, listed from north to south. Start out one evening beneath the striking castle-tower of 🄲 **Restaurant Café des Artistes** (740 Guadalupe Sanchez at Leona Vicario, tel. 322/222-3228 or 322/222-3229, 6–11:30 P.M. daily, reservations mandatory, latest at 10:30 P.M., entrees $10–30, most around $20). Romantics only need apply. Candlelit tables, tuxedoed servers, gently whirring ceiling fans, soothing live neoclassical melodies, and gourmet international cuisine all set a luxurious tone. You might start with your pick of soups, such as chilled cream of watercress or cream of prawn and pumpkin, and continue with a salad, perhaps the smoked salmon in puff pastry with avocado pine nut dressing. For a finale, choose honey-and soy-glazed roast duck or shrimp sautéed with cheese tortellini and served with a carrot custard and a spinach-basil puree.

Higher up the slope is the longtime favorite mid-priced **Restaurant Chez Elena** (Matamoros 520, tel. 322/222-0161, 6–10 P.M. daily, reservations recommended, closed Aug.–Sept., $8–14), on a quiet side street a few blocks above and north of the downtown church. Soft live guitar music and flickering candlelight in a colonial garden terrace set the tone, while a brief but solid Mexican-international menu, augmented by an innovative list of daily specialties, provides the food. On a typical evening, you might be able to choose between entrées such as *cochinita pibil* (Yucatecan-style shredded pork in sauce, $9), banana leaf-wrapped Oaxacan tamales ($6), or dorado fillet with cilantro in white sauce ($14). Chez Elena guests often arrive early for sunset cocktails at the rooftop panoramic view bar and then continue with dinner downstairs.

Finally, highest on the hill, treat yourself to dinner at Puerto Vallarta's most uniquely private restaurant, at the elegant, boutique fifteen-room **Hacienda San Ángel** hotel (Miramar 336, Puerto Vallarta, Jalisco 48300, tel. 322/222-2692 or 322/221-2277, www.hacienda sanangel.com, dinner 6–10 P.M.,). Personable owner Janice Chatterton initially created her restaurant for her in-house guests, but now extends her invitation to all lovers of fine fusion Mexican-Continental-North American cuisine. Some of her favorite recommendations include, for starters, smoked salmon *carpaccio* ($9) and/or grilled vegetables ($7). Continue with shrimp coconut cream soup ($7) and climax it all with roasted half chicken, stuffed with cuitlacoche. ($15).

Entertainment and Events

Puerto Vallarta is a town brimming with entertainments, most of them spontaneous. The glowing sunsets, the balmy evening sea breeze, the crowds of relaxed folks out and about, and the abundance of sidewalk stands, selling everything from paintings to popcorn, are continuous sources of impromptu diversions. Add to that the more formal entertainments, such as the *malecón*-front nightclubs, discos, Mexican fiesta tourist shows, quiet refined side-street bars, plus all the traditional festivals—Virgin of Guadalupe, Mexican Independence, Carnaval and much more—and you'll have enough to enjoy a party for every day you spend in Puerto Vallarta.

The *malecón*, where the sunsets seem the most beautiful in town, is a perfect place to begin the evening. Make sure you eventually make your way to the downtown central plaza by the Presidencia Municipal (City Hall). On both weekday and weekend nights, the city often sponsors free music and dance concerts beginning around 8 P.M. at the bayside **Los Arcos** (Arches) amphitheater. (For current listings, see the events calendar listing of tourist newspapers *Vallarta Today* or *Vallarta Tribune*.)

After the concert, join the crowds watching the impromptu antics of the *mimos* (mimes) on the amphitheater stage and the nearby street artists painting plates, watercolor country

Shady *palapas* line the beach just north of New Pier.

scenes, and fanciful, outer-galaxy spray-can spacescapes.

If you miss the Los Arcos concert, you can usually console yourself with a balloon, *palomitas* (popcorn), and sometimes a band concert in the plaza. If you're inconsolable, buy some peanuts, a roasted ear of sweet corn, or a hot dog from a vendor. After that, cool down with an *agua* or *jugo* (fruit juice) from the *juguería* across the bayside plaza corner, or a cone of ice cream from Baskin-Robbins (Morelos 420), a few blocks north of City Hall.

A tranquil south-of-Cuale spot to cool off evenings is the **Muelle Nuevo** (New Pier) at the foot of Francisca Rodríguez (beach side of Hotel Playa Los Arcos). On a typical evening you'll find a couple of dozen folks—men, women, and kids—enjoying the breeze and the swish of the surf, and, with nets or lines, trying to catch a few fish for sale or dinner.

NIGHTLIFE

The popularity of Puerto Vallarta's nightlife scene has given it an extra touch of sophistica-

tion that many other beach destinations don't share. There's something for everyone here: The offerings range from quiet neighborhood bars and numerous terraces with oceanview tables to ultra-cool rooftop lounges and pounding dance clubs. Since Puerto Vallarta is a top destination for Mexicans and foreigners alike, you can expect to find an international clientele at many of the trendy nightspots.

For the visitor, this means that a night out isn't the inexpensive fun it once was. It's much harder on the wallet these days, but on the other hand, you won't have any trouble finding a bartender who will pour you a wicked cosmopolitan or offer a lengthy martini or margarita menu with flavors that you hadn't dreamed existed. You'll need to dress up more than you might when clubbing in other beach destinations, but don't forget to wear comfortable shoes: There aren't just the long nights of dancing to consider, there are also the cobblestone streets. But some things are the same as the rest of Mexico: The action doesn't really start until after midnight.

PUERTO VALLARTA

The night scene isn't just for drinking and dancing anymore. In earlier decades, late-night dining options consisted of the corner taco stand or the other corner taco stand. Now the growing popularity of nightclubs with food on premises allows you more than just a toss-it-down snack. Whether it's sushi or tapas, it may be just what you needed to catch that second (or third) wind.

As the hot spot for gay travelers in Mexico, Puerto Vallarta has seen an increase in the range and refinement of the gay night-life choices as well. There are drag shows and friendly local bars, along with the pick-me-up, toss-me-down, shake-it-loose joints and strip clubs. Many gay bars are located in the Romantic Zone or Zona Romántica, a commonly used moniker for the area south of the Cuale River in downtown Puerto Vallarta. Home to street-side coffee shops, restaurants, clubs, shops and boutiques, this area is a great place to spend the evening just walking around the casual streets of the neighborhood.

All this sophistication doesn't mean that people looking for the serious party scene will be disappointed. Puerto Vallarta has a lot of raucous nightspots, especially along the *malecón* during spring break and the student month of June. Whatever your taste, you're bound to find something fun. Just get out there: The night lasts forever and the sun comes up late in Vallarta.

Bars and Lounges

Romantics might enjoy whiling away some time at the **Oceano Bar** (corner of Galeana, upstairs, overlooking the *malecón*), once the bar of the long-gone Oceano Hotel, Puerto Vallarta's first deluxe. Enjoy the ocean view and even maybe a palm-silhouetted sunset, and dream about those days long ago when lovers Richard Burton and Elizabeth Taylor enjoyed the same view when they stayed together in the hotel.

Farther north another block, traditionalists often enjoy **Restaurant Las Palomas** (corner of Aldama, tel. 322/222-3675), which features live marimba music 7–10 P.M. and a mariachi guitar trio after that.

The jungle never sleeps at **Mogambo** (Paseo Díaz Ordaz 644, *malecón,* tel. 322/222-3476, www.mogambo-vallarta.com, 5:30 P.M.–3 A.M. daily), where animal prints and spears decorate the walls and cover the furniture. The jukebox primarily turns out rock and pop and attracts the late crowds. Stop in early for a drink with friends, and you'll have the place to yourselves. The casual atmosphere and open windows that face the sea and the Malecón make for a nice impromptu stop when strolling the busy main street. A half block farther north, restaurant **La Dolce Vita** (corner of Domínguez, tel. 322/222-3852, 10 P.M.–midnight in season) entertains dinner customers with live Latin and Cuban music.

Those who desire a more refined, romantic ambience go to **Restaurant Café des Artistes** (tel. 322/222-3228) and take a table for dinner or a seat at the bar, where they enjoy soothing neoclassical flute–accompanied piano melodies nightly during high season, Friday and Saturday during low season. Find it by walking three blocks along Leona Vicario inland from the *malecón.*

Built high into the night sky of downtown Puerto Vallarta, the ultra-chic **Azul 96** (Morelos 696, Centro, tel. 322/222-1022, www.azul96.com, 6 P.M.–4 A.M. daily) rivals bars in New York and Mexico City. This third-floor beach club comes complete with sand, a view of the sea, and a retractable roof for stargazing. Nosh on sushi and other nibbles while choosing from the extensive cocktail and wine list with martini specials and swaying to the tune of international DJs. Dress trendy and join the scene of restless moneyed youth of urban Mexico.

For a romantic tête-à-tête, there's simply no place like **Costantini Wine Bar** (Guadalupe Sánchez 740, Centro, tel. 322/222-3228, www.cafedesartistes.com, 6 P.M.–1 A.M. daily): Its dark red interior with high-backed banquettes holds many hidden corners. Local pianist Enrique provides live piano music, and on weekends Don and Rhonda perform their review, full of singable melodies from the '70s. Free wine tastings are offered on Thursday nights

(6–7 P.M.), giving you the chance to discover new favorites from the unmatched wine list, accompanied by a full selection of *botanas* (snacks). This is also a downtown hotspot for business cocktails and can be a fun gathering place for friends or co-workers.

Founded by one of the band members of the international group Maná, **De Santos** (Morelos 771, Centro, tel. 322/223-3052, www .desantos.com.mx, 10 P.M.–6 A.M. Wed.–Sat.) tends to draw names from Mexico and abroad. Although it's also known as a restaurant, De Santos is one of the best nightspots in town. Relax with a cocktail at one of the prime tables or the long mirrored bar on the first floor, or climb the stairs to the upper terrace, where you can sip your martini on a gauze-curtained bed under the stars and the house music keeps things cool. Modern, trendy, and the place to be seen, De Santos also draws the late-night dance crowds with the hottest DJs.

Located just a block off the *malecón* on Morelos, **La Cantina** (Morelos 709, Centro, tel. 322/222-1734 or 322/-1629, www .etcbeach.com, 11:59 A.M.–2 A.M. Sun.–Tues., 11:59 A.M.–4 A.M. Wed.–Sat.) is a popular smoky hangout for students who need a break between classes or finals. La Cantina is genuine and doesn't give a thought to tourists, since not many of them find their way here. The dark interior feels homey, and the canned music, which ranges from *banda* to mariachi to ballads, adds to the very Mexican ambience, while the high ceilings lend a '40s-hacienda atmosphere. This place is best for talking with groups of friends rather than dancing or clubbing.

The international **Nikki Beach** (Hotel Westin Regina at Paseo de la Marina Sur 205, Marina Vallarta, tel. 322/226-1150, www .nikkibeach.com/pv, 10 A.M.–4 A.M. daily) lost no time in getting established in sophisticated Marina Vallarta, where the beachfront location offers everything not only to the nighttime reveler but also the daytime sun worshipper. Weekly fashion events, daily sunset parties, regular VIP invitations, and Sunday brunch make Nikki Beach the happening place all day, but it's after the sun goes

down that it really comes alive. While drinks are expensive, the crowd is sure to be beautiful, and the service is top-notch. There's also a limited late-hour menu.

In classy Mexican style, **Tequilas de Noche** (Galeana 104–101, *malecón*, tel. 322/222-2733, 6 P.M.—11 P.M. daily) offers an evening of traditional live mariachi from one of the best local groups. Two soloists, one male, one female, will twist your heartstrings with their renditions of classics olden and golden. Sipping a margarita made with the best tequila while watching the sun slip below the horizon from the second-floor balconies will make all seem right with the world. This is where to go when you want to feel like you're in Mexico without the tourist trappings. Even though tourists might be sitting at the next table, you can be sure locals visit this favorite.

Facing onto the *malecón* from an open second-floor balcony, the smashing new **Ztai** (Morelos 737, Centro, tel. 322/222-0306, www.ztai.com, 6 P.M.–5 A.M. daily) throbs with a beat of its own, fueled by heavy rock from a good sound system. Drinks are made with flash and presented with flourish. When the decibels are high, the crowd stays young, but on gentler nights earlier in the week, even 30-somethings will trip up those stairs for the seashore view. It's a pleasant place to have a cocktail either before dinner or after when you don't have dancing in mind.

The increasingly popular small entertainment district, spread along I. Vallarta, near the corner of L. Cárdenas, has acquired a number of lively spots, among them the popular **Mariachis Locos** bar/restaurant (tel. 322/223-2205). Inside, a mostly local straight clientele enjoys a lively nonstop mariachi show nightly from about 11 P.M. to the wee hours.

For good food with your entertainment, continue south on I. Vallarta a block, to the corner of Vallarta and Carranza and the longtime favorite **Restaurant El Torito** (tel. 322/222-3784, 10 P.M.–5 A.M. nightly); reasonably priced barbequed ribs are their specialty, with DJ music to boot.

A number of popular bars and night spots

entertain folks along Avenida Olas Altas. For example, many folks' nights wouldn't be complete without stopping in at the **Ándale** Mexican pub (Olas Altas 425, 322/222-1054, open until around 2 A.M.), whose atmosphere is so amicable and lively that few even bother to watch the nonstop TV. If the night is still young, continue a block to the beachfront foot of Francisca Rodríguez and restaurant **Cuates and Cuetes** for innovative live Latin jazz, beginning around 7:30 nightly.

Dance Clubs

Celebrating 30 years of existence, **Carlos O'Brian's** (Paseo Díaz Ordaz 796, *malecón*, tel. 322/222-1444, www.carlos-obrians .com, 11 A.M.–4 A.M. daily) is a local institution on the *malecón*. They used to say if you haven't been here, you haven't been to Vallarta. Today, it continues to be a popular place for tourists who want to party with people they don't know. The age range spans college-age youngsters to middle-aged empty nesters. Tall beers and energetic waiters add to the festive atmosphere, so be prepared to say hello to your neighbors as you share tequila shots.

At the time it was built, **Christine** (NH Krystal Hotel, Zona Hotelera, tel. 322/224-6990, 10 P.M.–6 A.M. daily; cover varies) was the best modern disco in town, and served tourists and visitors more than the local community. While still chic, Christine is now more democratic, but prices can still be high for locals. The indoor auditorium-style design allows for viewing the dance floor from any angle. With flashing lights and pounding music, this young persons' paradise is worth dancing the night away.

Hard Rock Cafe (Paseo Díaz Ordaz 652, *malecón*, tel. 322/222-2230, www.hardrock .com, 11 A.M.–2 A.M. daily), the Vallarta location of the international chain, offers friendly, efficient service with the same menu you've come to know if you're a fan. The music is loud, even in the daytime, but then that comes with the territory. On weekends there is usually live rock music from local and visiting bands, and a small dance floor will let you warm up since the space always seems to be chilly from strong air-conditioning. College-age tourists take over Hard Rock after midnight, but the atmosphere is more family-oriented during the earlier hours.

When **Hilo** (Paseo Díaz Ordaz 588, *malecón*, tel. 322/223-5361, www.hilobardance .com, 4 P.M.–4 A.M. daily) opened across from the *malecón*, the two-floor-high sculpture of a woman leaning out to peer toward the sea caused a sensation. The oceanview tables here are great for a drink at sunset. A high second-floor mezzanine might cause vertigo, but climb up to find yourself above the very Mexican sculptures. The dance floor gets crowded with tourists sometime after midnight, and the music pounds into the night at this fun club. The later it gets, the higher the decibels, so don't plan on talking once the dancing starts.

Pronounced "ho-ta-bei" for the letters JB in Spanish, **J&B** (Francisco Medina Ascencio 2043, Zona Hotelera, tel. 322/224-4616, www.jbdiscoclub.com, 10 P.M.–6 A.M. daily, cover $9) offers the best ambience for dancing to Latin music with locals. (The club actually opens at 8 P.M. for dance classes during the week. See www.tangobar-productions.com for information.) The night usually starts with DJ-spun music, but on weekends it alternates with live music. Try out your steps in salsa, rumba, merengue, cha-cha, tango, and more in this true community spot where most people get on the floor and dance. If you're part of a group, buy an entire bottle of liquor with mixers for a better deal.

Cuba staunchly holds its own in downtown Puerto Vallarta with **La Bodeguita del Medio** (Paseo Díaz Ordaz 858, *malecón*, tel. 322/223-1585, 8 A.M.–1 A.M. daily), which serves up not only the best *mojitos* in town but also the hottest live Latin music. The tiny dance floor doesn't deter reveling regulars. Revolutionary Cuba is reflected in the huge one-star flag that covers one wall, while the other walls are scribbled with notes, signatures, and epithets in pre-revolutionary style.

The rhythm of the Caribbean fills the large Big Band–style space of **Mambocafé**

(Plaza Marina, local A-50, Marina Vallarta, tel. 322/221-1940, www.mambocafe.com.mx, 10 P.M.–5 A.M. Wed.–Sat., cover $3–6), part of a national chain that has locations in all the coastal tourist destinations. This place was made for dancing, and that's exactly what the locals come to do: The floor hosts mambo, samba, cha-cha, and more, with live music to keep it all going. The crowd tends to be older, and the attire is on the classy side, with women in slinky dresses and men in slacks and shirts—and everyone is wearing good dance shoes. Avoid the drinks—they are not cheap and not even very good.

With the slogan "Please don't act your age," **Señor Frog's** (Venustiano Carranza 218, Zona Romántica, tel. 322/222-5177, www.senorfrogs.com/puertovallarta, 10 P.M.–4 A.M. Tues., Fri., and Sat., 10 P.M.–1 A.M. all other nights) is where to have a casual, raucous evening. Wet T-shirt contests say it all, but they're equal opportunity: There are wet-shorts nights as well. DJs usually keep the place hopping, but on special occasions there is live music with a cover charge. Drinks are large and run freely. Expect dancing on the bar, although not necessarily by those trained to do so. A limited menu is also available for patrons in need of a few more calories to keep the night going.

When you want to dance and conga line with strangers, the **Zoo** (Paseo Díaz Ordaz 630, malecón, tel. 322/222-4945, www.zoobardance.com, 11 A.M.–6 A.M. daily) is the perfect spot to release inhibitions that were in hiding until a couple of tequila shots jolted them loose. A 200-pound costumed gorilla may meet you on the street to invite you in, where a party of tourists will most likely become your new best friends. The decor of mounted animal heads and other zoo-like paraphernalia lives up to this nightspot's name.

Gay Venues

A comfortable street-side neighborhood bar, **Apaches** (Olas Altas 439, Zona Romántica, tel. 322/222-5235, apaches2000@yahoo.com, 4 P.M.–1 A.M. Mon.–Sat.) isn't trying to amaze or astound you, so expect to be able to relax,

whether with old or new friends. A longtime favorite of locals and repeat visitors to Vallarta, this lesbian-owned establishment always treats you like you matter. While it sometimes might be a bit dusty around the edges, it's always a great place to spend the afternoon or evening.

Los Amigos (Venustiano Carranza 239, Zona Romántica, tel. 322/222-7802, www.losamigosbar.com, 6 P.M.–4 A.M. daily) brings in those who are not necessarily on the prowl or trying to be chic. The friendly service convinces patrons to stick around this laid-back neighborhood hangout, despite the draw of two popular gay hangouts next door. Daily specials offered 6–8 P.M. include 20-peso cocktails and 10-peso beers.

In a well-located space that previously housed the popular Palms, **Bench and Bar** (Olas Altas 508, Zona Romántica, tel. 322/223-4818, www.bench-and-bar.com, 9 P.M.–2 A.M. Mon.–Thurs., 9 P.M.–4 A.M. Fri.–Sat.) produces hot Latin nights with men, music, and drink specials. Wi-Fi is free for patrons, and a full events calendar keeps the regulars entertained. The stage features Ida Slapter's popular drag show, and happy hour is 5–9 P.M. daily. Stop in early or stay late. Entertainment nights usually have a cover charge.

Primarily serving the guests of the Blue Chairs Resort, **Blue Sunset Roof Bar** (Hotel Blue Chairs Resort, Zona Romántica, tel. 322/222-5040, www.bluechairs.com, 7 P.M.–11 P.M. daily) is nevertheless accessible by elevator to the passing public. Ask about the entertainment—frequently a visiting chanteuse or reigning drag queen will put on a show on the weekends during the busy season. The friendly wait staff will keep that drink refreshed, and the casual atmosphere opens up the possibility of meeting new friends.

The Cheeky Monkey (Corona at the malecón, www.cheekymonkeypv.com, noon–4 A.M. daily) is the only gay-owned club on the popular malecón in downtown Vallarta. Climb to the third floor after locating the side door on Corona, just in from the corner of Paseo Díaz Ordaz. Good drinks and snacks are served with panache and a friendly flair. Don't take the raunchy website too seriously—this place is quite tame and friendly. It's no problem to bring your straight friends, either.

For years, **Paco Paco** (Ignacio L. Vallarta 278, Zona Romántica, tel 322/222-1899, www.club-pacopaco.com, 1 P.M.–6 A.M. daily) was the key dance club for all of Vallarta, gay or straight, offering the latest dance music, two drag shows nightly, and a strip show next door at The Ranch. Although it got going late like all clubs, this one also had a rooftop bar for drinks at sunset for early arrivals. During the busy season, live music was not unusual. Drinks were good and prices were cheap. But since the arrival of so many other intriguing clubs, Paco Paco is still trying to win back its previous popularity.

A heavy calendar of activities has built up a following at **Dewayne's Oasis** (Pilitas 156, Zona Romántica, tel. 322/223-5273, www .dewaynesoasis.com, 4 P.M.–2 A.M. daily), a friendly bar with a neighborhood Mexican atmosphere. There are regular drink specials, and the "famous" Papi Chulo dancers offer two shows Tuesday, Friday, and Saturday, with Sunday being Absolut Madness. The terrace and balcony offer only a view of the buildings that front the bay, but at least you can get some fresh air.

With lipstick-red interiors adorned with black-and-white Hollywood glossies from earlier days, neighborhood-y **Diva's** (Francisco Madero 388, Zona Romántica, tel. 322/222-7774, www.divaspv.com, 6 P.M.–2 A.M. daily) is a great place to go alone or with friends early in the evening before strapping on your dance shoes. The drinks are good, and the service is at your elbow without being in your face. And you don't have to worry about offending anyone if you don't feel like chatting up the regulars—the crowd will respect your privacy. You may have to search for the bar, however, as it's nearly hidden on a side street at the exit of the popular Cine Bahía.

Frida (Lázaro Cárdenas 361, Zona Romántica, no phone, www.fridaunbar.com, 1 P.M.–2 A.M. daily) would have been called a dive in other days, but is actually a quite-friendly neighborhood bar—a good place to go with old friends. The pool table takes your mind off the drink in your hands, but the jukebox can sometimes make it difficult to talk. Beer is the beverage of choice and rugged jeans are the preferred attire among the crowd here, primarily older locals and their young friends.

There are few places like **Garbo** (Púlpito 142, Zona Romántica, tel. 322/229-7309, www.bargarbo.com, 6 P.M.–2 A.M. daily), where you can sit and chat with friends in comfort or flirt with your neighbor with ease in the same breath. A regular spot for many local professionals, usually during happy hour, Garbo gives you space and respect but you're always welcome to join the party. Sit at the high bar or find a quiet four-top with chairs or banquettes. Weekends may bring the added benefit of live music, usually on piano, but it's not overwhelming.

Folks crowd in at **Rojan** bar and nightclub (at the southwest corner of Lazaro Cardenas and Ignacio Vallarta), where personable owner Robert Gonzales wants his patrons to enjoy a "truly Mexican experience." The name of his club comes from a legendary Olmec shaman that Robert brought back from 3,000 years of history and whom he illustrates by a mural in the downstairs bar. Upstairs, in the nightclub concert and dance hall, programs of live salsa, reggae, and rock entertain patrons from around 11 P.M. Friday, Saturday, and Sunday low season and Tuesday–Sunday high.

Although primarily known as a restaurant, **Kitkat** (Púlpito 120, Zona Romántica, tel. 322/223-0093, 6 P.M.–2 A.M. daily) broke into the night scene with weekend drag shows that romped right past the diners, gay and straight alike. Outdoor street-side tables allow for a romantic evening under starlit trees, while the interior is heavily air-conditioned with its own dramatic ambience. Drink specials include martinis.

A drink in a romantic corner is the specialty of **La Noche** (Lázaro Cárdenas 257, Zona Romántica, tel. 322/222-3364, www .lanochepv.com, 6 P.M.–3 A.M. daily), where the dimly lit air-conditioned interior removes you from the busy world and the lively music varies from Broadway to Latin. A hangout for a slightly older crowd, this neighborhood bar has cubicle-like seating that provides a private space for that budding romance or friendship, and the huge old-fashioned chandelier is a nice overhead touch.

When **Mañana** (Venustiano Carranza 290, Zona Romántica, tel. 322/222-7772, www.manana.com.mx, 10 P.M.–6 A.M. daily) opened, even local politicians showed up. It's the first club of this category that has been able to break into the local scene, changing it forever, probably. The charming hacienda has a private garden with patios; a swimming pool; air-conditioned disco; great shows featuring singers, drag queens, and strippers; VIP lounge; drink specials; and more. The normal $10 cover charge gives you unlimited Coronas or one free national drink. Besides all that, their prime location in the Zona Romántica allows easy access by local transportation.

When you're wandering around and just want to sit down and put up those feet, trip up to **Sama** (Olas Altas 510, Zona Romántica, tel. 322/223-3182, 5 P.M.–2 A.M. Tues.–Sun.), a sidewalk cocktail bar with shaded tables and nibbles to eat in case you're hungry. Service is quick and friendly, and the drinks are good and strong. While not a destination in itself, Sama nevertheless attracts a healthy clientele who decides to stick around for further drinks while enjoying the good people-watching.

Overstuffed couches, large bronze sculptures of goddesses, and a breezy interior cooled by huge fans give the **Uncommon Grounds Buddha Lounge** (Lázaro Cárdenas 625, Zona Romántica, tel. 322/223-3834, www.uncommon-grounds .com, 4 P.M.–close Tues.–Sun.) a comfortable feel. Stop in for a drink and chat with the owners, a vivacious lesbian couple from New Jersey who fell in love with Vallarta—these friendly women give this popular spot its character. Daily drink specials include such toothsome drinks as raspberry *mojitos* and mango margaritas. This is a good place to go either to meet friends for a drink early in the evening or to get to know someone new.

Jarabes ("sweet") courtship dances are almost always performed as part of Puerto Vallarta's tourist shows.

LIVE SHOWS AND CINEMA
Tourist Shows

Visitors who miss the real-life fiestas can still enjoy one of several local **Fiesta Mexicana** tourist shows, which are as popular with Mexican tourists as foreigners. The evening typically begins with a sumptuous buffet of salads, tacos, enchiladas, seafood, barbecued meats, and flan and pastries for dessert. Then begins a nonstop program of music and dance from all parts of Mexico: a chorus of revolutionary *soldaderas* and their Zapatista male compatriots; raven-haired señoritas in flowing, flowered Tehuantepec silk dresses; rows of dashing Guadalajaran *charros* twirling their fast-stepping *chinas poblanas* sweethearts, climaxing with enough fireworks to swab the sky red, white, and green.

The south-of-Cuale **Restaurant Iguana** (Calle Lázaro Cárdenas 311, btwn. Insurgentes and Constitución, tel. 322/222-0105) stages very popular and *auténtico* shows Thursday and Sunday around 5 and 7 P.M. (Sun. only in the low season, call ahead to confirm). Other reliable bets are tourist shows at the **Hotel NH Krystal** (tel. 322/224-0202, Tues. at 7 P.M.) and the **Sheraton** (tel. 322/226-0404, Thurs). Call ahead to confirm progarms. Tariff for these shows typically runs $40–50 per person with open bar. During holidays and the high winter season, reservations are generally necessary; best book through a travel or tour desk agent.

Live Music

Cover charges are not generally required at the hotel bars, many of which offer live music and dancing. Among the most reliable venues are the **Sheraton** (tel. 322/224-0202), the **Marriott** (tel. 322/226-0000), the **Fiesta Americana** (tel. 322/226-2100), and the **Playa los Arcos** (tel. 322/226-7100). Be sure to phone ahead to check programs.

Many Puerto Vallarta restaurants also offer low- to medium-volume live music accompaniment with your evening meal. For example, for Latin music try **La Palapa** (tel. 322/222-5225), on Playa los Muertos beach just north of the new pier. For Latin jazz, go to **Cuates y Cuetes** (tel. 322/222-9511), also on Playa los Muertos; and the **River Cafe** (modern classical-style, tel. 322/223-0788) on Isla Río Cuale, below the downstream Avenida Vallarta bridge; or **El Set** (tel. 322/221-5341) view restaurant, about a mile south of town. For more live music listings, see the nightlife and events pages in *Puerto Vallarta Today* and the *Vallarta Tribune*.

Movies

A number of movie houses entertain residents and visitors. South of Cuale, find the **Cine Bahía** (Insurgentes 63, btwn. Madero and Serdán, tel. 322/222-1717), which remains a typical 1950s-style small-town movie house. Managers run a mixture of Mexican and American pop horror, romantic comedy, and action. Another similar neighborhood movie house on the north side of town is the **Cine Versalles** on

side street Francisco Villa 799, a block north of the sports field, across the airport boulevard from the Hotel Sheraton.

FESTIVALS AND EVENTS

Puerto Vallarta residents enjoy their share of local fiestas. Preparations for **Semana Santa** (Holy Week) begin in February, often with a **Carnaval** parade and dancing on Shrove Tuesday, and continue for the seven weeks before Easter. Each Friday until Easter, you might see processions of people bearing crosses filing through the downtown for special Masses at neighborhood churches. This all culminates during Easter week, when Puerto Vallarta is awash with visitors, crowding the hotels, camping on the beaches, and filing in somber processions, which finally brighten to fireworks, dancing, and food on Domingo Gloria (Easter Sunday).

The town quiets down briefly until the **Fiesta de Mayo,** a countrywide celebration of sports contests, music and dance performances, art shows, parades, and beauty pageants.

On the evening of **September 15,** the Plaza de Armas (City Hall plaza) fills with tipsy merrymakers, who gather to hear the mayor reaffirm Mexican independence by shouting the Grito de Dolores—"Long Live Mexico! Death to the Gachupines!"—under booming, brilliant cascades of fireworks.

Celebration again breaks out seriously during the first 12 days of December, when city groups—businesses, families, neighborhoods—try to outdo each other with music, floats, costumes, and offerings all in honor of Mexico's patron, the Virgin of Guadalupe. The revelry climaxes on **December 12,** when people, many in native garb to celebrate their indigenous origins, converge on the downtown church to receive the Virgin's blessing. If you miss the main December Virgin of Guadalupe fiesta, you can still enjoy a similar but smaller-scale celebration in El Tuito (see the *Jalisco Coast* chapter) a month later, on January 12.

Sports and Recreation

Some people believe that Puerto Vallarta is too warm for sports; but that's not necessarily the case, especially since water sports couldn't be more perfect during the warm midday, while jogging, tennis and golf are best early mornings and late afternoons. Whatever the case, Puerto Vallarta affords plenty of opportunities for exercising your bliss.

SWIMMING, SURFING, AND BOOGIE BOARDING

While Puerto Vallarta's calm waters are generally safe for swimming, they are often too tranquil for surfing, bodysurfing, and boogie boarding. Sometimes strong, surfable waves rise along the southern half of **Playa los Muertos.** Another notable possibility is at the mouth of the Ameca River (north of the airport) where, during the rainy summer season, the large river flow helps create bigger-than-

normal waves. Surfing is more rewarding and common at Bucerías and Punta Mita.

SAILBOARDING AND SAILBOATING

A small but growing nucleus of local sailboarding enthusiasts practice the sport from Puerto Vallarta's beaches. They sometimes hold a **sailboarding tournament** during the citywide Fiesta de Mayo in the first week of May. For more information, contact Puerto Vallarta tourist information, tel. 325/223-2500, ext. 230 or 232.

Sail Vallarta (tel. 322/221-0096 or 221-0097), which operates from Marina Vallarta, takes parties out on sailing excursions, as does **Vallarta Adventures** (tel. 322/297-1212, from U.S., toll-free 888/303-2653, info@vallarta -adventures.com, www.vallarta-adventures.com) for $160 for two. Ask for a low-season discount.

© BRUCE WHIPPERMAN

Playa Olas Altas, which begins at the New Pier, is the northerly continuation of Playa los Muertos.

If you're seriously interested in learning to sail, check out **Vallarta Explorer** (cell tel. in Puerto Vallarta, 044-322/779-7526. www.vallarta explorere.com), who, in addition to taking you on a sailboat ride, offers comprehensive how-to-sail instruction.

SNORKELING AND SCUBA DIVING

Although Vallarta Adventures also offers scuba diving services, the biggest scuba instructor/outfitter in town is **Chico's Dive Shop** (malecón at Díaz Ordaz 770, btwn. Pípila and Vicario, tel. 322/222-1895, fax 322/222-2210, www .chicosdiveshop.com, 8 A.M.–10 P.M. daily). Chico's offers complete lessons, arranges and leads dive trips, and rents scuba equipment to qualified divers (bring your certificate). A beginning scuba lesson in the pool runs about $26, after which you'll be qualified to dive at Los Arcos. A day boat trip, including one 40-minute dive, costs $59 per person (two tanks, $80), gear included. Snorkelers on the same trip pay about $38. Chico's takes certified divers only to the **Marietas Islands,** the best site in the bay, for $100, including gear and two dives, and sandwiches and sodas for lunch.

PERSONAL WATERCRAFT, WATERSKIING, AND PARASAILING

These are available right on the beach at a number of the northside resort-hotels, such as the Sheraton, Las Palmas by the Sea, Fiesta Americana Puerto Vallarta, and NH Krystal.

The same sports are also seasonally available south of Cuale on Playa los Muertos, in front of the Hotels Playa los Arcos and Tropicana. Expect to pay about $50 per half hour for a personal watercraft, $75/hour for waterskiing, and $25 for a 10-minute parasail.

BOATING

The superb 350-berth **Marina Vallarta** (P.O. Box 350-B, Puerto Vallarta, Jalisco 48300, tel. 322/221-0275, fax 322/221-0722) has all possible hookups, including certified potable water, metered 110–220-volt electricity, phone, fax, showers, toilets, laundry, dock lockers, trash collection, and pump-out. Other amenities include 24-hour security, a yacht club, and complete repair yard. It is surrounded by luxurious condominiums, tennis courts, a golf course, and dozens of shops and offices. Slip rates run around $.75 per foot per day for 1–6 days, $.60 for 7–29 days, and $.50 for 30 or more days.

You can also drop by the Marina office (9 A.M.–2 P.M. and 4–7 P.M. Mon.–Fri., 9 A.M.–2 P.M. Sat.). Get there from the airport boulevard, northbound, by turning left at the main marina turnoff (marked by the huge Neptune sculpture on the building to the left.) After two blocks, bear left at the fork, on to Paseo Marina. Timón is the next street on the left. The marina office is at the foot of Timón, on the left, beneath the embarcadero-front portal.

The Marina also has a **public boat-launching ramp** where you can float your craft into the Marina's sheltered waters for a nominal fee. If the guard isn't available to open the gate, call the marina office for entry permission. To get to the launch ramp, follow the street marked Proa, next to the big pink and white disco, one block south of the main Marina Vallarta entrance (below the monumental Neptune statue on the corner building).

SPORTFISHING

At their present rate of attrition, sailfish and marlin will someday certainly disappear from Puerto Vallarta waters. Some captains and participants have fortunately seen the light and are releasing the fish after they're hooked, in accordance with IFGA (International Fish and Game Association) guidelines.

You can hire a *panga* (outboard launch) with skipper on the beach in front of several hotels, such as Los Arcos on Playa Los Muertos; the Buenaventura and Sheraton on Playa los Camarones; the Plaza Pelícanos, Las Palmas Resort, and Fiesta Americana Puerto Vallarta on Playa las Glorias; and NH Krystal on Playa de Oro. Expect to pay about $25/hour for a two- or three-hour trip that might net you and a few friends some jack, bonito, *toro,* or dorado for dinner. Ask your favorite local-style restaurant to fix your catch.

Another good spot for *panga* rentals is near the **Peines** (pay-EE-nays) docks, where the fishermen keep their boats. You may be able to negotiate a good price, especially if you or a friend speaks Spanish. Access to the Peines is along the dirt road to the left of the Isla Iguana entrance (just adjacent, south, to the fake roadside lighthouse a mile north of the Marina cruise ship terminal). The fisherfolk, a score or so members of the Cooperativa de Deportes Aquaticos Bahía de Banderas, have their boats lined up along the roadside channel to the left, a few hundred yards from the highway.

At the end-of-the-road dock complex (the actual Peines), behind the entrance gate, lie the big-game sportfishing boats that you can reserve only through agents back in town at the hotels. Agents such as American Express (tel. 322/223-2910, 322/223-2927, or 322/223-2955, fax 322/223-2926) customarily book reservations during high season on the big 40-foot boats. They go out mornings at 7:30 A.M. and return about seven hours later with an average of one big fish per boat. The tariff runs around $100 per person; food and drinks are available but cost extra. Big boats generally have space for 10 passengers, about half of whom can fish at any one time. Most everyone usually gets something, if not a big sailfish or marlin.

A local agency that rents sportfishing boats is the **Sociedad Cooperativa Progreso Turístico** (north end of the *malecón* at 31 de Octubre, across from Hotel Rosita, tel. 322/222-1202) which has 4 boats, ranging 32–40 feet. Rentals run $350–450 per day for a completely outfitted boat. It's best to talk to the manager, who is usually there 8 A.M.–noon and 4–8 P.M. Mon.–Sat.

A number of local English-speaking captains regularly take parties out on their well-equipped sportfishing boats. Alex Gómez, known as **Mr. Marlin** (tel. 322/221-0809 at the Tennis Club Puesta del Sol deli, info@mrmarlin.com, www.mrmarlin.com) and record-holder of the biggest marlin catch in Puerto Vallarta, acts as agent for more than 40 experienced captains.

Prices begin at about $300 for a 26-foot boat, $575 for a 35-foot boat, for a full day, including bait, ice, and fishing tackle.

Alternatively, go **Fishing with Carolina** and Captain Juan (call Candace Caroline Shaw for information and reservations, tel. 322/224-7250, local cell phone 044-322/292-2953, fishingwithcarolina@hotmail.com, www.mexonline.com/fishingwithcarolina.htm), who offer sportfishing, whale-watching, and snorkeling expeditions on their fully equipped diesel boat. Two anglers go all day for $125 per person, three for $350.

Call Mr. Marlin if you'd like to enter the Puerto Vallarta **Sailfish Tournament** (322/221-0809, info@fishingvallarta.com, www.fishvallarta.com); it's held annually in November (2007 marks the 52nd). The registration fee runs about $1,200 per participant, which includes the welcome dinner and the closing awards dinner. The five grand prizes usually include automobiles. The biggest sailfish caught was a 168-pounder in 1957.

Freshwater bass fishing is also an option, at lovely foothill Cajón de Peñas Reservoir (see the *Jalisco Coast* chapter), on your own or with **Viva Tours** (tel. 322/224-0410 or 322/224-0826, tel./fax 322/224-0182). For about $150 per person, minimum four persons, you get all transportation, breakfast and lunch, fishing license, guide, and gear. The lake record is 13 pounds.

JOGGING AND WALKING

Puerto Vallarta's cobbled streets, high curbs (towering sometimes to 6 feet!), and holey sidewalks make for tricky walking around town. The exception is the *malecón*, which can provide a good two-mile round-trip jog when it isn't crowded. Otherwise, try the beaches or the big public sports field, Unidad Deportiva on the airport boulevard north of downtown, across from the Sheraton hotel.

TENNIS AND GOLF

The friendly **John Newcombe Tennis Club** (Hotel Canto del Sol, tel. 322/226-0123, $16/hour) rents eight courts—four outdoor clay, four indoor. A sign-up board is available for players seeking partners. Also available are massage, steam baths, equipment sales and rentals, and professional lessons ($35/hour).

The **Hotel NH Krystal** (tel. 322/224-0202 or 322/224-2030, $15/hour) has several night-lit courts and offers equipment sales, rentals, and professional lessons ($20/hour). Other clubs, such as at the **Sheraton** (tel. 322/223-0404, 7:30 A.M.–dusk daily, $10/hr.) also rent their courts to the public.

The 18-hole, par-71 **Marina Vallarta Golf Course** (tel. 322/221-0545, www.foremexico .com/marina), designed by architect Joe Finger, is one of Mexico's best. It is open to the public for $110 mornings, $80 afternoons, which includes greens fee, caddy, and cart.

Alternatively, try the newer, very popular **Vista Vallarta** 18-hole golf course (tel. 322/329-2900, www.vistavallartagolf.com), in the country east of the Marina about three miles. Greens fees run about $150 morning, $99 after 2 P.M.

The green, palm-shaded 18-hole **Los Flamingos Golf Course** (Km 145, Highway 200, 8 mi./13 km north of the airport, from Puerto Vallarta, tel. 01-329/296-5006, 7 A.M.–5 P.M. daily, $60) offers an alternative. Open to the public, Los Flamingos services include carts ($28), caddies ($10), club rentals ($20), a pro shop, restaurant, and locker rooms. The greens fee includes the cart.

BICYCLING

Bike Mex (361 Guerrero, tel. 322/223-1834, bikemex@pvnet.com.mx, www.bikemex.com) offers mountain biking adventures in surrounding scenic country locations. It tailors trips according to individual interests and ability, from beginning to advanced levels. More advanced trips include outback spots Yelapa and Sayulita and mountain destinations, such as San Sebastián, Mascota, and Talpa. Participants enjoy GT Full Suspension or Kona mountain bikes (27 gears), helmets, gloves, purified water, and bilingual guides. Alternatively, contact **Ecoride** (382 Miramar, tel. 322/222-7912, www.ecoridemex.com), which, among others, offers an advanced, super-scenic bike trip around San Sebastián, in the mountains above Puerto Vallarta.

HORSEBACK RIDING

A pair of nearby ranches give visitors the opportunity to explore the Puerto Vallarta region's gorgeously scenic tropical forest, river, and mountain country. Options include English or Western saddles, and rides ranging from two hours to a whole day or a whole week. Contact either **Rancho Ojo de Agua** (tel. 322/224-0607, ranchojo@pvnet.com.mx, www.mexonline .com /ranchojo.htm) or **Rancho El Charro** (tel. 322/224-0114, aguirre@pvnet.com.mx, www .ranchoelcharro.com).

TOURS
Adventure Tours

A number of nature-oriented tour agencies lead off-the-beaten-track Puerto Vallarta-area excursions. **Vallarta Adventures** (tel. 322/297-1212, info@vallarta-adventures.com, www .vallarta-adventures.com) offers boat tours to the Islas Marietas wildlife sanctuary (sea turtles, manta rays, dolphins, whales, seabirds), a dozen airplane excursions, and a rugged all-day Mercedes-Benz truck ride (canyons, mountains, crystal streams, rustic villages) into the heart of Puerto Vallarta's backyard mountains.

The offerings of the ecologically aware **Expediciones Cielo Abierto** (Open Sky Expeditions; 339 Guerrero, two blocks north of the riverside Municipal Crafts Market, tel. 322/222-3310 or U.S./Can. toll-free 866/422-9972, openair@vivamexico.com, www.vallarta whales.com) include snorkeling around Punta Mita, hiking in the Sierra Cuale foothill jungle, bird-watching, cultural tours, dolphin encounters, and whale-watching.

Viva Tours (tel./fax 322/224-0410, info@ vivatours-vallarta.com, www.vivatours-vallarta .com) organizes a number of off-the-beaten-track adventures, including horseback riding, hiking, biking, fishing, and much more.

Finally, if you want to see a listing of all adventures possible in Puerto Vallarta, visit www .puertovallartatours.net, creation of web-savvy agents John and Sandra, who offer a long list of options, from booze cruises and golf, to visits to remote Huichol mountain villages and hot air ballooning.

Jungle Canopy Tours

Puerto Vallarta's first **jungle canopy adventure tour** (tel. 322/224-0699, $79) is for the fearless and fit only. You're suspended at treetop heights sailing downhill, like a bird, beneath the leafy tropical forest canopy. The local inventor is ecologically aware Jeff Coates ("Gringo Bob," as he's known to local folks), who's been receiving visitors for the last few years at his jungle preserve, a 45-minute drive south of Puerto Vallarta. Alternatively, you can try rival **Canopy Tour Los Veranos** (tel. 322/223-6060, www .canopytours-vallarta.com, $77) nearby.

Reach both of these by car or bus, via Hwy. 200 south, three miles (5 km) past Boca de Tomatlán. At Las Juntas, turn right onto the dirt side road. Continue about a mile to Jeff Coates's place, on the left; or continue a fraction of a mile farther to Canopy Tour Los Veranos at the end of the road. For more information, visit www.canopytours-vallarta.com.

Vallarta Adventures (see *Adventure Tours*) offers arguably the most professional of all canopy tours, at its camp nestled in the vine-hung tropical forest foothills along the road to San Sebastián. The actual canopy tour takes you through about ten sturdy forest perches, via 100- or 200-yard cable rides from perch to perch in a total of about an hour and a half.

GYMS

Puerto Vallarta has a number of good exercise gyms. One of the best is the women-only **Total Fitness Gym** (at the Marina, Tennis Club Puesta del Sol, tel. 322/221-0770), offering 40 machines, complete weight sets, professional advice, and aerobics workouts. Similar facilities and services are available for both sexes at the **Hola Puerto Vallarta** hotel and spa (tel. 322/226-4600, $15/day).

SPORTING GOODS STORES

Given the sparse and pricey local sporting goods selection, serious sports enthusiasts should pack their own equipment to Puerto Vallarta. A few stores carry some items. Among the most reliable is **Deportes Gutiérrez Rizo** (corner of Avenida Insurgentes and Avenida Serdán, tel. 322/222-2595, 9 A.M.–7 P.M. and 4–8:30 P.M. Mon.–Sat.). Although fishing gear—rods, reels, line, sinkers—is its strong suit, it also stocks a general selection including sleeping bags, inflatable boats, tarps, pack frames, wetsuits, scuba tanks, and water skis.

Shopping

Although Puerto Vallarta residents make few folk crafts themselves, they import tons of good—and some very fine—pieces from the places where they *are* made. Puerto Vallarta's scenic beauty has become an inspiration for a growing community of artists and collectors who have opened shops filled with locally crafted sculpture, painting, and museum-grade handicrafts gathered from all over Mexico. Furthermore, resort wear needn't cost a bundle in Puerto Vallarta, where a number of small boutiques offer racks of stylish, comfortable Mexican-made items for a fraction of stateside prices.

SOUTH OF RÍO CUALE

The couple of blocks of Avenida Olas Altas and side streets around the Hotel Playa los Arcos are alive with a welter of T-shirt and *artesanías* (crafts) stores loaded with the more common items—silver, onyx, papier-mâché, pottery—gathered from all over Mexico.

A few shops stand out, however. On Avenida Olas Altas, a block north of Hotel Playa los Arcos, find **Safari Accents** (Olas Altas 224, tel. 322/223-2660, 10 A.M.–10 P.M. daily). Inside, peruse a delightful trove of the baroque, including brilliant designer candles, angelic icons, bright metal-framed mirrors, a rainbow of glass lampshades, and gleaming candelabras.

For a different kind of excellence, head uphill from Avenida Olas Altas along Badillo. After a block and a half, on the south side of the street, step into **Galería La Indígena** (tel./fax 322/222-3007, 10 A.M.–8 P.M. Mon.–Sat.) for a brilliant display of fine native ceremonial crafts. Here, you can appreciate bright Huichol yarn paintings and masks; Tarascan art from Ocumichu, Michoacán; Nahua painted coconut faces from Guerrero; a host of masks, both antique originals and new reproductions; pre-Columbian replicas; and Oaxaca fanciful wooden *alebrijes* animal figures.

Continue half a block to the corner of I. Vallarta to admire the eclectic collection of designer **Patti Gallardo** (250 B. Badillo, tel./fax 322/222-5712 or 322/224-9658, 10 A.M.–6 P.M. Mon.–Sat., closed Sept.–Nov.). Although Patti's creations extend from fine art and jewelry to clothing and metal sculptures, she's especially proud of her collection of colorfully designed, handmade carpets.

Walk a few doors uphill and across the street to view the eclectic sculpture collection at **Galería Dante** (269 B. Badillo, tel. 322/222-2477, fax 322/222-6284, www.galleriadante .com, 10 A.M.–5 P.M. Mon.–Fri., 10 A.M.–2 P.M. Sat.). Exquisite wouldn't be too strong a description of the many museum-quality pieces, from neoclassic to abstract modern. Across the street, step into **Pirámide** (10 A.M.–2 P.M. and 6–9 P.M. Mon.–Sat.), which specializes in fine Huichol pre-Columbian reproductions.

Next to Pirámide, look into **Viva** (274 B. Badillo, tel. 322/222-4078, www.vivacollection .com, 10 A.M.–11 P.M. daily), the life project of designer Mary Sue Morris. Take your pick from lots of handmade men's and women's shoes and sandals, and one-of-a-kind designer jewelry.

Continue north to Insurgentes and **Arte Indias,** for an interestingly eclectic selection, including much women's cotton resort wear, one-of-a-kind jewelry, and Tiffany-style lamps. (Open daily 9 A.M.–9 P.M. near the southwest corner of Madero.)

Tucked away on a quiet residential street a block uphill from Insurgentes, find **Mando de**

Azulejos (Carranza 374, tel. 322/222-2675, fax 322/222-3292, info@talavera-tile.com, www. talavera-tile.com, 9 A.M.–7 P.M. Mon.–Fri., 9 A.M.–2 P.M. Sat.). It offers a treasury of made-on-site tile and Talavera-style pottery at reasonable prices. Unique, however, are the custom-made tiles—round, square, oval—inscribed and fired as you choose, with which you can adorn your home entryway or facade.

Detour back downhill along Lázaro Cárdenas, to **Olinalá Gallery** (274 Lázaro Cárdenas, tel. 322/222-4995, or by appointment, tel. 322/228-0659, 10 A.M.–2 P.M. and 5–8 P.M. Mon.–Sat.). Founded by Mexico-lovers Nancy and John Erickson, Olinalá Gallery is now in the hands of new owners/managers Brewster and Carmen Brockman. Although the "Olinalá" name originated from the famed Mexican lacquerware village where the Ericksons originally got most of their pieces, the present collection, a mini-museum of mostly ceremonial and festival masks—devils, mermaids, goddesses, skulls, crocodiles, horses, and dozens more—comes from all over southern and western Mexico. All offerings, moreover, are priced to sell.

ALONG THE RÍO CUALE

For the more ordinary, yet attractive, Mexican handicrafts, head any day except Sunday (when most shops are closed) to the Mercado Municipal at the north end of the Avenida Insurgentes bridge. Here, shops ordinarily initially ask prices two to three times higher than the going rate. You should counter with a correspondingly low offer. If you don't get the price you want, always be prepared to find another seller. If your offer is fair, the shopkeeper will often give in as you begin to walk away. Theatrics, incidentally, are less than useful in bargaining, which should merely be a straightforward discussion of the merits, demerits, and price of the article in question.

The Mercado Municipal is a two-story warren of dozens upon dozens of shops filled with jewelry, leather, papier-mâché, T-shirts, and everything in between. The congestion can make the place hot; after a while, take a break at a cool river-view seat at one of the *fondas*—permanent food stalls on the second floor.

One of the most unusual Mercado Municipal stalls is **Cabaña del Tío Tom** (Uncle Tom's Cabin), whose menagerie of colorful papiermâché parrots are priced a peg or two cheaper than at the tonier downtown stores.

It's time to leave when you're too tired to distinguish silver from tin and Tonalá from Tlaquepaque. Head downstream to the **Pueblo Viejo** complex on Calle Augustín Rodríguez between Juárez and Morelos, near the Avenida I. Vallarta lower bridge. This mall, with individual stores rather than stalls, is less crowded but generally pricier than the Mercado Municipal. Some shopkeepers will turn their noses up if you try to bargain. If they persist, take your business elsewhere.

If, on the other hand, you're in the market for **huaraches** cross the Avenida Vallarta (downstream river bridge) and continue to jewel-of-a-store **Huarachería Fabiola,** near the northeast corner of Vallarta and Aquiles Serdán (tel. 322/222-9154, 9 A.M.–9 P.M. daily). Inside, find festoons of every kind of huarache seemingly conceivable, for giants to leprechauns and styles from the latest chic to rubber-tire-soled models.

NORTH OF RÍO CUALE

A sizable fraction of Puerto Vallarta's best boutiques, galleries, and arts and crafts stores lie along the six downtown blocks of Avenida Juárez, beginning at the Río Cuale. The **María Bonita** boutique (Juárez 136, no phone, 11 A.M.–7:30 P.M. Mon.–Sat.) half a block north of the river heads the parade. The friendly, outgoing owner offers reasonably priced women's resort wear of her own design. (Also find much of the same at **Luisa's** (tel. 322/222-5042, 10 A.M.–8 P.M. Mon.–Sat.) next door.

Another block north, cross to the west side of the street to **Alberto's** (Juáez 185, 10 A.M.–8 P.M. Mon.–Sat., tel. 322/222-8317, albertos pv@albertos.com.mx, www.albertos.com.mx) arguably Puerto Vallarta's top class-act jewelry store. Here, owner-artisan Jaime Ballesteros and his son Emerson carry on the Puerto Vallarta tradition begun by Jaime's late father, Roberto ("Alberto") Ballesteros. They offer a treasury of unique pieces, mostly crafted by Jaime and Em-

Puerto Vallarta stalls and galleries exhibit a broad range of painting and sculpture.

erson, taken from designs passed down through three family generations. Considering their fine work, their prices are very reasonable.

Continue another block north, to **Galería Vallarta** (Juárez 265, tel./fax 322/222-0290, webart@galerialvallarta.com, www.galeriavallarta .com, 10 A.M.–6 P.M., low season Mon.–Sat., 10 A.M.–8 P.M. high, Sundays by appointment). Through the years, arts-and-crafts-lovers Barbara Peters and her late husband, Jean, collected so many Mexican handicrafts that they had to find a place to store their finds. Galería Vallarta, a small museum of singular paintings, ceremonial masks, lampshades, art-to-wear, and more, is the result. Be sure to visit the upstairs gallery room, where many of the best paintings are on display.

A few doors farther up the street, the store of renowned Guadalajara resident **Sergio Bustamante** (Juárez 275, tel. 322/223-1405, 10 A.M.–9 P.M. Mon.–Sat.) contains so many unique sculptures it's hard to understand how a single artist could be so prolific. (The answer: He has a factory-shop full of workers who execute his fanciful, sometimes unnerving, studies in juxtaposition.) Bustamante's more modest faces on eggs, anthropoid cats, and double-nosed clowns go for as little as $200; the largest, most flamboyant works sell for $10,000 or more.

For something different, continue next door from Bustamante, and take a look inside **Orígenes** (279 Juárez, 10 A.M.–9 P.M. Mon.–Sat., tel. 322/223-3952, www.davidluna.com) for a carefully selected out-of-the ordinary collection, from Mexico, Asia, and Africa. Examples include fine baskets, mystical glass, stone, and hardwood figurines, shiny glassware, rattan furniture, and exquisite Oaxaca-loomed wool rugs and hangings (*tapetes*) and colorful tinware picture frames and holiday decorations.

Back across the street, the government **Instituto de Arte Jaliscense** store (Juárez 284, tel. 322/222-1301, 9 A.M.–9 P.M. daily) displays examples of nearly every Jalisco folk craft, plus popular items from other parts, such as Oaxaca *alebrijes* (ahl-BREE-hays), fanciful wooden animals. Since it has a little bit of everything at relatively reasonable prices, this is a good spot for comparison shopping.

A few blocks farther on, at the northwest corner of Galeana, an adjacent pair of stores, **Querubines** (Juárez 501A, tel. 322/223-1727, 9 A.M.–9 P.M. Mon.–Sat., 10 A.M.–6 P.M. low season) and **La Reja** (Juárez 501B, 10 A.M.–2 P.M. and 4–8 P.M. Mon.–Sat., 10 A.M.–6 P.M. Mon.–Sat. winter season), display their excellent traditional merchandise—riots of papier-mâché fruit, exquisite blue pottery vases, gleaming pewter, clay trees of life, heavenly Baroque reproductions, rich Oaxaca and Chiapas textiles, shiny Tlaquepaque hand-painted pottery—so artfully they are simply fun to walk through.

Carefully cross to the east side of Juárez, at the corner of Galeana and Corona, and your reward will be **Olé** (tel. 322/222-2470, 9 A.M.–2 P.M. and 4–8 P.M. Mon.–Sat.), a hidden "must see" gem of a store, overflowing with fine wool woven *tapetes* (rugs) from Oaxaca. Kindly owner Juan Marcos Solórzano's merchandise ranges from small (but nevertheless fine) coasters for drinks, through long hall carpets, to simply stunning 8-by-10-foot area rugs, all priced to sell.

Re-cross Juáez and follow Corona downhill a few doors to ceramics gallery **Majolica** (183 Corona, tel. 322/222-5118, 10 A.M.–2 P.M. and 4–9 P.M. Mon.–Sat.), which uses the older name, after the Mediterranean island of Majorca, where the celebrated Talavera pottery style, a blend of Moorish, Chinese, and Mediterranean traditions, originated before migrating to Spain and Mexico. The later Talavera name comes from the town in Spain from which the potters, who eventually settled in Puebla, Mexico, emigrated. The personable owner/manager hand-selects the pieces, all of which come from the Puebla family workshops that carry on the Talavera tradition. Her prices reflect the high demand that the Talavera style of colorful classic elegance has commanded for generations.

Downhill a few doors, **Arte Mágico Huichol** (Corona 179, tel./fax 322/222-3077, 10 A.M.–2 P.M. and 4–8 P.M. Mon.–Sat., also 10 A.M.–2 P.M. Sun. in winter) displays an unusually fine collection of Huichol yarn paintings by renowned artists such as Mariano Valadéz, Hector Ortíz, and María Elena Acosta. Downhill, one door before the corner of Morelos, you'll find the unusual collection of **Casa de Feng Shui,** which specializes in the mysteriously quirky but glittering collectibles—onyx pyramids, geodes, blown-glass spheres, glass crystals—of the Chinese feng shui vogue.

Step west, across Morelos, to **Galería Uno** (Morelos 561, tel. 322/222-0908, galeria-uno@ pvnet.com.mx, www.mexonline.com/galeriauno.htm, 10 A.M.–8 P.M. Mon.–Sat.), one of Puerto Vallarta's longest-established fine art galleries. The collection—featuring internationally recognized artists with whom the gallery often schedules exhibition openings for the public—tends toward the large, the abstract, and the primitive. Check the website for the exhibition schedule.

For a similarly excellent collection, step one block north and around the uphill corner of Aldama, to **Galería Pacífico** (Aldama 174 upstairs, tel./fax 322/222-1982 or tel. 322/222-5502, 10 A.M.–10 P.M. daily, shorter hours in low season). Here, in an airy upstairs showroom, personable owner Gary Thompson offers a fine collection of paintings, prints, and sculptures of Mexican artists, both renowned and up-and-coming. The mostly realistic works cover a gamut of styles and feelings, from colorful and sentimental to stark and satirical. Gary often hosts Friday meet-the-artist openings, where visitors are invited to socialize with the local artistic community.

Finally, head a few blocks back south along Morelos to the Fábrica de Joyería Regina, or **Regina Jewelry Factory** (Morelos 434, on the *malecón*, tel. 322/222-2487, 10 A.M.–10 P.M. daily), for just about the broadest selection and best prices in town. Charges for the seeming acres of gold, silver, and jeweled chains, bracelets, pendants, necklaces, and earrings are usually determined simply by weight; from a dollar per gram for silver.

DEPARTMENT AND WAREHOUSE STORES

Among Puerto Vallarta's best department stores are Comercial Mexicana and locally owned Supermarket Gutiérrez Rizo. Comercial Mexicana's newest local branch is the **Megastore** (tel. 322/222-7708 and 222–7709, 7 A.M.–10 P.M. daily), on the beachfront boulevard, a quarter mile south of the Hotel Sheraton. The other branch is at **Plaza Marina** (Km 6.5, Highway 200, a few blocks south of the airport, beneath the McDonald's sign, tel. 322/221-0053 or 322/221-0490, open same hours).

SUPERMARKETS, BAKERIES, AND ORGANIC GROCERIES

The king of national supermarket chains is **Comercial Mexicana,** Mexico's K-Mart with groceries. The quality is generally good to excellent, and the prices match those in the United States and Canada.

Much closer to downtown is the big, locally owned **Supermarket Gutiérrez Rizo** (Constitución and Vallarta, just south of the Río Cuale, tel. 322/222-0222 or 322/222-6701, 6:30 A.M.–10 P.M. daily), a remarkably well-organized dynamo of a general store. Besides vegetables, groceries, film, socks, spermicide, and sofas, it stocks one of the largest racks of English-language newspapers and magazines (some you'd be hard-pressed to find back home) outside of Mexico City.

South of Cuale, don't miss stopping by the charming neighborhood bakery **Pays de Catalina** (317 Basilio Badillo, north side, tel. 322/223-2682, 8 A.M.–10 P.M. daily), a few doors up the street from Casa de los Hot Cakes. Here, the longtime owner-baker continues to put out a scrumptious menu of goods, from big, crunchy cookies and cinnamon rolls, to get-'em-while-they're-there croissants and crisp apple tarts. Also south of Cuale, pastry lovers enjoy visiting **Pie in the Sky** (Lázaro Cárdenas 247, near the corner of P. Suárez, tel. 322/222-8411, 8 A.M.–11 P.M. daily). The highlight here, besides good coffee, apple and mango pie, and chocolate cake, is the indulgently scrumptious brownies.

On the north side of town, rival **Panadería los Chatos** (8 A.M.–8 P.M. Mon.–Sat.) offers a comparably fine selection at two locations: in the Hotel Zone (Francisco Villa 359, tel. 322/223-0485) across from the Hotel Sheraton; and farther north, in the Marina (tel. 322/221-2540).

Health-food devotees have an excellent south-of-Cuale option in **Agro Gourmet** (corner of Basilio Badillo and Pino Suárez, tel. 322/222-5155 and 322/222-5357, 8 A.M.–8 P.M. A.M. Mon.– Sat., 9 A.M.–6 P.M. Sun.). Besides home-grown lettuces and other vegetables and herbs, it also offers a trove of hard-to-get cheeses, breads, ravioli, pesto, tahini, hummus, and much more.

PHOTOGRAPHY

Cameras are an import item in Mexico and consequently expensive. Even the simplest point-and-shoot cameras cost half again as much as in the United States or Canada. You're better to bring your own.

A number of downtown stores sell cameras and photo supplies and do one-hour negative and digital developing and printing at U.S. prices. Try **Fotográfico del Puerto** (Libertad 330, tel. 322/222-0937, 9 A.M.–9 P.M. daily) or another branch a few blocks away (Morelos 490, tel. 322/222-9855, same hours).

Information

Because Puerto Vallarta is an up-to-date city, information is as close as your hotel telephone (or if you don't speak Spanish, your hotel desk clerk) or one of the hundreds of publicly available Internet connections.

TOURIST INFORMATION OFFICES

The downtown tourist information office (tel. 322/223-2500 ext. 230 or 232, fax ext. 233, 8 A.M.–9 P.M. Mon.–Fri., 9 A.M.–2 P.M. Sat.) is on the northeast corner of the central plaza. They provide assistance and information, and dispense whatever maps, pamphlets, and copies of *Vallarta Today* and *Puerto Vallarta Lifestyles* they happen to have.

PUBLICATIONS

New books in English are not particularly common in Puerto Vallarta. Nevertheless,

TIPS FOR GAY AND LESBIAN TRAVELERS

Puerto Vallarta has a particular draw for national and international gay and lesbian travelers for a number of reasons, among them the strong support system within the local community that goes beyond nightlife and beaches. Certainly Puerto Vallarta doesn't match Mexico City in terms of organization within the gay community, as it tends to attract more vacationers than residents, and there is no gay and lesbian center per se. Nevertheless, a strong gay community has existed here as early as the 1970s, and in the last few years, numerous gay-owned businesses have opened – and, more important, are unabashed about their gay friendliness. For more information, take a look at www.gayguidevallarta.com for tips on activities, venues, and more. In addition, most of the websites of the gay-friendly realtors include interesting facts and figures. Pick up the gay-friendly bimonthly, bilingual *Bay Vallarta*, which lists events for guests and locals: culture, art, music, and sports.

Locals have always adopted the "live and let live" attitude about Vallarta's nightlife. But it's important not to lose sight of the fact that there are locals who may not be open to shows of public affection between same-sex couples. Also, be aware that during this time of rapid growth in Puerto Vallarta, many people you might assume are locals are not locals at all but come from other areas in Mexico, some of which are not as liberal or as used to turning a blind eye.

Beyond the town of Puerto Vallarta, you can expect to find open and friendly people throughout the Bay of Banderas. In some of the smaller towns, however, it's not that they won't be as friendly, but their curiosity to see foreign-appearing visitors may get the better of them. Their actions are not necessarily aggressive, just curious. As always, speaking Spanish will be helpful.

As laws in Mexico are in the process of change (two states have voted to accept same-sex relationships and allow legal rights and benefits), those very changes may occasionally spark reactions. Resort towns are usually more open, in that the population tends to be more aware not only of differences but of the economic importance of tourism. Be aware that nudity is not officially allowed on beaches in Mexico.

With regard to safety, most visitors should avoid areas that are unlit at night, whether in the Zona Romántica or elsewhere. Be aware that young men sometimes try to attract the interested foreigner with the intention of mugging or worse. If you've had too much to drink, don't open yourself to trouble. Tell your friends where you're going or who you're planning to go with. And if you've met someone special during your vacation, be sure to protect yourself by wearing a condom as well as maintaining your common sense at all times – even after that third (who's counting!) margarita.

Supermercado Gutiérrez Rizo (south of Cuale, corner of Constitución and Aquiles Serdán, tel. 322/222-0222) stocks an excellent American magazine selection, some new paperback novels, newspapers, including the Miami *Herald* Mexico edition and sometimes *USA Today* and the *Los Angeles Times*.

Also, a number of small stores and stalls, such as the no-name **newsstand** (420 Olas Altas, until 9 or 10 P.M. daily), regularly sell at least one U.S. newspaper.

Vallarta Today (tel. 322/225-3323, fax 322/224-1186, vallartatoday@yahoo.com, www.vallartatoday.com) and **Vallarta Tribune** (tel. 322/223-0585 or 322/223-1302, gerencia@ vallarta tribune.prodigy.net.mx, www.vallarta tribune.com), both unusually informative tourist dailies, are handed out free at the airport and travel agencies, restaurants, and hotels all over town (contact them directly if you can't find a copy). Besides detailed information on hotels, restaurants, and sports, both include a local events and meetings calendar and interesting historical, cultural, and personality feature articles.

Equally excellent is **Puerto Vallarta Lifestyles**

GAY-FRIENDLY TOUR OPERATORS

Whether or not you're staying at the Blue Chairs Resort, the **Blue Chairs Concierge** (Blue Chairs Resort, 322/222-5040, www .bluechairs.com) is more than happy to help you find the gay tour or outing you're looking for to pass the time, get to know the area, or just meet new friends. They can arrange for anything from home-visit massages to horseback rides.

Speaking of horses, **Boana Horseback Riding** (322/222-0999, www.boana.net/tours .htm) is a great way to get to know the area beyond the highway, bars, and beaches – the lushness of the jungle once you go beyond the beaten track is breathtaking.

While **Diana's Tours** (322/222-1510 or 322/222-6506, www.bluechairs.com/ cruisepay.htm) began as a specialty, offering a day-cruise for women, they can help you with any local tour that sounds interesting, and will steer you in the direction that's right for your comfort level. Call them first or stop in at Blue Chairs Resort.

The very lavender **Doin' It Right** (U.S./Can. tel. 800/808-4486 or 800/936-3646, www .doinitright.com) offers a list of gay travel adventures in Mexico as well as Costa Rica. Locally, they represent a number of gay-owned and gay-friendly establishments.

The marine biologist Oscar Frey of **Ocean Friendly Whale Watching** (322/225-3774, www.oceanfriendly.com) is available for private tours catering to the gay community. While most other tours are gay-friendly, there's nothing wrong with having a gay guide who knows what he's talking about. He specializes in groups, so if you have one, call him first.

For sailing, try **Coming About Sailing School** (Pat Henry, 322/222-4119, www.coming-about. com). Pat Henry sailed around the world in eight years and wrote the book about it. She'll talk about her adventures if you ask, but what she really likes to do is to help you to connect with the amazing sea that she was so intimately related to for so long on her solo trip.

At **Spanish Experience Center** (República de Chile 182, 5 de Diciembre, 322/223-5864, www.spanishexperiencecenter.com), you can learn Spanish while taking a cooking class or a tour of the city. The owners believe in getting you involved in the community, since that's where you'll learn the language more quickly. Easy class schedule with rolling rates based on daily, weekly, or monthly attendance.

The gay-owned **Unique Concierge** (Basilio Badillo 429, Zona Romántica, 322/222-6233, www.uniqueconcierge.com) will provide those services that you either may not want to do for yourself, such as visa extensions and paying bills, or making the contacts for party planning and maintenance. They also run a consignment shop.

(Calle Timón 1, tel. 322/221-0106, 9 A.M.–7 P.M. Mon.–Fri.), the quarterly English-language magazine, which also features unusually detailed and accurate town maps. If you cannot find a copy at the airport or your hotel contact *PuertoVallarta Lifestyles* directly.

Also potentially very useful is the class-act **Gay Guide Vallarta** that lists many gay and gay-friendly hotels, restaurants, real estate offices, bars and nightclubs, plus an events calendar and much more. Visit the website, www.gayguidevallarta.com, or pick up a copy at one of their advertisers, notably the Blue Chairs Beach Resort (tel. 322/222-2176 or 322/222-5040) on Playa Los Muertos, south end, or call the editor, at 322/222-7980, email editor@gayguidevallarta.com.

A new **Puerto Vallarta Library** (Francisco Villa 1001 in Colonia Los Mangos, director Ricardo Murrieta, tel. 322/224-9966, or Jimmie Ellis, tel. 322/222-1478), built and now operated by the volunteer committee Pro Biblioteca Vallarta, has accumulated a sizable English and Spanish book collection. Get there by taxi or car along Villa, which diagonals northerly and inland at the sports field across the airport boulevard from the Hotel Sheraton. Or take a bus marked Pitillal and Biblioteca.

SPANISH INSTRUCTION

The **University of Guadalajara Study Center for Foreigners** (Libertad 105 downtown, tel. 322/223-2082, fax 322/223-2982, cepv@prodigy.net.mx, www.cepe.udg.mx) offers one-, two-, and four-week total immersion Spanish language instruction, including home stays with local families.

VOLUNTEER WORK

A number of local volunteer clubs and groups invite visitors to their meetings and activities. Check with the tourist information office or see the events calendar and directory pages in *Vallarta Today* or *Vallarta Tribune.*

The International Friendship Club, or **Club Internacional de la Amistad** (Parian del Puente office complex, local 13, P.O. Box 604, Puerto Vallarta, Jalisco 48350, tel. 322/222-5466, ifcpv@pvnet.com.mx, www.pvmexico.com, 8:30 A.M.–12:30 P.M. Mon.–Fri.), an all-volunteer service club, sponsors a number of health, educational, and cultural projects. It welcomes visitors to the (usually second Monday) monthly general membership meeting. For more information, see the events calendar section of *Vallarta Today* or the directory page of the *Vallarta Tribune,* or drop by the office behind the HSBC bank, above the north bank of the Río Cuale Avenida Insurgentes (upper) bridge.

The **Ecology Group of Vallarta,** a group of local citizens willing to work for a cleaner Puerto Vallarta, welcomes visitors to its activities and regular meetings. Contact Ron Walker (tel. 322/222-0897, rc_walkermx@yahoo.com.mx) for more information.

The **S.O.S. Animal** (local cell tel. 044-322/227-5519 or 322/221-0078) protection association is working to humanely reduce the number of stray and abandoned animals on Puerto Vallarta streets. Call for more information, or see the directory page of the *Vallarta Tribune.*

Services

Banks with ATMs, street telephones, Internet stores, pharmacies, doctors, hospitals, and much more are available ready to smooth your Puerto Vallarta visit.

MONEY EXCHANGE

Banking has come to the Olas Altas district, with the branch of **Banorte** (Av. Olas Altas btwn. B. Badillo and Carranza, tel. 322/222-4040, 9 A.M.–4 P.M. Mon.–Fri., 10 A.M.–2 P.M. Sat.). After hours, use its ATM. Or you can use the HSBC bank ATM on upper Olas Altas (corner of Rodríguez, two blocks south of Hotel Playa Los Arcos).

Most downtown banks cluster along Juárez, near the plaza. One exception is **HSBC** (tel. 322/222-0027 or 322/222-0277, 8 A.M.–7 P.M. Mon.–Sat.), on Libertad, corner of Carranza, just north of the Insurgentes bridge and open the longest hours of all.

Banamex (176 Zaragoza, at Juárez, south side of the of the town plaza, tel. 322/222-0911) changes U.S. and Canadian cash and travelers checks at the best rates in town. For money exchange, go to the special booth (9 A.M.–4 P.M. Mon.–Fri., 10 A.M.–2 P.M. Sat.) to the left of the bank main entrance.

If the lines at Banamex are too long, try **Scotiabank Inverlat** (Juárez, half a block north of the plaza, tel. 322/223-1224, money exchange hours 9 A.M.–5 P.M. Mon.–Fri.) or **Bancomer** across the street (at the corner Juárez and Mina, tel. 322/222-1919 or 322/222-3500, 8:30 A.M.–4 P.M. Mon.–Fri.).

Additionally, scores of little **casas de cambio** (exchange windows) dot the cobbled old town streets, especially along the south end of the *malecón* downtown, and along Avenida Olas Altas and Insurgentes south of the Río Cuale. Although they generally offer about $2 per $100 less than the banks, they compensate with long hours, often 9 A.M.–9 P.M. daily. In the big hotels, cashiers will generally exchange your money at rates comparable to the downtown exchange booths.

The local **American Express** (Morelos 160, corner of Abasolo, tel./fax 322/223-2955 or 322/223-2910, 9 A.M.–6 P.M. Mon.–Fri., 9 A.M.–1 P.M. Sat.) agency cashes American Express travelers checks and offers full member services, such as personal-check cashing (up to $1,000, every 21 days; bring your checkbook, your ID or passport, and your American Express card). The office is downtown, one block inland from the Hard Rock Cafe.

COMMUNICATIONS

Puerto Vallarta has a number of branch post offices. The main *correo* (Mina 188, tel. 322/223-1360, 9 A.M.–5 P.M. Mon.–Fri., 9 A.M.–1 P.M. Sat.), with secure Mexpost mail service, is downtown, two blocks north of the central plaza, just off Juárez. There's a branch at the Edificio Maritima (Maritime Building), near the cruise liner dock (tel. 322/224-7219, 8 A.M.–2 P.M. Mon.–Fri., 9 A.M.–1 P.M. Sat.), but the airport has lost its post office branch; deposit postcards and letters in the airport mailbox *(buzón)*.

The cheapest and often most convenient telephone option is to buy a **tarjeta de teléfono** (Ladatel public phone card) and use it at street telephones. Lacking a telephone card, call from your hotel. Lacking a hotel (or if you don't like its extra charges), go to one of the many **casetas de larga distancia** (long-distance telephone offices), sprinkled all over town.

Puerto Vallarta has a flock of public **Internet** stores. However, they change as often as the Puerto Vallarta breeze. At this writing, I saw many, mostly concentrated downtown: several south of the Río Cuale, along Avenida Olas Altas, and several more north of the Río Cuale along Juárez. Ask your hotel desk clerk for the closest.

HEALTH AND EMERGENCIES

In an emergency, go to one of the Puerto Vallarta Hospitals that have 24-hour service: **Amerimed,** in the Marina, tel. 322/221-0023, **Medasist,** south of Cuale, tel. 322/223-0444, and **San Javier** tel. 322/226-1010, also in the Marina.

If, however, you prefer to go to Puerto Vallarta's newest hospital, with a load of diagnostic equipment and a raft of specialists to use it, go to **Cornerstone Hospital,** behind the Gigante store at north-side Plaza Caracol, tel. 322/224-9400. Alternatively go to the respected **Hospital CMQ** (Centro Médico Quirúrgico; 366 Basilio Badillo, btwn. Insurgentes and Aguacate, tel. 322/223-1919 ground floor or 322/223-0011 second floor), south of the Río Cuale.

If you need to have an American-trained English-speaking doctor, Puerto Vallarta visitors enjoy the services of at least two IAMAT (International Association for Medical Assistance to Travelers) doctors: Consult either Dr. Alfonso Rodríguez, at Lucerna 148, tel. 322/293-1991, or Dr. Mark Engleman, at Amerimed Hospital, just off the airport boulevard, in the Marina, tel. 322/293-1991.

For round-the-clock prescription service, call or go to the well-stocked 24-hour **Farmacia Guadalajara** on the Avenida Insurgentes corner of Avenida Lazaro Cardenas, south of Cuale, tel. 322/222-0101. Alternatively, try one of the five branches of **Farmacia CMQ;** for example, south of Cuale (B. Badillo 367, tel. 322/222-1330 or 322/222-2941) or on the north side (Peru 1146, tel. 322/222-1110).

Furthermore, legions of loyal customers swear by the diagnostic competence of Federico López Casco, of **Farmacia Olas Altas** (Av. Olas Altas 365, two blocks south of Hotel Playa Los Arcos, tel. 322/222-2374), whom they simply know as "Freddy." Although a pharmacist and not a physician, his fans say he is a wizard at recommending remedies for their aches and pains.

For **police** emergencies, call the emergency number, either 322/290-0507 or 322/290-0512. In case of fire, call the *bomberos*—the fire department (tel. 322/224-7701.)

IMMIGRATION, CUSTOMS, AND CONSULATES

If you need an extension to your tourist card, you can most likely get a total of 180 days at the local branch of **Instituto Nacional de Migración.** Present your existing tourist card at the office (on the cruise ship dock entrance road, next to the gas station, at street number 2755, upstairs, tel. 322/224-7653 or 322/224-7970, fax 322/224-7719, 9 A.M.–1 P.M. Mon.–Fri.).

Alternatively, you can go to Migración at the airport (tel. 322/221-1380, 322/224-7653, or 322/224-7970, fax 322/224-7719). If you lose your tourist card, avoid last-minute trouble by going to airport Migración several hours before your flight, with your passport or picture identification, and some proof of the day you arrived in Mexico, such as a copy of the original permit or your arrival airplane boarding pass or a copy of your round-trip ticket.

Both the U.S. and Canadian Consuls have moved out of downtown. They have retained their local Puerto Vallarta telephone numbers, however. The U.S. Consul issues passports and does other essential legal work for U.S. citizens at the consular office on the main Nuevo Vallarta beachfront boulevard (Plaza Paraíso, Paseo de los Cocoteros #1, tel./fax 322/222-0069 or 322/223-0074, 8 A.M.–12:30 P.M. Mon.–Fri.). In an emergency after hours, call the U.S. Consul General in Guadalajara (tel. 33/3268-2100 or 33/3268-2200).

The Canadian honorary consul, who has moved to the hotel zone on the airport boulevard (at Edificio Obelisco, suite 108, Bulevar Francisco Ascencio 1951, tel. 322/293-0098, or 322/293-0099, fax 322/293-2894, 9 A.M.–3:30 P.M. Mon.–Fri.), provides similar services for Canadian citizens. In an emergency or after hours call the Canadian Embassy in Mexico City (toll-free in Mex. tel. 01-800/706-2900).

ARTS AND MUSIC COURSES

The private, volunteer **Centro Cultural Vallartense** periodically sponsors theater, modern dance, painting, sculpture, aerobics, martial arts, and other courses for adults and children. From time to time it stages exhibition openings for local artists, whose works it regularly exhibits at the gallery/information center at Plaza del Arte on Isla Río Cuale. For more information, look for announcements in the events pages of

Vallarta Today or the *Vallarta Tribune,* or drop by and talk to the volunteer in charge at the Plaza del Arte gallery and information center, at the upstream end of Isla Río Cuale.

Sharing the Plaza de Arte is the **Centro Cultural Cuale** building and adjacent class-rooms, where, late weekday afternoons, you may hear the strains of students practicing the violin, guitar, piano, flute, and pre-Columbian instruments. Such lessons are open to the general public; apply in person during the late afternoon or early evening.

Getting Around

BY TOWN BUS

Since nearly all through traffic flows along one long thoroughfare, Puerto Vallarta bus transportation is a snap. Puerto Vallarta is blessed by a large squadron of buses, operated by both private companies and bus drivers' cooperatives. They run north-south, beginning at their south-of-Cuale terminus on the east (Calle Pino Suárez) side of Plaza Lázaro Cárdenas. From Plaza Lázaro Cárdenas, all buses head north. Most of them (marked "Centro") pass through the downtown center northbound along Avenida Juárez. A few other buses, marked "Tunel," bypass the downtown center via a town bypass tunnel uphill, east of downtown, and continue along the foothill *libramiento* boulevard and rejoin the main-route buses on the north-bound main Boulevard Francisco Ascencio at the Zona Hotelera. From there, the major bus terminals (marked prominently on the bus windshields) are at Pitillal (at the north end of the Zona Hotelera), the Marina, and the Las Palmas, Juntas, and Ixtapa suburbs, farther north.

The Puerto Vallarta bus system is a simple learn-as-you-go (no tourist passes, transit maps, nor set schedules) expanded version of the original village system of two generations ago. However, it's efficient and very safe, except perhaps for an occasional pick-pocket when crowded. Be sure to keep your purses buttoned and your wallets secure in your waist belt.

Buses run daily between about 5:30 A.M. and about 11 P.M., at two-minute intervals during peak hours, 5- or 10-minute intervals, non-peak. Have enough coins *(monedas)* in hand to pay your $.40 tariff to the driver, who can usually change small bills. All buses eventually return to their south-end terminus, at Plaza Lázaro Cárdenas a few blocks south of the River Cuale. Northbound, from Plaza Lázaro Cárdenas, buses retrace their routes to one of several important stops scrawled across their windows. Destinations on the north side, from closest in to farthest north, are the Centro (town center, 1–2 miles, 5 minutes), Zona Hotelera (Hotel Zone, 3–5 miles, 10–15 minutes), Pitillal (5 miles, 15 minutes), Marina Vallarta (7 miles, 20 minutes), the airport (8 miles, 22 minutes), Camionera Central (long-distance bus station, 10 miles, 24 minutes), Las Palmas (11 miles, 25 minutes), Juntas (13 miles, 28 minutes), and Ixtapa (15 miles, 33 minutes). Since the buses headed to the destinations farthest north stop at all of the intermediate destinations, you can go everywhere you are likely to want to go by hopping on to a Las Palmas, Juntas, or Ixtapa-marked bus.

Hint: If you're headed to the downtown north of the River Cuale, be sure to take a "Centro"-marked bus. (And not a "Tunel"-marked bus that bypasses the town center by going through the tunnel and along the uphill *libramiento* bypass.) On the other hand, from south of Cuale, if you want to get to north side (Zona Hotelera, Marina, airport) destinations in a hurry, you should take the "Tunel" marked bus.

Two other local bus terminals serve Puerto Vallarta. For south-end destinations of Mismaloya and Boca de Tomatlán, catch one of the minibuses marked Mismaloya or Boca that leave from the south-of-Cuale corner of Constitución and Calle Basilio Badillo, just below Insurgentes.

On the other hand, for the northwesterly Bay of Banderas destinations of Bucerías, Cruz de Huanacaxtle, and Punta de Mita, go by **Autotransportes Medina** buses that you can conveniently catch either at the downtown, north-side station (1410 Brasil, tel. 322/212-4732 or 322/222-7279) or on the main boulevard, northbound side, across from the Hotel Sheraton.

BY TAXI, CAR, AND OTHER ALTERNATIVES

Taxis, on the other hand, are all private, much more convenient, and safe, but not cheap (about $2–6 per trip within the city limits, verify rates at your hotel desk). Most taxi drivers will quote you the correct going rate. If not, bring the driver to his senses by hailing another taxi. Under any circustances, don't get in until the price is settled.

Congestion and lack of parking space (or even parking garages) reduce the desirability of doing much driving of your own or a rental car around downtown Puerto Vallarta. Nevertheless, for excursions outside of town, a car adds flexibility, convenience, and economy over the price of a guided tour, especially if you share costs with other passengers. Expect to pay about $40–50 a day for the cheapest rental, including legally required liability insurance. Car rental companies have booths at the airport.

If however, you must drive and park downtown, avoid driving along the very congested downtown *malecón* southbound. If you're coming into town along the ingress boulevard from the north, instead follow the *libramiento* downtown bypass that forks left at the big "Barra de Navidad" sign over the main boulevard heading south. It leads you quickly to the less-congested south-of-Cuale old town neighborhood. There, either park your car and walk, or take a taxi. If you still insist on driving, go north along one-way Avenida Insurgentes, cross the River Cuale bridge, bear left three blocks along Libertad, then right into the town center along Juárez, where you will eventually be able to find a parking place.

Walking is by far the best alternative for getting around downtown Puerto Vallarta. The heart of the old town, north and south of the river, stretches barely a mile and a half (2.5 km), a 30-minute walk north-south; and a half mile (0.6 km), or 10-minute walk, east-west. Bicycles, while available for rent ($10/day) downtown, are not a very safe alternative, given the many buses and fast drivers, who either don't see or ignore bicycles. Moreover, bicycles are a burden in Puerto Vallarta's hilly old-town neighborhoods.

Getting There and Away

Dozens of air departures, hundreds of long-distance buses, and a good paved highway network speed thousands of travelers to and from Puerto Vallarta daily.

BY AIR
Major Carriers

Several major carriers connect Puerto Vallarta by direct flights with United States and Mexican destinations.

Mexicana Airlines (reservations, tel. 322/221-1266 or toll-free Mex. tel. 01-800/502-2000; flight info, tel. 322/224-8900) flights connect daily with Mexico City and Guadalajara. **Aerocalifornia Airlines** (tel. 322/209-0328) connects with Los Angeles and Mexico City. **Aeroméxico** (tel. 322/224-2777) flights connect daily with Los Angeles, Tijuana, Guadalajara, Acapulco, León, Monterrey, and Mexico City.

Alaska Airlines (reservations, toll-free Mex. tel. 001-800/426-0333) flights connect with Los Angeles, San Francisco, San Jose, and Seattle; for arrival and departure information, call the airport (tel. 322/221-1350 or 322/221-2610).

American Airlines (toll-free Mex. tel. 01-800/362-7000) flights connect with Dallas-Ft. Worth and Chicago seasonally.

U.S. Airways, formerly America West Airlines, flights connect with Phoenix and Los Angeles. (For reservations in Mexico, dial toll-free U.S. 001-800/235-9292, for flight information call the airport at tel. 322/221-1927, or 322/221-1333.)

Minor Carriers

United Airlines flights connect with San Francisco (reservations via toll-free Mex. tel. 01-800/003-0777, flight information, tel. 322/222-3264).

Frontier Airlines flights connect with Denver. For reservations and information, contact a travel agent, such as American Express, tel. 322/223-2955, or 322/223-2910.

Continental Airlines (tel. 322/221-1025 or toll-free Mex. tel. 01-800/900-5000) flights connect daily with Houston.

Aerocalafia Airlines connects with Los Cabos (reservations, toll-free Mex. 01-800/560-3949, for flight information call the airport at 322/221-1333).

Aviacsa airlines connects with Mexico City (reservations call toll-free Mex. tel. 01-800/560-3949; flight information, call 322/221-3095, or 322/221-2624).

Seasonal Charter Carriers

West Jet and Air Tran charter flights connect with several Canadian cities (Toronto, Winnipeg, Saskatoon, Regina, Calgary-Edmonton, and Vancouver), mostly during the winter. For reservations call Noli Tours, toll-free tel. 800/666-8881.

Other charters that connect with Puerto Vallarta from a number of U.S. cities seasonally are **USA 3000** (www.usa3000) and **Apple Vacations** (www.applevacations.com).

Puerto Vallarta Airport Arrival and Departure

Air arrival at Puerto Vallarta Airport (code-designated PVR, officially the Gustavo Díaz Ordaz International) is generally smooth and simple. After the cursory (if any) customs check, arrivees can avail themselves of two 24-hour ATMs and a money exchange counter open 9 A.M.–6 P.M. daily.

A lineup of **car rental booths** includes Advantage (tel. 322/221-1499, advantagepvr@ prodigy.net.mx), Alamo (tel. 322/221-3030), Avis (tel. 322/221-1112), Budget (toll-free Mex. tel. 01-800/700-1700), Dollar (tel. 322/223-1354), National (tel. 322/209-0356), and Thrifty (toll-free Mex. tel. 01-800/021-2277, local tel. 322/321-2984 or 321-2485). You might also save money with an air-and-car package or by reserving with a discount (ask for AARP, AAA, senior, airline, credit card, or other) before you leave for Mexico.

Transportation to town is easiest by *colectivo* (collective taxi-vans) or *taxi especial* (individual taxi). Booths sell tickets at curbside. The *colectivo* fare runs about $6 per person to the northern hotel zone, $7 to the center of town, and $8 or more to hotels and hamlets south of town. Individual taxis (for up to four passengers) run about $15, $16, and $25 for the same rides.

Taxis to more distant northern destinations, such as Sayulita (30 mi./50 km), San Francisco (32 mi./53 km), Rincón de Guayabitos (39 mi./62 km), and San Blas or Tepic (100 mi./160 km), run about $50, $60, $108 and $170, respectively. A much cheaper alternative is to hire a taxi (no more than $10) from the airport to the new bus terminal a mile north of the airport, where you can continue by very frequent buses.

Airport departure is as simple as arrival. Save by sharing a taxi with departing fellow hotel guests. Agree on the fare with the driver before you get in. If the driver seems too greedy, hail another taxi.

If you've lost your tourist card, arrive early and be prepared with a copy or you may have to pay a fine unless you've gotten a duplicate through Immigration (Migración). In any case, be sure to save enough pesos or dollars to pay your **$12 departure tax** (unless your ticket already includes it).

BY CAR OR RV

Three road routes connect Puerto Vallarta north with Tepic and San Blas, east with Guadalajara, and south via Melaque-Barra de Navidad with Manzanillo.

To Tepic, **Mexican National Highway 200** is all asphalt and in good condition most of its 104 miles (167 km) from Puerto Vallarta. Traffic is ordinarily light to moderate, except for some slow going around Tepic, and over a few low passes about 20 miles north of Puerto Vallarta. Allow three hours for the southbound trip and half an hour longer in the reverse direction for the winding 3,000-foot climb to Tepic.

A shortcut connects San Blas directly with Puerto Vallarta, avoiding the oft-congested uphill route through Tepic. Heading north on Highway 200, at Las Varas, turn off west on to Nayarit Highway 16 to Zacualpan and Platanitos, where the road continues through the coastal tropical forest to Santa Cruz village on the Bay of Matanchén. From there you can continue along the shoreline to San Blas. In the opposite direction, heading south from San Blas, follow the signed Puerto Vallarta turnoff to the right (south) a few hundred yards after the Santa Cruz de Miramar junction. Allow about three hours, either direction, for the entire San Blas-Puerto Vallarta trip.

The story is similar for Mexican National Highway 200 along the 172 miles (276 km) to Manzanillo via Barra de Navidad (134 mi./214 km). Trucks and a few potholes may cause slow going while climbing the 2,400-foot Sierra Cuale summit south of Puerto Vallarta, but light traffic should prevail along the other stretches. Allow about four hours to Manzanillo, three from Barra de Navidad, and the same in the opposite direction.

The Guadalajara route is nearly as easy. From Puerto Vallarta, follow Highway 200 as if to Tepic, but, just before Compostela (80 mi./129 km from Puerto Vallarta), follow the 22-mile

(36 km) Guadalajara-bound toll *(cuota)* short-cut east, via Chapalilla. From Chapalilla, connect seamlessly east via **Mexican National Highway 15 D** toll *(cuota)* expressway *autopista*. Although expensive (about $20 per car, much more for motor homes), the expressway is a breeze compared to the narrow, winding, and congested *libre* Highway 15. Allow around five hours at the wheel for the entire 214-mile (344 km) Guadalajara-Puerto Vallarta trip, either way (7 hours by the old *libre route*).

BY BUS

Many bus lines run through Puerto Vallarta. The major long-distance bus action is at the new **Camionera Central** (Central Bus Station) a few miles north of the airport. Reservations and ticketing are efficiently computerized, and most major lines accept credit cards. The shiny, air-conditioned complex resembles an airline terminal, with a cafeteria, juice bars, a travel agency, a long-distance telephone and fax service, luggage storage lockers, a gift shop, and a hotel reservation office (tel. 322/290-1014). The buses are usually crowded; don't tempt people with a dangling open purse or a bulging wallet in your pocket.

Mostly first- and luxury-class departure ticket counters line one long wall. First-class **Élite** line and its parent **Estrella Blanca** (tel. 322/290-1001), with its affiliated lines Turistar, Futura, Transportes Norte de Sonora, and Transportes Chihuahenses, connect the entire northwest-southeast Pacific Coast corridor. Northwesterly destinations include La Peñita (Rincón de Guayabitos), Tepic, San Blas, Mazatlán, all the way to Nogales or Mexicali and Tijuana on the U.S. border. Other departures head north, via Tepic, Torreón, and Chihuahua to Ciudad Juárez, at the U.S. border. Still others connect northeast, via Guadalajara, Aguascalientes, Zacatecas, and Saltillo, with Monterrey, where quick connections are available with the east Texas border at Matamoros. In the opposite direction, departures connect with the entire southeast Pacific Coast, including Melaque-Barra de Navidad, Manzanillo, Playa Azul junction, Lázaro Cárdenas,

Ixtapa, Zihuatanejo, and Acapulco (where you can transfer to Oaxaca-bound departures). Additionally, **Transportes Norte de Sonora** (TNS) departures connect north with San Blas via the coastal (Tepic bypass) shortcut.

New competing first-class line **TAP** (tel. 322/290-0119 or 322/290-1001), Transportes y Autobuses del Pacífico, provides about the same first-class northwest Pacific service as both Elite and Transportes Pacífico.

Transportes Pacífico (tel. 322/290-1008) offers first-class departures (for cash only) that also travel the northwest Pacific route, via Tepic and Mazatlán to Nogales, Mexicali, and Tijuana. Transportes Pacifico provides additional first-class connections east with Guadalajara and Mexico City direct, and others to Guadalajara by expressway shortcut *(corta)*.

Transportes Pacífico also provides very frequent second-class daytime connections north with Tepic, stopping everywhere, notably Bucerías, Sayulita, Guayabitos, La Peñita, Las Varas, and Compostela en route. The Bucerías bus fare should run less than $2, Sayulita $4, Guayabitos about $5, and Tepic or San Blas $7 (for San Blas, go by Transportes Norte de Sonora direct or Transportes del Pacifico second-class and transfer at Las Varas).

Affiliated lines **Autocamiones del Pacífico** and **Transportes Cihuatlán** (tel. 322/290-0994) provide many second-class and some first-class departures along the Jalisco Coast. Frequent second-class connections stop at El Tuito, Tomatlán, El Super, Careyes, Melaque, Barra de Navidad, and everywhere in between. They also connect with Guadalajara by the long southern route, via Melaque, Autlán, and San Clemente (a jumping-off point for Talpa, Mascota, and San Sebastián). Primera Plus, its luxury-class line, provides a few daily express connections southeast with Manzanillo, with stops at Melaque and Barra de Navidad.

A separate luxury-class service, a subsidiary of Flecha Amarilla, also called **Primera Plus** (tel. 322/290-0716, or toll-free 01-800/375-7587), also provides express connections, southeast, with Melaque, Barra de Navidad, Manzanillo, and Colima. Other Primera Plus departures connect east with Lake Chapala and Guadalajara, continuing to Aguascalientes, Irapuato, Celaya, Querétaro, and León. Affiliated line **Autobuses Costa Alegre** provides frequent second-class connections southeast along the Jalisco Coast, via El Tuito, El Super, Careyes, Melaque, Barra de Navidad, and all points in between.

Additionally, **ETN** (Enlaces Transportes Nacional, tel. 322/223-2999 or 322/290-0997) provides first-class departures connecting east with Guadalajara and Mexico City, offering continuing connections in Guadalajara with several Michoacán destinations.

Around the Bay of Banderas

As a destination city, Puerto Vallarta is packed with all the services, food, and accommodations a quality resort can supply. What Puerto Vallarta sometimes cannot offer, however, is peace and quiet.

But an out exists. The diadem of rustic retreats—fishing villages, palm-shadowed sandy beaches, diminutive resorts—that ring the Bay of Banderas can provide a day-, week-, or month-long respite from the citified tourist rush.

The southern-arc beach gems consist of Mismaloya, Boca de Tomatlán, Las Animas, Quimixto, and Yelapa.

The northern arc—Nuevo Vallarta, Bucerías, and Punta Mita—begins as Highway 200 crosses the Ameca River and enters the state of Nayarit. Here clocks shift from central to mountain time; heading north, set your watch back one hour.

NUEVO VALLARTA

The Nuevo Vallarta development, just north of the river Ameca, is Nayarit's design for a grand

© BRUCE WHIPPERMAN

a condominium complex on the broad Bay of Banderas

resort, potentially comparable to the Puerto Vallarta Zona Hotelera 10 miles south. The spurt of activity that began in the mid-1990s has continued until Nuevo Vallarta now has a green golf course, a marina, a flock of luxurious new homes, and many beachfront resort hotels and condominium complexes. At this writing, however, development continues at some spots, with the associated construction noise competing with the whoosh of the waves on Nuevo Vallarta's creamy beachfront.

Nevertheless, the **Club de Playa Nuevo Vallarta,** the core of the original development, finished for more than a decade, is indeed a pretty place—perfect for a relaxing beach afternoon. Get there by turning left at Avenida Nuevo Vallarta, about 5 miles (8 km) north of the airport, about a mile past north of the Ameca River bridge. At the end of the 1.4-mile entrance drive you'll come to the Club de Playa, where, past the parking lot (entrance fee about $15 per car), is the beach club with a public pool, snack bar, and seemingly endless beach, fine for a day's relaxation.

The miles-long beach is the main attraction. The nearly level golden white sand is perfect for beachcombing, and the water is excellent for surf fishing, swimming, bodysurfing, and boogie boarding. Beginning or intermediate surfing might be possible for those who bring their own boards.

Accommodations

Adjacent to the Club de Playa is Nuevo Vallarta's first world-class hotel, the palmy, Mediterranean-style, French-Canadian–owned twin development, with its older (circa-1990) section, the **Club Suites Marival,** beside the new, shinier **Grand Marival** (Blvd. Nuevo Vallarta, esq. Paseo Cocoteros, Nuevo Vallarta, Nayarit 63573, tel. 322/297-0100 or 322/226-8200, or toll-free Mex. tel. 800/326-6600, fax 322/297-0160, servicioh@clubmarival.com, www .gomarival.come, all-inclusive $200/day for two, low season, $270 high; Club section $10 less per person). The hotels sometimes invite the public to drop in on their continuous party ($50/day pp), which includes sports, crafts, games, and food and drink. All-inclusive packages include food, lodging, and activities. The cheaper Club section is half a block from the beach. If you reserve through an agent, be sure to ask for a package or promotional price.

Along the beach boulevard, Paseo de Cocoteros, about two miles south of the original development, a line of big new hotels woo vacationers with a plethora of facilities and long, velvety beaches. The 344-room **Vallarta Palace Resort** (Paseo de los Cocoteros 19, Nuevo Vallarta, Nayarit 63732, tel. 322/226-8470, Mex. toll-free tel. 01-800/672-5223, fax 322/226-8471, www.palaceresorts.com, all-inclusive $260 for two, kids 4–17 about $80) is the most established. Arrival there feels like approaching a small Elysium. Above the reception area rises an airy, angular atrium. Nearby, a garden of lovely ceramic fruits decorates whitewashed stairs leading down to a buffet loaded with salads, fruit, poultry, fish, meats, and desserts spread on one side of a spacious, guest-filled dining area. Outside are pools beneath palm trees along the beach, where crowds enjoy nightly dancing and shows. By day, guests lounge, swim, and frolic amid a varied menu of activities, from water aerobics and yoga to beach volleyball, bicycling, and kayaking.

Rates include all food, drinks, activities, and a deluxe ocean-view room with everything. If the season is right, you may be able to secure a reduced-rate package via the Internet or a travel agent. Be aware that this is partly a timeshare property and the management is always interested in selling you a timeshare.

Next door to the south, the **Occidental Grand Nuevo Vallarta** (Paseo de los Cocoteros 18, Nuevo Vallarta, Nayarit 63732, tel. 322/297-0400, fax 322/297-0082, www.occidental-hoteles.com, U.S-Canada toll-free tel. 800/858-2258, Mex. toll-free tel. 01-800/907-9500, $190 for two in low season, $230 high; kids under 6 free, kids 6–12 $50 in low season, $70 high) offers a similar all-inclusive vacation package; day passes, including all in-house, food, drinks, sports and entertainment, run about $40 per adult; night about $50. Bargain packages are often available by Internet reservation or through agents during non-peak seasons.

BUCERÍAS

The scruffy roadside clutter of Bucerías (Place of the Divers) is deceiving. Situated 12 miles (19 km) north of the Puerto Vallarta airport, Bucerías (pop. 5,000) residents and visitors enjoy the longest, creamiest beach on the Bay of Banderas. Local people have long flocked to Bucerías on Sunday for beach play, as well as for fresh seafood from one of several beachfront *palapa* restaurants (which, however, may be mostly closed weekdays).

For arrivals seeking at least a quiet week in the sun or at most a comfortable retirement, Bucerías offers many inviting possibilities. The town has developed continuously from its beginning as a fishing village of a few long dusty streets running parallel to the beach. Visitors from Puerto Vallarta began arriving and the town gradually aquired a sprinkling of small businesses—grocery stores, bakeries, and local-style restaurants. Recently, the wealth brought in by the growing expatriate colony supports several excellent restaurants and many good lodgings, from moderate hotel rooms, suites, and apartments, to luxurious beachfront villas.

Despite its burgeoning popularity, the original charm of Bucerías remains: lots of old-fashioned local color, especially around the lively town center market and the adjacent rickety mid-town footbridge over the creek (which blocks through traffic and divides Bucerias into a pair of tranquil, virtually traffic-free sub-villages), and the seemingly endless beach, with slowly breaking waves and soft, golden-white sand, perfect for swimming, bodysurfing, boogie boarding, surfing, and surf fishing. Tent camping is customary on the beach, especially during the Christmas and Easter holidays.

Accommodations

At the town's serene north end is the Playas de Huanacaxtle subdivision, with big flower-decorated villas, owned by well-heeled Mexicans and North Americans. Sprinkled among the intimate, palm-shaded *retornos* (cul-de-sacs)

PUERTO VALLARTA

are a number of good bungalow-style beach-side lodgings.

As you move southward from the north edge of town, the top-value accommodations begin with the **Vista Vallarta Suites** (Av. de los Picos s/n, Playas de Huanacaxtle, Bucerías, Nayarit 63732, tel. 329/298-0361 or 329/298-0360, U.S.-Canada toll-free tel. 888/888-9127, Mex. toll-free tel. 01-800/570-7292, info@vistavallartsuites.com, www.vistavallartasuites.com, $70 d, $130 q low season; $95 d, $165 q high). Here, three stories of comfortably furnished stucco and tile apartments cluster intimately around a palm-tufted beachside pool and patio. A loyal cadre of longtime guests—mostly U.S. and Canadian retiree-couples—return year after year to enjoy the big blue pool, the *palapa* restaurant, walks along the beach, and the company of fellow vacationers. All enjoy fully furnished two-bedroom suites with dining room, kitchenette, living room, cable TV, and private ocean-view balconies. Maids clean rooms daily, while downstairs, friendly, English-speaking clerks manage the desk and rent cars, boogie boards, and surfboards. Discounts may be negotiable for long-term rentals.

A block south, the family-style **Bungalows Princess** (Retorno Destiladeras, Playas Huanacaxtle, Bucerías, Nayarit 63732, tel. 329/298-0100 or 329/298-0110, fax 329/298-0068, bungalows_princess@hotmail.com, www.vallarta-info.com/rentals/princess.html, rooms $55 low season, $75 high, and up) looks out on the blue Bay of Banderas beneath the rustling fronds of lazy coco palms. Their several two-story, detached beachfront bungalows provide all the ingredients for a restful vacation for a family or group of friends. Behind the bungalows, beside an interior pool-patio, a stone's throw from the beach, a motel-style lineup of rooms and suites fills the economy needs of couples and small families.

A total of 36 bungalows, suites and rooms are available. The big, semideluxe (two-bedroom, two-bath) beachfront housekeeping bungalows rent, high season, for about $200, 160 low. A row of about six "interior" beachfront poolside (two-bedroom, two-bath) housekeeping bunga-

low apartments go for about $165 high season, $120 low. Away from the beach, facing a second pool-patio, a lineup of junior suites and rooms, rent, respectively, for about $110 high season, $90 low and $75 high, $55 low. Discounts and cheaper long-term rates are often available during the low months of January, May–June, and September–November. All rooms feature TV with HBO, phone, and air-conditioning; hotel amenities include desk service, a minimarket, and two pools, and credit cards are accepted.

Continuing south, nearby **Bungalows Los Picos** (Av. los Picos and Retorno Pontoque, Playas Huanacaxtle, Bucerías, Nayarit 63732, tel. 329/298-0470, fax 329/298-0131, lospicos@lospicos.com.mx, www.lospicos.com.mx, kitchenette suite $80 low, $95 high, and up) shares the same palm-shadowed Bucerías beachfront. The rambling, Mexican family-style complex centers around a big inner pool/patio, spreading shoreward, to a second motel-style bungalow wing beside a breezy beachside pool area. The most desirable units are the big three-bedroom ocean-front kitchenette bungalows (about $200 high, $160 low, with choice of a/c or fans, sleeping up to eight). Other units, off the beach, around a nevertheless inviting interior pool-patio include one-bedroom kitchenette apartments (about $125 high, $100 low, with choice of fans or a/c, sleeping four); and adjacent smaller, four-person kitchenette suites ($95 high, $80 low, all with a/c). A few smaller fan-only rooms ($50 high, $42 low) are also available. All units are clean and comfortably furnished. Amenities include cable TV, snack restaurant, lounge, Internet café, two pools; parking, and credit cards accepted. During low seasons, the management sometimes offers such promotions as three nights for the price of two; discounts for long-term rentals are usually available. Bargain under all conditions.

About a mile south, near the good restaurants, on the opposite of town, consider the inviting, gay-friendly, moderately priced **C Casa Tranquila** (Morelos 7A, Bucerías, Nayarit 63732, tel. 329/298-1767, cell 322/728-7519, home@casatranquila-bucerias.com, or casatranquila@prodigy.net.com, www.casa

tranquila-bucerias.com, $40–55 d). Welcoming owners Patricia Mendez and Joan Quickstad offer five compact one-bedroom kitchenette apartments that open to a lovely tropical pool-patio garden. All of the apartments are clean, comfortable, and individually decorated (themes are Aztec, Gringo, Vaquero, Suzie Wong, and Quimixto). Rates range depending on season and whether you prefer a/c or fan. Amenities include the bookstore-coffee shop next door, massage, laundry service, airport pickup, and services and good restaurants close by.

Around the corner, less than a block away, find the inviting **C Hotel Palmeras** (35 Lázaro Cárdenas, Bucerías, Nayarit 63732, from U.S. and Canada direct, dial tel. 1-647/722-4139, local tel./fax 329/298-1288, hotelpalmeras35@yahoo.com, www.hotel palmeras.com, $35 1br low season, $55 high; $65 low 2br, $90 high; and up). Here you have all the basics for a cozy tropical beach vacation: about 20 comfortable, attractively decorated one- and two-bedroom kitchenette apartments, built around a tranquil and spacious tropical pool-patio, just a block from the beach. If some of the apartments seem a bit dark, ask for one upstairs for more light and privacy. Recent construction has added a new wing of apartments. Prices, moreover, are right, with the one-bedrooms in the old wing running about $35 low season, $55 high, two bedrooms about $65 low, $90 high for four persons, all with a/c, fans, and kitchenettes. The newer wing apartments, all either studios or one-bedroom, run about $65 low season, $80 high ($90 and $105 for the penthouse); all with a/c, fans, and cable TV. Amenities include lounge with satellite TV, wireless Internet, and good restaurants close-by.

About four blocks farther south is the popular **Bungalows Arroyo** (500 Lázaro Cárdenas, Bucerías, Nayarit 63732, tel./fax 329/298-0076, bungalowsarroyo@hotmail.com, $100/ day low season, $120 high). The dozen-odd roomy, two-bedroom apartments are clustered beside a palmy swimming pool and garden half a block from the beach. The units are comfortably furnished, each with king-sized beds,

private balcony, kitchen, and living and dining room. Discounts are available for monthly rentals. They're popular; get your winter reservations in months early.

(Note: Development has eliminated both of Bucerías' trailer parks. As of this writing, the closest trailer parks are south in Puerto Vallarta, and north in Sayulita.)

RENTAL AGENTS

If you can't find your ideal Bucerías vacation retreat by yourself, try savvy and personable Bucerías resident **Victoria Pratt** (Retorno Flamingos 20, tel. 329/298-1644, fax 329/298-0932, buceriasvillas@pvr.cybercable.net.mx), on the sorth side of town, a block north of the big Decameron resort complex. She manages rentals for a number of choice Bucerías villas, houses, and apartments. Other competent Bucerías real estate/rental agents are easy to contact ahead of time through the Internet or locally. For more information, contact **Las Palmas Travel** (tel. 329/298-0060, fax 329/298-0061, www.las-palmas-travel.com) or **The Real Estate Group** (tel. 329/298-1212, www.move2mexico.com).

Food

A number of good restaurants serve Bucerías's cadre of discriminating diners. Most of the restaurants lie between the cross streets of Galeana and Morelos, along Calle Lázaro Cárdenas, the street that runs parallel to the beach, beginning just south of the town-center Puente de los Besos (Bridge of the Kisses). The two best and most popular restaurants are probably Sandrina's and ocean-view Claudio's Meson Bay.

Find **C Sandrina's** (btwn. Galeana and Morelos, tel. 329/298-0273, 3–10:30 P.M. Wed.–Mon., entrees $8–15), just south of Hotel Palmera, the labor of love of Victoria, B.C., expatriates Andrew and Sandra Neumann. They serve a varied late-lunch and dinner Mediterranean fusion menu with lots of Greek specialties (antipastos, salads, souvlaki, lasagna) and exquisite mahimahi fish fillet dinners, in an inviting inside-outside garden setting.

Especially popular and equally enjoyable for

lunch or dinner, [C] **Claudio's Meson Bay** (tel. 329/298-1634, 2–10 P.M. daily, entrees $8–18) is a block farther north on the beach side. Here the welcoming owner has everything in place in his large airy beachfront *palapa,* perfect for evening happy-hour sunsets. Offerings include super-fresh catch-of-the-day fish, lobster, prawns, clams, and oysters ($8–14), plus a bountiful meat barbecue ($8–18), and a generous salad bar ($5). This all climaxes every Wednesday night with an overflowing all-you-can-eat barbecue ($15).

After trying the above, you might also check out a number of other reliably recommended restaurants in the same neighborhood. Moving south to north, first comes **Karen's Place** (corner of Lázaro Cárdenas and Juárez, tel. 329/298-1499, 8:30 A.M.–10 P.M. Mon.–Sat., 8:30 A.M.–3 P.M. Sun., $5–12), in the big Costa Dorada condo complex, serving breakfast, lunch, early dinner, and Sunday champagne brunch. Continue north a block to gourmet **Expressions** (across Lázaro Cárdenas from Hotel Palmera, $12–14) with light, Asian-Continental fusion cuisine, such as sesame chicken and veal picata; next door comes the **Red Apple** (corner of Morelos, tel. 329/298-1235, 8:30 A.M.–10 P.M. Mon.–Sat., 8 A.M.–4 P.M. Sun., $5–15), an upstairs ocean-view palapa, specializing in garlic shrimp, fajitas, and hearty *ranchero* breakfasts. For more options, check out **Café Magna** (just north of Morelos), a sports bar serving finger-lickin' ribs and fish and chips. For more popcorn and beer camaraderie, try the **Gecko Pub** (half a block east on Morelos).

Even if you're only passing through Bucerías, don't miss **Pie in the Sky** (tel. 322/298-0838 or toll-free 01-800/849-2339, 9 A.M.–8 P.M. daily), the little bakery that's developed a thriving business soothing the collective sweet tooth of Puerto Vallarta's expatriate and retiree colony. Their chocolate-nut cookies have to be tasted to be believed. Watch for the sign on the inland side of the highway just south of town.

ROAD TO PUNTA MITA

A day trip on the road to Punta Mita takes you past white-sand beaches, fishing villages,

and waterfront *palapa* restaurants. A few miles north of Bucerías the Punta Mita highway splits left (west), and passes over Highway 200. Drivers, mark your mileage (or reset your odometer). Within a mile (2 km), look downhill on the left and you'll see the formerly drowsy, now developing, little town of **Cruz de Huanacaxtle** above a small fishing harbor. Although the town has stores, a good café, a few lodgings, and a protected boat and yacht anchorage, it lacks a decent beach.

Playa Manzanillo and Hotel Piedra Blanca

Half a mile (at around Mile 2/Km 3) farther on, a rough side road to the left leads to beautiful Playa Manzanillo and the Hotel Piedra Blanca. The beach itself, a carpet of fine, golden-white coral sand, stretches along a little cove sheltered by a limestone headland—thus Piedra Blanca (White Stone). This place was made for peaceful vacationing: snorkeling at nearby **Playa Piedra Blanca** on the opposite side of the headland; fishing from the beach, rocks, or by boat launched on the beach or hired in the Cruz de Huanacaxtle harbor.

The **Hotel Piedra Blanca** (Alcatraz 36, Cruz de Huanacaxtle, Nayarit 63732, tel. 329/295-5489 or 329/295-5493, reserva_hotel pblanca@hotmail.com, $56 d year-round, $37 for more than two weeks) is an unpretentious, family-managed resort. The best of the big, plain but comfortable suites offer upstairs ocean views. All the ingredients—a tennis court, a shelf of used paperback novels, and a rustic *palapa* restaurant beside an inviting beach-view pool and patio-are perfect for a season of tranquil relaxation. The 41 suites have kitchenettes, air-conditioning, and cable TV; credit cards are not accepted.

Past Piedra Blanca, the highway winds for 12 miles (19 km) to Punta Mita through the bushy summer-fall green jungle country at the foot of the Sierra Vallejo. Although pristine only a few years ago, this stretch is now pocked with condo and villa developments that unfortunately restrict access to the emerald-forested and coral-studded shoreline. Let's hope aroused local citizens will coax authorities to establish public access.

Rock coral, the limestone skeleton of living coral, becomes gradually more common as you move west along the Punta Mita coast, thus tinting the water aqua and the sand white. As the highway approaches Punta Mita, the living reef offshore becomes intact and continuous.

Playa Destiladeras

A pair of ocean-side *palapa* restaurants (at Mile 5/Km 8) mark Playa Destiladeras, a beach-lover's heavenly mile of white sand. Two- to five-foot waves roll in gently, providing good conditions for bodysurfing and boogie boarding. Surfing gets better the closer you get to the end of the headland at **Punta el Burro** (known also as Punta Veneros), where good left-breaking waves make it popular with local surfers.

The intriguing label *destiladeras* originates with the fresh water dripping from the cliffs past Punta el Burro, collecting in freshwater pools right beside the ocean. Campers who happen upon one of these pools may find their water problems solved.

Restaurant Amapas

For a treat, stop in at the friendly, family-run Restaurant Amapas (Mile 8/Km 13, 9 A.M.–sunset daily). Homesteaded when the Punta Mita road was a mere path through the jungle, Restaurant Amapas still retains a country flavor. Ducks waddle around the yard, *jabali* (wild pigs) snort in their pen, and candles flicker during the evening twilight as the elderly owner recalls her now-deceased husband hunting food for the table: "We ate deer, javelina, ducks, coatimundi, rattlesnake, iguana…whatever we could catch." Although local hunters supply much of the game, she and her daughter-in-law do all the cooking, and their many loyal customers still enjoy the same wild fare.

PUNTA MITA

In the early 1990s, the Mexican government concluded a deal with private interests to build the Four Seasons resort development at Corral de Riscos, at the end of the Punta Mita highway. The idyllic Corral de Riscos inlet, however, was *ejido* (communally owned) land and base of operations for the local fishing and boating cooperative, Cooperativa Corral de Riscos. In 1995 the government moved the people, under protest, into modern housing beside a new anchorage at nearby Playa Anclote. Now the *ejido* people seem to have grudgingly accepted their new housing and harbor (which they've even named "Nuevo Corral de Riscos"). At approximately Mile 12, a private gate on the right leads to the super-exclusive 18-hole golf course and 100-room Four Seasons Hotel.

The Hotel Four Seasons was only the first step in government plans for Punta Mita development. Real estate offices show (with pride) a map of about five projected large hotels and several condominium complexes (some already built, others under construction). Although all of this ferment bodes well for employment prospects of local people, the question of whether it will transform Punta Mita for the better or the worse will become more apparent after the dust of construction settles.

The name Punta Mita (actually Punta de Mita) encompasses the entire northwestern headland of the Bay of Banderas. Important sections include the Emiliano Zapata village (pop. about 1,000) on the bluff above the beach; Nuevo Corral de Riscos (pop. about 500), the new town that the government built for the displaced *ejido* people, adjacent, west of Emiliano Zapata; and the boat harbor and beachfront *palapa* restaurant strip, called Playa Anclote, or simply "Anclote," by local folks.

The hotel people are trying to erase Corral de Riscos, the lovely west-side fishing inlet and location of the original *ejido* village, from memory. "Corral de Riscos doesn't exist," they claim.

Corral de Riscos

I'm hopeful that someday, public land access will be restored to the lovely sand crescent that borders the petite, gorgeous Corral de Riscos inlet, former anchorage of the Corral de Riscos fishing cooperative.

PUERTO VALLARTA

If you want to visit Corral de Riscos now, you have to hire a launch and a captain (check with English-speaking guide Rudi Hofer at the office of the Caseta Cooperative Punta Mita Servicios Turísticos), who might be able, or can recommend someone, to guide you.

When land access is again established, then families will again be able to swim and picnic on the golden sand, in view of the two small bare-rock islands, **Isla del Mono** on the left, and **Isla de las Abandonadas** on the right, that shelter the scenic lagoon. The name of the former comes from a *mono* (monkey) face people see in one of the outcroppings; the latter label springs from a legend of fishermen who went out to sea and never returned. Las Abandonadas were their wives, who waited on the islet for years, vainly searching the horizon for their lost husbands.

◖ Playa Anclote

Head left, downhill, at the highway's end (Mile 13/Km 21) toward Playa Anclote (An-

chor Beach), which gets its name from the galleon anchor displayed at one of the beachside *palapa* restaurants. The beach itself is a broad, half-mile-long curving strand of soft, very fine coral sand. The water is shallow for a long distance out, and the waves are gentle and long-breaking, good for beginning surfing, boogie boarding, and bodysurfing.

A few hundred yards downhill from the highway, a block left of the road T at the beach-front, stands the **Caseta Cooperativa Corral de Riscos Servicios Turísticos** (Av. Anclote 17, tel./fax 329/291-6298, cooperativapuntamita@prodigy.net.mx). This former fishing cooperative, now tourism provider, offers a number of services, such as sightseeing and snorkel tours at the Marietas Island, an hour offshore, fishing for ($40/hour), whale-watching (Dec.–March), and surf instruction. One of the guiding lights of the Cooperativa whom you might ask for at the office is personable Austrian-English-German-Spanish guide Rudi Hofer, who among other things leads visitors on sea-mammal, birdwatching, snorkel, and fishing excursions ($100 for two–eight people) especially during the wildlife-rich winter months.

Alternatively, look up the veteran surf instructor and guide **Eduardo del Valle Ochoa** (Langostina 3, Cruz de Huanacaxtle, tel. 329/295-5087 or in Punta Mita 329/291-6633, acciontropical@hotmail.com www.acciontropical.com.mx), who welcomes visitors daily across the street at his Acción Tropical shop, west of the *cooperativa* office. Besides offering surfing lessons, Eduardo arranges sportfishing launches (Dec.–May, 3 hours about $110, complete) and snorkeling, wildlife-watching, and photography boat tours to the pristine offshore wildlife sanctuaries of Islas Las Marietas. During a typical half-day trip, visitors may glimpse dolphins, sea turtles, and often whales, as well as visit breeding grounds for brown and blue-footed boobies, Heerman's gulls, and other birds.

Another surf lessons option is to go with Oscar, veteran surf instructor, whose surf equipment rental shop, **Oscar's Rentals** (www.puntamita.com/oscarsrentals), is next door to the Casa Cooperativa Corral de Riscos.

© BRUCE WHIPPERMAN

Playa Anclote curves southward toward Punta Mita.

Accommodations

If you decide to stay, Punta Mita offers a number of comfortable accommodations. In the town of Emiliano Zapata, on the bluff above Playa Anclote, you have your choice of a comfortable apartment complex, a small bed-and-breakfast, and a modest hotel. Most comfortable is **Casa Las Palmas** (Calle Francisco Madero, Emiliano Zapata, Punta de Mita, Nayarit 63734, tel. 329/291-6304, elas_palmas72@hotmail.com, www.casalaspalmas.net, $50 d low season, $70 high; $70 2br low season, $90 high), tucked on a quiet side street. Owner/builders David and Irene Forbes offer about 10 spacious apartments, in two sections, one built around an inviting inner garden on one side of the street and an inviting pool patio on the other. Inside, the immaculate, commodious one-bedroom and two-bedroom apartments are finished in pleasingly rustic brick and stucco, with soft chairs, gleaming bathrooms, and soft beds. Discounts are available for long-term rentals. Guests are welcome to use the beautiful blue pool and whirlpool hot tub across the street.

Alternatively, consider the downscale **Hotel Punta de Mita** (Hidalgo 5, Fracc. E. Zapata, Punta de Mita, Nayarit 63734, tel. 329/291-6269. www.hotelpuntamita.com, $35), overlooking the bay in Emiliano Zapata. Here, what you see is what you get: about 15 small, plain motel-style rooms around an inviting, kid-friendly grassy pool/patio. Rates run about $35 per room, with air-conditioning, bunk bed for children, and small kitchenette.

Informal tent **camping** and RV parking around Punta Mita is possible when not prohibited by the government because of construction; ask at the Playa Anclote restaurants if it's okay to camp under big trees at either end of the beach. Stores nearby and on the highway in Emiliano Zapata (commonly known as Punta Mita) back on the highway a quarter-mile east can furnish the necessities, including drinking water.

If you must stay on the beach, you can do it, at luscious Playa Anclote's first (and only at this writing) beachfront hotel, the **Hotel**

Mesón de Mita (Av. Anclote, Corral de Riscos Nuevo, Nayarit 63734, tel. 329/291-6330, mesondemita@yahoo.com.mx, $65 d low season, $80 high). Owners offer eight spacious, comfortably furnished rooms, with shiny baths and a/c; some with ocean views, all overlooking the hotel's beachfront restaurant and pool patio.

Increased visitor arrivals now support a sprinkling of mid- to high-end accommodations. Among the loveliest is **(Casa Las Brisas** (Playa Cayero, Punta de Mita, Nayarit 63734, tel. 329/298-4114, fax 329/298-4112, toll-free U.S. tel. 1-206/219-0671, visit www.casalasbrisas.com, all-inclusive $415 for two) of friendly owner/manager/builder Mark Lindskog. Mark personally makes sure that his guests enjoy the best of all possible tropical worlds: a breezy creamy-sand beach, gourmet cuisine, fine wines, spacious art- and antique-decorated rooms, and plenty of peace and quiet, around an azure pool-patio. For the active, Mark provides a universal gym station, and optional fishing, horseback riding, surfing, golf, and more. All lodging, food, and drinks are included. (You may also reserve Casa las Brisas accommodations through Mexico Boutique Hotels, toll-free in U.S. and Can. 800/728-9098, or in Mex. 01-800/508-7923, info@mexicoboutiquehotels.com, www.mexicoboutiquehotels.com.)

For an equally unusual, but completely different, lodging experience, look into the **(Huerta de la Paz** (Km 4, Carretera Higuera Blanca, Punta de Mita, Nayarit 63764, sandra@huertalapaz.com, www.huertalapaz.com, $125 larger cabanas, $55 and $85 smaller). This ecoretreat is the life project of artist-pioneer Sandra Richards, formerly of San Francisco, California. In 10 years of solid work, Sandra has carved her version of paradise out of the Punta Mita foothill tropical forest. Now, her bucolic acreage encompasses mini-groves of mandarin orange and mango trees, and an all-organic vegetable garden. Besides her horticultural work, Sandra enjoys both cooking and company, so she has added four comfortable guest cabanas to her paradise. Two of the cabanas she describes as "rustic-elegant." Indeed; they are spacious, art- and antique-decorated and enjoy luxurious panoramic forest and ocean views. The other two cabanas are also comfortable, with panoramic views, but more modestly (although invitingly) furnished. Sandra asks $125 with breakfast for two (fruit, baked bread, scones, coffee, tea, juice) for the larger cabanas, and $55 and $85, also with breakfast, for the smaller. She closes down during the buggier, rainy season (July 1–Oct. 15).

Access directions for both Casa Las Brisas and Huerta de la Paz are similar. For both, from the Punta Mita Highway at Mile 11 (Km 18) follow the Higuera Blanca road fork north. (If you reach the Four Seasons Hotel gate, turn around; you've gone too far.) Heading north, within a mile, cross two bridges. For Casa Las Brisas, turn left on to the dirt road after the second bridge. Continue about half a mile to the beach, where you bear left at the fork. Continue another approximately quarter mile to Casa Las Brisas, marked by a small tile plaque, on the right.

For Huerta de la Paz, after the second bridge, continue straight ahead. Follow the signs, to the Higuera de la Paz entrance driveway, a total of 3.0 miles (4.8 km) from the Punta Mita highway turnoff.

RENTAL AGENTS

A number of real estate agents handle villa, house, and condo rentals in Punta Mita. If you're looking for a high-end villa ($200/day and up), you might check out **Punta Mita Realty** (tel. 329/291-6420, fax 329/291-6421, www.puntarealty.com), on beachfront Avenida Anclote by the restaurant El Dorado. For more affordable ($40 and up) apartments, condominiums, and houses, visit **www.puntamita .com,** which lists more modest owner-managed rentals. Bucerías rental agents also manage Punta Mita rentals.

Food

On the beachfront street, you'll find one of Playa Anclote's oldest and best seafood restaurants, ☕ **El Dorado** (tel. 329/291-6296 or 329/291-6297, 9:30 A.M.– 9:30 P.M. daily). Take a table in the airy upstairs ocean-view seating area. The menu ($5–18) is based on meat, poultry, and the bounty of super-fresh snapper, scallops, oysters, and lobsters that local fisherfolk bring onto the beach.

For something a bit fancier, try **Tino's** restaurant (tel. 329/291-6473, 11 A.M.–9:30 P.M. daily, $6–22), next door to El Dorado. This is the newest member of a chain of three restuaurants, the original in the Puerto Vallarta Pitillal district, next in Nuevo Vallarta, and now in Punta Mita. Here it's nearly all seafood, from Marlin tacos and shrimp salad to mixed fish kebab and oysters Nuevo Vallarta.

Other good Punta Mita restaurant choices are **Rocio's** on Playa Anclote and **Vito's** Italian restaurant, on Calle Pez Vela, uphill in Emiliano Zapata.

GETTING TO NUEVO VALLARTA, BUCERÍAS, AND PUNTA MITA

Autotransportes Medina (1410 Brasil, tel. 322/212-4732 or 322/222-7279) buses complete a flood of daily round-trips between Playa Anclote (Restaurant El Dorado terminal) and the Puerto Vallarta station, north of the *malecón*. In Puerto Vallarta, walk or hire a taxi to the terminal, or catch the bus as it heads north along the airport boulevard through the Zona Hotelera. Stops en route include Bucerías, Cruz de Huanacaxtle, Piedra Blanca, and Destiladeras. The last bus returns to Puerto Vallarta at about 9 P.M.

THE JALISCO COAST

The country between Puerto Vallarta and Barra de Navidad is a landscape ripe for travelers who enjoy getting away from the tourist track. Development has scarcely penetrated its vast tracts of mountainous jungle, tangled thorny scrub, and pine-tufted summit forests. Few footprints mark its many miles of curving, golden beaches.

Cabo Corrientes, Mexico's great western cape, defines the Jalisco Coast. Beginning at Puerto Vallarta, the Bay of Banderas's shoreline juts 40 miles (64 km) southwest into the Pacific, forming Cabo Corrientes. Like a giant's great protecting chin, Cabo Corrientes regularly deflects Pacific northbound storms past Puerto Vallarta.

South of the cape, the coastline curves gently southeast, indented by a trio of broad, beach- and islet-studded bays—Chamela, Tenacatita, and Navidad—all havens for lovers of sun, sand, and surf. Consquently, for most visitors, the Jalisco Coast's major attractions are its magnificent seclusion and outdoor beach and ocean pleasures. Topping the list are abundant fishing (fresh water, deep ocean, and surf), beachcombing, wildlife viewing, off-road adventuring, and scuba diving, snorkeling, and surfing.

The ripe plums at the Jalisco Coast's southern border with the state of Colima are the twin country beach resorts of Melaque and Barra de Navidad, long favorites of a legion of international travelers seeking paradise at a moderate price. Excepting Melaque and Barra de Navidad, the Jalisco Coast is nearly all pioneer country, with only a few villages.

HIGHLIGHTS

Tehualmixtle: Idyllic Tehualmixtle cove, including nearby **El Maito** beach and **Tlalpuyeque** hot spring, might be perfect for those prepared travelers who enjoy off-the-tourist-trail adventures (page 269).

El Careyes Beach Resort: This uniquely lovely hotel and spa, perched like a gem on a headland-enfolded little bay, is good for at least a stop for lunch, which you may be tempted to stretch out for a memorably relaxing week in the sun (page 279).

Playa el Tecuán: The north end of this wild, white-sand beach offers an abundance of bird-watching opportunities. Most other outdoor activities are also available, including kayaking on the mangrove lagoon, surf fishing, and advanced surfing (page 281).

Playa Tenacatita: For campers and RVers, this big, lovely beach has nearly everything, from informal RV parking, a shady palm grove, a river (the Río Purificación), a mangrove lagoon for wildlife-viewing and kayaking, abandoned *palapas* for tenters, beachfront *palapa* restaurants, a coral reef for snorkeling and scuba diving from the shore, and much more. It's a delight just to visit for a day and gets better the longer you stay (page 281).

Laguna de Navidad: The far reaches of the Laguna de Navidad are home to dozens of common species, and others, such as bright parrots, tanagers, orioles, wildcats, and crocodiles, that are not so common. Hire a guide and make a whole day of it (page 289).

Boat Trip to Colimilla: A prime Barra de Navidad diversion is to ride a boat across the mirror-smooth Laguna de Navidad for a superfresh seafood lunch or early dinner (page 293).

LOOK FOR **C** TO FIND RECOMMENDED SIGHTS, ACTIVITIES, DINING, AND LODGING.

Fortunately, however, everyone who travels south of Puerto Vallarta doesn't have to be a Daniel Boone. The coastal strip within a few miles of the highway has acquired some amenities—stores, trailer parks, campgrounds, hotels, and a scattering of small resorts, some humble and some posh—all enough to become well known to Puerto Vallarta people as the Costa Alegre (Happy Coast).

PLANNING YOUR TIME

Let's consider the posh first. Moving from Puerto Vallarta south along the luxurious path less traveled, you might first stay at least an overnight in one of the Italian designer-chic cabañas of the **Hotelito Desconocido** on its pristine seaside lagoon. Continue on for an overnight at **Las Alamandas,** surfing resort for movie stars, moguls, and maharajas. Next, at least stop for lunch or dinner at regally elegant **El Careyes Beach Resort,** tucked on a patch of sand on its own exceptionally lovely, wildlife-rich little bay. Finally, before Barra de Navidad, lodge a night or two as you explore the sylvan forested swales, meandering golf course, and luxuriously isolated beaches of the **El Tamarindo** jungle country club and vacation home paradise for the rich and famous.

On the other hand, for travelers seeking the moderately priced, home-grown delights of south-seas Mexico, the Costa Alegre offers what local people have known for years: plenty of sun, fresh seafood, clear blue water, and sandy beaches, some of which stretch for miles, while others are tucked away in little rocky coves like pearls in an oyster.

First out of Puerto Vallarta, follow the detour into rustically pristine Cabo Corrientes country, to the bucolic **Tehualmixtle** fishing hamlet, and enjoy a one- or two-day idyll, sharpened by the local memory of galleons, shipwrecks, the turn-of-the-20th-century cocaine trade, and a visit to a community hot spring.

Farther south, beachcomb and surf-fish the curving, sandy reach of islet-dotted **Chamela Bay** by day while lodging at a friendly local trailer park or homey hotel by night. Continue

Horses are often seen on the streets of Barra de Navidad.

and spend a day or two in a small beachfront hotel or your own camp at the scuba, snorkel, and fisherfolks' haven of **Tenacatita.** Continue for more of the same at gorgeous **Boca de Iguana** mangrove jungle lagoon and beach, and then hop a few miles farther south to petite **La Manzanilla** beach resort town, where you can enjoy days dining on super-fresh seafood and cozy nights being lulled to sleep by the swish of the friendly La Manzanilla waves.

Whatever your style of travel, the reward at the end of the Road to Barra de Navidad are the manifold surprises of the small twin beach-resort towns of **Barra de Navidad** and **San Patricio-Melaque.** Here, multiple pleasures beckon if you linger for two days or more: strolling the beach, gazing out at the languid wave-washed shoreline from beneath a shady palapa, wildlife-watching in the broad mirror-smooth Laguna de Navidad, fishing for wild tuna and *dorado,* and enjoying fine fare, from steaming streetfront tacos to nouvelle gourmet restaurant cuisine.

THE JALISCO COAST

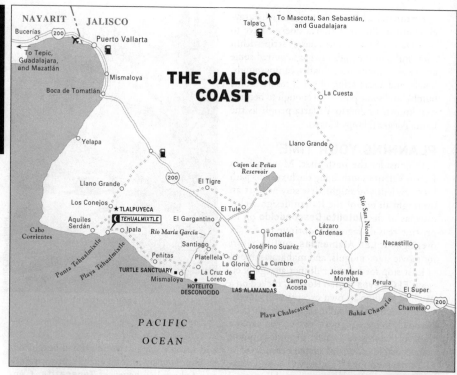

Road to Barra de Navidad

If you're driving, note your odometer mileage (or reset your tripmeter to zero) as you pass the Pemex gas station at Km 214 on Highway 200 at the south edge of Puerto Vallarta. In the open southern country, mileage and roadside kilometer markers are a useful way to remember where your little paradise is hidden.

If you're not driving, simply hop on one of the many southbound Autocamiones del Pacífico or Transportes Cihuatlán buses just before they pass at the south-end gas station. Let the driver know a few minutes beforehand where along the road you want to get off.

CHICO'S PARADISE

The last outpost on the Puerto Vallarta tour-bus circuit is Chico's Paradise (at Km 192,

tel. 322/223-6005 or 322/223-6006, 9 A.M.–7 P.M. daily), 13 miles (22 km) from the south edge of Puerto Vallarta in the lush jungle country. Here, the clear, cool Río Tuito cascades over a collection of smooth, friendly granite boulders. Chico's restaurant is a big multi-level *palapa* that overlooks the entire beautiful scene—deep green pools for swimming, flat warm rocks for sunning, and gurgling gentle waterfalls for splashing. Although a few homesteads dot the streamside nearby, the original Chico's still dominates, although its reputation rests mainly on the beauty of the setting rather than the quality of its menu.

The forest-perfumed breezes, the gurgling, crystal stream, and the friendly, relaxed ambience

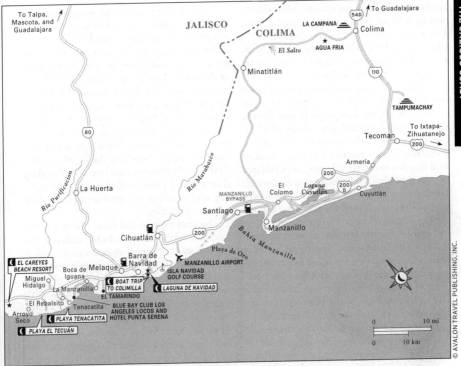

© AVALON TRAVEL PUBLISHING, INC.

are perfect for shedding the cares of the world. Although as yet there are no formal lodgings, a number of potential camping spots border the river, both up- and downstream. Stores at either the nearby upstream Las Juntas village or Boca de Tomatlán, three miles downhill, can provide supplies.

Adventurers can hire local guides (ask at Chico's restaurant) for horseback rides along the river and overnight treks into the green, jungly **Sierra Lagunillas** that rises on both sides of the river. If you're quiet and aware, you may be rewarded with views of chattering parrots, dozing iguanas, feisty javelinas (wild pigs), clownish *tejones* (coatimundis), and wary *gatos de montaña* (wildcats).

Alternatively, try a **jungle canopy tour** (tel. 322/223-0649, $79). For the fearless and fit only; you ride at treetop heights like a bird through the tropical forest. The local inventor is

ecologically aware Jeff Coates ("Gringo Bob," as he's known to local folks), who's been receiving visitors since about 2000 at his forest preserve, uphill past Chico's Paradise. Or you can try rival **Canopy Tour los Veranos** (tel. 322/223-6060, www.canopytours-vallarta.com, $77) nearby.

Get to both of these by car or bus, via Hwy. 200 south, about a mile uphill past Chico's Paradise. At Las Juntas village, turn right on to the dirt side road. Continue about a mile to Jeff Coates's place; or continue a fraction of a mile farther to Canopy Tour los Veranos at the end of the road.

CABO CORRIENTES COUNTRY
El Tuito

The town of El Tuito, at Km 170 (27 mi./44 km from Puerto Vallarta), looks from the highway like nothing more than a bus stop (although it has finally acquired a gas station). Most visitors pass by without even giving a second glance. This is a pity, because El Tuito (pop. 3,500) is a friendly little colonial-era town that spreads along a long main street to a pretty town square about a mile from the highway.

El Tuito enjoys at least two claims to fame: Besides being the mescal capital of western Jalisco, it's the jumping-off spot for the seldom-visited coastal hinterland of Cabo Corrientes, the southernmost lip of the Bay of Banderas. This is pioneer country, a land of wild beaches and sylvan forests, unpenetrated by paved roads. Wild creatures still abound: Turtles come ashore to lay their eggs, hawks soar, parrots swarm, and the faraway scream of the jaguar can yet be heard in the night.

The rush for the **raicilla,** as local connoisseurs call El Tuito *mescal,* begins on Saturday when men crowd into town and begin upending bottles around noon, without even bothering to sit down. For a given individual, this cannot last too long, so the fallen are continually replaced by fresh arrivals all weekend.

Although El Tuito is famous for the *raicilla,* it is not the source. *Raicilla* comes from the sweet sap of the maguey plants, a close relative of the cactuslike century plant, which blooms once and then dies. The *ejido* (cooperative farm) of Cicatán (see-kah-TAHN), eight miles out along the dirt road as you head to the coast west of town, cultivates the maguey.

Along the Road to Aquiles Serdán

You can get to the coast with or without your own wheels. If you're driving, it should be a strong, high-clearance vehicle (pickup, jeep, very maneuverable RV, or VW van) filled with gas; if you're not driving, trucks and VW taxivans (*combis* or *colectivos*) make daily trips from the El Tuito town plaza (at this writing around 2 P.M.; returning from Tehualmixtle at 9 A.M.). Their destinations include the coastal hamlet of Aquiles Serdán, the storied fishing cove of Tehualmixtle, and the farming village of Ipala beside the wide Bahía de Tehualmixtle. Fare runs several dollars per person; inquire at the west end of the El Tuito central plaza.

Getting there along the bumpy, rutted, sometimes steep 23-mile (37 km) dirt track is half the fun of Aquiles Serdán (pop. 200). If you're driving, mark your odometer where the road takes off from the southwest corner of the town plaza. About eight miles (13 km) from the plaza, you'll pass through the lands of the Cicatán mescal liquor cooperative, marked only by a crumbling thatch house on the right. On the left, you'll soon glimpse a field of maguey in the distance. A few dozen families (who live in the hills past the far side of the field) quietly go about their business of tending their maguey plants and extracting, fermenting, and distilling the precious sap into their renowned *raicilla.*

The road dips up and down the rest of the way, over sylvan hillsides dotted with oak *(robles),* through intimate stream valleys perfect for parking an RV or setting up a tent, and past the hardscrabble rancho-hamlets of Llano Grande (Broad Plain; 14 mi./22 km), with stores, *comedores* (places to eat), and a *Centro de Salud;* and **Los Conejos** (The Rabbits; 19 mi./30 km). At Los Conejos, a signed road forks left 5 miles (8 km) to **Tlalpuyeque** hot spring and and sacred site. Obey local custom and refrain from nude bathing.

You can't get lost, because there's only one route until a few miles past Los Conejos, where a fork (23 mi./37 km) marks your approach to Aquiles Serdán. The left branch continues south a few miles to Maito and Tehualmixtle. A mile and a half to the north along the right branch you'll arrive at the Río Tecolotlán. Aquiles Serdán stands on the far bank, across 100 yards of watery sand. Fortunately the riverbed road is concrete-bottomed, and, if it's in good repair, you can drive right across the streambed any time other than after a storm. If you can't drive across, roll up your pants legs and walk across, like most of the local folks do.

Aquiles Serdán

The Aquiles Serdán villagers see so few outsiders that you'll become their attraction of the week. Wave and say *hola,* buy a *refresco,* and stroll around town. After a while, the kids will stop

Tehualmixtle, basking behind its sheltering headland, is the reward to travelers who are willing and able to stray from the well-worn path.

crowding around and the adults will stop staring when they've found out that you, too, are human. By that time, someone may even have invited you into his or her tree branch-walled, clean, dirt-floored house for some hot fish-fillet tacos, fresh tomatoes, and beans. Accept, of course.

Aquiles Serdán basks above the lily-edged river lagoon, which during the June–October rainy season usually breaks through the beach-sandbar and drains directly into the surf half a mile below the town. During the dry season, the ocean plugs the hole in the sandbar, and the lagoon wanders lazily up the coast for a few miles. In any case, the white-sand beach is easily accessible only by boat, which you can borrow or hire at the village.

If you do, you'll have miles of untouched white sand and surf all to yourself for days of camping, beachcombing, shell collecting, surf fishing, wildlife-watching, and, if the waves permit, swimming, surfing, boogie boarding, and snorkeling. The town's two stores can provide your necessities.

Back at the fork (23 mi./37 km from the highway), continue along the left branch about two miles through Maito (pop. 100), which has two stores and a friendly **auto mechanic.** His name is Arias Gonzales, and his establishment is marked by a fence hung with dozens of eerie cow skulls.

A right fork just after Maito leads a quarter mile to **Playa Maito,** a surf-fishing and beach-combers' haven, where you can either park your RV or tent on the beach or stay at the excellent, family-friendly beachfront **Hotel Maito** (Guadalajara tel. 33/3177-2184, or leave a message with the local Tehualmixtle telephone operator, tel. 200/126-8990 or 200/126-8991, or 200/126-8992, $55 d, kids $10). Amenities include eight simply furnished but clean and comfortable rooms, most with two beds, a big swimming pool, shady palm grove, green lawn, fishing tours, horses to ride, hammocks, and a restaurant.

Tehualmixtle
Back on the main road, continue about two miles to another fork (at 26 mi./42 km). The right branch goes steeply up and then down a

rough track to the right, which soon levels out on the cliff above the idyllic fishing cove of Tehualmixtle. Here, a headland shelters a blue nook, where a few launches float, tethered and protected from the open sea. To one side, swells wash over a submerged wreck, while an ancient, moss-stained warehouse crumbles above a rocky little beach. At the end of the road downhill, a pair of beachside *palapas* invite visitors with drinks and fresh-out-of-the-water oysters, lobster, dorado, and red snapper.

Candelario ("Candle"), owner/operator of the right-side *palapa*, is the moving force behind this pocket paradise. After your repast and a couple more bottles of beer for good measure, he might tell you his version of the history of this coast—stories of sunken galleons or of the days when the old warehouse stored cocaine for legal shipment to the United States, when Coca-Cola got its name from the cocaine that was added to produce "the pause that refreshes."

Nowadays, however, Tehualmixtle serves as a resting point for occasional sailors, travelers, fisherfolk, and those who enjoy the rewards of clear-water snorkeling and scuba diving around the sunken shrimp trawler and the rocky shoreline nearby. Several level spots beside the cove invite camping or RV parking. Candelario and his wife and daughters will gladly supply you with your stomach's delight of choice seafood and drinks.

Furthermore, Candelario and his family, led by friendly, outgoing, English-speaking daughter Gaby (who heads the local tourism delegation), have built a small **hotel** ($25 s, $30 d, $35 t). They offer four clean, simply furnished rooms with shiny white bathrooms, view windows, and ceiling fans. Additionally, they rent out a comfortable view bungalow ($45/night) sleeping five, that's fine for groups, with a kitchenette, good bathroom, and ceiling fans; discount for one-week stay. For reservations, leave a message with the local radio telephone operator (tel. 200/126-8990 or 200/126-8991, or 200/126-8992).

For those who stay a few days, Candelario offers his services as a **guide** for turtle-watching (during summer-fall season), fishing trips,

and for equipped snorkelers and scuba divers to investigate nearby sites, especially the submerged wreck right offshore. Farther afield, he can also lead parties inland a few miles, by foot or horseback, to hot spring **Tlalpuyeque,** where, years ago, a French company operated a logging concession.

Southeast of Tehualmixtle

Returning back up the road above the cove, you'll catch a glimpse southward of the azure Bay of Tehualmixtle washing the white-sand ribbon of the Playa de Tehualmixtle. The village of **Ipala,** three miles down the road, is supply headquarters (unleaded gasoline available) for the occasional visitors drawn by the good fishing, surfing, beachcombing, and camping prospects of the Playa de Tehualmixtle. Being on the open ocean, its waves are usually rough, especially in the afternoon. Only experienced swimmers who can judge undertow and surf should think of swimming here.

From Ipala (29 mi./47 km), you can either retrace your path back to the highway at El Tuito, or continue down the coast (where the road gets rougher before it gets better) through the hamlet and beach of **Peñitas** (36 mi./58 km), which has a few stores, beach cabañas for rent, and restaurants. Next you'll pass **Mismaloya** (46 mi./74 km), site of a University of Guadalajara turtle-hatching station. To get there, turn right onto the rough dirt road just before the concrete bridge over the broad Río María Garcia.

From Mismaloya, return to the bridge, ford the river (during low water) three miles farther, and you'll soon be back in the 21st century at **Cruz de Loreto** (49 mi./79 km), equipped with many stores, sidewalks, electric lights, and phones.

Hotelito Desconocido

After all the backcountry hard traveling, treat yourself to at least one night at luxury eco-resort **C Hotelito Desconocido** (toll-free U.S. tel. 800/851-1143 or toll-free Mex. 01-800/013-1313, local 322/281-4010, hotelito@hotelito .com, www.hotelito.com, $340 d low season,

$450 high, and up). The accommodations, deluxe (but rustically candle-lit) thatched cabañas on stilts beside an idyllic lagoon, rent from $340 d low season, $450 high for the least expensive, to about $650 for the most, with breakfast. Add $75 per person for lunch and dinner. Inquire locally for directions, or follow the signs west to the hotel at the lagoon and beach nearby; reservations are strongly recommended.

If you decide not to stay at Hotelito Desconocido, return to Highway 200 directly from Cruz de Loreto, by heading east 10 miles (via Santiago and El Gargantino) to the highway at the Km 133 marker, just 23 miles (37 km) south of where you started at El Tuito.

CAJÓN DE LAS PEÑAS RESERVOIR

The lush farms of the Cabo Corrientes region owe much of their success to the Cajón de Peñas dam, whose waters enable farmers to profit from a year-round growing season. An added bonus is the recreation—boating, fishing, swimming, camping, and hiking—the big blue lake behind the dam makes possible.

With a car, the reservoir is easy to reach. Trucks and cars are frequent, so hikers can easily thumb rides. At Highway 200 Km 131, about a mile south of the Cruz de Loreto turnoff, head left (east) at a signed, paved road. After about five miles the road turns to gravel. Continue another four miles to a road fork atop a complex of three rock-fill dams, separated by a hill. The left road continues over the smaller two dams to a dead end. The right fork leads to a sign reading "Puerto Vallarta Bass Club" and a left fork just before the largest dam. Turn left and continue downhill to **La Lobina**, a modest family-run restaurant *palapa* and boat landing. The friendly husband-wife team maintains the little outpost in hopes of serving the trickle of mostly holiday and weekend visitors. Besides their children, who help with chores, their little settlement consists of two parrots, a brood of turkeys, and a flock of chickens that flies into the nearby forest to roost at night. The couple's cooking, based mostly upon freshly caught *lobina* (large-mouth bass), is basic but wholesome. Their parking lot above the lake has room for a number of self-contained RVs, while the forested knoll nearby might serve for tent camping. They offer their boat for lake sightseeing and fishing excursions for about $15 an hour. Otherwise, you could swim, kayak, or launch your own motorboat right from the lakeshore below the restaurant.

Head back, turn left at the uphill fork and continue over the larger dam, counterclockwise around the forested, sloping lakeshore. Within about two miles (3 km) you'll arrive at the boat-cooperative village, where several downscale *palapa* restaurants and boat landings provide food and recreational services for visitors. For a fee—ask at one of the restaurants, *"¿Hay una tarifa para campar?"* ("Is there a fee to camp?")—you can usually set up a tent or park your RV under a nearby lakeside tree.

PLAYA CHALACATEPEC

Playa Chalacatepec (chah-lah-kah-tay-PEK) lazes in the tropical sun just six miles from the highway at Km 88. Remarkably few people know of its charms except a handful of local youths, a few fisherfolk, and occasional families who come on Sunday outings, and the resident volunteers of the beachfront Tortuguera Verde Valle (Green Valley Turtle Encampment).

Playa Chalacatepec, with three distinct parts, has something for everyone: on the south side, a wild, arrow-straight, miles-long strand with crashing open-ocean breakers; in the middle, a low, wave-tossed, rocky point; and on the north, a long, tranquil, curving fine-sand beach. One of the few natural amenities that Playa Chalacatepec lacks is drinking water, however. Bring your own from the town back on the highway.

The north beach, shielded by the point, has gently rolling breakers good for surfing, bodysurfing, and safe swimming. Shells seasonally carpet its gradual white slope, and visitors have even left a pair of *palapa* shelters. These seem ready-made for camping by night and barbecuing fish by day with all of the driftwood lying around for the taking.

The point, Punta Chalacatepec, which

THE JALISCO COAST

© BRUCE WHIPPERMAN

A cactus-crowned outcropping separates Playa Chalacatepec into foamy, open ocean on the south side and a sheltered, sandy beach suitable for child's play on the north side.

separates the two beaches, is good for pole fishing on its surf-washed flanks and tidepooling in its rocky crevices.

Folks with RVs can pull off and park either along the approach road just above the beach or along tracks (beware of soft spots) downhill in the tall acacia scrub that borders the sand.

Getting There

Just as you're entering little José María Morelos (pop. 2,000), 100 feet past the Km 88 marker, turn right at the signed dirt road toward the beach at the corner. (Note the telephone booth.) If you're planning to camp, stock up with water and groceries at the stores in the town down the road, south.

The road, although steep in spots, is negotiable by passenger cars in good condition and small-to-medium RVs. Owners of big rigs should do a test run. On foot, the road is an easy two-hour hike—much of which probably won't be necessary because of the many passing farm pickups.

Mark your odometer at the highway. Con-

tinue over brushy hills and past fields and pastures, until mile 5.2 (Km 8.4), where the main road veers right. Instead, continue straight ahead, over the dune, to the beach, at mile 5.4 (Km 8.7), where the road turns left (south) and parallels the beach. Pass turtle encampment Tortuguera Verde Valle, at mile 5.9 (Km 9.5). Steer right downhill to Playa Chalacatepec at mile 6 (Km 9.7). The present bad news is that a squad of itinerant fisherfolk have junked up the beach; the good news is twofold: Several choice parking sites are available in the high brush bordering the beach (be careful of soft sand), and you may have the good company of the turtle-saving volunteers (most likely during the July–October turtle season), who would probably appreciate any help you can give them.

LAS ALAMANDAS

After roughing it at Playa Chalacatepec, you can be pampered in the luxurious isolation of Las Alamandas (Quémaro, Km. 83 Carretera Puerto Vallarta-Barra de Navidad, Jalisco

48850, local tel. 322/285-5500, U.S./Can. 888/882-9616, info@alamandas.com or info alamandas@aol.com, www.alamandas.com, $425 studios low season, $520 high, and up), a deluxe 1,500-acre retreat a few miles down the road.

The small Quémaro village sign at Km 83 gives no hint of the pleasant surprises that Las Alamandas conceals behind its guarded gate. Solitude and elegant simplicity seem to have been the driving concepts in the mind of Isabel Goldsmith when she acquired control of the property in the late 1980s. Although born into wealth (her grandfather was the late tin tycoon Antenor Patiño, who developed Manzanillo's renowned Hotel las Hadas; her father was the late multimillionaire Sir James Goldsmith, who bought the small kingdom her family now owns at Cuitzmala, 25 miles south), she was not idle. Isabel converted her dream of paradise—a small, luxuriously isolated resort on an idyllic beach in Puerto Vallarta's sylvan coastal hinterland—into reality. Now, her guests (28 maximum) enjoy accommodations that vary from luxuriously simple studios to a villa sleeping six. Activities include a gym, tennis, horseback riding, bicycling, fishing, kayaking, snorkeling, and lagoon and river excursions.

The hotel's luxurious facilities—restaurant and veranda, bars, book and video library, sitting and reading areas, pool-patio, gym, pavilions, and much more—are gracefully sprinkled throughout a plumy, grass-carpeted, beachfront palm grove. Powerful waves, good for intermediate and advanced surfing, on the south and north shoals, rise about 100 yards out and break rather quickly at the creamy, yellow-sand beach. With about twice as many employees as guests, hotel service is personal. Staff are attentive and focused on the goal of complete guest relaxation.

Daily rates range from about $425 low season ($520 high) for garden-view studios, up to about $1,600 low season ($2,200 high) for a three-unit beachfront villa for six, all with full breakfast. Three meals, prepared to your order, cost about $100 more per day per person. For reservations, contact Las Alamandas directly or book through the agent, Mexico Boutique Hotels (toll-free U.S./Can. 800/728-7098, info@mexicoboutiquehotels.com, www.mexicoboutiquehotels.com).

Get there by car, taxi (about $100), bus, or rental car from the Puerto Vallarta airport via Highway 200. At the Km 83 highway marker, 81 miles (130 km) south of Puerto Vallarta, turn right at the signed Quémaro village side road. Continue about three miles west, passing through Quémaro village, to the Alamandas gate. Don't arrive unannounced; unless you're a recognizable celebrity, the guard will not let you through the gate without a reservation in hand or an advance appointment. Alternatively, you can arrive by charter airplane, using the Las Alamandas's private airstrip. If you don't have a plane, contact a travel agent.

CHAMELA BAY

Most longtime visitors know Jalisco's Costa Alegre through Barra de Navidad and two big, beautiful, beach-lined bays: Tenacatita and Chamela. Tranquil Bahía de Chamela, the more northerly of the two, is broad, blue, dotted with islands, and lined by a strip of fine, honey-yellow sand.

Stretching five miles south from the sheltering Punta Rivas headland near Perula village, Chamela Bay is open but calm. A chain of intriguingly labeled rocky *islitas,* such as Cocinas (Kitchens), Negrita (Little Black One), and Pajarera (Place of Birds), scatter the strong Pacific swells into gentle billows by the time they roll onto the beaches.

Besides its natural amenities, Chamela Bay has three bungalow-complexes, one mentionable motel, two trailer parks, and an unusual "camping club." The focal point of this low-key resort area is the Km 72 highway corner (88 mi./142 km, from Puerto Vallarta; 46 mi./74 km, to Barra de Navidad). This spot, which on many maps is incorrectly marked Chamela (actually the village is at Km 63), is known simply as **"El Super"** by local people. Though the supermarket and neighboring bank have closed and are filled with the owner's dusty antique car collection, El Super nevertheless lives on in the minds of the local folks.

Beaches and Activities

Chamela Bay's beaches are variations on one continuous strip of sand, from Playa Rosadas in the south through Playa Chamela in the middle to Playas Fortuna and Perula at the north end.

Curving behind the sheltering headland, **Playa Perula** is the broadest and most tranquil beach of Chamela Bay. It is best for children and a snap for boat launching, swimming, and fishing from the rocks nearby. A dozen *pangas* usually line the water's edge, ready to take visitors on fishing excursions (expect to pay about $60 for a half-day trip, after bargaining) and snorkeling around the offshore islets. A line of seafood *palapas* provides the food and drinks for the fisherfolk and mostly Mexican families who know and enjoy this scenic little village/cove.

Playas Fortuna, Chamela, and Rosada: As you head south, the beach gradually changes character. The surf roughens, the slope steepens, and the sand narrows from around 200 feet at Perula to perhaps 100 feet at the south end of the bay. Civilization also thins out. The dusty village of stores, small eateries, vacation homes, and beachfront *palapa* restaurants that line Playa Fortuna give way to farmland and scattered houses at Playa Chamela. Two miles farther on, grassy dunes above trackless sand line Playa Rosada.

The gradually varying vigor of the waves and the isolation of the beach determine the place where you can indulge your own favorite pastimes. For bodysurfing and boogie boarding, Rosada and Chamela are best; and while sailboarding is usually possible anywhere on Chamela Bay, it will be best beyond the tranquil waves at La Fortuna. For surf-fishing, try casting beyond the vigorous, breaking billows of Rosada. And Rosada, being the most isolated, will be the place where you'll most likely find that shell-collection treasure you've been wishing for.

The five-mile curving strand of Chamela Bay is perfect for a morning hike from Rosada Beach. To get there, ride a Transportes Cihuatlán second-class bus to around the Km 65 marker, where a dirt road heads a half-mile to the beach. With the sun comfortably at your back, you can walk all the way to Perula if you want, stopping

Sheltered Playa Perula is one of Pacific Mexico's most child-friendly beaches.

© BRUCE WHIPPERMAN

for refreshments at any one of several *palapas* along the way. The firm sand of Chamela Bay beaches is likewise good for jogging, even for bicycling, provided you don't mind cleaning the sand out of the gears afterwards.

Accommodations
EL SUPER

Three accommodations serve travelers near the El Super corner: an emergency-only motel on the highway, bungalows, and a "camping club," **Paraíso Costa Alegre** (Km 72, Carretera 200, Barra de Navidad a Puerto Vallarta, El Super, Jalisco 48854, tel. 315/333-9778 or 315/333-9777, www.paraisocostalegre.com.mx, $45 cabaña for one or two, $100 for four; $20/day, $600/month RV site). The owners of Paraíso Costa Alegre, who live in Guadalajara, don't call it a campground because, curiously, in the past their policy has been instead of allowing campers to use their own tents, to rent out one of their stuffy, concrete, tent-shaped constructions. Unfortunately these have fallen out of repair and are unusable. Nevertheless, it's worth asking about it, for Paraíso Costa Alegre would be a beautiful tent camping spot, where the beach and bay set the mood: soft, golden sand, island-silhouetted sunsets, tranquil surf, abundant birds and fish, sometimes whales and dolphins, and occasionally great manta rays leaping from the water offshore.

Even without your own tent you can still enjoy staying in the outdoors by renting one of Paraíso Costa Alegre's several recently renovated open-air oceanfront Swiss Family Robinson-style cabañas, each with a cooking and eating area and toilet and shower downstairs, and a pair of thatch-roofed bedrooms with soft floor-sleeping pads upstairs.

In addition, you could rent one of the 15 shady spaces in its **trailer park** with all hookups, right next to the communal showers and toilet. Moreover, the lovely, palm-shadowed complex has two tall, elaborate *palapa* restaurant/bars, a minimarket, drinkable water, hot water, and a laundry.

A minor drawback to all this, besides there being no pool for guest use, are the somewhat steep rates: the open-air cabañas go for the same price as a hotel room. The. gainable and discounts (sta asking price) any time oth

Right across the lane Alegre stands the **Bungalo** (Km 72, Carretera Puertc Jalisco 48854, tel. 315/333-. ..., φ+υ u, φ/5 for four), where 18 spacious kitchenette-bungalows with fans (no a/c) surround an attractive inner garden and a palmy, banana-fringed pool and patio. Although the blue meandering pool and palmy grounds are very inviting, the bungalows themselves have suffered from past neglect. Look inside three or four and make sure that everything is in working order before moving in. If so, the bungalows' pool and garden setting and the long, lovely Chamela beach just a block away might be perfect for a week or month of tranquil relaxation. If you're passing through, it might be worthwhile to take a look. Monthly discounts are available. For reservations (usually not necessary), telephone the on-site manager, or the owner, Gabriel Yañez G. (Obregón 1425 S.L., Guadalajara, Jalisco, tel. 33/3644-0044).

Note: The late summer and fall season is pretty empty on the Chamela Bay beaches. Consequently, food is scarce on the beach around Paraíso Costa Alegre and Bungalows Mayar Chamela. Meals, however, are available a mile away at the El Super highway corner restaurant and the few small groceries nearby, or in San Mateo village a mile south.

PERULA

At Km 74, a sign marks a paved road to Playas Fortuna and Perula. About two miles downhill, right on the beach, you can't miss the bright yellow stucco **Hotel, Bungalows, and Trailer Park Playa Dorada** (Perula, Km 76, Carretera 200 Melaque-Puerto Vallarta, Jalisco 48854, tel. 315/333-9710, fax 315/333-9709, pdorada@ cybercable.net.mx, www.playa-dorada.com .mx, $55 rooms, $75 with kitchenette; $18/day, $500/month RV site). More a motel than bungalows, its three tiers of simply decorated rooms and suites with kitchenettes are nearly empty except on weekends and Mexican holidays.

Playa Dorada's two saving graces, however,

AVING TURTLES

Sea turtles were once common on Puerto Vallarta beaches. Times have changed, however. Now a determined corps of volunteers literally camps out on isolated strands, trying to save the turtles from extinction. This is a tricky business, because their poacher opponents are poor, determined, and often armed. Since turtle tracks lead right to the eggs, the trick is to get there before the poachers. The turtle-savers dig up the eggs and hatch them themselves, or bury them in secret locations where they hope the eggs will hatch unmolested. The reward – the sight of hundreds of new hatchlings returning to the sea – is worth the pain for this new generation of Mexican ecoactivists.

Once featured on a thousand restaurant menus from Puerto Angel to Mazatlán, turtle meat, soup, and eggs are now illegal commodities. Though not extinct, the Mexican Pacific's three scarcest sea turtle species – green, hawksbill, and leatherback – have dwindled to a tiny fraction of their previous numbers.

The **green turtle** (Chelonia mydas), known locally as tortuga verde or caguama, is more black than green. Its name comes from the light green tint of its fat. Although officially threatened, the prolific green turtle remains relatively numerous, with about 100,000 nesting females worldwide. Females can return to shore up to eight times during the year, depositing 500 eggs in a single season. When not mating or migrating, the vegetarian green turtles can be spotted most often in lagoons and bays, especially the Bay of Banderas, nipping at seaweed with their beaks. Adults, usually three or four feet long and weighing 300-400 pounds, are easily identified out of water by the four big plates on either side of their shells. Green turtle meat was once prized as the main ingredient of turtle soup.

The severely endangered **hawksbill** (Eretmochelys imbricata), with only about 20,000 nesting females worldwide, has vanished from many Mexican Pacific beaches. Known locally as the tortuga carey, it was the source of both meat and the lovely translucent tortoiseshell. Adult careys, among the smaller of sea turtles, run two to three feet in length and weigh 100-150 pounds. Their usually brown shells are readily identified by shingle-like overlapping scales. During late summer and fall, females come ashore to lay clutches of eggs (around 100) in the sand. Careys, although preferring fish, mollusks, and shellfish, will eat most anything, including seaweed. When attacked, careys can be plucky fighters, inflicting bites with their eagle-sharp hawksbills. Playa Teopa, under the care of the El Careyes Beach Resort, is one of the its few nesting sites on the Mexican Pacific Coast.

You'll be fortunate indeed if you glimpse the rare **leatherback** (Dermochelys coriacea), the world's largest turtle. Until recent years even experts knew little about the leatherback, tortuga de cuero, but now they estimate that it's severely endangered with only about 35,000 nesting females worldwide. Tales are told of fisherfolk netting seven- or eight-foot leatherbacks weighing nearly a ton apiece. If you see even a small one, you'll recognize it immediately by its back of smooth, tough skin (instead of a shell), creased with several lengthwise ridges.

Prospects are better for the more abundant (800,000 nesting females), although still endangered, **olive ridley** or golfina turtle, which nests at a number of Pacific Mexico beaches. With a noticeably narrow head, it's one of the smallest of sea turtles, adults averaging only about 90 pounds, and 2 feet in length. Its name derives from the adult turtle's olive-green shell. Partly due to the persistence of a corps of dedicated volunteers, the olive ridley seems to making a comeback in the Puerto Vallarta region. Nesting sites in the Puerto Vallarta region are on the Jalisco Coast (at Playa Mismaloya, in Cabo Corrientes country, near Cruz de Loreto), and on the Nayarit Coast at San Francisco (north of Sayulita) and Playa Tortuga (north of Las Varas, on the road to San Blas). The group of volunteers at San Francisco (www.project-tortuga.org) reports more than a ten-fold increase (of several hundred) nest sites during the past 20 years.

are the beach, which curves gracefully to the scenic little fishing nook of Perula, and its inviting palm-shaded pool and patio. The best-situated accommodations are on the top floor, overlooking the ocean. The 46 attractively painted rooms sleep up to four; 15 kitchenette units also sleep four, all with a/c and parking. Discounts are customarily available for weekly and low-season rentals.

Folks who take one of the dozen trailer spaces in the bare lot across the street are welcome to lounge all day beneath the palms of the pool and patio. Spaces include all hookups and showers and toilets.

It's easy to miss the low-profile **Hotel Punta Perula** (Perula, Km 76, Carretera 200, Melaque-Puerto Vallarta, Jalisco 48854, tel. 315/333-9782, $25 d in one bed, $37 d or t in two beds), just one block inland from the Bungalows Playa Dorada. This homey place seems like a scene from Old Mexico, with a rustic white stucco tier of rooms enclosing a spacious green garden and venerable tufted grove (with no pool, however). Its 14 clean, gracefully decorated, colonial-style, fan-equipped rooms are priced higher during Christmas and Easter holidays. Bargain for lower, long-term rates.

Also occupying the same luscious beach-front nearby is **Red Snapper RV Park and Restaurant** (P.O. Box 42, Melaque, Jalisco 48980, tel. 315/333-9784, redsnapper@hotmail.com, $14/day, $80/week, $325/month RV site), life project of friendly North American owners Harry, Carmen, and Bonnie Adams. Here, what you see is what you get: a dozen largely shadeless, fenced-in spaces with all hookups (including 30-amp a/c power), showers, toilets, washing machine, beachfront restaurant *palapa* on gorgeous Chamela Bay, ripe for surf or boat fishing (launch right from the beach), surfing, and sailboarding. A 15-foot, 25-horsepower Zodiac is available for fishing.

CENTRO VACACIONAL CHAMELA SECCIÓN 47

Four miles south of El Super, at Rosada Beach,

The attractive pool patio at Centro Vacacional Chamela Sección 47 sits right on the Chamela Bay beachfront.

© BRUCE WHIPPERMAN

THE JALISCO COAST

sharing the same luscious Chamela Bay strand, is the **Centro Vacacional Chamela Sección 47,** a teachers' vacation retreat that rents its unoccupied units to the general public. The two modern, apartment-style tiers enfold an invitingly lovely grassy pool-patio and park. An outdoor *palapa* stands by the pool, and another airy open room invites cards and conversation. The units themselves are large, bright one-bedrooms, sleeping four, with sea views and kitchens. Rentals ($60/day) are on a drop-in basis. Telephone the manager around noon at 315/333-9878 or 315/333-9777 in Spanish to see if he can rent you an apartment. Arrive before about 4 P.M., when the manager is usually around to check things before going home for the night. On nonholiday weekdays, the place is often nearly empty. Have a look by following the upper of two side roads at the big 47 sign near the Km 66 marker. Within a few hundred yards you'll be there. Ask one of the teachers to explain the significance of 47.

CAMPING
For RVs, the best spots are the trailer parks at **Paraíso Costa Alegre,** the **Hotel, Bungalows and Trailer Park Playa Dorada,** and **Red Snapper Restaurant and RV Park.**

If you can walk in, you can probably set up a tent anywhere along the bay you like. One of the best places would be the grassy dune along pristine Playa Rosada a few hundred yards north of the Centro Vacacional Chamela Sección 47 (Km 66). Water is available from the manager (offer to pay) at the Centro Vacacional.

Playa Negrita, the pristine little sand crescent that marks the southern end of Chamela Bay, offers still another picnic or camping possibility. Get there by following the dirt road angling downhill from the highway at the south end of the bridge between Km 63 and Km 64. Turn left at the Chamela village stores beneath the bridge, continue about two miles, bearing left to the end of the road, where a restaurant *palapa* stands at beachside. This is the southern of two islet-protected coves flanking the low Punta Negro headland. With clear, tranquil wa-

ters and golden-sand beaches, both coves are great for fishing from the rocks, snorkeling, sailboarding, and swimming. The gorgeous south-end beach, Playa Negrita, is offered seasonally as a campground, with plenty of room for tenting and RV parking; a friendly caretaker usually collects about $2.50 per day per car. Weekends and holidays the restaurant serves drinks and seafood lunches and dinners.

Food
Groceries are available at stores near the **El Super** corner (Km 72) or in the villages of **Perula** (on the beach, turn off at Km 74), **San Mateo** (Km 70), and **Chamela** (walk north along the beach, or follow the side road, downhill, at the south end of the bridge between Km 64 and 63).

Hearty country Mexican food, hospitality, and snack groceries are available at the **Tejeban** truck stop/restaurant (breakfast until 10:30 P.M. daily, tel. 315/333-9705) at the El Super corner. Two popular local roadside seafood spots (8 A.M.–9 P.M. daily, $5–10) are the **La Viuda** (The Widow; Km 64) and **Don Lupe Mariscos** (Km 63), on opposite ends of the Río Chamela bridge. They both have their own divers who go out daily for fresh fish, octopus *(pulpo)*, conch, clams, oysters, and lobster.

Information and Services
The closest **bank** is 34 miles north at Tomatlán (turnoff at La Cumbre, Km 116). A card-operated **telephone** is outside at the El Super corner, in addition to long-distance telephones inside the adjacent Tejeban restaurant and at the centro de salud at Pueblo Careyes, the village behind the soccer field at Km 52.

Until someone resurrects the **Pemex** *gasolinera* at El Super, the closest unleaded gasoline is 27 miles north at La Cumbre (Km 116) or 50 miles (80 km) south at Melaque (Km 0).

If you get sick, the closest health clinics are in Perula (Km 74, one block north of the town plaza, no phone, but a pharmacy) and at Pueblo Careyes at Km 52 (medical consultations 8 A.M.–2 P.M. daily; doctor on call around the clock for emergencies).

Local special **police,** known as the Policia Auxiliar del Estado, are stationed in a pink roadside house at Km 46, and also in the house above the road at Km 43. The local *preventiva* (municipal police) are stationed about a half mile (one km) north of the El Super corner.

◖ EL CAREYES BEACH RESORT

One of the hidden gems of Pacific Mexico, this is really two hotels in one. After Christmas and before Easter, the El Careyes Beach Resort brims with well-to-do Mexican families letting their hair down. The rest of the year the hotel is a tranquil, tropical retreat basking at the edge of a pristine, craggy cove.

The natural scene sets the tone: a majestic palm grove opens onto a petite sandy beach set like a pearl between craggy cliffs. Offshore, the water, deep and crystal clear, is home for dozens of kinds of fish. Overhead, hawks and frigate birds soar, pelicans dive, and gulls and terns skim the waves. During their summer-fall nesting season, sea turtles carry out their ancient ritual by silently depositing their precious eggs on nearby beaches where they were born.

As if not to be outdone by nature, the hotel itself is an elegant, tropical retreat. A platoon of gardeners manicure lush spreading grounds that lead to gate and reception area. Past the desk, tiers of ochre-hued Mediterranean-chic lodgings enclose an elegant inner courtyard where a blue pool meanders beneath majestic, rustling palms. At night, the grounds glimmer softly with lamps. They illuminate the tufted grove, light the path to a secluded beach, and lead the way up through the cactus-sprinkled hillside thorn forest to a romantic restaurant high above the bay.

Note: Even if you don't plan to stay overnight, be sure to stop for at least few hours, strolling the beach after taking breakfast, lunch or early dinner ($20–30 for two), at the refined but relaxing beachview restaurant; call the hotel desk ahead for a reservation. Car arrival (bus travelers, hail a taxi on the highway to take you the extra mile downhill) is mandatory to smooth your way past the guards at the hotel gate.

Hotel Activities

Hotel guests enjoy a plethora of sports facilities, including tennis courts, riding stables, and a polo field. Aquatic activities include snorkeling, scuba diving, kayaking, sailing, and deep-sea fishing. Boats are available for picnic-excursions to nearby hidden beaches, wildlife-viewing, and observing turtle nesting in season. A luxury spa with view pampers guests with massage, facials, sauna, whirlpool tub, and exercise machines. Evenings, in season, live music brightens the cocktail and dinner hours at the elegant beach-view restaurant/bar.

The hotel was named for *carey* (kah-RAY), the native word for an endangered species of sea turtle (the hawksbill) that used to lay eggs on the little beach of Careyitos that fronts the hotel. Saving the *carey* turtles that still nest at nearby Playa Teopa, accessible only through hotel property, has now become a major hotel mission. Guards do, however, allow access to serious outside visitors during the summer-fall hatching season; follow the dirt road between Km 49 and Km 50 to the gate and beach; no camping, please. Check with the hotel desk for information and permission.

Hotel Information

The luxurious rooms and suites, depending on location and size, run about $335–575 d in low season, and $375–670 d high. All accommodations have air-conditioning, TV, and direct-dial phones. Additional hotel facilities and services include fiber-optic telecommunications, a 100-person meeting room, a number of shops and boutiques, library, small theater, babysitters, heliport, private landing strip, and a range of business services.

For reservations and information, contact the hotel directly (local tel. 315/351-0000, fax 315/351-0100, careyes@careyeshotel.com, www.elcareyesresort.com) or through its agent, Mexico Boutique Hotels (toll-free U.S./Can. 800/728-7098, info@mexicoboutiquehotels .com, www.mexicoboutiquehotels.com).

Getting There

El Careyes is a few minutes' drive down a

cobbled entrance road (bear left all the way) at Km 53.5 (100 mi./161 km from Puerto Vallarta, 34 mi./55 km from Barra de Navidad, and 52 mi./84 km from the Manzanillo International Airport).

PLAYA CAREYES

At Km 52, just south of a small bridge and a bus stop, a dirt side road (beach side) leads past a gated guard station with a sign labeled Costa Careyes to the lovely honey-tinted crescent of Playa Careyes. The guard, whose job is to provide security for the beach *palapa* restaurants and the houses atop the neighboring headlands, will let you through if you ask. Beyond the gate, bear left to the car-negotiable track (beware of sandy soft spots) that continues along the dune, where you could enjoy at least a pleasant day on the beach. Beyond the often powerful waves (swim with caution), the intimate, headland-framed bay brims with outdoor possibilities. Bird- and wildlife-watching can be quite rewarding; notice the herons, egrets, and cormorants in the lagoon just south of the dune. Fishing is good either from the beach, by boat (launch from the sheltered north end), or the rocks on either side. Water is generally clear for snorkeling and, beyond the waves, good for either kayaking or sailboarding. If you have no boat, no problem—the local fishing cooperative (boats beached by the food *palapa* at north end) would be happy to take you on a fishing trip. Figure about $20 per hour, with bargaining. Afterward, they might even cook up the catch for a big afternoon dinner at the tree-shaded *palapa* of the Cocodrilo Azul restaurant nearby. If you want to camp, you can set up your tent or park your camper by one of the restaurant *palapas* at the right, north end of the beach.

As for services, **Pueblo Careyes** (inland, behind the soccer field at Km 52) has a Centro de Salud, with a pharmacy and long-distance telephone, tel. 335/351-0170.

Access to the neighboring **Playa Teopa** is more carefully guarded. The worthy reason is to save the hatchlings of the remaining *carey* turtles that still come ashore during the late summer and fall to lay eggs. For a closer look at Playa Teopa, you could walk south along the dunetop track, although guards might eventually stop you. They will let you through (entry gate on dirt road between Km 49 and 50) if you get official permission at the desk of the El Careyes Beach Resort.

The pristine tropical deciduous woodlands that stretch for miles around Km 45 are no accident. They are preserved as part of the **Fideicomiso Cuitzmala** (Cuitzmala Trust), the local kingdom of beach, headland, and forest held by the family of late multimillionaire Sir James Goldsmith. Local officials, many of whom were not privy to Sir James's grand design (which includes a sprawling sea-view mansion complex), say that a team of biologists are conducting research on the property. A ranch complex, accessible through a gate at Km 45, is Fideicomiso Cuitzmala's most obvious highway-visible landmark.

RANCHO AND PLAYA EL TECUÁN

Little was spared in perching the former Hotel el Tecuán above the Rancho el Tecuán, its small kingdom of beach, lagoon, and palm-brushed rangeland. The hotel was to be the centerpiece of a sprawling vacationland, with marina, golf course, and hundreds of houses and condos. Although those plans have yet to materialize, the hotel, unoccupied and for sale, still stands proudly on its hilltop, seeming more like an African safari lodge than a Mexican beach resort.

Masculinity bulges out of its architecture. Its corridors are lined with massive, polished tree trunks, fixed by brawny master joints to thick, hand-hewn mahogany beams. The view restaurant was built, patterned after the midships of a Manila galleon, complete with a pair of varnished tree-trunk masts reaching into the inky darkness of the night sky above. If the restaurant could only sway, the illusion would have been complete.

Wildlife-Watching, Hiking, and Jogging

It is perhaps fortunate that the former hotel

and its surroundings, part of the big **Rancho el Tecuán,** may never be developed into a residential community. Being private, public access has always been limited, so the Rancho has become a de facto habitat-refuge for the rapidly diminishing local animal population. Wildcats, ocelots, small crocodiles, snakes, and turtles hunt in the mangroves edging the lagoon and the tangled forest that climbs the surrounding hills. The lagoon itself nurtures hosts of water birds and shoals of *robalo* (snook) and *pargo* (snapper).

At this writing, visitors were still being allowed to pass along the entrance road and enjoy wildlife-watching opportunities. If such visitors tread softly, clean up after themselves, start no fires, and refrain from fishing or hunting, the present owners may continue to allow access. This would be ideal, because wildlife-watching here is superb. First, simply walk along the lagoon-front below the hotel hilltop, where big white herons and egrets perch and preen in the mangroves. Don't forget your binoculars, sun hat, mosquito repellent, telephoto camera, and identification book. Try launching your own rowboat, canoe, or inflatable raft for an even more rewarding outing.

The environs offer plenty of jogging and walking opportunities. For starters, stroll along the lagoonside entrance road and back (3 mi./4.8 km) or south along the beach to the Río Purificación and back (4 mi./6.4 km). Take water, mosquito repellent, sunscreen, a hat, and something to carry your beachcombing treasures in.

◖ Playa el Tecuán

The focal point of the long, wild, white-sand Playa el Tecuán is at the north end, where, at low tide, the lagoon's waters stream into the sea. Platoons of water birds—giant brown herons, snowy egrets, and squads of pelicans, ibises, and grebes—stalk and dive for fish trapped in the shallow, rushing current.

On the beach nearby, the sand curves southward beneath a rocky point, where the waves strew rainbow carpets of limpet, clam, and snail shells. There the billows rise sharply, angling shoreward, often with good intermediate and advanced surfing breaks. Casual swimmers beware; the surf is much too powerful for safety.

Getting There

The former Hotel el Tecuán is six miles (10 km) along a paved entrance road marked by a monumental but fake white lighthouse at Km 33 (112 mi./181 km from Puerto Vallarta, 22 mi./35 km from Barra de Navidad).

◖ PLAYA TENACATITA

Imagine an ideal tropical paradise: free camping on a long curve of clean white sand, right next to a lovely little coral-bottomed cove, with all the beer you can drink and all the fresh seafood you can eat. That describes Tenacatita, a place that old Mexican Pacific hands refer to with a sigh: Tenacatitaaahhh . . .

Folks usually begin to arrive sometime in November; by Christmas some years there's room only for walk-ins. Which anyone who can walk can do: Carry in your tent and set it up in one of the many RV-inaccessible spots.

Tenacatita visitors enjoy three distinct beaches: the main one, Playa Tenacatita; the little one, Playa Mora; and Playa la Boca, a breezy, palm-bordered sand ribbon stretching just over three km north to the *boca* (mouth) of the Río Purificación.

Playa Tenacatita's strand of fine white sand curves from the north end of Punta Tenacatita along a long, tall packed dune to **Punta Hermanos,** a total of about two miles. The dune is where most visitors—nearly all Americans and Canadians—park their RVs. The water is clear with gentle waves, fine for swimming and sailboating. Being so calm, it's easy to launch a boat for fishing—common catches are *huachinango* (red snapper) and *cabrilla* (sea bass)—especially at the very calm north end.

Food and Accommodations

Playa Tenacatita's sheltered north-end cove has acquired a village of *palapas* that service the winter camping population. One of the

© BRUCE WHIPPERMAN

house for rent, Tenacatita

veteran establishments is **El Puercillo,** run by longtimer José Bautista. He and several other neighbors take groups out in his launches ($80 total/half-day, bring your own beer) for off-shore fishing trips and excursions.

On the other hand, for some of the best food and highest standards on the beach, go to very well-established **Fiesta Mexicana** *palapa* restaurant, on the Tenacatita beach south end, across the beachfront from the trailer park. (Alternatively, you can also check out neighboring Restaurant Chito and Restaurant Cato, especially for the local fish specialty *rollo del mar.*)

A pair of recommendable hotels and a trailer park (also with hotel rooms) also serve Tenacatita visitors. The most deluxe is **Hotel las Villitas** (Av. Tenacatita 376, Tenacatita, Jalisco 48895, reserve by Barra de Navidad toll-free tel. 01-800/980-7060, or local tel. 315/355-5353 or 315/355-7078, brenda_ruenes@hotmail.com, $95 rooms, $160 suites), actually a petite boutique resort, where owners have spared little in providing a restaurant, oceaniew pool patio,

tennis courts, comfortably appointed deluxe rooms, and spacious kitchenette suites. Rentals come with fans, a/c, a library of paperback novels, and plenty of ocean views. At this writing, the only possible drawback to all this is the hotel's isolation, about a mile along the road south from the main settlement, and the sometimes lack of sufficient solar-powered electricity to run the pump and keep the swimming pool from getting murky green.

A plainer, but still acceptable closer-in choice is the beachfront **Hotel Paraiso de Tenacatita** (Av. Tenacatita 32, Tenacatita, Jalisco 48895, dobie@prodigy.net.mx, $30 d, $40 with a/c), with 23 clean, simply decorated rooms, with fans, some with a/c, and a ocean-view restaurant and pool-patio.

RvVers and campers enjoy a good option at the ☾ **Tenacatita Trailer Park** and hotel (Av. Tenacatita, Tenacatita, Jalisco 48895, tel. Guadalajara local cell 044/33-3115-5406, long distance tel. 01-33/3115-5406, emmarortega@hotmail.com, $20–25 RV site, $28 d, $46 t or q room). Here, find around 20 spaces, about half of them shaded, with several big enough to accommodate large motor homes. Rates run about $20 for smaller RVs, $25 for larger, with all hookups, wastewater dump, a/c power, and lavish showers and toilet facilities, all in a big, grassy, securely fenced-in yard, kept green by a private, piped-in fresh-water supply.

The trailer park's **four hotel rooms** (out front, on the beachfront road) are equally well-equipped and attractive. Here, you get a clean, comfortably semi-deluxe oceanview room with a pair of double beds, for $28 d, $46 t or q, with fan and hot-water shower bath, right across the street from the good Fiesta Mexicana *palapa* restaurant.

Playas Mora and La Boca

Jewel of jewels Playa Mora is accessible by a steep, but short, uphill dirt road (at this writing in need of repair and and only jeep-negotiable) running north from Playa Tenacatita past the *palapas.* Playa Mora itself is salt-and-pepper black sand dotted with white coral, washed by water sometimes as smooth as glass. Just 50 feet from the beach the reef begins. Corals, like heads of cauliflower, some brown, some green, and some dead white, swarm with fish: iridescent blue, yellow-striped, yellow-tailed, some silvery, and others brown as rocks. (Be careful. Moray eels like to hide in rock crannies, and they bite. Don't stick your hand anywhere you can't see.)

If you get to Playa Mora by December, you may be early enough to snag one of the roughly dozen car-accessible camping spots. If not, plenty of tent camping spaces accessible on foot exist; also, a few abandoned *palapa*-thatched huts are usually waiting to be resurrected.

North-side Playa la Boca (fronting the palm grove to the right of the ingress road) is the overflow campground for Tenacatita. It's not as popular because of its rough surf and steep beach. Its isolation and vigorous surf, however, make Playa la Boca the best for driftwood, beachcombing, shells, and surf-fishing.

Wildlife-Watching

Tenacatita's hinterland is a spreading, wild-life-rich mangrove marsh. From a lagoon-side landing inland from the Tenacatita dune, you can float a boat, rubber raft, or canoe for a wildlife-watching excursion. Local guides (ask for Adan at restaurant Chito) furnish boats and lead trips ($30) from the same spot. Animals often viewable are coatimundis, crocodiles, iguanas, ilamacoa (boa constrictors) and flocks of herons (grey and white), cormorants, anhingas, and much more, especially in the winter. Take your hat, binoculars, camera, telephoto lens, and plenty of insect repellent.

Tenacatita Bugs

That same marshland is the source for swarms of mosquitoes and *jejenes,* "no-see-um" biting gnats, especially around sunset. At that time, no sane person at Tenacatita should be outdoors without having slathered on some good repellent. (Note: For more useful information about Tenacatita, visit www.tomzap.com/tenaca.html.)

Rebalsito Village Services and Food

The village of **El Rebalsito,** on the Highway 200-Tenacatita road, 1.5 miles back from the beach, is Tenacatita's supply and service center. It has two or three fair *abarroterías* (groceries) that carry meat and vegetables. Best of all these is friendly **Minisuper la Morenita,** on the highway, with a little bit of everything and long-distance phones (tel. 315/355-5214). Additional services include a *gasolinera* that dispenses gasoline from drums, a water *purificadora* that sells **drinking water** retail. Connect to the Internet in Rebalsito, at the small store at José Vargas Vigil 14, a block and a half from the church (9 A.M.–2 P.M. and 4–9 P.M. Mon.–Fri., 9 A.M.–2 P.M. Sat.).

If you want a diversion from the fare of Tenacatita's seafood *palapas* and El Rebalsito's single restaurant, you can drive or thumb a ride seven miles (11 km) to **Restaurant Yoli** (7 A.M.–8 P.M. daily) at roadside Miguel Hidalgo village (Km 30 on Highway 200) for some country-style enchiladas, tacos, *chiles rellenos,* tostadas, and beans.

Getting There and Away

By bus from Manzanillo and Barra de Navidad, catch the single Transportes Cihuatlán bus that makes one return trip per day between El Rebalsito and Manzanillo. It leaves El Rebalsito daily at the crack of dawn (for departure times, inquire locally in Rebalsito and the bus stations at Barra de Navidad tel. 315/355-5200, or Melaque tel. 315/355-5003), and returns from the Manzanillo central bus station around 3 P.M., arriving back at El Rebalsito around 6 P.M.

By car, leave Highway 200 at the big Tenacatita sign and interchange (at Km 27) half a mile south of the big Río Purificación bridge. El Rebalsito is 3.7 miles (6 km), Tenacatita 5.4 miles (8.7 km), by a good paved road.

BLUE BAY CLUB LOS ANGELES LOCOS

Although the Blue Bay resort chain has been operating the former Hotel los Angeles Locos as an all-inclusive resort for several years, the curious name Los Angeles Locos (which had nothing to do with crazy people from Los Angeles) lives on in minds of local people. Once upon a time, a rich family built an airstrip and a mansion by a lovely little beach on pristine Tenacatita Bay and began coming for vacations by private plane. The local people, who couldn't fathom why their rich neighbors would go to so much trouble and expense to come to such an out-of-the-way place, dubbed them *los ángeles locos* (the crazy angels), because they always seemed to be flying.

The beach is still lovely and Tenacatita Bay, curving around Punta Hermanos south from Tenacatita Beach, is still pristine. Now Los Angeles Locos makes it possible for droves of sun-seeking vacationers to enjoy it en masse. Continuous music, open bar, plentiful buffets, and endless activities set the tone at Los Angeles Locos, the kind of place for folks who want a hassle-free week of fun in the sun. The guests are typically working-age couples and singles, mostly Mexicans during the summer, Canadians and some Americans during the winter. Very few children seem to be among the guests, although they are welcome.

Activities

Although all sports and lessons—including tennis, snorkeling, sailing, sailboarding, horseback riding, volleyball, aerobics, exercises, and water-skiing—plus dancing, disco, and games cost nothing extra, guests can, if they want, do nothing but soak up the sun. A relaxed attitude will probably allow you to enjoy yourself the most. Don't try to eat, drink, and do too much to make sure you get your money's worth. If you do, you're liable to arrive back home in need of a vacation.

Although people don't come to the tropics to stay inside, Los Angeles Locos' rooms are quite comfortable. They're completely private, decorated in pastels, and air-conditioned, each with cable TV, phone, and private balcony overlooking either the ocean or palmy pool and patio.

Information

For information and reservations, contact a travel agent or the hotel (Km 20, Carretera Federal 200, Tenacatita, Jalisco 48989, toll-free U.S. 800/483-7986, toll-free Mex. tel. 01-800/713-3020, local tel. 315/351-5020, fax 315/351-5412, www.losangeleslocos.com). Low-season all-inclusive rates for the 201 rooms and suites run a bargain-basement $65 per person per day midweek, $85 weekends, double occupancy; $100 high season. Children under 7 with parents stay free; kids 7–12, $30. For a bigger, better junior suite, add about $30 per room; prices include everything—food, drinks, entertainment—except transportation.

Getting There

Los Angeles Locos is about four miles (6 km) off Highway 200 along a signed cobbled entrance road near the Km 20 marker (120 mi./194 km from Puerto Vallarta, 14 mi./23 km from Barra de Navidad, and 32 mi./51 km from the Manzanillo International Airport). If you want to simply look around the resort, don't drive up to the gate unannounced. The guard won't let you through. Instead, call ahead and make an appointment for a "tour." After your guided looksee, you have to either sign up or mosey along. The hotel doesn't accept day guests.

Hotel Punta Serena

Part of the original Los Angeles Locos development, but separate in concept and location, is Punta Serena (through Blue Bay Club los Angeles Locos switchboard tel. 315/351-5020 ext. 4013 or 4011, fax 315/351-5412, www .puntaserena.com). Perched on a breezy hilltop overlooking the entire broad sweep of Tenacatita Bay, this is an adults-only romantic retreat, with all meals and in-house activities included, plus a big blue ocean-view pool/patio, sauna, sea-vista hot tub, gym, and clothing-optional settings. You can also enjoy all of the lively sports, discoing, and beach action of Los Angeles Locos on the beach downhill, at no extra cost. Added-cost amenities include spa services such as a native-Mexican *temazcal* hot room and massage.

Paths radiate to the tile-roofed lodging units, spread over the palmy summit-park like a garden of giant mushrooms. The units themselves are designer spartan, in white and blue, with modern baths, luxuriously high ceilings, and broad ocean vistas from view balconies.

All-inclusive tariffs for the 70 accommodations, all with air-conditioning, run about the same as Hotel los Angeles Locos. Directions and address are identical to Los Angeles Locos, but turn right at the signed Punta Serena entrance driveway before heading downhill to Los Angeles Locos.

PLAYA BOCA DE IGUANAS

Playa Boca de Iguanas curves for six miles along the tranquil inner recess of the Bay of Tenacatita. The cavernous former beachfront Hotel Bahía Tenacatita, which slumbered for years beneath the grove, is being reclaimed by the jungle and the animals that live in the nearby mangrove marsh.

The beach, however, is as enjoyable as ever: wide and level, with firm white sand good for hiking, jogging, and beachcombing. Offshore, the gently rolling waves are equally fine for bodysurfing and boogie boarding. Beds of oysters, free for those who dive for them, lie a few hundred feet offshore. A rocky outcropping at the north end invites fishing and snorkeling while the calm water beyond the breakers invites sailboarding. Bring your own equipment.

Get to Playa Boca de Iguanas by following the signed paved road at Km 17 for 1.5 miles (2.4 km).

Accommodations

For hotel-style lodging, go to **◖ Coconuts-by-the-Sea** (tel. 314/338-6315, cocos42@ starband.net, www.coconutsbythesea.com, $75 d low season, $90 d high). Owners Bob and Clessie Jones offer four spacious kitchenette guest rooms with fans, air-conditioning, king-sized beds, fans and a/c, satellite TV with HBO, and hot showers with plenty of water in a big hillside house. It features view verandas, hammocks, a pool, and just a short downhill walk from creamy Boca de Iguanas beach.

Second choice goes to nearby **◖ Camping Trailer Park Boca Beach** (Km 16.5 Carretera Melaque-Puerto Vallarta, P.O. Box 18, Melaque, Jalisco 48987, tel. 317/381-0393, fax 317/381-0342, bocabeach@hotmail.com, $17–26 RV site, $7 tent site), with about 50 camping and RV spaces shaded beneath a majestic, rustling grove. Friendly owners Michel and Bertha Billot (he's French, she's Mexican) have built up their little paradise, surviving hurricanes and a 1995 ten-foot tidal wave by trying harder. Their essentials are in place: electricity, water, showers, toilets, and about 40 spaces with sewer hookups. Much of their five acres is undeveloped and would be fine for tent campers who prefer privacy with the convenience of fresh water, a small store, and congenial company at tables beneath the trailer park's rustic beachfront *palapa* snack restaurant. RV rates run about $17 per day, back from the beach, $26 on the beach, $500 per month for motor home, trailer, or van, including electricity for a/c. Camping runs $7 for two, $10 including two kids.

The original Boca de Iguanas pocket paradise, **Camping and Trailer Park Boca de Iguanas** (Km 16.5, Carretera Melaque-Puerto Vallarta, P.O. Box 93, Melaque, Jalisco 48987, $28 q bungalow, $14 RV site, $5 pp tent site), got everything started here by succeeding where the big old hotel down the beach failed. Instead of fighting the jungle, the manager is coexisting with it. A big crocodile lived in the mangrove-lined lotus marsh at the edge of the trailer park. "When the crocodile gets too close to my ducks," the manager told me, "I drive him back into the mangrove where he belongs. This end of the mangrove is ours, the other side is his." (At this writing, the big crocodile has disappeared; but another probably will soon appear to take his place.)

The trailer park offers 40 sandy, shaded spaces for tents and RVs, including electricity, well water for showering, flushing, and laundry, bottled water for drinking, and a dump station. A loyal cadre of American and Canadian regulars stay here all winter. The trailer park includes an "authentically rustic" run-down kitchenette bungalow that sleeps four for $28 per day. Reserve by mail, generally necessary only during Christmas or Easter week. Rates run about $14 per RV for two persons. Add $5 per additional person. Tent camping runs $5 per person.

PLAYA LA MANZANILLA

The little fishing town of La Manzanilla (pop. 2,000) drowses at the opposite end of the same long, curving strip of sand that begins at the Boca de Iguanas trailer parks. Here the beach, Playa la Manzanilla, is as broad and flat and the waves are as gentle, but the sand is several shades darker. Probably no better fishing exists on the entire Costa Alegre than at La Manzanilla. A dozen seafood *palapas* on the beach manage to stay open by virtue of a trickle of foreign visitors and local weekend and holiday patronage.

Besides its gorgeous beachfront, the only other La Manzanilla sight is the town's family of toothy **crocodiles**, at the south end of main street María Asunción. (As you enter the town, a block before the beach, turn right.) About six individuals are usually visible, basking in the mangrove-fringed pond, waiting for handouts. The king of the heap, a 12-foot (four-meter) grandfather, periodically defends his seniority by fiercely chasing off potential junior rivals.

La Manzanilla has become a haven for a small but growing community of North American and Mexican winter vacationers and full-time residents. A growing cadre of restaurants and services, including vacation rentals and home sales, fishing excursions, adventure biking, hiking and horsebacking, cater to visitor's needs. For more information of all of this ferment, visit www.tomzap.com/manza.html, www .lamanzanilla.biz, and www.lamanzanilla.info.

Accommodations
UNDER $50

A handful of moderately priced recommendable hotels accommodate guests. Just a block from the north end of main street Calle María Asunción, find downscale **Hotel Posada del Cazador** (María Asunción 183, La Manzanilla, Jalisco 48988, tel. 315/351-5000, fax 315/351-5212, $18 s or d, $30 d in two beds low season, $30 and $45 high; kitchenette suites $40 low season, $50 high), where visitors enjoy friendly husband-wife management, a lobby for sitting and socializing, a shelf of used paperback novels, and a long-distance telephone. They offer seven plain but clean rooms, plus kitchenette suites that sleep four. Find it on the main street on the left, as you enter town.

On the opposite, sleepy south-end beachfront edge of town, the **Hotel Puesta de Sol** (Calle Playa Blanca 94, La Manzanilla, Jalisco, tel./fax 315/351-5033, $20 s or d, $30 t low season; $30 and $45 d high) offers 17 basic rooms around a cool, leafy central patio. Discounts for longer-term rentals.

One of the class-act La Manzanilla accommodations is the beautiful **Posada Tonalá** (María Asunción 75, La Manzanilla, Jalisco, tel./fax 315/351-5474, posadatonala@hotmail.com, $33 s or d, $30 d, $43 t, with a/c, fans, hot water shower baths, add about $15 during Christmas and Easter holidays), life project of kindly owner/builder Alfonso Torres López. Señor López retired from his auto parts business in Guadalajara and returned to realize his lifelong dream, to contribute to his hometown. You must at least come and look at his handiwork: the graceful teak *(granadillo)* stairway, the vines cascading on one side of the airy lobby, all topped by a uniquely lovely *palapa* roof. His rooms are immaculate and spacious, with modern shower baths and plenty of attractive tile, as well as handsome, dark, hand-carved furniture and colorful, handmade bedspreads. Find it on the town's main street, right in the center of town.

$50-100

Enjoy that vacation feeling with a stay at secluded, sea-view **Villa Montaña** (46 Calle los Angeles Locos, La Manzanilla, Jalisco 48988, $65 d low season, $89 d high) on the hillside above and behind the town. Discounts are available for long-term stays. For more information and reservations, contact Dan Clarke (P.O. Box 16343, Seattle, Washington 98116, tel. 206/937-3882, lamanzanilla@ hotmail.com, www.lamanzanilla.biz).

For an equally enjoyable, but completely different experience, stay right on the beach, at **Tranquilidad Bungalows** (Calle María Asunción 150, La Manzanilla, Jalisco 48980, tel. 315/351-5063, roberto@rkimsey.com, www .rkimsey.com, $75 low season, $95 d high), pride of local residents Robera and Tonia Kimsey. They offer four one-bedroom apartments (two upper-floor, two lower) tastefully decorated in modern spartan-chic style with queen-sized bed, fans, full kitchen, gleaming tile bath, living-dining room, and private ocean-view patios.

Get to La Manzanilla accommodations by following the La Manzanilla-signed paved road at Km 13 for one mile. The Hotel Cazador is on the left, one block after you turn left onto the main beachfront street. The Posada Tonalá and Tranquilidad Bungalows are a block farther, across the street from each other, while Hotel Puesta de Sol is a quarter-mile farther along; bear right past the town plaza for a few blocks along the beachfront street, Calle Playa Blanca. Villa Montaña is prominent on the hill (ask locally for directions), a quarter mile north of the town center.

RENTAL AGENTS

A number of agents manage **vacation rentals** for the many attractive homes that sprinkle La Manzanilla's shady lanes and golden beachfront. Dan Clarke, owner of Villa Montaña is probably the most experienced; check out his website www.lamanzanilla.biz, or telephone him in Seattle, 206/937-3882.

Alternatively, contact personable Daniel Hallas's **Costa Alegre Properties** office on the main street, María Asunción, beach side, or call him, in La Manzanilla, at 315/351-5059, or visit www.lamanzanilla.info.

Food

Two local restaurants stand out. For good comfort food, such as pizza, hamburgers, fish fillets, and Mexican plates, go to **Palapa Joe's** (María Asunción 163, tel. 315/351-5348, noon–10 P.M. Tues.–Sat., $3–8),

On the other hand, savor the breeze and the swish of the waves at **Martin's** (south end of beachfront Calle Playa Blanca, tel. 315/351-5348, 8 A.M.–10 P.M. daily). Let the romantic *palapa* setting enhance a delicious menu, including salads (watercress with bacon, $5), soups (vegetable, $3), fish (salmon and herbs, $12) and much more.

EL TAMARINDO

The Costa Alegre's newest big development occupies the lush, green peninsula that forms the southernmost point of Tenacatita Bay. Plans, virtually complete at this writing, project a giant, exclusive jungle country club, based on sales of about 100 parcels averaging 20 acres (8 hectares) apiece. Owners have access to extensive resort facilities, including a gorgeous jungle golf course, tennis courts, hotel, full spa with *temazcal* hot room, fine restaurant, heliport, skeet range, equestrian paths, beach club, and small marina. Plans require owner commitment to leaving a sizable fraction of the present forest in its original, pristine state.

The plan seems to be on track. The Tamarindo hinterland remains home to myriad wild creatures, from possumlike armadillos and snorting *jabali* (wild pigs) to feisty raccoons and warm and fuzzy but wily coatimundis.

Virtually all of the resort facilities are top quality; the meandering, forest-fringed golf course is

© BRUCE WHIPPERMAN

sunset at Hotel el Tamarindo

a wonder all in itself, designed by renowned Robert Trent Jones and David Fleming. It winds for thousands of yards, traversing lush lawns, tricky sand traps, serene ponds, and verdant, vine-hung thickets. Greens fee runs about $150 for in-house guests, more than $200 for outside clients from such plush hotels as Grand Bay, Cabo Blanco, Los Angeles Locos, Punta Serena, Las Alamandas, El Careyes, and Las Hadas.

Accommodations at **Hotel el Tamarindo** (tel. 315/351-5032 or 315/351-5052, toll-free Mex. tel. 800/909-4800, fax 315/351-5070, eltamarindoresort.com, $500–800 d) are in airy, pastel stucco and tile, super-deluxe jungle-edge housekeeping villas. For reservations, call Mexico Boutique Hotels toll-free U.S./Can. 800/728-7098, info@mexicoboutiquehotels .com, www.mexicoboutiquehotels.

Get there via the signed side road at Km 8, five miles north of Melaque. After about two miles of winding through the tropical forest, you arrive at the gate, where you must have either a reservation in hand or an appointment before the guard will let you through.

Barra de Navidad and Melaque

The little Jalisco country beach town of Barra de Navidad (pop. 5,000), whose name literally means Bar of Christmas, has unexpectedly few saloons. However, this bar has nothing to do with alcohol; it refers to the sandbar upon which the town is built. That lowly spit of sand forms the southern perimeter of the blue Bay of Navidad, which arcs to Barra de Navidad's twin town of San Patricio Melaque (pop. 10,000), a few miles to the west.

Barra and San Patricio Melaque, locally known as Melaque (may-LAH-kay), may be twins, but they're nevertheless distinct. Barra has the cobbled, shady lanes and friendly country ambience; Melaque is the business metropolis of the two, with most of the stores and services and also the better beach, long and lovely Playa Melaque.

HISTORY
The sandbar is called "Navidad" because the Viceroy Antonio de Mendoza, the first viceroy Mexico ever had, disembarked there on December 25, 1540. The occasion was auspicious for two reasons. Besides being Christmas Day, Don Antonio had arrived to personally put down a bloody rebellion raging through western Mexico that threatened to burn New Spain off the map. Unfortunately for the thousands of native people who were torched, hung, or beheaded during the brutal campaign, Don Antonio's prayers on that day were soon answered. The rebellion was smothered, and the lowly sandbar was remembered as Barra de Navidad from that time forward.

A generation later, Barra de Navidad became the springboard for King Philip's efforts to make the Pacific a Spanish lake. Shipyards built on the bar launched the vessels that carried the expedition of conquistador Miguel López de Legazpi and Father André de Urdaneta in search of God and gold in the Philippines. Urdaneta came back a hero one year later, in 1565, having discovered the northern circle route, whose favorable easterly winds propelled a dozen subsequent generations of the fabled treasure-laden Manila galleons home to Mexico.

By 1600, however, the Manila galleon was landing in Acapulco, which provided much quicker land transport to the capital for their priceless Asian cargoes. Barra de Navidad went to sleep and didn't wake up for more than three centuries.

Now Barra de Navidad only slumbers occasionally. The townsfolk welcome crowds of beach-going Mexican families during national holidays, and a steady procession of North American and European budget vacationers during the winter.

SIGHTS AND ACTIVITIES

A sizable fraction of Barra hotels and restaurants lie on one oceanfront street named, uncommonly, after a conquistador, Miguel López de Legazpi. Barra's other main street, Veracruz, one short block inland, has most of the businesses, groceries, and small, family-run eateries.

Head south along Legazpi toward the steep **Cerro San Francisco** in the distance and you will soon be on the palm-lined walkway that runs atop the famous sandbar of Barra. On the right, ocean side, the **Playa Barra de Navidad** arcs northwest to the hotels of Melaque, which spread like white pebbles along the far end of the strand. The great blue water expanse beyond the beach, framed at both ends by jagged, rocky sea stacks, is the **Bahía de Navidad.**

Laguna de Navidad

Opposite the ocean, on the other side of the bar, spreads the tranquil, mangrove-bordered expanse of the Laguna de Navidad, which forms the border with the state of Colima, whose mountains (including nearby Cerro San Francisco) loom beyond it. The lagoon's calm appearance is deceiving, for it is really an *estero* (estuary), an arm of the sea, which ebbs and

© BRUCE WHIPPERMAN

A line of rocky islands and a headland shelter the beach at Melaque.

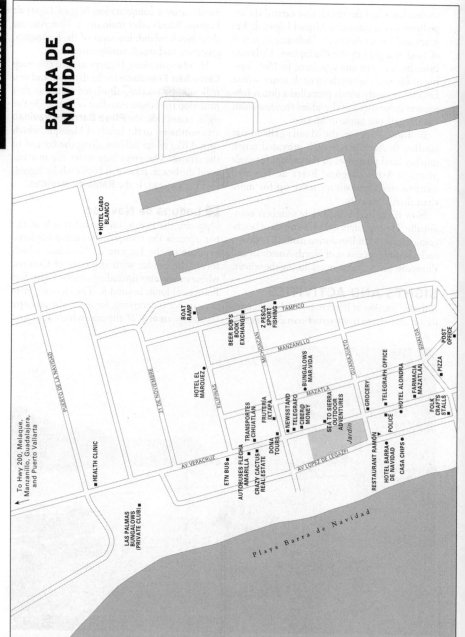

BARRA DE NAVIDAD

To Hwy 200, Melaque, Manzanillo, Guadalajara, and Puerto Vallarta

HOTEL CABO BLANCO

PUERTO DE LA NAVIDAD

21 DE NOVIEMBRE

FILIPINAS

HEALTH CLINIC

LAS PALMAS BUNGALOWS (PRIVATE CLUB)

AV VERACRUZ

ETN BUS

AUTOBUSES FLECHA AMARILLA

TRANSPORTES CIHUATLAN

CRAZY CACTUS REAL ESTATE

DOÑA TOURS

FRUTERIA IXTAPA

HOTEL EL MARQUEZ

BOAT RAMP

BEER BOB'S BOOK EXCHANGE

MICHOACAN

MANZANILLO

TAMPICO

Z PESCA SPORT FISHING

NEWSSTAND

TELEGRAFO

CIBER@ MONEY

MAZATLA

BUNGALOWS MAR VIDA

SEA TO SIERRA OUTDOOR ADVENTURES

GUANAJUATO

Jardín

AV LOPEZ DE LEGAZPI

RESTAURANT RAMON

HOTEL BARRA DE NAVIDAD

CASA CHIPS

POLICE

GROCERY

TELEGRAPH OFFICE

HOTEL ALONDRA

FARMACIA MAZATLAN

FOLK CRAFTS STALLS

SINALOA

POST OFFICE

PIZZA

Playa Barra de Navidad

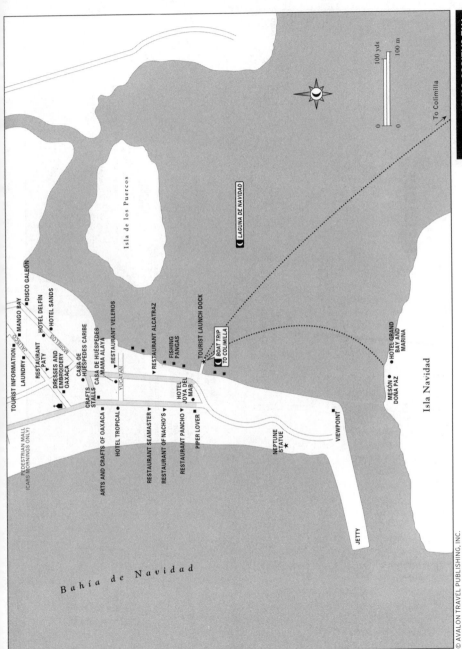

Bahía de Navidad

Isla de los Puercos

LAGUNA DE NAVIDAD

To Colimilla

Isla Navidad

TOURIST INFORMATION
LAUNDRY
MANGO BAY
DISCO GALEÓN
HOTEL DELFÍN
HOTEL SANDS
RESTAURANT PATY
DRESSES AND EMBROIDERY OAXACA
CASA DE HUÉSPEDES CARIBE
CASA DE HUÉSPEDES MAMA ALAYA
RESTAURANT VELEROS
RESTAURANT ALCATRAZ
FISHING PANGAS
TOURIST LAUNCH DOCK
BOAT TRIP TO COLIMILLA
JALISCO
MORELOS
YUCATÁN
CRAFTS STALLS
ARTS AND CRAFTS OF OAXACA
HOTEL TROPICAL
RESTAURANT SEAMASTER
RESTAURANT OF NACHO'S
RESTAURANT PANCHO
HOTEL JOYA DEL MAR
PIPER LOVER
HOTEL GRAND BAY AND MARINA
MESÓN DOÑA PAZ
NEPTUNE STATUE
VIEWPOINT
JETTY
PEDESTRIAN MALL (CARS MORNINGS ONLY)

100 yds
100 m
0
0

© AVALON TRAVEL PUBLISHING, INC.

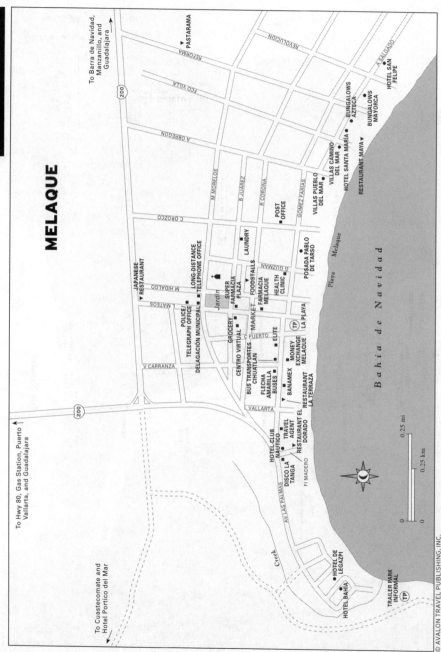

MELAQUE

To Barra de Navidad, Manzanillo, and Guadalajara

To Hwy 80, Gas Station, Puerto Vallarta, and Guadalajara

To Cuastecomate and Hotel Portico del Mar

PASTARAMA
REFORMA
ECO VILLA
REVOLUCION
A OBREGON
A SALGADO
HOTEL SAN FELIPE
BUNGALOWS AZTECA
BUNGALOWS MAYORCA
VILLAS CAMINO DEL MAR
HOTEL SANTA MARIA
RESTAURANT MAYA
VILLAS PUEBLO DEL MAR
B JUAREZ
R CORONA
GOMEZ FARIAS
M MORELOS
POST OFFICE
C OROZCO
JAPANESE RESTAURANT
M HIDALGO
LONG-DISTANCE TELEPHONE OFFICE
LAUNDRY
POSADA PABLO DE TARSO
MATEOS
POLICE/TELEGRAPH OFFICE
DELAGACION MUNICIPAL
Jardin
SUPER FARMACIA PLAZA
FOODSTALLS
FARMACIA MELAQUE
HEALTH CLINIC
G GUZMAN
GROCERY
MARKET
Playa Melaque
V CARRANZA
CENTRO VIRTUAL
C PUERTO
ELITE
LA PLAYA
TP
BUS TRANSPORTES CHUATLAN
MONEY EXCHANGE MELAQUE
FLECHA AMARILLA BUSES
BANAMEX
RESTAURANT LA TERRAZA
VALLARTA
HOTEL CLUB NAUTICO
TRAVEL AGENT
RESTAURANT EL DORADO
FI MADERO
DISCO LA TANGA
AV LAS PALMAS
Bahia de Navidad
Creek
HOTEL DE LEGAZPI
HOTEL BAHIA
TRAILER PARK INFORMAL
TP

0.25 mi
0.25 km
0

© AVALON TRAVEL PUBLISHING, INC.

flows through the channel beyond the rock jetty at the end of the sandbar. Because of this natural flushing action, local folks still dump fishing waste into the Laguna de Navidad. Fortunately, new sewage plants route human waste away from the lagoon, so with care, you can usually swim safely in its inviting waters. *Do not,* however, venture too close to the lagoon-mouth beyond the jetty or you may get swept out to sea by the strong outgoing current.

On the sandbar's lagoon side, a *panga* and passenger dock hum with daytime activity. From the dock, launches ferry loads of passengers for less than half a dollar to the Colima shore, which is known as **Isla Navidad,** where the marina and hotel development has risen across the lagoon. Back in the center of town, **minibuses** enter town along Veracruz, turn left at Sinaloa by the crafts stalls, and head in the opposite direction, out of town along Mazatlán, Veracruz, and Highway 200, three miles (4.8 km) to Melaque.

San Patricio and Melaque

The once-distinct villages of San Patricio and Melaque now spread as one along the Bay of Navidad's sandy northwest shore. The business district, still known locally as San Patricio (from the highway, go west two blocks toward the beach), centers around a plaza, market, and church bordering the main shopping street López Mateos.

Continue two more blocks to beachfront Calle Gómez Farías, where a lineup of hotels, eateries, and shops cater to the vacation trade. From there, the curving strand extends toward the quiet Melaque west end, where *palapas* line a glassy, sheltered blue cove. Here, a rainbow of colored *pangas* perch upon the sand, sailboats rock gently offshore, pelicans preen and dive, and people enjoy snacks, beer, and the cooling breeze in the deep shade beneath the *palapas.*

Boat Trip to Colimilla

A boat trip across the lagoon for super-fresh seafood at the palm-studded village of Colimilla is a primary Barra pastime. While you sit enjoying an oyster cocktail, ceviche, or broiled whole-fish dinner, gaze out on the

refreshments at the lagoon dock, a jumping-off point for Colimilla

mangrove-enfolded glassy expanse of the Laguna de Navidad. Far away, a canoe may drift silently, while white herons quietly stalk their prey. Now and then a launch will glide in and deposit its load of visitors, or an angler will head out to sea.

One of the most pleasant Colimilla vantage spots is the **La Colimilla Restaurant** (8 A.M.– 8 P.M. daily, $5–10), whose *palapa* extends into the lagoon. Take mosquito repellent, especially if you're staying for dinner. Launches routinely ferry as many as six passengers to Colimilla from the Barra lagoonside docks for about $5 round-trip. Tell them when you want to return, and they'll pick you up.

From the same Barra lagoonside dock, launches also shuttle passengers for $1.50 round-trip across the lagoon to **Isla Navidad** and its new Hotel Grand Bay, marina, vacation home development, and golf course.

Playa Coastecomate

On another day, explore this hidden beach tucked behind the ridge rising beyond the north edge of Melaque. The dark, fine-sand beach arcs along a cove on the rampart-rimmed big blue **Bahía de Coastecomate** (kooah-stay-koh-MAH-tay). Its very gentle waves and clear waters make for excellent swimming, sailboarding, snorkeling, and fishing from the beach itself or the rocks beneath the adjacent cliffs. A number of *palapa* restaurants along the beach serve seafood and drinks.

The Coastecomate beachside village itself, home to a number of local fisherfolk and a few North Americans in permanently parked RVs, has a collection of oft-empty bungalows on the hillside, a small store, and about three times as many chickens as people.

To get there, drive, taxi, or bus via the local minibus or Transportes Cihuatlán to the signed Melaque turnoff from Highway 200. There, a paved side road marked Hotel Real Costa Sur heads northwest into the hills, winding for two miles (3.2 km) over the ridge through pasture and jungle woodland to the village. If you're walking, allow an hour and take your sun hat, insect repellent, and water.

Other Beaches

Although a continuous strand of medium-fine golden sand joins Barra with Melaque, it changes character and names along its gentle, five-mile arc. At Barra de Navidad, where it's called **Playa de Navidad,** the beach is narrow and steep, and the waves are sometimes very rough. Those powerful swells often provide good intermediate surfing breaks adjacent to the jetty. Fishing by line or pole is also popular from the jetty rocks.

Most mornings are calm enough to make the surf safe for swimming and splashing, which, along with the fresh seafood of beachside *palapa* restaurants, make Barra a popular Sunday and holiday picnic-ground for local Mexican families. The relatively large number of folks walking the beach unfortunately makes for slim pickings for shell collectors and beachcombers.

For a cooling midday break from the sun, drop in to one of the beachfront restaurants (such as Seamaster) at the south end of Legazpi and enjoy the bay view, the swish of the waves, and the fresh breeze streaming beneath the *palapa.*

As the beach curves northwesterly toward Melaque, the restaurants and hotels give way to dunes and pasture. At the outskirts of Melaque, civilization resumes, and the broad beach, now called **Playa Melaque,** curves gently to the west.

Continuing past the Melaque town center, a lineup of rustic *palapas* and *pangas* pulled up on the sand decorate the tranquil west-end cove, which is sheltered from the open sea behind a tier of craggy sea stacks. Here, the water clears, making for good fishing from the rocks.

Barra-Melaque Hike

You can do this four-mile stroll either way, but starting from Barra early in the morning, the sun will be behind you and the sky and ocean will be at their bluest and best. Take insect repellent, sunscreen, and a hat. At either end, enjoy lunch at one of the seaside restaurants. At the Melaque end you can continue walking north to the cove on the far side of town. The trail, now a concrete *andador* beneath the cliff, leads to spectacular wave-tossed tide pools and rugged sea rocks at the tip of the bay. At the Barra end, you can hire a launch to Colimilla for lunch or dinner. End your day leisurely by taxiing or busing back from the bus station at either end.

Bird- and Wildlife-Watching

The wildlife-rich upper reaches of the Laguna de Navidad stretch for miles and are only a boat ride away. Besides the ordinary varieties of egrets, terns, herons, pelicans, frigate birds, boobies, ducks, and geese, patient bird-watchers can sometimes snare rainbow flash-views of exotic parrots and bright tanagers and orioles.

As for other creatures, quiet, persistent observers are sometimes rewarded with mangrove-edge views of turtles, constrictors, crocodiles, coatimundis, raccoons, skunks, deer, wild pigs, ocelots, and wildcats. The sensitivity and experience of your boatman/guide is, of course, crucial to the success of any nature outing. Ask at the tourist information office or the dock-office of the **Sociedad Cooperativa de Servicios Turísticos** (40 Av. Veracruz) on the lagoon front. You might also ask Tracy Ross at Crazy Cactus Real Estate (Veracruz 165, tel. 315/355-6091), across from the bus station, or Nan Niemela and/or Enrique Palominos of Sea to Sierra Outdoor Adventures (Veracruz 204, across from the *jardín*) to recommend a good guide, or even a complete wildlife-watching excursion.

BARRA ACCOMMODATIONS

Whether on the beach or not, all Barra hotels (except the world-class Hotel Grand Bay) fall in the budget or moderate categories. Note: The Barra de Navidad waves during fall storm season sometimes hit the sand with a boom. If you're a light sleeper, best come prepared with earplugs. Otherwise, choose one of Barra's many good off-beach hotels.

Under $50

Find the budget traveler's perennial favorite, **¢ Casa de Huéspedes Caribe** (Sonora 15, Barra de Navidad, Jalisco 48987, tel. 315/355-

5952, $15 s, $20 d, and $25 t), tucked along a side street. The family owners offer their devoted following of long-term customers 11 plainly decorated bare-bulb but clean rooms, with twin, double, or both types of beds, but all with bath and hot water. Amenities include a homey downstairs garden sitting area, and more chairs and hammocks for snoozing on an upstairs porch.

Return north a block, then east another block, where its loyal international clientele swears by the family-operated **¢ Hotel Delfín** (Morelos 23, Barra de Navidad, Jalisco 48987, tel. 315/355-5068, info@hotel-delfinmx.com, www.hoteldelfinmx.com, $36 s or d, $55 t low season; $45 s or d, $60 t high season). Its four stories of tile-floored, balcony-corridor rooms (where curtains, unfortunately, must be drawn for privacy) are the cleanest and coziest of Barra's moderate hotels. The Delfín's tour de force, however, is the cheery patio buffet where guests linger over the breakfast offered every morning (8:30–10:30 A.M. daily, $6) to all comers. Overnight guests, however, must put up with the moderate nighttime noise of the disco half a block away. For maximum sun and privacy, take one of the top-floor rooms, many of which enjoy lagoon views. The Delfín's 30 rooms come with fans, small pool, and parking; credit cards are accepted.

$50-100

Right across the street, bordering the lagoon, the most charmingly tropical of Barra hotels, the drowsy, old-Mexico **Hotel Sands** (Morelos 24, Barra de Navidad, Jalisco 48987, tel./fax 315/355-5018, $32 s, $48 d low season; $51 s, $65 d high; with kitchenette, $90 q low season, $125 q high), offers a bit of class at moderate rates. A pair of three-story room tiers enclose an inner courtyard lined with comfortable airy sitting areas that open on to a lush green garden of leafy vines and graceful coconut palms. A right-side garden walkway leads to a panorama of Barra's colorful lineup of lagoon-front fishing launches. On the other side, past the swim-up bar, a big curving pool and outer patio lead to a grand, airy vista of the placid,

THE JALISCO COAST

© BRUCE WHIPPERMAN

view of Isla Navidad from the palm garden of
the Hotel Sands

mangrove-bordered Laguna de Navidad. The
pool-bar (happy hour 4–6 P.M. daily, winter
season) and the airy sitting areas afford inviting places to meet other travelers.

Despite its many charming pluses, the Sands
also has some mentionable minuses. Many of
the rooms are too dark for most tastes, and,
despite the fans, sometimes too warm. Furthermore, rock and salsa music from the disco, half
a block down the street, sometimes (especially
holidays and some long weekends) thumps
away until around 2 A.M. (Either join the fun,
rent a room as far away from the source as possible, or be prepared with earplugs.)

The Sands' 43 rooms and bungalows, all
with fans (but with slow-to-arrive hot water
in some rooms—check before moving in) are
clean and furnished with dark varnished wood
and tile. Credit cards (with a 6 percent sur-
charge) are accepted, and parking is available.

Return south three blocks along Veracruz
(and jog half a block uphill, west) to a relative newcomer, white-stuccoed **Hotel Joya**

del Mar, formerly Hotel Buenos Aires (Veracruz 209, Barra de Navidad, Jalisco 48987,
tel./fax 315/355-6967, hoteljoyadelmar@
yahoo.com.mx, $42 s, $47 d, $51 t low sea-
son, and up). The Mexican on-site owner offers
three floors of eight simply but comfortably
furnished rooms and suites, topped by a pair
of view suites. The building's height affords
upper-floor guests the benefit of either lagoon
or ocean sunset views and cooling afternoon
westerly breezes. Rooms rent, low season, from
$42 s, $47 d, and $51 t, for the bottom floor;
$52, $57, and $61 for the second-floor rooms.
The third-floor suites go for about $85 s, $90
d. Add about $10 to all rates for high season.
With fans, air-conditioning, no smoking in
rooms, and credit cards accepted. Make your
winter season reservations early.

An attractive new (post-hurricane) addition
to Barra's sprinkling of beachfront lodgings is
◖ **Casa Chips** (198 López de Legazpi, Barra
de Navidad, Jalisco 48987, tel. 315/355-5555,
barrachips@earthlink.net, www.casachips
.com; or P.O. Box 882004, San Francisco, California 94188-2004, U.S. tel. 415/671-3816,
$45–85 d low season, $50–110 high) tucked
above the beach in the middle of town. Here,
owners have packed a lot of hotel into a small
space. They offer an assortment of seven invitingly decorated rustic-chic lodgings, ranging
from double-bed rooms to one-bedroom suites,
all the way up to an entire deluxe two-bedroom
upstairs view apartment. All are decorated with
color-coordinated bedspreads and drapes, attractive tile, and hand-hewn wood furniture.
An important extra here is an airy beachfront
restaurant, fine for relaxing dining, socializing, and sunset-watching. Add $10 and $15 low
and high season, respectively, per extra person.
All with fans, air-conditioning, and hot water
showers; the larger lodgings have kitchenettes.

Folks interested in tennis, boating, and/or
fishing might appreciate Barra's original deluxe
lodging, the stucco-and-tile, four-star **Hotel
Cabo Blanco** (P.O. Box 31, Barra de Navidad, Jalisco 48987, tel./fax 315/355-5103, fax
315/3556494, Mexico toll-free tel. 01-800/710-
5690, email@hotelcaboblanco.com, www.hotel

caboblanco.com, $50 d low season, $65 d high). The 125-room low-rise complex (named after the 1970s Barra de Navidad-filmed Hollywood thriller *Cabo Blanco,* starring Charles Bronson) anchors the vacation-home development along the three marina-canals that extend about five blocks north from the Barra lagoon. Within its manicured garden-grounds, Hotel Cabo Blanco offers night-lit tennis courts, restaurants, bars, two pools, kiddie pools, and deluxe sportfishing yachts-for-hire. The deluxe, pastel-decorated rooms run about $50 d (except $65 d July and August, holidays and some weekends), all with air-conditioning, cable TV, and phones; with a folkloric dance show, many water sports, and credit cards accepted. Bring your repellent; during late afternoon and evening mosquitoes and gnats from the nearby mangroves seem to especially enjoy the Cabo Blanco's posh ambience.

Tucked four short blocks from the beach at Barra's north end is the very worthy family-friendly, three-star 【 Hotel el Márquez (Calles Filipinas and Manzanillo, Barra de Navidad, Jalisco 48987, tel./fax 315/355-5304, elmarquez@esmas.com, www.costalegre.ca/barra_hotels.htm, $35 d low season, $55 high). Inside the gate, guests enjoy about 30 comfortable, semideluxe rooms around an invitingly intimate inner pool patio. Air-conditioning is $9 extra; there's a kiddie playground and parking.

If the Marquéz is full, try similarly comfortable but smaller three-star neighbor **Bungalows Mar Vida** (Mazatlán 168, Barra de Navidad, Jalisco 48987, tel. 315/355-5911, fax 315/355-5349, marsha@marshaewing.com, www.tomzap.com/marvida.html, $55 d May-Nov., $60 d high season), one block west and one block south. Friendly owner and real estate agent Marsha Ewing has five comfortable, semi-deluxe rooms, with air-conditioning and small pool patio.

The second of Barra's two recommendable beachfront lodgings is the white stucco three-story **Hotel Barra de Navidad** (Av. L. de Legazpi 250, Barra de Navidad, Jalisco 48987, tel. 315/355-5122, fax 315/355-5303, hotel_barra@yahoo.com.mx, $62 s, $72 d, $78

t low season, $68, $78, $80 high) on the beach side of the town plaza. Guests in the seaside upper two floors of comfortable, semi-deluxe rooms enjoy palm-fringed ocean vistas from private balconies. A shady, plant-decorated interior courtyard, inviting pool and patio, and good Bananas Restaurant upstairs complete the compact but attractive picture. Rates for the 57 rooms include air-conditioning. Ask for one of the sunnier, quieter, ocean-view rooms. Credit cards are accepted.

Over $100

Barra's hottest new accommodation is the ecologically correct **Coco Cabañas** (Kilometer 8.2, on the road between Hwy. 200 and Isla Navidad hotel and golf course, tel. 335/004-2686, U.S. tel. 281/205-4100, contactus@ecocabanas.com, www.ecocabanas.com, $100 d low season, $125 high), perched on pristine and breezy Playa los Cocos, a couple of miles south of Barra de Navidad. Both guests and reviewers rave about this place. This is clearly a place for those who enjoy solitude: no telephones, no cable TV, no exercise room, but with a good restaurant, perhaps a few other guests, miles of luscious beach to explore, and plenty of opportunities for reading and relaxing in the pool that meanders in front of the cabañas. The cabañas can sleep as many as four adults and two kids: two downstairs in a sofa bed, kids on a foam mattress, and two more adults in a king-sized bed in the loft. Add $5 per extra person; rates include breakfast, hot water, and solar-generated electricity (leave your hair dryer at home).

Note: If you're not driving, the easiest way to get to Hotel Coco Cabáns is by rented launch ($15), from the dock on the Barra de Navidad south-side lagoon front.

In complete contrast nearby stands Barra's plushest hotel by far, the class-act **Hotel Grand Bay** (P.O. Box 20, Barra de Navidad, Jalisco 48987, tel. 315/331-0500, fax. 315/355-0560, reservaciones@islaresort.com.mx, www.islanavidad.com, $200 d and up), a short boat ride to the Isla Navidad development across the lagoon. Builders spared little expense to create the appearance of a *gran epoch* resort. The 198 rooms are elaborately furnished with marble floors, French Provincial furniture reproductions, and Italian jade-hued marble bathroom sinks. Accommodations run from spacious "superior" rooms for about $200 d except holidays and some weekends; master suites about $300 d, through grand four-room executive suites that include their own steam rooms, from about $1,000. With all possible amenities, including three pools, three elegant restaurants, tennis, volleyball, children's club, marina, and a wonderfully breezy oceanfront golf course.

The owners of the Hotel Grand Bay also offer a more private, personal option, the **Mesón Doña Paz** (tel. 315/337-9002 or 315/337-9000, fax 314/337-9015, reservaciones@ mesondonapaz.com, www.mesondonapaz .com, $270 d low season, $340 high, and up) Originally built as the owners' private manor house (which they now use only at Christmas), the Mesón Doña Paz is a maharaja's mansion of spacious super-luxurious suites, elegantly decorated in the marble-French Provincial mode of the neighboring Hotel Grand Bay. The load of conveniences include elaborate telephone-equipped bathrooms (with separate rooms for tubs and showers), airy, private view patios, an exclusive restaurant, dining veranda, bar, and boat landing. Upstairs, a regal penthouse view salon, perfect for executive meetings (up to about 50 people) adds an attractive business-friendly option. Offering rates, beginning at $270 d (about $340 holidays and some weekends); $350 ($500) for junior suites; $520 ($640) for master suites, are reasonable, considering the luxurious exclusive facilities. Reserve for Mesón Doña Paz either directly or through its agent, Mexico Boutique Hotels (toll-free U.S./Can. 800/728-7098, info@mexicoboutiquehotels.com, www .mexicoboutiquehotels).

Note: Security is tight at Hotel Grand Bay and Mesón Doña Paz. Guards at the hotel lagoonside boat dock (and the separate Mesón Doña Paz dock) only allow entrance to guests and prospective guests. If you want to look around, you have to be accompanied by an in-house guide. Call the desk beforehand for an appointment.

MELAQUE ACCOMMODATIONS

In contrast to Barra de Navidad, San Patricio-Melaque has many beachfront hotels. Although the majority of them, especially in the old San Patricio town center, are mediocre at best, visitors enjoy a number of well-managed, comfortable, even deluxe exceptions, most of them in the sleepy **south-of-town** neighborhood. All of the following enjoy beachfront locations, although few, except those noted, accept credit cards.

Under $50

Melaque's best-buy budget lodging is the ◖ **Hotel Santa María** (Abel Salgado 85, P.O. Box 188, San Patricio-Melaque, Jalisco 48980, tel. 315/355-5677, fax 315/355-5553, $25 d and up). Long popular with cost-conscious Canadians and Americans in winter, the Santa María's 46 accommodations, all one-bedroom kitchenette apartments, are arranged in two motel-style wings, around an invitingly green and tranquil inner patio. All are close enough to the water for the waves to lull guests to sleep. Units vary; uppers are brighter, so look at a few before you move in. All-season prices for the spartan but generally tidy apartments begin at about $25 d per day, $160/week, $355/month, with TV, fans, hot water showers, and pleasantly sunny beachfront pool patio.

North a few blocks, closer to the town center, is the well-kept, colonial-chic **Posada Pablo de Tarso** (Av. Gómez Farías 408, San Patricio-Melaque, Jalisco 48980, tel./fax 315/355-5707 or 315/355-5717, $43 d and up), named after the apostle Paul of Tarsus. Guests enjoy many attractive (although at this writing somewhat worn) details, including art-decorated walls, hand-carved bedsteads and doors, and a flowery beachside pool and patio. The main drawback to all this lies in the motel-style corridor layout, which requires guests to pull the dark drapes for privacy. Year-round rates for the 27 rooms and bungalows begin at about $43 d ($23 daily rate for one-month rental) except possibly for some holidays; a kitchen raises the tariff to about $85 d, fan, a/c, TV, and phones. You may also reserve with their Guadalajara office (tel./fax 333/811-5262 and 333/811-4273).

A sprinkling of hotels in the sleepy Melaque **north-end** neighborhood offer comfortable accommodations at budget-to-moderate rates. One of Melaque's tidiest accommodations is the 🄲 **Hotel Bahía** (Calle Legazpi 5, tel./ fax 315/355-6894, www3.telus.net/public/ a7a84441/hotelbahia/index.html, $32 q low season, $40 high) of kindly owner-managers Evelia and Rafael Galvez Moreno, just half a block off the beach. The hotel's 21 rooms and two kitchenette bungalows line a pair of two-floor tiers that enclose an intimate inner patio and a pool in a second patio off to one side and an airy upstairs veranda, fine for relaxing and socializing. The rooms are spic-and-span and attractively decorated with flowery curtains and matching bedspreads. A common kitchen is available downstairs for guest use. Room rates run from about $32 (for one–four), about $40 high; kitchenette bungalows about $50, with TV, fans, hot water showers, and filtered drinking water.

The neighboring homey, downscale-modern, white stucco **Hotel de Legazpi** (Av. de las Palmas 3, P.O. Box 88, San Patricio-Melaque, Jalisco 48980, tel./fax 315/355-5397, hotelde legazpi@prodigy.net.mx, $30 s or d, $35 t low season; $39, $44, $49 high) offers relaxing vacation options right on the beachfront. A number of the hotel's spacious, clean, and comfortable front-side rooms have balconies with palmy ocean and sunset views. Downstairs, guests enjoy a small restaurant and a rear-court pool and patio. The hotel's beach-side entrance leads through a jungly front garden straight to the idyllic Melaque west-end sand crescent. Here, good times bloom among an informal club of longtime winter returnees beneath the *palapas* of the popular La Sirenita, Cabo Blanco, and Viva María restaurants. The hotel's 16 fan-only rooms (two with kitch-

enette) come with a TV room, and hot water shower baths.

$50-100

Classy in its unique way is the **Villas Camino del Mar** (Calle Francisco Villa, corner Abel Salgado, P.O. Box 6, San Patricio-Melaque, Jalisco 48980, tel. 315/355-5207, fax 315/355-5498, www.villascaminodelmar.com.mx, $49 d and up). Only a few signs in the humble beach neighborhood about a quarter-mile on the Barra side of the Melaque town center furnish any clue that this gem of a lodging hides at the beach end of a bumpy Melaque street. (Note: Recently, owners have added an annex across the street, which, although inviting, crams in more accommodations in a smaller space than the original building. Specifically ask for a room in the original building in your written or faxed reservation request.)

A five-story white stucco monument draped with fluted, neoclassic columns and hanging pedestals, the original Villas Camino del Mar hotel offers a lodging assortment from simple double rooms through deluxe suites with kitchenettes to a rambling penthouse. The upper three levels have sweeping ocean views, while the lower two overlook an elegant blue pool and patio bar and shady beachside palm grove. The clientele is split between Mexican middle-class families who come for weekends and holidays year around, and quiet, mostly middle-aged Canadians and Americans who come to soak up the winter sun for weeks and months on end. Reserve early, especially for the winter. Rates for the 37 rooms and suites run as little as $49 ($43 per day for a week, $34 per day for a month) for small but comfortable ocean-view room for two; $79 ($71 weekly, $55 monthly) for a studio with kitchenette; $95 ($85 weekly, $66 monthly for medium one-bedroom with two queen beds and kitchenette); and $120 ($108 weekly, $88 monthly) for deluxe two-bedroom, two-bath suites with kitchen; all with fans only. All rates are discounted 10 percent during low occupancy (usually May–June and Sept.–Nov.).

Camino del Mar's nearby upscale **Villas Pueblo del Mar,** set in a spacious, grassy beachfront compound with its own pool, offers much more luxury and space. The nine one- and two- bedroom kitchenette apartments go for $95–135; a one-week rental gets an 8 percent discount; one month 30 percent. Reserve early, through the Villas Camino del Mar contact numbers.

Close by is the sky-blue and white **Bungalows Azteca** (P.O. Box 57, San Patricio-Melaque, Jalisco 48980, or tel./fax 315/355-5150, $37 1 br low season, $50 high, and up). Auto court-style cottages line both sides of a cobbled driveway-courtyard-garden that spreads to a lazy, lovely beachfront pool-patio. The 14 spacious kitchenette cottages, in one-bedroom or three-bedroom versions, are plainly furnished but clean. The nine one-bedroom units rent, low season, for about $37/day, $220/week, $540/month ($50, $300, $800 high season). The five three-bedrooms rent for about $65/day, $400/week, $1,200/

the pool-patio-garden of Melaque's Bungalows Azteca

month, low season ($90, $550, $1400 high). Get your reservation in early, especially for the winter.

Less than a block south, the open, park-like grounds, spacious blue pool with kiddie pools, and beachside palm garden of the **Bungalows Mayorca** (Abel Salgado 133, Colonia Villa Obregón, P.O. Box 157, San Patricio-Melaque, Jalisco 48980, tel./fax 315/355-5219, bungalowsmayorca@hotmail .com, bungalowsmayorca@prodigy.net.mx, www.tomzap.com/mayorca.html, $60 d low season, $76 high) invite unhurried outdoor relaxation. Its stacked, Motel 6-style layout, attractively draped with tropical greenery, has aged gracefully. Here, groups and families accustomed to providing their own atmosphere find the kitchens and spacious (but dark) rooms of the Bungalows Mayorca appealing. The 21 two-bedroom bungalows, all with air-conditioning and TV rent for about $60 d, $230/week, $890/month low season ($76, $330, and $1,020 high). If you're in the mood for a splurge, ask for one of their three beachfront suites, with view balconies and jacuzzis, for about 20 percent additional.

If you prefer hotel high-rise ambience with privacy, a sea-view balcony, and a disco (holidays and some weekends) next door, you can have it right on the beach at the **Hotel Club Náutico** (Av. Gómez Farías 1A, San Patricio-Melaque, Jalisco 48980, tel. 315/355-5770 or 315/355-5766, fax 315/355-5239, club_nauticomx@ yahoo.com, www.clubnauticoeldorado.com, $34 s, $60 d, $74 t low season). The 40 simply but attractively decorated rooms, in blue, pastels, and white, angle toward the ocean in sunset-view tiers above a smallish pool and patio. The upper-floor rooms nearest the beach are likely to be quieter with the best views. The hotel also has a good beachside restaurant whose huge *palapa* both captures the cool afternoon sea breeze and frames the blue waters of the Bay of Navidad. The hotel's main drawback is lack of exterior space, being sandwiched, with a small pool-patio on one side, into a long, narrow beachfront lot. Add about 30 percent during Christmas and Easter holidays; ask for a discount during times of low occupancy. With air-conditioning, TV, phones, and good view restaurant/bar; credit cards are accepted.

The five-star **Hotel Portico del Mar** (formerly the Hotel Real Costa Sur; P.O. Box 12, San Patricio-Melaque, Jalisco 48980, toll-free Mex. tel. 01-800/710-5690, tel./fax 315/355-5085, $70 d low season, $90 q high) on Playa Coastecomate a few miles north of Melaque offers a moderately priced resort alternative. Built as a luxury hotel, it fell into disrepair and was closed for a spell in 2002. Nevertheless, new owners have re-opened for business. The hotel's low-rise view guest cabañas spread like a giant mushroom garden in the jungly palm-forest hillside above the beach. Patrons—mostly Canadians and Americans in winter, Mexicans in summer and holidays—enjoy air-conditioned view rooms with cable TV, tennis courts, sailing, sailboarding, pedalboats, snorkeling, volleyball, and a broad pool and sundeck right on the beach. During low-occupancy seasons, hotel cleanliness in the past has been less than desirable and the rooms have been musty due to lack of ventilation. Check before moving in.

Apartments, Houses, and Long-Term Rentals

If you're planning on a stay longer than a few weeks, you'll get more for your money if you can find a long-term house or apartment rental. Check out the good **Vacation Rentals by Owner** website (www.vrbo.com/vacation-rentals/mexico/mexican-riviera) that had five solid Barra-Melaque rental choices at this writing. Alternatively, contact longtime Barra realtors Peggy and Tracye Ross at **Crazy Cactus Real Estate** (165 Veracruz, tel./fax 315/355-6091 or 315/355-6099, crazycactusmx@yahoo.com, www.casademarco.com) in Barra across from the bus station; or Marsha Ewing Hernandez, operator of **Mar Vida Real Estate** (tel. 315/355-5911, fax 315/355-5349, marshahernandez@yahoo.com).

Trailer Parks and Camping

Barra-Melaque's best trailer park is **La Playa** (P.O. Box 59, Av. Gómez Farías 250, San Patricio-Melaque, Jalisco 48980, tel. 315/355-5065, $19 RV site), right on the beach in downtown Melaque. Although the park is a bit cramped and mostly shadeless, longtimers nevertheless get their winter reservations in early for the choice beach spaces. The better-than-average facilities include a small store, fish-cleaning sinks, showers, toilets, and all hookups. The water is brackish—drink bottled. Boat launching is usually easy on the sheltered beach nearby. The Trailer Park la Playa's 45 spaces rent for about $19/day, $100/week or $350/month.

Scores of winter returnees enjoy Melaque's north-end shoreline **informal RV-trailer park-campground** with room for about 50 rigs and tents, operated by the Emiliano Zapata *ejido* community. The cliff-bottom lot spreads above a calm rocky cove, ripe for swimming, snorkeling, and sailboarding. Other extras include super fishing and a sweeping view of the entire Bay of Navidad. All spaces are usually filled by Christmas and remain that way until March. The people are friendly, the price ($3 per tent or $5 per RV per day, $15/week, $70/month, plus a small garbage haul-away fee, collected by the *ejido* folks) is certainly right, and the beer and water trucks arrive regularly throughout the winter season. Please dump your waste in sanitary facilities while staying here; continued pollution of the cove by irresponsible occupants in the past has led to complaints. Get there by the dirt road that co continues from Avenida del Palmar, at the the northwest end of Melaque.

Wilderness campers might appreciated the solitude of **Playa de Cocos,** the miles-long golden sand beach, south of Barra de Navidad, that borders the ocean side of the Isla Navidad golf course. Playa de Cocos has an intimate hidden north-end sandy cove, perfect for an overnight or a few barefoot days of bird-watching, shell collecting, beachcombing, and dreaming around your driftwood campfire. The restaurants and stores in the village of Colimilla are available for food and water. Mosquitoes come out around sunset. Bring plenty of good repellent and a mosquito-proof tent.

The easiest way to get to Playa de Cocos is by hiring a launch at the Barra de Navidad lagoonfront that will drop you off right on the Playa de Cocos beach. You can also go by hiring a taxi from Barra de Navidad, or by your own car from Highway 200. From Barra de Navidad, head south on Highway 200 a few miles to the signed Isla Navidad right turn-off. Continue through the golf course, bearing left, toward the ocean, to the golf course's northwest corner and an oceanfront parking lot at the beach.

FOOD
Breakfast, Snacks, and Stalls

An excellent way to start your Barra day is at the intimate *palapa*-shaded patio of the **Hotel Delfín** (Av. Morelos 23, tel. 315/357-0068, 8:30–10:30 A.M. daily, $4–6). While you dish yourself fruit and pour your coffee from its little countertop buffet, the cook fixes your choice of breakfast options, from savory eggs and omelettes to French toast and luscious, tender banana pancakes. Alternatively, in Barra, for an equally satisfying breakfast ($3–6), go to the ocean-view restaurant **(Bananas**, upstairs at the Hotel Barra de Navidad, tel. 315/355-5122.

In Melaque, for breakfast with a bit of class, go to the **(Restaurant el Dorado** ($4–7) at the Hotel Club Náutico. For good, plain eating, and what some say are the best breakfasts in town, go to **Pastarama** (on Abel Salgado, tel. 315/355-6123, open daily, $3–5) on the Melaque south side, near the Hotel Saul de Tarso.

Also, plenty of good daytime eating in Melaque goes on at the lineup of small, permanent **fondas** ($2–4) in the alley that runs south from Avenida Hidalgo, half a block toward the beach from the southwest plaza corner. You can't go wrong with *fonda* food, as long as it's made right in front of you and served piping hot.

For light evening meals and snacks, Barra

has plenty of options. Here, families seem to fall into two categories: those who sell food to sidewalk passersby, and those who enjoy their offerings. The three blocks of Avenida Veracruz from Morelos to the city *jardín* (park) are dotted with tables ($1–3) that residents nightly load with hearty, economical food offerings, from tacos *de lengua* (tongue) and pork tamales to *pozole Guadalajara* and *chiles rellenos*. The wholesomeness of their menus is evidenced by their devoted followings of longtime neighbor and tourist customers.

Barra Restaurants

One local family has built its sidewalk culinary skills into a thriving Barra storefront business, the **Restaurant Paty** (corner of Veracruz and Jalisco, tel. 315/355-5907, 8 A.M.–11 P.M. daily, entrees $2–5). It offers the traditional menu of Mexican *antojitos*—tacos, quesadillas, tostadas—plus roast beef, chicken, and very tasty *pozole* soup. For a variation, try expatriate favorite **Pizzeria Yvette** nearby.

Among Barra's favorite eateries is the **(Restaurant Ramón** (260 Legazpi, tel. 315/355-6435, 7 A.M.–11 P.M. daily, entrees $5–12), across the street from the Hotel Barra de Navidad. Completely unpretentious and making the most of the usual list of international and Mexican specialties, friendly owner/chef Ramon and his hardworking staff continue to build their already sizable following. Choose whatever you like—chicken, fish, *chiles rellenos*, guacamole, spaghetti—and you'll most likely be pleased. Meals include gratis salsa and chips to start, hearty portions, and often a healthy side of cooked veggies on your plate.

One of Barra's most entertainingly scenic restaurants is **Veleros** (Veracruz 64, tel. 315/355-5907, noon–10 P.M. daily, entrées $7–15), right on the lagoon. If you happen to visit Barra during the full moon, don't miss watching its shimmering reflection from the restaurant *palapa* as it rises over the mangrove-bordered expanse. An additional Veleros bonus is the fascinating school of darting, swirling fish attracted by the spotlight shining on the water. Finally comes the food, which you can

© BRUCE WHIPPERMAN

A sprinkling of restaurants and boat docks decorate the lagoon-front in Barra de Navidad.

select from a menu of carefully prepared and served shrimp, lobster, octopus, chicken, and steak entrées. The brochettes are especially popular; credit cards are accepted.

Alternatively, for a singularly romantic option, try refined lagoon-front ❰ **Restaurant Alcatraz** (Veracruz 12, tel. 315/355-7041, noon–10 P.M. daily, $8–20), named by friendly owners Sergio and Susana Aguilar for the Mexico native lily that grows only in the Mexican altiplano. (But is nevertheless very common in California gardens.) Susana, who manages the restaurant, offers a delicious menu, from soups and salads, to meats, fish fillets, shrimp, and lobster. During winter high season, reservations are recommended.

Shift your scene one block away, to **Restaurant Seamaster** (López de Legazpi 140, no phone, 8 A.M.–11 P.M. daily $6–10), on the beach side of the sandbar, where guests enjoy a refreshing sea breeze every afternoon and a happy-hour sunset every evening. Besides super-fresh seafood selections, Seamaster features savory barbecued chicken and rib plates.

Restaurant Pancho (Legazpi 53, 8 A.M.–8 P.M. daily, $6–10), a few doors away, is one of Barra's original *palapas*, which old-timers can remember from the days when *all* Barra restaurants were *palapas*. The reputation for super-fresh seafood, built up by the original (but now late) Pancho, who saw lots of changes in the old sandbar in his 80-odd years, is now continued by his wife and son.

Melaque Restaurants

In Melaque, jazz and nouvelle cuisine first arrived at ❰ **Restaurant Maya** (foot of southside Calle Obregon, 6 P.M.–11 P.M. Tues.–Sat., brunch 10:30 A.M.–2 P.M. Sun., entrées around $14), favorite of a loyal cadre of American and Canadian vacationers and expatriates. Its private, sheltered beachfront garden and the murmur of the Melaque surf set the stage for the good music and food. For example, start out with a Maya Martini ($4), continue with curried fish cakes ($5), follow up with linguine with pesto, cream, and prawns ($14), and finish off with the chef's dessert creation of the day ($5). Winter high-season reservations highly recommended.

Besides good breakfasts, longtimers rave about the fish and chips ($4) at the **Pastarama** restaurant (on Abel Salgado, tel. 315/355-6123, open daily, $3–5), formerly Bananarama, on the Melaque south side, near the Hotel Saul de Tarso.

Restaurant el Dorado (Calle Gómez Farías 1A, tel. 315/355-5770, 8 A.M.–11 P.M. daily, moderate-expensive), under the big beachside *palapa* in front of the Hotel Club Náutico, provides a cool breezy place to enjoy the beach scene during breakfast or lunch. Service is crisp and the specialties are carefully prepared; credit cards are accepted.

ENTERTAINMENT AND EVENTS

Most entertainments in Barra and Melaque are informal and local. *Corridas de toros* (bullfights) are occasionally held during the winter-spring season at the bullring on Highway 200 across from the Barra turnoff. Local *vaqueros* (cowboys) sometimes display their pluck in spirited *charreadas* (Mexican-style rodeos) in neighboring country villages. Check with your hotel desk or the Barra tourist information office for details.

The big local festival occurs in Melaque during the St. Patrick's Day week of March 10–17. Events include blessing of the local fishing fleet, folk dancing, cake eating, and boxing matches.

Nightlife

Folks enjoy the Bahía de Navidad sunset colors evenings during the happy hours at **Restaurant Seamaster, Hotel Alondra top-floor bar,** or the **Casa Chips** hotel restaurant bar, half a block south of the Hotel Barra de Navidad.

The same is true at the beachside Restaurant Maya and Restaurant Dorado at Hotel Club Náutico in Melaque. You can prepare for this during the afternoons (Dec.–Feb. mostly) at the very congenial 4–6 P.M. happy hour around the swim-up bar at Barra's Hotel Sands. Lovers of pure tranquility, on the other hand, enjoy

the breeze and sunset view from the end of Barra's rock jetty.

Perhaps the friendliest bar in Barra or Melaque is **Piper Lover,** owned by a man whose father loved his Piper Cub airplane (tel. 315/355-6747, 4 P.M.–2 A.M. daily). Here you can cool off and kick back, enjoying the breeze and the swish of the waves outside the bar's air upstairs *palapa* perch. Find it at the south, sandbar end of Avenida Lopez de Legazpi.

If discoing is your thing, huge speakers begin thumping away, lights flash, and the fogs ooze from the ceilings around 10 P.M. at disco **El Galeón** (tel. 315/355-5018) of the Hotel Sands (young local crowd) and at **La Tanga** (Gómez Farías, entrance $7) across the street from Hotel Club Náutico (mixed young and older, local and tourist crowd). Hours vary seasonally; call for details.

SPORTS AND RECREATION
Swimming, Surfing, and Boogie Boarding

The roughest surf on the Bahía de Navidad shoreline is closer to Barra, the most tranquil closest to Melaque. Swimming is consequently best and safest toward the Melaque end, while, in contrast, the most popular local surfing spot is where the waves rise and roll in beside the Barra jetty. Bodysurfing and boogie boarding are best somewhere in between. At least one shop in Barra, Farmacia Zurich (on Legazpi, south corner of Jalisco, tel. 315/355-6135), sells boogie boards, surfboards, fishing poles, tackle and lures.

Sailing and Sailboarding

Sailing and sailboarding are best near the Melaque end of the Bay of Navidad and in the Bay of Coastecomate nearby. Bring your own equipment, however; none is available locally.

Snorkeling and Scuba Diving

Local snorkeling is often rewarding during the dry winter season, especially at Playa Tenacatita, off Highway 200, about 20 miles (32 km) miles north. Snorkel and scuba tours and instruction are available in Barra de Navidad through **Sea to Sierra Outdoor Adventures** (tel. 315/355-8582, info@seatosierra.com) at Av. Veracruz 204, across from the town *jardín*. Although Sea to Sierra has no scuba instructor, they partner with the professional PADI-trained instructors of **Nautimar** dive shop at the Hotel Grand Bay (tel. 315/331-0500).

The best organized and most professional regional dive shop is **Underworld Scuba** (P.O. Box 295, Santiago, Colima 28860, tel./fax 314/333-0642 or 314/333-3678, Carlos's mobile tel. 044-314/358-0327, Susan's cellular tel. 044-314/358-5042, scuba@gomanzanillo .com, www.divemanzanillo.com or www.go manzanillo.com/scubamex) is run by Manzanillo-based Susan Dearing and her partner, NAUI-certified instructor Carlos Cuellar.

Tennis and Golf

The Hotel Cabo Blanco tennis courts (tel. 315/355-5182, fax 315/355-64-94) are customarily open for public rental for about $4 per hour. Evenings, be prepared with mosquito repellent. Lessons may also be available; call ahead to check. The Hotel Portico del Mar (tel. 315/355-6495), at Playa Coastecomate, also rents tennis courts to outside visitors ($3/hr).

The plumy, breezy 18-hole **Isla Navidad Golf Course** is open to the public for a fee upwards of around $100 per person. Call the Hotel Grand Bay (tel. 315/331-0500, www.isla navidad.com) and ask for the Club de Golf for information. Get there by regular launch from the Barra launch dock on the lagoon (to the Casa Club landing, about $5 round-trip). By car, turn right from Highway 200 at the Ejido la Culebra (or Isla Navidad) sign as the highway cuts through the hills at Km 51 a few miles south of Barra. Follow the road about three miles (4.8 km) to a bridge, where the road curves right, paralleling the beach. After about two more miles (3.2 km), you pass through the golf course gate. After winding through the golf course another mile (1.6 km), turn right at the traffic circle at the north edge of the golf course. Continue another mile (1.6 km), between the golf course and the adjacent hillside, to the big golf clubhouse on the right.

Sportfishing

The captains of the Barra Boat Cooperative **Sociedad Cooperativa de Servicios Turísticos** (Av. Veracruz 40, mobile tel. 315/354-3792 or 044-315/354-3792) routinely take parties on successful marlin and swordfish hunts for about $28 per hour, including bait and tackle. Ask at their lagoonside office-dock.

Alternatively, you can arrange a fishing trip through highly recommended **Z Pesca** sportfishing (Reservations office, Hotel Alondra, no. 8, tel. 315/355-6464, U.S. tel. 949/643-1560, fax 949/643-8825, info@zpesca.com, www.zpesca.com, boat dock tackle shop and office staffed by Captain Chaparro, at Tampico 71.) Depending on the size of the craft, fees run from about $200 and up.

Sea to Sierra Outdoor Adventures (tel. 315/355-8359) also can probably arrange a fishing excursion for you.

Fishing trips will typically net *dorado* (mahi-mahi), albacore, rooster fish, snapper, or other delicious eating fish. Local restaurants will generally cook a banquet for you and your friends if you give them the extra fish caught during such an outing.

If you'd like to enter one of a pair of annual Barra de Navidad **International Fishing Tournaments** (billfish, tuna, and *dorado* in January and May; father and son/daughter tournament in January), contact captain Chaparro of Z Pesca, or the tourist information office.

Boat Launching

If you plan on mounting your own fishing expedition, you can do it from the Barra **boat-launching ramp** (end of Av. Filipinas, 8 A.M.–4 P.M. Mon.–Fri.) near the Hotel Cabo Blanco. The fee, about $10 per day, covers parking your boat in the canal and is payable to the boatkeeper, whose headquarters is inside the boatyard adjacent to the ramp.

Sports Equipment Sales and Rentals

The **Farmacia Zurich** (on Legazpi, south corner of Jalisco, tel. 315/355-8582, 9 A.M.–10 P.M.

daily) sells boogie boards, surfboards, fishing poles, tackle and lures. **Sea to Sierra Outdoor Adventures** in Barra (Av. Veracruz 204, tel. 313/355-8359) rents mountain bikes.

SHOPPING
Handicrafts

While Melaque has many stores crammed with humdrum commercial tourist curios, Barra has a few interestingly authentic sources. A number of Nahuatl-speaking families from Guerrero operate small individual shops, at the south end of Legazpi. Some of the shops near the corner of Sinaloa and Legazpi, behind the church, are mini-museums of delightful folk crafts, made mostly by *indígena* country craftspeople. Pick what you like—lustrous lacquerware trays from Olinalá, winsome painted pottery cats, rabbits, and fish, a battalion of wooden mini-armadillos, and polished dark hardwood swordfish from Sonora.

You can pick from an equally attractive selection at **Arts and Crafts of Oaxaca,** across Legazpi diagonally southwest from the church. Besides a fetching collection of priced-to-sell Oaxacan *alebrijes* (fanciful wooden animals), *tapetes* (woven wool rugs), and masks, you'll also find a host of papier mâché and pottery from Tlaquepaque and Tonalá, fine *sombreros* from Zitácuaro in Michoacán, and much more.

Across the street, a lineup of other shops, such as **Artestanías Nahuatl** and **Artesanías Guerrero** have similarly attractive offerings, on the south end of Veracruz, near the corner of Morelos. Although bargaining is customary, don't bargain too hard. Many of these folks, far from their country villages, are strangers in a strange land. Their sometimes-meager earnings often support entire extended families back home.

Fruit, Vegetable, and Grocery Stores

There are no large markets, traditional or modern, in Barra. However, a few minimarkets and *fruterías* stock basic supplies. Best is probably **Frutería Ixtapa** (northeast corner of Veracruz and Michoacán, tel. 315/355-6443,

8 A.M.–10 P.M. Mon.–Sat.). Drop by and find out the produce delivery day, so you can get them when they're fresh.

In Melaque, nearly all grocery and fruit shopping takes place at the **central market** or at several good stores on main street López Mateos, which runs away from the beach past the west side of the central plaza.

INFORMATION
Tourist Information Office

The small Barra-Melaque regional office of the **Jalisco Department of Tourism** (Jalisco 67, tel./fax 315/355-5100, setujalcostalegre@ prodigy.net.mx, www.costalegre.com, 9 A.M.– 5 P.M. Mon.–Fri., 9 A.M.–2 P.M. Sat.) is tucked near the east end of Jalisco across the street from the Terraza upstairs bar. Staff distributes maps and literature and answers questions during office hours. The office is a good source of information about local civic and ecological issues and organizations.

Publications

The Barra **newsstand** (corner of Veracruz and Michoacán, 7 A.M.–10 P.M. daily) may seasonally stock some English-language newspapers and magazines. The liquor store Fatima, north across Michoacán, next to the Transportes Cihuatlán bus station, stocks the *Miami Herald.*

Perhaps the best English-language lending library in all of Pacific Mexico is **Beer Bob's Book Exchange** (Calle Tampico, btwn. Pilipinas and Michoacán) on a Barra back street. Many hundreds of vintage paperbacks, free for borrowing or exchange, fill the shelves. Chief librarian and Scrabble devotee Bob (a retired counselor for the California Youth Authority) manages his little gem of an establishment just for the fun of it. "It's not a store," he says. Just drop your old titles in the box and take away the equivalent from his well-organized collection. If you have nothing to exchange, simply return whatever you borrow before you leave town.

In Melaque, the **Librería Saifer** (on the southwest corner of the central plaza, by the church, 9 A.M.–3 P.M. and 5–10 P.M. daily) stocks the *Miami Herald.*

Ecotouring

Friendly and enterprising local guides Nan Niemela and Enrique Palominos, through their **Sea to Sierra Outdoor Adventures**, guide and arrange a number of tours for nature lovers. These include snorkel, scuba, fishing, mountain bike trips, and more. Contact them at their Barra shop (Av. Veracruz 204, across from the town *jardín* tel. 315/355-8582, info@seatosierra.com, www.seatosierra.com).

SERVICES
Money Exchange

Although Barra has no bank, it does have a **Banamex ATM,** at the Barra plaza, southeast corner. Melaque does have a bank, **Banamex** (tel. 315/355-5217 or 315/355-5217, 9 A.M.– 4 P.M. Mon.–Fri., 10 A.M.–2 P.M. Sat.), with ATM, across the street and half a block north of the main bus station. Barra's friendliest money exchange is Ciber@Money, at 212 Veracruz. With even longer hours, the **Vinos y Licores Barra de Navidad** (on Legazpi, across from Hotel Barra de Navidad, 8:30 A.M.– 11 P.M. daily) exchanges both Canadian and American traveler's checks and cash.

After bank hours in Melaque, use the Banamex ATM, or go to **Money Exchange Melaque** (Gómez Farías 27A, tel. 315/355-5343, 9:30 A.M.– 7 P.M. Mon.–Sat.), across from the bus terminal. It exchanges both American and Canadian travelers checks and cash, but the tariff often amounts to a steep $3 per $100 above bank rate.

Communications

Barra and Melaque each have a small *correo,* and Barra has a *telégrafo.* The **Barra post office** (8 A.M.–3 P.M. Mon.–Fri.) is on Veracruz, south side of the town *jardín.*

The **Melaque post office** (13 Clemente Orozco, between G. Farías and Corona, tel. 315/355-5230, 8 A.M.–3 P.M. Mon.–Fri.) is three blocks south of the plaza, a block and a half from the beach.

The Barra **telégrafo** (on Veracruz, tel. 315/355-5262, 9 A.M.–2 P.M. Mon.–Fri.), which handles money orders, is half a block north of Barra plaza.

In Barra, go to friendly **Ciber@Money** (212 Veracruz, tel. 315/355-6177, 9 A.M.– 6 P.M. Mon.–Sat.) for public telephone, Internet access, and money exchange. Or connect to the Internet at **Mango Bay** café (70 Jalisco), across the street from the *turismo.*

In Melaque, go to the **long-distance telephone office** (corner of Morelos and Hidalgo, tel. 315/355-8608, 8 A.M.–3 P.M. and 5–10 P.M. daily) on the *jardín* northeast corner. Also in Melaque, you have a pair of Internet choices: **Ciber@Net** (9 A.M.–2:30 P.M. and 4–8 P.M. Mon.–Sat.), on Gómez Farías across from the bus terminal and next to the money exchange; or **Centro Virtual** (in the market, across the lane from the food stalls, mobile tel. 315/355-5044, 9 A.M.–10 P.M. Mon.–Sat.), half a block toward the beach from the plaza.

Health and Emergencies

In Barra, the government **Centro de Salud** (corner Veracruz and Puerto de la Navidad, tel. 315/355-6220), four blocks north of the town plaza, has a doctor 24 hours a day. The **Melaque Centro de Salud** (Calle Gordiano Guzman 10, tel. 315/355-5880), off the main beachside street Gómez Farías two blocks from the trailer park, also offers access to a doctor 24 hours a day.

In a medical emergency, call for a Red Cross (Cruz Roja) **ambulance** (tel. 315/355-2300) to whisk you to the well-equipped hospitals in Manzanillo.

Otherwise, for over-the-counter remedies, in Barra, go to **Farmacia Zurich** (on Legazpi, across from the church, at the south corner of Jalisco, tel. 315/355-6135); or in Melaque, try **Super Farmacia Plaza** (on López Mateos, tel. 315/355-5167), at the northwest corner of the town plaza.

Police

The Barra police (179 Veracruz, tel. 315/355-5399) are on 24-hour duty at the city office adjacent to the *jardín.*

For the Melaque police, either call (tel. 315/355-5080) or go to the headquarters behind the plazafront *delegación municipal*

(municipal agency) at the plaza corner of L. Mateos and Morelos.

Travel Agent

For airplane tickets, fishing trips, tours, and other vacation arrangements in Barra, contact **Viajes Dona Tours** (Veracruz 220, corner of Michoacán, tel./fax 315/355-5667, dona tours@hotmail.com, 11 A.M.–8 P.M. Mon.–Fri., 11 A.M.–5 P.M. Sat.). In Melaque, go to their branch office (Gómez Farías 27A, tel. 315/355-5615).

Laundries

Barra and Melaque visitors enjoy the services of a number of *lavanderías*. In Barra, try **Lavandería Jardín** (Jalisco 69, 9 A.M.–2 P.M. and 4–7 P.M. Mon.–Fri., 9 A.M.–noon Sat.), next to the *turismo*. In Melaque, step one block east (parallel to beach) along Juárez from the plaza, to **Lavandería Frances.**

GETTING THERE AND AWAY
By Air

Barra de Navidad is air-accessible either through **Puerto Vallarta Airport** or the **Manzanillo Airport,** only 19 miles (30 km) south of Barra-Melaque. While the Puerto Vallarta connection has the advantage of many more flights, transfers to south coast are time-consuming. If you can afford it, the quickest option from Puerto Vallarta is to rent a car. Alternatively, ride a local bus or hire a taxi from the airport to the new central bus station, north of the airport. There, catch a bus, preferably **Autocamiones del Pacífico** (tel. 322/290-0716) or Flecha Amarilla's luxury service **Primera Plus** (tel. 322/221-0994) to Barra or Melaque (three hours).

On the other hand, arrival via the Manzanillo airport, half an hour from Barra-Melaque, is much more direct, provided you can get a flight there through the relatively few carriers that serve the airport.

For Puerto Vallarta and Manzanillo airport flight, arrival and departure details, see the respective *Getting There and Away* sections in the *Puerto Vallarta* and *Manzanillo and Colima* chapters.

By Bus

Several regional bus lines cooperate in connecting Barra and Melaque north with Puerto Vallarta; south with Cihuatlán, Manzanillo, Colima, Playa Azul, Zihuatanejo, and Acapulco; and northeast with Guadalajara, via Highway 80, and Morelia and Mexico City, via the expressway. They arrive and leave so often (about every half-hour during the day) from the three little Barra de Navidad stations, clustered on Avenida Veracruz a block and a half north of the central plaza, that they're practically indistinguishable.

Of the various companies, affiliated lines **Transportes Cihuatlán** and **Autocamiones del Pacífico** (on the east side of Veracruz, tel. 315/355-5200), provide the most options: super-first-class Primera Plus buses connect (several per day) with Guadalajara, Manzanillo, and Puerto Vallarta. In addition to this, they offer about two dozen second-class buses per day in all three directions. These often stop anywhere along the road if passengers wave them down.

Across the street, other lines, affiliated with bus giant **Flecha Amarilla,** provides similar services, including a different Primera Plus luxury-class service to Manzanillo, Puerto Vallarta, Guadalajara, and León, out of its separate little station (Veracruz 269, tel. 315/355-6111), across and half a block up the street.

Also, next door to Flecha Amarilla, **ETN** (Enlaces Transportes Nacionales; tel. 315/355-8400) buses leave from a small air-conditioned station to connect with Manzanillo, Colima, Morelia, and Mexico City.

With the exception of Elite, which stops only in Melaque, all the buses that stop in Barra also stop in Melaque. All Autocamiones del Pacífico and Transportes Cihuatlán buses stop at the Melaque main terminal, **Central de Autobuses** (on Gómez Farías at V. Carranza, tel. 315/355-5003; open 24 hours daily).

In Melaque, Flecha Amarilla maintains its own fancy new air-conditioned station (tel. 315/355-6110) across the street, where you can ride its luxury-class Primera Plus buses, in addition to regular second-class Autobuses Costa Alegre, north to Puerto Vallarta, south to Manzanillo, and with expanded service, to Guadalajara, León, and Mexico City.

However, one line, first class **Elite** does not stop in Barra. It maintains its own little Melaque station (Gómez Farias 257, tel. 315/355-5177), a block south of the main station, across from the Melaque Trailer Park. From there, Elite connects by first-class express north (two daily departures) all the way to Puerto Vallarta, Mazatlán, and Tijuana; and south (two daily departures) to Manzanillo, Zihuatanejo, and Acapulco.

Note: Nearly all Barra de Navidad and Melaque bus departures are *salidas de paso,* meaning they originate somewhere else and arrive already full of riders. Although seating cannot usually be confirmed until the bus arrives, seats are generally available, except during super-crowded Christmas and Easter holidays.

By Car or RV

Three highway routes access Barra de Navidad: from the north via Puerto Vallarta, from the south via Manzanillo, and from the northeast via Guadalajara.

To and from Puerto Vallarta, Mexican National Highway 200 is all asphalt and in good condition (except for some potholes) along its 134-mile (216 km) stretch to Barra de Navidad. Traffic is generally light, but it may slow a bit as the highway climbs the 2,400-foot Sierra Cuale summit near El Tuito south of Puerto Vallarta; the light traffic and the good road make passing, with caution, safely possible. Allow about three hours for this very scenic trip.

From Manzanillo, the 38-mile (61 km) stretch of Highway 200 is nearly all countryside and all level. It's a snap in under an hour.

The longer, but quicker and easier, Barra de Navidad-Guadalajara road connection runs through Manzanillo along *autopistas* (superhighways) 54D, 110, and 200 D. In Guadalajara, start out at the Minerva Circle (at the intersection of Avenida López Mateos and Guadalajara west-side Avenida Vallarta). Mark your odometer and follow Avenida López Mateos south. After about 10 miles (32 km), at Guadalajara's country edge, continue, following the signs for Colima that direct you along the four-lane combined Mexican National Highways 15, 54, and 80 heading southwest. At 19 miles (30 km) from the Minerva Circle, as Highway 15 splits right for Morelia and Mexico City, continue straight ahead, following the signs for Colima and Barra de Navidad. Nearly immediately, follow the Highway 80-Highway 54 D right fork for Barra de Navidad-Colima. Two miles farther, follow the Highway 54 D branch left toward Colima. Continue on Highway 54 D straight ahead for about two hours, bypassing Colima. About 10 miles south of Colima, Highway 54 D changes, continuing as Highway 110 expressway. On the outskirts of Tecomán, Highway 110 curves right, north, and becomes Highway 200 D expressway, which you follow another hour, bypassing Manzanillo (via the Manzanillo Highway 200 *cuota* toll bypass) all the way to Barra de Navidad. Easy grades allow a leisurely 55 mph (90 km/hour) most of the way for this 192-mile (311 km) trip. Allow about 4.5 hours, either direction.

The same is not true of the winding, scenic two lane, 181-mile (291 km) Highway 80 route between Barra de Navidad and Guadalajara. Start out from the Minerva Circle, as described above, but south of the city, instead of forking left on Highway 54 D to Colima, continue straight ahead on Highway 80 toward Barra de Navidad. The narrow, two-lane road continues through a dozen little towns, over three mountain ranges, and around curves for another 160 miles (258 km) to Melaque and Barra de Navidad. To be safe, allow about six hours' driving time uphill to Guadalajara, five hours in the opposite direction.

MANZANILLO AND COLIMA

Manzanillo (pop. 100,000) is a small city tucked at the southern corner of a large bay, so broad that it has room for a pair of five-mile-wide junior bays. From the north spreads the Bahía de Santiago, separated by the jutting Península de Santiago from its twin Bahía de Manzanillo on the south.

Manzanillo's importance as a port has continued since the conquest. Even its name comes from its fortunate harborfront location, where *manzanillos*—trees whose inedible yellowish-red fruit resembles a small apple, or *manzanillo*—flourished beside the original wharves.

Splendid local fishing led to an unexpected bonus: flocks of visitors, drawn by Manzanillo's renown as the sailfish capital of the world. The balmy winters and the golden beaches drew even more visitors, until, by the 1980s, a string of small hotels, condos, and world-class resorts, notably the celebrated Las Hadas, lined Manzanillo's long, soft strands.

Finally, Hollywood arrived in Manzanillo, in the person of Bo Derek, starring in her fabulously successful movie *10,* the popularity of which increased Manzanillo's steady visitor stream to a flood.

Manzanillo's residents and vacationers now enjoy a range of good restaurants, entertainments, and diversions, both man-made and natural: on the water, snorkeling, scuba diving, sailboarding, and surfing; and on the land, tennis, golf, and the fine museums, fetching handicrafts, and fascinating archaeological sites of Colima, the prosperous and refined small capital of Colima state.

Right off the 60-mile (100-km) upcountry

HIGHLIGHTS

◖ Cerro Vigía Chico: Feast your eyes on town, bay, and mountain views from the lower summit of Manzanillo's highest hill. For something even more spectacular, continue your climb another 600 feet (200 meters) higher to the top of Cerro Cruz (page 315).

◖ Museo Universitario de Arqueología: Manzanillo's archaeological museum displays a fine collection of local finds, including ancient shellwork and charming human and animal figurines (page 318).

◖ Playa Audiencia: This small, rock-enfolded stretch of sand is a popular Sunday family beach and is also a good place for snorkeling right off the shore (page 319).

◖ El Salto: Bus or drive into Manzanillo's green mountain country to this weekend-popular shady mountain waterfall park and picnic ground. The verdant beauty of the place might persuade tent or RV campers to linger a night or two in the adjacent informal campground (page 341).

◖ Agua Fria: At Agua Fria natural spring, cool, crystal-clear water wells up into a large, waist-deep pond, perfect for swimming, frolicking, and simply relaxing. Families picnic at lakeside *palapa*-shaded tables; some set up tents in a nearby campground (page 342).

◖ Museo de Culturas del Occidente: In Colima, the museum's outstanding displays climax in what is perhaps Mexico's most charming pre-Columbian pottery collection, starring a delightful chorus of Colima's irresistible ceramic dogs (page 346).

◖ La Campana Archaeological Zone: With the sacred, smoking cone of Colima's Volcano of Fire high in the distance, explore the reconstructed pyramids, platforms, and ceremonial plazas of Colima's former capital, which reached its apex around A.D. 800 (page 346).

◖ Hacienda Noguera: Travel to the cool foothills above Colima to the University of Colima's Hacienda Noguera, wander the garden, have a snack at the café, and enjoy viewing the fine art and artifact collection of artist-benefactor Alejandro Rangel Hidalgo (page 353).

◖ Museo de Sal: Here, in an ancient wooden salt warehouse, a fascinating model, old photos, and artifacts demonstrate Cuyutlán's venerable tradition of salt manufacture. Afterward, go to the **Campamento Tortuguero** (Turtle Encampment) to see the rescued young turtles, iguanas, and crocodiles (page 357).

LOOK FOR ◖ TO FIND RECOMMENDED SIGHTS, ACTIVITIES, DINING, AND LODGING.

MANZANILLO AND COLIMA

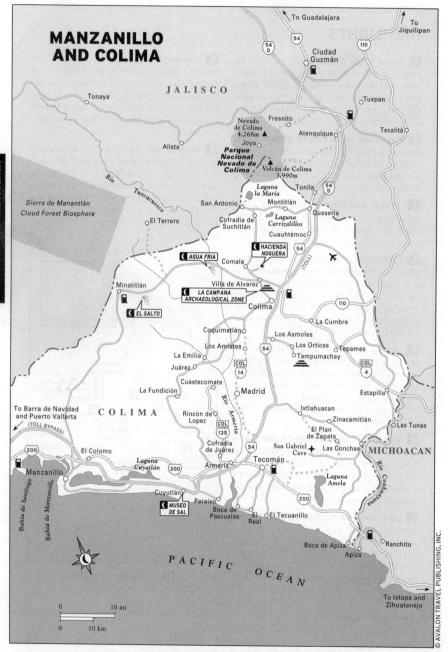

MANZANILLO AND COLIMA

To Guadalajara

To Jiquilipan

54 D   54

110

Ciudad Guzmán

JALISCO

Tonaya

Tuxpan

Nevado de Colima 4,268m ▲   Fresnito

Tecalitá

Atenquique

Alista

Joya

Parque Nacional Nevado de Colima

Volcán de Colima 3,990m ▲

Tonila

54 D

Sierra de Manantlán Cloud Forest Biosphere

Laguna la María

Montitlán

Río Tuxcacuesco

San Antonio

Queseria

El Terrero

Cofradia de Suchitlán

Laguna Carrizalillos

Cuauhtémoc

AGUA FRIA   Comala

HACIENDA NOGUERA   54

Minatitlán

Villa de Alvarez

LA CAMPANA ARCHAEOLOGICAL ZONE

EL SALTO

Colima

110

La Cumbre

Coquimatlán

Los Asmoles

Los Amiates   54   Los Ortices   Tepames

La Emilia

Juárez

COL 14

Tampumachay

COL 4

Cuastecomate

Madrid

La Fundición

Rincón de Lopez   Río Armería

Ixtlahuacan

Zinacamitlán

COL 135

Estapilla

Las Tunas

To Barra de Navidad and Puerto Vallarta (TOLL BYPASS)

COLIMA

Cofradía de Juárez   54

El Plan de Zapata

MICHOACAN

200

El Colomo

Laguna Cuyatlán   200

San Gabriel Cave   Las Conchas

Tecomán

Río Coahuayana

Manzanillo

Cuyutlán

MUSEO DE SAL   Paraíso

Armería

Laguna Amela

Bahía de Santiago

Bahía de Manzanillo

Boca de Pascuales   El Real   El Tecuanillo

200

Boca de Apiza   Ranchito

Apiza

PACIFIC OCEAN

0   10 mi

0   10 km

To Ixtapa and Zihuatanejo

© AVALON TRAVEL PUBLISHING, INC.

back road connecting Manzanillo with Colima, visitors can explore a trio of Colima gems: the cool, gushing El Salto waterfall, the verdant, moss-draped Manantlán cloud forest ecoreserve, and crystalline Agua Fria natural spring and picnic and camping ground.

Farther on, towering above Colima town, are Colima's volcanos, the fiery 13,087-foot (3,989-meter) Volcán de Fuego, among the world's most active, and his dormant snowcapped brother, 14,220-foot (4,334-meter) Nevado de Colima. The volcanos draw an increasing stream of adventurous nature lovers, who trek through hushed tropical forests, explore dark lava-tube caves, rappel down moss-strewn volcanic cliffs, and camp beside sylvan lakes, overlooking the sun-dappled panorama of Colima's lush valley and mountain hinterland.

South of Manzanillo, the Mexican Pacific Coast Highway follows the southern Colima coast, well known for its beaches, surf, and abundant fresh seafood.

PLANNING YOUR TIME

You can enjoy exploring Manzanillo's downtown sights in a leisurely day, starting on the harbor-front plaza, known locally as the *jardín*. Include in your tour the cathedral, the downtown market, the view from atop **Cerro Vigía Chico,** and a stop at the **Museo Universitario de Arqueología.**

On another day, start out at **Playa Audiencia** for a swim, some sun, and maybe some snorkeling. In the afternoon, head all the way northwest around to scenic La Boquita, the narrow estuary that connects the Laguna Jaluapan to the sea. Stop for a refreshment at the restaurant overlooking the picturesque estuary footbridge. Continue uphill for a sunset splurge dinner (or at least a cocktail) at **Restaurant L'Recife.**

A few days more could be spent exploring the city of **Colima** and its lush hinterland. Enjoy the first day visiting Colima's museums and its **La Campana Archaeological Zone.** On a succeeding day, head uphill and visit the charming foothill village of Comala, one of a handful of nationally designated Pueblos Mágicos (Magic Villages), and its nearby

Hacienda Noguera, museum of artist Alejandro Rangel Hidalgo. Continue uphill for a picnic and perhaps an overnight at sylvan mountain lake Laguna la María.

A good way to return to Manzanillo is by the back road, through the lush Colima foothill country via Minatitlán. Along the way, enjoy a cool swim at **Agua Fria spring** and a picnic at **El Salto waterfall.** With an additional day, head uphill to Terrero village, in the Manantlán cloud forest, for a picnic and/or a camping overnight.

HISTORY
Before Columbus

One of the earliest records of Manzanillo comes from a story of Ix, king of ancient Coliman, now the state of Colima. The legend states that Ix received visits from Chinese trader-emissaries at a shore village, which became the present town of Salagua, on Tzalahua Bay (now the Bay of Manzanillo). It's not surprising the dream of riches gained by trade propelled the Chinese across the Pacific hundreds of years before the Spanish conquest. The same goal drew Columbus across the Atlantic and pushed Hernán Cortés to this gateway to Asia a generation later.

Conquest and Colonial Times

Cortés heard of the legend of the Chinese at Manzanillo Bay from the emperor of the Tarascan kingdom in Michoacán. With the riches of China tantalizingly within his grasp, Cortés sent his lieutenants to conquer Pacific Mexico, on whose sheltered beaches they would build ships to realize Columbus's elusive quest.

In 1522, Gonzalo de Sandoval, under orders from Cortés, reconnoitered Manzanillo Bay, looking for safe anchorages and good shipbuilding sites. Before he left a year later, Sandoval granted an audience to local chieftains at the tip of the Santiago Peninsula, which to this day retains the name Playa Audiencia.

Cortés himself visited Manzanillo Bay twice, in pursuit of a Portuguese fleet rumored to be somewhere off the coast. Cortés massed his forces at the northern bay of Manzanillo, which he christened Bahía de Santiago on July

24, 1535. Although Cortés's enemy failed to appear, the foreign threat remained. Portuguese, English, Dutch, and French corsairs menaced Spain's galleons as they repaired, watered, and unloaded their rich cargoes for 10 generations in Manzanillo and other sheltered Pacific harbors.

Independence

The hope generated by independence in 1821 soon dissipated in the turbulent civil conflicts of the next half century. Manzanillo languished until President Porfirio Díaz's orderly but heavy-handed rule (1876–1910) finally brought peace. The railroad arrived in 1889; telephone, electricity, drainage, and potable water soon followed. During the 1950s and '60s, the harbor was modernized and deepened, attracting ships from all over the Pacific and capital for new industries. Anticipating the demand, the government built a huge, oil-fueled (but unfortunately smelly and smoky) generating plant, which powered a fresh wave of factories. By the 1970s, Manzanillo had become a major Pacific manufacturing center and port, providing thousands of local jobs in dozens of mining, agricultural, and fishing enterprises.

Recent Times

Although Mexican tourists had been coming to Manzanillo for years, international arrivals grew rapidly after the opening of the big Club Maeva and Las Hadas resorts in the 1970s. The new jetport north of town increased the steady flow to a flood; then came the 1980s and the Manzanillo-filmed Hollywood movie *10*, which rocketed Las Hadas and Manzanillo to the stars as an international vacation destination.

Sights

Longtimers know two Manzanillos: the old downtown, clustered around the south-end harborfront *jardín,* and the rest—greater Manzanillo—spread northerly along the sandy shores of Manzanillo Bay and Santiago Bay. The downtown has most of the banks, the government services, and the busy market district, while most of the hotels, restaurants, and tourist businesses dot the northern beachfronts.

Everything north of downtown is measured from the **El Tajo** junction (Km 0), marked by the downtown Pemex station. Here, along bayfront **Avenida Niños Héroes,** the Barra de Navidad-Puerto Vallarta highway starts north just a few blocks from the *jardín.*

The shoreline highway curves past foothills and marshland, crossing the mirror-smooth waters of the **Valle de las Garzas** (Valley of the Herons) between Km 5 and Km 7. The soaring white concrete sailboat sculpture at the traffic circle (Km 7) marks the *crucero* Las Brisas, known locally as the "suicide crossing." Here, the **Las Brisas Highway** forks left, curving southward, through a quiet neighborhood of condos, homes, and small hotels fronting Playa las Brisas.

Back on the main highway, now the **Boulevard Costera Miguel de la Madrid,** continue north past the hotels and restaurants that dot the long Playa Azul beachfront. Just after the dusty little town *jardín* of **Salagua** around Km 11, a golf course and big white gate mark the Las Hadas *crucero* (crossing) at Km 12. There, **Avenida Audiencia** leads uphill along the plush, condo-dotted **Santiago Peninsula,** flanked by the Las Hadas resort on its south side and Hotel Tesoros Manzanillo on Playa Audiencia on the north.

Back on the main road, continuing north, you pass the Pemex gas station at Km 13. Soon comes the Río Colorado creek bridge, then the **Santiago** town *jardín,* on the right, across from the restaurants, banks, and stores of Plaza Santiago shopping center (Km 13.5) on the left.

From there, traffic thins out as you pass scattered beachfront condos along Playa Olas Altas (Km 15–16). Soon the **Club Maeva** spreads, like a colony of giant blue and white mush-rooms, along the hill above Playa de Miramar at Km 17. Finally, another golf course and entrance gate at Km 19 mark the vacation-home community of **Playa Santiago.**

Visitors can easily drive, taxi (share to make it affordable), or bus to their favorite stops along Manzanillo's long shoreline. Dozens of local buses run along the highway through Las Brisas, Salagua, and Santiago (destinations marked on the windshields), all eventually returning to the downtown *jardín.* Fares (in pesos) run less than half a dollar. Hop on with a supply of small change and you're in business.

A Walk Around Downtown

A pair of busy north-south streets—Avenida México and Avenida Carrillo Puerto—dominate the downtown. Avenida Carrillo Puerto traffic runs one-way from the *jardín,* while Avenida México traffic does the reverse. The corner of Avenida México and Avenida Juárez, adjacent to the *jardín,* is a colorful slice of old Mexico, crowded with cafés, storefronts, and street vendors. A dignified Porfirian kiosk presides nearby at the center of the *jardín,* while, on the far side, boats queue obediently at dockside Avenida Morelos. In the distance, drab gray cutters and destroyer escorts line the **Base Naval** (BAH-say nah-VAHL) wharfs.

Walk a pair of blocks along Avenida Juárez (which becomes B. Dávalos) past Avenida México to the cathedral, officially the **Parroquia Nuestra Señora de Guadalupe,** after Manzanillo's patron saint. Inside, four shining stained-glass panels flanking the main altar tell the story of Juan Diego and the miracle of the Virgin of Guadalupe.

During the first 12 days of December, a colorful clutter of stalls lines the streetfront, where families bring their children, girls in embroidered *huipiles* and *chinas poblanas,* and boys in sombreros and serapes. After paying their respects to the Virgin, they indulge in their favorite holiday foods and get themselves photographed in front of a portrait of the Virgin.

Steep knolls punctuate Manzanillo's downtown. Residents climb precipitous cobbled al-

Downtown Manzanillo's prosperity is due to its busy port and the visitors who come to enjoy its suburban beaches.

leyways, too narrow for cars, to their humble (yet luxuriously perched) homes overlooking the city. For an interesting little detour, climb one of the staircase lanes that angle uphill off Avenida Juárez, around City Hall.

☾ Cerro Vigía Chico

An even steeper hill rises behind the cathedral—the brushy slope of Cerro Vigía Chico, where colonial soldiers kept a lookout for pirates. Above and beyond that towers the cross-decorated summit of **Cerro Cruz,** the highest point (about 1,000 feet) above the Bay of Manzanillo; climb up for a sunset view on the west, merging with broad panorama of the town, Manzanillo's two bays, and finally the verdant, cloud-tipped slopes of the Sierra Madre on the eastern horizon. Every May 3, the **Día de la Santa Cruz,** pilgrims climb to its summit.

Mercado

A Manzanillo downtown walk wouldn't be complete without including a stroll down

MANZANILLO AND COLIMA

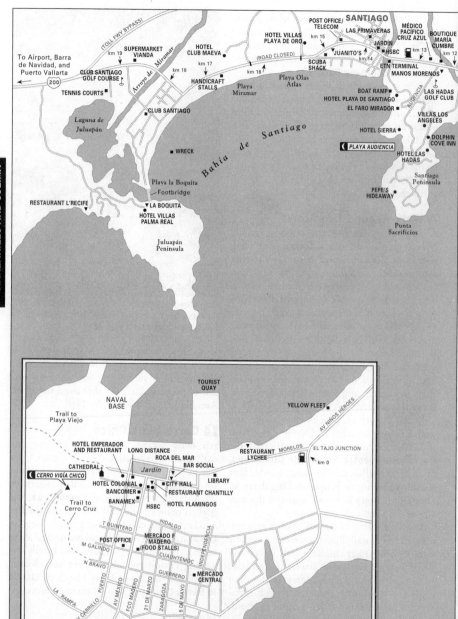

Upper map — Bahía de Santiago area:

To Airport, Barra de Navidad, and Puerto Vallarta — 200

(TOLL FWY BYPASS)

km 19
SUPERMARKET VIANDA
CLUB SANTIAGO GOLF COURSE
TENNIS COURTS
Arroyo de Miramar
km 18
HOTEL CLUB MAEVA
km 17
HANDICRAFT STALLS
CLUB SANTIAGO
Laguna de Juluapán

POST OFFICE/ TELECOM
SANTIAGO
HOTEL VILLAS PLAYA DE ORO
km 15
LAS PRIMAVERAS
MÉDICO PACÍFICO CRUZ AZUL
BOUTIQUE MARÍA CUMBRE
km 12
JARDÍN
JUANITO'S
HSBC
km 13
km 14
ETN TERMINAL
MANOS MORENOS

(ROAD CLOSED)
SCUBA SHACK
km 16
Playa Miramar
Playa Olas Atlas

BOAT RAMP
HOTEL PLAYA DE SANTIAGO
EL FARO MIRADOR
LAS HADAS GOLF CLUB
VILLAS LOS ANGELES
DOLPHIN COVE INN
HOTEL SIERRA

WRECK

Bahía de Santiago

PLAYA AUDIENCIA
HOTEL LAS HADAS
Santiago Peninsula

Playa la Boquita
Footbridge
RESTAURANT L'RECIFE
LA BOQUITA
HOTEL VILLAS PALMA REAL

PEPE'S HIDEAWAY

Juluapán Peninsula

Punta Sacrificios

Lower map — downtown Manzanillo:

NAVAL BASE
TOURIST QUAY
YELLOW FLEET
AV NIÑOS HÉROES

Trail to Playa Viejo

HOTEL EMPERADOR AND RESTAURANT
LONG DISTANCE
ROCA DEL MAR
BAR SOCIAL
RESTAURANT LYCHEE
MORELOS
EL TAJO JUNCTION
km 0

CATHEDRAL
CERRO VIGÍA CHICO
Jardín
HOTEL COLONIAL
BANCOMER
BANAMEX
HSBC
CITY HALL
LIBRARY
RESTAURANT CHANTILLY
HOTEL FLAMINGOS

Trail to Cerro Cruz

T QUINTERO
HIDALGO
POST OFFICE
M GALINDO
N BRAVO
LA RAMPA
AV CARRILLO PUERTO
AV MÉXICO
FCO MADERO
21 DE MARZO
ZARAGOZA
5 DE MAYO
MERCADO F MADERO (FOOD STALLS)
CUAUHTÉMOC
GUERRERO
INDEPENDENCIA
MERCADO CENTRAL

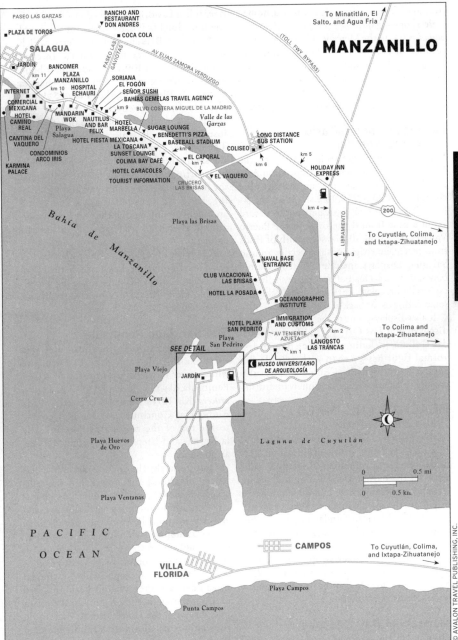

MANZANILLO

PASEO LAS GARZAS
PLAZA DE TOROS
RANCHO AND RESTAURANT DON ANDRES
COCA COLA
To Minatitlán, El Salto, and Agua Fría
(TOLL FWY BYPASS)
SALAGUA
JARDÍN
km 11
BANCOMER
PLAZA MANZANILLO
PASEO LAS GAVIOTAS
AV ELIAS ZAMORA VERDUZGO
INTERNET
km 10
SORIANA
EL FOGÓN
SEÑOR SUSHI
BAHÍAS GEMELAS TRAVEL AGENCY
HOSPITAL ECHAURI
COMERCIAL MEXICANA
HOTEL CAMINO REAL
MANDARIN WOK
NAUTILUS AND BAR FELIX
km 9
BLVD COSTERA MIGUEL DE LA MADRID
Valle de las Garzas
Playa Salagua
HOTEL MARBELLA
SUGAR LOUNGE
CANTINA DEL VAQUERO
HOTEL FIESTA MEXICANA
BENEDETTI'S PIZZA
LONG DISTANCE BUS STATION
CONDOMINIOS ARCO IRIS
LA TOSCANA
BASEBALL STADIUM
km 8
km 5
SUNSET LOUNGE
COLISEO
KARMINA PALACE
COLIMA BAY CAFÉ
EL CAPORAL
km 7
km 6
HOLIDAY INN EXPRESS
HOTEL CARACOLES
TOURIST INFORMATION
CRUCERO LAS BRISAS
EL VAQUERO
km 4
200
LIBRAMIENTO
Playa las Brisas
Bahía de Manzanillo
NAVAL BASE ENTRANCE
km 3
To Cuyutlán, Colima, and Ixtapa-Zihuatanejo
CLUB VACACIONAL LAS BRISAS
HOTEL LA POSADA
OCEANOGRAPHIC INSTITUTE
HOTEL PLAYA SAN PEDRITO
IMMIGRATION AND CUSTOMS
AV TENIENTE AZUETA
km 2
LANGOSTO LAS TRANCAS
To Colima and Ixtapa-Zihuatanejo
Playa San Pedrito
km 1
SEE DETAIL
MUSEO UNIVERSITARIO DE ARQUEOLOGÍA
Playa Viejo
JARDÍN
Cerro Cruz
Laguna de Cuyutlán
Playa Huevos de Oro
0   0.5 mi
0   0.5 km
Playa Ventanas
PACIFIC
OCEAN
CAMPOS
To Cuyutlán, Colima, and Ixtapa-Zihuatanejo
VILLA FLORIDA
Playa Campos
Punta Campos

MANZANILLO AND COLIMA

© AVALON TRAVEL PUBLISHING, INC.

Avenida México, past a dozen old-fashioned little shops—*papelerías, farmacias, dulcerías, panaderías*—to the Mercado (Calle 5 de Mayo); turn left at Cuauhtémoc. Here you can wander among the mounds of bright produce, admire the festoons of piñatas, say a good word to the shrimp-sellers, and stop to listen to the harangue of a sidewalk politician or evangelist.

Museo Universitario de Arqueología

Manzanillo's new archaeology museum, the Museo Universitario de Arqueología (on Avenida Niños Héroes, near the San Pedrito traffic circle, tel. 314/332-2256, 10 A.M.–2 P.M. and 5–8 P.M. Tues.–Sat.), on the waterfront boulevard about a mile from downtown, in the Puerto Vallarta direction, displays a wealth of finds from recent investigations, especially around Salagua. Displays include painted ceramic bowls, jars, and a load of decorative shellwork, especially bracelets, earrings, and necklaces, some dating as far back as 2,000 years.

It also displays some of the remains recently discovered at Los Ortices, south of present-day Colima, including charming human and animal figurines—a man with a headache, flutes, dogs, whistles—some masterfully crafted to an alabaster-like stoneware finish.

BEACHES AND HIKES
Playa San Pedrito

Manzanillo's closest-to-downtown beach, Playa San Pedrito, although now a bit polluted, remains a tranquil little strip of sand right on the harbor along Avenida Teniente Azueta (which angles off Niños Héroes half a mile from the El Tajo junction Pemex station). The perfect Mexican Sunday beach, San Pedrito has lots of golden sand, seafood *palapas*, and a few big trees for shade. Although its very gentle waves are fine for swimming and sailboarding (with your own equipment), Playa San Pedrito is too close to the harbor for much good fishing or snorkeling.

Manzanillo Bay Beaches

From either the *jardín* or the Las Brisas *cru-cero,* ride a Las Brisas–marked bus to end-of-the-line Hotel la Posada at the southern end of **Playa las Brisas.** From the jetty, which marks the entrance to the Puerto Interior (Inner Harbor), a 100-foot-wide sand ribbon seems to curve north without end. It changes its name to **Playa Azul,** then **Playa Salagua** along its five-mile length, ending finally at Las Hadas at the base of the Santiago Peninsula. The beach, while wide, is also steep. The usually gentle waves break suddenly at the sand, allowing little chance for surfing, bodysurfing, or boogie boarding. Sailboarding (bring your own equipment) and surf fishing, however, are popular, as are snorkeling and scuba diving among the fish that swarm around the corals and rocks of the south-end jetty.

A number of restaurants along the beaches provide refreshments. They include the Hotel la Posada, Carlos 'n Charlie's, the big adobe-colored Fiesta Mexicana on Playa Azul, and Hotel Marabella on Playa Salagua.

The Santiago Peninsula

One of Manzanillo's loveliest views is from the hillside topped by **El Faro,** the white tower at the summit of the Santiago Peninsula. At the Highway 200 Las Hadas *crucero* (Km 12) turn onto the cobbled Avenida Audiencia. Continue past the golf course to the top of the rise, turn right at Calle la Reyna, and keep winding upward as far as possible.

Unfortunately, the condo community has fenced off the El Faro tower, but the still-accessible views, especially from the topmost lane beneath the summit's north side, are nevertheless memorable. From the emerald ridge of the **Juluapan Peninsula** and the 4,000-foot (1,300-meter) Cerro Toro bull's hump on the north, the panorama sweeps past green sierra and the blue bays to the white downtown spread beneath the pyramid-peak of Cerro Cruz on the southern horizon. On the ocean side, due west, the Hotel Tesoros Manzanillo rises above the diminutive sand ribbon of Playa Audiencia.

© BRUCE WHIPPERMAN

Soft sand, clear water, and gentle billows account for the weekend popularity of Playa Audiencia.

Playa Audiencia

Once a secluded, idyllic cove, Playa Audiencia has lost its isolation since it became the home of the ultramodern gleaming white tower of the Hotel Tesoros Manzanillo (which qualifies as a sight in itself).

Nevertheless, Playa Audiencia retains its lovely ambience, which you can best appreciate by avoiding the weekend crowd. Face the sea, to best appreciate what local families have enjoyed for years: plenty of golden sand, deep blue water, rolling surf, all enfolded by rocky, palm-shadowed crags on both sides.

Beach concessionaires (right on the beach, 9 A.M.–6 P.M. daily) rent kayaks, sailboards, personal watercraft, banana boats, and boogie boards. Instructors from the hotel often guide snorkeling and scuba diving parties from the beach to the shoals on either side.

Santiago Bay Beaches

The beaches of Santiago Bay stretch for five golden miles north of the Santiago Peninsula to Playa la Boquita, the lagoon-mouth beneath the Juluapan Peninsula's headland. The beaches are all continuous variations of the same wide carpet of yellow, semicoarse sand.

First, at around Km 14, **Playa Santiago** reaches the Río Colorado creek, where it becomes **Playa Olas Altas.** Here, although the sand drops steeply into the surf, it levels out offshore, so the waves roll in gradually, providing excellent surfing, bodysurfing, and boogie boarding breaks.

Playa Miramar continues past Club Maeva, marked by the highway pedestrian overpass. The beach itself is popular and cluttered with umbrellas, horses for rent, and vendors. The usually gentle surf is good for bodysurfing and boogie boarding. Concessionaires rent boogie boards for about $3 an hour.

Finally, at Km 17.5, the highway veers north, but the beach curves south on the ocean side of Club Santiago, where a village of seafood *palapas* and fishing boats decorate the strand, now called **La Boquita** (The Little Mouth). The sand is wide and firm, and the surf is as tranquil as a huge kiddie pool. Offshore, a 200-foot wreck swarms with fish a few feet beneath the surface, excellent for snorkeling and scuba diving. On the other side of the beach, the **Laguna de Juluapan,** a wildlife-rich tidal wetland, winds along miles of forest-edged shallows and grassy marshes.

Hikes

The adventurous can seek out Manzanillo's many hidden corners, beginning right downtown. **Playa Viejo** is often missed, tucked in a little cove over the hill and accessible on foot only. Wear walking shoes and a hat, and take your bathing suit, water, and a picnic lunch. Walk uphill along Calle Balbino Dávalos past the downtown cathedral. Bear left up the narrow street (which narrows to a

Playa Viejo is a hidden gem tucked on the bay just 15 minutes by foot from downtown.

sidewalk) and climb the steep concrete staircase (on the left) to the hilltop basketball court. Continue down the other side along a forest-shaded concrete arroyo trail to the beach. The dark sand beach is strewn with shells and surf-rounded rocks. If you're fortunate, you may find a high, dry perch, good for overnight tenting (bring mosquito repellent) above the surf.

Also beginning from downtown, the steep trail to **Cerro Vigía Chico,** continuing to Cerro Cruz, will challenge fit hikers. It leads to the top of the highest point in Manzanillo for a breezy panoramic view of the city, bay, and ocean below. Allow about 1.5 hours round-trip for Cerro Vigía Chico, about twice that for the steep continuation to Cerro Cruz. Take plenty of water and avoid midday heat by going early in the morning or late afternoon.

Head south along Avenida Carrillo Puerto from the *jardín.* Notice the *sastrería* (tailor shop) Vasquéz at No. 213 on the left-hand side, where the master tailor sews suits by hand. Turn the corner at the *tortillería* at Nícolas Bravo and head along the upward lane, past little hillside-perched houses. Ask the local people if you get lost. Say *"¿A Cerro Vigía, por favor?"* They'll help keep you on the right track.

You'll know you've arrived when you see the white FM radio transmitter station atop the hill.

Unfortunately the direct old route to Cerro Cruz has been blocked by a fence. An easier route is accessible by proceeding downhill along the stone and concrete automobile access road. After about 100 yards, you'll see a trail angling right from the road. Go about 4 P.M. to both avoid the midday heat and enjoy the sunset. From the summit, a majestic panorama spreads below: from the Gibraltar-like headland of Juluapan in the north, past golden beaches, over the villa-studded Santiago Peninsula, past the white city to the huge expanse of the Laguna de Cuyutlán, where power stanchions leapfrog across the lagoon from the gargantuan, smoke-spewing seaside power plant.

Accommodations

DOWNTOWN
Near cafés, food stalls, bountiful shopping, and easy transportation, Manzanillo's downtown offers a colorful and lively slice of old Mexico.

Under $50
A prime budget stop is the **◖ Hotel Emperador** (B. Dávalos 69, Manzanillo, Colima 28200, tel. 314/332-2374, $14 s, $17 d, $26 t), a stack of 28 rooms around a dim interior patio, which, at first glance, appears uninviting. Inside, however, the grandmotherly owner, María Trinidad Bautista, her son and their staff keep the corridors and stairways shining. The rooms too, although very plain, are very clean, with hot-water shower baths, ceiling fans, TV, and a good restaurant downstairs. It's half a block from the *jardín*, on the quiet westward extension of B. Dávalos, just before the church.

If Hotel Emperador is full, try the good economical alternative, **Hotel Flamingos** (Madero 72, Manzanillo, Colima 28200, tel. 314/332-1037, $18 s, $20 d, higher during fiestas). Find it on the dead-end street, Madero, that leads inland uphill from the *jardín*. Its quiet side-street location makes the Hotel Flamingos very worthy of consideration. Upstairs, past the small front desk, the approximately 30 rooms in four floors are clean, mostly spacious, and simply but thoughtfully decorated with maroon Asian-motif bedspreads to match the ruddy tile floors and handsome rustic wood furniture and doors. Rates are a bargain at ordinary (nonfestival) rates. The only drawback here is lack of privacy and ventilation of the hotel's inside rooms, whose only windows face the hallways. Ask for an outside room for more air, quiet, and privacy.

The **◖ Hotel Colonial** (Bocanegra 28, at Avenida México, Manzanillo, Colima 28200, tel./fax 314/332-0668, 314/332-1134, or 314/332-1230, credit cards accepted, $28 s, $37 d), Manzanillo's most distinguished downtown hotel, is built around dignified interior courtyard Restaurant Candiles. Dating from the 1940s, the Colonial, one block from the *jardín*, is replete with old-fashioned touches—bright-hued tile staircases, stained-glass windows, and sentimental tile wall scenes. The rooms, although worn, have traditional high ceilings, hand-hewn leather chairs, and wrought-iron lamp fixtures. They open to shady, street-view corridors, lined with chairs for sitting. Try for a room on the relatively quiet Bocanegra Street side of the hotel. The 38 rooms have hot-water baths and a/c.

If, on the other hand, you prefer a beach location, walk or taxi east of downtown along the waterfront about 0.6 mile (1 km) to the **Hotel Playa San Pedrito** (Av. Teniente Azueta 3, Manzanillo, Colima 28200, tel. 314/332-0535, credit cards not accepted, $25 s, $32 d, low season; $28 s, $37 d during fiestas). The hotel offers a homey close-in alternative, right on locally popular Playa San Pedrito. This unpretentious Mexican family hotel rambles amid a flowery garden, edged with colorful tropical plants and centering on a free-form blue swimming pool. A worn but usable tennis court stands at one side, and beyond that, waves lap the sandy beach. With all those outdoor attractions, the plainness of the rooms and the dust in their corners matter little. Request one of the *piso arriba* (upper-floor) rooms for privacy and sea views from a front balcony-corridor. The 33 rooms include fans and parking.

LAS BRISAS AND PLAYA AZUL
A number of very recommendable accommodations, many bungalow-style with kitchenettes, sprinkle the breezy and golden shoreline of Manzanillo Bay. The Las Brisas beachfront district, along the (cul-de-sac) Avenida Lázaro Cárdenas (Las Brisas Highway), is an especially tranquil location.

Under $50
The **◖ Condominios Arco Iris** (Km 9.5, P.O. Box 359, Manzanillo, Colima 28200, tel./fax

314/333-0168, arcoiris@colima.com, $47 1br, $95 2br, higher during fiestas) in Salagua, about a block from the beach, more resembles a garden bungalow complex than condominiums. The Arco Iris (Rainbow), favorite of a loyal cadre of Manzanillo longtimers, is a spacious, leafy manicured tropical park, with inviting blue pool-patio and *palapa*. The units, most at ground level, with kitchenettes and either one or two bedrooms, are immaculate and attractively furnished in 1970s-modern style. The two-bedroom, two-bath units can sleep four. Discounts are generally available for monthly (or perhaps even weekly) rentals. Get your winter reservation in early.

$50-100

The swish of the waves on the sand, long walks at dusk, and easy access to good restaurants highlight the attractions of the "passionate pink" **(Hotel la Posada** (Av. Lázaro Cárdenas 201, P.O. Box 135, Manzanillo, Colima 28201, tel. 314/333-1899, fax 314/333-6690, posada@bay.net.mx, www .hotel-la-posada.info, or www.gomanzanillo .com/hotels/posada, credit cards accepted, $38 s, $58 d low season, $58 s, $78 d high), a durable jewel among Manzanillo's small hotels. Every detail—leafy potted plants, rustling palms, brick arches, airy beach-view *sala,* resplendent bay-view sunsets—adds to La Posada's romantic ambience. Most customers, both longtimers and new, tend to prefer the upstairs rooms, some of which have private balconies and bay views. Get your winter reservations in early. Some of the 23 comfortable semideluxe rooms come with a/c for $5 extra, add $20 for a kitchenette studio, with a/c, all including a good breakfast. The hotel has a bar-cart, snack restaurant, comfortable sitting area, good pool, and street parking.

A few doors northwest along the beach, the family-friendly **Club Vacacional las Brisas** (Av. L. Cárdenas 207, Fracc. las Brisas, Manzanillo, Colima 28200, tel. 314/333-1747, fax 314/334-0086, clubvacac@prodigy.net.mx, credit cards accepted, $37 s, $67 d low season, higher during fiestas) likewise enjoys platoons of

repeat customers. Attentive on-site management keeps the garden manicured, the pool inviting, and the beach beyond the gate clean and golden. The best rooms, white-walled and comfortable and well-maintained but not fancy, are on the ocean-view upper floors. The 30 rooms and suites, most with kitchenettes, go up in price by about 30 percent during Christmas and Easter holidays and July–August. With fans, a/c, and parking.

Although on the busy main beach boulevard, the petite **Hotel Caracoles** (Blv. Miguel de la Madrid 875, Km 8, Manzanillo, Colima 28200, tel. 314/334-2302 and 314/334-2303, Mex. toll-free long distance tel. 01-800/710-1492, hotel_caracolemzllo@hotmail.com, credit cards accepted, $58 d low season, $82 high; $66 and $90 with ocean view) offers an attractive beachfront option, convenient to good restaurants and entertainment. The main attraction here is the breezy beachfront, delightfully enjoyable from the hotel's oceanview pool patio. Upstairs, the approximately 25 rooms, many with private sea-view balconies, are attractively decorated in soothing pastels and furnished with large, soft beds and shiny, modern-standard shower baths, plus a/c, cable TV, kiddie pool, restaurant-bar, and street parking.

About half a mile farther north, away from downtown, stands the beachfront **Hotel Marbella** (Km 8.5, Playa Azul, P.O. Box 554, Manzanillo, Colima 28200, tel. 314/333-1102, 314/333-1105, tel./fax 314/333-1222, informacion@ hotelmarbella.com.mx, www.hotelmarbella .com.mx, credit cards accepted, $50 s or d, $65 and up high season). All the ingredients seem to be in place—a sea-view pool-patio, rustling palms, a good breakfast restaurant, sand, and surf—for a restful Manzanillo week in the sun. Of the approximately 150 rooms, the best are the oceanview balcony rooms on the upper floor of the original two-story low-rise beachfront wing. A pair of new wings added many more deluxe rooms, but most without ocean views. The all-inclusive *"plan marinero"* runs about $50 per person, kids $15. If an airy ocean-view balcony is what you want, specify reservations in the old wing with an ocean view—*sección vieja con vista del mar.* Parking is available.

SANTIAGO PENINSULA

The Santiago Peninsula's sea-view villas, condo developments, and resorts are luxuriously isolated, generally requiring a car or taxi to get anywhere.

$100-200

Manzanillo visitors weary of sky-high hotel rates but who still crave a luxurious location can choose the hilltop **Villas Los Angeles** (Av. de Cima, Península de Santiago, Manzanillo, Colima 28200, tel. 314/333-1702 or 314/333-1703, fax 314/334-0283, info@villaslosangeles .com, www.villaslosangeles.com, $95 d, $115 1br high season, and up). Here, owners Patricia and Michael La Pointe have built a hilltop cluster of deluxe rooms and suites perched artfully above an airy panoramic-view pool and patio. Inside, rooms are immaculate, luxuriously light and private, comfortably furnished, and decorated with handicrafts and original wall art. Guests in most rooms enjoy sweeping bay or mountain vistas. Their most economical option is one of their several "hotel suite" rooms for $95 d high season; $115 gets you a larger one-bedroom apartment with kitchenette. Two bedrooms and larger run $150–250. Low season (roughly June–Oct.) rentals get a 30 percent discount. High-season stays of more than a week receive a 10 percent discount; all with a/c, TV, and parking. Reserve early, especially during the winter.

The **Dolphin Cove Inn** (down by the beach, tel. 314/334-1692 or 314/334-1515, toll-free U.S. tel. 866/360-9062, toll-free Canada tel. 866/4441577, fax 314/334-1689, reservations@dolphin coveinn.com, www.dolphin coveinn.com, credit cards accepted, $110 d and up) offers deluxe view lodgings, spread artfully above a spectacularly scenic shorefront, adjacent to Hotel las Hadas. Inside, guests in the approximately 30 low-rise studios and suites enjoy attractive designer white and blue decor, with luxuriously marbled baths and floors, 1990s-standard kitchenettes and baths and

panoramic bay views. (A short walking path leads to Las Hadas Resort shops, restaurants, and beach sports. To get through the Las Hadas Resort gate from Dolphin Cove Inn, however, guests must buy a $25 day pass per adult, kids under 12 free, $10 usable toward food and beverages.) Dolphin Cove Inn room rates run from a reasonable $110 d ($670/week) for a standard studio with balcony, breakfast included; during holidays add about 20 percent. (In the past, seniors over 60 have customarily gotten a 20 percent discount.) Amenities include breakfast, a/c, cable TV, lovely oceanfront pool-patio, restaurant, and kiddie pool.

On the southwest side of the peninsula, the shining white **Hotel Tesoro Manzanillo** (Av. la Audiencia 1, Península de Santiago, Manzanillo, Colima 28200, tel. 314/333-2000 or 314/333-2200, toll-free Mex. tel. 01-800/216-5500, toll-free U.S./Can. tel. 866/99-TESORO, fax 314/333-22223, reservations01@tesororesorts .com, www.tesororesorts.com, credit cards

© BRUCE WHIPPERMAN

The white sun-tents of the towering Hotel Tesoro Manzanillo line the Playa Audiencia beachfront.

OWNING PARADISE

Droves of repeat visitors have fled their northern winters and bought or permanently rented a part of their favorite Pacific Mexico paradise. They happily reside all or part of the year in individual homes or developments both in town and up and down the coast, from Barra de Navidad to San Blas. Deluxe vacation homes, which foreigners can own through special trusts, run from about $100,000 up; condos begin at about half that. Timeshares start at about $5,000.

Probably the most important difference between buying real estate in the United States or Canada and in Mexico is the unavailability of real estate loans in Mexico. Real estate in Mexico is generally sold for cash only; although their numbers are growing slowly, only a few companies finance real property sales with loans. This will be no problem, however, for folks who arrive with a bundle of cash from the sale of their North American home.

TRUSTS

In the past, Mexicans have feared, with some justification, that foreigners were out to buy their country. As a consequence, present laws prohibit foreigners from holding direct title to property within 30 miles (50 km) of a beachfront or within 60 miles (100 km) of a national border.

However, Mexican law does permit *fideicomisos* (trusts), which substitute for outright foreign ownership. Trusts allow you, as the beneficiary, all the usual rights to the property, such as use, sale, improvement, and transfer, in exchange for paying an annual fee to a Mexican bank, the trustee, which holds nominal title to the property.

Otherwise, *bienes raíces* (real estate) in Mexico works a lot like in the United States and Canada. Agents handle multiple listings, show properties, assist negotiations, track paperwork, and earn commissions for sales completed. If you're interested in buying a Mexican property, work with one of the many honest and hardworking agents in Mexico, preferably one recommended through a reliable firm back home or trustworthy, property-savvy friends in Mexico.

Once you find a good property and have a written sales agreement in hand, your agent should recommend a *notaria pública* (notary) who, unlike a U.S. notary public, is an attorney skilled and licensed in property transactions. A Mexican notary, functioning much as a title company does in the United States, is the most important person in completing your transaction. The notary traces the title, ensuring that your bank/trustee legally receives it, and making sure the agreed-upon amounts of money get transferred between you, seller, bank, agent, and notary.

You and your agent should meet jointly with the notary early on to discuss the deal and get the notary's computation of the closing costs. For a typical trust-sale, closing costs (covering permit, filing, bank, notary, and registry fees) are considerable – typically 8-10 percent of the sale amount. After that, you will continue to owe property taxes and an approximately 1 percent annual fee to your bank/trustee.

TIMESHARES

Started in Europe, timesharing has spread all over the globe. A timeshare is a prepaid rental of a resort condo for a specified time period per year. Agreements usually allow you to temporarily exchange your timeshare rental for similar lodgings throughout the world.

The basic appeal is your investment – say $10,000 cash for a two-week annual stay in a deluxe beach condo – will earn you a handsome profit if you decide to sell your rights sometime in the future. What they don't mention is that, in recent years, timeshares have become increasingly difficult to sell, and the interest you could get for your $10,000 cash would go far toward renting an equally luxurious vacation condo every year without entailing as much risk.

And risk there is, because you would be handing over your cash for a promise only. Read the fine print. Shop around, and don't give away anything until you inspect the condo you would be getting and talk to others who have invested in the same time-share. It may be a good deal, but don't let them rush you into paradise.

accepted, $220 for two all-inclusive) towers futuristically above gemlike Playa Audiencia. The hotel's large (350-room) size doesn't seem to bother the guests, whose activities focus upon the spreading ocean-view pool and patio. There, around the swim-up bar, drinks flow, music bounces, and water volleyball and polo fill the sunny days. No matter if guests tire of pool frolicking. The bar offers nightly live music, fine crafts and designer clothes fill the boutiques, while dozens of books and the latest U.S. magazines line the shop shelves. The all-inclusive rates, which include all in-house food and entertainment, run about $220 for two, except for Christmas–New Year and Easter holidays. Children under 6 free; 7–12, about $30 per day. All rooms have a/c, cable TV, phones, and minibars; all water sports, tennis, golf, and wheelchair access included.

Over $200

Hotel las Hadas Golf Resort and Marina
(P.O. Box 158, Manzanillo, Colima 28200, tel. 314/331-0101, toll-free Mex. tel. 01-800/713-3233, toll-free U.S./Can. tel. 800/559-4329, fax 314/331-0121, hadas.reserv@brisas.com.mx, www.brisas.com.mx, $240 d and up) is a self-contained small city with a host of pleasurable amenities. Las Hadas, now operated by the big Mexican Las Brisas hotel chain, spreads over so much ground that only a fraction of its rooms are near the water, and most are a small hike to the beach. Furthermore, when guests finally get there, they find no waves on the sheltered Las Hadas cove, and their views are cluttered by the white Arabian-style tents of a regiment of fellow vacationers. Las Hadas nevertheless offers plenty of interest, at extra charge: three restaurants, a sportfishing marina, a sunset cruise, horseback riding, a golf course, a squadron of tennis courts, and a dozen aquatic sports. The approximately 300 luxurious white-and-blue motif suites, villas, and deluxe rooms rent from about $240 d; larger junior suites run from about $300 d. All amenities included, including complete wheelchair access.

By contrast, intimacy is one of the features of petite **Pepe's Hideaway** (tel. 314/333-

0616, www.pepeshideaway.com, $200–220 pp double all-inclusive), a miniretreat of six palm-shadowed, comfortable rattan-furnished comfortable *cabañas* perched above a hidden rocky cove on the Santiago Peninsula's southern tip. For romantics and honeymooners, this is paradise found, in luxurious south-seas style, with panoramic ocean views, dreamy sunset, a whirlpool bath and pool, and gourmet meals included. Year-round rates, except for Thanksgiving and Christmas, are about $200 (pool area), or $220 (overlooking the ocean) per person, double occupancy. Adults only.

A contrasting but worthy all-inclusive option for those who can afford it is the **Barceló Karmina Palace** (about a quarter mile along the shoreline northeast of Las Hadas, tel. 314/334-1313, toll-free U.S./Can. tel. 800/237-2256, fax 314/334-1108, reservations@barcelokarminapalace.com, www.barcelo karminapalace.com, credit cards accepted, all-inclusive $180 pp double low season, $240 pp high). The hotel's 320 superluxurious accommodations enfold an oceanfront mini-paradise of palm-shaded pools, fountains, and spreading green lawns. The Barceló Karmina Palace offers all possible facilities, including nearby golf access, for about $240 per person, double occupancy during the winter high season, and about $180 other times, excepting Christmas and Easter holidays, including all food, drinks, entertainment and much more.

SANTIAGO BAY

A sprinkling of recommendable hotels decorate the half-moon arc of broad, mountain-backed Santago Bay.

$50-100

The once-grand but now relatively humble 1950s-genre **Hotel Playa de Santiago** (Balneario de Santiago s/n, Bahía de Santiago, P.O. Box 147, Santiago, Colima 28860, tel. 314/333-0055, fax 314/333-0344, hoplsan@prodigy.net.mx, credit cards accepted, $55 d, $100 1br low season, $62 d, $120 1br high) on the south side of Santiago Bay offers much for budget-conscious travelers. Besides spacious, private balcony sea-view rooms overlooking the hotel's placid cove and beach, guests enjoy a palmy, seaside pool and sundeck, sunset views, a tennis court, a boat ramp, and friendly management. High-season prices for the 61 rooms and suites begin at about $62 d, two-bedroom suites go for about $120; low season, about $55 and $100. All with phones and fans only.

$100-200

At the sylvan northernmost corner of Santiago Bay, guests at **Hotel Villas Palma Real** (tel./fax 314/335-0000, Guadalajara reservation office tel. 33/3880-0700, fax 33/3121-6232, www.palmareal.com.mx, $135 1br low season, $170 1br high, and up) enjoy Santiago Bay's entire beach, ocean, and mountain panorama from the comfort of their private, shaded balconies. A 32-unit hybrid condo, timeshare, and hotel tucked at the foot of a jungly mountain ridge, Villas Palma Real offers luxurious tropical living at relatively modest rates. Apartments vary from spacious one-bedroom junior suites without kitchens to huge three-bedroom, three-bath apartments sleeping eight. All suites and apartments are simply but elegantly appointed, with creamy tile floors, decorator pastel sofas and bedspreads, designer lamps, king-sized beds, and modern tiled baths. All but the junior suites have full kitchenettes. Here, you can have Las Hadas luxury for a fraction of the price. Rates for the one-bedroom junior suites run about $135 low season, $170 high; one-bedroom suites with kitchenette, about $190 low season, $220 high. Two-bedroom apartments run about $290 low season, $350 high. During low season (May–June and Aug. 15–Dec. 15), the hotel often offers bargain three-night packages. The hotel is adjacent to scenic La Boquita beach and wildlife-rich Laguna de Juluapan; bring your binoculars and bird book. Amenities include cable TV, phones, a/c, fans, view balconies, pool, good airy *palapa* restaurant, minimarket, and laundry.

Over $200

Manzanillo's all-inclusive fun-in-the-sun colony, the **Club Maeva** (P.O. Box 440, Manzanillo, Colima 28200, tel./fax 314/331-0800,

toll-free Mex. tel. 800/523-8450, www.club maeva.com, credit cards accepted, $70 pp d low season, and up) spreads for a whitewashed quarter mile on the hillside above Santiago Bay. Club Maeva, whose clientele is mostly Mexican in the summer, Canadian and American during the winter, demonstrates the power of numbers. Its staff of 700 serves upward of 1,000 guests who enjoy a plethora of aquatic, field, court, and gym activities at no extra cost. Months would be needed to take full advantage of the extensive activity menu, which includes snorkeling, tennis, horseback riding, volleyball, softball, aerobics, table games—cards, backgammon, checkers, and chess—Spanish lessons, and a tranquil adults-only solarium and pool-bar. Moreover, Club Maeva guests enjoy continuous open bar and restaurant service, nightly theme shows, a disco, a miles-long beach, sunning beside Latin America's largest pool, and a complete water-slide park. Inclusive rather than exclusive, Club Maeva resembles a huge comfortable summer camp. Children are more than welcome, with a special miniclub for ages 4–12. The rooms, actually clusters of small villas, are an unusual luxurious-spartan combination, snow white and royal blue with private view balconies and marble floors, but with no movable furniture. All shelves, cabinets, bed platforms, and seats are attractive but indestructible white concrete built-ins. Rates for the 550 rooms and suites begin at about $70 per person, low season double occupancy, $90 per person mid-season, $120 midweek high season, about $160 high season weekends. Kids under 7 stay free; 7–12 $40, 13–17 $65. All rooms have a/c, but no phones or TV.

CAMPING

The closest good country campsites are about a dozen miles north, three miles off Highway 200, at **Playa de Oro,** from the signed cobbled (but very rough in parts) side road near Km 31, five miles north of El Naranjo. The caretaker at the entrance portal told me that the owners welcome campers. He pointed out some good camping and parking spaces and a shady *ramada* by the south-side headland.

A land development turned sour, Playa de Oro has returned to the wild: an endless sandy beach with many drive-in sites, good for RVs and tents. The surf, while often not too rough, has some undertow—don't swim alone. Boogie boarding and surfing are possible for cautious beginners and intermediates. Surf fishing is excellent, and the waves deposit carpets of shells and miles of driftwood, perfect for a week of beachcombing. You'll share the beach with a colony of sand crabs, which, like a legion of arthropodic prairie dogs, jealously guard their individual sand holes. Bring everything; the closest stores are in El Naranjo.

Although the Mexican name Playa de Oro (Beach of Gold) is as common as tacos in Taxco, this particular Playa de Oro is not just another developer's label. The story goes back to 1862, when the paddle-wheeled steamship *Golden Gate,* loaded with 337 passengers and more than a million dollars in California gold,

caught fire and sank not far off the beach. Only 80 people were saved and none of the gold. Although a salvage operation two years later netted some of the treasure, most remained until an enterprising American, a now-retired former Manzanillo hotel owner, arrived on the scene during the 1950s. He promoted a powerful suction dredge, brought from the United States, which harvested the lost treasure. Despite the giant underwater vacuum cleaner's efficiency, local folks tell stories of occasional shiny coins still washing up on the "Beach of Gold."

Note: The cobbled access road, excellent when new many years ago, appears unmaintained and consequently has developed a number of rough spots, especially on steep sections. These make the road marginally usable by bulky RVs and passenger cars. It's best to be prepared to drive in with a maneuverable, high-clearance, preferably four-wheel-drive truck or SUV.

Food

DOWNTOWN
Snacks and Stalls

The cluster of *fondas* (permanent foodstalls) at the **Mercado Francisco Madero** is the downtown mecca for wholesome homestyle cookery. Each *fonda* specializes in a few favorite dishes, which vary from rich *pozole* and savory stewed pork, beef, or chicken, to ham and eggs and whole grilled fish.

One of the favorites, the **Menudería Paulita** (off Avenida México, at the F. Madero and Cuauhtémoc corner, 5 A.M.–10 P.M. daily), tended by a jolly squad of women five short blocks from the *jardín.* One of them enjoys the singular job of crafting and baking unending stacks of hot tortillas, which their mostly workingmen customers use to scoop up the last delectable morsels.

Besides sit-down meals, the same downtown neighborhood is a source of on-street desserts. These include *churros* (long doughnuts) and

pastries, sold from carts late afternoons along Avenida México about four blocks from the *jardín,* and velvety ice cream from the **Bing** ice cream chain's downtown branch on the east end of the *jardín.*

A famously popular downtown snack spot is the **Bar Social** (on the *jardín,* diagonally across the street from the Presidencia Municipal), where folks gather 2–9 P.M. daily except Sun., for drinks, live music and free (2–5 P.M.) *botanas* (appetizers.)

Restaurants

One of Manzanillo's prime people-watching cafés is the **Restaurant Chantilly** (on the *jardín* corner adjacent to City Hall, tel. 314/332-0194, 7:30 A.M.–10:30 P.M. daily except Sat.). The completely unpretentious Chantilly offers its mostly local clientele prompt service, an extensive economical menu, and long moments lingering over several varieties of café espresso.

The *comida corrida* (five-course set lunch, $6) highlights many patrons' downtown day.

The dignified, airy ambience of the Hotel Colonial's restaurant **Los Candiles** (on Avenida México, just south of the *jardín*, 7 A.M.–10 P.M. daily) offers another attractive option. Besides its high-beamed ceiling, softly whirring ceiling fans, and a tranquil adjoining open-air patio, the lunch and dinner menu offers an unusually long selection of seafood, from broiled marlin and tuna ($6–8) to jumbo butterflied shrimp ($10) and pan-fried squid ($8).

The crowd of midafternoon customers alerts budget-minded diners to the value and quality of the restaurant at the **Hotel Emperador** (B. Dávalos 69, tel. 314/332-2374), half a block west of the *jardín*. Although *desayuno, comida,* and *cena* are all good at the Emperador, the favorite is the $3 *comida corrida* set lunch, beginning around 1 P.M.

A different cadre of loyal customers enjoys the **Café Roca del Mar** (at the east end of the *jardín*, tel. 314/332-0302, 7 A.M.–10 P.M. daily). With approximately the same menu and prices ($3–8) as the Chantilly, the Roca del Mar, whose tables spread to the shady sidewalk, is a bit more relaxed.

Restaurant Lychee (Niños Héroes 397, local cell tel. 044-314/3058-8268, 2–10 P.M. Tues.–Sun.), on the dock-front, two blocks east, serves bountiful plates of tasty Chinese-style specialties. Although the meat and fish dishes ($5–8) are tasty enough, it's the mounds of stir-fried broccoli, bean sprouts, snow peas, and bok choy ($5–6) that spell welcome relief for vegetable-hungry palates.

NORTH SIDE
Breakfast and Snacks

No local vacation would be complete without breakfast or lunch at **Juanito's** (Km 13.5, a few blocks north of Santiago Plaza in Santiago, tel. 314/333-1388, 8 A.M.–10 P.M. daily), Manzanillo's friendly refuge from high prices. The longtime American owner and his family feature tasty, modestly priced hometown fare, such as ham and eggs any style, hotcakes, hamburgers, milk shakes, and apple pie. For a generation of repeat customers, Juanito's is home away from home, with satellite TV, a shelf of used paperbacks, a long-distance telephone, and bottomless cups of coffee.

Alternatively, try the intimately homey restaurant at **Hotel la Posada** (8–10 A.M. sharp daily), which offers hearty North American–style breakfasts for both in-house guests and drop-ins.

Another good spot to start the day is the restaurant at the **Hotel Marbella** (at around Km 8.5 on Playa Azul, tel. 314/333-1103). Here, bright sun streams into the ocean-view bay windows while waitresses bring hearty breakfasts of eggs with potatoes, pancakes with maple syrup, and bottomless cups of coffee.

Regulars flock nightly to petite **Don Quixote's** (on the boulevard in front of the Hotel Marbella, 7 P.M.–1 A.M. daily), which specializes in mouthwatering barbecued beef, roast chicken, and pork loin tacos. Another popular taco stand option is **Garamelas** (adjacent to the Las Brisas traffic circle, at Km 7, open 6 P.M.–6 A.M.).

CRUCERO LAS BRISAS-PLAYA AZUL
Restaurants

Right at the Crucero las Brisas (Km 7) stands **El Vaquero** (a few doors east of the intersection, south side of the street, tel. 314/333-1654, about noon–midnight daily), Manzanillo's enduring cowboy B-movie set. An apparently exact replica of a 1900 Arizona (or maybe Sonora?) mining-town saloon, all that El Vaquero seems to have missing is the tinkling of an old upright piano. Leave all dietary pretensions aside and enjoy the hearty chuck-wagon cuisine: grill-roasted onions, real-thing chili and beans (*frijoles charros*), and a load of meat, from mere hamburgers and *arrachera* (thin-cut sirloin steak) to choice two-pound filet mignon and porterhouse steaks, all grilled to order in the outside patio.

Tops for zany personality is Carlos 'n Charlie's **Colima Bay Café** (Highway 200, Km 8, tel. 314/333-1150 or 314/333-1890, 2 P.M.–1 A.M. Mon.–Sat. high season, low-season hours may be shorter), the Manzanillo branch of late owner

Carlos Anderson's goofy worldwide chain. The fun begins at the entrance, where a sign announces: "Colima Bay Café, since 1800." Inside, the outrageous decorates the ceilings while a riot of photos—romantic, poignant, sentimental, and brutal—covers the walls. Meanwhile, the waiters (who, despite their antics, are gentle sorts) entertain the customers. The menu, with items such as "Moo," "Peep," and "Pemex," cannot be all nonsense, since many of them, such as Oysters 444, TBC Salad, and the tangy barbecued ribs, are delicious.

Sea breeze, soft lights, and the swish of the waves set the romantic tone of (**La Toscana** Italian-Mexican restaurant (Hwy. 200, Km 8.5, tel. 314/333-2515, 6 P.M.–midnight daily, entrees about $12); the tasty offerings of owner-chef Jean Francois La Roca provides the finale. For example, start out with fishermen's cream of mussel soup, or *ensalada mama mía*, both $8, continue with fish, such as catch-of-the-day *robalo* in mango and ginger sauce, $12, and finish with apple tart ($3.50) and good espresso coffee ($2).

Continue west to find (**Señor Sushi** (on the inland side of Highway 200, at Km 9.5, just half a block past the Chrysler dealer, 8 A.M.–10 P.M.). Although it specializes in about 30 kinds of sushi ($3–5), it also offers a full Japanese food menu. Enter the open-air *palapa*-roofed enclosure, and soon the colorful, fluttering banners, the waiters, garbed as if out of old Osaka, and aperitif cups of warm *o-sake* begin to create an illusion of Japan. The impression becomes more vivid with the arrival of the food: *gyoza* (pot stickers, $4), yakitori (chicken kebabs, $7), tempura (breaded, deep-fried vegetables, $7), and *teppanyaki* (diced-in-front-of-you grilled meat and vegetables, $9), all of which seems a minor miracle half a world away from the source. Appearances, however, are only the beginning. The miracle becomes complete as you taste the sticky rice, with its grains individual yet just exactly sticky enough, and very correctly served with a dab of pungent green wasabi (horseradish sauce).

At (**El Fogón** (across the adjacent street, west, noon–11 P.M. daily), a completely different illusion awaits. It's best to go at night, when the very artful, subdued lighting enhances the effect, of an old-time Rancho Grande somewhere up north, where meat was (and is) both the staple and king. Appetizers—chorizo, or spicy sausage, fondue, quesadillas, salads (shrimp, mixed), and soups (Azteca)—quickly lead to meats, from tongue *(lengua)* and pork loin *(lomo)* to main events, such as *arrachera* (steak, often tough), several styles of *molcajetes* (steaming meat and vegetables), and T-bone steaks.

Mandarin Wok (across the street, tel. 314/334-0590, approximately 2 P.M.–midnight daily) offers pretty fair standard Chinese cuisine—good hot-and-sour soup, sweet-and-sour pork, and spring rolls ($4–7). Mandarin Wok's customers enjoy the added plus of handsome decorations, a refined but festive atmosphere, and attentive, very professional service.

Among the best of Manzanillo restaurants is (**Manos Morenos** (Brown Hands; Blv. Costera Miguel de la Madrid Km 12, Salagua, tel. 314/333-0323, 8 A.M.–10 P.M. daily), whose owner's mission is to demonstrate the best of Mexican culture: arts and crafts, music, and cuisine. She's certainly proved herself by her cuisine, which is gourmet Mexican at its best, such as *chiles* stuffed with cheese and potato, fish fillet with mango sauce, and *arrachera* in mushroom sauce. Close your eyes and put your forefinger to the menu, and whatever you touch will be bound to please. Make up a party of four to share and sample as much as possible. Good for breakfast, too.

A treat is in store for those who venture off the busy Costera to the quiet country-ambience restaurant (**Rancho Don Andres** (tel. 314/334-6667, noon–9 P.M. daily). The family owners have collected a small flock of ostriches, guinea fowl, ducks and chickens, all free to wander an adjacent large grassy field. They invite their guests to take a seat beneath their airy hacienda roof and enjoy the best of grilled meats, fowl, and seafood, such as rib-eye steak ($10), pork chop ($6), or shrimp kabob ($11), and much more, with all the country fixins. Best go by taxi, following Paseo las Garzas inland, from the Salagua town plaza. The signed Rancho Don Andres driveway is on the left after about a mile (1.6 km). If you reach the big Coca-Cola factory, turn, around; you went a quarter mile too far.

For romantics, a Manzanillo trip wouldn't be complete without a visit to the showplace **(Restaurant L'Recife** (end of Avenida Cerro de Cenicero, at the breezy tip of north-end Juluapan Península, tel. 314/335-0900, 5–11 P.M. daily, Nov.–May only). Although its dazzling clifftop location is at least half the attraction, the tasty food—salads ($6–10), seafood ($15–20), and steaks ($20–30)—would alone make the trip worthwhile. Taxi or drive northwest along the beach boulevard. Pass the Club Santiago; within a mile, turn left at the La Boquita road. After about two miles winding along the lagoon, follow the signed L'Recife road fork uphill right. Continue another quarter mile to road's end. Be sure to arrive before 5:30 P.M., in time to enjoy the sunset. Reservations are mandatory.

Entertainment and Events

BOTANERAS

A number of *botaneras,* beer and entertainment halls, have big local followings. As soon as you order a drink, the *botanas*—small plates of ceviche, beans, pickled vegetables, and guacamole—begin to flow. Although the clientele is mostly male, a sprinkling of accompanied wives, girlfriends, sisters, and cousins make the atmosphere comfortable for women also.

One of the most popular local *botaneras* is the **El Caporal** near the Crucero las Brisas. It opens quietly at around 1 P.M. By 3 P.M., mariachis begin strumming away, more bottles pop open, and more *botanas* arrive. By 4 P.M., the place is often packed for the first show at 4:30. If you stay till 7 P.M. you'll probably need someone to stuff you into a taxi home. El Caporal is behind the Superior beer distributor at Km 8, across the highway from the beach; noon–7 P.M. daily.

A more refined and intimate *botanera* is the very popular downtown **(Bar Social** (on the *jardín,* diagonally across the street from the Presidencia Municipal), where folks gather daily except Sun. 2–9 P.M., for drinks, free *botanas* (2–5 P.M.), and live music.

SUNSETS, STROLLING, AND SIDEWALK CAFÉS

Playa las Brisas and Playa Azul provides the best vantage for viewing Manzanillo's often spectacular sunsets. For liquid refreshment and atmosphere to augment the natural light show, try one of the romantic beachside spots, such as Hotel la Posada, Carlos 'n Charlie's Colima Bay Café, Restaurant la Toscana, Hotel Playa Santiago, and especially Restaurant L'Recife. Sunset views from the plush terraces at Hotels las Hadas and Karmina Palace are unfortunately obstructed by intervening headlands.

Las Hadas provides an out, however. Its catamaran yacht, **Explorer,** departs high season from the Las Hadas marina at around 4:30 P.M. for a *crucero de atardecer* (sunset cruise). The $26 per-person tariff includes drinks. For schedule and tickets, contact the hotel, tel. 314/331-0101, ext. 3210, or a travel agent, such as Agencia Bahías Gemelas, tel. 314/333-1060, 314-333/3100, or 314/333-3160, fax 314/333-0649.

Early evenings are great for enjoying the passing parade around the downtown *jardín.* Relax over dessert and coffee at bordering sidewalk cafés, such as **Chantilly,** corner Avenida México, closed Saturday, or **Roca del Mar,** east end of the *jardín.*

An unmissable downtown spectacle is the swarm of swallows *(golondrinas)* who fly in around sunset and crowd upon the overhead telephone and power lines around the *jardín.* They first scream and squack as they squabble for the choice perches. Later, after much cackling and preening, they settle down for the night.

North of downtown, the **Salagua** (Km 11.5) and **Santiago** (Km 14) village plazas offer similar, even more *típica* sidewalk diversions.

NIGHTLIFE
Tourist Shows

The **Club Maeva** seasonally hosts a lively Saturday **Mexican Fiesta,** including swirling dancers, mariachis, rope dance, and rooster fights. Other nights, it stages theme parties where guests become part of the entertainment, such as International Gala Night, a journey to the world's great cities; or Brazilian Night, a glittering Río de Janeiro Carnaval; or amateur Night of the Stars, your chance to shine on the stage. Club Maeva parties, customarily open to the public, begin with a big buffet at 8 P.M. and cost about $30 per person, half price for kids under 12. For reservations, phone the hotel at tel. 314/331-0800.

Dancing and Live Music

The big hotels, such as Las Hadas, tel. 314/331-0101, and Hotel Tesoros Manzanillo, tel. 314/333-2000, offer seasonal live dance music in their lobby bars and restaurants. Call for times and programs.

Mexican rancho atmosphere at its welcoming best fills low-key *botanas* restaurant-bar **Cantina del Vaquero** (tel. 314/333-1769, 2–11 P.M. daily except Sun.) at Highway 200 Km 10, about two blocks south of Comercial Mexicana in Salagua. Relax with friends over drinks and/or ranch-style supper plates to the soothing live melodies of strolling guitarists.

Discos

Discomania reigns regularly at a sprinkling of clubs along beach boulevard Highway 200. Call to verify hours, which vary with season. Bring earplugs, just in case. Some of the longer-lasting spots, from south to north:

The very popular **Bar Felix** (Km 9 on Playa Azul, tel. 314/333-1875 or 314/334-1444) has relatively low-volume recorded music, soft couches, and no cover, with a two-drink minimum at $3 apiece.

Music is much less subdued, however, at its companion club, **Club Nautilus,** next door. There, lights begin gyrating and the woofers begin thumping around 10:30 P.M. Cover runs around $10.

FESTIVALS AND EVENTS

Manzanillo's longest yearly party is the **Fiesta de Mayo,** celebrated for two weeks, beginning late April and ending around May 10. A continuous schedule of events, including sports tournaments, art exhibitions, parades, concerts, folkloric dancing in the *jardín,* and a carnival by the downtown market, brightens Manzanillo days and nights.

The **Fiesta de Guadalupe** honors Manzanillo's—and all Mexico's—patron saint, the Virgin of Guadalupe. Shrines to the Virgin, with flower and food offerings beneath her traditional portrait, begin appearing everywhere, especially downtown, by the end of November. For 12 evenings beginning December 1, floats parade and native-costumed dancers twirl around the *jardín.* Afternoons, people (women and girls, especially) proudly display their ancestry by dressing up in indigenous clothing—*huipiles, enredos,* and *fajas*—and heading to the cathedral. Nearing their destination, they pass through lanes crowded with stalls offering Indian food, curios, toys, souvenirs of the Virgin, and snapshots of people beside the Virgin's portrait.

Manzanillo hosts an occasional winter-season *corrida de toros* (bullfight) at either the **Salagua** or the **El Coloma bullring** (on Highway 200, four miles south of town). Watch for posters. For dates, call a travel agent, such as Bahías Gemeles, tel. 314/333-1060, or Manzanillo city tourism, tel. 314/332-1004, at the booth in front of City Hall on the *jardín,* open 9 A.M.–7 P.M. daily.

Sports and Recreation

All of the beaches of Manzanillo and Santiago bays are fine for walking. The sand, however, is generally too soft for jogging, except along the wide, firm, north-end Playa de Miramar. On the south side, the last mile of the no-outlet Las Brisas Highway asphalt serves as a relatively tranquil and popular jogging course.

WATER SPORTS
Swimming, Surfing, and Bodysurfing

With the usual safety precautions, Manzanillo's beaches are generally safe for swimming, except on occasional days of high waves, when all but the most foolhardy avoid the surf. The safest swimming beaches are Playa San Pedrito and Playa de Miramar at the protected south and north ends, respectively.

The best surfing breaks occur along Playa Olas Altas (High Waves Beach), where, most any day, a sprinkling of surfers ride the swells 100 yards offshore.

Bodysurfing and boogie boarding are much more common, especially on Playas Audiencia, Olas Altas, and Miramar, where concessionaires often rent boogie boards.

Sailing, Sailboarding, and Kayaking

Manzanillo's waters are generally tranquil enough for kayaking, but also windy enough for good sailing and sailboarding. A few concessionaires rent equipment at fairly hefty prices. At **Playa Audiencia,** the beach concessionaire, Deportes Aquáticos del Pacífico, tel. 314/331-0101 (Las Hadas Resort number), ext. 3804, rents kayaks ($18/hour) to any able body. The same concessionaire, at **Las Hadas Resort** beachside, rents sailboard outfits and kayaks to Las Hadas guests and those of other

Playa Miramar is good for most beach activities, including surfing.

© BRUCE WHIPPERMAN

hotels who buy a Las Hadas beach day pass ($25 adults, $15 kids).

Snorkeling and Scuba Diving

Manzanillo waters are generally clear. Visibility runs from about 30 feet onshore to 60–80 feet farther out. Manzanillo has three standout shore-accessible spots: the jetty rocks (depth 5–25 feet) at the south end of Playa las Brisas; rocks in mid-bay and shoals on both sides of Playa Audiencia; and the wrecked (1959 hurricane) frigate 200 yards off north-end Playa la Boquita. All of these swarm with schools of sponge- and coral-grazing fish.

The veteran YMCA-method-certified dive director Susan Dearing and her NAUI-certified partner, Carlos Cuellar, operate **Underworld Scuba** from their dive shop on Highway 200 in Santiago. With thousands of accident-free dives between them, Susan and Carlos rank among Pacific Mexico's best-qualified scuba instructors. They offer all levels and many types of certification, including PADI, YMCA, CMAS, NAUI, and SSI.

Susan and Carlos start you out with a free qualifying lesson at the pool. After enough free practice, they'll guide you in onshore dives (for about $60 for a two-hour outing, including one half-hour fully equipped dive). They guide experienced divers (bring your certificate) much farther afield, including super sites such as Roca Elefante at the Juluapan Peninsula's foamy tip.

Contact them at their **Scuba Shack** headquarters (on Highway 200, Km 15 in Santiago, just north of Juanito's restaurant, tel./fax 314/333-3678; Carlos's cell phone: dial locally 044-314/358-0327, long-distance 01-314/358-0327, scuba@gomanzanillo.com, www.dive manzanillo.com).

TENNIS AND GOLF

Manzanillo has no free public tennis courts. **Hotel Tesoros Manzanillo,** tel. 314/333-2000, rents its six superb courts to nonguests for about $8 hourly during the day and $10

at night. The hotel's teaching pro offers lessons for about $25 per hour. Most other large hotels, notably Club Maeva and Las Hadas, have many courts but do not rent them to the public.

You might also be able to take advantage of the three excellent tennis courts of the **Club Santiago,** tel. 314/335-0370, open about 7 A.M.–6 P.M., about $6/hour. Get there by turning off Highway 200 at the side road, signed Canchas de Tenis, just north of the golf course. The Club Santiago nine-hole golf course (office just inside the Club Santiago gate at Highway 200, Km 19) is available for public use 8 A.M.–5 P.M. daily. The nine-hole greens fee runs about $48 ($55 for 18 holes), add about $40 for a golf cart. Caddies work nine holes for about $10 ($18 for 18 holes).

The renowned 18-hole **Las Hadas** course (off Avenida Audiencia, at the Km 12.5, Highway 200, *crucero Las Hadas*) is open to the public. The greens fee (cart included) runs about $110 for nine holes and about $130 for 18 holes. Caddys work for about $12 for nine holes, $18 for 18; club rental $33. Call Las Hadas, tel. 314/331-0101, ext. 3703 for details and reservations.

ECO-ADVENTURING

A number of guides lead groups on outdoor explorations of Manzanillo's wildlife-rich mountain, tropical forest, and coastal hinterlands.

Scuba instructor and Colima lover Susan Dearing also leads ecotours. Her "Wild Expeditions" itineraries can range from dolphin- and crocodile-watching and exploring the antique resort of Cuyutlán and the neighboring turtle hatchery, to basking in idyllic Agua Fria spring and hiking the spectacular Colima volcanoees. For more details, click on "Wild Expeditions" in her www.gomanzanillo .com website.

Join friendly English-speaking French geophysicist and volcano lover Gilles Arfeuille for **volcano tours** (outside Colima, long-distance tel. 01-312/310-5015, 01-312/310-7483, or in Colima, tel. 044-312/310-5015 or 044-312/310-7483, volcano@colimamagic .com, www.colimamagic.com) year-round on the slopes of the Volcán de Fuego (Volcano of Fire) near Colima. Itineraries vary, from moderate hikes and modest rapelling, to rugged treks to the top of 14,334-foot dormant Nevado de Colima (Oct.–June).

The Association of Guides of Manzanillo (tel. 314/332-1185) collectively specializes in a Mountain Tour Adventure, leading hikers through mountain tropical forest where they visit a coffee plantation, catch their own fresh-water prawns and shrimps, and swim in a waterfall-fed natural pool.

Alternatively, go with **Robert Sandoval** (Manzanillo local cellular tel. 044-314/352-3536, guides association tel. 314/332-1185, localbeto@hotmail.com), a member of the Association of Guides of Manzanillo, on an exploration into the La Floreña stalagmite-and stalactite-rich limestone cavern and the neighboring pristine tropical forest.

SPORTFISHING

Manzanillo's biggest sportfishing operation is the **Flota Amarilla** (Yellow Fleet), whose many captains operate cooperatively through their association, Sociedad Cooperativa de Prestación de Servicios Turísticos Manzanillo. You can see their craft anchored off their dockside office on Avenida Niños Héroes, a long block north (away from downtown) of the El Tajo Pemex gas station. Their eight-person boats run about $300 high season, $200 low, for a day's billfish (marlin, sailfish) hunting, with three fishing lines. Larger, plusher 12-person, six-line boats go for about $400 high season, $250 low, complete with ice and no-host bar. All boats are insured and equipped with CB radios and toilets. For information and reservations, call tel. 314/332-1031, or write Flota Amarilla-Soc. Coop. de P. de Servicios Turísticos Manzanillo, Niños Héroes frente al 638, Manzanillo, Colima 28200, or drop into the dockside office.

A local Texas-bred couple, Sam and Marilyn Short, offer a duo of highly recommended

sportfishing boats (reservations tel./fax 314/335-0605, cellular tel. 044-314/357-0717 in Manzanillo, 314/357-0717 from elsewhere, fish@bay.net.mx, www.mexonline.com/ opafish.htm). The smaller is the 26-foot **Rosa Elena;** the larger is the 40-foot **S.F. Marlin.** The captains, Hector and Hugo, veteran trophy winners in past fishing tournaments, try hard to get their clients big catches. The *Rosa Elena,* with room for six passengers and up to four lines, runs about $235 per day, complete. The *S.F. Marlin* can handle 10 passengers and eight lines, and costs about $375.

Other alternatives are available through travel agents, such as the Agencia Bahías Gemelas, tel. 314/333-1000.

YACHT BERTHING AND BOAT LAUNCHING

Las Hadas Hotel's excellent **marina** has about 100 berths (up to 80 feet) rentable for about $.75 per foot per day, including potable water and 110/220-volt electrical hookup. Reservations recommended, especially during the winter; call the marina direct at tel. 314/331-0114, or hadasmarina@brisas.com.mx, or call the hotel, at tel. 314/331-0101 (ask for the marina, ext. 3706). You may also send in your reservation request via fax 314/331-0127.

Las Hadas marina also has a boat ramp, available for a $12 fee. Make a telephone appointment with the marina before you arrive, however, or you might have to do some fast talking to get past the guard at the gate. At Highway 200, Km 12, follow Avenida Audiencia past the hilltop, turn left at the Las Hadas sign. At the gate, the guard will direct you.

On north-side Santiago Bay, you can also use the steep ramp (smaller boats only) at the **Hotel de Playa Santiago,** tel./fax 314/333-0055 or 314/333-0344, for a $3 fee. Get there from Highway 200, Km 13.5, just south of the Los Colorados creek bridge, just north of the gas station, follow the side road running next to the ETN bus terminal, along the peninsula's north shore to the hotel at road's end.

Shopping

DOWNTOWN

Manzanillo's colorful, untouristed **Mercado Municipal** district clusters around the main market at Cuauhtémoc and Independencia (five short blocks along Avenida México from the *jardín,* turn left and go four blocks). Southbound Mercado-marked buses will take you right there.

Wander through the hubbub of fish stalls, piled with dozens of varieties, such as big, fresh-caught *sierra* (mackerel) or slippery *pulpo* (octopus). Among the mounds of ruby tomatoes, green melons, and golden papayas, watch for the exotic, such as nopales (cactus leaves) or spiny green *guanábanas,* the mango-shaped relative of the Asian jackfruit. On your way out, don't miss the spice stalls, with their bundles of freshly gathered aromatic cinnamon bark and mounds of fragrant dried *jamaica* flower petals (for flavoring *aguas* drinks). Be sure to arrive a few hours before 3 P.M., when the inside section shuts down.

SALAGUA

In Salagua, handicrafts lovers mustn't miss the **María Cumbe** (a block south of the Las Hadas crossing, tel. 314/333-0561, mariacumbe@latinmail.com, www.gomanzanillo.com, 10–6 P.M. Mon.–Sat.), a boutique that offers a diverse, carefully selected from a highly skilled cadre of Mexican and international artisans.

Choose from a treasury of handsome women's apparel, ranging from traditional embroidered *huipiles* to designer pastel resort wear, and supple leather purses, belts, and woven hats. Delicate embroidery, in napkins and tablecloths, and Mexican and Indonesian batik is the best, as is the fine stoneware and the small gallery of paintings, ranging from sentimental country scenes to evocative vignettes of Mexican folks at work and play.

SANTIAGO

In **Santiago,** on Saturday, from around 10 A.M., join the folks who gather for the **Market,** beneath *tianguis* (awnings) that spread along Avenida V. Carranza, two blocks north of the Santiago town plaza. Although merchandise tends toward dime-store-grade clothes and hardware, it's worth a stroll if only for the color and the occasional exotica (wild herbs and fruits, antiques, bright parrots) that may turn up. (A similar market also draws big crowds from around the same time Sunday mornings in Salagua, not far from the town plaza.)

For a host of traditional folkcrafts, head to nearby **Centro Artesanal las Primaveras** (Juárez 40, tel. 314/333-1699, 8 A.M.–8 P.M. Mon.–Sat., 8 A.M.–2 P.M. Sun.), two blocks from the highway, a couple of blocks north of the Santiago town *jardín.* There, scattered amid a rambling dusty clutter, a warehouse of many attractive handicrafts—blown glass, crepe flowers, pre-Columbian-motif pottery, leatherwork, papier-mâché clowns and parrots—languish, waiting for someone to rescue them.

As you exit Las Primaveras, cross the street to the modest **Arts and Crafts of Oaxaca** (9 A.M.–6 P.M. Mon.–Sat., 9 A.M.–3 P.M. Sun.) shop, with a fetching all-Mexico handicrafts collection, such as bright metal picture frames and holiday ornaments, wool carpets, and *alebrijes,* fantastic wooden animals.

For a treat, back on the highway, just a few doors north of the Santiago *jardín,* take a look inside **El Palacio de las Conchas y Caracoles** shell emporium (tel. 314/333-0260, 9 A.M.–9 P.M. Mon.–Sat., 9 A.M.–2 P.M. Sun). Bring your shell book. Hosts of glistening, museum-quality specimens—iridescent silver nautiluses, luscious rose conches, red and purple corals—line a multitude of shelves. Buy them (from $1,000 on down) singly or choose from an array of jewelry: necklaces, earrings, brooches, and rings.

As you near Club Maeva on the highway, stop about 100 yards south of the Club Maeva pedestrian overpass and look over the offerings of the **Mercado de Artesanías** (Handicrafts Market) on the beach side of the highway. Here, a dozen families sell crafts, many made by family and friends in their native villages in the mountains of Guerrero, Michoacán, Oaxaca, and Chiapas. They're poor but proud people. You should bargain, but gently.

SUPERMARKETS AND PHOTOGRAPHY

The big **Soriana** Kmart look-alike department store is Manzanillo's latest big shopping venue, unmissable, in Salagua, Km 9.5, inland side of Highway 200 (tel. 314/333-9053 or 314/334-0253, 8 A.M.–11 P.M. daily). Everything, from motor scooters and computers to screwdrivers, socks, and groceries seems to be on sale. Also in the same complex are banks (Banamex, Banorte, and Bital), all with ATMs, and fast food lunch spots serving tacos, cookies, ice cream and much more.

Also in Salagua, the Manzanillo branch of

the big **Comercial Mexicana** (tel. 314/333-0005, 8 A.M.–11 P.M. daily), marked by the orange pelican sign, anchors the American-style Plaza Manzanillo shopping center at Km 10.5. It offers everything—from appliances and cosmetics to produce, groceries, and a bakery—spread along shiny, well-stocked aisles.

At the entrance to the same Plaza Manzanillo complex, drop off your film for quick finishing at up-to-date **Foto Sol** (tel. 314/333-1860, 9 A.M.–9 P.M. daily). Foto Sol also sells popular films and stocks some camera accessories.

Downtown, **Photo Studio Cárdenas** offers film and some cameras and accessories on the *jardín* (at Balvino Dávalo 52, tel. 314/332-1160, 9:30 A.M.–2 P.M. and 5–10 P.M. daily). Alternatively, go to the downtown branch of **Foto Sol,** two doors away, on Avenida Mexico (tel. 314/332-4343, 9 A.M.–9 P.M. Mon.–Sat.)

Information and Services

TOURIST INFORMATION OFFICES

Downtown, Manzanillo city maintains a tourist information *modulo* (booth) in front of City Hall, on the inland side of the *jardín* (tel. 314/332-1004, 7 A.M.–7 P.M. daily).

At the local Colima state Secretary of Tourism (SECTUR) (tel. 314/333-2277 or 314/333-2264, toll-free 01-800/505-8164, www.manzanillo.com.mx, 8:30 A.M.–7 P.M. Mon.–Fri., 9 A.M.–2 P.M. Sat.), office staff answers questions and hands out brochures and maps at their office on the beach boulevard around Km 8, next to the Hotel Caracol

PUBLICATIONS

Downtown, two branches of **Revistas Saifer** (Av. México 117, no phone, across the corner from the Hotel Colonial; and Av. México 207, one block down the street from the *jardín)* usually stock the *Miami Herald* and several American magazines, such as *Time, Newsweek, National Geographic, Popular Science* and *Brides;* 9 A.M.–10 P.M. daily. The same is ap-

proximately true for Saifer's Plaza Manzanillo shopping center branch (in Salagua, Km 11, 9 A.M.–10 P.M. daily).

The *tabaquería* at **Hotel Tesoros Manzanillo** (tel. 314/333-2000) has one of the most extensive stock of U.S. newspapers, magazines, and English-language paperbacks in Manzanillo.

Additionally, the **Supermarket Vianda** (tel. 314/335-0450, 8 A.M.–9 P.M. Mon.–Sat., 8 A.M.–6 P.M. Sun.), across Highway 200 from Club Santiago at the northwest end of town, stocks some American magazines and the *Miami Herald* (October through April only).

MONEY EXCHANGE

Several banks, all with ATMs, serve downtown customers. **Banamex** (Banco Nacional de Mexico) exchanges both U.S. and Canadian traveler's checks and cash at its office three blocks from the *jardín* (Av. México 136, tel. 314/332-0115, 9 A.M.–4 P.M. Mon.–Fri., 10–2 P.M. Sat.). The **Banorte,** a few doors south, does the same (8:30 A.M.–4 P.M. Mon.–Fri., 10–2 P.M. Sat.). If both are closed or too crowded, the **HSBC** bank (tel. 314/332-0950, 8 A.M.–7 P.M., Mon.–Sat.) across the street a block toward the *jardín* changes U.S. traveler's checks and cash and has even longer hours After hours and on Sunday, use the banks' ATMs.

Banks, all with ATMs, along the Highway 200 suburbs also change money. At the Crucero las Brisas try the **Scotiabank Inverlat,** 9 A.M.–5 P.M. Mon.–Fri.

In Salagua, go to **Banco Serfin,** or **Banamex,** both in the Manzanillo Plaza shopping center west of Comercial Mexicana. Alternatively, go across the highway and a block north to **Bancomer,** tel. 314/334-0102.

In Santiago, choose from **HSBC** bank, tel. 314/333-0813 (8 A.M.–7 P.M. Mon.–Fri., 8 A.M.–3 P.M. Sat.), on the highway, or **Banco Santander Serfin** (tel. 314/333-0738, 9 A.M.–4 P.M. Mon.–Fri.), on Juárez, two blocks inland from the highway. Both banks have ATMs.

TRAVEL AGENCIES

The former Manzanillo American Express agency **Agencia de Viajes Bahías Gemelas,** Highway 200 Km 9, on the inland side of the boulevard, tel. 314/333-1000 or 314/333-1060, fax 314/333-0649, idali48@hotmail.com, 9 A.M.–2 P.M. and 4–6 P.M. Mon.–Fri., 9 A.M.–2 P.M. Sat.) no longer offers any American Express financial services. However, it remains a full-service travel agency, booking air tickets, local tours, hotel reservations, and more.

An alternative travel agency option is **Acuario,** at Av. Mexico 207, downtown, tel. 314/332-4577, turisticozlo@hotmail.com.

COMMUNICATIONS

The downtown combined *correo* and express mail **Mexpost** office, tel. 314/332-0022, is on Calle Galindo, between Avs. Mexico and Carrillo Puerto, about four blocks inland from the *jardín.* Find it open 9 A.M.–4 P.M. Mon.–Fri., 9 A.M.–1 P.M. Sat.

Telecomunicaciones, the high-tech telegraph office at Carrillo Puerto 135, about two blocks south from the *jardín,* sends telegrams, telexes, fax messages, and money orders. Open Mon.–Fri. 8 A.M.–7:30 P.M., Sat.–Sun.

9 A.M.–12:30 P.M. *Giros* (money order) hours are shorter: Mon.–Fri. 9 A.M.–1 P.M. and 3–5 P.M. only.

In Santiago, the post office, tel. 314/334-1130, and *telecomunicaciones* offices stand side by side on Venustiano Carranza nos. 2 and 4, across Highway 200 from Juanito's restaurant. Both have the same hours: Mon.–Fri. 9 A.M.–3 P.M.

Manzanillo's *larga distancia* telephone offices are conveniently spread from the downtown north along Highway 200. Everyone's favorite downtown stop is homey **Restaurant del Río,** 330 Av. Mexico, tel. 314/332-2525 or 314/332-2575, about three blocks inland from the *jardín,* where you can enjoy a country-style enchilada, *torta,* or *hamburguesa* while you await your call. Open Mon.–Sat. 8 A.M.–9 P.M.

However, if you're in the mood for economy and efficiency, buy a widely available Ladatel telephone card (drug stores and groceries often sell them; look for the blue and yellow Ladatel sign) and use a street telephone.

Internet access stores are popping up all over town. For example, on the Las Brisas Highway (Av. Lázaro Cárdenas) a block south of the Las Brisas crossing, answer your email at **Papeleria Damcol,** open Mon.–Sat. 9 A.M.–8 P.M.; in Salagua, **Cyber Café Enredos,** in the Manzanillo Plaza Shopping Center (marked by the big Comercial Mexicana sign), in Salagua, open daily 11 A.M.–10 P.M., about $3.50 per hour; and in Santiago, at **Juanito's** restaurant, at Km 15 in Santiago, tel. 314/333-1388, $4 per hour.

HEALTH AND EMERGENCIES

In a medical emergency, call a taxi to take you to either **Centro Médico Quirúrgico Echauri** at Km 9.7, Blvd. Miguel de la Madrid, tel. 314/334-0001, or **Médico Pacífico Cruz Azul** (and Super-Farmacia, tel. 314/333-3047), at Av. Palma Real 10, Km 13, a block just south of the gas station, tel. 314/334-0385. Manzanillo's newest and best-equipped private hospitals, they each have round-the-clock service, including a laboratory and several specialists on call you can also visit for routine consultations.

For police emergencies, call the **Tourist Police,** tel. 314/332-1004. For fire emergencies, call the *bomberos* (fire station) at 314/332-1254, or 314/332-3054.

IMMIGRATION

Migración (the Immigration Office) occupies the third floor in the **Edificio Federal Portuario** (Federal Port Building) on San Pedrito Beach, at the foot of Avenida Teniente Azueta. The cooperative, efficient staff, tel.

314/332-1730, fax 314/332-0030, can replace a lost tourist card. (Make a a copy of your tourist card, just in case.) Lacking this, go to them with your passport and some proof, such as an airline ticket, of your arrival date in Mexico. Open Mon.–Fri. 9 A.M.–1 P.M. for business and around the clock for questions.

You can accomplish the same business at the Migración (tel. 315/335-3689 or 315/335-3690) office at the Manzanillo airport, open daily 8 A.M.–8 P.M.

Getting There and Away

BY AIR

The **Manzanillo airport,** officially the Playa de Oro International Airport (code ZLO), is 28 easy highway miles (44 km) from downtown Manzanillo, and only about 22 miles (35 km) from most Manzanillo beachside hotels. From the other direction, the airport is 19 miles (30 km) south of Barra de Navidad.

Manzanillo Airport Flights

Alaska Airlines (U.S. toll-free number direct from Mexico, tel. 001-800/426-0333) flights connect daily with Los Angeles.

U.S Airways (formerly America West) flights connect with Phoenix during the winter-spring season. For local reservations, call the airline via U.S. toll-free number direct from Mexico (dial 001-800/235-9292).

Aerocalifornia Airlines (tel. 314/334-1414) flights connect with Los Angeles and Mexico City; call for local reservations and flight information.

Aeromar Airlines flights connect daily with Mexico City, where many U.S. connections are available. For reservations and flight information, contact its airport office (tel. 314/333-0151, or 314/334-0532) or the Manzanillo downtown office (tel. 314-334/8356 or 314/334-8355, or toll-free Mex. tel. 01-800/237-6627).

Magnicharter airlines connects directly with Mexico City, and **Northwest Airlines** connects with Minneapolis January through April. For reservations, contact a travel agent.

Airport Arrival and Departure

The terminal, although small for an international destination, does have a money exchange counter, open 10 A.M.–6 P.M. daily. Also it has a few gift shops for last-minute purchases, snack stands, a good upstairs restaurant, some car rentals, and a *buzón* (mailbox) just outside the front entrance. However, the airport has no hotel booking service, so you should arrive with a hotel reservation or you'll be at the mercy of taxi drivers who love to collect fat commissions on your first-night hotel tariff. Upon departure, be sure to save enough cash to pay the approximately $12 **departure tax** (if your ticket doesn't already include it).

After the usually rapid immigration and customs checks, independent arrivees have their choice of a car rental or taxi tickets from a booth just outside the arrival gate. *Colectivos* head for Barra de Navidad and other northern points seasonally only. Taxis, however, will take three passengers to Barra, Melaque, or Hotel Real Coastecomate for about $34 total; to El Tamarindo, $52; Hotel

Blue Bay Los Angeles Locos, $54, El Careyes, $75; Chamela-El Super, $84; or Las Alamandas, $120. *Colectivo* tickets run about $10–12 per person to any Manzanillo hotel, while a *taxi especial* runs about $25–34, depending on destination.

No public buses serve the Manzanillo airport. Strong, mobile travelers on tight budgets could save pesos by hitching or hiking the three miles to Highway 200 and flagging down one of the frequent north- or southbound second-class buses (fare about $2 to Barra or Manzanillo). Don't try it at night, however.

As for airport **car rentals,** you have a choice of Alamo (tel. 314/333-0611, fax 314/333-1140, alamomanzanillo@prodigy .net.mx), Hertz (tel. 314/333-3191, 314/333-3141, or 314/333-3142), Thrifty (tel. 314/334-3282 or 314/334-3292, autzs@prodigy.net .mx), and Budget (tel./fax 314/333-1445 or 314/334-2270, budgetmzo@prodigy.net.mx). Unless you don't mind paying upward of $50 per day, shop around for your car rental by calling the car rentals company's U.S. and Canada toll-free numbers at home *before* you leave.

Don't lose your tourist card; if somehow you do, arrive early enough to get a replacement (bring proof of arrival date, such as air ticket or copy of the lost document) at the Manzanillo airport *migracion* (tel. 315/335-3689 or 315/335-3690).

BY CAR OR RV

Three main highway routes connect Manzanillo with the outside world: from the north via Puerto Vallarta and Barra de Navidad; from the northeast via Guadalajara and Colima; and from the southeast via Ixtapa, Zihuatanejo, and Playa Azul (Lázaro Cárdenas).

From the north, Mexico National Highway 200 glides 172 mostly smooth asphalt miles (276 km) from Puerto Vallarta via Barra de Navidad. The only steep (and possibly slow) section is at the north end, about half an hour south of Puerto Vallarta, where the highway climbs to the mountain summit (about 2,000 feet, 600 meters) near El Tuito. Otherwise, it's mostly easy going along this foothill-, forest-, and beach-studded route. Allow about four hours to or from Puerto Vallarta, about one hour to or from Barra de Navidad.

The safety and ease of the Guadalajara-Colima *autopista* (combined National Highways 54 D, 110, and 200) more than compensates for the (approximately $20 per car) tolls. Head southwest from the Glorieta Minerva circle in Guadalajara along Avenida López Mateos south (Highway 15, 54, and 80) for around 27 miles (45 km) until Acatlán de Juárez, and follow the *cuota* toll) Highway 54 D freeway south for Colima. Two or three highway hours later, after bypassing Colima, the expressway 54 D continues as expressway Highway 110, continuing south to just before Tecomán, where Highway 110 becomes Highway 200 as it splits off right, northwest, to Manzanillo. Figure about 4.5 driving hours for this easy, 190-mile (311-km) trip, either way.

The same cannot be said for the winding 238 miles (390 km) of coastline Highway 200 between Zihuatanejo and Manzanillo. Keep your gas tank filled; the spectacularly scenic but sparsely populated 100-mile stretch from the Colima border to Caleta de Campos, Michoacán, has no gas stations. Allow a full eight-hour day, in broad daylight, either way. Best don't try it at night.

Drivers just passing through who want to avoid the long, sometimes congested Manzanillo Bay beachfront strip should follow the **Manzanillo town bypass.** Southbound, watch for signs around Km 20, just past the village of Naranjo, where you should bear left at the bypass road fork. Northbound, approaching Manzanillo from the south, follow the Cihuatlán signed turnoff after you cross the Laguna Cuyutlán bridge on the Highway 200 *cuota* (toll) expressway.

BY BUS

Several bus lines serve Manzanillo from the **Central de Autobús** (central bus station) at

Oceano Pacific 20, in the neighborhood by the big auditorium, one block off the main old Highway 200 boulevard around kilometer 6. Get there via taxi or ride a Central de Autobus (or Camionera Central-marked bus.

All departures listed below are local *(salidas locales)* unless noted as *salidas de paso.* Choose first class whenever you can; its service, speed, and *asientos reservados* (reserved seats) far outweigh the small additional ticket cost. The bus lines divide roughly into northwest-southeast (coastal), north, and northeast (Mexico City-Michoacán) categories.

Northwest-Southeast (Coast Route) Bus Lines: Elite, tel. 314/336-7617, provides first-class *salidas de paso* service north with Melaque, Puerto Vallarta, Mazatlán, and Tijuana, and south with Playa Azul junction, Lázaro Cárdenas, Zihuatanejo, and Acapulco. Other first-class Futura departures also connect northeast with Colima and Mexico City.

Transportes Cihuatlán, tel. 314/332-0515, and associated line Autocamiones del Pacífico provide Manzanillo's most frequent service northwest and north. A few first-class departures connect along the coast with Puerto Vallarta; several first-class departures connect with Guadalajara via Highway 80 (through Melaque and Autlán) daily. Many other second-class buses follow the same routes, stopping everywhere.

Autobuses Nuevo Horizonte second-class buses, tel. 314/332-3900, connect round the clock with Guadalajara via Colima. A few buses per day also connect south along the Michoacán Coast, with the Playa Azul junction and Lázaro Cárdenas.

The interurban second-class **Sociedad Cooperativo de Autotransportes** buses connect half-hourly with south Colima destinations of Armería, Cuyutlán, Tecomán, and Colima.

Northern Buses: Major carrier **Omnibus de Mexico** (tel. 314/336-8402) provides wide-ranging long-distance first-class connections

north, mostly through Guadalajara, with Zacatecas, Fresnillo, Durango, Aguascalientes, and Monterey, with many buses continuing all the way to the U.S. border at either Ciudad Juárez, Nuevo Laredo, Reynosa, or Matamoros.

Northeast Buses: More than a dozen **Autovías del Occidente** (AO) second-class buses, tel. 314/332-0123, connect round the clock with Mexico City through Michoacán via Morelia. At Morelia, you can continue to Pátzcuaro. Many second-class buses connect daily with subsidiary Michoacán destinations of Apatzingan, Zamora, and Uruapan.

Also in the same booth as Autovias del Occidente, **Linea Plus** first-class buses connect Colima, Guadalajara, and Mexico City (Observatorio Terminal), and Michoacán destinations of Morelia, Uruapan, Nueva Italia, and Apatzingan.

Flecha Amarilla, tel. 314/336-4801 or 314/336-0205, and its subsidiary lines combine under the "Servicios Coordinados" blanket to offer a host of departures. Many luxury-class "Primera-plus" buses connect direct with Guadalajara and Mexico City. Other "Primera-plus" connections continue past Guadalajara as far as Aguascalientes and Querétaro. A few departures connect with Mexico City (Norte) through Colima and Morelia. Several second-class departures connect north with Minatitlán, Colima, Zamora, Salamanca, Irapuato, and Morelia. Some second-class departures connect northwest with Barra de Navidad-Melaque and Puerto Vallarta and all intermediate Highway 200 points.

Independent, airline-style luxury **Enlaces Transportes Nacionales** (ETN), tel. 314/334-1050, operates out of its separate terminal in Santiago, across from the Pemex station. ETN provides frequent connections northwest with Barra de Navidad and Melaque, and Puerto Vallarta; northeast, with the Guadalajara airport, and east through Colima, Michoacán, all the way to Mexico City (Norte).

Excursions from Manzanillo

Manzanillo provides a convenient base for some rewarding excursions. Although sharing a rental car is the easiest way to go, you can also get most anywhere quickly via early-morning buses from the main bus station (Central de Autobuses). One of the most enjoyable excursions leads to El Salto waterfall, Minatitlán, and Agua Fria spring in the northeast foothills. Manzanillo is also a base for trips to Cuyutlán and El Paraíso beaches in south Colima state.

Start out on your excursion early by Minatitlán-bound bus from the Manzanillo Central de Autobus, or by car. Drivers, set your odometer to zero at the northbound all-paved Minatitlán highway, across the big traffic circle near the Km 4 Pemex gas station.

The road quickly rises, winding past ranches and farms that soon give way to lush, summer-green tropical deciduous forest. Along the way, you pass a **double spring** that cascades by the road on the right (at Mile 26, Km 42). At the same spot, on the left, you can view the scar of the **Peña Colorada** (Red Rock) iron strip mine on a mountaintop to the north. An entire mountain of iron ore is being extracted and sent via a 17-mile (27-km) ore-slurry-filled pipe to the processing mill on Manzanillo's north side. There, the ore is made into pellets and sent by ship to the giant Las Truchas mill in Lázaro Cárdenas, Michoacán, and other Pacific Rim locations to be made into steel.

Continue another three miles (5 km) to the prim company town Peña Colorada, with all up-to-date facilities—bank, hospital, schools, houses—for the miners' families, built by the Japanese-Mexican consortium that developed the mine.

(El Salto

In another mile (at Mile 30, Km 48) you come to **El Salto Park** and new picnic ground to the right, below the highway. Bear left after you enter, another 100 yards, to the more intimate old park just overlooking the waterfall. Here, butterflies flutter and orchids grow among great mossy rock

© BRUCE WHIPPERMAN

El Salto waterfall gushes into a pristine, rock-walled canyon.

outcroppings. A rustic swimming pool and kiddie pool delight picnicking families.

Follow the steps down to the base of the El Salto (the Jump) waterfall, which cascades in a pair of 30-foot leaps to a turbulent pool below. The best time to arrive is during the dry late autumn, winter, and spring. During the rainy summer and early autumn El Salto may be an uninviting muddy brown. From the base of the falls, adventurers can float down the deep, slow creek 100 yards to a beach downstream. Bring a picnic, or maybe even a tent or your RV for an overnight. Weekdays the park isn't usually crowded. Sundays and holidays, however, are for those who like company. Then, the place will likely be crowded with frolicking families, mariachis, and taco vendors.

Minatitlán and El Terrero

From El Salto, continue to Minatitlán, half a mile off the highway intersection at Mile 32 (Km 53). It's a typically pleasant Mexican mountain *municipio,* with a modicum of stores and services. Stop for a break or a meal at the welcoming and very clean **Cocina la Herradura** (tel. 314/336-0294), where you'll find *tacos de chorizo, adobado, cabeza, puerco, burrito tuxpeño,* and beef, pork, and chicken soups and stews *(caldos y guisados).*

Continue ahead downhill toward Agua Fria spring. Another eight miles (13 km) along, at Mile 40 (Km 64), near kilometer marker 41 from Colima, a sign at Rastrujitos crossroad marks a gateway to the **Manantlán Biosphere,** a unique ice-age remnant cloud-forest habitat. A cobbled, car-negotiable road leads uphill; fork right after about a mile, before El Sauz Rancho, and continue another 10 steep but easy miles (16 km) to **El Terrero** hamlet in the cloud forest around the 7,000-foot summit. There, folks are prepared for visitors, with a cabin shelter for about 10 campers, a small grocery store, a health center, a potable water faucet, and a pine-shaded campground park with picnic tables and and outhouse, at around Mile 11, just past the town (for more information, call tel. 312/320-8888, Spanish only).

Back on the main road, continue another 13 miles (21 km) downhill, where a signed side road (around Mile 53, 85 km from Manzanillo), near kilometer 20 marker from Colima, leads to **Agua Dulce.** (Here, an old-timer told me that Agua Dulce (Sweet Water) got its name from the single potable natural spring—among the many foul ones—discovered here.)

🄲 Agua Fria

Finally, another mile later, you reach Agua Fría on the right, an idyllic cluster of cool, clear ponds that meander among rustic picnic *palapas.* Here, you can have it all: food and drinks from the restaurants, plenty of relaxing shade, lots of space for informal tent and RV camping. When so much pleasure gets boring, you can top it all by slipping, for a cooling break, into a crystal-clear spring-fed pool.

Continue ahead another 15 miles (24 km), following the signs, and you'll arrive in downtown Colima in about half an hour.

The cool, crystal-blue waters of Agua Fria are very popular with local families.

© BRUCE WHIPPERMAN

Colima and Vicinity

Legends say that from atop their thrones of fire and ice high above the Valley of Colima, the gods look down upon their ancient domain. The name "Colima" itself echoes the tradition: from the Nahuatl "Colliman" (*colli:* ancestors or gods, and *maitl:* domain of).

Approaching from Manzanillo, visitors seldom forget their first view of the sacred mountains of Colima: the serene, snowcapped 14,220-foot (4,334-meter) Nevado de Colima, above his fiery, tempestuous younger brother, the 13,087-foot (3,989-meter) Volcán de Fuego (Volcano of Fire). The heat from that heavenly furnace rarely reaches down the green slopes to the spring-fed valley, where the colonial city invites coastal visitors to its more temperate (1,600-foot) heights for a refreshing change of pace.

HISTORY
Before Columbus
Although Colima (pop. 180,000) is the smallish capital of a diminutive agricultural state, it is much more than a farm town. Visitors can enjoy the residents' obvious appreciation of their arts and their history—twin traditions whose roots may extend as far south as Ecuador and Peru and as far west as the Gulf coast's mystery-shrouded monument builders, the Olmecs.

Colima's museums display a feast of ceramic treasures left behind by the many peoples—Nahua, Tarascan, Chichimec, Otomi—who have successively occupied the valley of Colima for upward of 3,000 years. Much more than mere utilitarian objects, the Colima pottery bursts with whimsy and genius. Acrobats, musicians, and dancers frolic, old folks embrace, mothers nurse, and most of all, Colima's famous dogs scratch, roll, snooze, and play in timeless canine style, as if they could come alive at any moment.

Conquest and Colonization
By 1500, the ruler of Colima, in order to deter his aggressive Tarascan neighbors to the north, had united his diminutive kingdom with three neighboring coastal provinces. This union, now known as the Chimalhuacan Confederation, did not prevail against Spanish horses and steel, however. Many local folks take ironic pride that Colima is one of Mexico's earliest provinces. Their ancestors fell to the swords of conquistador Gonzalo de Sandoval and his 145 soldiers, who, in an anticlimax to their bloody campaign, founded the city on July 25, 1523.

Two years later, Cortés appointed his nephew, Francisco Cortés de Buenaventura, mayor and head of a settlement of about 100 Spanish colonists and 6,000 native tributaries.

Cortés himself, in search of Chinese treasure in the Pacific, repeatedly visited Colima on his way to and from the Pacific coast during the 1530s, most notably during January 1535, en route to his exploration of Baja California.

Scarcely a generation after the Great Circle route to the Orient was finally discovered in the 1560s, the Spanish king bypassed Colima by designating Acapulco as the prime Pacific port. This, along with a series of disasters—earthquakes, volcanic eruptions, hurricanes, and pirates—kept Colima in slumber until President Porfirio Díaz began building the railroad to the beaches and from the port of Manzanillo during the 1890s.

Modern Times
The destructive 1910–1917 Revolution and the hard economic times of the 1930s kept Colima quiet until the 1950s, when burgeoning mining and Pacific Rim shipping, fishing, and tourism brought thousands of new jobs. Manzanillo became a major port and manufacturing center, boosting Colima to a government and university headquarters and trading hub for the bounty (meat, hides, milk, fruit, vegetables, copra, sugar) of rich valley and coastal plantations, farms, and ranches.

SIGHTS
Colima's central district is a simple, one-mile square. The street grid runs north-south

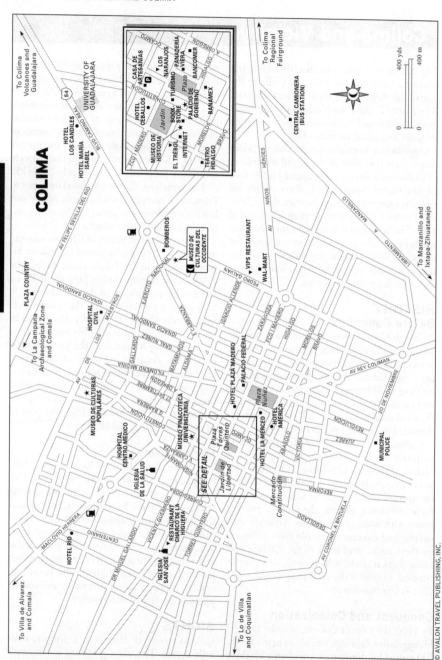

COLIMA

(north, toward the volcanoes; south, toward the coast) and east-west. Nearly all sights and services are reachable by a few minutes' walk or short taxi ride from the central plaza, the **Jardín de Libertad.**

A Walk Around Downtown

An ambience of refined prosperity—fashionable storefronts, shady portals, and lush, manicured greenery—blooms in the blocks that spread from Jardín de Libertad. The landmark **Catedral de San Felipe de Jesús** and **Palacio de Gobierno** statehouse stand side by side on Avenida Constitución, bordering the *jardín.* For a colonial town, the buildings are not old, having replaced the original earthquake-weakened colonial-era structures generations ago. Most prominent is the cathedral, the latest (1894) incarnation of a succession of churches built on the same spot since 1527.

A number of local celebrations begin from the *jardín,* the hub of commercial and community activities. The mayor shouts the **Grito de Dolores** (independence cry, evening of Sept. 15), and crowds celebrate the **Fiesta Charrotaurina** (Feb. 7).

Other landmarks dot the portals around the square. As you move counterclockwise from the cathedral, next comes the renovated **Hotel Ceballos** (corner of Constitución and Avenida Francisco I. Madero). At the succeeding corner rises the **Presidencia Municipal** (Madero and north-south Avenida V. Carranza). And finally, on the south side, stands the state and city **Museo de Historia** (Av. 16 de Septiembre, corner of Constitución, tel. 312/312-9228, open 9 A.M.– 6 P.M. Tues.–Sat., Sun 5–8 P.M.). Step into the museum for excellent examples of Colima's famous pre-Columbian pottery and go next door to a good bookstore offering a number of excellent local art, history, and picture guidebooks.

Next stroll across the *jardín* corner to the **Palacio de Gobierno** and head through its big, open front door and enjoy the calm, classic elegance of the inner patio. Take a minute or two to admire the stairwell mural, completed in 1953 by muralist Jorge Chaves Carrillo to commemorate the 200th anniversary of *insurgente*

Colima's second plaza is named in honor of a beloved local teacher, Torres Quintero.

Miguel Hidalgo's birth. Continue out the other side and into Colima's second square, named after Torres Quintero (1866–1934), a beloved Colima teacher whose statue decorates the tree-shaded park. (Note: Since the Colima state offices were removed to the suburbs a few years back, the Palacio de Gobierno serves a largely ceremonial function. The exception is the tourist information office, open daily except Sunday, 9 A.M.–8 P.M.).

Back on the Jardín de Libertad, at the cathedral-front, head north across Madero and explore the little block-long **Andando Constitución** pedestrian mall, one of Colima's charming little corners. Here you will find several interesting shops, and at the north end an excellent crafts store with a bountiful selection of reasonably priced folkcrafts. These include fine ceramic reproductions of Colima's beloved dogs.

Continue one block farther on Constitución to the University of Colima's art musuem, **Pinocoteca Universitaria** (corner of Guerrero, tel. 312/312-2228, 10 A.M.–2 P.M. and 5–8 P.M. Tues.–Sat., 10 A.M.–1 P.M. Sun.). Besides a permanent collection of historical works by local and nationally noted artists, including Sofia Bassi, José Clemente Orozco, and Dr. Atl, the museum schedules showings of contemporary paintings and photography.

Museo de Culturas Populares

For a look at more excellent regional crafts, continue along Constitución three more blocks north to Gallardo and then east a block to G. Barrera to the Museo de Culturas Populares (Calle Aldama and Avenida 27 de Septiembre, tel. 312/312-6869, 10 A.M.–2 P.M. and 4:30–7 P.M. Tues.–Sat.). Besides a folk-art sales shop (pottery, gourds, baskets, a loom, glassware) and several intriguing displays of masks (don't miss the scary horned crocodile-man) and ceremonial costumes, you can often watch potters and other artisans at work in the little house to the right of the museum entrance on Gallardo. The full name of the museum is Museo Universitario de Culturas Populares María Teresa Pomar.

◖ Museo de Culturas del Occidente

The prime repository of Colima's archaeological treasures is the landmark Museo de Culturas del Occidente (Museum of Cultures of the West; Ejercito Nacional, tel. 312/312-8431 or 312/312-3155, 9 A.M.–3 P.M. Mon.–Sat.). Walk or taxi northeast along the diagonal street E. Carranza to side street Ejercito Nacional, less than a mile (about one kilometer) from the town center. Inside the modern building, a spiral walkway leads you past artifact-illustrated displays of the history of Colima and surrounding regions. The exposition climaxes on the top floor with choirs of delightful classical Colima figurines: musicians tapping drums and fingering flutes, dancers circling, wrestlers grappling, and hosts of animals, including the all-time favorites, Colima dogs.

◖ La Campana Archaeological Zone

If you're not driving, walk or take a taxi a couple of miles northwest of the city center to the recently restored La Campana (The Lookout) Archaeological Zone (Av. Tecnología, tel. 312/313-4946, 10 A.M.–6 P.M. daily except Mon.). Head north about a mile from the city center; at main street Avenida Tecnología, turn left and continue about another mile, past the technological institute, to the archaeological zone on the right (north) side of the boulevard.

Although untold generations of local people, especially those of Villa Alvarez, have known that La Campana was a special place, serious studies of the site didn't get under way until about 1920. Engineer José María Gutiérrez first mapped the site in 1917, clearing the way for archaeologist Miguel Galindo, who led the first systematic excavation in 1922. Now, with the perspective of half a century of digging, investigators believe that La Campana reached its heyday around A.D. 800, when it was a complete town with ceremonial platforms, markets, a commercial area, schools, priests' and nobles' quarters, and residential zones for several thousand commoners. From physical remains—mainly pottery shards, implements, and small stone sculptures—experts furthermore conclude that the predominant culture of Campana's former inhabitants was Nahua (Aztec-speaking), although signs of other cultures are present.

The entire archaeological zone extends over an area of more than 120 acres, although the restored structures cover only about one-tenth of that. The main monument, the **Adoritorio Central,** is a 15-foot-high (five-meter), 50-foot (15-meter) square-based stone platform. Here, archaeologists uncovered a ritually interred skeleton, apparently a human sacrifice. A pair of secondary (lower, but larger in area) rectangular platform-complexes flank the Adoritorio. Experts believe that all of these platforms supported shrines dedicated to yet unknown gods or goddesses. Earthquakes, most investigators believe, led to the abandonment of La Campana by the time of the conquest.

Plenty is yet to be uncovered here, however. From atop the Adoritorio, between 100 and 300 yards toward the northeast, you might be able to make out the approximately eight additional unexcavated mounds scattered over the archaeological zone.

The Volcanoes

Although taller by about 1,130 feet, Nevado (Snowy One) de Colima is far quieter than his younger brother, Volcán de Fuego, one of the world's most active volcanoes. The **Volcán de Fuego** (Volcano of Fire, elev. 13,087 feet/3,989 meters) has erupted more than a dozen times since the conquest, continuously belching a stream of smoke and ash and frequently burping up red-hot boulders. The government seals the access road when a serious eruption is imminent.

If you want a close-up look at Volcán de Fuego, check with the state tourism office (in the plaza-front Palacio de Gobierno, downtown Colima, tel./fax 312/312-4360) for advice, pack everything you're going to need, and head out along Highway 54 *libre* (old nontoll route) northeast of Colima. Drive a high-clearance truck or van or ride a second-class bus from the Colima bus station. Pass Tonila (19 miles/30 km from Colima) to a dirt turnoff road 35 miles (near the Km 56 marker) from Colima. There, at a Telmex (Teléfonos de Mexico) *microndas* (microwave relay station) sign, take a sharp left toward the mountain. The Volcanic National Park boundary is a bumpy 17 miles (27 km) farther (although at this writing the road was closed at 11 kilometers from the entrance). How close you can actually get to the volcano depends on the authorities. A guided tour may get you closer.

The approach to the much quieter **Nevado de Colima** (elev. 14220 feet (3481 meters) is considerably more certain. The clear, dry winter months, when the views and the weather are the best, are Colima climbers' season of choice. This is wilderness mountain country, so you'll need to pack everything—winter sleeping bags, tents, alpine equipment, water, and food—that you'll require.

(An experienced guide, English-speaking French geophysicist Gilles Arfeuille, leads parties on Colima volcano explorations. For details, see *Ecoadventuring* in the *Manzanillo* section.)

The ascent, which begins at La Joya hut at around the 11,000-foot level, is not particularly difficult for experienced, fit hikers. The trail starts out leading for an easy hour to the microwave station at the tree line. Then it continues for a few hours of steep walking, except for a bit of scrambling at the end. Ice is a possibility all year-round, however, so carry crampons and ice axes and be prepared to use them. Climbers often tent overnight at La Joya, get an early morning start, and arrive at the summit before noon.

To get to Nevado de Colima, go by bus or drive a jeep, pickup, or rugged, high-clearance van. Head out northeast along Highway 54 *libre* past Tonila. Continue 39 miles (63 km) from Colima (a couple of miles past the Atenquique mining village), where Highway 54 *libre* interchanges with the Colima-Guadalajara *cuota* (toll) freeway 54 D. Fork left on Highway 54 *libre* toward Ciudad Guzmán (rather than straight ahead, toward Jiquilipan). After paralleling the freeway for about two miles, a small sign reading Fresnito at Km 66 marks a good gravel uphill road (about eight miles, 13 km)) to Fresnito. At Fresnito, head left another 17 very rough miles (27 km) farther to the Environmental Information Center (open Mon.–Fri. only at this writing). About two miles (three km) farther, you reach the gate at the Volcanic Observatory. Admittance may be possible by pre-arrangement with authorities in Ciudad Guzmán. Check with Colima Tourism, in Colima, for contact details.

Alternatively, on Highway 54, you can continue past the Fresnito sign several miles. Pass over the freeway 54 D. After a few more miles, turn left at the El Grullo sign. Pass under the freeway 54 D and continue until you see a Parque Nacional Nevado de Colima sign, where you turn left and continue 17 rough miles to La Joya.

By bus, from the Colima bus station, ride an early Autotransportes Sur de Jalisco or other bus to Ciudad Guzmán; transfer to a local bus to Fresnito, where you can thumb your way by truck uphill to La Joya.

ACCOMMODATIONS

Untouristed Colima has a sprinkling of good hotels. Some are city-style, downtown near the central plaza, and others are motel-style, in the suburbs. The prices quoted may be subject to discounts, which, under any conditions, you should always ask for: Say *"¿Hay descuento, por favor?"*

Under $50

Travelers looking for old-Mexico ambience on a budget might enjoy staying at posada-style **Hotel la Merced** (188 Hidalgo, Colima, Colima 28000, tel. 312/312-6969 or 312/314-2734, gerencia @hotellamerced.com.mx, $25 s or $30 d), just off shady Plaza Nuñes, five blocks west of the city center. Here, travelers have a choice of two connected sections: at Hidalgo 188, a dozen plainly furnished high-ceilinged rooms with baths around a homey, traditional inner patio, and at Juárez 82, a more conventional, modest, but still clean hotel with reception desk. Look at rooms in both sections.

If the Merced is full, for another budget choice, go about four blocks north (to Aldama), about eight blocks diagonally northwest (along Maclovio Herrera) to Centenario and the motel-style ("Don't look for stars") basic but clean **Hotel Río** (Centenario 289, Colima, Colima 28000, tel./fax 312/312-9607, $22 s, $26 d, $30 t, with a/c; $16 s, $22 d, $26 t, with fan only). Rooms, built around an inner garden patio, include hot water and parking.

Just two blocks east of the *jardín*, on busy city-center Madero, check out **Hotel Plaza Madero** (Madero 165, Colima, Colima 28000, tel. 312/330-2895, fax 312/330-2878, $37 s or d in one bed, $46 d in two beds, $59 t). The 16 newly decorated rooms open to a corridor that overlooks an inner commercial foyer-patio. Although dark, they are comfortably furnished and decorated with blue, handmade bedspreads, floor tile, attractive hand-hewn rustic wooden furniture, and shiny modern-standard shower baths. Tariffs include a/c, phones, and TV.

$50-100

Many business travelers stay at popular **Hotel América** (Morelos 162, Colima, Colima 28000, tel./fax 312/312-9596 or 312/314-4425, hotelamericacolima@hotmail.com, credit cards accepted, $60 for one–four standard grade, $92 for deluxe), three blocks from the city center. Outside, the facade is colonial; inside a two-story warren of rooms hides among a maze of glass-and-steel tropical terrariums. The rooms are spacious, carpeted, and comfortable. Lack of a pool is partially compensated for by a sauna (use of which is limited to mornings, however). One of Hotel América's pluses is its good restaurant, where patrons enjoy snappy service and tasty food at reasonable prices. The 70 rooms have king-sized or two beds, cable TV, a/c, phones, and parking, and limited lower-level wheelchair access.

The Best Western █ **Hotel Ceballos** (Portal Medillin 12, Colima, Colima 28000, tel. 312/312-4444, fax 312/312-0645, ventas@hotelceballos.com, www.hotelceballos.com, credit cards accepted, $80 s or d), right on the central plaza, offers a class-act alternative. Although recently renovated, the hotel retains its high ceilings and graceful colonial ambience. Ceballos offers tastefully decorated, clean, and comfortable air-conditioned rooms with TV. Rooms vary in size and ventilation; ask to see more than one before choosing. The owners have recently upgraded the hotel amenities considerably, adding a lovely top-floor sundeck, petite pool, airy sitting room, and small kiddie playground. Parking is included.

(You may also reserve the Hotel Ceballos from the U.S. and Canada, through Best Western toll-free tel. 800/782-7234, or www .bestwestern.com.)

█ **Hotel Los Candiles** (Blvd. Camino Real 399, Colima, Colima 28010, tel. 312/312-3212, fax 312/313-1707, www.hotelloscandiles .com, ventascandiles@hotmail.com, credit cards accepted, $58 economy s or d, $75 deluxe, suite $130) is about two miles northeast of the city center. It avoids the usual cluttered motel parking lot atmosphere by putting the swimming pool and patio at the center and the cars off to the side. An attractive tropical garden-style hotel is the result. Recently increased prices have led to greatly improved room quality, especially in the lower-priced standard-grade economy rooms. You more or less get what you pay for: Standard rooms, while clean and comfortable, are about Motel 6 size and decor. The deluxe grade are larger and more plush. All come with TV, phones, and restaurant breakfast included.

Neighboring motel-style **Hotel María Isabel** (Blvd. Camino Real 351, corner of Avenida Felipe Sevilla del Río, Colima, Colima 28010, tel. 312/312-6262 or 312/316-0750, fax 312/316 0751, gerencia@hotelmariaisabel.com.mx, www .hotelmariaisabel.com.mx, credit cards accepted, $87 standard s or d, $165 luxury) also appeals to families and RV and car travelers. Moreover, desk management, general hotel cleanliness, and accommodation quality have greatly improved in recent years. The double-story room tiers line a long parking lot edged on one side by a lawn and tropical foliage. A large pool and airy restaurant occupy one side near the entrance. The rooms come in standard and luxury versions. The standard rooms, although smaller, are nevertheless clean and deluxe. The luxury rooms are larger, with tonier decor. All come with parking.

FOOD
Breakfast, Snacks, and Bakery

A good place to start out the day is the restaurant at the **Hotel América** (Morelos 162, tel. 312/312-9596), open daily at 7 A.M. for breakfast, dinner served till 10 P.M., where the servers greet you with hot coffee and a cheery *"Buenos días."* The menu affords plenty of familiar fare, from fresh eggs any style to pancakes and fruit ($4–6).

After a few hours among the downtown sights, take a break at one of the sidewalk cafés bordering the Jardín de Libertad. First choice goes to the airy **Café de la Plaza** (at the Hotel Ceballos on the Jardín de Libertad, 7 A.M.– 10 P.M. daily). Here, high ceilings, graceful arches, and, if you choose, sidewalk tables add a touch of leisurely refinement to your breakfast or midday lunch break. The relatively short menu of breakfasts ($3–5), sandwiches,

tacos, and *tortas* ($3–5), and juices, desserts, and coffees ($1–3) is crisply served and reasonably priced.

Alternatively, you can sample the possibilities on the opposite side of the *jardín,* such as **Restaurant Portales** (south side of the *jardín*), where patrons enjoy either shady sidewalk tables or an upstairs balcony perch from which to take in the passing scene.

If you're in the mood for dessert, head east two blocks and sample the luscious baked offerings of **Panadería Viera** (east side of Plaza Torres Quintero, tel. 312/313-0017 9 A.M.– 9 P.M. Mon.–Sat., 9 A.M.–6 P.M. Sun.).

Restaurants

Starting downtown, at the southwest *jardín* corner, the strictly local **Restaurant El Trébol** (at the plaza's southwest corner of Degollado and Torres Quintero, tel. 312/312-2900, 8 A.M.– 11 P.M. Mon.–Sat.) offers hearty breakfasts, lunches, and dinners. Especially popular with the downtown shopping and business crowd is the *comida corrida* (traditional multiple-course set lunch, about $4), and *antojitos* and *pozole* nights.

Equally good for breakfast, lunch, or dinner is the mid- to upper-class (**Los Naranjos** (The Orange Trees; 34 Gabino Barreda, between Madero and Zaragoza, tel. 312/312-7316 or 312/312-0029, 8 A.M.–11:30 P.M. daily). Los Naranjos's relaxed, refined ambience— try the airy back patio—and eclectic menu (salads, sandwiches, tacos, enchiladas, meats, and poultry $3–10), professionally prepared and presented, have ensured a legion of loyal customers since 1956.

Unpretentiously lovely restaurant (**El Charco de la Higuera** (at old San José church, six blocks west from the *jardín*, along the westward extension of Madero, tel. 312/313-0192, 8 A.M.–midnight daily) is a perfect spot for soaking up the charm of traditional Mexico. Its graceful setting at the leafy edge of an old church plaza, with a bubbling fountain and a shady veranda, and its long list of *típico* Mexican specialties provide all the ingredients for a leisurely breakfast, lunch, or dinner ($5–12).

If, however, you hanker for familiar food in polished, air-conditioned surroundings, head for the local branch of **VIPs** (on east-side Calz. Galvan, just a block downhill from Allende, in front of the Wal-Mart, tel. 312/313-0633, 7 A.M.–11 P.M. Sun.–Thurs., 7 A.M.–2 A.M. Fri.–Sat., entrées $4–8), the Mexican (although classier) version of Denny's.

ENTERTAINMENT AND EVENTS
Fiestas
Local folks compensate for the lack of night-life by whooping it up during Colima's major local festivals. Don't miss them if you happen to be in town.

For nine days beginning Jan. 23, people celebrate the **Fiesta de la Virgen de la Salud,** which climaxes on Feb. 2. The church (Iglesia de la Salud) neighborhood, near Avs. Gallardo and Corregidora, blooms with colorful processions, bands, food, and crafts stalls, and the church plaza resounds with music, folk dancing, and fireworks.

Ever since 1820 the Villa de Alvarez (a suburb a few miles northwest of the city center) has staged **Fiesta Charrotaurina,** a 15-day combination rodeo/bullfight/carnival. The celebration wouldn't be as much fun if the Villa de Alvarez people stayed to themselves. Every day, however, Feb. 7–23 around noon, a troupe of Villa de Alvarez musicians, cowboys, cowgirls, papier-mâché bulls, and a pair of *mojigangos* (giant effigies of the Colima governor and spouse) assemble on Colima's downtown Jardín de Libertad. The music begins, the *mojigangos* start whirling, and a big crowd of bystanders follows them back to Villa de Alvarez.

Visitors who miss the Virgen de la Salud in January can get in on the similar **Fiesta de San José,** which culminates on March 19 in the west-side neighborhood of the Iglesia de San José (corner Quintero and Suárez) with a host of traditional foodstalls, regional folk dancing, and religious processions.

During the fall, Colima heats up again for the **Feria Todos Santos/Día de los Muertos** (All Saints/Day of the Dead) fair, from the last Saturday of October to the second Sunday of November. Most events and merrymaking take place at the Parque Niños Héroes, known locally as El Rodeo, about three miles (five km) east of town along the extension of Avenida Niños Héroes.

Live Music and Dance
Right downtown, some cafés and restaurants offer live music around the plaza. The most reliable is the **Café de la Plaza,** tel. 312/312-4444, that offers guitar and keyboard melodies nightly, beneath the plaza-front portal of Hotel Ceballos.

The University of Colima has an active folkloric ballet group that performs seasonally. Check with the tourist information office (pick up its "Agenda Cultural" events schedule; see *Information and Services*), or call the ballet director, tel. 312/312-5140, for information.

SHOPPING
Handicrafts
Reliable downtown shops sell a wide variety of local and all-Mexico handicrafts. Most renowned are the locally crafted ceramic reproductions of Colima's charming pre-Columbian animal and human figurines.

One of the best sources is the state-operated **Casa de las Artesanías** (at the uphill end of Andando Constitución, corner of Avenida Zaragoza, tel. 312/314-4790, 10 A.M.–2 P.M. and 5–8 P.M. Mon.–Sat., 10 A.M.–2 P.M. Sun.), near the Jardín de Libertad. They stock a wealth of locally crafted figurines, plus shelves of handicrafts gathered from all over Mexico, such as sombreros, *huipiles,* serapes, toys, and Christmas decorations. Other local items include Colima coffee beans, regional cuisine cookbooks, and coconut candy.

A few doors down the Andador Constitución, a pair of privately owned shops, **El Mejor** (tel. 312/312-8350, 10 A.M.–2:30 P.M. and 5–8:30 P.M. Mon.–Sat., 11 A.M.–2 P.M. Sun.) and **Casa Méxicana** (no phone, 10 A.M.–2 P.M. and 4–9 P.M. Mon.–Sat., 11 A.M.–2 P.M. Sun.) also offer attractive handicrafts selections.

Across the *andador,* take a look inside at the broad and unusual handicrafts selection at **Big Dog** (tel. 312/312-0005, 10 A.M.–2 P.M. and

4:30–8:30 P.M. Mon.–Sat.), with much women's wear, from handsome embroidered *huipiles* and eye-catching blouses, pants, and dresses, to cool, pastel resort wear. As a bonus, check out the shelf of English used paperback books.

Finally, arrive at the andador's downhill end, at **Artesanías Ceballos,** an annex of the adjacent Hotel Ceballos. Here, pick from a treasury of women's wear, both traditional and up-to-date chic, and also select your favorite dozen from the seemingly endless collection of appealing Colima ceramic figurines.

If, however, you prefer to buy your ceramics directly from the artisan, go to the **Museo de Culturas Populares** (Avs. Gallardo and Barreda, tel. 312/312-6869, 10 A.M.–2 P.M. Tues.–Fri., 10 A.M.–1 P.M. Sat.), four blocks north of the *jardín*. Here, you can sometimes watch potters reproducing Colima's captivating animal and human figurines. If no artisans are available, the museum shop inside sells their work, plus many other folk crafts, including wooden toys and plenty of ceremonial masks.

Photography

Get your film developed in an hour and buy film and basic camera supplies at **Foto Carmen,** on the *jardín* (northwest corner of Degollado and Madero, tel. 312/314-0066, 9 A.M.–2 P.M. and 4:30–8 P.M. Mon.–Sat.)

INFORMATION AND SERVICES
Tourist Information Office

The efficient and helpful staff of the *oficina de turismo,* inside the Palacio de Gobierno, east side of the *jardín* (tel. 312/316-2021, fax 312/312-4360, turiscol@correo.col.gob.mx, www.visita colima.com.mx, 9 A.M.–8 P.M., daily except Sun.) answer questions and hand out a good Colima map and excellent color brochures.

Publications

English newspapers and magazines are rare in Colima. Nevertheless, the plaza-front newsstand, Las Palmeras, tucked four doors down the block from the Hotel Ceballos stocks the English-language *Miami Herald* and several American magazines. Find it open daily 8 A.M.–11 P.M.

Money Exchange

Several banks, all with ATMs, serve downtown customers. The **Banamex** downtown branch, at Hidalgo 90, just two blocks east of the *jardín,* tel. 312/312-9820, exchanges U.S. and Canadian currency and traveler's checks Mon.–Fri. 9 A.M.–4 P.M. If Banamex lines are too long, walk a block north to **Bancomer,** at Madero 106, corner of Obregón, tel. 312/314-6843, open Mon.–Fri. 8:30 A.M.–4 P.M., Sat. 10 A.M.–2 P.M.; or another block east to **HSBC,** at Madero 183, tel. 312/312-3623 or 312/312-3624, open Mon.–Sat. 8 A.M.–7 P.M.

After bank hours, try one of the nearby *casas de cambio,* on Madero, such as **Casa de Cambio USA-Mex.,** tel. 312/312-9230, at the corner of 27 de Septiembre and Madero, open Mon.–Sat. 9 A.M.–8 P.M. and Sun. 9 A.M.–2 P.M.

Communications

The main *correo* (post office), tel. 312/312-0033, is open Mon.–Fri. 8 A.M.–6 P.M., Sat. 8 A.M.–noon, on Madero at Plaza Nuñez, four blocks east of the *jardín,* by the Palacio Federal. For simple letter mailing, use the *buzón* (mailbox) on the Andador Constitución.

For **telephone,** local or long-distance, buy a **Ladatel** phone card (look for the small blue and yellow signs) on the plaza and use it in the public street telephone. (For long-distance in Mexico, first dial 01, then the area code and local number. For Canada and the United States, first dial "001," then the number.)

Or you can use the *larga distancia* and fax in the little office (open daily 7 A.M.–10 P.M.) beneath the portal on the south side of the *jardín;* or the Caseta Colima in the Andador Constitución, tel. 312/314-1664, open Mon.–Sat. 8:30 A.M.–8:30 P.M.

Connect to the Internet at **CI@ Internet,** Reforma 63 upstairs, just downhill from the southwest plaza corner, tel. 312/330-1547, open daily 8 A.M.–9 P.M.

MANZANILLO AND COLIMA

Health, Police, and Emergencies

The respected private hospital, **Centro Médico,** at Maclovio Herrera 140, a quarter mile north of Jardín de Libertad, tel. 312/312-4044, 312/312-4045, or 312/312-4046, has emergency service and many specialists on 24-hour call.

The **Super Farmacia,** tel. 312/312-0031 or 312/312-5537, on the *jardín,* offers a large stock of medicines and drugs. Open Mon.–Sat. 7 A.M.–11 P.M., Sun. 8 A.M.–10:30 P.M.

The **Cabercera Policia** (police headquarters), tel. 312/313-1434, is on the north side of town, at (take a taxi) Roberto Esperón 1152, in Colonia Trabajadores.

For **fire** emergencies, call the *bomberos* (firefighters), tel. 312/312-5858, off Ejercito Nacional, a block north of the Museum of the Cultures of the West.

Travel Agency

For tickets, tours, and car rentals, go to the excellent **Vamos A** (We're Going) travel agency, tel. 312/314-9600 or 312/314-9700, open Mon.–Fri. 9 A.M.–2 P.M. and 4–7:30 P.M., Sat. 9 A.M.–2 P.M., at Independencia 51, two blocks south of the *jardín.* Alternatively, try **Turisste Colima** on the Andador Constitución, northeast corner of the *jardín,* tel. 312/314-3592 or 312/314-3593; open Mon.–Fri. 9 A.M.–6 P.M.

GETTING THERE AND AWAY
By Car or RV

The Manzanillo-Colima combined Highways 200 and 110 *autopista* makes Colima safely accessible from Manzanillo in about 1.5 hours. From Manzanillo, follow the *cuota* (toll) Highway 200 (34 miles, 54 km) southeast to the Highway 110 junction near Tecomán. Branch north, continuing on Highway 110 for another 25 miles (40 km) to Colima.

To Guadalajara from Colima, drive to the east side of town, where entrance ramps lead you on to the combined Highway 110-54D *autopista* freeway for an easy drive three hours north to Guadalajara.

For southeast coastal destinations, such as Playa Azul and Zihuatanejo, follow Highway 110 south, then fork southeast to Highway 200 at Tecomán and continue along the coast about six hours to Playa Azul (eight to Zihuatanejo).

By Bus

The airy, airport-style *central camionera* (central bus station), on the Highway 110 *libramiento* (bypass) east of town, is the Colima point of departure for several good first- and luxury-class bus lines. The terminal has a number of services, including a tourist information booth, hotel reservations, trinket shops, travel agent, and luggage storage. The ticketing is efficiently computerized, and major lines accept credit cards. A continuous procession of **local** and **semilocal buses,** destinations marked on their windshields, stop out in front.

Estrella Blanca and its associated lines, **Elite,** and **Futura** (tel. 312/312-8499) provide connections northwest, with Mexicali and Tijuana at the U.S. border via Ciudad Guzman, Tepic, and Mazatlán, and northeast (via Futura), with Mexico City (Norte) direct.

First-class **Omnibus de Mexico** buses (tel. 312/314-7190 or 312/312-1630) connect north with Guadalajara. From there they continue north via Durango to the U.S. border at Ciudad Juárez, or northeast via Aguascalientes, Monterrey, and Matamoros and Nuevo Laredo at the U.S. border.

La Linea buses (tel. 312/314-8179) provide frequent first-class connections with Manzanillo in the southwest, Guadalajara in the north and Mexico City (Observatorio) via Michoacán destinations of Uruapan and Morelia. It also provides first-class connections, via Tecomán, southeast, with La Mira (Playa Azul) and Lázaro Cárdenas. Autovias del Occidente, furthermore, provides connections northeast, through northern Michoacán, via Mazamitla, Jiquilipan, Zamora, Quiroga, and Morelia.

Flecha Amarilla (tel. 312/314-8067) and its subsidiary *servicios coordinados* lines provide "Primera-plus" luxury-class and first-class direct connections north with Guadalajara, Aguascalientes, and León, northeast with Mexico City, and southwest with Manzanillo, continuing, via Barra de Navidad-Melaque, to Puerto Vallarta. Second-class departures also connect frequently northwest with Jalisco and Michoacán destinations of Tamazula, Mazamitla, Jiquilipan,

Zamora, and Irapuato, continuing via Querétero, to Mexico City. Other second-class departures connect southwest via Tecomán, with Manzanillo, and southeast, with San Juan de Alima.

The airline-style, luxury-class buses of **Enlaces Transportes Nacionales (ETN)** (tel. 312/312-5899 or 312/314-1060) connect directly north with Guadalajara, southwest with Manzanillo and Puerto Vallarta, and east with Michoacán destinations of Uruapan and Morelia, continuing to Mexico City (Norte).

Autotransportes Sur de Jalisco (tel. 312/312-0316) provides regional second-class connections northeast with Guadalajara via Ciudad Guzman, southwest with Manzanillo, and southeast with La Mira (Playa Azul) and Lázaro Cárdenas, where you can continue to Zihuatanejo and Acapulco.

NORTH-SIDE FOOTHILL COUNTRY EXCURSION

By car or local bus from downtown, head out on the Comala road toward the foothills north-

© BRUCE WHIPPERMAN

Strolling mariachis entertain at Comala's plaza-front restaurants.

west of the city, where your first reward will be ever-closer views of the volcanoes. **Comala town,** nestling above a lush stream valley about six miles from Colima, has always been a local Sunday favorite.

◖ Hacienda Noguera

If you have an extra hour, reverse your path downhill and turn left at the Hacienda Noguera–signed road that heads left (east) just downhill from town. In a few miles, you'll come to the venerable 18th-century Hacienda Noguera, where the University of Colima has established a new campus, centering on historical, archaeological, and anthropological studies. An especially exquisite small museum, the **Museo Alejandro Rangel Hidalgo** (tel. 312/315-6028, 10 A.M.–2 P.M. and 4:30–7 P.M. Tues.–Fri., 10 A.M.–6 P.M. Sat. and Sun.), features artifacts and art from the estate of Comala collector/artist Alejandro Rangel Hidalgo. The exhibitions climax in a collection of exceptionally fine and lovable Colima ceramic dogs.

Hacienda San Antonio

Continuing uphill from Comala, the road leads past green pastures and groves, through the village of Cofradia de Suchitlán. Soon the road divides. Take the left fork and continue down a jungly, lava-cliffed canyon to Hacienda San Antonio, about 20 miles (32 km) from Colima.

(Unfortunately, the recently restored hacienda is marked only by a guarded gate. A roadside earth levee hides a trove of charming old-Mexico scenes inside: Water gurgles from the ancient aqueduct, a stone chapel dedicated to San Antonio stands intact, and a massive gate and wall, like a medieval keep, still protect the inhabitants from long-forgotten marauders.)

The latecomer owners, family of the late British multimillionaire Sir James Goldsmith, have recently renovated the hacienda into a superexclusive hotel, replete with restored old-world details.

Paying guests at Hacienda San Antonio (tel. 312/316-0300, toll-free Mex. tel.

01-800/590-3845, toll-free U.S. tel. 866/516-2611, fax 312/316-0301, reservations@ haciendadesanantonio.com, www.haciendade sanantonio.com, $650 d low season, and up daily), of course, get to see all the hidden treasures. Low-season (June 1–Sept. 30) rates, including all meals, beverages, and in-house activities, run about $650 d for standard suites and $1,000 d for grand suites; medium-season (Oct. 1–Dec. 15), about $800 and $1,400, and high season (Dec. 16–May 30) $850 and $1,600.

Ejido and Laguna la María

A gravel road continues uphill from Hacienda San Antonio a few miles farther to the mountainside Shangri-La Ejido la María (tel. 312/320-8891, $50– 60 bungalow, $8 RV site, $8 tent site). Past a gate (where you pay $1 per person to park), a walking trail downhill leads past tidy vegetable fields to the idyllic shoreline of natural Laguna la María. Here, weekend and holiday visitors enjoy picnicking and camping beneath the spreading boughs of a venerable lakeside grove. At other times, walk-in campers often enjoy nearly complete solitude. Bring everything, including water-purifying tablets, insect repellent, and tents for possible rain, especially during the summer. The 4,000-foot (1,200-meter) elevation produces usually balmy days and mild nights.

For noncampers, the *ejido* (communal farm) offers five clean, rustic bungalows on the hillside above the lake, with complete kitchens (bring your food), flush toilets, and hot water for $50 to $60 per night. Call for reservations (ask for a discount). Self-contained RVs may park hereabouts (but not at the lake) for about $8 per car; tent spaces go for the same. Given the general friendliness of the local *ejido* folks, visitors who enjoy the sunny outdoors by day and mountain stillness by night could spend a few very enjoyable days at Laguna la María.

Centro Turístico Carrizalillos

Centro Turistico Carrizalillos (Little Reeds Tourist Center; tel. 312/320-9596, $5 tent/RV site) offers yet another outdoor possibility. Back at the fork, two miles uphill past Cofradia de Suchitlán, head right. After about two more miles, follow the signed driveway off to the right. The Carrizalillos campsites spread for about a mile around the circumference of an oak-studded ridge that encloses a small volcanic crater lake. The few dozen developed campsites (picnic tables, water, pit toilets), some suitable for small-to-medium RVs, rent for about $5 a day. A rustic view **Restaurant Portales del Volcán** occupies a lakeside hilltop, and a dozen unkempt (at this writing) housekeeping cabins overlook the lake. In season—Easter and Christmas weeks and July–August—horses ($10/hour) and boats ($4/hour) are available. Given the magnificent mountain and valley views, the volcano's reflections in the azure lake (if the water level is up), and the fresh air, Carrizalillos might be just right for a cool, restful change of pace.

Handicrafts

On your stroll around the Comala plaza, a trio of **handicrafts** shops that deserve a look include **Jaime's,** at the plaza corner of V. Carranza and Aquiles Serdán; **Artesanías la Mexicanía,** at Llerenas (Yay-RAY-nahs) number 2, on the left, as you face the plaza churchfront, open daily except Monday, 11 A.M.–7 P.M., tel. 312/315-6040; and **Artesanías Regional,** down the street, at 42 Llerenas, open 9 A.M.–3 P.M. and 5–7 P.M. daily except Sun.

Also, on the Colima road, at the downhill edge of town, be sure to stop by the roadside stalls of the local woodworkers' cooperative **Cooperativa Artesanal Pueblo.** Their specialty is furniture, adorned with the flower-, bird-, and children-motif decorations of painter Alejandro Rangel Hidalgo.

Accommodations

If you decide to linger overnight, a number of distinguished family homes have been refurbished as *hostales* (small inns) and **bed and breakfasts.** Although all are recommendable, with modern-standard baths and hot water, some do stand out. Breakfast is included in all of the following:

The young enterprising husband-wife owners of the fancy (but smallish) Casa Alvarada (105 Obregón, Colima 28450, cellular tel. 312/315-5229, dial locally 044-312/111-6198, casa_alvarada@hotmail.com, www.casaalvarada.com, $55 d) offer two lovely, art-decorated rooms, with a/c.

Also consider homey and spacious **Hostal El Naranjo** (Ocampo 39, Comala, Colima 28450, tel. 312/315-5541 and 312/315-5759, $35 d), with three comfortable rooms, set around around a garden of fragrant orange and lemon trees; likewise you might check out the similarly airy **Hostal Comalli** (near the Casa de Cultura, six blocks from the plaza on Reforma 193, Comala, Colima 28450, Colima, tel. 312/315-5729, in the uphill district, $55 d). The family owners offer two large, comfortable villa-suites, one with an airy private balcony, opening to a lovely inner fruit-tree garden patio.

Food and Entertainment

Continue from Colima, uphill about six miles (nine km) to the Comala town center, where cares seem to float away in the orange blossom—scented air around the picture-perfect old plaza. Mariachis stroll every afternoon and airy plaza-front restaurants serve *botanas* (snacks) free with drinks (which should include at least one obligatory glass of local *ponche* fruit wine.)

Perhaps take a table beneath the portal of the most popular (often with lots of mariachi trumpets) block-long restaurant **Don Comalón,** or alternatively, the smaller, more subdued **Los Portales** at the adjacent corner.

For dessert, sample some *típico* **Comala sweet bread,** and a good cup of coffee (.$50 solo, $1 with a shot of *rompope* egg nog) and perhaps pick up some fresh-roasted local coffee beans ($2/pound), at **Cafetería Comala** (Degollado 25, 9 A.M.–9 P.M. daily).

SOUTHERN EXCURSIONS

The valley of Colima has a number of important archaeological sites. One of the most accessible and scenic is at **Tampumachay,** near the village of Los Ortices, eight miles south of Colima city.

The **Centro Turístico Tampumachay** (P.O. Box 149, Colima, Colima 28000, cellular tel. 044-312/317-2381 or 044-312/339-3235, $33d, $38 q), a shady green miniresort, accommodates visitors with a modest five-room hotel, two swimming pools, a rope bridge, a restaurant, and a camping area. It was developed originally by archaeologist Fidencio Perbez of Colima, and the present owners continue his policy of careful custodianship of the nearby ruins.

The archaeological zone surrounds the hotel, whose grounds perch at the edge of a spectacularly deep, rock-studded river gorge. Paths wind past intriguing animal- and human-motif petroglyph-sculptures and descend into tombs littered with grave pottery and human bones. Guides point out the remains of an unexcavated ceremonial platform on the opposite side of the canyon. The tombs and petroglyphs are well preserved, since local people, fearing dire ghostly consequences, generally leave the site alone.

Other local excursions include exploration of a limestone cave a couple of miles past the archaeological zone and wildlife-viewing hikes down into the gorge by a trail near the hotel. The Tampumachay resort itself is a lovely, tree-shaded garden, with artifact-dotted paths, a Tarzan-style rope suspension bridge, view gazebos, and pool-decks perfect for snoozing. (**Note:** Recently, access to the archaeological zone that surrounds the Tampumachay resort has been closed to non-guided visitors. Groups with properly certified guides may be permitted, however. Check with the government Tourist Information Offices in Manzanillo and Colima, and see the *Ecoadventuring* section in the *Manzanillo* section for guide recommendations.)

The five thoughtfully decorated, rustic beamed-ceilinged rooms rent for about $33 d (in one double bed), $38 (two double beds for up to four people), with shower and fan. A four-room cabin with communal kitchen and campsites for tents and (self-contained) RVs are also available. Reservations are usually not necessary except during holidays.

Getting There

Eight miles (13 km) along Highway 110 south of Colima city, at the Km 12 marker, just past the gas station, turn left, east, at the big Los Asmoles sign. Head uphill toward Los Ortices for 2.5 miles (4 km), and then turn right at a dirt road just before Los Ortices village. After about 200 yards, a sign directs you left to Tampumachay.

Northbound, toward Colima, take the right turnoff near Km 14, signed Los Asmoles. Continue about one mile (1.5 km), past the signed Rancho; turn right at the next paved side road.

An interesting western excursion from Colima could include Agua Fria natural spring, the Manantlán cloud forest ecoreserve, and El Salto waterfall near Minatitlán.

South Colima Beaches

The road south of Manzanillo leads the way to a necklace of south Colima minihavens for lovers of easy tropical living. First along the path is Cuyutlán, an antique little downscale resort, rich in history, and with something for everyone, from wildlife-viewing and beach RVing and tenting to good eating and old-fashioned peace and quiet.

Antique, wooden salt warehouses still store the salt harvests on the lagoon in Cuyutlán.

CUYUTLÁN

Little Cuyutlán (pop. 2,000) is heaven for lovers of nostalgia and tranquility. No raucous hangouts clutter its lanes; no rock, techno, or rap bounces from its few cafés. Sun, sand, and gentle surf are its prime amenities. Rickety wooden walkways lead across its hot dark sands to a line of beachfront umbrellas, where you can rent a chair for the day, enjoy the breeze, and feast on the seafood offerings of seaside kitchens.

Most of Cuyutlán's hotels, restaurants, and services lie along a single street: Hidalgo, which runs from the *jardín* (on the Manzanillo-Armería road) a few blocks, crossing Avenida Veracruz and ending at the beachfront *malecón*.

The shady, cobbled side streets of Cuyutlán invite impromptu exploring. Near the beach, lanes lead past weathered wooden houses and *palapas* (some for rent). On the inland side of the *jardín* near the rail station, kerosene lamps flicker at night through the wood-stick walls of village houses. The station itself is an antique out of the Porfirian age, with the original iron columns still supporting its moss-streaked, gabled platform roof. Nearby, hulking wooden (exotically unusual in Mexico) salt warehouses line an earthen street. Those ancient repositories are reminders of the old tradition of salt harvesting at the edges of nearby Cuyutlán lagoon. Peek through the cracks in the rickety warehouse walls and you'll see the salt—huge white piles, looking exactly like *nieve* (snow) from the heights of the Nevado de Colima.

© BRUCE WHIPPERMAN

◖ Museo de Sal

Local authorities have, very appropriately, turned one of those old warehouses into a museum, the Museo de Sal (The Salt Museum), a block north of the *jardín*. Around the walls inside, displays describe the last 1,000 years of local history, and a model in the middle of the room demonstrates the laborious salt-extraction process. First, workers filled pottery jars with salt-laden brine from *tajos* (shallow wells) near the naturally salty Laguna de Cuyutlán. By hand, they lifted the brine several feet to the top of a *cujete* (leaching bed). After percolating through the *cujete,* the enriched brine gathered in a ground-level *toza* (collection basin). Workers then carried jars full of brine to nearby rectangular salt-diked *planes* (concentration pans) where the sun evaporated the remaining water, leaving pure white sea salt. They sell bags of it in the museum for less than a dollar.

The Green Wave

Cuyutlán's latter-day claim to fame is the mysterious Green Wave, which is said to occasionally rise offshore and come crashing down from a height of 20, 30, or even 50 feet. (The later at night the story is told, it seems, the greater the height.)

The origin of the Green Wave's color is also a mystery, although some local aficionados speculate that an offshore algae bloom might be responsible.

The source of the legend is real, however. On June 22, 1932, a gigantic 60-foot-high *maremoto* (tsunami) came close to washing Cuyutlán off the map. The wave reared from the sea, smashing everything on the beach and flooding the rest of the town.

Although several faithful still apprehensively scan the horizon during the most likely month of May, nothing like the 1932 tidal wave has occurred since. Some suggest that the 1978 local earthquake may have shifted the ocean bottom and quieted the Green Wave (temporarily, at least). The Hotel Morelos, at the corner of Hidalgo and Veracruz, displays, in addition to its lobby gallery of James Dean and Marilyn Monroe photos, a snapshot of an alleged 20-foot Green Wave by local photographer and enthusiast Eduardo Lolo.

Campamento Tortuguero de Cuyutlán

Cuyutlán has its own member of the growing roll of Pacific Mexico turtle-saving encampments. Find it by following main street Avenida Veracruz south; after about eight blocks, jog right, then left, and continue (where the street becomes Avenida López Mateos) for a total of 2.5 miles (4 km). At the end of the road you'll arrive at the government-sponsored encampment, known officially as the **Centro de Desarrollo Productivo, Recreativo, y Ecológico de Cuyutlán** (Cuyutlán Center for Productive, Recreative, and Ecological Development; south end of Avenida López Mateos, 8:30 A.M.–5 P.M. daily, admission $1.50).

Inside the gate, the center staff gladly explain their manifold educational, scientific, economic, and ecological mission. They have made an excellent start. They have been returning more than 50,000 hatchling turtles to the sea annually since the program started in 1995. The turtle hatchery (which now includes iguanas and crocodiles), where they incubate

the eggs that they rescue from poachers, is beneath the big tent on the beach.

Three turtle species arrive during the July–November hatching season: the **olive ridley** (*golfina*, or *Lepidochelys olivacea); the* **Pacific green** (*tortuga negra*, or black turtle, as it's known in Mexico—*Chelonia agassizi*); and, most notably, the **leatherback** (*tortuga de cuero—Dermochelys coriacea*). (See the sidebar *Saving Turtles* in *The Jalisco Coast* chapter.)

Project staff also try to educate everyone—most important, a steady flow of local schoolchildren and teachers—both about saving turtles specifically and threatened plants and wildlife in general. Animal enclosures and tanks of a (thankfully) few fish, turtles, crocodiles, iguanas, and more serve as examples.

The Campamento Tortuguero's efforts also extend to guiding visitors on **wildlife-viewing boat tours** in the adjacent lagoon ($4 adults, $3 kids—watch for the 10-foot crocodiles!) during the Dec.–May waterfowl season. Visitors are invited to take a dip in the Campamento's **blue swimming pools,** have a *refresco,* and enjoy a picnic lunch beneath the *palapa.*

Beaches

Cuyutlán's wide and seemingly endless beach invites a number of activities and sports. The nearly level offshore slope produces little undertow, so wading and swimming conditions are ideal. The waves, which roll in gradually, are fine for boogie boarding, bodysurfing, and all levels of surfing, depending on the size of the swells. Bring your own surfboard, although boogie board rentals are available on the beach. Shells become more common the farther you stroll away from the few picked-over blocks of beach.

As for fishing, the shallow slope decreases the chances for successful surf-casts. Hire or launch your boat (easy in calm weather) and head to the happy fishing grounds beyond the waves.

Accommodations

Bargain-rate **Hotel Posada San Miguel** (Av. Hidalgo, Cuyutlán, Colima 28350, tel. 313/326-4062, posadasanmiguel@prodigy

© BRUCE WHIPPERMAN

Quaint wooden walkways lead to the beach in Cuyutlán.

.net.mx, $10 pp low season, $15 high), across Hidalgo from the Hotel Morelos, has bright, comfortable upstairs rooms that open onto a shady sitting porch overlooking the street. The eight rooms come with hot water and fans.

Across the street, the **Hotel Morelos** (Hidalgo 185, Cuyutlán, Colima 28350, tel. 313/326-4013, $12 s, $24 d low season, $30 pp all-inclusive in during fiestas), founded in the 1890s, continues Cuyutlán's antique century-old antique tradition with its long (quaintly downhill-sloping) lobby, decorated with plastic flowers and white Grecian columns. The hotel has added an inviting new patio, built around a designer blue pool. Rooms, moreover, have been redecorated with elegant, hand-carved wooden beds and doors. Most rooms, however, are dark, and many are stuffy; look at more than one before moving in. The family owners top all this off with hearty local-style food, which they serve in the hotel restaurant. The Morelos's 40 rooms come with hot water and fans. During the superhigh Christmas and Easter weeks, and the Mother's Day weekend

in June, rates run $30 per day per person, including three meals.

Across the street toward the beach stands the also venerable ((**Hotel Fénix** (Hidalgo 201, Cuyutlán, Colima 28350, tel./fax 313/326-4082, hotelfenixcuyutlan@yahoo.com, www.cuyutlandirectory.com, credit cards accepted, $13 s, $26 d, $40 d with a/c), whose patrons likewise enjoy a good open-air, street-level restaurant. Olivia and Geoffrey, husband-wife owners (she's Mexican, he's American), have completely redecorated the two dozen rooms, scattered along upstairs corridors, in attractive natural wood with billowing white cotton curtains. The result is pleasingly light, airy, and traditional. Rooms have fans and hot-water shower baths. For more light and privacy, ask for one of the upstairs rooms.

New owners have likewise rejuvenated Cuyutlán's biggest hostelry (formerly the Hotel Ceballos), now the **Hotel María Victoria** (Veracruz 10, Cuyutlán, Colima 28350, tel. 313/326-4004, fax 313/326-4023, $43 s, $47 d; $85 during fiestas), fronting the beach at the foot of Hidalgo. Inside, the airy, cream-tinted lobby towers to a fluted concrete roof-shell like a giant spaceship hangar. It encloses a curious cylindrical central tier of rooms that resemble a flying saucer waiting to whisk a few chosen guests to an Encounter of the Third Kind. But never mind; simply rent one of the many comfortable, attractive pink-and-white pastel rooms that surround the entire lobby in three stories. Ask for a room on the oceanfront *(frente el mar)* side, and enjoy your own breezy sea-view balcony. The 80 rooms rent for about $43 s, $47 d all year, except around Christmas and Easter, when tariffs rise to about $85 per room for up to four people, with hot water, fans, beachview restaurant, and a small beach-front pool.

Down the beach, a block south of the Hotel María Victoria, stands the luxuriously situated beachfront **C Hotel San Rafael** (Av. Vera-cruz y Piño Suárez, Cuyutlán, Colima 28350, tel. 313/326-4015, fax 312/312-0319, info@ hotelsanrafael.com, www.hotelsanrafael.com/ cuyutlan.html, $43 s, $46 d). Besides its invit-ing big blue swimming pool, the hotel offers 30 simply furnished rooms (a few with hand-carved wood and reading lamps), six of which have spacious, breezy, semiprivate second- and third-floor ocean-view porches. Downstairs, a shady open-air restaurant overlooks the beach and waves beyond. Rooms come with fans and hot water; bargain for a lower long-term rate. Reserve your room *arriba con vista del mar* (up-stairs with ocean view).

LONG-TERM APARTMENT AND HOUSE RENTALS

If you'd like to linger in Cuyutlán a few weeks or more, contact the co-owner of the Hotel Fénix, **Olivia Ramírez** (tel./fax 313/326-4082, hotelfenixcuyutlan@hotmail.com, www .cuyutlandirectory.com), who manages a num-ber of beachfront rental properties.

CAMPING AND RV PARKING

Tent campers who desire company stay at the beachfront **Centro Turístico las Cabañas** (about six blocks southeast of the town cen-ter), on the way to the Campamento Tortu-guero. Tariffs run about $10 per group, with showers, toilets, shady picnic *palapas,* a kiddie pool, and a mini-mart.

On the other hand, campers who hanker for privacy can follow dirt roads that lead to miles of open beach, good for camping or park-ing, on both sides of town. (Be careful of soft sand, however.) Cuyutlán, being a generally friendly, upright, country place, will ordinarily present no security problem. If in doubt, how-ever, don't hesitate to ask local shopkeepers. Say, *"¿Está bueno acampar acá?"* (ehs-TAH boo-EY-noh ah-kam-PAHR ah-KAH?).

Food

Besides the good restaurants at the Hotels Mo-relos, Fénix, and San Rafael, the main Cuyutlán eateries are the many seafood vendors, whose semipermanent umbrella-covered establish-ments do big business on holidays and week-ends. Quality of the fare—oyster cocktails, grilled or boiled shrimp and lobster, and fried fish—is generally excellent, since many of them depend on loyal repeat customers.

For groceries, try **Abarrotes Baby** (at the *jardín,* corner Hidalgo).

Information and Services

Most of Cuyutlán's businesses are spread along Hidalgo between the beach and the *jardín.* At the *jardín,* corner Hidalgo, is the **Farmacia Carmen,** open daily 9 A.M.–2 P.M. and 4–9 P.M. Up the street, at 144 Hidalgo, the mu-nicipal *policía* (police), tel. 313/326-4114, are on duty round the clock. Downhill, a block from the *jardín,* Manzanillo direction, is the **Centro de Salud** (health center), open rou-tinely until 5 P.M., but only in emergencies after that. If you get seriously ill, a special am-bulance is available by radio (see the police) to whisk you to hospitals in Colima and/or Manzanillo. Long-distance telephone service is available at Ladatel card–operated street phones around the *jardín.* Buy cards at the Farmacia Carmen or the grocery. Connect to the **Internet** at the upstairs store (tel. 313/326-4041, 10 A.M.–2 P.M. and 4–10 P.M. Mon–Sat., noon–2 P.M. and 4–10 P.M. Sun.) on the southeast side of the town *jardín*.

Getting There

Manzanillo taxis take three or four passengers to and from Cuyutlán for about $30 one-way. If this is too expensive, local buses make the Manzanillo-Cuyutlán connection approximately every hour until around 8 P.M. via Armería (transfer point on Highway 200), half an hour by bus from Manzanillo's Central de Autobús bus station.

By car or RV from Manzanillo, follow the Highway 200 *cuota* (toll) branch superhighway 17 miles (28 km) to Cuyutlán. Or, for a more scenic alternative, from Manzanillo, follow main street Avenida Carrillo Puerto south from the *jardín* through downtown Manzanillo and continue along the west end of placid Laguna Cuyutlán. This route passes the giant smoking power plant chimneys, through miles of *ciruela* orchards, then along a breezy barrier dune and wild beach, eventually joining the toll highway about 10 miles before Cuyutlán. In the reverse direction from Cuyutlán, follow Avenida Hidalgo east, past the Cuyutlán *jardín* to the Highway 200 expressway entrance, Manzanillo direction. Continue about 10 miles to the first exit, and proceed west.

EL PARAÍSO

El Paraíso (pop. 1,000) is just seven miles south from Cuyutlán, via the local highway; turn at the right fork, four miles from the Cuyutlán *jardín*. Its beach is especially popular on Sunday and holidays with families, who eat their fill at the dozen shorefront seafood *palapas* lining the bumpy main street. El Paraíso's long strand, which extends for miles on both sides, is similar to Cuyutlán's: warm (sometimes hot) dark sand and generally gentle, rolling surf, with little or no undertow, excellent for safe wading, swimming, bodysurfing, boogie boarding, and surfing.

The good beach and seafood account for the success of the restaurant and **Hotel Paraíso** (Playa Paraíso, Armería, Colima 28300, tel. 313/322-4305 or 313/325-5094, Colima tel./fax 312/312-1032, credit cards accepted,

$25–29 d), which perches above the surf at the south end (left as you arrive) of the beachfront street. Guests in many of the hotel's plain but clean rooms enjoy the same airy oceanfront vista as the popular restaurant. The adjacent pool and sundeck is yet another reason for spending a day or two there. The approximately 20 rooms in the older section by the ocean rent from about $25 d (room-temperature water only). The 26 rooms in the new three-story section across the street rent for about $29 d, with hot water and fans. Reserve, especially during holidays and weekends, by writing or calling the hotel or contacting its agent in Colima.

Guided **mangrove jungle boat trips** ($5 per person, kids half price) take off from the dock (on the right, just before entering town) daily at about 9 A.M. and 11 A.M. (and 1 and 3 P.M. if there are customers). Along the way, you're likely to see crocodiles and turtles, and (during the high winter bird season) swarms of ducks, geese, egrets, herons, cormorants, flamingo-like roseate spoonbills, anhingas, ibis, lily walkers, parrots, and more. How much you see depends upon the sensitivity of the boatman. If he insists on plowing ahead, scattering droves of animals and birds, tell him to slow down. Bring your repellent, a hat, binoculars, and your copy of Steve Howell's *Bird-Finding Guide to Mexico.*

BOCA DE PASCUALES AND EL REAL

Local folks know this twin duo of downscale beachside *palapa* havens well for their gentle surf, abundant seafood, and wide-open spaces for tent and RV camping. Drivers can get to them along good paved roads from Highway 200. For bus travelers, Tecomán's town market, adjacent to the *camionera central* central bus station, is the point of departure for local buses, which run frequently until around 6 P.M. After that, you might have to take a taxi.

Boca de Pascuales, eight paved miles (13 km) from Highway 200, is literally the *boca* (mouth) of the Armería River, whose waters, which begin on the snowy slope of Nevado de Colima, widen to a broad estuary. Here, they nourish schools of fish and flocks of seabirds—pelicans, cormorants, herons—which dive, swoop, and stalk for fry in the rivermouth lagoon. Fishermen wade in and catch the very same prey with throw-nets.

The beach itself is broad, with semicoarse gray sand. The waves roll gradually shoreward over a near-level, sandy shelf, and recede with little or no undertow. Consequently, swimming, boogie boarding, and bodysurfing are relatively safe, and surfing (only for the experienced) is common during the fall hurricane season. Driftwood litters the sandbar seasonally, and several rentable fishing *lanchas* lay pulled up along the beach. A quarter-mile lineup of seafood *ramadas* (the best is **Hamacas del Mayor,** with a big lovely pool; tenting, but no RV space is available at the *palapa* restaurant La Loba) provide shade and food for the local families who crowd in on Sundays and holidays.

If you decide to stay overnight, the downscale beachfront **Hotel Paco** (long-distance radio tel. 01-200-124/736-2363, $37 for one to four, with a/c), or the rough surfer favorite **Hotel Real de Pasquales** (tel. 313/108-3253, $33 s, d, or t, with a/c), dark and stuffy but with surfing shop, will probably have room to accommodate you.

Get to Boca de Pascuales by car at the north end of Tecomán. On the Highway 200 far right-hand lateral lane, southbound, turn right, at the Boca de Pascuales sign and pedestrian overpass by the big Bodega warehouse store. Continue (on Calle Ramón Pedro Ortí) one mile and turn right at the signal at Calle 20 de Noviembre. Continue another seven miles to Boca de Pascuales.

For more lovely beach and surf, head from Boca de Pascuales along the two miles of beachfront road to **El Real** (marked La Mascota on some maps). The paved road passes a file of shoreline weekend homes. Several restaurants, notably the popular **En Ramada Boca de Río and En Ramada Sobre las Olas** (Above the Waves) which have added pools and water slides, dot the two miles to El Real. There, a few more seafood *ramadas* crowd the corner

where the road heads back about seven miles (11 km) to Highway 200 at Tecomán.

TECUANILLO, BOCA DE APIZA, AND APIZA

For **Tecuanillo,** head seaward from Highway 200 at the signed paved turnoff road about a mile south of the Tecomán (south end) Pemex station. Continue about five miles, passing the roadside aquaculture ponds of the former Bara Bara restaurant (which has given up cooking for cultivating shrimp, prawns, and fish) on the right.

At the beach, turn left and continue along the beachfront road. Besides its long, wide strand and good surf fishing, visitors to the hamlet of Tecuanillo enjoy the fresh offerings of a long lineup of seafood *ramadas*. Stores can supply food and drinks for picnickers, and there's space for beach tenters (sorry, no room for RVs). A hotel, the plain **Hotel las Palmas** (lovely beachfront, tel. 313/329-9222 or 313/328-8089, $20 d, $40 t or q), with about six clean, simply furnished rooms (pick room 5 upstairs for breezy ocean views), will most likely be able to put you up for the night. The road ends at Estero Tecuanillo, with lagoon-front *palapa* restaurants, and **lanchas,** available for **wildlife-viewing** excursions.

Boca de Apiza, at the mouth of the Río Coahuayana (which forms the Colima-Michoacán border), has surfing potential, driftwood, and possible tenting spots next to a wild, mangrove jungle-lined beach. Get there by following Colima Highway 139, the signed, paved turnoff road about 21 miles (34 km) south of Tecomán. About three miles from the highway, past a mangrove channel bridge, the road splits. Ahead is a beach with some informal camping spots. Follow the left fork through a mangrove jungle (bring insect repellent) for about a mile to a second beach. Near a weekend and seasonal *palapa* restaurant, with a shady, fenced-off informal campground, look seaward for the powerful surfing waves that seasonally rise sharply and break both left and right. In the rainy summer and early fall, Coahuayana river outflow stains the water an uninviting brown, but during the rest of the year, parking, tenting, fishing, beachcombing, and surfing might be fine here, providing it's safe. If in doubt, check with storekeepers back on the highway.

Although the fishing hamlet of Apiza is in Michoacán, it's barely so, being just south of the Río Coahuayana. It's reachable by the paved side road about a mile south of the river bridge. A dozen seafood *ramadas,* complete with tables and hammocks, spread along the road's end 2.5 miles from the highway. The long, dark-sand beach spreads seemingly without limit on the south side, while on the other, a bamboo-hut south-seas village spreads quaintly along the boat-lined estuary bank. With a store for supplies, tenters and self-contained RV campers could fish, beachcomb, and bodysurf here for a month of Sundays.

If you'd prefer a hotel stay, try the **Hotel Sarahi** (on the road as you enter town, tel. 313/327-9029 or 313/327-9120, $33d). Owners offer clean but plain rooms (number 1 upstairs is the best) with toilet, shower and fans.

TECOMÁN

Tecomán (pop. 80,000), on Highway 200, 37 miles (59 km) southeast of Manzanillo, three miles south of the Colima (Highway 110) junction, is south Colima's major transportation hub and service center. All services are not far from Avenida Insurgentes, the Highway 200 through-town main boulevard, which splits, diverting city-center traffic into a pair of one-way northbound (Manzanillo-Colima) and southbound (Michoacán) streams.

Accommodations

If you're planning to stay overnight, Tecomán offers a pair of good hotels. You'll find reasonably priced semideluxe amenities at the **Hotel Plaza** (Insurgentes 502, tel. 313/324-3574, fax 313/324-2648, fax 313/324-2675, $40 s or d, $70 t or q), two blocks closer to town than the fancier Hotel Real. Here, comfortable doubles come with a/c, TV, parking, restaurant, and phone.

For something fancier, choose the refined four-star **Hotel Real** (Av. Insurgentes, corner of Lic. M. Gudiño, Tecomán, Colima 28110, tel. 313/324-0100, fax 313/324-1581, realhotel@ prodigy.net.mx, $56 s, $70 d), on Highway 200 about eight blocks north of the city center. Rates for the 80 comfortable rooms include a/c, phones, satellite TV, pool, good restaurant, and parking.

Information and Services

A number of banks, all with ATMs, dot the downtown plaza-front streets. **HSBC** bank, with the longest hours (tel. 313/324-6364 or 313/324-6641, 8 A.M.–7 P.M. Mon.–Fri., 8 A.M.–3 P.M. Sat.), changes money on the north side of the main plaza. Alternately, try **Banamex,** one block west of the plaza's north side, tel. 313/324-1413; or **Bancomer,** on Avenida Insurgentes, tel. 313/324-0568, about three blocks north of the main plaza.

For a doctor, go to 24-hour diagnostic **Clínica Centro Médico,** at 592 E. Zapata, a block off Insurgentes, about six blocks north of the main plaza, tel. 313/324-3560. Alternatively, try the **Clínica de Especialidades,** tel. 313/324-2718, with many specialists on call.

For simple remedies and medicines, go to one of the plaza-front *farmacias,* such as **Farmacia America,** southeast side, tel. 313/324-0071, or **Farmacia Moderna,** on the opposite, northeast, side, tel. 313/324-1094.

The *correo,* tel. 313/324-1939, is at B. Dávalos 35, two blocks north of the main plaza. Long-distance telephone service is available from many Ladatel card–operated telephones around the central plaza. Buy a card ($3, $5, or $10) from one of many local minimarkets or drugstores.

Bus Service

A trio of cooperating long-distance bus networks operates out of the *camionera central* (central bus terminal), at the Plaza Progreso shopping mall, about four blocks west and two blocks north of the main plaza. Local buses, which connect to nearby communities, such as Armería, Cuyutlán, El Paraíso, Tecuanillo, Boca de Pasquales, Boca de Apiza, and Apiza, line up on the curb in front of the town market, adjacent to the central bus terminal. **Autotransportes Sur de Jalisco,** tel. 313/324-0795, offers many daily first- and second-class departures, connecting north with Colima, Ciudad Guzmán, and Guadalajara. Northwest-southeast departures connect with Manzanillo in the northeast end and Lázaro Cárdenas in the southeast. Companion line **Autovias del Occidente,** same phone number, offers first-class connections northeast with Michoacán, via Jiquilipan, Paracho, Uruapan, Pátzcuaro, and Morelia. Cooperating line **La Linea** offers luxury-class connections with Guadalajara, and with Michoacán destinations of Nueva Italia, Uruapan, Morelia, continuing all the way to Mexico City.

In an adjacent booth, agents, tel. 313/324-6166, sell tickets for first-class **Flecha Amarilla** and "Primera-plus" luxury-class departures, which connect, along both northerly routes, with Colima, Manzanillo, Guadalajara, Celaya, and Querétaro and northeasterly routes, with Michoacán destinations, of Jiquilipan and Zacapu, continuing to Mexico City.

Next door, first-class **Elite,** tel. 313/324-6027, coordinates its services with its Estrella Blanca companion lines. It offers several *salidas de paso* that connect daily along the Highway 200 corridor, southeast with Acapulco, via the Playa Azul junction (of Hwy. 200 and Hwy. 37), and Zihuatanejo and northwest, with the U.S. border (via Manzanillo, Melaque, Puerto Vallarta, and Mazatlán).

THE MICHOACÁN COAST AND PÁTZCUARO

Heading southeast out of Colima state, the Mexican Pacific Coast Highway hugs the shoreline as it pierces the little-traveled wild coast of Michoacán.

That last lonely Michoacán coastal link was completed in 1984. Local people still remember when, if they wanted to travel to Manzanillo, they had to walk half the way. What they saw along the path is still there: mountainsides of great vine-draped trees and seemingly endless pearly, driftwood-strewn beaches, fringed by verdant palm groves and enfolded by golden sandstone cliffs. From ramparts high above the foaming surf, gigantic headlands seem to file in procession along the shore and fade into the sea-mist a thousand miles away. Along the highway, coatimundis peer from beneath bushes, iguanas slither along the shoulder, and, in the spring,

a rainbow of blossoms, yellow, red, pink, and violet, blooms beside the roadside.

Near the small resort of Playa Azul, Highway 37 branches north, climbing into the Sierra Madre, where Michoacán becomes another country, the land of the Purépecha (sometimes known as the Tarascans), the proud inheritors of an empire never conquered by the Aztecs. The Purépecha (poo-RAY-pay-cha) highland is a vast pine- and spruce-tufted landscape, dotted with dormant volcanos, lakes both grand and intimate, vibrant market towns such as Pátzcuaro and Uruapan, monumental ruins of ancient imperial cities, petite villages, precious antique churches, and lush semitropical valleys of mango, citrus, and avocado.

Although the Purépecha were ravaged and scattered to the hills by brutal Spanish soldiers

© BRUCE WHIPPERMAN

HIGHLIGHTS

◖ Ex-Colegio San Nicolás: Pátzcuaro's oldest building is famous for its three-bell belfry facade, constructed in 1540. Exhibits display fine examples of local masks, lacquerware, basketry, copperware, and woodwork (page 386).

◖ Casa de Once Patios: A former Dominican convent, built within a maze of patios, the House of 11 Patios now hosts a number of handicrafts stores and workshops, where you can watch the craftspeople paint, weave, and carve for-sale handicrafts (page 388).

◖ Ex-Templo San Agustín: A former convent and church, the Ex-Templo now houses a remarkable 1942 work by renowned muralist Juan O'Gorman that depicts Pátzcuaro's history in a single grand panorama (page 388).

◖ Janitzio Island: This is an unmissable Pátzcuaro diversion, starting with a panoramic boat ride to the island, where a colossal sculpture of José María Morelos crowns the hilltop (page 388).

◖ Ihuatzio: Two grand truncated pyramids amid a field of unreconstructed mounds mark the heart of the former capital of an invincible Purépecha empire (page 390).

◖ Tzintzuntzán: After Ihuatzio, Tzintzuntzán (Place of the Hummingbirds) rose and defeated the mighty Aztec legions. A grand abandoned city remains, marked by the Great Platform, embellished by a row of five semicircular *yácata* pyramids (page 391).

◖ Santa Clara de Cobre: Handcrafted copperware decorates the shops around the town plaza. Be sure to stop in the Museo de Cobre (Copper Museum) and the factory store El Arte del Cobre (page 409).

◖ Parque Nacional Lic. Eduardo Ruiz: Uruapan's incomparably lovely national park occupies the verdant, vine-hung valley of the Río Cupatitzio. Stroll through a paradise of waterfalls and gushing cliffside springs (page 416).

◖ Angahuan and Volcán Paricutín: While exploring this 100 percent indigenous Purépecha town, don't miss a visit to the 1577 village church, with its unmistakably Moorish facade. If you have time to take the volcanic zone hike (or horseback ride), be sure you see the lava-buried church and climb the cinder-strewn volcanic crater of Paracutín (page 424).

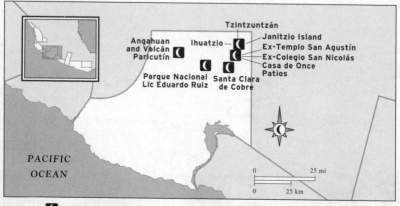

LOOK FOR ◖ TO FIND RECOMMENDED SIGHTS, ACTIVITIES, DINING, AND LODGING.

THE MICHOACÁN COAST

during the 1520s, a gritty, compassionate band of Franciscan padres, led by still-beloved Father Vasco de Quiroga, soon arrived to help them restore their homes and land. The padres established schools and colleges and taught the Purépecha to adapt their native skills to handicrafts traditions that today result in the trove of wool weavings, lacquerware, embroidery, copperware, and masks and woodcarving that overflows Michoacán's shops and markets.

PLANNING YOUR TIME

A minimum of a week would be required to see the best of Michoacán. If you prefer beaches, beach camping, seafood, and surfing, you could easily spend all of that along the coast, in sleepy downscale resorts, such as **San Juan de Alima, Caleta de Campos,** and **Playa Azul,** or in tiny miniparadises, such as **Faro de Buceriás, Maruata, Barra de Nexpa,** and **La Soledad.**

Lovers of colonial-era charm, handicrafts, lake vistas, and pine-scented breezes would enjoy spending most of their time in the highlands, maybe four days around **Pátzcuaro** and one or two days in **Uruapan.** By car, heading south from Manzanillo, Colima, or Cuyatlán, start out early, and enjoy the luscious coastal scenery for half a day. Then, at Lázaro Cárdenas, turn upcountry via the expressway to Uruapan and/or Pátzcuaro. Allow 10 hours at the wheel for the whole trip to Uruapan or Pátzcuaro. Bus travelers who start very early can follow the same route in a total of maybe 12 hours, transferring at Lázaro Cárdenas to an Uruapan- or Pátzcuaro-bound bus.

The quickest route to the highlands is to skip the Michoacán Coast entirely and, from Manzanillo, drive the expressway via Colima, then fork northeast at Atenquique to Tamazula and Mazamitla. Just past Mazamitla, fork east on to paved backcountry Highway 42, via Valle de Juárez, Cotija, Tocumbo, Los Reyes, Periban, Angahuan, and finally Uruapan, a total of about seven hours at the wheel from Manzanillo. Bus travelers should probably allow another day and go past Mazamitla

© BRUCE WHIPPERMAN

THE MICHOACÁN COAST

mountain-rimmed Lake Pátzcuaro as seen from the Janitzio island summit

to Jiquilipan, where they can transfer to an Uruapan-bound bus.

Many visitors go to Michoacán during the **Day of the Dead** (Nov. 1–2) festivities. Although this is a fascinating time to visit, it's very popular, and hotel reservations should be made months in advance.

HISTORY
Before Columbus

The great Río Balsas, whose watershed includes Michoacán and five other Mexican states, has repeatedly attracted outsiders. Some of the first settlers to the Río Balsas basin came thousands of years ago, from perhaps as far away as Peru. They left remains—pottery, of unmistakable Andean influence—and their language, roots of which remain in the native dialects of highland Michoacán.

The major inheritors of this ancient Andean heritage became known as the Tarascans. They founded a powerful Michoacán empire, centered at highland Lake Pátzcuaro, which rivaled the Aztec empire at the time of the conquest.

Conquest and Colonial Era

Although the Tarascans were never subdued by the Aztecs, they quickly fell prey to the Spanish conquistadors, who were also drawn to the riches of the Southern Sea (as the Pacific was known to him), Hernán Cortés sent his captains Juan Rodríguez and Ximón de Cuenca to the mouth of the Río Balsas, where they founded the Villa de la Concepción de Zacatula in 1523. But, like all the early Pacific ports, Zacatula was abandoned in favor of Acapulco by 1600.

Recent Times

The Michoacán-Colima coast slumbered until the 1880s, when railroad building began at the reawakened port of Manzanillo. Although places like Cuyutlán were receiving train traffic, and the resulting economic activity, by 1887, neighboring coastal Michoacán had to wait for the dust of the 1910–1917 Revolution

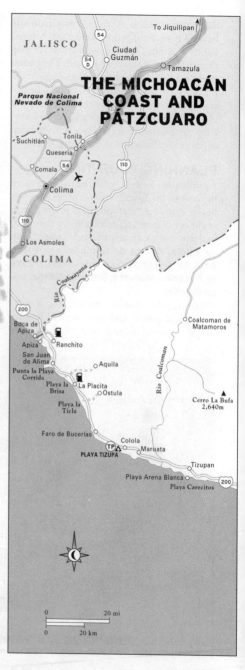

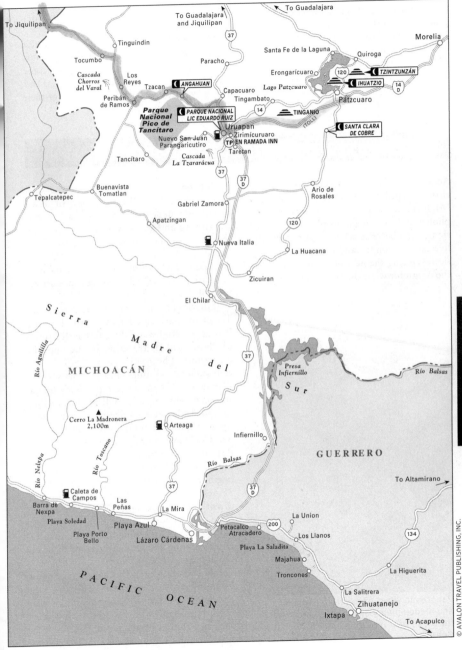

to settle before getting its own development project. Again the Río Balsas drew outsiders. Dam builders came to harness the river's hydropower to make steel out of a mountain of Michoacán iron ore. In succession came the new port, Lázaro Cárdenas, the railroad, the dam, then finally the huge Las Trucas steel mill. Concurrently, Playa Azul, Michoacán's planned beach resort on the Pacific, was developed nearby.

The new facilities, however, never quite lived up to expectations. Although a few ships and trains still arrive, and some tourists come weekends and holidays, Lázaro Cárdenas and Playa Azul drowse fitfully, dreaming of their long-expected awakening.

Northwestern Michoacán Beaches

Adventure often draws travelers along the thinly populated, pristine northwestern Michoacán Coast. Mostly lacking telephones and electricity, people live by natural rhythms. They rise with the sun, tend their livestock, coconuts, and papayas, take shady siestas during the heat of the day, and watch the ocean for what the tides may bring.

Panoramic views of towering headlands and hidden plumy beaches are the reward for those who venture along the Michoacán Coast.

Outsiders often begin to enjoy the slow pace. They stop at little beaches, sit down for a soda beneath a *ramada*, ask about the fishing and the waves, and stroll along the beach. They wander, picking up shells and driftwood and saying hello to the kids and fisherfolk along the way. Charmed and fully relaxed, they sometimes linger for months.

If driving, fill up with unleaded gas at the Tecomán south side Pemex or the La Mira Pemex on Highway 200 a few miles south of Playa Azul (if traveling in the opposite direction). The road's empty middle section stretches 93 miles (149 km) between La Placita and Caleta de Campos with no gas station except only a few village stores selling unleaded Magna from drums. If you're driving south, note your odometer mileage at the Río Coahuayana bridge (Highway 200, Km 231) at the Colima-Michoacán border. (The northbound kilometer markers, incidentally, begin with zero at the junction with Highway 37 near Playa Azul, thus giving the distance directly from that point.) In such undeveloped, untouristed country, road mileage will help you find and remember your own favorites among Michoacán's dozens of lovely beach gems.

Bus travelers enjoy the best connections at Manzanillo *camionera central,* Tecomán in the northwest, and Lázaro Cárdenas and La Mira (near Playa Azul) in the southeast. Bus lines, such as Autotransportes Sur de Jalisco, Flecha Amarilla, and Elite, run a few daily first-class local departures from both Manzanillo and Lázaro Cárdenas.

San Juan de Alima

Once-sleepy San Juan de Alima (at Km 211, 12 miles, 19 km southeast of the Colima border) has now been discovered and is developing. Parallel to the highway, a wide new concrete main street has been built. Energized by growing numbers of visitors, especially fall-season surfers, enterprising residents have built new stores, added tiers of shiny new rooms to old hotels, and opened brand-new lodgings on the beachfront.

San Juan de Alima's popularity comes from its long, creamy sand beach, framed between a pair of rocky headlands. Very surfable breakers roll in from about 100 yards out and recede with little undertow. All beach sports are relatively safe, except during the fall hurricane season, when the waves are 10 or 15 feet tall and surfers are as common as coconuts.

ACCOMMODATIONS AND FOOD

The side-by-side south-end hotels Parador and Miramar, each with about 25 rooms and its own sea-view *palapa* restaurant, are open all year. Mutual rivalry keeps their standards and prices on an approximate par. At the hotel **Miramar** (on the left as you face the beach, tel. 313/327-9048, $19 s or d, $38 t), you can find a simply furnished but comfortable room for two with toilet and shower. Add about $20 for a/c.

The **Hotel Parador** (next door, tel. 313/327-9038 $25 d, $28 d king-sized, $35 d with a/c) also has the most popular restaurant in town. The family members who run it take special pride in the cooking, which invariably includes the fresh catch of the day. They're friendly, and the view from their shady tables is blue and breezy.

In third place is the rival motel-style **Hotel San Juan** and beach *palapa* restaurant, which has gained a niche on the north side of town. The 20 simply furnished but clean rooms with showers rent for about $25 s or d, with fan only, $35 d for a/c.

Trying harder to become San Juan de Alima's upscale destination of choice is the new

Hotel Puerta del Mar (at the far north edge of town, Ranchito tel. 313/327-9120, $23 d). Watch for the hotel sign and dirt road turnoff on the highway, right side, as you're heading south. Guests in all of the simply furnished but comfortable rooms (with fans and hot water, but no a/c) enjoy panoramic ocean views from private balconies. (However, bring your own clippable lamp shade, book light, or reading lamp—bare bulbs predominate here.) Downstairs past the reception is a patio (with a pool maybe to be built) that leads past a small restaurant overlooking the beach and waves beyond. For reservations (not generally necessary), contact the owner in Ranchito.

Playa la Brisa

At Km 207, 16 miles (26 km) south of the Colima-Michoacán line, Highway 200 reaches a breezy vista summit, where a roadside *mirador* (viewpoint) affords a look southeast. Far below, a foam-bordered white strand curves from a little palm grove, past a lagoon to a distant misty headland. This white strand is Playa la Brisa, where, beneath the little grove, the Rentería-Álvarez family members manage their miniature utopia.

Their shady grove is made for tent or self-contained RV **camping.** People often ask them how much they charge. "Nothing," they say. "As long as you have a little lunch or dinner in our *palapa* here, stay as long as you like."

On the very broad beach beyond the grove, the waves roll in, breaking gradually both right and left. With little or no undertow, the surf is good for swimming, boogie boarding, and bodysurfing. Furthermore, taking your clue from the name "La Brisa," you know that sailboarding is frequently good here, too.

Additionally, the **mangrove lagoon,** a mile south down the beach, affords opportunities for wildlife-viewing, aided by your own kayak or portable rubber boat. Fishing is also often rewarding either from the rocks beneath the headland, or by boat (your own or local *panga*) launched from the beach.

The mod **Hotel El Paraíso Las Brisas** (tel. 313/327-9055 or 313/327-9056, fax 313/327-9067, hotelparaisolasbrisas@hotmail.com, credit cards accepted, $38 s, $45 d, $60 t low season) crowds the beach, 100 yards north of the Rentería-Alvarez grove. From the outside, it's a big, white stucco motel of about 30 rooms (uppers have sea-view balconies) around an inner parking patio with a kiddie pool. Inside, the rooms are thoughtfully decorated in 1990s-mode pastels and shiny, modern-standard bathrooms with shower. However, they are smallish and lack light and natural ventilation. Consequently, some rooms are usually musty and in need of airing out. Look at more than one room before moving in. Rentals include good cable TV, a/c, hot water, telephones, and restaurant.

Getting There: Follow the dirt road at Km 205 at the base of the hill one mile to the beachfront palm grove and hotel (on the right) at Playa la Brisa.

La Placita

The dusty town of La Placita (pop. 3,000) sits at Km 199 four miles south of Playa la Brisa. If it's past your bedtime, bare-bones rooms are available in the Reyna, a small hotel next to the north-end bridge. A restaurant, the Zuñiga, and pharmacies are on the highway at the central plaza; a government Centro de Salud (health center) is on the street that borders the south edge of the plaza; a *larga distancia* phone is on the plaza; and a *gasolinera,* at the south end of town, has unleaded gasoline.

Playa la Ticla

The broad, gray-white sands of La Ticla attract visitors—mostly surfers—for one good reason: its big, right-breaking rollers. Besides the surfing waves, a clear, sandy-banked river, fine for freshwater swimming, divides the beach in two. The town has stores and a health center. The beach has plenty of room for RV parking and tents and appears fine for camping. Unfortunately, drugs have led to problems in the past, but lately the situation appears to have improved. Check with a local storekeeper to see if this is still true.

GETTING THERE

Turn off at the signed dirt side road at Km 183,

31 miles from the Colima border (notice the big La Ticla government billboard). At mile 1.7 (Km 2.7), just past the big warehouse, fork left downhill to the village square. Jog right, then left, around the square, and continue downhill, passing the red Playa sign at the next corner. Continue to the beach at Mile 2.2 (Km 3.5).

Faro de Bucerías

Idyllic perfectly describes Faro de Bucerías: a crystalline yellow-sand crescent and clear blue waters sheltered by offshore islets. The name Bucerías (Divers) suggests what local people already know: Faro de Bucerías is a top **snorkeling and scuba** location. Favorable conditions, such as minimal local stream runoff and a nearly pure silica-sandstone shoreline, combine to produce unusually clear water. Chance intervened to make it even better, in the form of a wreck beside the offshore Morro Elefante (Elephant Isle), where multicolored fish swarm among the corals.

Several petite sandstone bays and beaches dot the coast around the main beach, Playa de Faro de Bucerías, which has all the ingredients for a relaxing stay. The beach itself is a lovely half-mile arc, where the waves rise and crash immediately at the water's edge and recede with strong undertow. Wading is nevertheless generally safe and swimming ideal in a calm south-end nook, protected by a rocky, tidepool-laced outcropping.

ACCOMMODATIONS AND FOOD

For accommodations and food, beachside *palapas* serve seafood during holidays, the store Abarrotes Mauricia supplies groceries, while the well-organized **Kalaki Alt Tlayekantik** restaurant/campground at the middle of the beach serves visitors on a daily basis. You set up your tent or park your self-contained RV beneath its beachfront camping *ramada* for about $5 per person per night, with toilets, freshwater showers, and drinking water.

Alternatively, try the nearby government-sponsored **Parador Turístico,** with a beach restaurant and comfortable sea-view *cabañas* (about $55 d) at Playa la Manzanilla, a quarter mile north.

Faro de Bucerías is heaven for fresh seafood lovers. Local divers (their spots marked by floating inner tubes) bring up daily troves of octopus, conches, clams, oysters, and lobsters, which you can buy on the spot and have cooked in the restaurant. If you prefer, catch your own from the rocks or hire a local fisherman to take you out for half a day.

For more local diversions, poke around in tidepools or climb to the white lighthouse *(faro)* perched atop the southeast rocky point. Another day you can walk in the opposite direction and explore little Playa la Manzanilla and other hidden coves beyond the stony northeast headland.

GETTING THERE

A big El Faro sign over the highway at Km 173 marks the Faro de Bucerías turnoff, 37 miles (60 km) south of the Colima border. Continue 0.9 mile (1.4 km) from the highway; after the village plaza, turn right, pass the town grocery, Abarrotes Mauricia, on the left and continue about 300 yards to a T intersection. Turn right for the Parador Turístico **cabañas** at Playa la Manzanilla and left for Kalaki Alt Tlayekantik campground, on the beach, at the end of the track.

Playa Maruata

This unique seaside refuge has formed where a mountain river tries to empty into the sea but is partially blocked by a pair of big rocks. Sand has collected, so the rocks appear as islands in sand rather than water. The ocean has worn away sea tunnels, which surging waves penetrate, pushing air and water, gushing and spouting. onto the shore. At times, a dry sand beach builds up next to the rocks, where campers can build an evening fire and be soothed to sleep by the gurgling, booming, and whistling lullaby of Maruata.

Maruata visitors enjoy three distinctly different beaches. On the northwest, right-side, thunderous, open-ocean breakers (advanced surfing) pound a long, steep beach. A small middle beach, protected between the rocks, has oft-swimmable (with caution) water. The southeast, left-side beach is long and sheltered by the sea rocks, enclosing a shallow rivermouth lagoon. Its usually gentle waves are generally safe for wading, swimming, and boat launching. In addition, snorkeling off the rocks is often very good during the winter-spring dry season.

What's even better, the Nahuatl-speaking *ejido* owners of Playa Maruata, who once fished for turtles for living, have joined the green revolution and now maintain a turtle sanctuary, protecting the turtle eggs from poachers. The local community has organized, under the banner of **Maruata 2000,** with the goal of preserving and protecting local wildlife and habitat in the 21st century and beyond. They back up their ideals with deeds by not allowing personal watercraft (such as Jet Skis) and other power sports, which they write, "could alter the view and freedom for swimmers and scuba divers."

As part of their plan, they encourage visitors to stay in their improved facilities. They run a number of permanent *palapa* restaurants beneath the sleepy beachfront grove and rent rustic tourist *palapas* ($4 per person). They've developed a campground where tenters can set up for about $3 per person per night and motorized folks can set up a self-contained RV for about the same.

Moreover, community members are ready with horse rentals ($10 per person), motor *lanchas* for fishing or snorkeling ($50 per trip), and boat tours ($5 per person).

GETTING THERE

Playa Maruata is 50 miles (80 km) southeast of the Colima line at Km 150. Just south of a big bridge, a dirt turnoff road descends from the southbound lane. Continue straight across the airstrip to a gravel road, heading into the village. Turn right (north) at the village square, go about 100 yards, then left at the road that borders the village square's north side. Continue through a stream to the palm grove and *palapa* restaurant-campgrounds by the beach.

Playa Tizupa

Between kilometer markers 103 and 104, Highway 200 skirts a picture-perfect dune-sprinkled beach, home for the new **Playa Tizupa Trailer Park and Campground.** The beach is decorated offshore by the monumental snorkel and scuba haven **Morro Chino** sea rock and on-shore by a swatch of gorgeous golden sand (much of which disappears seasonally during the Nov.–April storm season, only to return May–Oct.).

Nevertheless, the waves remain constant, rolling in from about 100 yards out, and breaking perfectly for beginning and intermediate surfing. Soak in all this, and much more, with at least an overnight or two or three Prices ($15 RV site, $3 pp tent site) include all hookups, dump station, showers, toilets, a mini-mart and small restaurant.

Playas Arena Blanca, Carecitos, and Pichilinguillo

Near Km 93, the rugged coastal mountains open to a stream valley, where (by a small roadside store) a narrow dirt lane winds down from the highway through a small village to **Playa Arena Blanca.** Here a creamy strand faces a broad blue bay, which arcs gracefully for a mile to a wave-splashed south-end headland. Prospects appear excellent for swimming, beachcombing, and surf- and rock-casting. During calm mornings boat-launching wouldn't be difficult, as evidenced by the *pangas* pulled up on the beach. Seafood lovers are in heaven here, with the fish, octopuses, and oysters that local fisherfolk and divers bring in and sell right on the beach. During the summer-fall turtle-hatching season, your beach neighbors will be the dedicated volunteers and workers of a local **turtle conservation and research station.** For water and limited additional supplies, little stores and restaurants in the village and on the highway (a half mile north at the truck stop) are available.

Even prettier and more intimate is neighboring **Playa Carecitos,** a crescent of yellow sand enfolded by sandstone cliffs, accessible from Playa Arena Blanca by ducking around the north-end cliff corner. Recently someone has built a big house on the beach, but that doesn't block access. Big rolling surfable breakers rise in the middle of a petite bay, while tranquil billows lap the sand on the sheltered northwest end. The sand curves a few hundred yards past scattered shoreline rocks, where snorkeling and fishing (by either surf- or rock-casting) appear promising, while shells and driftwood enrich the beach possibilities.

Playa Carecitos might be good for at least a pleasant afternoon, perhaps more. Temporary palm-thatch *ramadas,* apparently ready for new camper-occupants, often stand on the beach.

If you get to Carecitos, you might also check out petite **Pichilinguillo** bay and beach just half a mile north. On the left (south) side of the beach, an enterprising owner-builder has built a basic *palapa* restaurant and a pair of rough rooms that, at this writing, appear to be mostly rented by the hour, but are also rentable overnight for about $20. Even if you don't stay overnight, you should explore the petite south-side beach (visible from the restaurant) called **Playa el Tunel,** for the long swimmable (by the experienced with care under calm conditions) sea tunnel-cave that leads some 200 feet beneath the headland to the open ocean.

Barra de Nexpa

While known as one of Pacific Mexico's best surfing beaches, Barra de Nexpa's appeal is not limited to surfers. Don Gilberto, the grandfatherly founder of this pocket paradise, will gladly tell you all about it (in Spanish, of course). As more people arrived, facilities were added. First, Don Gilberto built *palapas,* a well, and showers. Then he built a restaurant, which his son now runs. Next door, another family, the Mendozas, built a laid-back RV and tenting park along the palmy shoreline of the adjacent freshwater lagoon. Gradually they put together a line of Robinson Crusoe–style rustic driftwood beach houses along the sandbar.

Although Don Gilberto's and the Mendozas' enterprises grew, the natural setting remained unchanged. The breakers (10-footers are common) still roll in, often curling into tubes, to the delight of both surfers and surf-watchers. Nexpa's big waves, however, need not discourage waders and swimmers, who splash and paddle in the freshwater lagoon instead. Beachcombers savor many hours picking through driftwood and shells, while bird-watchers enjoy watching dozens of species preen, paddle, stalk, and flap in the lagoon. And finally, when tired of all of these, everyone enjoys the hammocks, which seem to hang from every available Nexpa post and palm.

At the height of the fall-winter season, when lots of surfers and campers crowd in, the atmosphere is generally communal and friendly. At the *palapa* **restaurant,** on the beach, or in the shade beneath the palms and the *ramadas,* you won't lack company. (Note: Palmy surfing havens such as Barra de Nexpa are sometimes marred by one or two light-fingered individuals. Don't forget to safely stow your valuables.)

Although Don Gilberto and his son are still renting only rustic *palapas* for about $7 per person, with shared toilet and showers, Jorge Mendoza and his English wife, Helen, next door (left as you enter) offer more. Besides their driftwood beach *cabañas*, they've built comfortable, modern-standard **hotel rooms** (helennex@ hotmail.com, www.surf-mexico-rio-nexpa.com, $25 d, $35 d with a/c, $8 cabaña, $3 pp RV/tent site), each with room-temperature shower baths, all beside a green, grassy beachfront garden, a kiddie playground, and *palapa* **restaurant.** The adjacent **RV-camping park,** managed by Jorge's brother Chicho, charges about $3 per person per night, $8 for his *cabañas* also. Additionally, Jorge and Chicho rent surfboards, kayaks, boogie boards, and arrange fishing excursions by *lancha,* from the beach.

GETTING THERE

At Km 56, 109 miles (175 km) southeast of the Colima border, follow the unmarked dirt road turnoff, beach side (which northbound, requires a sharp left turn from the highway), following an uphill slope. It continues bumping and winding downhill about half a mile to the beach. The road appears negotiable when dry by ordinary cars and RVs, even perhaps big motor homes. If in doubt, do a preliminary run.

Caleta de Campos

Caleta de Campos (pop. 3,000) is at the signed turnoff of Km 50, 112 miles (181 km) southeast of the Colima border. Sometimes called Bahía de Bufadero (Blowhole Bay), Caleta de Campos is the metropolis and service center for this corner of Michoacán. Caleta's main attraction is a long, golden-sand beach beside a blue bay, haven for both touring visitors and commercial fishing launches. Snorkeling and pole casting prospects appear excellent off the rocky shelf and breakwater jetty beneath the north-side headland. Likewise, tenting, RV parking, beachcombing, good surfing, and surf-fishing prospects appear equally fine, on the beach's palm-shaded far south end.

A lineup of seafood *palapas* in the middle of the beach serve superfresh seafood meals for visitors. Fishing *pangas* may be hired on the beach. A half-day excursion (about $75) typically returns with 50 pounds of *huachinango* (snapper), *cabrilla* (sea bass), *sierra* (mackerel), *robalo* (snook), and *atún* (tuna). Anyone can launch a boat on the beach's protected northwest end. Get to the beach, via the access road, right, southbound, about a quarter mile south of the main signed town entrance.

ACCOMMODATIONS

Caleta's most visible hotel, the **❰ Hotel Yuritzi** (tel./fax 753/531-5010, fax 753/531-5020, webmaster@hotelyuritzi.com, www .hotelyuritzi.com, $22 s, $28 d with fan, $33 s, $40 d with a/c) perches on the hill above the beach. The family owners have remodeled and rebuilt their originally plain establishment into something more upscale and comfortable, adding about 10 modern-standard rooms and an inviting view pool-patio and a restaurant. A big yard within the fenced hotel compound can also accommodate large RVs (no hookups, however). The 26 rooms, all have hot-water shower baths. Add about 30 percent during Christmas–New Year and Easter holidays, when you should make early reservations. The friendly family owners of Hotel Yuritzi take special pride in their don't-miss-it **homemade ice cream,** which they make in luscious chocolate, vanilla, coconut, and strawberry flavors. If you do nothing else, be sure to stop by for a sample.

Across the street from Hotel Yuritzi, American expatriate-surfer "Gringo John" and his Mexican wife, Alfa, operate **Surf y Espuma**

(Surf and Foam) laundry and surfing shop. Besides surfboard ($8) and boogie board ($6) rentals and sales, beach clothes, hats, and friendly information, they offer accommodations—four comfortable rooms with fans and kitchen privileges and a one-bedroom kitchenette apartment—in attractive **Villa Tropical** (tel./fax 753/531-5255, surfyespuma@hotmail .com, $50 d; $65 d apartment; $250 entire house), with pool, luxuriously perched on an ocean-vista slope nearby.

Lower profile **Hotel Los Arcos** (Heróica Escuela Naval 5, Caleta de Campos, Michoacán, tel. 753/531-5038, $23 s or d, $28 t with fans; $32 d, $37 t with a/c) stands on the hillside downhill, one block west, of the Hotel Yuritzi. The on-site husband-wife owners offer three breezy floors of 32 clean but simply furnished bare-bulb rooms, many with panoramic ocean views, some even with a view of the famous spouting *bufadora* (blowhole). Rooms all have hot water showers. Add about 50 percent during holidays.

(Get to Hotels Yuritzi and Los Arcos via the main town entrance street. Turn left after two blocks, then after a block, turn right at the Los Arcos sign, continue straight ahead another block to Hotel Yuritzi.)

Note: For lots more information about Caleta de Campos, including more rentals, visit www.caletadecampos.com.

FOOD AND SERVICES

Most of Caleta's restaurants, stores, and services are scattered along its single main street, which leads directly from the signed highway entrance. A new pavement, which replaced the former bumpy, dusty surface, is a source of so much community pride that shopkeepers sweep the storefront concrete clean both morning and night. There you'll find a *larga distancia* telephone office, tel./fax 753/531-5129, a *farmacia,* a grocery, a dentist, doctors, and a Centro de Salud (health center) on a side street nearby.

Of the several town eateries, Alfa, knowledgeable co-owner of Surf y Espuma, recommends either **Lonchería la Bahía,** across from the Hotel Yuritzi, or restaurant **Adela**

(7:30 A.M. to 10 P.M. daily), on the main town street. If you're staying at the Hotel Yuritzi, you might also check out its restaurant, **El Faro.**

Buses stop frequently at either the Highway 200 crossing or the small station on the main street by the town plaza a block uphill. They include La Linea first-class, Galeana second-class, and Sur de Jalisco second-class, all running between Manzanillo and Lázaro Cárdenas, and two or three few first-class Elite, running the nearly the entire Pacific Coast route, from the U.S. border to Acapulco. Executive-class "Plus" buses run between Lázaro Cárdenas and Guadalajara; and local Michoacanos minibuses run to and from Lázaro Cárdenas, via La Mira and the Playa Azul junction. Drivers of mini- and second-class buses will generally let you off anywhere along the highway you request.

Around Caleta de Campos

A number of plumy havens north and south of Caleta are lately offering more reasons to stop, take a look, and perhaps linger. Worth investigating is **Playa Las Cabañas,** at Km 52, barely a mile north of Caleta, beneath a long, gorgeous beach and grove. At this writing there were several very rough thatched *cabañas,* a restaurant, and some simply furnished hotel rooms (about $40 double with a/c) around an invitingly blue pool-patio. A mile of luscious, palm-shadowed beach invites **RV and tent camping** ($10 per car or tent, includes use of pool, showers and toilets). For more information, call 753/531-5074 in Lázaro Cárdenas. (If, however, you prefer something fancier, check out the several deluxe *cabaña*-bungalows: each with two bedrooms with a/c and kitchenette, about $75, atop the south-end bluff.)

You might also check out **Playa la Soledad,** at Km 36, about nine miles (14 km) south of Caleta, where a paved side road leads downhill to the beach. There, a colony of several permanent *palapa* restaurants laze in the shade beneath the palms while a creamy, rock-enfolded beach decorates the shoreline. A **six-room house** (Casa Live) with a palm-shaded green lawn and tank pool, is available for rent either entirely for $180, or for $50 per bedroom, with a/c and private hot-water shower baths. For more information, see the manager of the *palapa* Conchita on the beach, or call tel. 753/539-3100 or 333/191-9251, or cellular local 044-753/103-0249, long distance 01-753/103-0249.

Three miles (4 km) farther south, at Km 32, at Chuquiapan (choo-kee-AH-pan), a signed concrete side road leads a quarter mile to **Playa Porto Bello,** a beach hamlet of several permanent *palapa* seafood restaurants beneath a shorefront palm grove. Very surfable waves roll in from 100 yards out to break gradually on a soft gray-sand beach. No hotel has been built at this writing, but two or three fenced-in *palapa* restaurants (one, Las Muchachitas, with a small pool) and some open spaces were available for tenting and RV parking on the south end.

Hotel Villa Dorada

Developers working to establish a luxury beach vacation-home community have built Hotel Villa Dorada (tel./fax 753/535-1084, Morelia office tel. 443/314-8102, toll-free Mex. tel. 800/719-8587, fax 443/314-8309, villadorada@hotmail.com, www.mexonline.com/villa-dorada.htm, $75) as the anchor of a big planned shoreline subdivision, a few miles north of Playa Azul. The hotel, envisioned

as a beach club for a regiment of well-heeled retirees and vacationers, offers 21 palm-shaded modern kitchenette bungalows built around a gorgeously spacious beachfront pool-patio. The attractive deluxe units are decorated with white stucco walls, colorful Mexican tile, and furnished with handsome hand-hewn wood furniture and up-to-date appliances. Guests in beachfront units enjoy ocean views.

The lavish facilities include tennis and basketball courts, a soccer field, table games, a kiddie pool and playground, and a restaurant. This is a great spot for families with kids, who stay free with parents, for about $75 per night (ask for a promotional rate, especially May–June and Sept.–Dec. 15). The main drawback to Hotel Villa Dorada appears to be isolation; weekdays, the place is usually nearly empty. However, you can easily drive or taxi into Playa Azul for the excitement and color of real Mexico, then retire to the peace and quiet of your Hotel Villa Dorada refuge.

Get to Hotel Villa Dorada by car or local bus, at the signed side road at Km 7.5, about 25 miles (42 km) south of Caleta de Campos, about five miles (7.5 km) north of Playa Azul. Continue 1.4 miles (2.5 km), to a village; jog left, then right, toward the beach. Continue another mile south along the beach to the hotel.

Playa Azul

It's easy to see how Playa Azul (Blue Beach) got on the map of Pacific Mexico. The beach is long and level, the sand is yellow and silky. The waves roll in slowly, swish gently, and stop, leaving wet, lazy arcs upon the sand. At sunset, these glow like medallions of liquid gold.

Playa Azul (pop. 5,000) is a small town on a big beach with a mile of *palapa* seafood restaurants. Four bumpy streets, Carranza, Madero, Independencia, and Justo Sierra, parallel the beachfront *malecón* walkway. Much of the activity clusters on or near a fifth street, Aquiles Serdán, which bisects the other four and ends at the *malecón* beach

walkway. Here the atmosphere—piquant aromas of steaming *pozole* and hot tacos, the colorful mounds of papayas and tomatoes, the language and laughter of the people—is uniquely and delightfully Mexican.

The Playa Azul beach is fine for just about everything. The waves, big enough for surfing as they break far offshore, roll shoreward, picking up boogie boarders and bodysurfers along the way, finally rippling around the ankles of waders and splashers at the sand's edge. Concessionaires rent chairs, umbrellas, and boogie boards, but few, if any, surfboards. The weekend crowds keep the

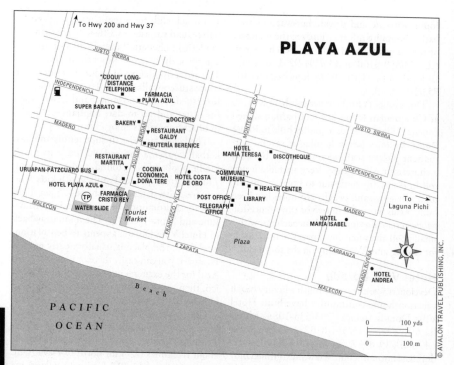

beach relatively free of shells and driftwood, although pickings will be better farther out along the beach (which stretches many miles in either direction).

Eating is another major Playa Azul occupation. Fruit vendors stroll the sand, offering luscious cut pineapple, watermelon, and mangoes-on-a-stick, while semipermanent beach stands and dozens of *malecón* restaurants offer fresh *cóctel de ostión* (oyster cocktail, $6), *langostina al gusto* (prawns any style, $9), and *langosta al vapor* (steamed lobster, $12).

Playa Azul's long, creamy beach is interrupted only during the summer rainy season, when the **Laguna Pichi** (follow main street Independencia about a mile east of town) overflows and spills into the ocean. Most of the time, however, Laguna Pichi is a big blue freshwater lake, bordered by palms and *palapa* restaurants. The lagoon provides visitors

with a variety of diversions, such as superfresh seafood, wading and swimming, fishing, and viewing the battalion of waterbirds that cackle, paddle, and preen in the clear waters. The prepared can set up tents for camping along the sandy shore (bring insect repellent) and venture out in their kayaks and rubber boats (or lacking those, hire a boat) for bird-watching and wildlife-viewing in the lagoon's mangrove wilderness reaches.

ACCOMMODATIONS

Playa Azul has about ten hotels, one with a trailer park. All of the following have hot water, an important plus for many winter vacationers.

Under $25

Budget-conscious vacationers will appreciate the **Hotel Costa de Oro** (Av. F. Madero s/n, Playa Azul, Michoacán 60982, tel. 753/536-

0393, no phone, $20 s or d with fan, $30 with a/c), a block east of A. Serdán, two blocks from the beach. The 14 plainly furnished but tidy rooms have hot water shower baths, but no pool.

$25-50

For a bit more relaxed resort ambience, consider the **Hotel María Isabel** (Av. F. Madero s/n, Playa Azul 60982, Michoacán, tel. 753/536-0016, $25 s, $30 d, $35 t with fans, $45 s or d with a/c low season), four blocks east of the center of town. Its two stories of approximately 20 simply but comfortably furnished motel-modern rooms, with hot water, cluster around an interior pool and patio one block from the beach. Add about 15 percent holidays.

The newish **Hotel Andrea** (E. Zapata 879, Playa Azul, Michoacán 60982, tel. fax 753/536-0251, $32 s or d), corner of Librado Rivera, just a block from beach, has a dozen spartan but clean accommodations, with fans and hot water.

For something yet more refined, check out the 🄲 **Hotel María Teresa** (Av. Independencia 626, Playa Azul, Michoacán 60982, tel. 753/536-0005, tel./fax 753/536-0055, hotel@vacza_international.com, credit cards accepted, $30 s, $40 d, and $50 t with fan; $39 s, $50 d, and $60 t with a/c). The hotel, three short blocks from the beach, stands within an airy garden compound, with parking on one side and an attractive *palapa* restaurant and sunny pool and patio tucked on the other. Its discotheque, Playa Azul's only one, is nearly always quiet, but it may occasionally heat up on the holidays. If this is the case, request a room on the relatively *tranquilo* wing farthest from the disco. The 42 comfortable, semi-deluxe rooms, all with TV and phones come with parking and some wheelchair access. Add about 25 percent holidays.

One block from the beach, the triple-storied main building of the **Hotel Playa Azul and Trailer Park** (Av. V. Carranza s/n, Playa Azul, Michoacán 60982, tel./fax 753/536-0024, www.mexonline.com/hotel-playa-azul

.htm, credit cards accepted, $48 s or d with fan; $60 with a/c; $5 per extra person) surrounds a lovely patio, decorated with stately palms, rubber trees, and giant-leafed vines. A spacious blue swimming pool curves artfully in the middle, while the bar and restaurant are tucked beneath a soaring beamed *palapa* on one side. The shady patio invites quiet relaxation; other rooms offer TV and table tennis. Families especially enjoy the hotel's water-slide minipark (beachside, behind the main building past the trailer park). The 70-odd rooms, spacious and comfortable but some a bit worn, may have a low-season promotional rate—ask for it. Parking is included, and some ground-level rooms are wheelchair-accessible.

THE MAR DEL SUR

It's surprising to many travelers that Pacific Mexico runs farther east than it does south. From the Michoacán Coast southward (or more accurately, eastward) the Pacific Mexico coastline, instead of running mostly north-south as in Mazatlán and Puerto Vallarta, runs essentially east-west. Here, the Pacific Ocean becomes truly the Mar del Sur (Ocean of the South) that the early Spanish explorers named it. Consequently, in Playa Azul, Zihuatanejo, Acapulco, and on the entire Oaxaca coast, streets that run parallel to the shore run east-west, and those perpendicular to the shore run north-south.

You can convince yourself of this by simply observing sunrise or sunset on the beach. For example, in Playa Azul and points south, notice that the sun rises and sets in direction roughly parallel to the shoreline. Since it's true that the sun rises generally in the east and sets in the west, worldwide, it follows that the southerly compass direction, 90 degrees counterclockwise from west, must coincide with the direction of the Pacific Ocean.

The Hotel Playa Azul's **trailer park,** with about a dozen spaces crowded behind the hotel, is nevertheless popular, since guests have access to the hotel pools and restaurant. Cramped spaces (for up to about 30-footers) rent for about $16 per day with all hookups, including power for air-conditioning, toilets, and hot showers. Discounts for lower power and weekly and monthly stays are available. Contact the hotel for reservations, which are mandatory for the trailer park during the winter.

FOOD

Avenida Aquiles Serdán (at the Hotel Playa Azul corner) offers several possibilities. Evenings, a squad of taco stalls open. Their steaming tacos of *res* (roast beef), chorizo (spicy sausage), and *lengua* (tongue) wrapped in hot tortillas and spiced with piquant salsas make perfect appetizers.

At the same corner, budget-minded travelers will appreciate the prices of sit-down **Cocina Económica Doña Tere** (7 A.M.–11 P.M. daily). Come early for breakfast eggs or pancakes, $2, or join the crowd afternoons for the hearty four-course *comida corrida* set lunch, $2.

For an equally tasty second course, walk down Serdán past the corner of Madero and take a streetside table at ▢ **Restaurant Galdy** (7 A.M.–11 P.M. daily) begun in 1968. Now retired, the original Galdy rests while her daughter Alexandra continues Galdy's tradition. Alejandra recommends that her customers order the house specialty, *frijoles charros,* a rich meat, vegetable, chile, and bean stew, simmered to perfection, served Friday, Saturday, and Sunday only. For a final course any day, pick one of the hearty country specialties for which Galdy's hardworking all-women cadre of cooks and waitresses is well-known, such as its hearty *pozole* (soup), *pierna* (roast pork), and *platos Mexicanos* (combination plates).

For dessert, step back to the Madero corner to **Frutería Berenice** (6:30 A.M.–9 P.M. daily) for a succulent selection of fruit. Local mangoes (in spring and summer), pineapple, and *platanos* (bananas) will be familiar, but *guanabanas* (green and scaly, like an artichoke) and *ciruelas* (yellow and round, like a plum) might not be.

To top everything off, cross Serdán to the **panadería** and pick up some cake, cookies, or *donas* (7 A.M.–noon and 7–10 P.M. Mon.–Sat.).

For a change of scene, go to the fanciest restaurant in town, beneath the big inner-patio *palapa* of the **Hotel Playa Azul** (Av. V. Carranza s/n, 7:30 A.M.–10 P.M. daily). Your reward will be tasty appetizers, salads, pizza, pasta, meat, seafood, and chicken entrées, professionally prepared and served.

ENTERTAINMENT AND SHOPPING

Playa Azul's evening entertainment begins with the sunset, views of which are unobstructed year-round. The effect is doubly beautiful, for the sky's golden glow is reflected from both the ocean and Playa Azul's shoreline swaths of flat wet sand. Sunset is also an excellent time for joggers and walkers to take advantage of the cool sea breeze and Playa Azul's level, firm sand.

The **tourist market,** beneath the awnings stretched over Aquiles Serdán next to the Hotel Playa Azul, has several stands that offer beach balls, T-shirts, and bathing suits. Some of the more common crafts, such as painted ceramic animals and papier-mâché, may be available also.

The friendly **Super Barato** grocery (Av. Aquiles Serdán, at the Hotel Playa Azul corner and Madero, 7:30 A.M.–9 P.M. daily) has a little bit of everything, from cheese and milk to mops and *espirales mosquitos* (mosquito coils).

INFORMATION AND SERVICES

Playa Azul has only a few services. Go to Lázaro Cárdenas, 14 miles (22 km) east along Highway 200, for what Playa Azul lacks.

If you get sick, consult one of the town **doctors,** either Dr. Mayolo Martínez Razo or gynecologist Dr. Ricardo J. Quintas, tel. 753/536-0197, who maintain offices on Independencia, a few doors east of the

Aquiles Serdán corner, or go to the very modest Centro de Salud on the town plaza. Alternatively, hire a taxi to take you to either the 24-hour **Centro de Salud** in La Mira (five miles, at the Highway 200 and Highway 37 intersection, tel. 753/535-0004), or the big **Seguro Social General Hospital** (tel. 753/532-0900, 753/532-0901, or 753/532-0902), in Lázaro Cárdenas.

For routine drugs and medications, go to the **Farmacia Cristo Rey** (corner of Carranza and Aquiles Serdán, across the street from the Hotel Playa Azul, 9 A.M.–9 P.M. Mon.–Sat.)

The Playa Azul **correo** (post office) is open 9 A.M.–3 P.M. Mon.–Fri., in the park behind the Centro de Salud, two blocks from the beach and two blocks south from Aquiles Serdán. The **telégrafos** (tel. 753/536-0158, 9 A.M.–3 P.M. Mon.–Fri.) is next door. For telephone, go to the private *larga distancia* "Cuqui" (on Independencia, one block west of the Aquiles Serdán corner, tel. 753/536-0122 or 753/536-0123).

GETTING THERE AND AWAY
By Bus
None of the buses that run along Highway 200 stop in Playa Azul except **Parhikuni**. If you're going to Playa Azul, ask your driver to drop you at Km 0, the Highway 200-Highway 37 Playa Azul junction (three miles from Playa Azul, two miles from La Mira), where a taxi or local minibus can take you the rest of the way.

Long-distance bus departure has been greatly simplified by **Parhikuni** buses that leave twice daily for Morelia, via Uruapan and Pátzcuaro (at 7 A.M. and 10 P.M. respectively), from the ticket office across the street from the Hotel Playa Azul, tel. 753/536-0151.

For other departures, go to La Mira (five miles by local minibus or taxi) and wait at the intersection of Highways 200 and 37. Although most Manzanillo-, Pátzcuaro-, and Zihuatanejo-bound buses stop and pick up passengers frequently at La Mira during daylight hours, reserved seats are available only at the Lázaro Cárdenas stations.

By Car or RV
Paved Highway 200 connects Playa Azul with Manzanillo in the northwest (195 miles, 314 km). Although the route is in good condition and lightly traveled most of the way, its twists and turns through rugged oceanside canyons and along spectacular shoreline ridges make it considerably slow going. Allow six hours for safety. If the Playa Azul Pemex is open, fill up with gasoline as you start out (otherwise gas up at La Mira or maybe Caleta), since the first reliably available Magna (unleaded) heading northeast is in La Placita, 125 miles or 199 km from Playa Azul.

Between Playa Azul and Ixtapa and Zihuatanejo in the southeast, the route is relatively short and straight, although trucks sometimes slow progress. Allow 2.5 hours for the 76-mile (122-km) trip.

For Pátzcuaro and central Michoacán in the north, you have a pair of options. The quicker by far is new toll *autopista* 37 D, about 3.5 hours (157 miles, 253 km) to Uruapan, four hours (196 miles, 317 km) to Pátzcuaro, and five hours (239 miles, 384 km) to Morelia. Connect with the *autopista* in the northern outskirts of Lázaro Cárdenas. Drive east from Playa Azul along Highway 200 about 12 miles (19 km); fork right on to the signed Lázaro Cárdenas entrance boulevard. Continue approximately one mile to the first signalled intersection. Turn left, and after another mile you arrive at the expressway entrance toll gate, at the first Río Balsas bridge.

Alternatively, old Highways 37 and 14 connect Pátzcuaro and Central Michoacán in the north, with Playa Azul, over 191 miles (307 km) of winding mountain highway. Although paved all the way, this route, over the pine-shadowed Sierra Madre crest, through the cactus-studded Río Balsas basin, is often potholed and sometimes congested. Allow at least seven hours for safety. Magna unleaded gasoline is available only at Arteaga, Nueva Italia, and Uruapan, so keep filled. Stick to the main highway for security. Some mountain folks cultivate marijuana and opium. They're understandably suspicious of wandering strangers.

Pátzcuaro

The high road from Playa Azul leads inland to Pátzcuaro (pop. 70,000), a city brimming with inspirations. Pine- and cedar-brushed mountains ring it, an islet-studded lake borders it. Its air is fresh and clean and the sky always seems blue. Visitors come from all over the world to wander through narrow colonial lanes, buy fine copper and lacquerware, and gaze at grand, mystery-shrouded monuments of long-forgotten emperors.

HISTORY
Before the Conquest

The valley and lake of Pátzcuaro, elev. 7,500 feet (2,280 meters), have nurtured civilizations for millennia. The Tarascans, whose king, Tariácuri, rebuilt the city during the 1370s, were the last and the greatest dynasty. To them the lake and surrounding grounds were sacred: the door to the land of their ancestors. They chose the venerated foundation stones of already-ancient temples as the new city's cornerstones, marking the symbolic door to the land of the dead: *tzacapu-amúcutin-pátzcuaro* (stone door where all changes to blackness). The last part of that original name remains in use today.

The founders of Pátzcuaro did not call themselves Tarascans. This was from the Spanish word meaning "son-in-law." Before the conquest, Pátzcuaro people called (and still call) themselves the Purépecha (poo-REH-pehchah). After they arrived in 1521, the Spanish increasingly applied their own label as they intermarried with the Pátzcuaro people.

Before the conquest, the Valley of Pátzcuaro was the center of a grand Purépecha empire, which extended beyond the present-day borders of the state of Michoacán. Local folks are still proud that their ancestors were never subjects of the Aztecs, whose armies they defeated and slaughtered by the tens of thousands on the eve of the conquest.

Conquest and Colonization

As Hernán Cortés approached the Valley of Mexico, the jittery Aztec emperor Moctezuma sent ambassadors to Tzintzuntzán (seen-soon-SAHN), the Purépecha capital on the shore of the lake a dozen miles northwest of Pátzcuaro. The ambassadors implored King Zuangua, known by his imperial title *caltzonzin,* to send an army to help repel Cortés. The *caltzonzin* refused, hastening Moctezuma's downfall and perhaps his own.

The first Spaniards, a few seemingly harmless travelers, wandered into the Valley of Pátzcuaro in 1521. The smallpox they unwittingly brought, however, was far from harmless. Zuangua soon succumbed to the ugly disease, along with tens of thousands of his subjects.

The Spanish military threat, in the person of conquistador Cristóbal de Olid and 70 mounted cavalry, 200 foot soldiers, and thousands of native allies, arrived at Tzintzuntzán in 1522. As the new *caltzonzin,* Tangaxoan II, fled to Uruapan, Olid quickly appropriated the imperial treasure and the gold and jewels from the temples. After a short resistance, Tangaxoan II pledged his homage to Cortés and was soon baptized, accepting the Christian name of Pedro. By 1526, most of his subjects had followed suit.

Peace reigned, but not for long. Cortés was called back to Spain, and the gold-hungry opportunist Nuño de Guzmán took temporary control in Mexico City. In late 1528, Guzmán had the *caltzonzin* tortured and killed. The Spanish royal government, alarmed by Guzmán's excesses, sent an official panel, called the Second Audiencia, to replace him. Guzmán, one jump ahead of them, cleared out in command of a battalion of like-minded adventurers, hell-bent to find another Tenochtitlán in western Mexico. They pounced upon the Purépecha, burning, raping, and pillaging the Valley of Pátzcuaro.

Vasco de Quiroga

The Purépecha fortunes began to improve when Father Vasco de Quiroga, a member of

© BRUCE WHIPPERMAN

statue of Bishop Vasco de Quiroga (1470–1565)

the Second Audiencia, arrived in 1533. At the age of 63 he began his life's work on the shore of Lake Pátzcuaro. Through his kindness, compassion, and tireless energy, Don Vasco gained the confidence of the Purépecha. He immediately established a hospital for the care of the poor. Named Santa Fe de la Laguna, it still stands by the lakeshore.

Appointed bishop in 1538, Don Vasco moved the episcopal seat from Tzintzuntzán to Pátzcuaro, which had already become the provincial government headquarters. Pressing ahead, he immediately began the Colegio San Nicolás. Its features became the model for many more: a hospital for the care of the poor, a school to educate young Tarascans, and a seminary for training bilingual Tarascan priests.

Pátzcuaro's rich handicrafts heritage is partly due to Don Vasco. He moderated the Tarascans' *encomienda* obligations so that they had time to become self-sustaining on their communal and individual plots. Entire villages be-

came centers of specific skills and trades. Such traditions remain: Santa Clara turns out fine copperware; Tzintzuntzán, furniture. Other valley communities produce elaborate baskets, delicate lacquerware, and handsome saddles.

Don Vasco toiled until his death in 1565 at the age of 95. Pátzcuaro people still adore him. Children often leave flowers at the foot of his statue in the plaza at the very heart of the city.

IN-TOWN SIGHTS

From the good bishop's tree-shaded bronze image in the main **Plaza Don Vasco de Quiroga,** shaded by a grove of grand elm-like *fresno* trees, the city spreads out along half a dozen north-south and east-west main streets. **Avenida Mendoza** runs from the northwest plaza corner one long block north to the city's second square, **Plaza Gertrudis Bocanegra,** named for the city's renowned independence heroine. The **market** spreads from the northwest side of Plaza Bocanegra, while past the south end, Avenida la Paz runs uphill (east) two blocks to the **basilica.**

Back at the main plaza's northeast corner, a second main thoroughfare, **Avenida Amuhada,** runs north, becoming Avenida Lázaro Cárdenas, the main highway-access route. It continues about two miles to the east-west Uruapan-Morelia highway and the railroad station. Crossing the railroad tracks at the station, a branch road leads about a mile north to the **Lake Pátzcuaro** embarcadero, where boats depart for Janitzio and other islands.

Virtually everything downtown is within a few blocks of the Plaza Don Vasco de Quiroga. For trips out of the city, hail a taxi or ride a white *colectivo* van of your choice, for about $.30 (read the destinations on the windows), from in front of the Hotel Los Escudos at the Plaza Don Vasco de Quiroga corner of Ibarra and Mendoza or on the Plaza Bocanegra in front of the market.

If you'd rather ride, you can enjoy a quick introduction to Pátzcuaro on the **Tranvia Pátzcuaro** motorized trolley (tel. 434/342-0117, paradatura@yahoo.com). Hourly tours

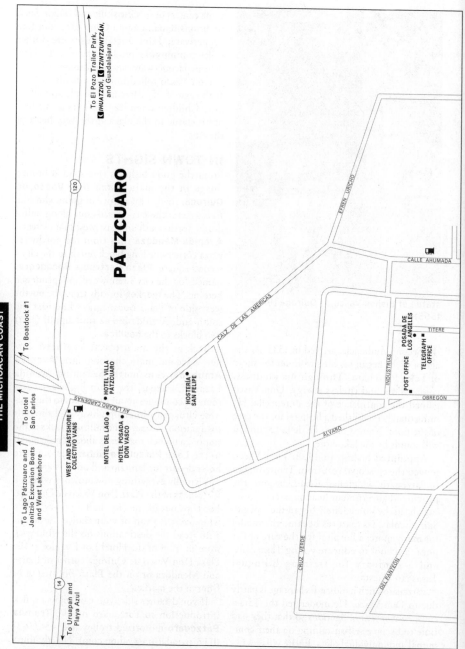

PÁTZCUARO

To El Pozo Trailer Park,
IHUATZIO, TZINTZUNTZÁN,
and Guadalajara

120

To Boatdock #1

To Hotel
San Carlos

To Lago Pátzcuaro and
Janitzio Excursion Boats
and West Lakeshore

14

To Uruapan and
Playa Azul

WEST AND EASTSHORE
COLECTIVO VANS

HOTEL VILLA
PÁTZCUARO

MOTEL DEL LAGO

HOTEL POSADA
DON VASCO

AV. LÁZARO CÁRDENAS

HOSTERÍA
SAN FELIPE

CALZ. DE LAS AMÉRICAS

EFRÉN URICHO

CALLE AHUMADA

INDUSTRIAS

POST OFFICE

POSADA DE
LOS ANGELES

TELEGRAPH
OFFICE

TITERE

OBREGÓN

ÁLVARO

CRUZ VERDE

DEL PANTEÓN

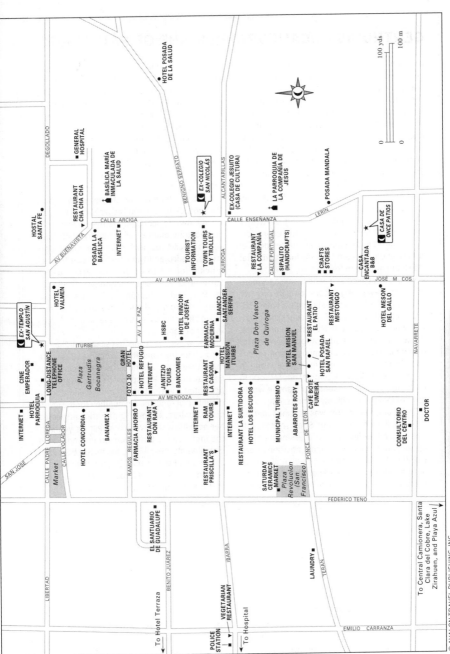

THE MICHOACÁN COAST

© AVALON TRAVEL PUBLISHING, INC.

GERTRUDIS BOCANEGRA, HEROINE OF PÁTZCUARO

Independence heroine Gertrudis Bocanegra de Lazo de la Vega was born into a well-to-do Pátzcuaro family on April 11, 1765. Her outspoken nature emerged at an early age. Once, as a young child, on her family balcony overlooking Pátzcuaro's main plaza, she was horrified at the sight of an unruly mob beating a helpless beggar with sticks. She cried out from the top of her lungs, but the crowd took little notice. She retreated inside, sobbing, to her mother's arms. The incident indelibly marked her; from then on, the oppressed had a ready defender in Gertrudis Bocanegra.

As she was growing up, young Gertrudis, like many of her Mexican criollo generation, was inspired by the European liberal ideas of liberty and justice and the daring deeds that led to the American Revolution.

When she arrived at marriageable age, more than just a few young suitors competed for her affections. Pedro Lazo de la Vega, a young criollo second lieutenant of the local army garrison, won Gertrudis's heart with a secret note, declaring his fervent admiration. Soon he proposed marriage, but she imposed one severe condition: she would not marry someone in the service of Mexico's colonial oppressors; in exchange for her consent, her fiancée would have to resign his military commission.

For young Pedro, this was no small matter. Criollos (Mexican-born of Spanish descent) such as he had few good professional career options; the most prestigious positions were traditionally reserved for *peninsulares*, Spanish-born colonists, derisively known as *gachupines*. Even after Pedro promised to quit the army,

Gertrudis's father refused to give the couple his blessing, citing no better reason than the fact that Pedro had black hair and a swarthy complexion. Finally, however, the father was unable resist his daughter's pleadings and Pedro's obvious love for her.

Seven children resulted from their union, four sons and three daughters. For 20 years, the young family enjoyed the modicum of success accorded Mexican criollos under the rule of the Spanish-born colonials.

But they chafed under the *peninsular* yoke. On Sept. 15, 1810, when Father Miguel Hidalgo cried "Viva Mexico! Death to the *gachupines!*" he had immediate allies in hundreds of thousands of criollos, including Pedro and Gertrudis. Pedro and their teenage son Manuel quickly joined the insurgent army, which suffered disastrous defeat on Jan. 17, 1811, at the Puente de Calderón, east of Guadalajara. They returned and joined the guerrilla campaign being waged against the Spanish forces in Michoacán.

Meanwhile, Gertrudis never wavered in her support for them and the *insurgente* cause. She made their Pátzcuaro house a secret rebel intelligence, finance, and supply headquarters. She promoted contributions of money and a small mountain of food and ammunition for the *insurgente* fighters. Although authorities suspected her activities, she avoided arrest for years as the increasingly bitter war ground on. Rebel guerrillas attacked, killed, and tortured Spanish soldiers and their sympathizers; the royalists responded with equal ferocity. Eventually both Pedro and Manuel died of battle wounds.

(adults $4, kids $3) depart between 10 A.M. and 7 P.M. every day, from its ticket office, at 32 Arciga, across from the Ex-Colegio San Nicolás.

A Walk Around Old Pátzcuaro

The natural place to start is at the center of the main plaza, beneath the statue of the revered Don Vasco de Quiroga (1470–1565). As first bishop of Pátzcuaro he reversed the despair and destruction wrought by the conquistadors.

Colonial buildings, some dating to the 17th century, rise behind the portals that spread around the square. The portals are themselves named and localize individual addresses (such as the Hotel Los Escudos, Portal Hidalgo 73).

◖ Ex-Colegio San Nicolás

Walk east, uphill, one block to Pátzcuaro's oldest colonial building, the former Colegio

Gertrudis nevertheless redoubled her efforts. She traveled tirelessly, gathering support for her compatriots. On one such trip, she left a family friend, a retired sergeant whom she had once saved from the gallows, to watch her house. When she returned, Gertrudis found some valuables missing. She questioned him, and, in retaliation, he denounced her to the authorities.

The local military commander quickly arrived at her house. During a chess party, before her compatriot-guests, he took Bocanegra into custody, placing her under arrest in the house at 14 Calle Ibarra, just around the corner from her childhood home. Her execution was summarily ordered; on Oct. 10, 1817, a military guard escorted her, blindfolded, to the corner square (now Plaza Revolución) in front of San Francisco church. The priest accompanying her asked that she be allowed to stop and pray for a few moments. His request was granted, but she was not allowed to go inside the church to her family altar, for it traditionally had been a place where the persecuted had found refuge from civil authorities.

The guards conducted her to gallows that had been set up in the adjacent small plaza. The streets were empty of passersby; neighbors shut their windows, refusing to witness the execution. Bells rang out in protest from every church tower. At the last moment, the official in charge received an order to take Gertrudis to the main town plaza and execute her by firing squad. There, in front of the jail, she was to become an example for many of her comrades who were being held inside.

First the soldiers tried to rope her to a tree, but she protested such a humiliation. Left standing free, she removed her shawl, then a fine comb from her hair. This, along with a gold watch, Bocanegra handed over to her executioner, requesting that they be given to her three daughters so that they would remember her and not be shamed by their mother, who had been executed for defending the cause of liberty. Then Bocanegra produced a gold peso, saying, "Here's all I have left," as she threw it to the soldiers of her execution squad. She pulled off her blindfold and began addressing the small crowd of friends and compatriots. Her fervent message so stirred the onlookers that the official in charge was forced to disperse the gathering.

A single fusillade ended her life. Her body fell and lay for hours, until her blood caked and crusted in the sun and a swarm of flies gathered on the corpse. Guards finally had to douse it with a bucket of water and cover it with her shawl. The next day, her family was allowed to take her body home for vigil, then burial at the nearby church of the Compañía de Jesús.

The people of Pátzcuaro have never forgotten Bocanegra's sacrifice. During his 1934-1940 presidency, Lázaro Cárdenas ordered that a statue of the defiant Gertrudis at her moment of execution be erected in Plaza San Agustín (now Plaza Bocanegra) in Pátzcuaro. Every year, on the Oct. 10 anniversary of her death, the people of Pátzcuaro gather beside her statue and honor Gertrudis Bocanegra's memory with overflowing bouquets of flowers.

San Nicolás, begun by Don Vasco in 1540. Pass inside beneath its quaint three-bell Spanish classic facade to the venerable inner garden. Now called the **Museo de Arte Popular** (tel. 434/342-1029, 9 A.M.–7 P.M. Tues.–Sat., 9 A.M.–2:30 P.M. Sun.), its corridors lead past rooms filled with fine regional crafts. In a rear courtyard, be sure to see the stair-step foundations of the original Tarascan temple, exposed on the hillside. Turn around and inspect a wall inscribed with the marks of prisoners counting the days.

As you exit the museum, glance left at the curious little doorway emerging from the outside uphill lane. Behind that door, Pátzcuaro people say, is an aqueduct that Don Vasco built to supply the poor with water during times of drought.

Ex-Colegio Jesuito

Walk ahead past the big courtyard and church

on the left, a former Jesuit College, now restored as a community cultural center. It maintains an art museum upstairs and offers classes in theater, painting, drawing, and music, both instrumental and choral. Watch for posters announcing events. The old church at the far end of the bare courtyard, **La Parroquia de la Compañía de Jesús,** is the final resting place of renowned Pátzcuaro independence heroine Gertrudis Bocanegra, who was executed on October 10, 1817, for her staunch defense of the *insurgente* cause.

Casa de Once Patios
Continue along Calle Enseñanza. After two blocks, turn right, downhill, to the former Dominican Convent of Santa Catarina de Sena, commonly known as the Casa de Once Patios (House of 11 Patios; 9 A.M.–2 P.M. and 4–7 P.M. daily) on the left. Most of its inner labyrinth of gardens, corridors, and rooms are restored and open to the public. Dozens of artisans have set up display workshops where they paint, weave, polish, and carve handicrafts for sale. Especially interesting are the factory shops, such as the *local de laca* (lacquerware section), where visitors can observe master artisans at work.

Basílica María Inmaculada de la Salud
Return past the former Colegio San Nicolás and continue two blocks along Calle Arciga to the big Basílica María Inmaculada de la Salud, begun by Don Vasco during the mid-16th century. In addition to Don Vasco's tomb, the basilica is noted for its four-century-old main altar image of the Virgin, made according to a pre-Columbian recipe of cornstalk paste and orchid glue.

Ex-Templo San Agustín
Follow diagonal Avenida Buenavista downhill and continue a block along Lloreda to the former monastery, Ex-Templo San Agustín, now housing the public library, **Biblioteca Gertrudis Bocanegra** (at the northeast corner of Plaza Bocanegra, tel. 434/342-5441, 9 A.M.–7 P.M. Mon.–Fri., 9 A.M.–1 P.M. Sat.). The library's main attraction is its huge mural, the first by Juan O'Gorman, completed in 1942. In this panorama of the history of the Valley of Pátzcuaro, O'Gorman is nearly as critical of the Tarascans' slaughter of 30,000 Aztec prisoners as of Nuño de Guzmán (scowling like a demon in armor) as he tortures the last *caltzonzin* (emperor). All is not lost as O'Gorman shows the murdered emperor's niece, Erendira, riding out to warn the people (and becoming the first Native North or South American to ride a horse). Don Vasco, the savior, appears at the bottom, assuring a happy ending as he brings utopia to Pátzcuaro.

The librarian has both a CD explanation of the mural, for $5, and a Spanish copy of the mural guide signed by O'Gorman, who appears with his wife at the mural's left side. Additionally, the librarian will duplicate a copy of a brief but informative Spanish biography of independence heroine Gertrudis Bocanegra, whose statue stands in the adjoining plaza. The library's respectable book collection includes many Spanish-language reference works and several shelves of English-language fiction and nonfiction.

JANITZIO ISLAND
An excursion to the island of Janitzio (hah-NEET-seeoh) is *de rigueur* for first-time Pátzcuaro visitors. The breezy launch trip takes about half an hour. Waves splash, spray, and rock the bow; gulls wheel above the stern as the pyramidal volcanic island-village of Janitzio grows upon the horizon. The Janitzio villagers believe themselves to be the purest of the Purépecha. Only the young speak Spanish; the old, some of whom have never visited the mainland, hold fast to their language and traditional ways.

Fishing for the tasty Pátzcuaro *pescado blanco* (whitefish) used to be the major Janitzio occupation. Overfishing has unfortunately reduced the famous *mariposas* (butterfly nets), which Don Vasco introduced long ago, to mere ceremonial objects. Long, cumbersome nets are now needed for the increasingly meager catches. The price (about $10) of a succulent whitefish platter, the specialty of the dozen-

view of Janitzio Island with the grand, 200-foot statue of José María Morelos at its summit

© BRUCE WHIPPERMAN

odd embarcadero restaurants, has inflated beyond the reach of most Pátzcuaro families.

Fortunately, government and local cooperative conservation measures show promise of eventually replenishing the whitefish population. Progressive rules limit the commercial fishing season to the months of January–April, during which only fish larger than nine inches (23 centimeters) are allowed to be taken. Meanwhile, the *mariposas* still come out for display during tourist-show regattas on weekends and holidays.

A steady procession of handicrafts shops lines the steep lane that winds to the island's summit. Although many items are common, some unusual finds in baskets, masks, papier-mâché, lacquerware, cottons, and woolens await those willing to look and bargain.

From the hillcrest, you can see the still more isolated islets of Tecuen, Yuñuen, and La Pacanda dotting the lake's northern reaches, while in the opposite direction, the city of Pátzcuaro basks at the foot of a distant pine-tufted green sierra. Gather up your energy for

the five-minute upstairs climb to the tip-top of the colossal José María Morelos statue, lined along the inside staircase with a continuous mural of scenes from the fiery independence hero's life.

Yuñuen Island

Lake Pátzcuaro's other islands, notably Yuñuen, also welcome visitors. The community maintains a cluster of rustic *troje,* native-style wooden kitchenette **C guest cabins** (tel. 434/342-4473, fax 434/342-3969, $40 d) in an airy hilltop poinsettia-adorned garden. Inside, the cabins are immaculate, cozy, and comfortable, with a number of amenities, including a good pool table in a handsome game room, and a small store, and no cars, and no noise except the crowing of roosters and sunrise and sunset for entertainment. Active visitors can stroll around the island, go fishing (in season) or kayaking, and try some Purépecha language lessons. Call for reservations and more information. Alternatively, you may make reservations at the Yuñuen booth at the

the main dock *(muelle general)* approximately 9 A.M.–5 P.M. daily.

Getting There

Ride a taxi or take the white *colectivo* VW van (about $.40, from the corner by the Hotel Los Escudos on Plaza Don Vasco de Quiroga, or the market corner, Plaza Bocanegra) to the main dock embarcadero.

If you're driving, head downhill (north) a couple of miles along Avenida Lázaro Cárdenas and turn left at the Uruapan-Morelia highway. Within a few hundred yards, turn right at the road crossing the rail tracks at the rail station. After about half a mile, bear right at a fork, and soon you'll see the main dock parking lot (about $1). Round-trip boat tickets, available from a dock-front booth, cost about $2 for Janitzio, $5 or more for Yuñuen, Pacanda, and Tecuen, in advance of departure. The last boat returns from the islands around 5 P.M.

C IHUATZIO

Pre-Columbian ruins dot the Pátzcuaro Valley. Most remain unexcavated grassy mounds except the most famous: Ihuatzio (ee-WAHT-seeoh) and Tzintzuntzán, both near the lakeshore northeast of the city.

Pátzcuaro dominated the valley during the latter-1300s golden-era reign of King Tariácuri. When he died, the valley was divided between his younger son and his nephews, Hiripan and Tangaxoan (ancestor of Tangaxoan II, the last Tarascan emperor). According to Vasco de Quiroga's 16th-century narrative, *Relación de Michoacán,* squabbling broke out among the heirs. Hiripan won out, and, by A.D. 1400, had concentrated power at Ihuatzio.

Exploring the Archaeological Site

The remains of Ihuatzio (Place of the Coyotes; around 10 A.M.–6 P.M. daily; entry fee about $2) spread over a rectangular area about half a mile long by a quarter mile wide. Nearly all ruins are mound-dotted unexplored fields, closed to the public. The open part, the so-called **Parade Ground,** is about the size of four football fields and enclosed by a pair of ceremonial stepped-wall raised causeways. These lead toward a pair of hulking truncated pyramids that tower above the Parade Ground's west

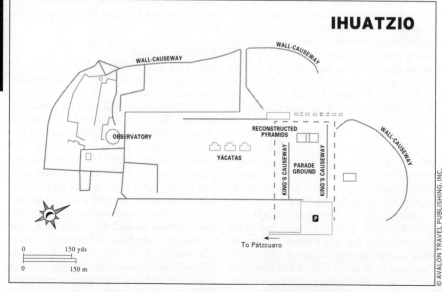

end. These, Ihuatzio's most prominent structures, lost nearly all of their original stone sheathing to colonial construction projects, although a remnant appears on the right pyramid's face as you approach from the Parade Ground.

Climb carefully (the steps are steep) to the top for a view of the surrounding unexcavated ruins. Along the Parade Ground's north and south sides, notice the **King's Causeways,** a pair of long stepped mounds, presumably used as the *caltzonzin's* ceremonial approach road.

About a quarter mile due south rises another mound, which marks the **Observatory,** a mysterious unrestored 100-foot-wide cylindrical structure whose name merely represents an educated guess about its possible function. In nearly the same direction as the Observatory, but much closer, stands the rubbly mound of the *yácatas,* three half-cylindrical truncated pyramids, whose original forms are unrecognizable because of repeated ransackings. Their shapes, however, are certain, because of a number of other excavated local examples, most notably Tzintzuntzán, five miles to the north. The Ihuatzio site has no facilities except a lavatory. Bring your hat and drinking water.

Getting There

By car or taxi, take Highway 120 from Pátzcuaro northeast (Morelia direction) about five miles (8 km) to the signed Ihuatzio turnoff. After 1.1 miles (1.8 km) bear right at the fork and continue a total of 3.1 miles (5 km) from the highway to a small plaza on the left. Turn right on to the cobbled, then rough dirt entrance road and continue another 0.7 mile (1 km) to the site parking lot.

By bus, ride one of the blue and white *urbano* buses, which all pass the central bus station front entrance on the southwest edge of town and continue to north-side Highway 120 at the foot of Avenida Lázaro Cárdenas. Hop on the bus marked Ihuatzio on the windshield. Alternatively, you can go by one of the *colectivo* vans that leave from the *gasolinera* by the railroad track at the downhill end of Avenida Lázaro Cárdenas.

About 20 minutes later, when the van or bus turns from the highway on to the Ihuatzio side road, tell the driver *"ruinas, por favor"* and you'll soon get dropped off at the small plaza on the left near town. Follow the dirt entrance road that takes off across, north, from the plaza, about a kilometer to the site.

TZINTZUNTZÁN

Ihuatzio's power waned during the 1400s, gradually giving way to nearby Tzintzuntzán (Place of the Hummingbirds). Within a generation, Tzintzuntzán became the hub of an expanded Tarascan empire, which included nearly all of present Michoacán and half of Jalisco and Guanajuato. When the Spanish arrived in 1521, authority was concentrated entirely in Tzintzuntzán, an imperial city whose population had swelled to perhaps as much as 100,000.

The present town (pop. 5,000), a dozen miles northeast of Pátzcuaro, is a mere shadow of its former glory. The Great Platform, although long abandoned, still towers in proud relief on the hill above the dusty modern town.

Exploring the Archaeological Site

The entire archaeological zone (open about 10 A.M.–5 P.M. daily, entry fee about $3)—of which the **Great Platform** occupies a significant but very small area—spreads over nearly three square miles. The excavated part, open to the public, represents only a 50th of the total, being confined within a rectangle perhaps 500 yards long and half that in width. The visitor's entrance leads you toward the rear of the Great Platform from the east through a tree-shadowed grassy park. You first see the Great Platform spreading from right (north) to left, with the town and lake below the far front side.

The Great Platform is singularly intriguing because of its five side-by-side *yácatas:* massive, semicylindrical ceremonial platforms. The *yácatas* are built of huge cut basalt (lava) stones, like a giant child's neat stacks of black building blocks. When the Spanish arrived, a temple to the legendary god-king Curicaueri perched upon the *yácata* summit.

Although the Great Platform itself was purely ceremonial in function, excavations in outer sections of the zone reveal that

TZINTZUNTZÁN

To Pátzcuaro

ENTRANCE RAMP

WALL

BUILDING A

BUILDING C

5

BUILDING B

THE PALACE

P

BUILDING D

RECONSTRUCTED STEPPED WALLS

4

ENTRANCE AND MUSEUM

3

BUILDING E

ENTRANCE RAMP

THE YÁCATAS

2

GREAT PLATFORM

1

0   50 yds
0   50 m

imperial Tzintzuntzán was an entire city, housing all classes from kings to slaves. Within the city, people lived and worked according to specialized occupations—farmers, artisans, priests, warriors, and nobles. Most experts agree that such urban organization required a high degree of sophistication, including excess wealth, laws and efficient government, and an accurate calendar.

Tzintzuntzán grew through a number of stages from its founding around A.D. 900. Excavations beneath the Great Platform masonry reveal earlier *yácatas* overlaid, like layers of an onion, above earlier constructions with similar, but smaller, features. (Look, for example, at the archaeological test hole between *yácatas* 4 and 5.)

Other intriguing structures dot the Great Platform. **Entrance ramps,** apparently built as boat-traffic terminals, appear beneath the Great Platform's 20-foot-high stepped retaining wall. Records reveal that, at the time of the conquest, lake waters lapped beaches at the foot of these ramps.

The Palace (Building B), a group of rooms surrounding an inner patio, stands about 100

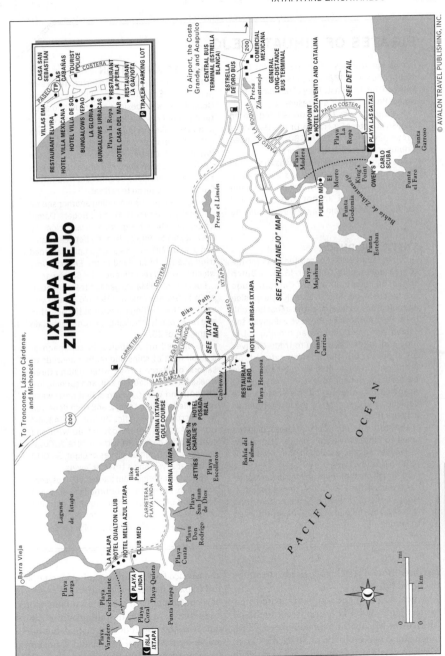

IXTAPA AND ZIHUATANEJO

To Troncones, Lázaro Cárdenas, and Michoacán

To Airport, the Costa Grande, and Acapulco

CENTRAL BUS TERMINAL (ESTRELLA BLANCA)

ESTRELLA DE ORO BUS

COMMERCIAL MEXICANA

GENERAL LONG-DISTANCE BUS TERMINAL

Presa Zihuatanejo

Presa el Limón

Presa de la Boquita

PASEO DE LA BOQUITA

Playa Madera

VIEWPOINT

HOTEL SOTAVENTO AND CATALINA

PASEO COSTERA

Playa La Ropa

SEE DETAIL

PLAYA LAS GATAS

PUERTO MÍO

El Morro

King's Point

OWEN'S

CARLO SCUBA

Punta Godomia

Punta el Faro

Punta Garroso

Bahía de Zihuatanejo

SEE "ZIHUATANEJO" MAP

Playa Majahua

Punta Esteban

Playa Hermosa

Punta Carrizo

PACIFIC   OCEAN

PASEO DE LOS PELICANOS

Bike Path

PASEO IXTAPA

SEE "IXTAPA" MAP

HOTEL LAS BRISAS IXTAPA

PASEO DE LAS GARZAS

RESTAURANT EL FARO

Cableway

CARRETERA

MARINA IXTAPA GOLF COURSE

HOTEL POSADA REAL

CARLOS 'N CHARLIE'S

JETTIES

Playa Escolleros

MARINA IXTAPA

Bahía del Palmar

Playa San Juan de Dios

Bike Path

Playa Don Rodrigo

CARRETERA A PLAYA LINDA

Playa Cuata

LA PALAPA

HOTEL QUALTON CLUB

CLUB MED

PLAYA LINDA

Laguna de Ixtapa

Barra Vieja

Playa Larga

Playa Cuachalalate

Playa Varadero

Playa Corral

ISLA IXTAPA

Playa Quieta

Punta Ixtapa

Detail (inset, top left)

COSTERA

PASEO

CASA SAN SEBASTIAN

VILLAS EMA

LAS CABAÑAS

TOURIST POLICE

RESTAURANT ELVIRA

HOTEL VILLA MEXICANA

BUNGALOWS YEPAO

LA GLORIA

BUNGALOWS URRACAS

Playa La Ropa

RESTAURANT LA PERLA

HOTEL CASA DEL MAR

RESTAURANT LA GAVIOTA

TRAILER-PARKING LOT

© AVALON TRAVEL PUBLISHING, INC.

0   1 mi

0   1 km

PIRATES OF ZIHUATANEJO

For 10 generations, from the late 1500s to independence in 1821, corsairs menaced the Mexican Pacific Coast. They often used Zihuatanejo Bay for repair and resupply.

The earliest was the renowned and feared English privateer Sir Francis Drake. During his circumnavigation of 1577-1580, Drake raided a number of Spanish Pacific ports.

The biggest prize, however, was the Manila galleon, for which he searched the Mexican coast for months. Finally, low on water and food, he dropped anchor and resupplied briefly at Zihuatanejo Bay before continuing northwest.

ENTER THE DUTCH

Dutch corsairs also scoured the seas for the Manila galleon. In October 1624, a Dutch squadron, commanded by Captain Hugo Schapenham, grouped in a semicircle outside Acapulco Bay to intercept the departing galleon. Port authorities, however, delayed the sailing, and the Dutch began running out of food and water. They tried to trade captives for supplies, but the Spanish refused, offering only inedible gold for the captives. In desperation, Schapenham tried to attack the Acapulco fort directly, but his vessels were damaged and driven off by the fort's effective artillery fire.

The starving Dutch sailors retreated up the coast to Zihuatanejo Bay where, after a few weeks, rested and resupplied, they set sail for Asia on Nov. 29, 1624.

Although most of them arrived in the Moluccas Islands in the East Indies, they disbanded. Most of them, including Schapenham, who was dead by the end of 1625, never returned to Europe.

DAMPIER AND ANSON

A much more persistent and fortunate galleon hunter was English captain William Dampier (1652-1715), who, besides accumulating a fortune in booty, was renowned as a navigator and mapmaker. Lying in wait for the Manila galleon, Dampier anchored in Zihuatanejo Bay in 1704. On Dec. 7, Dampier came upon the Manila galleon *Nuestra Señora del Rosario*. However, a ferocious Spanish defense forced Dampier's squadron to retreat.

Six years later, commanding another squadron jointly with captain Woodes Rogers, Dampier captured both the galleon *Encarnación* and the *Nuestra Señora de Begoña* between Jan. 1 and Jan. 5, 1710. Rogers and Dampier returned triumphantly to England in the *Encarnación*, which they had rechristened the *Batchelor*.

Luckiest of all Manila galleon treasure hunters was George Anson (1697-1762), who volunteered for the English navy at the age of 15 and rose rapidly, attaining the rank of captain at the age of 25.

He arrived off Acapulco, in command of a small fleet of ships and many hundreds of sailors, on March 1, 1742. After waiting three weeks for the galleon to sail, and running low on food and water, Anson sailed northwest, resupplied at Zihuatanejo, and then departed west across the Pacific. On July 1, 1743, off Guam, Anson's forces caught up with and captured the galleon *Nuestra Señora de Covadonga*, with 1.3 million pieces of eight, 35,000 ounces of silver, and a trove of jewels.

Although suffering from the loss of 90 percent of his men, Anson finally returned to England in command of his last remaining ship, carrying booty worth 800,000 pounds sterling, a fortune worth many tens of millions of dollars today.

increased from a trickle to a steady stream by the mid-1990s.

A decade later, the long-anticipated new express highway 54 D, south, from highland Mexico via Michoacán was completed. With much quicker access to the south Pacific Coast, Mexican vacationers from as far as Guadalajara

and Mexico City began streaming in, especially to Ixtapa. The new influx attracted a wave of new construction, in hotels, restaurants, stores, and services, that began spilling over to Zihuatanejo, so that, by 2006, the distinct but inseparable twin resorts of Ixtapa and Zihuatanejo (combined pop. 100,000) were attracting a steadily growing stream of both Mexican and foreign vacationers.

SIGHTS

Both Ixtapa and Zihuatanejo are small and easy to know. Zihuatanejo's little **Plaza de Armas** town square overlooks the main beach, Playa Municipal, just beyond the palm-lined pedestrian walkway, Paseo del Pescador. From the plaza looking out toward the bay, you are facing south. On your right is the *muelle* (moo-AY-yay), and on the left, the bay curves along the outer beaches Playas la Ropa, Madera, and finally Las Gatas beneath the far Punta El Faro (Lighthouse Point).

Turning around and facing inland (north), you see a narrow waterfront street, **Juan Álvarez,** running parallel to the beach past the plaza, crossing the main business streets (actually tranquil shady lanes) Cuauhtémoc and Guerrero. A third street, busy Benito Juárez, one block to the right of Guerrero, conducts traffic several blocks to and from the shore, passing the market and intersecting a second main street, Avenida Morelos. There, a right turn will soon bring you to Highway 200 and, within five miles, Ixtapa.

Nearly everything in Ixtapa lies along one three-mile-long boulevard, Paseo Ixtapa, which parallels the main beach, hotel-lined Playa del Palmar. Heading westerly from Zihuatanejo, you first pass the **Campo de Golf,** then the big Hotel Barceló on the left, followed by a succession of other high-rise hotels. Soon come the **Zona Comercial** shopping malls and the Paseo de las Garzas corner on the right. Turn right for either Highway 200 or the outer beaches, Playas Cuata, Quieta, Linda, and Larga. At Playa Linda, boats continue to heavenly Isla Ixtapa.

If, instead, you continued straight ahead back at the Paseo de las Garzas corner, you would soon reach the **Marina Ixtapa** condo development and yacht harbor.

Getting Around

In downtown Zihuatanejo, shops and restaurants are within a few blocks' walking distance

© BRUCE WHIPPERMAN

Fishing *lanchas* (motorized boats) line Zihuatanejo's main beach, Playa Municipal.

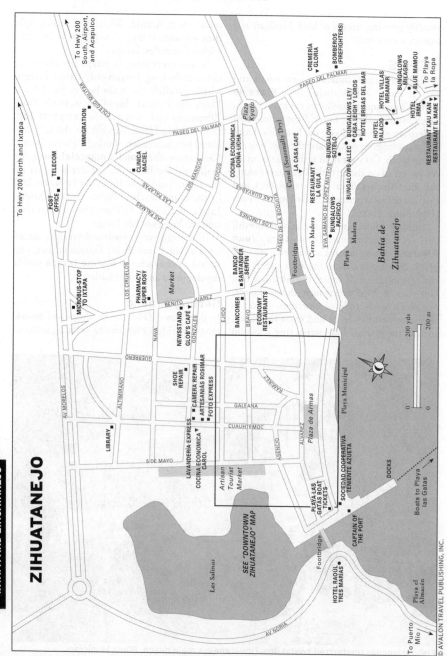

IXTAPA AND ZIHUATANEJO

ZIHUATANEJO

To Hwy 200 North and Ixtapa

To Hwy 200 South, Airport, and Acapulco

COLEGIO MILITAR

POST OFFICE
TELECOM

IMMIGRATION

PASEO DEL PALMAR

CREMERIA GLORIA
BOMBEROS (FIREFIGHTERS)

PASEO DEL PALMAR

Plaza Kyoto

CLINICA MACIEL

LOS MANGOS

COCOS

COCINA ECONOMICA DOÑA LICHA

LA CASA CAFÉ

Canal (Seasonally Dry)

BUNGALOWS MILAGRO
HOTEL VILLAS MIRAMAR
HOTEL IRMA
BLUE MAMOU
To Playa la Ropa

BUNGALOWS LEY
CASA LEIGH Y LOROS
HOTEL BRISAS DEL MAR

BUNGALOWS SOTELO

RESTAURANT LA GULA

HOTEL PALACIO

MICROBUS-STOP TO IXTAPA

PHARMACY/ SUPER ROSY

Market

LAS PALMAS
LOS CIRUELOS

NAVA

GUERRERO

AV MORELOS

ALTIMIRANO

LIBRARY

BENITO
JUAREZ
GONZALES

NEWSSTAND
GLOB'S CAFÉ

SHOE REPAIR

LAVANDERÍA EXPRESS
COCINA ECONOMICA CAROL

CAMERA REPAIR
ARTESANÍAS ROSIMAR
FOTO EXPRESS

5 DE MAYO

EJIDO
BANCOMER
BRAVO

BANCO SANTANDER SERFIN

ECONOMY RESTAURANTS

RAMIREZ

GALEANA

CUAUHTEMOC

ASENCIO

ALVAREZ

Plaza de Armas

Artisan Tourist Market

SEE "DOWNTOWN ZIHUATANEJO" MAP

PLAYA LAS GATAS BOAT TICKETS

SOCIEDAD COOPERATIVA TENIENTE AZUETA

LAS GUAYABAS
LOS LIMONES

PASEO DE LA BOQUITA

Footbridge

Cerro Madera

EVA SAMANO DE LOPEZ MATEOS

BUNGALOWS ALLEC
BUNGALOWS PACIFICO

Playa Madera

RESTAURANT KAU KAN
RESTAURANT IL MARE

Bahía de Zihuatanejo

Playa Municipal

DOCKS

CAPTAIN OF THE PORT

Footbridge

Las Salinas

HOTEL RAOUL TRES MARIAS

AV NORIA

To Puerto Mío

Playa el Almacén

Boats to Playa las Gatas

200 yds
200 m

0

0

© AVALON TRAVEL PUBLISHING, INC.

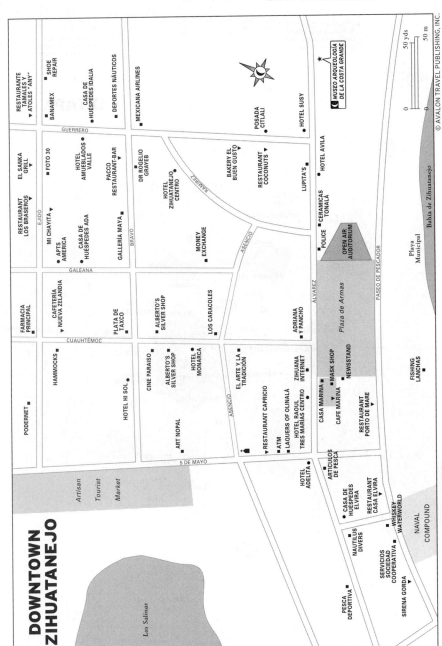

DOWNTOWN ZIHUATANEJO

Las Salinas

Artisan Tourist Market

PESCA DEPORTIVA
SIRENA GORDA
SERVICIOS SOCIEDAD COOPERATIVA
NAUTILUS DIVERS
WHISKEY WATERWORLD
CASA DE HUÉSPEDES ELVIRA
RESTAURANT CASA ELVIRA
ARTICULOS DE PESCA
HOTEL ADELITA
NAVAL COMPOUND

PODERNET
HAMMOCKS
FARMACIA PRINCIPAL
RESTAURANT LOS BRASEROS ▼
EL SANKA GRILL ▼
RESTAURANTE TAMALES Y ATOLES "ANY" ▼
SHOE REPAIR

ART NOPAL
HOTEL HI SOL
CAFETERÍA NUEVA ZELANDIA
CINE PARAISO
ALBERTO'S SILVER SHOP
HOTEL MONARCA
PLATA DE TAXCO
MI CHAVITA ▼
APTS AMERICA
CASA DE HUÉSPEDES ADA
GALLERIA MAYA
FOTO 30
HOTEL AMUEBLADOS VALLE
PACCO RESTAURANT-BAR ▼
BANAMEX
CASA DE HUÉSPEDES IDALIA
DEPORTES NÁUTICOS

GUERRERO
EJIDO
GALEANA
CUAUHTÉMOC
5 DE MAYO

ALBERTO'S SILVER SHOP
LOS CARACOLES
MONEY EXCHANGE
HOTEL ZIHUATANEJO CENTRO
DR ROGELIO GRAYEB
BAKERY EL BUEN GUSTO ▼
RESTAURANT COCONUTS ▼
MEXICANA AIRLINES
POSADA CITLALI
HOTEL SUSY

BRAVO
ASENCIO
RAMIREZ

EL ARTE Y LA TRADICIÓN
RESTAURANT CAPRICIO ▼
ATM
LAQUERS OF OLINALÁ
HOTEL RAOUL TRES MARIAS CENTRO ▼
ZIHUANA INTERNET
ADRIANA Y PANCHO
LUPITA'S
HOTEL AVILA

CERAMICAS TONALA
POLICE

CASA MARINA
CAFE MARINA
MASK SHOP
NEWSSTAND
RESTAURANT PORTO DE MARE

OPEN AIR AUDITORIUM
ALVAREZ
ASENCIO

Plaza de Armas

PASEO DE PESCADOR

Playa Municipal

FISHING LANCHAS

★ **MUSEO ARQUEOLOGÍA DE LA COSTA GRANDE**

Bahia de Zihuatanejo

0   50 yds
0   50 m

© AVALON TRAVEL PUBLISHING, INC.

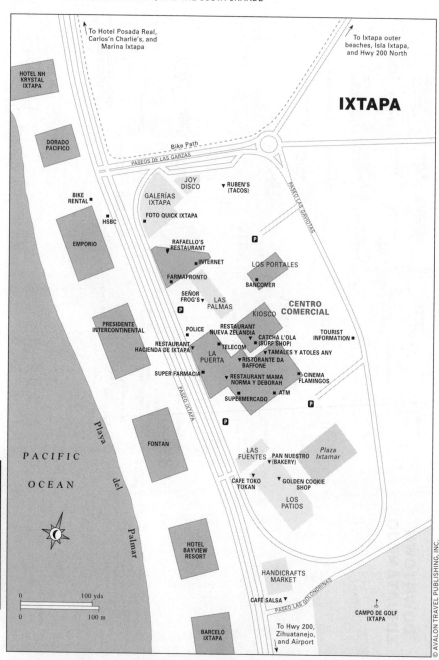

To Hotel Posada Real,
Carlos'n Charlie's, and
Marina Ixtapa

To Ixtapa outer
beaches, Isla Ixtapa,
and Hwy 200 North

HOTEL NH
KRYSTAL
IXTAPA

IXTAPA

DORADO
PACIFICO

Bike Path
PASEOS DE LAS GARZAS

PASEO LAS GAVIOTAS

JOY
DISCO

RUBEN'S
(TACOS)

BIKE
RENTAL

GALERÍAS
IXTAPA

HSBC

FOTO QUICK IXTAPA

EMPORIO

RAFAELLO'S
RESTAURANT

INTERNET

LOS PORTALES

FARMAPRONTO

BANCOMER

SEÑOR
FROG'S

LAS
PALMAS

CENTRO
COMERCIAL

KIOSCO

PRESIDENTE
INTERCONTINENTAL

POLICE

RESTAURANT
NUEVA ZELANDIA

TOURIST
INFORMATION

RESTAURANT
HACIENDA DE IXTAPA

CATCHA L'OLA
(SURF SHOP)

TELECOM

TAMALES Y ATOLES ANY

LA
PUERTA

RISTORANTE DA
BAFFONE

SUPER FARMACIA

RESTAURANT MAMA
NORMA Y DEBORAH

CINEMA
FLAMINGOS

SUPERMERCADO

ATM

FONTAN

LAS
FUENTES

PAN NUESTRO
(BAKERY)

Plaza
Ixtamar

PACIFIC

OCEAN

CAFE TOKO
TUKAN

GOLDEN COOKIE
SHOP

LOS
PATIOS

Playa del Palmar

HOTEL
BAYVIEW
RESORT

PASEO IXTAPA

HANDICRAFTS
MARKET

0   100 yds
0   100 m

CAFÉ SALSA

PASEO LAS GOLONDRINAS

CAMPO DE GOLF
IXTAPA

BARCELÓ
IXTAPA

To Hwy 200,
Zihuatanejo,
and Airport

© AVALON TRAVEL PUBLISHING, INC.

inland from the beachfront Plaza de Armas. For the beaches, walk along the beachfront *andador* (walkway) to Playa Madera, take a taxi ($3) to Playa la Ropa, and a launch from the pier ($4) to Playa las Gatas. For Ixtapa or the outer beaches, take a taxi (about $5) or ride one of the very frequent minibuses, labeled by destination, which leave from the east corner of Juárez and Morelos. In Ixtapa itself, walk or ride the minibuses that run along Paseo Ixtapa.

Museo Arqueología de la Costa Grande

The small but very fine Museo Arqueología de la Costa Grande (on the beachfront side of Álvarez, near the corner of Guerrero, 9 A.M.–8 P.M. Tues.–Sun.) details the archaeological history of the Costa Grande. Maps, drawings, small dioramas, and artifacts—many donated by local resident and innkeeper Anita Rellstab—illustrate the development of local cultures, from early hunting and gathering to agriculture and, finally, urbanization by the time of the conquest.

BEACHES AROUND ZIHUATANEJO BAY

Ringed by forested hills, edged by steep cliffs, and laced by rocky shoals, Zihuatanejo Bay would be beautiful even without its beaches. Five of them line the bay. On the west side is narrow, tranquil **Playa el Almacén** (Warehouse Beach), mostly good for fishing from its nearby rocks. Moving past the pier toward town comes the colorful, bustling **Playa Municipal.** Its sheltered waters are fine for wading, swimming, and boat launching (which fishers, their motors buzzing, regularly do) near the pier end.

For maximum sun and serenity, walk away from the pier along Playa Municipal past the usually dry creek outlet where a concrete *andador* winds about 200 yards along the beachfront rocks that mark the beginning of Playa Madera. If you prefer, you can hire a taxi to take you to Playa Madera, about $1.

Playa Madera

Playa Madera (Wood Beach), once a loading point for lumber, stretches about 300 yards, decorated with rocky nooks and outcroppings, and backed by the lush hotel-dotted hill **Cerro Madera.** The beach sand is fine and gray-white. Swells enter the facing bay entrance, breaking suddenly in two- or three-foot waves, which roll in gently and recede with little undertow. Madera's usually calm billows are good for child's play and easy swimming. Bring your mask and snorkel for glimpses of fish in the clear waters. Beachside restaurant/bars Kau Kan, La Bocana, and the Hotel Irma, above the far east end, serve drinks and snacks. (Lately some pollution overflow had fouled Playa Madera; authorities, however, were at work enlarging waste-treatment facilities.)

Playa la Ropa

Zihuatanejo Bay's favorite resort beach is Playa la Ropa (Clothes Beach), a mile-long crescent of yellow-white sand washed by oft-gentle surf. The beach got its name centuries ago from the apparel that once floated in from a galleon wrecked offshore. From the bay's best *mirador* (viewpoint) at the summit of **Paseo Costera,** the La Ropa approach road, the beach sand, relentlessly scooped and redeposited by the waves, appears as an endless line of half-moons.

On the 100-foot-wide beach, vacationers bask in the sun, personal watercraft buzz beyond the breakers, rental sailboats ply the waves, and sailboard outfits recline on the sand. The waves, generally too gentle and quick-breaking for surf sports, break close-in and recede with little undertow. Joggers come out mornings and evenings. Restaurants at the several beachfront hotels provide food and drinks.

Playa las Gatas

Secluded Playa las Gatas (Cat Beach), reachable by very rough shoreline rock-hopping or easily by launch from the town pier, lies sheltered beneath the south-end Punta El Faro headland. Once a walled-in royal Tarascan bathing pool, the beach got its name from a species of locally common, small, whiskered nurse sharks. Generally calm and quiet, often with superclear offshore waters, Playa

© BRUCE WHIPPERMAN

Ixtapa is enjoying a tourism revival due to improved highway access.

las Gatas is both a snorkeling haven and a jumping-off spot for dive trips headed for prime scuba sites. Beach booths rent gear for beach snorkelers, and a professional dive shop, **Carlos Scuba** right on the beach, instructs and guides both beginner and experienced scuba divers.

For a treat, pass the beach restaurant lineup and continue to **Owen's** *palapa* restaurant, visible on **King's Point,** the palm-shaded outcropping past the far curve of the beach. There, enjoy some refreshment, watch the surfers glide around the point, and feast on the luscious beach, bay, and hill view.

IXTAPA BEACHES

Ixtapa's 10 distinct beaches lie scattered like pearls along a dozen miles of creamy, azure coastline. As you move from the Zihuatanejo direction, **Playa Hermosa** comes first. The elevators of the superluxurious clifftop Hotel Brisas Ixtapa make access to the beach very convenient. At the bottom

you'll find a few hundred yards of seasonally broad white sand, with open-ocean (but often gentle) waves usually good for most water sports except surfing. Good beach-accessible snorkeling is possible off the shoals at either end of the beach. Extensive rentals are available at the beachfront aquatics shop. A poolside restaurant serves food and drinks. Hotel access is only by car or taxi.

For a sweeping vista of Ixtapa's beaches, bay, and blue waters, ride the *teleférico* (cable tramway, 7 A.M.–7 P.M. daily) to El Faro restaurant (at the south end of Ixtapa's main beach, Playa del Palmar, tel. 755/555-2510, 8 A.M.–10 P.M. daily—hours may be seasonally shortened).

Long, broad, and yellow-white, **Playa del Palmar** could be called the "Billion-Dollar Beach" for the investment money it attracted to Ixtapa. The confidence seems justified. The broad strand stretches for three gently curving miles. Even though it fronts the open ocean, protective offshore rocks,

© BRUCE WHIPPERMAN

Parasailing is a prime pastime on Playa del Palmar.

islands, and shoals keep the surf gentle most of the time. Here, most sports are of the high-powered variety—parasailing ($15), personal watercraft riding and water-skiing ($40), banana-boating ($10)—although boogie boards are rentable for $5 an hour on the beach.

Challenging surfing breaks roll in consistently off the jetty at **Playa Escolleros,** at Playa del Palmar's far west end. Bring your own board.

◖ Playa Linda

Playa Linda, an open-ocean yellow-sand beach, extends for miles beyond the road's end. Flocks of sandpipers and plovers skitter at the surf's edge; pelicans and cormorants dive offshore, while gulls, terns, and boobies skim the wavetops. Driftwood and shells decorate the sand beside a green-tufted palm grove that seems to stretch endlessly to the north.

In addition to the beach, mangrove-fringed **Laguna de Ixtapa,** an arm of which extends

to the bridge before the Playa Linda parking lot, is becoming an attraction. The lagoon's star actors are **crocodiles,** which often sun and doze in the water and along the bank beneath the bridge.

Officially, the bicycle path ends at the bridge, but you can continue on foot or by bicycle about 1.5 miles to Barra Vieja village. Take a hat, water, insect repellent, your binoculars, and your bird-identification book.

The friendly downscale **La Palapa** beach restaurant, at pavement's end, offers beer, sodas, and seafood, plus showers, toilets, and free parking. Neighboring stable **Rancho Playa Linda,** managed by friendly "Spider-man" Margarito, provides horseback rides at about $15 per hour.

The flat, wide Playa Linda has powerful rollers often good for surfing. Boogie boarding and bodysurfing—with caution, don't try it alone—are also possible. Surf fishing yields catches, especially of *lisa* (mullet), which locals have much more success netting than hooking.

◖ Isla Ixtapa

Every few minutes (9 A.M.–5 P.M. daily; $3 round-trip), a boat heads from the Playa Linda embarcadero to mile-long Ixtapa Island. Upon arrival, you soon discover the secret to the preservation of the island's pristine beaches, forests, and natural underwater gardens. "No trash here," the *palapa* proprietors say. "We bag it up and send it back to the mainland."

It shows. Great fleshy green orchids and bromeliads hang from forest branches, multicolored fish dart among offshore rocks, shady native acacias hang lazily over the shell-decorated sands of the island's little beaches. Boats from Playa Linda arrive at **Playa Cuachalatate** (koo-ah-chah-lah-TAH-tay), the island's most popular beach, named for a local tree whose bark is said to relieve liver ailments. Many visitors stay all day, splashing, swimming, and eating fresh fish, shrimp, and clams cooked at any one of a dozen *palapas*. Visitors also enjoy the many sports rentals: water skis, banana boat rides, boats for fishing, aquatic bicycles ($6/hour), snorkel gear ($3/hour), and kayaks ($5/hour).

For a change of scene, follow the short concrete walkway over the west-side (right as you arrive) forested knoll to **Playa Varadero** and **Playa Coral** on opposite flanks of an intimate little isthmus. Varadero's yellow-white sand is narrow and tree-shaded, its waters calm and clear. Behind it lies Playa Coral, a steep coral-sand beach fronting a rocky blue bay. Playa Coral is a magnet for beach lovers, snorkelers, and the scuba divers who often arrive by boat to explore the waters around the offshore coral reef.

Scuba diving is so rewarding here that a dive shop, **Oliverio,** is maintained by the sons of the late founder, near the west end of Playa Cuachalatate. Other shops in Zihuatanejo (see *Sports and Recreation*) are better equipped to provide the same services, however.

Isla Ixtapa's fourth and smallest beach, secluded **Playa Carey,** is named for the sea-turtle species (see the sidebar *Saving Turtles*

Isla Ixtapa, accessible by boat from the Ixtapa mainland, is perfect for a day excursion.

© BRUCE WHIPPERMAN

in *The Jalisco Coast* chapter). For access, hire a boat from Playa Cuachalatate.

Ixtapa Outer Beaches

Ixtapa's outer beaches spread among the coves and inlets a few miles northwest of the Hotel Zone. Drive, bicycle (rentals by bank Bital, in front of the Hotel Emporio), taxi, or take a "Playa Linda" minibus along the Paseo de las Garzas (drivers, turn right just past the shopping mall), then fork left again after less than a mile. After the Marina Golf Course (watch out for crocodiles crossing the road, no joke), the road turns toward the shoreline, winding past a trio of development-blocked beach gems, **Playa San Juan de Dios, Playa Don Rodrigo,** and **Playa Cuata.**

Although Mexican law theoretically allows free public oceanfront access, guards might try to shoo you away from Playa Cuata, on the open-ocean side, even if you arrive by boat. If somehow you manage to get there, you will discover a cream-yellow strip of sand, nestled between rocky outcroppings, with oft-gentle waves with correspondingly moderate undertow for good swimming, bodysurfing, and boogie boarding. Snorkeling and fishing are equally good around nearby rocks and shoals.

On the peninsula's sheltered northern flank, **Playa Quieta** (Quiet Beach) is a place that lives up to its name. A ribbon of fine yellow sand arcs around a smooth inlet dotted by a regatta of Club Med kayaks and sailboats plying the water. Get there via the north-end access stairway from the parking lot, signed "Playa Quieta Acceso Público." Stop by the beachfront restaurant for refreshment or fresh seafood lunch.

ACCOMMODATIONS
Zihuatanejo Downtown

Zihuatanejo's hotels divide themselves by location (and largely by price) between the budget to moderately priced places downtown and moderate to expensive Playas Madera-La Ropa. (For more information and updates on many of the following lodgings, in Ixtapa, Zihuatanejo, north in Troncones, and south in Barra de Potosí, visit the excellent www.zihuatanejo.net.)

Many more lodgings are available out of town, in the increasingly popular but still sleepy small beach resorts of **Troncones** about 45 minutes north of Ixtapa, and **Playa Blanca** and **Barra de Potosí,** 30–45 minutes south of Zihuatanejo. (For Troncones details, see the *Michoacán Coast and Pátzcuaro* chapter; for the others, see the *Costa Grande* section of this chapter.)

UNDER $50

Many of Zihuatanejo's best-buy hotels are near or on Avenida Álvarez, just a block from the beach. One of the most enduring is **Casa de Huéspedes Elvira** (Paseo del Pescador 9, Zihuatanejo, Guerrero 40880, tel. 755/554-2061, 10 s or d, $20 t low season, $11 s, $15 d, $22 t high), operated since 1956 by its founder, Elvira R. Campos. Every day, Elvira looks after her little garden of flowering plants, feeds rice to her birds—both wild and caged—and passes the time of day with friends and guests. She tells of the "way it used to be" when all passengers and supplies arrived from Acapulco by boat, local *almejas* (clams) were as big as cabbages, and you could pluck fish right out of the bay with your hands. Her petite eight-room lodging divides into an upper section, with more light and privacy, and a lower, with private baths. The leafy, intimate lower patio leads upward, via a pair of quaint, plant-decorated spiral staircases, to the airy upper level. The 22 rooms themselves are small, authentically rustic, and clean. The four upper rooms share a bathroom and toilet. If nighttime noise bothers you, bring earplugs; noise from Elvira's adjoining restaurant continues until about 11 P.M. most evenings during the winter season.

A few blocks east, **Hotel Susy** (corner Guerrero and Álvarez, Zihuatanejo, Guerrero 40880, tel. 755/554-2339, viajesbravo@yahoo.com, $28 s, $33 d, $45 t low season, $32 s, $38 d, $50 t high) offers three floors of rooms surrounding a shady inner patio. The seven upper-floor bayside rooms have private view balconies. Inside corridors unfortunately run past room windows, necessitating closing curtains for privacy, a drawback in these fan-only rooms.

Avoid traffic noise by requesting an upper-floor room away from the street. The 20 clean but plain rooms have fans and hot water.

A better choice, if you don't mind a bit of morning noise from the adjacent school, is the popular ℂ **Posada Citlali** ("Star" in Nahuatl; Guerrero 4, tel./fax 755/554-2043, citlali@zihuatanejo.com.mx, $30 s, $35 d, $40 t low season, $35 s, $40 d, $45 t high). The hotel rises in a pair of three-story tiers, around a shady, plant-decorated inner courtyard. The 20 plain, rather small but clean rooms are all thankfully removed from direct street traffic hubbub. Guests on the upper floors have less corridor traffic and consequently enjoy more privacy. Reservations are mandatory during the high winter season and strongly recommended at other times. Rates include hot water and fans.

Back on the west side of town, find the sleepy, enduring **Hotel Raoul Tres Marías** (Noria 4, Colonia Lázaro Cárdenas, Zihuatanejo, Guerrero 40880, tel. 755/554-2191, $18 s, $28 d, $33 t low season, $38 s, $47 d, $58 t high season), across the lagoon-channel by footbridge from the end of Paseo del Pescador. The hotel's longtime popularity derives from its low prices and the colorful lagoon-front boat scene, visible from porches outside some of its 25 rooms. Otherwise, facilities are strictly bare-bones, without even hot water, but with fans.

Guests at the **Hotel Raoul Tres Marías Centro** (Juan Álvarez and Cinco de Mayo, Zihuatanejo, Guerrero 40880, tel./fax 755/554-6706, reservatresmarias@prodigy.net.mx, www.ixtapa-zihuatanejo.net, $43 s or d, $50 t low season, $65 d and $76 t high), on the west side, near the end of Álvarez, enjoy a sprinkling of amenities, including the long-popular Restaurant Garrobos downstairs. Some of the 18 rooms have private balconies looking out on the usually quiet street below. Being close to the pier, the new branch is popular with fishing parties. Newcomers might pick up some local fishing pointers around the tables after dinner. Rooms include breakfast in high season; all have hot water and a/c.

$50-100

The popularity of **Hotel Ávila** (Juan Álvarez 8, Zihuatanejo, Guerrero 40880, tel./fax 755/554-2010, credit cards accepted, $60 s or d with view and $50 without, low season; $70 with view, $60 without, high season), downtown Zihuatanejo's only beachfront hostelry, is due mainly to its location. Rooms, although simply decorated, are comfortable. Of its 27 accommodations, the several beachfront rooms, with airy private-patio bay and beach views, are the best. If possible, avoid taking a room on the noisy streetfront side. All rooms have fans, TV, a/c, and hot water.

Right in the middle of everything is **Hotel Zihuatanejo Centro** (Ramírez 2, Zihuatanejo, Guerrero 40880, tel. 755/554-2669, fax 755/554-6897, zihuacenter@prodigy.net.mx, www.ixtapa-zihuatanejo.com/zihuacenter, credit cards accepted, $80 d low season, $90 high), a favorite of Mexican families. Although it's right smack downtown, guests are nevertheless sheltered from the hubbub by rooms that face inward onto an inviting inner pool-courtyard. The 79 rooms rising in four stories are clean and simply but comfortably furnished in pastels and vinyl floor tile. Some rooms have two double beds, others have one king- or queen-sized bed. For more air and light, ask for a room with a balcony. Rooms have a/c, fans, TV, hot water showers, parking, and restaurant.

Zihuatanejo Playa Madera

Another sizable fraction of Zihuatanejo's lodgings spreads along Playa Madera on the east side of the bay, easily reachable during the dry season, by foot from the town plaza, via the scenic beachfront *andador* (walkway). Several hotels cluster on Cerro Madera, the bayside hill just east of town. Because of Zihuatanejo's east-side creek channel and one-way streets (which fortunately direct most noisy traffic away from downtown), getting to Cerro Madera is a bit tricky. (See access directions at the end of this section.)

$50-100

A choice Cerro Madera view location is the main attraction of the aging, 1960s-era

Bungalows Allec (Cerro Madera, Calle Eva Samano de López Mateos, Zihuatanejo, Guerrero 40880, tel./fax 755/554-2002, reservar@ bungalowsallec.com, www.bungalowsallec .com, $40 d low season, $55 d high; $65 2br low season, $95 d high). Comfortable, light, and spacious, although worn, the 12 clean fan-only apartments have breezy bay views from private balconies. Six of the units and very large, with two bedrooms sleeping up to six; he others, smaller doubles for two to four, don't have kitchenette. No pool, but Playa Madera is a few steps downhill. Long-term discounts may be negotiable.

Back downhill on Avenida Adelita, right above the beach, is the longtime Mexican family-run **Hotel Palacio** (Av. Adelita, Playa Madera, P.O. Box 57, Zihuatanejo, Guerrero 40880, tel./fax 755/554-2055, $55 s or d with fan, $65 with a/c low-season; $75–85 high season), a beachfront maze of rooms connected by meandering, multilevel walkways. Room windows along the two main tiers face corridor walkways, where curtains must be drawn for privacy. Upper units fronting the quiet street avoid this drawback. The rooms themselves are clean, renovated, brightly decorated and comfortable, with fans or a/c and hot water. Guests enjoy a small but very pleasant bay-view pool, kiddie pool, and sundeck, which perches above the waves at the hotel beachfront. Street parking only.

Nearby, a couple of blocks off the beach, find the homey **(Bungalows El Milagro** (Av. Marina Nacional s/n, P.O. Box 71, Playa Madera, Zihuatanejo, Guerrero 40880, tel. 755/554-3045, klausbuhrer@hotmail.com, www .ixtapa-zihuatanejo.net/elmilagro, $75 d, $95 q high season), the life project of physician Dr. Klaus Bührer and his wife, Lucina Gomes. A hacienda-like walled compound of cottages and apartments clustering around a shady pool, the Bungalows El Milagro is winter headquarters for a cordial group of German longtime returnees. Both the friendly family atmosphere, the inviting pool and garden and the very clean, kitchenette lodgings (that vary in style from rustic to 1950s Bavarian motel) account for

the El Milagro's success. Owners offer three rental categories according to size. High-season rentals run about $75/day ($800/month) for a one-bedroom, two-person suite; $95 ($1100/ month) for a two-bedroom four-person suite, and $120 ($1,500/month) for an even larger, six-person suite. Subtract about 30 percent for low season. All have kitchenettes, hot water, fans, pool, and parking, but no credit cards accepted.

Back overlooking the beach, the **(Hotel Irma** (Av. Adelita, Playa Madera, Zihuatanejo, Guerrero 40880, tel. 755/554-8003 or 755/554-8472, toll-free U.S./Can. tel. 800/262-4500, fax 755/554-3738, info@mcrx.com, www .mcrx.com, $70–80 s or d low season, $82–95 high) is a favorite for longtime lovers of Zihuatanejo, if for no reason other than its location. The best news is that fresh, revitalized management has renovated the hotel throughout. Now, guests enjoy very comfortable upgraded deluxe rooms, a passably reliable sunset-view terrace restaurant and bar, and a pair of blue pools perched above the bay. A short walk downhill and you're on creamy Playa Madera. Best of all, many of the upstairs-wing rooms have private balconies with just about the loveliest view on Playa Madera. The 70 rooms rent for about $80 s or d low season, $95 high, with view ($70 and $82 without view), all with a/c, TV, and hot water. Add about 30 percent Christmas-New Year and Easter holidays. (Even when the hotel is nearly empty, bargaining for a better price, although not impossible, is like pounding on a brick wall here. Offering to put up cash in advance for a one-week stay may grease the wheels, however.)

Several more medium-priced bungalow complexes cluster along the scenic Cerro Madera hilltop street. Although their details differ, their basic layouts—which stair-step picturesquely downhill to private beach-front gardens—are similar. Prominent among them is **Bungalows Sotelo** (Calle Eva Samano de López Mateos13, Zihuatanejo, Guerrero 40880, tel./fax 755/554-6307, reservar@ bungalowssotelo.com or silviasm6335@ bungalowssotelo.com, www.bungalowssotelo .com, $45 d low season, $80 high, and up).

Guests in several of the clean stucco-and-tile apartments enjoy spacious private or semiprivate terraces with lounge chairs, bay views, and private whirlpool tubs. Rents for the smallest (refrigerator, but no kitchenette) units run about $45 d low season, $80 high; larger one-, and two- bedroom kitchenette suites rent, respectively, for about $90 d low season, $120 high, and $160 low, $200 high. Rentals vary; look at more than one before moving in. No pool, street parking only, but with some king-sized beds, and a/c; get your winter reservations in early.

A few doors east is the very attractive ◖ Bungalows Ley (Calle Eva Samano de López Mateos s/n, Playa Madera, P.O. Box 466, Zihuatanejo, Guerrero 40880, tel. 755/554-4087, bungalowsley@prodigy.net.mx, www .zihua.net/bungalosley, $75 d low season, $90 high, fan only; $130 q low season, $160 high with a/c). Here, several white stucco studio apartments stair-step directly downhill to heavenly Playa Madera. Their recent redecorations show nicely. Bathrooms shine with flowery Mexican tile, hammocks hang in spacious, rustic-chic, *palapa*-roofed view patios, and bedrooms glow with wall art, native wood details, and soothing pastel bedspreads. Except for a two-bedroom kitchenette unit at the top, all are kitchenette studios. No pool, but the beach is straight down the steps from your door. Longterm low-season discounts (of 15–20 percent for 6–21-night stays) may be available.

Back down on Avenida Adelita, the ◖ Hotel Villas Miramar (Playa Madera, Avenida Adelita, P.O. Box 211, Zihuatanejo, Guerrero 40880, tel. 755/554-2106, fax 755/554-2149, toll-free Mex. tel. 01-800/570-6767, reservaciones@ hotelvillasmiramar.com, www.hotelvillas miramar.com, credit cards accepted, $60 d low season, $100 high, garden view; $70 d low, $110 high ocean view) clusters artfully around gardens of pools, palms, and leafy potted plants. The gorgeous, manicured layout makes maximum use of space, creating both privacy and intimacy in a small setting. The designer rooms have high ceilings, split levels, built-in sofas, and large, comfortable beds. The street divides the hotel into two different but equally lovely sections, each with its own pool. The restaurant, especially convenient for breakfast, is in the shoreside section but still serves guests who sun and snooze around the luxurious, beach-view pool patio on the other side of the street. All rooms have phones and a/c. Reservations strongly recommended during the winter season.

$100-200

Atop Cerro Madera, find yet another option, **Hotel Brisas del Mar** (Calle Eva Samano de López Mateos s/n, Cerro Madera, Zihuatanejo, Guerrero 40880, tel./fax 755/554-8332 or 755/554-2142, brisamar@prodigy.net.mx, www.hotelbrisasdelmar.com, $100 d low season, $125 high; $110 and $120 family suites, $130 and $160 master suites). New owners have completely renovated the original hotel and have added a big new wing of a dozen spacious, rustic-chic view suites to the original 20 apartments, all with private sea-view balonies and deluxe amenities, hammock, bath with tub, satellite TV, and a/c. Guests enjoy use of a lovely beachfront club, with restaurant, shady *palapas,* lounge chairs, and big blue pool.

Also on Cerro Madera, perched atop Bungalows Ley, with the same address but completely separate, is upscale **Casa Leigh y Loros** (Calle Eva Samano de López Mateos s/n, Playa Madera, P.O. Box 466, Zihuatanejo, Guerrero 40880, tel. 755/554-3755, zihua01@earthlink .net, www.zihuatanejo-rentals.com, $225 d with fans, $255 with a/c, high season), the lovely life project of friendly California resident Leigh Roth and her pet parrot, Loros. Casa Leigh y Loros, which Leigh rents when she's away, is a multilevel, art-decorated, white-stucco-and-tile, two-bedroom, two-bath villa with roof garden, airy bay-view balconies, and up-to-date kitchen appliances. High winter season (except Christmas) rent runs about $225 d, with fans, $255 with a/c (Nov. 15–April 30), $155 and 180 May 1–Nov. 14. With cable TV, and daily maid service; a cook is available at extra charge. Leigh also manages rentals for many other luxurious villas, apartments, and condominiums. For a more economical option, ask Leigh (or Lila, as she's known locally) about **Casa de Bambu** (across the street from Casa Leigh y Loros), which she also rents, for about $100.

OVER $400

A few hundred yards farther southeast along the Paseo Costera is **La Casa Que Canta** (Camino Escénico at Playa la Ropa, Zihuatanejo, Guerrero 40880, tel. 755/554-7100 or 755/554-7026, toll-free Mex. tel. 800/710-9345, toll-free U.S. tel. 888/523-5050, fax 755/554-7040, information@lacasaquecanta .com, www.lacasaquecanta.com, $485 room, $510 grand suite, and $725 master suite low season), which is as much a work of art as a hotel. The pageant begins at the lobby, a luxurious soaring *palapa* that angles gracefully down the cliffside to an intimate open-air view dining-room. Suite-clusters of naturalistic adobe-concrete, sheltered by thick *palapa* roofs, cling artfully to the craggy precipice decorated with riots of bougainvillea and gardens of cactus. From petite pool terraces perched above foamy shoals, guests enjoy a radiant aqua bay panorama in the morning and brilliant ridge-silhouetted sunsets in the evening. The 18 art-bedecked, rustic-chic suites, all with private view balconies, come in three grades: superdeluxe "terrace" rooms, more spacious "grand suites," and even more spacious and luxurious "master suites," the latter two options with their own small pools. Low-season rentals run respectively, about $485, $510, and $725; high season, about $550, $650, and $850; all with a/c, fans, phone, parking, no TV, and no kids under 16 allowed. Furthermore, Casa Que Canta offers the best of all possible upscale worlds within its present grounds: **El Murmullo,** a superprivate 10,000-square-foot four-villa inner sanctum compound, built for a maharaja, with complete all-exclusive staff, from gardener, chambermaids, and butler, to waiters, kitchen staff, and gourmet chefs, all for only $4,000 daily. Make reservations (winter especially) very early.

Get to Cerro Madera either by walking along the beach east from downtown or by car via Plaza Kyoto, the traffic circle-intersection of Paseo de la Boquita and Paseo del Palmar a quarter mile east of downtown. If you're at the wheel, keep a sharp eye out and follow the small Zona Hotelera signs. At Plaza Kyoto, marked by a big red Japanese *torii* gate, bear right (heading inland) off the traffic circle, across the east-side canal bridge and turn right at the first street. Continue straight ahead for another block to Avenida Adelita, the address of several Playa Madera hotels and which runs along the base of Cerro Madera. At Adelita, jog right, then left at the first street, which will lead you uphill to the lane, Calle Eva Samano de López Mateos, that runs atop Cerro Madera.

Zihuatanejo Playa La Ropa
$50-100

At the far south end of the beach, find the **Hotel Casa del Mar** (Playa la Ropa, Zihuatanejo, Guerrero 40880, tel./fax 755/554-3873, reserv@ zihua-casadelmar.com, www.zihua-casadelmar .com, $65 with fan, $70 with a/c low season, $70 and $75 high). In the mid-1990s, former owners Juan and Margo Barnard Avila renovated an old hotel, cleaned up the adjacent mangrove lagoon, and nurtured its wildlife (dozens of bird species and a number of crocodiles) back to health. Now, new owners continue with the 14-room lodging, right on gorgeous Playa la Ropa, where guests can watch the birds and snoozing crocodiles, relax at the restaurant, and sample the good snorkeling, scuba diving, kayaking, and fishing available right from the beach. Choose your room from one of two sections: beachview in front, or garden view in back. All rooms are immaculate and simply but comfortably furnished with handsomely handcrafted wooden beds, lamps, and cabinets. Rentals include hot water, parking, and tank pool. Reservations mandatory in winter.

In the middle of the Playa la Ropa, and picturesquely unusual, is **C Bungalows las Urracas** (Playa la Ropa, Zihuatanejo, Guerrero 40880, tel. 755/555-2053, fax 755/554-2049, www.ixtapa-zihuatanejo.com, $60 d low season, $80 high), about 15 petite brick cottages, like proper rubber planter's bungalows out of Somerset Maugham's

Malaysian Stories, nestling in a shady jungle of leafy bushes, trees, and vines. Inside, the illusion continues: dark, masculine wood furniture, spacious bedrooms, shiny tiled kitchenettes and baths, and overhead, rustic beamed ceilings. From the bungalows, short "jungle" paths lead to the brilliant La Ropa beachfront. About eight additional bungalows occupy beachfront view locations in front. Amenities include private, shady front porches (use insect repellent in the evenings), hot water, and fans. Ask for a long-term discount. Get your winter reservations in early.

A few hundred yards farther along the beach, consider **Bungalows Vepao** (Playa la Ropa, Zihuatanejo, Guerrero 40880, tel. 755/554-3619, fax 755/554-5003, vepaozg@prodigy.net.mx, www.vepao.com, $65 d low season, $80 high). Here you have your basic clean and pleasant beach lodging, simply but architecturally designed, with floor-to-ceiling drapes, modern-standard kitchenettes, tiled floors, shower baths, white stucco walls, and pastel bedspreads and shaded lamps, plus fans and parking. Guests in each apartment enjoy front patios (upper ones have some bay view) that lead right to the hotel's private beachfront row of *palapas* a few steps away. Long-term discounts are possible. Reserve by email or by calling the owner, Gonzalo Ramírez, 9 A.M.–8 P.M. Central time please.

Luscious Playa la Ropa begins at **Beach Resort Sotavento** (P.O. Box 2, Zihuatanejo, Guerrero 40880, tel. 755/554-2032 or 755/554-2024, fax 755/554-2975, toll-free U.S. tel. 877/699-6685, Canada 877/667-3702, info@hotelsotavento.com.mx, www.beachresortsotavento.com, credit cards accepted, $87 low season, $99 midseason, $152 high season, and lower). Good hands-on management keeps the rambling complex, which perches on a leafy bayview hillside, healthy. The Sotavento is a 70-room mod-style warren that stair-steps five stories (with no elevator) down the slope. Each floor of rooms opens to a broad, hammock-hung either communal or semi-private terrace, some with unobstructed ocean views. Inside, the Sotavento's rooms are spartan 1960s-style,

clean and comfortable, many with king- or queen-sized beds and all with ceiling fans.

Rates vary according to season: low season is Easter–mid-July and mid-August–November; midseason is mid-July–mid-August and Nov.–Dec. 15; high season is Dec. 15–Easter. Accommodations (all including hot breakfast) come in three variations: large upper-level *terraza* suites, virtually all with ocean views, suitable for a couple up to a family of six ($87 low season, $99 midseason, $152 high season); mid-sized middle-level *playa* studios, some with ocean views, with two beds, for up to four ($76, $87, and $122); and smaller beach-level *oceano* rooms, shaded by the beachfront forest, very few ocean views, with two beds, for up to three ($76, $76 and $82). (Note: Views, light, and shade depend on your room's vertical position in the stack. Guests in upper rooms enjoy expansive bay and sunset vistas, while guests in less pricey lower-level rooms nevertheless enjoy intimate tropical verdure-framed sunset vistas of the bay beyond. Maybe look at both kinds of rooms before choosing.) The Hotel Sotavento's amenities include a beachside pool, room fans, and parking, a restaurant, and a beach aquatics shop but no elevator or wheelchair access.

$100-200

On the gorgeous beachfront front corner of the Bungalows Vepao property are the four apartments of **Casa la Gloria María** (Playa la Ropa, Zihuatanejo, Guerrero 40880, tel. 755/554-2055 or 755/554-3510, gloriamaria@zihuatanejo.net, www.zihuatanejo.net/casagloriamaria/, $90 low season, $110 high). Each of the deluxe units (two upstairs and two down) is attractively decorated with native rustic tile floors, bright floral tile baths, and whimsical hand-painted wall designs at the head of the two queen-sized beds, plus parking and fans. Each unit has its own kitchenette on an outdoor beachview patio. For more breeze and privacy, ask for one of the top-floor units. Make winter reservations very early.

A few blocks north, at the beginning of the Playa la Ropa, **Villas Ema** (contact through Posada Citlali, Av. Guerrero 4, Zihuatanejo,

Guerrero 40880, tel./fax 755/554-2043, home tel. 755/554-4880—Spanish only, villasema@ zihuatanejo.com.mx, $75 d low season, $105–110 high) perches at the top of a flowery hillside garden a block from the beach. Here, the enterprising husband-wife owners of downtown Posada Citlali have built kitchenette apartments, invitingly furnished with white tile floors, matching floral drapes and bedspreads, modern-standard shower baths, plenty of windows for light, and sliding doors leading to private view porches for reading and relaxing. Amenities include a/c or fans, hot water, a beautiful blue pool, and the murmur of the waves on Playa la Ropa a block away. Rates for the nine smaller units, with kitchen in common, run about $75 d low season, $110 high. The three top-level units, although sunnier and consequently warmer, have the best views and most privacy. A pair of larger, ground-level "villitas," each with its own kitchen and patio, sleeping four, rent for about $75 d low season, $105 high. Reservations highly recommended in winter; to avoid confusion with Posada Citlali, be sure to specify your reservation is for Villas Ema.

The 40-odd lodgings of the hillside **((Catalina Beach Resort** (tel. 755/554-2137 or 755/554-9321 through 755/554-9325, toll-free U.S. tel. 877/287-2411, toll-free Can. tel. 866/485-4312, fax 755/554-9327, info@catalina beachresort.com, www.catalinabeachresort .com, $88 room, $116 suite, $130 bungalow, $134 honeymoon suite low season, and up), next to the Hotel Sotavento, stair-step picturesquely all the way down to the beach. The Catalina's comfortably appointed, 1960s-era tropical-rustic accommodations maximize privacy, with individual view terraces and hammocks. The lodgings, all clean and deluxe, vary, from large to huge; look until you find the one that suits you. Most have fans only (not necessarily a minus on this airy hillside); some do have a/c, however. At the bottom of the hill, a beach aquatics shop offers sailing, sailboarding, snorkeling, and other rentals; those who want to simply rest enjoy chairs beneath the shady boughs of a beach-

side grove. The Catalina's food and drink facilities include a view restaurant, perching in the middle of the complex, a snack bar down at the beach, and an airy upper-level terrace bar. Access to all of this requires lots of stair climbing, which fitness aficionados would consider a plus. The Catalina's high-season rates for two run as follows: small casitas (large room) $120 fan only; standard casita (suite) $150 fan only; deluxe bungalow (even larger suite) $187 fan only; deluxe honeymoon suite with a/c $219; all with cable TV and phone. Low-season rates for the same categories run about $88, $116, $130, and $134.

OVER $300

German expatriate Helmut Leins left Munich and came to create paradise on Playa la Ropa in 1978. The result is the 90-suite superluxurious **((Hotel Villa del Sol** (Playa la Ropa, P.O. Box 84, Zihuatanejo, Guerrero 40880, tel. 755/555-5500 or 755/554-3239, toll-free U.S./Can. tel. 888/389-2645, fax 755/554-2758, info@hotel villadelsol.net, reservations@hotelvilladelsol .net, www.hotelvilladelsol.net; or contact the agent, Mexico Boutique Hotels, toll-free U.S. tel. 800/278-8018, info@mexicoboutique hotels.com, www.mexicoboutiquehotels.com; credit cards accepted, $300 s or d, low season, $365 high, and up). Here, in Helmut's exquisite beachside mini-Eden, a corps of well-to-do North American, European, and Mexican clients return yearly to enjoy tranquility and the elegance of the Villa del Sol's crystal-blue pools, palm-draped patios, and classic *palapas.* The lodgings themselves are spacious, with shining floor tile, handcrafted wall art, tropical-canopy beds, and private patios with hammocks. The plethora of extras includes restaurants, bars, pools, night tennis courts, a newsstand, art gallery boutique, beauty salon, and meeting room for about 30 people. Lodgings depend on size and location. Most economical are the superior suites, beginning at about $300 s or d, low season, $365 high. Superplush options include more bedrooms and baths, ocean views, and small private soaking pools, included for around $700 low season, $940 high and up; all with with cable TV, phones, a/c, and parking, but children in two-bedroom suites only.

Ixtapa
$100-200

Ixtapa's dozen-odd hotels line up in a luxurious strip between the beach and boulevard Paseo Ixtapa. Best buy among them is the Best Western ◖ **Hotel Posada Real** (Paseo Ixtapa s/n, Ixtapa, Guerrero 40880, tel. 755/553-1625 or 755/553-1745, toll-free U.S./Can. tel. 800/528-1234, fax 755/553-1805, ixtapa@posadareal.com.mx, www.posadareal.com.mx, credit cards accepted, $110 d low season, $160 high), at Paseo Ixtapa's far west end. Get there via the street, beach side, just past the restaurant with the tower on the left. With a large grassy football field instead of tennis courts, the hotel attracts a seasonal following of soccer enthusiasts. Other amenities include a large airy beachfront restaurant and two luscious pools. Although the 110 (most rather small) rooms are clean and comfortable, many lack ocean views. Rooms rent for about $110 d low season, $160 high, often with extended-stay or low-season discounts, such as third night free. Kids under 12 with parents are free; with a/c, satellite TV, phones, wheelchair access, and parking.

Another good buy is the Spanish-owned **Hotel NH Krystal Ixtapa** (Paseo Ixtapa s/n, Ixtapa, Guerrero 40880, tel. 755/553-0333, toll-free U.S. tel. 888/726-0528, from Canada toll-free 866/299-7096, fax 755/553-0216, nhkrystalixtapa@nh-hotels.com.mx, www.nh-hotels.com, credit cards accepted, $125 d low season, $160 high), which towers over its spacious garden compound. The hotel's innovative wedge design ensures an ocean view from each room. Relaxation centers on the blue pool, where guests enjoy watching each other slip from the water slide and duck beneath the waterfall all day. The 260 tastefully appointed deluxe rooms and suites have private view balconies, satellite TV, a/c, and phones. Rooms rent from a low of about $125 d low season, to about $160 high. Check for additional discounts through extended-stay or other packages. Extras include tennis courts,

racquetball, an exercise gym, parking, and wheelchair access.

OVER $200

If the NH Krystal is full, try the nearly-as-good **Hotel Dorado Pacífico** (Paseo Ixtapa s/n, P.O. Box 15, Ixtapa, Guerrero 40880, tel. 755/553-2025, fax 755/553-0126, U.S. toll-free tel. 888/738-4205, Canada toll-free tel. 866/295-6971, reserv@doradopacifico.com.mx, www.doradopacifico.com.mx, credit cards accepted, $180 d low season, $220 high) next door. Besides the gorgeous ocean and beachfront, three palm-shaded blue pools, water slides, a swim-up bar, and three restaurant/bars keep the guests happy. Upstairs, the rooms, all with sea-view balconies, are pleasingly decorated with sky-blue carpets and earth-tone designer bedspreads. The 285 rooms include buffet breakfast, with a/c, phones, and TV, and two children under 12 with parents stay free. Low-season and extended stay discounts may be available. Other extras include tennis courts, parking, and wheelchair access.

The ◖ **Hotel Barceló Ixtapa Beach** (Paseo Ixtapa s/n, Ixtapa, Guerrero 40880, tel. 755/555-2000, fax 755/553-2438, U.S.-Canada toll-free tel. 800/227-2356, reservas@barcelo ixtapa.com.mx, www.barceloixtapa.com, $175 pp double occupancy all-inclusive low season, $220 high), across from the golf course at the east end of the beach, rises around a soaring lobby/atrium, both grand and intimate, with soft chairs and sofas, made for pleasant relaxation. The Barceló (formerly the Sheraton), which operates, at this writing, **only on an all-inclusive** basis, offers a long list of resort facilities, such as multiple pools, many sports, an exercise gym, several restaurants and bars, cooking and arts lessons, live music and dancing, and a Fiesta Mexicana show Wednesdays. The more than 300 rooms and suites (which include either mountain- or ocean-view private balconies) are spacious and tastefully furnished in designer pastels and include a/c, phones, and satellite TV. The all-inclusive tariffs run about $175 per person double occupancy, low season, $220 high, kids under 6 free with parents,

6–12 $45, including all in-house drinks, food, and entertainment.

From the adjacent jungly hilltop, the **Ⓒ Hotel las Brisas Ixtapa** (Paseo de la Roca, P.O. Box 97, Ixtapa, Guerrero 40880, tel. 755/553-2121, toll-free Mex. tel. 01-800/227-4727 or 01-800/713-3233, toll-free U.S./Can. tel. 888/559-4329, fax 755/553-1038, ixtapa@brisas.com.mx, www.brisas.com.mx, $180 d low season, $350 high, and up) slopes downhill to the shore like a latter-day Aztec pyramid. The monumentally stark hilltop lobby, unadorned except for a clutch of huge stone balls, contrasts sharply with its surroundings. The hotel's severe lines immediately shift the focus to the adjacent jungle. The fecund forest aroma wafts into the lobby and the terrace restaurant, where, at breakfast, during the winter and early spring, guests sit watching iguanas munch hibiscus blossoms in the nearby treetops. The hotel entertains guests with a wealth of luxurious resort facilities, including pools, four tennis courts, a gym, aerobics, an intimate shoal-enfolded beach, restaurants, bars, and nightly piano bar music. The standard rooms, each with its own spacious view patio, are luxuriously spartan, floored with big designer tiles, furnished in earth tones, and equipped with big TVs, small refrigerators, phones, and a/c. More luxurious options include suites with individual pools and hot tubs. The 427 rooms begin at about $180 for a standard low-season double, $350 high, and run about twice that for the superluxurious suites.

RV Parking and Tent Camping

Ixtapa and Zihuatanejo has one small long-time RV park and one newcomer park. The longtimer is **Camping Park las Cabañas** (P.O. Box 197, Zihuatanejo, Guerrero 40880, tel. 755/554-4718, $12 RV site, $6 tent site), a block from Playa la Ropa. Here, you can find out what it's like to park or camp in someone's shady backyard. Friendly, retired owner-managers María Elena and Hernán Cabañas, in order to make ends meet, decided to rent out their front and back yards. The result is enough space for a dozen tents or four medium-sized

RVs in back, and one in front, with electricity, water, showers, and toilets. The price is certainly right—about $6 per person for tents, RVs $12—and it's only a block from one of the loveliest resort beaches in Pacific Mexico.

The bare-bones newcomer place to park your RV (at far end of Playa la Ropa, Zihuatanejo, Guerrero, 40880, by the mangrove lagoon between the Hotel Casa del Mar and the Restaurant El Manglar, tel. 755/554-3752, $8 RV or tent site). Here, the restaurant owners who run the trailer park offer parking space for about half a dozen self-contained RVs. Facilities, if any, are minimal. Figure about $8 a night to set up a tent or park your RV. Bring your insect repellent.

House, Apartment, and Condo Rentals

Zihuatanejo residents sometimes offer their condos and homes for rental through agents. Contact highly recommended real-estate agent **Judith Whitehead** (tel. 755/554-6226, cellular tel. 044-755/557-0078, fax 755/5531212, judith@paradise-properties.com.mx, www.paradise-properties.com.mx).

FOOD
Zihuatanejo
BREAKFAST AND ECONOMY MEALS

Downtown Zihuatanejo has a good bakery, the **Buen Gusto** (Guerrero 11, 8 A.M.–10 P.M. daily), on the east side of the street, a few doors up the street from Coconuts Restaurant. Choose from a simply delicious assortment of fruit and nut tarts and cakes: pineapple, coconut, peach, strawberry, pecan, with coffee to go with them all.

For something cool, stop by the ice shop **Paletería y Nevería Michoacana** (across from the Zihatanejo beachfront plaza). Besides ice cream, popcorn, and safe *nieves* (ices), it offers delicious *aguas* (fruit-flavored drinks), which make nourishing, refreshing non-Pepsi alternatives.

Tasty, promptly served breakfasts are the specialty of the downtown **Cafetería Nueva Zelandia** (on Cuauhtémoc, corner of Ejido, tel.

© BRUCE WHIPPERMAN

Zihuatanejo has its share of late-night taco stands, where you can get two or three tacos for a dollar.

753/554-2340, 8 A.M.–10 P.M. daily). Favorites include hotcakes, eggs any style ($3–5), fruit, juices, and espresso coffee. Nueva Zelandia serves lunch and supper also.

Playa Madera's crowd-pleasing breakfast spot is family-run **(La Casa** (Calle Adelita 7, tel. 755/554-3469, 8 A.M.–1 P.M. daily except Mon.) Dad, mom, and the kids put out a steady stream of omelettes, pancakes, breakfast burritos, fruit, tamales, sausage, ham, and fried potatoes ($3–6) to a continuous stream of satisfied customers.

Economy meals in Zihuatanejo are invariably local style. The most concentrated collection of local food eateries (known as *fondas*) line the short east-side lane that connects beachfront Avenida Álvarez north to Calle Bravo. Here, you can enjoy your heart's desire of hearty tacos, enchiladas, *chiles rellenos,* and *guisados* (stews) ($2–5).

Also on the east side of town, half a block off Paseo del Palmar, local folks swear by **(Cocina Economica Doña Licha** (Calle Cocos #8, tel. 755/554-3933, 7 A.M.–11 P.M.

daily). The reason is clear: tasty local-style food, served promptly in an airy, spic-and-span setting. Here customers have it all: for breakfast *huevos Mexicanos* ($3) or pancakes ($2); for *lonche,* go for the four-course *comida corrida* set lunch ($5); for *cena* (supper), try tacos, enchiladas, *chiles rellenos,* and *pozole* ($2–5). To get there, from Plaza Kyoto, follow the canal east one block, and turn left on to Diamante.

Back downtown, families fill the tables at petite **Cocina Economica Carol** (on Cuauhtémoc, west side, between Gonzales and Ejido, tel. 755/556-6463, 8 A.M.–8 P.M. Mon.–Sat.). They enjoy country-style breakfasts (*chilaquiles, huevos a la Mexicana* $2–3), *comida* (soup, rice, meat entrée, and dessert, $3), and supper (*tacos, enchiladas, tostadas,* $2–3).

RESTAURANTS
Local chefs and restaurateurs, long accustomed to foreign tastes, operate a number of good restaurants, mostly in Zihuatanejo, where, in contrast to Ixtapa, most of the serious eating occurs *outside* hotel dining rooms. (Some

restaurants popular with foreign visitors, noted below, close during low-season months of September and October.)

Zihuatanejo has a pair of moderately priced, genuinely local-style restaurants in the downtown area. **❰ Tamales y Atoles "Any"** (corner Guerrero and Ejido, tel. 755/554-7373, 9 A.M.–11 P.M. daily), Zihuatanejo's clean, well-lighted place for Mexican food, is the spot to find out if your favorite Mexican restaurant back home is serving the real thing. Tacos, tamales, quesadillas, enchiladas, *chiles rellenos* ($4–8) and such goodies are called *antojitos* in Mexico. At Tamales y Atoles "Any," they're savory enough to please even demanding Mexican palates. Incidentally, "Any" (AH-nee) is the co-owner, whose perch is behind the cash register, while her friendly husband cooks and tends the tables.

Restaurant los Braseros (Ejido 21, 4 P.M.– 1 A.M. daily), half a block along Ejido between Cuauhtémoc and Guerrero, is similarly authentic and popular. Waiters are often busy after midnight even during low season, serving seven kinds of tacos and specialties such as Gringa, Porky, and Azteca ($2–6) from a menu it would take three months of dinners (followed by a six-month diet) to fully investigate.

Longtime **Casa Elvira** (on waterfront Paseo del Pescador, by the naval compound, tel. 755/554-2061, 1–10 P.M. daily, entrees $4–12), founded long ago by now-octogenarian Elvira Campos, is as popular as ever, still satisfying the palates of a battalion of loyal Zihuatanejo longtimers. Elvira's continuing popularity is easy to explain: a palm-studded beachfront, strumming guitars, whirling ceiling fans, and a list of superfresh salads, soups, fish, meat, and Mexican specialties, expertly prepared and professionally served. Reservations recommended during the high season.

If Elvira's is full, an excellent alternative half a block east is **Porto di Mare** (Paseo del Pescador 56, corner of Cinco de Mayo, tel. 755/555-3902, noon–11 P.M. daily, closed Sept.–Oct., entrees $8–14), the labor of love of its Italian architect owner, who designed and crafted its elegant open-air interior himself. As would be expected, his specialties are Italian-style pastas blended with the superbly fresh local seafood.

For hot sandwiches and pizza on the downtown beach, try the **Café Marina** (Paseo del Pescador, just west of the plaza, tel. 755/554-2462, noon–10 P.M. Mon.–Sat., closed approximately June–mid-Sept., entrees $6–$8) The friendly, hardworking owner features specials, such as a ribs and potato salad ($8) or a spaghetti party—either bolognese, pesto, or primavera ($6)—Wednesday night and maybe chili on Friday ($3). The shelves of books for lending or exchange are nearly as popular as the food.

A local vacation wouldn't be complete without dropping in to the **Sirena Gorda** (Fat Mermaid; near the end of Paseo del Pescador across from the naval compound, tel. 755/554-2687, 8 A.M.–11 P.M. daily except Wed., entrees $3–7). Here the fishing crowd relaxes, trading stories after a tough day hauling in the lines. The other unique attractions, besides the well-endowed sea nymphs who decorate the walls, are tempting shrimp-bacon and fish tacos, juicy hamburgers, fish *mole,* and conch and nopal (cactus leaves, minus the spines) plates.

No guide to Zihuatanejo restaurants would be complete without mention of the restaurant **❰ Coconuts** (on Guerrero, a block from the beach, across from Posada Citlali, tel. 755/554-2518, noon–midnight daily in season, closed approximately July–Oct., entrées $8–15). Here, the entrées—seafood, pasta, chicken, and steaks ($8–15)—although tasty, appear to be of equal importance to its airy garden setting and good cheer generated among the droves of Zihuatanejo longtimers who return year after year.

On the other side of downtown, the up-and-coming owners of **Restaurant Caprichio** (on Cinco de Mayo, next to the church, tel. 755/554-3019, noon–midnight daily, entrees $7–16) have used the successful example of Coconuts as a model. Soft background jazz, fairy lights, and a tropical plant-festooned patio set the scene, while the cuisine, especially good seafood pastas, steaks, and hamburgers provide the main event.

Restaurant Kau Kan (on the road above

Playa Madera, half a block uphill from Hotel Irma, tel. 755/554-8446, noon–6 P.M. and 7 P.M.–midnight daily, call to confirm hours, closed Sept.–Oct., entrees $15–30) continues to be popular for both its romantic view location and its excellent food and service. While music plays softly and bay breezes gently blow, waiters scurry, bringing savory appetizers ($4–7), romaine Caesar salad ($7), and cooked-to-perfection *dorado,* lobster, steak, and shrimp; high-season reservations mandatory.

At least as worthy is Mediterranean boutique 🍴 **Restaurant Il Mare** (right next door, tel. 755/554-9067, 1–11 P.M. daily high season, approximately 4 P.M.–11 P.M. low, entrees to $20). Enter and let the luscious ambience—soothing Italian arias, waves crashing against the rocks far below, the golden setting sun—transport you somewhere to the southern Amalfi coast: *O! Sole mio!* The menu extends the impression; first with *bruschetta alla Romagna* ($4); follow with soup *brodetta di pesce* ($7); salad *pomodoro cipolla rossa con gorgonzola* ($6); and *scampi al vino bianco* ($20), accompanied by a bottle of good Chilean Sendero chardonnay ($19). Finish off with lemon liqueur Sogna di Sorrento ($5). Reservations necessary in high season.

For a nouvelle variation, sample the "fusion" cuisine of hot new **Restaurant la Gula** (Playa Madera, tel. 755/554-8396, 5–11:30 P.M. daily, closed Sept.–Oct., entrees $12–30). Here, chefs refine the art of small portions and artful presentation of seafood (clams, lobster, shrimp, scallops, $15–30), and steaks and chicken ($12–25). Reservations strongly recommended.

Ixtapa
BAKERIES AND BREAKFAST
The perfume wafting from freshly baked European-style yummies draws dozens of the faithful to the nearby 🍴 **Golden Cookie Shop** (on the upper floor of the Los Patios shopping complex, tel. 755/553-0310, 8 A.M.–3 P.M. Mon.–Fri., 8 A.M.–1 P.M. Sat., closed May through Oct.), brainchild of local German expatriate Helmut (and his late wife, Esther) Walter. He carries on, satisfying homesick palates with a continuous supply of scrumptious cinnamon

rolls, pies, and hot buns, and hearty American-style breakfasts ($4–6) daily. In recent years, Helmut has served an authentic German buffet ($8) every Friday; call to confirm.

Alternatively, sample the good coffee and baked offerings of **Pan Nuestro** (Our Bread) bakery, also in the Los Patios complex (tel. 755/553-3563, 8 A.M.–11 P.M. daily).

The 🍴 **Café Toko Tucán** (on the west front corner of the Los Patios shopping complex, across the boulevard from Hotel Bay View Resort, tel. 755/553-0717, 9 A.M.–10 P.M. daily), offers a refreshing alternative to hotel breakfasts. White cockatoos and bright toucans in a leafy patio add an exotic touch as you enjoy the fare, which, besides the usual juices, eggs, hotcakes, and French toast, includes lots of salads, veggie burgers, and sandwiches ($2–7).

RESTAURANTS
Restaurants in Ixtapa have to be exceptional to compete with the hotels. One such, the **Bella Vista** (in the Las Brisas Ixtapa, tel. 755/553-2121, 7 A.M.–11 P.M. daily, credit cards accepted, entrées $8–16), is *in* a hotel, being the Las Brisas Ixtapa's view-terrace café. Breakfast buffet ($12) is the favorite time to watch the antics of the iguanas in the adjacent jungle treetops. These black, green, and white miniature dinosaurs crawl up and down the trunks, munch flowers, and sunbathe on the branches. The food and service, incidentally, are quite good. Call ahead to reserve a terrace-edge table.

An Ixtapa restaurant that has customers even when others don't is 🍴 **Restaurant Mama Norma and Deborah** (La Puerta shopping center, in the rear, by Da Baffone Italian restaurant, tel. 755/553-0274, 11 A.M.–11 P.M. Mon.–Sat., 3–11 P.M. Sun., closed Wed., entrees $10–25). Canadian-born proprietor Deborah Thompson manages with aplomb, working from a menu of delicious specialties familiar to North American and European palates. Whatever your choice, be it Greek salad ($5), lobster ($25), steak ($15), or fettuccine Alfredo ($10), Deborah makes sure it pleases.

Those hankering for Italian-style pastas and seafood walk to 🍴 **Ristorante Da Baffone** (next door, tel. 755/553-1122, about noon–midnight daily during high season, 5–11 P.M. low, entrees $12–18). The friendly owner, a native of the Italian isle of Sardinia, claims his restaurant is the oldest establishment in Ixtapa. He's probably right: He served his first meal here in 1978, simultaneous with the opening of Ixtapa's first hotel, right across the boulevard. While Mediterranean-Mex decor covers the walls, marinara-style shrimp and clams with linguini, calamari, ricotta-and-spinach-stuffed cannelloni ($12–18) and glasses of chianti and chardonnay ($5–7) load the tables. Call for reservations.

The Ixtapa visitor influx has resulted in more recommendable Ixtapa restaurants. Favorite Zihuatanejo eateries have added branches here, notably **Tamales y Atoles "Any,"** (on the north edge of La Puerta shopping complex, behind Restaurant Mama Norma and Deborah, tel. 755/553-3370, daily 8 A.M.–8 P.M.), and Nueva Zelandia (tel. 755/553-0038, in shopping Plaza Kiosko, 8 A.M.–8 P.M. daily).

Ruben's hamburger and taco hall is Ixtapa's most popular eatery, especially with the flocks of new Mexican vacationers (at the north end of the Ixtapa Centro Comercial shopping complex, behind the corner Galerias Ixtapa center, about a block inland from boulevard Paseo Ixtapa, tel. 755/553-0027, 8 A.M.–midnight daily). Ruben's is a phenomenon as much as it is a restaurant, outdoing traditional *taquerías* (taco stalls) at their own game, with superfine and fresh ingredients and snappy service by a squadron of eager young servers. Favorite choices are mesquite charcoal-grilled Sonora top sirloin, in steaks, hamburgers and tacos, in a dozen variations ($3–5).

(Other Ixtapa restaurants, popular for their party atmosphere, are described under *Entertainment and Events*.)

ENTERTAINMENT AND EVENTS

In Zihuatanejo, visitors and residents content themselves mostly with quiet pleasures. Afternoons, they stroll the beachfront or the downtown shady lanes and enjoy coffee or drinks with friends at small cafés and bars. As the sun goes down, however, folks head to Ixtapa for its sunset vistas, happy hours, shows, clubs, and dancing.

Sunsets

Sunsets are tranquil and often magnificent from the 🄲 **Restaurant/Bar El Faro,** tel. 755/553-1027, which even has a cableway that you can ride uphill from the south end of the Ixtapa beach, 7 A.M.–7 P.M. Many visitors stay to enjoy dinner and the relaxing piano bar. The restaurant is open low season, around 5:30–10 P.M. daily, longer hours high season; reservations are recommended winter and weekends. Drive or taxi via the uphill road toward the Hotel las Brisas Ixtapa, east of the golf course; at the first fork, head right for El Faro.

For equally brilliant sunsets in a lively but refined setting, try the **lobby bar** of the **Hotel las Brisas Ixtapa.** Happy hour runs 6–7 P.M.; piano bar or seasonal live music for dancing begins around 7:30 P.M. (call tel. 755/553-2121 to confirm programs.) Drive or taxi, following the signs, along the uphill road at the golf course, following the signs to the crest of the hill just south of the Ixtapa beach.

Zihuatanejo Bay's west-side headland blocks most Zihuatanejo sunset views, except for spots at the far end of Playa la Ropa. Here, guests take in the longtime beachfront favorite **Restaurant la Perla** (tel. 755/554-2700, 10 A.M.–10 P.M.).

Cruises

Those who want to experience a sunset party while at sea ride the 75-foot catamaran **Picante,** which leaves from the Zihuatanejo pier (call to confirm schedule) around 5:30 P.M. daily, returning around 8 P.M. The tariff runs about $50 per person, including open bar.

The *Picante* also heads out daily on a Sunshine Cruise around 10 A.M., returning around 2:30 P.M. Included are open bar, lunch, and snorkeling, for about $75 per person. Book tickets for both of these cruises, which customarily include transportation to and from your hotel, through your hotel travel agent. Tickets are also available directly, through the *Picante* office, tel. 755/554-2694 or 755/554-8270, picante@picantecruises.com, www.picante cruises.com, at Puerto Mío, the small marina about half a mile across the bay from town. Get there via the road that curves around the western, right-hand shore of Zihuatanejo Bay.

Tourist Shows

Ixtapa hotels stage **Fiesta Mexicana** extravaganzas, which begin with a sumptuous buffet and go on to a whirling skirt-and-sombrero folkloric ballet. After that, the audience becomes part of the act, with piñatas, games, cockfights, dancing, while enjoying drinks from an open bar. In the finale, fireworks often boom over the beach, painting the night sky in festoons of reds, blues, and greens.

Entrance runs about $30–40 per person, with kids under 12 usually half price. Shows (often seasonally only) Sat., at the **Presidente Intercontinental,** tel. 755/553-0018; at the **Dorado Pacífico,** tel. 755/553-2025; and Wed. at the **Barceló,** tel. 755/555-2000, are the most reliable and popular. Usually open to non-guests; call ahead for confirmation and reservations.

Bars and Clubs

Nightlife lovers are blessed with a broad range of enjoyable choices, sprinkled around Ixtapa and Zihuatanejo. In Ixtapa, options vary from the zany Carlos 'n Charlie's to the relaxed piano bar at El Faro restaurant. Zihuatanejo choices run from the big-name jazz club Blue Mamou to restful Restaurant Coconuts lounge bar.

Clubs and bars in Ixtapa are spread along main boulevard Paseo del Palmar, and have the highest-volume, latest-night options. Most of the Zihuatanejo choices are downtown (and usually close before midnight) and can be best discovered on a night-time stroll while looking and listening for what you want.

Beginning in **Ixtapa,** high on the list is the part restaurant and part wacky seasonal nightspot **Carlos 'n Charlie's** (on the beachfront, about half a block on the driveway road west past the Hotel Posada Real, tel. 755/553-0085, noon–midnight daily). It's as wild and as much

fun as all of the other Carlos Anderson restaurants from Puerto Vallarta to Paris. Here, you can have your picture taken on a surfboard in front of a big wave for $3, or have a fireman spray out the flames from the chili sauce on your plate. Loud recorded rock music ($10 minimum) goes on 10 P.M.–4 A.M. during the winter season.

For more of the same, but even more loud and outrageous, go to **Señor Frog's** (in the Ixtapa shopping plaza, across from the Hotel Presidente Intercontinental, tel. 755/553-2282).

Other Ixtapa choices include **Liquid** late-night cocktail bar (behind Rafaello's restaurant, at the north end of the Ixtapa Commercial Center, opens about midnight) with a DJ spinning techno-rock-progressive music; and the piano-bar at **El Faro** restaurant (atop the lighthouse in Marina Ixtapa, tel. 755/553-2090).

Continuing to **Zihuatanejo** the hottest choice is **Blue Mamou** (tel. 755/544-8025, www .bluemamou.com, winter-spring 9 P.M.–2 A.M. daily), "Zihuatanejo's new home for jazz," on Paseo del Palma, on the way to Playa la Ropa. Here, you can enjoy cocktails, barbeque, and snacks ($5–15) with professional name-band jazz in a stylish blue-motif night club setting. Find it in the big blue building on the right, past the curve where the road climbs the hill. For programs, call, visit www.bluemamou .com, or see the local tourist newspapers.

In Zihuatanejo downtown, check out open-air **Restaurant Bandidos** (on Cinco de Mayo near the church, tel. 755/553-8072), colorfully decorated in faux-1910 Revolution style, with plenty of old Pancho Villa and Emiliano Zapata *bandido* photos. Guests sing along to the music, both live and recorded, nightly high season, weekends low season until around midnight. Call to confirm hours.

More Zihuatanejo choices (in declining order of volume) include **Black Bull** (corner of N. Bravo and V. Guerrero, tel. 755/554-2230), a younger-crowd disco; **Rick's** (on Cuauhtémoc downtown, tel. 755/554-2535), with live music nightly, from around 6 P.M., and sometimes shows, popular with sailboaters; the **Bay Club** (on the cliff-top road to Playa la Ropa, tel. 75/554-4844), with panoramic bay view and live evening jazz; and the upscale **Coconuts Lounge-Bar** and restaurant (on Guerrero, a block from the beach, tel. 755/554-2518), in a relaxing garden setting, with hammocks, sofas, and videos.

Dancing and Discos

Several Ixtapa hotel lobbies bloom with dance music from around 7 P.M. during the high winter season. Year-round, however, good medium-volume groups sometimes play for dancing evenings, at the **Presidente Intercontinental,** tel. 755/553-0018; the **Barceló,** tel. 755/555-2000, and the **Las Brisas,** tel. 755/553-2121. Programs change, so call ahead to confirm.

Christine, Ixtapa's big-league discotheque in the Hotel NH Krystal, offers fantasy for a cover charge of $10 women, $20 men. From 10 P.M., patrons warm up, listen to relatively low-volume rock, watch videos, and talk while they can still hear each other. That stops around 11:30 P.M., when the fogs descend, the lights begin flashing, and the speakers boom forth their 200-decibel equivalent of a fast freight train roaring at trackside. Call to verify times, tel. 755/553-0333.

Also, check out clubs **Liquid, Black Bull,** and **Rick's** in the *Bars and Clubs* section for music for dancing.

SPORTS AND RECREATION
Walking and Jogging

Zihuatanejo Bay is strollable from the Playa Madera all the way west to Puerto Mío. A relaxing half-day adventure could begin by taxiing to the Hotel Irma, Avenida Adelita, on Playa Madera, for breakfast. Don your hats and follow the stairs down to Playa Madera and walk west toward town. At the end of the Playa Madera sand, head left along the *andador* (walkway) that twists along the rocks, around the bend toward town. Continue along the beachfront Paseo del Pescador; at the west end, cross the lagoon bridge, and head left along the bayside road to **Puerto Mío** resort

and marina for a drink at the hotel's La Cala restaurant and perhaps a dip in the pool. Allow three hours, including breakfast, for this two-mile walk; do the reverse trip during late afternoon for sunset drinks or dinner at the Irma.

Playa del Palmar, Ixtapa's main beach, is good for similar strolls. During high winter-spring season, start in the morning with breakfast (not served low season) at the Restaurant/Bar El Faro, tel. 755/555-2510) atop the hill at the south end of the beach; high-season breakfast hours 6–11 A.M. daily. Ride the cableway or walk downhill. With the sun at your back, stroll the beach, stopping for refreshments at the hotel pool patios en route. The entire beach stretches about three miles to the marina jetty, where you can often watch surfers challenging the waves and where taxis and buses return along Paseo Ixtapa. Allow about four hours, including breakfast.

The **reverse walk** would be equally enjoyable during the afternoon. Time yourself to arrive at the El Faro cableway about half an hour before sundown (7:30 P.M. summers, 5:30 P.M. winters) to enjoy the sunset over drinks and/or dinner. Get to El Faro by driving or taxiing via Paseo de la Roca, which heads uphill off the Zihuatanejo road at the golf course. Follow the first right fork to El Faro.

Adventurers who enjoy ducking through underbrush and scrambling over rocks might enjoy exploring the acacia forest and pristine beaches of the uninhabited west side of **Isla Ixtapa.** Take water, lunch, and a good pair of walking shoes.

Joggers often practice their art either on the smooth, firm sands of Ixtapa's main beachfront or on Paseo Ixtapa's sidewalks. Avoid crowds and midday heat by jogging early mornings or late afternoons. For even better beach jogging, try the flat, firm sands of uncrowded Playa Quieta, about three miles by car or taxi northwest of Ixtapa. The mile-long Playa la Ropa can be enjoyed by early morning and late-afternoon joggers.

Golf and Tennis

Ixtapa's 18-hole, professionally designed

Campo de Golf is open to the public. In addition to its manicured, 6,898-yard course, patrons enjoy full facilities, including pool, restaurant, pro shop, lockers, and tennis courts. Greens fee runs about $65, cart $30, club rental $25, 18 holes with caddy $20. Play goes on 7 A.M.–5:30 P.M. daily. The clubhouse, tel. 755/553-1062, is off Paseo Ixtapa, across from the Barceló. Reservations are accepted; morning golfers, get in line early during the high winter season.

The **Marina Golf Course,** tel. 755/553-1410 or 755/553-1424, offers similar services (greens fee $55, cart $30, club rental $30, caddy $20).

Ixtapa has virtually all of the local **tennis** courts, all of them private. The Campo de Golf has some of the best. Rentals run about $7/hour days, $10 nights. Reservations, tel. 755/553-1062, may be seasonally necessary. A pro shop rents and sells equipment. A teaching professional offers lessons for about $25 per hour.

Several hotels also have tennis courts, equipment, and lessons. Call the **Barceló,** tel. 755/555-2000; **Dorado Pacífico,** tel. 755/553-2025; **NH Krystal,** tel. 755/553-0333; and the **Las Brisas,** tel. 755/553-2121, for information.

Horseback Riding

"Spiderman" Margarito, manager of the stable at **Playa Linda,** rents horses daily for beach riding for about $15 per hour, low season, $20 high. Travel agencies and hotels offer the same, though for higher prices.

Bicycling

Ixtapa's popular pastime is bicycling along the new 10-mile round-trip *ciclopista* bike path to Playa Linda. The main rental station is on the main boulevard, Paseo Ixtapa, in front of the Hotel Emporio by Banco Internacional. Bargain for a discount from the steep $10/hour asking rate.

The *ciclopista* takes off north, across the street from the Banco Internacional rental station, at the Paseo las Garzas intersection. Officially the *ciclopista* ends five miles west, at the wooden bridge and crocodile-viewing point at the Playa Linda parking lot, but you can go another 1.5 miles farther to Barrio Viejo village at the lagoon's edge. Be sure to take a hat, water, and insect repellent.

If, on your return approach to Ixtapa, you haven't enjoyed your fill of bicycling, you can rack up more mileage along the Zihuatanejo *ciclopista* leg: Heading back to Ixtapa, about 100 yards after the intersection that directs traffic left to Highway 200, bear left at Paseo de los Pelicanos and follow the Zihuatanejo *ciclopista* leg past the back (northwest) side of the golf course, another eight miles (13 km) two hours (leisurely), to Zihuatanejo and return.

Swimming and Surfing

Calm Zihuatanejo Bay is fine for swimming and sometimes good for boogie boarding and bodysurfing at Playa Madera. On Playa la Ropa, although waves generally break too near shore for either bodysurfing or boogie boarding, swimming beyond the breakers is fine. Surfing is very rewarding at Playa las Gatas, where swells sweeping around the south-end point give good, rolling left-handed breaks.

Heading northwest to more open coast, waves improve for bodysurfing and boogie boarding along Ixtapa's main beach Playa del Palmar, while usually remaining calm and undertow-free enough for swimming beyond the breakers. As for surfing, good breaks sometimes rise off the Playa Escolleros jetty at the west end of Playa del Palmar.

Surfing lessons have arrived in Zihuatanejo, at **Catcha L'Ola** (Alvarez 37, tel. 755/553-1384, local cellular 044-755/557-1442, catchalola333@prodigy.net.mx, www.ixtapasurf.com), across the street from the Zihuatanejo beachfront plaza. In Ixtapa, go the **Centro Comercial Kiosko,** behind Mama Norma and Deborah restaurant. Besides surfing lessons and luxury camping trips to all the best local surfing beaches, they offer board and equipment rentals and repair, and for-sale accessories equipment, information, and cheap beer.

Along Ixtapa's outer beaches, swimming is

© BRUCE WHIPPERMAN

Playa las Gatas, accessible only by boat, is great for surfing, snorkeling, and scuba diving right from the beach.

great along very calm Playa Quieta; surfing, bodysurfing, and boogie boarding are correspondingly good but hazardous in the sometimes mountainous open-ocean surf of Playa Larga farther north.

Snorkeling and Scuba Diving

Clear offshore waters (sometimes up to 100-foot visibility during the dry winter-spring season) have drawn a steady flow of divers and nurtured professionally staffed and equipped dive shops. Just offshore, good snorkel and scuba spots, where swarms of multicolored fish graze and glide amoung the rocks and corals, are accessible from **Playa las Gatas** and **Playa Carey** on Isla Ixtapa.

Many boat operators take parties for offshore snorkeling excursions. On Playa la Ropa, contact the aquatics shop at the foot of the hill beneath Hotel Sotavento. Playa las Gatas, easily accessible by boat for $4 from the Zihuatanejo pier, also has snorkel and excursion boat rentals. In Ixtapa, similar services are available at beachfront shops at many of the hotels, such

as the Posada Real, the NH Krystal, and the Presidente Intercontinental.

Other even more spectacular offshore sites, such as Morros de Potosí, El Yunque, Bajo de Chato, Bajo de Torresillas, Piedra Soletaria, and Sacramento, are accessible with the help of professional guides and instructors.

A pair of local scuba dive shops stand out. In Zihuatanejo, licensed longtime instructors Carlos Bustamante and L. Ricardo Gutiérez carry on Zihuatanejo's professional scuba tradition, with **Nautilus Divers** (at Juan Álvarez 33, two blocks west of the Zihuatanejo beachfront plaza, tel. 755/554-9191, nautilusdivers@hotmail.com, www.nautilus-divers.com). They begin with the resort course, with two hours of pool instruction and a guided dive, for $80. Open-water NAUI certification takes three or four days and runs about $450. For certified divers (bring your certificate) they offer night, shipwreck, deep-water, and marine biology dives at more than three dozen coastal sites.

Carlo Scuba (Playa las Gatas, tel./fax 755/554-6003, carloscuba@yahoo.com, www.carloscuba.com) also offers professional scuba services. The PADI-trained instructors offer a resort course, including one beach dive, for $60; a five-day open-water certification course, $400; and a two-tank dive trip for certified participants, $80, one-tank $55. They also conduct student referral courses and night dives. Contact the manager-owner, friendly Jean-Claude Duran (known locally as Jack Cousteau), and his son Thierry, on las Gatas beach.

Sailing, Sailboarding, and Kayaking

The tranquil waters of Zihuatanejo Bay, Ixtapa's Playa del Palmar, and the quiet strait off Playa Quieta are good for these low-power aquatic sports. Shops on Playa la Ropa (at Hotel Sotavento and Catalina) in Zihuatanejo Bay and at beachfront at Ixtapa hotels, such as the NH Krystal, Presidente Intercontinental, and Dorado Pacifico, rent small sailboats, sailboards, and kayaks hourly.

Lagoon Kayaking and Bird-watching

The grand Laguna de Potosí and the smaller, more remote Estero Valentin, abour 10 and 20 miles (16 and 32 km), respectively, southeast of Zihuatanejo, have become prime wildlife viewing sites, due to the enterprise of Ixtapa-based Zoe Kayak Tours (contact Brian in Ixtapa, at 755/553-0496, zoe5@aol.com, www.zoekayaktours.com). The earnest, wildlife-sensitive operators conduct thoroughly professional excursions, designed to maximize the quality of participants' wildlife-viewing experience and appreciation. Itineraries vary from half-day outings to extended overnights and more.

Fishing

Surf or rock casting with bait or lures, depending on conditions, is generally successful in local waters. Have enough line to allow casting beyond the waves (about 50 feet out on Playa la Ropa, 100 feet on Playa del Palmar and Playa Linda).

The rocky ends of Playas la Ropa, la Madera, del Palmar, and las Gatas on the mainland, and Playa Carey on Isla Ixtapa, are also good for casting.

For deep-sea fishing, you can launch your own boat or rent one. *Pangas* (launches) are available for hire from individual fishermen on the beach, or from the boat cooperative at Zihuatanejo pier, or the aquatics shops of the Hotel Sotavento on Playa la Ropa or the Hotels las Brisas Ixtapa, Barceló, NH Krystal, and others on the beach in Ixtapa. Rental for a seaworthy *panga,* including tackle and bait, should run about $20 per hour, depending upon the season and your bargaining skill. An experienced boatman can help you and your friends hook, typically, six or eight big fish in about four hours, which local restaurants are often willing to serve as a small banquet for you in return for your extra fish.

Big-Game Sportfishing

Zihuatanejo has long been a center for billfish (marlin, swordfish, and sailfish) hunting. Most local captains have organized themselves into cooperatives, which visitors can contact either directly or through town or hotel travel agents. Trips begin around 7 A.M. and return 2–3 P.M. Fishing success depends on seasonal conditions. If you're not sure of your prospects, go down to the Zihuatanejo pier around 2:30 P.M. and see what the boats are bringing in. During good times they often return with one or more big marlin or swordfish per boat (although captains are increasingly asking that billfish be set free after the battle has been won). Fierce fighters, the sinewy billfish do not make the best eating and are often discarded after the pictures are taken. On average, boats bring in two or three other large fish, such as *dorado* (dolphinfish or mahimahi), yellowfin tuna, and roosterfish, more highly prized for the dinner table.

The biggest local sportfishing outfitter is the blue and white fleet of the **Sociedad Cooperativa Teniente Azueta** (office at the foot of the pier, tel./fax 755/554-2056, 6 A.M.–6 P.M. daily), named after the naval hero Lieutenant José Azueta. You can see adjacent to the Zihuatanejo pier many of its several dozen boats bobbing at anchor.

Arrangements for fishing parties can be made through hotel travel desks or at its office at the foot of the pier. The largest 36-foot boats, with four or five lines, go out for a day's fishing for about $275 low season, $350 high. Twenty-five-foot boats with three lines run about $150 per day low season, $250 high. Smaller *pangas* go out for about $100 low season, $150 high.

The smaller (18-boat) **Servicios Sociedad Cooperativa Triangulo del Sol** (office across from the naval compound, near the west end of Paseo del Pescador, tel./fax 755/554-3758, 9 A.M.–7 P.M. daily) is trying harder. Its 36-foot boats for six start around $350; a 25-foot boat for four, about $150. Contact the office across from the naval compound, near the west end of Paseo del Pescador.

On the adjacent corner, next door, newest and trying even harder, is **Whisky Water World** (Paseo del Pescador 20, tel./fax 755/554-0147, local cell 044-755/556-6488, long-distance cell 01-755/556-6488, email whiskey@prodigy.net.mx, www.zihuatanejosportfishing.com), which claims to employ only sober captains. Its top-of-the-line-only boats run from 30 feet and $300, including license, bait, and drinks. Jack Daniel's is extra. Captains will take two people fishing, 7 A.M.–2 P.M., for $40 apiece (six-person minimum). Proud members of the IGFA (International Game Fishing Association), captains follow sailfish, tuna, and dorado catch-and-release policy.

Prices quoted by providers often (but don't necessarily) include fishing licenses, bait, tackle, and amenities such as beer, sodas, ice, and on-board toilets. Such details should be pinned down (ideally by inspecting the boat) before putting your money down.

Sportfishing Tournament

Twice a year, usually in May and January, Zihuatanejo fisherfolk sponsor the **Torneo de Pez Vela,** with prizes for the biggest catches of sailfish, swordfish, marlin, and other varieties. Entrance fee runs around $800, and the prizes usually include a new Dodge pickup, cars, and other goodies. For information, con-

tact the local sportfishing cooperative, Sociedad Cooperativa Teniente José Azueta, Muelle Municipal, Zihuatanejo, Guerrero 40880, tel. 755/554-2056, or the fishing tournament coordinator, Crecencio Cortés, tel. 755/554-8423, or Whiskey Water World.

Marina and Boat Launching

Marina Ixtapa, at the north end of Paseo Ixtapa, offers excellent boat facilities. The slip charge runs about $.90 per foot per day, for 1–6 days ($.65 for 7–29 days), subject to a minimum charge per diem. This includes use of the boat ramp, showers, pump-out, electricity, trash collection, mailbox, phone, fax, and satellite TV. For reservations and information, contact the marina 9 A.M.–2 P.M. and 4–7 P.M. daily, at the harbormaster's office in the marina-front white building on the right a block before the big white lighthouse, tel./fax 755/553-2180, 755/553-0222, 755/553-2365, or email info@marinaixtapa.com. For more information, visit www.marinaixtapa.com.

The smooth, gradual Marina Ixtapa **boat ramp,** open to the public for a modest fee, is on the right-hand side street leading to the water, just past the big white lighthouse. Get your ticket beforehand from the harbormaster.

Sports Equipment Shops

Deportes Náuticos (corner of N. Bravo and Guerrero in downtown Zihuatanejo, tel. 755/554-4411, 10 A.M.–2 P.M. and 4–9 P.M. Mon.–Sat.) sells snorkel equipment, boogie boards, tennis racquets, balls, and a load of other general sporting goods.

A pair of shops on Álvarez, near the pier, sell fishing equipment and supplies. Check out **Pesca Deportiva** (Sportfishing; at the far west end of Álvarez, corner of Armada de Mexico, tel. 755/554-3651, 9 A.M.–2 P.M. and 4–7 P.M. Mon.–Sat.), which specializes in rods, reels, lines, weights, and lures.

Alternatively, a block east, across the street **Articulos de Pesca** (Álvarez 35, tel. 755/554-6451, 9 A.M.–2 P.M. and 4–8 P.M. Mon.–Sat.) offers a similar selection of heavy-duty fishing goods.

SHOPPING
Zihuatanejo

Every day is market day at the Zihuatanejo **Mercado** on Avenida Benito Juárez, four blocks from the beach. Behind the piles of leafy greens, round yellow papayas, and huge gaping sea bass, don't miss the sugar and spice stalls. There you will find big cones of raw *panela* (brown sugar), thick, homemade golden honey, mounds of fragrant *jamaica* petals, crimson dried *chiles,* and forest-gathered roots, barks, and grasses sold in the same pungent natural forms as they have been for centuries.

For more up-to-date merchandise, go to the big Walmart-style **Comercial Mexicana** behind the bus terminals, on Highway 200, about a mile east (Acapulco direction) of downtown, tel. 755/554-8321 or 755/554-8384, 8 A.M.–11 P.M. daily. Its shelves are stacked with a plethora of quality goods, from bread and bananas, to flashlights and film.

For convenience shopping downtown, by the beach, go to the small grocery **Adriana y**

Pancho, at the plaza-front corner of Álvarez and Cuauhtémoc.

ZIHUATANEJO HANDICRAFTS SHOPPING TOUR

Although stores in the Ixtapa Centro Comercial shopping center and the adjacent tourist market (at the south-end corner, across from the Hotel Barceló) sell many handicrafts, Zihuatanejo shops offer the best overall selection and prices.

Sometime along your tour, be sure to visit the Zihuatanejo **Artisan Tourist Market** stalls, filled with a flood of attractive handicrafts brought by families who come from all parts of Pacific Mexico. Their goods—delicate Michoacán lacquerware, bright Tonalá birds, gleaming Taxco silver, whimsical Guerrero masks, rich Guadalajara leather—spread for blocks along Avenida Cinco de Mayo on the downtown west side. Compare prices; although bargaining here is customary, the glut of merchandise makes it a one-sided buyer's market, with many sellers barely managing to scrape by. If you err in your bargaining, kindly do it on the generous side.

Private downtown Zihuatanejo shops offer an abundance of fine handicrafts. The best place to start is the **Casa Marina** shopping complex, tel. 755/554-2373, a family project started by late community leader Helen Krebs Posse. Her adult children and spouses own and manage stores on the bottom floor of the two-story building, just west of the beachfront town plaza.

The original store, **Embarcadero,** on the lower floor, streetside, has an unusually choice collection of woven and embroidered finery, mostly from Oaxaca. In addition to walls and racks of colorful, museum-quality traditional blankets, flower-embroidered dresses, and elaborate crocheted *huipiles,* they also offer wooden folk-figurines and a collection of intriguing masks.

Other stores in the Casa Marina that you should visit include **La Zapoteca,** specializing in weavings from Teotitlán del Valle in Oaxaca. Also very worthwhile are **Metzli,** featuring

Camels are an unusual but attractive motif for Talavera ware.

all-Mexico crafts and resort wear selection, **El Jumil** (laquerware and masks), and **Costa Libre** (one-of-a-kind crafts and hammocks). Zapotec indigenous weavers from Oaxaca demonstrate their craft, often in the Embarcadero and La Zapoteca stores, mornings and afternoons, November through April. The entire complex is open 10 A.M.–2 P.M. and 4–8 P.M. Mon.–Sat.; credit cards are generally accepted.

Two blocks farther west, toward the pier, be sure to visit **Marea** clothing shop on Paseo del Pescador, across from the naval compound (tel. 755/554-6733, 8 A.M.–10 P.M. daily). It would be easy to pass because of its mounds of ho-hum T-shirts out front. But if you look inside, you'll find racks of many fetching hand-crocheted *huipiles* and blouses from backcountry Guerrero and Oaxaca.

Return east two blocks along Avenida Álvarez and turn inland at the corner of Cinco de Mayo to find **Artesanías Olinalá** (2 Cinco de Mayo, tel. 755/554-6733, 9 A.M.–9 P.M. daily). Inside, you can enjoy a virtual museum of the venerable Guerrero laquerware tradition, showcased by a seemingly endless collection of glossy boxes, trays, gourds, plates, and masks, all painstakingly crafted by age-old methods in the remote upcountry town of Olinalá.

After exiting Artesanías Olinalá, you could conveniently visit the **Artisan Tourist Market** stalls on the other side of Cinco de Mayo.

Continue up Cinco de Mayo, past the church, to **Art Nopal** (tel./fax 755/554-7530, 9 A.M.–9 P.M. daily high season, 10:30 A.M.– 9 P.M. low season),), the joy of the of the owner, who likes things from Oaxaca, especially baskets. He fills his shop with an organized clutter, including unique woven goods and ceramics.

Next, head right (east) at the next street, Bravo, one block to Cuauhtémoc, for a look through several more interesting shops.

At the corner, turn left, and continue a block, passing Ejido. A few doors farther, on the right, step into **Rosimar** (tel. 755/554-2864, 9 A.M.– 9 P.M. daily), the creation of Josefina and Manuel Martínez. Inside, they offer a large priced-to-sell collection of Tonalá and Tlaquepaque pottery, papier-mâché, glassware and more.

Head back down Cuauhtémoc. Turn left at Bravo, continuing another block, past Galeana, to **Galería Maya** (tel. 755/554-4606, 10 A.M.– 2 P.M. and 5–9 P.M. Mon.–Sat.) in mid-block, on the left. Here, owner Tania Scales displays a multitude of one-of-a-kind folk curios from many parts of Mexico. Her wide-ranging, carefully selected collection includes masks, necklaces, sculptures, purses, blouses, *huipiles,* ritual objects, and much more. Furthermore, be sure not to miss Tania's favorites: regal sculptures that represent a number of indigenous female deities: Ixta Bay, Maya jungle goddess; Coyolxauhqui, Aztec moon goddess; and Cihuateteo, representing all the women of Zihuatanejo.

Return to Cuauhtémoc, to **Alberto's** (tel. 755/554-2161, 9 A.M.–9 P.M. daily, credit cards accepted) pair of shops, a few doors below the corner of Bravo, on opposite sides of the street, which offer an extensive silver jewelry collection. As with gold and precious stones, silver prices can be reckoned approximately by weight, at between $1 and $1.25 per gram. The cases and cabinets of shiny earrings, chains, bracelets, rings, and much more are products of a family of artists, taught by a master craftsman Alberto, formerly of Puerto Vallarta, now deceased. Many of the designs are original, and, with bargaining, reasonably priced.

Continue another block downhill, past the corner of Ascencio, to **El Arte y Tradición** (tel. 755/554-4625, 10 A.M.–2 P.M. and 5–8 P.M. daily, credit cards accepted), where you can admire a lovely Talavera stoneware collection. This prized ceramic style, the finest of which is made by a few families in Puebla, comes in many shapes, from plates and vases, to pitchers and tea cups. Talavera's colorful floral motifs originate from a fusion of traditions, notably Moorish, Italian, Turkish, and Persian, from the Mediterranean basin.

Now that you're again near the beachfront, head east along Avenida Álvarez, half a block past the plaza, to **Cerámicas Tonalá** (at number 12B, beach side, tel. 755/554-2161, 9 A.M.–2 P.M. and 4–8 P.M. Mon.–Sat., credit cards are accepted) to view one of the finest Tonalá ceramics collections outside of the renowned source itself. Here, friendly owner Eduardo López's graceful glazed vases and plates, decorated in traditional plant and animal designs, fill the cabinets, while a menagerie of lovable owls, ducks, fish, armadillos, and frogs, all seemingly poised to spring to life, crowd the shelves.

Ixtapa

Ixtapa's **Centro Comercial** complex stretches along the midsection of Paseo Ixtapa across from the hotels. Developers built about ten sub-complexes within the Centro Comercial, but several of them remain virtually empty. The good news is that the increasing stream of visitors to Ixtapa is adding new life to the Centro Comercial. At this writing, about six subcomplexes, most fronting the boulevard, are welcoming customers.

Moving from south to north, first come the **Los Patios** and **Las Fuentes** subcomplexes, where designer stores occupy the choice boulevard frontages. Behind them, many small handicrafts stores and ordinary crafts and jewelry shops wait for customers along back lanes and inside patios.

Some stores stand out, however. Especially worth a look is the **La Fuente** (The Source) store on the ground floor, at the northeast corner of the Los Patios complex (tel. 755/553-0812, 9 A.M.–9 P.M. daily). The expertly selected all-Mexico handicrafts collection includes a treasury of picture frames, ranging from polished hardwood to mother-of-pearl; droll Day of the Dead figurines, lots of tinkling glass and ceramic bells, and a trove of women's blouses, dresses, and skirts, both traditional and stylishly up-to-date.

Also in Los Patios, you'll find at least three good Taxco silver shops and a gem of an embroidery store, **Artesanías Deshilados** (tel. 755/553-0221), with lovely tablecloths, curtains, *huipiles,* and much more.

At the **La Puerta** subcomplex 100 yards farther on, a sprinkling of good restaurants, a cinema, and a Supermercado (tel. 755/553-1514 or 755/553-1508, 8 A.M.–11 P.M.daily), stocking veggies, fruit, groceries, wine, plus telecom money orders and fax, ATM, and pharmacy, are for business.

Behind the Los Patios, find the up-and-coming **El Kiosko** subcomplex, with a number of good restaurants and a surf shop.

Next comes the boulevard-front **police station,** and, after that, the **Las Palmas** subcomplex (Señor Frog's, pharmacy, restaurant, Internet connection) and finally, the busy **Las Galerías** (mini-super, photo store, restaurant), at the corner of Paseo de las Garzas.

Photography

In Zihuatanejo, **Foto 30** (on Ejido, between Galeana and Guerrero, two blocks from the plaza, tel. 755/554-7610) offers 30-minute develop-and-print service and stocks lots of film and accessories. These include a host of cameras, including SLRs, and film, including 120 print, 35mm slide, and sheet film, plus filters, tripods, and flashes. 9 A.M.–2 P.M. and 4–8 P.M. Mon.–Sat.

In Ixtapa, **Foto Quick** (in shopping center Galerias Ixtapa, across the boulevard from the Hotel Emporio, tel. 755/553-1956, 9 A.M.–9 P.M. daily) offers development servics and a modest selection of cameras, film, and supplies.

INFORMATION
Tourist Information Office

The local **Convention and Visitors Bureau** (Oficina de Convenciones y Visitantes, or OCV) information office is in Ixtapa near the south end of Avenida Gaviotas, the street that runs behind the Ixtapa Centro Comercial shopping complex (tel. 755/553-1270 or 755/553-1540, fax 755/553-0819, info@visit-ixtapa-zihuatanejo.org, www .visit-ixtapa-zihuatanejo.org, 9 A.M.–2 P.M. and 5:30–8 P.M. or so Mon.–Sat.). Call ahead to confirm hours. The generally helpful and knowledgable staff answers questions, dispenses literature and maps, and can recommend tour agencies and guides.

Publications

The best local English-language book and

magazine selection in town fills the many shelves of the **Hotel las Brisas** shop (9 A.M.–9 P.M. daily). Besides dozens of new paperback novels and scores of popular U.S. magazines, it stocks the *Miami Herald* and *USA Today* and a small selection of Mexico coffee-table books of cultural and historical interest.

In Zihuatanejo, the **newsstand** across Juárez from the town market (near the corner of Gonález) sells the *Miami Herald*. A second newsstand, west end of the beachfront town plaza, may in high season stock some popular U.S. newspapers and magazines8 A.M.–8 P.M. daily.

The small Zihuatanejo **Biblioteca** (public library) also has some shelves of English-language paperbacks. on Cuauhtémoc, five blocks from the beach, 9 A.M.–8 P.M. Mon.–Fri., 9 A.M.–5 P.M. Sat.

SERVICES
Money Exchange

Several banks, all with ATMs, cluster on the east side of downtown. Find **Banamex** (tel. 755/554-7293 or 755/554-7294, at the corner of Guerrero and Ejido, two blocks from the beach, 9 A.M.–4 P.M. Mon.–Fri., 10 A.M.–2 P.M. Sat.) offers money exchange. If the Banamex lines are too long, use the ATM or walk a long block east to Juárez and Ejido and then a short block south, to the corner of Bravo and Juárez. There, find **Bancomer** (tel. 755/554-7492 or 755/554-7493, 8:30 A.M.–4 P.M. Mon.–Fri., 10 A.M.–3 P.M. Sat.); or **Banco Santander Serfin** (tel. 755/554-3941, 9 A.M.–4 P.M. Mon.–Fri., 10 A.M.–2 P.M. Sat.) across the street.

After hours, go back to the center of town to **Casa de Cambio Guibal** (at Galeana and Ascencio, two blocks from the beach, tel. 755/554-3522, fax 755/554-2800, 8 A.M.–8 P.M. daily), with long-distance telephone and fax, to change U.S., Canadian, French, German, Swiss, and other currencies and traveler's checks. For the convenience, it offers you a few percent less for your money than the banks.

In Ixtapa, for long money-changing hours, go to **HSBC** bank in front of the Hotel Em-

porio (on Paseo Ixtapa, tel. 755/553-0641, 755/553-0642, or 755/553-0646, 8 A.M.–7 P.M. Mon.–Fri., 8 A.M.–3 P.M. Sat.). Alternatively, go to **Bancomer** in the Los Portales complex behind the shops across the boulevard from the Hotel Presidente Intercontinental, tel. 755/553-0535, or 755/553-0525, 8:30 A.M.–4 P.M. Mon.–Fri.

Communications

A single *correo* (post office), tel. 755/554-2192, serves Zihuatanejo and Ixtapa; it's in Zihuatanejo at Centro Federal, in the northeast corner of downtown, five blocks from the beach and about three blocks east of the Ixtapa minibus stop at Juárez and Morelos 8 A.M.–6 P.M. Mon.–Fri., 9 A.M.–1 P.M. Sat. Also in the post office is a sub-office of the very reliable government **Mexpost** (like U.S. Express Mail) upgraded, secure mail service.

Next door is **Telecomunicaciones,** which offers long-distance telephone, public fax (755/554-2163), telegrams, and money orders 8 A.M.–7 P.M. Mon.–Fri. Another similar telecommunications office serves Ixtapa, in the La Puerta shopping center (rear side), across Paseo Ixtapa from the Hotel Presidente Intercontinental.

Money changer Casa de Cambio Guibal is also Zihuatanejo's private *larga distancia* telephone and fax office. It's on Galeana, the lane parallel to Cuauhtémoc, corner of Bravo, tel./fax 755/554-3522, 8 A.M.–8 P.M. daily.

In both Ixtapa and Zihuatanejo, many streetside public phone booths provide economical national and international (call the United States for about $1 per three minutes) long-distance service, using a Ladatel telephone card. Cards are readily available in grocery, drug, and liquor stores everywhere. First dial 001 for calls to the United States and Canada, and 01 for Mexico long-distance.

Get on the Internet in Zihuatanejo at **Internet Zihuana** (Álvarez 42, near the Cinco de Mayo corner by the plaza, tel. 755/554-6525, 9 A.M.–2 P.M. and 4–9 P.M. Mon.–Sat.). Pick up your copy of the good *Paradise* tourist magazine here; the proprietor is the magazine's designer.

In Ixtapa, answer your email at **Internet**

Connection Ixtapa in the Las Palmas sub-complex, behind Señor Frog's (tel. 755/553-2253, 8 A.M.–11 P.M. daily).

Health, Police, and Emergencies

For medical consultations in English, contact U.S.-trained IAMAT associate Dr. Rogelio Grayeb, in Zihuatanejo (Bravo 71A, beach side, between Guerrero and Galeana, tel. 755/554-3334, 755/553-1711, or 755/554-2040, cellular tel. 044-755/551-3335, fax 755/554-5041).

Another Zihuatanejo medical option is the very professional Clínica Maciel (12 Palmas, two blocks east, one block north of the market, tel. 755/554-2380 or 755/554-0517), which has a dentist, pediatrician, gynecologist, surgeon, and general practitioner on 24-hour call.

Neither Ixtapa nor Zihuatanejo has any state-of-the art private hospitals. However, many local people recommend the state of Guerrero Hospital General (on Avenida Morelos, corner of Mar Egeo, just off Highway 200, tel. 755/554-3965, 755/554-3650, or 755/554-3436), for its generally competent, dedicated, and professional staff.

For medicines and drugs in Zihuatanejo, go to one of the several downtown pharmacies, such as Farmacia la Principal (on Cuauhté-moc, two blocks from the beach, tel. 755/554-4217, 9 A.M.–9 P.M. Mon.–Sat.) In Ixtapa, go to Farmapronto pharmacy (tel. 755/553-2423, 8 A.M.–11 P.M. daily), in the Las Palmas sub-complex across the parking lot, north, from Señor Frog's. It has a delivery service.

For police emergencies in Ixtapa and Zihuatanejo, contact the cabercera de policía headquarters in Zihuatanejo, on Calle Limón, near Highway 200, tel. 755/554-2040. Usually more accessible are the police officers at the caseta de policía 24-hour police booth at the Zihuatanejo plaza-front, and in Ixtapa on Paseo Ixtapa, across from the Hotel Presidente Intercontinental. On Playa la Ropa, go to the small police station on the Paseo Costera, at the north-end intersection by the Hotel Villa del Sol.

Immigration

If you lose your tourist permit, go to Migración,

on Colegio Militar, about five blocks northeast of Plaza Kyoto, on the northeast edge of downtown (tel. 755/554-2795; 9 A.M.–3 P.M. Mon.–Fri.). Bring your passport and some proof of the date you arrived in Mexico, such as your airline ticket, stamped passport, or a copy of your lost tourist permit. Although it's not wise to let such a matter go until the last day, you may be able to accomplish the needed paperwork at the airport Migración office (tel. 755/554-8480, 8 A.M.–9 P.M. daily). Call first, however.

Laundry and Dry Cleaning

In Zihuatanejo, take your laundry to Lavandería Express (on Cuauhtémoc, near the corner of González, five blocks from the beach, tel. 755/554-4393, 8 A.M.–8 P.M. daily.

If you also need something dry-cleaned, take it to Lavandería Premium, across the street, 8:30 A.M.–8 P.M. daily.

GETTING THERE AND AWAY
By Air

Four major carriers connect Ixtapa and Zihuatanejo directly with U.S. and Mexican destinations year-round; two more operate during the fall-winter season.

Many Aeroméxico flights (reservations tel. 755/554-2018 or 755/554-2019; flight information tel. 755/554-2237 or 755/554-2634). connect daily with Mexico City, where connections with U.S. destinations may be made.

Mexicana Airlines (reservations tel. 755/554-2208 or 755/554-2209; flight information tel. 755/554-2227) flights connect directly with Mexico City.

Alaska Airlines connects with Los Angeles, San Francisco, and Seattle. For flight information and reservations, call a travel agent or Alaska's toll-free U.S. tel. 800/426-0333.

US Airways (formerly America West Airlines) connects with Phoenix. For flight information and reservations, call a travel agent or America West's toll-free U.S. number by dialing direct from Mexico, 001-800/235-9292.

Continental Airlines connects with Houston seasonally during the late fall, winter, and spring. Call a travel agent or toll-free Mex.

tel. 800/900-5000 for flight information and reservations.

A number of **seasonal and charter flights** operated by airlines such Air Canada, Frontier, American, and Northwest connect with U.S. northern and Canadian destinations during the winter. For more information, contact a travel agent or the airlines' respective websites.

Air Arrival and Departure

Ixtapa and Zihuatanejo are quickly accessible, only about twenty minutes, seven miles (11 km), north of the airport via Highway 200. Arrival is generally simple—if you come with a day's worth of pesos and hotel reservations. Although the terminal does have an ATM (by the exit door near the car rentals), it has neither tourist information booth nor hotel-reservation service. Best arrive with a hotel reservation, and not leave the choice up to your taxi driver who will probably deposit you at the hotel that pays him a commission on your first night's lodging.

Transportation to town is usually by *taxi especial* (private taxi) or *colectivo* van. Tickets are available at booths near the terminal exit. Tariff for a *colectivo* is $6–9 per person (depending on destination); for a taxi, $19–26 for three or four people. Taxis to Troncones run about $48. Mobile budget travelers can walk the few hundred yards to the highway and flag down one of the frequent daytime Zihuatanejo-bound buses (very few, if any, continue to Ixtapa, however). At night, spend the money on *colectivo* or taxi.

Several major **car rental** companies staff airport arrival booths. Avoid problems and save money by negotiating your car rental through the agencies' toll-free numbers before departure. Agents at the airport include Hertz (tel. 755/554-2590, tel./fax 755/554-3050), Budget (tel. 755/554-4837 or 755/553-0397, budget@cdnet.com), and Alamo (tel. 755/553-0206).

Departure is quick and easy if you have your passport, tourist permit (which was stamped on arrival), and $19 cash (or the equivalent in pesos) international departure tax if your air ticket doesn't already cover it. Departees who've lost their tourist permits can avoid trouble and a fine by getting a duplicate from Zihuatanejo Immigration at the airport a few hours prior to departure. Simplify this procedure by being prepared, with your passport, a copy of the lost permit, or at least some proof of their date of arrival, such as an airline ticket.

For last-minute postcards and shopping, the airport has a mailbox and a several gift shops and a pretty fair magazine stand.

By Car or RV

Three routes, two easy and one formerly unsafe but now marginally recommended, connect Ixtapa and Zihuatanejo with Playa Azul and Michoacán to the northwest, Acapulco to the southeast, and Ciudad Altamirano and central Guerrero to the northeast.

Traffic sails smoothly along the 76 miles (122 km) of Highway 200, either way, between Zihuatanejo and Lázaro Cárdenas/Playa Azul. Allow about an hour and a half. Several miles before Lázaro Cárdenas the new Highway 37 D *cuota* toll expressway allows easy access to highland central Michoacán (190 miles, 312 km, 4.5 hours to Uruapan, add another half-hour to Pátzcuaro) from Zihuatanejo. The same is true of the 150-mile (242-km, allow four hours) Highway 200 southern extension to Acapulco.

The story is different, however, for the winding, sparsely populated, cross-Sierra Highway 134 (intersecting with Highway 200 nine miles north) from Zihuatanejo to Ciudad Altamirano. Rising along spectacular, jungle-clad ridges, the paved but sometimes potholed road leads over cool, pine-clad heights and then high, dry valley of the grand River Balsas after about 100 miles (160 km). The continuing leg to Iguala on the Acapulco-Mexico City highway is longer, about 112 miles (161 km), equally winding, and sometimes busy. Allow about eight hours westbound and nine hours eastbound for the entire trip. Keep filled with gasoline, and be prepared for emergencies, especially along the Altamirano-Zihuatanejo leg, where no hotels and few services exist. *Warning:* This route, unfortunately, was once plagued by robberies and nasty drug-related incidents. Inquire locally—your hotel, the tourist information office, the bus station—to see if authorities deem the road safe before attempting this trip.

By Bus

Zihuatanejo has three major bus terminals. They stand side-by side on Highway 200, on the Acapulco-bound, east side of town. The biggest and busiest is the big Estrella Blanca **Central de Autobús** station. Inside its shiny airline-style terminal, there are few services available: a battery of Ladatel card-operated telephones, a left-luggage service, and only a small snack bar. If you're going to need supplies for a long bus trip, stock up with water and food before you get to the station.

Estrella Blanca, tel. 755/554-3477, computer-coordinates the service of its subsidiaries, including first-class Elite, Estrella Blanca, Futura, and luxury-class Turistar.

Most buses run along the Highway 200 corridor, connecting with Lázaro Cárdenas/Playa Azul and northwestern points, and with Acapulco and points south and east.

Several luxury- and first-class buses and some second-class buses connect daily with Acapulco. A number of them continue to Mexico City, and at least one continues east along the Oaxaca coast all the way to Salina Cruz. In the opposite direction, many luxury-, first-, and second-class buses (at least one an hour during the day) connect with Lázaro Cárdenas, Playa Azul junction, and northwest points.

Other departures connect north, via Michoacán. Among them, at least one daily departure connects north with points of Uruapan and Morelia, via the new expressway. Another departure connects north via the expressway, via Uruapan, continuing northwest, via Guadalajara, Mazatlán, all the way to the U.S. border at Mexicali and Tijuana.

Competing major bus carrier **Estrella de Oro,** tel. 755/554-2175, operates out of its separate station, on the adjacent, west side of the Estrella Blanca station. It offers some long-distance first-class connections southeast along the coast via Acapulco, thence inland, via Chilpancingo, Iguala, and Taxco, with Mexico City.

Transportes Autobuses del Pacífico (TAP) departures, tel. 755/554-2175, also operating out of the Estrella de Oro station, connect northwest, via Uruapan, Guadalajara, and Mazatlán, with Mexicali and Tijuana at the U.S. border.

A third major terminal, adjacent, west of the Estrella de Oro station, offers mostly first- and luxury-class departures, via a number of competent, well-equipped carriers, all of which are reservable via tel. 755/112-1002, or tel. 755/544-8723:

La Linea Plus luxury-class departures connect north with Guadalajara via Uruapan and also northwest, with Puerto Vallarta, via Lázaro Cárdenas and Manzanillo; **Autovias** first-class departures connect northeast, with Mexico City, via Morelia and Toluca; **Parhikuni** first-class departures connect northeast, with Morelia, via Uruapan; **Omnibus de Mexico,** first-class departures connect north with Monterrey; and **Primera Plus** luxury-class departures connect northeast, with Irapuato, León, and Aguascalientes.

The Costa Grande

Although the 150-mile (242-km) Zihuatanejo-Acapulco stretch of Highway 200 is smooth and easy, resist the temptation to hurry through. Your reward will be a bright string of little pearls—idyllic South Seas villages, miles of strollable and fishable beaches, wildlife-rich *esteros,* lovely small hotels, and a tranquil little beach resort on the hidden edge of Acapulco.

If you're driving, mark your odometer at the Zihuatanejo southside Pemex, near Km 240 on Highway 200. Or, if driving north, do the same at the Acapulco *zócalo* (old town square) Km 0, and head out on the northbound coast road past Pie de la Cuesta. Road mileages and kilometer markers are helpful in finding the paths to hidden little beaches.

Bus travelers, if you're going straight through to Acapulco, take a first-class bus from the Zihuatanejo Estrella Blanca station. If you're planning to linger, take a second-class bus and ask the driver to drop you at your chosen haven.

PLAYA LAS POZAS AND PLAYA BLANCA

These pocket paradises have arrived on the map of Guerrero. Las Pozas, a swimming, boogieboarding and surf-fishing haven, is reachable via the Zihuatanejo airport road. The reward is a lagoon full of bait fish, space for RV or tent camping (be careful of soft sand), a wide beach, and good beachside *palapa* restaurants. Farther east, the beach changes to Playa Blanca, where a delightfully luxurious new hotel welcomes travelers willing to stray a few miles off the beaten track.

Get to Playa las Pozas by following the well-marked airport turnoff road at Km 230. After one mile, turn right at the cyclone fence just before the terminal and follow the bumpy but easily passable straight level road 1.1 miles (1.8 km) direct to the beach. Continue one mile (1.6 km) two miles along the beach road to Playa Blanca and Hotel las Palmas.

But first, back at Playa las Pozas, the beach itself is 100 yards wide, of yellow-white sand, and extends for miles in both directions. It has driftwood but not many shells. Fish thrive in its thunderous, open-ocean waves. Consequently, casts from the beach can yield five-pound catches by either bait or lures. Local folks catch fish mostly by net, in the surf and the nearby lagoon. During the June–September rainy season, the lagoon breaks through the bar. Big fish, gobbling prey at the outlet, can be netted or hooked at the same spot themselves.

Camping is popular here on weekends and holidays. Other times you may have the place to yourself. As a courtesy, ask the friendly Neto family restaurant (on the west end, by the lagoon), the best of the *palapa* restaurants, if it's okay to camp nearby.

Hotel las Palmas

In 2001, the welcoming on-site owner-builders, from Phoenix, Arizona, decided to create heaven on lazy, lovely Playa Blanca. The result was Hotel las Palmas, replete with precious architecture-as-art, including polished natural tree trunk-beamed ceilings, elegant tropical hardwood shutters, and massive overhanging thatched *palapa* roofs. A recipe for paradise? Yes, but even more: a big blue pool, good restaurant and bar, all set in cool green grassy grounds overlooking a long, creamy, yellow-white strand. Their six super-comfortable, hand-crafted rooms, four with a/c, two with ceiling fans, rent for $225 d high season, $150 low (June–Oct.), with breakfast, but without TV, phones, credit cards, or kids under 18. Reserve directly at the hotel (tel. 755/557-0634, locally dial tel. 044-755/557-0634, hotel laspalmas@hotmail.com). Reservations are also possible through the owners' Arizona agent (Gold Coast Travel, 335 W. Virginia St., Phoenix AZ 85003-1020, fax 602/253-3487, email goldcoasttravel@hotmail.com). For more information, visit www.zihuatanejo .net/laspalmas. Get there by continuing about 1.5 miles (2.5 km) along the beach road from Playa las Pozas to Playa Blanca and Hotel las Palmas.

BARRA DE POTOSÍ

At Achotes, on Highway 200, nine miles (15 km) south of Zihuatanejo, a Laguna de Potosí sign points right to Barra de Potosí, an idyllic fishing hamlet at the sheltered south end of the Bahía de Potosí. After a few miles through green, tufted groves, the paved road parallels the bayside beach, a crescent of fine white sand, with a scattering of houses a comfortable bed-and-breakfast, and one modest beachfront hotel.

The waves become even more tranquil at the beach's southeast end, where a sheltering headland rises beyond the village and the adjacent broad lagoon. Beneath its swaying palm grove, the hamlet of Barra de Potosí (pop. 1,000) has all the ingredients for tranquil living. Several broad, hammock-hung *palapa* restaurants (here called *enramadas*) front the bountiful lagoon.

The Laguna de Potosí offers both camping and wildlife-viewing.

© BRUCE WHIPPERMAN

Sights and Recreation

Home for flocks of birds and waterfowl and shoals of fish, the **Laguna de Potosí** stretches for miles to its far mangrove reaches. Adventure out with your own boat or kayak, or go with Orlando (ask for him at the lagoon-front *palapa* Restaurant Teresita), who regularly takes parties out for fishing or wildlife-viewing tours. Bring water, a hat, and insect repellent.

If you want to do more but don't have your own kayak, Ixtapa-based **Zoe Kayak Tours** (contact owner-manager Brian in Ixtapa, tel. 755/553-0496, zoe5@aol.com, www.zoekayaktours.com) leads kayaking trips on the Laguna de Potosí's pristine waters.

Bait fish, caught locally with nets, abound in the lagoon. Fishing is fine for bigger catches (jack, snapper, mullet) by boat or casts beyond the waves. Launch your boat easily in the lagoon, then head, like the local fishermen, past the sandbar.

Accommodations and Food

In the village, at least two bed-and-breakfast-style hotels offer lodging. First consider the charming flower-bedecked **Casa del Encanto** (House of Enchantment) on a village side street (reservations tel. 755/100-1446, locally, dial 044-755/100-1446, lauragecko2@hotmail.com, www.casdelencanto.com, $65 d low, $85 d, high season); ask for owner Laura Nolo. Lovingly decorated roomshere include private hot-water bath and full breakfast. High season runs Nov.–May.

Beneath the plumy grove a few blocks away, guests at **Casa Frida** (reservations, local tel. 044-755/556-0049, long distance in Mexico 01-755/556-0049, from the U.S. 011-52-755/556-0049, casa-frida@zihuatanejo.net, www.zihuatanejo.net/casafrida, $80 d, including breakfast), life project of Mexican-French couple Annabel and François, enjoy fondly decorated rooms within a charmingly compact pool-patio garden. Room furnishings, based on a Frida Kahlo theme, include handcrafted art and furniture, mosquito curtains over the double beds, and bright Talavera-tiled hot-water bathrooms. Adults only, no pets, closed May 1–Nov. 1.

About a mile out of the village, back toward Zihuatanejo, the downscale **Hotel Barra de**

Potosí (tel. 755/554-7060 or 755/554-556-8434, reserve with owner Rafael Guzman direct, at tel./fax 755/554-3445, info@hotel-barra depotosi.com, www.hotel-barradepotosi.com, $50 d with kitchenette, $40 d studio) perches right on the beach. The surf is generally tranquil and safe for swimming near the hotel, although the waves, which do not roll but break rather quickly along long fronts, do not appear good for surfing. The hotel, once neglected, has been somewhat restored. Rooms have been renovated and the pool has been returned to a brilliant blue. The owner says that the restaurant will be open during the high winter season, but will close during the low summer and fall. The beach, nevertheless, remains inviting year-round. Kitchenette apartments rent for about $50 d, studios $40 d, but with only tepid room-temperature water. All lamps are bare-bulb; bring your own lampshade or booklight.

About a mile farther from town, on the same luscious beachfront, just south of the spot where the road from Achotes arrives at the beach, **Bernie's Bed and Breakfast** (cell tel. 755/556-6333; locally, dial 044-755/556-6333; playacalli@hotmail.com, www.berniesbedand breakfast.com, $110 d low season, $110 d high) offers three comfortable, semi-deluxe rooms with "no TV or piped-in-music" (says friendly owner Bernie Wittstock), and a palmy ocean-front pool and patio. Rentals run about $110 d high season (Dec.–April), $100 low, including full breakfast. If you give him a day's notice, Bernie will cook a light lunch or dinner for you.

Camping is common by RV or tent along the uncrowded edge of the lagoon. Village stores can provide basic supplies.

Prepared food is available at about a dozen permanent lagoon-side *palapa* restaurants. **Restaurant Teresita** is especially recommended.

For more information about Barra de Potosí, visit www.barra-potosi.com.

Getting There and Away
By car, get to Barra de Potosí by following the signed turnoff road from Highway 200, at Km 225, nine miles (14 km) south of Zihuatanejo, just south of the Los Achotes River bridge. Continue along the good mostly paved road; pass the hotel at Mile 5 (Km 8) and continue to the village at Mile 5.5 (Km 8.9).

By bus, follow the same route via a Petatlán-bound bus (Omnibus de Mexico, Estrella Blanca) either from one of the Zihuatanejo bus stations, or the local Petatlán bus from the station on Zihuatanejo Avenida las Palmas, across from Bancrecer. In either case, ask the driver to let you off at the Barra de Potosi turnoff at Achotes and wait for the Barra de Potosi-bound covered pickup truck (about every 30 minutes daytime).

Alternatively, you can get to Barra de Potosí by continuing east about three miles along the beach road from Hotel las Palmas at Playa Blanca.

SOLEDAD DE MACIEL ARCHAEOLOGICAL ZONE
Find this important archaeological zone, five miles (8 km) south of Highway 200, via the good gravel signed side road at Km 214, about 31 miles southeast of Zihuatanejo. It was first explored by

© BRUCE WHIPPERMAN

IXTAPA AND ZIHUATANEJO

a stone ball-ring, unearthed at the Soledad de Maciel Archaeological Zone

INAH (National Institute of Archaeology and History) investigators around 1925. From time to time excavations have continued, although none of the structures has been yet restored. It is only recently that local folks (who call their site "El Chole") have begun to benefit from it. They now welcome visitors to their small artifact museum, introduce them to the monumental "King of Chole" monolith, and offer tours.

Investigators have identifed a classic-era (circa A.D. 300) town and ceremonial zone that extends over at least a square mile (2.6 square km) around the present Soledad de Maciel village. Excavated structures include three pyramids, ceremonial mounds and courtyards, a ball court, and extensive former habitation zones. Many artifacts have been uncovered; examples include pottery, on display at the Zihuatanejo archaeological museum, the two monoliths at the Petatlán downtown *parque,* and two ball rings beside Highway 200 in town.

Other artifacts are on display at the modest village **museum,** also the point of departure for local tours (mostly in Spanish). Find the museum, on the right, at the first intersection in the village. The major local artifact is the "King of

Chole" monolith, in front of the village church, adjacent to the museum. It represents a personage with two faces, looking in opposite right and left directions. One face, representing death, is emaciated; the other, representing life, is vital.

Local guides can lead you on a one- or two-hour tour of the environs. Highlight of the tour is the 200-foot, forested **Cerro de las Peñas** (Hill of the Rocks). At the airy summit, the broad hinterland of corn and tobacco (for locally made cigars) fields and communal coconut groves spreads to the ocean, visible on the southern horizon. Also uphill, you will find a monumental *organo* (organ cactus), some petroglyphs (of the "Lord of the Hill"), and a small cave, complete with bats and more petroglyphs. Bring a flashlight.

Among the available guides (ask at the museum), **Adan Belez Romero** (cellular local tel. 044-755/551-4851) is among the best qualified. Offer $10–20 for a two-hour tour.

PAPANOA

The small town with the Hawaiian-sounding name of Papanoa (pop. 3,000) straddles the highway 47 miles (75 km) south of Zihuatanejo

© BRUCE WHIPPERMAN

On Highway 200 (near km 193 and 194), you can see salt workers harvesting salt from the local lagoon.

and 103 miles (165 km) north of Acapulco. The town itself has a few snack restaurants, a pharmacy, a doctor, groceries, a *gasolinera* that stocks unleaded gas, first-class bus stops, and a long-distance telephone.

At least two recommdable hotels offer accommodations. At the center of town, a block north of the highway, on Calle Telecino Moreno, stands the spiffy, family-run ◖ **Hotel la Sirenita** (Papanoa, Guerrero 40907, tel. 742/422-2029, $20 d, $35 with a/c) Here you get a very spacious, clean and comfortable room, with hot water shower bath and ceiling fan, with parking in the patio.

Alternatively, stay at the resort-style **Hotel Club Papanoa** (Papanoa, Guerrero 40907, tel. 742/422-0150, info@hotelpapanoa.com, www .hotelpapanoa.com, $55 s or d low season, $75 high). The hotel has about 30 large rooms with a/c, a restaurant, and a big pool set in spacious ocean-view garden grounds. Intended to be luxurious but now a bit worn around the edges, the hotel is nearly empty most nonholiday times.

The hotel grounds adjoin the beach, **Playa Cayaquitos.** The wide, breezy, yellow-gray strand stretches for two miles, washed by powerful open-ocean rollers with good left and right surfing breaks. Additional attractions include surf fishing beyond the breakers and driftwood along the sand. Beach access is via the off-highway driveway just north of the hotel. At the beach, a parking lot borders a seafood restaurant. Farther on, the road narrows (but is still motor home–accessible) through a defunct beachside home development, past several brush-bordered informal RV parking or tent camping spots.

Playa Ojo de Agua

Nestled in the little nook between the headlands, about half a mile southeast of the Hotel Club Papanoa, is the petite half-moon beach named Playa Ojo de Agua for its cooling and cleansing fresh-water spring. Local families flock here on weekend afternoons to play in the surf, eat fresh seafood at the beachfront *palapas,* and rinse themselves in the community spring (*ojo de agua,* literally "eye of water") that trickles from the hillside above the beach.

PUERTO VICENTE GUERRERO AND PLAYA ESCONDIDA

Puerto Vicente Guerrero, a small workaday fishing port and naval training center, 97 miles (156 km) from Acapulco and 52 miles (84 km) from Zihuatanejo, hides a pearl of a beach, appropriately known as Playa Escondida, beyond its southeast headland.

Two miles from the signed highway turn-off, continue through the port village, bearing left (east), uphill, at the village-center road fork overlooking the harbor. Pass the naval training center at the road's summit, and continue a few blocks downhill to the Playa Escondida beach.

Beyond the several permanent *palapa* restaurants that populate the beachfront spreads a wide yellow sand beach, sheltered on both sides by rocky headlands. Strong waves break and roll in along a nearly level shoreline, receding with only mild undertow.

Playa Escondida (also known locally as Playa Secreta) appears ideal for every kind of beach entertainment, from kiddie play and beachcombing to intermediate surfing and scuba diving. The beach even has ample room for tent camping, especially on the east side.

Accommodations and Food

New lodgings are receiving a growing number of visitors. Most prominent is ◖ **Hotel and Restaurant los Arcos** (at the end of the entrance road, right on the beach at Playa Escondida, cellular tel. 044-742/427-0252, $35 s, $40 d, $50 t). Its dozen-odd light and comfortably furnished rooms, with hot-water shower-baths, a/c, and cable TV encircle an inviting pool and parking patio. On the beach side, guests also enjoy an airy beach-view restaurant.

Folks interested in big-game fishing and other water sports might enjoy the **Bahía de la Tortuga Fishing Lodge** (on Playa Escondida, tel. 742/455-6931, U.S. tel. 956/455-6931, escape@escapeixtapa.com, www.escapeixtapa .com, packages start at $745). It offers three-night/ four-day packages for two, including two days sportfishing, all meals and drinks, and airport pickup. Also offered are kayaking, snorkeling, scuba diving, surfing lessons, and whale- and turtle-watching, in season.

PIEDRA TLACOYUNQUE

At Km 150 (56 miles, 90 km from Zihuatanejo, or 94 miles, 151 km from Acapulco) a signed Restaurant las Carabelas side road heads seaward to Piedra Tlacoyunque and the **Carabelas Restaurant.** About a mile down the paved road, the restaurant appears, perching on a bluff overlooking a monumental sandstone rock, Piedra Tlacoyunque. Below, a wave-tossed strand, ripe for beachcombing and surf fishing, stretches for miles. Powerful breakers with fine right-hand surfing angles roll in and swish up the steep beach. For fishing, buy some bait from the net fishermen on the beach and try some casts beyond the billows crashing into the south side of the Piedra. Later, stroll through the garden of eroded rock sea stacks on the north side. There you can poke among the snails and seaweeds in a big sheltered tidepool, under the watchful guard of the squads of pelicans roosting on the surrounding pinnacles.

At the downscale Carabelas Restaurant on the bluff above, you can take in the whole breezy scene while enjoying the recommended catch of the day. The name Carabelas (Caravels) comes from the owner's admiration of Christopher Columbus. He christened his restaurant's three petite ocean-view gazebos after Columbus's three famous caravels: the *Niña,* the *Pinta,* and the *Santa María.*

For an overnight or a short stay, ask the restaurant owners if it's okay to set up your tent or park your (self-contained) RV in the restaurant lot or by the beach below the restaurant.

HOTEL RESORT VILLAS SAN LUIS

Little was spared to embellish this pretty hacienda-like corner of a big mango, papaya, and coconut grove (Carretera Zihuatanejo-Acapulco, Km 143, Buenavista de Juárez, Guerrero 40906, tel. 742/427-0282, fax 742/427-0235, credit cards not accepted, $43 s or d, $65 d in two beds). It appears as if the owner, tiring of all work and no play, built a park to entertain his friends. Now, his project blooms with lovely swimming and kiddie pools, a big *palapa* restaurant, a smooth *palapa*-covered dance floor, a small zoo, basketball and volleyball courts, and an immaculate hotel.

Ideal for a lunch/swim break or an overnight or a respite from hard Mexico traveling, the 40 immaculate and attractively furnished hotel rooms all have hot water shower baths and a/c. Add about 10 percent to the rate during holidays. If you'll be arriving on a weekend or holiday, write, phone, or fax for a reservation. It's on the southbound side of the road near Km 142, 61 miles (98 km) southeast of Zihuatanejo, 89 miles (143 km) northwest of Acapulco.

PIE DE LA CUESTA

The translation of the name Pie (pee-YAY) de la Cuesta (Foot of the Hill) aptly describes this downscale resort village. Tucked around the bend from Acapulco, on the broad, palmy sandbar between a wide, open-ocean beach and placid Laguna Coyuca, Pie de la Cuesta appeals to those who want both the excitement that Acapulco offers and the tranquility it doesn't.

excursion boats on the Laguna Coyuca, in Pie de la Cuesta

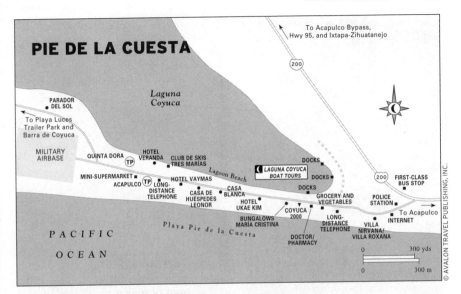

PIE DE LA CUESTA

To Acapulco Bypass, Hwy 95, and Ixtapa-Zihuatanejo

Laguna Coyuca

PARADOR DEL SOL

To Playa Luces Trailer Park and Barra de Coyuca

MILITARY AIRBASE

QUINTA DORA

HOTEL VERANDA

CLUB DE SKIS TRES MARIAS

Lagoon Beach

DOCKS

LAGUNA COYUCA BOAT TOURS

DOCKS

MINI-SUPERMARKET

ACAPULCO

LONG-DISTANCE TELEPHONE

HOTEL VAYMAS

CASA DE HUÉSPEDES LEONOR

CASA BLANCA

HOTEL UKAE KIM

DOCKS

GROCERY AND VEGETABLES

FIRST-CLASS BUS STOP

POLICE STATION

To Acapulco

INTERNET

COYUCA 2000

BUNGALOWS MARIA CRISTINA

LONG-DISTANCE TELEPHONE

VILLA NIRVANA/ VILLA ROXANA

Playa Pie de la Cuesta

DOCTOR/ PHARMACY

PACIFIC

OCEAN

0   300 yds

0   300 m

© AVALON TRAVEL PUBLISHING, INC.

Laguna Coyuca, kept full by the sweet waters of the Río Coyuca, has long been known for its fish, birdlife, and tranquil, palm-lined shores. During the early 1400s, the Purépecha kings (who ruled from the Michoacán highlands) established a provincial capital near the town of Coyuca. After the Aztecs drove out the Purépecha a century later (and the Aztecs in turn were defeated by the Spanish), Pie de la Cuesta and its beautiful Laguna Coyuca slumbered in the shadow of Acapulco.

Sights

Laguna Coyuca is a large sky-blue sandy-bottomed lake, lined by palms and laced by mangrove channels. It stretches 10 miles along the shoreline, west from Pie de la Cuesta, which occupies the southeast (Acapulco) side. The barrier sandbar, wide Playa Pie de la Cuesta, separates the lagoon from the ocean. It extends a dozen miles west to the river outlet, which is open to the sea only during the rainy season. A road runs along the beach west the length of Laguna Coyuca to the tourist hamlet of Barra de Coyuca. There, *palapas* line the beach and serve seafood to busloads of Sunday visitors.

Playa Pie de la Cuesta, a seemingly endless, 100-yard-wide stretch of yellow sand, is fine for surf fishing, beachcombing, jogging, and long sunset walks. However, its powerful open-ocean waves are unsuited for surfing and frequently hazardous for swimming. They often break thunderously near the sand and recede with strong, turbulent undertow.

On the other side of the bar, the tranquil Acapulco (east) end of Laguna Coyuca is an embarkation point for lagoon tours and the center for water-skiing and personal watercraft riding. Among the best equipped of the shoreline clubs that offer powerboat services is the **Restaurant and Club de Skis Tres Marías**, tel. 744/460-0013. Besides a pleasant lake-view shoreline *palapa* restaurant, it offers water-skiing at about $43/hour and personal watercraft (such as Jet Skis) for about $75/hour.

If you want to launch your own boat, you can do so easily at Club Tres Marías and others for about $15. The boat traffic, which confines itself mostly to midlagoon, does not deter swimming in the lagoon's clear waters. Slip on your bathing suit and jump in anywhere along the sandy shoreline.

IXTAPA AND ZIHUATANEJO

The Laguna Coyuca boat tours customarily stop for lunch at idyllic Isla Montosa.

© BRUCE WHIPPERMAN

Laguna Coyuca Boat Tours

Lagoon tours begin from several landings dotting the Pie de la Cuesta end of the lagoon. Half-day regular excursions (maximum 10 people, about $10 per person) push off daily around 11 A.M., noon, and 1:30 P.M. Along the way, they pass islands with trees loaded with nesting cormorants, herons, and pelicans. In midlake, gulls dip and sway in the breeze behind your boat while a host of storks, ducks, avocets, and a dozen other varieties paddle, preen, and forage in the water nearby. Other times, your boat passes through winding channels hung with vines and lined with curtains of great mangrove roots. At midpoint, tours usually stop for a bite to eat at Isla Montosa. (Ask ahead of time, because you shouldn't miss it.) Here, roosters crow, pigs root, bougainvillea blooms, and a colony of fishing families live, unencumbered by 21st-century conveniences, beneath their majestic shoreline palm grove.

Barra de Coyuca

On another day, drive your car or ride one of the frequent buses that head from Pie de la Cuesta to Barra de Coyuca village at the west end of the lagoon. Along the way, you will pass several scruffy hamlets and a parade of fenced lots, some still open meadows where horses graze while others are filled with trees and big houses. Lack of potable water, local residents complain, is a continuing problem on this dry sandbar.

At road's end, 10 miles from Pie de la Cuesta, a few tourist stores, a platoon of T-shirt vendors, and hammock-equipped beach *palapa* restaurants serve holiday crowds. Boats head for tours from lagoonside, where patrons at the **Restaurant Dos Vistas** enjoy a double view of both beach and lagoon.

Hotels and Guesthouses

Approximately 20 bungalows, *casas de huéspedes* (guesthouses), and hotels line Pie de la Cuesta's single beachside road. Competition keeps cleanliness high, management sharp, and prices low. They all cluster along a one-mile roadfront, enjoying highly visible locations right on the beach. Telephone, fax, or email for reservations, especially for the winter season and holidays. Many, but not all of them, have tepid, room-temperature bath water only and do not accept credit cards; exceptions are noted below. (Note: Although all hotels line the single road through Pie de la Cuesta, some owners specify the road differently in the addresses they give, mostly either simply "Pie de la Cuesta" or "Avenida Fuerza Aerea.")

Note: Some unscrupulous Acapulco taxi drivers are trying to squeeze commissions from Pie de la Cuesta lodgings in return for bringing customers to their doorsteps. Typical tactics include outright refusal to take customers to places that don't pay commissions, or telling customers that the hotel they request *"no sirve"* ("is not running"). You can combat this, before you get into the taxi, by making sure that the driver agrees to take you to the hotel of your choice. Once in Pie de la Cuesta, make sure that he follows through or don't pay.

UNDER $50

In approximate order of increasing price, first comes **Casa de Huéspedes Playa Leonor** (63 Pie de la Cuesta, Guerrero 39900, tel. 744/460-0348, $30 d low season, $38 high), which is very popular with a loyal cadre of Canadian winter returnees. They enjoy camaraderie around the tables of the *palapa* restaurant that occupies the beachside end of a large parking-lot garden. The several breezy, more private, upper-floor, plain but clean units are most popular. All 10 rooms have two beds, showers, and fans.

More picturesque are the **Bungalows María Cristina** (P.O. Box 607, Acapulco, Guerrero 39300, tel. 744/460-0262, $35 d, $80 bungalow), with eight units (four rooms, four kitchen-equipped bungalows) set between a streetside parking lot and a palmy beachside restaurant/garden. The clean, fixed-up, and painted rooms with toilets and hot-water showers rent for about $35 d (except for holidays). The kitchenettes, most of which face the ocean, run about $80 for up to four people.

The enduringly lovely ◖ **Villa Nirvana** (302 Playa Pie de la Cuesta, P.O. Box 950, Acapulco, Guerrero 39300, tel. 744/460-1631, fax 744/460-3573, nirvana@acabtu.com, www.lavillanirvana.com, $35 d and up, $80 suite) attracts a steady stream of repeat guests. A look around and the reason becomes clear: clean, comfortable semi-deluxe accommodations in an attractive garden beachfront compound, with beachfront pool and patio, restaurant, and parking intelligently screened beyond the tall garden wall, in an adjacent lot. Personable owners Daniel Reams and Pamela Fox offer a wide range in their 14 accommdations, from compact garden-view rooms, for about $35 d, to an airy, spacious ocean-view suite accommodating up to eight, for about $80. Discounts for long-term rentals are available.

The adjacent **Villa Roxana** (302 Playa Pie de la Cuesta, P.O. Box 950, Acapulco, Guerrero 39300, tel. 744/460-3252, $30 low season, $48 high), managed by owner Roxana and her daughter Alexis, also offers attractive choices. Their dozen-odd clean, comfortable rooms sit in two stories around a flowery garden with pool.

Guests at the **Hotel and Restaurant Casa Blanca** (Av. Fuerza Aerea 370, Pie de la Cuesta, Guerrero 39900, tel. 744/460-0324 or fax 744/460-4027, casablanca@prodigy.net.mx, credit cards accepted, $48 s-q) enjoy a tranquil, car-free tropical garden, small blue beachfront pool and restaurant, and French management. The 15 or so very clean and comfortable rooms all have toilets and hot-water showers and a/c. Discounts may be available for monthly or low season (May–Oct.) rentals.

$50-100

Ten comfortable rooms, a lagoon-front view location, coupled with an invitingly palmy pool-patio and airy *palapa* restaurant are the prime offerings of **Hotel Veranda I** (Av. Fuerza Aerea 41, Pie de la Cuesta, Guerrero 399000, tel. 744/460-3624, lorena_hava@hotmail.com, www.hotelveranda.com.mx, $45 d low season, $60 d winter, $90 during fiestas). Rooms are tiled and white stucco throughout, and simply but comfortably furnished with double or king-sized beds. Two rooms have hot water; others have tepid (not hot) water only. Upstairs rooms away from the highway (numbers 1, 2, 3, 4, and 5) have tranquility and especially scenic lagoon views. Rentals run about $60 d during the winter season, drop to around $45 d during low fall season, and rise to around $90 during the Christmas–New Year and Easter holidays.

Pie de la Cuesta's class-act upscale lodging is the innovative boutique (**Hotel Vaymas** (378 Playa Pie de la Cuesta, Pie de la Cuesta 39900, tel. 744/460-2882 or 744/460-5260, fax 744/460-0697, email vayma@vayma.com .mx, www.vayma.com.mx, $60 d, $200 suite). Here, guests enjoy the best of all possible rustic chic, including a grandly intimate blue pool, romantically illuminated at night with flickering torches, and 20 individually designed superdeluxe rooms, with names, such as Ravel, Berlioz, Débussy, and Pause I and Pause II. Charming Afghan-born owner-manager Parwin Kojani has decorated her rooms richly, with soft, roomy beds, exotic dark brown hardwood accents, designer lamps, and richly tiled bathrooms. Rentals, which are often occupied by Parwin's friends—diplomats, entertainers, politicos and business executives—from all over Mexico and the world, rent from abround $60 d upwards to about $200 for the largest suites.

Trailer Parks and Camping

RV-equipped Pie de la Cuesta vacationers have three recommendable trailer park choices. First to consider is the homey and popular **Acapulco Trailer Park** (P.O. Box 1, Acapulco, Guerrero 39300, tel. 744/460-0010, fax 744/460-2457 or 744/485-6086, acatrailerpark@hotmail .com, $20 RV site, $10 tent site), with about 60 palm-shaded beachfront and choice lagoonside spaces, with all hookups. A congenial atmosphere, good management, and many extras, including a secure fence and gate, keep the place full most of the winter. Facilities include a boat ramp, blue pool, a store, a security guard, and clean restrooms and showers. The spaces rent for about $20 or $350 per month; tent spaces, $10. Get your winter reservation in early.

The security guard at the Acapulco Trailer Park is a reminder of former times, when muggings and theft were occurring with some fre-

quency on Playa Pie de la Cuesta. Although bright new night lights on the beach (which marines patrol, while local police patrol the streets) have greatly reduced the problem, some (but not all) local folks still warn against camping or walking on the beach at night.

Next in line is the homey but somewhat neglected **Quinta Dora Trailer Park** (across the road from the Acapulco Trailer Park, tel. 744/460-1138 or 744/460-0600, $11 RV site). Its pluses are an azure, palm-shaded lagoonfront location and boat ramp. Spaces come with electricity and water only, no sewer connection.

(**Trailer Park Playa Luces** (tel./fax 744/444-4483, playaluces@hotmail.com, $20–26 RV site, $5–16 tent site) is about 2.5 miles (4 km) west out of Pie de la Cuesta village, along the Barra de Coyuca road, past the air force base. Formerly a KOA Kampground, Playa Luces is a large park, undoubtedly the best equipped on the beach, and it offers some shade. Although most spaces are not right on the beach, everyone is a stone's throw from the long, silky Pie de la Cuesta beach, fine for shells, beachcombing, and surf fishing. Facilities include a snack restaurant, ministore, security fence, laundry, playground, pool, and kiddie pool. Big motor-home spaces with all hookups run $27 by the beach, $20 in the shade away from beach, and tent spaces go for $16; all get a 20 percent discount for monthly rentals. Tents alone rent for $5.

Food

Most Pie de la Cuesta restaurants are beachfront *palapas* that line Pie de la Cuesta road. One of the most reliable, especially for breakfast on the lagoon, is the lakeview *palapa* of the (**Restaurant and Club de Skis Tres Marias** (Av. Fuerza Aerea 375, tel. 744/460-0013, 8 A.M.–8 P.M. daily, entrees $5–10). Here, you can start the day off right with an omelette, or pancakes, or eggs over easy with ham ($4–6). In the afternoon kick back and pick your favorite from their long list of superfresh seafood entrees ($5–10).

If you prefer an oceanfront location, you can have it right across the street at **Hotel and**

Restaurant Tres Marias (tel. 744/460-0178, 8 A.M.–8 P.M. daily), offering similar attentive service, good breakfasts, and seafood and Mexican plates.

Gourmet cuisine has arrived in Pie de la Cuesta, at upscale █ **Restaurant Vayma** (tel. 744/460-5260 or 744/460-2882, 8 A.M.–11 P.M. daily), where you can enjoy fine food while being soothed by the murmur of the waves and the romantic flicker of tiki torches at night. Start with Niçoise salad ($6), or super-fresh oysters Rockefeller ($10), or a tasty broccoli-zucchini-tomato-mozzarela pizza ($10), or a fine rib-eye steak ($15). Finish off with tiramisu ($5) accompanied by a savory-smooth Graham's 10-year-old Portuguese port.

On the other hand, a few steps down the economic scale, but equally choice, especially for enjoying the cooling afternoon offshore breeze, or watching the sunset, try local favorite **Coyuca 2000** (8 A.M.–10 P.M. daily). Here, hearty snack food is the specialty, such as chicken fajitas, rich guacamole ($3) and a load of tropical margaritas (strawberry, guava, pineapple, $4) to choose from.

Entertainment and Events

Pie de la Cuesta's big fiesta honors the local patron, the **Virgin of Guadalupe,** with Masses, processions, fireworks, and dances on Dec. 10, 11, and 12. The fiesta's climax, de rigueur for visitors, is the mass pilgrimage around the lake by boat.

The deluxe all-inclusive resort **Parador del Sol** (about a mile west of Pie de la Cuesta village—turn right at the Barra de Coyuca fork, tel./fax 744/444-4050 or 744/444-4049, fax 744/444-4214, parador@acabtu.com.mx, www.paradordelsol.com.mx, $90 pp d low season all-inclusive, $100 high) invites visitors to buy day and/or evening guest memberships for about $47 per adult (children ages 4–11,

half price) per eight-hour day session (10 A.M.–6 P.M.) and evening session (7 P.M.–1 A.M.). Day guests enjoy breakfast (10–11 A.M.), lunch (12–1 P.M.), open bar, and free use of the pools, beach club, kiddie playground, exercise gym, and basketball, volleyball, minigolf course, and tennis courts. The evening program kicks off at 7 P.M., with sports (including night-lit tennis) and swimming, continuing with supper (8:30–9:30 P.M.), bar, and dancing at the discotheque until after midnight.

Services

Although most services are concentrated half an hour away in Acapulco, Pie de la Cuesta nevertheless provides a few essentials. For medical consultations, see either Doctora Patricia Villalobos or her husband, Doctor Luis Amados Rios (tel. 744/460-0923), at their pharmacy where the lagoon begins, right in the middle of the village. Between them, they understand both English and French.

A scattering of minimarkets supply food. Two public long-distance phones are available, one in front of the Acapulco Trailer Park and the other on the highway by the doctors' pharmacy. In emergencies, go to the *policía,* at the small station near the intersection of the Pie de la Cuesta road and the highway to Acapulco.

Getting There and Away

Pie de la Cuesta is accessible via the fork from Highway 200 near Km 10, 144 miles (232 km) southwest of Zihuatanejo. First- and second-class buses from both Zihuatanejo and Acapulco will drop you at fork, where you can either walk, taxi, or ride one of the very frequent microbuses less than a mile to most of the hotels.

From Acapulco, the same Pie de la Cuesta–Highway 200 intersection is six miles (10 km) by car, taxi ($5), or local bus from near the Acapulco old town plaza.

ACAPULCO AND TAXCO

All over Mexico and half the world, Acapulco (pop. 1.5 million) means merrymaking, good food, and palm-shaded beaches. Despite half a century of continuous development, its popularity is as deserved as ever. The many Acapulcos—the turquoise bay edged by golden sands and emerald hills, the host of hotels, humble and grand, the food, both traditional and nouvelle, the spontaneous entertainments, the colorful market, the shady old town square—continue to draw millions of yearly visitors from all over the world.

Those legions of folks who love Acapulco come for manifold reasons. Many come for the Las Vegas–style glitz and neon glitter of the Costera, the beachfront boulevard. Still others come for Acapulco's natural beauty, which they can begin to savor only a block

from the Costera, at the gorgeous golden edge of Acapulco's half-moon bay. There, on late afternoons, after the sunbathers have cleared out, the onshore breeze cools the sand and the setting sun casts long dark shadows on the shoreline.

Some people come to enjoy the delights of Acapulco's hidden corners, such as the leafy Palma Sola archaeological zone of petroglyphs set in a shady hillside ecological park; or forested Isla Roqueta, with its tiny hidden beaches and inviting, crystal-clear waters; or vintage Hotel los Flamingos with its clifftop gazebo, perfect for a sunset cocktail.

The list goes on: the venerable 17th-century Fuerte de San Diego, now restored to a museum of Acapulco's fascinating 450-year history; nearby the Casa de la Máscara, with

© BRUCE WHIPPERMAN

HIGHLIGHTS

◖ Acapulco *Zócalo*: This is Acapulco's old hidden heart, where you can relax beneath the grand old *higuera* trees, browse the bookstands, and have coffee at a sidewalk café (page 493).

◖ Fuerte de San Diego: This monumentally austere old fort deterred pirate attacks during its 300-year colonial history. Today it serves as a monument and museum of old Acapulco (page 493).

◖ Casa de la Máscara: Here, a kind benefactor and lover of Acapulco maintains a fascinating seven-room treasury of masks, which from red devils and pink cherubs to yawning crocodiles and fierce jaguars (page 497).

◖ La Quebrada: Come see Acapulco's intrepid divers, who plummet more than 100 feet into a precipitously narrow, rock-lined tidal channel (page 497).

◖ Isla Roqueta: Ride a glass-bottomed tour boat from Playa Caleta across the crystal-clear Boca Chica channel to Isla Roqueta. Here, you can have lunch, simply sunbathe, and/or snorkel. Or, stroll the cross-island trail to the lighthouse and return clockwise around the sea-view clifftop trail. Along the way, relax at hidden little Playa las Palmitas, then continue, stopping for a snack at relaxing view Restaurant Palao (page 498).

◖ Santa Prisca: Your first stop in Taxco should be Santa Prisca, the grand 18th-century church built with the profits from Taxco's fabulous silver lode (page 529).

◖ Museo Guillermo Spratling: This fine history and archaeology museum is as interesting as the man for whom it's named, William Spratling, who helped the local community revive its silversmithing tradition during the late 1920s (page 530).

◖ Cableway *(Teleférico)* to Hotel Monte Taxco: This cable ride puts you high above the panorama of old Taxco, enfolded by ruddy, green-dappled rock ramparts on one hand, and verdant valleys that rise to misty mountains on the other (page 532).

◖ Grutas de Cacahuamilpa: Here, you can visit what is arguably the world's greatest limestone cave complex – a veritable forest of stone, all climaxing in an underground grotto that towers hundreds of feet and meanders half a mile (page 541).

◖ Xochicalco: This monumental U.N. World Heritage site is a regal complex of grand excavated pyramids, sunken ball courts, and broad ceremonial plazas (page 543).

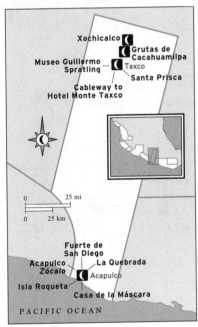

LOOK FOR ◖ TO FIND RECOMMENDED SIGHTS, ACTIVITIES, DINING, AND LODGING.

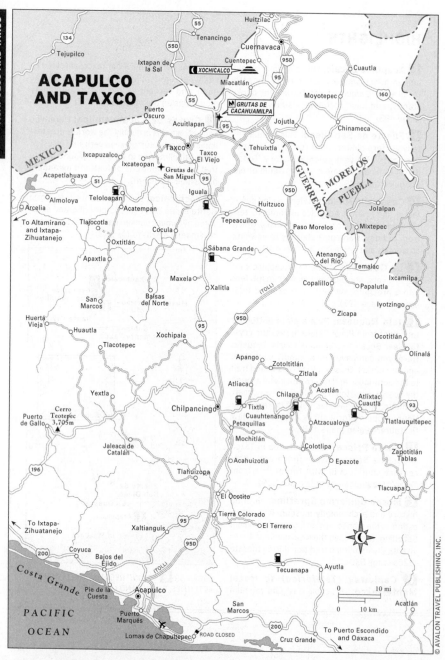

ACAPULCO AND TAXCO

its all-Guerrero mask collection—some scary, some funny, some very strange.

Acapulco's appeal overflows beyond its metropolitan limits: south to the breezy, driftwood-strewn strands of Playa Larga; and north to plumy south-seas islands, such as Isla Montosa, in wildlife-rich Laguna Coyuca; and the palmy, charmingly out-of-date downscale resort village of Pie de la Cuesta.

And finally, all Acapulco roads seem to lead to Taxco, the silver-rich colonial gem, a mere three hours by expressway, in the cool, pine-tufted Sierra Madre. Stroll Taxco's winding cobbled lanes, admire its grand colonial monuments, and visit some of the many shops of Taxco's silver-crafting families. And not to be missed nearby are the marvelous limestone caves of the national park Grutas de Cacahuamilpa and the fascinating legendary ruined city Xochicalco, a United Nations World Heritage site.

© BRUCE WHIPPERMAN

the ball court at Xochicalco, with the stone ball-ring in mid-court intact as it was found

PLANNING YOUR TIME

The recipe for enjoying Acapulco is to spend less of your time on the noisy glitzy Costera and more in Acapulco's charming old-Mexico corners. If you're driving, park your car in a garage and spend a day visiting the sights by taxi or one of the swarm of local buses that stop along the Costera. Along this route, you could spend at least two days poking around old town, visiting the **Fuerte de San Diego,** the **Casa de la Máscara,** the *zócalo,* and **Isla Roqueta.** Be sure to end one of your old-town days with sunset cocktails at the clifftop gazebo in the **Hotel los Flamingos** and later dinner in the adjacent restaurant. Spend another old-town evening watching the **cliff divers** perform at **La Quebrada.**

Farther afield, you can go southeast, also by bus, or by car, past Playa Larga, for a day on the beach at **Barra Vieja,** and maybe hire a boat for wildlife-viewing on the adjacent **Laguna Tres Palos.** Another day, go northwest via taxi or bus to Pie de la Cuesta for a wildlife-viewing boat tour on glassy, mangrove-tufted Laguna Coyuca. This might be a good time to spend

a night or two by the beach in a small Pie de la Cuesta hotel.

With a few more days, head inland, via car or, better, by bus, to Taxco for at least two nights. Spend a day strolling around, visiting some silver shops, the **Museo Guillermo Spratling,** the **Santa Prisca church,** and the fascinating **market.** The next day, go by public van to the monumental limestone **Grutas de Cacahuamilpa,** and if you go early enough, continue by tour or car to the ruins at **Xochicalco.**

HISTORY
Before Columbus

Despite its modern facade, Acapulco has been well known as a traveler's crossroads for at least a millennium. Its name comes from the Nahuatl (Aztec) words that mean "Place of Dense Reeds."

The earliest discovered local remains, stone metates and pottery utensils, were left behind by seaside residents around 2500 B.C. Much later, sophisticated artisans fashioned curvaceous female figurines, which archaeologists unearthed at Las Sabanas near Acapulco during the mid-20th century. Those unique finds added fuel to speculation of early Polynesian or Asian influences in Pacific Mexico as early as 1,500 years before Columbus.

Other discoveries, however, resemble artifacts found in highland Mexico. Although undoubtedly influenced by Tarascan, Mixtec, Zapotec, and Aztec civilizations and frequented by their traders, Acapulco never came under their direct control but instead remained subject to local chieftains until the conquest.

Conquest and Colonization

The Aztecs had scarcely surrendered when Cortés sent expeditions south to build ships and find a route to China. The first such explorers sailed out from Zacatula, near present-day Lázaro Cárdenas on the coast 250 miles northwest of Acapulco. They returned, telling Cortés of Acapulco Bay. By a royal decree dated April 25, 1528, "Acapulco and her land...where the ships of the south will be built . . ." passed directly into the hands of the Spanish Crown.

Voyages of discovery set sail from Acapulco for Peru, the Gulf of California, and to Asia. None returned from across the Pacific, however, until Father Andrés de Urdaneta discovered the northern Pacific tradewinds, which propelled him and his ship, loaded with Chinese treasure, to Acapulco in 1565.

From then on, for more than 200 years, a special yearly trading ship, renowned as the Nao de China and in England as the Manila galleon, set sail from Acapulco for the Orient. Its return sparked an annual merchant fair, swelling Acapulco's population with traders jostling to bargain for the Manila galleon's shiny trove of silks, porcelain, ivory, and lacquerware.

Acapulco's yearly treasure soon attracted marauders, too. In 1579, Francis Drake threatened, and in 1587, off Cabo San Lucas, Thomas Cavendish was the first to capture the Manila galleon, the *Santa Ana*. The cash booty alone, 1.2 million gold pesos, severely depressed the London gold market.

After a Dutch fleet invaded Acapulco in 1615, the Spanish rebuilt their fort, which they christened Fuerte de San Diego in 1617. Destroyed by an earthquake in 1776, the fort was rebuilt by 1783. But Mexico's War of Independence (1810–1821) stopped the Manila galleon forever, sending Acapulco into a century-long slumber.

Modern Acapulco

In 1927, the government paved the Mexico City–Acapulco road; the first cars arrived on Nov. 11. The first luxury hotel, the Mirador, at La Quebrada, went up in 1933; soon airplanes began arriving. During the 1940s President Miguel Alemán (1946–1952) fell in love with Acapulco and thought everyone else should have the same opportunity. He built new boulevards, power plants, and a superhighway. Investors responded with a lineup of high-rise hostelries. Finally, in 1959, Presidents Dwight Eisenhower and Adolfo López Mateos convened their summit conference in a grand Acapulco hotel.

Thousands of Mexicans flocked to fill jobs in the shiny hotels and restaurants. They built shantytowns, which climbed the hills and spilled over into previously sleepy communities nearby. The government responded with streets, drainage, power, housing, and schools. By 2000, more than 1.5 million people were calling Acapulco home.

But, by the 1980s overdevelopment was beginning to tarnish Acapulco's luster. Hotels had aged; some had become run-down. Untreated sewage was beginning to pollute Acapulco's once-pristine bay.

Soon, however, the government acted to reverse Acapulco's decline. New sewage works were built, clearing up the pollution. New streets and parks were constructed, and dozens of middle-aged hotels were returned to their former grandeur.

By the year 2000 Acapulco had been largely restored and was attracting new investments. Its sky was again blue, its azure waters were again clean, and it had become a magnet for a fresh generation of lovers of Acapulco's enjoyments, from its comfortable hotels, fine restaurants, and exciting nightlife to its hidden natural delights and the traditional-Mexico charm of its historic old town neighborhood.

Sights

In one tremendous sweep, Acapulco curves around its dazzling half-moon bay. Face the open ocean and you are looking due south. West will be on your right hand, east on your left. One continuous beachfront boulevard, appropriately named the **Costera Miguel Alemán** (the "Costera," for short), unites old Acapulco, west of the Parque Papagayo amusement zone, with new Acapulco, the lineup of big beach hotels that stretches around the bay to the Las Brisas condo headland. There, during the night, a big cross glows and marks the hilltop lookout, Mirador la Capilla, above the bay's east end.

On the opposite, old-town side of Parque Papagayo, the Costera curves along the palmy, uncluttered *playas* Hornos and Hamacas to the steamship dock. Here the Costera, called the *malecón* as it passes the *zócalo* (town plaza), continues to the mansion-dotted hilly jumble of Península de las Playas.

Buses run nearly continuously along the Costera. Fare averages the equivalent of about $.30. Bus routes—indicated by such labels as Base (BAH-say, the naval base on the east end), Centro *(zócalo),* Caleta (the beach, at the far west end), Cine (movie theater near the beach before the *zócalo*), and Hornos (the beach near Parque Papagayo)—run along the Costera.

Taxis, on the other hand, cost between $1.50 and $5 for any in-town destination. They are not metered, so agree upon the price *before* you get in. If the driver demands too much, hailing another taxi often solves the problem.

A WALK AROUND OLD ACAPULCO

In old Acapulco, traffic slows and people return to traditional ways. Couples promenade along the *malecón* dockfront, fishing boats leave and return, while in the adjacent *zócalo,* families stroll past the church, musicians play, and tourists and businesspeople sip coffee in the shade of huge banyan trees.

(ZÓCALO

Discover the heart of Acapulco. Start your walk beneath those *higuera* trees, and under their pendulous air roots, browse the bookstalls, relax in one of the cafés; at night, watch the clowns perform, listen to a band concert, or join in a pitch-penny game. Take a look inside the mod-style **cathedral** dedicated to Our Lady of Solitude. Admire its angel-filled sky-blue ceiling and visit the Virgin to the right of the altar.

Outside, cross the boulevard to the *malecón* dockside; in midafternoon, you may see huge marlin and swordfish being hauled up from the boats.

(FUERTE DE SAN DIEGO

Head out of the *zócalo* and left along the Costera past the steamship dock to the 18th-century fort atop its bayside hill, Fuerte de San Diego (tel. 744/482-3828, 10:30 A.M.–4:30 P.M. Tues.–Sun.). Engineer Miguel Costansó completed the massive, five-pointed maze of moats, walls, and battlements in 1783.

Inside, galleries within the original fort storerooms, barracks, chapel, and kitchen illustrate local pre-Columbian, conquest, and colonial history. The excellent, unusually graphic displays include much about pirates (such as Francis Drake and John Hawkins, known as "admirals" to the English-speaking world); Spanish galleons, their history and construction; and famous visitors, notably Japanese Captain Hasekura Tsunenaga, who in 1613 built a ship and sailed from Sendai, Japan, to Acapulco; thence he continued overland to Mexico City, by sea to Spain, to the pope in Rome, and back again through Acapulco to Japan.

Fuerte de San Diego puts on a regular sound and light show that dramatizes Acapulco's history (showtimes at 7 P.M. Sat. low season, Thurs.–Sat. high). Confirm at the museum or at the tourist information office (tel. 744/484-4416 or 744/484-4583).

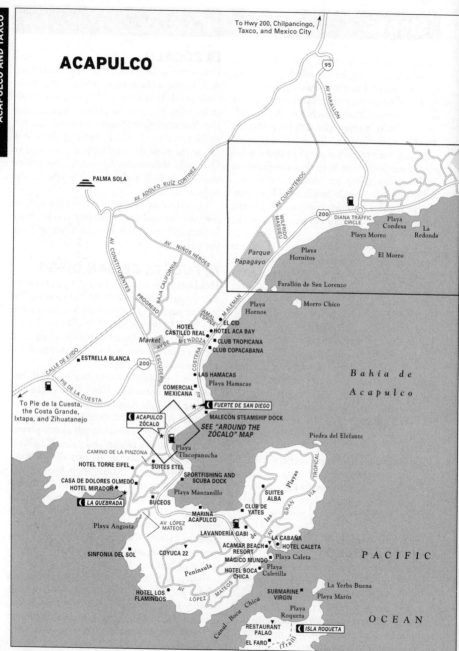

ACAPULCO

To Hwy 200, Chilpancingo, Taxco, and Mexico City

95

AV. FARALLON

AV. CUAUHTÉMOC

WILFRIDO MASSIEU

AV. ADOLFO RUÍZ CORTINEZ

PALMA SOLA

200   DIANA TRAFFIC CIRCLE

Playa Condesa

La Redonda

Playa Morro

AV. NIÑOS HEROES

Parque Papagayo

Playa Hornitos

El Morro

AV. CONSTITUYENTES

PROGRESO

BAJA CALIFORNIA

Farallón de San Lorenzo

CALLE DE EJIDO

Market

AMAL ESTINA

M. ALEMAN

Playa Hornos

Morro Chico

ESTRELLA BLANCA

200

AVDE MENDOZA

ESCUDERO

HOTEL CASTILLO REAL

EL CID

HOTEL ACA BAY

CLUB TROPICANA

CLUB COPACABANA

PIE DE LA CUESTA

To Pie de la Cuesta, the Costa Grande, Ixtapa, and Zihuatanejo

LAS HAMACAS

Playa Hamacas

COSTERA

Bahía de Acapulco

COMERCIAL MEXICANA

FUERTE DE SAN DIEGO

ACAPULCO ZÓCALO

MALECÓN STEAMSHIP DOCK

SEE "AROUND THE ZÓCALO" MAP

Piedra del Elefante

CAMINO DE LA PINZONA

Playa Tlacopanocha

HOTEL TORRE EIFEL

SUITES ETEL

SPORTFISHING AND SCUBA DOCK

CASA DE DOLORES OLMEDO
HOTEL MIRADOR

LA QUEBRADA

BUCEOS

Playa Manzanillo

SUITES ALBA

Playas

VIA TROPICAL

AV. GRAN

MARINA ACAPULCO

CLUB DE YATES

las

Playa Angosta

AV. LÓPEZ MATEOS

LAVANDERÍA GABI

de

LA CABAÑA

AV.

SINFONIA DEL SOL

COYUCA 22

ACAMAR BEACH RESORT

HOTEL CALETA

PACIFIC

MÁGICO MUNDO

Playa Caleta

Peninsula

HOTEL BOCA CHICA

Playa Caletilla

HOTEL LOS FLAMINGOS

AV. LÓPEZ MATEOS

SUBMARINE VIRGIN

La Yerba Buena

Playa Marín

Playa Roqueta

Canal Boca Chica

RESTAURANT PALAO

ISLA ROQUETA

OCEAN

EL FARO

(Trail)

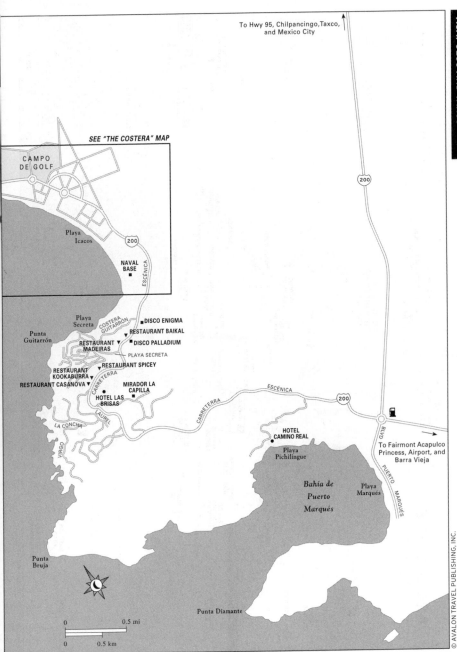

To Hwy 95, Chilpancingo, Taxco,
and Mexico City

SEE "THE COSTERA" MAP

CAMPO
DE GOLF

Playa
Icacos

200

NAVAL
BASE

Playa
Secreta

Punta
Guitarrón

COSTERA GUITARRÓN

■ DISCO ENIGMA

▼ RESTAURANT BAIKAL

RESTAURANT ▼
MADEIRAS

■ DISCO PALLADIUM

PLAYA SECRETA

▼ RESTAURANT SPICEY

RESTAURANT
KOOKABURRA ▼

RESTAURANT CASANOVA ▼

MIRADOR LA
CAPILLA

HOTEL LAS
BRISAS

CARRETERRA

ESCÉNICA

CARRETERRA

ESCÉNICA

200

LAUREL

LA CONCHA

VIRGO

HOTEL
CAMINO REAL

Playa
Pichilingue

Bahía de
Puerto
Marqués

Playa
Marqués

To Fairmont Acapulco
Princess, Airport, and
Barra Vieja

BLVD PUERTO MARQUES

Punta
Bruja

Punta Diamante

0   0.5 mi

0   0.5 km

© AVALON TRAVEL PUBLISHING, INC.

ACAPULCO AND TAXCO

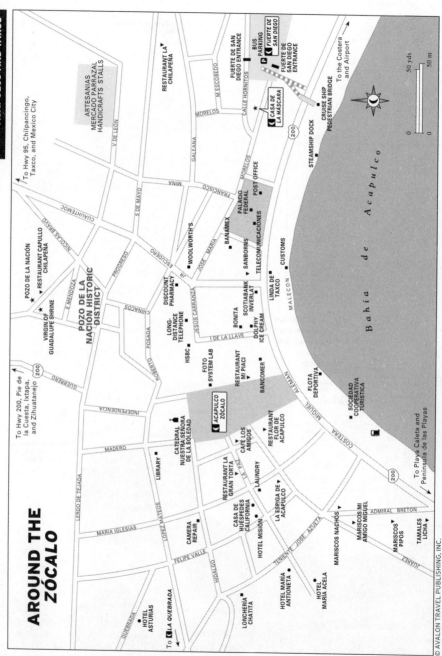

AROUND THE ZÓCALO

To Hwy 200, Pie de la Cuesta, Ixtapa, and Zihuatanejo

To Hwy 95, Chilpancingo, Taxco, and Mexico City

POZO DE LA NACIÓN HISTORIC DISTRICT

POZO DE LA NACIÓN

RESTAURANT CAPULLO CHILAPEÑA

ARTESANIAS MERCADO PARRAZAL HANDICRAFTS STALLS

RESTAURANT LA CHILAPEÑA

VIRGIN OF GUADALUPE SHRINE

E. MENDOZA

NICOLAS BRAVO

CUAUHTEMOC

V. DE LEÓN

5 DE MAYO

GALEANA

MORELOS

M. ESCOBEDO

CALLE HORNITOS

FUERTE DE SAN DIEGO ENTRANCE

BUS PARKING

FUERTE DE SAN DIEGO

FUERTE DE SAN DIEGO ENTRANCE

CASA DE LA MÁSCARA

To the Costera and Airport

CRUISE SHIP PEDESTRIAN BRIDGE

STEAMSHIP DOCK

MINA

FRANCISCO

PALACIO FEDERAL

POST OFFICE

MORELOS

JR.

ESCUDERO

WOOLWORTH'S

JOSE MARIA

BANAMEX

SANBORNS

TELECOMUNICACIONES

CUSTOMS

PROGRESO

CHINACOS

DISCOUNT PHARMACY

JESÚS CARRANZA

SCOTIABANK INVERLAT

BONITA

LINDA DE TAXCO

MALECON

LONG-DISTANCE TELEPHONE

I DE LA LLAVE

DOLPHY ICE CREAM

POSADA

HSBC

FOTO SYSTEM LAB

RESTAURANT MI PIACI

BANCOMER

Bahía de Acapulco

GUERRERO

ROBERTO

INDEPENDENCIA

ACAPULCO ZÓCALO

ALEMAN

FLOTA DEPORTIVA

SOCIEDAD COOPERATIVA TURISTICA

LEBRO DE TEJADA

LIBRARY

CATEDRAL NUESTRA SEÑORA DE LA SOLEDAD

MADERO

RESTAURANT FLOR DE ACAPULCO

CAFÉ LOS AMIGOS

MIGUEL

COSTERA

LOPEZ MATEOS

RESTAURANT LA GRAN TORTA

LA PAZ

LAUNDRY

MARIA IGLESIAS

CAMERA REPAIR

CASA DE HUESPEDES CALIFORNIA

LA ESPIGA DE ACAPULCO

HOTEL MISIÓN

FELIPE VALLE

HIDALGO

TENIENTE JOSE AZUETA

MARISCOS NACHOS

MARISCOS MI AMIGO MIGUEL

ADMIRAL BRETON

QUEBRADA

HOTEL ASTURIAS

To LA QUEBRADA

LONCHERIA CHATITA

HOTEL MARIA ANTONIETA

HOTEL MARIA ACELA

MARISCOS PIPOS

TAMALES LICHA

JUAREZ

To Playa Caleta and Península de las Playas

Bahía de Acapulco

50 yds

50 m

© AVALON TRAVEL PUBLISHING, INC.

C CASA DE LA MÁSCARA

Don't miss visiting the Casa de la Máscara (House of the Mask; just outside the old fort's exit, a block west, on the pedestrian walkway west of the museum's bus parking lot, 10 A.M.–4 P.M. Tues.–Sun.). Inside, enjoy a fascinating museum of indigenous masks, from squinting pink El Viejitos and grinning red devils, to scary crocodiles and angelic cherubs, all hand-crafted for the myriad age-old traditional fiestas celebrated in towns and villages all over Mexico.

C LA QUEBRADA

From the Fuerte de San Diego, head back to the *zócalo* and continue past the cathedral. After three short blocks to Avenida López Mateos, continue uphill to the divers' point La Quebrada (The Burned Place; marked by the big parking lot at the hillcrest; dive times at 1 P.M. and evenings hourly 7:30–10:30 P.M.). There, Acapulco's energy focuses five times a day as tense crowds watch the divers plummet more than 100 feet to the waves below. Admission is about $2, collected by the divers' cooperative. Performers average less than $100 per dive from the proceeds. If the public viewing is too crowded, you can go to the Hotel Plaza las Glorias (the former Hotel Mirador, by the parking lot), which charges about $10 cover per person to view the dives from its terrace.

PALMA SOLA ARCHAEOLOGICAL SITE

On a high hillside above Acapulco's west-side neighborhood, a trove of recently uncovered petroglyphs have been excavated for public viewing. The site (adjacent to ridgetop El Veladero ecological park, 8 A.M.–5 P.M. daily), at an elevation of about 1,200 feet (400 meters) displays a number of big monoliths (3–20 feet) inscribed with geometric-, animal-, and human-form petroglyphs. Created by ancient yet-unidentified people, the stones date from between 200 B.C. and A.D. 600. Get there most easily by taxi ($5), up Avenida Palma Sola to road's end before the hilltop, where a shady stone pathway meanders uphill for about half a mile. Don't miss the climax, at a cave shel-

The petroglyphs at the Palma Sola Archaeological Site date from 200 B.C. and A.D. 600.

© BRUCE WHIPPERMAN

tering a large petroglyph depicting an Adam and Eve-like creation myth. Continue upward for another hundred yards for a rewardingly airy panoramic view of all Acapulco. Take a hat, water, and walking shoes. Local guides will most likely be available on-site. You may also want to arrange a tour through a travel agent, such as American Express, tel. 744/435-2200. For more information, contact the tourist information office (tel. 744/484-4416 or 744/484-4583).

OLD TOWN BEACHES

These start not far from the *zócalo*. At the foot of the Fuerte de San Diego, the sand of **Playa Hamacas** begins, changing to **Playa Hornos** (Ovens) and curving northeast a mile to a rocky shoal-line called Farallón de San Lorenzo. Hornos is the Sunday favorite of Mexican families, where boats buzz beyond the very tranquil waves and retirees stroll the wide, yellow sand while vendors work the sunbathing crowd.

Kids love to play at Playa Caleta.

© BRUCE WHIPPERMAN

Moving south past the *zócalo* and the fishing boats, you'll find **Playa Tlacopanocha,** a petite strip of sand beneath some spreading trees. Here, bay-tour launches wait for passengers, and kids play in the glassy water, which would be great for swimming if it weren't for the refuse from nearby fishing boats.

From there, cross the Costera and hop on a bus marked Caleta to gemlike **Playa Caleta** and its twin **Playa Caletilla** on the far side of the hilly peninsula (named, appropriately, Península de las Playas). With medium-coarse yellow sand and blue ripples for waves, Caleta and Caletilla are for people who want company. They are often crowded, sometimes nearly solid on Sundays. Boats offer banana-tube rides, and snorkel gear is rentable from beach concessionaires. Dozens of stalls and restaurants serve food and refreshments. Prominent among them is the stall of Arturo "Chocolate" Castro and his oyster divers, who serve their own catch-of-the-day mussels, oysters, and octopus right on the west end of the beach.

The water park **Mágico Mundo** (tel. 744/483-1215, 9 A.M.–5 P.M. daily, admission $3 adult, $2 child)—with an aquarium, neglected museum, restaurant, water slides, cascades, and more—perches on a petite, bridge-accessible, island between the beaches.

◖ ISLA ROQUETA

An Isla Roqueta ticket tout will often try to snare you as you get off the Caleta bus. Best ignore them, and ride one of the several Isla Roqueta tour boats that dock at the little **Mágico Mundo** island between the beaches. The round-trip runs around $4; make sure your boat has a glass bottom, through which you can peer at the fish as they peer back from their aqua underwater world.

If you have about an hour and a half extra time, get the full **boat tour** (about $5 per person). The full tour boats leave a few times daily. Trips include viewing underwater life, shoreline vistas, the *Virgen Submarina* (a statue submerged in the Isla Roqueta channel), movie stars' homes along the shoreline, a stop on the island, and snorkeling. Beer and soft drinks are sold onboard.

On the other side, get off and relax on sunny little Playa Roqueta, have lunch at one of several beachside *palapas* or Restaurant Palao.

Other Isla Roqueta options include hiking the **mid-island trail** uphill from Playa Roqueta a few hundred yards through the shady hillside tropical deciduous forest to the **lighthouse** (*faro*) at the island summit. The few marines who guard the place might welcome company. Say hello through the gate and they may let you in for a look around.

Afterward, you could cool off with a swimming, snorkeling, and sunning excursion at one of the island's intimate hidden beaches. For example, from the lighthouse, continue uphill a few hundred yards, then at the clifftop trail, fork right, and stroll downhill about a mile, where you can cool off, paddling in the tidepools at Playa las Palmitas, at Roqueta's secluded western tip. (Bring your snorkel, mask, and sunscreen.)

An especially nice spot to linger and kick back after your Isla Roqueta exertions is Polynesian-style **Restaurant Palao** (noon–6 P.M. daily) which perches invitingly above the island's west side channel-front. If you've got an appetite, satisfy it with their melt-in-your mouth Hawaiian-style pork ribs.

PLAYA ANGOSTA

Back on the mainland, you can visit another hidden beach nearby, Playa Angosta (Narrow Beach), the only Acapulco strand with an unobstructed sunset horizon. A breezy dab of a beach, tucked between a pair of sandstone cliffs, Angosta's ocean waves roll in, swishing upon the sand. A food *palapa* occupies one side of the beach and a few fishing launches and nets are on the other. With caution, swimming, bodysurfing, and boogie boarding are sometimes possible here; otherwise, Angosta is best for scenery and picnics.

Just uphill, a few hundred yards along the southbound cliffside boulevard, is **Sinfonía del Sol** sunset amphitheater. Here, local folks begin gathering around 5 P.M. daily during the

winter (6:30 P.M. in the summer) to watch the sun go down.

COSTERA BEACHES

These are the hotel-lined golden shores where affluent Mexicans and foreign visitors stay and play in the sun. They are variations on one continuous curve of sand. Beginning at the west end with **Playa Hornitos** (also known as Playa Papagayo), they continue, changing names from **Playa Morro** to **Playa Condesa** and finally, **Playa Icacos,** which curves and stretches to its sheltered east end past the naval base. All of the same semicoarse golden silica sand, the beaches begin with fairly broad 200-foot-wide Playa Papagayo and Playa Morro. They narrow sharply to under 100 feet at Playa, then broaden again to more than 200 feet along Playa Icacos.

The surf is usually gentle, breaking in one- or two-foot waves and receding with little undertow. This makes for safe swimming within float-enclosed beachside areas, but it's

The balloon at Playa Icacos marks the CICI water park.

too tranquil for bodysurfing, boogie boarding, or surfing. Beyond the swimming floats, motorboats hurry along, pulling parasailers and banana-tube riders, while personal watercraft cavort and career over the swells.

Such motorized hubbub lessens the safety and enjoyment of quieter sports off most new town beaches. **Sailboaters** and **sailboarders** with their own equipment might try the remote, more tranquil east end of Playa Icacos.

Waterskiing, officially restricted to certain parts of Acapulco Bay, has largely moved to Laguna Coyuca northwest of the city. Laguna Coyuca also has enough space for many good motorboat-free spots for sailboaters and sailboarders.

Rocky outcroppings along the *playas* Papagayo, Morro, and Condesa add interest and intimacy to an already beautiful shoreline. The rocks are good for tidepooling and fishing by pole-casting (or by net, as locals do) above the waves.

BEACHES SOUTHEAST OF TOWN

Ride a Puerto Marquez- or Lomas-marked bus or drive along the Costera eastward. Past the naval base entrance on the right, the road climbs the hill, passing a number of panoramic bay viewpoints. After the Las Brisas condo-hotel complex, the road curves around the hill shoulder and heads downward past picture-perfect vistas of **Bahía de Puerto Marquez.** At the bottom-of-the-hill intersection and overpass, a road branches right to Puerto Marquez.

The rough little bayside town is mainly a Sunday seafood and picnicking retreat for Acapulco families. Dozens of *palapa* restaurants line its motorboat-dotted sandy beach. One ramshackle hotel, at the far south end of the single main beachfront street, offers lodgings.

If you're **driving,** mark your odometer at the hill-bottom intersection overpass and head east toward the airport. If traveling **by bus,** continue via one of the Lomas buses, which continue east from Acapulco about once an hour. About a mile farther, a turnoff road goes right to the Fairmont Acapulco Princess and

the Pierre Marquez hotels and golf course on Playa Revolcadero.

Beach access is by side roads or by walking directly through the hotel lobbies. If you come by bus, hail a taxi from the highway to the Hotel Princess door for the sake of a good entrance.

Playa Revolcadero, a broad, miles-long, yellow-white strand, has the rolling open-ocean billows that Acapulco Bay doesn't. The sometimes-rough waves are generally good for boogie boarding, bodysurfing, and even surfing near the rocks on the northwest end. Because of the waves and sometimes hazardous currents, the hotel provides lifeguards for safety. The Playa Revolcadero breeze is also brisk enough for sailing and sailboarding with your own boat or board. Some rentals may be available from the hotel beach concession.

PLAYA LARGA AND BARRA VIEJA

About seven miles (11 km) from the Puerto Marquez traffic intersection, the Barra Vieja road forks right and heads along breezy, wild Playa Larga. About two miles from the fork, you will pass the lovely retreat **Villas San Vicente,** a collection of five small villas and two studio cottages, all nestled in their own palmy, private beachside park.

For the past several years, a hardy group of ecovolunteers has patrolled Playa Larga (Long Beach), Playa Revolcadero's dozen-mile-long eastern extension to Barra Vieja. At this writing, they were camped out at around 10 miles (16 km) from the fork for the summer-fall turtle season at "Campamento Tortuguero Playa Larga." If you see them, stop and say a word of encouragement and perhaps donate some food or money to help them sustain their lonely vigil. Even better, set up your own tent nearby and volunteer your help recovering, incubating, and finally releasing the turtle hatchlings.

If you do camp, you'll share in the wide, breezy strand, whose rolling waves, with ordinary precautions, appear to be good for boogie boarding, bodysurfing, and possibly surfing. The sun sets on an unobstructed horizon, and the crab-rich beach is good for surf fishing (or by boat if you launch during morning calm). The firm, level sand is excellent for jogging, walking, and beachcombing.

At about 12 miles (19 km) from the Barra Vieja fork, the stores (groceries and long-distance phone) and modest houses of fishing village Barra Vieja dot the roadside. Many seafood *palapas* line the beachside. The better among them include Don Beto's and Gloria del Mar, both with pools.

In addition to the beach, Barra Vieja visitors enjoy access to the vast **Laguna Tres Palos** mangrove wetland from the *estero* at the east end of town before the bridge. From there,

boatmen (ask for José Organes, Beto Godoy, or Felipe Sala) take parties on fishing and wildlife-viewing excursions for about $25 per hour for six. Horseback rides are also available, for about $20/hour.

The road continues over a new lagoon bridge, two miles later, passes scruffy Lomas de Chapultepec and then crosses the new bridge across the grand Río Papagayo. Three miles (5 km) farther, it connects with Highway 200, where, if you hanker for more adventure, you can either drive ahead or hop on to a bus that will take you all the way through the Costa Chica to the Oaxaca state line and beyond.

Accommodations

Location largely determines the price and style of Acapulco hotels. In old Acapulco, most hotels are either clustered around the *zócalo* or perched on the hillsides of Península de las Playas. They are generally not on the beach and are cheaper and less luxurious. Most new town hotels, by contrast, lie along the Costera Miguel Alemán right on the beach. Guests often enjoy a wealth of resort amenities and luxury view rooms at correspondingly luxurious prices.

Many lodgings, however, defy categorization. Acapulco offers numerous choices to suit individual tastes and pocketbooks. In all cases, and especially in the luxury hotels, you can often save money by requesting low-season, package, and weekly or monthly discounts. For winter high-season lodgings, call or write for early reservations.

For many more budget beachfront lodgings than are listed here, check out the sleepy Pie de la Cuesta downscale beach resort village on placid Laguna Coyuca (about six miles by the oceanfront Highway 200 northwest from the Acapulco *zócalo*). There, you'll find plenty of inexpensive palm-shaded shoreline hotels and bungalows, as well as trailer parks and campsites.

NEAR THE *ZÓCALO*

A number of clean, budget- to moderately priced hotels cluster in the colorful working-class neighborhood between the *zócalo* and La Quebrada divers' point.

Under $50

Three blocks west of the *zócalo* on the quiet cul-de-sac end of Avenida la Paz stands the spartan three-story **Hotel María Acela** (Av. la Paz 19, Acapulco, Guerrero 39300, tel. 744/482-0661, $8 s, $13 d low season, $11 and $18 high, with fans). Its family management lends an atmosphere more like a guesthouse than a hotel. The 21 austerely furnished rooms, although clean enough (but not immaculate), lack hot water. Guests enjoy a small lobby library of paperback books.

On the same street nearby, half a block closer to the *zócalo*, the 1960s-modern **Hotel María Antioneta** (Teniente Azueta 17, Acapulco, Guerrero 39300, tel. 744/482-5024, credit cards not accepted, $8 s, $16 d fronts the busy store- and restaurant-lined Avenida Azueta. The 34 plainly furnished, somewhat worn rooms, with a/c, hot water, and fans, are nevertheless light, especially on the upper floor. Bathrooms could use a good scrubbing, however. Most rooms are fortunately recessed along the leafy

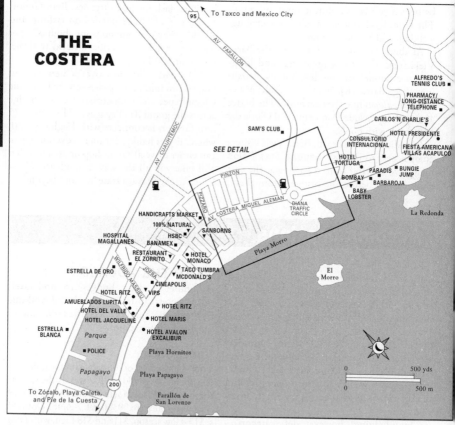

THE COSTERA

To Taxco and Mexico City

ALFREDO'S TENNIS CLUB

PHARMACY/ LONG-DISTANCE TELEPHONE

CARLOS'N CHARLIE'S

SAM'S CLUB

HOTEL PRESIDENTE

CONSULTORIO INTERNACIONAL

FIESTA-AMERICANA VILLAS ACAPULCO

SEE DETAIL

HOTEL TORTUGA

PARADIS ■ BUNGIE JUMP

BOMBAY

BARBAROJA

BABY LOBSTER

La Redonda

HANDICRAFTS MARKET

100% NATURAL

SANBORNS

OHANA TRAFFIC CIRCLE

Playa Morro

El Morro

HOSPITAL MAGALLANES

HSBC

BANAMEX

RESTAURANT EL ZORRITO

HOTEL MONACO

ESTRELLA DE ORO

TACO TUMBRA

MCDONALD'S

CINÉAPOLIS

HOTEL RITZ

VIPS

AMUEBLADOS LUPITA

HOTEL RITZ

HOTEL DEL VALLE

HOTEL JACQUELINE

HOTEL MARIS

ESTRELLA BLANCA

Parque

HOTEL AVALON EXCALIBUR

■ POLICE

Playa Hornitos

Papagayo

Playa Papagayo

To Zócalo, Playa Caleta, and Pie de la Cuesta

Farallón de San Lorenzo

0   500 yds

0   500 m

inner courtyard, away from street noise. Guests have the use of a handy communal kitchen and a potentially attractive upstairs terrace.

Several blocks west, uphill, overlooking the La Quebrada parking lot, is **Hotel Torre Eiffel** (Inalambrica 110, Acapulco, Guerrero 39300, tel. 744/482-1683, fax 744/483-5727, hoteltorreeiffel@hotmail.com, $9 s, $18 d, $27 t except holidays). Above a hillside garden overlooking the La Quebrada divers' point tourist mecca, guests enjoy 25 simply but comfortably furnished rooms, with fans, hot water, and parking, overlooking an inviting pool-patio. Guests in the uppermost rooms enjoy breezy sea views and a sunset horizon. (Note: The hotel's Inalambrica address is misleading:

find it at the corner of Avenida Pinzona, one block uphill, on the right from the La Quebrada parking lot.)

Three blocks west, uphill from the *zócalo,* the **Hotel Asturias** (Quebrada 45, Acapulco, Guerrero 39300, tel./fax 744/483-6548, cerardoancera@aol.com, $18 s, $32 d, $42 t with fans; $28 s, $56 d, and $70 t with a/c) offers a relaxing atmosphere at moderate rates. Its two stories of 15 plain but tidy rooms surround a plant-decorated pool and patio with chairs for sunning. Get an upper room for more light and privacy. Find it four short blocks west of the cathedral, between Ramírez and Ortiz.

Arguably the most charming of *zócalo*-area hotels is the authentically colonial-era **Hotel**

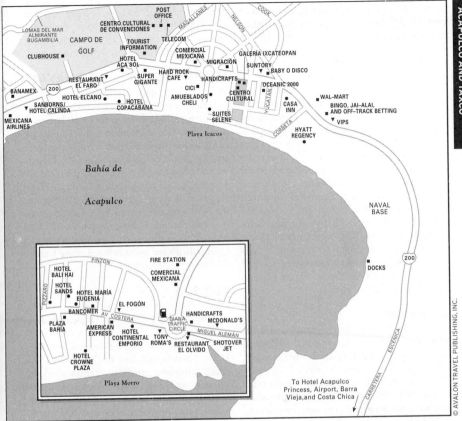

© AVALON TRAVEL PUBLISHING, INC.

Misión (Felipe Valle 12, Acapulco, Guerrero 39300, tel. 744/482-3643, fax 744/482-2076, hotelmision@hotmail.com, $14 s, $28 d, low season, $23 and $46 high), corner of La Paz, two blocks west of the *zócalo*. The owner, María Elena Sayago, relates the history of her hotel-home. From 1930 to 1966, it was a school, the Colegio Acapulco. When she began repairs several years ago, her workers uncovered broken antique Chinese porcelain, most likely brought from Asia by the colonial-era Manila galleons. She says that before the 1910–1917 Revolution, the place housed army offices, and before that, it was a banklike *estango* (depository) for valuables. The front-section walls and rooms were preserved in the original adobe, and the columns

in the original stone. Most of the 28 guest rooms, however, she had rebuilt, in two stories around a plant-decorated patio, shaded by a spreading mango tree. When the mangoes ripen in April, guests get their fill of the fragrant fruit. With fans, hot water, and parking, in an adjacent lot.

$50-100

Five blocks west of the *zócalo*, up winding Avenida Pinzona, the **Hotel Etel Suites** (Av. Pinzona 92, Acapulco, Guerrero 39390, tel. 744/482-2240 or 744/482-2241, fax 744/483-8094, etelsuites@terra.com.mex, www.etelsuites.com, credit cards accepted, $32 s or d low season, $55 high, with fans, a/c, and hot water, and up) perches on the view hillside above old Acapulco. Well managed by friendly owner Etel Sutter Álvarez (great-granddaughter of renowned Swiss-California pioneer Johann A. Sutter) and her daughter, the three-building complex stair-steps downhill to a luxurious view garden and pool. Its airy hillside perch lends the Etel Suites a tranquil, luxurious ambience unusual in a moderately priced lodging. Chairs and sofas in a small street-level lobby invite relaxed conversation with fellow guests. The primly but thoughtfully furnished and well-maintained rooms range from singles to multibedroom view apartments. The dozens of rooms and suites rent from about $32 s or d low season, $55 high, with fans, a/c, and hot water. Completely furnished view apartments with kitchens go for about $55 low season, $90 high, with discounts negotiable for monthly rentals. With some parking. (Note: If you arrive in Acapulco on a crowded high-season weekend without a reservation, the Etel Suites will probably be the last decent place in town likely to have a room.)

Over $100

At the cliff-end of Calle Quebrada stands the *zócalo* area's only upscale hostelry, the 🄲 **Hotel el Mirador Acapulco** (Plazoleta la Quebrada 72, Acapulco, Guerrero, 39300, tel. 744/483-1155, toll-free U.S. tel. 866/toll-free Mex. tel. 01-800/021-7557, fax 744/483-8800, mirador_reservaciones@hotmail.com.mx, www.hotelel miradoracapulco.com.mx, $80 d low season, $150 high, for room; $230 d low season, $180 low, for suite). Acapulco's first deluxe hotel, El Mirador was built in the early 1930s. The hotel, appropriately, uses the La Quebrada diver in its logo. Directly below the hotel restaurant-bar, the divers accomplish their feat to the acclaim of hundreds of spectators five times daily. The hotel has much more to recommend than spectacle, however. Guests choose from a collection of about 50 semidetached picturesquely perched hillside lodgings. Inside, they are attractively furnished in dark masculine tones, shiny rustic floor tiles, decorator reading lamps, and deluxe bathrooms. Two airy, sunset-view restaurants, bars, and three swimming pools complete the attractive picture. All this for about $80 d stan-

dard, low season, $150 high; or $230 d low season, $180 low, for large suite with private view balcony and kitchenette; all with cable TV, a/c, some wheelchair access, and parking.

PENÍNSULA DE LAS PLAYAS

Many of old Acapulco's mid-range to high-end lodgings are spread along one continuous boulevard that winds through the plush Península de las Playas neighborhood. The boulevard starts as the Costera Miguel Alemán as it heads past the *zócalo*. A couple of miles farther southwest, the boulevard curves left as the Gran Via Tropical, rounding the Península de las Playas clockwise. Passing Caleta and Caletilla beaches, the boulevard changes to Avenida López Mateos and continues along the peninsula's sunset (southwest) side past Playa Angosta and La Quebrada divers' point before ending back in the *zócalo* neighborhood.

$50-100

On the peninsula's northeast side, apartment-style **Suites Alba** (Gran Via Tropical 35, Acapulco, Guerrero 39390, tel. 744/483-0073, fax 744/483-8378, U.S. toll-free tel. 866/805-4626, Canada toll-free tel. 877/428-1327, alba@suitesalba.com.mx, ventasacapulco@albasuites.com.mx, credit cards accepted, $60 d, $90 d holidays) rambles through its well-kept hilltop garden of palms and pools. During the winter, the mostly Canadian and American middle-class guests enjoy many facilities, including a pair of pools, a whirlpool bath, a restaurant, a minimart, some wheelchair access, and a bayside beach club with its own saltwater pool. The 292 comfortably furnished apartments have kitchenettes, a/c, and private garden-view balconies. Standard rentals (reserved through the hotel, not through travel agents) usually begin at around $60 d and rise to about $90 d holidays, with discounts available for monthly rentals, and parking is available.

A trio of recommendable deluxe hotels decorate the peninsula's luscious southeast-side oceanfront. (I've looked hard, but haven't been able to find a recommendable budget hotel in this neighborhood.) Most economical is the **Hotel Caleta** (Cerro San Martin 225, Playa Caleta, Acapulco, Guerrero 39300, tel. 744/483-9140, toll-free Mex. tel. 01-800/700-0979, fax 744/483-9121, hotelesposeidon.com.mx, meigaca@prodigy.net.mx, credit cards accepted, $70–90 d; all-inclusive $65 pp double occupancy low-season, $85 high), on the east headland bordering Playa Caleta. Hotel guests enjoy a big blue pool and view sundeck, an intimately private (but sometimes trash-strewn) rock-enfolded open-ocean beach, multiple restaurants and bars, lush green garden, and comfortable rooms, with private panoramic view balconies. Although renovated in the mid-1990s, the hotel is now showing a bit of wear around the edges. Prices for the 260 rooms are very reasonable, at about $70 d, rising to $90 high. All-inclusive rates run about $65 per person low-season double occupancy, $85 high, including all meals, drinks, and in-house sports and entertainment. All with a/c, phones, cable TV, some wheelchair access, and parking.

About four blocks farther west along the beach, guests of the **(Hotel Boca Chica** (Playa Caletilla s/n, Acapulco, Guerrero 39300, tel. 744/483-6601 or 744/483-6741, 744/434-1990, fax 744/483-9513, San Diego tel. 619/476-9493, hotelbocachica@gmail.com, www.bocachicahotel.com, credit cards accepted, $75 d low season, $120 high) enjoy an enviable beach vantage and semideluxe amenities. Views of Playa Caletilla on one side and the verdant Isla Roqueta beyond an azure channel on the other are stunning. The hotel perches on a rocky point, enfolded by a lush, leafy garden and swaying palms. Walk ten steps down from the pool deck and enjoy swimming and snorkeling in the clear aqua water that washes the hotel's surrounding rocky shoals. The 45 light, comfortably furnished rooms vary; if you have the option, look at two or three before you choose. Early reservations year-round are strongly recommended., Rooms come with phones, a/c, breakfast, some wheelchair access, bars, restaurants, in-house wireless Internet, and parking.

Half a mile farther west uphill, a contrasting, but equally attractive option is available at the **(Hotel los Flamingos** (P.O. Box 70,

the "Tarzan" pool, built by former owner Johnny Weissmuller, at the Hotel los Flamingos

Acapulco, Guerrero 39300, tel. 744/482-0690, 744/482-0691, or 744/482-0692, fax 744/483-9806, flamingoo@prodigy.net.mx, www.hotel losflamingos.com, credit cards accepted, $70, $80, and $90 d low season; $80, $100, and $115 d high season). The Los Flamingos is the place where oldsters reminisce and young-sters find out who John Wayne, Johnny Weiss-muller, and Rory Calhoun were. Personable owner-manager and musician Adolfo Santiago González enjoys playing his guitar and relat-ing his experiences with his famous guests of yesteryear. Vintage Hollywood photos decorate the open-air lobby walls, while pathways lead through a hilltop jungle of palm, hibiscus, and spreading mangoes. The 40-odd rooms, several with private, ocean-view balconies, perch on a cliffside that plummets into foaming break-ers hundreds of feet below. Soft evening gui-tar music in an open-air sunset-view restaurant and a luxurious clifftop pool and patio com-plete the lovely picture. The rooms, in stan-dard, superior, and junior suite grades, run about $70, $80, and $90 d low season, respec-tively, and $80, $100, and $115 high season; add about $25 for an extra person. The hotel also rents **Casa Redonda** (about $280 for up to six), a luxuriously secluded cliffside view house, the former Acapulco home of Johnny Weiss-muller (the most famous Tarzan), who passed away in 1984. All with parking, some a/c.

COSTERA WEST END

With few exceptions, these hostelries line both beach and inland sides of the busy boulevard, Costera Miguel Alemán, east of Papagayo amusement park. Hotels are nearly all either right on or just a short walk from the beach.

Under $50

Among the most inviting is the modest **Hotel del Valle** (G. Gomez Espinosa 8, Acapulco, Guerrero 39670, tel. 744/485-8336 and 744/485-8388, $42 s or d, $55 high, $75 Christmas-New Year and Easter), across the street from Papagayo amusement park. Three motel-style floors of 18 invitingly redecorated rooms border a small but attractive pool patio.

A kitchen for guests is available for $6. On a side street away from the noisy boulevard, the del Valle is a tranquil winter headquarters for retirees and youthful budget travelers, with hot water and fans.

If the Hotel del Valle is full, you might try its more moderately priced (but without pools) petite next-door neighbors, the **Hotel Jacqueline** (tel./fax 744/485-9338, $45 d) and the **Amueblados Lupita** (tel. 744/485-9412, $37 d).

Several blocks farther east, check out best-buy **Hotel Sands** (Costera Miguel Alemán 178, P.O. Box 256, Acapulco, Guerrero 39670, tel. 744/484-2260 through -2264, toll-free Mex. tel. 01-800/710-9800, fax 744/484-1053, sands@ sands.com.mx, www.sands.com.mx, credit cards accepted, $47 d *cabaña,* $55 d room). In addi-tion to a pool-patio and restaurant next to the main 1960s-modern building, the hotel's spa-cious grounds encompass a shady green park in the rear that leads to an attractive hidden cluster of garden *cabañas.* Of the main build-ing rooms, the uppers are best; many have been redecorated with light, comfortable furnishings. *Cabaña* guests, on the other hand, enjoy taste-ful browns, tile decor, and big windows look-ing out into a leafy garden. *Cabañas* 1–8 are the most secluded. The 90-odd accommodations run about $47 d for the *cabañas* and $55 d for the hotel rooms. Holidays such as Christmas and Easter are higher. Low-season promotional packages weekdays and for longer stays may be available; be sure to ask. All with a/c, cable TV, and phones. Parking and use of squash courts are included.

On the beach side of the street, two blocks east of McDonald's, the petite, three-story **Hotel Monaco** (Av. Costera Miguel Alemán 137, Aca-pulco, Guerrero 39670, tel./fax 744/485-6467, 744/485-6415, or 744/485-6518, monac_otel@ hotmail.com, $46 d, $54 holidays) offers a tropi-cal miniretreat from the Costera noise and bus-tle. Past the small lobby, a big, round blue pool, decorated with shade umbrellas and edged by palms and leafy greenery, invites relaxation. (The patio's attractiveness, however, leads to its drawback: For peace and quiet, spend your time on the beach during the weekends, when families love to frolic in the pool. Weekdays by the pool are usually more tranquil.) Upstairs, the rooms are plain but clean, with the basics: hot showers and two double beds, with a/c, phone, TV, and parking; it's close to everything, just a block from the beach.

$50-100

Back near the west end, the renovated, longtime **(C Auto-tel Ritz** (corner of Costera M. Alemán and Wilfrido Massieu, Acapulco, Guerrero 39670, tel. 744/486-2081, 744/485-5242, or 744/485-8939, toll-free Mex. tel. 01-800/716-2159, panorami@aca-novenet.com.mx, www.hotelesposeidon.com.mx, $60 d low season, $85 high) stands just a block from the beach. The downstairs, with its chandeliered but dowdy lobby, leads nevertheless to an invitingly tropical pool and patio, climaxed by plumy, exotic fan palms. The rooms (get one upstairs for more privacy) are likewise attractive: light and clean, with big double beds, marble baths, and airy, private patio-view balconies. Rates include a/c, cable TV, and parking.

Just half a block from the Auto-tel Ritz and right on the beach stands the midrise **Hotel Maris** (Av. Costera M. Alemán 59, Acapulco, Guerrero 39670, tel. 744/485-8596, fax 744/485-8492, hotelmaris@hotmail.com, $90 d, $130 during holidays). Here, guests enjoy 85 spacious rooms with private view balconies at reasonable rates. Lobby-level amenities include a small pool above the beach club *palapas,* with bar and restaurant. (You may want to ask the staff to turn down the TV volume.) With a/c, cable TV, and phones. Street parking only.

Head a few blocks east (on the beach about three blocks past McDonald's) to the **Hotel Maralisa** (Alemania s/n, Acapulco, Guerrero 39670, tel. 744/485-6677 or 744/485-7363, fax 744/485-9228, hotelmaralisa@hotmail.com, www.hotelesposeidon.com.mx, credit cards accepted, $70 d low season, $86 high), which nestles among its towering beachfront condo neighbors. The Maralisa is a luxuriously simple retreat, where guests, after their fill of sunning beside the palm-lined pool patio, can

step down onto the sand for a jog or stroll along the beach. Later, they might enjoy a light meal in the hotel's beachside café and go out for dancing in nearby resort hotels. Several of the Maralisa's 90 comfortable rooms, tastefully decorated in whites and warm pastels, have private balconies. Ask for a discount or package. Up to two kids under 12 stay free; with a/c, cable TV, phones, and parking.

Over $100

A mile farther east, the popular longtime luxury **(C Fiesta Americana Villas Acapulco,** formerly the Fiesta Americana (Av. Costera M. Alemán 1220, Acapulco, Guerrero 39690, tel. 744/435-1600, toll-free U.S./Can. tel. 800/FIESTA-1–800/343-7821–fax 744/484-1828, resfaca@posadas.com, www.fiestamericana.com, credit cards accepted, $200 d and up) presides atop its rocky shoreline perch smack in the middle of the Costera action. Boulevard traffic roars nonstop past the front door, and nightclubs rock (on the west side; the east side is quiet) nearby. By day during the winter, ranks of middle-class American and Canadian vacationers sun on the hotel's spacious pool deck and downstairs at its *palapa*-shaded beach club. Resort facilities include restaurants and bars, shops, auto rental, golf nearby, and all aquatic sports. Rooms, most with private bay-view balconies, are furnished in soothing pastels, rattan, and designer lamps. Rooms rent from about $200 d year-round except holidays, with a/c, cable TV, phones, parking, and full wheelchair access. Low-occupancy season promotions or discounts (ask for the senior discount) may be available.

COSTERA EAST SIDE

East of the golf course stretches the newest, shiniest part of Acapulco, where seemingly every enterprise, from Wal-Mart and McDonald's to Hooters and Hyatt Regency, has strained to locate during the recent past. Despite the hubbub, corners of tranquility do exist, especially among many of the high-rise hostelries and condominiums that occupy the golden beachfront.

Under $50

A few vintage east-side remnants of Acapulco "the way it used to be" live on, seemingly oblivious of the fast-lane world around them. At the CICI water park corner, walk straight toward the beach, along Calle Cristóbal Colón. Just before the beach, on the left, find **Suites Selene** (Colón 175, Acapulco, Guerrero 39860, tel./fax 744/484-2977 or 744/484-3643, suitesselene @hotmail.com, $45, $55 with kitchenette). Here, just half a block from the beach, by a shady street's-end park, stands a complex of 24 modest apartments. Exterior amenities include a leafy garden, a blue pool and patio, and parking sensitively situated in the rear, away from the garden and apartments. Most of the somewhat worn but clean units have one bedroom with two double beds, a living-dining room, bathroom, and a kitchenette, with stove, refrigerator, utensils, and dishes and purified water in a five-gallon *garafón* (demijohn) for cooking. The remaining six units have everything but the kitchenette. Low-season rentals usually go for $45 per day without kitchenette, $55 with. Discounts may be negotiable for weekly or monthly rentals.

Walk away from the beach two doors and find neighbor complex **Amueblados Cheli** (Colón 155, Acapulco, Guerrero 39860, tel. 744/484-3160 or 744/484-2019—Spanish only, $50), also scarcely a block from the beach. The complex (titled "Amueblados," meaning, literally, "Furnished") consists of about 20 apartments in two floors, set around a lovingly tended tropical garden and parking patio. On the south, beach side of the apartments is an inviting pool patio for guest use. The whole place is set behind a sturdy security fence, probably mostly to keep beachgoers from wandering in at all hours. The only possible drawback here might be the music and noise from the CICI water park (10 A.M.–6 P.M. daily) across the street. Although most apartments are rented by the month, vacant rentals are often rented for about $50 per day.

$50-100

For a very worthy, moderately priced hotel alternative, just a block and a half from the beach, return directly back to the Costera and the classy, small **Hotel Aca Sol** (Costera Miguel Alemán 53B, Acapulco, Guerrero 39690, tel. 744/484-2782, fax 744/484-0977, ventas@ turismointersol.com, www.hotelacasol.com, credit cards accepted, $70 s or d). Enter the petite but invitingly chic lobby and continue to an airy, palm-decorated rear pool-patio. To one side, an attractive small restaurant, shielded from street noise, serves guests. Upstairs, the 35 rooms in four floors enfold the patio. Inside, rooms are white, marbled, and squeaky clean. Guests in most rooms enjoy exterior balconies. Get a room overlooking Almendro, the adjacent quiet side street. Rentals, excluding Easter, Christmas, and July and August, usually run about $70 s or d, sometimes fourth night free, with a/c, parking, cable TV, telephones, and tennis court.

Over $100

On the other hand, those who hanker for a party can have it on the beach, at **Hotel Copacabana** (Tabachines 2, Fracc. Club Deportivo, Acapulco, Guerrero 39690, tel. 744/484-3260, tel./fax 744/484-6268, U.S. toll-free tel. 800/562-0197, toll-free Mex. tel. 01-800/710-9888, acapulco@hotel copacabana.com, www.hotelcopacabana.com, credit cards accepted, $107 d and up). Past the midsized, attractive lobby, guests enjoy a live music restaurant-bar, a beachview pool deck, and a squadron of private beachfront *palapas*. Everywhere inside, the marble, brass, and rattan are polished, the guests are youngish, and the mood is upbeat. Upstairs, the 18 floors of 400-plus rooms are deluxe, comfortable, marble-floored and cheerily decorated in yellows and whites, with bamboo furniture and bedsteads. All this for the standard promotional rate (except holidays and July and August) of about $107 d (add $10 per extra person), with a/c, cable TV, parking, and boogie boards, kayaks, water polo, aerobics, and volleyball at no extra cost. Other downstairs amenities include shops, travel agent, and business center.

Favorite among lovers of peace and quiet is the grand, dignified **Hotel Elcano** (Av. Costera Miguel Alemán 75, Acapulco, Guerrero 39690, tel./fax 744/435-1500 or 744/484/2230, elcano@hotel-elcano.com .mx, www.hotel-elcano.com, $130 d low season, $320 high), two blocks removed—and with rooms facing away from the Costera traffic. The hotel was named after Ferdinand Magellan's navigator, Sebastián Elcano (who actually was the one who first circumnavigated the globe; Magellan died en route but got the credit). Hotel Elcano is austerely luxurious, hued in shades of nautical blue, from the breezy, gracefully columned lobby and the spacious turquoise beachside pool to the 180 immaculate, marble-tiled view rooms. Unlike some of Acapulco's beachfront hostelries, the Elcano has plenty of space for guests to enjoy its load of extras, which include two restaurants, three bars, poolside hot tub, beach club, kiddie pool, gym, nine-hole golf course three blocks away, and video games center. Rooms, all with private ocean-view balconies, rent for a very reasonable $130 d low season (but $320 high). Be sure to ask for possible promotional packages, or midweek or weekly rates.

Towering over the Costera's east end is the 20-story high-rise of the **⟨ Hyatt Regency Acapulco** (Costera M. Alemán 1, Acapulco, Guerrero 39869, tel. 744/469-1234, toll-free Mex. tel. 800/005-0000, toll-free U.S./ Can. tel. 800/223-1234, fax 744/484-3087, acara-reservations@hyattintl.com, Mexico toll-free tel 01-005-0000, credit cards accepted, $180 d low season, $225 high). Its lavish beachfront facilities include spacious gardens, blue lagoon swimming pool, a Tarzan jungle waterfall, a squadron of personal beach *palapas*, restaurants, bars, frequent live music, shops, all aquatic sports, tennis, and golf nearby. The 690 rooms, all with private view balconies, are large and luxurious. Standard rooms rent from about $180 d low season, $225 high, with a/c, cable TV, phones, parking, and full wheelchair access.

EAST OF TOWN

A number of luxury hostelries spread along the Playa Revolcadero shore, on the beach side of the airport road.

Over $100

One of the most reasonably priced yet most heavenly is the **Villas San Vicente** (downtown office tel. 744/486-4037, fax 744/485-6846, hotel direct tel. 744/462-0120, sanvicente villas@aol.com, casas@casasyvillas.com.mx, www.villassanviecnte.com.mx, $120 studios, and up), a miniparadise for lovers of peace and quiet. Plenty of space, sweeping green lawns, swaying palms, and a long gorgeous strand, where you can have it all: afternoons in splendid isolation, reading by the pool, long walks on the beach, savoring the tropical breeze, and watching the sun go down. Guests in the five spacious, super deluxe minivillas enjoy two bedrooms, with king-sized beds, and two baths, designer living-dining room, completely equipped kitchen, hot tub, a/c, and a small private pool. The two smaller units are more modest but still comfortable studios, with bath, kitchenette, and a/c, set at the upper edge of the property, a bit farther from the beach. All residents share a lusciously inviting main pool and patio, with bar, tennis courts, and parking, all on about 10 palm-shaded beachfront acres. Rates run about $120 for the studios, upward from $250 to about $400 for the minivillas, depending on location and amenities. Holiday rates are about 30 percent higher. Reservations (necessary in high season, strongly recommended low) are available by either contacting the Villas' in-town office, or the Villas San Vicente directly. Get to Villas San Vicente by following the airport road, eastbound about seven miles (11 km) past the hill-bottom Puerto Marquez traffic interchange. Instead of heading straight ahead to the airport, fork right toward Barra Vieja. After a mile or two, you'll reach the Villas San Vicente gate, on the right.

Closer in (only about a mile east of the Puerto Marquez interchange) along the airport road, the showplace **Hotel Fairmont Acapulco Princess** (Playa Revolcadero, P.O.

Box 1351, Acapulco, Guerrero 39300, tel. 744/469-1000, toll-free U.S./Can. tel. 800/866-5577, fax 744/469-1012, aca.reservations @fairmont.com, www.fairmont.com/acapulco, credit cards accepted, $210 d low season, $230 high) provides an abundance of resort facilities (including an entire 18-hole golf course), spreading from luscious beachfront garden grounds. Although the hotel centers on a pair of hulking neopyramids (1,019-room total), the impression from the rooms themselves is of superluxury; from the garden it is of Eden-like jungle tranquility—meandering pools, gurgling cascades, strutting flamingos, swaying palms—which guests seem to soak up with no trouble at all. Rooms, all deluxe with a plethora of up-to-date amenities, rent from about $210 d low season, $230 high, including breakfast and dinner high season; guests enjoy a host of facilities, all sports, and full wheelchair access.

Alternatively, consider the **Vidafel Mayan Palace** (Av. Costera del las Palmas, Fracc. Playa Diamante, Acapulco, Guerrero 39300, tel./fax 744/469-6000, toll-free Mex. tel. 800/711-2165, toll-free U.S./Can. tel. 800/292-9446, reservacionesaca@mayan-palace .com.mx, www.mayanresorts.com.mx, $238 d low season, $470 high), about a mile farther along the beach from the Fairmont Acapulco Princess. Here, in a palace like the Mayan kings never had, you can have an 18-hole golf course, 12 clay tennis courts, a kilometer-long swimming pool (no kidding), five bars, three restaurants, fountains, waterfalls, and an entire blue lagoon, all overlooking a gorgeous, breezy beach. Hotel rates run from about $238 d low season, $470 high, for a luxurious and spacious marble and pastel room with everything. Ask for a discount or promotional package.

RENTALS AND REAL ESTATE

A good source of Acapulco long-term rentals and real estate is the (Spanish-language) website **www.acabtu.com,** electronic descendant of the former community newspaper *Acapulco Heat.* (Curiously, "btu" refers to the "British thermal unit" commonly used to measure quantity of heat energy.) Go directly to the acabtu real estate *(bienes raices)* section by typing in www.acabtu.com.mx/acaweb/ bienesraices.html.

Another very useful Internet site is **Vacation Rentals by Owner** (www.vrbo.com) which links to a broad range of individual Acapulco rentals, from moderate to expensive.

For folks less familiar with the Internet, some of the more useful rental sources can also be contacted by telephone. For example, in Acapulco, check out **Bachur Real Estate** (Av. Costera Miguel Aleman 20, Hotel Tropicana, Fracc. Costa Azul, Acapulco, Guerrero 39300, tel./fax 744/484-1333, www.bachur.com.mx), specializing in condos and villas.

Furthermore, some U.S. and Canadian real estate networks have Acapulco branches. One of the most active is the Century 21 local branch, **Century 21 Realty Mex** (in the eastern Costera neighborhood, at Calle Alonso Martín 43, Fracc. Magellanes, Acapulco, Guerrero 39670, tel. 744/485-9090 or 744/486-6110, fax 744/486-4187, www .century21acapulco.com.mx). Although it specializes in high-end villas and condominiums, the staff also may be able to get you a moderately-priced house or villa rental (or suggest someone who can).

Finally, don't forget the three moderately priced apartment complexes recommended under *Accommodations* in this chapter: **Hotel Etel Suites, Amueblados Cheli,** and **Suites Selene.**

Food

NEAR THE ZÓCALO
Breakfast and Snacks

Eat well for under $3 at 【 **Lonchería Chatita** (Av. Azueta, corner of Hidalgo, 8 A.M.–10 P.M. daily), where a friendly female kitchen squad serves mounds of wholesome, local-style specialties. On a typical day, these may include savory *chiles rellenos,* rich *puerco mole de Uruapan, pozole* (savory hominy soup), or potato pancakes.

Something fancier is available at **La Flor de Acapulco** (on the upstairs balcony overlooking the *zócalo,* cell tel. 044-744/421-7639) 8 A.M.–10 P.M. Mon.–Wed., 8 A.M.–midnight Thurs.–Sun.). Formerly Restaurant la Parroquia, it's good for a snack or a light lunch ($4–7) as you soak in the scene below, with the bonus of live music Thurs.–Sun. 9 P.M.–midnight.

For something creamy and cool, go for ice cream to **Dolphy** (one block along the Costera, from the *zócalo* toward the steamship dock, 9 A.M.–11 P.M. daily).

Continue another block to air-conditioned **Sanborn's** (a block east of the *zócalo,* at the Costera corner of Escudero, tel. 744/482-4095, 7:30 A.M.–11 P.M. daily) for soup and salads ($4), ham and eggs and hamburgers ($3–5), and apple pie (4$).

Woolworth's (one block from the Costera, behind Sanborn's, tel. 744/480-0072) also offers air-conditioned ambience and similar fare at lower prices.

Finally, for dessert, head back over to the other side of the *zócalo* to the bakery **La Espiga de Acapulco** (on Juárez, a block west of the *zócalo,* tel. 744/482-2699, 7 A.M.–10 P.M. daily) for a tasty tart or piece of cake.

COSTERA
Breakfast and Snacks

Snack food concentrates in Acapulco around at least two branches of **McDonald's** (the original one at the corner of Esclavo and Avenida Costera M. Alemán, a few blocks east of the landmark Hotel Ritz; and also farther east, on the Costera, east of the Diana fountain and traffic circle, 8 A.M.–11 P.M. daily). Here, you have it all, from breakfast Egg McMuffins to Chicken McNuggets and the Big Mac, priced about a third higher than back home.

For an interesting contrast, visit **Taco Tumbra** (across the adjacent street from the original McDonald's, tel. 744/485-7621, 6:30 P.M.–2 A.M. Sun.–Thurs., 6:30 P.M.–4 A.M. Fri.–Sat.). Here, piquant aromas of barbecued chicken, pork, and beef and strains of Latin music fill the air. For a treat, order three of the delectable tacos along with a refreshing fruit juice *(jugo)* or fruit-flavored *agua.*

Restaurant el Zorrito (Little Fox; about a block east of McDonald's and across the street, tel. 744/485-3735, 24 hours Wed.–Mon., 6 A.M.–1 P.M. Tues.) packs in the crowds with just about the tastiest Mexican food in town. If you're in the mood for some serious eating,

fresh-caught oysters and octopus for sale on Playa Caleta

fill up with a Filete Tampiqueña ($11) (beef fillet Tampico style), or *chiles rellenos* ($7) big enough for two, or *lomo* (pork loin roast, $6). **Sanborn's** (across the street, tel. 744/485-5360, 7–1 A.M. daily) provides a blessedly cool, refined refuge from the busy boulevard. Here (formerly Denny's), you can sample an international menu of either North American favorites (eggs, pancakes, bacon, and bottomless coffee, $5) or hearty Mexican specialties ($4–8). Sanborn's also offers a rack of American magazines, such as *Time, Glamour,* and *National Geographic,* and an ATM.

In competition, **100 Percent Natural** (directly across the Costera from Sanborn's, tel. 744/485-3982, 24 hours daily) offers appropriately contrasting fare: many veggie and fruit drinks ($1–2; try the Conga, made of papaya, guava, watermelon, pineapple, lime, and spinach), several egg breakfasts ($3–5), breads, sandwiches, tacos, and enchiladas ($3–5). You can also find two more branches of 100 Percent Natural: mid-Costera (next door to Carlos 'n Charlie's across from Hotel Presidente, tel. 744/484-6447, 7 A.M.–11 P.M.), and on the east side (next to Baby O disco, tel. 744/484-8440, same hours).

Two miles farther along the Costera, find the central Costera branch of **Sanborn's** (at Hotel Calinda, tel. 744/481-2426, 7–1 A.M. daily), offering the same Sanborn's refined atmosphere, good food, and a big book and gift store.

Restaurants

At **VIPs** (on the Costera, a block from Papagayo Amusement Park, tel. 744/486-8574, 7 A.M.–midnight daily, credit cards accepted), you can glimpse the Mexico of the future. Here, Mexican middle-class families flock to a south-of-the-border–style Denny's that beats Denny's at its own game. Inside, the air is as fresh as a spring breeze; the windows, water glasses, and utensils shine like silver; the food is tasty (but rather pricey, entrées $5–10); and the staff is both amiable and professional. (Also visit VIPs' newer Costera locations, beach side, near the Hotel Calinda, and east side, across the boulevard from the Hyatt Regency.)

Although these days sometimes overlooked, enduring open-air terrace **[Restaurant el Olvido** (The Forgotten One; on the mid-Costera, rear of Plaza Marbella, beach side of the Diana Circle, tel. 744/481-0214 or 744/481-0236, 6 P.M.–2 A.M. daily) remains one of Acapulco's best. It seems the model by which some of Acapulco's now-trendy eateries were created. What's remarkable is that such a tranquil tropical mini-island could exist so close to the smoggy roar of the Costera traffic. By day, guests enjoy a palm-tufted airy bay view, and by night an ebony star-studded sky bordered below by myriad twinkling city lights. The excellent cuisine, however, provides the main attraction. Choose from a very recognizable menu of lots of pasta ($5–8), meat ($6–15), and fish ($8–18), including a number of nouvelle international specialties. For example, start off with Boston lettuce with watercress and strawberries ($6), continue with black fettuccine with smoked Norwegian salmon ($13) or quail with honey and pineapple ($14), and finish off with *tiramisu* ($5). Reservations recommended, especially on weekends.

No tour of Acapulco restaurants would be complete without a stop at **Carlos 'n Charlie's** (on the Costera, across from and a block east of the Hotel Fiesta Americana, tel. 744/484-0039, 2 P.M.–midnight daily, credit cards accepted), which, like all of the late Carlos Anderson's worldwide chain, specializes in the zany. The fun begins with the screwy decor, continues via the good-natured, tongue-in-cheek antics of the staff, and climaxes with the food and drink, which is organized on the menu by categories, such as "Slurp" ($3), "Munch" ($4), "Peep" ($8), "Moo" ($9), and "Zurts" ($2–12), and is very tasty.

Another successful culinary experiment is the Acapulco branch of the worldwide Japanese restaurant chain **[Suntory** (across from the Oceanic 2000 building, east end of the Costera, tel. 744/484-8088, 2 P.M. to midnight daily, credit cards accepted). Although a Japanese restaurant in Mexico seems as difficult to create as a Mexican restaurant in Japan, Suntory, the giant beer, whiskey, and wine manufacturer, carries it off with aplomb. From the outside, the clean-lined wooden structure appears authentically classic Japanese, seemingly lifted right out of 18th-century Kyoto. The impression continues in the cool interior, where patrons enjoy a picture-perfect tropical Zen garden, complete with moss, a stony brook, sago palm, and feathery festoons of bamboo. Finally comes the food, from a host of choices—vegetables, rice, fish, and meat ($6–14)—which chefs (who, although Mexican, soon begin to look Japanese) individually prepare for you on the grill built into your table.

Restaurant el Faro (The Lighthouse; at Hotel Elcano, tel. 744/435-1500, 8 A.M.–11 P.M. daily) has raised Acapulco to new heights of culinary fantasy, at least equal to that of its rotating beacon high above the Costera. The cool subdued interior is reminiscent of a 1940s Hollywood supper club, tinted in suave greens and blues. The numerous nautical accents climax in an overhead stained-glass submarine mural. The total impression is as if you and your fellow diners were inhabitants of a grand aquarium, visible only to the poor exterior denizens through the street-level porthole windows. The cuisine is no less than you'd expect: mostly seafood, some exotic, such as *koktoxas* of grouper (fish cheeks, $22), or more recognizable, such as cod a la Vasque ($20), or grilled shrimp with vegetables and wild rice, sautéed in sesame oil ($24). Meat lovers, nevertheless, will do quite well, with entrées such as lusciously tender rib-eye steak ($28), or lamb ribs in their own juice, marinated in oils of wild grass, apple puree, and shallots ($22). High-season reservations strongly recommended.

ZÓCALO AND PENÍNSULA DE LAS PLAYAS
Restaurants

Even though Acapulco has seemingly zillions of restaurants, only a fraction may suit your expectations. Local restaurants come and go like the Acapulco breeze, though a handful of solid longtime eateries continue, depending on a steady flow of repeat customers.

For plain good eating and old-Mexico sidewalk atmosphere morning and night, try outdoor ◖ **Café los Amigos** (Calle la Paz, a few steps off the *zócalo*, tel. 744/483-8732, 7 A.M.–7 P.M. daily). Shady umbrellas beneath a spreading *higuera* (wild fig) tree and many familiar favorites, from tuna salad ($3) and chili ($3) to waffles ($3), T-bone steak ($8), and breaded shrimp ($6), attract a friendly club of Acapulco Canadian and American longtimers.

La Gran Torta (La Paz 6, tel. 744/483-8476, 8 A.M.–11 P.M. daily), one block west from the *zócalo*, is an old-town headquarters for hearty local-style food at local-style prices. Specialties here are *tortas* (hearty sandwiches, $2–3), often of *pierna* (roast pork), chorizo (spicy sausage), or *pollo* (chicken) with tomato and avocado stuffed in a *bolillo* bun. Additional favorites include hearty *pozole* ($3–4) Thursday and Friday.

Good, reasonably priced seafood restaurants are unexpectedly hard to come by in Acapulco. An important exception is the lineup of local-style seafood eateries along Avenida Azueta three blocks west from the *zócalo*. Situated right where the boats come in, they get the freshest morsels first. Local longtimers swear by the excellence of seafood served at ◖ **El Amigo Miguel** (corner of Juárez and Azueta, 10 A.M.–9:30 P.M. daily), where continuous patronage assures daily fresh shrimp, prawns, half a dozen kinds of fish ($5–10), and lobster (big, $14, smaller, $10). Doing nearly as good a job is very worthy **Mariscos Nachos** (across the street, about the same hours).

If you prefer something a bit fancier, head a block farther from the *zócalo* to tourist favorite **Mariscos Pipos** (3 Almirante Breton, tel. 744/482-2237, around noon–9 P.M. daily). The freshest of everything ($6–15) is cooked and served to please.

A few steps away, seekers of home-style Mexican cooking need go no farther than ◖ **Tamales Licha** (Costera M. Alemán 322, corner of Almirante Breton, tel. 744/482-2021, 5–11 P.M. daily). Here, appetizing south-of-the-border specialties—succulent tamales, savory *pozole*, crunchy tostadas, and tangy enchiladas ($2–5)—reign supreme. Portions are generous, ambience is relaxed, and hygiene standards are impeccable.

Although the very clean, strictly local-style **Restaurant la Chilapeña** (Cinco de Mayo 36, tel. 744/482-0498, 10 A.M.–11 P.M. daily) requires a walk of a few blocks east from the *zócalo,* it's worth it. Friendly owner Consuela Araiz de Rosario welcomes everyone to sample her Guerrero-style *antojitos* cooked the way she learned from her mother years ago in up-country Chilapa. It's best to organize a party so you can sample everything. Besides the tostadas, tacos, enchiladas, and *chalupas* ($2–4), be sure to order the house specialty, *pozole* ($3–4)—which Señora Consuela claims was invented in Chilapa; see the *Origin of Pozole* wall painting—complete with its bountiful vegetable plate. Additionally, Señora Consuela is very proud of her *pata* (leg of pork vinaigrette) with carrots *zanahoria* ($2). Get to La Chilapeña (see the map *Acapulco: Around the Zócalo*) from the *zócalo* by walking east two blocks to the Avenida Escudero corner (at Sanborn's). Turn left and walk along the east side of the street (passing Woolworth's) three blocks north to Cinco de Mayo. Turn right and walk a block and a half to Restaurant la Chilapeña on the right.

Many visitors' Acapulco vacations wouldn't be complete without a dinner at the luxuriously scenic clifftop *palapa* restaurant at the **Hotel los Flamingos** (Av. López Mateos s/n, tel. 744/482-0690, 8 A.M.–10:30 P.M. daily, credit cards accepted), about a mile uphill, west from Playa Caleta. Here all the ingredients for a memorable evening—attentive service, tasty seafood ($7–12), chicken ($6), and meat ($6–12) entrées, airy sunset view, and soft strumming of guitars—come together. (A bonus here is the family of raccoons that shows up for meals as regularly as the paying customers.)

Longtime favorite **Coyuca 22** (Calle Coyuca 22, tel. 744/482-3468 or 744/483-5030, 7 P.M.–midnight daily Nov. 1–April 30, credit cards accepted) is both the name and the address of the restaurant so exclusive and popular it manages to close half the year. The setting is a spacious hillside garden, where tables spread down an open-air bay- and city-view terrace. Arrive early (around 5:30 P.M. winter, 7 P.M. summer) to enjoy the sunset sky lighting up and painting the city ever-deepening colors, ending in a deep rose as finally the myriad lights shimmer and stars twinkle overhead. After that, the food (prime rib, $30; lobster tails, $40) and wines seem like dessert. Find it on Calle Coyuca, a side street off Blv. López Mateos on the Peninsula las Playas. Reservations are required. Dress is elegant resortwear.

The east-end bayview Las Brisas district has acquired a sprinkling of stylish restaurants. One of *the* places to be seen is **Kookaburra's** (tel. 744/446-6020 or 744/446-6039, noon –midnight daily), where, among the beautiful people, you can gaze out on yet another view of Acapulco. In the cool of the evening, from afar, the heat, fumes, and congestion of the Costera give way to a curtain of twinkling lights like a galaxy, sliced by the curving ebony line of the bay. The food (for example, start with crab cakes, $7, continue with roast duck with mandarin sauce, $20, and finish with almond cake, $5) only embellishes the effect. Reservations are required.

Acapulco's top "must do" restaurant among the rich and famous is **Baikal** (Carretera Escenica 22, tel. 744/446-6867, 6 P.M.– midnight daily), right in the middle of the Las Brisas bayview strip, across from landmark Palladium disco. Join the well-heeled mostly Mexico City crowd and soak in the relaxed elegance—massive white columns, draped windows, looking out on the gleaming galaxy of the Acapulco night—all to the soothing strains of live jazz. Start off with a fine overview of the entire scene, accompanied by appetizers, at the upper bar, and then take a main-floor table for your entrée and dessert. After such an introduction, the food may seem like an afterthought. For example, for appetizer, try fresh mussels, $18; for salad, arugula with pear, $13; and entrée, salmon in honey and balsamic vinaigrette, $27. Reservations strongly recommended any time.

Entertainment

The old *zócalo* is the best place for strolling and people-watching. Bookstalls, vendors, band concerts, and, on weekend nights especially, pitch-penny games, mimes, and clowns are constant sources of entertainment. When you're tired of walking, take a seat at a sidewalk café, such as La Flor de Acapulco or Café los Amigos, and let the scene pass *you* by for a change.

West-side hills block Acapulco Bay's sunset horizon. Sunset connoisseurs remedy the problem by gathering at ocean-view points on the west-side Península de las Playas, such as the **Sinfonía del Sol** sunset amphitheater (see *Playa Angosta*), La Quebrada, Playa Angosta, and the cliffside restaurant and gazebo/bar of the **Hotel Flamingos** (see *Accommodations*) before sunset.

Far east-side beach locations around the Hotel Hyatt Regency and the east-end Las Brisas Scenic Highway (Carretera Escénica) restaurants such as **Kookaburra's** also provide unobstructed sunset-viewing horizons.

NIGHTLIFE
Music and Dancing

Acapulco's hottest new dance nightclub is the **Salon Q,** Acapulco's "Cathedral of Salsa" (Costera Miguel Alemán 3117, on the east end, tel. 744/484-3252 or 744/481-0114). The fun begins quietly at around 10 P.M., the live music starts, and by midnight a platoon of folks are rocking to *salsa*. The climax comes with the live show at 12:45 A.M. Admission (about $30) includes open bar.

Several of the Costera hotels have live music for dancing at their lobby bars. As you move east along the Costera, the better possibilities are: the **Hotel Crowne Plaza** (formerly Costa Club, tel. 744/440-5555), the **Copacabana** (tel. 744/484-3260), and the **Hyatt Regency** (tel. 744/469-1234). Call to verify times.

On the *zócalo,* a live trio at the **Flor de Acapulco** plays at medium volume (from live oldies-but-goodies to salsa and latin rock; call cell tel. 044-744/421-7649 to confirm) Thurs.–Sat. 8 P.M.–midnight.

On the other hand, lovers of quieter music enjoy the piano bar evenings, from 6:30 P.M., at the refined but moderately priced **Restaurant Pacífico** (entrees $6–10) of the Hotel Tortuga. Find it on the mid-Costera, inland side, between the Diana Circle and the Hotel Fiesta Americana (tel. 744/484-8889).

Discos and Hangouts

Discotheques usually monitor their entrances carefully and are consequently safe and pleasant places for a night's entertainment (provided you are either immune to the noise or bring earplugs). They open their doors around 10 P.M. and play relatively low-volume music and videos for starters until around 11 P.M., when fogs descend, lights flash, and the thumping

© BRUCE WHIPPERMAN

The Sinfonía del Sol amphitheater is one of the best places to enjoy a brilliant Acapulco sunset.

begins, continuing sometimes till dawn. Admission runs about $10 upwards to $30 or more for the tonier joints.

Acapulco's discos and music hangouts concentrate in two major east-side spots. As you move east, between the Diana Circle and the Hotel Fiesta Americana, a solid lineup of hangouts and discos occupies the Costera's beach side. During peak seasons, the dancing crowds spill onto the street. Stroll along and pick out the style and volume that you like.

Of the bunch, **O'Beach** disco is the loudest, brashest, and among the most popular. For the entrance fee of $5, the music and the lights go till dawn. Other neighboring discos, such as Bombay, Baby Lobster, Barba Roja, Crazy Lobster, Paraíso, Happy Lobster, and Mangos, while sometimes loud, are nevertheless subdued in comparison.

Rising above everything is the **Bungie Jump** (tel. 744/484-7529), where dozens of spectators get goosebumps watching one soul do his or her death-defying leap (for only $55, seniors half price) daily, until about midnight.

Another mile east, Planet Hollywood and Hard Rock Cafe, both of which actually serve food, signal the beginning of a second lineup on both sides of the street of about a dozen live-music or disco clubs. The energy they put out trying to outdo each other with brighter lights, louder music, and larger and flashier facades is exceeded only by the frequency at which they seem to go in and out of business. More or less permanently fixed are **Planet Hollywood** (10 P.M.–2 A.M., no cover, tel. 744/484-0717), with recorded music and videos; **Hard Rock Cafe** (10:30 P.M.–2 A.M., no cover, tel. 744/484-0047), with live music; **Baby O** (10:30 P.M.–4 A.M., cover $9 women, $20 men, tel. 744/484-7474) disco and concert hall; and **Nina's** (10 P.M.–4 A.M., cover about $20 for women, much higher for men) concert and *salsa* night club, across from the Acapulco Convention center.

Reigning above all of these lesser centers of discomania is **Palladium,** visible everywhere around the bay as the pink neon glow on the east-side Las Brisas hill. Go there, if only to

A clown takes a well-deserved rest in the *zócalo*.

© BRUCE WHIPPERMAN

look, though call for a reservation beforehand (tel. 744/446-5490), or you might not be let in. Inside, the impression is of ultramodern fantasy—a giant spaceship window facing outward on a galactic star carpet—while the music explodes, propelling you, the dancing traveler, through inner space. A mere $35 cover (women $20) gets you through the door; inside, cocktails are around $10, while French champagne runs upward of $300 a bottle. Open Tues., Thurs., Fri., and Sat. low season, Mon.–Sat. high.

Sports and Recreation

WALKING AND JOGGING

The most interesting beach walking in Acapulco is along the two-mile stretch of beach between the Hotel Fiesta Americana and the rocky point at Parque Papagayo. Avoid the midday heat by starting early for breakfast along the Costera (a good choice is Sanborn's Restaurant, tel. 744/481-2426, at the Hotel Calinda) and walking west along the beach with the sun to your back. Besides the beach itself, you'll pass rocky outcroppings to climb on, tidepools to poke through, plenty of fruit vendors, and *palapas* to rest in from the sun. Bring a hat, shirt, and sunscreen and allow two or three hours. If you get tired, ride a taxi or bus back. You can do the reverse walk just as easily in the afternoon after about 3 P.M. from Playa Hamacas just past the steamship dock after lunch on the *zócalo* (try the Café los Amigos).

Soft sand and steep slopes spoil most jogging prospects on Acapulco Bay beaches. However, the green open spaces surrounding the Centro Cultural de Convenciones (Acapulco Convention Center), just east of the golf course, provide a good in-town substitute.

TENNIS AND GOLF

Acapulco's tennis courts are all private and mostly at the hotels. Try the Crowne Plaza (tel. 744/485-9050, $6/hr. days, $9 nights); Acapulco Park (tel. 744/485-5437, $7/hr. days, $9 nights, on the Costera near the Crowne Plaza), and Hyatt Regency ($8/hr. days, $13 nights, tel. 744/484-1225). Lessons by in-house teaching pros customarily run $20–30 an hour.

The Acapulco **Campo de Golf** course (tel.

744/484-0781 or 744/484-0782), right on the mid-Costera, is open to the public on a first-come, first-served basis, 7 A.M.–5 P.M. daily. Exceptions are Wed. and Sat. after 1 P.M., when the course is limited to foursomes. Greens fee is about $45 for nine holes and $75 for 18 holes. Caddy costs $14, club rental $10.

Much more exclusive are the fairways at the **Club de Golf** of hotels Fairmont Acapulco Princess and Pierre Marques (tel. 744/469-1000), about five miles past the southeast edge of town. Here, the 18-hole greens fee runs $140, cart included; $85 after 3 P.M.

The **Vidafel Mayan Palace** (tel. 744/469-6000), farther east, past the Fairmont Acapulco Princess, also has a luxury beachfront golf course.

WATER ACTIVITIES
Swimming, Surfing, and Boogie Boarding

Acapulco Bay's clear green, and oft-tranquil waters usually allow safe swimming from hotel-front beaches. The water is often too calm and waves break too close to shore for surf sports, however. Strong waves off open-ocean Playa Revolcadero southeast of the city often give good rides. Be aware, the waves can be dangerous. The Fairmont Acapulco Princess on the beach provides lifeguards. Check with them before venturing in. Bring your own equipment; rentals may not be available.

Snorkeling and Scuba Diving

The best local snorkeling is off **Isla Roqueta**. Closest access point is by boat from the docks at Playa Caleta and Playa Tlacopanocha. Such trips usually run about $20 per person for two hours, equipment included. Snorkel trips can also be arranged through beachfront aquatics shops at hotels such as the Ritz, Crowne Plaza, Hotel Fiesta Americana, the Hyatt Regency, and the scuba shops below.

Although local water clarity is often not ideal, especially during the summer-fall rainy season, Acapulco does have a few professional dive shops. Contact instructor José Vasquez's **Acapulco Scuba Center** (PADI and NAUI, tel. 744/482-9474, reserve@acapulcoscuba.com, www.acapulco scuba.com) near the Bonanza tour boat dock, about half a mile west, past the old-town *zócalo*.

Another good option is the up-and-coming **Swiss Divers Association,** headquartered at the Hotel Caleta above Playa Caleta (tel./fax 744/482-1357, email info@swissdivers .com, or visit www.swissdivers.com). Their services range from beach dives ($40) to NAUI and PADI open-water certification courses (four days, $400).

Sailing and Sailboarding

Close-in Acapulco Bay waters (except off west-end Playa Icacos) are generally too congested with motorboats for tranquil sailing or sailboarding. Nevertheless, some beach concessionaires at the big hotels, such as the Hotel Crowne Plaza and Hyatt Regency, do rent (or take people sailing in) simple sailboats from $15 per hour.

Outside of town, tranquil **Laguna Coyuca,** on the coast about 20 minutes' drive northwest of the *zócalo,* offers good sailboarding and sailing prospects.

Personal Watercraft Riding, Water-Skiing, and Parasailing

Power sports are very popular on Costera hotel beaches. Concessionaires—recognized by their lineup of beached minimotorboats—operate from most big hotel beaches, notably around the Ritz, the Crowne Plaza, Fiesta Americana, and the Hyatt Regency. Prices run about $60 per hour for personal watercraft, $50 per hour

for water-skiing, and $20 for a 10-minute parasailing ride.

Sportfishing

Fishing boats line the *malecón* dockside across the boulevard from the *zócalo*. Activity centers on the dockside office of the 20-boat blue and white fleet of fishing boat cooperative **Sociedad Cooperativa Servicios Turístico,** whose dozens of licensed captains regularly take visitors for big-game fishing trips. Although some travel agents may book you individually during high season, the Sociedad Cooperativa Turísticas office (tel. 744/482-1099, 8 A.M.–11 P.M. daily), rents only entire, captained boats, including equipment and bait.

Rental prices and catches depend on the season. Drop by the dock after 2 P.M. to see what the boats are bringing in. In season, boats might average one big marlin or sailfish apiece. Best month for sailfish *(pez vela)* is October; for marlin, Jan. and Feb.; for dorado, March.

Big 40-foot boats with five or six fishing lines (and accommodating eight persons) rent for $350 per day. Smaller boats, with three or four lines and holding five or six passengers, rent from around $200. All of the Cooperativa boats are radio-equipped, with toilet, life preservers, tackle, bait, and ice. Customers usually supply their own food and drinks. Although the Cooperativa is generally competent, look over the boat and check its equipment before putting your money down.

Alternatively, some Internet-savvy experienced sportfishing outfitters can be contacted half a mile west along the Costera, at the dock just past the Bonanza cruise ship landing. A very solid option is **Fish-R-Us** (tel. 744/482-8282 or 744/487-8787, or long-distance toll-free in Mexico, tel. 01-800/347-4787, U.S. toll-free tel. 877/3-FISHRUS, reservations@fish-r-us.com, www.fish-r-us .com).

Another reliable sportfishing choice is **Divers of Mexico.** Personable expatriate American owner Cristina organizes fishing

© BRUCE WHIPPERMAN

boats of the local boat cooperative Sociedad Cooperativa Servicios Turístico

trips, tours, and snorkel and scuba trips, and offers tourist information at her dockside office (tel. 744/482-1398, cristina@funfishingfactory .com, www.funfishingfactory.com).

Sailfish and marlin are neither the only nor necessarily the most desirable fish in the sea. Competently captained *pangas* can typically haul in three or four large 15- or 20-pound excellent-eating *robalo* (snook), *huachinango* (snapper), or *atún* (tuna) in two hours just outside Acapulco Bay.

Such lighter boats are rentable from the Sociedad Cooperativa Turísticas cooperative for about $20 per hour or from individual fishermen on Playa las Hamacas (east, past the steamship dock at the foot of Fuerte de San Diego).

Marina and Boat Docking

A safe place to dock your boat is the **Club de Yates** (Av. Costera M. Alemán 215, Fracc. las Playas, Acapulco, Guerrero 39300, tel. 744/482-3859, fax 744/482-3846, cyates@acabtu.com.mx or gg@clubdeyatesaca .com.mx, www.clubdeyatesaca.com.mx) on the

Península de las Playas's sheltered inner shoreline. The slip rate is around $1.25 per foot per day (for up to 39 feet), use of the ramp for launching runs about $75. The many services include 110/220-volt power, pump-out, toilets, showers, restaurant, repair facilities, access to the swimming pool and more.

Get to the Club de Yates from the Gran Via Tropical on the inner, bay side of the Península de las Playas. Start out by following the Costera past the *zócalo*. About 2.5 miles southwest of the *zócalo*, where the boulevard splits at the gas station, fork left along Gran Via Tropical. Continue straight ahead about 300 yards, to the Club de Yates entrance gate on the left.

Bay Cruises

One popular way to enjoy the sunset and a party at the same time is by cruise aboard the steel excursion ship *Bonanza*. It leaves from its bayside dock on the Costera half a mile (toward the Península de las Playas) from the *zócalo*. Although schedules vary seasonally, cruise offerings usually include midday (11 A.M.–2 P.M.), sunset (4:30–7 P.M.), and moonlight (10:30 P.M.–1 A.M.) cruises. Tickets are available from hotels, travel agents, or at the dock (tel. 744/483-1803). Tickets run about $19 per person, kids 1.4 meters (about 4 feet 9 inches) tall and under go free.

Alternatively you can go by the smaller Catamaran **Aca Rey** (sunset and evening cruises (all daily) at 5:30 and 8 P.M. (May through Sept.), and 4:30 and 7 P.M. (Oct. through April), and *lunada* moonlight cruises 10:30 P.M. and 1 A.M. Get tickets ($20) at the boat dock across the Costera from the *zócalo*.

BULLFIGHTS AND OTHER SPECTATOR SPORTS

Bullfights are staged every Sunday at 5:30 P.M. seasonally, usually Jan.–March, at the arena (here called a *frontón*) near Playa Caletilla. Avoid congestion and parking hassles by taking a taxi. Get tickets at the arena (about $28) through a travel agent or the ticket office (tel. 744/483-9561).

About $10 gains you entrance to Acapulco's big **jai-alai *frontón*,** an indoor stadium—look for the Bingo sign—on the Costera, east end, across from the Hyatt Regency (Tues.–Sun. 9 P.M.–1 A.M., tel. 744/484-378). Here, it's hard not to ooh and aah at the skill of players competing in the ancient Basque game of jai-alai (Fridays and Saturdays, beginning at 9 P.M.). With a long, narrow, curved basket tied to one

arm, players fling a hard rubber ball, at lethal speeds, to the far end of the court, where it rebounds like a pistol shot and must be returned by an opposing player. You can place wagers on your favorite player or, in the adjacent room, join the home-town crowd of local folks playing bingo, or downstairs, bet on horse races and other sports events taking place far away.

KID-FRIENDLY ATTRACTIONS

CICI (short for Centro Internacional de Convivencia Infantil) is the biggest of Acapulco's water parks. An aquatic paradise for families, CICI has acres of liquid games, where you can swish along a slippery toboggan run, plummet down a towering kamikaze slide, or loll in a gentle wave pool. Other pools contain performing whales, dolphins, and sea lions. Sea mammal performances ($1.50 for adults) occur at 2, 4, and, in season, 5:30 P.M. Patrons also enjoy a restaurant, a beach club, and much more. CICI is on the east end of the Costera between the golf course and the Hyatt Regency (tel. 744/484-8210, 10 A.M.–6 P.M. daily, adults and kids over 3 admission $9).

Mágico Mundo (tel. 744/483-1215, 9 A.M.–6 P.M. daily, admission $3 adult, $2 child), Acapulco's other (but run-down) water park, is on the opposite side of town at Playa Caleta. In addition to its very scenic rocky shoal location, it offers an aquarium, restaurant, water slides, and cascades.

Shopping

MARKETS AND DEPARTMENT STORES

Acapulco, despite its modern glitz, has a very colorful traditional market, which is fun for strolling through even without buying anything. It is open daily, dawn to dusk. Vendors arrive here with grand intentions: mounds of neon-red tomatoes, buckets of nopales (cactus leaves), towers of toilet paper, and mountains of soap bars. As you wander through the sunlight-dappled aisles, past big gaping

fish, bulging rounds of cheese, and festoons of huaraches, don't miss **Piñatas Uva,** one of the market's friendliest shops. You may even end up buying one of Uva's charming paper Donald Ducks, Snow Whites, or Porky Pigs. The market is at the corner of Mendoza and Constituyentes, a quarter mile inland from Hornos Beach. Ride a Mercado-marked bus or take a taxi.

In the *zócalo* area, **Woolworth's,** tel. 744/480-0072, is a good source of a little bit of everything at reasonable prices, on Escudero, corner of Morelos, behind Sanborn's; 9:30 A.M.–8:30 P.M. daily. Its lunch counter provides a welcome refuge from the midday heat.

Comercial Mexicana, with two Acapulco branches, is a big Mexican Kmart, which, besides the expected film, medicines, cosmetics, and housewares, also includes groceries and a bakery. Its locations are on the Costera, by Playa las Hamacas, just east and dowhill from the Fuerte de San Diego, tel. 744/483-5449, 9 A.M.–11 P.M. daily; and on the Costera, across from CICI water park, tel. 744/484-3373, open 24 hours.

If you can't find what you want at Comercial Mexicana, try the huge **Sam's Club,** tel. 744/469-0202, just uphill from the Diana Circle Comercial Mexicana, and the giant **Wal-Mart,** at the far east end, across from the Hyatt Regency, tel. 744/485-3462.

HANDICRAFTS

Despite much competition, asking prices for Acapulco handicrafts are relatively high. Bargaining, furthermore, doesn't always bring them down to size. **Sanborn's,** tel. 744/482-4095, two blocks from the zócalo, at Costera M. Alemán and Escudero, is 8 A.M.–11 P.M. daily, with restaurant, bookstore, and handicrafts. The all-Mexico selection includes, notably, black Oaxaca *barra* pottery, painted gourds from Uruapan, Guadalajara leather, Taxco silver jewelry, colorful plates from Puebla, and Tlaquepaque pottery and glass.

With Sanborn's prices in mind, head one block toward the zócalo to **Bonita** handicrafts store, where, in the basement of the big old Edificio Oviedo, glitters an eclectic fiesta of Mexican jewelry. Find it at I. de la Llave and Costera M. Alemán, local 1, tel. 744/482-0590 or 744/482-5240; 9 A.M.–7 P.M. daily. Never mind if you find the place empty; cruise-line passengers regularly fill the aisles. Here you'll be able to see artisans adding to the acre of gleaming silver, gold, copper, brass, fine carving, and

lacquerware around you. Don't forget to get your **free margarita** (or soft drink) before you leave.

While you're still near the zócalo, for a treat, back at Sanborn's, walk directly across the Costera to class-act **Linda de Taxco** (adjacent to the cruise ship terminal, tel. 744/483-3347), a silver shop that amounts to a sight all by itself. Their amazingly huge solid-silver pieces, ranging from elephants and hippos, through giant crucifixes and noble, new-age gods and goddesses, are worth a visit even without buying.

Still another bountiful handicrafts source near the zócalo is the artisans' market **Mercado de Parrazal.** From Sanborn's, head away from the Costera a few short blocks to Vasquez de León and turn right one block. There, a big plaza of semipermanent stalls offers a galaxy of Mexican handicrafts: Tonalá and Tlaquepaque papier-mâché, brass, and pottery animals; Bustamante-replica eggs, masks, and humanoids; Oaxaca wooden animals and black pottery; Guerrero masks; and Taxco jewelry. Sharp bargaining is necessary, however, to cut the excessive asking prices down to size.

The best store in the Parrazal market is **Yazmin**, in the middle of the complex, 9 A.M.–6 P.M. daily. They have an unusual collection, with many one-of-a-kind jewelry, ceramics, woodwork examples. Bargaining is necessary, however, to lower the high asking prices.

On the new-town east side a number of handicrafts shopping centers line the Costera. Check out the pair of handicrafts arcades, **Dalia** and **Pueblito,** across the Costera from the Plaza Bahía shopping mall and the Hotel Crowne Plaza. Stalls along shady interior walkways display a host of moderately priced leather, silver, hand-embroidered dresses, *huipiles,* bedspreads, napkins, and ceramics, glass, stoneware, and much more.

For a grand selection of largely inexpensive, but still attractive, native-made handicrafts, go to the large indigenous *mercado de artesanías* warren of stalls, on the mid-Costera, just east of the Diana Circle, inland side.

Not far from the Costera's eastern end, the state of Guerrero operates **Casa Artesanal Guerrerense** handicrafts store, in the shady mango grove-now-park a couple of blocks east of the CICI water park. Step inside and peruse the modest all-Guerrero handicrafts selection, which usually includes Taxco bright silver, fierce jaguar masks from Chilapa, shiny lacquerware from Olinalá, and fetching *huipiles* from Xochistlahuaca, 10 A.M.–8 P.M. daily.

PHOTOGRAPHY

Acapulco visitors enjoy the services of a number of photo stores. One of the best is the very professional **Foto y Mechanica** (tel.

744/483-1603, 10 A.M.–2 P.M. and 4–7 P.M. Mon.–Fri., 10 A.M.–2 P.M. Sat.), corner of Iglesia and Hidalgo, one block west of the *zócalo*. Goods and services include film and development, cameras both film and digital, a number of digital services, and expert camera repair.

For more basic photo needs, right on the *zócalo*, go to **Foto System Lab** (on the corner of J. Carranza, right side as you enter the *zócalo* from the Costera, tel. 744/482-2112, 9 A.M.–10 P.M. daily), supplying photofinishing, a few cameras and accessories, and some popular film varieties.

At the east end of the Costera, among the several photo stores, try **Foto Imagen** (tel. 744/484-5770, daily 9 A.M.–9 P.M.), in the basement of Gigante supermarket, across the Costera, from the Acapulco Convention Center.

Information

An easily accessible local **tourist information office** is the *modulo* in front of the Convention Center, two blocks east of the golf course (tel. 744/484-4416 or 744/484-4583). Here, workers staff a small crafts shop, 8 A.M.–11 P.M. daily.

PUBLICATIONS

The best English-language magazine sources in town are **Sanborn's** three Acapulco branches. The first is on the beach side of the Costera, a few blocks from the east end (tel. 744/484-2035, 7:30–1 A.M. daily, ground floor of the eastside Oceanic 2000 shopping plaza). Alternatively, try Sanborn's mid-Costera branch (tel. 744/482-2426, at the Hotel Calinda); or its *zócalo* branch (tel. 744/482-4095, 7 A.M.–11 P.M. daily), on the Costera across from the steamship dock, which stocks a similar, but smaller assortment.

English-language newspapers, such as the *Miami Herald,* the *Los Angeles Times,* and

USA Today, are often available in the large hotel bookshops, especially the Fiesta Americana (tel. 744/435-1600) and the Hyatt Regency (tel. 744/469-1234). In old town, newsstands around the *zócalo* regularly sell the *Miami Herald.*

Pick up the commercial but handy and widely available American Express–sponsored tourist booklet *Acapulco Passport* free at a hotel, store, or travel agency.

Acapulco's former expatriate and tourist English-language newspaper *Acapulco Heat* has gone completely electronic, as www.acabtu.com.mx; on the home page, click on "Acapulco website." It provides many useful links to mostly midscale hotels, restaurants, community events and organizations, travel activities, and entertainment.

PUBLIC LIBRARY

The modest Acapulco *biblioteca* is near the *zócalo* adjacent to the cathedral (Madero 5, corner of Quebrada, tel. 744/482-0388,

9 A.M.–9 P.M. Mon.–Fri.). Its modest collection, used mostly by college and high school students in the airy reading room, is nearly all in Spanish.

LANGUAGE INSTRUCTION

Spanish-language instruction is available at the reputable private **Universidad Americana**

on the Costera, approximately across from the Hotel Crowne Plaza. For more information, contact the language department at the university (Costera Miguel Alemán 1756, Fracc. Magellanes, Acapulco 39670, tel. 744/486-5618, ext. 166, or 744/486-5619, ext. 166, uamerica@aca.uamericana.mx, www.uaa .edu.mx.)

Services

MONEY EXCHANGE

In the *zócalo* neighborhood, **HSBC** bank (no. 8 Jesús Carranza, the one-block side street, tucked near the *zócalo*'s northeast corner, tel. 744/483-5722, 8 A.M.–7 P.M. Mon.–Sat.) is the best bet. Alternatively, nearby, go to **Bancomer** (fronting the Costera, tel. 744/482-2097 or 744/480-1277, 9 A.M.–4 P.M. Mon.–Fri., 10 A.M.–2 P.M. Sat.) to change U.S. cash or traveler's checks only. Although the lines at **Banamex** (tel. 744/483-6425), nearby, two blocks from the *zócalo* next to Sanborn's, are usually longer, it exchanges major currencies 9 A.M.–4 P.M. Mon.–Fri. You can avoid the lines by using the bank **ATM machines,** which are routinely connected with international networks.

On the new side of town, also change money at **HSBC** bank (across from the west-end McDonald's, tel. 744/485-5309, 8 A.M.–7 P.M. Mon.–Sat.) or at **Bancomer** (a few blocks west of the Glorieta Diana, 9 A.M.–5 P.M. Mon.–Fri., 9 A.M.–2 P.M. Sat.).

After hours on the Costera, change money and traveler's checks at **Consultorio International,** in Galería Picuda shopping center, across the street and a block west from the Hotel Fiesta Americana (tel. 744/484-3108, 9 A.M.–6 P.M. Mon.–Fri., 9 A.M.–3 P.M. Sat.–Sun.).

American Express Office

The Acapulco American Express branch (tel. 744/435-2200), at the west end of the Hotel Continental Emporio, near the Diana Circle,

cashes American Express traveler's checks at near-bank rates and provides member financial services and travel agency services (9 A.M.–6 P.M. Mon.–Fri., 9 A.M.–1 P.M. Sat., although check-cashing hours may be shorter).

COMMUNICATIONS

The Acapulco main *correo* (post office) is in the Palacio Federal across the Costera from the steamer dock three blocks from the *zócalo*. It provides Mexpost fast, secure mail, and philatelic services (8 A.M.–8 P.M. Mon.–Sat.). A branch **post and telegraph office** is at the Estrella de Oro bus terminal, Cuauhtémoc and Massieu (9 A.M.–8 P.M. Mon.–Fri., 9 A.M.–noon Sat.).

Telecomunicaciones (tel. 744/482-2622 or 744/482-0103), also in the Palacio Federal, provides money order, telegram, telex, and fax services (8 A.M.–8 P.M. Mon.–Fri., 9 A.M.–noon Sat.–Sun.).

In mid-Costera, go to the small branch post office (tel. 744/484-8029), and neighboring Telecom (tel. 744/484-6976), at the Centro de Convenciones (Convention Center), both open 8:30 A.M.–4 P.M. Mon.–Fri.

For lowest **telephone** rates, use the widely available Ladatel cards in the many public street telephones. First dial 001 for long distance to the United States and Canada and 01 for Mexico. Otherwise, near the *zócalo*, you can call *larga distancia* 8 A.M.–9 P.M. daily from the small office on J. Carranza at Calle de la Llave, next to the HSBC bank.

Connect to the **Internet** at one of the many streetfront stores scattered along the Costera and around the *zócalo*. For example, try **Big Master Net II**, at Hidalgo 6, half a block west of the *zócalo*'s northwest corner (the left side, facing the churchfront, 9 A.M.–10 P.M. daily).

HEALTH AND EMERGENCIES

If you get sick, ask your hotel to call a doctor for you or contact the **Hospital Magellanes,** one of Acapulco's most respected private hospitals, for both office calls and round-the-clock emergencies. Facilities include a lab, 24-hour pharmacy, and an emergency room with many specialists on call (tel. 744/485-6544 or 744/485-6597, ext. 119, for the pharmacy), at W. Massieu 2, corner of Colón, one block inland from the Hotels Maris and Ritz.

A group of American-trained **IAMAT** (International Association for Medical Assistance to Travelers) **physicians** offers medical consultations in English. Contact them at the medical department, Hotel Fairmont Acapulco Princess, tel. 744/469-1000, ext. 1309.

For routine medications near the *zócalo*, go to one of many pharmacies, such as at **Sanborn's** (corner of Escudero and the Costera, tel. 744/482-6167), or the big **Farmacia Moderna** (tel. 744/482-0804, 8 A.M.–10 P.M. daily), at Escudero and Carranza, across the street from Woolworth's.

For police emergencies, contact one of the **tourist police** (on the Costera, in safari pith helmets, tel. 744/485/0283), or call the officers at the **municipal police Papagayo station** (tel. 744/485-0490) at the end of Avenida Camino Sonora, on the inland side of Papagayo Park.

In case of fire, call the *bomberos* (fire station, tel. 744/484-4123).

IMMIGRATION AND CUSTOMS

If you lose your tourist card go to **Migración,** at the airport (sufficiently early on your day of departure), or on the east-side Costera, across the traffic circle CICI water park, tel. 744/435-0102, 9 A.M.–1 P.M. Mon.–Fri. Bring proof of your identity and some proof (such as your stamped passport, airline ticket, or a copy of your lost tourist card) of your arrival date in Mexico. If you try to leave Mexico without your tourist card, you may face trouble and a fine. Also report to Migración if you arrive in Acapulco by yacht.

CONSULATES

Acapulco has several consular agents and officers. The offices of the **U.S. consular officer,** Alexander Richards (tel. 744/481-1699, 744/484-0300, or 744/481-0100, fax 744/484-0300, consular@prodigy.net.mx) are in the Hotel Continental Emporio (10 A.M.–2 P.M. Mon.–Fri.). He's a busy man and asks that you kindly have your problem written down, together with a specific request for information or action. In genuine emergencies only, contact him at tel. 744/431-0094.

The **Canadian consul,** Diane McLean de Huerta (tel. 744/484-1305, fax 744/484-1306 or 744/481-1349, acapulco@canada.org.mx), holds office hours 9 A.M.–12:30 P.M. Mon.–Fri., at the Centro Comercial Marbella, suite 23. After hours, in an emergency, call toll-free Mex. tel. 01-800/706-2900.

For the **British consul,** Lorraine Bajas, call tel. 744/484-1735. Contact the **German consul** at Antone de Alamino 26, tel. 744/484-1860, fax 744/484-3801. The **Netherlands consul,** Ángel Díaz, can be reached by dialing tel. 744/486-6179.

For additional information and assistance, the consulates maintain a joint **Consular Corps** office (tel. 744/481-2533, 9 A.M.–2 P.M. Mon.–Fri.), in the Centro de Convenciones (Convention Center) just east of the golf course.

LAUNDRY

Near the *zócalo,* get your laundry done at **Lavandería Laradin** (corner of Iglesias and La Paz, one block west of the *zócalo,* 8 A.M.–10 P.M. Mon.–Sat.).

Alternatively, near Playa Caleta, get your laundry done at **Lavandería Gabi** (12 A Av. Lopez Mateos, two blocks inland from the beach, 9 A.M.–7 P.M. Mon.–Sat.).

Getting There and Away

BY AIR

Several airlines connect the **Acapulco airport** (code-designated ACA, officially the Juan N. Álvarez International Airport) with U.S. and Mexican destinations.

Aeroméxico flights connect directly with Mexico City, Monterrey, Tijuana, and Guadalajara (reservations tel. 744/485-1625 or 744/485-1600, flight information, tel. 744/466-9296 or 744/466-9109).

Mexicana Airlines flights connect five times daily with Mexico City and once daily with Guadalajara via associated Aerolitoral airline (reservations tel. 744/486-7587, or toll-free Mex. tel. 01-800/502-2000, flight information tel. 744/466-9136 or 744/466-9138).

U.S. Airways (formerly America West) flights connect with Phoenix; for reservations and information, call toll-free U.S. tel. 001-800/235-9292; or call a local travel agent, such as American Express, tel. 744/435-2200.

Continental Airlines flights connect with Houston (reservations toll-free Mex. tel. 01-800/900-5000, flight information tel. 744/466-9063).

American Airlines flights connect with Dallas during the winter season (reservations toll-free Mex. tel. 01-800/904-6000, flight information tel. 744/466-9227).

Aviacsa Airlines flights connect with Guadalajara, Mexico City, Tijuana and Oaxaca (reservations tel. 744/481-3240 or 744/481-3242, flight information tel. 744/466-9209, 744/466-9223, or 744/466-9225).

Delta Air Lines Aéromexico affiliate charter flights connect with Los Angeles, Portland, and Dallas during the winter season. For reservations, call a travel agent or Delta at toll-free Mex. tel. 800/902-2100.

Air Arrival and Departure

After the usually quick immigration and customs checks, Acapulco arrivees enjoy airport car rentals, efficient transportation for the 15-mile trip to town, post box *(buzón)*, and ATMs.

Airport car rental booths often open for arriving flights include **Hertz** (tel./fax 744/485-8947 or 744/485-6889), **Avis** (tel. 744/466-9190 or 744/485-5720, antonio.gonzales@avis.com.mx), **Alamo** (tel. 744/466-9444 or 744/484-3305), **Budget** (tel. 744/481-2433, or 744/466-9103, acapulco@budget.com), and **SAAD jeep rentals** (tel. 744/484-3445 or 744/484-5325, fax 744/484-5132, saad@acapulcorentacar.com). You can ensure availability and often save money by bargaining for a reservation with agencies via their toll-free numbers before you leave home.

Tickets for **ground transport** to town are sold by agents near the terminal exit. Options include collective GMC Suburban station wagon (about $8), that deposits passengers at individual hotels. Compact *Taxis especiales* run about $11–22, on distance. GMC Suburbans can also be hired *"especial"* as private taxis for $35–45 for up to seven passengers.

On your departure day, save money by sharing a taxi with fellow departees. Don't get into the taxi until you settle the fare. Having already arrived, you know what the airport ride should cost. If the driver insists on greed, hail another taxi.

Simplify your departure by saving $17 or its peso equivalent for your international (or $12 national) departure tax, if your ticket doesn't already cover it. If you lost your tourist permit (which immigration stamped upon your arrival) either go to Migración, in town (see *Immigration and Customs,* under *Services)* before your departure date, or arrive early enough at the airport to iron out the problem with airport Migración officials before departure. Bring some proof of your date of arrival, either a stamped passport, airline ticket copy, or a copy of your lost tourist permit.

The Acapulco air terminal building has a number of shops upstairs for last-minute handicrafts purchases, a *buzón* (mailbox), stamp vending machine, public telephones and a restaurant.

BY BUS

Major competitors Estrella Blanca and Estrella de Oro operate three separate long-distance *centrales de autobús* (central bus terminals), one Estrella Blanca (the Ejido) station on the west side and two (both Estrella Blanca and Estrella de Oro) stations on the east side of town.

Estrella Blanca (tel. 744/469-2028 or 744/469-2030), coordinates the service of its subsidiary lines Elite, Flecha Roja, Autotransportes Cuauhtémoc, Turistar, Futura, and Gacela at two separate terminals. credit cards accepted. Most first- or luxury-class departures use the big west-side **Ejido** terminal at Av. Ejido 47. The airy station is so clean you could sleep on the polished onyx floor and not get dirty; bring an air mattress and blanket. Other conveniences include left-luggage lockers, food stores across the street, a deluxe and midscale hotel booking agency, and Sendatel 24-hour *larga distancia* and fax office daily 6 A.M.–10 P.M.

Also from the Ejido station, scores of Estrella Blanca *salidas locales* (local departures) connect with destinations in three directions: northern interior, Costa Grande (northwest), and Costa Chica (southeast) coastal destinations. Most connections are first-class Elite, Turistar, and Futura. Specific northern interior connections include Mexico City (dozens daily, some via Taxco), Toluca, Morelia via Chilpancingo and Altamirano (six daily), and Guadalajara (three daily).

Many first-class (about 10 per day) and second-class (hourly) departures connect northwest with Costa Grande destinations of Zihuatanejo and Lázaro Cárdenas. Southeast Costa Chica connections with Puerto Escondido, some continuing to Huatulco and Salina Cruz, include four first-class daily (one via Ometepec) and several second-class connections per day.

Also from the Avenida Ejido Estrella Blanca terminal, one or two daily departures connect with the U.S. border (Mexicali and Tijuana) via the entire Pacific Coast route, through Zi-

huatanejo, Manzanillo, Puerto Vallarta, and Mazatlán. Other departures connect with the U.S. border at Ciudad Juárez, via San Luis Potosí, Zacatecas, Torreón, and Chihuahua.

Many additional first- and luxury-class buses depart from Estrella Blanca's separate west-side big **Papagayo** terminal, on Avenida Cuauhtémoc, tel. 744/469-2081. Facilities and services include an a/c waiting room, left-luggage service, a snack bar, and hotel reservations. From the Papagayo terminal, luxury-class and first-class buses connect with northeast Mexico and the U.S. border, via Querétaro, San Luis Potosí, Monterrey, and Nuevo Laredo. Other departures connect northwest, with Guadalajara, León, Celaya, and Irapuato; and north with Puebla and Mexico City bus stations Norte and Sur; and northwest, with Zihuatanejo.

About five blocks east of the Estrella Blanca terminal, is the busy, modern **Estrella de Oro,** at Cuauhtémoc and Massieu, tel. 744/485-8758, 744/485-8705, or 744/485-9360. They provide connections only with the Mexico City corridor (Chilpancingo, Iguala, Taxco, Cuernavaca, Mexico City) and northwest Costa Grande destinations via Zihuatanejo and Lázaro Cárdenas. Services include left-luggage lockers, but no food except sweets, chips, and drinks. *Correo* (9 A.M.–8 P.M. Mon.–Fri., 9 A.M.–noon Sat.) and *telecomunicaciones* (telephone, fax, and money orders 8 A.M.–9 P.M. Mon.–Sat.) offices are on the outside upstairs walkway, west end.

Estrella de Oro departures include dozens of first- and luxury-class with Mexico City and intermediate points. Several connect directly through Taxco. Four departures connect daily with Costa the Grande, three with Zihuatanejo, one only with Lázaro Cárdenas. Estrella de Oro offers no Costa Chica (Puerto Escondido) connections southeast.

BY CAR OR RV

Good highways connect Acapulco north with Taxco and Mexico City, northwest with the Costa Grande and Michoacán, and southeast with the Costa Chica and Oaxaca.

MEXICO CITY DRIVING RESTRICTIONS

To reduce smog and traffic gridlock, authorities have limited which cars can drive on which days in Mexico City, depending upon the last digit of their license plates. If you violate these rules, you risk getting an expensive ticket. On Monday, no vehicle may be driven with final digits 5 or 6; Tuesday, 7 or 8; Wednesday, 3 or 4; Thursday, 1 or 2; Friday, 9 or 0. Weekends, all vehicles may be driven.

The Mexico City Highway 95 D *cuota* (toll) superhighway would make the connection via Chilpancingo easy (73 miles, 117 km, about and hour and half) if it weren't for the Acapulco congestion. Avoid congestion by going via the toll tunnel *(túnel cuota)*. The uncluttered extension (another 125 miles, 201 km) to Cuernavaca is a breeze in 2.5 hours. For Taxco, stay on the Mexico City-bound expressway north past Chilpancingo a total of about 100 miles to a "Taxco cuota" (toll) turnoff and follow the signs about

another 25 miles (40 km) uphill to Taxco. From Cuernavaca, the over-the-mountain leg to Mexico City (53 miles, 85 km) would be simple except for possible Mexico City gridlock, which might lengthen it to two hours. Better allow a minimum of around 5.5 driving hours for the entire 251-mile (404-km) Acapulco–Mexico City trip.

The Costa Grande section of Highway 200 northwest toward Zihuatanejo is generally uncluttered and smooth (except for occasional bumps and potholes). Allow about four hours for the 150-mile (242-km) trip.

The same is true for the Costa Chica stretch of Highway 200 southeast to Pinotepa Nacional (157 miles, 253 km) and Puerto Escondido (247 miles, 398 km total). Allow about four driving hours to Pinotepa, 6.5 hours total to Puerto Escondido.

Avoid congestion heading east by going via the coastal **Barra Vieja** bypass, across the new Río Papagayo bridge that connects directly to Highway 200, Costa Chica direction, about 20 miles (32 km) east of town. From downtown, drive east along the Costera as if you were heading to the airport. But, two miles before the airport, fork right at the big, monument-decorated Barra Vieja intersection. Continue another 15 miles (24 km) through Barra Vieja, across the Papagayo bridge to Highway 200 and the Costa Chica.

Taxco

As Acapulco thrives on what's new, Taxco (pop. 150,000) luxuriates in what's old. Nestling beneath forest-crowned mountains and decorated with monuments of its silver-rich past, Taxco now enjoys an equally rich flood of visitors who stop en route to or from Acapulco. They come to enjoy its fiestas and clear, pine-scented air and to stroll the cobbled hillside lanes and bargain for world-renowned silver jewelry.

And despite the acclaim, Taxco preserves its diminutive colonial charm *because* of its visitors, who come to enjoy what Taxco offers. They stay in venerable, family-owned lodgings,

walk to the colorful little *zócalo*, where they admire the famous baroque cathedral, and wander among the awning-festooned market lanes just downhill.

HISTORY

The traditional hieroglyph representing Taxco shows athletes in a court competing in a game of *tlatchtli* (still locally played) with a solid, natural rubber *(hule)* ball. "Tlachco," the Nahuatl name representing the place that had become a small Aztec garrison settlement by the eve of the conquest, literally translates as "Place of the Ball Game." The Spanish, more

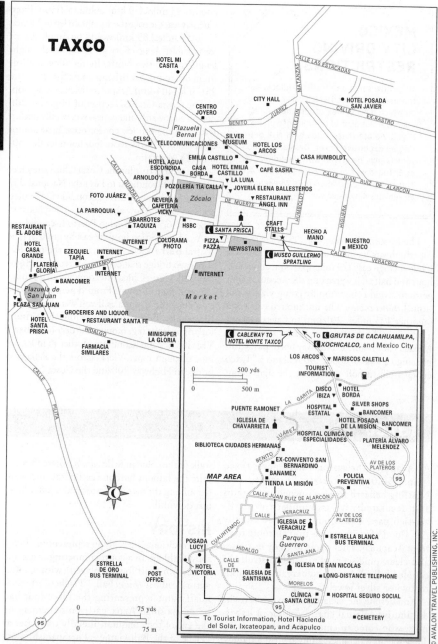

TAXCO

HOTEL MI CASITA

CITY HALL

HOTEL POSADA SAN JAVIER

CENTRO JOYERO

Plazuela Bernal

SILVER MUSEUM

HOTEL LOS ARCOS

CELSO

TELECOMUNICACIONES

CASA HUMBOLDT

EMILIA CASTILLO

HOTEL AGUA ESCONDIDA

CASA BORDA

HOTEL EMILIA CASTILLO

CAFÉ SASHA

ARNOLDO'S

POZOLERÍA TÍA CALLA

LA LUNA

JOYERÍA ELENA BALLESTEROS

FOTO JUÁREZ

NEVERÍA & CAFETERÍA VICKY

Zócalo

RESTAURANT ÁNGEL INN

LA PARROQUIA

ABARROTES TAQUIZA

HSBC

SANTA PRISCA

CRAFT STALLS

HECHO A MANO

RESTAURANT EL ADOBE

INTERNET

COLORAMA PHOTO

PIZZA PAZZA

NEWSSTAND

NUESTRO MEXICO

HOTEL CASA GRANDE

EZEQUIEL TAPÍA

INTERNET

MUSEO GUILLERMO SPRATLING

PLATERÍA GLORIA

INTERNET

INTERNET

BANCOMER

Plazuela de San Juan

PLAZA SAN JUAN

GROCERIES AND LIQUOR

RESTAURANT SANTA FE

Market

HOTEL SANTA PRISCA

MINISUPER LA GLORIA

FARMACIA SIMILARES

ESTRELLA DE ORO BUS TERMINAL

POST OFFICE

CALLE LAS ESTACADAS

CALLE EX-RASTRO

CALLE JUAN RUIZ DE ALARCON

CUAUHTEMOC

HIDALGO

CALLE DE PILITA

95

0   75 yds
0   75 m

(Inset map)

CABLEWAY TO HOTEL MONTE TAXCO

To *GRUTAS DE CACAHUAMILPA*, *XOCHICALCO*, and Mexico City

LOS ARCOS

MARISCOS CALETILLA

TOURIST INFORMATION

DISCO IBIZA

HOTEL BORDA

PUENTE RAMONET

SILVER SHOPS

HOSPITAL ESTATAL

BANCOMER

IGLESIA DE CHAVARRIETA

HOTEL POSADA DE LA MISIÓN

BANCOMER

HOSPITAL CLÍNICA DE ESPECIALIDADES

PLATERÍA ÁLVARO MELENDEZ

BIBLIOTECA CIUDADES HERMANAS

EX-CONVENTO SAN BERNARDINO

BANAMEX

AV DE LOS PLATEROS

MAP AREA

TIENDA LA MISIÓN

POLICIA PREVENTIVA

95

CALLE JUAN RUIZ DE ALARCÓN

CALLE

VERACRUZ

AV DE LOS PLATEROS

IGLESIA DE VERACRUZ

POSADA LUCY

Parque Guerrero

ESTRELLA BLANCA BUS TERMINAL

HIDALGO

SANTA ANA

HOTEL VICTORIA

CALLE DE PILITA

IGLESIA DE SANTISIMA

IGLESIA DE SAN NICOLAS

LONG-DISTANCE TELEPHONE

MORELOS

CLÍNICA SANTA CRUZ

HOSPITAL SEGURO SOCIAL

95

CEMETERY

To Tourist Information, Hotel Hacienda del Solar, Ixcateopan, and Acapulco

0   500 yds
0   500 m

© AVALON TRAVEL PUBLISHING, INC.

interested in local minerals than in linguistic details, shifted the name to Taxco.

Colonization

In 1524, Hernán Cortés, looking for tin to alloy with copper to make bronze cannon, heard that people around Taxco were using bits of metal for money. Prospectors hurried out, and within a few years they struck rich silver veins in Tetelcingo, now known as Taxco Viejo (Old Taxco), seven miles downhill from present-day Taxco. The Spanish crown appropriated the mines and worked them with generations of native forced labor.

Eighteenth-century enlightenment came to Taxco in the person of José Borda, who, arriving from Spain in 1716, modernized the mine franchise his brother had been operating. José improved conditions and began paying the miners, thereby increasing productivity and profits. In contrast to past operators, Borda returned the proceeds to Taxco, building the monuments that still grace the town. His fortune built streets, bridges, fountains, arches, and his masterpiece, the church of Santa Prisca, which included a special chapel for the miners, who before had not been allowed to enter the church.

Independence and Modern Times

The 1810–1821 War of Independence and the subsequent civil strife within a generation reduced the mines to but a memory. They were nearly forgotten when William Spratling, an American artist and architect, moved to Taxco in 1929 and began reviving Taxco's ancient but moribund silversmithing tradition. Working with local artisans, Spratling opened the first cooperative shop, Las Delicias.

Spurred by the trickle of tourists along the new Acapulco highway, more shops opened, increasing the demand for silver, which in turn led to the reopening of the mines. Soon silver demand outpaced the supply. Silver began streaming in from other parts of Mexico to the workbenches of thousands of artisans in hundreds of family- and cooperatively owned

shops dotting the still-quaint hillsides of a new, prosperous Taxco.

SIGHTS

Although the present city, elev. 5,850 feet (1,780 meters), spreads much farther, the center of town encompasses the city's original seven hills, wrinkles in the slope of a towering mountain.

For most visitors, the downhill town limit is the *carretera*, the local stretch of old National Highway 95, now named Avenida de los Plateros, after the Taxco *plateros* (silversmiths) who put Taxco on Mexico's tourism map. The highway contours along the hillside from **Los Arcos** (The Arches) on the north, Mexico City, end of town about two miles, passing the Calle Pilita intersection on the south, Acapulco, edge of town. Along the *carretera*, immediately accessible to a steady stream of tour buses, lie the town's plusher hotels and many silver shops.

The rest of the town is fortunately insulated from tour buses by its narrow winding streets. From the *carretera*, the most important of them climb and converge, like bent spokes of a wheel, to the *zócalo* (main plaza). Beginning with the most northerly, the main streets (and directions they run) are La Garita (uphill), Alarcón (downhill), Veracruz (downhill), Santa Ana (downhill), Salubridad (uphill), Morelos (downhill), and Pilita (downhill).

Although walking is Taxco's most common mode of transport, taxis go anywhere within the city limits for about $2 days, $3 nights. White *combi* collective vans (fare about $.30) follow designated routes, marked on the windshields. Simply tell your specific destination to the driver. For side trips to nearby towns and villages, a fleet of **Flecha Roja** second-class local buses and *colectivo* vans leave frequently from the Estrella Blanca on the *carretera* terminal near the corner of Veracruz.

◖ Santa Prisca

All roads in Taxco begin and end on the *zócalo* at Santa Prisca church. French architect

© BRUCE WHIPPERMAN

Taxco's winding lanes all seem to end uphill at the zócalo in front of the Santa Prisca church (at top).

D. Diego Durán designed and built the church between 1751 and 1758 with money from the fortune of silver king Don José Borda. The facade, decorated with saints on pedestals, arches, and spiraled columns, follows the baroque churrigueresque style (after Jose Churriguera, 1665–1725, the "Spanish Michelangelo"). Interior furnishings include an elegant pipe organ, brought from Germany by muleback (via boat to Veracruz, thence overland) in 1751, and a riot of gilded side altars. The riot of interior elaboration climaxes in the towering gold-leaf main altar, which seems to drip with ornamentation in tribute to Santa Prisca, the Virgin of the Immaculate Conception, the Virgin of the Rosary, and San Sebastian (on the right), who bravely and piously endures his wounds.

Dreamy Bible-story paintings by Miguel Cabrera decorate a chamber behind the main altar, while in a room to the right, portraits of Pope Benedict XIV, who sanctioned all this, José Borda, who paid for it, and his brother,

Manuel Borda, Santa Prisca's first priest, hang at the head of a solemn gallery of subsequent padres.

Outside, landmarks around the plaza include the **Casa Borda** (visible, as you face away from the church facade, on the right side of the zócalo, and open 9 A.M.–9 P.M. daily). This former Borda family town house, built concurrently with the church in typical baroque colonial style, now serves as the Taxco Casa de Cultura, featuring exhibitions by local artists and artisans, in the upstairs gallery, 10 A.M.– 5 P.M. daily except Monday.

Downhill

Heading out and down the church steps, you can continue downhill in either of two interesting ways. If you walk left immediately downhill from the church, you reach the lane Calle los Arcos, running alongside and below the church. From there, reach the **market** by heading right before the quaint archway over the street, down the winding staircase-lane, where you'll soon be in a warren of awning-covered stalls.

If, however, you head right from the church steps, another immediate right leads you beside the church along legendary **Calle de Muerte** (Street of Death), so named because of the former cemetery where the workers who died constructing the church were buried. (Note the skeleton on the church-front corner facing Calle de Muerte.)

◖ Museo Guillermo Spratling

Continuing downhill, you'll find Museo Guillermo Spratling (fronting the little plaza behind the church, tel. 762/622-1660, usually 9 A.M.–5 P.M. daily except Monday, although hours may vary seasonally). William Spratling in the late 1920s was instrumental in helping the community revive its silversmithing tradition. On the main and upper floors of this history and archaeology museum named in his honor, the National Institute of Archaeology displays intriguing carvings and ceramics (including unusual phallic examples), such as a ball-game ring, animal masks, and a priestly statuette with knife in one hand, human heart in the other. The basement floor houses temporary historical, cultural, and archaeological displays.

Casa Humboldt

Nearby stands the Casa Humboldt (one block down Alarcón, the downhill extension of Calle de Muerte, tel. 762/622-5501, 10 A.M.–6 P.M. Tues.–Sat. 10 A.M.–2 P.M., Sun., although winter hours may be shorter). The museum is named after the celebrated geographer (who is said to have stayed only one night, however). Now the state maintains it as the Museum of Viceregal (read colonial) Art. Displays feature a permanent collection of historical artifacts, including the Manila galleon, colonial technology, and colonial religious sculpture and painting.

Museo Platería

Nearby, the Museo Platería (4 Alarcón, third floor, a few doors uphill, from the Hotel Emilio Castillo, tel. 762/622-0658, 10 A.M.–6 P.M. daily) illustrates a history of Taxco silver craft and displays a number of prizewinning pieces by renowned Taxco artists-in-silver. (Alternatively, you may enter the museum through the *zócalo*-front shopping Patio de las Artesanías, next to the Casa Borda.)

Other In-Town Sights

A short ride, coupled with a walk circling back to the *zócalo,* provides the basis for an interesting half-day exploration. Taxi or ride a *combi* to the Hotel Posada de la Misión, where the **Cuauhtémoc Mural** glitters on a wall near the pool. Executed by renowned muralist Juan O'Gorman with a riot of pre-Columbian symbols—yellow sun, pearly rabbit-in-the-moon, snarling jaguar, writhing serpents, fluttering eagle—the mural glorifies Cuauhtémoc, the last Aztec emperor. Cuauhtémoc, unlike his uncle Moctezuma, tenaciously resisted the conquest, but was captured and later executed by Cortés in

An old mine elevator derrick and chimney near Hotel Borda is a reminder of the honeycomb of tunnels that underlie present-day Taxco.

© BRUCE WHIPPERMAN

1525. His remains were discovered in 1949 in Ixcateopan, about 24 miles away by local bus or car.

Continue your walk a few hundred yards along the *carretera* (north, Mexico City direction) from the Hotel Posada de la Misión. There, a driveway leading right just before the gas station heads to the Hotel Borda grounds. Turn left on the road just after the gate and you'll come to an **antique brick chimney and cable-hung derrick.** These mark an inactive **mineshaft** descending to the mine-tunnel honeycomb thousands of feet beneath the town. The mines are still being worked from another entrance, but for mostly lead rather than silver. You can see the present-day works from the hilltop of the now-closed Hotel Hacienda del Solar on the south edge of town.

Now, return to the *carretera,* cross over and stroll the main town entry street, **Calle la Garita** about a mile back to the *zócalo.*

Of special interest along the way, besides a number of crafts stores and stalls, are the **Iglesia de Chavarrieta,** the **Ex-Convento San Bernardino,** and the **Biblioteca Taxco-Canoga Park** (library; 9 A.M.–1 P.M. and 3–7 P.M. Mon.–Fri., 9 A.M.–1 P.M. Sat.) with many English-language novels and reference books.

Farther on, a block before the *zócalo,* pause to decipher the stone mosaic of the **Taxco Hieroglyph,** which decorates the pavement in front of the Palacio Municipal (City Hall). Inside, climb the stairs for a balcony-front view of the hieroglyph and the wall mural for a graphic review of Mexican history. See the main actors, from left to right: stolid Benito Juárez ("Respect for the rights of all is peace"); elderly General Porfirio Díaz gives away church and communal land to foreigners; banderilla-laden Emiliano Zapata declares his Plan de Ayala; President Lázaro Cárdenas in overalls expropriates foreign oil companies; and Aldolfo López Mateos declares free school textbooks;

The Taxco Hieroglyph is set in the street stones in front of the Palacio Municipal.

© BRUCE WHIPPERMAN

while Juárez, John F. Kennedy, Henry Kissinger, Charles de Gaulle, and Jawarlal Nehru look on.

In-Town Vistas

You needn't go as far afield as the Hotel Monte Taxco or the Cristo del Monte to get a good view of the city streets and houses carpeting the mountainside. Vistas depend not only on vantage point but time of day, since the best viewing sunshine (which frees you from squinting) should come generally from *behind.* Consequently, spots along the highway (more or less east of town), such as the patios of the Hotel Posada de la Misión and the *mirador* atop the Hotel Borda, provide good morning views, while afternoon views are best from points west of town, along the extension of Cuauhtémoc past the Plazuela San Juan uphill by (or in the hilltop garden of) the Hotel Rancho Taxco Victoria.

◖ Cableway *(Teleférico)* to Hotel Monte Taxco

A cableway above the highway (on the north side of town, where the *carretera* passes beneath Los Arcos, 8 A.M.–7 P.M. daily, round-trip tickets about $6, kids half price) lifts passengers to soaring vistas of the town on one side and ponderous, pine-studded mesas on the other. The ride ends at the Hotel Monte Taxco, where you can make a day of it golfing, horseback riding, playing tennis, eating lunch, and sunning on the panoramic-view pool deck. Return by taxi if you miss the last car.

Cristo del Monte

Above the opposite, west, side of town, about two miles uphill from the *zócalo,* stands the colossal new stone statue of Jesus, where folks enjoy an airy panoramic town view framed by lush, green looming mountains. Get there on foot (if you relish a 1,500-foot climb, wear a hat and carry water) or by taxi (about $2.50), *colectivo* (to Casahuates village), or car, west from the *zócalo,* via Calle Cuauhtémoc, past the Hotel Victoria. After about two miles (3

© BRUCE WHIPPERMAN

The uphill park of Cristo del Monte is the best spot to view Taxco and its surrounding pine-decorated mountain landscape.

km), fork right at the Huixteco sign and continue past Casahuates village about 200 yards, where a dirt driveway leads right to the Cristo del Monte park.

ACCOMMODATIONS

Taxco's dry, temperate climate relegates air-conditioning, ceiling fans, and central heating to frills offered only in the most expensive hotels. All of the hotel recommendations below have hot water and private baths, however.

Taxco's low-end hotels (under $50, but nevertheless comfortable) cluster in the colorful *zócalo* neighborhood, while many of the high-end (Over $100) lodgings are scattered mostly along the *carretera*.

Under $50

Walk west of the *zócalo* half a block past Plazuela de San Juan to the **Posada Lucy** (Carlos J. Nibbi 8, Taxco, Guerrero 40200, tel./fax 762/622-1780, $30 s or d one bed; $56 for 2–4 in two double beds) on the left. Here,

owners offer 32 budget rooms in a rambling complex, fortuitously isolated below and away from street noise. Airy patios with chairs and tables invite quiet relaxation. Inside, rooms are simply but attractively decorated with color-coordinated curtains, bedspreads, and handmade wooden furniture.

Five blocks northwest of the *zócalo,* find the inviting ☾ **Hotel Posada San Javier** (Estacas 32, Taxco, Guerrero 40200, tel. 762/622-3177, tel./fax 762/622-2351, posadasanjavier@hotmail.com, $39 s, $42 d, 40 t, suites $55 d). Although it's a climb to the *zócalo,* this very popular hotel, built around a tranquil inner garden, offers about 40 immaculate rooms, a lovely patio with (unheated) blue pool, framed in lush verdure, and airy verandas for relaxing. All with parking, and an inviting reading room with lots of books. Reserve a week in advance.

Back by the *zócalo,* on Alarcón just downhill west of the *zócalo,* a pair of former colonial mansions, now popular hotels, face each other across the street. First choice goes to the refined ☾ **Hotel los Arcos** (J. Ruiz de Alarcón 4, Taxco, Guerrero 40200, tel. 762/622-1836, fax 762/622-7982, reserve@hotellosarcos.net, hotelosarcostaxco@yahoo.com, www.hotellos arcos.net, $34 s, $40 d). The 21 rooms rise in three vine-draped tiers around an inner patio, replete with reminders of old Mexico. The rooms have thoughtfully selected handmade polished wooden furniture, tile floors, rustic wall art, and immaculate hand-painted cobalt-on-white tile bathrooms.

Guests at the very compact **Hotel Emilia Castillo** (J.R. Alarcón 7, Taxco, Guerrero 40200, tel./fax 762/622-1396, reservations2@hotelemiliacastillo.com, www.hotelemilia castillo.com, $32 s, $36 d, $41 t) across the street, enjoy carved wood, paintings, sculptures and plants gracing every wall and corner. The 41 smallish rooms, in neocolonial decor, around an intimate upper balcony are clean and comfortable and thoughtfully furnished in old-world style. The owners also run a nearby silver boutique, whose displays decorate the downstairs lobby.

$50-100

Picturesquely tucked on an uphill lane, just two blocks north of the *zócalo,* find ☾ **Hotel Mi Casita** (Altos de Redondo #1, Taxco, Guerrero 40200, tel./fax 762/627-1777, email reservations@hotelmicasita.com, www.hotelmi casita.com, $50 s or d and up). A charmingly rustic retreat for a cadre of savvy lovers of Mexico, the Hotel Mi Casita blooms with a treasury of delightful Mexicana. Its 12 rooms and suites, most with panoramic balcony views of the surrounding city and cloud-tipped mountains, are individually decorated with fetching designer lamps, handpainted wall art, and colorful Talavera-tiled bathrooms. Rentals, some quaintly petite, ordinarily begin at about $50 s or d and range upward to about $80 for the largest suites. Add about 25 percent during holidays.

Head uphill, past the opposite, west, side of the plaza, and follow Cuauhtémoc to the Plazuela de San Juan and the adjacent **Hotel Santa Prisca** (Cena Obscura 1, P.O. Box 42, Taxco, Guerrero 40200, tel. 762/622-0080 or 762/622-0980, fax 762/622-2938, htl_staprisca@yahoo.com, credit cards accepted, $35 s, $51 d; superior-grade rooms, $57 s or d). This tranquil, dignified old hostelry surrounds an oft-fragrant garden of orange trees; its off-lobby dining room shines with graceful details, such as beveled glass, a fireplace, blue-white stoneware and ivy-hung portals. Its tile-decorated rooms, in two floors around the garden just outside, are clean and comfortable, with private baths and parking.

Taxco's only *zócalo*-front hostelry, the **Hotel Agua Escondida** (Calle Guillermo Spratling 4, Taxco, Guerrero 40200, tel. 762/622-0726 or 762/622-1166, fax 762/622-1306, hotelaguaesc@prodigy.net.mx, credit cards accepted, $51 s, $64 d, $85 t) stands on the diagonally opposite corner from the church. A multilevel maze of hidden patios, rooftop sundecks, and dazzling city views, the Agua Escondida has 76 clean, comfortable rooms. The name, which translates as "Hidden Water," must refer to its big swimming pool, which is tucked away in a far rooftop corner. Rooms vary; if you have the choice, look at several.

Try to avoid the oft-noisy streetfront rooms. If you don't mind climbing, some of the upper-floor rooms have airy, penthouse views.

The formerly neglected **Hotel Borda** (Cerro de Pedregal, P.O. Box 483, Taxco, Guerrero 40200, tel. 762/622-0225, fax 762/622-0617, hotelborda@prodigy.net.mx, www.hotelborda .com, credit cards accepted, $87 s or d, suites $110), off the *carretera* downhill, thanks to new owners is being fixed up to approximate the luxury hotel it once was. This is fortunate, for the hotel's magnificent assets—grand vistas, spacious garden, restaurant bar, and luxurious blue pool and patio—remain as attractive as ever. The 110 clean, comfortable, and invitingly decorated rooms come with fans, and parking.

Over $100

Resort-style ☾ **Hotel Monte Taxco** (Lomas de Taxco, Taxco, Guerrero 40200, tel. 762/622-1300 or 762/622-1301, fax 762/622-1428, reservaciones@montetaxco.com.mx, www .montetaxco.com.mx, credit cards accepted, $140 s or d; $110 Sun.–Thurs.) stands atop a towering mesa accessible by either a steep road or cableway *(teleférico)* from the highway just north of town. On weekends, the hotel is often packed with well-heeled Mexico City families, whose kids play organized games while their parents enjoy the panoramic poolside view or play golf and tennis. The 156 deluxe rooms, most with view balconies, come with a/c, phones, and TV; facilities include restaurants, shops, a piano bar, disco, weekend live music, parking, a gym, pool, sauna, and spa. The adjacent country club offers a nine-hole golf course, tennis courts, and horseback riding.

If you'd like to stay atop Monte Taxco, a good alternative to the hotel would be to rent one of the neocolonial-style apartments of the **Villas Monte Taxco** (adjacent to the golf course, 100 yards outside the Hotel Monte Taxco front door, tel. 762/622-2305, fax 762/622-5609, $110 1br). For about $110 per night (ask for a midweek discount), you get a deluxe, one-bedroom mountain-view apartment with kitchenette, living room, dining room, use of the pool, and access to the golf course, tennis courts, horseback riding, mountain trails, and the Hotel Monte Taxco's facilities next door.

Back down on the highway in town, the **Hotel Posada de la Misión** (Cerro de la Misión 32, Taxco, Guerrero 40200, tel. 762/622-0063 or 762/622-0533, fax 762/622-2198, hpmreserva@posadamision.com, www.posada mision.com, credit cards accepted, $200 d, $225 weekends) spreads over a view hillside. Its guests, many on group tours, enjoy cool, quiet patios, green gardens, plant-lined corridors, a sunny pool and deck, a view restaurant, and parking. Many of the semideluxe rooms have panoramic city views; some have fireplaces. All rooms have color TV and phones. Standard rooms rent for about $200 d, $225 weekends, including dinner and breakfast. Kids under 12 with parents are free in room, with half off on meals. Christmas and New Year's prices are higher. Some guests have complained about unkempt rooms; take a look before moving in. Find it just off the *carretera*, uphill side, 200 yards south of the Pemex gas station.

FOOD
Stalls and Snacks
The numerous *fondas* (foodstalls) atop the *artesanías* (ar-tay-sah-NEE-ahs) handicrafts section of the Taxco market are Taxco's prime source of wholesome country-style food. The quality of their fare is a matter of honor for the proprietors, since among their local patrons word of a little bad food goes a long way. It's very hard to go wrong, moreover, if your selections are steaming hot and made fresh before your own eyes (in contrast, by the way, to most restaurant and hotel fare).

Choose from a potpourri that might include steaming bowls of *menudo* or *pozole*, or maybe plates of pork or chicken *mole*, or *molcajetes* (big stone bowls) filled with steaming meat and broth and draped with hot nopal cactus leaves.

On the *zócalo*, stalls appear late afternoons, offering favorite evening snacks, including tacos, *pozole, menudo*, hot dogs, popcorn, po-

tato chips (deep-fried on the spot), and sweets, such as french-fried bananas and *churros*.

For a sit-down snack or light lunch or supper, go to the **Nevería and Cafetería Vicky** (above the *zócalo's* northwest corner, across from the Hotel Agua Escondida). Take a balcony seat and take in the fascinating *zócalo* view, with your espresso *café Americano* ($1) and/or fruit plate ($3), hamburger ($2), topped off with ice cream ($1.50). (Get there via the lane that heads steeply uphill across from the Hotel Agua Escondida. At the first street, turn a sharp left. Vicky's is one door past Arnoldo's mask shop.)

Restaurants
Although its restaurants are not what draws most of Taxco's visitors, Taxco nevertheless offers some very recommendable dining options. Of the *zócalo* choices, the upstairs **La Parroquia** (across the *zócalo* from the church, tel. 762/622-3096, 9 A.M.–10:30 P.M. daily, credit cards accepted) ranks high, for a light meal (guacamole, $4, hamburger, $5, tuna salad or tacos, $3). The front balcony tables are ideal perches for watching the people parade below.

Judging from its hundreds of daily customers, the ⟨ **Pozoleróa Tía Calla** (a block north of the churchfront, at the *zócalo's* northeast corner, downstairs, tel. 762/622-5602, 1–10 P.M. daily) is, very likely, Taxco's most popular restaurant. Everyone comes to feast on the delicious country-style tacos, enchiladas, *pozole* ($2–4) in multiple variations (and even salads—try the good tuna salad, full of crunchy veggies, enough for two, $4). Besides the budget prices, the final clincher here is the prompt, professional service, in an immaculate, family-friendly dining room setting.

Another good bet on the *zócalo* is **Pizza Pazza** (at the corner, right-hand side of the cathedral, upstairs, tel. 762/622-5500, noon–11 P.M. daily). Although the menu offers a little bit of everything Italian and more, the specialty is good pizza in about 15 varieties ($5–12); extras include relaxed ambience, professional service, checkered tablecloths, and airy, plaza-view balcony tables. If the TV bothers you, the staff won't mind turning it down to low volume *(volumen bajo),* if asked.

Join in a 30-year Taxco tradition at **Mario's** (Plaza Borda 1, south side of the *zócalo,* tel. 762622-7797, 10 A.M.–midnight daily). Favorites here are Sicilian burritos ($4), chili American-style ($3), spaghettis ($5–9) and pizzas in many varieties ($6–12). Musician owner Mario Esquivel (a '60s-era headliner) continues his long custom, entertaining at his piano bar along with a trio Saturdays and holidays (call to check program).

Recommendable for its refined old-world ambience, the restaurant **◖ Del Ángel Inn** (Calle de Muerte—now Celso Muñoz—4, second floor, tel. 762/622-5525, 8 A.M.–10:30 P.M. daily) adds an airy view and good food to the reasons for going there. Inside, rustic old-adobe walls, regal stone columns, and baroque statuary enhance the pleasing effect. As for food, choose from a very recognizable, tasty menu of appetizers, soups, and salads ($4–6), pasta ($6–7), Mexican specialties ($5–6), meats ($8–10), and more. Find it a few steps downhill from the Santa Prisca churchfront, left side.

A block from the *zócalo,* along Calle Cuauhtémoc overlooking Plazuela de San Juan, try Mexican-style **Restaurant el Adobe** (Plazuela de San Juan 13, tel. 762/622-1416, 8 A.M.–11 P.M. daily) for breakfast or a lunch break. For breakfast, you can enjoy juice, eggs, and hotcakes ($5); for lunch, hamburgers, tacos, enchiladas ($3–6), or, for dinner, steak Adobe-style and shrimp brochette ($8–12).

Of the restaurant options, one of the best for non-tourist ambience is the local favorite **Restaurant Santa Fe** (on the left a few doors downhill from Plazuela San Juan, tel. 762/622-1170, 8 A.M.–10 P.M. daily). Tasty, professionally prepared and served country fare keeps a battalion of faithful patrons happy. Although the long á la carte menu varies from *pozole* and soup to chicken and fish, the main event is the daily four-course *comida* of soup (try *crema de zanahoria*), spaghetti, main dish (try *chiles rellenos*), and dessert, about $5. Good for breakfast, too.

Customers at **Café Sasha** (on Callejón Matanzas, around the corner from Casa Hum-

boldt, tel. 762/101-1713, 8:30 A.M.–11 P.M. daily) enjoy both an inviting bohemian atmosphere and hearty comfort food. Pick from a unique and tasty menu of breakfasts, including home-fry potatoes ($4–6), salads (Roquefort and spinach, $4), pizzas, sandwiches, pastas ($4–8), and special plates, such as falafel, excellent chow mein, Thai chicken ($6–8), and apple pie ($2).

ENTERTAINMENT AND EVENTS

Taxco people mostly entertain each other. Such spontaneous diversions are most likely around the *zócalo,* which often seems like an impromptu festival of typical Mexican scenes. Around the outside stand the monuments of the colonial past, while on the sidewalks sit the native people who come in from the hills to sell their onions, tamales, and pottery. Kids run between them, their parents and grandparents watching, while young men and women flirt, blush, giggle, and jostle one another until late in the evening.

Nightlife

A number of night spots, around or near the *zócalo,* are popular with both local folks and visitors. For example, join the locals at **Bar Berta,** on the church corner, or bouncy music with the mostly tourist crowd at **Bar Estación** on Cuauhtémoc, by Bancomer, a block west of the *zócalo* (or for tranquility and conversation, head upstairs to **Restaurant la Parroquia** across the *zócalo* from the church).

Later, or on another day, continue your Taxco party via the jazzy recorded music pouring out of the speakers (live Saturdays) at the restaurant/bar **Concha,** upstairs at Hotel Casa Grande, at Plazuela de San Juan. At **Mario's** (see *Restaurants*), a piano accompanies a trio playing oldies but goodies Saturdays from around 9 or 10 P.M.

For more music in a refined, upscale setting, the **Hotel Monte Taxco,** tel. 762/622-1300 or 762/622-1301, offers a piano bar and discotheque and a trio weekends and seasonally. At the similarly upscale **Hotel Posada**

de la Misión, tel. 762/622-0063 or 762/622-0533, patrons enjoy a roving trio for lunch and a piano bar Friday and Saturday nights. Programs may vary seasonally; call to confirm.

Festivals

An abundance of local fiestas provide the excuses for folks to celebrate, starting on Jan. 17 and 18 with the **Festival of Santa Prisca.** On the initial day, kids and adults bring their pet animals for blessing at the church. At dawn the next day, pilgrims arrive at the *zócalo* for *mañanitas* (dawn Mass) in honor of the saint, then head for folk dancing inside the church.

During the year, Taxco's many neighborhood churches celebrate their saints' days (such as Chavarrieta, March 4; Veracruz, the four weeks before Easter; San Bernardino, May 20; Santísima Trinidad, June 13; Santa Ana, July 26; Asunción, Aug. 15; San Nicolás, Sept. 10; San Miguel, Sept. 19; San Francisco, Oct. 4; and Guadalupe, Dec. 12) with food, fireworks, music, and dancing.

Religious fiestas begin with **Carnaval** the few days before Ash Wednesday (usually in February), and climax six weeks later during Semana Santa (Holy Week, before Easter). On the Thursday and Good Friday before Easter, cloaked penitents proceed through the city, carrying gilded images and bearing crowns of thorns.

On the Monday after the Nov. 2 Día de los Muertos (Day of the Dead), Taxco people head to pine-shaded **Parque Huixteco** (PAR-kay weesh-TAY-koh) atop the Cerro Huixteco behind town to celebrate their unique **Fiesta de los Jumiles.** In a ritual whose roots are lost in pre-Columbian legend, people collect and feast on *jumiles* (small crickets)—raw or roasted—along with music and plenty of beer and fixings. Since so many people go, transportation is easy. Drive or ride a *colectivo* (Huixteco on windshield) along the west-side road (westward extension of Cuauhtémoc from the *zócalo*) uphill about two miles. Fork right at the Huixteco sign. Continue for several miles to the mountaintop Parque Huixteco.

Three weeks later, during the last week in November and/or early December the Taxco year-end holiday season kicks off in earnest, with the **National Silver Fair.** A month of partying continues, with the **Fiesta of the Virgin of Guadalupe** on Dec. 12, climaxing with a week of continuous Christmas and New Year merrymaking.

SPORTS AND RECREATION

Stay in shape as local folks do, by walking Taxco's winding, picturesque side streets and uphill lanes. And, since all roads return to the *zócalo,* getting lost is rarely a problem.

For more formal sports, the **Monte Taxco Country Club** has horses ready for riding ($15/hour), three good tennis courts ($14/hour), and a nine-hole golf course available for use by nonguests for $50 per person. Contact the country club sports desk, in the little house about 100 yards away from the Hotel Monte Taxco's front entrance, or call the hotel, tel. 762/622-1300. Informal *sendas* (hiking paths) head north, uphill, into the luscious pine- and cedar-forested mesa country. Take sturdy shoes, water, and a hat.

SHOPPING
Market

Taxco's big market day is Sunday, when the town is loaded with people from outlying villages selling produce and live pigs, chickens, and ducks. The market is just downhill from Los Arcos, the lane that runs below the right side of (as you face) the *zócalo* church. From the lane, head right before the arch and down the staircase. Soon you'll be descending through a warren of market stalls. Pass the small Baptist church on Sunday and hear the congregation singing like angels floating above the market. Don't miss the spice stall, **Yerbería Castillo,** piled with the intriguing wild remedies collected by owner Elvira Castillo and her son Teodoro.

Farther on you'll pass mostly scruffy meat stalls but also some clean juice stands, such as **Liquados Memo** (7 A.M.–6 P.M. daily), where you can rest with a delicious fresh *zanahoria* (carrot), *toronja* (grapefruit), or *sandía* (watermelon) juice.

Before leaving the market, be sure to ask for

jumiles (hoo-MEE-lays), live crickets that sell in bags for about a penny apiece, ready for folks to pop them into their mouths.

If *jumiles* don't suit your taste, you may want to drop in for lunch at one of the *fondas* above the market's *artesanías* (handicrafts) section.

Handicrafts

The submarket **Mercado de Artesanías** (watch for the white sign overhead as you descend the market staircase) offers items for tourist and local consumption, such as economical belts, huaraches, wallets, and inexpensive silver chains, necklaces, and earrings.

As you head out for tonier shops, don't miss the common but colorful handicrafts, such as the host of charming ceramic cats, turtles, doves, fish, and other figurines that local folks sell very cheaply. Find them everywhere, in the market, on street corners, and, especially in front of the Museo Guillermo Spratling. If you buy, bargain—but not too hard, for the people are poor and have often traveled far.

Masks are the prime attraction at **Tienda Arnoldo** (Palma 1, tel. 762/622-1272, 11 A.M.–3 P.M. and 6–8 P.M. Mon.–Fri., 11 A.M.–8 P.M. Sat.–Sun.), upstairs, across the uphill lane next to Hotel Agua Escondida, where the friendly proprietors, Arnoldo Jacobo and his son Raoul, can explain every detail about their fascinating array of merchandise. (Be sure to see his scrapbook of his travels looking for masks all over Guerrero.) Hundreds of masks from all over Guerrero—stone and wood, antique and new—line the walls like in a museum. All of the many motifs, varying from black men puffing cigarettes and blue-eyed sea goddesses to inscrutable Aztec gods in onyx and grotesque lizard-humanoids, are priced to sell.

Other shops nearby have similar offerings, such as Arnoldo's neighbor, **Celso** (4 Palma, just uphill, tel. 762/622-8485, 10 A.M.–6 P.M. daily).

For a good general Mexico handicrafts selection—Puebla Talavera ceramics, Tonalá papier-mâché, metalwork, pewter—take a look inside the shop, confusingly named **"Plaza San Juan"** (on the Plazuela San Juan, west side, beneath Restaurant Adobe, tel. 762/622-

1683, 10 A.M.–8 P.M. Mon.–Sat., 11 A.M.–5 P.M. Sun.).

Silver Shops

Among the many good silver shops that cluster around the *zócalo* and downhill on the highway, one of the most enduring is the family-owned shop of **Emilio Castillo** (J. R. Alarcón 7, tel. 762/622-3471, 10 A.M.–7 P.M. Mon.–Sat., 10 A.M.–4 P.M. Sun., credit cards accepted), adjacent to the lobby of the Hotel Emilia Castillo, downhill from the *zócalo*, to the right of the Hotel Agua Escondida. Run by a branch of the industrious and prolific Castillo family, the shop offers all in-house work, specializing in porcelain and silver, at reasonable prices. Here, unlike at many shops, you can bargain a bit.

Return uphill along Alarcón half a block to the **Centro Joyero** (10 A.M.–7 P.M. Mon.–Sat., 11 A.M.–5 P.M. Sun.) on the small Plazuela Bernal, just half a block downhill from the *zócalo*. Inside find a number of small shops with a number of fine but priced-to-sell pieces.

One of the more interesting silver shops, if only for a look around, is **Luna Collection** (in the *zócalo*-front complex, Patio de las Artesanías, next to the Casa Borda, tel. 762/622-6447, 9:30 A.M.–8 P.M. daily; credit cards accepted). The staff says, with a smile, that the Grutas de Cacahuamilpa were modeled after their shop. Inside, plaster stalagmites hang above small mountains of fine silver jewelry.

Continue to Calle Cuauhtémoc, on the *zócalo*'s west side, to the store of master silversmith **Ezequiel Tapia** (15 Cuauhtémoc, tel. 762/622-0416, 9 A.M.–8 P.M. daily), winner of two-dozen-odd national prizes. Besides an exquisite collection of one-of-a-kind earrings, necklaces, and cameos, his shop glows with huge, lovely sculptures in silver.

A few doors farther west to Cuauhtémoc 9, next to Hotel Casa Grande, check out the long-time (since 1950) **Arte Nacional** (tel. 762/622-1096, fax 762/622-2202, noon–8 P.M. daily), a grand selection of virtually everything silver. Specialties range from a museum-quality selection of gleaming table silver (chafing dishes, large platters, teas sets, candelabras) to a treasury of necklaces, bracelets, rings, and much much more.

For a very fitting silver-shopping finale, be sure to visit what must be Taxco's most elegantly extravagant silver shop, the **Joyería Elena Ballesteros** (Calle de la Muerte 4, tel. 762/622-3767, fax 762/622-3907, silver@ballesteros.com, www.ballesteros.com, 9 A.M.–7 P.M. daily). More than just a labor of love, her store amounts to a cathedral of silver, beginning with the simply exquisite, moving to dining-room tables loaded with enough plate for a maharajah's banquet, to gleaming, 10-pound $50,000 crucifixes, and a monumental gold tree of life.

Grocery and Photo Stores

Petite grocery store **La Plazuela** (2 Guadalupe, tel. 762/622-0633, 9 A.M.–10 P.M. daily), uphill, west, from the *zócalo,* has a little bit of everything.

Alternatively, go to **Minisuper la Gloria** (on Hidalgo, a long block downhill from Plazuela de San Juan, tel. 762/622-3878, 8 A.M.–10 P.M. daily).

The small photo shop **Foto Juárez** (Guadalupe 2, tel. 762/622-1072, 11 A.M.–9 P.M. Mon.–Sat., 2–9 P.M. Sun.) (from the *zócalo,* walk uphill past the Restaurant Parroquia a block), offers a modest stock of merchandise, such as batteries, point-and-shoot cameras, and popular print film.

Better-stocked **Tienda la Misión** (Benito Juárez 216, tel. 762/622-0116, 10 A.M.–8 P.M. Mon.–Sat., 11 A.M.–3 P.M. Sun.), downhill a few blocks past City Hall, on the right, next to Banamex, offers some cameras and accessories, and Kodak film, including Tri-X Pan, Plus-X, and Ektachrome. It also does Xerox photocopying, including enlargement and reduction.

INFORMATION AND SERVICES
Tourist Information Offices, Guides, and Travel Agents

Taxco has a pair of tourist information offices, both beside the highway at opposite ends of town, approximately 9 A.M.–7 P.M. daily. The knowledgeable and English-speaking officers readily answer questions and furnish whatever maps and

literature they may have. The north office, tel. 762/622-0798, is next to the north-end Pemex gas station; the south office is about a quarter mile south of the south-end Pemex station.

Personable, veteran Mexico guide **Benito Flores Batalla,** tel./fax 762/622-0542, who staffs the north-side tourist information office, offers his services as a guide. For starters, he offers a 3.5-hour city tour for $30, without car; $60 with car supplied. Longer trips might include the Grutas de Cachuamilpa, Xochicalco, and Ixcateopan. (See *Excursions from Taxco.*)

About the same is true for **Enrique Viveros,** who staffs the south-end information office, daily 9 A.M.–7 P.M., tel. 762/627-6245; or cellular, dial 044-762/626-3095 locally, or tel. 01-762/626-3095 long distance.

If Benito and Enrique are unavailable, they highly recommend guide **Juan Menatel** ($70 per day including car, home tel. 762/622-0986).

One of the most reliable travel agents in town is **Turismo Misión** (at the Hotel Posada de la Misión reception desk, tel. 762/622-1125 or 762/622-0063, info@posadamision.com), who provides tours plus all the usual travel agency services.

Publications

English-language books and newspapers are hard to find in Taxco. The most convenient place to find used paperbacks will probably be your hotel.

For newspapers and magazines, a pair of stores have carried a few English-language books and newspapers on and off in the past (although at this writing they didn't have any). Nevertheless, you might check with them. They are **Agente de Publicaciones Raoul Domínguez,** tel. 762/622-0794, on the Los Arcos lane, below the right side as you face the churchfront, and **Casa Domínguez** newsstand, tel. 762/622-0133, at Los Arcos 7, a few doors farther downhill.

The scarcity of English reading matter makes the collection at the small library **Biblioteca Taxco Canoga Park** (9 A.M.–1 P.M. and 3–7 P.M. Mon.–Fri., 9 A.M.–1 P.M. Sat.) even more precious. Browse its several shelves of English-language novels, nonfiction, magazines, and reference books . Most of the book collection has been donated by volunteers from Taxco's sister city, Canoga Park, California. The library is a five-minute walk downhill along Juárez, east, from the zócalo. About a block past the City Hall, turn right at an alley (watch for the Taxco-Canoga Park sign) and continue a few steps downhill to the library. (You might ask the librarian where you can get an English-language magazine or newspaper.)

Money Exchange

Banks near the zócalo and their ATMs are Taxco's cheapest source of pesos. The good longest-hours option is **HSBC** bank (to the right of the church, tel. 762/622-7300 or 762/622-7506, 8 A.M.–7 P.M. Mon.–Sat.). Alternatively, a block along Cuauhtémoc from the zócalo, try **Bancomer** (tel. 762/622-0287 or 762/622-0288, 9 A.M.–5 P.M. Mon.–Fri.); or the second Bancomer branch (tel. 762/622-2393, 8:30 A.M.–4 P.M. Mon.–Fri.), downhill on the carretera across from the Hotel Posada Misión.

Communications

The **town center correo** (tel. 762/622-8596, 9 A.M.–2 P.M. Mon.–Fri., 9 A.M.–12:30 P.M. Sat.), with an after-hours mailbox out front, is in the Presidencia Municipal on Juárez, downhill, east from the zócalo. The **highway branch** downhill (tel. 762/622-0501, 8 A.M.–2:30 P.M. Mon.–Fri.), is half a block north (Mexico City direction) of the Estrella de Oro bus station.

Telecomunicaciones, off the zócalo, behind the Casa Borda downhill (tel. 762/622-4885, fax 762/622-0001, 9 A.M.–3 P.M. Mon.–Fri), offers telex, money order, and public fax services.

Public street telephones all over the town center allow cheap, easy **long-distance** direct dialing with widely available Ladatel telephone cards. Get them everywhere, especially at pharmacies and liquor and grocery stores.

Internet access is available at **Interplaza** computer center, in the town market, 200 feet down the steps below the right (west) side of the church. 9:30 A.M.–9 P.M. Mon.–Sat., 10 A.M.–6 P.M. Sun., tel. 762/622-0789. If the Interplaza is closed, go to the hole-in-the-wall

Internet store on Cuauhtémoc, half a block west of the zócalo 11 A.M.–11 P.M. daily.

Health and Emergencies

Taxco has a pair of respected private hospitals, both on the carretera. The **Clínica de Especialidades,** 33 Av. de los Plateros, tel. 762/622-1111 or 762/622-4500, has a 24-hour emergency room, X-rays, a laboratory, a 24-hour pharmacy, and many specialists on call. The **Clínica Santa Cruz,** tel. 762/622-3012, offers similar services, also on Carretera Plateros, at the corner of Morelos, across from the government Seguro Social hospital.

For routine medicines and remedies, go to one of the good town-center pharmacies, such as **Farmacia de Ahorro** half a block west of the zócalo, on Cuauhtémoc, tel. 762/627-3444, 7 A.M.–11 P.M. daily, or **Farmacia Similares,** on Hidalgo, one block downhill from Plazuela San Juan, tel. 762/627-2214, 8 A.M.–9 P.M. Mon.–Sat., 8 A.M.–8 P.M. Sun. Alternatively, go to the good 24-hour pharmacy at the Clínica de Especialidades, on the carretera.

For police emergencies, contact the **policía,** either by tel. 762/622-0007, or on duty on the zócalo; at City Hall, two blocks downhill, at Juárez 6, tel. 762/622-0007; or at the substation on the side street Calle Fundaciones, one block below the carretera near the corner of Alarcón.

GETTING THERE AND AWAY
By Car or RV

National Highway 95 provides a major connection south with Acapulco in a total of about 159 miles (256 km) of driving via Iguala, accessible in 22 miles (36 km) via winding, old Highway 95. From there, continue south via two lane Highway 95, to Chilpancingo (for a total of about 86 miles, 138 km). For Acapulco, continue another 73 miles (117 km) via the cuota (toll) autopista. Allow about four and a half hours' driving time for the entire Taxco-Acapulco trip, either direction.

Alternatively, you can save about an hour to Acapulco by following toll expressways the whole way, by first heading north (Cuernavaca–Mexico City direction) out of town. Follow the

Mexico City *cuota* (toll) signs all the way about 25 miles (40 km) to the Mex. 95 D *cuota* expressway, where you fork south, Chilpancingo-Acapulco direction. Allow about three and a half hours for this longer but quicker 192-mile (310-km) Taxco-Acapulco route.

Highway 95 also connects Taxco north via Cuernavaca with Mexico City, a total of about 106 miles (170 km). The new leg of the Taxco–Mexico City cuota (toll) expressway splits off from old Highway 95 about two miles north of town. For those who want to save time, the expressway cuts about half an hour off the driving time. Otherwise, follow the winding old Highway 95 about 20 miles (32 km) to its intersection with Highway 95 D *cuota* (toll) superhighway. Congestion around Mexico City may lengthen the driving time to about three hours in either direction.

Note: Authorities limit driving your car in Mexico City according to the last digit of your license plate. (See the sidebar *Mexico City Driving Restrictions.*)

Highway 55 (junction at Cacahuamilpa) gives Michoacán- and Jalisco-bound drivers the desirable option of avoiding Mexico City by connecting Taxco directly with Toluca (and thence the fast east-west toll expressway 15 D, five hours to Guadalajara). The two-lane Highway 55 is paved and in good condition for its entire 74 miles (119 km). Fortunately, a faster, safer toll (cuota) expressway along the northern half of Highway 55 shortens the Taxco-Toluca driving time by at least an hour over the old winding, nontoll highway. Northbound, figure about 2.5 hours driving time to Toluca; southbound, allow about two hours.

By Bus

Competing lines **Estrella Blanca,** tel. 762/622-0131, and **Estrella de Oro,** tel. 762/622-0648, operate separate stations on the downhill *carretera* a few blocks apart. Both offer several luxury- and first-class connections north with Mexico City via Cuernavaca and south with Acapulco via Iguala and Chilpancingo.

Additionally, Estrella Blanca offers many local Flecha Roja bus with local towns, in addition to connections with Puebla, and the very

Walking, motorcycling, and motor-scootering are all good ways to get around in congested Taxco.

useful option for northwest-bound travelers of bypassing Mexico City via the superscenic Highway 55 route via Ixtapan del Sal (an interesting spa town) to Toluca. There, you can connect via Pátzcuaro, Michoacán, and Guadalajara, Jalisco, to the palmy Pacific Mexico beach destinations of Playa Azul, Manzanillo, Puerto Vallarta, San Blas, and Mazatlán.

EXCURSIONS FROM TAXCO

The monumental duo of the Grutas de Cacahuamilpa (caves) and the ruins of ancient Xochicalco makes for a fascinating, although long, day trip, by tour or car (two days if by public transportation). If you're going to do them both, start early; the Grutas are 15 miles (25 km) north (Mexico City direction) of town and Xochicalco is 25 miles (40 km) farther.

◖ Grutas de Cacahuamilpa

They're well worth the effort. The colossal Grutas de Cacahuamilpa (kah-kah-ooah-MEEL-pah; open daily, with hourly three-mile, two-hour

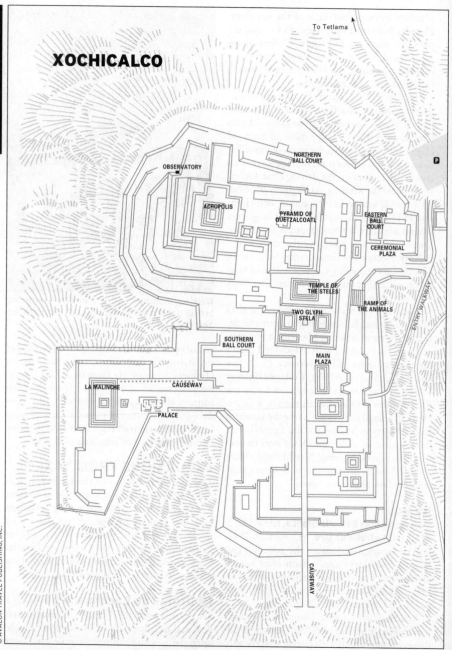

XOCHICALCO

To Tetlama

NORTHERN
BALL COURT

OBSERVATORY

ACROPOLIS

PYRAMID OF
QUETZALCOATL

EASTERN
BALL
COURT

CEREMONIAL
PLAZA

TEMPLE OF
THE STELES

RAMP OF
THE ANIMALS

TWO GLYPH
STELA

SOUTHERN
BALL COURT

MAIN
PLAZA

LA MALINCHE

CAUSEWAY

PALACE

CAUSEWAY

ENTRY WALKWAY

P

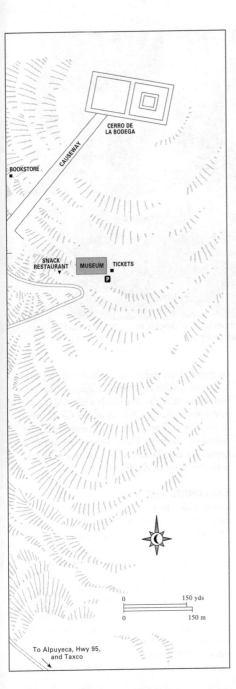

CERRO DE
LA BODEGA

CAUSEWAY

BOOKSTORE

SNACK
RESTAURANT   MUSEUM   TICKETS

P

0   150 yds

0   150 m

To Alpuyeca, Hwy 95,
and Taxco

walking tours in Spanish included in the $5 admission ($3 for kids), beginning at 10 A.M.) The *grutas* comprise one of the world's greatest cavern complexes. Forests of stalagmites and stalactites, in myriad shapes—Pluto the Pup, the Holy Family, a desert caravan, asparagus stalks, cauliflower heads—festoon a series of gigantic limestone chambers. The finale is a grand, 30-story hall that meanders for half a mile, like a fairyland in stone. A few gift shops sell souvenirs; snack bars supply food.

For the adventurous, experienced guides lead more extensive entire-day Cacahuamilpa cave tours ($50 per person), for robust, determined hikers only, during the Feb.–May dry season. Highlights include walking (and sometimes maybe crawling) about five miles (8 km) along sinuous, sometimes steep and slippery subterranean tunnels and paths, and wading waist-deep (and perhaps even shoulder-deep) in cool underground rivers. Make arrangements with guides a week ahead of time, either in person, at the cave's information and ticket booth, or by phone or email (tel. 734/346-1716, grutas_cacahuamilpa@hotmail.com), or with chief guide Lorenzo Amates Mura (tel. 777/129-9078 or 777/300-3695, amates_m@hotmail.com), or assistant guide Jo Paul (jopaul17@hotmail.com).

GETTING THERE

Combi collective vans leave hourly for the caves, beginning at 8:30 A.M., from just north of the Estrella Blanca bus station on the *carretera*. Watch for "Grutas" written on the windshields; expect to pay about $2 for a one-way fare. By car, get to the caves via Highway 95 north from Taxco; after 10 miles (16 km) from the northside Pemex station, fork left onto Highway 55 toward Toluca. Continue five more miles (8 km) and turn right at the signed Grutas de Cacahuamilpa junction. After a few hundred yards, turn right again into the entrance driveway.

◖ Xochicalco

Grand Xochicalco (soh-shee-KAHL-koh), an hour farther north from Cacahuamilpa, although lightly touristed, is a fountainhead of Mesoamerican legend. The archaeological

© BRUCE WHIPPERMAN

A remarkable bas-relief on the Pyramid of Quetzalcoatl, at Xochicalco, shows a hand (via a rope) joining two dates in the Mesoamerican calendar.

zone, officially designated as a United Nations World Heritage site, spreads over a half dozen terraced pyramid hilltops above a natural lake-valley, which at one time sustained a large population. Xochicalco flowered during the late classic period around A.D. 800, partly filling the vacuum left by the decline of Teotihuacán, the previously dominant Mesoamerican classic city-state. Some archaeologists speculate that Xochicalco at its apex was the great center of learning known in legend as Tamanchoan, where astronomer-priests derived and maintained calendars and where the Quetzalcoatl legend was born.

Your first stop should be the world-class **museum,** via the signed driveway east of the archaeolgical site. A grand entrance hall leads to six masterfully executed showrooms that illustrate the main currents of Xochicalco civilization: Earthly Gifts (flora, fauna, and trade); Warlords and Priests (don't miss the headless Lord-in-Red sun god); Xochicalco, Guardian of the People (centered around a pair of

calendar-glyph stelae that undoubtedly records a historic Xochicalco event); Creators and Artists (don't miss the sensitively executed jaguar and coyote pieces); World of the Gods (dramatic illustration of the ball court and ring found on the site); Daily Spaces (replica of a typical house, family altars and utensils and realistic "Lord of Xochicalco").

EXPLORING THE SITE

Leave at least two hours (mandatory visitor exit time 5:45 P.M.) to cover the site highlights. See the *Xochicalco* map. After visiting the excellent bookstore (closes 5 P.M.), your first stop should be the unmissable **Pyramid of Quetzalcoatl** on the site's north side. From the parking lot, head south uphill for about 100 yards, where a wide path forks right, uphill. After approximately another 100 yards, when you reach level ground again, turn right and pass the beautifully reconstructed **eastern ball court** on your right. Continue continue another 50 yards or so, until, on the wall about 200 feet your left, you see some stairs that you should climb, to the next upper level where the platform-like Pyramid of Quetzalcoatl (The Plumed Serpent) rises on the hilltop.

Vermilion paint remnants hint at the pyramid's original appearance, which was perhaps as brilliant as a giant birthday cake. In bas-relief around the entire base a serpent writhes, intertwined with personages, probably representing chiefs or great priests. Above these are warriors, identified by their helmets and *atlatl*, or lance-throwers.

Most notable, however, is one of Mesoamerica's most remarkable bas-reliefs, flanking the staircase. It shows the 11th week sign, *ozomatli* (monkey), being pulled by a hand (via a rope) to join with the fifth week sign, *calli* (house). Latter-day scholars generally interpret this as describing a calendar correction that resulted from a grand conclave of chiefs and sages from all over Mesoamerica, probably at this very spot.

About 100 yards south of the Pyramid of Quetzalcoatl rises the **Temple of the Steles,** so named for three large stone tablets found beneath the floor. They narrate the events of the Quetzalcoatl legend, wherein Quetzalcoatl (discoverer of corn and the calendar) was transformed into the morning star (the planet Venus); he continues to rule the heavens as the brightest star and the Lord of Time.

About 100 yards farther south, the **Main Plaza** was accessible to the common people via roads from below. This is in contrast to the sacrosanct **Ceremonial Plaza** by the eastern ball court nearby. South of the Ceremonial Plaza, the **Ramp of the Animals** (named for the carved animal-motif stones found along its length) slopes upward from east to west.

On the south end of the zone, a faintly visible

TLATCHTLI: THE BALL GAME

Basketball fever is probably a mild affliction compared to the enthusiasm pre-Columbian crowds felt for *tlatchtli*, the ball game that was played throughout Mesoamerica and is still played in some places. Contemporary accounts and latter-day scholarship have led to a partial picture of *tlatchtli* as it was played centuries ago. Although details varied locally, the game centered around a hard, natural rubber ball, which players batted back and forth across a center dividing line with leg-, arm-, and torso-blows.

Play and scoring was vaguely similar to tennis. Opponents, either individuals or small teams, tried to smash the ball past their opponents into scoring niches at the opposite ends of an I-shaped, sunken court. Players also could garner points by forcing their opponents to make wild shots that bounced beyond the court's retaining walls.

Courts were often equipped with a pair of stone rings fixed above opposing ends of the center dividing line. One scoring variation awarded immediate victory to the team who could manage to bat the *tlatchtli* through the ring.

As in tennis, players became very adept at smashing the ball at high speed. Unlike in tennis, the ball was solid and perhaps as heavy as two or three baseballs. Although protected by helmets and leather, players were usually bloodied, often injured, and sometimes even killed from opponents' punishing *tlatchtli*-inflicted blows. Matches were sometimes decided like a boxing match, with victory going to the opponent left standing on the court.

As with everything in Mesoamerica, tradition and ritual ruled *tlatchtli*. Master teachers subjected initiates to rigorous training, prescribed ritual, and discipline not unlike the ascetic life of a medieval monastic brotherhood.

Potential rewards were enormous, however. Stakes varied in proportion to a contest's ritual significance and the rank of the players and their patrons. Champion players could win fortunes in gold, feathers, or precious stones. Exceptional games could result in riches and honor for the winner, and death for the loser, whose heart, ripped from his chest on the centerline stone, became food for the gods.

causeway once connected the La Malinche pyramid, 200 yards to the southwest, with the Ceremonial Plaza.

That causeway passed the **southern ball court,** which is strikingly similar to ball courts as far away as Toltec Tula in the north and Maya Copan in Honduras, far to the south. On the opposite side of the causeway from the ball court lies the **Palace,** a complex marked by many rooms with luxury features such as toilet drainage, fireplaces, and steam baths.

On the far northwest side of the complex is the **Observatory,** a room hollowed into the hill and stuccoed and fitted with a viewing shaft for timing the sun and star transits essential for an accurate calendar.

GETTING THERE

It's best to get to Xochicalco by tour; for example, contact Misión Tours (Hotel Posada de la Misión, tel. 762/622-1125 or 762/622-0065). Or you can travel by taxi or car: Continue past the Grutas de Cacahuamilpa entrance. The route is straightforward, continuing by a single main road generally northeast, through Coatlá del Río (12 miles, 19 km), Mazatepec (20 miles, 33 km) and finally Miacatlán (23 miles, 37 km). There you bear right (east) at a fork (watch for Xochicalco signs) and continue past Rodeo hamlet (and lake on the right) to the Xochicalco signed left side road that leads a mile or two uphill to the archaeological site, a total of 29 miles (46 km) about an hour, from Cacahuamilpa, or 48 miles (77 km), two hours, from Taxco. The ruins are daily are daily 9 A.M.–6 P.M. (last visitor entry at 5 P.M., however). Admission (get tickets at the museum) runs about $5. Since caretakers shoo all visitors out by 5:45 P.M., arrive early enough to allow a couple of hours to explore the ruins. Although there is a restaurant by the museum, you should probably be prepared with some food and drinks, and for sure, bring a hat, water, and comfortable walking shoes.

Ixcateopan

The picturesque little furniture-making town of Ixcateopan (eeks-kah-tay-OH-pan—

Land of Cotton) has become famous for the remains of the last Aztec emperor, Cuauhtémoc, which archaeologists discovered there on Sept. 26, 1949.

EXPLORING IXCATEOPAN

The renown has been beneficial. The town streets and plaza are smartly cobbled with the local white marble, and houses and shops are neatly painted and whitewashed. At the center of all this stands Cuauhtémoc's resting place, the venerable **Iglesia de Santa María de la Asunción** church, beside the town plaza. Inside, city workers maintain the sanctuary and its small adjoining museum (9 A.M.–3 P.M. and 4–5 P.M. Mon.–Sat., 9 A.M.–3 P.M. Sun.). Cuauhtémoc's relics themselves, which were subjected to thorough investigation when they were unearthed, were believed to authentic (although lately some doubters dispute this claim). The bones lie in a glass case directly over the spot where they were buried beneath the altar stones more than four centuries ago.

The museum next door details the story of Cuauhtémoc's heroic defense of the Aztec capital, Tenochtitlán, and his capture, torture, and subsequent execution by Cortés on Feb. 28, 1525. Copies of pictograms, known as codices, such as the codex *Vatican-Ríos* (1528), displayed in the museum, represent Cuauhtémoc (literally, "The Descending Eagle") with an inverted, stylized eagle above his head. The museum sells an excellent booklet ($3) in Spanish, which details the fascinating story of the discovery and authentication of his ancestor's remains.

Outside the church, be sure to take a look about three blocks downhill past the church, on main street Calle Guerrero, at the town **archaeological site** (Wed.–Sun. 10 A.M.– 5 P.M.). The main remains, called the "Temple of Cotton," echoing the name Ixcateopan, reveal a ceremonial complex, including a pair of pedestals, royal rooms, and a former spring leading through what appear to be wash basins (presumably for the cotton the high priests may have ritually processed there).

Farther afield, you might be able to find

a guide to show you the limestone caves, **Grutas de San Miguel,** near neighboring San Miguel village (two or three miles, 15 minutes by car or better high-clearance truck or SUV); off the highway back to Taxco, fork right at the dirt road, at Plaza del Gallo (Plaza of the Rooster), with a few houses, about seven miles from Ixcateopan.

FESTIVALS
Customarily sleepy Ixcateopan wakes up for three annual fiestas. The fun kicks off in February, when folks celebrate their indigenous roots, with a weeklong party of daily flower processions, indigenous dances, fireworks, all climaxing around the Feb. 23 birthday of Cuauhtémoc.

The customary arrival of the governor of Guerrero, the Acapulco Symphony, and maybe even the president of Mexico on Sept. 26, the discovery date of Cuautémoc's remains, culminates another week of celebrating.

Finally, townsfolk bring in the New Year in grand style with a combined Christmas-carnival-New Year celebration of their patron Santo Niño de Atocha.

ACCOMMODATIONS AND FOOD
Besides its historic interest, Ixcateopan and its environs—the rustic old church and garden, the tranquil plaza, the surrounding lush oak-forested hills—invite lingering. Moreover, the amiable, frankly curious townsfolk, who are definitely not overwhelmed by tourists, are ready for visitors. They operate some pretty fair plaza-front country eateries, such as Cocinas Económicas Amanec, at the south side of the plaza.

Accommodations are available on the main street, at the **Posada de los Reyes** (Calle V. Guerrero 14, Ixcateopan, Guerrero 40430, tel. 736/366-2368, $15 s, $25 d), a block past the plaza, across the street from the church. The welcoming family-owners offer eight clean rooms, around a tranquil inner patio, furnished with attractive, locally crafted wood furniture and homespun bedspreads, plus private hot-water shower baths.

GETTING THERE
Get to Ixcateopan via *colectivo* van ($3, one way) labeled Ixcateopan.Catch it in front of the Estrella Blanca bus station in Taxco, or at any point on the *carretera* before the south-side, signed, turnoff road to Ixcateopan.

Drivers, follow the signed fork, west (turn right if traveling south) from the *carretera,* past the Pemex *gasolinera* about a mile south of town. Mark your odometer. Continue about an hour along the very scenic (a pair of waterfalls, good for picnicking and splashing, at Mile 4.5, Km 7.2, and Mile 11, Km 17.7), sometimes potholed, paved road for 23 miles (37 km) to the town plaza.

THE COSTA CHICA

In reality, the Costa Chica, the "Little Coast," which includes the state of Guerrero south of Acapulco and the western half of the adjoining coast of Oaxaca, isn't so little. Highway 200, heading out of the Acapulco hubbub, requires 300 miles (500 km) to traverse the scattered groves, forests, fields, and villages to the Costa Chica's southern bulge, where the coastline curves, like the belly of a dolphin, to its most southerly point near Puerto Ángel.

In the main resorts of the Costa Chica—Puerto Escondido, Puerto Ángel, and the Bays of Huatulco—the beaches face south, toward the Mar del Sur, the Pacific Ocean. On the other hand, if travelers head inland, they go north, over the verdant, jungle-clad Sierra Madre del Sur and into the Valley of Oaxaca, the native heartland of southern Mexico.

In addition to its abundance of picture-perfect golden beaches and pristine wildlife-rich coastal lagoons, the indigenous people (*indígenas*, een-DEE-hay-nahs) of the Costa Chica are another major reason for lingering on the Costa Chica. They make up a fascinatingly diverse family of about a million folks, spread along the coasts of eastern Guerrero and western and central Oaxaca, and speaking at least six separate languages, in at least a dozen distinct local dialects.

To a sizable fraction of the Costa Chica's indigenous people, Spanish is a foreign language. Many of them—Zapotecs, Mixtecs, and four smaller groups: Tlapanec, Amusgo, Chatino, and Chontal—live in remote foothill

© BRUCE WHIPPERMAN

HIGHLIGHTS

◖ Museo de las Culturas Afromestizos:
Be sure to schedule a stop at this uniquely fascinating museum and community center, with many fine displays depicting the history and cultural contributions of Mexico's African-Mexican people (page 556).

◖ Pinotepa Market: Morning is the best time to browse the old-fashioned goods and people-watch at this colorful market. Among the fresh vegetables, herbal remedies, and piñatas, you might be lucky enough to find a *pozahuanco* (Mixtec wraparound skirt) for sale (page 558).

◖ Laguna Manialtepec: This spreading mangrove-tufted lagoon is home to many dozens of animal and bird species, such as the anhinga and the red *papagayo* parrot (page 566).

◖ Playa Zicatela: Join the dozens, sometimes hundreds, of onlookers watching daredevil surfers trying to conquer the thundering

breakers at Puerto Escondido's Playa Zicatela (page 569).

◖ Playa Manzanillo: This petite strand of golden sand, at the inner recess of Puerto Escondido's Bahía Puerto Angelito, seems perfect for a holiday outing. It has good seafood *palapas* for eating, oft-gentle waves for child's play, clear water for good off-beach snorkeling, and fishing *lanchas* for hire (page 572).

◖ Playa Estacahuite: This picture-perfect sheltered little nook, just five minutes by taxi from Puerto Ángel, has something for nearly everyone: sand and gentle waves, a couple of restaurants, snorkeling from the beach, and boats for fishing (page 589).

◖ Centro Mexicano de la Tortuga: This combined aquarium and museum – ironically housed in a former turtle-processing factory – is dedicated to restoring Mexico's sea turtle populations (page 592).

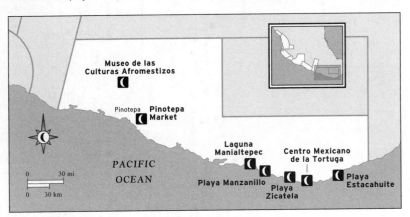

LOOK FOR ◖ TO FIND RECOMMENDED SIGHTS, ACTIVITIES, DINING, AND LODGING.

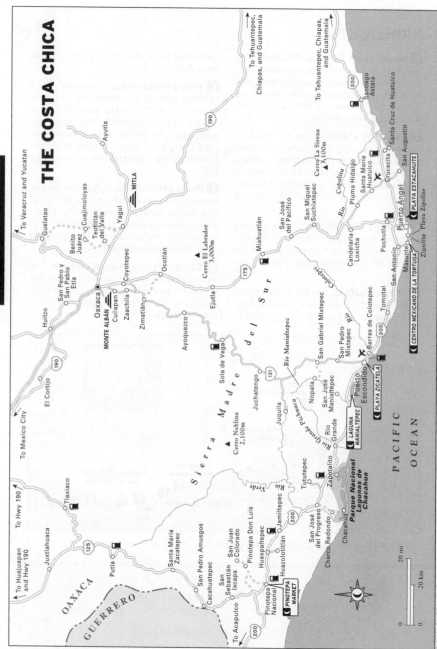

THE COSTA CHICA

© AVALON TRAVEL PUBLISHING, INC.

and mountain villages, subsisting as they always have on corn, beans, and squash, with few, if any telephones, sewers, schools, or roads. Those who live near towns often speak the Spanish they have learned by coming to market. In the Costa Chica town markets, you will brush shoulders with them, men sometimes in pure-white cottons and women in colorful embroidered *huipiles* or *pozahuancos,* saronglike handwoven striped skirts.

Besides the native people, on the Costa Chica, you will often see African Mexicans—*morenos* (brown ones)—known locally as *costeños* because their isolated settlements are near the coast. Descendants of African slaves imported hundreds of years ago, the *costeños* subsist on the produce from their village gardens and the fish they catch.

Costa Chica *indígenas* and *costeños* have a reputation for being unfriendly and suspicious. If true in the past (although it's certainly less so in the present), they have had good reason to be suspicious of outsiders, who in their view have been trying to take away their land, gods, and lives for 400 years.

Communication is nevertheless possible. Your arrival, for the residents of a little mountain or shoreline end-of-road village, might be the event of the day. People are going to wonder why you came. Smile and say hello. Buy a soda at the store or *palapa.* If kids gather around, don't be shy. Draw a picture in your notebook. If a child offers to do likewise, you've succeeded.

PLANNING YOUR TIME

Although travelers following the chapters of this book south and east along the Pacific Mexico coast necessarily arrive on the Costa Chica last, they should plan spending at least a week in this fascinating southeast corner of Mexico. Traveling east, out of Acapulco by either bus or car, the first highlights are the colorful **market towns**, both indigenous (Ometepec, Pinotepa Nacional, and

Jamiltepec) and *costeño* (Cuajinicuilapa), around the Oaxaca-Guerrero border. For travelers on a limited time budget, **Pinotepa Nacional** would be the best choice, being conveniently right off Highway 200. For *costeño* local flavor, **Cuajinicuilapa** is hands-down best, for a stroll around its vibrant midtown market and a visit to the unique and excellent town museum **(Museo de las Culturas Afromestizos)** of Afro-Mexican heritage and culture.

Divide the rest of your time between the petite downscale resorts of Puerto Escondido (two days, gorgeous little beaches, good restaurants, and **Playa Zicatela,** Mexico's hallowed ground of surfing). Continue to Puerto Ángel (three days, lovely blue bay, great snorkeling and fishing) and neighboring golden Playas **Zipolite** and **Mazunte** and its fine **turtle museum.**

Add a second week, and you'd gain the time to really kick back, starting in **Puerto Escondido,** with plenty of sunning, swimming, snoozing by the pool, and a day of beachcombing on Playa Zicatela. You could savor both Oaxaca- and Italian-style dinners, enjoy some wildlife-viewing with an extended tour around **Laguna Manialtepec** and/or horseback riding to the **Atotonilco** hot spring and sacred site.

With a couple more days around **Puerto Ángel** you could do a day of snorkeling at **Playa Estacahuite** and maybe even a **waterfall excursion, fishing,** or some surfing and boogie boarding at Playa Zipolite, and day trip or overnight at the breezy, coral-strewn **Bays of Huatulco,** and a stroll around the intimate **Crucecita** town plaza (good restaurants, handicrafts) and the **Santa Cruz de Huatulco** boat harbor (Bays of Huatulco catamaran tours).

Note: An alternative, very popular way to visit the Costa Chica would be to head south to the Oaxaca coast after a Oaxaca City visit.

Road to Puerto Escondido

If **driving** from Acapulco, mark your odometer at the traffic circle where Highways 95 and 200 intersect over the hill from Acapulco. If, on the other hand, you bypass that congested point via the Barra Vieja coastal bypass, set your odometer to zero at the point where you join with Highway 200 east, then simply subtract 20 miles (32 km) from the mileages along Highway 200 from Acapulco given in this chapter.

Fill up with gas before starting out in Acapulco. After that, Magna (unleaded) is available at Cruz Grande (56 miles, 91 km), Pinotepa Nacional (157 miles, 253 km), Puerto Escondido (247 miles, 398 km), and near Puerto Ángel (291 miles, 469 km).

If you're going **by bus,** ride one of the several daily first-class or second-class buses from the Estrella Blanca (Av. Ejido) terminal in Acapulco.

PLAYA VENTURA

Three miles east of the small town of Copala, 77 miles (123 km) from Acapulco, a roadside sign points toward Playa Ventura. Four miles down a paved road, which a truck-bus from Copala traverses regularly, you arrive pavement's-end at Ventura village. From there, a mile-long golden-sand beach arcs gently east. Past a lighthouse, the beach leads to a point, topped by a stack of granite rocks, known locally as Casa de Piedra (House of Stone).

Playa Ventura can provide virtually everything for a restful day or week on the beach. Several good tent camping or RV spots (for maneuverable medium-size rigs, vans, or campers) sprinkle the inviting, outcropping-dotted shoreline east of the village. Shady *palapas* set up by former campers stand ready for rehabilitation and reuse by new arrivals.

Surf fishing (with net-caught bait fish) is fine from the beach, while *pangas* can be hired for deep-sea catches. Good surfing breaks angle in from the points, and, during the rainy season, the behind-the-beach lagoon is good for fishing, shrimping, and wildlife-viewing. (Bring your kayak or inflatable raft.)

The palm-lined beach stretches southeast for miles. Past the picturesque Casa de Piedra outcropping, an intimate *palapa-* and *panga-*lined sandy cove curves invitingly to yet another palmy point, Pico del Monte. Past that lies still another, even more pristine, cove and beach.

Playa Ventura now has a small **community museum** (10 A.M.–5 P.M. Tues.–Sun.) with displays of locally discovered artifacts, pottery and local flora and fauna.

Accommodations and Food

Besides the village stores, food is available at a number of *loncherías* and beach *palapa* restaurants. Pioneer among all of these is the **Restaurant and Cabaña Pérez** . If anyone dispels the rumor that *costeño* folks are unfriendly, it's the hospitable family of father Bulmaro, mother Virginia, Inés, son Luis and his wife Inés, and daughter Hortencia Pérez, who were first to put together the modest beginnings of a little resort. Bulmaro and his family invite visitors to park (small) RVs in their lot, where they offer a friendly word, showers, a homemade swimming pool, kiddie pool, and a bit of shade for a reasonable $3 per person per day. For tenters, they rent spaces beneath their shady beachfront *ramada* for the same price.

Others have followed the Pérez example. From the Pérez compound, moving east (Oaxaca direction) along the beach, find plumy **Las Palmeras** with a shady, spacious grove for RV parking or tenting. Continue next door to beachfront restaurant and campground **Doña Maura,** with plenty of space for small-to-medium self-contained RVs and tents beneath shady palm-frond *ramadas*. Next comes a couple of inviting restaurants, first **El Faro,** with a working lighthouse, and finally the thatched **Jay** restaurant.

Most of **Playa Ventura's lodgings** are on the west, Acapulco side. Past the Pérezes', find the restaurant and hotel **Doña Celsa,** with

THE MIXTECS

Sometime during the 1980s, the Mixtecs regained their preconquest population of about 350,000. Of that total, around one-third speak only their own language. Their villages and communal fields spread over tens of thousands of square miles of remote mountain valleys north, west, and southwest of Oaxaca. Their homeland, the Mixteca, is divided into three distinct regions: Mixteca Alta, Mixteca Baja, and the Mixteca Costera.

The **Mixteca Alta** centers in the mountains about 100 road miles due west of Oaxaca city, in the high, cool roof of Oaxaca, centering on the market towns of Tlaxiaco and Juxtlahuaca.

Mixteca Baja communities, such as San Miguel Tequistepec, Tonalá, and Juxtlajuaca, dot the dry northwestern Oaxaca mountains and valleys, centering roughly on Huajuapan de León on Highway 190.

In the **Costera,** important Mixtec communities exist in or near Pinotepa Nacional, Huaxpaltepec, and Jamiltepec, all along Highway 200 in southwestern Oaxaca.

The Aztec-origin name Mixtecos (People of the Clouds) was translated directly from the Mixtec's name for their own homeland: Aunyuma (Land of the Clouds). The Mixtec's name for themselves, however, is Nyu-u Sabi (People of the Rain).

When the conquistadors arrived in Oaxaca, the Mixtecs were under the thumb of the Aztecs, who, after a long, bitter struggle, had wrested control of Oaxaca from combined Mixtec-Zapotec armies in 1486. The Mixtecs naturally resented the Aztecs, whose domination was transferred to the Spanish during the colonial period, and, in turn, to the mestizos during modern times. The Mixtecs still defer to the town Mexicans, but they don't like it. Consequently, many rural Mixtecs, with little state or national consciousness, have scant interest in becoming Mexicanized.

In isolated Mixtec communities, traditions still rule. Village elders hold final authority, parents arrange marriages through go-betweens, and land is owned communally. Catholic saints are thinly disguised incarnations of old gods such as Tabayukí, ruler of nature, or the capricious and powerful *tono* spirits that lurk everywhere.

In many communities, Mixtec women exercise considerable personal freedom. At home and in villages, they often still work barebreasted. And while their men get drunk and carry on during festivals, women dance and often do a bit of their own carousing. Whom they do it with is their own business.

about 20 clean, modern rooms, with tiled baths and hot-water showers, for about $25 d, $40 holidays. Alternatively, check out the nearby lineup of similar rustic lodgings, Cabañas Condesa, Hermoso Pacheco, and **Tomy** (tel. 744/501-8172, $18 d, 28 t or q), the best of the bunch, with about 20 very clean rooms, some upstairs with sea views, all with fans and private shower baths. Inviting extras include a breezy beachfront restaurant and pool.

About 1.5 miles farther down the beach, the **Restaurant el Profe** invites guests, with a petite palm-shaded grove, and a tent and small RV campground. Near that, **Cabañas la Perla Coyacuyul** (tel. 744/438-6145, $18 d, $27 with ocean view) offers rustic but comfortable

accommodations, with a pool, kiddie pool, and beachfront *palapa* restaurant.

SAN MARCOS, OMETEPEC, AND CUAJINICULAPA

A few larger towns along the road can provide a number of essential services, along with some sights worth seeing.

San Marcos

Thirty-six miles (58 km) east of Acapulco, San Marcos (pop. 10,000) has a bank (Banamex, tel. 745/453-0036, 9 A.M.–3 P.M. Mon.–Fri., with 24-hour ATM); a motel (**Le Carma,** tel./fax 745/453-0037, with about 24 rooms around an inviting pool and patio, for $23 d with fan

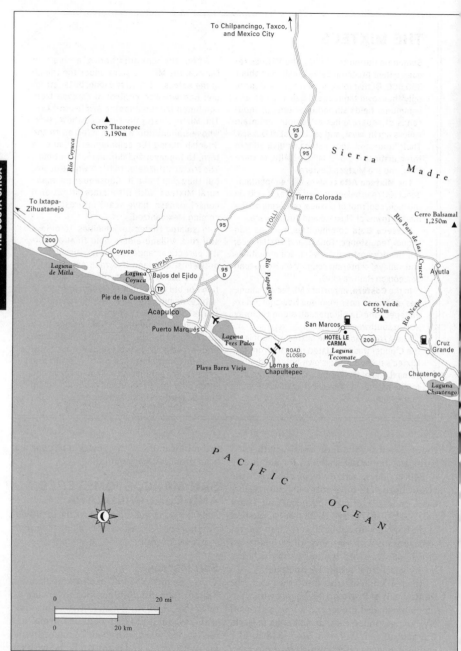

To Chilpancingo, Taxco, and Mexico City

95 D

95

Sierra Madre

Cerro Tlacotepec 3,190m

Río Coyuca

Tierra Colorada

Cerro Balsamal 1,250m

To Ixtapa-Zihuatanejo

95

200

(TOLL)

Río Paso de las Cruces

Coyuca

BYPASS

Ayutla

Laguna de Mitla

95 D

Laguna Coyuca

Bajos del Ejido

TP

Río Papagayo

Pie de la Cuesta

Cerro Verde 550m

Río Nexpa

Acapulco

San Marcos

Puerto Marqués

HOTEL LE CARMA

200

Cruz Grande

Laguna Tres Palos

ROAD CLOSED

Laguna Tecomate

Playa Barra Vieja

Lomas de Chapultepec

Chautengo

Laguna Chautengo

P A C I F I C   O C E A N

0   20 mi

0   20 km

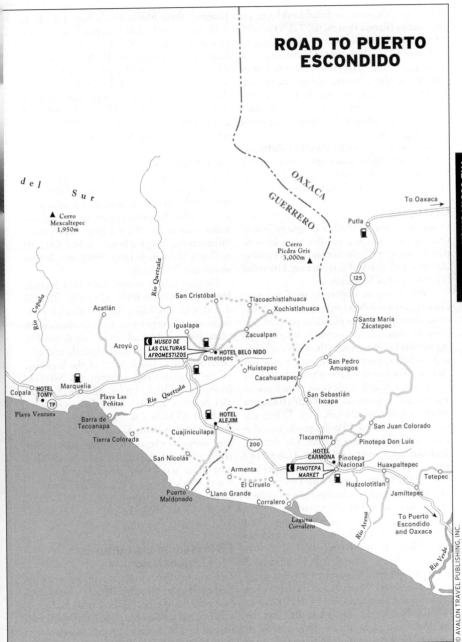

ROAD TO PUERTO ESCONDIDO

To Oaxaca

d e l S u r

▲ Cerro
Mexcaltepec
1,950m

Cerro
Piedra Gris
3,000m ▲

OAXACA
GUERRERO

Putla

125

Río Quetzala

Río Copala

San Cristóbal

Acatlán

Igualapa

Tlacoachistlahuaca
Xochistlahuaca

Santa María
Zácatepec

Azoyú

MUSEO DE
LAS CULTURAS
AFROMESTIZOS

Zacualpan

HOTEL BELO NIDO
Ometepec

San Pedro
Amusgos

Huistepec
Cacahuatapec

Marquelia

Copala

HOTEL
TOMY

TP

Playa Las
Peñitas

Río Quetzala

San Sebastián
Ixcapa

Playa Ventura

Barra de
Tecoanapa

Tierra Colorada

Cuajinicuilapa

HOTEL
ALEJIM

200

Tlacamama

San Juan Colorado

Pinotepa Don Luis

San Nicolás

HOTEL
CARMONA

Pinotepa
Nacional

Huaxpaltepec

Armenta

PINOTEPA
MARKET

Tetepec

El Ciruelo

Huazolotitlan

Jamiltepec

Puerto
Maldonado

Llano Grande

Corralero

To Puerto
Escondido
and Oaxaca

Laguna
Corralero

Río Arena

Río Verde

$32 with a/c); Centro de Salud health center; pharmacies (Farma Pronto, tel. 745/453-1697, 8 A.M.–10 P.M. Mon.–Fri.); a doctor (Mauricio Ibarra); street-front Ladatel card–operated telephones; and *telecomunicaciones* (long-distance telephone, money orders, and fax, tel. 745/453-0130). Find the pharmacy, bank, doctor, and more on the town *jardín*, on main street Hidalgo, about 0.3 mile (0.5 km) north of the highway.

For food, try homey **Restaurant Ruth** and **Restaurant Edith** across the street, on the highway, both open about 8 A.M.–9 P.M. daily, two blocks east of the Le Carma hotel.

Ometepec

Ometepec (pop. 15,000), a couple of hours' drive farther east, is accessible via a 10-mile paved road, which branches north off Highway 200 at a well-marked intersection 110 miles (175 km) east of Acapulco.

Besides being an important service center, Ometepec (elev. 2,000 feet) enjoys a cooler climate, drawing crowds of native peoples, notably Amusgos, from outlying villages to its big Sunday markets, one at the town entrance, and the other, mostly handicrafts, a mile farther on, downtown by the plaza. Many local buses follow paved roads from Ometepec to more remote centers, such as **Xochistlahuaca** (so-chees-tlah-hoo-AH-kah, pop. 3,000), the Amusgo town about 30 miles northeast, with a very colorful Sunday market. On the way Xochistlahuaca, not far off the road (about five miles north of town, turn left at the sign) you can visit **Cochoapa**, a town with a community museum that displays a number of very ancient Olmec-style stelae and sculptures.

In Ometepec itself, accommodations, food and essential services include recommendable hotels 【 **Hotel Belo Nido** (tel. 741/412-0141 or 741/412-0134, about $20 d), with fans and hot-water shower baths and an inviting pool-patio; and **Hotel Venus II** (on the left before the town entrance arch, tel. 741/415-8026 or 741/415-8027); restaurants **Las Delicias,** by the downtown plaza, 8 A.M.–10 P.M. daily, or homey all-female-run **Amparito** on side-street

Jiménez, three blocks north from the plaza, 7:30 A.M.–9 P.M. daily; banks with ATMs (Banamex, tel. 741/412-0880, 9 A.M.–4 P.M. Mon.–Fri., and long-hours HSBC, tel. 741/412-2878, 8 A.M.–7 P.M. Mon.–Fri., 8 A.M.–3 P.M. Sat.); a private hospital (De la Amistad, tel. 741/412-0985, with 24-hour emergency); public Seguro Social clinic (tel. 741/412-0392); and *telecomunicaciones* (tel. 741/412-0386) and post office (9 A.M.–3 P.M. Mon.–Fri.).

Cuajinicuilapa

Back on Highway 200, Cuajinicuilapa (kwah-hee-nee-kwee-LAH-pah, pop. 10,000), 125 miles (199 km) from Acapulco, is a major market town for the sprinkling of *costeño* communities, such as San Nicolás (pop. 5,000, eight miles south), along the beach road (at Km 201) to Punta Maldonado (pop. 1000), the drowsy south-seas fishing port.

Cuajinicuilapa accommodations include **Marin** (tel. 741/414-0021, $16 s with fan, $20 d with with fan, $23 s, $29 d with a/c), a few doors east of the town-center basketball court-plaza, comfortable and attractively decorated; and the tranquil, orchard-shaded, and spacious **Alejim** (a block north of the highway, on the Acapulco edge of town, tel. 741/414-0310, $16 s, $20 d with fan, $23 s, $28 d with a/c). Services include a bank (Banamex, with 24-hour ATM, 9 A.M.–4 P.M. Mon.–Fri.); a **Regional Hospital,** about half a mile (0.8 km) north of the town center; pharmacies (such as Farmapronto, tel. 741/414-1074); a post office (across the highway from the plaza, 8 A.M.–3 P.M. Mon.–Fri.); and *telecomunicaciones* a few doors away (tel. 741/414-0337, 9 A.M.–3 P.M. Mon.–Fri., 9 A.M.–12:30 P.M. Sat.–Sun.).

【 Museo de las Culturas Afromestizos

In Cuajinicuilapa, make it a priority to stop at this singular museum (10 A.M.–2 P.M. and 5–7 P.M. daily except Mon.) with many excellent displays depicting the Afro-Mexicans' origins in Africa, forced immigration to Mexico, plantation life, and their cultural heritage.

The museum houses a uniquely precious Afro-Mexican library, and also sponsors community dance, theater, instrumental music, and handicrafts workshops.

PINOTEPA NACIONAL

Pinotepa Nacional (pop. about 50,000; 157 miles, 253 km, east of Acapulco; 90 miles, 145 km, west of Puerto Escondido) and its neighboring communities form the hub of an important coastal indigenous region. Mixtec, Amusgo, Chatino, and other peoples stream into town for markets and fiestas in their traditional dress, ready to combine business with pleasure. They sell their produce and crafts—pottery, masks, handmade clothes—at the market, then later get tipsy, flirt, and dance.

The Name

So many people asked the meaning of their city's name that the town fathers wrote the explanation on a wall next to Highway 200 on the west side of town. Pinotepa comes from the Aztec-language words *pinolli* (crumbling) and *tepetl* (mountain); thus "Crumbling Mountain." The second part of the name came about because, during colonial times, the town was called Pinotepa Real (Royal). This wouldn't do after independence, so the name became Pinotepa Nacional, reflecting the national consciousness that emerged during the 1810–1821 struggle for independence.

The Mixtecs, the dominant regional group, disagree with all this, however. To them, Pinotepa has always been Ñií Yo-oko (Little Place). Only within the town limits do the Mexicans (mestizos), who own most of the town businesses, outnumber the Mixtecs. The farther from town you get, the more likely you are to hear people conversing in the Mixtec language, a tongue that uses a number of subtle tones to make meanings clear.

Getting Oriented

On Pinotepa's west (Acapulco) side, Highway 200 splits into the town's two major arteries,

THE COSTA CHICA

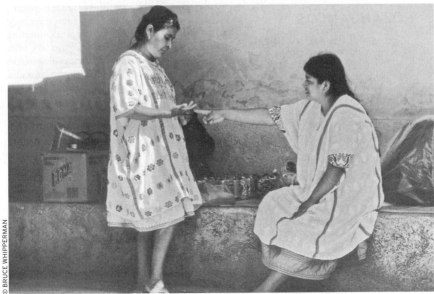

Amusgo women wear *huipiles* with designs distinctive of their home village.

© BRUCE WHIPPERMAN

which rejoin on the east (Puerto Escondido) side. The north, west-bound branch is called Aguirre Palancares; the south, east-bound branch, the more bustling of the two branches, passes between the town-center plaza and church and is called Avenida Porfirio Díaz on the west side and Avenida Benito Juárez on the east. The main north-south street, Avenida Pérez Gasga, runs past both the church front, which faces west, and the Presidencia Municipal (City Hall), which faces east, toward the town plaza.

C Pinotepa Market

Highway 200 passes a block north of the main town market, by the big, fenced-in secondary school, on the west side about a mile west of the central plaza. Despite the Pinotepa market's oft-exotic goods—snakes, iguanas, wild mountain fruits, forest herbs, and spices—its people, nearly entirely Mixtec, are its main attraction, especially on the big **Wednesday** and **Sunday** market days. Men wear pure-white loose cot-

---

POZAHUANCOS

To a coastal Mixtec woman, her *pozahuanco* is a lifetime investment symbolizing her maturity and social status, something that she expects to pass on to her daughters. Heirloom *pozahuancos* are wraparound, horizontally striped skirts of hand-spun thread. Women dye the thread by hand, always including a pair of necessary colors: a light purple *(morada)*, from secretions of tidepool-harvested snails, *Purpura patula pansa*, and scarlet red, dyed with cochineal, extracted from the beetle *Dactylopius coccus*, cultivated in the Valley of Oaxaca. Increasingly, women are weaving *pozahuancos* with synthetic thread, which has a slippery feel compared to the hand-spun cotton. Consider yourself lucky if you can get a traditionally made *pozahuanco* for as little as $100. If someone offers you a lookalike for $20, you know it's an imitation.

---

tons, topped by woven palm-leaf hats. Women wrap themselves in their lovely striped purple, violet, red, and navy blue *pozahuanco* sarong-like, horizontally striped skirts. Many women carry a polished tan *jicara* gourd soup bowl atop their heads, which, although it's not supposed to, looks like a whimsical hat. Older women (and younger ones with babies at their breasts) go bare-breasted with only their white *huipil* draped over their chests as a concession to mestizo custom. Others wear an easily removable *mandil*, a light cotton apron-halter above their *pozahuanco*. A few women can ordinarily be found selling beautiful handmade *pozahuancos*. (Alternatively, Artemio López Clavel, in his market shop, sells *pozahuancos*, both machine- and genuine hand-made.)

Festivals

Although the regular Pinotepa market days are big, they don't compare to the week before Easter (Semana Santa). People get ready for the finale with processions, carrying the dead Christ through town to the church each of the seven Fridays before Easter. The climax comes on Good Friday (Viernes Santa), when a platoon of young Mixtec men paint their bodies white to portray Jews, and while intoning ancient Mixtec chants shoot arrows at Christ on the cross. On Saturday, the people mournfully take the Savior down from the cross and bury him, and on Sunday gleefully celebrate his resurrection with a riot of fireworks, food, and folk dancing.

Although not as spectacular as Semana Santa, there's plenty of merrymaking, food, dancing, and processions around the Pinotepa *zócalo* church on July 25, the day of Pinotepa's patron, Santiago (St. James).

Accommodations

All of Pinotepa's recommendable hotels are basic but clean, and cost less than $30 d. None accepts credit cards. In approximate order of desirability:

The motel-style **Hotel Carmona** (Av. Porfirio Díaz 127, Pinotepa Nacional, Oaxaca 71600, tel. 954/543-2322, $22 s, $28 d, $34 t fan only; $30, $38, and $45 for a/c), about three blocks west of the plaza, offers three stories of 50 clean, not fancy but comfortable rooms with hot water shower bath and cable TV, with a big backyard garden with pool and sundeck. For festival dates, make reservations.

If the Carmona is full, check the two high-profile newer hotels, Pepe's and Las Gaviotas, beside the highway on the west side of town. Of the two, **Pepe's** (Carretera Pinotepa Nacional-Acapulco Km 1, Pinotepa Nacional, Oaxaca 71600, tel./fax 954/543-4347, tel. 954/543-3602, $18 s or d fan only, $32 with a/c) is the better choice. It offers 35 spacious, semideluxe rooms with good TV, hot water, restaurant, and parking. **Hotel las Gaviotas** (tel. 954/543-2838, fax 954/54320-56, $14 s, $20 d with fan; $22 and $28 with a/c) is more basic.

Next choice goes to clean **Hotel Marisa** (Av. Juárez 134, north side of the street, tel. 954/543-2101 or 954/543-3190, $14 s, $16 d t, $25 t with fan; $23 s or d, $30 t with a/c), downtown on the highway. All rooms have hot-water shower baths and parking.

Campers enjoy a tranquil spot (best during the dry late fall-winter-spring season) on the **Río Arena** about two miles east of Pinotepa. Eastbound, turn right onto the track just before the river bridge, and continue to the riverbank. Your neighbors will usually be poor but friendly sand collectors, set up on the riverside. You can also reach the opposite riverbank by turning left (eastbound) just after the bridge. Continue along the dirt track a few hundred yards, past a pumphouse on the left, to a fork that heads down to the riverbank. Notice the waterfall cascading down the rocky cliff across the river (which would be excellent for kayaking if you arrange some way of returning back upstream).

Food

For a light lunch or supper, try the very clean, family-run **Burger Bonny** (at the southeast corner of the main plaza, tel. 954/543-2016, 9 A.M.–10 P.M. Mon.–Sat., 5–10 P.M. Sun.) Besides several varieties of good hamburgers, Burger Bonny offers *tortas,* tacos, hot dogs ($1–3), and french fries, microwave popcorn, and *refrescos* ($1 or less).

Also worthy is traditional-style **Fonda Toñita** (a block north of the church-front, at the corner of Aguirre Palancares, 7 A.M.–9 P.M. Mon.–Sat.). Local folks flock here for the hearty afternoon *comida* ($4, pick the entrée, and you get rice and tortillas thrown in free); it's also good for basic breakfasts (eggs any style, pancakes, toast, jam, and coffee, $2–4).

Third restaurant choice goes to restaurant **Tacos Orientales** (on Pérez Gasga, half a block north of the churchfront, 6–11 P.M. daily) with 15 styles of tacos, from fish to *carnitas,* three for $2.50.

On the other hand, consider next-door *marisquería* **Peñitas,** which specializes in fresh seafood ($6–8) however you like it: fried, baked, breaded, *al mojo,* and more, 8 A.M.–midnight daily.

For a quick and convenient on-the-road breakfast, lunch, or dinner, stop by the restaurant of high-profile **Pepe's Hotel** (west of town, 8 A.M.–10 P.M. daily).

Shopping and Services

It's best to visit the market on Wednesday and Sunday when it's biggest. For film and film and digital processing, step into the **Arlette** photo shop (tel. 954/543-2766, 8 A.M.–8 P.M. Mon.–Sat., 8 A.M.–3 P.M. Sun.), on the south side of the plaza.

Exchange money over the counter or use the ATM at all Pinotepa banks. Try **Bancomer** (corner of Díaz and Progreso, two blocks west of the plaza, tel. 954/543-3022 or 954/543-3190, 8:30 A.M.–4 P.M. Mon.–Fri.); or **Banamex** across the street (9 A.M.–4 P.M. Mon.–Fri.). Alternatively, try **HSBC** bank (tel. 954/543-3949 or 954/543-3969, 8 A.M.–7 P.M. Mon.–Fri., 8 A.M.–3 P.M. Sat.), also on Avenida Progreso, but across Porfirio Díaz and uphill a block from Bancomer.

The *correo* (post office) is open 8 A.M.–7 P.M. Mon.–Fri., about half a mile west of downtown, a block past Hotel Pepe's and across the street. Find the *telecomunicaciones* office (tel. 954/543-2019) for money orders, public telephone, and fax, one block north of the plaza church, on Avenida Pérez Gasga (8 A.M.–7:30 P.M. Mon.–Fri., 9 A.M.–noon Sat.–Sun.). For telephone, use Ladatel card-operated street telephones or go to the *larga distancia* Lada Central telephone and fax office (tel. 954/543-2547, 9 A.M.–9 P.M. daily) on the plaza, south side.

For a doctor, go to the **Clínica Rodríguez** (503 Aguirre Palancares, tel. 954/543-2330), one block north, two blocks west of the central plaza church-front. Get routine medications at one of several town pharmacies, such as the 24-hour *farmacia* on Díaz, a block west, downhill, from the central plaza church-front.

Check your email at Switch **Internet** store, at the plaza's southeast corner, 10 A.M.–9 P.M. daily.

Getting There and Away
BY CAR OR RV
Highway 200 connects west to Acapulco (160 miles, 258 km) in an easy 4.5 hours' driving time. The 89-mile (143-km) connection to Puerto Escondido can be done safely in about 2.5 hours. Additionally, the 239-mile (385-km) Highway 125-Highway 190 route connects Pinotepa Nacional to Oaxaca, via Putla de Guerrero and Tlaxiaco (136 miles, 219 km). Although winding most of the way and potholed at times, the road is generally uncongested. It's safely driveable in a passenger car with caution, from Pinotepa to Oaxaca (follow the toll *autopista* near Oaxaca) in about eight hours (under dry conditions) at the wheel, and seven hours in the reverse, downhill, direction from Oaxaca.

BY BUS
From the new **Camionera Central** (Central Bus Station), about a mile west of downtown, several long-distance lines connect Pinotepa Nacional with destinations north, northwest, east, and west. **Estrella Blanca,** tel. 954/543-3194, via subsidiaries Turistar, Elite, Cuauhtémoc, Gacela, and Flecha Roja, offers several daily first- and second-class *salidas de paso* (departures passing through) along coast Highway

200: west to Acapulco, Zihuatanejo, Lázaro Cárdenas, and Mexico City; and east to Puerto Escondido, Pochutla (Puerto Ángel), Bahías de Huatulco, and Salina Cruz.

Other independent, mostly second-class lines also operate out of the same terminal. **Fletes y Pasajes,** tel. 954/543-6016, connects with inland points, via Putla de Guerrero, Tlaxiaco, and Teposcolula along Highway 125, continuing along Highway 190 via Nochixtlán, to Oaxaca. **Estrella del Valle,** tel. 954/543-5476, also connects with Oaxaca, but in the opposite direction, via Highway 200 east to Puerto Escondido and Pochutla, thence north along Highway 175 via San José del Pacífico and Miahuatlán to Oaxaca. **Estrella Roja del Sureste,** tel. 954/543-6017, connects by yet another route with Oaxaca, along Highway 200 east to Puerto Escondido, thence north along Highway 131, via El Vidrio (Juquila) and Sola de Vega, to Oaxaca.

EXCURSIONS NORTH OF PINOTEPA
The local patronal festival year begins early, on Jan. 20, at **Pinotepa Don Luis** (pop. 5,000), about 15 miles, by back roads, northeast of Pinotepa Nacional, with the uniquely Mixtec festival of San Sebastián. Village bands blare, fireworks pop and hiss, and penitents crawl, until the finale, when dancers whirl the local favorite dance, Las Chilenas.

Yet another exciting time around Pinotepa Nacional is during **Carnaval,** when nearby communities put on big extravaganzas. Pinotepa Don Luis, sometimes known as Pinotepa Chica (Little Pinotepa), is famous for wooden masks the people make for their big Carnaval festival. The celebration usually climaxes on the Sunday before Ash Wednesday, when everyone seems to be in costume and a corps of performers gyrates in the traditional dances: Paloma (Dove), Tigre (Jaguar), Culebra (Snake), and Tejón (Badger).

Pinotepa Don Luis bubbles over again with excitement during Semana Santa, when the faithful carry fruit- and flower-decorated trees to the church on Good Friday, explode Judas effigies on Saturday, and celebrate by dancing most of Easter Sunday.

San Juan Colorado, a few miles north of Pinotepa Don Luis, usually appears as just another dusty little town until Carnaval, when its festival rivals that of its neighbors. Subsequently, on Nov. 29, droves of Mixtec people come into town to honor their patron, San Andres. After the serious part at the church, they celebrate with a cast of favorite dancing characters such as Malinche, Jaguar, Turtle, and Charros (Cowboys).

Amusgo Country

Cacahuatepec (pop. about 5,000; on Highway 125 about 25 miles north of Pinotepa Nacional) and its neighboring community **San Pedro Amusgos** are important centers of the Amusgo-speaking people. Approximately 20,000 Amusgos live in a roughly 30-mile-square region straddling the Guerrero-Oaxaca state border. Their homeland includes, besides Cacahuatepec and San Pedro Amusgos, Xochistlahuaca, Zacoalpán, and Tlacoachistlahuaca on the Guerrero side.

The Amusgo language is linguistically related to Mixtec, although it's unintelligible to Mixtec speakers. Before the conquest, the Amusgos were subject to the numerically superior Mixtec kingdoms until the Amusgos were conquered by the Aztecs in 1457, and later by the Spanish.

Now, most Amusgos live as subsistence farmers, supplementing their diet with occasional fowl or small game. Amusgos are best known to the outside world for their lovely animal-, plant-, and human-motif *huipiles,* which Amusgo women always seem to be hand-embroidering on their doorsteps.

Although Cacahuatepec enjoys a big market each Sunday, that doesn't diminish the importance of its big Easter weekend festival, the day of Todos Santos (All Saints' Day), Nov. 1, and Day of the Dead, Nov. 2, when, at the cemetery, people welcome their ancestors' return to rejoin the family.

San Pedro Amusgos celebrations are among the most popular regional fiestas. On June 29, the day of San Pedro, people participate in religious processions, and costumed participants dressed as Moors and Christians, bulls, jaguars, and mules dance before crowds of men in traditional whites and women in beautiful heirloom *huipiles.* Later, on the first Sunday of October, folks crowd into town to enjoy the traditional processions, dances, and sweet treats of the fiesta of the Virgen de la Rosario (Virgin of the Rosary).

Even if you miss the festivals, San Pedro Amusgos is worth a visit to buy *huipiles* alone. Three or four shops sell them along the main street through town. Look for the sign of **Trajes Regionales Élia,** the little store run by Edin, the welcoming wife of late Élia Guzmán, tel. 954/582-8697. Besides dozens of beautiful embroidered garments, she stocks a few Amusgo books and offers friendly words of advice and local information.

EXCURSIONS EAST OF PINOTEPA

For 30 or 40 miles east of Pinotepa Nacional, where road kilometer markers begin at zero again near the central plaza, Highway 200 stretches through the coastal Mixtec heartland, intriguing to explore, especially during festival times. The population of **San Andres Huaxpáltepec** (oo-wash-PAHL-tay-payk), about 10 miles east of Pinotepa, sometimes swells from about 5,000 to 20,000 or more during the three or four days before the day of Jesus the Nazarene, on the fourth Friday of Lent (or in other words, the fourth Friday after Ash Wednesday). The entire town spreads into a warren of shady stalls, offering everything from TVs to stone metates. (Purchase of a corn-grinding metate, which, including *mano* stone roller, sells for about $25, is as important to a Mixtec family as a refrigerator is to an American. Mixtec husband and wife usually examine several of the concave stones, deliberating the pros and cons of each before deciding.)

The Huaxpaltepec Nazarene fair is typical of the larger Oaxaca country expositions. Even the highway becomes a lineup of stalls;

whole native clans camp under the trees, and mules, cows, and horses wait patiently around the edges of a grassy trading lot as men discuss prices. (The fun begins when a sale is made, and the new owner tries to rope and harness his bargain steed.)

Even sex is customarily for sale within a quarter of very tightly woven no-see-through grass houses, patrolled by armed guards. Walking through, you may notice that, instead of the usual women, one of the houses offers men, dressed in low-cut gowns, lipstick, and high-heeled shoes.

Huazolotitlán

At nearby Santa María Huazolotitlán (pop. 3,000), several resident woodcarvers craft excellent masks. Local favorites are jaguars, lions, rabbits, bulls, and human faces. Given a photograph (or a sitting), one of them might even carve your likeness for a reasonable fee. (Figure perhaps $40–60.) Near the town plaza, ask for José Luna, Lázaro Gómez, or Idineo Gómez (tel. 954/518-3115), all of whom are related and live in *barrio* Ñií Yucagua.

Textiles are also locally important. Visit the *palacio municipal* on the town plaza, and see the for-sale display of colorfully embroidered animal and floral motif *huipiles*, *manteles*, and *servilletas* (native smocks, tablecloths, and napkins). You might also be able to bargain for a genuine heirloom *pozahuanco* (handwoven wrap-around skirt) for a reasonable price.

Besides all the handicrafts, Huazolotitlán people celebrate the important local **Fiesta de la Virgen de la Asunción** around Aug. 13–16. The celebrations customarily climax with a number of favorite traditional dances, in which you can see why masks are locally important, especially in the dance of the Tiger and the Turtle. The finale comes a day later, celebrated with the ritual dance of the Chareos, dedicated to the Virgin.

Get to Huazolotitlán (ooah-shoh-loh-teet-LAN) in about two miles along the paved road that forks south uphill from Highway 200 in Huaxpaltepec. Drive, or hitchhike

(with caution), ride the local bus, or hire a taxi for about $3.

Santiago Jamiltepec

About 18 miles (at Km 30) east of Pinotepa Nacional is the hilltop town of Santiago Jamiltepec (hah-meel-teh-PAYK, for short). Two-thirds of its 20,000 inhabitants are Mixtec. A grieving Mixtec king named the town in memory of his infant son, Jamilly, who was carried off by an eagle from this very hilltop.

The market, while busy most any day, is biggest and most colorful on Thursday. The town's main fixed-date festivals are celebrated on Sept. 1, Jan. 1, and Feb. 15. In addition, Jamiltepec celebrates its famous pre-Easter (week following Domingo de Ramos, or Palm Sunday) festival, featuring neighborhood candlelight processions accompanied by 18th-century music. Hundreds of the faithful bear elaborate wreaths and palm decorations to the foot of their church altars.

Jamiltepec is well worth a stop if only to visit the handicrafts shop **Yu-uku Cha-kuaa** (Hill of Darkness) of Santiago de la Cruz Velasco. Personable Santiago runs both his home shop and a better stocked one at the Jamiltepec plaza market, because the government cluster of shops (Centro Artesanal de la Costa, on the highway) was closed down, victim of a dispute over control.

Some of their crafts—masks, *huipiles*, carvings, hats—occupy the shelves and racks in Santiago's shop. Find it, signed "Artesanía Yu-uku Cha-kuaa," in the town center warren of stalls (ask for Santiago by name and someone will probably offer to guide you there). He usually stays open until about 4 P.M.

If you want to linger overnight, Jamiltepec has a couple of recommendable hotels. Check out the mod **Hotel Mirador** (down on the highway, west side of town, tel. 954/559-2448, $17 d with fans, $25 with a/c) with about 20 comfortable, albeit dark, rooms. Also worthy downtown is **Hotel Díaz** (in the town center, tel. 954/582-9103, fax 582-9104, $12 d), with about 10 clean but a bit worn upstairs patio rooms, with fans.

LAGUNAS DE CHACAHUA NATIONAL PARK AND VICINITY

The Lagunas de Chacahua National Park spreads for about 20 miles of open-ocean beach shoreline and islet-studded jungly lagoons midway between Pinotepa Nacional and Puerto Escondido. Tens of thousands of birds typical of a host of Mexican species fish the waters and nest in the mangroves of the two main lagoons, Laguna Pastoría on the east side and Laguna Chacahua on the west.

The fish and wildlife of the lagoons, overfished and overhunted during recent years by local people, are now recovering. Commercial fishing is now strictly licensed. A platoon of Marines patrols access roads, shorelines, and the waters themselves, making sure catches are within legal limits. Crocodiles were hunted out during the 1970s, but the government is restoring them with a hatchery on Laguna Chacahua.

For most visitors, mainly Mexican families on Sunday outings, access is by boat, except for one rugged dirt road, impassable in the wet season, and rutted and dusty in the dry. From east-side Zapotalito village, the local fishing cooperative offers full- and half-day boat excursions to the beaches, Playa Hermosa on the east side and Playa Chacahua on the west.

Exploring Lagunas de Chacahua

Zapotalito, on the eastern shore of Laguna Pastoría, is the busiest access point to the Lagunas de Chacahua. (San Jose Progreso is another one.) Get to Zapotalito (3 miles, 5 km) from the signed turnoff at Highway 200 Km 82, 51 miles from Pinotepa and 41 miles from Puerto Escondido. (Taxis and local buses run from Río Grande all the way to Zapotalito on the lagoon, while second-class buses from Puerto Escondido and Pinotepa Nacional will drop you on the highway.)

From the Zapotalito landings, the boat

cooperative, Sociedad Cooperativa Turística Escondida, enjoys a monopoly for transporting visitors on the lagoons. Their standard full-day trip goes all the way to **Playa Chacahua,** at the far western corner of the Chacahua lagoon, for sunning, beach play, and feasting in beachfront *palapa* restaurants.

The boatmen used to make their livings fishing; now they mostly ferry tourists. Having specialized in hauling in fish, they are generally neither wildlife-sensitive nor wildlife-knowledgeable. Canopied power-boats, seating about 10, make long, full-day trips for about $70 per boat. (For a cheaper option, go by **Cooperativa Faro de Chacahua**

LAGUNAS DE CHACAHUA ALTERNATIVES

Few roads penetrate the thick tropical deciduous forest surrounding the lagoons. Well-prepared adventurers can try to thumb a ride or drive a rugged high-clearance vehicle (dry season only) along the very rough 18-mile forest track to Chacahua village from San José del Progreso, which is on Highway 200, 36 miles (58 km) from Pinotepa Nacional. Before setting out, check with local residents or storekeepers about safety and road conditions.

If you have a boat or kayak, you can try launching your own excursion on Laguna Pastoría. The Cooperativa members, being both poor and protective of their interests, may ask you for a "launching fee," whether they're entitled to it or not.

Some of the islands in Laguna Pastoría are high and forested and might be bug-free enough during the dry Nov.-Feb. months for a relaxing few days of wilderness camping, kayaking, and wildlife viewing. Another alternative is to pay a boatman to drop you at your choice of islands and pick you up at a specified later time. Take everything, especially drinking water and insect repellent.

boat collective, $5 per person Chacahua tour, on the shoreline, about 200 yards past the main landing.)

An alternate, more economical (about $30 per boat) half-day excursion takes visitors to nearby idyllic **Playa Cerro Hermosa** at the mouth of Laguna Pastoría for a couple of hours' beach play and snorkeling—if you bring your own snorkeling gear. On the other hand, you can save yourself $30 and drive, taxi, or walk the approximately two miles along the shoreline road from Zapotalito to Playa Cerro Hermosa. Here you'll find a lovely open-ocean beach good for surf-fishing and beach sports, camping, a wildlife-rich lagoon mangrove wet-land, and several *palapa* restaurants.

A much cheaper, but slower, transportation-only option exists. Take the local *colectivo* boat (about $2 one-way) that leaves every hour from the main Zapotalito landing. It drops you at the El Corral dock on Chacahua island, from which you can ride a truck (about $2) to Chacahua village. Unless you start early, count on an overnight at Chacahua village.

On the other hand, the full-day private excursion to Playa Chacahua, about 14 miles distant, unfortunately seems to necessitate a fast trip across the lagoon. It's difficult to get the boat drivers to slow down. They roar across broad Laguna Pastoría, scattering flocks of birds ahead of them. They wind among the islands, with names such as Escorpión (Scorpion), Venados (Deer), and Pinuelas (Little Pines), sometimes slowing for viewing multitudes of nesting pelicans, herons, and cormorants. They pick up speed again in the narrow jungle channel between the lagoons, roaring past idyllic, somnolent El Corral village, and break into open water again on Laguna Chacahua.

The tour takes you first to the **crocodile hatchery,** at Chacahua west-side village on the west side of the lagoon, home to about two dozen local *costeño* families, a shabby hotel, and a pair of lagoonside *palapa* restaurants. Past the rickety crocodile caretaker's quarters are a few enclosures housing about 100 crocodiles segregated according to size, from hatchlings to six-foot-long toothy green adults.

© BRUCE WHIPPERMAN

Playa Chacahua has very surfable waves.

The tour climaxes at the east-side half of Chacahua village and beach across the estuary. **Playa Chacahua,** lovely *because* of its isolation, is formed of golden-white sand, washed by gently rolling waves, and seems perfect for all beach activities. You can snorkel off the rocks nearby, fish in the breakers, and surf the intermediate breaks that angle in on the west side. A few beachfront hotels offer rough, non-recommendable accommodations. A line-up of *palapas* provide food and drinks (don't miss María's enchiladas) and, for beachcombers, wildlife-viewers, and backpackers (who carry their own water), the breezy, jungle-backed beach spreads for 10 miles east.

The best hotels are on the uncrowded lagoon-front, a short walk north from the beach. Here, palms line the placid lagoon, shading the **Restaurant and Hotel Siete Mares** (Seven Seas; tel. 954/588-1340, $10 pp negotiable) south-seas tourist *cabañas.* The hotel's owner-chef, friendly Doña Meche, offer a quiet, rustic tropical retreat, with about 20 cabins with showers and toilets. She cooks hearty meals in her small restaurant.

Doña Meche's son, Reynaldo and his wife, Juana, also rent rustic but comfortable cabañas for about the same rates. Reynaldo's **Los Almendros** plain but comfortable rooms rent for about $20 d, with private toilets and showers. Reynaldo also arranges lagoon wildlife-viewing boat tours, for about $20 per person.

Juana's accommodations, **Cabañas Delfines** (tel. 954/588-3800, $20 d with fans, $30 for a/c, #3 tent site), are more deluxe and inviting. She also welcomes tenters to her **campground,** including hammock-hung **palapa** shelters and showers.

Some groceries and fruits and vegetables are available at **Abarrotes Nayeli** store, on the lagoon-front, by Hotel Siete Mares.

Río Grande

Río Grande (pop. 15,000), five miles east of the Lagunas de Chacahua-Zapotalito access road, is a transportation, supply, and service point for the region. Right on the highway are *abarroterías* (groceries), pharmacies and doctors, and Ladatel card–operated street telephones.

The downscale **Hotel Río** (Av. Puebla, Río Grande, Oaxaca 71830, tel. 954/582-6033, $11 s, $13 d with fans, $18 with a/c) is the big white building off the highway's north side, at the west end of town. It offers 22 plain but clean rooms on two floors, encircling a spacious parking courtyard. The rooms have toilets, but tepid (not hot) water.

A pair of restaurants that stand side-by-side across the street offer good eating options. Fancier is **Finca de los Abuelos** (Grandparents' Farm; tel. 954/582-6033, 7 A.M.–10 P.M. daily). Here, in a rustic faux rancho atmosphere, you can select from a long menu of breakfasts, Oaxaca specialties, soups, salads, seafood, and steaks ($3–8).

Next door, the friendly, family-run **Restaurant Río Grande** (7 A.M.–10 P.M. daily) provides good cheer and hearty meals, especially a delicious four-course set lunch *comida corrida* (soup, rice, entrée, and dessert, $4) afternoons.

A good second choice, with pool, good for a rest, lunch, and swimming stop, is **Balneario las Delicias** water park, with shaded tables and snack bar, at Km 102.

Las Delicias Balneario Restaurant and Hotel

Las Delicias (Carretera 200, Km 107, Río Grande, tel. 954/559-2480, 8 A.M.–7 P.M. daily, $5 pp entrance, rooms $20 d with fan, $30 with a/c), a grassy palm- and *palapa*-shaded *balneario,* or pool park, provides a relaxing food and lodging option only a few miles east of Río Grande. For about $5 entrance per person, families can stay the whole day, enjoying a big blue pool, kiddie pool, playground equipment, and plenty of shady room to run around within a fenced garden park. The restaurant serves from a long, reconizable menu with plenty of (but not exclusively) breakfast and seafood selections ($3–10). The several simply decorated but clean and comfortable hotel rooms are located thoughtfully away from highway noise and have hot-water shower baths. If you're arriving on a weekend or holiday, best reserve at least a week in advance.

◖ LAGUNA MANIALTEPEC

Sylvan, mangrove-fringed Laguna Manialtepec, about 10 miles west of Puerto Escondido,

LAGUNA MANIALTEPEC

To Río Grande and Pinotepa Nacional — **200**

Río Manialtepec

Tropical

Deciduous

Forest

El Zacatal

El Corozal

El Carnero

Las Negras

◖ LAGUNA MANIALTEPEC

HOTEL ISLA EL GALLO

Isla El Gallo

La Alejandria   Las Hamacas

200

To Puerto Escondido

Tropical

Deciduous

La Salina

Forest

Sandy   Beach

PACIFIC OCEAN

0   1 mi
0   1 km

© AVALON TRAVEL PUBLISHING, INC.

is a repository for a trove of Pacific Mexico wildlife. Unlike Lagunas de Chacahua, Laguna Manialtepec is relatively deep and fresh most of the year, except occasionally during the rainy season when its main source, the Río Manialtepec, breaks through its sandbar and the lagoon becomes a tidal estuary. Consequently lacking a continuous supply of ocean fry for sustained fishing, Laguna Manialtepec has been left to local people, a few Sunday visitors, and its wildlife.

Laguna Manialtepec abounds with birds. Of the hundreds of species frequenting the lagoon, 40 or 50 are often spotted in a morning outing. Among the more common are the olivaceous cormorant and its relative, the anhinga; and herons, including the tricolored, green-backed, little blue, and black-crowned night heron. Other common species include ibis, parrots, egrets, and ducks, such as the Muscovy and the black-bellied whistling duck. Among the most spectacular are the huge great blue herons, while the most entertaining are the northern *jacanas,* or lily walkers, who scoot across lily pads as if they were the kitchen floor.

Manialtepec tours can be arranged through travel agencies in Puerto Escondido. Although most of these advertise so-called "ecotours," genuine options include **Hidden Voyages Ecotours,** led by Canadian ornithologist Michael Malone, and **Lalo's Ecotours** guides, trained by Michael Malone. (For contact details, see *Tours* under *Excursions from Puerto Escondido* in the *Puerto Escondido* section.)

Las Hamacas, La Alejandria, and Isla El Gallo

Laguna Manialtepec is ripe for kayaking, boating, and camping along its shoreline. Bring plenty of repellent, however. Alternatively, RV and tent campers can settle in for a few days in one of a handful of shady restaurant compounds along the shore.

The most developed of these is Las Hamacas (tel. 954/588-8552) at the lake's eastern end, near the Km 126 marker, about 10 miles (16 km) west of Puerto Escondido. The owners

have gotten off to a good start in creating their version of paradise, with a minifarm of ducks, goats, sheep, cattle and rabbits, a lakeshore *palapa* restaurant, kayak and sailboat rentals, and lagoon tours.

One kilometer farther west is the sleepy little family-run pocket Eden of **La Alejandria** (cell tel. dial 044-954/550-2873 locally, 01-954/550-2873 long-distance), which nestles along its 100 yards of lakefront, shaded by palms and great spreading trees. It's so idyllic that the *Tarzan* TV series picked La Alejandria for its setting, adding a rustic lake tree house (now destroyed by hurricanes) to the already gorgeous scene. Embellishing all this is a homey restaurant/bar, screened in from bugs, decorated with animal trophies, and reminiscent of an old-time East African safari lodge.

La Alejandria rents a basic cabin (check for mildew) with toilet and shower for up to four, for $15; also about six palm-shaded self-contained RV spaces with electricity and water (be prepared with your own long extension and hose) for about $10, $15 with electricity. Camping spaces go for $10; launch your boat from their boat ramp for $10.

Another kilometer west of La Alejandria is lakefront restaurant and dock **Isla el Gallo** (tel. 954/588-7280 or 954/588-3650), perfect for a day or a week exploring the lagoon. At least stop for lunch at the restaurant, then follow up on more local options, such as snoozing in a hammock, volleyball, swimming, kayaking and bird-watching along the mangrove-decorated shoreline, launching your own canoe or boat ($5), or hiring one of El Gallo's boatmen to take you on a lagoon excursion from the dock.

If you decide to linger, Isla el Gallo offers 18 modern, invitingly furnished lakefront rooms. The lower rooms' windows, unfortunately don't open for fresh air. Ask for one of the upper-floor rooms, with doors opening to private balconies and lake views. Tariffs run $46 s or d, $50 t, $55 q, with hot water shower baths and a/c.

Puerto Escondido

Decorated by intimate coves and sandy beaches, and washed by jade-tinted surf, Puerto Escondido enjoys its well-deserved popularity. Despite construction of a jet airport in the 1980s, Puerto Escondido remains a place where most everything is within walking distance, no high-rise blocks anyone's sunset view, and moderately priced accommodations and good food remain the rule.

Puerto Escondido (Hidden Port) got its name from the rocky Punta Escondida that shelters its intimate half-moon cove, which perhaps would have remained hidden if local farmers had not discovered that coffee thrives beneath the cool forest canopy of the lush seaward slopes of the Sierra Madre del Sur. They began bringing their precious beans for shipment when the port of Escondido was established in 1928.

When the coast highway was pushed through during the 1970s, Puerto Escondido's then-dwindling coffee trade was replaced by a growing trickle of vacationers, attracted by the splendid isolation, low prices, and high waves. With some of the best surfing breaks in North America, a permanent surfing colony soon got established. This led to more non-surfing visitors, who, by the 1990s, were arriving in droves to enjoy the comfort and food of a string of small hotels and restaurants lining Puerto Escondido's still-beautiful but no longer hidden cove.

AROUND TOWN
Getting Oriented

Puerto Escondido (pop. 55,000) seems like two towns separated by Highway 200, which runs along the bluff above the beach. The upper town is where most of the local folks live and go about their business, while in the town below the highway, most of the restaurants, hotels, and shops spread along a sin-

on the beach at dusk, Puerto Escondido

© BRUCE WHIPPERMAN

gle, touristy, beachfront street mall, **Avenida Pérez Gasga** (known locally as the **adoquín,** ah-doh-KEEN), where motor traffic is allowed only before noon. Afternoons, chains go up, blocking cars at either end.

Beyond the west-end chain, Pérez Gasga leaves the beach, winding uphill to the highway, where it enters the upper town at the *crucero,* Puerto Escondido's only signaled intersection. From there, Pérez Gasga continues into the upper town as Avenida Oaxaca, National Highway 131.

Getting Around

In town, walk or take a taxi, which should cost no more than $2 to anywhere. For longer excursions, such as to Lagunas Manialtepec and Chacahua (westbound), and as far as Pochutla (near Puerto Ángel) eastbound, ride one of the very frequent *urbano* minibuses that stop at the *crucero,* or rent a car from Budget (on the west side, a couple of blocks east of the airport, tel./fax 954/582-0312 or 954/582-0315, budget33@hotmail.com).

BEACHES AND ACTIVITIES

Puerto Escondido's bayfront begins at the sheltered rocky cove beneath the wave-washed lighthouse point, Punta Escondida. The shoreline continues easterly along Playa Principal, the main beach, curving southward at Playa Marineros, and finally straightening into long, open-ocean Playa Zicatela. The sand and surf change drastically, from narrow sand and calm ripples at Playa Principal to a wide beach pounded by gigantic rollers at Zicatela.

Playa Principal

The best place to appreciate Puerto Escondido is not from the cluttered *adoquín,* but from one of the shady restaurants that front Playa Principal. It's here that Mexican families love to frolic on Sunday and holidays and sun-starved winter vacationers doze in their chairs and hammocks beneath the palms. The sheltered west side is very popular with local people who arrive afternoons

with nets and haul in small troves of silvery fish. The water is great for wading and swimming, clear enough for casual snorkeling, but generally too calm for anything else in the cove. However, a few hundred yards east around the bay the waves are generally fine for bodysurfing and boogie boarding, with a minimum of undertow. Although it's not a particularly windy location, sailboarders do occasionally bring their own equipment and practice their art here. Fishing is fine off the rocks or by small boat, easily launched from the beach. Shells, generally scarce on Playa Principal, are more common on less-crowded Playa Zicatela.

Playa Marinero

As the beach curves toward the south, it increasingly faces the open ocean. Playa Marinero begins about 100 yards from the "Marineros," the east-side rocky outcroppings in front of the Hotel Santa Fe. The rocks' jutting forms are supposed to resemble visages of grizzled old sailors. Here the waves can be rough. Swimmers beware: Appearances can be deceiving. Intermediate surfers practice here, as do daring boogie boarders and bodysurfers.

Turn around and gaze inland at the giant Mexican flag, waving in the breeze on the hill above the east-side beach. At dawn every rainless day soldiers of the 54th infantry battalion raise the colossal banner, which measures about 82 by 59 feet (18 by 25 meters) and is so heavy that it takes 25 of them to do it.

◖ Playa Zicatela

Past the Marinero rocks you enter Mexico's hallowed ground of surfing, Playa Zicatela. The wide beach, of fine golden-white sand, stretches south for miles to a distant cliff and point. The powerful Pacific swells arrive unimpeded, crashing to the sand with awesome, thunderous power. Both surfers and non-surfers congregate year-round, waiting for the renowned Escondido "pipeline," where grand waves curl into whirling liquid tunnels, which expert surfers skim through like

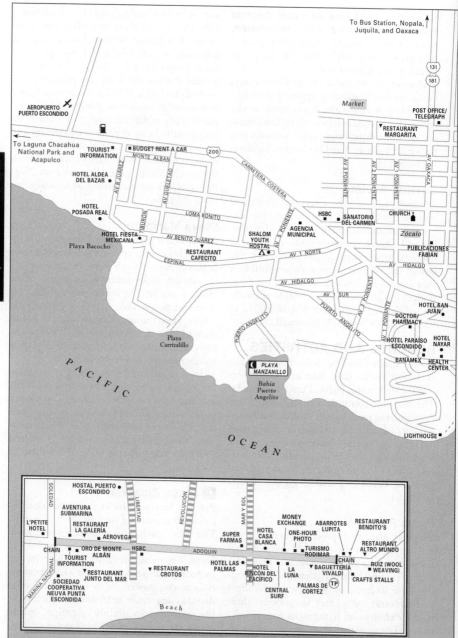

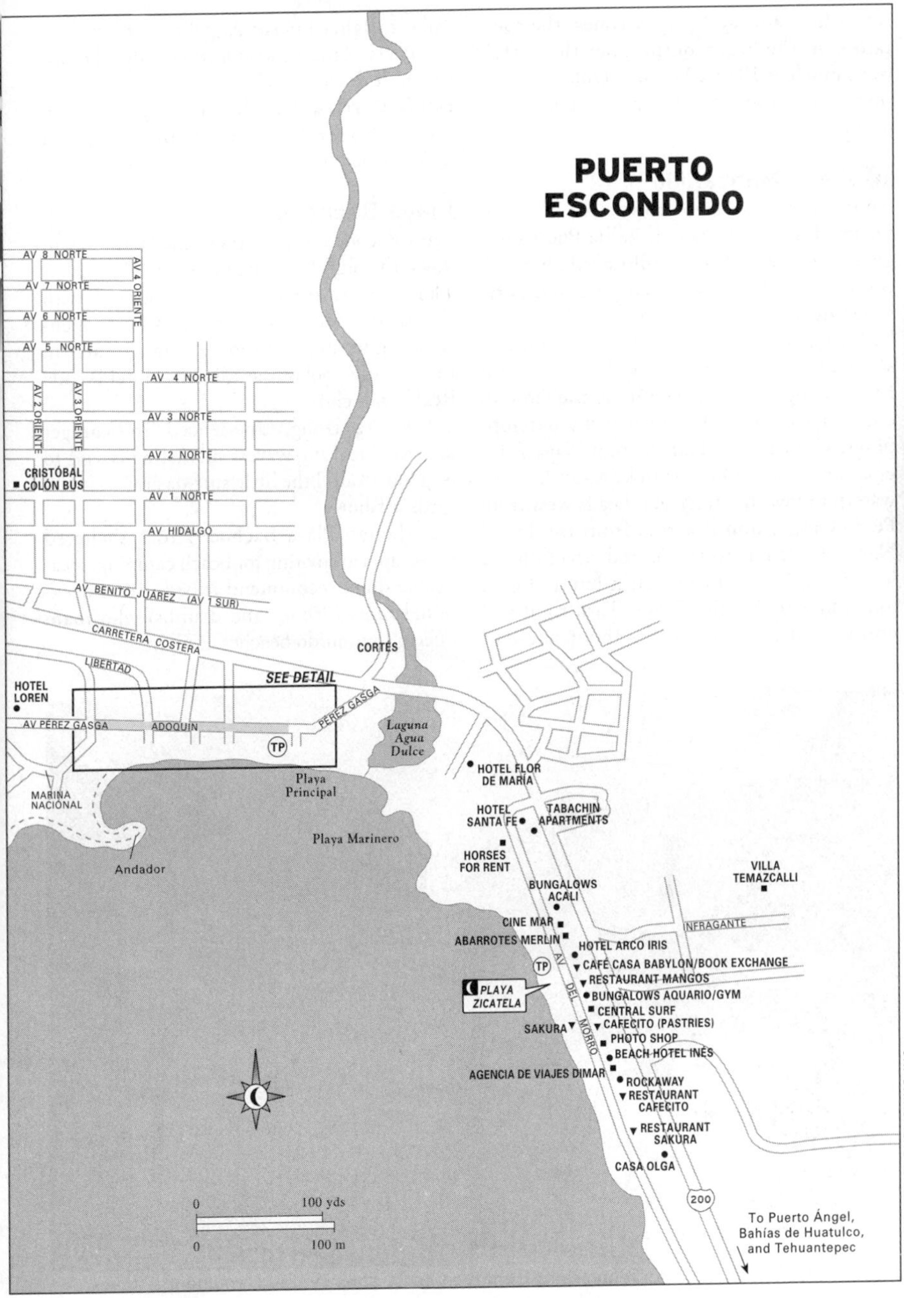

PUERTO ESCONDIDO

AV 8 NORTE
AV 7 NORTE
AV 6 NORTE
AV 5 NORTE
AV 4 ORIENTE
AV 3 ORIENTE
AV 2 ORIENTE
AV 4 NORTE
AV 3 NORTE
AV 2 NORTE
AV 1 NORTE
AV HIDALGO
CRISTÓBAL COLÓN BUS
AV BENITO JUÁREZ (AV 1 SUR)
CARRETERA COSTERA
LIBERTAD
HOTEL LOREN
AV PÉREZ GASGA
ADOQUIN
SEE DETAIL
CORTÉS
PÉREZ GASGA
TP
Laguna Agua Dulce
Playa Principal
MARINA NACIONAL
Andador
Playa Marinero
HOTEL FLOR DE MARÍA
HOTEL SANTA FE
TABACHÍN APARTMENTS
HORSES FOR RENT
BUNGALOWS ACALI
CINE MAR
ABARROTES MERLIN
VILLA TEMAZCALLI
INFRAGANTE
HOTEL ARCO IRIS
CAFÉ CASA BABYLON/BOOK EXCHANGE
RESTAURANT MANGOS
TP
PLAYA ZICATELA
BUNGALOWS AQUARIO/GYM
CENTRAL SURF
CAFECITO (PASTRIES)
PHOTO SHOP
SAKURA
BEACH HOTEL INÉS
AGENCIA DE VIAJES DIMAR
AV DEL MORRO
ROCKAWAY
RESTAURANT CAFECITO
RESTAURANT SAKURA
CASA OLGA
200
To Puerto Ángel, Bahías de Huatulco, and Tehuantepec
0   100 yds
0   100 m

trains in a subway. At such times, the spectators on the beach outnumber the surfers by as much as 10 or 20 to one. Don't try surfing or swimming at Zicatela unless you're expert at both.

Playa Manzanillo

About a mile west of town, the picture-postcard little blue bays of Bahía Puerto Angelito and Bahía Carrizalillo nestle beneath the seacliff. Their sheltered gold-and-coral sands are perfect for tranquil picnicking, sunbathing, and swimming. Here, snorkeling and scuba diving are tops, among shoals of bright fish grazing and darting among the close-in coral shelves and submerged rocky outcroppings. Get there by launch from Playa Principal or by taxi. On foot (take a sun hat and water), follow the street that heads west from Pérez Gasga, uphill across from the Hotel Nayar. Continue to the second street on the left, Avenida 1 Poniente, turn left and go a long block to Avenida 5 Sur. Turn right and continue straight ahead for about one-half

mile to Bahía Puerto Angelito, which shelters Playa Manzanillo at its inner edge. Follow the path down the cliff. Even more pristine, **Bahía Carrizalillo,** a petite strip of golden sand with a few *palapa* restaurants, is another mile farther west.

Playa Bachoco

Playa Bachoco, yet another mile farther west, down the bluff from the Hotel Posada Real, is a long, scenic strip of breeze-swept sand, with thunderous waves and correspondingly menacing undertow. Swimming is much safer in the inviting pool of the adjacent Hotel Posada Real beach club.

If you're strong, experienced, and can get past the breaking waves, snorkeling is said to be good around the little surf-dashed islet 100 yards offshore.

Although Playa Bachoco's rock-sheltered nooks appear inviting for beach camping, local people don't recommend it because of occasional *rateros* (thugs and drunks) who roam Puerto Escondido beaches at night.

Playa Manzanillo offers snorkeling right from the beach, good seafood, and gentle waves.

Beach Walking

The *andador* concrete walkway, which circles the lighthouse point, provides a pleasant, breezy afternoon (or sunset) diversion. From the west-end chain, follow the street that heads toward the beach. Soon, on the left, stairs lead left down on to the beach cove, where, in front of the Capitania del Puerto building, the *andador* heads left along the rocks. It continues, above the spectacularly splashing surf, for about half a mile. Return by the same route, or loop back through side streets to Pérez Gasga.

For a longer walk, you can stroll as far out of town along on **Playa Zicatela** as you want, in outings ranging from an hour to a whole day. Avoid the heat of midday, and bring along a sun hat, shirt, drinks, and snacks (and perhaps sunglasses) if you plan on walking more than a mile past the last restaurant down the beach. Your rewards will be the acrobatics of surfers challenging the waves, swarms of shorebirds, and occasional finds of driftwood and shells. After about three miles you will reach

a cliff and a sea arch, which you can scamper through at low tide to the beach on the other side, **Playa Barra de Colotepec.**

Playa Barra de Colotepec's surf is as thunderous as Zicatela's and the beach even more pristine, being a nesting site for sea turtles. The beach continues for another mile to the jungle-fringed lagoon of the Río Colotepec where, during the dry winter season, a host of birds and wildlife, both common and rare, paddle and preen in the clear, fresh water.

You could break this eight-mile round-trip into a pair of more leisurely options: Hike A could cover Zicatela only. On Hike B you could explore Playa Barra de Colotepec and the Laguna de Colotepec by driving, taxiing, or busing straight to La Barra, the beach village just west of the Río Colotepec. Access is via the signed side road just before (west of) the Río Colotepec bridge.

Boat Tours

Travel agencies and the local boat cooperative, **Sociedad Cooperativa Punta Escondida,**

THE COSTA CHICA

Puerto Escondido's bay-front walkway continues above the splashing surf for about half a mile.

© BRUCE WHIPPERMAN

offer trips for parties of several passengers to beautiful local bays, including Carrizalillo and Puerto Angelito, plus Manzanillo, Puesta del Sol, and Coral. The minimum one-hour trip takes you to a number of sandy little coves east of town, including Carrizalillo (Little Reeds), Manzanillo (Little Apple, in Puerto Angelito Bay), Coral, and Puesto del Sol (Sunset). Take drinks, hats, sunscreen, and perhaps sunglasses, and don't go unless your boat has a sunroof. Trips can be extended (about $15 per additional hour) to your heart's content of beach picnicking, snoozing, and snorkeling.

ACCOMMODATIONS

The successful hotels in Puerto Escondido are appropriate to the town itself: small, moderately priced, and near the water. They dot the beachfront from Playa Zicatela around the bay and continue up Avenida Pérez Gasga to the highway. Most are either on the beach or within a stone's throw of it, which makes sense, because it seems a shame to come all the way to Puerto Escondido and not stay where you can soak up all the scenery.

Beach lovers and surfing enthusiasts enjoy staying on Playa Zicatela, the creamy strand that stretches east and south of the busy *adoquín*. Here, folks relax, in street-side cafes and restaurants and strolling and sunning on the beach as they watch the surfers conquer (or try to conquer) Zicatela's awesome, oft-thunderous open-ocean waves.

Under $50

Moving downhill, from the highway, first find the immaculate, best-buy ◖ **Hotel San Juan** (Felipe Merklin 503, Puerto Escondido Oaxaca 71980, tel. 954/582-0518, sanjuanhotel@ prodigy.net.mx, www.sanjuanhotel.com.mx, $24 s or d, $33 t midseason) For those who like saving money and don't mind (or would enjoy) a ten-minute downhill walk to the beach, this is the place. Rooms, in four levels, enclose an intimate inner pool-patio. They are squeaky clean and invitingly furnished with wall paintings, reading lamps, and color-coordinated drapes and bedspreads. Medium season July–

Aug. and Dec.–April (excepting Christmas-New Year and Easter holidays), tariffs for the 32 rooms run about $24 s or d in one double bed, $33 t in two beds; low-season (May–June, Oct.–Nov.), $23 s or d, $30 t. Add $13 for a/c with a private ocean-view balcony. Rooms come with private hot-water shower baths, fans, in-house wireless Internet access, morning coffee, restaurant, and parking.

Also perched on the same view hillside, three blocks above the beach, the 1960s-genre **Hotel Nayar** (Pérez Gasga 407, Puerto Escondido, Oaxaca 71980, tel. 954/582-0113, fax 954/582-0319, hotel_nayar@hotmail.com, www.oaxaca-mio.com/hotelnayar.htm, $31 s, $45 d, $50 t high season) spreads from its inviting pool patio past the reception to a viewpoint restaurant. Its spacious, simply but comfortably furnished air-conditioned rooms have private balconies, several with ocean views. The Nayar's 40 rooms run about $31 s, $45 d, $50 t high season, about 25 percent less low season, with reading lamps, hot-water shower baths, fans, and a/c, and in-house wireless Internet.

The popular **Hotel Loren** (Av. Pérez Gasga 507, Puerto Escondido, Oaxaca 71980, tel. 954/582-0057, fax 954/582-0591, credit cards accepted, $28 s or d, $36–41 t with fan), downhill just two blocks from the beach, offers 30 or so rooms spread through two three-story buildings. Guests in the front-building rooms enjoy private, ocean-view balconies. (All rooms, however, could use a good scrubbing.) The good news is the hotel's inviting blue pool-patio and the short five-minute walk to the beach. Reserve a *cuarto con vista* in the front-building view room. Reservations are often necessary, especially in the winter. The 24 basic but comfortable fan-only rooms rent for about $28 s or d, $36–41 t, add $10 for a/c; with parking.

Tucked in its own corner, away from the tourist mall bustle, the compact, newly built ◖ **Le P'tit Hotel** (at the west-end intersection of Soledad and Pérez Gasga, Puerto Escondido, Oaxaca, 71980, tel. 954/582-3178, michel kobryn@tutopia.com, $32 s, $42 d) offers an attractive lodging option. Personable French-born owner-builder Michel Kobryn offers 16 rooms and thatched south-seas-style bungalows, all lovingly adorned with colorful tile, original wall art, decorator reading lamps, and sparkling bathrooms, with a/c, cable TV, restaurant, and inviting small pool-patio.

Right on the beach amid the tourist-mall hullabaloo is the enduring **Hotel las Palmas** (Av. Pérez Gasga s/n, Puerto Escondido, Oaxaca 71980, tel. 954/582-0230, fax 954/582-0303, credit cards not accepted, $25 s, $30 d, 35 t). Its main plus is the palmy, vine-strewn patio where you can sit for breakfast every morning, enjoy the breeze, and watch the boats, the birds, and families frolicking in the billows. The big drawback, besides sleepy management and no pool, is lack of privacy. Exterior walkways pass the room windows, which anyone can see through unless you close the curtains, which unfortunately makes the 40 or so (smallish, fan-only) rooms dark and hot. This doesn't seem to bother the legions of return customers, however, since they spend little time in their rooms anyway. There's a restaurant.

The **Hotel Rincón del Pacífico** (Av. Pérez Gasga 900, Puerto Escondido, Oaxaca 71980, tel. 954/582-0056 or 954/582-0193, fax 954/582-1812, reservaciones@rincondelpacifico .com.mx, credit cards accepted, but not American Express, $30 s, $35 d, $45 t with fan; $40, $46, and $65 with a/c; $70 suite), next door to the Hotel las Palmas, offers about the same. The two tiers of 28 clean, comfortable rooms enfold a shady patio that looks out onto the lively beachfront. As at the Hotel las Palmas, you must draw drapes for privacy in the hotel's glass-front rooms. This is nevertheless a very popular hotel. Reserve early. Ask for a discount during low-occupancy season (May–June and Sept.–Oct.) Four larger suites with TV and a/c rent for about $70; with a restaurant, but no parking nor pool.

Although it's not right on the beach like its neighbors across the street, the rooms of the **Hotel Casa Blanca** (Av. Pérez Gasga 905, Puerto Escondido, Oaxaca 71980, tel. 954/582-0168, fax 954/582-3120, imariabc@ hotmail.com, www.ptohcasablanca.com, Visa and MasterCard accepted, $20 s, $27 d low season, $35 s, $45 d high) are larger, cooler, and much more private. Some rooms even have private balconies, fine for people-watching on the street below. Guests report noise is not a problem since cars and trucks are banned on Gasga noon–7 A.M. Other amenities include a shelf of used paperback books, and, beyond the graceful arches that border the lobby, a petite, inviting pool and patio. The 21 clean, comfortable rooms have fans and hot-water shower baths, but no parking.

Moving south from **Playa Zicatela's** north-end beginning, first find 【 **Bungalows Acali** (Av. del Morro, P.O. Box 11, Puerto Escondido, Oaxaca 71980, tel. 954/582-0754, bungalowsacali@puertoconnection.com, www .puertoconnection.com/acali, credit cards accepted, room $30 s, $32 d, $38 t; bungalow $36 fan only, $55 with a/c and kitchen). Here, a small colony of rustic *cabañas* clusters around a blue pool in a banana, palm, and mango mini-jungle. The *cabañas* themselves, like a vision out of a south-seas tale, are built with walls made of sticks (non-see-through) and sturdy plank floors, raised above ground level. Rentals are clean, fan-equipped, with mosquito nets and good bathrooms. They run about $30 s, $32 d, $38 t year-round except Christmas-New Year and Easter holidays, with fan, hot water shower, small refrigerator, and parking included.

Additionally, the hotel offers a few rustic hammock-hung, sunset-view bungalows sleeping 1–4, perched on its bamboo- and mango-decorated hillside. Rentals go for about $36 fan only, $55 with a/c and kitchen.

About two long blocks farther south down the beach comes **Beach Hotel Inés** (Av. del Morro, P.O. Box 44, Playa Zicatela, Puerto Escondido, Oaxaca 71980, tel. 954/582-0792, fax 954/582-2344 or 954/582-0416, pedrovoss@yahoo.com, www.hotelines.com, from $25 d room to $120 d suite), the life project of German expatriate Peter Voss and his daughter, Inés. Their 45 units occupy the palmy periphery of a lush, pool-café-garden layout, which climaxes with an attractive, stuccoed, two-story complex of rooms at the back side. At the poolside tables, longtime repeat guests linger for coffee and conversation after late-morning breakfasts, stroll the beach in the afternoon, and return for a balmy sunset happy hour. Other days they sunbathe au naturel or relax in the petite but luxurious health club, which provides massage and hot tub. Most of the rentals are hotel-style rooms, in deluxe and superdeluxe grades, with clean, light interiors, comfortable furnishings, and well-maintained bathrooms. They rent six levels of accommodation, from smallish, but comfortable, hotel-style rooms for about $25 d; larger deluxe rooms for $35 and $45 d; super-deluxe suites $60 and $70 d; to about $120 d for large super-deluxe suites.

A few doors farther south stands the very economical and tidy "surfer village" **Rockaway** (Av. del Morro, Playa Zicatela, Puerto Escondido, Oaxaca 71980, tel. 954/582-0668, rockhomemx@yahoo.com, www.mexonline .com/rockaway.htm or www.hotelrockaway .com, $11 s, $16 d *cabaña* ; $28 s, $37 d, 47 t room), a fenced-in cluster of about 10 clean, concrete-floored bamboo and thatch *cabañas*. Plainly decorated but clean, spacious, and fan-equipped, they sleep up to four and come with private showers and toilets, mosquito nets, and shady, hammock-hung front porches. An inviting, leafy pool-patio occupies the center, while a squad of new air-conditioned rooms stands to one side. *Cabaña* rentals run, low season, about $11 s, $16 d, $24 per *cabaña* for up to four. The sparely furnished but comfortable new a/c rooms go for about $28 s, $37 d, 47 t. Weekly or monthly discounts are negotiable, with parking and adjacent pizzeria.

Tucked only a block inland from the beach, at the south end of the Zicatela development, is **Casa Olga** (Av. del Morro, olga_hmex@ yahoo.com, $25 s, $30 d, $40 d, $50 q) that the friendly Mexican owner likes to call "your home away from home." And yes, it could easily be, with five attractively decorated, comfortable rooms on hammock-hung porches overlooking a lovely green lawn, garden and

blue swimming pool. The upper-story rooms, with two and three beds, are the most invitingly private, with airy ocean view and awning-draped shade. Rates begin at about $25 s, $30 d for the smaller rooms, rising to $40 d, $50 q for the large, except during Christmas and Easter holidays, when rates approximately double. All have private hot-water shower baths, fans, and use of an outdoor kitchen adjacent to the pool-patio.

$50-100

Back uphill, two blocks below the highway on a short side street off Pérez Gasga, is the **Hotel Paraíso Escondido** (Calle Union 1, Puerto Escondido, Oaxaca 71980, tel./fax 954/582-0444, credit cards not accepted, $63 s, $72 d). A tranquil colonial-chic refuge, the hotel abounds in unique artistic touches—Mixtec stone glyphs, tiny corner chapels, stained glass, and old-world antiques—blended into the lobby, corridors, and patios. The two levels of rooms nestle around a lovely view pool and restaurant patio. The rooms themselves are large, with view balconies and designer tile bathrooms, wrought-iron fixtures, and hand-crafted wooden furniture. Very popular with North American and German winter vacationers; get reservations in early. The 24 rooms customarily rent for about $63 s, $72 d, with a/c, pool, kiddie pool, and parking.

It's easy to miss the **Hotel Flor de María** (at Primera Entrada Playa Marinero, Colonia Marinero, Puerto Escondido, Oaxaca 71980, tel. 954/582-0536, fax 954/582-2617, pajope@ hotmail.com, www.mexonline.com/flordemaria .htm, $37 d, $56 d view low season; $55 and $65 high), tucked on a quiet side street above east-side Playa Marinero. That would be a pity, for the Flor de María is an attractive, reasonably priced hotel. Rooms rise in two stories around a tranquil, leafy interior patio. At rooftop, a breezy sundeck-bar, with a small but inviting pool and a hammock-hung *palapa*, overlooks a beach-and-bay vista. The approximately dozen immaculate deluxe rooms are simply but thoughtfully decorated, each with two double beds with flowery violet covers and modern-standard hot-water shower baths. Additionally, the hotel offers a pair of similarly inviting but more spacious second-floor ocean-view suites and a very good restaurant. Accommodations rent, low season, from about $37 d standard, $56 d with ocean view; high season $55 and $65, with fans.

Go about three blocks south along Avenida del Morro, which runs along Playa Zicatela, to the three-story **Hotel Arco Iris** (Av. del Morro s/n, Colonia Marinero, Puerto Escondido, Oaxaca 71980, tel./fax 954/582-1494, fax 954/582-0432, arcoiris@hotel-arcoiris .com.mx, www.hotel-arcoiris.com.mx, $45 s or d room low season, $70 s or d suite) A flowery, shady green garden surrounds the hotel, leading to a gorgeous rear pool and patio. For those who love sunsets, sand, and waves (and don't mind their sometimes insistent pounding), one of the spacious, simply furnished top-floor view rooms might be just the ticket. The Arco Iris's proximity to the famous Puerto Escondido "pipeline" draws both surfers and surf-watchers to the third-floor restaurant La Galera, which seems equally ideal for wave-watching at breakfast and sky-watching at sunset. Low-season (May–June, Sept.–Nov. 15) asking rates for the 26 rooms run $45 s or d; suites with kitchen, about $70 s or d (add about 15 percent during the high winter season).

Over $100

Puerto Escondido's class-act hostelry is the 🄲 **Hotel Santa Fe** (Av. del Morro, Playa Marinero, Puerto Escondido, P.O. Box 96, Puerto Escondido, Oaxaca 71980, tel. 954/582-0170 or 954/582-0266, fax 954/582-0260, from U.S. toll-free tel. 888/649-6407, info@hotel santafe.com.mx, www.hotelsantafe.com.mx, credit cards accepted, $80 s, and $95 d, $100 d suites low season, and up). Built in graceful neocolonial style, with gracefully curving staircases, palm-shaded pool patios, and flower-decorated walkways, the Santa Fe achieves an ambience both intimate and luxuriously private. Its restaurant is outstanding. The rooms, spacious, high-ceilinged and comfortable, are thoughtfully appointed with hand-painted tile,

rustic wood furniture, and regional handicrafts. Moreover, a room wing that owners added lately has enhanced the hotel's ambience, with an airy and tranquil elevated pool patio, connecting the recent wing with the original section. The 50 rooms rent, high season, for about $105 s, $120 d, $130 t; about 10 kitchenette suites go, high season, for around $85 s, $140 d, 160 t, kids free. During the low season, rooms go for about $80 s, and $95 d, suites about $100 d. All accommodations have a/c, phones, and parking, but no TV.

Apartments and Long-Term Rentals

If you're planning on a stay of two weeks or more, you may be able to save money and yet have all the comforts of home in an apartment rental. First look over the classifieds in the English-Spanish newspaper *El Sol de la Costa* (tel./fax 954/582-2230, elsol@escondido.com .mx, www.elsoldelacosta.com), edited by Warren Sharpe.

Also check with local realtors; the best for rentals is Vicki Cole of **Zicatela Properties** (tel. 954/582-2495, info@zicatelaproperties .com, www.zicatelaproperties.com). Vicki also provides help—real-estate matters, immigration papers, residency—for newcomers.

Alternatively, for rentals, you might also contact Nolan Van Way, of **PEP Realty** (tel. 954/582-0085, nvpep@yahoo.com, www .pep-realty.com).

Trailer Park, Camping, and Hostel

Occasional muggings and robberies on the beach have eliminated virtually all camping on Puerto Escondido beaches (with the possible exception of Easter week, when such large crowds flock into town that they spill onto the beaches).

Nevertheless, beachfront camping space is available in small palm-shaded, trailer park **Palmas de Cortés** (once closed, now reopened, at the east side of Puerto Escondido's Playa Principal, half a block downhill from the chain, cortes@ptoescondido.com.mx, $15–25 RV site, $5 pp tent site). Facilities include security fence, night watchman, brand-new showers and toilets, all hookups, and room for about a dozen RVs and maybe some tents. Tariffs run $15–25 for RVs, depending on size, and about $5 per person for tents.

A good alternative for tenters and hostelers is **Shalom** Hostel (in Rinconada subdivision, west side of town, on the east end of Calle Benito Juárez, tel. 954/582-3234, rigeloo@yahoo.com, $6 dorm bed, $8 pp *cabañas*, $4 pp tent site). Besides tenting ($4 per person) in their shady, green back garden, with heavenly pool-patio, they offer rustic *cabañas* with shared baths ($8 per person) and dorm beds for $6, with snack restaurant and parking out front.

FOOD
Breakfast and Snacks
Mornings you can enjoy breakfast with the baked offerings of Carmen's pastry and coffee shop **Cafecito** (on Zicatela beach, next to Bungalows Acuario). Here, you can savor a cappuccino and one of her goodies as you watch the surfers conquering the waves.

Carmen has aquired some competition, at **Baguettería Vivaldi** (middle of beachfront Avenida Pérez Gasga, across the street from the Hotel Casa Blanca, tel. 954/582-0800, 7:30 A.M.–11 P.M. daily), the labor of love of friendly Jenny Sinnhuber, who, besides lots of homemade bread, serves a wide selection of delicious breakfasts and sandwiches for lunch.

You can also get your day started right with breakfast, while watching the beachfront scene, at leafy **Restaurant los Crotos,** on the *adoquín*, west end.

Restaurants
Many of Puerto Escondido's good restaurants line the *adoquín*. One major exception is immaculate, strictly home-cooking-style ▐ **Margaritas,** where all you need is to love good Mexican food. Find it in the upper town, near the market, at Ave. 8 Norte, few doors east of Calle 2 Poniente, tel. 954/582-0212, 8 A.M.–6 P.M. daily. Although the long country menu, including eggs in several styles ($3), tacos, tamales and quesadillas ($2–3), fish and

shrimp any style ($6–10), and broiled steaks ($8–12) reveals nothing unusual, everything arrives at your table delicious. The day's main event is the *comida corrida* set lunch, including soup, entrée choices such as savory beef or pork *guisado* stew, or *mole* chicken, or *chiles rellenos* and dessert and drink. Choose from half a dozen delicious fruit *aguas* (strawberry, lemonade, melon, orange, and more). All this for $3.50!

Back down on the *adoquín*, ▐ **Restaurant la Galería** (just inside the west end chain, on the inland side of Pérez Gasga, tel. 954/582-2039, 8 A.M.–midnight daily) usually has customers even when most other eateries are empty. The reason is the excellent Italian fare—crusty, hot pizzas, rich pastas and lasagna, bountiful salads, and satisfying soups—which the European-expatriate owner puts out for her batallion of loyal customers.

Try the excellent, airy **Restaurant Junto del Mar** ("Next to the Beach": just inside the *adoquín* west-end chain, tel./fax 954/582-0025, credit cards accepted, 8 A.M.–11 P.M. daily), which offers good breakfasts—rich bottomless coffee, fresh fruit, omelettes, and French toast ($2–5)—and many delectable lunch and dinner options. Specialties include shrimp-stuffed fillets ($9), lobster and shrimp brochettes ($11–14), and whole garlic-stuffed fish ($9). Mornings are brightened by the always-changing beach scene; evenings, the setting turns romantic, with soft candlelight and strumming guitars.

Breakfast patrons at beachfront **Restaurant Crotos** (a block farther east, tel. 954/582-0025, 8 A.M.–11 P.M. daily) sit at shady view tables, enjoying the fascinating morning beachside scene. Later, at lunch and dinner, back beneath the luxuriously breezy, palm-fringed *palapa*, the house specialties—jumbo shrimp, broiled lobster, and superfresh pompano, attractively presented, competently served, and delicious— seem like an added bonus.

Devotees of authentic Italian food find paradise at **Restaurant Altro Mundo** (half a block outside the east-end chain, tel. 954/582-1455, dinner only, 6 P.M.–midnight daily). Here, white tablecloths and wine glasses set the stage. Start off, perhaps, with *crema* Altro Mundo ($4), continue with an *insalata mista* ($5), share a plate of lasagna *di calamari* ($10), and climax with fettuccine *flameante* ($10) and/or *filete di dorado* ($12).

Alternatively, next door, try the tasty creations ($7–14) of Napolitano owner-chef Bendito at completely unpretentious **Restaurant Bendito** (tel. 954/588-2186, 8 A.M.–midnight Mon.–Sat.). Napoli-style neighborhood cooking is the specialty here. Make up a party and enjoy sampling spaghetti *putanesca* ($5), spinach raviolis ($5), mushroom fetuccine ($7), and pizza *zavarieta* ($8).

If you have dinner at the restaurant of the **Hotel Santa Fe** (on Avenida del Morro, east side of the bay, tel. 954/582-0170, 7:30 A.M.–11 P.M. daily), you may never go anywhere else. Savory food, impeccably served beneath a luxurious *palapa* and accompanied by softly strumming guitars, brings travelers from all over the world. Although everything on the menu is delicious, the restaurant is proudest of its Mexican favorites, such as rich tortilla soup ($4), bountiful plates of *chiles rellenos* ($9), and succulent snapper, Veracruz style ($11).

Restaurant Mangos (next to Hotel Acuario on Zicatela beach, tel. 954/582-3805, 8 A.M.–midnight daily) packs in a steady stream of youngish customers, with a long menu of innovative breakfasts (crepes, three-egg omelettes, $4), salads (plenty of alfalfa sprouts, $3–5), sandwiches (*cuerno*, large horn croissant, $5), and Mexican specialties (fish-stuffed chiles rellenos, $6).

Farther south a few blocks past Hotel Rockaway **Restaurant Cafecito** (tel. 954/582-0516, 6:30 A.M.–10 P.M. daily, not to be confused with pastry shop Cafecito) is headquarters for a loyal platoon of local surfers and Canadian and American residents. Breakfasts ($3–5), hamburgers ($3–4), and fresh seafood plates ($6–8) are bountiful and tasty.

Customers at **Sakura** sushi bar and Japanese restaurant (on Zicatela, south end, tel. cell 044-954/559-0239, 8 A.M.–11 P.M. daily) enjoy a menu so correct that it seems straight out of the owner's Yokohama hometown. He offers a trove of delectable options, such as *miso* soup ($2), *wakame* (seafood salad, $4), chicken *teri-yaki* ($6), vegetable *tempura* ($5), and *teppan-yaki* ($5–10). *Daijobu des neh!* (Wonderful!)

ENTERTAINMENT AND EVENTS
Sunsets and Happy Hours
Many bars have sunset happy hours, but not all of them have good sunset views. Since the Oaxaca coast faces south (and the sun sets in the west), bars and restaurants along west-facing Zicatela Beach, such as the Hotel Santa Fe, Hotel Arco Iris, Bar and Café Casa Babylon, and Restaurant Cafecito, are some of those that can offer unobstructed sunset horizons.

If, on the other hand, you prefer solitude, stroll the bayfront *andador* walkway to near the lighthouse. Start on the Playa Principal (main beach), west side, past the Capitán del Puerto office. There, from breezy perches above the waves, you'll enjoy an equally panoramic sunset.

Strolling the *Adoquín*
The amusements along the *adoquín* mall are Puerto Escondido's prime after-dinner entertainment source. By around 9 P.M., some people get weary of walking and, since there are few benches, begin sitting on the curb and sipping bottles of beer near the west-end chain.

The main attraction of curb-sitting is watching other people sitting on the curb, while listening to the music blasting nightly from the open-air bars of **Blue Station** and **Wipe Out,** nearby. The music is so loud that little can be gained except hearing impairment by actually taking a seat in the bars themselves.

Those who prefer to gyrate to the beat go to the *adoquín* **discos.** Besides Wipe Out and Blue Station, one of the reliable is the longtime Latin-beat **Tequila Sunrise** (where, if your eyes are still open, you can actually witness sunrise), half a block along the lane, Marina Nacional, that juts toward the beach at the west-side *adoquín* chain. From 10 P.M. Wed.–Sun.

For softer musical offerings, check out the guitarists who play evenings at the Hotel Santa Fe Restaurant Bar, and/or the **El Son y**

la Rumba nightclub, with Mayka y Amigos, entertaining nightly in season, across the street, from the Hotel Santa Fe.

For more entertainment picks, ask friendly **Gina Machorro,** who staffs the information booth just inside the adoquín west-end chain.

Cinema

If you're hankering for a good movie, go to **Cine Mar** (tel. 954/588-2166, 10 A.M.–11 P.M. daily except Wed.), Puerto Escondido' mini-movie-house, on Playa Zicatela's northern side, about half a block north of the Hotel Aquario. Here, Cine Mar's friendly proprietor, Paul Yacht, lives out his bliss selling and exchanging used and new books, and renting, selling, and screening a wide range of videos and DVDs for a loyal cadre of movie-lovers.

Festivals

Puerto Escondido pumps up with a series of fiestas during the low-season (but excellent for vacationing) month of November. Scheduled "Fiestas de Noviembre" events invariably include surfing and usually sportfishing,cooking, and beauty contests, and notably, the dance festival, **Fiesta Costeño,** when a flock of troupes—from Pochutla, Pinotepa Nacional, Jamiltepec, Tehuantepec, and more—perform regional folk dances.

Visitors who hanker for the old-fashioned color of a traditional fiesta, make sure you arrive in Puerto Escondido before Dec. 8, when seemingly the whole town takes part in the fiesta of the **Virgen de Soledad.** Besides being the patron saint of the state of Oaxaca, the Virgen de Soledad is also protectress of fishermen. To honor her, the whole town accompanies the Virgin by boat around 3 P.M. out to the bay's far reach, and then returns with her to the church plaza for dancing, fireworks, and bullfights.

If you can't be in Puerto Escondido in time to honor the Virgin in December, perhaps you may be able enjoy the Puerto Escondido's **Carnaval** or take a day trip a couple of hours west of Puerto Escondido to enjoy the more traditionally colorful native Carnaval

fiestas at one of the small towns around Pinotepa Nacional, with parades, fireworks, and masked traditional dances, on the weekend before Ash Wednesday, the beginning of Lent (46 days before Easter Sunday, 47 during a leap year).

SPORTS AND RECREATION

Walking, Jogging, and Horseback Riding

In addition to the *adoquín*, Playa Zicatela is Puerto Escondido's most interesting walking or jogging course. Early mornings, before the heat and crowds, are good for jogging along the *adoquín*. In addition to Playa Zicatela itself, Avenida del Morro, which parallels Playa Zicatela, is good for jogging, also best during early morning or late afternoons.

Ease your hiking by riding horseback along Zicatela beach. Rentals are available on the beach in front of Hotel Santa Fe.

Gym and Tennis

The **Acuario Gym** on Playa Zicatela, at the Bungalows Acuario, tel. 954/582-0357, has a roomful of standard exercise equipment. Single visits run about $2, one-month passes $17.

Probably the only tennis courts in town available for public rental ($9/hour, daytime only) is at the **Hotel Posada Real** above the beach, on the west side of town. Call the hotel at tel. 954/582-0133 for a reservation.

Surfing, Snorkeling, and Scuba Diving

Although surfing is de rigueur for the skilled in Puerto Escondido, beginners often learn by bodysurfing and boogie boarding first. Boogie boards and surfboards are for sale and rent ($7/day) at a few shops along the *adoquín,* such as **Squad,** half a block inside the west-end chain. Surf equipment is more abundant at several shops along Playa Zicatela, however. For example, try **Central Surf** (which also offers surfing lessons), at Bungalows Acuari, tel. 954/582-2285, www.centralsurfshop.com, high season 9 A.M.–2 P.M. and 4–7 P.M. daily.

Beginners practice on the gentler billows of

Playa Principal and adjacent **Playa Marinero,** while advanced surfers go for the powerful waves of **Playa Zicatela,** which regularly slam foolhardy inexperienced surfers onto the sand with backbreaking force.

Local aficionados organize **surfing tournaments** during the summer-fall surfing season. Dates depend on when the surf is up. For surfing tournament information, best contact **Gina Machorro,** who staffs the Pérez Gasga information booth, tel. 954/582-0276, ginainpuerto@yahoo.com.

Clear blue-green waters, coral reefs, and swarms of multicolored fish make for good local snorkeling and diving, especially in little **Puerto Angelito** and **Carrizalillo** bays just west of town. A number of *adoquín* stores sell serviceable resort-grade snorkeling equipment.

A professional dive shop, **Aventura Submarina,** has gained a foothold in Puerto Escondido. It's run by friendly veteran PADI instructor Jorge Pérez Bravo, at Pérez Gasga 601 A, at the west-end chain. tel. 954/582-2353, asubmarina@yahoo.com.mx. Introductory lesson, including one offshore dive, runs about $75, including equipment. For certified (bring your certificate) open-water divers, a one-tank night dive costs about $60, a two-tank day dive, about $120.

Alternately, check out equally professional **Puerto Dive Shop** a block farther east, at the corner of Libertad steps, across from the HSBC ATM (tel. 954/102-67, info@puertodivecenter .com, www.scuba-diving-mexico.com).

Sportfishing

Puerto Escondido's offshore waters abound with fish. Launches go out mornings from Playa Principal and routinely return with an assortment including big tuna, mackerel, snapper, sea bass, and snook. The sheltered west side of the beach is calm enough to easily launch a mobile boat with the help of usually willing beach hands.

The local **Sociedad Cooperativa Nueva Punta Escondida,** www.tomzap.com/ pe-coop.html, which parks its boats right on Playa Principal, regularly take fishing parties

of three or four out for about $25 an hour, including bait and tackle. Check with boatmen right on the beach, or at El Pescador restaurant, a few steps along Calle Marina Nacional, the street that heads toward the beach from the west-end adoquín chain.

Another good choice is **Captain Charles Guma** (tel. 954/582-1303, guerra445@ hotmail.com), with a 25-foot boat ($100 for four-hour excursion), fine for catching good-eating *dorado,* tuna, and roosterfish. Also, you might check out **Omar's Sportfishing** (cellular, dial locally tel. 044-954/588-4975, or find Omar on the beach at Puerto Angelito bay), which offers fishing excursions for similar prices.

Travel agencies, such as Viajes Dimar (Av. Pérez Gasga 905, tel. 954/582-0734 or 954/582-0737, viajesdimar@hotmail.com), arrange such trips at somewhat higher prices.

SHOPPING
Market and Handicrafts

As in most Mexican towns, the place to begin your Puerto Escondido shopping is the local **Mercado,** between Avenida 9 and Avenida 10 Norte, one long block west of the electric station on upper Avenida Oaxaca. Although produce occupies most of the space, a number of stalls at the south end offer authentic handicrafts. These might include pearly San Bártolo Coyotepec black pottery, fetching floral-motif pottery from Atzompa; endearing multicolored pottery animals from Iguala and Zitlala in Guerrero; beautiful *huipiles* from San Pedro Amusgos and colorfully embroidered "Oaxaca Wedding Dresses" from San Antonino Castillo Velasco in the Valley of Oaxaca.

Back downhill on the *adoquín,* the prices increase along with the selection. Perhaps the most fruitful time and place for handicraft shopping is during the cooler evenings, within the illuminated cluster of crafts stalls along the *staircase lanes* that head uphill from the *adoquín* or the cluster of stalls just beyond the east-side chain.

Watch for one or two shops at that spot,

© BRUCE WHIPPERMAN

Huipiles made in San Pedro Amusgos are among the most desired handicrafts.

with genuine handwoven wool rugs *(tapetes)* and serapes from Teotitlán del Valle near Oaxaca city. Fine-quality *tapetes* are the most tightly woven—typically about 20 strands per centimeter (50 per inch).

Oaxaca's venerable jewelry tradition is well represented at the very professional **Oro de Monte Albán,** on the *adoquín,* ocean side, inside the west-end chain (tel. 954/582-0530, 10 A.M.–2 P.M. and 5–10 P.M. Mon.–Sat., 5–10 P.M. Sun.). Here find museum-grade replicas of the celebrated Mixtec trove discovered in Monte Albán's tomb 7.

The Uribe silversmithing family reflects its Taxco tradition very well, at its **Platería Ixtlán** (tel. 954/582-1672, 10 A.M.–10 P.M. Mon.–Sat., 5–10 P.M. Sun.), a few doors east. Choose from a host of fetching floral, animal, and abstract designs, in silver and turquoise, garnet, jade, and other semiprecious stones.

Also, around the middle of the *adoquín,* step into elegant **Oasis** (tel. 954/582-3557, 10 A.M.–2 P.M. and 5–10 P.M. Mon.–Sat., 5–

10 P.M. Sun.), with carefully selected Mexican-modern-motif fine furniture and lamps.

Groceries

Abarrotes Lupita, a fairly well-stocked small grocery, offers meats, milk, ice, and vegetables; 10 A.M.–11 P.M. daily. Out on Playa Zicatela, **Abarrotes Merlin,** tel. 954/582-1130, offers a modest grocery and wine selection; 8 A.M.–midnight daily.

Photography

Foto Express Figueroa, tel. 954/582-0526, on Gasga next to Viajes Dimar, offers fast film and digital photofinishing services, Kodak color print and slide film, and a moderate stock of accessories, including point-and-shoot digital cameras. 9 A.M.–9 P.M. daily.

On Playa Zicatela, **Centro Fotográfico** tel. 954/582-3307, stocks a modest selection of film, digital and film cameras, accessories color and and digital and film developing and printing services, 9 A.M.–9 P.M. daily.

For a better camera selection, visit **Foto Discuento** (Av. Oaxaca 110, tel. 954/582-0354, 9 A.M.–8 P.M. Mon.–Sat., 9 A.M.–noon Sun.), in the upper town.

INFORMATION
Tourist Information Office, Guides, and Language Instruction

Most months of the year, personable **Gina Machorro** staffs a small **information booth** (tel. 954/582-0276, ginainpuerto@yahoo .com, 9 A.M.–2 P.M. and 4–6 P.M. Mon.–Fri.) on the *adoquín,* just inside the west-end chain. She also conducts a walking tour of Puerto Escondido, including an important local archaeological site.

You can also consult the friendly, well-informed *oficina de turismo* staff (tel./fax 954/582-0175), who distribute a map of Oaxaca. Open 8 A.M.–5 P.M. Mon.–Fri., 9 A.M.–2 P.M. Sat., just off Highway 200, in the little office on the beach side of the highway, a couple of blocks toward town from the airport Pemex gas station.

Hidden Voyages Ecotours of the Canadian husband-wife team of Michael Malone and Joan Walker offer a number of excellent out-of-town birdwatching/wildlife viewing excursions (roughly $50 per person), especially around Laguna Manialtepec.

Alternatively, try one of the tours guided by experienced and well-equipped **Lalo Tours.** Their several tours (full day tours, about $40 per person, half-day $20) include Laguna Manialtepec bird and wildlife viewing by boat; or the same by footpath in Laguna Manialtepec's barrier sandbar forest; an ocean sunset cruise, and a fascinating night exploration by boat of the ghostly glow of Laguna Manialtepec's phosphorescent waters.

(For contact details for the Malones and Lalo's, see *Tours* in the *Excursions from Escondido* section.)

The Puerto Escondido **Language Institute** (tel. 954/582-2055, brian@puerto school.com, www.puertoschool.com) offers private and group lessons ($12 and $8 per hour), homestays, tours, rock climbing,

surfing lessons and more, across the highway from Cruz Azul cement store, on Highway 200, above Playa Zicatela.

At least two individual English-speaking teachers offer Spanish lessons: **Sheila Clarke,** tel. 954/582-0276, and **Yolanda Park,** tel. 954/582-0837.

Publications

One of the few local outlets of English-language newspapers or magazines in Puerto Escondido is **Publicaciones Fabian** (tel. 954/582-1334, 8 A.M.–9 P.M. Mon.–Sat.), in the upper town, at the corner of main-street Avenida Oaxaca and Calle 1 Norte. Usually available are the daily *Miami Herald* and magazines, such as *Time, Newsweek,* and *Scientific American,* and maybe some new paperback novels.

The local English-Spanish tourist newspaper, *El Sol de la Costa,* provides an abundance of useful information, including community events, unusually informative cultural features, emergency numbers, house and apartment rental listings, and many service advertisements. Pick up a free copy from one of its many advertisers along the Pérez Gasga mall. If you can't find a copy, contact editor Warren Sharpe, tel. 954/582-2230, elsol@escondido .com.mx, www.elsoldelacosta.com.

English-language books are available at a few spots (in addition to the shelves of paperbacks in most hotels) in Puerto Escondido. Check out **Café-Bar Casa Babylon,** on Playa Zicatela, a few doors north of the Hotel Bungalows Acuario, and also **Cine Mar,** a few doors farther north, where friendly proprietor Paul Yacht sells paperback books and screens, rents, and sells movie DVDs and videos.

Safety

Occasional knifepoint robberies and muggings have marred the once-peaceful Puerto Escondido nighttime beach scene. Walk alone and you invite trouble, especially along Playa Bachoco and the unlit stretch of Playa Principal between the east end of Pérez Gasga and the Hotel Santa Fe. If you have dinner alone at the Hotel Santa Fe, avoid the beach by returning by taxi or walking along the highway to Pérez Gasga back to your hotel.

Fortunately, such problems seem to be confined to the beach. Visitors are quite safe on the Puerto Escondido streets themselves, often more so than on their own city streets back home.

SERVICES
Money Exchange
Banamex (Pérez Gasga 314, with ATM, uphill from the Hotel Nayar, tel. 954/582-0626), changes U.S. and Canadian cash and traveler's checks (9 A.M.–4 P.M. Mon.–Fri., 10 A.M.–2 P.M. Sat.). You can also use the HSBC 24-hour ATM, around the midpoint of the *adoquín,* next to the Hotel las Palmas.

After bank hours, the small **casa de cambio** (money exchange) office on the *adoquín,* next to the Hotel Casa Blanca, tel. 954/582-1928, also exchanges cash and traveler's checks 10 A.M.–3 P.M. and 5:30–9 P.M. Mon.–Fri., 10 A.M.–2 P.M. Sat.–Sun. Another *casa de cambio* offers similar services, on Playa Zicatela, next to Bungalows Acuario, tel. 954/582-0592, 9 A.M.–6 P.M. daily except Sun.

Communications
The **correo** and **telégrafo** are side by side on Avenida 7 Norte, corner Avenida Oaxaca, seven blocks into town from the *crucero* : the post office (tel. 954/582-0959, 8 A.M.–3 P.M. Mon.–Fri., 9 A.M.–1 P.M. Sat.) and the *telégrafo* (tel. 954/582-0232, 8 A.M.–7:30 P.M., Mon.–Fri., 9 A.M.–noon Sat.) which has public fax.

For local and long-distance **telephone,** save money and buy a Ladatel public telephone card at one of many *adoquín* stores and use it in street telephones. First dial 001 for calls to the United States and Canada, and 01 for long-distance calls within Mexico.

Alternatively, ask to use your hotel's desk telephone; or on Playa Zicatela, you can use the public long-distance telephone at the desk of the Bungalows Acuario.

Internet, fax, and long-distance telephone is available at **Coffee Net** (across from the HSBC bank ATM in the middle of the *adoquín,* tel. 954/582-0797, 11 A.M.–10:30 P.M. daily). On Playa Zicatela, Internet connection is also available at **Hotel Bungalows Acuario** (9 A.M.–11 P.M. daily).

Health, Police, and Emergencies
If you need a doctor, go to the small hospital **Sanatorio del Carmen** (tel. 954/582-1876 or 954/582-0174), three blocks west of the *crucero,* uphill from the highway on Calle 3 Poniente between Calles 2 and 3 Norte. You'll find a number of doctors, including general practitioners and specialists, such as pediatrician, family medicine, opthamologist, and internist, plus a pathology laboratory.

You could also consult with English-speaking general practitioner **Dr. Mario Francisco de Alba** on the *adoquín,* outside the east-end chain, at his pharmacy **San Lucas** (tel. 954/582-3581 or local cell tel. 044-954/588-4018).

Another option is the 24-hour government health clinic, **Centro de Salud,** on Avenida Pérez Gasga, just uphill from the Hotel Loren.

Get over-the-counter remedies and prescriptions at one of the good tourist-zone pharmacies, such as the 24-hour **Farmacia la Moderna,**, tel. 954/582-0698 or 954/582-2780, on Pérez Gasga, a block below the *crucero,* or **Super Farmas,** tel. 954/582-0112, on the *adoquín,* across from Hotel las Palmas, 8 A.M.–2 P.M. and 5–10 P.M.

For police emergencies, call the **municipal police,** tel. 954/582-0498, or go to the headquarters in the Agencia Municipal on Highway 200, about four blocks west of the Pérez Gasga *crucero.* For **fire emergencies,** call the *bomberos* (tel. 954/582-3538).

Meditation and Massage
Healing is the mission of partners Patricia Heuze and Alejandro Villanuevo, who operate **Villa Temazcalli** meditation and massage center, Zicatela side of town, on Avenida Infragante, two blocks uphill from the highway. Facilities include rustic hot baths, an

indigenous-style *temazcal* hot room, and massage room in an invitingly tranquil tropical garden setting. Prices run about $45 each for massage and the hot tub, and about $30 for one, $40 for two, and $60 for three, in the *temazcal*. For information and appointments, call tel. 954/582-1023, or masaje@ temazcalli.com; for more information, visit www.temazcalli.com.

Travel Agent and Car Rentals

One of the most respected travel agents in town is **Viajes Dimar,** at the middle of the tourist mall (Avenida Pérez Gasga 906, P.O. Box 22, Puerto Escondido, Oaxaca 71980, tel./fax 954/582-0734 or 954/582-0737, viajesdimar@hotmail.com) or their Playa Zicatela office by Hotel Inés (tel. 954/582-0737).

Rent a car at **Budget Rent a Car** on Calle Juárez, beach side of Highway 200, in the Bachoco suburb, by the airport (tel. 954/582-0312). Alternatively, you can rent a car at **Rutas de Aventuras** tour desk, at the Hotel Santa Fe (tel. 954/582-1246).

Laundry

Get your laundry done (8 A.M.–8 P.M. Mon.–Sat., 8 A.M.–5 P.M. Sun.) at the **Lavamático del Centro,** two doors downhill from Banamex, on Pérez Gasga, about two blocks uphill, from the west-end chain.

GETTING THERE AND AWAY
By Air

The small jetport, officially the **Aeropuerto Puerto Escondido** (code-designated PXM), is just off the highway a mile west of town. The terminal, only a plain waiting room with check-in desks, has no services save a small snack bar. Out in front, *colectivo* vans to hotels in town run $2 per person. Arrivees with a minimum of luggage, however, can walk a block to the highway and flag down one of the many eastbound local minibuses, which all stop at the main town highway crossing. Arrive with a hotel in mind (better yet, a hotel reservation in hand), unless you prefer letting your taxi driver choose one, where he

will probably collect a commission for depositing you there.

Although **car rental agents** may not routinely meet flights, they will meet you if you have a reservation. Call **Budget** (tel. 954/582-0312 or 954/582-0315, budget33@ hotmail.com).

If you lose your tourist card, avoid trouble or a fine by taking your passport and some proof of your arrival date (such as a stamped passport, a copy of your lost tourist card, or an air ticket) to **Migración** at the airport, tel. 954/582-3369, for help *before* your day of departure.

A few regularly scheduled flights connect Puerto Escondido with other Mexican destinations.

One Mexicana affiliate **Click Airlines** flight connects daily with Mexico City. For reservations, contact a travel agent or call toll-free 01-800/122-5425. For flight information, call the airport at tel. 954/582-2023.

If the above flight does not take you where you want to go, contact **Aerovega,** the dependable local air-taxi service, tel./fax 954/582-0151 (or in Oaxaca city, tel. 951/516-4982), aerovegapto@hotmail.com, www.oaxaca-mio .com/aerovega.htm. Aerovega flights routinely connect Puerto Escondido, Huatulco, and Oaxaca city.

By Car or RV

National Highway 200, although sometimes winding, is generally smooth and un-congested between Puerto Escondido and Pinotepa Nacional (89 miles, 143 km, 2.5 hours) to the west. From there, continue another 160 miles (258 km, 4.5 hours) to Acapulco. Stay on the safe side by filling up at Puerto Escondido before you leave, although gasoline is customarily available at several points along the route.

Traffic sails between Puerto Escondido and Puerto Ángel, 44 miles (71 km) apart, in an easy hour. (Actually, Pochutla is immediately on the highway; Puerto Ángel is an additional six miles to the right, downhill from the junction.) Santa Cruz de Huatulco is an easy 27 miles (45 km) farther east from the Pochutla junction. (Puerto Ángel is alternatively accessible via the very scenic paved shortcut, via the miniresorts of Mazunte and Zipolite, from Highway 200, at San Antonio village, Km 198.)

To or from Oaxaca city, all paved but sometimes roughly potholed National Highway 131 connects directly north, along main street Avenida Oaxaca, via its winding but spectacular 158-mile (254-km) route over the pine-clad Sierra Madre del Sur. The route, which rises 9,000 feet through Chatino foothill and mountain country, can be chilly in the winter and has only a modicum of rough restaurants, few if any guesthouses, and no gas stations (but Magna gasoline sold from drums) on the long 100-mile middle stretch between San Gabriel Mixtepec and Sola de Vega. Take water and blankets, and be prepared for emergencies. Allow about nine hours at the wheel from Puerto Escondido, eight hours the other way, from Oaxaca city. Fill up with gasoline at the airport Pemex stations on either end before heading out.

By Bus

Several long-distance bus lines serve Puerto Escondido from the new bus station on Highway 131 uphill, a mile beyond the north edge of town. The terminal provides a few services, including card-operated telephones, an a/c first-class waiting room, a snack store with only bottled drinks and sandwiches (but no fruit), and luggage storage.

Many of the lines offer first-class service. Biggest and busiest is **Estrella Blanca** and its subsidiary lines (luxury and first-class Elite and Futura and others), tel. 954/582-3878 or 954/582-0086, that travel the Highway 200 Acapulco-to-Isthmus coastal corridor. More than two dozen daily *salidas de paso* come through en route both ways between Acapulco and Pochutla and Huatulco (Crucecita) and Salina Cruz. A few additional buses pass through, connecting with either Ixtapa and Zihuatanejo or Mexico City via Acapulco.

Independent **Fletes y Pasajes** (tel. 954/582-3873) has second-class departures that connect north with Oaxaca, via Pochutla and Highway 175.

Cooperating lines **Autobúses Estrella del Valle** and **Autotransportes Oaxaca Pacífico,** tel. 954/582-0050, provide both first- and second-class connections with Oaxaca city, via both Highway 175 through Pochutla and Highway 131 directly north from Puerto Escondido.

Minor lines **Autobúses Estrella Roja del Sureste** and **Transol** buses, tel. 954/582-0603, connect first-class (via pilgimage town Juquila) along Highway 131 from Puerto Escondido, directly north, with Oaxaca.

Cristóbal Colón, the other major first-class bus line, tel. 954/582-1073, serves the Oaxaca east coast, from its own separate bus terminal, at 207 Calle 1 Norte, about three blocks above the highway, and two blocks east of main street Avenida Oaxaca. Beginning in Puerto Escondido, several buses connect daily along Highway 200 east, all the way to San Cristóbal las Casas in Chiapas and Tapachula at the Guatemala border. Separate departures connect north with Oaxaca, some continuing to Mexico City and Puebla, via Tehuantepec on the Isthmus. Intermediate destinations for all buses include Pochutla, Huatulco (Crucecita), Salina Cruz, and Tehuantepec, all along Highway 200 east.

EXCURSIONS FROM PUERTO ESCONDIDO

Whether you go escorted or independently, outings away from the Puerto Escondido resort can reveal rewarding glimpses of flora and fauna, local cultures, and idyllic beaches seemingly half a world removed from the *adoquín* tourist hubbub.

Farthest afield, beginning two hours drive west of Puerto Escondido, are the festivals, markets, and handicrafts of Mixtec towns and villages around **Jamiltepec and Pinotepa Nacional** and the crystalline beaches and wildlife-rich mangrove reaches of the **Lagunas de Chacahua National Park.** To the east lie the hidden beaches of **Mazunte, Zipolite,** and the picture-book **Bay of Puerto Ángel,** with their turtle museum, au naturel sunbathing on Playa Zipolite, and very accessible off-beach snorkeling at Puerto Ángel. A bit farther beckon the nine breezy Bays of Huatulco, ripe for swimming, scuba diving, wildlife viewing, biking, and river rafting.

Closer at hand, especially for wildlife lovers and beachgoers, are the jungly lagoons and pristine strands of the **Laguna de Manialtepec** and the nearby hot springs and Chatino sacred site of Atotonilco.

Atotonilco Hot Springs

Also on the west side, the Aguas Termales Atotonilco hot springs, a Chatino sacred site, provides an interesting focus for a day's outing. The jumping-off point is the village of San José Manialtepec, about half an hour by bus or car west of Puerto Escondido.

At the village, you should hire someone to show you the way, up the canyon of the Río Manialtepec. The trail winds along cornfields, beneath forest canopies, and past Chatino native villages. Finally you arrive at the hot spring, where a large basin bubbles with very hot (bearable for the brave), clear, sulfur-smelling water.

Get there by driving or busing to the Highway 200 turnoff for San José Manialtepec, around Km 116, just east of the Río Manialtepec bridge. Village stables provide horses and guides to the hot springs. It's a very easy two-mile walk, except in times of high water on the river, which the trail crosses several times.

Tours

Puerto Escondido agencies arrange outings to all of the above and more. Among the very best are the tours of the Canadian husband-wife team of Michael Malone and Joan Walker, **Hidden Voyages Ecotours** (Viajes Dimar travel agency, Avenida Pérez Gasga 906, tel./fax 954/582-0734 or 954/582-2305, viajesdimar@hotmail.com; or next to Hotel Inés, Playa Zicatela, tel. 954/582-0737). Working through the competent **Viajes Dimar** travel agency, ornithologist Michael and artist/ecologist Joan lead unusually informative beach, lagoon, and mountain tours seasonally, mid-December through Easter. In addition, they offer a sunset lagoon wildlife and beach excursion, and a birdwatching and beach tour by boat at Lagunas de Chacahua. Their trips ordinarily run about $50 per day, per person. For more details, visit www .peleewings.ca, or email them michael@ peleewings.ca, or (May–November) call them at 519/326-5193 in Canada.

Other Dimar tours include a full-day jaunt east to the turtle museum at Playa Mazunte, continuing to Playa Zipolite, lunch, then an afternoon of snorkeling around Puerto Ángel. Evenings during the dark of the moon, trips can include night snorkeling when algae coats everything underwater with an eerie bioluminiscent glow. The cost runs about $30 per person. Additionally, they offer an all-day hiking, picnic, and swimming excursion at a luxuriously cool mountain river and cascade in the sylvan Sierra Madre foothill jungle above Pochutla for about $40 per person, $80 two days, one night (minimum four people).

Alternatively, try one of the tours guided by very experienced and well-equipped **Lalo Tours**, tel. 954/582-2468, laloecotours@ hotmail.com, www.lalo-ecotours.com. Their several tours (full day tours, about $40 per person, half-day $20) include Laguna Manialtepec birdwatching by boat, or birdwatching by footpath in Laguna Manialtepec's barrier sandbar forest, an ocean sunset cruise, and a fascinating night exploration by boat of the ghostly glow of Laguna Manialtepec's phosphorescent waters.

Personable **Gina Machorro** (tel. 954/582-0276, ginainpuerto@yahoo.com) of Puerto Escondido *turismo,* who often staffs the booth at the west-end Pérez Gasga chain, also leads local walking tours, including an important archaeological site.

Puerto Ángel and Vicinity

During his three presidencies, Oaxaca-born Benito Juárez shaped many dreams into reality. One such dream was to better the lot of his native brethren in the isolated south of Oaxaca by developing a port for shipping the lumber and coffee they could harvest in the lush Pacific-slope jungles of the Sierra Madre del Sur. The small bay of Puerto Ángel, directly south of the state capital, was chosen, and by 1870 it had become Oaxaca's busiest port.

Unfortunately, Benito Juárez died two years later. New priorities and Puerto Ángel's isolation soon wilted Juárez's plan, and Puerto Ángel lapsed into a generations-long slumber.

In the 1960s, Puerto Ángel was still a sleepy little spot connected by a single frail link—a tortuous cross-Sierra dirt road—to the rest of the country. Adventure travelers saw it at the far south of the map and dreamed of a south-seas paradise. They came and were not disappointed. That first tourist trickle has grown steadily, so that it now supports the sprinkling of modest lodgings, restaurants, and services not only around Puerto Ángel's tranquil little blue bay, but also in the neigboring palm-shadowed villages on the gorgeous golden Playas Zipolite, San Agustinillo, and Mazunte.

BEACHES AND SIGHTS

Puerto Ángel is at the southern terminus of Highway 175 from Oaxaca, about six miles (9 km) downhill from its intersection with Highway 200. It's a small place, where nearly everything is within walking distance along the beach, which a rocky bayfront hill divides into two parts: Playa Principal, the main town beach, and sheltered west-side Playa Panteón, the tourist favorite. A scenic boulder-decorated shoreline *andador* (watch out for gaps and holes in the concrete) connects the two beaches.

A paved road winds west from Puerto Ángel along the coastline a couple of miles to Playa Zipolite, lined by a colony of hammock-and-bamboo beachfront *cabañas,* popular with an

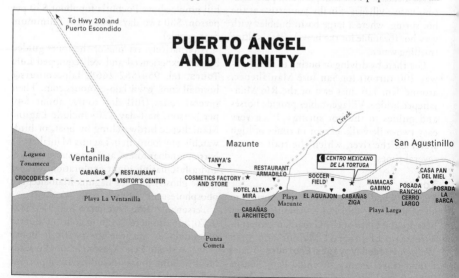

PUERTO ÁNGEL AND VICINITY

international cadre of budget-minded seekers of heaven on earth. Continuing west, the road passes the former turtle-processing village beaches of Playa San Agustinillo and Playa Mazunte. From there it goes on another four miles, joining with Highway 200 (and thence Puerto Escondido) at San Antonio village at Km 198.

The major local service and transportation center is **Pochutla** (pop. 35,000), a mile north along Highway 175 from its Highway 200 junction.

Local *colectivo* taxis ferry passengers frequently between Pochutla and Puerto Ángel (fare, about $.70) 6 A.M.–8 P.M., stopping at the Highway 200 intersection. Some taxis continue to Zipolite after stopping on Boulevard Uribe, Puerto Ángel's main bayfront street. To continue to Playa San Agustinillo and Playa Mazunte, you must transfer to another *colectivo* (arriving from the opposite direction) in Zipolite. Private taxis also routinely make runs between Puerto Ángel and either Zipolite or Pochutla for about $5.

You can also get around (more expensively) by boat. Captains routinely take parties of up to eight for sightseeing, snorkeling, and picnicking to a number of nearby beaches. Bargain at Playa Panteón.

Playas Principal and Panteón

Playa Principal's 400 yards of wide golden sand decorate most of Puerto Ángel's bayfront. Waves can be strong near the pier, where they often surge vigorously onto the beach and recede with some undertow. Swimming is more tranquil at the sheltered west end toward Playa Panteón. The clear waters are good for casual snorkeling around the rocks, on both sides of the bay.

Sheltered Playa Panteón (Cemetery Beach) is Puerto Ángel's sunning beach, lined with squadrons of beach chairs and umbrellas in front of beachside restaurants. **Playa Oso** (Bear Beach) is a little dab of sand beside a rugged seastack of rock beyond Playa Panteón, fun to swim to from Playa Panteón and explore the small cave in the rocks by the beach.

◖ Playa Estacahuite

Just outside the opposite (east) side of the Bay of Puerto Ángel, Playa Estacahuite is actually three beaches in one: a trio of luscious

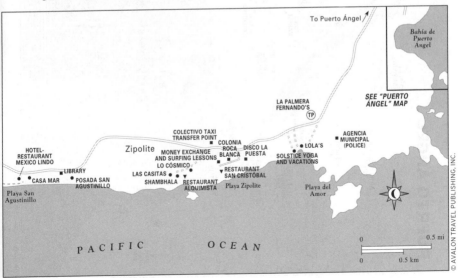

THE COSTA CHICA

© AVALON TRAVEL PUBLISHING, INC.

PUERTO ÁNGEL

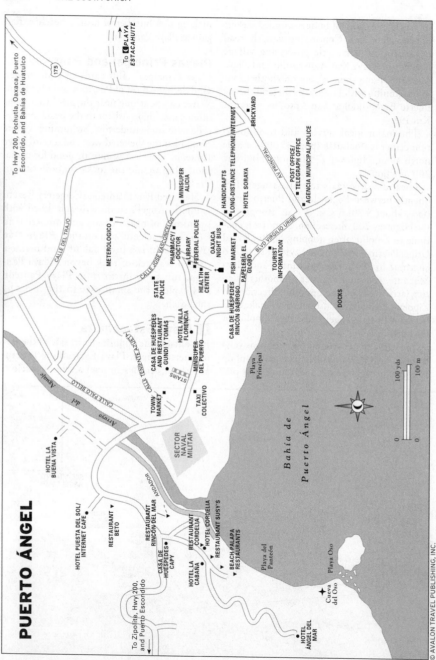

To Hwy 200, Pochutla, Oaxaca, Puerto Escondido, and Bahías de Huatulco

To ◆PLAYA ESTACAHUITE

175

CALLE DEL TRAJO

CALLE JOSE VASCONCELOS

METEROLOGICO

MINISUPER ALICIA

HANDICRAFTS

LONG-DISTANCE TELEPHONE/INTERNET

HOTEL SORAYA

BRICKYARD

AV. PRINCIPAL

POST OFFICE/ TELEGRAPH OFFICE

AGENCIA MUNICIPAL/POLICE

STATE POLICE

PHARMACY/ DOCTOR

LIBRARY

FEDERAL POLICE

OAXACA NIGHT BUS

FISH MARKET

PAPELERÍA EL GLOBO

BLVD VIRGILIO URIBE

HEALTH CENTER

CASA DE HUÉSPEDES AND RESTAURANT GUNDI Y TOMÁS

HOTEL VILLA FLORENCIA

CASA DE HUÉSPEDES RINCÓN SABROSO

TOURIST INFORMATION

DOCKS

CALLE TENIENTE AZUETA

Arroyo del Aguaje

CALLE PALO BELLO

MINISUPER DEL PUERTO

STAIRS

TOWN MARKET

TAXI COLECTIVO

SECTOR NAVAL MILITAR

Playa Principal

Bahía de Puerto Ángel

HOTEL LA BUENA VISTA

HOTEL PUESTA DEL SOL/ INTERNET CAFÉ

RESTAURANT BETO

RESTAURANT RINCÓN DEL MAR

ANDADOR

RESTAURANT CORDELIA

HOTEL CORDELIA

RESTAURANT SUSY'S

CASA DE HUÉSPEDES CAPY

HOTEL LA CABAÑA

BEACH PALAPA RESTAURANTS

Playa del Panteón

Playa Oso

Cueva del Oso

To Zipolite, Hwy 200, and Puerto Escondido

HOTEL ANGEL DEL MAR

100 yds

100 m

0

0

© AVALON TRAVEL PUBLISHING, INC.

© BRUCE WHIPPERMAN

Clear blue water, good snorkeling, and restaurants make Playa Estacahuite one of Pacific Mexico's best beaches.

coral-sand nooks teeming with fish grazing the living reef just offshore. A pair of *palapa* restaurants perched picturesquely above the beaches provide food and drinks. There's plenty of soft sand and usually gentle waves, due to the reef's protecting rocky perimeter. Snorkel equipment is customarily for rent on the beach, and a few *lanchas* are usually available for fishing excursions. Get there in less than a mile by taxi or on foot via the dirt road that forks right off Highway 175 about 400 yards uphill from beachfront Boulevard Uribe.

Playa Zipolite

Playa Zipolite is a wide, mile-long strand of yellow-white sand enfolded by headlands and backed by palm groves. It stretches from the gorgeously intimate little cove and beach of **Playa del Amor** (now very gay-friendly), tucked on its east side to towering seacliffs rising behind the new-age Shambala retreat on the west end. The Playa Zipolite surf, although usually tranquil in the mornings (but always with significant undertow), can turn thunder-

ous by the afternoon, especially when offshore storms magnify both the swells and the undertow. Experienced surfers love these times, when everyone but experts should stay out.

Good surfing notwithstanding, Zipolite's renown stems from its status as one of the very few nude beaches in Mexico. Bathing au naturel, practiced nearly entirely by visitors and a few local young men, is tolerated only grudgingly by local people, many of whose livelihoods depend on the nudists. If you're discreet and take off your clothes at the more isolated west end (behind the big rock), no one will appear to mind (and women will avoid unwelcome voyeuristic attention).

Playa Zipolite has evolved from a lineup of stick and thatch beachfront *cabañas* to sturdy concrete (cheap, and mostly scruffy) hotels, most with oceanview *palapa* restaurants. Many of these share a new, paved two-block main streetfront along with a procession of restaurants and small businesses, from grocery and pharmacy, to surf shop, laundry, and money exchange. All of this, locally known as either

© BRUCE WHIPPERMAN

San Agustinillo residents enjoy a beach that faces both east and west at the same time.

Colonia Roca Blanca or the *adoquín* (as in Puerto Escondido), is now Zipolite's new town center. (Get there, heading west, from Puerto Ángel, by turning toward the beach after the children's school, at the library on the corner.)

Playas San Agustinillo and Mazunte

About a mile west of Zipolite, a wide, mile-long, yellow-sand beach curves past the village of San Agustinillo. On the open ocean but partly protected by offshore rocks, its surf is much like that of Zipolite, varying from gentle to rough, depending mostly upon wind and off-shore swells. Small village groceries and beach-side *palapa* restaurants supply food and drinks to the occasional Zipolite overflow and local families on weekends and holidays. Fishing is excellent, either in the surf, from nearby rocks, by rented *lancha*, or your own boat launched from the beach. Beach camping is custom-ary, especially at a few rustic, hammock-hung roadside *ramadas*, such as **El Paraíso,** at the east (Zipolite) end of the beach.

Remnants of the local turtle industry can be found at the rusting former processing factories on Playa San Agustinillo (west end) and Playa Mazunte two miles farther west.

The half-mile-long, yellow-sand Mazunte Beach, like San Agustinillo, is semisheltered and varies from tranquil to rough. Fishing is likewise good, beach camping is customary (as a courtesy, ask nearby business owners if it's okay), and local stores and seafood *palapa* res-taurants sell basic supplies and food.

Mazunte people have also been renovating their houses and building sturdy hotels and *cabañas* to accommodate an increasing num-ber of visitors. Some have even begun to adver-tise on the Internet. Signs along the road and at the beach advertise their homespun lodg-ings and restaurants. (For details, see *Mazunte* under *Accommodations,* and visit www.tomzap .com/mazunteb.html.)

⬧ Centro Mexicano de la Tortuga

The former turtle-processing plant at Mazunte lives on as the National Mexican Turtle

Center (on the main road, east end of the village, P.O. Box 16, Puerto Ángel, Oaxaca 70902, tel. 958/584-3055, fax 958/584-3603, www .tomzap.com/turtle.html, 10 A.M.–4:30 P.M. Wed.–Sat., 10 A.M.–2:30 P.M. Sun.). At the museum, which includes an aquarium, study center, and turtle hatchery, you can peruse displays illustrating the ongoing turtle research and conservation program and see members of most of Mexico's turtle species paddling in tanks overlooking the beach where their ancestors once swarmed.

Cosmetics Factory and Store

About half a mile farther west along the main road through Mazunte village, stop by the store and works of the **Fábrica Ecología de Cosméticos Naturales de Mazunte.** Initially funded mostly by the Body Shop Foundation, and spearheaded by the community, local workers make and sell all-natural shampoo, skin cream, hair conditioner, and more. Staff are working hard to assure that the effort catches on, so that locally grown products, such as coconut, corn, and avocado oils and natural aromatics will form the basis for a thriving cottage cosmetics industry.

Playa la Ventanilla

Continue about 1.5 miles west along the main road over the low hill west of Mazunte and turn left at the signed dirt road to pristine wildlife haven Playa and Laguna la Ventanilla. Now protected by local residents, swarms of birds, including pelicans, cormorants, and herons, nest there, and a population of wild *cocodrilos* and *lagartos* is making a comeback in a bushy mangrove wetland.

Boatmen headquartered at the sturdy *visitors center palapa* past the beach village road's end parking lot guide visitors on a two-hour ecotour ($4 per adult, kids half price), which includes a stop for refreshment at a little mid-lagoon island. The boatmen are known for their wildlife sensitivity and allow no motor vehicles within 100 yards of their communally owned lagoon-sanctuary.

(Note: A second latecomer cooperative,

which does nothing for conservation, but only conducts lagoon tours, may try to intercept you in the parking lot. Simply avoid them and continue to the original conservation cooperative's beachfront visitors center to get your boat-tour ticket.)

The Playa la Ventanilla community has also taken responsibility for protecting the turtles that arrive on their beach against poachers. During both February and June through October, hundreds of sea turtles come ashore to lay eggs. If necessary, community volunteers help the exhausted turtles up the steep beach, where they lay their eggs. Volunteers then gather the eggs and rebury them in a secure spot. After the hatchlings emerge about a month and a half later, volunteers nurture them for about three months and release them safely back into the ocean. For more information, visit www .tomzap.com/ventanil.html.

Besides boat tours and conservation, the La Ventanilla cooperative maintains an excellent beach-view **restaurant,** 8 A.M.–7 P.M. daily. Furthermore, the La Ventanilla cooperative invites visitors to stay in their rough-and-ready, rustic but sturdy, concrete-floored *cabañas* with beds. (Bring your own mosquito net.)

ACCOMMODATIONS

The Puerto Ángel area offers dozens of accommodations, most of which are modest, home-grown guesthouse-style lodgings. The successful ones have given their legion of savvy repeat customers what they want: clean, basic, tepid-water accommodations in tranquil, television-free settings where Puerto Ángel's natural isolation and tropical charm set the tone for long, restful holidays.

Visitors have their choice of several neighborhoods. In Puerto Ángel itself, hotels and guesthouses dot the hillside above the main town beach, the pier, and the single main business street. The Playa Panteón (Cemetery Beach) lodgings, by contrast, are on the sleepier west side of the bay, above the lineup of rustic *palapa* restaurants along petite Playa Panteón.

Outside of Puerto Ángel, visitors also have

many choices, mostly right on the beach but others atop breezy view hillsides, above the plumy, west-side country beachfront hamlets of Zipolite, San Agustinillo, and Mazunte.

Main Town
UNDER $25

One of Puerto Ángel's most welcoming lodgings is the exceptional **Ⓒ Casa de Huéspedes Gundi y Tomás** (P.O. Box 6, Puerto Ángel, Oaxaca 70902, tel. 958/584-3068, gundtoma@ hotmail.com, www.puertoangel-hotel.com, $20 s or $25 d; with bath $35 d; bungalow $40), the life project of friendly German-born Gundi Ley. Her homey, rustic-aesthetic complex rambles up a leafy hillside to a breezy bay-view *palapa* where patrons relax, socialize, and enjoy food and drink from the kitchen. Just above that, guests enjoy a double row of several clean, simply furnished rooms, shaded by a shared hammock-hung view porch. Besides all this, the staff changes U.S. dollar traveler's checks, volunteers information about local sights, offers telephone service, does laundry, and arranges activities and excursions for guests. Gundi's sons, Bastián and Fabián, also offer surfing lessons. The accommodations, which include the Almendro tropical garden guesthouse near the beach downhill, consist of 16 rooms and a kitchenette bungalow. Rooms with shared showers and toilets cost about $20 s or $25 d; larger rooms with private shower and toilet run about $35 d, the bungalow, $40 d, all with fans and a good restaurant. Get there via the lane that stair-steps uphill near the west end of Puerto Ángel's main beachfront street.

At the splendidly isolated **Casa de Huéspedes Rincón Sabroso** (Puerto Ángel, Oaxaca 70902, tel. 958/584-3095, $18 s or d, $20 t tepid water; $27 s or d, $30 t hot water), atop a bay-vista hill, guests enjoy lodgings that open onto a hammock-hung view breezeway adorned by luscious tropical greenery. Inside, the 10 rooms are very clean (but dark), with white walls, tile floors, shiny bathrooms, natural wood furnishings, and fans.

$25-50

Travelers who enjoy being right in the middle of the Puerto Ángel beachfront street scene choose the petite **Hotel Villa Florencia** (Blv. Virgilio Uribe s/n, Puerto Ángel, Oaxaca 70902, tel./fax 958/584-3044, villaserenaoax@ hotmail.com, $28 s, $32 d, $40 t, add $3 for a/c). Here, in the shady interior lobby-patio, past the good streetfront restaurant, tranquility reigns as soft classic songs and instrumental music play in the background, while guests read and relax on comfortable chairs and couches. Upstairs, the approximately 15 rooms, with bath, are immaculate and thoughtfully decorated with local art and handicrafts.

Another very worthy Puerto Ángel accommodation is **Ⓒ Hotel la Buena Vista** (P.O. Box 48, Puerto Ángel, Oaxaca 70902, tel./fax 958/584-3104, reservations@labuenavista .com, www.labuenavista.com, rooms $42 s, $48 d and $55 t; $60 d on top floors), tucked on the hillside that rises just west of the midtown Arroyo de Aguaje bridge. The hotel's five levels of accommodations level stair-step artfully (but steeply) up the forested slope. First- and second-level rooms look out onto verdure-framed bay views. On the third level are more rooms and a luxuriously airy restaurant *palapa* that opens to a picture-perfect bay vista. The hotel climaxes with several large onyx-tile-floored fourth- and fifth-floor rooms that share a their own view patio with hammocks. All guests can share another luxurious **view pool-patio** up here. Rooms are immaculate, light, and simply but tastefully furnished, with spotless bathrooms. Customary rates (holidays excepted) for the approximately 20 rooms are about $42 s, $48 d and 55 t for the first-, second-, and restaurant-level rooms, several of which have private hammock-hung view balconies. The larger, newer, and more deluxe fourth- and fifth-level rooms by the pool run about $60 d. All with fans, mosquito curtains, and good breakfast and supper restaurant, but with room-temperature water only.

Back on the east side of town, find the

1960s motel-style **Hotel Soraya** (Priv. José Vasconcelos 2A, Puerto Ángel, Oaxaca 70902, tel./fax 958/584-3009, $35 s or d, $40 t high season), perched on the bluff above the pier. The well-managed hotel includes a restaurant with an airy bay view, fine for bright morning breakfasts and sunset-glow dinners. Outside, two tiers of spartan but light and comfortable rooms enclose a parking patio. Although some rooms have a/c, the fan-only ones are preferable, since they avoid the a/c noise and oft-associated mildew. Check before moving in. Rent on the upper story for more privacy and air. The 32 rooms rent for about $35 s or d, and $40 t high season; ask for a discount low season.

Playa Panteón
UNDER $25

Heading around the curve of the bay to the Playa Panteón neighborhood, you'll find one of Puerto Ángel's old standby budget lodgings, **Casa de Huéspedes Capy** (Playa Panteón, P.O. Box 44, Puerto Ángel, Oaxaca 70902, tel./fax 958/584-3240, hotel_capy@hotmail.com, $10 s, $15 d one bed; $18 d, $20 t two beds), sitting on the bay-view hillside by the road fork to Zipolite. Rooms, in two tiers with views toward Playa Panteón, are basic but clean with fans and cool-water private baths. Good family management is the Capy's strong suit. This shows in the shady view restaurant, Arcely, where good food in a friendly atmosphere encourages guests to linger, reading or talking, for hours. The family also watch the community TV at night; if it bothers you, ask them to turn it down.

$25-50

Downhill stands Puerto Ángel's only truly beachfront lodging, **Hotel Cordelia** (right on Playa Panteón, Puerto Escondido, Oaxaca 70902, tel. 958/584-3109, fax 958/584-3232, azul_profundomx@hotmail.com, $27 s or d). The Cordelia's seven rooms, most with bay views, are sparely but pleasingly decorated with rustic whitewashed walls, attractive native floor tiles, natural wood furniture, and artful

tile touches in the modern-standard baths. No phone, no TV, just the murmur of the gentle Playa Panteón surf to lull you to sleep. Rooms rent for about $27 s or d, except holidays. With fans and good restaurant downstairs.

OVER $50

Visitors who long for the delights of a hidden south seas hideaway can have it at **Bahía de la Luna** (on the coast about two miles east of Puerto Ángel, tel. 958/589-5020, info@bahiadelaluna.com, www.bahiadelaluna.com, $75 s or d and up). New owners have revitalized this mini-paradise, set on a petite, palm-shaded half-moon strand, lapped by gentle waves and enfolded by rocky headlands. They offer about a dozen comfortable rustic-chic thatched, adobe *cabañas*, some with panoramic views, on the forested hillside above the beach, and others, tucked in the leafy shade, right on the beach below. Rentals begin at $75 s or d high season, for one room with big bed, reading lamps, and private tepid-water shower bath; there's a good restaurant, hammocks for snoozing, shady beach *palapas* and recliners, and snorkeling equipment for guest use. A pair of larger similarly comfortable units: a suite accommodating four, and a villa accommodating six, go for about $125 and $190 high season, respectively. (Get there via the signed but rough side road, east off of Highway 175, about five miles (8 km) downhill from the Highway 200 Pochutla junction, or two miles (3 km) uphill from Puerto ángel. After about two bumpy miles from the turnoff, the road steepens and becomes impassable for all but a sturdy four-wheel drive vehicles. Best go by taxi.)

Zipolite
UNDER $25

Shambhala (P.O. Box 68, Pochutla, Oaxaca 70900, shambhala_vision@excite.com, www.advantagemexico.com/shambhala, $23), on Zipolite's west-side forested headland, is as it sounds—a tranquil Buddhist-style retreat. Shambhala's driving force is the articulate owner-community leader Gloria Esperanza Johnson, who arrived in Zipolite by accident in 1970 and decided to stay, eventually adopting Mexican citizenship.

Shambhala is a quiet, alcohol-free haven for lovers of reading, sunbathing, hiking, yoga, and meditation. It sits atop an enviable few acres at the edge of a sylvan hinterland. Adjacent cactus-studded cliffs plummet spectacularly to surf-splashed rocks below, while paths fan out through lush tropical deciduous forest. An excellent macrobiotic panoramic vista restaurant completes the attractive picture.

Gloria has built Shambhala from the ground up, until she now offers five rustic view *cabañas* (on a no-reservation, first-come-first-served basis only), two on the beach and three in the leafy (green summer-fall, early winter) forest overlooking lovely Zipolite beach. All accommodations rent for about $23 per night. Choices include two beachfront *cabañas,* one accommodating two and the other accommodating four, with shared bath; two small view *cabañas,* tucked in the uphill forest, each with private shower baths; and a larger view *cabaña,* also in the uphill forest, accommodating three, with shared bath. All *cabañas* come with fans, and mosquito nets.

The *cabañas* of **Lo Cósmico** (at Playa Zipolite, P.O. Box 36, Pochutla, Oaxaca 70900, admin@locosmico.com, www.locosmico.com, $15–30 d *cabaña,* $25 d room) nestle on a cactus-decorated rocky knoll adjacent to Shambhala. White spheres perched on their thatched-roof peaks lend a mystical accent to the *cabañas'* already picturesque appearance. In the restaurant atop the knoll, you're likely to find Regula and Antonio Nadurille, Lo Cósmico's European-Mexican owners. Regula manages the restaurant, specializing in a dozen varieties of tasty crepes, while Antonio supervises the hotel. Their hillside and beach-level *cabañas* are clean, candle-lit, and equipped with hammocks and concrete floors, for about $15–30 d. Recently, Antonio has built a number of sturdy, rock-walled, hurricane-proof designer rooms on his view hillside. Figure about $25 d for these. Note: All of Lo Cosmico's toilet and shower facilities are separate from the accommodations, a short walk downhill.

Get to both Shambhala and Lo Cósmico by turning from the main road onto the dirt driveway just west of the arch at Zipolite's west end. Bear right at the first fork, then left at the next for Lo Cósmico, right for Shambhala.

$25-50

If you arrive from Puerto Ángel, Zipolite's line of lodgings starts at **Lola's** (on the east end of the beach, Playa Zipolite, Puerto Ángel, Oaxaca 70902, tel. 958/584-3201 or 958/584-3203, $20 s or d low season, $30 high). The friendly, now-elderly owner continues her decades-long good management (although her equally personable daughter, Lola Chica, does the day-to-day work of her mother's enterprise).

The scene at Lola's is all relaxation, with the restaurant right on the beach, where guests enjoy late breakfasts, stroll out for swims, read thick novels, and kick back and enjoy convivial conversation with mostly North American and European fellow vacationers. Although past hurricanes wiped out her former rustic wood *cabañas,* they've been replaced with modern-standard stucco units that rent for about $20 s or d low season, $30 high, with fan and private shower baths.

Alternatively, consider **◖ Solstice Yoga and Vacations** (at Playa Zipolite, P.O. Box 18, Puerto Ángel, Oaxaca 70902, info@solstice-mexico.com, www.solstice-mexico.com, $27-33 d low season, $33-39 high, $8-10 dorm bed), next door, west, from Lola's. Friendly European expatriate owners Brigette Longueville and Guy Hamaekers have built an inviting, authentically rustic minicolony of two-story *cabañas* on the gorgeous Zipolite beachfront. Accommodations are in Robinson Crusoe–style huts, in all natural wood, with ladders leading to upstairs sleeping-lounging areas, with serape-draped beds, hung with gauzy mosquito nets. Guests are about evenly divided between beach vacationers and yoga devotees, who attend sessions in the in-house studio.

Accommodations rent for about $27 d low season, $33 high, for the one smaller unit, and about $33 low, $39 high for the three larger units; $5 per extra person, with private bathroom with toilet and tepid-water shower baths and breakfast included. Dormitory accommodations are also available, for $8 per person low season, $10 high. Brigette and Guy offer Hatha yoga classes, for $7 per 1.5 hours.

Bungalows **Las Casitas** (on Zipolite's west end, occupying the same hilltop, but west, of Shambhala, info@las-casitas.net, www.las-casitas .net, $40 d and up) are the labor of love of friendly builders-owners Daniela and Bruno Canibus, who have created their version of paradise in Zipolite's summer-green tropical forest. They offer four housekeeping bungalows, meticulously hand-built of all-natural materials, in a lovingly tended naturalistic garden of meandering stone pathways, sea views, and refreshing breezes, with a rustic *palapa* restaurant, fine for enjoying leisurely meals and conversation with fellow guests. A path leads downhill to Zipolite beach.

The four bungalows, all different, come with kitchenettes equipped with gas stove, utensils, and purified water. Two of the bungalows, El Organo and La Tortuga, have one room each that accommodates two people, with private shower bath, for about $40 d, that would be fine for couples. The other two bungalows, Los Platanos and La Ceiba, each have three bedrooms with shared kitchen and bathroom and accommodate six and nine people respectively. The three rooms in the Los Platanos bungalow, for one, two, and three people each, rent for $20, $25, and $30 respectively. The rooms in the larger La Ceiba bungalow, for two, three and four people, rent for about $40, $50, and $60. (Get to Las Casitas via the dirt road to Lo Cósmico, which you should pass. Continue uphill about two hundred yards more to the Las Casitas gate.)

San Agustinillo
$25-50
A few mostly ordinary lodgings sprinkle the San Agustinillo oceanfront. The gem among them, however, is **Casa Mar** (tel. 958/589-2401–Spanish only, havasluis@hotmail.com, $45 and $35 d, $60 with kitchenette), a sturdy brick house and beachview *palapa*, perched

right on the edge of the gorgeous, sheltered shoreline. The welcoming retired (primarily Spanish-speaking) owners, Luis and Guadalupe Havas, built Casa Mar because they wanted to live right by the beach. Now, they enjoy sharing their airy oceanfront haven with other lovers of sun, sea, and sand. They offer three comfortable and clean accommodations, two invitingly furnished but smallish rooms downstairs, accommodating two in a double bed, with private bath, for about $45 and $35 d, respectively. Best of all is the airy view kitchenette apartment upstairs, accommodating four, with private bath and its own panoramic ocean-view patio, for about $60. Here, you can enjoy it all: Mexican beach village ambience, stores and small restaurants nearby, and a hammock-hung veranda with a gorgeous view of the foaming San Agustinillo surf and hundreds of yards of golden sand to wander upon.

A few doors west, walk out your door right onto the sand at San Agustinillo beachfront option **Mexico Lindo** (fafinyleila@latinmail .com, $50 d) hotel and restaurant. Owner Fausto offers five spacious individually decorated *cabañas* in two stories, with soft beds and private shower baths. Rates run about $50 d, with fans and a good (but sometimes noisy) restaurant downstairs.

OVER $50
Casa Pan de Miel (about a third of a mile west of San Agustillo, tel. 958/589-5844, casapandemiel@yahoo.com.mx, www.casa pandemiel.com, $80 d, $100 q), the lifelong dream-come-true of French-born co-owner Anne Gillete, perches on its airy hilltop above the blue Pacific. Only superlatives can describe the architecturally designed amenities: spacious veranda breakfast restaurant, a blue designer pool, soft couches and chairs for sitting inside, lounge chairs and umbrellas by the pool, and panoramic ocean views east, toward San Agustinillo; south, out to sea; and west toward Mazunte's gracefully curving strand. Guests enjoy four spacious, comfortable, and artfully decorated deluxe rooms, for about $80 d, $100 for four, higher during holidays, with

private view porches, hot water bathrooms, fans, and a/c, but credit cards not accepted, and no children, please.

Outstandingly innovative **Posada Rancho Cerro Largo** (P.O. Box 121, Pochutla, Oaxaca 70900, ranchocerrolargomx@yahoo.com.mx, $60 s, $70 d), half a mile farther west, is the creation of ecoactivist Mario Corella, descendant of a longtime Hermosillo, Sonora, hotel family. After knocking around in the hospitality trade for several years, Mario decided to create his own version of utopia. Mario says that he wanted to "be in contact with nature and live among the community with as little impact as possible."

He's done it, with a reception-restaurant and six rustically charming tile-floored, wood-and-adobe *cabañas,* furnished with hand-loomed bedspreads and opening to hammock-hung ocean-view verandas. The entire complex nestles in a summer-green and gorgeous hillside deciduous forest, linked by a path that meanders, between panoramic ocean viewpoints, to a gorgeously isolated, wave-washed sandy beach below. Rates run a reasonable $60 s, $70 d, including dinner and breakfast. Email for reservations, necessary in winter, highly recommended anytime. Get to Rancho Cerro Largo via the signed driveway on the Puerto Ángel-Mazunte road, four miles (6.4 km) from the Puerto Ángel bus stop.

Mazunte

Mazunte folks offer a number of lodgings, from rough beachfront *cabañas* to semideluxe architecturally designed thatched *palapas.*

$25-50

Star of the Mazunte beachfront accommodations is **(Cabañas Ziga** (no phone, no email, $20 d shared bath, $25 d private bath), just west of the turtle museum, with 17 rooms in three floors and a palm-shaded beachview restaurant just above the waves. The plainly decorated, spacious, and clean tile-floored rooms go for about $25 d, with private bath, $20 d with shared bath, all with fans and mosquito nets. As of this writing Cabañas Ziga accepts

no reservations. Show up before noon to be sure you get a room, especially during the busy winter season.

Another invitingly rustic lodging that you might check out on the palm-shadowed Mazunte beachfront is **Posada del Arquitecto,** on Playa Rinconcito (at the far, west end of the Mazunte beach, tel. 958/583-8982, guidocco@ yahoo.com.mx, $35, dorm bed $4 pp, camping hammock $4 pp). Owners offer nine clean, *palapa*-sheltered cabañas with mosquito nets, fans, and private shower baths for about $35. They also have dormitory rooms with bunks for $4 per person, and a campground with *palapa* shelters and hammocks, also $4 per person. (Find it at the beach end of Calle Rinconcito, a block west of the bridge in Mazunte.)

The fanciest accommodation in Mazunte and sister to the Hotel La Buena Vista in Puerto Ángel is the lovely hillside **(Alta Mira Bungalows** (reserve via the Buena Vista in Puerto Ángel: P.O. Box 48, Puerto Ángel, Oaxaca 70902, tel./fax 958/584-3104, reservations@ buenavista.com, www.labuenavista.com/ alta_mira, $45 d low season, $50 d high). Guests enjoy a lovely hillside oceanview setting with restaurant, the murmur of the waves, and a stepped path down to glorious Mazunte beach. The approximately 10 rooms are comfortable rustic chic, with handcrafted furniture, soft beds and hurricane lamps, with private shower baths, and mosquito nets. At this writing the Alta Mira's main drawback was low-power (solar-panel) electricity, which results in weak fans and dim light bulbs.

Get to Alta Mira Bungalows from the main through-town road. A block west of the bridge, turn toward the beach at the side road, Calle Rinconcito. Continue about a block where you turn right at a signed uphill fork road. Continue 300 yards to Alta Mira's signed driveway on the left.

Trailer Park and Camping

The homey café and **Trailer Park la Palmera Fernando's** (Carretera Playa Zipolite-Puerto Ángel, Oaxaca 70902, $8-20 RV site, $6 tent site) has about 20 parking (big rigs possible) or camping spaces beneath a shady, tufted grove by the road at the east end of Playa Zipolite. A spirit of camaraderie often blooms among the tents and assorted RVs of travelers from as far away as Miami, Medicine Hat, and Murmansk. About $8 for small RV, $12 large, $20 very large, gets you a space for two people, including electricity, shared dump station, shower, and toilets. Tent spaces cost $6 for two people.

One of Zipolite's best beach tenting spots is on the beach below Shambhala (with fine food from neighboring Restaurant Alquimista or Shambhala's restaurant uphill). The friendly owner, Gloria Johnson, will probably allow you to use Shambhala's showers and toilets for a small fee. Ask at the Shambhala office if it's okay to camp.

Camping is also customary in **Mazunte** on the beach, in front of Palapa Omar and Cabañas Yuri, or for a $4 per-person fee, at Posada del Architecto.

FOOD
Main Town

For a country place, Puerto Ángel has surprisingly good food, starting with the **Hotel Villa Florencia** (right on the main beachfront street, 8 A.M.–11 P.M. daily). Lulu, the wife of the late Italian-born owner/chef, carries on his tradition, specializing in antipasti and salads ($3–5), and meat and seafood pastas ($5–12). As in any good country Italian restaurant, service is crisp and presentations are attractive. The modest wine list has, in the past, included some good old-country imports, and the pastas al dente and cappuccino are among the best on the coast.

Most welcoming of all Puerto Ángel places to eat is the relaxingly simple restaurant at **Casa de Huéspedes Gundi y Tomás** (uphill on the west end of Puerto Ángel's beachfront street, tel. 958/584-3068, 8 A.M.–9 P.M. daily); see the streetside sign. Owner Gundi Ley offers hearty breakfasts, light lunches, and one or two tasty dinner entrées.

The unpretentiously elegant view *palapa* restaurant at the **Hotel la Buena Vista** (tel.

958/584-3104, 7:30–11 A.M. and 6–10 P.M. daily) is one of the best spots in town for a leisurely, intimate dinner. The menu includes salads, soups ($4), pastas ($4–7), and fresh broiled fish and meats ($7–9).

For simply good *comida casera* (home-cooked food) head straight to **Beto's** (tel. 958/584-3011, 4 P.M.–midnight daily), two blocks west of the town center, a block uphill, past the west-side creek bridge. It's strictly a family operation, with Edilbert Espinosa, owner; Teresa Guzman, his mother, doing the cooking; and Felipe Guzman, his uncle, lending a helping hand. Over more than 20 years, they've built a loyal clientele, who return year after year for their tasty *ceviche* ($3) and healthy specialties, such as avocado stuffed with tuna ($3) and *pescado veracruzana* (*huachinango*, mahimahi, or tuna, veracruz style, $4).

For a spectacular view with late lunch or early dinner (or even just a drink), visit the family-run **Restaurant Rincón del Mar** (on the west-side headland overlooking the bay, 4–10 P.M. daily). Follow the *andador* toward the beach from the beachfront Avenida Uribe bridge, just west of the naval compound. At the restaurant sign, follow the stairway up the rocky headland. The star of the show (aided by a husband-daughter team) is the wife, Mari, who crafts a short but tasty menu of soups and salads ($3–5), pastas ($4–7), and seafood and meats ($5–12).

Zipolite and San Agustinillo

Zipolite also has some good eating places. For hearty macrobiotic-style fare and a breezy beach view, go to the restaurant at **Shambhala** (on the Playa Zipolite west-end headland above the beach, 8 A.M.–8 P.M. daily). Personable owner Gloria Johnson runs a very tidy kitchen, which serves good breakfasts ($3–6), soups and salads ($3–4), and sandwiches ($3–5). No alcohol.

Regula, the European co-owner of **Lo Cósmico** (on the knoll just east of Shambhala, 8 A.M.–7 P.M. daily high season), cooks from a similar macrobiotic-style menu, although she specializes in several variations of crepes, including egg, meat, cheese, and vegetable ($3–6). Shorter hours and closed Monday during the low season.

A regiment of satisfied patrons of 🅒 **Restaurant Alquimista** (right on the Shambhala-Lo Cósmico beachfront, 4–10 P.M. daily low season; noon–midnight high season) choose from a seemingly mile-long menu of appetizers (hummus, guacamole $3–5), soups (onion, cream of carrot $3–6), salads (Greek, romaine, $4–6), *tortas* (egg, ham, cheese, $3–5), fish (10 styles of fillet, $6–12), pastas (*al burro*, cream, Bolognese, $4–8), hamburgers (fish, beef, chicken, $4), and much, much more.

Restaurant San Cristóbal (on the beach, a few steps from Zipolite's main street in Colonia Roca Blanca, 8 A.M.–9 P.M. daily) is one of the best. Especially good are the breakfasts: scrambled eggs with bacon ($4), vegetable soup ($3), and hamburger with french fries ($4).

In **San Agustinillo,** longtimers like shady beachfront *palapa* **Restaurant Mexico Lindo** (at the east, Mazunte end of the beach, 8 A.M.–10 P.M. daily). Owner Fausto and his wife serve from a short but tasty menu of salads ($3), sandwiches ($2–4), tacos and tostadas ($2–4), and seafood ($5–10); closed Sept.–Oct.

Mazunte

In Mazunte, tasty vegetarian-style goodies are the specialty at **Tanya's** (on the west end, up-hill, above the cosmetics factory-store). Besides superfresh seafood ($5–10), Tanya offers plenty of hearty juices ($2–3), salads ($3–5), and soy burgers ($3–4).

A fortunate addition to Mazunte's growing list of good restaurants is **Armadillo** restaurant and bakery (no phone, armadillo.mazunte@yahoo.com.mx, 8 A.M.–11 P.M. daily high season, 3–11 P.M. daily low season). Armadillo is the life project of a personable Mexican-French husband-wife team, who, beneath their sculpture-decorated *palapa* (he's the sculptor), offer a delicious, eclectic menu, including breakfasts (omelettes, $3), lunch (tuna salad, $4), and, for dinner, the Armadillo specialty, stuffed fish fillet ($9). Find them a block and a half down Calle Rinconcito, the street that heads toward the beach, a block west of the Mazunte bridge.

ENTERTAINMENT AND SPORTS

Puerto Ángel's entertainments are mostly spontaneous. If anything exciting is going to happen, it will most likely be on the beachfront Boulevard Uribe, where people tend to congregate during the late afternoon and evenings. A small crowd may accumulate in the adjacent restaurant Villa Florencia for coffee, talk, or something from the bar.

For more lively nightlife, head west to Zipolite and Mazunte. In Zipolite, follow the youthful folks who (especially Saturdays) crowd into **Disco la Puesta** (on the Zipolite *adoquín*, 9 P.M. until the wee hours, Tues.–Sat.).

Alternatively, in Mazunte, join the regulars who relax at hangout **La Barrita** with drinks and dancing (to usually recorded music) in the garden-patio 6 P.M.–midnight nightly. Find it in mid-village, on Calle Barrita, by the beach.

For additional nighttime diversions, head west to Puerto Escondido or east to Bahías de Huatulco, each about an hour by car or bus, for more and livelier entertainments.

Hotel Ángel del Mar sometimes provides music for dancing during the highest seasons, most likely between Christmas and New Year and the week before Easter.

The town's major scheduled event is the big **Fiesta de San Miguel Arcangel** on Oct. 1 and 2. Then the *mascaritas* (masked children) dancers romp, carnival games and rides light up the streetfront, and a regatta of fishing boats parades around the bay.

Sunset-watchers get their best chance from the unobstructed hilltop perch of the Hotel Ángel del Mar, or Lola's, on the beach in Zipolite, where the bar and restaurant at each place can provide something to enliven the occasion even if clouds happen to block the view.

Jogging and Horseback Riding

Potholed streets, rocky roads, and lack of grass sharply curtail Puerto Ángel jogging prospects. The highway, however, which runs gradually uphill from near the pier, does provide a continuous, more or less smooth surface. Avoid the midday heat by confining your jogging to early morning and late afternoon, and take water along.

You can also avoid the heat by renting a horse for riding on Playas Zipolite and Ventanilla, for about $10/hr.

Swimming and Surfing

Swimming provides cooler local exercise opportunities, especially in the sheltered waters off Playa Panteón. Off Playa Zipolite, bodysurfing, boogie boarding, and surfing can be rewarding, depending on wind and swells. Be super-careful of undertow, which is always a threat, even on calm days at Zipolite. If you're inexperienced, don't go out alone. Novice and even experienced swimmers sometimes drown at Zipolite. If you get caught in a current pulling you out to sea, don't panic. Experts advise that you simply float and paddle parallel to the beach a hundred yards or so, to a spot where the offshore current is not so severe (or may even push you back toward the beach). Alcohol and surf, moreover, don't mix. On rough days, unless you're an expert, forget it. Bring your own board, or rent one at one of the sprinkling of shops along the beach and the Zipolite *adoquín.*

Sailboarding

If you have your own carryable boat or windsurfing gear, sheltered **Playa Panteón** would be a good place to put it into the water, although the neighboring headland may decrease the available wind. Calm mornings at **Playas Zipolite, San Agustinillo,** or **Mazunte,** or afternoons, with more wind but rougher waves, might also be fruitful.

Snorkeling and Scuba Diving

Rocky shoals at the edges of Puerto Ángel Bay, especially just off **Playa Panteón,** are fine for casual snorkeling. **Playa Estacahuite,** on the open ocean just beyond the bay's east headland, is even better. Snorkel rentals are available on the beach, at both Playa Estacahuite and Playa Panteón.

Puerto Ángel has a well-equipped professional **Profundo Azul** (Deep Blue) scuba diving shop (tel. 958/584-3109, azulprofundomx@hotmail .com, www.tomzap.com/azulprofundl.html), at Playa Panteón, run by very experienced Juan José de Nova Reyes, known locally as "Chepe." Besides scuba dives, and instruction, from the basics all the way up to a complete open-water certification, Chepe also offers snorkeling and fishing trips.

Fishing

The bayfront pier is the best place to bargain for a boat and captain to take you and your friends out on a fishing excursion. Prices depend on season, but you can figure on paying about $100 for a half-day excursion for three or four persons with bait and two or three good rods and reels. During a three-hour outing a few miles offshore, a competently captained boat will typically bring in three or four big, good-eating *dorado (mahi-mahi) huachinango* (snapper), *atún* (tuna), or pompano. If you're uncertain about what's biting, go down to the dock around 2 or 3 p.m. in the afternoon and see what the boats are bringing in.

SHOPPING
Market

The biggest local market is the Monday *tianguis,* which spreads along the Pochutla main street, Highway 175, about seven miles from Puerto Ángel, one mile inland from the Highway 200 junction. It's mostly a place for looking rather than buying, as throngs of vendors from the hills line the sidewalks, even crowding into the streets, to sell their piles of onions, mangoes, forest herbs, carrots, cilantro, and *jícama.*

On other days, vendors confine their displays to the permanent Mercado 5 de Octubre, east side of the main street, between Calles 1 and 2 Sur.

In Puerto Ángel, fruit and vegetables are available (the earlier the better), at the small Puerto Ángel market, at the corner of main beachfront street Bulevar Uribe and the westside bridge.

Groceries and Photo

The best-stocked grocery store on the Puerto Ángel coast is **Minisuper Alicia** (on Vasconcelos, tel. 958/584-3237, 7 A.M.–9 P.M. daily), on the right, two blocks directly uphill from the pier. Also, a few little-bit-of-everything stores in Zipolite, San Agustinillo, and Mazunte sell cheese, bread, wine, vegetables, and more.

The best local photo store is professional **Foto García,** in Pochutla, on the main street (Lázaro Cárdenas 76, tel. 958/584-0735, 8 A.M.–2 P.M. and 4–8 P.M. Mon.–Sat.). They offer digital and film development service, and stock lots of film and digital point-and-shoot cameras and other supplies.

Handicrafts

For fine custom-made hammocks, visit local craftsman Gabino Silva at his country shop, off a jungly stretch of the road between Zipolite and San Agustín. He also rents two very rough *cabañas.* (However, he does have a solid seaview *palapa,* apparently orginally intended to be a restaurant, that would be fine for camping if you have mosquito repellent.) Watch for his sign labeled Hamacas and Cabaña on the beach side of the road, 4.2 miles (6.7 km) from the Puerto Ángel village center.

A handful of handicrafts have arrived in Puerto Ángel, at La Primavera beachware store, on Vasconcelos, directly uphill from the pier, tel. 958/584-3251, 9 A.M.–10 P.M. daily.

A few stores sell some unique handicrafts in Pochutla. Best-stocked is the Pochutla *larga distancia,* **Caseta Cybeltel** (between Calles 1 and 2 Norte, tel. 958/584-0706, 7 A.M.–10 P.M.), across the street from the Hotel Izola, which customarily offers a varied collection of mostly Guatemalan hand-embroidered purses, *huipiles,* shirts, vests, and 1960s-style tie-dyed apparel.

INFORMATION AND SERVICES
Money Exchange and Tourist Information

In Puerto Ángel, only a few folks change money. Owner Gundi Ley, at her guesthouse Casa de Huéspedes Gundi y Tomás, cashes U.S. dollars cash and travelers checks.

Otherwise, go to the banks in **Pochutla.** Best bet is **HSBC** bank, on the Pochutla main street, Lázaro Cárdenas, tel. 958/584-0698, Mon.–Fri. 8 A.M.–7 P.M., Sat. 8 A.M.–3 P.M. Alternatively, go to **Bancomer,** corner of Lázaro Cárdenas and Avenida 3A Norte, tel. 958/584-0259, Mon.–Fri. 8:30 A.M.–4 P.M.; or a few doors south, **Scotiabank Inverlat,** tel. 958/584-0145, Mon.–Fri. 9 A.M.–5 P.M.

Oaxaca tourism runs a **tourist information booth** on the second floor, at the foot of the Puerto Ángel pier. in season, daily 9 A.M.–2 P.M. and 4–8 P.M.

Communications

The Puerto Ángel *correo* and *telecomunicaciones* stand side by side at the Agencia Municipal at the foot of Highway 175. Both are open 9 A.M.–3 P.M. Mon.–Fri.

The Puerto Ángel *larga distancia* telephone, fax office, and **Gela Net** Internet access is on Calle José Vasconcelos, just uphill from main street Uribe, tel. 958/584-3046 or 958/584-3054, fax 958/584-3210, shenalo@ hotmail.com, 7 A.M.–10 P.M. daily.

Internet access is also available at Hotel Puesta del Sol and Cyber café, about half a block west of the Blv. Uribe bridge, and **Caseta Cybeltel,** in Pochutla, tel. 958/584-0706 on the main street, across from the Hotel Izola.

Internet access has also arrived in Zipolite (tel. 958/584-4343, 8 A.M.–10 P.M. daily), a few doors east of the Zipolite library (by the corner that leads to the Zipolite beach and *adoquín*).

Health and Emergencies

Puerto Ángel's **doctor,** Dr. Constancio Aparicio Juárez, holds consultation hours 7 A.M.–2 P.M. and 5–9 P.M. Mon.–Sat., and also manages the **pharmacy** (off Avenida Vasconcelos uphill a few doors and around the corner, tel. 958/584-3058). For serious illness requiring diagnostic specialists, Dr. Juárez recommends you go to the government Hospital Regional in Pochutla, tel. 958/584-0204, or the Seguro

Social in Crucecita (Bays of Huatulco) tel. 958/587-0124 or 958/587-0264.

Another option is to go to the small government **Centro del Salud** health clinic, which concentrates on preventative rather than diagnostic medicine, on the hill behind the church. Go up Vasconcelos a long curving block, go left at the first corner, and continue another block to the health center.

For police emergencies, contact the municipal police, uphill on Vasconcelos, tel. 958/584-3207, or call the **policía preventiva,** at the Presidencia Municipal, in Pochutla, on the town plaza, one block east of the main north-south town thoroughfare, tel. 958/584-0273.

GETTING THERE AND AWAY
By Air
Scheduled flights to Mexican destinations connect daily with airports at **Huatulco,** 19 miles (30 km) east, or **Puerto Escondido,** 44 miles (71 km) west, by road from Puerto Ángel.

By Car or RV
National highways connect Puerto Ángel to the west with Puerto Escondido and Acapulco, north with Oaxaca, and east with the Bahías de Huatulco and the Isthmus of Tehuantepec.

Highway 200 connects westward with Puerto Escondido in an easy 44 miles (71 km), continuing to Pinotepa Nacional (135 miles, 217 km, three hours) and Acapulco in a total of seven hours (291 miles, 469 km) of driving. In the opposite direction, Bahías de Huatulco (actually Crucecita town), 28 miles (45 km), is reachable in about 45 minutes. The continuation to Salina Cruz stretches another 92 miles (148 km), or around 2.5 additional hours of driving time.

North to Oaxaca, paved but narrow and winding National Highway 175 connects 148 miles (238 km) over the Sierra Madre del Sur from its junction with Highway 200 at Pochutla. The road climbs to around 9,000 feet through cool (chilly in winter) pine forests and hardscrabble Chatino and Zapotec native villages. Fill up with gas in Pochutla. Unleaded gasoline is available at the Pochutla Pemex

stations, both on through-town Highway 175: about 300 yards toward town from Highway 200, and on the north, uphill, edge of town. Carry water and blankets, and be prepared for emergencies. The first gas station after Pochutla is at Miahuatlán, 90 miles north. Allow about eight hours behind the wheel from Puerto Ángel to Oaxaca, about seven in the opposite direction.

By Bus or Van
Virtually all long-distance bus connections must be made in Pochutla. The sole exception is one second-class Oaxaca City-bound bus that leaves Puerto Ángel nightly around 10 P.M. from the corner of Vasconcelos and Uribe, just uphill from the pier. Get your ticket at Papelería el Globo, at the bus stop.

In Pochutla, operating out of five separate stations, several long-distance bus lines and two van shuttle services connect with points west, east, and north. The stations cluster less than a mile north from the Highway 200 junction along Avenida Lázaro Cárdenas, the Highway 175 main street into Pochutla.

As you enter the Pochutla business district, first you'll see first-class **Cristóbal Colón** station on the left (at L. Cárdenas 84, tel. 958/584-0274). Several departures per day connect east with Crucecita. Some continue east, connecting with Salina Cruz and Tehuantepec, continuing to Chiapas destinations of Tuxtla, Gutiérrez, San Cristóbal, and Tapachula, at the Guatemala border. A few buses connect north with Oaxaca via the long, relatively level, Isthmus route, via Salina Cruz and Tehuantepec. During the dry season, buses also connect with the trans-Sierra but shorter Highway 175. One bus connects daily with Puebla and Mexico City. A few buses also connect daily west with Puerto Escondido.

Next, a few doors farther north, tel. 958/584-0380, **Estrella Blanca** subsidiary-line buses (such as first-class Elite, luxury-class Turistar, Flecha Roja, and Autotransportes Cuauhtémoc) connect west daily with Puerto Escondido, continuing to Acapulco and Lázaro Cárdenas in Michoacán, there continuing along the entire Mexican Pacific Coast, all the way to the U.S. border. They also connect east (many per day) with Bahías de Huatulco destinations of Crucecita and Santa Cruz de Huatulco and Salina Cruz on the Isthmus. A few "plus" (say "ploos") luxury-class buses connect daily all the way to Mexico City.

About a block farther, across the main street, **Autobuses Estrella del Valle, Autobuses Oaxaca Pacífico,** and **Fletes y Pasajes** (tel. 958/584-0138 or 958/584-0349) operate out of their joint central bus station

central de autobus. Frequent second-class and some first-class service is offered, connecting west with Puerto Escondido and Pinotepa Nacional; north with Oaxaca, Puebla, and Mexico City; and east with Huatulco, Salina Cruz, and the Chiapas border.

Farther north, at Lázaro Cárdenas 62, across from Scotiabank Inverlat, **Atlantida** shuttle vans, tel. 958/584-0116, connect north, via Highway 175, about every two daylight hours, with Oaxaca. Next door, **Eclipse** vans, also offer frequent Oaxaca connections.

Bays of Huatulco and Vicinity

The nine azure Bahías de Huatulco (ooah-TOOL-koh) decorate a couple of dozen miles of acacia-plumed rocky coastline east of Puerto Ángel. Between the bays, the ocean joins in battle with jutting, rocky headlands, while in their inner reaches the ocean calms, caressing diminutive crescents of coral sand. Inland, a thick hardwood forest seems to stretch in a continuous carpet to the Sierra.

Ecologists shivered when they heard that these bays were going to be developed. Fonatur, the government tourism development agency, says it has a plan, however. Relatively few (but all upscale) hotels will occupy the beaches; other development will be confined to a few inland centers. The remaining 70 percent of the land will be kept as pristine ecological zones and study areas.

Although this story sounds sadly familiar, Fonatur, which developed Ixtapa and Cancún, seems to have learned from its experience. Up-to-date sewage treatment was installed *ahead of time;* logging and homesteading were halted; and soldiers patrol the beaches, stopping turtle poachers. If all goes according to the plan, the nine Bahías de Huatulco and their 100,000-acre forest hinterland will be both a tourist and ecological paradise, in addition to employing thousands of local people, when complete in 2020. If this Huatulco dream ends as well as

it has started, Mexico should take pride while the rest of the world should take heed.

HISTORY

Long before Columbus, the Huatulco area was well-known to the Aztecs and their predecessors. The name itself, from Aztec words meaning "Land Where a Tree (or Wood) Is Worshipped," reflects one of Mexico's most intriguingly persistent legends—of the Holy Cross of Huatulco.

When the Spanish arrived on the Huatulco coast in the 1520s, the local native people showed them a huge cross they worshiped at the edge of the sea. A contemporary chronicler, Ignacio Burgoa, conjectured the cross had been left by an ancient saint—maybe even the Apostle Thomas—15 centuries earlier. The cross remained as the Spanish colonized the area and established headquarters and a port, which they named San Agustín, at the westernmost of the Bays of Huatulco.

Spanish ports and their treasure-laden galleons from the Orient attracted foreign corsairs—including Francis Drake in 1579 and Thomas Cavendish in 1587. Cavendish arrived at the bay now called Bahía Santa Cruz, where he saw the cross the natives were worshiping. Believing it was the work of the devil, Cavendish and his men tried to chop, saw, and burn it down. Failing at all of these, Cavendish looped his ship's mooring ropes around the cross and with sails unfurled tried using the force of the wind to pull it down. Frustrated, he finally sailed away, leaving the cross of Huatulco still standing beside the shore.

By 1600, pilgrims were chipping pieces from the cross, so much so that in 1612, Bishop Juan de Cervantes had to rescue it. He brought the cross to Oaxaca, where he made four smaller two-foot crosses of it. He sent one specimen each to church authorities in Mexico City, Rome, and Santa María de Huatulco, head town of the Huatulco *municipio*. Cervantes kept the fourth copy in the cathedral in Oaxaca, where it has remained, venerated and visible in a side chapel, to the present day.

SIGHTS
Getting Oriented
With no road to the outside world, the Bahías de Huatulco remained virtually uninhabited and undeveloped until 1982, about the time that coastal Highway 200 was pushed through. A few years later, Huatulco's planned initial kernel of infrastructure was complete, centering on the brand-new residential service town, Crucecita (pop. 10,000), and nearby Santa Cruz de Huatulco boat harbor and hotel village on Bahía Santa Cruz.

The Bays of Huatulco decorate the coastline both east and west of Santa Cruz. To the east, a paved road links Bahías Chahue, Tangolunda, and Conejos. To the west lie Bahías el Organo, el Maguey, and Cacaluta. Of the latter three, only Bahía el Maguey is accessible by paved road. El Organo and Cacaluta are accessible only with the help of a guide; the former on foot or by horseback, the latter by truck or SUV. Isolated farther west are Bahías Chachacual and San Agustín, with no road from Santa Cruz (although a good dirt road runs to San Agustín from Highway 200 near the airport).

Besides Bahía Santa Cruz, the only other bays that have been extensively developed are Chahue, a mile east, and Tangolunda, four miles east. Chahue now has a marina and a sprinkling of small-to-medium-sized, medium-priced hotels. Tangolunda has a green and lovely golf course, small restaurant/shopping complex, and six resort hotels (Las Brisas, Quinta Real, Crown Pacific, Barceló, Club Gala Resort, and Zaashila) that have all been fully operational since the mid-1990s.

Getting Around
Frequent public **collective taxis** connect Crucecita and Bahías Santa Cruz, Chahue, and Tangolunda. Find the terminal, on Guaumuchil, two blocks east of plaza, at the corner where the boulevard heads south to Chaue. The taxis make the same trips for about $2 by day, $3 at night. No public transportation is available to the other bays. Taxi drivers are willing to drive you for a picnic to west-side bay El Maguey, or Playa Entrega (an isolated beach on Santa Cruz Bay), for about $5 one-way, from Crucecita or Tangolunda; figure about $4 for the trip to Bahía Conejos.

For an extended day trip to all road-accessible bays, figure on about $20–30 for a taxi, about $50 for a rental car. Call Alamo (in Tangolunda, tel. 958/581-0409 or 958/581-0058) or Budget (in Crucecita at Octillo and Jazmín, tel. 958/587-0010, fax 958/587-0019).

Another option is to go by boat. The local boat cooperative (Sociedad Cooperativa Turístico Tangolunda) runs a daily excursion on the 100-passenger catamaran **Fiesta** around 10:30 A.M., $20 per person, kids 5–9 half price, to all nine bays, including open bar, bilingual guide, and snacks; snorkeling is $5 extra. Reserve directly through its dock office (tel. 958/587-0081). Alternatively, tour by the similarly big catamaran **Tequila** (from the same dock, tel. 958/587-2303), or contact a travel agent such as Paraíso Huatulco (tel. 958/587-0181) or Prometur (tel. 958/587-0413, or 958/587-0199.)

The cooperative also rents entire boats for all-day tours for up to 10 people for about $100. Drop-off runs to the nearest beach are about $10 per boat round-trip; to the more remote, around $20–30.

Local travel agents offer other tour options: several hours of sunning, swimming, picnicking,

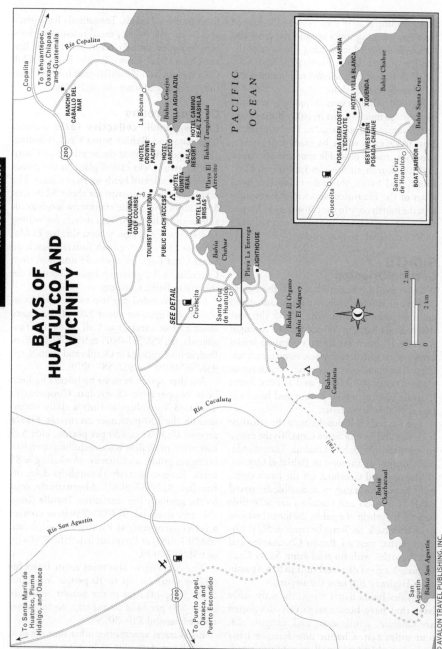

THE COSTA CHICA

BAYS OF HUATULCO AND VICINITY

To Tehuantepec, Oaxaca, Chiapas, and Guatemala

Copalita

Río Copalita

RANCHO CABALLO DEL MAR

200

La Bocana

Bahía Conejos

VILLA AGUA AZUL

HOTEL CAMINO REAL ZAASHILA

Bahía Tangolunda

HOTEL CROWN PACIFIC

HOTEL BARCELO

GALA RESORT

HOTEL QUINTA REAL

TANGOLUNDA GOLF COURSE

TOURIST INFORMATION

PUBLIC BEACH ACCESS

HOTEL LAS BRISAS

Playa El Arrocito

PACIFIC OCEAN

Crucecita

SEE DETAIL

Bahía Chahue

Santa Cruz de Huatulco

Playa La Entrega

LIGHTHOUSE

Bahía La Entrega

Bahía El Organo

Bahía El Maguey

Río Cacaluta

Trail

Bahía Cacaluta

Bahía Chachacual

Río San Agustín

San Agustín

Bahía San Agustín

Trail

200

To Santa María de Huatulco, Pluma Hidalgo, and Oaxaca

To Puerto Angel, Oaxaca, and Puerto Escondido

2 mi

2 km

Detail inset:

MARINA

Bahía Chahue

POSADA EDEN COSTA/ L'ECHALOTE

HOTEL VILLA BLANCA

XQUENDA

BEST WESTERN POSADA CHAHUE

Crucecita

Santa Cruz de Huatulco

BOAT HARBOR

Bahía Santa Cruz

© AVALON TRAVEL PUBLISHING, INC.

and snorkeling at a couple of Bahías de Huatulco beaches runs around $20 per person. Tours to Puerto Ángel, Puerto Escondido, and wildlife-rich lagoons go for $30–50 per person. For reservations, call Paraíso Huatulco or Prometur.

Another option is to get your own guide. An inexpensive way to do this is to hire an English-speaking taxi driver to take you wherever you want to go for several hours, up to a whole day, for $30–50, depending on the season.

Professional guides are another option.

Crucecita and Santa Cruz

Despite its newness, Crucecita (Little Cross, pop. 10,000) resembles a traditional Mexican town, with life revolving around a central plaza and adjacent market. Crucecita is where the people who work in the Huatulco hotels, businesses, and government offices live. Although pleasant enough for a walk around the square and a meal in a restaurant, it's nothing special, mostly a place whose modest hotels and restaurants accommodate business travelers and weekenders who can't afford the plush hotels near the beach.

While in Crucecita, be sure to step into the church on the plaza's west side to admire the heavenly **ceiling mural** of the Virgin of Guadalupe. The mural, the largest of Guadalupe in Mexico, is the work of local artists José Ángel del Signo and Marco Antonio Contreras, whose for-sale art is on display locally. Besides the heavenly Virgin overhead, the muralists have decorated the space above the altar with the miraculous story of Don Diego and the Virgin of Guadalupe.

The several deluxe hotels and the mostly travel-oriented businesses of Santa Cruz de Huatulco (on Bahía Santa Cruz about two miles from Crucecita) cluster near the boat harbor. Fishing and tour boats come and go, vacationers sun themselves on the tranquil yellow-sand Playa Santa Cruz (beyond the restaurants adjacent to the boat harbor), while T-shirt and fruit vendors and boatmen hang around the quay watching for prospective customers. After

THE COSTA CHICA

© BRUCE WHIPPERMAN

At the Santa Cruz de Huatulco harbor you can board a Bays of Huatulco excursion boat, hire a fishing *lancha,* or arrange a scuba diving lesson.

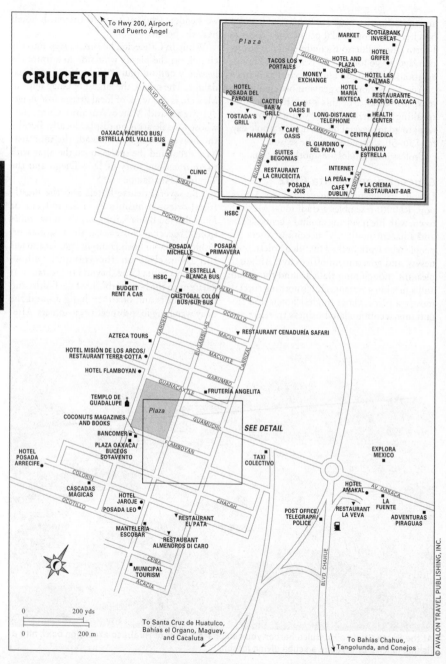

CRUCECITA

To Hwy 200, Airport, and Puerto Ángel

BLVD CHAHUE

JAZMIN

OAXACA PACÍFICO BUS/
ESTRELLA DEL VALLE BUS

CLINIC

SIBALI

POCHOTE

HSBC

POSADA MICHELLE
POSADA PRIMAVERA

PALO VERDE

ESTRELLA BLANCA BUS

HSBC

PALMA REAL

BUDGET RENT A CAR

CRISTÓBAL COLÓN BUS/SUR BUS

GARDENIA

OCOTILLO

AZTECA TOURS

HOTEL MISIÓN DE LOS ARCOS/
RESTAURANT TERRA COTTA

BUGAMBILIAS

MACUIL

CARRIZAL

RESTAURANT CENADURÍA SAFARI

MACUITLE

HOTEL FLAMBOYAN

GARUMBO

GUANACAXTLE

FRUTERÍA ANGELITA

TEMPLO DE GUADALUPE

Plaza

COCONUTS MAGAZINES AND BOOKS

GUAMUCHIL

BANCOMER

SEE DETAIL

PLAZA OAXACA/
BUCEOS SOTAVENTO

FLAMBOYAN

HOTEL POSADA ARRECIFE

COLORIN

TAXI COLECTIVO

EXPLORA MEXICO

CASCADAS MÁGICAS

OCOTILLO

HOTEL JAROJE

POSADA LEO

CHACAH

HOTEL AMAKAL

AV. OAXACA

LA FUENTE

POST OFFICE/
TELEGRAPH/
POLICE

RESTAURANT LA VEVA

ADVENTURAS PIRAGUAS

RESTAURANT EL PATA

MANTELERÍA ESCOBAR

RESTAURANT ALMENDROS DI CARO

CEIBA

MUNICIPAL TOURISM

ACACIA

BLVD CHAHUE

0   200 yds

0   200 m

To Santa Cruz de Huatulco,
Bahías el Organo, Maguey,
and Cacaluta

To Bahías Chahue,
Tangolunda, and Conejos

Detail

Plaza

MARKET

SCOTIABANK INVERLAT

GUAMUCHIL

TACOS LOS PORTALES

HOTEL AND PLAZA CONEJO

HOTEL GRIFER

MONEY EXCHANGE

HOTEL LAS PALMAS

HOTEL POSADA DEL PARQUE

HOTEL MARIA MIXTECA

RESTAURANTE SABOR DE OAXACA

CACTUS BAR & GRILL

CAFÉ OASIS II

LONG-DISTANCE TELEPHONE

HEALTH CENTER

TOSTADA'S GRILL

FLAMBOYAN

PHARMACY

CAFÉ OASIS

CENTRA MÉDICA

SUITES BEGONIAS

EL GIARDINO DEL PAPA

LAUNDRY ESTRELLA

BUGAMBILIAS

RESTAURANT LA CRUCECITA

INTERNET

CARRIZAL

LA PEÑA

LA CREMA RESTAURANT-BAR

POSADA JOIS

CAFÉ DUBLIN

© AVALON TRAVEL PUBLISHING, INC.

the sun goes down, not much usually happens in Santa Cruz. Tourists quit the beach for their hotels and workers return to their homes in Crucecita, leaving the harbor and streets empty and dark.

EXPORING THE BAYS OF HUATULCO

Isolation has left the Huatulco waters blue and unpolluted, the beaches white and clean. Generally, the bays are all similar: tropical deciduous (green July–Jan.) forested rocky headlands enclosing yellow-white coral sand crescents. The water is clear and good for snorkeling, scuba diving, sailing, kayaking, and sailboarding during the often-calm weather. Beaches, however, are typically steep, causing waves to break quickly near the sand, generally unsuitable for bodysurfing, boogie boarding, or surfing.

Your preparations depend on which bays you plan to explore. For the five developed or partially developed bays, Santa Cruz, Chahue, Tangolunda, El Maguey, and San Agustín, you'll need nothing more than transportation, a hat, and sunscreen. Restaurants and stores can supply everything else.

By contrast, the four undeveloped Huatulco bays of El Organo, Cacaluta, Chachacual, and Conejos have neither restaurants, stores, drinking water, nor lots of shade, since they're so pristine coconut palms haven't even gotten around to sprouting there. When exploring, bring food, drinks, hats, sunscreen, and mosquito repellent.

East Side

Bahía Chahue, about a mile from both Crucecita and Santa Cruz, is wide and blue, with a steep yellow dune above the beach, stretching to the marina jetty at the east end. Some scattered hotels and restaurants and a couple of bars and hangouts are sprinkled along the main Boulevard Benito Juárez, but Chahue beach, three blocks beyond the boulevard, is uncrowded even on weekends and holidays and nearly empty the rest of the time.

About four miles farther east is the breezy and broad **Bahía Tangolunda.** Although hotels front much of the beach, a signed Playa Pública public access road borders the western edge of the golf course (turn right just past the creek bridge). Except for its east end, the Tangolunda beach is steep and the waves break quickly right at the sand. *Palapa* restaurants at the public beach serve food and drinks; or, if you prefer, stroll a quarter mile along the beach for refreshments at the luxurious poolside beach clubs of the Barceló and Club Gala Resort.

Over the headland about two miles farther east, **Punta Arena** (Sand Point), a forested thumb of land, juts into wide **Bahía Conejos.** Three separate steep beaches spread along the inner shoreline. The main entrance road arrives at high-duned Playa Punta Arena. Playa Tejoncito (Little Coatamundi) is beyond the rocks far to the right; Playa Conejos (Rabbits) is to the left on the other side of Punta Arena. A few palm-frond *ramadas* for shade and a saltwater flush toilet lavatory occupy the Playa Punta Arena dune. Trees behind the dunes provide a few shady spots for RV or tent campers. (Playa Conejos is becoming a rapidly developing residential zone. By the time you read this, most of the accessible wild dunes and beach may be occupied by houses.)

Beyond **La Bocana,** near the mouth of the Río Copalita, less than a mile farther on, a long, broad beach with oft-powerful surfing rollers (novices beware) stretches for at least a mile east. Beachfront *palapas* serve drinks and very fresh seafood and rent surfboards for about $14 per day. A spring-fed lagoon above the beach (bring your kayak) appears ripe for wildlife-viewing.

After La Bocana, the road bends inland, paralleling the **Río Copalita wildlife sanctuary,** perfect for adventurous exploring. Several operators guide visitors on river ecotours: José Aussenac, owner of Posada Michelle (tel. 958/587-0535), organizes and guides outdoor adventure-tours. Options include bird- and animal-watching walks along riverine forest trails, kayaking river rapids, rafting, and mud baths at a riverside ranch.

West Side

Bahía Santa Cruz has a pair of beaches, **Playa**

a lazy afternoon at the Santa Cruz de Huatulco harbor

© BRUCE WHIPPERMAN

Entrega, and the more-visited **Playa Santa Cruz,** beyond the shops and restaurants, to the right (facing the ocean) of the boat harbor. During high season and weekends, kids play and tourists improve their tans at Playa Santa Cruz.

Playa Entrega is a small, hidden stretch of sand slipped into the west side of Bahía Santa Cruz. It is the infamous spot where, on January 20, 1831, Vicente Guerrero, president and independence hero, was brought ashore in custody of arch-villain Francisco Picaluga and sent to be murdered in Oaxaca a few months later.

Quarter-mile-long Playa Entrega is the ideal Sunday beach, with calm, clear water and clean yellow sand. Swimming, kayaking, and often snorkeling, sailing, and sailboarding possibilities are excellent. A number of shoreline restaurants serve fresh seafood plates and drinks daily, until around 8 P.M.

Get there via the main street, Boulevard Santa Cruz, which passes the Santa Cruz boat harbor. Continue west, bearing left, at the Y intersection at the Hotel Binneguenda (mark

your odometer) on the right. After 0.8 mile (1.3 km) the road bends left and winds uphill, past panoramic viewpoints of Bahía Santa Cruz. Follow the signs and you'll soon be at Playa Entrega.

If, instead of curving left to La Entrega, you follow the highway that continues straight ahead at the same spot, you'll be headed for the Bahías El Maguey, El Organo, Cacaluta, and Chachacual. The planned roads to the latter three of these four bays had not yet been completed as of this writing. Until authorities get around to finishing them, land access to the Bays of El Organo, Cacaluta, and remote Chachacual will be achievable only by hikers or experienced drivers in off-road vehicles who know the myriad dirt tracks that wind through the tropical deciduous forest west of Santa Cruz. If in doubt, hire a jeep and a guide, or take a boat tour.

Bahía el Organo is closest. About 1.1 miles (1.8 km) along the highway from the hotel, look on the left side for the (one-foot-high, 30-foot-long) raised concrete curb. The easy,

© BRUCE WHIPPERMAN

The beach at Bahía San Agustín is one of the most popular Bays of Huatulco beaches.

unofficial half-mile (0.8 km) foot trail to El Organo takes off downhill through the forest from there. The beach is isolated, intimate, and enfolded by rocky shoals on both sides, and sprinkled with driftwood and green verbena vines. Stroll the quarter-mile long beach, enjoy the antics of the spouting blowhole on the left-side shoal, and with caution, swim beyond the close-in surf. Surf fishing appears to be fine here. Some trees behind the dune provide shade. Bring food, water, and everything else, including insect repellent.

Back out on the road, continuing straight ahead, the paved highway forks again (about 1.8 miles from the hotel). Either continue straight ahead downhill to El Maguey, or fork right to Cacaluta. The sandy crescent of **Bahía el Maguey** is bordered by tidepools tucked beneath forested headlands. Facing a protected fjordlike channel, the Maguey beach is usually calm, nearly waveless and fine for swimming, snorkeling, diving, and sailing. It would be a snap to launch a kayak or a rubber boat here for fishing in the bay. Beach access is on foot only,

via a downhill staircase. A procession of permanent seafood *palapas* line the beach. Most days, especially weekends and holidays, picnickers arrive and banana towboats and *aguamotos* (mini-motorboats) buzz the beach and bay.

Bahías Cacaluta, Chachuacal, and San Agustín

At this writing, the paved road that forks right toward **Bahía Cacaluta** ends at a barrier, about 0.7 mile (1.1 km) past the fork, at an unsigned sandy but firm track, negotiable by car or bicycle, or on foot. It continues past the barrier and winds and bumps ahead through the shady tropical forest, past two signed forks that, if you bear left all the way, will lead you to Playa Cacaluta after about 1.2 miles (1.9 km) from the pavement's end.

There, the bay spreads along a mile-long, heart-shaped beach, beckoningly close to a cactus-studded offshore islet. Swimmers beware, for waves break powerfully, surging upward and receding with strong undertow. Many shells—limpets and purple- and brown-daubed clams—speckle the beach. Surf-fishing prospects, either from the beach itself or from rocks on either end, appear excellent.

Bahía Chachacual, past the Río Cacaluta, about four miles farther west from Bahía Cacaluta, is a sand-edged azure nook accessible only with a guide, via forest tracks.

Bahía San Agustín, by contrast, is well known and easily reachable by Pochutla-bound bus, then by the good dirt road just across the highway (one-way taxi from the highway runs about $10, *colectivo* van $1.30) from the fork to Santa María Huatulco (at Km 236, a mile west of the airport). After about seven miles along a firm track, accessible by all but the bulkiest RVs, bear right to road's end to a modest, but very crowded village of *palapas* at the bay's sheltered west end. From there, the beach curves eastward along two miles of forest-backed dune.

Besides good swimming, sailing, sailboarding, and fishing prospects, Bahía San Agustín offers some RV or tent camping options. On your way in, follow the first of two left forks immediately before the road's end. After about a mile, you arrive at **El Playon** (Big Beach). Facilities, besides a long, lovely curving beach, include several beachfront *palapa* restaurants and several lots, ripe for for RV and tent camping.

Back on the entrance road, follow the second left fork, and after a soccer field, you arrive at **El Sacrificio,** a sheltered, family-friendly beach, lapped by gentle waves, lined by *palapa* restaurants, and picturesquely decorated by big, friendly rocks.

Another choice is to turn right about 100 yards before the end of the road and explore the wild, rough, and very fishable, campable, and surfable open-ocean beach.

A few small stores and the road's-end village *palapas* can, at least, supply seafood and drinks and maybe some water and basic groceries.

ACCOMMODATIONS

In Huatulco as in other resorts, hotels on the beach are the priciest. Tangolunda's are most expensive, Santa Cruz and Chahue hotels fall in between, and Crucecita's hotels are the cheapest. Virtually all Huatulco lodgings are of modern standard, with private baths with hot water. Many, but not all, have air conditioning, a plus, especially in the warm spring. More information about most of the hotels listed below is available through the Huatulco Hotel and Motel Association, toll-free U.S tel. 800/866-416-0555, www.hoteleshuatulco.com.mx.

Huatulco accommodation rates are highly seasonal. Hotels below are arranged by approximate ascending order of high season (customarily Dec. through Easter) price for two people in one double bed with fans only. Holiday (Christmas and Easter) prices average about 30 percent more than those listed below.

Crucecita

Nearly all Crucecita lodgings are within a few blocks of the central plaza. They are generally clean, well-managed posada-style hotels, but mostly without restaurants and even fewer (none in the recommendations below) with pools.

UNDER $50

First, the **Posada Primavera** (Palo Verde 5, corner of Gardenia, Crucecita, Oaxaca 70980, tel./fax 958/587-1167 fax 958/-1169, $23 s or d low season, $35 high), a few blocks north of the plaza, offers six simply furnished but clean, light, high-ceilinged upstairs rooms with bath and fans. Windows look out onto the palmy, bougainvillea-adorned surrounding neighborhood.

At the adjacent corner, **Hotel Posada Michelle** (Gardenia 8, Crucecita, Oaxaca 70980, tel./fax 958/587-0535, $23 d low season with fan, $35 d high; $30 d low season with a/c, $65 high), run by personable eco-tour guide José Aussenac, offers about a dozen smallish but clean and comfortable rooms with big beds, baths, and good satellite TV. Some of the rooms are airy and light; others, although dark because of their half-mirrored windows (for privacy), do have white walls and open to a breezy, second-story walkway that leads to a pleasant, hammock-hung, shady view porch. Rooms with fans only cost about $23 low season and $35 high; rooms with a/c (a very desirable option for the rooms that face the afternoon sun) run about $30 d low season, $65 high.

A couple of blocks south of the plaza, budget-minded visitors should check out the new-ish **Posada Leo** (Bugambilias 302, Crucecita, Oaxaca 70980, tel. 958/587-0372 or 958/587-2601, posadaleo.hux@hotmail.com, $20 s, $25 d low season, $25 and $37 high). The six rooms, although a bit small for their two double beds, are attractively tiled and furnished with hand-woven bedspreads, and shiny modern shower baths, plus cable TV; all with fans, some with a/c. Guests enjoy an airy upstairs patio for reading and relaxing.

Nearby, just a block south of the plaza, find **Posada Jois** (Chacah 209, Crucecita, Oaxaca 70980, tel. 958/587-0781, joishuatulco@hotmail.com, $20 d low, $35 d high, and up), between Carrizal and Bugambilias. Past the welcoming female owner's storefront are seven differing rooms on both ground and upper floor. The most attractive are upstairs. One is semideluxe, with king-sized bed and bath, for $25 d low season, $40 high; another room for four with two double beds and bath goes for $33 low and $55 high. A pair of rooms with shared baths rent for $20 d low, $35 d high; all rooms have hot water, TV, and fans. A major plus here is an inviting, shady terrace for guest use, with tropical plants and soft chairs for relaxing.

On Guamuchil, just half a block east of the plaza, the **Hotel los Conejos** (Calle Guamuchil 208, tel./fax 958/587-0054, fax 958/587-0009, informacion@turismoconejo.com, www.turismoconejo.com, $30 s, $35 d low season, $35 and $40 high) offers 10 spic-and-span rooms built around the upstairs balcony of a tranquil, intimate interior patio. The rooms are attractively decorated with ceramic tile floors, white stucco walls, and tasteful, color-coordinated curtains and bedspreads. Rates begin at about $30 s, $35 d low season, and $35 and $40 high, with choice of a/c or fans. All with cable TV, private hot-water shower baths, Internet café, and small restaurant, but no parking.

About three blocks farther east from the Crucecita plaza hubbub, the **Hotel Amakal** (Av. Oaxaca 1, Crucecita, Bahías de Huatulco, Oaxaca 70980, tel. 958/587-1500, toll-free Mex. tel. 800/667-5343, fax 958/587-2338, amakal@prodigy.net.mx, credit cards accepted, $32 s or d with fan low season, $46 high; $37 d with a/c low season, $50 high) offers semideluxe, modern-standard rooms at reasonable prices. A stairway from the small, spartan lobby leads upstairs to 26 clean, light, white-tile-floored, invitingly decorated rooms with modern-standard baths. With beach club, but street parking only.

$50-100

The **Hotel Suites Begonias** (Bugambilias 503, Crucecita, Oaxaca 70980, tel. 958/587-0390, fax 958/587-1390, getosa@prodigy.net.mx, credit cards accepted, $33 s or d low season, $55 high), at the southeast plaza corner, offers a semideluxe, family-run alternative. The rooms, although clean and comfortable, have motel-style walkways passing their windows, decreasing privacy. Rates for the 13 rooms include fan, a/c, and TV.

Two blocks south of the plaza, at the corner of Colorin, **Hotel Jaroje** (hah-RO-hay; Bugambilias 304, Crucecita, Oaxaca 70980, tel./fax 958/583-4801, jaroje@yahoo.com.mx, $30 d low season, $55 high) offers 12 comfortable rooms, simply but attractively decorated with color-coordinated drapes, bedspreads, and shiny-tiled baths, plus a/c, cable TV, and breakfast.

A very worthy addition to Crucecita's lodging options is the new, refined **Hotel Misión de los Arcos** (Gardenia 902, tel. 958/587-0165, fax 958/587-1904, reservations@misiondelosarcos.com, www.misiondelosarcos.com, $60 d, junior suites $75 d), a block north of the plaza's northwest corner. Owners offer 14 spacious, rustic-chic white-and-beige rooms and suites. Guests in many rooms enjoy views toward the leafy park next door. Some rooms have airy balconies and/or private patios. Room rentals begin at about $60 d, junior suites $75 d, about 30 percent higher holidays; all with large luxurious baths, cable TV, a/c, credit cards accepted, and an excellent restaurant downstairs, but street parking only.

Owner of the Restaurant Sabor de Oaxaca has turned profits into investment in lovely C Hotel María Mixteca (Guamuchil 204, Crucecita, Oaxaca 70989, tel. 958/587-2336 or 958/587-2337, fax 958/587-2338, andrea100@ prodigy.net.mx, www.travelbymexico.com/ oaxa/mariamixteca, credit cards accepted, $45 d low season, $70 high), just a block east of the plaza. The 14 rooms, around an invitingly tranquil inner patio, reflect the owner's love of the Mixteca region of Oaxaca. All rooms are named individually, mostly for Mixteca towns, such as Juquila, Tlaxiaco, and Juxtlahuaca. Rooms are high-ceilinged and attractively decorated in pleasant pastels, tile, and native art. One room has a queen-sized bed, the rest have two double beds, many have airy private balconies and all have a/c and cable TV.

Santa Cruz
Although no Santa Cruz hotels are actually on the beach, they all have inviting pools-patios on their own grounds, and are within a five-minute walk of the lovely golden strand of Playa Santa Cruz.

$50-100
Three blocks west of the Santa Cruz harbor and beach, stands the inviting **Hotel Meicer Binneguenda** (Blv. Santa Cruz 201, Santa Cruz de Huatulco, Oaxaca 70900, tel. 958/587-0077 or 958/587-0078, fax 958/587-0284, binniguenda@ prodigy.net.mx, www.meicerhotels.com, credit cards accepted, $85 s or d low season, $100 high). Neocolonial arches, pastel stucco walls, and copper and ceramics handicrafts decorate the interiors, while in the adjacent leafy patio, guests sun themselves around the elaborate cascade pool. Upstairs, the 90-odd neocolonial decor rooms are spacious, comfortable, and equipped with phones, TV, a/c, and restaurant-bar, with parking. Ask for a discount package, especially during times of low occupancy.

OVER $100
Another good Santa Cruz hotel choice is the

40-room **Hotel Marina** (Tehuantepec 112, Santa Cruz de Huatulco, Oaxaca 70989, tel./ fax 958/587-0830 or 958/587-0963 through -0968, hotelmarinaresort@yahoo.com, www .hotelmarinaresort.com, credit cards accepted, $110 d high season), which perches attractively on the east side of the Santa Cruz harbor-marina. Rooms are comfortable and deluxe, with phones, a/c and cable TV; and bar, restaurant, attractive pool-patio, and a discotheque a block away.

Another smaller-hotel option is the renovated **Hotel Marlin** (Paseo Mitla 107, Santa Cruz de Huatulco, Oaxaca 70989, tel. 958/587-0055, toll-free Mex. tel. 800/712-7373, fax 958/587-0546, hmarlin@prodigy.net.mex, www.oaxaca-mio.com/marlin.htm, credit cards accepted, $75 s or d low season, $120 high), only two blocks from the beach. From street level, the small lobby leads to an appealingly intimate coral-hued inner pool patio and adjacent restaurant, enfolded by three stories of accommodations. Upstairs, the approximately three dozen rooms are thoughtfully decorated with colorful colorful bedspreads, floor-length drapes, attractive, rustic tile floors, and deluxe modern-standard bathrooms. Rates run from about $75 s or d low season, $120 high, with a/c, cable TV, phones. The drawback of this hotel is its very compact size. If you can't get a discount, best take your business elsewhere.

On the main Boulevard Santa Cruz, a block inland from the boat harbor, the **Hotel Castillo Huatulco** (Blv. Santa Cruz 303, Santa Cruz de Huatulco 70980, tel. 958/587-0135 or 958/587-0144, toll-free Mex. tel. 800/903-4900, fax 958/587-0131, ventas@hotelcastillohuatulco .com, www.hotelcastillohuatulco.com, credit cards accepted, $100 s or d low season, $120 high) offers a recommendable alternative. Its 106 rooms, although deluxe and comfortable, are crowded into a smaller space than the Binneguenda's 90. They are nevertheless popular with families on weekends and holidays but nearly empty during quieter seasons. Low-season asking rates run about $100 s or d, $120 high, with phones, cable TV, a/c, palmy pool-patio, restaurant, and parking. Ask for a discount, especially during times of low occupancy. (Note: The hotel is a five-minute walk to the beach, despite how it appears in the lead photo in the hotel website, which is of the hotel's beach club.)

Chahue

The Bahía Chahue vicinity has, in recent years, acquired a number of new hotels that dot the mostly undeveloped land a few blocks from the beach. At present, however, underdevelopment and isolation make Chahue a less attractive beach neighborhood than either Santa Cruz or Tangolunda. Nevertheless, if you can get a low promotional rate, you might consider staying at one of the hotels recommended here.

$50-100

A block inland from the bayfront boulevard, find the semideluxe **Hotel Real Aligheri** (Calle Zapoteco, Bahía Chahue, Bahías de Huatulco, Oaxaca 70989, tel. 958/587-1242, toll-free Mex. tel. 800/737-0783, fax 958/587-1243, hrealigheri@prodigy.net.mx, www.oaxaca-mio .com/hrealalighri.htm, $55 d). It offers about 20 clean, comfortable rooms for about $55 d year-round except holidays, with pool, a/c, cable TV, and beach club access.

Nearby, on the same quiet side street, my hurrahs go out to the petite **☾ Posada Eden Costa** (Calle Zapoteco, tel./fax 958/587-2480, info@edencosta.com, www.edencosta.com, $60 d), behind the larger Hotel Villablanca. Here the husband-wife owners—he's French, she's Southeast Asian—set the international theme. The nine rooms and three kitchenette suites, all with a pair of double beds, are simply beautiful, with rustic-chic tiled floors and gorgeous *talavera*-accented bathrooms. Rooms go for about $60 d, except holidays, with cable TV, fans, attractive pool-patio, and good on-site restaurant L'Echalote.

Not so gorgeous, but nevertheless very recommendable next door is the relaxing **Hotel Villablanca Huatulco** (Blv. Benito Juárez, corner of Zapoteco, tel. 958/587-1717, toll-free Mex. tel. 01-800/712-7757, toll-free U.S. tel. 888/844-7429, fax 958/587-0660, hotelvillablanca@prodigy.net.mx, www

.hotelesvillablanca.com.mx, $85 s or d). Hotel Villablanca guests, mostly upper-middle-class Mexican weekenders, enjoy simply but comfortably furnished semi-deluxe rooms and junior suites. Amenities include attractively rustic tiled floors, blue curtains and bedspreads, modern-standard baths, and private balconies overlooking a palmy pool-patio. Rates for standard rooms are about $85 s or d, except holidays; two kids under 12 with parents are free; third night is customarily free; all with air-conditioning, phones, cable TV, and restaurant-bar, but street parking only.

Tangolunda

Several **luxury resort hotels** spread along the Tangolunda shoreline. The Hotel las Brisas dominates the sheltered western-side bay, with four stacklike towers that make the place appear, from a distance, like a big ocean liner. As you move east, next comes the elegant Hotel Quinta Real, perching atop its bayview hillside. The Hotel Barceló and Club Gala Resort stand side by side on the bay's inner recess next to the golf course. The Camino Real Zaashila Resort spreads gracefully to its east-end cove, while in the middle, away from the beach, the gleaming white Crown Pacific stair-steps up the hillside.

The emphasis of all Tangolunda resorts is on facilities, such as multiple pools, bars, and restaurants, full wheelchair access, live music, discos, shows, and sports such as tennis, golf, sailing, kayaking, sailboarding, snorkeling, diving, and swimming. Other amenities may include shops, baby-sitting, children's clubs, and Spanish and arts and crafts instruction.

OVER $100

Of the Tangolunda luxury hotels, the most economical (and with some of the largest rooms) is the **Hotel Crown Pacific** (Blv. Benito Juárez 8, Bahía Tangolunda, Bahías de Huatulco, Oaxaca 70989, tel. 958/581-0044, toll-free Mex. tel. 800/711-0044, fax 958/581-0221, reservaciones@crownpacifichuatulco .com, www.crownpacifichuatulco.com, $100 pp d all-inclusive low season). Perhaps these large rooms were meant to compensate for the drawback that it's not actually on the beach: Guests must either walk or shuttle a couple of blocks to the beach club. The biggest plus of the Crown Pacific is the price, which, low season, runs only about $100 per person, double occupancy, including all meals, drinks, sports, kid's miniclub, and in-house entertainment, all with a/c. During high season, the same costs about $120 per person.

The **((Club Gala Resort Huatulco** (Blv. Benito Juárez 4, P.O. Box 227, Bahías de Huatulco, Oaxaca 70989, tel. 958/583-0400 or 958/581-0220, toll-free Mex. tel. 800/712-7401, toll-free U.S./Can. tel. 877/888-GALA–877/888-4252, fax 958/581-0220, infomex@ galaresorts.com.mx, reservhux@galaresorts .com.mx, www.galaresorts.com.mx, $125 pp d all-inclusive low season), originally built and operated by the competent Mexican Club Maeva chain, ranks among Mexico's better all-inclusive resorts. The beach setting is gorgeous, the tile floors in the halls and rooms shine, and bright bedspeads, immaculate bathrooms, and private ocean-view balconies grace the accommodations. All-inclusive rates run about $125 per person, low season, $140 high; kids 7 years or under go free; 8–11 half price.

The **Barceló Huatulco** (Blv. Benito Juárez, Bahía Tangolunda, Oaxaca 70989, tel. 958/581-0055, or 958/581-0039, toll-free U.S./Can. tel. 800/227-2356, fax 958/581-0113, reservas@barcelohuatulco.com, www .barcelohuatulco.com, $120 pp d all-inclusive low season), originally a Sheraton hotel, is now a worthy member of the worldwide Spanish Barceló chain. Rooms are comfortable, deluxe, and decorated in soothing pastels, with private bay-view balconies, phones, cable TV, and a/c. All-inclusive (all lodging, food, drinks, and in-house entertainment included) runs about $120 per person low season, $150 high. Kids 2–12 stay for about $50.

Perched at the west end of Bahía Tangolunda, the **Hotel las Brisas Huatulco** (Lote 1, Bahía de Tangolunda, Huatulco, Oaxaca, 70989, tel./fax 958/583-0200, fax 958/583-0240, toll-free Mex. tel. 01-800/227-4727,

toll-free U.S./Can. tel. 888/559-4329, lasbrisas.huatulco@brisas.com.mx, www .brisas.com.mx, $160 s or d and up), formerly Club Med, is now owned and operated by the Mexican Las Brisas hotel chain. Judging from the longstanding fine reputation of existing Las Brisas hotels in Acapulco, Ixtapa, and Puerto Vallarta, we should be able to expect the same excellence for the Las Brisas Huatulco. The place is huge, spreading from its grand open-air lobby, from which carts ferry guests to hundreds of spartan-deluxe view rooms equipped with all modern amenities. Hotel facilities include many sports, three pools, gym, secluded beaches and coves, kiddie activities, and much more. Rates run from about $160 s or d; two kids under 12 go free with parents, breakfast is included.

If the **((Camino Real Zaashila Huatulco** (Blv. Benito Juárez Lote 5, Bahía de Tangolunda, Huatulco, Oaxaca 70989, tel. 958/581-0460 or 958/581-0461, toll-free Mex. tel. 800/910-2300, toll-free U.S./Can. tel. 800/7-CAMINO or 800/722-6466, fax 958/581-0461, zaa@caminoreal.com.mx, zaares@ prodigy.net.mx, www.caminoreal.com/ zaashila, $200 d low season and up) hasn't yet gotten an architectural award, it should soon. Builders have succeeded in creating a modern luxury hotel that has an intimate feel. This begins right at the reception, a plush round *palapa*, where arriving guests are graciously invited to sit in soft chairs while being attended to by personable clerks, who are also seated behind rustic, designer desks. Outside, you walk to your room through manicured tropical gardens, replete with gurgling fountains, splashing brooks, and cascading, green lawn terraces. If the Zaashila has a drawback, it's in some of the 148 rooms, which, although luxurious and comfortable, are entirely tile-floored and could use more color and warmth. However, the arrangement of separate units, nested like a giant child's building blocks, resembles a space-age Hopi Native pueblo, each unit uniquely perched among the whole, affording much privacy and light, especially in upper-floor units. Outside, a few steps downhill, past the big, meandering blue pool, comes the superb beachfront: acres of luscious, billow-washed yellow sand, intimately enclosed between wave-sculpted rocks on one side and a jungly headland on the other. Low-season rentals begin at about $200 d, or about $375 if you must have your own little private pool. Corresponding high-season rates are around $380 and $500, with access to all water sports, tennis, golf, and three restaurants.

Bahía Conejos

A personable North American couple, Richard and Brooke Gazer, have built ◖ **Villa Agua Azul** (overlooking Playa Conejos, tel. 958/581-0265, guarei@hotmail.com, www.huatulco .com.mx/aguaazul, $130 and $150 s or d) with six elegantly lovely and comfortable guestrooms into their home. The luxuriously private accommodations, for nonsmoking adults only, stair-step down from the main house to an airy ocean-vista garden pool patio. Rates currently run between $130 and $150 s or d year-round, including a hearty breakfas; for the Christmas-New Year holiday, add 25 percent. With fans and a/c, and a short downhill walk to a private, intimate beach.

Camping

Authorities permit tent camping and RV parking at some of the Bahías de Huatulco. Self-contained RV parking or tenting is allowed in the big Bahía Tangolunda public beach access lot for about $2 per person per day. Although the beach is beautiful and the partly palm-shaded lot is pleasant enough, facilities are limited to toilets and possibly cold-water showers. Get there along the road along the beach to Tangolunda. Turn right at the signed Playa Pública public access road bordering the western edge of the golf course.

Other Huatulco beaches, such as Playa el Maguey, may be available for RV or tent camping. For more information, visit the **Huatulco National Park office** (adjacent, beach side, to the boat harbor, Santa Cruz de Huatulco, tel. 958/587-0446, 8 A.M.–5 P.M. Mon.–Fri., 8 A.M.–1 P.M. Sat.), which issues camping per-

mits. Alternatively, contact one of the tourist information offices.

FOOD

Aside from the Tangolunda hotels, most of the good Huatulco eateries are near the Crucecita plaza.

Breakfast and Snacks

For inexpensive homestyle cooking, try the *fondas* at the Crucecita *mercado* (market), between Guamuchil and Guanacastle, half a block off the plaza.

The market stalls are good for fresh fruit during daylight hours, as is the **Frutería Angelita** (just across Guanacastle, 7 A.M.– 9 P.M. daily).

Also nearby, the **Panadería San Alejandro** (at the southeast plaza corner of Flamboyan and Bugambilias, tel. 958/587-0317, 7 A.M.– 10:30 P.M. daily) offers mounds of scrumptious baked goodies.

In Crucecita, pineapples and watermelons fresh from the field go for about a dollar a piece.

The crowd of satisfied customers will lead you to Crucecita's best-bet snack shop, **❰ Los Portales Taco and Grill** (corner of Guamuchil and Bugambilias, right on the plaza, tel. 958/587-0070, 8–2 A.M. daily). Breakfasts ($2–3), a dozen styles of tacos ($2–3), Texas chili (or, as in Mexico, *frijoles charros*–cowboy beans, $2), and barbecued ribs ($5) are the specialties. Beer is inexpensive, to boot.

For a relaxing drink or a sandwich in Santa Cruz, go to the **Cafe Huatulco** (at the bandstand in the shady Santa Cruz town plaza, a block west of the marina embarcadero, tel. 958/587-1228, cafehuatulco@hotmail.com, 8 A.M.–10 P.M. daily). The mission of the friendly owner, Salvador López de Toledo, and his wife (who operates the kitchen) is to promote the already well-deserved popularity of Huatulco's mountain-grown coffee, which they grind fresh daily for their good cappuccinos and café lattes. Furthermore, Salvador is a good source of information on Huatulco coffee and the mountain *fincas cafeteleras* (coffee farms) where it's grown.

Restaurants

The refined sidewalk atmosphere of **❰ Cafe Oasis** (at the southeast plaza corner, Bugambilias and Flamboyan, tel. 958/587-0045, 8 A.M.–midnight daily) has made it Crucecita's plaza-front restaurant of choice. Beneath cooling ceiling fans, customers watch the passing plaza scene while enjoying a full bar and a professionally prepared and served menu of breakfast ($4–6), good espresso, fruit and salads ($2–5), hamburgers ($3–5), Mexican and international specialties ($5–10), and much more.

Lovers of fine Italian cuisine can't miss enjoying a meal at Crucecita's class-act restaurant, **El Giardino del Papa** (The Pope's Garden; Flamboyan 204, tel. 958/587-1763, 2 P.M.–midnight daily), brainchild of owner Rossana Pandolfini, of Amalfitano, and chef Mario Saggese of Salerno. Mario, who was once the pope's bodyguard, immigrated to Mexico to follow his passion for cooking. Rossana asked Mario to come to Huatulco because she craved pasta al dente the way it's "supposed to be" in the old country. Although Mario's suggestions include calamari criollo ($12), scampi al brandy ($15), *insalata* Mediterrenea ($5), and spaghetti a la Mario ($12), whatever you get will be tasty. Call for reservations, especially during the winter. Find the restaurant one block west of the plaza's southwest corner.

Diagonally across the plaza, half a block north of the plaza's northwest corner, step into the cool, airy interior of **Restaurant Terra Cotta** (at the Hotel Misión de los Arcos, Gardenia 902, tel. 958/587-0165, 8 A.M.–11 P.M. daily). Kick back and enjoy the leafy green bay-window view while you choose from a list of tasty breakfasts (eggs any style $3.50, omelets $4, waffles $3), salads (Caesar $6), baguettes (barbequed pork loin $7), and Mexican specialties (*mole negro* on chicken $8, baby back ribs with luscious tamarind sauce $10).

A worthy new addition to the Crucecita plaza-front restaurant options is **Tostada's Grill** (on the south side, tel. 958/587-1697, 7 P.M.–midnight daily). Although it offers plenty of good soups, salads, and pastas ($3–6), the house specialties come hot off the grill: barbecued ribs ($9), whole lobster ($14), surf and turf brochette ($11), and barbecued snapper, tuna, or *dorado* ($10).

Good, economically priced, local-style food in an open-air, TV-free setting is the specialty of refined but relaxing **❰ Restaurant la Crucecita** (501 Bugambilias, corner of Chacah, tel. 958/587-0906, 8 A.M.–11 P.M. daily), one block south of the plaza. A platoon of loyal local customers arrives daily to enjoy the afternoon five-course *comida corrida*. Pick an entrée (such as *guisado de res, costilla en mole verde,* or *chiles rellenos*) and you get bottomless fruit *agua* (lemon, orange, pineapple, *jamaica*), soup, rice, cooked veggies or salad, and dessert, all for $5. The *comida* is served noon–4:30 P.M.

For late lunch or *comida,* local folks crowd into the airy *palapa* of **Restaurant Almendros di Caro** (three blocks south, one block east of the plaza's southeast corner, on Ocotillo, just west of Carrizal, tel. 958/587-0645, 8 A.M.–8:30 P.M. daily), life project of friendly Carina Enriquez Gutiérrez. Here, the big draw is the four-course set lunch, but with plenty of options. Choose your soup, main plate (of pasta, or meat, or seafood, or *antojito*), and you get rice, a drink, and dessert thrown in, all for $5. Also good for breakfast.

Fine dining in Huatulco has received a big boost at █ **Restaurant L'Echalote** (on Calle Zapateco behind the big Hotel Villablanca in Chahue, tel. 958/587-2480, info@edencosta .com, 2–11 P.M. daily except Mon., reservations highly recommended). Although the cooking of owner-chefs Thierry Faivre and his Laotian wife, Tina, derives from an entire world of cuisine experience, their creations invariably come with a French touch. Ask Thierry to put on Edith Piaf and it will be better than Paris. Everything they serve is good, from the soup (*caldo camarón* $9), salad with goat cheese ($7), and Thai fondue for two ($22). *Vive la France!*

ENTERTAINMENT
Nightlife

Huatulco entertainments center on the Crucecita plaza. Although the hubbub cools down weekdays and low seasons (and hot clubs seem to change as often as the Huatulco breeze), many spots heat up significantly during the high winter season.

A growing platoon of visitors and local expatriates gather for a little bit of Ireland in Huatulco at **Café Dublin** (Calle Carrizal, noon–after midnight daily low season, 6 A.M.–2 A.M. daily high season), a block east and half a block south of the Crucecita plaza's southeast corner. Good imported beer, Irish coffee, spaghetti and meatballs, hamburgers, satellite TV, and good fellowship keeps the customers happy. In a cozy upstairs room, patrons settle in for the evening, socializing, enjoying recorded music, and watching videos.

Next door to the Café Dublin is the very worthy low- to medium-volume jazz, guitar, and vocal nightspot **La Peña** (Carrizal 504, cell 044-958/587-6986, 7–11 P.M. except Sun.).

One of the longest lasting Crucecita nightclubs is the **La Crema Restaurant-Bar,** on Carrizal, across from Café Dublin and La Peña bar. In high season, it's open nightly, with food and drink, videos, flashing lights, and high-volume *salsa* music for dancing.

In Santa Cruz, on the east side of the harbor, pass in front of the Hotel Marina and continue about a block, to the road's end and hot **Zalamandra** disco, which offers continuous recorded reggae, salsa, and Latin rock from about 11 P.M. To verify programs, call the Hotel Marina (tel. 958/587-0963).

A pair of promising new nightspots have opened up in Chahue. The original was the cleverly decorated disco **La Mina,** fixed up to resemble a coal mine, in the basement of the **Hotel Real Aligheri** (tel. 958/587-1242). Programs (call to verify) include mostly salsa, tango, and '70s and '80s rock. Find it on Zapoteco, about a block north of main Boulevard Benito Juárez.

Newer and hotter is **Disco Papaya,** on main east–west Bulevar Benito Juárez, beach side, approximately two blocks east of the intersection to Crucecita, most nights, and especially weekends and holidays, beginning around 10 P.M.

Sunset Cruises, Live Music, and Tourist Shows

Lovers of quieter diversions might enjoy going on a wine, snack, and soft-music sunset cruise on the sailboat *Luna Azul* (tel. 958/587-0509). For higher-volume entertainments with your sunset view, go by the catamaran *Tequila* (tel. 958/587-2303) from the Santa Cruz boat harbor.

The **Club Gala Resort** in Tangolunda is one of the most reliable sources of hotel nightlife. Live music often plays before dinner (about 6–8 P.M.) in the lobby bar, and "Gala Night" tourist buffet and shows rev up at least weekly year-round. Contact a travel agent or call the hotel direct at 958/583-0400 for details and reservations (about $55 per person, including everything). Other hotels, such as the Crown Pacific, tel. 958/581-0044, and Barceló ("Caribe Tropical" and "Broadway" nights, tel. 958/587-0055) may also offer similar buffet and show entertainments in season.

Travel agents customarily can get you tickets to cruises and shows. Contact your hotel desk, or an experienced agent such as **Paraíso**

Huatulco (tel. 958/587-0181) or **Prometur** (tel. 958/587-0413).

SPORTS AND RECREATION

Huatulco's open spaces and smooth roads and sidewalks afford plenty of walking and jogging opportunities. One of the most serene spots is along the Tangolunda Golf Course mornings or evenings. Also, an interesting sea-view forest trail takes off from Bahía Conejos.

Tennis and Golf

If you're planning on playing lots of tennis, best stay at one of the Tangolunda luxury resorts. Otherwise, the Barceló, tel. 958/581-0055 or 958/581-0005, and the Tangolunda Golf Course, tel. 958/581-0037, fax 958/581-0059, rent tennis courts for about $7/hour. Call for rental information and reservations.

The breezy green **Tangolunda Golf Course**, tel. 958/581-0037, fax 958/581-0059, designed by the late architect Mario Chegnan Danto, stretches for 6,851 yards down Tangolunda Valley to the bay. The course starts from a low building complex (watch for bridge entrance) off the Highway 200-Tangolunda highway across from the sanitary plant. Greens fee runs about $60, cart $32, club rental $17, caddy $20. The tennis courts, maintained by the same government corporation that owns the golf course, are next to the clubhouse on the knoll at the east side of the golf course.

The luxury **Xquenda** (sh-QUEN-dah, "soul" in Zapotec) spa and athletic club, in Chahue, west side (on the Santa Cruz-Tangolunda road, tel. 958/583-4448, -4449, xquenda@huatulco spa.com, visit www.huatulcospa.com, 9 A.M.– 6 P.M. daily), offers tennis, paddle tennis, and a lap swimming pool. Spa services include massage, facials, *temazcal* ceremonial hot room, and more.

Horseback Riding

Rancho Caballo del Mar (tel. 958/589-9387, local cell 044-958/587-4886, reservaciones@ ranchocaballodelmar, www.ranchocaballodel mar.com) guides horseback trips along the ocean-view forest trail that stretches from its corral through the eco-preserve zone by the Río Copalita. The four-mile tour, which costs about $35 per person, begins at the ranch site, on the road (best go by car or taxi) on the road several miles east past Tangolunda, about a mile before (south of) Highway 200.

Adventure Tours

José Aussenac, owner-operator of **Copalita River Tours,** organizes and guides outdoor adventure tours in the east-side Río Copalita wildlife sanctuary. Options include bird- and animal-watching walks along riverine forest trails, kayaking river rapids, and mud baths at a riverside ranch. Contact him, at his Hotel Posada Michelle, tel. 958/587-0535, for more information and reservations.

Another good choice is to go with **Cascadas Magicas** to the luscious tropical foothill forest headwaters of the Río Copalita and hike forest trails for a refreshing swim and picnic (about $25 per person) in the waterfalls of Copalilla creek. For more details, drop by the Cascada Magicas office at Colorin 404, two blocks south of the Crucecita plaza, tel. 958/587-1470, cascadasmagicas@hotmail.com.

Swimming, Snorkeling, and Scuba Diving

Swimming is ideal in the calm corners of the Bahías de Huatulco. Especially good swimming beaches are at **Playa Entrega** in Bahía Santa Cruz and **Bahía el Maguey.**

Generally clear water makes for rewarding snorkeling off the rocky shoals of all of the Bays of Huatulco. Local currents and conditions, however, can be hazardous. Novice snorkelers should go on trips accompanied by strong, experienced swimmers or professional guides. Bring your own equipment if you can; gear purchased locally can be expensive at best and unusable at worst.

Huatulco scuba divers enjoy the services of well-equipped and professional **Hurricane Divers** scuba shop (tel. 958/587-1107, email@ hurricanedivers.com, www.hurricanedivers .com, 9 A.M.–6 P.M. Mon.–Fri., 9 A.M.–4 P.M. Sat.), in the small complex between the Santa

Cruz main beach and boat harbor. They start novices out with a pool mini-course, followed by a three-hour ($80) resort dive in a nearby bay. Snorkelers go for about $50, with good equipment furnished. Hurricane Divers' open-water certification course takes about four days and runs about $300, complete. The shorter, two-day 12-meter course runs about $200. With your open-water certificate, you are qualified for the advanced (one-tank $50; two-tank $80) dives. After that, you may be ready for more advanced trips, which might include local shipwrecks, night dives, and marine flora, fauna, and ecology tours.

Alternatively, try very experienced (since 1988 in Huatulco) **Buceos Sotavento,** which offers similar services. Contact them either at the Plaza Oaxaca complex, upstairs, shop #18, on the Crucecita plaza, southwest corner of Flamboyan and Gardenia, tel./fax 958/587-2166, scubasota@hotmail.com, www.tomzap .com/sotavento.html; or in Tangolunda, tel. 958/581-0051, across from the Hotel Barceló.

Fishing and Boat Launching

The local boat cooperative **Sociedad Servicios Turísticos Bahía Tangolunda** takes visitors out for fishing excursions from the Santa Cruz boat quay. Contact them at their ticket office (for catamaran *Tequila,* tel. 958/587-2303) at the Santa Cruz boat dock.

For a launch with two lines and bait, figure on paying about $40 minimum for a three-hour excursion. For big-game fishing, rent a big 40-foot boat, with lines for several persons, for about $400. More reasonable prices might be obtained by asking around among the individual fishers at the Santa Cruz boat harbor or the village at San Agustín.

Alternatively, go fishing in the 30-foot motor yacht *Fortuna* (tel. 958/581-0491 or 958/587-1381, toll-free Mex. tel. 01-800/624-6161, fortunahuatulco@msn.com), with about four lines and room for about six.

On the other hand, you can leave the negotiations up to a travel agent, who will arrange a fishing trip for you and your friends. You can stop afterward at a beachside *palapa,*

which will cook up a feast with your catch. Save money by bringing your own tackle. Rates for an approximately three-hour trip for three run about $60 if you supply your own tackle, $120 if you don't. Contact the agent at your hotel travel desk, or an outside agent such as **Paraíso Huatulco** (in the Hotel Flamboyan on the Crucecita plaza, tel. 958/587-0181, fax 958/587-0190).

Huatulco's best **boat-launching site** is at easily reachable Bahía Chahue marina, with about 40 slips and an excellent heavy-duty boat ramp. Go to the marina office (tel. 958/587-2652, 8 A.M.–3 P.M. and 4–6 P.M. Mon.–Fri.) for permission to launch ($15) and slip rental information. Slip rates run about $0.55 per foot per day (between 35 and 80 feet) at the dock. Electricity and water cost extra. Find it from the east–west Chahue beachfront boulevard, follow the sign for remolques (trailers) to the big parking lot and ramp.

SHOPPING
Market and Handicrafts

Crucecita has a small traditional market (officially the Mercado 3 de Mayo) east of the plaza, between Guanacastle and Guamuchil. Although produce, meats, and clothing occupy most of the stalls, a few offer Oaxaca handicrafts. Items include black *barra* pottery, hand-crocheted Mixtec and Amusgo *huipiles,* wool weavings from Teotitlán del Valle, and whimsical duck-motif wooden bowls carved by an elderly, but sharp-bargaining, local gentleman.

In Santa Cruz, just west of the boat harbor, a warren of dozens of stalls offer nearly everything, from T-shirts and Taxco silver, to carved wooden fish and lacquerware.

Steep rents and lack of business force many local silver, leather, art, and other handicrafts shops to hibernate until tourists arrive in December. The few healthy shops with good selections cluster either around the Crucecita plaza, the Santa Cruz boat harbor, or in the Punta Tangolunda shopping complex adjacent to the Hotel Barceló (or shops in the hotel itself).

In Crucecita, one of the most reliable crafts stores is **Plata de Taxco** (9 A.M.–9 P.M. daily), next to Hotel Suites Begonias, a few doors south of the plaza's southwest corner. Here you can select from an all-Mexican assortment: shiny *barro negro* (black pottery) from the Valley of Oaxaca, pottery moon and sun faces from Tonalá, Jalisco, *talavera* ware from Puebla, *alebrijes* from Arrazola, near Oaxaca City, and lots of glistening silver jewelry from Taxco.

Alternatively, for a fine all-Taxco silver collection, especially rings, go to **Platería Maitl** (tel. 958/587-1223, 9 A.M.–9 P.M. daily) on the Crucecita plaza, west side, between Guanacastle and Guamuchil.

One of the few local handicrafts workshops is the charmingly traditional **Mantelería Escobar** (Ocotillo 217, tel. 958/587-0532, 8 A.M.–8 P.M. Mon.–Sat.) at the corner of Bugambilias, three blocks south of the Crucecita plaza. This factory uses century-old looms to create lovely all-cotton *manteles* (tablecloths). Besides their own work, they also sell plenty—blouses, skirts, *huipiles,* and ceramics—from all over Oaxaca.

Another worthwhile Crucecita handicrafts option is **Artesanías Paradiso** (tel. 958/587-0268, 9 A.M.–10 P.M. Mon.–Sat., 5–10 P.M. Sun.), just past the plaza's northwest corner, on Gardenia, corner of Guarumbo. Among the many carefully selected treasures, find masks from Huazaolotitlán, black pottery from San Bartolo Coyotepec, dolls from San Miguel de Allende, *alebrijes* from San Martén Tilcajete, and a whole roomful of fetching one-of-a-kind dresses, blouses, and skirts ranging from traditional to chic.

Supermarket, Laundry, and Photography

The supermarket **La Fuente** (tel. 958/587-0222, 8 A.M.–10 P.M. daily), in Crucecita on east-side Avenida Oaxaca, a block east of the Pemex station, offers a large stock of groceries, an ice machine, and a little bit of everything else.

Take your washing to the **Lavandería Aragon** (8 A.M.–8 P.M. Mon.–Sat.). Find it five short blocks north of the Crucecita plaza, on Flamboyan, corner of Gardenia and Palma Real.

For quick digital and film processing and printing, go to **Foto Conejo** (tel. 958/587-0054, 9 A.M.–8 P.M. Mon.–Sat., 9 A.M.–5 P.M. Sun.), just off the Crucecita plaza, across Guamuchil from the market. Besides a photo-portfolio of the Bahías de Huatulco, the friendly owner stocks point-and-shoot cameras and both film and digital supplies and accessories.

SERVICES
Money Exchange

For cash, you may either use the ATMs available at all of Huatulco's banks, or go inside. In Crucecita, try long-hours **HSBC** (8 A.M.–7 P.M. Mon.–Sat.), at the corner of Bugambilias and Sibali, eight short blocks north of the plaza. Otherwise, go to **Scotiabank Inverlat** and ATM, with shorter hours (9 A.M.–4 P.M. Mon.–Fri.), a block west of the plaza at the corner of Guamuchil and Carrizal. After hours, use either the Banamex ATM, on Carrizal a block west of the plaza a few doors north of the Hotel Grifer, or the Bancomer ATM, on the Crucecita plaza's southwest corner by the newsstand.

Other banks are in Santa Cruz: **Banamex** (tel. 958/587-0322, 9 A.M.–4 P.M. Mon.–Fri.) on the main street Avenida Benito Juárez, corner of Pochutla, exchanges both U.S. and Canadian travelers checks. **Bancomer** (tel. 958/587-0305, 8:30 A.M.–4 P.M. Mon.–Fri.), on the adjacent corner, across Pochutla, does about the same thing.

Post and Telecommunications

The Huatulco *correo* (tel. 958/587-0551, 8 A.M.–3 P.M. Mon.–Fri., 9 A.M.–1 P.M. Sat.) and *telecomunicaciones* (tel. 958/587-0894, 8 A.M.–7 P.M. Mon.–Fri., 9 A.M.–12:30 P.M. Sat.) stand side by side, across from the Pemex gas station on east-side Blv. Tangolunda.

For telephone, buy a **Ladatel** telephone card and use it at public telephones, or go to one of the *larga distancia* businesses on Carrizal, near the Hotel Grifer, such as **Caseta Telefónica Gemenis,** tel. 958/587-0735 or 958/587-0736, 8 A.M.–9:30 P.M. daily.

Internet connection is available at Cuijosnet store, at Carrizal 504, between Flamboyan and Chaca, next to the Irish Pub, tel. 958/587-1569, 10 A.M.–10 P.M. daily.

Health and Emergencies

Among the better of Huatulco private clinics is **Clínica Médico,** with 24-hour emergency service, tel. 958/587-0600 or 958/587-0687. Find them at 403 Sibali, corner of Gardenia, about eight blocks north of the Crucecita plaza.

For an English-speaking, U.S.-trained doctor, go to IAMAT (International Association for Medical Assistance to Tourists) member and general practitioner Dr. Andrés González Ayvar, at the Hotel Barceló (tel. 958/581-0055), or his cellular 044-958/587-6065. Regular consultation hours are 11 A.M.–1 P.M. and 6–9 P.M. Mon.–Sat.

Alternatively, go to the 24-hour government **Centro de Salud** clinic, tel. 958/587-1421, on Carrizal, a block east of the Crucecita plaza, or the big modern-standard **Seguro Social** hospital, tel. 958/587-1182 or 958/587-1183, in Crucecita, on the boulevard to Tangolunda, a quarter mile south of the Pemex gas station.

For routine medications, Crucecita has many pharmacies, such as **Farmacia del Centro,** plaza corner of Flamboyan and Bugambilias, tel. 958/587-0232, 8 A.M.–10 P.M. Mon.–Sat., 9 A.M.–2 P.M. and 5–10 P.M. Sun., at street level, below the Hotel Begonias.

For police emergencies, call the Crucecita **policía,** tel. 958/587-0210, in the Agencia Municipal behind the post office, across the Tangolunda boulevard from the Pemex *gasolinera.*

Immigration and Customs

Both Migración and the Aduana are at the Huatulco airport. If you lose your tourist card, try to avoid trouble or a fine at departure by presenting Migración with proof of your date of arrival—stamped passport, an airline ticket, or preferably a copy of your lost tourist permit—a day (or at least three hours) before your scheduled departure.

INFORMATION
Tourist Information Offices
The Huatulco office of the **Oaxaca Secretary**

of Tourism (tel./fax 958/581-0176, 8 A.M.–5 P.M. Mon.–Fri. high season, hours vary in the low season, call ahead) is in the Tangolunda hotel zone, inland side, west edge of the hotel-shopping complex.

Alternatively, go to **Huatulco Municipal Tourism** (tel. 958/587-1871 or 958/587-1070, fax 958/587-1777, 9 A.M.–5 P.M. Mon.–Fri., 9 A.M.–2 P.M. Sat.) in the Casa de Cultura, in Crucecita, at the corner of Bugambilias and Ceiba, four blocks south of the plaza.

Publications

The small **newsstand** (tel. 958/587-0279, 8 A.M.–10 P.M. daily) at the southwest Crucecita plaza corner stocks a number of North American magazines, such as *Newsweek, People,* and *Scientific American,* in addition to the daily *Miami Herald.*

Also, pick up a copy of *Huatulco Magazine,* the handy commercial tourist booklet, at your hotel or a store or travel agent, or at the magazine's office (Cerrada de Tlacolula no. 3, tel. 958/587-0342) in Santa Cruz.

GETTING THERE AND AWAY
By Air
The **Huatulco airport** (officially the Aeropuerto Internacional Bahías de Huatulco, code-designated HUX) is just off Highway 200, eight miles (13 km) west of Crucecita and 19 miles (31 km) east of Puerto Ángel. The terminal is small, with a pair of snack bars, a few handicrafts and trinket shops and a small book and magazine store, with some English-language paperback novels, and an ATM.

A number of scheduled air carriers connect with Mexican and international destinations:

The most direct U.S. flight is via *Continental Airlines,* connecting daily non-stop with Houston. For information and reservations, call toll-free Mexico tel. 800/900-5000 or contact a travel agent.

Mexicana Airlines flights connect daily with Mexico City. For reservations, call Mexicana's office at the Plaza Chahue shopping center, tel. 958/587-0223 or 958/587-0243, or toll-free in Mexico tel. 800/502-2000. For flight information, call the airport at tel. 958/581-9008 or 958/587-9007.

Aerocaribe airlines connects with Oaxaca. For reservations, call a travel agent or dial toll-free 800/623-4518.

A number of winter-spring seasonal charter flights connect Huatulco with U.S. and Canadian destinations, such as Toronto, Winnipeg, Calgary, Vancouver, New York, Chicago, Denver, Seattle, and many more. For more information and reservations, contact a travel agent.

Furthermore, British **First Choice** (www .firstchoice.co.uk/mexico) charter airlines connects Huatulco with certain English destinations during the fall, winter, and spring months.

Of the long-distance Mexican charter airlines, **Magnicharter** is the most frequent, connecting with Mexico City daily except Tuesday. For reservations and flight information, call a travel agent or dial local tel. 958/584-581-9072.

Also, experienced local light charter airline **Aerotucan** regularly connects Huatulco with Oaxaca City, Puebla and Veracruz. For information and reservations dial toll-free 800/640-4148. Or in Huatulco, dial local tel. 958/587-2427; or in Oaxaca City, 951/501-0530 or 951/501-0532. For many more details, log on to www.aero-tucan.com.

Huatulco **air arrival** is usually simple. Since the terminal has no hotel booking agency or money-exchange counter (although there is an ATM), come with a hotel reservation and sufficient pesos to last until you can get to the bank in Santa Cruz or Crucecita. After the typically quick immigrations and customs checks, arrivees have a choice of efficient ground transportation to town. Agents sell tickets for collective GMC Suburbans to Crucecita, Santa Cruz, and Tangolunda (about $9). A private *taxi especial* outside the airport gate only, for three, possibly four passengers, runs about $40 to the same destinations. Prices to Puerto Ángel vicinity run about double these.

Mobile travelers on a budget can roll their suitcase the couple of blocks from the terminal to Highway 200 and catch one of the frequent public **taxi** *colectivos* (about $1–2) headed either way to Crucecita (east, left) or the Pochutla (Puerto Ángel) junction (west, right).

Car rental agents are usually on duty for flight arrivals. Make a reservation ahead of time to ensure they will meet your flight: **Budget** in Crucecita, tel. 958/587-0010, fax 958/587-0019; **Thrifty** in Tangolunda, across from the Hotel Barcelo, tel. 958/581-0058; **Hertz**, tel. 958/581-9092; or **Europecar 1,** tel. 958/581-9094 or 958/581-0552. During the winter especially, make reservations at home prior to departure.

By Car or RV

Paved highways connect Huatulco east with the Isthmus of Tehuantepec, west with Puerto Ángel and Puerto Escondido, and north with Oaxaca.

Highway 200, the east-west route, runs an easy 100 miles (161 km) to Tehuantepec, where it connects with Highway 190. From there, it continues northwest to Oaxaca or east to Chiapas and the Guatemala border. (A new $2 toll cutoff, fork left about five miles west of, before, Salina Cruz, cuts the time to Tehuantepec and, thence Oaxaca, by at least half an hour.)

In the opposite direction, the Highway 200 route is equally smooth, connecting Huatulco with Pochutla (Puerto Ángel), 25 miles (40 km) west, and Puerto Escondido, 70 miles (113 km), continuing to Acapulco in a long 322 miles (519 km). Allow about three hours to Tehuantepec, 1.5 hours to Puerto Escondido, and to Acapulco, a full nine hours' driving time, either direction.

Highway 175, the cross-Sierra connection north with the city of Oaxaca, although paved, is narrow, winding, and oft-potholed, with few services in the 80-mile high Sierra stretch between its junction with Highway 200 at Pochutla (22 miles west of Crucecita) and Miahuatlán in the Valley of Oaxaca. The road climbs to 9,000 feet into pine-tufted, winter-chilly Chatino and Zapotec country. Be prepared for emergencies. Allow eight hours northbound, seven hours southbound, for the entire 175-mile (282-km) Huatulco-Oaxaca trip. (You can save an hour by road Huatulco-

Oaxaca by taking the new shortcut, from Highway 200, a couple of miles west of the Huatulco airport, via Santa Cruz de Huatulco and Pluma Hidalgo, to Highway 175 and thence to Oaxaca.)

By Bus

Four main long-distance bus lines connect Huatulco with destinations east, west, and north. They depart from three small separate terminals in Crucecita, several blocks north of the plaza.

Many daily **Cristóbal Colón** first-class buses (terminal located on Gardenia, corner of Ocotillo, four blocks north of the plaza, tel. 958/587-0261, toll-free in Mexico, 800/702-8000) connect west with Pochutla

(Puerto Ángel) and Puerto Escondido. Buses also connect east with the Salina Cruz and Tehuantepec on the Isthmus, continuing either east to San Cristóbal las Casas and Tapachula in Chiapas, or northwest to Mexico City via Oaxaca and Puebla.

One block farther north, corner of Palma Real, a few **Estrella Blanca** affiliate buses (tel. 958/587-0103), such as first-class Elite connect west with Pinotepa Nacional and Acapulco via Pochutla and Puerto Escondido, and east with Salina Cruz.

A few second- and first-class **Estrella del Valle** and **Autobuses Oaxaca Pacífico** buses connect daily with Oaxaca via Pochutla, from Jazmin, corner Sabali, nine blocks north of the plaza, tel. 958/587-0193 or 958/587-0354.

OAXACA CITY AND VALLEY

A visit to the city of Oaxaca (pop. 400,000, elev. 5,110 feet, 1,778 meters) and its rich surrounding Valley of Oaxaca is truly a journey not to be missed. Oaxaca City, the state capital, with its sun-splashed, year-round spring-like weather, precious, traffic-free central plaza—its cherished *zócalo*—is just about the most charming and relaxing colonial city in Mexico. The city's rich treasuries of handicrafts, beloved old churches, fascinating museums, renowned festivals, fine-arts galleries, wonderfully varied cuisine, both traditional and nouvelle, and abundance of comfortable hotels, both moderate and luxurious, have made Oaxaca a favorite destination for a world-wide legion of savvy travelers.

The city of Oaxaca's appeal, however, spreads beyond its city limits, into the surrounding Val-

ley of Oaxaca. In reality, the Valley of Oaxaca is three valleys, which diverge, like the thumb, index finger, and middle finger of a hand, from a single strategic point. Aztec conquerors called that hilltop spot Huaxyacac (oo-AHSH-yah-kahk, Point of the Guaje) for the forest of pod-bearing trees that still carpets its slopes. The Spanish, who founded the city at the foot of the hill, shifted that name to the more-pronounceable Oaxaca (wah-HAH-kah).

The people of the Valley of Oaxaca, walled in by mountains from the rest of Mexico, both benefited and suffered from their long isolation. They are proud but mostly poor inheritors of rich traditions that live on despite centuries of Spanish occupation.

A large proportion of Oaxacans are pure native Mexicans who speak one of dozens of

HIGHLIGHTS

◖ Catedral de Oaxaca: Arguably the bulkiest of Oaxaca's churches, the Oaxaca Cathedral is famous because it preserves one of the four replicas made from the enigmatic Holy Cross of Huatulco (page 637).

◖ Centro Cultural de Santo Domingo: This Oaxacan pride and joy is two sights in one: The Museo Regional de las Culturas de Oaxaca is a first-rate museum, while the lovingly restored Templo y Ex-Convento de Santo Domingo climaxes overhead with a spectacularly ornate Sistine Chapel-like barrel ceiling (page 638).

◖ El Tule: The townsfolk of Santa María del Tule have literally built their village around El Tule tree, the most massive tree in Latin America. Known to botanists as a Mexican bald cypress, the 2,000-year-old El Tule is a genetic cousin of the renowned giant redwood trees of the California Sierra Nevada mountains (page 663).

◖ Teotitlán del Valle: Featuring many dozens of home factory stores offering a treasury of brilliant *tapetes* (Mexico's finest wool weavings), this is a prime stop on any Oaxaca handicrafts shopping tour (page 664).

◖ Tlacolula: Seemingly all of Oaxaca converges here every Sunday for the market. Be sure to include a visit to the precious old chapel, the Capilla del Señor de Tlacolula, and the Pensamiento mescal shop in your visit (page 666).

◖ Mitla: This renowned ruined city lives on in the present town, built over the houses of its ancient inhabitants. The columns, platforms, burial chambers, and especially the intricate *greca* fretwork facades are prime signatures of Mitla (page 666).

◖ Zaachila: Thursday is the choicest time

to visit, when thousands of Zapotec-speaking country folks stream into the town's spectacularly colorful weekly market. While there, be sure to include a visit exploring the tombs of the famous Zaachila archaeological site just uphill from the market (page 671).

◖ Monte Albán: Monte Albán, probably Mesoamerica's first true metropolis, reigns atop a mountain above Oaxaca City. The fine on-site museum provides a good introduction to this majestic site (page 674).

LOOK FOR ◖ TO FIND RECOMMENDED SIGHTS, ACTIVITIES, DINING, AND LODGING.

OAXACA CITY AND VALLEY

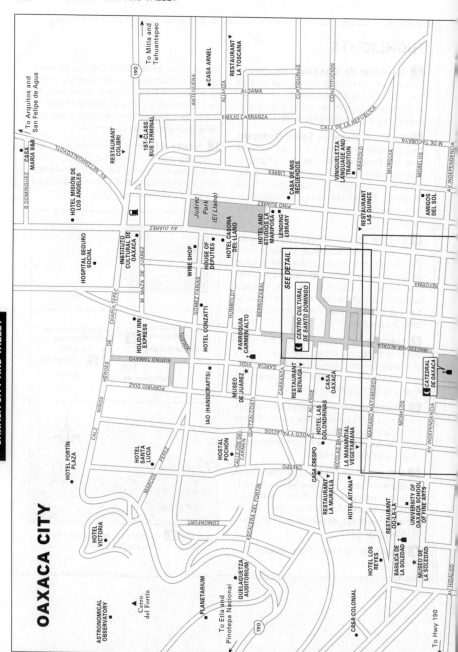

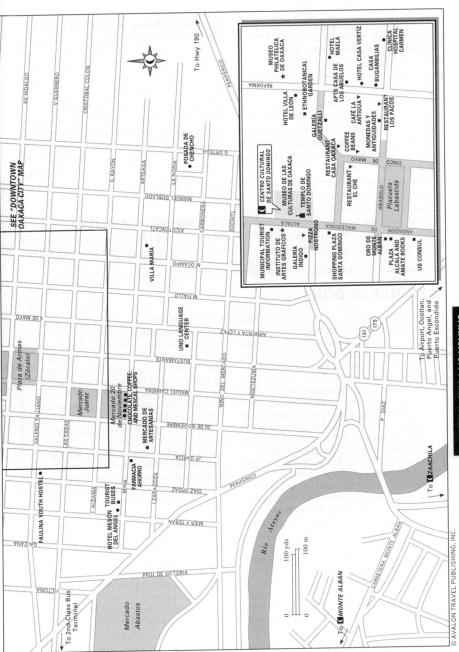

SEE "DOWNTOWN OAXACA CITY" MAP

To Hwy 190

PERIFERICO

REFORMA

MUSEO PHILATELICA DE OAXACA ★

HOTEL MAELA

HOTEL CASA VERTIZ

CLINICA HOSPITAL CARMEN

APTS CASA DE LOS ABUELOS

CASA BUGAMBILIAS

HOTEL VILLA DE LEÓN

ETHNOBOTANICAL GARDEN

GALERIA QUETZALLI

CAFÉ LA ANTIGUA

RESTAURANT LOS PACOS

MONEDAS Y ANTIGUIDADES

RESTAURANT CASA OAXACA

COFFEE BEANS

CINCO DE MAYO

CENTRO CULTURAL DE SANTO DOMINGO

MUSEO DE LAS CULTURAS DE OAXACA

RESTAURANT EL CHE

TEMPLO DE SANTO DOMINGO

Plazuela Labastida

ABASOLO

ANDADOR

MUNICIPAL TOURIST INFORMATION

INSTITUTO DE ARTES GRÁFICOS ★

PIZZA NOSTRONO

ALCALA

MACEDONIA

GALERIA INDIGO

SHOPPING PLAZA SANTA DOMINGO

ORO DE MONTE ALBAN

PLAZA ALCALA AND AMATE BOOKS

US CONSUL

DE MACEDONIA

AV. HIDALGO

V. GUERRERO

CRISTÓBAL COLON

IL RAYON

ARTEAGA

LA NORIA

MANUEL DOBLADO

CARBONERA

XOCHITL

G. ORTEGA

POSADA DE CHENCHO

XICOTENCATL

M. OCAMPO

VILLA MARÍA

M. FIALLO

ARMENTA Y LOPEZ

UNO LANGUAGE CENTER

131

175

To Airport, Ocotlan, Puerto Angel, and Puerto Escondido

5 DE MAYO

BUSTAMANTE

MIGUEL CABRERA

NIÑO DEL MERCADO

MOCTEZUMA

P. DIAZ

PERIFERICO

Plaza de Armas (Zócalo)

Mercado Juarez

VALERIO TRUJANO

LAS CASAS

GALEANA

Mercado 20 de Noviembre

CHOCOLATE, COFFEE, AND MESCAL SHOPS

MERCADO DE ARTESANIAS

20 DE NOVIEMBRE

JP GARCIA

FARMACIA AHORRO

DIAZ ORDAZ

IZTAPALAPA

MINA

ALDAMA

PAULINA YOUTH HOSTEL

TOURIST BUSES

HOTEL MESON DEL ANGEL

ZARAGOZA

MIER Y TERAN

To 2nd-Class Bus Terminal

VICTORIA

PROL DE VICTORIA

Mercado Abastos

Rio Atoyac

To ZAACHILA

CARRETERA MONTE ALBAN

To MONTE ALBÁN

0   100 yds
0   100 m

© AVALON TRAVEL PUBLISHING, INC.

native languages and dialects. Significant numbers speak little or no Spanish at all. Even in the valley around Oaxaca city itself they make up a sizable fraction of the people. Far out in the country, they *are* the people. Mostly speaking dialects of Zapotec or Mixtec, they harvest their corn for tortillas and their maguey for *pulque* and *aguardiente* (fire water). They spin their wool, hoe their vegetables, and then go to market and sit beside their piles of blankets and mounds of onions, wondering when their luck is going to change.

And their luck has been changing, for the better. Authorities have recognized the potential value of the Valley of Oaxaca's fortunate location for both its residents and the travelers who visit Oaxaca. The government has responded vigorously, with new infra-structure, including modern-standard roads. They lead out from the city in all directions to famous handicrafts and market villages such as Teotitlán del Valle, Tlacolula, Coyotepec, Ocotlán, Arrazola, and Etla, and to the legendary archaeological sites, such as at Mitla, Zaachila, and Monte Albán. All of these places and more are drawing an increasing flow of visitors, both local and foreign, to the town markets and crafts villages, to sell, to browse, and to buy; and to the Valley's ruined cities, to explore and wonder at the ancient but still regal monuments of Oaxaca's glorious past.

PLANNING YOUR TIME

In a whirlwind five to seven days, you could explore the major highlights for which Oaxaca

---

PRINCESS DONAJI

The fabled marriage of King Cosijoeza of the Zapotecs to Coyollicatzin, daughter of Emperor Moctezuma II of the Aztecs, around 1490 was a happy one. It resulted in five children, the youngest of whom was a charming little girl.

The king asked his soothsayers what their divinations told of his little daughter's future. They replied that her life would be filled with tragic events and that she would finally sacrifice herself for her people. The king, saddened by the news, but happy that she would turn out to be so selfless, named her Donaji (Great Soul).

Earlier, Cosijoeza (koh-see-ho-AY-zah), who ruled the Zapotec Isthmus domains from his capital at present-day Tehuantepec, had been an uneasy ally of his old enemy, King Dzahuindanda (zah-ween-DAHN-dah) of the Mixtecs. In 1520, with the Aztec threat diminished by the Spanish invasion, Cosijoeza recklessly attacked the fierce Mixtecs, losing the initial battle and then nearly his life as the Mixtecs pressed their advantage.

However, the Spanish, in the person of Hernán Cortés's lieutenant Francisco Orozco, soon imposed a Mixtec-Zapotec treaty in which Dzahuindanda received Princess Donaji as a hostage to guarantee the peace.

Having Donaji as a prisoner at Monte Albán (known as Danni Dipaa in those days) was not exactly an advantage to Dzahuindanda, for he suspected that she was as much a spy as a hostage. His guess was right. Donaji gleaned intelligence vital to the Zapotec counterattack her father Cosijoeza was planning. At the moment Dzahuindanda's forces were most vulnerable, she sent her father a secret message to attack, which he did, with complete success, except for one thing.

With the treaty broken, the outraged Mixtecs decided to do away with Donaji. They decapitated her and buried her body before her father could rescue her. Later, some Zapotecs found Donaji's remains on the bank of the Atoyac river. They were surprised to see a lovely violet wild iris blossoming from her blood. Even more surprising, they found the flower's roots growing around her head, which was without any sign of decomposition.

Three hundred years later, the Oaxaca government decided to honor the heroine who sacrificed herself for her people by adding an image of Donaji's head to the Oaxacan coat of arms, where it remains to the present day.

City and Valley are famous. On your first day in town, spend the morning at a sidewalk café soaking in the relaxing *zócalo* (central plaza) ambience. While there, be sure to visit the **Oaxaca Cathedral,** especially the **Holy Cross of Huatulco,** inside.

Then stroll up the **Macedonio Alcalá** pedestrian street mall, browsing through handicrafts shops, visiting some of the famous art-rich landmarks, such as the **Teatro Alcalá,** the **Museum of Contemporary Art,** and the **Ex-convento de Santa Catalina.** But most of all, be sure to spend a couple of hours inside the beloved gem-like **Templo y Ex-Convento de Santo Domingo** church and the unrivaled **Museo Regional de las Culturas de Oacaxa** next door.

On subsequent days, best divide your time between City and Valley sights, browsing some of the city's many excellent museums, handicrafts shops, and venerable churches, but also spending some days heading out into the Valley of Oaxaca to at least some of the colorful weekly markets, handicrafts villages, and archaeological sites.

And by all means, you must save half of one of your days for a visit to the 2,500-year-old **Monte Albán** archaeological site, America's first true metropolis, that still reigns on the mountain-top not far southwest of the city.

On a Sunday, it would be best to go to the Valley's east side, to the **Teotitlán del Valle** carpet-weaving village, continuing to the **Tlacolula** Sunday market, and finally visiting the renowned, unmissable **Mitla** archaeological site.

Similarly, on Thursday, if possible, you should venture southwest, straight to the archaeological site and the famously colorful Thursday market at **Zaachila** village. On your return north, stop by the monumental (but curiously unfinished) 16th-century church at **Cuilapan de Guerrero,** followed by a side visit to **Arrazola** *alebrijes* woodcrafts village.

Subsequently, on Friday, you could venture south from the city, in the morning, straight to the grand Friday market at Ocotlá. Afterwards,

return north, via the crafts villages of **Jalieza** (embroidery), **Tilcajete** (*alebrijes* woodcrafts), and **Coyotepec** (pearly black pottery).

HISTORY

Evidence of human prehistory litters the river bottoms and hillsides of the Valley of Oaxaca. Cave remains near the ancient city-state of Mitla tell of hunters who lived there as long as 8,000 years ago. Several thousand years later, their descendants, heavily influenced by the mysterious Olmecs of the Gulf coast, were carving gods and glyphs on stone monuments in the Valley of Oaxaca. Around 600 B.C., people speaking a Zapotec mother tongue, similarly influenced by the Olmecs, founded Monte Albán on a mountaintop above the present city of Oaxaca.

Monte Albán ruled the Valley of Oaxaca for more than a millennium, climaxing as a sophisticated metropolis of perhaps 40,000, controlling a large and populous area of southern Mexico and enjoying diplomatic and trade relations with distant kingdoms. But, for reasons unknown, Monte Albán had declined to a shadow of its former glory by A.D. 1000.

Mixtec-speaking people filled the vacuum. They took over Monte Albán, using it mostly as a burial ground. Their chiefs divided up the Valley of Oaxaca and ruled from separate feudalistic city-states, such as Mitla, Yagul, Mazatlán, and Zaachila, for hundreds of years.

The Mixtecs in turn gave way to the Aztecs, whose invading warriors crossed the mountains and threatened Oaxaca during the A.D. 1440s. In A.D. 1486 the Aztecs established a garrison on the hill of Huaxyacac (now called Cerro del Fortín), overlooking the present city of Oaxaca, ruling their restive Zapotec and Mixtec subjects for less than two generations. On Nov. 21, 1521, conquistador Francisco de Orozco and his soldiers replaced them on the hill of Huaxyacac, scarcely four months after the Spanish tide had flooded the Aztecs' Valley of Mexico homeland.

Conquest and Colonization

Spanish settlers began arriving soon after

the conquistadors. At the foot of the hill of Huaxyacac, they laid out their town, which they christened Antequera after the old Spanish Roman city. Soon, however, the settlers came into conflict with Cortés, whom the king had named marquis of the Valley of Oaxaca, and whose entire valley domain surrounded the town. Townspeople had to petition the queen of Spain for land on which to grow vegetables: they were granted a one-league square in 1532.

For hundreds of years, Cortés's descendants reigned, the church grew fat, the colonists prospered, and the natives toiled, in cane and corn, in cattle pastures and mulberry groves.

Independence, Reform, and the Porfirian Era

In contrast to its neighbors in the state of Guerrero, conservative Oaxaca was a grudging player in the 1810–1821 War of Independence. But, as the subsequent republican tide swept the country, local fervor produced a new state constitution, including a state legislature and governmental departments, as well as public instruction and an Institute of Arts and Sciences.

By the 1850s, times had changed. Oaxacans were leading a new national struggle. Benito Juárez, a pure Zapotec native Mexican, was rallying liberal forces in the civil War of the Reforms against the oligarchy that had replaced colonial rule. Born in Guelatao, north of the valley, Juárez at age 12 was an orphan sheepherder. A Catholic priest, struck by the boy's intelligence, brought him to the city as a servant and taught him Spanish in preparation for the priesthood.

Instead, Benito became a lawyer. He hung out his shingle in Oaxaca, first as a defender of the poor, then state legislator, governor, chief justice, and finally the president of Mexico. In his honor, the city's official name was again changed—to Oaxaca de Juárez—in 1872.

In 1861, after winning the three-year civil war, Juárez's Reformista forces had their victory snatched away. France, taking advantage

of the United States's preoccupation with its own civil war, invaded Mexico and installed an Austrian Hapsburg prince as Emperor Maximilian of Mexico.

It took Juárez five years to prevail against Maximilian and his conservative Mexican backers. Although Maximilian and Juárez paradoxically shared many of the same liberal ideas, Juárez had Maximilian executed after his defeat and capture in 1867. Juárez bathed Mexico in enlightenment as he promulgated his "Laws of the Reform" (which remain essentially in force). Although the country rewarded him with reelection, he died of exhaustion in 1871.

Another Oaxacan of native Mexican descent, General Porfirio Díaz, vowed to carry Juárez's banner. Díaz, the hero who defeated the French in the battle of Puebla on Cinco de Mayo (May 5) of 1862, was elected president in 1876. *"No Reelección"* was his campaign cry. Although he did step down to become governor of Oaxaca in 1880, he subsequently ruled Mexico for 26 years.

Under Díaz's "Order and Progress," Mexico, and to a lesser degree, Oaxaca, was modernized at great human cost. As railroads, factories, and mines mushroomed, property ownership increasingly became concentrated among rich Mexicans and their foreign friends. Smashed protest marches, murdered opposition leaders, and rigged elections returned Díaz to office time and again.

Modern Oaxaca

But Díaz couldn't last forever. The revolution that ousted him in 1911 has, in theory, never ceased. The PRI, the Institutional Revolutionary Party, presided over a uniquely imperfect Mexican form of democracy. Under three generations of PRI rule, from 1929 to 2000, the lives of native Oaxacans improved gradually. Although native families now go to government health centers and more of their children attend government rural schools, the price for doing so is to become less *indígena* and more Mexican.

Times in the Valley of Oaxaca nevertheless

seem to be getting gradually better. In the late 1980s, UNESCO recognized Oaxaca as one of several world sites belonging to the "Cultural Patrimony of Mankind." The government took notice and began preparing Oaxaca for an influx of visitors. Museums were built, monuments refurbished, and the venerable buildings restored. Burgeoning tourism since the mid-1990s has visibly improved the economic well-being of many Oaxaca families.

Increased international and national awareness seems to have contributed to other improvements. Some longstanding grievances are being recognized. In 1995, moderate PRI governor Diodoro Carrasco Altamirano pushed through an unprecedented "Usos y Costumbres" law, which legalized Oaxacan native rights to their indigenous language and their traditional, town-meeting form of government.

Still, by developed-world standards, most Oaxaca city families remain very poor, and the political system is far from perfect. Nevertheless, since his inauguration in December 2000, the clean, increasingly transparent administration of opposition President Vicente Fox has excited new hope in the minds and hearts of Oaxacans: They hope and pray that grievances stemming from bad former governments—police bruality, corruption, and political assassination—will diminish and finally become things of the past.

Unfortunately, despite President Fox's efforts at the national level, serious political trouble surfaced in Oaxaca in mid-2006. It started mildly enough. In May 2006, Oaxaca's statewide teachers union went on their perennial strike for much-needed higher wages. They accused PRI governor Ulises Ruiz of diverting millions of dollars in education funds to his controversial pet public works projects.

By mid-June, when teachers began barricading streets around the *zócalo,* Ruiz sent in his police, who brutally manhandled the non-violent demonstrators. The protest escalated quickly. The teachers allied themselves with their left-leaning supporters, forming an umbrella protest organization, the A.P.P.O. (Popular Assembly of the People of Oaxaca), and added the demand that Governor Ruiz must step down.

During the summer months of July, August, and September, the protests turned violent. Highways were blocked, buses were burned, a radio station was occupied, and several people were shot to death. By October, downtown Oaxaca City resembled a ghost town. Tourism evaporated, and consequently, many businesses, including hotels and restaurants, shut their doors.

In late October, President Vicente Fox, spurred by the killing of an American news reporter, acted. He sent a brigade of federal troops and police to Oaxaca, who removed the street barricades and dispersed the protestors while inflicting only minimal injuries. The local townspeople, breathing a sigh of relief, turned out, and in two days they swept up the mess, painted over the accumulated graffiti, opened their businesses, and filled the streets, buying flowers to celebrate the Nov. 1–2 Day of the Dead holiday.

At this writing, in late January 2007, the teachers have gotten their raise and returned to work, and peace has continued in Oaxaca. Although it's still quiet around the *zócalo,* visitors are beginning to return. Merchants and restauranteurs are serving a trickle of customers, and hotels are placing lodging discounts on their websites and accepting reservations.

And lastly, what's very important for visitors to realize is that, through all of the recent politcal trouble, the people of Oaxaca have overwhelmingly remained appreciative of visiting travelers and are now increasingly looking forward to again sharing their celebrated handicrafts, delicious cuisine, and beloved fiestas with all visitor who come to their lovely city and surrounding valley.

Sights

The streets of Oaxaca City still run along the same simple north-south grid the city fathers laid out in 1529. If you stand at the center of the old *zócalo* and look out toward the *catedral* across the Avenida Hidalgo, you will be looking north. Diagonally left, to the northwest, you'll see the smaller plaza, **Alameda de León,** and directly beyond, in the distance, the historic hill of Huaxyacac, now called **Cerro del Fortín.**

Along the base of that hill, the Pan-American Highway (National Highway 190) runs generally east-west through the northern suburbs. Turn around and you'll see the porticoed facade of the **Palacio de Gobierno,** where Oaxaca's governor tends to the state's business. Half a mile behind that (although you can't see it from the *zócalo*) the **periférico** (peripheral) boulevard loops around the town's

MARGARITA MAZA: A LIFE OF COURAGE AND CONVICTION

Calle M. Maza, a modest two-block lane on Oaxaca's northern downtown edge, memorializes Margarita Maza, both the wife of Mexico's revered president Benito Juárez and the heroine who gave her all for love and country. Her greatness and that of her husband were inextricably intertwined by their own strong liberal ideals and their collective fate. Years before Margarita was born, Benito, of pure Zapotec blood, came to Oaxaca city seeking both

his sister and his fortune. He found his sister working as a cook in the household of Italian immigrant and merchant Antonio Maza and his wife, Petra Parada.

Benito also found refuge and warmth in the Maza household; through the Mazas, Benito got work and social connections that led to education and introduction into Oaxacan society. Benito was 20 years old when Margarita was born, the Mazas' youngest child. He bounced the baby on his knee and played with her like an older brother as she matured and while Benito's career as a lawyer, then Oaxaca state legislator, blossomed.

By the time Margarita was 17, their mutual affection had bloomed into love, and Benito, a successful attorney at 37, proposed marriage. They were married in the church of San Felipe de Neri, in Oaxaca, on July 31, 1843. Even today such a match would be unusual; in the Oaxaca of 1843 it was unheard of. That he, a poor, dark brown Zapotec, and she, a lily-white daughter of a prominent merchant, were even able to associate, much less to marry, is testament to the Mazas' liberal views.

The same liberal views and their iron determination to do something about them marked the last half of Benito and Margarita's 26 years of married life. From around 1854, when Benito was driven into exile in New Orleans, civil war, foreign invasion, and assassination attempts forced the family to be nearly always on the

south end. There it passes the yawning but oft-dry wash of the **Río Atoyac** and the sprawling **Mercado Abastos** market and second-class bus terminal on the southwest. Finally, if you find a clear vantage point you'll see the hill of **Monte Albán** looming 1,000 feet (450 meters) above the southwest horizon.

A WALK AROUND TOWN

The venerable restored downtown buildings and the streets, some converted to traffic-free malls, make a delightful strolling ground for

discovering traditional Mexico at its best. The *zócalo* itself sometimes seems to be a place of slow, leisurely motion, perfect for sitting at one of many sidewalk cafés and watching the world glide by.

Step to the *zócalo*'s south side and give the guards at the front door of the **Palacio de Gobierno** a cheery *"buenos días"* or *"buenas tardes"* and step under the entrance arch. Straight ahead, across the courtyard, you'll see the main mural, by Arturo Bustos, completed during the 1980s. It depicts the struggles of

move, living in unfamiliar and trying circumstances, hounded and threatened by enemies, and continually lacking money.

One of the most dangerous episodes came in 1858, when Margarita, at the age of 32, had to move her brood of five children and entire household from Oaxaca to Veracruz, where Benito was running the liberal Mexican government-in-exile. Fearing spies and assassins, Margarita took the torturous, roundabout route over the heart of the Sierra Madre, traveling at night, on foot beside their burro-train, disguising herself in native *huipil* and sleeping by day in farmhouses of friendly Zapotec campesinos.

Later, Benito and Margarita enjoyed two years of peace together, beginning in 1861, after the liberal triumph in the civil War of the Reforms. Their marriage, although severely tried by hardship and separation, was a supremely happy one. Twelve children resulted; seven – six girls and a boy – outlived their parents. Two boys and three girls died when still young. Their love, although profoundly deep, had few pretensions. Benito called her his "old lady." She called him "Juárez" and, when asked, replied that "he is very homely but good."

Their peace together was short-lived. The French invasion forced Benito to travel the country, managing the government in a black carriage, one jump ahead of the French army. Margarita took the family on a hopscotch path

into northern Mexico and finally to New York and Washington, DC. There, she reached the depths of despair when two of her three sons died. She wrote to Benito: "The loss of my sons is killing me.... I prefer death a thousand times more than life.... I do not blame persons who kill themselves.... If I had been braver I should have done it a year ago."

Eventually Margarita recovered her equilibrium, buoyed by the birth of her first grandchild, a baby girl, and the admiring attention of American society, including General Ulysses S. Grant and President Andrew Johnson.

On June 19, 1867, Juárez had the French-installed Emperor Maximilian executed. This was Margarita's signal to return home. A month later, with her party of 14, she arrived in Veracruz, showered by bouquets as she walked down the gangplank.

Reunited for three happy years with Margarita in Mexico City, Benito worked like a demon to turn his dreams for Mexico into reality. But overwork took its toll, and Benito suffered a stroke in October 1870. He recovered partially to discover that Margarita was fatally ill. She died on Jan. 2, 1871, of cancer. Although weak, Benito strained with all of his strength and with tears in his eyes to lift her body into the coffin. All of Mexico, both friends and former enemies, joined in grief with their president for their beloved Margarita Maza, who had given as much as any heroine could for both love and country.

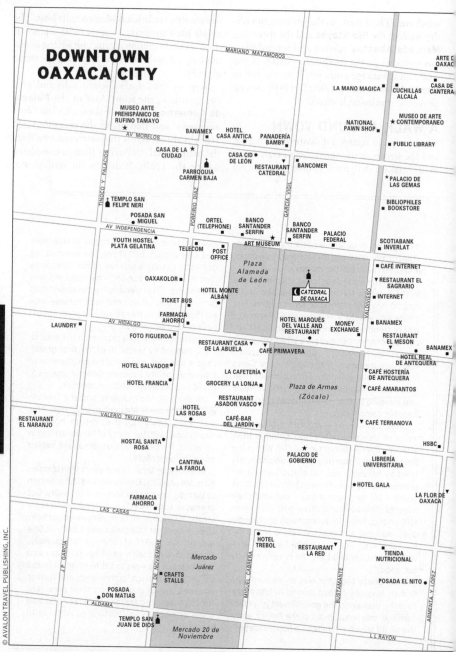

DOWNTOWN OAXACA CITY

MARIANO MATAMOROS

ARTE DE OAXACA

LA MANO MAGICA ■   ■ CUCHILLAS ALCALÁ   ■ CASA DE CANTERA

MUSEO DE ARTE ★ CONTEMPORANEO

MUSEO ARTE PREHISPÁNICO DE RUFINO TAMAYO ★

NATIONAL PAWN SHOP ■

■ PUBLIC LIBRARY

AV. MORELOS

BANAMEX ■   ■ HOTEL CASA ANTICA   PANADERÍA BAMBY ■

CASA DE LA ★ CIUDAD

CASA CID DE LEÓN ●

★ PALACIO DE LAS GEMAS

PARROQUIA CARMEN BAJA

RESTAURANT ▼ CATEDRAL

■ BANCOMER

BIBLIOPHILES ■ BOOKSTORE

■ TEMPLO SAN FELIPE NERI

POSADA SAN ● MIGUEL

ORTEL (TELEPHONE) ●

BANCO SANTANDER SERFIN ■

BANCO SANTANDER SERFIN ■

PALACIO FEDERAL ■

SCOTIABANK ■ INVERLAT

AV. INDEPENDENCIA

YOUTH HOSTEL ● PLATA GELATINA

ART MUSEUM ■

■ CAFÉ INTERNET

TELECOM ■

■ POST OFFICE

Plaza Alameda de León

▼ RESTAURANT EL SAGRARIO

OAXAKOLOR ■

■ INTERNET

CATEDRAL DE OAXACA

HOTEL MONTE ALBÁN ●

TICKET BUS ■

■ BANAMEX

FARMACIA AHORRO ■

HOTEL MARQUÉS DEL VALLE AND RESTAURANT ●

MONEY EXCHANGE ■

RESTAURANT EL MESON ▼

■ BANAMEX

LAUNDRY ■

AV. HIDALGO

FOTO FIGUEROA ●

RESTAURANT CASA ▼ DE LA ABUELA

CAFÉ PRIMAVERA ▼

HOTEL REAL DE ANTEQUERA ●

HOTEL SALVADOR ●

LA CAFETERÍA ▼

▼ CAFÉ HOSTERÍA DE ANTEQUERA

HOTEL FRANCIA ●

GROCERY LA LONJA ▼

Plaza de Armas (Zócalo)

▼ CAFÉ AMARANTOS

RESTAURANT ASADOR VASCO ▼

▼ RESTAURANT EL NARANJO

VALERIO TRUJANO

HOTEL ● LAS ROSAS

CAFÉ-BAR ▼ DEL JARDÍN

▼ CAFÉ TERRANOVA

HOSTAL SANTA ● ROSA

PALACIO DE GOBIERNO ★

HSBC ■

CANTINA ▼ LA FAROLA

LIBRERÍA UNIVERSITARIA ■

● HOTEL GALA

FARMACIA AHORRO ■

LA FLOR DE OAXACA ▼

LAS CASAS

HOTEL TREBOL ●

RESTAURANT ▼ LA RED

TIENDA NUTRICIONAL ■

Mercado Juárez

● POSADA EL NITO

■ CRAFTS STALLS

POSADA ● DON MATIAS

ALDAMA

TEMPLO SAN JUAN DE DIOS

Mercado 20 de Noviembre

L L RAYÓN

HOTEL CAMINO REAL
(EX-CONVENTO DE
SANTA CATALINA)

■ FARMACIAS AHORRO

MURGUIA

STATE OF OAXACA
TOURIST
INFORMATION

● HOTEL
PRINCIPAL

WOMEN ARTESANS OF THE
■ REGIONS OF OAXACA (MARO)

POSADA DEL
VIRREY

AV MORELOS

LUZ MARÍA
B&B

5 DE MAYO

REFORMA

AV JUÁREZ

● SUITES
LA FE

PASTELERÍA LA
VASCONIA

PROVEEDORA
■ ESCOLAR (BOOKS)

AV INDEPENDENCIA

★ TEATRO MACEDONIO
ALCALÁ

AV HIDALGO

V GUERRERO

TEMPLO
SAN AGUSTÍN

M.FIALLO

M. OCAMPO

FLORES MAGÓN

0   100 yds

0   100 m

Oaxaca's independence, reform, and revolutionary heroes. In the center is Oaxaca's favorite son and Mexico's revered *presidente,* Benito Juárez, and his wife, Margarita Maza. Below them is Juárez's *reformista* cabinet (notice the young, restive General Porfirio Díaz with the sword on the right), which struggled through two bloody wars, finally emerging, with Juárez, triumphant in 1867.

◖ CATEDRAL DE OAXACA

Head to the *zócalo*'s opposite, north side, for a look at the present Catedral de Oaxaca (Oaxaca Cathedral). It replaced the 1550 original, demolished by an earthquake in 1696. Finished in 1733, with appropriately burly twin bell towers, the present cathedral is distinguished by its Greek marble main altar, where a polished Italian bronze Virgin of the Assumption is being drawn upward to the cloud-tipped heavenly domain of the Holy Spirit (the dove) and God (the sunburst). Notice the glass

The Catedral de Oaxaca's thick walls and side buttresses reflect the city's earthquake-prone environment.

images of noble, bearded St. Peter and St. Paul, flanking opposite sides of the altar.

Of considerable historical interest is the **Santa Cruz de Huatulco** (Holy Cross of Huatulco), enshrined in a chapel at the middle, south (right) side of the nave. The cross, about two feet high, is one of four made in 1612 by Oaxaca bishop Juan Cervantes from the original cross worshipped by the natives on the southern Oaxaca coast long before the conquest. An explanation, in Spanish, gives three versions of the story of the cross—which, the natives reported to the *conquistador* Pedro Alvarado in 1522, was erected long before by a strange, white-robed holy man, who soon departed and never returned. Bishop Cervantes sent the three other copies to authorities at Santa María Huatulco town, Mexico City, and Rome.

ANDADOR DE MACEDONIO ALCALÁ

Continue behind the cathedral north along the tranquil Andador de Macedonio Alcalá pedestrian mall, named after the composer of the Oaxacan hymn "Dios Nunca Muere" (God Never Dies). Paved with Oaxaca greenish *cantera* stone in 1985 and freed of auto traffic, the mall connects the *zócalo* with a number of distinguished Oaxaca monuments.

Among them is the **Teatro Alcalá** (900 Independencia, tel. 951/516-8312, 9 A.M.–5 P.M. daily except Sunday); from the back of the cathedral head right one block along Independencia to the corner of Independencia and 5 de Mayo. Christened by a 1909 opening performance of *Aïda,* the Teatro Alcalá houses a treasury of Romantic-era art. Above the entry foyer, a sumptuous marble staircase rises to a bas-relief medallion allegorizing the triumph of art. Inside, soaring above orchestra, a heavenly ceiling blooms with floating angels, frolicking cherubs, and elegantly robed muses, representing the arts.

Continuing north along the Alcalá street mall, you soon pass the so-called **Casa de Cortés,** now the **Museo de Arte Contemporaneo de Oaxaca** (Macedonio Alcalá 202, tel. 951/514-2818 or 951/514-2228, 10:30 A.M.–8 P.M. daily except Tues.). Past the excellent bookstore

(mostly Spanish but some English-language history, art, guidebooks, and lovely postcards), exhibitions feature works of local and nationally known modern artists. Although named popularly for Hernán Cortés, the building is at least 100 years too new for Cortés to have lived there. The coat of arms on the facade above the door reveals it to have been the 17th-century home of a different Oaxaca family.

Half a block farther uphill, at Murguia, detour a block right, to the **Ex-Convento de Santa Catalina,** the second-oldest women's convent in New Spain, founded in 1576. Although the quarters of the first initiates were spare, the convent grew into a sprawling chapel and cloister complex decorated by fountains and flower-strewn gardens. Juárez's reforms drove the sisters out in 1862; the building has since served as city hall, school, and movie theater. Now, it stands beautifully restored as the Hotel Camino Real. Note the native-motif original murals that the renovation revealed on interior walls.

C CENTRO CULTURAL DE SANTO DOMINGO

Return to the Alcalá street mall and continue another block uphill to Oaxaca's pride, the Centro Cultural de Santo Domingo, which contains two main parts, side by side: the **Museo Regional de las Culturas de Oaxaca** (Museum of the Cultures of Oaxaca) and the **Templo y Ex-Convento de Santo Domingo** (Church and Ex-Convent of Santo Domingo), both behind the broad Plaza Santo Domingo maguey garden and pedestrian square.

Inside, Santo Domingo church (7 A.M.– 1 P.M. and 5–8 P.M. daily) glows with a wealth of art. Above the antechamber spreads the entire genealogical tree of Santo Domingo de Guzmán, starting with Mother Mary and weaving through a score of noblemen and women to the saint himself over the front door.

Continuing inside, the soaring, Sistine Chapel-like nave glitters with saints, cherubs, and Bible-story paintings. The altar climaxes in a host of cherished symbols—the Last Supper, sheaves of grain, loaves and fishes, Jesus and Peter on the Sea of Galilee—in a riot of gold leaf.

The Templo y Ex-Convento de Santo Domingo has been lovingly restored, both inside and out.

© BRUCE WHIPPERMAN

Continue to the museum (next door, tel. 951/516-2991, 10 A.M.–7:30 P.M. daily except Mon.), which occupies the completely restored convent section of the Santo Domingo church. Exhibitions begin on the bottom floor in rooms adjacent to the massive convent cloister, restored in 1998 to all of its original austere glory. A downstairs highlight is the long-neglected but now safely preserved **Library of Francisco Burgoa,** which you can walk right through and examine some of the more important works on display. The collection, 23,000 titles in all, includes its earliest work, a 1484 commentary on the works of Aristotle by Juan Versor.

A Museo sign points you upstairs, via a gorgeously restored, towering domed chamber, adorned overhead with the Dominican founding fathers, presided over by Santo Domingo de Guzmán himself.

It's hard not to be impressed by the seeming miles of meticulously prepared displays, divided into about a dozen long rooms covering respective historical periods. One room exhibits priceless Monte Albán–era artifacts, including one of the most important of the original so-called *danzantes,* with the typically mutilated sex organs. The highlight comes in the Tesoros of Tomb 7 room, where the entire gilded trove discovered at Monte Albán Tomb 7 is on display. Besides a small mountain of gold and turquoise ornaments, notice the small but masterfully executed golden head of Ecéchatl, god of the wind, made eerie by the omission of facial skin over the jaw, to produce a nightmarishly skeletal piece of jewelry.

The museum maintains an **ethnobotanical garden** in its big backyard. Staff customarily conduct both English and Spanish tours. The schedule varies, and reservations are generally necessary. For information, check with the museum front desk (see preceding, tel. 951/516-2991) or the ethnobotanical garden library (at the garden entrance corner of Reforma and Constitución, two blocks behind the Santo Domingo churchfront, 10 A.M.–7 P.M. Mon.–Fri., 10 A.M.–2 P.M. Sat.).

OTHER MUSEUMS

Back outside the museum, step across the street and a few doors uphill, into the rust-colored colonial-era building, now tastefully restored as the museum of the **Instituto de Artes Gráficos de Oaxaca** (Alcalá 507, tel. 951/516-6980, fax 951/516-7672, 10 A.M.–8 P.M. daily except Tues.). Inside, displays exhibit mostly contemporary etchings, wood-block prints, and paintings by artists of both national and international renown. Exhibits change approximately monthly.

Head west one block (along the Plazuela Carmen mall, off Alcalá across from the museum) to the **Casa de Juárez museum** (609 Garcia Vigil, tel. 951/516-1860, 10 A.M.–7 P.M. daily except Mon.). The modest but beautifully restored house was the home of Juárez's benefactor, priest and bookbinder Father Antonio Salanueva. Rooms decorated with homey mid-19th-century furnishings realistically illustrate the life and times of a man as revered in Mexico as is his contemporary, Abraham Lincoln, north of the border.

OAXACA CITY AND VALLEY

SIGHTS WEST AND SOUTH OF THE *ZÓCALO*

The **Museo Arte Prehispánico de Rufino Tamayo** (503 Morelos, tel. 951/516-4750, 10 A.M.–2 P.M. and 4–7 P.M. Mon. and Wed.–Sat., 10 A.M.–3 P.M. Sun.), two blocks west and north of the *zócalo*, exhibits the brilliant pre-Columbian artifact collection of celebrated artist Rufino Tamayo (1899–1991). Displays include hosts of animal motifs—Colima dogs, parrots, ducks, snakes—whimsically crafted into polychrome vases, bowls, and urns.

Continue three blocks west, past the University of Oaxaca School of Fine Arts and the airy Plaza of Dances, to the baroque **Basílica de Nuestra Señora de la Soledad.** Inside, the Virgin of Solitude, the patron of Oaxaca, stands atop the altar with her five-pound solid gold crown, encrusted with 600 diamonds. Step into the **Museo de la Soledad** (at the downhill side of the church, rear end, tel. 951/516-5076, 7:30 A.M.–2 P.M. and 4–8 P.M. daily). A multitude of objects of adornment—shells, paintings, jewelry—crowd cabinets, shelves, and aisles of musty rooms. Large stained-glass panels tell of the images of Jesus and the Virgin that arrived miraculously in 1620, eventually becoming Oaxaca's patron symbols.

Return to the vicinity of the *zócalo* and the traditional **Juárez Market,** which occupies the one-block square that begins just one block southwest of the *zócalo*. Stroll around for fun and perhaps a bargain in the honeycomb of traditional leather, textile, and clothing stalls.

Basílica de Nuestra Señora de la Soledad

For a treat, continue from the Juárez market's southwest corner of Aldama and 20 de Noviembre. Cross Aldama to the **Church of San Juan de Dios** and take a look inside, at the gallery of several large, antique paintings around the nave that record little-known but fascinating slices of Oaxaca history, such as Oaxaca's first mass on Nov. 25, 1521, on the bank of the Río Atoyac; the mysterious Holy Cross of Huatulco; and the baptism of Cosijoeza, the Zapotec king of Oaxaca.

Accommodations

Oaxaca offers a wide range of good lodgings. Air-conditioning is not particularly necessary in temperate Oaxaca, although hot-water showers (furnished by all lodgings listed below) feel especially comfy during cool winter mornings and evenings. The less expensive hotels, which often do not accept credit cards, are mostly near the colorful, traffic-free *zócalo*.

With few exceptions, Oaxaca's plush, resort-style hostelries dot the northern foothill edge of town. During holidays and festivals (Easter week, July, August, late October–early November, Dec. 15–Jan. 4) many Oaxaca hotels raise their prices 20–30 percent above the numbers listed. (For other lodging options, see the *Youth Hostel and Bed-and-Breakfasts* and *Apartments and Long-Term Rentals* sections.)

DOWNTOWN
Under $50

For strict economy, consider the simple, nine-room **Hotel Salvador** (20 de Noviembre 204, Oaxaca, Oaxaca 68000, tel. 951/516-4008, $30 s, $35 d, $40 t), a block west of the *zócalo*, next door north of the Hotel Francia. Here, you can get a spartan, but clean and comfortable upstairs room with bath, with the plus of a good restaurant downstairs.

Even closer to the *zócalo* is the petite and popular **Hotel las Rosas** (Trujano 112, Oaxaca, Oaxaca 68000, tel./fax 951/514-2217, credit cards not accepted, $37 s, $41 d, $45 t), just half a block west of the *zócalo*. Climb a flight of stairs to the small lobby, relatively tranquil by virtue of its side-street, second-floor location. Beyond that, a double tier of rooms surrounds a homey inner patio. Adjacent to the lobby is a cheery sitting room with big, beautiful tropical aquarium. In the rear, guests enjoy an airy terrace for reading and relaxing. The rooms themselves, although plainly furnished, are clean and tiled (except some bathrooms, which could use an extra scrubbing). Prices, while not the bargain they once were, are relatively reasonable for such a well-situated hotel. With fans, cable TV, parking, but no wheelchair access.

Conveniently situated just east of the *zócalo*'s northeast corner, the colonial-era **Hotel Real de Antequera** (Hidalgo 807, Oaxaca, Oaxaca 68000, tel./fax 951/516-4020 or 951/516-4635, hra5109@prodigy.net.mx, credit cards accepted, $42 s or d, $53 t) offers plenty for reasonable rates. The 29 comfortable rooms around an inviting old-world-style restaurant-patio have bath, fans, cable TV, phones, and parking.

On the far northwest side of downtown, about three blocks west of the Santo Domingo church, is the very inviting and superpopular **Hotel las Golondrinas** (Tinoco y Palacios 411, Oaxaca, Oaxaca 68000, tel. 951/514-3298 or tel./fax 951/514-2126, lasgolon@prodigy.net.mx, $39 s, $45 d, $53 t, $50 honeymoon suite). Rooms enfold an intimate garden, lovingly decorated with festoons of hothouse verdure. Leafy bananas, bright bougainvillea, and platoons of potted plants line pathways that meander past an intimate fountain patio in one corner and lead to an upstairs panoramic vista sundeck on the other. The care also shows in the rooms, which are immaculate and adorned with spartan-chic pastel earth-toned curtains and bedspreads and natural wood furniture. Guests enjoy use of laundry facilities, a TV sitting room, a shelf of paperback books, and a breakfast restaurant 8–10 A.M. In addition to the 27 regular rooms, two honeymoon suites rent for about $50 each. Street parking only, however.

A block west of the *zócalo*'s southwest corner, find the **Hóstal Santa Rosa** (Trujano 201, Oaxaca, Oaxaca 68000, tel. 951/514-6714 or 951/514-6715, credit cards not accepted, $39 s, $48 d, $55 t). The streetside lobby leads past an airy restaurant to the rooms, recessed along a meandering inner passageway and courtyard. Inside, the rooms are very clean, comfortably furnished, and decorated in pastels. Rents, although raised, continue to be reasonable, except during festivals and holidays, when they might rise as much as 40 percent. It offers cable, TV, phones, parking, limited wheelchair access, and an in-house travel-tour agency.

$50-100

Just a block south of the *zócalo*'s southwest corner, the **Hotel Trebol** (at Flores Magón 201, tel./fax 951/516-1256, reservacioneshotrebol@prodigy.net.mx, www.oaxaca-mio.com/trebol.htm, $50 s, $55 d, $60 t) remains an enduring jewel among Oaxaca's close-in moderately priced hotels. Guests can choose from about 50 accommodations, artfully sprinkled in three stories around an airy, plant-decorated inner patio. The recently renovated rooms are comfortably furnished with rustic tile, hand-hewn wooden furniture, table lamps, and color-coordinated bedspreads and shiny, modern-standard shower baths, plus fans, telephone, cable TV, parking, travel agent, and good restaurant. Rates are $60, $65, $70 during festivals.

Walk just a block west from the *zócalo*'s

southwest corner, to the longtime **(Hotel Francia** (20 de Noviembre 212, Oaxaca, Oaxaca, 68000, tel. 951/516-4811 or 951/516-4120, fax 951/516-4251, reservaciones@hotel francia.com.mx, www.hotelfrancia.com.mx, credit cards accepted, $59 s or d, $72 t). Savvy new managers have brightened up the Francia with fresh white paint, a bright chandelier, potted palms, shiny lobby tile, and a new restaurant. They have also added a renovated colonial-era section (once a separate hotel next door), built around an invitingly traditional interior patio. Rooms are clean and spacious, with high ceilings and old-world dark wood furniture. Rates for the 62 rooms include baths, hot water, fans, TV, and phones; parking is $4/day.

At the *zócalo*'s southeast corner, consider popular '80s-mod **Hotel Gala** (Bustamante 103, Oaxaca, Oaxaca 68000, tel. 951/514-2251 or 951/514-1305, fax 951/516-3660, galaoaxaca@oaxaca-hotel-group.com, www.oaxaca-hotel-group.com/gala.htm, credit cards accepted, $55 s, $64 d rooms; $71 d junior suite). Here, guests enjoy comfortable, modern, deluxe accommodations at relatively moderate prices right in the middle of the *zocaló* action. The 36 rooms and junior suites, although tastefully decorated and carpeted, are smallish. Get one of the quieter ones away from the street. With phones, TV, fans, and a restaurant, but parking is not included.

Jump six blocks (three south, three west) from the *zócalo*, to **Hotel Rivera del Ángel** (Mina 518, Oaxaca, Oaxaca 68000, tel. 951/516-6666, fax 951/514-5405, reservaciones@hotelriveradelangel.com, www.hotelrivera delangel.com, credit cards accepted, but cash gets you a 10 percent discount, $50 s, $60 d low season), which offers several advantages, including secure parking. Downstairs, an airy, shiny, but busy lobby and restaurant area offers nothing special, but through the lobby windows, feast your eyes on the inviting big blue pool and sunny central patio. Upstairs you'll find the rooms semideluxe, clean, spacious, and comfortable, many with private terraces overlooking the pool patio. The hotel's main drawback, besides the questionable neighbor-hood (streetwalkers, low-life bars, and drunks at night), is street noise, from buses along Mina. Ask for a *tranquilo* off-street room, next to or above the inner pool-patio. Asking rates run about $60 and $75 during holidays, with TV, fans, phones, restaurant, parking, travel agency, and tour buses to Mitla and Monte Albán.

$100–$200

Next, consider the reliable standby *zócalo*-front **(Hotel Marques del Valle** (Portal Clavería, P.O. Boxes 13 and 35, Oaxaca, Oaxaca 68000, tel. 951/514-0688 or 951/516-3474, fax 951/516-9961, reservaciones@hotelmarquesdelvalle.com.mx, www.hotelmarquesdelvalle.com.mx, credit cards accepted, $85 s, $105 d, and $130 t), beside the cathedral, on the northeast side of the *zócalo*. Guests enter a restored lobby, with bright chandeliers, mirrors, and shiny dark wood paneling. Upstairs, however, massive wrought-iron fixtures cast gloomy nighttime shadows through the soaring, balconied central atrium. The 96 rooms, nevertheless, retain their original 1940s polish, with handcrafted cedar furniture and marble-finished baths. Rents rise to about $100, $120, and $150 during holidays; with fans, cable TV, carpets, restaurant/bar, some balconies looking out on to the *zócalo*, and limited wheelchair access.

Over $200

Oaxaca's classiest downtown hotel, the **(Camino Real** (Calle 5 de Mayo 300, Oaxaca, Oaxaca 68000, tel. 951/516-0611, toll-free U.S./Can. tel. 800/7-CAMINO or 800/722-6466, fax 951/516-0732, oax@caminoreal.com, credit cards accepted, $215 s, $250 d), occupies the lovingly restored former convent of Santa Catalina, four blocks north, one block east of the *zócalo*. Flowery secluded courtyards, massive arched portals, soaring beamed ceilings, a big blue pool, and impeccable bar and restaurant service combine to create a refined but relaxed old-world atmosphere. Rooms are large, luxurious, and invitingly decorated with antiques and folk crafts and furnished with a plethora of modern conveniences. If street noise is likely to bother you, get a room away from bustling Calles Abasolo and 5 de Mayo; if not, bring earplugs. The hotel entertains guests and the paying public (about $35 per person) with a weekly class-act in-house buffet and folkloric dance performance. Room rates go up to $320 s or d holidays. With phones and cable TV, but parking not included.

NORTH-SIDE

A trio of worthy suburban hostelries border the north, uphill, side of Highway 190, Avenida Niños Héroes.

Over $100

The **Hotel Fortín Plaza** (Av. Venus 118, Oaxaca, Oaxaca 68040, tel. 951/515-7777, fax 951/515-1328, reservaciones@ hotelfortinplaza.com.mx, www.hotelfortinplaza.com.mx, credit cards accepted, $100 s or d) is hard to miss, especially at night. Its yellow-lit six-story profile tops everything else in town. The hotel offers the usual modern facilities—restaurant/bar, pool, live music most nights, parking—in a compact, attractively designed layout. Upstairs, guests enjoy deluxe, clean, and comfortable rooms with private view balconies (whose tranquility is reduced, however, by considerable highway noise—sk for a more *tranquilo* rear-side mountain-view room). With phones, cable TV, wheelchair access, and parking. Room rates rise to $130 holidays; ask for a discount or a package *(paquete)*, especially during weekdays and low-occupancy months of January, May, June, and September.

C Hotel Misión de los Angeles (Calz. Porfirio Díaz 102, Oaxaca, Oaxaca 68050, tel./fax 951/502-0100, mision@oaxaca-hotel-group .com, www.hotel-mision-oaxaca.com, credit cards accepted, $110 d, $160 d suite) rambles like a hacienda through a spreading oak- and acacia-decorated garden-park two blocks uphill from Highway 190, about a mile north of the city center. After a rough few days on the sightseeing circuit, it's an ideal place to kick back beside the big pool or enjoy a set or two of tennis. The rooms and suites are spacious and comfortable, decorated in earth tones and pastels, and the choicest have big garden-view windows and/or balconies. Upper rooms are quieter and more private. (Some rooms, however, may not be as favorably situated; ask for a garden view—*vista del jardín*—room. Look at more than one before deciding.) The 162 rooms and suites come with phones, cable TV, parking, gym, and restaurant.

Just two blocks west, uphill, from the Fortín Plaza, the **C Hotel Victoria** (Km 545, Carretera Panamericana, Oaxaca, Oaxaca 68070, tel. 951/515-2633, fax 951/515-2411, reservaciones@ hotelvictoriaoax.com.mx, www.hotelvictoria oax.com.mx, credit cards accepted, $150 d room, $200 d suite, $215 d villa) spreads over a lush hillside garden of panoramic vistas and luxurious resort amenities. The '60s-modern lobby extends from an upstairs view bar downhill past a terrace restaurant to a flame tree– and jacaranda-decorated pool patio. As for rooms, the most luxurious are in the newer view wing detached from the lobby building. There, the junior suites are spacious, comfortable, and luxuriously appointed, with double-size bathrooms and private view balconies. The 150 rooms, junior suites, and villas rent for about $150, $200, and $215 d, respectively; with TV, phones, a/c, tennis court, live music Tues.–Sat. evenings, handicrafts shop, parking, and wheelchair access.

YOUTH HOSTEL AND BED-AND-BREAKFASTS

A number of Oaxacan residents have discovered the North American bed-and-breakfast tradition and now offer comfortable lodgings, mostly in residential neighborhoods outside the immediate *zócalo* area.

Under $50

One major location exception is the beautifully restored **Paulina Youth Hostel** (V. Trujano 321, Oaxaca, Oaxaca 68000, tel. 951/516-2005, reservations@ paulinahostel.com, $25 s, $28 d, $12 dorm bed), which offers a good bed-and-breakfast option just three blocks west of the *zócalo*. The Paulina Youth Hostel offers the best of all possible hostelling worlds, with a good cafeteria and inviting, spacious common areas, all within attractive garden grounds. The comfortable, squeaky-clean rooming options include separate male and female dorms for $12 per person and private rooms with shower baths for $25 s, $28 d, all with orthopedic mattresses, roof terrace, hot water, and hearty breakfast. Get your reservations in early.

One of the more attractive Oaxaca bed-and-breakfasts, also near the town center, is homey but exclusive **Casa Luz María** (1002 Morelos, Oaxaca, Oaxaca 68000, tel. 951/516-2378, f_fagoaga@hotmail.com, credit cards not accepted, price on request). Since it's her home, the owner chooses her clients carefully. If you qualify, your reward will be one of her five comfortable, immaculate, modern rooms (or her one kitchenette apartment), all built around a pair of flowery, sunny interior patios. Two of the rooms have private baths, three are shared; with hot water, fans, no phone nor TV. Rentals include a hearty breakfast, with coffee, tea, fruit, bread, eggs, and sweet rolls. The owner assured me that her prices, which she declined to state, are both flexible and moderate (probably around $35 d).

$50-100

From the *zócalo* northeast (cathedral) corner, walk four blocks east along Independencia, to Pino Suárez, then left, five blocks uphill, north, to the bed-and-breakfast gem ⬛ **Casa de Mis Recuerdos** (House of My Memories; Pino Suárez 508, Oaxaca, Oaxaca 68000, tel./fax 951/515-5645, U.S. toll-free tel. 877/234-4706, or U.S tel. 713/429-1057, email misrecue@hotmail.com, www.misrecuerdos.net, credit card accepted, $50 s, $60 d and up). Enter the front gate and continue through a blooming, bougainvillea-festooned garden to the private home of the Valenciana family, which has been accommodating students and foreign visitors for years. The rented rooms occupy rear and front sections. The four front rooms, immaculate, spacious, and lovingly decorated with folk art and furnished with handmade wooden furniture, have two bathrooms between them. They are closer to the busy streetfront than the five similarly furnished rear rooms, which, although they have private baths, are smaller. Guests also have the use of an airy, shaded roof-

top gazebo for reading and relaxing. Breakfast, included with rentals, is served in the inviting downstairs family dining room. Rooms normally rent from around $50 s and $60 d, rising to around $75 and $85 during festivals and holidays, with fans, some a/c, with all linens and cleaning service included. Discounts are negotiable for long-term low-season stays.

On the northwest side of downtown, abut ten blocks from the *zócalo* (but only four blocks west of Santo Domingo) consider the petite, gay-friendly **Casa Crespo** bed-and-breakfast Crespo 415, Oaxaca, Oaxaca 68000, tel. 951/514-1102, casacrespo@go-oaxaca.com, www.casacrespo .com, $90 s or d). Personable owner-operator-artist Oscar Carrizosa offers two large, elegantly appointed rooms that open to a tranquil inner fountain patio and are traditionally decorated with polished hand-hewn furniture, antiques, paintings, and reading lamps. For all this, rentals run about $90 s or d, with full breakfast, wireless internet connection, shiny, tile-deccorated bathrooms, big beds, fans, and cooking classes at a 20 percent discount for guests.

Only a few bed-and-breakfast lodgings dot the south and west sides of town. Here are two gems, however.

Start with **Posada de Chencho** (4 Privado Noria 115, Oaxaca, Oaxaca 68000, tel./fax 951/514-0043, pchencho@prodigy.net.mx, www.mexonline.com/chencho.htm, $45 s, $60 d), several blocks southeast of the *zócalo*. Part of the attraction here is the sparkplug owner, Inocencio "Chencho" Velasco, a friendly Mixtec version of Santa Claus. Such a stream of visitors from all over the world stay at his place that he seems to know someone everywhere. Moreover, very well-informed English-speaking Chencho is a treasury of information about Oaxaca, both local and statewide. His compound, 22 immaculate rooms in two stories, surrounds an inviting, green garden patio. The rooms themselves are comfortably and thoughtfully decorated, with Western-standard baths. Downstairs, guests enjoy a dining room and a big sitting room/library, besides patio nooks for reading and relaxing. Some rooms in the sun might get hot during the summer. If heat bothers you, be sure to select one in the shade, with a ceiling fan. If your room has no fan, ask Chencho to supply one. Rates customarily run about $45 s, $60 d, including full breakfast. Holiday rates are higher. A full-board single costs about $75. Ask for a cheaper long-term rate. Get to Chencho's by walking east, along Guerrero, from the southeast corner of the zócalo. After four blocks, at Xicotencatl (shee-koh-tayn-KAH-tuhl), turn right and continue another four blocks south to Calle la Noria; 4 Privado la Noria is one of the one-block streets to your left that run south from La Noria.

On the western edge of downtown, about 10 blocks due west of the zócalo, stands (**Casa Colonial** (Calle Miguel Negrete 105, tel./fax 951/516-5280, toll-free U.S./Can. tel. 800/758-1697, colonial@spersaoaxaca.com.mx, reservations@casa-colonial.com, www.mexonline.com/colonial.htm, $55 s to $105 d). Personable owners Jane and Thornton Robison, who seem to know everyone in town, call their domain the "posada with no sign" because they don't advertise, and accept guests only with reservations. Upon arrival, you immediately see why Casa Colonial is such a favorite among savvy visitors. Low-rise rooms and apartments enfold a spacious, gracefully lovely inner garden. Rooms vary from high-ceilinged antique-decorated Victorians to smaller, one-person gardenside units. Besides the leisurely tropical ambience, guests enjoy the use of a spacious, refined but homey living room with a fine library and Internet connection. Room prices vary according to size and elegance from $55 s to about $105 d. They welcome long-term guests at a discount after Easter through October.

APARTMENTS AND LONG-TERM RENTALS

The handiest sources of rental information are the classified sections (available on their websites) of the English-language newspapers *Oaxaca Times* and *Go-Oaxaca,* which usually advertise a number of nonhotel-style rentals. Both papers are often available at hotels, shops, and the downtown tourist information office. You may also find copies at the **Oaxaca Times**

office (in the Plaza Alcala, across the street downhill from Santo Domingo church, at 307 Alcalá, tel. 951/516-3443, fax 951/516-3265, info@oaxacatimes.com, www.oaxacatimes.com). Likewise, find the **Go-Oaxaca office** at Crespo 415, tel./fax 951/514-1102, info@go-oaxaca.com, www.go-oaxaca.com).

Other websites, such as www.mexonline.com, customarily advertise Oaxaca lodgings. (See the *Internet Resources* section of this book.) Moreover, both the downtown state and municipal **tourist information offices** list a number of economical home-style lodgings. And **language schools** (see *Language Instruction and Courses* in the *Services* section) arrange homestays with families.

About half a mile (or a fifteen-minute walk) north and east of the zócalo just before Los Llanos park, find (**Hotel and Studios las Mariposas** (Pino Suárez 517, Oaxaca, Oaxaca 68000, tel. 951/515-5854, ventas@lasmariposas.com.mx, www.lasmariposas.com.mx, $40 s, $45 d room, $45 s, $50 d suite), good for either short or long-term stays. Welcoming and knowledgable owner Teresa Dávila offers six comfortable studio kitchenette suites with private baths, for about $45 s, $50 d, in her restored 19th-century family house. In addition, seven rooms with bath rent for about $40 s, $45 d. Ask for a discount for a long-term stay. Besides lots of happy customers, pluses include use of fax machine, Internet connection, coffee, and optional breakfast and TV.

In the southeast quarter of town, an easy five-block walk to the zócalo, you'll find the attractive (**Villa María** (Arteaga 410 A, Oaxaca, Oaxaca 68000, tel. 951/516-5056, fax 951/514-2562, emailvillamaria22@hotmail.com, $45–65 d). Villa María is the labor of love of a trilingual (English, French, Spanish) owner-manager María Garcia, so welcoming that you immediately feel at home. Step inside her domain and you'll see the other reason for Villa María's popularity: about 15 apartments (that she manages along with her also personable sister Mari Carmen) surround an inviting, plant-adorned inner patio, where stairways rise to rooftop sundecks furnished with comfortable chairs and shady umbrellas.

The immaculate, thoughtfully decorated one-bedroom housekeeping apartments, with themes such as "Mixteco" and "Zapoteco" are completely furnished, including dishes, silverware, and maid service. Apartments vary in cost, $45–65 d per night, $400–600 per month, depending on location, size, and amenities.

TRAILER PARKS AND CAMPING

Oaxaca has two trailer-camping parks. The best choice for tenting and for rigs 25 feet or under (and capable of climbing a steep hill) is **San Felipe del Agua Trailer Park** (Camino de la Chigolera 10, San Felipe del Agua, P.O. Box 252, Oaxaca, Oaxaca 68000, home tel. 951/516-0654, fax 951/516-4239, trailer park 951/520-0947, info@oaxacanstuff.com, www.oaxacanstuff.com, $10 RV site, $5 tent site). It perches atop a valley-view knoll in foothill San Felipe del Agua village, about three miles (5 km) north of downtown. The California-born owner (and former Oaxaca consular agent) Roberta French and her son, Doug French, offer all hookups for about 10 rigs in a large country lot with few trees, but lots of room for tents. A small clubhouse with kitchenette, shower, and toilet is also available for resident use. Owners charge about $5 per party for camping, $10 for RVs, including water, electricity, and drainage. For reservations (probably not necessary), write, call, fax, or email them. For more information, visit their interesting website.

Their hilltop location appears ideal for hikers and backpackers, at the park jumping-off point to rugged horseback and steep, informal steep trails, past waterfalls and meadows, en route to the summit of towering, pine-tufted Cerro San Felipe (elev. 10,300 feet, 3,140 meters). The trailer park manager might (or might know someone who would) serve as your guide for hikes around the mountain. Figure on paying about $30 for a day's outing. The summit itself is accessible only by rough, uphill scrambles; attempt the full summit climb only in the company of an experienced guide.

Get there by bus, taxi, or car to San Felipe del Agua village. By bus, ride a "San Felipe"-marked local bus from the corner of Independencia and Reforma, two blocks east of the *zócalo*, thence following Pino Suárez uphill, past El Llano park. Get off at the San Felipe del Agua village plaza (see the old church on the right) and follow drivers' directions below. (Note: The end-of-the-line bus turnaround is a few blocks farther uphill from the village plaza. From there you can hike a quarter mile to the **Parque Comunal San Felipe** guard station and trailhead.)

For drivers, the jumping-off point for San Felipe del Agua is Avenida Netzahualcoyotl (nay-tzah-oo-wahl-coh-YOH-tuhl), which heads uphill at the big green "San Felipe" sign from its intersection with Highway 190 (Av. Niños Héroes), one block east of the Pemex station. Continue uphill about two-thirds of a mile (1 km), bear left at the hotel sign, then right one block and left one long block, and right again. You'll be on your way, heading uphill along Calzada San Felipe, which parallels the old stone aqueduct (on your left). In a few miles the road becomes San Felipe village's Calle Hidalgo. Just before the San Felipe plaza, at the restaurant on the right, turn left (west) on to Calle Iturbide, then right again at the first street, Morelos, then another quick left on to the "Prologation of Iturbide." After another long block or two downhill, at the arroyo bottom, turn right on to Chigolera; continue, winding uphill 0.4 mile (0.6 km) to the trailer park sign and gate on left.

Much more accessible is the worn (but still functioning at this writing) **Oaxaca Trailer Park** (900 Av. Violetas, Oaxaca, Oaxaca 68000, tel. 951/515-0376, $18 RV site, $14 van site, $9 tent site), at the far northeast side of town. Once an excellent, popular facility, the Oaxaca Trailer Park was allowed to deteriorate during construction of an adjacent office building. Still, dozens of all-hookup spaces remain, many with shade, and including showers, toilets, security fence, and night watchman.

Get there by turning left, eastbound, at Violetas, at its intersection with Highway 190, marked by McDonalds, and the baseball stadium, several blocks east of Highway 190 gas station. Continue uphill six long blocks to the signed trailer park on the left.

Food

SNACKS, STALLS, AND COFFEEHOUSES

During fiestas, snack stalls along Hidalgo at the cathedral-front Alameda de León square abound in local delicacies. Choices include *tlayudas,* giant crisp tortillas loaded with avocado, tomato, onions, and cheese, and *empanadas de amarillo,* huge tacos stuffed with cheese and red salsa. For dessert, have a *buñuelo,* a crunchy, honey-soaked wheat tortilla.

At nonfiesta times, you can still fill up on the sizzling fare of taco, *torta,* hamburger, and hot dog (eat 'em only when they are served hot) stands that set up in the same vicinity.

For very economical, wholesome local-style fare, go to the acre of foodstalls inside the **Mercado 20 de Noviembre** (two blocks south of the *zócalo*'s southwest corner). Here, adventurous eaters will be in heaven among a wealth of both delicious and economical ($2–4) *chiles rellenos;* piquant *moles* (moh-LAYS); fat, banana leaf–wrapped *tamales Oaxaqueños;* and savory *sopas* and *guisados* (soups and stews). Insist, however, that your selection is served hot.

A OAXACAN MENU

Oaxacan food adds another layer to the already rich Mexican food tradition. Oaxacan menus start off with appetizers, such as *quesillo a la plancha,* Oaxaca's famous white cheese, served melted, with guacamole and black beans. An appetizer list wouldn't be truly Oaxacan without *chapulines,* small grasshoppers grilled with minced onion in oil until crunchy.

Next come the Oaxacan *sopas* (soups), such as *sopa de guias,* a delicious stewed medley of squash flowers, tender baby squash, small corn dumplings, corn, and tender vine shoots. Other typically served soups include *caldillo de nopales,* a broth of fleshy cactus leaves, often cooked with bits of pork, chicken, or small shrimp, and *sopa de frijoles,* black bean soup, with cheese chunks and tortilla chips.

Main courses must include *moles* (MOH-lays), the most Oaxacan of all dishes. Very typical is *mole negro* (black *mole*), a spicy-sweet mixture of chocolate, chilies, garlic, peanuts, and a score of spices and other flavorings, cooked to a sauce, then baked with chicken or turkey. The turkey variation, called *mole de pavo,* is so *típica* that it's widely regarded as the national dish.

The *mole* list goes on, through *mole amarillo* (yellow *mole*) to *mole colorado* (red *mole*), a sauce of chilies, sesame seeds, almonds, raisins, bananas, tomatoes, and spices, served over chicken with rice seasoned with *chepil,* a wild local herb.

Oaxacan main-dish sauces are not necessarily chili-based. Some menus feature fruit- and nut-based sauces, such as *almendrado,* an almond sauce spiced with tomatoes, green olives, and herbs and served over chicken.

Oaxacans also enjoy local variations on the usual Mexican *antojitos,* such as *chiles rellenos de picadillo.* Here the cook replaces the usual *chiles rellenos* cheese stuffing with minced, spiced pork, beef, or chicken and serves them with guacamole, grilled onion, and refried black beans.

Menu meat selections often include *cecina* (say-SEE-nah), thin slices of spicy cured pork, frequently served with bean sauce and cheese, or *tasajo,* thinly sliced grilled beef, often dished up with *chilaquiles* (tortillas cooked in chili-tomato sauce).

Finally, top off your meal with a local dessert, such as flan (egg custard), and a drink, such as *té de poleo,* a tea brewed from *poleo,* a local, mint-like herb, or *café de la olla,* a rich regional coffee sweetened with *panela,* the dark brown sugar that market vendors sell by the chunk.

The airy, tranquil interior patio of **Hostería Alcalá** (Alcalá 307, 8:30 A.M.–11 P.M. daily) is ideal for a relaxing refreshment or lunch break from sightseeing along Alcalá mall.

For coffee and dessert, you have a number of downtown choices, notably **Coffee Beans** (Cinco de Mayo 400), five blocks north of the zócalo; or nearby **Café la Antigua** (Reforma 401, tel. 951/511-5761), a block east, just uphill from Abasolo.

For baked goods by themselves, a trio of good carry-out bakeries stand within a stone's throw of the zócalo. First, try the sweet offerings of **Tartamiel Pastelería Frances** (Trujano 118, half a block west from the Del Jardín café southwest zócalo corner, tel. 951/516-7330, 7 A.M.–8 P.M. Mon.–Sat., 11 A.M.–7 P.M. Sun.). Continue clockwise, north of the zócalo a block, to **Panadería Bamby** (northwest corner of G. Vigil and Morelos, tel. 951/516-2510, 7 A.M.–9 P.M. Mon.–Sat.). Finally, stop by the **Pastelería la Vasconia** (Independencia 907, tel. 951/516-2677, 7 A.M.–8 P.M. daily), a block east of the zócalo between Cinco de Mayo and Reforma.

RESTAURANTS
Around the Zócalo

Oaxaca visitors enjoy many good eateries right on or near the zócalo. In fact, you could spend your entire Oaxaca time enjoying the fare of the several zócalo-front sidewalk cafés. Of the seven cafés, six offer recommendable food and service. Moving counterclockwise from the northwest corner, they are **Primavera, La Cafetería, Del Jardín, Terranova, Amarantos, Hostería Antequera,** and the zócalo-front café of the **Hotel Marques del Valle.**

First place overall goes to the pricier, upper-class **Terranova** at the southeast corner, and the **Hotel Marqués del Valle** on the north side, for their professionally prepared and served lunch and dinner entrées. For good, economical breakfasts, however, go to **Primavera,** at the northeast (Hidalgo) corner. The adjacent west-side **La Cafetería** and **Del Jardín** (with loud marimba music most nights) rate generally good for food (notably Del Jardín's tummy-

warming apple strudel), but their service can be spotty. While service at **Amarantos** is usually good, its food is only fair, while the reverse is true at Hostería Antequera. They all are open long hours, about 8 A.M.–midnight, and serve from very recognizable menus.

Note: The zócalo's west side is generally shadier, cooler, and more pleasant during the warm March, April, and May dry season. On the other hand, the east side, which gets the afternoon sun, is the warmer and often the more pleasant side during the cooler months of November, December, and January. As for zócalo-front seating, nonsmokers can escape to the open-air tables, thus avoiding the cigarette and cigar smoke beneath the portal.

The one drawback of zócalo-level eating is the persistent flow of vendors, which can be unnerving. If, however, you refuse (or bargain for) their offerings gently and with humor, you might begin to accept and enjoy them as part of the entire colorful scene. (If they really get to you, best take an inside table or retreat to the two restaurants that shoos them away, the Terranova and the Marques del Valle.)

Oaxaca veteran travelers swear by the Oaxacan specialties at **Casa de la Abuela** (at the zócalo's northwest corner, above the Primavera café, tel. 951/516-3544, 1–10 P.M. daily). Here, you can enjoy tasty, professionally prepared regional dishes ($6–12) and airy zócalo vistas from the balcony. Call for reservations and a good view table.

For many loyal local business and upper-class patrons, **Restaurant Catedral** (Garcia Vigil 105, corner of Morelos, tel. 951/516-3285, 8 A.M.–8 P.M. daily), two blocks north of the zócalo, serves as a tranquil refuge from the street hubbub. Here, the refined ambience—music playing softly in the background, tables set around an airy, intimate fountain patio crowned by the blue Oaxaca sky above—is half the show. The finale is the very correct service and quality food for breakfast, lunch, or supper. The Aguilar family owners are especially proud of their *moles* (MOH-lays), sauces that flavor their house specialties. These include fillets, both meat and fish ($6–14), and regional dishes such as banana leaf–wrapped *tamales Oaxaqueños* ($7).

Back downhill a block, on Hidalgo, just past the *zócalo*'s northeast corner, the spotless little *fonda* ◖ **El Mesón Oaxaqueño** (Hidalgo 805, tel. 951/516-2729, 8 A.M.–11:30 P.M. daily) specializes in breakfast and lunch buffets. For about $5, you can select your fill of fresh fruit, eggs, pancakes, chilaquiles, and more for breakfast; and salads, chili beans, and several entrées, including roast beef and pork, chicken, *moles,* tacos, tamales, and enchiladas for lunch. For lighter appetites, they offer plenty more delicious a la carte choices ($2–4).

More good eating, in a genteel but relaxed atmosphere, awaits you at the very popular **Restaurant el Sagrario** (120 Valdivieso, tel. 951/514-0303 or 951/514-0303, 8 A.M.–midnight daily, credit cards accepted), around the corner behind the church. Here, mostly local, youngish upper-class customers enjoy either a club/bar atmosphere (lower level), pizza parlor booths (middle level), or restaurant tables (upper level). At the restaurant level during the evening, you can best take in the whole scene around you—chattering, upbeat crowd, live guitar, flute, or jazz melodies, elegantly restored colonial details. Then, finally, comes the food: beginning, perhaps, with an appetizer, continuing with a soup or salad, then an international or regional specialty, which you top off with a light dessert and a savory espresso coffee. Music volume goes up later in the evening.

North of the *Zócalo*

Devotees of light, vegetarian-style cuisine get what they're hungering for at ◖ **La Manantial Vegetariana** (Tinoco y Palacios 303, tel. 951/514-5602, 9 A.M.–9 P.M. Mon.–Sat., 9 A.M.–6 P.M. Sun,), on the west side of the street, just above Matamoros, two blocks west and three blocks north of the *zócalo.* The tranquil patio ambience sets the tone for the specialty, a set lunch *comida.* Typically it might offer soup (onion or cream of zucchini), salad (mixed greens or tomato cucumber), stew (mushroom or soya steak), bread, fruit drink, dessert, and coffee or tea. About $4

until 7 P.M., $5 after that. (When they have few customers, the employees are in the habit of playing the radio loudly. Nevertheless, if you ask, they'll gladly turn it off.

La Manantial Vegetariana has done so well that you have a second branch to try out, in the commercial Plaza Santo Domingo, ground floor, diagonally southwest, across Alcalá, from the Santo Domingo church, tel. 951/501-0685, 8 A.M.–9 P.M. Mon.–Sat., 8 A.M.–6 P.M. Sun.

If you're unfamiliar with (or unconvinced about) Oaxaca's *mole* sauces, the place to go is ◖ **Restaurant los Pacos** (Abasolo 121, tel. 951/516-1704, 12:30–10 P.M. daily except Sun.), two blocks east of the Santo Domingo church front. Your meal automatically comes with a *mole* appetizer sampler, which treats you to six (*coloradito, verde, negro, estofado, amarillo,* and *chichilo*) of Oaxaca's *moles* right off the bat. It only gets better after that, especially if you continue with one of the good salads, from Caesar to tomato ($3–6), then follow up with a traditional Oaxaca specialty such as *enchiladas coloradito con picadillo* ($8), or *espinazo de puerco con mole verde* ($10), or *entomatadas* either *solas* or with beef ($9).

South of the *Zócalo*

A few good sit-down restaurants sprinkle the south *zócalo* neighborhoods.

Local folks strongly recommend the no-nonsense, country-style (but refined) ◖ **La Flor de Oaxaca** (Armenta y López 311, tel. 951/516-5522, 8 A.M.–8 P.M. Mon.–Sat., 9 A.M.–3 P.M. Sun., credit cards accepted), a block east and half a block south from the *zócalo*'s southeast corner. Here, along with spotless linen and very correct service, you'll get the customary bottomless plate of warm corn tortillas to go with your entrée. The *mole*-smothered regional specialties come mostly in four styles, *con tasajo* (with a thin broiled steak), *con pollo* (chicken), *con cesina* (roast pork), or *sola* (without meat), $8–12. Besides those, you can choose from an extensive menu of equally flavorful items such as *tamales Oaxaqueños* (wrapped in banana leaves), pork chops, several soups, spaghetti, and much more ($6–12). Vegetable lovers get started off right with the crisp *ensalada mixta* (sliced tomato, cucumber, onions, avocado, and lettuce with vinegar and oil dressing, $5).

If, however, you hanker for some nouveau variations on the Oaxaca regional theme, head to **Restaurant el Naranjo** (The Orange Tree; Trujano 203, tel. 951/514-1878, 1–10 P.M. Mon.–Sat.), two blocks west of the *zócalo*'s southwest corner. Here, the quiet, genteel patio atmosphere sets the tone, and the long, inviting menu tempts the palate. Choose among soups, salads, and Oaxaca's seven *moles,* one for each day of the week. Use them to flavor any one of a host of stuffed *chiles,* tamales, stewed chicken, roast pork, and much, much more ($10–20).

A block west and two blocks south of the *zócalo*'s southwest corner, **⊂ Restaurant Tayu** (20 de Noviembre 416, tel. 951/516-5363, 8 A.M.–5 P.M. daily) allows you to step back to Oaxaca "as it used to be." Take a table and relax in the refined, old-world TV-free ambience. Mornings, select from a host of tasty breakfasts ($2.50–4); afternoons, choose one of their four-course $4 *comidas* that include a choice of several hearty entrees, such as short ribs, chicken, *chiles rellenos,* with soup, rice and dessert included. Arrive 2:30–4:30 P.M. and enjoy their live instrumental music.

Lovers of fresh seafood can join the loyal brigade of local folks who frequent the airy and unpretentious **Restaurant la Red** (The Net, one of five Oaxaca branches, at the corner of Bustamante and Colón, tel. 951/514-8840, noon–8 P.M. daily), one block south of the *zócalo* southeast corner. Customers get their heart's delight of generous seafood cocktails ($4), heaping bowls of shrimp ($14), fish fillets ($8), octopus ($10), and much more.

Entertainment and Events

Many Oaxaca institutions, such as the **Museo de Arte Contemporáneo de Oaxaca,** the **Teatro Macedonio Alcalá,** the **Instituto de Artes Gráficos de Oaxaca,** the **Cinema el Pochote** (at 817 Garcia Vigil, tel. 951/514-9080, near the corner of Humboldt, one block west and about three blocks north from the Santo Domingo churchfront plaza) and others sponsor many first-rate cultural events. See the excellent monthly calendars of events in the English-language newspapers *Oaxaca Times* and *Go-Oaxaca* for details.

AROUND THE *ZÓCALO*

The Oaxaca *zócalo,* years ago relieved of traffic, is ideal ground for spontaneous diversions. A concert or performance seems to be going on nearly every evening. When it isn't, you can run like a kid over the plaza, bouncing an eight-foot-long *aeroglobo* into the air. (Get them from vendors in front of the cathedral.) If you're in a sitting mood, watch the world go by from a *zócalo* sidewalk café. Later, take in the folk-dance performance at the Hotel Monte Albán on the adjacent Plaza Alameda de León (west side, opposite the cathedral front, 8:30 A.M.–10 P.M. nightly, about $8). After that, return to a *zócalo* café and enjoy the musicians who entertain most every evening until midnight.

FOLKLORIC DANCE SHOWS

If you miss the Lunes del Cerro festival, some towns and villages stage smaller Guelaguetza celebrations at other times. So do some hotels and clubs, the most frequent of which occurs nightly at 8:30 P.M., $8 per person, at the Hotel Monte Albán, on Plaza de León, tel. 951/516-2777, adjacent to the *zócalo*. At other venues, days may change, so call ahead to confirm: Hotel Camino Real, tel. 951/516-0611, show with dinner, $30, not including drinks; Restaurant Casa de Cantera, Murguia 102, tel. 951/514-7585 or 951/514-9522, at 8:30 P.M., $15 per person.

NIGHTLIFE

When lacking an official fiesta, you can create your own at a number of nightspots around town.

Perhaps the most sizzling in-town nightclub is **Candela**, which jumps with hot salsa and African-Latin rhythms, usually Thurs.–Sat. Arrive at about 10 P.M., for dance lessons, at Murguia 413, corner of Pino Suárez, tel. 951/514-2010.

Another jumping nightspot among 20-somethings is the class-act **Bar la Pasión** (hidden beyond the rear of Restaurant Mayordomo, Alcalá 303) with flat-screen TV, studio lighting, and loud, live music. On Friday, Saturday, and Sunday, you can recognize it easily after about 8 P.M. by the large crowd out in front.

Besides many of the sidewalk cafés around the *zócalo,* a number of restaurants also offer live music. Try the El Sagrario, tel. 951/514-0303, evenings beginning at about 7 P.M., and the Hotel Marqués del Valle, tel. 951/516-3474, restaurant on the *zócalo.*

The big hotels customarily have live music in their lobby bars. Call to confirm programs: Camino Real, tel. 951/516-0611; Fortín Plaza, tel. 951/515-7777; and the Victoria, tel. 951/515-2633.

FESTIVALS

There seems to be a festival somewhere in the Valley of Oaxaca every week of the year. Oaxaca's wide ethnic diversity explains much of the celebrating. Each group celebrates its own traditions. Sixteen languages, in dozens of dialects, are spoken within the state. Authorities recognize around 500 distinct regional costumes.

All of this ethnic ferment focuses in the city during the July **Lunes del Cerro** festival. Known in preconquest times as the Guelaguetza (gay-lah-GAY-tzah, or Offering), it was a time when tribes reunited for rituals and dancing in honor of Centeotl, the god of corn. The ceremonies, which climaxed with the sacrifice of a virgin who had been fed hallucinogenic mushrooms, were changed to tamer mixed Christian-native rites by the Catholic Church. Lilies replaced marigolds,

Oaxacans often invite musicians to perform at small parties, such as the birthday gathering shown here.

© BRUCE WHIPPERMAN

the flower of death, and saints sat in for the native gods.

Now, for the weeks around the two Mondays following July 16, the Virgin of Carmen day, Oaxaca is awash with native Mexicans in costume from all seven traditional regions of Oaxaca. The festivities, which include a crafts and agricultural fair, climax with dances and ceremonies at the Guelaguetza open-air auditorium on the Cerro del Fortín hill northwest of the city. Entrance to the Guelaguetza dances runs about $40; bring a hat and sunglasses. Make hotel reservations months ahead of time. For more information, contact the downtown tourist information office, tel./fax 951/516-0123, info@aoaxaca.com, www.aoaxaca.com, or www.guelaguetza-oax.com at Murguia 206, two blocks north and two blocks east of the cathedral-front, between 5 de Mayo and Constitución.

Note: If the first Monday after July 16 happens to fall on July 18, the anniversary of Benito Juárez's death, the first Lunes del

Cerro shifts to the next succeeding Monday, July 25.

On the Sunday before the first Lunes del Cerro, Oaxacans celebrate their history and culture at the Plaza de Danzas adjacent to the Virgen de la Soledad church. Events customarily include a big sound, light, and dance show and depictions in tableaux of Oaxacan history, including the story of Donaji, Oaxaca's beloved princess-heroine.

Besides the usual national holidays, Oaxacans celebrate a number of other locally important fiestas. The first day of spring, March 20, kicks off the **Flower Games** (Juegos Florales). Festivities go on for 10 days, including crowning of a festival queen at the Teatro de Alcalá, poetry contests, and performances by renowned artists and the National Symphony.

On the second Monday in October, residents of Santa María del Tule venerate their ancient tree in the **Lunes del Tule** festival. Locals in costume celebrate with rites, folk dances, and feats of horsemanship beneath the boughs of their beloved great cypress.

As in many southern-Mexico communities, Oaxaca people celebrate a robust **Día de los Muertos** Day of the Dead (actually Days of the Dead) centering around Nov. 1 and 2. Traditionally, townsfolk form a processesion, accompanied by the village or city parish band, and visit neighbors' homes for offerings of food and drink. Then, in the afternoons and evenings of both Nov. 1 and 2, families gather at cemeteries (in the city, especially at west-side Panteón General, Main Cemetery, at the corner of Refugio and Blv. Eduardo Vascocelos), where they decorate the graves of their departed with flowers and favorite foods of the deceased, and then light choirs of candles to light the paths of their beloved ancestors to happily reunite (albeit temporarily) with the family once again.

Oaxacans venerate their patron, the **Virgin of Solitude** (Soledad), Dec. 16–18. Festivities, which center on the Virgin's basilica (on Independencia six blocks west of the *zócalo*), include fireworks, dancing, food, and street processions of the faithful bearing the Virgin's gold-crowned image decked out in her fine silks and satins.

For the **Festival of the Radishes** (Fiesta de los Rábanos) on December 23, celebrants fill the Oaxaca *zócalo*, admiring displays of plants, flowers, and figures crafted of giant, bulging radishes. Ceremonies and prizes honor the most innovative designs. Foodstalls nearby serve traditional delicacies, including *buñuelos* (honey-soaked fried tortillas), plates of which are traditionally thrown into the air before the evening is over.

Oaxaca people culminate their Posada week on **Nochebuena** (Christmas Eve) with candlelit processions from their parishes, accompanied by music, fireworks, and floats. They converge on the *zócalo* in time for a midnight cathedral Mass.

Sports and Recreation

JOGGING AND WALKING

For jogging, try the public **Ciudad Deportiva** (Sports City) fields on the west side of Highway 190 about two miles (3 km) north of the town center. Closer in, you might also jog around the big **Parque Paseo Juárez** (El Llano), on Avenida Juárez, three blocks east and about 10 blocks north of the *zócalo*.

For an invigorating in-town walk, climb the **Cerro del Fortín.** Your reward will be a breezy city, valley, and mountain view. The key to getting there through the maze of city streets is to head to the **Escalera del Fortín** (staircase), which will lead you conveniently to the instep of the hill. For example, from the northeast *zócalo* corner, walk north along the Alcalá mall. After five blocks, in front of the Santo Domingo Church, turn left onto Allende, continue four blocks to Crespo, and turn right. After three blocks, you'll see the staircase on the left. Continue uphill, past the Guelaguetza open-air auditorium, to the road (Av. Nicolás Copernicus) heading north to the **Planetarium** (open Nov.–May, 7–10 P.M.). After that, enjoying the panorama, you can keep walking along the hilltop for at least another mile. Take a hat and water. The round-trip from the *zócalo* is a minimum of two miles (3 km); the hilltop rises only a few hundred feet. Allow at least a couple of hours.

SWIMMING, TENNIS, AND SPORTING GOODS

Swimmers can do their laps and laze the afternoon away by the big pool (unheated but swimmable) at in-town **Hotel Rivera del Ángel** (Mina 518, tel. 951/516-6666, $10 adults, $5 kids 5 and under). Alternatively, you can spend the whole day at the country club–style **Club Brenamiel** (at the intersection of High-

way 190 and Calle San Jacinto, on the left just past the Hotel Villas del Sol, about three miles north of the town center, tel. 951/512-6822, clubbrenamiel@hotmail.com, $14 adults, $7 kids), which, besides a luscious blue swimming pool and umbrella-shaded patio, has an exercise gym, sauna, and restaurant to boot.

For both swimming and tennis, stay at either the **Hotel Victoria** or the **Misión de los Angeles,** which have courts. Otherwise, call the **Club Brenamiel** and reserve a court for about $7 per hour.

A modest sporting goods and clothing selection is available at **Deportes Ziga,** with two branches: one on the southwest corner of Alcalá and Matamoros, next to La Mano Mágico handicrafts shop, tel. 951/514-1463, and the main branch, at J.P. Garcia 400, tel. 951/514-6616. Both are open 9 A.M.–3 P.M. and 5–9 P.M. Mon.–Sat., 11 A.M.–2 P.M. Sun.

Shopping

The city of Oaxaca is renowned as a handicrafts shopper's paradise. Prices are moderate, quality is high, and sources—in both large traditional markets and many dozens of private stores and galleries—are manifold. In the city, however, vendors do not ordinarily make the merchandise they sell. They buy wholesale from family shops in town, the surrounding valley, and remote localities all over the state of Oaxaca. If your time is severely limited, buy from the good in-town sources, many of which are listed below. If, on the other hand, you have the time to shop the villages, it's to your benefit—both because of lower prices and person-to-person contact with the artisans. (Consult the *Around the Valley of Oaxaca* section for sources of local village handicrafts.)

TRADITIONAL MARKETS

The original town market, **Mercado Juárez,** covers the entire square block just one block south and one block west of the *zócalo*. Many dozens of stalls offer everything; cotton and wool items—such as dresses, *huipiles,* woven

wool carpets and serapes—are among the best buys. Despite the overwhelming festoons of merchandise, bargains are there for those willing to search them out.

Before diving into the Juárez market's cavernous interior, first orient yourself by browsing the lineup of stalls on the market's west side, along the block of 20 de Noviembre, between Las Casas and Trujano. Here, you'll be able to select from a reasonably priced representative assortment—baskets, pottery, tinware, *huipiles,* dolls, *alebrijes* (fanciful wooden animals), gourds and jewelry—of much that Oaxaca offers.

After your Juárez market tour, walk a block west, to J.P. Garcia, and 3.5 blocks south, between Mina and Zaragoza, for a look inside the **Mercado Artesanías** handicrafts market. Here, you'll find more of the same: tons of textiles—*huipiles, camisas* (shirts), and *blusas* (blouses)—plus *alfarería* (pottery), *alebrijes,* some for-tourist masks, and *tapetes* (rugs and serapes; visit stall 74, of José Tranquilo Jiménez, for some especially fine examples).

baskets for sale, downtown Oaxaca

PRIVATE HANDICRAFTS SHOPS

Although pricier, the private shops generally offer the choicest merchandise. Here you can select from the very best: *huipiles* from San Pedro de Amusgos and Yalalag; richly embroidered "wedding" dresses from San Antonino de Castillo Velasco; rugs and hangings from Teotitlán del Valle; pottery—black from San Bártolo Coyotepec and green and floral from Atzompa; carved *alebrijes* animals from Arrazola and Tilcajete; whimsical figurines by the Aguilar sisters of Ocotlán; mescal from Tlacolula; and masks from Huazolotitlán.

Most of the best individual shops lie scattered along three streets, Cinco de Mayo, Macedonio Alcalá, and García Vigil, which run uphill, north of the *zócalo*.

First, head north along the Alcalá mall; two blocks north of Independencia, you'll arrive at a Oaxaca favorite, the **Palacio de las Gemas** (corner of Morelos and Alcalá, tel. 951/514-4603, 10:30 A.M.–2 P.M. and 4:30–8:30 P.M. Mon.–Sat.). Although specializing in semiprecious stones and jewelry, it has much more, including a host of charming hand-painted tinware Christmas decorations, Guerrero masks, and pre-Columbian reproductions in onyx and turquoise.

Go a block east to Cinco de Mayo, then turn left (north) half a block to the big house on the right, No. 204, headquarters of ◖ MARO, **Mujeres Artesanas de las Regiones de Oaxaca** (Craftswomen of the Regions of Oaxaca; 204 Cinco de Mayo, Oaxaca, Oaxaca 68000, tel./fax 951/516-0670, 9 A.M.–8 P.M. daily). Here a remarkable all-Oaxaca grassroots movement of women artisans has gotten the government to stake them to a building, where they sell their goods and demonstrate their manufacturing techniques. The artisans are virtually pure native Mexicans from all parts of Oaxaca, and their offerings reflect their unique effort. Hosts of gorgeous handicrafts—wooden masks, toys, carvings; cotton *traje* native clothing, such as *huipiles, pozahuancos,* and *quechquémitles;* wool serapes, rugs, and hangings; woven palm hats, mats, and baskets; fine steel knives, swords, and machetes; tinplate mirrors, candlesticks, and ornaments; leather saddles, briefcases, wallets, and belts—fill the shelves of several rooms. Don't miss it; better still, do a major part of your Oaxaca city shopping at this store.

Walk a block west along Murguia back to Alcalá and stop at **La Mano Mágico** on the west side, just below the corner of Murguia (at Alcalá 203, tel./fax 951/516-4275, 10:30 A.M.–3 P.M. and 4–7:30 P.M. Mon.–Sat.). The shop offers a colorful exposition of crafts from all over Mexico and a patio workshop, where artisans work, dyeing wool and weaving examples of the lovely, museum-quality rugs and serapes that adorn the walls; other rooms display a small treasury of one-of-a-kind handicrafts: lacquerware, Day of the Dead skulls and skeletons, and *alebrijes.*

Across the street, step into **Cuchillos Alcalá** (206 Alcalá, tel. 951/514-7943, 9 A.M.–2 P.M. and 4–8:30 P.M. Mon.–Sat.) and view the best knives, swords, scissors and more from the venerable Oaxaca family Martínez cutlery tradition.

Continue uphill on Alcalá, a block farther north, to the **Plaza Alcalá** complex, southwest corner of N. Bravo, which has both a tranquil courtyard restaurant and some good shops. Outstanding among them is the excellent ◖ **Librería Amate** bookstore (Alcalá 307, tel. 951/516-6960, 10:30 A.M.–2:30 P.M. and 3:30–7:30 P.M. Mon.–Sat.). Its extensive and expertly selected offering of English-language books about Mexico includes guides, literature, ethnography, archaeology, history, cookbooks, maps, postcards, and much more. Upstairs, Librería Amate's brother shop, **Corazón del Pueblo** (Heart of the People; tel. 951/514-1808, same hours) accomplishes the same with a fine, eclectic collection of Mexican handicrafts.

Half a block farther uphill, be sure to look inside ◖ **Oro de Monte Albán** jewelry store (Alcalá 403, daily 10 A.M.–8 P.M., tel. 951/514-3813), just downhill half a block from the Santo Domingo church-front. This extraordinary family-run enterprise carries on Oaxaca's venerable goldsmithing tradition as the sole licensed manufacturer of replicas from the renowned treasure trove of Monte Albán Tomb 7. Besides the luscious, museum-quality reproductions, Oro de Monte Albán offers a fine assortment of its own silver and gold earrings, charm bracelets, necklaces, brooches, and much more.

Rewards await shoppers who are willing to walk a few long blocks farther uphill, to the state-run **IAO** (Instituto Oaxaqueño de Artesanías, 809 Garcia Vigil, tel. 951/514-0992 or 951/514-0735, 9 A.M.–8 P.M. Mon.–Sat., 10 A.M.–5 P.M. Sun.). There, you can pick from a broad, authentic, and very traditional selection of masks, *huipiles,* wedding dresses, carved animals, ceramics, tinware, and much more. Prices vary: cheap on some items and high on others.

FINE ARTS GALLERIES

The tourist boom has stimulated a Oaxaca fine arts revival. Several downtown galleries bloom with the sculpture and paintings of masters such as Rufino Tamayo, Rudolfo Mo-rales, Francisco Toledo, and a host of up-and-coming local artists. Besides La Mano Mágico, listed above, a number of galleries stand out. Foremost among them is **Arte de Oaxaca,** the gallery of the Rudolfo Morales Foundation (Murguia 105, between Alcalá and 5 de Mayo, tel. 951/514-2324 or 951/514-0910, www.arte deoaxaca.com, 11 A.M.–6 Mon.–Sat.).

Also outstanding is **Galería Quetzalli,** local outlet for celebrated artist Francisco Toledo, opposite the south wall-flank of Santo Domingo church, at Constitución 104, between Reforma and 5 de Mayo, tel. 951/514-2606, fax 951/514-0735, 10 A.M.–2 P.M. and 5–8 P.M. Mon.–Sat.

Also well worth visiting is **Galería Arte Mexicano** (tel./fax 951/514-3815, 10 A.M.–2 P.M. and 4–8 P.M. Mon.–Sat., 11 A.M.–5 P.M. Sun.) in the Santo Domingo shopping complex, southwest corner of Alcalá and Allende, across Alcalá from the Santo Domingo church.

GROCERIES AND HEALTH FOOD

For fruits and vegetables, the cheapest and freshest are in the Juárez and 20 de Noviembre markets, which take up the two square blocks immediately southwest of the *zócalo.*

For simpler, straightforward grocery shopping, stop by **Abarrotes Lonja** (on the *zócalo* west side, middle of the block, by café La Cafeteria, 8 A.M.–9:30 P.M. daily).

Local natural food devotees get their heart's content of teas—arnica, anise, manzanilla—and ginseng, organic grains, granola, and soy burgers two blocks west of the *zócalo* at **Tienda Naturista Trigo Verde** (J. P. Garcia 207, tel. 951/516-2369, 8:30 A.M.–9 P.M. Mon.–Sat., 10 A.M.–6 P.M. Sun.).

PHOTOGRAPHY

Downtown has some good photo shops, most on 20 de Noviembre, a block west of the *zócalo.* Best of all is **Oaxakolor** (20 de Noviembre 108, tel. 951/516-3487, 9 A.M.–8:30 P.M. Mon.–Sat.), perhaps the best-stocked photo store in Oaxaca. It carries dozens of cameras— 35 mm film and digital point-and-shoot,

SLRs, professional medium format—as well as an abundance of film, and a host of digital accessories.

Express Kolor (half a block farther down at 20 de Noviembre 225, tel. 951/516-1492, 9 A.M.–8 P.M. Mon.–Sat.) is also well stocked, with scores of point-and-shoot cameras and many Minolta, Vivitar, and Olympus accessories. It also stocks plenty of Konica, Fuji, and Kodak film and digital supplies.

Information

TOURIST INFORMATION OFFICE

The Oaxaca state tourism secretariat maintains a good information office, one block north and two blocks east of the cathedral-front (Murguia 206, between 5 de Mayo and Constitución, tel./fax 951/516-0123 or 951/514-9341, info@aoaxaca.com, www.aoaxaca.com, 8 A.M.–8 P.M. daily). Among their services they maintain lodging listings, recommend tour guides, and have plenty of literature to hand out, including their very handy and compact Oaxaca City tourist guide booklet.

PUBLICATIONS

One of Mexico's richest sources of new English-language books about Mexico is the **Librería Amate** bookstore on the ground floor of Plaza Alcalá (Alcalá 307, four blocks north of the zócalo, tel. 951/516-6960; 10:30 A.M.–2 P.M. and 4–8 P.M. Mon.–Sat.).

Another possible book source is **Librería Universitaria** (Guerrero 104, half a block east of the zócalo, tel. 951/516-4243, 9:30 A.M.–2 P.M. and 4–8 P.M. Mon.–Sat.). It has English paperbacks, both used and new, a number of indigenous language dictionaries, and guides, cookbooks, art, and history books.

The daily English-language *Miami Herald* Mexico edition is usually available late morning at stands near the southwest corner of the zócalo, by the café-bar del Jardín.

Get a copy of the informative tourist newspaper, the **Oaxaca Times,** at your hotel, the tourist information office, or at the publisher, the Instituto de Comunicación y Cultura, tel. 951/516-3443, info@oaxacatimes.com, at 307 Alcalá, 2nd floor. The newspaper covers cultural and historical features, tourist hints, and a list of local events. The classified rental section, accessible at www.oaxacatimes.com, is especially handy.

Alternatively, pick up a copy of the similarly useful and available newspaper, **Go-Oaxaca,** with office at the Hotel Crespo (Calle Crespo 415, tel./fax 951/514-1102, info@go-oaxaca .com, www.go-oaxaca.com).

LIBRARIES

The city **biblioteca** (public library), in a lovingly restored ex-convent, is worth a visit, if only for its graceful, cloistered Renaissance interiors and patios. At the corner of Morelos and Alcalá, two blocks north of the zócalo, 9 A.M.–8:30 P.M. Mon.–Sat.

Visitors starving for a good read will find satisfaction by borrowing (or buying upstairs) at least one of the thousands of volumes at the **Oaxaca Lending Library** (519 Pino Suárez, tel. 951/518-7077, library@oaxlibrary.com, www.oaxlib.com, 10 A.M.–2, P.M. and 4–7 P.M. Mon.–Fri., 10 A.M.–1 P.M. Sat.).

Services

MONEY EXCHANGE

Several banks, all with ATMs, dot the downtown area. The **HSBC bank** (tel. 951/512-9753 or 951/512-9754, 8 A.M.–7 P.M. Mon.–Sat.) is a block east of the *zócalo*'s southeast corner, at the intersection of Guerrero and Armenta y López. The most conveniently located downtown branch is **Banamex** (tel. 951/514-5747, 9 A.M.–4 P.M. Mon.–Fri.), on one-block Valdivieso, behind the cathedral. A second branch serves customers just one block due east of the *zócalo* (Hidalgo and Cinco de Mayo, tel. 951/516-5900), with money exchange hours 9 A.M.–4 P.M. Mon.–Fri., 10 A.M.–2 P.M. Sat.). If it's too crowded, go to **Banco Santander Serfin** on the Independencia corner just north of the cathedral (tel. 951/516-1100, 9 A.M.–4 P.M. Mon.–Fri., 10 A.M.–2 P.M. Sat.).

After bank hours, go to **Casa de Cambio Internacional de Divisas** (tel. 951/516-3399, Mon.–Sat. 9 A.M.–6 P.M.), on the Alcalá street mall just north of the *zócalo*, behind the cathedral. Although it may pay about a percent less than banks, it changes many major currencies and traveler's checks.

COMMUNICATIONS

The Oaxaca *correo* (tel. 951/516-1291, 8 A.M.–7 P.M. Mon.–Fri., 9 A.M.–5 P.M. Sat.) is across from the cathedral at the corner of the Alameda de León square and Independencia.

Telecomunicaciones (tel. 951/516-4902, 8 A.M.–7:30 P.M. Mon.–Fri., 9 A.M.–4 P.M. Sat., 9 A.M.–noon Sun.), a block west, at the next corner of Independencia (at 20 de Noviembre), offers money orders, telephone, and public fax.

For long-distance and local **telephone service,** buy a Ladatel phone card (widely available in stores; look for the yellow Ladatel sign) and use it in public street telephones. Lacking that, take advantage of the efficient **Ortel** long-distance phone and public fax office on Independencia, across from the Plaza Alameda de León (tel. 951/514-8084, 7 A.M.–10 P.M.).

Connect to the **Internet** at any one of a number of downtown spots. For example, try the warren of small stalls and telephone booths at Valdivieso 120, next to Restaurant Sagrario (tel. 951/514-9277, 9 A.M.–11 P.M. daily), a block north of the *zócalo*.

HEALTH, POLICE, AND EMERGENCIES

If you get sick, ask your hotel desk to recommend a doctor. Otherwise, go to **Clínica Hospital Carmen,** staffed by English-speaking IAMAT (International Association for Medical Assistance to Travelers) Doctors Horacio Tenorio S. and Germán Tenorio V., at Abasolo 215, tel./fax 951/516-0027.

For routine medicines and drugs, go to one of many pharmacies, such as the **Farmacias Ahorro,** tel. 951/516-8001, corner of Las Casas and 20 de Noviembre, two blocks west of the *zócalo* cathedral, 7 A.M.–11 P.M. daily.

For police and fire emergencies, call the emergency number, tel. 066, or contact one of the police officers in the *zócalo* or have a taxi take you to the Dirección de la Seguridad (Police Station), at Aldama 108, a block north of the *zócalo*.

CONSULATES AND IMMIGRATION

The **U.S. consular agent,** tel. 951/514-3054 or 951/518-2853, fax 951/516-2701, holds hours 10 A.M.–3 P.M. Mon.–Fri. upstairs, at Plaza Santo Domingo, Alcalá 407, across from the Santo Domingo church. The **Canadian Consul** does the same for Canadian citizens 11 A.M.–2 P.M. Mon.–Fri., at 700 Pino Suárez, local 11B, tel. 951/513-3777, fax 951/515-2147. In an emergency, call the Canadian Embassy in Mexico City, toll-free Mex. tel. 800/706-2900.

Other consuls that may be available in Oaxaca are the **Italian,** Alcalá 400, tel. 951/516-5058; and the **Spanish,** Porfirio Díaz 340, tel. 951/515-3525 or 951/518-0031. For more information, look for consulate contact

OAXACA CITY AND VALLEY

numbers in the *Oaxaca Times* or the telephone directory Yellow Pages, under *Embajadas, Legaciones, y Consulados,* or call the U.S. or Canadian Consuls above for information.

If you lose your tourist permit, make arrangements with **Migración** at least several hours before your scheduled departure from Mexico. Take proof of arrival date in Mexico—stamped passport, airline ticket, or copy of lost permit—to the airport Migración, tel. 951/511-5733.

TRAVEL AGENCIES AND TOUR SERVICES

A reliable and experienced downtown travel agent is **Viajes Turísticos Mitla,** branch office at Hóstal Santa Rosa, Trujano 201 (a block west of the plaza's southwest corner), tel. 951/514-7800 or 951/514-7806. It offers tours, usually around the Valley of Oaxaca, including guide and transportation, for small or medium sized-groups. Its main office is at the Hotel Rivera del Ángel, at F. J. Mina 518 (two blocks south, three blocks west of the plaza), tel. 951/514-7806 or 951/516-6175, fax 951/514-3152, vmitla@prodigy.net.mx. It also provides economical bus-only tourist transportation to Oaxaca Valley sights. For more information and reservations, contact the bus departure ticket desk at the Hotel Rivera del Ángel, tel. 951/516-5327.

Another worthy travel and tour agency is **Viajes Xochitlán** (M. Bravo 210A, tel. 951/514-3271 or 951/514-3628, fax 951/514-2556, oaxaca@xochitlan-tours.com.mx, open 9 A.M.–7 P.M. Mon.–Fri., 9 A.M.–3 P.M. Sat.). Go in comfort to all and any Oaxaca City and Valley sites and villages, such as Monte Albán, Mitla, Teotitlán del Valle, Tlacolula, and much more. They specialize in both individuals and groups, tourist and business services, and travel agent services, such as air and bus tickets and hotel bookings.

For more extensive backcountry adventure bicycling, hiking, and camping in the mountains north of Oaxaca city, contact **Expediciones Sierra Norte** (210 M. Bravo, tel. 951/514-8271, www.sierranorte.org.mx,

9:30 A.M.–7 P.M. Mon.–Fri., 9:30 A.M.–2 P.M. Sat.).

A Oaxaca regiment of private individual guides also offer tours. Among the most highly recommended is English-fluent **Juan Montes Lara,** and his wife, Karin Schutte. Besides cultural sensitivity and extensive local knowledge, they can also provide comfortable transportation in a large Chrysler van or Mercury Sable sedan. Contact them at their home (Prol. de Eucaliptos 303, Colonia Reforma, Oaxaca, Oaxaca 68050, tel. 951/513-0126, jmonteslara@yahoo.com).

Moreover, satisfied customers give guide **Sebastián Chino Peña** rave reviews for his guided tours ($20/hour) anywhere you would like in the city or Valley of Oaxaca. Contact him in town (cell 044-951/508-1220, fax 951/562-1405) or email him at sebastian_oaxaca@hotmail.com.

For more guide recommendations, go to the government tourist information office, north of the *zócalo* (Murguia 206, tel. 951/516-0123, info@aoaxaca.com, www.aoaxaca.com).

LANGUAGE INSTRUCTION AND COURSES

A long list of satisfied clients attests to the competence of the language instruction of **Instituto Cultural de Oaxaca** (tel. 951/515-3404 or 951/515-3404, and fax 951/515-3728, inscuoax@prodigy.net.mx or visit www.instculturaloax.com.mx), in a lovely garden campus at the north-side corner of Niños Héroes (Highway 190) and Juárez.

Also very highly recommended is the **Becari Language School** (N. Bravo 210, tel./fax 951/514-6076, becarioax@prodigy.net.mx, becari@becari.com.mx, www.becari.com.mx). Offerings include small-group Spanish instruction, as well as cooking and dancing classes. If you desire, the school can arrange homestays with local families.

Similarly experienced is the **Vinigulaza Language and Tradition** (Vinigulaza Idioma y Tradición) school, associated with the local English-language Cambridge Academy (at Abasolo 503, corner of Los Libres about six blocks east, four blocks north of the plaza, tel. 951/513-2763, info@ vinigulaza .com, www.vinigulaza.com). Offerings include informative (and even fun) small-group Spanish instruction. Schedules are flexible, and prices are reasonable.

Getting There and Away

BY AIR
The **Oaxaca Airport** (code-designated OAX) has several daily flights that connect with Mexico City and other Mexican and international destinations. Many of the Mexico City flights allow same-day connections between Oaxaca and many U.S. gateways.

The most direct flight connection to the U.S. is via **Continental Airlines,** which connects non-stop with Houston daily; for reservations and flight information, call Mexico toll-free tel. 800/900-5000, or contact a travel agent.

Mexicana Airlines flights connect a number of times daily with Mexico City. For reservations or flight information, call toll-free Mexico tel. 800/849-1524, or 800/502-2000. For flight information, call the airport tel. 951/511-5229 or 951/511-5337.

Aeroméxico and flights connect several times daily with Mexico City, and once with Tijuana. For reservations, call toll-free Mexico tel. 800/021-4050 or 800/021-4000, or local tel. 951/516-1066; for flight information, call tel. 951/511-5055.

Aviacsa Airlines connects once daily with Mexico City, once daily with Tijuana via Mexico City, and also with Acapulco, continuing to Tijuana. For reservations, call toll-free Mex. tel. 800/006-2200, or 951/518-4577. For flight information, call tel. 951/511-5039.

Azteca Airlines connects with Mexico City, Guadalajara, and Tijuana. For reservations, call toll-free Mex. tel. 800/229-8322, or local tel. 951/501-0190, or 951/501-0192. For flight information, call the airport, at tel. 951/503-3400.

Aerotucan light charter airline connects daily with the Puerto Escondido and Huatulco on the Oaxaca Pacific Coast. For reservations and flight information, call Mexico toll-free tel. 800/640-4148, or 951/501-0530 or 951/501-0532. For many more details, contact a travel agent, or visit www.aero-tucan.com.mx or email info@aerotucan.com.mx.

The Oaxaca airport provides a modicum of services, such as a good upstairs view restaurant, several shops, international newsstand, car rentals, a helpful tourist information office that will call hotels for you free (tel. 951/511-5040, 7 A.M.–8 P.M. daily), a bank (tel. 951/503-3188, 8 A.M.–7 P.M. Mon.–Sat.), and an ATM.

Arrival transportation for the six-mile trip into town is easy. Fixed-fare collective taxi tickets run about $3 per person for downtown ($7 to north-side Hotels Misión de los Angeles, Fortín Plaza, and Victoria). For the same trip, a *taxi especial* (private taxi) ticket runs about $12 for four people; larger GMC Suburbans, $25 for up to eight people. No public buses run between the airport and town.

Car rental agents operating at the Oaxaca Airport are **Hertz** (tel. 951/516-2434, fax 951/516-8268, hertz_oax@hotmail.com), **Alamo** (tel./fax 951/514-8534, fax 951/514-8686, oaxalamo@hotmail.com), and **Europecar** (www.europcar.com).

On **departure,** save taxi money by getting your *colectivo* airport transportation ticket ahead of time, at **Transportación Terrestres** (tel. 951/514-4350, open daily 9 A.M.–2 P.M. and 5–8 P.M.) on the west side of Plaza Alameda de León, across from the cathedral.

Furthermore, keep enough dollars or pesos for your $12 international departure tax (which may be collected in Mexico City) if your air ticket doesn't already cover it. If you lose your tourist permit, make arrangements with **Migración** several hours before departure from

OAXACA CITY AND VALLEY

Mexico. Take proof of arrival date in Mexico, such as stamped passport, airline ticket, or copy of lost permit, to airport Migración (tel. 951/511-5733), or in town (Pensamientos 104, uphill, in Colonia Reforma, tel. 951/518-4011, 9 A.M.–1 P.M. Mon.–Fri.).

BY CAR OR RV

Paved (but mostly long, winding, and sometimes potholed) roads connect Oaxaca city with all regions of Oaxaca and neighboring states.

South to the coast via the southern Sierra, narrow National Highway 175 connects along 148 winding, sometimes potholed, miles (238 km) over the Sierra Madre del Sur with its junction with Highway 200 at Pochutla (thence six miles to Puerto Ángel). The road climbs to more than 9,000 feet through winter-chilly pine forests and indigenous Chatino and Zapotec villages. Fill up with gas at the last-chance Pemex in Mihuatlán heading south and at Pochutla (north edge of town) heading north; carry water and blankets and be prepared for emergencies. Under dry, daylight conditions, count on about seven hours at the wheel, south from Oaxaca to Puerto Ángel, about eight hours in the opposite direction. Note: You can cut about an hour off the trip to Huatulco by following the cutoff to Highway 200, via Pluma Hidalgo and Santa María de Huatulco.

About the same is true for the paved National Highway 131 route south from Oaxaca, which splits off Highway 175 two miles (three km) south of San Bártolo Coyotepec. On your way out of town, fill up with gasoline at the airport Pemex. Continue, via Zimatlán and Sola de Vega (fill again with Magna here), over the pine-clad Pacific crest, a total of 158 miles (254 km) to Puerto Escondido. Under dry, daylight conditions, allow about seven hours southbound, about eight hours in the opposite direction. Unleaded gasoline is regularly available, midroute, at the Sola de Vega Pemex only.

The 229-mile (368-km) Highway 190-Highway 125 route connects Oaxaca southwest with coastal Pinotepa Nacional, via the Mixtec country destinations of Yanhuitlán,

Teposcolula, and Tlaxiaco. Although winding most of the way, the generally uncongested road is safely driveable (subject to some potholes, however) from Oaxaca in about eight driving hours if you use the *cuota* (toll) Highway 190 *autopista* northwest of Oaxaca city. Add an hour for the 5,000-foot climb in the opposite direction.

The 350-mile (564-km) winding Highway 190-160 from Oaxaca to Cuernavaca and Mexico City via Huajuapan de León requires a very long day, or better, two, for safety. Under the best of conditions, the Mexico City-Oaxaca driving time runs 11 hours either way. Take it easy and stop overnight en route. (Make sure you arrive in Mexico City on a day when your car is permitted to drive. (See the sidebar *Mexico City Driving Restrictions* in the *Acapulco and Taxco* chapter.)

Alternatively, you can cut the Mexico City-Oaxaca driving time significantly via the Mexico City-Puebla-Oaxaca **autopista,** combined 150 D-135 D, which, southbound, takes off from the southeast end of Mexico City's Calz. General Ignacio Zaragoza. Northbound, follow the signs on Highway 190 a few miles north of Oaxaca. Allow about six hours driving time at a steady 60 mph (about 100 kph). Tolls, which are worth the increased speed and safety, run about $30 for a car, much more for a big RV.

BY BUS
Luxury and First Class

Omnibus Cristóbal Colón and Autobuses del Oriente, Oaxaca's major luxury- and first-class carriers, and a number of associated lines, operate out of the modern terminal on Highway 190 (Calz. Héroes de Chapultepec 1036, at Carranza, on the north side of town). All bus lines accept credit cards and cooperate through their reservations-information connection, toll-free Mex. tel. 800/702-8000, of their "Ticket Bus" agency (www.ticketbus.com.mx). You may also get information and tickets at a convenient downtown Oaxaca "Ticket Bus" outlet (20 de Noviembre 103D, tel. 951/514-6655, or toll-free Mex. tel. 800/702-8000, a block west of the *zócalo,* 8 A.M.–10 P.M. daily except Sun.).

At the main Héroes de Chapultepec 1036 terminal, passengers enjoy a squad of public telephones out in front, a snack stand, luggage lockers, and cool, refined Restaurant Colibri, across the street, or the inviting coffee shop in Hotel Veracruz, next door, west.

Omnibus Cristóbal Colón offers luxury and first-class service to most major points in Oaxaca. Buses connect northwest with Mexico City (Taxqueña terminal) by the quick expressway route via Puebla; or by the slower Mixteca route, via destinations of Nochixtlán, Tamazulapan, and Huajapan de León, continuing to Puebla and Mexico City. Westerly, they connect with the Mixteca Alta, via Teposcolula, Tlaxiaco, Juxtlahuaca, Putla de Guerrero, and Pinotepa Nacional on the coast. Northerly, they connect, via Tuxtepec, with Villahermosa, on the Gulf coast. Southerly, they connect (via the surer, but long, Isthmus route) with Puerto Escondido, via Huatulco and Pochutla (Puerto Ángel); and southeasterly, with Tehuantepec, Chiapas, and Guatemala.

Autobúses del Oriente, offers both first class and "GL" luxury class connections, mostly along the Highway 190 corridor, connecting northwest with Mexico City (Tapo, Norte, and Taxqueña terminals), via the *"corta"* (shortcut) Puebla-Mexico City expressway route. Other departures connect north with Veracruz, Coatzacoalcos, Villahermosa, Palenque, and Mérida, while still others connect south with Huatulco via Salina Cruz, and also southeast via Tehuantepec with Chiapas destinations of Tuxtla Gutiérrez, San Cristóbal las Casas, and Tapachula on the Guatemala border.

Regional **Cuenca** first- and second-class buses connect with Northern Oaxaca points along Highway 175, including Ixtlán de Juárez, Valle Nacional, and Tuxtepec, continuing all the way to Veracruz.

Sur first- and second-class departures connect with Mexico City Taxqueña station, along old Highways 190 and 160, via Huajuapan de León, Izucar de Matamoros, Puebla, and Cuautla, Morelos.

Autobúses Unidos departures connect with Mexico City along the fast *autopista* expressway, via Nochixtlán, Coixtlahuaca, and Puebla; and also along the old Highway 135 via Cuicatlán, Teotitlán del Camino, Tehuacán, and Puebla.

Second Class

A swarm of long-distance second-class buses runs from the *camionera central segunda clase* southwest of downtown, just north of the Abastos market. It's best to get there early by taxi, or by walking due west about eight blocks from the *zócalo,* to the west end of Calle las Casas. Cross the *periférico* (peripheral boulevard) straight across the railroad tracks; keep walking the same direction along the four-lane street for two more blocks, where you'll see the terminal gate on the right. Inside, you'll find an orderly array of snack stalls, a cafeteria, luggage lockers, a long-distance telephone and fax, Internet access, a photography shop, and a squad of *taquillas* (ticket booths).

Cooperating **Auto Transportes Oaxaca-Pacífico** and **Autobúses Estrella del Valle,** tel. 951/516-2908, travel the Highway 175 north-south route between Oaxaca and Pochutla-Puerto Ángel. Both lines continue, connecting along east-west coastal Highway 200 with Bahías de Huatulco, Puerto Escondido, and Pinotepa Nacional.

Estrella Roja del Sureste second-class and first-class buses, tel. 951/516-0694, connect along Highway 131 north-south via Sola de Vega and Juquila, directly with Puerto Escondido. From there, you can make coastal connections with Pochutla-Puerto Ángel, Bahías de Huatulco, and Pinotepa Nacional.

Fletes y Pasajes, tel. 951/516-2270, offers very broad second-class (but with generally old and worn equipment) and some first-class service, connecting with nearly everywhere in Oaxaca. Three separate booths sell tickets: westerly, with Mixteca destinations of Nochixtlán, Tamazulapan, Huajuapan, and Tlaxiaco, connecting all the way, via Highway 125, with Pinotepa Nacional on the coast; easterly, with Mitla and Mixe destinations of Ayutla, Zacatepec, and Juquila Mixes; and southeasterly, with Isthmus destinations of Tehuantepec, Juchitán, and Salina Cruz.

Several other semilocal lines connect mostly

OAXACA CITY AND VALLEY

with Oaxaca Valley points. **Choferes del Sur** (tel. 951/514-4903) connects with northwest Oaxaca Valley Hwy 190 points, from San Lorenzo Nazarena to Etla. **Autobúses de Oaxaca** (no booth, pay on the bus) connects south with Cuilapan and Zaachila. **Sociedad Cooperativa Valle del Norte** (tel. 951/514-9820), connects west with Teotitlán del Valle. Finally, if you want a bone-jangling (but scenic) backroads adventure, ride **Flecha de Zempoatepetl**, tel. 951/516-6342, northeast to remote Zapotec mountain native market towns of Villa Alta and Yalalag (Tuesday market) via Tlacolula and Cuajimoloyas.

Around the Valley of Oaxaca

Oaxaca offers a world of interest—archaeological sites, crafts villages, ecoadventures, weekly markets, venerable Dominican missionary churches—outside the city. Valley market towns each have a market day, when local color is at a maximum and prices are at a minimum. Among the choices, starting on the east side, are **Teotitlán del Valle,** half an hour east, Saturday; **Tlacolula,** 45 minutes east, Sunday; **Ocotlán,** 45 minutes south, Friday; **Zaachila,** half an hour southwest, Thursday; **Zimatlán,** one hour southwest, Wednesday; and **Etla,** half an hour northwest, Wednesday.

These market visits can be combined with stops at handicrafts villages, ruins (notably Mitla, on the east side, and Monte Albán, west), and other sights along the way.

Getting Around

Droves of second-class buses from the Abastos terminal run everywhere in the Valley of Oaxaca. Those with plenty of time could spend a week or a month of weeks exploring the valley this way.

For those on a limited time budget, it's best to rent a car, ride a tourist bus, or see a travel agent for a tour. For car rentals, call **Hertz** (tel. 951/516-2434, fax 951/516-0009, hertz_oax@ hotmail.com); or **Alamo** (tel./fax 951/514-8534, fax 951/514-8686, oaxalamo@hotmail .com), or contact a travel agent.

For **tourist buses,** ride one of the many leaving daily from the Hotel Rivera del Ángel (F. J. Mina 518, bus desk tel. 951/516-5327), two blocks south, three blocks west of the plaza. Other hotels also provide such tour arrangements. See your desk clerk.

TOWN NAMES

Town names in Oaxaca (and in Mexico) generally come in two pieces: an original native name, accompanied by the name of the town's patron saint. Very typical is the case of San Jerónimo Tlacochahuaya, a sleepy but famous little place covered in this chapter. Combining both the saint's name (here, San Jerónimo) and the native name often makes for very unwieldy handles, so many towns are known only by one name, usually the native name. Thus, in the Oaxaca Valley, west side, San Jerónimo Tlacochahuaya, Santa María del Tule, Tlacolula de Matamoros, and San Pablo Villa de Mitla, for example, are commonly called Tlacochahuaya, El Tule, Tlacolula, and Mitla, respectively.

Nevertheless, sometimes a town's full name is customarily used. This is especially true when a single name – such as Etla, northwest of Oaxaca city – identifies an entire district, where many towns, such as San Agustín Etla, San Sebastián Etla, and San José Etla must necessarily be identified with their full names. In this book, although we may mention the formal name once on a map or in the text, we generally conform to local, customary usage for town names.

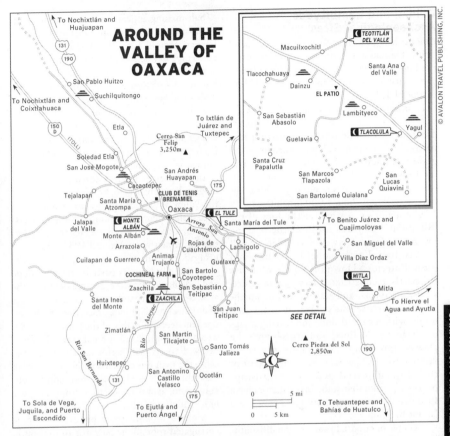

EL TULE, TEOTITLÁN DEL VALLE, AND TLACOLULA

Enough attractions lie along this route for weeks of exploring. For example, you could visit El Tule and the Teotitlán market on Saturday, continuing for an overnight at Mitla. Next morning, explore the Mitla ruins for a couple of hours, then return, stopping at the hilltop Yagul ruins and the Sunday market at Tlacolula. In either direction going or coming from the city, you could pause for an hour's exploration of the Dainzu and Lambityeco roadside archaeological sites. One more day would allow more time to venture past Mitla, to the remarkable mountainside springs and mineral deposits at Hierve de Agua.

El Tule

El Tule is a gargantuan Mexican cypress (*ahue-huete*), probably the most massive tree in Latin America. The townsfolk of Santa María del Tule celebrated their beloved El Tule's 1,000th birthday in October 2002.

Its gnarled, house-sized trunk divides into a forest of elephantine limbs that rise to festoons of bushy branches reaching 15 stories overhead. The small town, nine miles (14 km) east of the city on Highway 190, seems built around the tree. A crafts market, a church, and the town plaza, where residents celebrate their El Tule with a fiesta around Oct. 10, all surround the beloved living giant.

Dainzu and Lambityeco Archaeological Sites

Among the Valley of Oaxaca's dozen-odd buried cities, Dainzu and Lambityeco, both beside the highway, are the most accessible. Dainzu comes first, on the right about six miles (9 km) east of El Tule.

Dainzu (in Zapotec, Hill of the Organ Cactus; 10 A.M.–5 P.M. daily) spreads over an approximate half-mile square, consisting of a partly restored ceremonial center surrounded by clusters of unexcavated mounds. Beyond that, on the west side, a stream runs through fields, which, at Dainzu's apex (around A.D. 300) supported a town of about 1,000 inhabitants.

The major excavation, at the foot of the hill about 100 yards south of the parking lot, reveals more than 30 bas-reliefs of ball players draped with leather head, arm, and torso protectors. Downhill, to the west, lies the partly reconstructed complex of courtyards, platforms, and stairways. The northernmost of these was excavated to reveal a tomb, with a carved door supporting a jaguar head on the lintel and arms—note the claws—extending down along the stone doorjambs. The jaguar's face, with a pair of curious vampire teeth and curly nostrils, appears so batlike that some investigators have speculated that it may represent a composite jaguar-bat god.

A couple of hundred yards diagonally southwest you'll find the ball court, running east-west, in the characteristic capital I shape, with a pair of "scoring" niches at each end and flanked by a pair of stair-step stone-block grandstand-like "seats." Actually, archaeologists know that these were not seats, because the blocks were once stuccoed over, forming a pair of smooth inclined planes that flanked the central playing area.

Lambityeco (10 A.M.–5 P.M. daily), six miles (10 km) farther, is on the right, a few miles past the Teotitlán del Valle side road. The excavated part, only about 100 yards square, is a small but significant part of Yegui (Small Hill, in Zapotec), a large buried town of 200 mounds, covering about half a square mile.

Salt-making appears to have been the main occupation of Yegui people during the town's heyday, around A.D. 700. The name Lambityeco probably derives from the Arabic-Spanish *alambique,* the equivalent of English "alembic," or distillation or evaporation apparatus. This would explain the intriguing presence of the more than 200 local mounds. It's tempting to speculate that they are the remains of *cujetes,* raised leaching beds, still used in Mexico for concentrating brine, which workers subsequently evaporate into salt.

In the present small restored zone, archaeologists have uncovered, besides the remains of the Valley of Oaxaca's earliest known *temazcal* (ritual-therapeutic hot room), a number of fascinating ceramic sculptures. Next to the parking lot, a platform, Mound 195, rises above ground level. If, after entering through the gate, you climb up its partially restored slope and look down into the excavated hollow in the adjacent east courtyard, you'll see stucco friezes of a pair of noble, lifelike faces, one male and one female, presumably of the personages who were found buried in the regal grave (Tomb 6) below. Experts believe this to be the case, because the man was depicted with the symbol of his right to rule—a human femur bone, probably taken, as was the custom, from the grave of his chieftain father.

Mound 190, sheltered beneath the large corrugated roof about 50 yards to the south, contains a restored platform decorated by pair of remarkably lifelike, nearly identical divine stucco masks. These are believed to be of Zapotec rain god Cocijo (see the water flowing from the mouths). Notice also the rays, probably lightning, representing power, in one hand, and flowers, for fertility, in the other.

Teotitlán del Valle

Teotitlán del Valle, nine miles east of El Tule, at the foot of the Sierra, means "Place of the Gods" in Nahuatl; before that, it was known as Xa Quire, or "Foot of the Mountain," by the Zapotecs who settled it around A.D. 1000. Dominican missionaries introduced the first sheep, whose wool, combined with local traditional skills, results in the fine serapes, carpets, and blankets that seem to fill every shop in town.

Nearly every house is a minifactory where people card, spin, and dye wool, often using traditionally cultivated cochineal and hand-gathered natural indigo and moss dyes. Every step of wool preparation is laborious; getting pure water is even a chore—families typically spend two days a week collecting it from mountain springs. The weaving, on traditional hand looms, is the fun part.

In Teotitlán you have many choices. First, visit the weaving shops. Don't miss the shop of friendly master weaver **Isaac Vasquez** (on entrance road, Juárez No. 44, on the left, or main cross street, Hidalgo, No. 30, tel. 951/514-4122, 10 A.M.–6 P.M. daily). Another shop you should visit is the **Cooperativa Mujeres Tejedoras** (Women Weavers Cooperative; Juárez 86), 0.6 kilometer from the highway, signed "Mujeres Que Tejan."

Later, you can select from the hosts of fine offerings at the market itself, by the church, south end of Hidalgo. The best weaving is generally the densest, typically packing in about 45 strands per inch (18 strands per centimeter); ordinary weaving has about half that. Please don't bargain too hard. Even the highest prices typically bring the weavers less than a dollar an hour for their labor.

While you're at the Teotitlán market, stop by the **Community Museum** (in Zapotec, the Balaa Xtee Guech Gulal—House of the Old Town; in the brick building near the plaza-market end of Hidalgo, 10 A.M.–6 P.M. daily except Mon.) Ask for a copy of the museum's excellent English-language brochure (*folleto-foh-YAY-toh*). Exhibits detail the Teotitlán weaving tradition, archaeological artifacts, and traditions surrounding the traditional Zapotec marriage ceremony.

The museum would also be a good spot to arrange a visit to some **home weaving workshops.** At the museum desk, ask for a volunteer to guide you around town. Offer to pay, perhaps $5 or $10 for an hour's tour.

For **food,** sample Teotitlán's best, at the

© BRUCE WHIPPERMAN

In Teotitlán del Valle, wool is spun into thread with the time-honored spinning wheel.

OAXACA CITY AND VALLEY

charmingly traditional restaurant **Tlamanalli** (1–4 P.M. daily, longer hours when more people stop by). The menu of made-to-order Zapotec specialties, such as rich *sopa de calabaza* (squash soup) and savory *guisado de pollo* (chicken stew) ($4–7), is limited but highly recommended by Oaxaca city chefs. If Tlamanalli is closed, go to the good alternative **Restaurant el Descanso** (Juárez 51), which also offers plain but clean **accommodations** if you'd like to linger overnight.

Alternatively, stop by the class-act **◖ Restaurant el Patio** (out on the highway, 0.8 mile/1.2 km east of the Teotitlán entrance road, tel. 951/514-4889, 10 A.M.–6 P.M. daily.) The restaurant centers around an airy patio, decorated by antique country furniture and a fetching gallery of scenes from the 1940s-era films of the Mexican Golden Age of Cinema. The finale is the food, of tasty traditional Oaxacan dishes, such as *ensalada Oaxaqueña* ($4), Zapotec soup ($3), and the house specialty *botana Don Pepe* ($7).

Tlacolula

The Zapotecs who founded Tlacolula (24 miles, 38 km, from Oaxaca) around A.D. 1250 called it Guichiibaa (Town of Heaven). At its big Sunday market, half of the people and half of the speech are pure Zapotec, and a comparable share of the goods are strictly old-world: stone *manos* and *metates* for grinding corn, wood pack frames for burros, sheepskins, and yokes for oxen. Besides its market, its 1523 chapel, **Capilla del Señor de Tlacolula** (with a headless St. Paul), and its adjacent 1531 church, Tlacolula is famous for mescal liquor. Get a good free sample at the welcoming **Pensamiento** mescal shop (at Juárez 9, tel. 951/562-0017, 8 A.M.–7 P.M. daily), on the right as you head from the highway toward the market. Besides a selection of local handicrafts, Pensamiento offers mescal in 27 flavors, 20 for women and seven for men.

Yagul Archaeological Zone

The Yagul (Zapotec for "Old Tree") ruined city stands regally on its volcanic hilltop, 28 miles (45 km) east of Oaxaca city. Although only six miles from Mitla and sharing architectural details, such as Mitla's famous *greca* fretwork, the size and complexity of Yagul's buildings suggests that Yagul was an independent city-state. Local folks call the present ruin the Pueblo Viejo and remember it as the forerunner of the present town of Tlacolula. Archaeological evidence, which indicates that Yagul was occupied for about 1,000 years, until at least around A.D. 1100 or 1200, bears them out.

One of Yagul's major claims to fame is its **Palace of Six Patios,** actually three nearly identical but separate complexes of two patios each. In each patio, rooms surround a central courtyard. The northerly patio of each complex is more private, and probably was the residence, while the other, more open, patio served administrative functions.

South of the palace sprawls Yagul's huge **ball court,** the second largest in Mesoamerica, shaped in the characteristic Oaxaca I configuration. Southeast of the ball court is Patio 4, of four mounds, surrounding a courtyard.

A boulder sculpted in the form of a frog lies at the base of the east mound. At the courtyard's center, a tomb was excavated; descend and explore its three *greca-* style fretwork-decorated chambers.

If it's not too hot, gather your energy and climb to the hilltop **citadel** above the parking lot for a fine view of the ruin and the entire Valley of Oaxaca. The name for this prominence probably was accurately descriptive, for Yagul's defenders long ago added rock walls to enhance the hilltop's security.

MITLA

The ruins at Mitla (about 31 miles/50 km from Oaxaca city, 8 A.M.–5 P.M. daily), are a "must" for Valley of Oaxaca sightseers. Mitla (Liobaa in Zapotec, the "Place of the Dead") flowered late, reaching a population of perhaps 10,000 during its apex around A.D. 1350. It remained occupied and in use for generations after the conquest.

During Mitla's heyday, several feudalistic, fortified city-states vied for power in the Valley of Oaxaca. Concurrently, Mixtec-speaking people arrived from the north, perhaps under pressure from Aztecs and others in central Mexico. Evidence suggests that these Mixtec groups, in interacting with the resident Zapotecs, created the unique architectural styles of late cities such as Yagul and Mitla. Archaeologists believe, for example, that the striking *greca* (Grecian-style) frets that honeycomb Mitla facades result from the Mixtec influence.

Exploring the Site

In a real sense, Mitla lives on. The ruins coincide with the present town of San Pablo Villa de Mitla, whose main church actually occupies the northernmost of five main groups of monumental ruins. Virtually anywhere archaeologists dig within the town they hit remains of the myriad ancient dwellings, plazas, and tombs that connected the still-visible landmarks.

Get there by forking left from main Oaxaca Highway 190 onto Highway 176. Continue about two miles to the Mitla town entrance, on the left. Head straight through town, cross a bridge, and, after about a mile, arrive at the site.

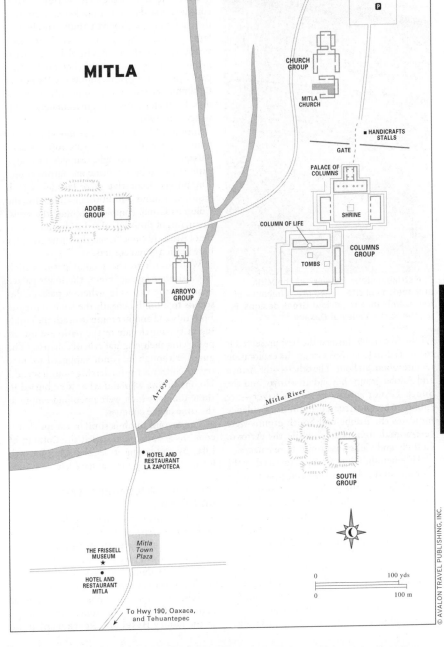

© BRUCE WHIPPERMAN

The striking stone fretwork at the Mitla archaeological site, called *greca* because of its resemblance to ancient Greek designs, is unique to the Valley of Oaxaca.

Of the five ruins clusters, the best preserved is the fenced-in Columns Group. Its exploration requires about an hour. The others—the Arroyo and Adobe groups beyond an arroyo, and the South Group across the Mitla River—are rubbly, unreconstructed mounds. Evidence indicates the Adobe and South groups were ceremonial compounds, while the Arroyo, Church, and Columns groups were palaces.

Although the Church Group (marked by the monumental columns that you pass first on your right after the parking lot) has suffered from past use by the local parish, it deserves a few minutes look around inside. It consists of a pair of regal courtyards, labeled A and B, adjacent to the triple red-domed 16th-century church. You first enter courtyard B, enclosed by monumental stone-framed doorways. A passageway leads on to smaller courtyard A, where you can see the fascinating remnants of the red hieroglyphic paintings of personages, name-dates, and glyphs that once covered its walls.

Back outside, on the main entrance path, continue past the tourist market and through the gate, to the **Columns Group** . Inside, two large patios, joined at one corner, are each surrounded on three sides by elaborate apartments. A shrine occupies the center of the first patio. Just north of this stands the **Palace of Columns,** the most important of Mitla's buildings. It sits atop a staircase, inaccurately reconstructed in 1901.

Inside, a file of six massive monolithic columns supported the roof. A narrow "escape" passage exits out the right rear side to a large patio enclosed by a continuous narrow room. The purely decorative *greca* facades, which required around 100,000 cut stones for the Columns Group complex, decorate the walls. Remnants of the original red and white stucco that lustrously embellished the entire complex hide in niches and corners.

Walk south to the second patio, which has a similar layout. Here, the main palace occupies the east side, where a passage descends to a tomb beneath the front staircase. Both this and another tomb beneath the building at the north side of the patio are intact, preserving their original crucifix shapes. (The guard, although he is not supposed to, may try to collect a tip for letting you descend.) No one knows who and what were buried in these tombs, which were open and empty at the time of the conquest.

The second tomb is similar, except that it contains a stone pillar called the **Column of Life;** by embracing it, legend says, you will learn how many years you have left.

Museum, Accommodations, and Food

The University of the Americas (Mexico City) houses an exceptionally fine Oaxaca artifact collection at the **Frissell Museum** (just west of, or left as you enter, the Mitla town plaza, 9 A.M.–5 P.M. daily). Displays include a host of finely preserved ceramic figurines, yet-to-be-deciphered Zapotec glyphs, and a Zapotec marriage certificate in stone. For food, go to the homey **Hotel and Restaurant Mitla** (across the street from the museum, tel. 951/568-0112).

Note: At this writing the museum was closed for repairs. Local folks, however, say that plans are nearly complete for re-opening it.

Across the plaza from the museum stands the new four-star neo-colonial style **Don Cenobio Banquet Salon and Hotel** (3 Calle Juárez, Mitla, Oaxaca 70450, tel. 951/568-0330, fax 951/568-0050, informas@hoteldoncenobio .com, www.hoteldoncenobio.com, $70 d), with about 20 beautifully decorated rooms built around a large, inviting grassy green pool patio. It has a wealth of facilities, including a restaurant and banquet hall for 500 people. Rooms rent for about $70 d, with a/c, cable TV, queen and king-sized beds, and much more. The only drawback to all of this is that they probably rent the place out to hundreds very often. Best check before reserving.

Otherwise, a few blocks back toward the ruins, just before the Mitla River bridge, **Hotel la Zapoteca** (5 de Febrero 12, Mitla, Oaxaca 70430, tel. 951/568-0026, $17 s, $25 d, $30 t) offers both a good restaurant and clean, reasonably priced lodgings, fine for an overnight. The 20 rooms come with hot water and parking.

Get to Mitla by Fletes and Pasajes second-class bus from the second-class bus central bus station, *camionera central segunda clase,* southwest of downtown Oaxaca.

Hierve el Agua Mineral Springs

Although the name of this place translates as "boiling" water, the springs that seep from the side of the limestone mountain less than an hour's drive east of Mitla are not hot. Instead, they are loaded with minerals. These minerals, over time, have built up into rockhard deposits, forming great algae-painted slabs in level spots and, on steep slopes, accumulating into what appear to be grand frozen waterfalls.

Get there by driving or riding an Hierve el Agua–marked colectivo van or truck bus east out of Mitla along Highway 179, the road that branches east from Highway 190, two miles before the town of Mitla. After another

© BRUCE WHIPPERMAN

At Hierve el Agua, calcium-rich water dribbling down the cliff-face deposits limestone that from a distance appears to be a grand waterfall, but is actually solid rock.

approximately 11 miles (18 km), follow the gravel road that branches right another five miles (8 km), through San Lorenzo village to Hierve de Agua.

Although the road's end may be crowded on weekends and holidays, you'll probably have the place nearly to yourself on weekdays. A tourist Yu'u ("lodging," in Zapotec, now called "Cabaña Ecoturistica") offers six newish housekeeping bungalows with baths for about $15 d, $45 for housekeeping cabin for up to six, with pool, and a lineup of snack and curio stalls by surrounds the cliffside parking lot. (Note: At this writing, the Cabaña Ecoturistica was closed because of a local political dispute. For an update, and maybe a reservation, check with the tourist information office in Oaxaca, Murguia 206, tel. 951/514-0123, info@aoaxaca.com, www.aoaxaca.com.)

Part of the appeal of Hierve el Agua is the panoramic, sun-dappled mountain and valley vista. On a clear day on the eastern horizon rises **Zempoateptl,** the grand holy mountain range of the Mixe people.

A trail leads downhill to the main spring, which bubbles from the mountain and trickles into a huge basin that the operators have dammed as a swimming pool. Bring your bathing suit.

From the pool, agile walkers can hike farther down the hill, following deposits, curiously accumulated in the shape of limestone minidikes that trace the mineral water's downhill path. Soon you'll glimpse the towering limestone formation, like a giant petrified waterfall, appearing to ooze from the cliff on the right.

COYOTEPEC, TILCAJETE, JALIEZA, AND OCOTLÁN

These crafts towns, all along Highway 175 south of Oaxaca city, make a nice quartet to visit on Ocotlán's Friday market day. Note: Since markets are best in the morning, **first go straight to visit Ocotlán,** then return, north, spending perhaps an hour each, visiting Jalieza, Tilcajete, and Coyotepec, in that order, on your way back to Oaxaca city.

San Bártolo Coyotepec

First along the highway comes San Bartolo Coyotepec (Hill of the Coyote) on Highway 175, 14 miles (23 km) south of Oaxaca, famous for its pottery and its Aug. 24 festival, when masked villagers, costumed half-man, half-woman in tiaras, blond wigs, tin crowns, and velvet cloaks, dance in honor of their patron, San Bártolo.

Their pottery, the renowned black *barra* sold all over Mexico, is available at a number of cottage factory-shops (watch for signs) off the highway on both the east and west sides of the highway. Especially prominent is the sign directing passersby to the pottery Mercado on the west side (right, traveling south), and the shops along east-side Juárez Street.

Doña Rosa, who died in 1980, pioneered the technique of crafting lovely, big, round jars without a potter's wheel. With the local clay, Doña Rosa's descendants and neighbor families regularly turn out acres of glistening black plates, pots, bowls, trees of life, and fetching animals for very reasonable prices (figure on $25 for a pearly three-gallon vase, and perhaps $2 for a cute little black rabbit).

San Martín Tilcajete and Santo Tomás Jalieza

San Martín Tilcajete (teel-kah-HAY-tay), about 21 miles (37 km) south of Oaxaca City (on the west side of Highway 175, not far north of the Highway 131 right fork), is a prime source of *alebrijes,* the fanciful wooden creatures occupying the shelves of crafts stores the world over. Both it and Santo Tomás Jalieza (south of the Highway 131 fork), a mile or two farther south, can be visited as a pair on any day.

The label *alebrije,* a word of Arabic origin, implies something of indefinite form, and that certainly characterizes the fanciful animal figurines that a generation of Oaxaca woodcarvers

Alebrijes, fanciful animal figurines, are made almost exclusively in the villages of Tilcajete and Arrazola.

© BRUCE WHIPPERMAN

has been crafting from soft *copal* wood. Dozens of factory-stores sprinkle Tilcajete town. Start on the front main street, but also be sure to wander the back lanes and step into several cottage workshops, whose occupants will be happy to show you what they have and demonstrate how they make them.

Jalieza, on the other hand, is known as the town of embroidered *cinturones* (belts). Townsfolk, virtually all of whom practice the craft, concentrate all of their selling in a single many-stalled market in the middle of town. Step inside and you'll be tempted not only by hundreds of hand-embroidered leather belts, but by a wealth of lovely hand-loomed and embroidered purses, shawls, dresses, blouses, small backpacks, and much more. Furthermore, asking prices are very reasonable. Open about 9 A.M.–5 P.M. daily.

Ocotlán de Morelos

Ocotlán (Place of Pines), 26 miles, 42 km south of Oaxaca, has the equally interesting trio of shops run by the Aguilar sisters, Irene, Guillerma, and Josefina. Watch for the signs at the edge of town on the right as you arrive from Oaxaca. Their creations include a host of fanciful figures in clay: vendors with big ripe strawberries, green and red cactus, goats in skirts, and bikini-clad blondes.

About a quarter mile farther north, by the town plaza, your main Ocotlán attraction (unless you're lucky enough to arrive during the May 18 fiesta) will be the big Friday market. Since markets are best in the morning, make Ocotlán your *first* Friday stop.

As for **food**, take a seat at the airy plaza-view veranda of the 🅲 **Restaurant Celebración** (cell 044-951/544-4254, 7 A.M.–10 P.M. daily), on the upstairs floor of the Plaza las Portales, on the east side of the central plaza.

For **accommodation** the best hotel in Ocotlán is the clean and modern **Hotel Rey David** (16 de Septiembre 248, tel. 951/571-1248, $20 s or d, $30 t). The hotel offers about 20 comfortable, attractively decorated rooms. Find it on the south-side Highway 175 ingress-egress avenue, Avenida 16 de Septiembre,

where it runs east–west, about three blocks east of the market and central plaza.

ZAACHILA, CUILAPAN, AND ARRAZOLA

This excursion is best on Thursday, when you can begin fresh in the morning at the big weekly market and ruins in Zaachila, then reverse your path back to the ex-convent Santiago Apostol near Cuilapan. On the final reverse leg, stop to see the *alebrijes* (fanciful animals) being crafted in Arrazola village.

Get there by tour bus, or bus from the Camionera Central Segunda Clase, or by car heading toward Monte Albán (look for the big road sign) southwest over the Atoyac River from the *periférico* at the south edge of town. Just after crossing the bridge, fork left (south) from the Monte Albán road onto the Zaachila road.

🅲 Zaachila

Your destination is the town plaza market in Zaachila, about 10 miles south of Oaxaca. Like Mitla, Zaachila overlies the ruins of its ancient namesake city, which rose to prominence after the decline of Monte Albán. Although excavations have uncovered many Mixtec-style remains, historical records nevertheless list a number of Zapotec kings who ruled Zaachila as a virtual Zapotec capital. On the eve of the conquest, it was a Mixtec noble minority who dominated the Zapotec-speaking inhabitants, whose leaders the Mixtec warriors had sent fleeing for their lives to Tehuantepec.

The big forested hill that rises north of the plaza market is topped by a large, mostly unexplored pyramid. Several unexcavated mounds and courtyards dot the hill's north and south flanks. The site parking lot and entrance gate are adjacent to the colonial church just north of the plaza.

In 1962, archaeologist Roberto Gallegos (guarded by soldiers against hostile villagers) uncovered a pair of unopened tombs beneath the summit of the Zaachila pyramid. They yielded a trove of polychrome pottery, gold jewelry (including a ring still on a left hand), and jade fan handles. Tomb 1, which is open

© BRUCE WHIPPERMAN

the unfinished ex-convent of Saint James in Cuilapan de Guerrero

for public inspection, descends via a steep staircase to an entrance decorated with a pair of ornamental cat heads. On the antechamber walls a few steps farther on are depictions of owls and a pair of personages (perhaps former occupants) inscribed respectively with name-dates (month-week) 5 Flower and 9 Flower. Do not miss the bas-reliefs on the tomb's back wall, which depict a man whose torso is covered with a turtle shell and another whose head is emerging from a serpent.

The narrow tomb staircase is negotiable by only a few people at a time and often requires an hour for a tour bus crowd to inspect it. Rather than wasting your market time standing in line, go downhill, stroll around the market, and return when the line is smaller. If driving, arrive early, around 9 A.M. on Thursday, to avoid tour-bus crowds.

The Thursday *tianguis* (native market) is Zaachila's weekly main event. It spreads for blocks below the archaeological site and church. Thousands of Zapotec-speaking country people stream into town to buy, sell,

gossip, flirt, and fill up with their favorite delicacies. For a breezy change of pace, hop into one of the buzzing *moto-taxis* (motorized rickshaws) for a 10-minute jaunt (for about $1.50) around town.

If you're in the mood for food, wholesome (make sure you get it served hot) country fare is available at the regiment of *fondas* in the permanent, roofed section of the market. Alternatively, enjoy lunch at the showplace **Restaurant la Capilla.** Get there on foot or by asking your *moto-taxi* driver to let you off at La Capilla (kah-PEE-yah), on the main east–west Oaxaca ingress street, a few blocks west of the market.

Cuilapan de Guerrero

Cuilapan de Guerrero, a few miles back north toward Oaxaca, is known for its elaborate unfinished ex-convent of Saint James (Santiago), visible from the highway, where President Guerrero was executed in 1831. Although the project was started in 1535, the basilica and associated monastery's costs began to balloon. In 1550, King Philip demanded humility and moderation of the builders, whose work was finally ended by a 1570 court ruling. The extravagances—soaring, roofless basilica, magnificent baptismal font, splendid Gothic cloister, and elaborate frescoes—remain as national treasures.

Arrazola

Arrazola, a few miles farther north, is the original source of the intricately painted *alebrijes* (ah-lay-BREE-hays), fanciful wooden creatures that have been turning up in shops all over Mexico and foreign countries during recent years. To get there, turn west (left) onto Highway 145 a few miles north of Cuilapan, or 3.2 miles (5.1 km) miles south of the Atoyac River Bridge. Pass through San Javier village and continue from the turnoff, a total of three miles (5 km), to just before the Arrazola town plaza. Turn right onto E. Zapata, then turn left after one block, at Independencia. After one more block, you will be at Calle Obregón, where everyone seems to be making *alebrijes.*

Although every family along the street crafts its own variations, **Pepe Santiago** and his Santa's workshop of craftspeople appear to have the edge. Inside the Santiago compound (on the right, just below the hilltop), men saw and carve away, while a cadre of young women painstakingly add riots of painted brocade to whimsical dragons, gargoyles, armadillos, giraffes, rabbits, and everything in between.

MONTE ALBÁN AND ETLA

Monte Albán is among Mesoamerica's most regal and spectacular ruined cities. The original name is lost in antiquity. "Monte Albán" was probably coined by a local Spaniard because of its resemblance to a similarly named Italian hill town.

Monte Albán's people cultivated corn, beans, squash, chiles, and fruits on the hillsides and adjacent valleys, occasionally feasting on meat from deer, small game, and perhaps (as did other ancient Mexicans) domesticated dogs. Tribute from surrounding communities directly enriched Monte Albán's ruling classes, and, by extension, its artisans and farmers.

Monte Albán reigned for at least 1,200 years,

between 500 B.C. and A.D. 750, as the capital of the Zapotecs and the dominant force between Teotihuacán in the Valley of Mexico and the Maya empires of the south.

Archaeologists have organized the Valley of Oaxaca's history from 500 B.C. to the conquest in five periods, known as Monte Albán I through V. Over those centuries, the hilltop city was repeatedly reconstructed, with new walls, plazas, and staircases, which, like peels of an onion, now overlie earlier construction.

Remains from Monte Albán Period I (500 B.C.–A.D. 0) reveal an already advanced culture, with gods, permanent temples, a priesthood, writing, numerals, and a calendar. Sharply contrasting house styles indicate a differentiated, multilayered society. Monte Albán I ruins abound in graceful polychrome ceramics of uniquely Zapotec style.

Concurrent Olmec influences have also been found, notably in the buildings known as the **Danzantes** (Dancers), decorated with bas-reliefs similar to those unearthed along the Veracruz and Tabasco coasts.

Monte Albán II people (A.D. 0–300), by contrast, came under heavy influence from Chiapas and Guatemala in the south. They built strange, ship-shaped buildings, such as Monte Albán's Building J, and left unique remains of their religion, such as the striking jade bat-god now on display in the Anthropology Museum in Mexico City.

Monte Albán reached its apex during Period III (A.D. 300–800), attaining a population of perhaps 40,000 in an urban zone of about three square miles, which spread along hilltops (including the El Gallo and Atzompa archaeological sites) west of the present city of Oaxaca.

Vigorous Period III leaders rebuilt the main hilltop complex as we see it today. Heavily influenced by the grand Teotihuacán styles, the buildings were finished with handsome sloping staircases, corniced walls, monumental carvings, ball courts, and hieroglyph-inscribed stelae depicting gods, kings, and heroic scenes of battle.

By A.D. 750 few foreign influences were continuing to enrich Monte Albán's uniquely Zapotec pottery styles. Quality declined until they seemed like mere factory copies. Concurrently, the Zapotec pantheon expanded to a horde of gods, as if mere numbers could protect the increasingly isolated Valley of Oaxaca from the outside world.

In A.D. 800, Monte Albán, mysteriously cut off from the rest of Mesoamerica, was declining in population and power. By A.D. 1000, the city was nearly abandoned. The reasons—whether drought, disease, or revolt—and the consequent loss of the necessarily imported water, wood, salt, and food supplies, remain an enigma.

During Periods IV and V, Mixtec peoples from the north invaded the Valley of Oaxaca. They warred with valley Zapotecs and, despite their relatively small numbers, became a ruling class in a number of valley city-states. The blend of Mixtec and Zapotec art and architecture sometimes led to new forms, especially visible at the west-valley sites of Yagul and Mitla.

Monte Albán, meanwhile, although abandoned, was not forgotten. It became both a refuge and a venerated burial place. In times of siege, local people retreated within the walls of a fortress built around Monte Albán's South Platform. At other times, Mixtec nobles opened tombs and reused them as burial vaults right down until the eve of the conquest.

◖ Monte Albán

Visitors to Monte Albán (9 A.M.–5 P.M. daily) enjoy a panoramic view of green mountains rising above the checkerboard of the Valley of Oaxaca. Monte Albán is fun for a picnic; alternatively, it is an auspicious place to perch atop a pyramid above the grand Main Plaza, etched by lengthening afternoon shadows, and contemplate the ages.

As you enter past the visitors' center, north is on your right, marked by the grand **North Platform,** topped by clusters of temples. Wheelchair access is by the elevator to the right of the entry path.

The **Ball Court** will soon appear below on your left. Twenty-foot-high walkways circumscribe the sunken I-shaped playing field. To ensure true bounces, builders spread smooth

© BRUCE WHIPPERMAN

The Ball Court at Monte Albán was used for highly ritualized contests using a hard natural rubber ball.

stucco over all surfaces, including the slopes on opposite sides (which, contrary to appearances, did not seat spectators). This, like all Oaxacan ball courts, had no stone ring (for supposed goals), but rather four mysterious niches at the court's opposite I-end corners.

The **Main Plaza,** 1,000 feet long and exactly two-thirds that wide, is aligned along a precise north-south axis. Probably serving as a market and civic-ceremonial ground, the monumentally harmonious Main Plaza was the Zapotec "navel" of the world.

Monte Albán's oldest construction, the **Danzantes** (surmounted by newer Building L, on the west side of the plaza between Buildings M and IV), dates from Period I. Its walls are graced with a host of personages, known commonly as the *danzantes* (dancers) from their oft-contorted postures—probably chiefs vanquished by Monte Albán's armies. Their headdresses, earplugs, bracelets, and necklaces mark them among the nobility, while glyphs around their heads identify each individual.

Building J (circa A.D. 0), one of the most remarkable in Mesoamerica, stands nearby in midplaza at the foot of the South Platform. Speculation has raged since excavators unearthed its arrow-shaped base generations ago. It is not surprising that Alfonso Caso, Monte Albán's principal excavator, theorized it was an astronomical observatory. In the mind's eye, it seems like some fantastic ocean (or space?) vessel, being navigated to some mysteriously singular southwest destination by a ghostly crew oblivious of its worldly, earthbound brother monuments.

The **South Platform,** especially during the late afternoon, affords Monte Albán's best vantage point. Starting on the right-hand, palace complex side, **Building II** has a peculiar tunnel on its near side, covertly used by priests for privacy or perhaps some kind of magical effect. To the south stands Building P, an undistinguished multiroom palace.

The South Platform itself is only marginally explored. Looters have riddled the mounds on its top side. Its bottom four corners were embellished by fine bas-reliefs, two of which had their engraving intentionally buried from view. You can admire the fine sculpture and yet-undeciphered Zapotec hieroglyphs on one of them, along with others, at the South Platform's plaza-edge west side.

Still atop the South Platform, turn southward, where you can see the 7 Deer complex, a few hundred yards away, labeled for the name-date inscribed on its great lintel.

Turning northward again, look just beyond Building J to Buildings G, H, and I at plaza center, erected mostly to cover a rocky mound impossible to remove without the then-unavailable dynamite. Between these buildings and the palace complex on the right stands the small chapel where the remarkable bat-god jade sculpture was found.

On Monte Albán's northern periphery stand a number of tombs which, when excavated, yielded a trove of artifacts, now mostly housed in museums. Walking west from the Northern Platform's northeast base corner, you will pass Building X on the right. A few hundred yards

farther comes the **Tomb 104** mound, presided over by an elaborate ceramic urn representing Cojico, the Zapotec god of rain. Just north of this is **Tomb 172,** with the skeletons and offerings left intact.

Heading back along the northernmost of the two paths from Tomb 104, you will arrive at **Tomb 7** a few hundred feet behind the visitors center. Here, around A.D. 1450, Mixtec nobles removed the original 8th-century contents and reused the tomb, burying a deceased dignitary and two servants for the netherworld. Along with the bodies they left a fabulous treasure in gold, silver, jade, alabaster, and turquoise, now visible in Oaxaca at the Museo Regional de las Culturas de Oaxaca.

A few hundred feet toward town on the opposite side of the road from the parking lot is a trail, leading past a small ball court to the Cerro de Plumaje (Hill of Plumage), site of **Tomb 105.** A magnificent entrance door lintel, reminiscent of those at Mitla, welcomes you inside. Past the patio, descend to the mural-decorated tomb antechamber. Inside the cruciform tomb itself, four figures walk in pairs toward a great glyph, flanked by a god and goddess, identified by their name-dates.

Visitors Center

The Monte Albán Visitors Center (tel. 951/516-1215, 8 A.M.–6 P.M.) has an excellent museum, good café with airy terrace, and information counter. Also, a well-stocked store offers many books—guides, histories, art, folklore—on Mesoamerica. First, take a look inside the museum, which displays a number of Monte Albán's famous finds. Most notable are several of the original *danzantes* monolith reliefs, recognizable by their mutilated genitals.

In the bookstore (tel. 951/516-9180), you might purchase a copy of the very useful *Guide to Monte Albán,* by Monte Albán's director, Neli Robles. You might also pick up a copy of the very authoritative, in-depth *Oaxaca, the Archaeological Record,* by archaeologist Marcus Winter, that covers many Oaxaca archaeological sites, including the Valley sites of Dainzu, Lambityeco, Mitla, San José el Mogote, and

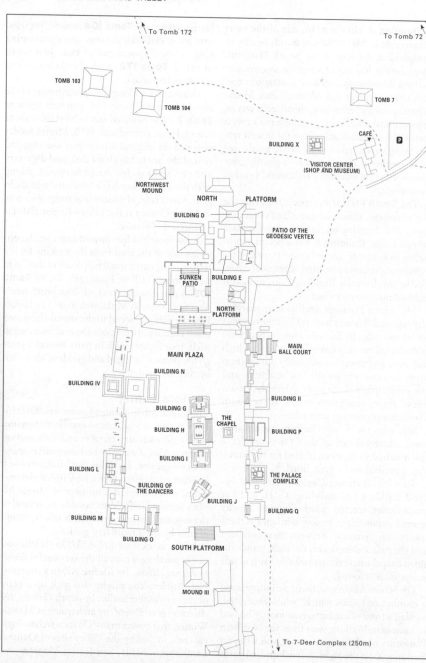

To Tomb 172

To Tomb 72

TOMB 103

TOMB 104

TOMB 7

CAFÉ

P

BUILDING X

VISITOR CENTER
(SHOP AND MUSEUM)

NORTHWEST
MOUND

NORTH PLATFORM

BUILDING D

PATIO OF THE
GEODESIC VERTEX

SUNKEN
PATIO

BUILDING E

NORTH
PLATFORM

MAIN
BALL COURT

MAIN PLAZA

BUILDING N

BUILDING IV

BUILDING II

BUILDING G

THE CHAPEL

BUILDING H

BUILDING P

BUILDING I

BUILDING L

THE PALACE
COMPLEX

BUILDING OF
THE DANCERS

BUILDING J

BUILDING M

BUILDING Q

BUILDING O

SOUTH PLATFORM

MOUND III

To 7-Deer Complex (250m)

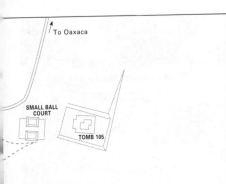

MONTE ALBÁN

Suchilquitongo and several other important sites in the Mixteca.

Getting There

Get to Monte Albán economically and very conveniently by one of the **tourist buses,** tel. 951/516-5327, run by Viajes Turísticos Mitla, that departs many times daily from downtown Hotel Rivera del Ángel (Mina 518), five blocks west of the *zócalo* in Oaxaca City.

By car, get to Monte Albán by following Highway 190 northwest from downtown Oaxaca City. After just about two miles (three kilometers) from the city center (look for a Monte Albán sign), curve left, around the big monument and traffic circle, reversing your direction, then immediately turn right (west) and continue across the Río Atoyac bridge. Follow the signs about six more miles (10 kilometers) uphill to Monte Albán.

Alternatively, by car, you can get to Monte Albán from the south side, at the *periférico,* about a mile due south from the *zócalo* past the end of southbound Calle M. Cabrera. Watch for a Monte Albán sign. Go south across the *periférico,* then bear right (southwest) and immediately cross over the Río Atoyac bridge. Continue straight ahead, following another Monte Albán sign. Continue, following the signs, about five miles (8 km), uphill, to Monte Albán.

Etla

The untouristed, very colorful Wednesday market at Villa de Etla, northwest of Oaxaca, could be visited either separately or in coordination with a visit to Monte Albán. Although Etla's market invariably has stalls overflowing with its famous white cheese, vendors offer much other old-fashioned merchandise. (How would you like, for example, some fresh sheepskins, burro packframes, green Atzompa pottery, or red Oaxaca tamales?)

Preferably visit the market in the forenoon and Monte Albán in the midafternoon. Arrive at Monte Albán by 2 P.M. to allow enough leisure to tour the ruins before they close at 5 P.M.

© BRUCE WHIPPERMAN

A good way to tour Etla is by moto-taxis, which line up in front of the Etla market steps.

For a fun change of pace, ride the circuit around town via one of the many **moto-taxis** ($1 round-trip) that line up in front of the Etla market steps.

For lunch treat, head to country-style *comedor* **La Fonda** of elderly Señora Julia Angulo, adjacent to the market's east side. Alternatively, try **Restaurant Chefy,** for a wholesome, home-style breakfast or lunch, on the left side of the main street as you enter town from the highway.

GETTING THERE

By car, head north along Highway 190 about nine miles (15 km) from the city center and turn left at the Etla sign, just before the Pemex station. The Etla market is in a handsome stone building, about half a mile from the highway, on the right, where the street ends at the rail-road station.

By bus, ride one of the many Etla-marked Choferes del Sur buses from the Abastos second-class terminal, or ride a tour bus from the hotel Rivera del Ángel (Mina 518, bus desk tel. 951/516-5327, two blocks south, three blocks west of the *zócalo.*

BACKGROUND

Land and Sea

On the map of North America, Mexico appears as a grand horn of plenty, spreading and spilling to its northern border with the United States. Mexico encompasses a vast landscape, sprawling over an area as large as France, Germany, England, and Italy combined. Besides its size, Mexico is high country, where most people live in mountain valleys within sight of towering, snowcapped peaks.

Travelers heading south of the Río Grande do not realize the rise in elevation, however. Instead, brushy, cactus-pocked plains spread to mountain ranges on the far blue horizon. Northern Mexico is nevertheless a tableland—the altiplano—that rises gradually from the

Río Grande to its climax at the very heart of the country: the mile-high Bajio (BAH-hee-oh) Valley around Guadalajara and the even loftier Valley of Mexico.

Here, in these fertile vales, untold generations of Mexicans have gazed southward at an awesome rampart of smoking mountains, a grand volcanic seam stretching westward from the Gulf of Mexico to the Pacific. In a continuous line along the 19th parallel, more than a dozen volcanoes have puffed sulfurous gas and spewed red-hot rock for an eon, building themselves into some of the mightiest peaks in the Americas. Most easterly and grandest of them all is Orizaba (Citlaltépetl, the Mountain of the

© BRUCE WHIPPERMAN

Acapulco's rugged west-side coastline affords ideal perches for viewing ocean sunsets.

Star), rising 18,856 feet (5,747 meters) directly above the Gulf. Then, in proud succession, the giants march westward: Malinche, 14,640 feet (4,462 meters); Popocatépetl, 17,888 feet (5,452 meters); Nevado de Toluca, 15,016 feet (4,577 meters); until finally the most active of all—the 13,087-foot (3,989-meter) Volcán de Fuego (Volcano of Fire)—fumes next to its serene twin, the Nevado de Colima (14,220 feet, 4,334 meters) above the long, plumy shoreline of Pacific Mexico.

PACIFIC MEXICO

This sun-drenched western coastland stretches along 1,000 miles of sandy beaches, palm-strewn headlands, blue lagoons, verdant foothills, high Sierra peaks, and upland valleys, from Mazatlán in the north and curving to the southeast past Acapulco to the new vacation land of Bahías de Huatulco in Oaxaca.

Pacific Mexico is a land washed by the ocean and sheltered by the western mountains: Sierra Madre Occidental and its southern extension, the Sierra Madre del Sur.

Everywhere, except in the north where the coastal plain is broad, these green jungle-clad sierras rise quickly, sometimes precipitously, above a narrow coastal strip. Few rivers and roads breach these ramparts, and where roads do, they wind through deep *barrancas,* over lofty passes to temperate, oak-studded highland valleys.

Climate

Elevation rules the climate of Pacific Mexico. The entire coastal strip (including the mountain slopes and plateaus up to 4,000 or 5,000 feet) basks in the tropics, never feeling the bite of frost. The seashore is truly a land of perpetual summer. Winter days are typically warm and rainless, peaking at 80–85°F (26–28°C) and dropping to 60–70°F (16–21°C) by midnight. The north-to-south variation on this theme is typically small: Mazatlán will be a few degrees cooler; Acapulco, a few degrees warmer.

Summers on the Pacific Mexico beaches are warmer and wetter. July, August, and September forenoons are typically bright and warm, heating to the high 80s (around 30°C) with afternoon clouding and short, sometimes heavy, showers. By late afternoon, clouds part, the sun dries the pavements, and the breeze is often balmy and just right to enjoy a sparkling Pacific Mexico sunset.

The highlands around Guadalajara, Pátzcuaro, Taxco, and Oaxaca experience similar, but more temperate seasons. Midwinter days are mild, typically peaking around 70°F (21°C). Expect cool, but frost-free, winter nights between 40° and 50°F (9–14°C). Highland summers are delightful, with afternoons in the 80s (27–32°C) and pleasant evenings in the mid-70s (21–26°C), perfect for strolling. May, before the rains, is often the warmest, with June, July, and August highs being moderated by afternoon showers. Many Guadalajara, Pátzcuaro, Taxco, and Oaxaca residents enjoy the best of all possible worlds: balmy summers at home and similarly balmy winters in vacation homes along the Pacific Mexico coast.

Flora and Fauna

Fascinating hothouse verdure—from delicate orchids and bulbous, fuzzy succulents to giant hanging philodendrons—luxuriates at some roadside spots of Pacific Mexico, as if beckoning admirers. Now and then visitors stop, attracted by something remarkable, such as a riot of flowers blooming from apparently dead branches or what looks like grapefruit sprouting from the trunk of a roadside tree. More often, travelers pass long stretches of thorny thickets, viny jungles, and broad, mangrove-edged marshes. A little knowledge of what to expect can blossom into recognition and discovery, transforming the humdrum into something quite extraordinary, even exotic.

VEGETATION ZONES

Mexico's diverse landscape and fickle rainfall have sculpted its wide range of plant forms. Botanists recognize at least 14 major Mexican vegetation zones, eight of which occur in Pacific Mexico.

Directly along the coastal highway, you often pass long sections of three of these zones: savanna, thorn forest, and tropical deciduous forest. The other five are less accessible.

Savanna

Great swaths of pasturelike savanna stretch along the roadside south of Mazatlán to Tepic. In its natural state, savanna often appears as a palm-dotted sea of grass—green and marshy during the rainy summer, dry and brown by late winter.

Although grass rules the savanna, palms give it character. Most familiar is the **coconut,** the *cocotero (Cocos nucifera)*—the world's most useful tree—used for everything from lumber to candy. Coconut palms line the beaches and climb the hillsides, drooping, slanting, rustling, and swaying in the breeze like troupes of hula dancers. Less familiar, but with as much personality, is the Mexican **fan palm,** or *palma real (Sabal mexicana)*, festooned with black fruit and spread flat like a señorita's fan.

The savanna's list goes on: the grapefruit-

Gigantic "El Tule" (a Mexican bald cypress) near Oaxaca is one of the world's most massive trees.

like fruit on the trunk and branches identify the **gourd tree,** or *calabaza (Crescentia alata)*. The mature gourds, brown and hard, have been carved into *jícaros* (cups for drinking chocolate) for millennia.

Orange-sized, pumpkinlike gourds mark the **sand box tree,** or *jabillo (Hura polyandra)*, so-named because they once served as desktop boxes full of sand for drying ink. The Aztecs, however, called it the exploding tree, because the ripe gourds burst their seeds forth with a bang like a firecracker.

The waterlogged seaward edge of the savanna nurtures forests of the **red mangrove,** or *mangle colorado (Rhizophora mangle)*, short trees that seem to stand in the water on stilts. Their new roots grow downward from above; a time-lapse photo would show them marching, as if on stilts, into the lagoon.

Thorn Forest

Lower rainfall leads to the hardier growth of the thorn forest, the domain of the pea family—the **acacias** and their cousins, the **mimosas.** Among the most common is the **long spine acacia,** with fluffy, yellow flower balls, ferny leaves, and long, narrow pods; less common, but more useful, is the **fishfuddle,** with pink pea-flowers and long pods, a source of fish-stunning poison. Take care around the acacias; some of the long-thorned varieties harbor nectar-feeding, biting ants.

Perhaps the most spectacular and famous member of the thorn forest community is the **morning glory tree,** which announces the winter dry season's end by blooming a festoon of white trumpets atop its crown of seemingly dead branches. Its gruesome Mexican name, *palo del muerto* (tree of the dead), is exceeded only around Taxco, where folks call it *palo bobo* (fool tree), because they believe if you take a drink from a stream near its foot, you will go crazy.

The cactuses are among the thorn forest's sturdiest and most spectacular inhabitants. In the dry Río Balsas basin (along Highway 95 inland from Acapulco) the spectacular **candelabra cactus** *(cordón espinosa)* spreads as much as 60 feet tall and wide.

Tropical Deciduous Forest

In rainier areas, the thorn forest grades into tropical deciduous forest. This is the "friendly" or "short-tree" forest, blanketed by a tangle of summer-green leaves that fall in the dry winter to reveal thickets of branches. Some trees show bright fall reds and yellows, later blossoming with brilliant flowers—spider lily, cardinal sage, pink trumpet, poppylike yellowsilk *(pomposhuti),* and mouse-killer *(mata ratón),* which swirl in the spring wind like cherry-blossom blizzards.

The tropical deciduous forest is the lush jungle coat that swathes much of coastal Pacific Mexico. And often, where the mountains rush directly down to the sea, the forest likewise spills right over the headland into the ocean. Vine-strewn thickets often overhang the highway, like the edge of some lost prehis-

© BRUCE WHIPPERMAN

Colima palms, known locally as the *guaycoyul* or *cohune,* are very common in the coastal areas of Nayarit, Jalisco, and Colima.

toric world, where you might expect a remnant dinosaur to rear up at any moment.

The biological realities here are nearly as exotic. A four-foot-long green iguana, looking every bit as primitive as a dinosaur, slithers across the pavement. Beside the road, a spreading, solitary **strangler fig** *(Ficus padifolia)* stands, draped with hairy, hanging air roots (which, in time, plant themselves in the ground and support the branches). Its Mexican name, *matapalo* (killer tree), is gruesomely accurate, for strangler figs often entwine themselves in death embraces with less aggressive tree-victims.

Much more benign is my favorite in the tropical deciduous forest: the **Colima palm** *(Orbygna guacuyule), guaycoyul,* or *cohune,* which means magnificent. Capped by a proud cock-plume, it presides over the forest singly or in great, graceful swaying groves atop seacliffs. Its nuts, harvested like small coconuts, yield oil and animal fodder.

Excursions by jeep or foot along shaded, off-highway tracks through the tropical deciduous forest can bestow delightful jungle scenes; however, unwary travelers must watch out for the poison-oaklike *mala mujer* (evil woman) tree. The oil on its large five-fingered leaves can cause an itchy rash.

Pine-Oak Forest

A couple of hours' drive inland (especially on the mountain roads from the coast to Guadalajara, Taxco, and Oaxaca), the tropics give way to the temperate pine-oak forest, Pacific Mexico's most extensive vegetation zone. Here, most of Mexico's 112 oak and 39 pine species thrive. At the lower elevations, bushy, nut-yielding piñon pines sometimes cover the slope; then come the tall pines, often Chihuahua pine and Montezuma pine, both yellow varieties, similar to the ponderosa pine of the western United States.

Interspersed with them are oaks, in two broad classifications—*encino* (evergreen, small-leafed) and *roble* (deciduous, large-leafed)—both much like the oaks that dot California hills and valleys. Clustered on their branches and scattered in the shade are the *bellota* (acorns) that distinctly mark them as oaks.

Mesquite Grassland

Although much of Pacific Mexico's mesquite grassland has been tamed for agriculture, outlying districts, notably in the highlands northeast of Guadalajara, still exhibit its typical landscape, similar to the semiarid plateau land of the U.S. Southwest.

Despite its seemingly monotonous roadside aspect, the mesquite grassland nurtures surprisingly exotic and unusual plants. Among the most intriguing is the **maguey** (mah-GAY), or century plant, so-called because it's said to bloom once, then die, after 100 years of growth, although its lifetime is usually closer to 50 years. The maguey and its cactuslike relatives—such as the very useful **mescal**, **lechuguilla**, and **sisal**, all of the genus *Agave*—each grow as a rose-like cluster of leathery, long, pointed gray-green leaves, from which a single flower stalk eventually blooms.

Century plants themselves, which can grow several feet tall and equally wide, thrive either wild or in cultivated fields in ranks and files like a botanical army on parade. These fields, prominently visible from National Highway 15 west of Guadalajara, are eventually harvested, the leaves crushed, fermented, and distilled into fiery 80-proof tequila, the most renowned of which comes from the town of Tequila near Highway 15.

Watch for the mesquite grassland's **candelilla** (*Euphorbia antisyphillitica*), an odd cousin of the poinsettia, also a Mexico native. In contrast to the poinsettia, the *candelilla* resembles a tall (two- to three-foot) candle, decorated with small white flowers scattered upward along its single vertical stem. Abundant wax on the many pencil-sized stalks that curve upward from the base is useful for anything from polishing your shoes to lubricating your car's distributor.

Equally exotic is the *Japtropha dioica*, called the **sangre de dragón** (dragon blood), which also grows in a single meaty stem producing two-inch-long lobed leaves with small white flowers. Break off a leaf and out oozes a clear sap, which soon turns blood-red.

High Coniferous Forest

Pacific Mexico's least accessible vegetation zone is the high coniferous forest, above about 9,000 feet, which swathes the slopes of the area's tallest peaks, notably the Nevado de Colima, elev. 14,220 feet (4,334 meters), and Tancítaro, elev. 12,665 feet (3,860 meters), in Michoacán. These pristine green alpine islands, accessible only on horseback or by foot, nurture stands of magnificent pines and spruce and grassy meadows, similar to the higher Rocky Mountain slopes in the United States and Canada. Reigning over the lesser species is the regal **Montezuma pine** (*Pinus montezumae*), distinguished by its long, pendulous cones and rough, ruddy bark, reminiscent of the sugar pine of the western United States.

© BRUCE WHIPPERMAN

Giant ferns (shown above the roadside) are a sure marker of the cloud forest vegetation zone.

Arid Tropical Scrub and Cloud Forest

Pacific Mexico's two rarest and most exotic vegetation zones are far from the coastal tourist centers. You can conveniently see the great cactus forests of the arid tropical scrub habitat (which occupies the wild, dry canyonland of the Río Balsas intermountain basin) either along Highway 95 inland from Acapulco, or along Highway 37 or the toll *autopista* between Playa Azul and Pátzcuaro. Finally, travelers who drive to high, dewy mountainsides, beginning around 7,000 feet, can explore the plant and wildlife community of the cloud forest. Oaxaca's northern Sierra (two hours' drive north of Oaxaca city, about 15 miles north of Ixtlán de Juárez) and the Sierra de Manatlán (in the roadless wilderness 40 miles northeast of Manzanillo, near Minatitlán) preserve such habitats. There, abundant cool fog nourishes forests of tree ferns, lichen-draped pines, and oaks above a mossy carpet of orchids, bromeliads, and begonias. For more details, consult M.

Walter Pesman's delightful *Meet Flora Mexicana* (which is out of print, but major libraries often have a copy). Also informative is the popular paperback *Handbook of Mexican Roadside Flora,* by Charles T. Mason Jr. and Patricia B. Mason. (See *Suggested Reading.*)

WILDLIFE

Despite continued habitat destruction—forests are logged, wetlands filled, and savannas plowed—Pacific Mexico still abounds with wildlife. In the temperate pine-oak forest zone of Pacific Mexico live most of the familiar birds and mammals—mountain lion, coyote, jackrabbit, dove, quail—of the American Southwest.

The tropical coastal forests and savannas, however, are home to species seen only in zoos north of the border. The reality of this often dawns on travelers when they glimpse something exotic, such as raucous, screeching swarms of small green parrots rising from the roadside, or a coati nosing in the sand just a few feet away at the forested edge of some isolated Pacific Mexico beach.

Armadillos, Coatis, Spider Monkeys, and Tapirs

Armadillos are cat-sized mammals that act and look like opossums but carry reptilianlike shells. If you see one, remain still, and it may walk right up and sniff your foot before it recognizes you and scuttles back into the woods.

A common inhabitant of the tropics is the raccoonlike coatimundi *(tejon, pisote).* In the wild, coatis like shady stream banks, often congregating in large troops. They are identified by their short brown or tan fur, small round ears, long nose, and straight, vertically held tail. With their endearing and inquisitive nature, coatis are often kept as pets; the first coati you see may be one on a string offered for sale at a local market.

If you are lucky, you may glimpse a band of now-rare brownish-black spider monkeys *(monos)* raiding a forest-edge orchard. And deep in the jungle fastness of southeast Oaxaca, you may find a tracker who can lead you to a view of the endangered tapir. On such

Although humans have died of wounds inflicted by cornered jaguars, there is little or no hard evidence they eat humans, despite legends to the contrary.

BIRDS

The coastal lagoons of Pacific Mexico lie astride the Pacific flyway, one of the Americas' major north-south paths for migrating waterfowl. Many of the familiar American and Canadian species, including pintail, gadwall, baldpate, shoveler, redhead, and scaup, arrive Oct.–Jan., when their numbers will swell into the millions. They settle near food and cover—sometimes to the frustration of farmers—even at the borders of cornfields. Among the best places to see their spectacle is the **Marismas Nacionales** marsh complex around the Sinaloa-Nayarit border, west of coast Highway 15 between Mazatlán and Acaponeta.

Besides the migrants, swarms of resident species—herons, egrets, cormorants, anhingas, lily-walkers, and hundreds more—stalk, nest, and preen in the same lagoons.

Few spots are better for observing seabirds than the beaches of Pacific Mexico. Brown pelicans and huge black-and-white frigate birds are among the prime actors. When a flock of pelicans spots a school of their favorite fish, they go about their routine deliberately: singly or in pairs they circle and plummet into the waves and come up, more often than not, with fish in their gullets. Each bird then bobs and floats over the swells for a minute or two, seemingly waiting for its dozen or so fellow pelicans to take their turns. This continues until they've bagged a big dinner of 10 to 15 fish apiece.

Frigate birds, the scavengers par excellence of Pacific Mexico, often profit by the labor of the teams of fisherfolk who haul in fish right on village beaches by the netful. After the fishermen auction off the choice morsels—perch, tuna, red snapper, octopus, shrimp—to merchants, and the villagers have scavenged everything else edible, the motley residue of small fish, sea snakes, skates, squids, slugs, and sharks is often thrown to a screeching flock of frigate birds.

Although the coatimundi, common in Pacific Mexico's coast and foothill zones, looks and acts like a racoon, it's also related to the grizzly bear.

© BRUCE WHIPPERMAN

an excursion, if you are really fortunate, you may even hear the chesty cry of—or even see—a jaguar, the fabled *tigre.*

El Tigre

"Each hill has its own *tigre,*" a Mexican proverb says. With black spots spread over a tan coat, stretching five feet (1.5 meters) and weighing about 200 pounds (90 kilograms), the typical jaguar resembles a muscular spotted leopard. Although hunted since prehistory, and now endangered, the jaguar still lives throughout Pacific Mexico, where it hunts along thickly forested stream bottoms and foothills. Unlike the mountain lion *(puma),* the jaguar will eat any game. Jaguars have even been known to wait patiently for fish in rivers and to stalk beaches for turtle and egg dinners. If they have a favorite food, it is probably the piglike wild peccary *(jabalí).* Experienced hunters agree that no two jaguars will, when examined, have the same prey in their stomachs.

(For more details on Mexico's mammals and birds in general, check out Starker Leopold's very readable classic, *Wildlife of Mexico,* and other works in the *Suggested Reading* section.)

REPTILES AND AMPHIBIANS
Snakes and Gila Monsters

Mexico has 460-odd snake species, the vast majority shy and nonpoisonous; they will generally get out of your way if you give plenty of warning. In Mexico, as everywhere, poisonous snakes have been largely eradicated in city and tourist areas. In brush or jungle areas, carry a stick or a machete and beat the bushes ahead of you, while watching where you put your feet. When hiking or rock-climbing in the country, don't put your hand in niches you can't see.

You might even see a snake underwater while swimming offshore at an isolated Puerto Vallarta–region beach. The **yellow-bellied sea snake** *Pelamis platurus* (grows to about two feet), although shy, can inflict fatal bites. If you see a yellow and black snake underwater, get away, pronto.

Some eels, which resemble snakes but have gills like fish and inhabit rocky crevices, can inflict nonpoisonous bites and should also be avoided.

The Mexican land counterpart of the *Pelamis platurus* is the **coral snake** *(coralillo),* which occurs as about two dozen species, all with multicolored bright bands that always include red. Although relatively rare, small, and shy, coral snakes occasionally inflict serious, sometimes fatal, bites.

More aggressive and generally more dangerous is the Mexican **rattlesnake** *(cascabel)* and its viper relative, the **fer-de-lance** *(Bothrops atrox).* About the same in size (to six feet) and general appearance as the rattlesnake, the fer-de-lance is known by various local names, such as *nauyaca, cuatro narices, palanca,* and *barba amarilla.* It is potentially more hazardous than the rattlesnake because it lacks a warning rattle.

The Gila monster (confined in Mexico to northern Sonora) and its southern tropical relative, the yellow-spotted, black **escorpión** *(Heloderma horridum),* are the world's only poisonous lizards. Despite its beaded skin and menacing, fleshy appearance, the *escorpión* bites only when severely provoked; even then, its venom is rarely, if ever, fatal.

Crocodiles

The crocodile, *cocodrilo* or *caimán,* once prized for its meat and hide, came close to vanishing in Mexican Pacific lagoons until the government took steps to ensure its survival. Now officially protected, crocodiles live in the wild in a few isolated breeding populations, while government and private hatcheries are breeding more for the eventual repopulation of lagoons where they once were common. Hatcheries open for touring are in San Blas, Nayarit, and Lagunas de Chacagua, Oaxaca.

Two crocodile species occur in the region. The true crocodile *Crocodilus acutus* has a narrower snout than its local cousin, *Caiman crocodilus fuscus,* a type of alligator *(lagarto).* Although past individuals have been recorded at up to 15 feet long (see the stuffed specimen at the Tepic anthropology and history museum or the live ones at the Mazatlán aquarium), wild native crocodiles are usually young and two feet or less in length.

Turtles

The story of Mexican sea turtles is similar: They once swarmed ashore on Pacific Mexico beaches to lay their eggs. Prized for their meat, eggs, hide, and shell, the turtle population was severely devastated. Now officially protected, sea turtles come ashore in numbers at a few isolated locations. Of the three locally occurring species, the green turtle *tortuga verde* is among the most common. From tour boats, it can often be seen grazing on sea grass offshore in the Bay of Banderas. (For more sea turtle details, see the sidebar *Saving Turtles* in *The Jalisco Coast* chapter.)

FISH AND MARINE MAMMALS

Shoals of fish abound in Pacific Mexico waters. Four billfish species are found in deep-sea grounds several miles offshore: **swordfish,** sailfish, and **blue** and **black marlin.** All are spirited fighters, though the sailfish and marlin are generally the toughest to bring in. The blue marlin is the biggest of the four; in the past, 10-foot specimens weighing more than 1,000 pounds were brought in at Pacific-coast marinas. Lately, four feet and 200 pounds for a marlin, and 100 pounds for a sailfish, are more typical. Progressive captains now encourage victorious anglers to return these magnificent "tigers of the sea" (especially the sinewy sailfish and blue marlin, which make for poor eating) to the deep after they've won the battle.

Billfish are not the only prizes of the sea, however. Serious fish lovers also seek varieties of tunalike **jack,** such as **yellowtail, Pacific amberjack, pompano, jack crevalle,** and the tenacious **roosterfish,** named for the "comb" atop its head. These, and the **yellowfin tuna, mackerel,** and *dorado,* which Hawaiians call mahimahi, are among the delicacies sought in Pacific Mexican waters.

Accessible from small boats offshore and by casting from shoreline rocks are varieties of **snapper** *(huachinango, pargo)* and **sea bass** *(cabrilla).* Closer to shore, **croaker, mullet,** and **jewfish** can be found foraging along sandy bottoms and in rocky crevices.

Sharks and **rays** inhabit nearly all depths, with smaller fry venturing into beach shallows and lagoons. Huge **Pacific manta rays** sometimes appear to be frolicking, their great wings flapping like birds, not far off Pacific Mexico shores. Just beyond the waves, local fisherfolk bring in **hammerhead, thresher,** and **leopard sharks.**

Also common is the **stingray,** which can inflict a painful wound with its barbed tail. Experienced swimmers and waders avoid injury by both shuffling (rather than stepping) and watching their feet in shallow waters with sandy bottoms. (For more on fishing and the species encountered in Pacific Mexico waters, see the *Sports and Recreation* section in the *Essentials* chapter.)

Seals, Sea Lions, Porpoises, and Whales

Although seen in much greater numbers in Baja California's colder waters, fur-bearing species, such as seals and sea lions, do occasionally hunt in the tropical waters and bask on the sands of island beaches off the Pacific Mexico coast. With the rigid government protections that have been in force for a generation, their numbers appear to be increasing.

The **California Gulf porpoise**—*delfín* or *vaquita* (little cow)—is much more numerous. The smallest member of the whale family, it rarely exceeds five feet. Its playful diving and jumping antics can occasionally be observed from Puerto Vallarta–based tour and fishing boats, and even sometimes right from Bay of Banderas beaches.

Although the **California gray whale** has a migration pattern extending only to the southern tip of Baja California, occasional pods stray farther south, where deep-sea fishermen and cruise and tour boat passengers see them in deep waters offshore.

Larger whale *(ballena)* species, such as the **humpback** and **blue** whale, appear to enjoy tropical waters even more, ranging the north Pacific tropics from Puerto Vallarta west to Hawaii and beyond.

Offshore islands, such as the nearby Marietas and María Isabel (accessible from San Blas), and the Revillagigedo (ray-vee-yah-hee-HAY-doh) Islands 300 miles due west of Puerto Vallarta, offer prime viewing grounds for Mexico's aquatic fauna.

History

Once upon a time, maybe as early as 40,000 years ago, the first bands of hunters, following great game herds, crossed from Siberia to the American continent. For thousands of years they drifted southward, many of them eventually settling in the rich valleys and plains of North and South America.

Many thousands of years later, perhaps around 10,000 B.C., and in what would later be called Mexico, people began gathering and grinding the seeds of a hardy grass that required only the summer rains to thrive. They selected and planted the larger seeds, and their grain eventually yielded tall plants with long ears and many large kernels. This grain, which they eventually called *teocentli* (sacred seed, which we call maize or corn), led to prosperity.

EARLY MEXICAN CIVILIZATIONS

Plentiful food gave rise to leisure classes— artists, architects, warriors, and ruler-priests— who had time to think and create. With a calendar, they harnessed the constant wheel of the firmament to life on earth, defining the days to plant, to harvest, to feast, to travel, and to trade. Eventually, grand cities arose.

Teotihuacán

Teotihuacán, with a population of perhaps 250,000 around the time of Christ, was one of the world's great metropolises, on a par with Rome, Babylon, and Chang'an. Its epic monuments still stand not far north of Mexico City: the towering Pyramid of the Sun at the terminal of a grand, 150-foot-wide ceremonial avenue faces a great Pyramid of the Moon. Along the avenue sprawls a monumental temple-court surrounded by scowling, ruby-eyed effigies of Quetzalcoatl, the feathered serpent god of gods.

Teotihuacán crumbled mysteriously around A.D. 650, leaving a host of former vassal states from what would be the Yucatán to Pacific Mexico free to tussle among themselves. These included Xochicalco, not far from present-day Taxco, and the great Zapotec center of Monte Albán farther southwest in Oaxaca. From its regal hilltop complex of stone pyramids, palaces, and ceremonial ball courts, Monte Albán reigned all-powerful until it, too, was abandoned around A.D. 1000.

The Living Quetzalcoatl

Xochicalco, however, was flourishing; its wise men tutored a young noble who was to become a living legend. In A.D. 947, Topiltzín (literally, Our Prince) was born. Records recite Topiltzín's achievements. He advanced astronomy, agriculture, and architecture and founded the city-state of Tula in A.D. 968, north of old Teotihuacán.

Contrary to the times, Topiltzín opposed human sacrifice; he taught that tortillas and butterflies, not human hearts, were the food of Quetzalcoatl. After ruling benignly for a generation, Topiltzín's name became so revered that the people began to know him as the living Quetzalcoatl, the plumed serpent-god incarnate.

Quetzalcoatl was not universally loved, however. Bloodthirsty local priests, desperate for human victims, tricked him with alcohol; he awoke groggily one morning in bed with his sister. Devastated by shame, Quetzalcoatl banished himself from Tula with a band of retainers. In A.D. 987, they headed east, toward Yucatán, leaving arrows shot through saplings, appearing like crosses, along their trail.

Although Quetzalcoatl sent word he would reclaim his kingdom during the 52-year cyclical calendar year of his birth, Ce Acatl, he never returned. Legends say that he sailed east and rose to heaven as the morning star.

The Aztecs

The civilization that Topiltzín founded, known to historians as the Toltec (People of Tula), was eventually eclipsed by others. These included the Aztecs, a collection of seven aggressive immigrant subtribes. Migrating from a mysterious western land of Aztlán (Place of the Herons) into the lake-filled valley that Mexico City now occupies, around A.D. 1300, the Aztecs survived by being forced to fight for every piece of ground they occupied. Within a century, the Aztecs' dominant tribe, whose members called themselves the México, had clawed its way to dominion over the Valley of Mexico. With the tribute labor that their emperors extracted from local vassal tribes, the México founded a magnificent capital, Tenochtitlán, on an island in the middle of the valley-lake. From there, Aztec armies, not unlike Roman legions, marched out and subdued kingdoms for hundreds of miles in all directions. They returned with the spoils of conquest: gold, brilliant feathers, precious jewels, and captives, whom they sacrificed by the thousands as food for their gods.

Among those gods they feared was Quetzalcoatl, who, legends said, was bearded and fair-skinned. It was a remarkable coincidence, therefore, that the bearded, fair-skinned Castilian Hernán Cortés landed on Mexico's eastern coast on April 22, 1519, during the year of Ce Acatl, exactly when Topiltzín, the Living Quetzalcoatl, had vowed he would return.

THE CONQUEST

Although a generation had elapsed since Columbus founded Spain's West Indian colonies, returns had been meager. Scarcity of gold and of native workers, most of whom had fallen victim to European diseases, turned adventurous Spanish eyes westward once again, toward rumored riches beyond the setting sun. Cortés, then only 34, had left his base in Cuba in February 1519, with an expedition of 11 small ships, 550 men, 16 horses, and a few small cannon. By the time he landed in Mexico, he was burdened by a mutinous crew. His men, mostly soldiers of fortune hearing stories of the great Aztec empire west beyond the mountains, had realized the impossible odds they faced and became restive.

Cortés, however, cut short any thoughts of mutiny by burning his ships. As he led his

---

MALINCHE

If it hadn't been for Doña Marina (whom he received as a gift from a local chief), Cortés might have been a mere historical footnote. Doña Marina, speaking both Spanish and native tongues, soon became Cortés' interpreter, go-between, and negotiator. She persuaded a number of important chiefs to ally themselves with Cortés against the Aztecs. Smart and opportunistic, Doña Marina was a crucial strategist in Cortés' deadly game of divide and conquer. She eventually bore Cortés a son and lived in honor and riches for many years, profiting greatly from the Spaniards' exploitation of the Mexicans.

Latter-day Mexicans do not honor her by the gentle title of Doña Marina, however. They call her Malinche, after the volcano – the ugly, treacherous scar on the Mexican landscape – and curse her as the female Judas who betrayed her country to the Spanish. *Malinchismo* has become known as the tendency to love things foreign and hate things Mexican.

---

grumbling but resigned band of adventurers toward the Aztec capital of Tenochtitlán, Cortés played Quetzalcoatl to the hilt, awing local chiefs. Coaxed by Doña Marina, Cortés's native translator, mistress, and confidante, local chiefs began to add their armies to Cortés's march against their Aztec overlords.

Moctezuma

While Cortés looked down upon the shimmering Valley of Mexico from the great divide between the volcanoes, Moctezuma, the emperor of the Aztecs, fretted about the returned "Quetzalcoatl." It is no wonder that the Spanish, approaching on horseback in their glittering, clanking armor, seemed divine to people who had never known steel, draft animals, or the wheel.

Inside the gates of the Venicelike island-city it was the Spaniards' turn to be dazzled: by gardens full of animals, gold, and palaces, and a great pyramid-enclosed square where tens of thousands of people bartered goods gathered from all over the empire. Tenochtitlán, with perhaps a quarter of a million people, was the great capital of an empire as large and as rich as any in Europe.

Moctezuma, the lord of that empire, was frozen by fear and foreboding, however. He quickly surrendered himself to Cortés's custody. After a few months, his subjects, enraged by Spanish brutality and Moctezuma's timidity, rioted and mortally wounded the emperor with a stone. With Moctezuma dead, the riot turned into a counterattack against the Spanish. On July 1, 1520, Cortés and his men, forced by the sheer numbers of rebellious Aztecs, retreated along a lake causeway from Tenochtitlán while carrying Moctezuma's treasure with them. Many of them drowned beneath their burdens of stolen Aztec gold, while others hacked a bloody path through thousands of screaming Aztec warriors to safety on the lakeshore.

That infamous night is now known as Noche Triste (Sad Night). Cortés, with half of his men dead, collapsed and wept beneath a great *ahuehuete* cypress tree (which still stands) in Mexico City.

A year later, reinforced by fresh soldiers, horses, a small fleet of armed sailboats, and 100,000 Indian allies, Cortés retook Tenochtitlán. The stubborn defenders, led by Cuauhtémoc, Moctezuma's nephew, fell by the tens of thousands beneath a smoking hail of Spanish grapeshot. The Aztecs, although weakened by smallpox, refused to surrender. Cortés found, to his dismay, that he had to destroy the city to take it.

The triumphant conquistador soon rebuilt it in the Spanish image: Cortés's cathedral and main public buildings—the present *zócalo*, central square of Mexico City—still rest upon the foundations of Moctezuma's pyramids.

NEW SPAIN

With the Valley of Mexico firmly in his grip, Cortés sent his lieutenants south, north, and west to extend the limits of a domain that eventually expanded to more than a dozen times the

POPULATION CHANGES IN NEW SPAIN		
GROUP	EARLY COLONIAL (1570)	LATE COLONIAL (1810)
peninsulares	6,600	15,000
criollos	11,000	1,100,000
mestizos	2,400	704,000
indígenas	3,340,000	3,700,000
negros	22,000	630,000

size of old Spain. He wrote his king, Charles V, "…the most suitable name for it would be New Spain of the Ocean Sea, and thus in the name of your Majesty I have christened it."

The Missionaries

While the conquistadores subjugated the local people, missionaries began arriving to teach, heal, and baptize them. A dozen Franciscan brothers impressed native Mexicans and conquistadores alike by trekking the entire 300-mile stony path from Veracruz to Mexico City in 1523.

The missionaries were a more humane counterbalance to the brutal conquistadores. Missionary authorities generally enjoyed a sympathetic ear from Charles V and his successors, who earnestly pursued Spain's Christian mission, especially when it dovetailed with their political and economic goals.

The King Takes Control

After 1525, the crown, through the Council of the Indies, began to wrest power away from Cortés and his conquistador lieutenants. Many of them had been granted rights of *encomienda*: taxes and labor of an Indian district. In exchange, the *encomendero*, who often enjoyed the status of feudal lord, pledged to look after the welfare and souls of his native Mexican charges.

From the king's point of view, though, tribute pesos collected by *encomenderos* translated into losses to the crown. Moreover, many *encomenderos* callously exploited their native wards for quick profit, sometimes selling them as slave labor in mines and on plantations. Such abuses, coupled with European-introduced diseases, began to reduce the indigenous population at an alarming rate.

After 1530, the king and his councillors began to realize that the native Mexicans were in peril, and without their labor, New Spain would vanish. They acted decisively: new laws would be instituted by a powerful new viceroy.

Don Antonio de Mendoza, the Count of Tendilla, arrived in 1535. He set the precedent for an unbroken line of more than 60 viceroys who, with few exceptions, served with distinction until independence in 1821. Village after village along Mendoza's winding route to Mexico City tried to outdo each other with flowers, music, bullfights, and feasts in his honor.

Mendoza wasted no time. He first got rid of the renegade opportunist (and Cortés's enemy) Nuño de Guzmán, whose private army, under the banner of colonization, had been laying waste to a broad western belt of Pacific Mexico, now Jalisco, Michoacán, Nayarit, and Sinaloa. (Guzmán, during his rapacious five years in Pacific Mexico, did, however, manage to found several towns: Guadalajara, Tepic, and Culiacán, among others.)

Hernán Cortés, the Marqués del Valle de Oaxaca

Cortés, meanwhile, had done very well for himself. He was one of Spain's richest men, with the title of Marqués del Valle de Oaxaca. He received 80,000 gold pesos a year from hundreds of thousands of native subjects on 25,000 square miles from the Valley of Mexico through the present states of Morelos, Guerrero, and Oaxaca.

Cortés continued tirelessly on a dozen projects: an expedition to Honduras, a young wife

whom he brought back from Spain, a palace (which still stands) in Cuernavaca, sugar mills, and dozens of churches, city halls, and presidios. He supervised the exploits of his lieutenants in Pacific Mexico: Francisco Orozco subdued the Zapotecs in Oaxaca, while Pedro de Alvarado accomplished the same with the Mixtecs, then continued south to conquer Guatemala. Meanwhile, Cristóbal de Olid subjugated the Purépecha in Michoacán, then moved down the Pacific Coast to Zacatula on the mouth of the Río Balsas. There (and at Acapulco and Tehuantepec), Cortés built ships to explore the Pacific. In 1535, he led an expedition to the Gulf of California (hence the Sea of Cortez) in a dreary six-month search for treasure along the Baja California coast.

Disgusted with Mendoza's meddling and discouraged by his failures, Cortés returned to Spain, where he got mired in lawsuits, a minor war, and his daughter's marital troubles, all of which led to his illness and death in 1547. Cortés's remains, according to his will, were eventually laid to rest in a vault at the Hospital de Jesús, which he founded in Mexico City.

COLONIAL MEXICO

In 1542, the Council of the Indies, through Viceroy Mendoza, promulgated its liberal New Laws of the Indies. The New Laws rested on high moral ground: The only Christian justification for New Spain was the souls and welfare of the indigenous people. Colonists had no right to exploit the natives. Slavery, therefore, was outlawed and *encomienda* rights were to revert to the crown at the death of the original grantees.

Despite uproar and near-rebellion by the colonists, Mendoza (and his successor in 1550, Don Luis Velasco) kept the lid on New Spain. Although some *encomenderos* held on to their rights into the 18th century, chattel slavery was abolished in Mexico, 300 years before Abraham Lincoln's Emancipation Proclamation.

Peace reigned in Mexico for 10 generations. Viceroys came and conscientiously served, new settlers arrived and put down roots, friars preached and built country churches, and the conquistadores' rich sons and daughters played while the native Mexicans worked.

The Role of the Church

The church somewhat moderated the natives' toil. On feast days, they would dress up and parade their patron saint through the streets and later eat their fill, drink *pulque,* and ooh and aah at the fireworks.

The church profited from the status quo, however. The biblical tithe—one-tenth of everything, from crops and livestock to rents and mining profits—filled church coffers. By 1800, the church owned half of Mexico. Moreover, the clergy (including lay church officers) and the military were doubly privileged. They enjoyed right of *fuero* (exemption from civil law) and could be prosecuted by ecclesiastical or military courts only.

Trade and Commerce

In trade and commerce, New Spain existed for the benefit of the mother country. Spaniards enjoyed absolute monopolies by virtue of the complete prohibition of foreign traders and goods. Colonists, as a result, paid dearly for oft-shoddy Spanish manufactures. The Casa de Contratación, the royal trade regulators, always ensured the colony's yearly balance of payments would result in deficit, which would be made up by bullion shipments from New Spain mines (from which the crown raked 10 percent off the top).

Despite its faults, New Spain lasted three times longer than the Aztec empire. By most contemporary measures, New Spain was prospering in 1800. The native labor force was completely subjugated and increasing, and the galleon fleets were carrying home growing tonnages of silver and gold worth millions. The authorities, however, failed to recognize that Mexico had changed in 300 years.

Criollos: The New Mexicans

Nearly three centuries of colonial rule gave rise to a burgeoning population of more than a million criollos—Mexican-born European descendants of Spanish colonists, many rich and educated—to whom power was denied.

High government, church, and military office had always been the preserve of a tiny but powerful minority of *peninsulares*—whites born in Spain. Criollos could only watch in disgust as unlettered, unskilled *peninsulares* (derisively called *gachupines*—wearers of spurs) were boosted to authority over them.

Although the criollos stood high above the *mestizo,* native Mexican, and *negro* underclasses, that seemed little compensation for the false smiles, the deep bows, and the costly bribes that *gachupines* demanded.

Mestizos, Indígenas, and African Mexicans

Upper-class luxury existed by virtue of the sweat of Mexico's mestizo, *indígena* (native, or indigenous), and *negro* laborers and servants. African slaves were imported in large numbers during the 17th century after typhus, smallpox, and measles epidemics had wiped out most of the native population. Although the African Mexicans contributed significantly (crafts, healing arts, dance, music, drums, and marimba), they had arrived last and experienced discrimination from everyone.

INDEPENDENCE

The chance for change came during the aftermath of the French invasion of Spain in 1808, when Napoléon Bonaparte replaced King Ferdinand VII with his brother Joseph on the Spanish throne. Most *peninsulares* backed the king; most criollos, however, inspired by the example of the recent American and French revolutions, talked and dreamed of independence. One such group, urged on by a firebrand parish priest, acted.

El Grito de Dolores

"¡Viva México! Death to the gachupines!" **Father Miguel Hidalgo,** shouting his impassioned *grito* from the church balcony in the Guanajuato town of Dolores on September 16, 1810, ignited action. A mostly *indígena,* machete-wielding army of 20,000 coalesced around

Hidalgo and his compatriots, Ignacio Allende and Juan Aldama. Their ragtag mob raged out of control through the Bajío, massacring hated *gachupines* and pillaging their homes.

Hidalgo advanced on Mexico City but, unnerved by stiff royalist resistance, retreated and regrouped around Guadalajara. His rebels, whose numbers had swollen to 80,000, were no match for a disciplined, 6,000-strong royalist force. Hidalgo (now "Generalisimo") fled north but was soon apprehended, defrocked, and executed. His head and those of his comrades—Aldama, Allende, and Mariano Jiménez—were hung from the walls of the Guanajuato granary (site of the slaughter of 138 *gachupines* by Hidalgo's army) for 10 years as grim reminders of the consequences of rebellion.

The 10-Year Struggle

Others carried on, however. A mestizo former student of Hidalgo, **José María Morelos,** led a revolutionary shadow government in the present states of Guerrero and Oaxaca for four years until he was apprehended and executed in December 1815.

Morelos's compatriot **Vicente Guerrero** continued the fight, joining forces with criollo royalist **Brigadier Agustín de Iturbide.** Their Plan de Iguala promised "Three Guarantees"—the renowned Trigarantes: Independence, Catholicism, and Equality—which their army (commanded by Iturbide, of course) would enforce. On September 21, 1821, Iturbide rode triumphantly into Mexico City at the head of his army of Trigarantes. Mexico was independent at last.

Independence, however, solved little except to expel the *peninsulares.* With an illiterate populace and no experience in self-government, Mexicans began a tragic 40-year love affair with a fantasy: the general on the white horse, the gold-braided hero who could save them from themselves.

The Rise and Fall of Agustín I

Iturbide—crowned Agustín I by the bishop of Guadalajara on July 21, 1822—soon lost his charisma. In a pattern that became sadly predictable for generations of topsy-turvy Mexican politics, an ambitious garrison commander issued a *pronunciamiento,* a declaration against the government. Supporting *pronunciamientos* followed, and old revolutionary heroes Guerrero, Guadalupe Victoria, and Nicolás Bravo endorsed a "plan"—the Plan of Casa Mata (not unlike Iturbide's previous Plan de Iguala)—dethroning Iturbide in favor of a republic. Iturbide, his braid tattered and brass tarnished, abdicated in February 1823.

Antonio López de Santa Anna, the eager 28-year-old military commander of Veracruz, whose *pronunciamiento* had pushed Iturbide from his white horse, maneuvered to gradually replace him. Throughout the late 1820s the government teetered on the edge of disaster as the presidency bounced between liberal and conservative hands six times in three years. During the last of these upheavals, Santa Anna jumped to prominence by defeating an abortive Spanish attempt at counterrevolution at Tampico in 1829. "The Victor of Tampico," people called Santa Anna.

The Disastrous Era of Santa Anna

In 1833, the government was bankrupt; mobs demanded the ouster of conservative President Anastasio Bustamante, who had executed the rebellious old revolutionary hero Vicente Guerrero. Santa Anna issued a *pronunciamiento* against Bustamante; Congress obliged, elevating Santa Anna to "Liberator of the Republic" and "Conqueror of the Spaniards," and naming him president in March 1833.

Santa Anna would pop in and out of the presidency like a jack-in-the-box 10 more times before 1855. First, he foolishly lost Texas to rebellious Anglo settlers in 1836. He later lost his leg (which was buried with full military honors) fighting the emperor of France.

Santa Anna's greatest debacle, however, was to declare war on the United States with just 1,839 pesos in the treasury. With his forces poised to defend Mexico City against a relatively small 10,000-man American invasion force, Santa Anna inexplicably withdrew. United States Marines surged into the "Halls of Montezuma," Chapultepec Castle, where Mexico's six beloved Niños Héroes cadets fell in the losing cause on September 13, 1847.

In the subsequent treaty of Guadalupe Hidalgo, Mexico lost nearly half of its territory—the present states of New Mexico, Arizona, California, Nevada, Utah, and Colorado—to the United States.

For Santa Anna, however, enough was not enough. Called back as president for the last and 11th time in 1853, Santa Anna, now "His Most Serene Highness," financed his final extravagances by selling off a part of southern New Mexico and Arizona, in what was known as the Gadsden Purchase, for $10 million.

REFORM, CIVIL WAR, AND INTERVENTION

Mexican leaders finally saw the light and exiled Santa Anna forever. While conservatives searched for a king to replace Santa Anna, liberals (whom Santa Anna had kept in jail) plunged ahead with three controversial reform laws: the Ley Juárez, Ley Lerdo, and Ley Iglesias. These *reformas,* augmented by a new Constitution of 1857, directly attacked the privilege and power of Mexico's landlords, clergy, and generals: Ley Juárez abolished *fueros,* the separate military and church courts; Ley Lerdo forbade excess corporate (read: church) landholdings; and Ley Iglesias reduced or transferred most church power to the state.

Conservative generals, priests, and *hacendados* (landholders), along with their mestizo and *indígena* followers, revolted. The resulting War of the Reform (not unlike the U.S. Civil War) ravaged the countryside for three long years until the victorious liberal army paraded triumphantly in Mexico City on New Year's Day 1861.

Juárez and Maximilian

Benito Juárez, the leading *reformista,* had won the day. Juárez's similarity to his contemporary, Abraham Lincoln, is legend: Juárez had risen from humble Zapotec origins to become a lawyer, a champion of justice, and the president who held his country together during a terrible civil war. Like Lincoln's, Juárez's triumph didn't last long.

Imperial France invaded Mexico in January 1862, initiating a bloody five-year imperialist struggle, infamously known as the **French Intervention.** After two costly years, the French forces pushed Juárez's liberal army into the hills and installed the king whom Mexican conservatives thought the country needed. Austrian Archduke Maximilian and his wife, Carlota, the very models of modern Catholic monarchs, were crowned emperor and empress of Mexico in June 1864.

The naive Emperor Maximilian I was surprised that some of his subjects resented his presence. Meanwhile, Juárez refused to yield, stubbornly performing his constitutional duties in a somber black carriage one jump ahead of the French occupying army. The climax came in May 1867, when liberal forces besieged and defeated Maximilian's army at Querétaro. Juárez, giving no quarter, sternly ordered Maximilian's execution by firing squad on June 19, 1867.

RECONSTRUCTION AND THE PORFIRIATO

Juárez worked day and night at the double task of reconstruction and reform. He won reelection but died, exhausted, in 1871. The death of Juárez, the stoic partisan of reform, signaled hope to Mexico's conservatives. They soon got their wish: **General Don Porfirio Díaz,** the "Coming Man," was elected president in 1876.

Pax Porfiriana

Don Porfirio is often remembered wistfully, as old Italians remember Mussolini: "He was a bit rough, but, dammit, at least he made the trains run on time."

Although Porfirio Díaz's humble Oaxaca mestizo origins were not unlike Juárez's, Díaz was not a democrat: When he was a general, his officers often took no captives; when he was president, his country police, the *rurales,* shot prisoners in the act of "trying to escape."

Order and progress, in that sequence,

Revolutionary Generals Alvaro Obregón and Pancho Villa meet U.S. General John "Blackjack" Pershing, circa 1913.

ruled Mexico for 34 years. Foreign investment flowed into the country; new railroads brought the products of shiny factories, mines, and farms to modernized Gulf and Pacific ports. Mexico balanced its budget, repaid foreign debt, and became a respected member of the family of nations.

The human price was high. Don Porfirio allowed more than 100 million acres—one-fifth of Mexico's land area (including most of the arable land)—to be acquired by wealthy Mexicans and foreigners. Poor Mexicans suffered the most. By 1910, 90 percent of the *indígenas* had lost their traditional communal land. In the spring of 1910, a smug, now-cultured, and elderly Don Porfirio anticipated with relish the centennial of Hidalgo's Grito de Dolores.

REVOLUTION AND STABILIZATION
¡No Reelección!
Porfirio Díaz himself had first campaigned on this slogan. It expressed the idea that the president should step down after one term. Although Díaz had stepped down once in 1880, he had gotten himself reelected for 26 consecutive years. In 1910, **Francisco I. Madero,** a short, squeaky-voiced son of rich landowners, opposed Díaz under the same banner.

Although Díaz had jailed him before the election, Madero refused to quit campaigning. From a safe platform in the United States, he called for a revolution to begin on November 20.

Villa and Zapata
Not much happened, but soon the millions of poor Mexicans who had been going to bed hungry began to stir. In Chihuahua, followers of Francisco (Pancho) Villa, an erstwhile ranch hand, miner, peddler, and cattle rustler, began attacking the *rurales,* dynamiting railroads, and raiding towns. Meanwhile, in the south, horse trader, farmer, and minor official Emiliano Zapata and his *indígena* guerrillas were terrorizing rich *hacendados* and forcibly recovering stolen ancestral village lands. Zapata's movement gained steam and by May had taken the Morelos state capital, Cuernavaca.

EMILIANO ZAPATA

Although the multitude of streets, towns, *ejidos,* and monuments named after Emiliano Zapata (1879-1919) mark him as a true national hero, his name is not free of controversy. Although his Zapatista revolutionary guerrillas, often crude and cruel, committed their share of atrocities, all the warring factions of the 1910 Revolution share the same guilt.

Emiliano Zapata's legacy nevertheless remains, embedded in both Mexican law and the hearts and minds of all Mexicans who have benefited from his selfless struggle to realize his broad social vision.

For Emiliano Zapata, achievement didn't come easy. He was born of poor mestizo parents, in Anenecuilco (ah-nay-nay-koo-IL-koh), Morelos, on Aug. 8, 1879. The modest thatched-roof home of his birth still stands, restored as a museum, three miles south of the main market town of Cuautla. Young Emiliano, orphaned when he was still a child, grew up in the care of relatives. As a youth he experienced firsthand the results of then-president Porfirio Díaz's land policies, which resulted in ancestral village fields' being gobbled up, both legally and illegally, by rich *hacendados.* Consequently, by 1900, thousands of Zapata's campesino neighbors were toiling as virtual serfs on the very land that had been stolen from them.

When he was a young man, Emiliano's intelligence, blunt honesty, and natural leadership earned him considerable community standing. Although determined to correct local injustices, he started out by working within the established order, accepting the presidency of the Anenecuilco municipal government. When conciliatory measures to address the local campesinos' grievances against the landholders failed, Zapata took justice into his own hands and organized posses to forcibly eject the offending *hacendados.* This earned Zapata the ire of the Díaz government, which sent Zapata fleeing for his life into the mountains with his guerrilla band of followers.

At the same time, in late 1910, Francisco Madero had been agitating for revolution from Texas. Zapata sent messengers north and liked what they told him about Madero. When, in early 1911, Madero crossed the Rio Grande and joined Pancho Villa's forces to capture Ciudad Juárez, Zapata's growing guerrilla regiment moved quickly, seizing Cuernavaca, the Morelos state capital, by mid-May.

Pressed on all sides, Díaz's army and government quickly fell apart, and on May 25,

---

Meanwhile, Madero crossed the Río Grande and joined with Villa's forces, who took Ciudad Juárez.

The *federales,* government army troops, began deserting in droves, and on May 25, 1911, Díaz submitted his resignation.

As Madero's deputy, **General Victoriano Huerta,** put Díaz on his ship of exile in Veracruz, Díaz confided, "Madero has unleashed a tiger. Now let's see if he can control it."

The Fighting Continues

Emiliano Zapata, it turned out, was the tiger Madero had unleashed. Meeting with Madero in Mexico City, Zapata fumed over Madero's go-slow approach to the "agrarian problem," as Madero termed it. By November, Zapata had denounced Madero. *"¡Tierra y Libertad!"* ("Land and Liberty!") the Zapatistas cried, as Madero's support faded. Federal troops in Mexico City rebelled; Huerta forced Madero to resign on February 18, 1913, put him under house arrest, and then had him murdered four days later.

The rum-swilling Huerta ruled like a Chicago mobster; general rebellion, led by the "Big Four"—Villa, Alvaro Obregón, and Venustiano Carranza in the north, and Zapata in the south—soon broke out. Pressed by the rebels and refused U.S. recognition, Huerta fled into exile in July 1914.

The Constitution of 1917

Fighting sputtered on for three years as authority

1911, Díaz resigned. As Madero, Pancho Villa, and (now General) Zapata rode in triumph into Mexico City, Díaz fled into exile in France.

Immediately, however, Zapata began quarreling with Madero's cautious, legalistic approach toward the problem of land and justice for Zapata's poor followers. "The land belongs to only those who work with their hands," Zapata asserted. Exasperated with Madero and his elite advisers (Zapata could barely read), Zapata stormed out of Mexico City in front of his Zapatista cavalry, openly breaking with Madero in November 1911.

In an attempt at conciliation, Madero came to Morelos to persuade Zapata to lay down his arms. Before the proceedings were over, however, federal troops, under orders from Madero's treacherous military commander, Victoriano Huerta, invaded Morelos. Fed up, Zapata rearmed his troops, and despite recommendations that he execute Madero on the spot, sent him packing back to Mexico City.

So, for seven more bloody years, Zapata's guerrillas, which by 1914 had grown to a formidable "Liberating Army of the South," battled government forces in Morelos, Guerrero, Puebla, and Oaxaca.

Despite the continued killing and chaos, and his personal exhaustion, Zapata remained incorruptibly dedicated to his credo, codified as the famous Plan of Ayala, that declared "¡Tierra y Libertad!" ("Land and Liberty!") for all must be the overriding goal of any just Mexican government.

Finally, by 1919, "Constitutionalist" forces, under the leadership of "First Chief" Venustiano Carranza and General Alvaro Obregón, had promulgated a constitution and, from Mexico City, controlled most of Mexico. Zapata, who never trusted the Constitutionalists, despite their liberal Constitution of 1917, remained a thorn in Carranza's side. Carranza got one of his officers, Colonel Jesús Guajardo, to feign surrender of his entire well-equipped regiment to Zapata, at Chinameca Hacienda, south of Cuautla. Zapata, desperate for supplies and reinforcements, fell for the bait, and was gunned down by a platoon of snipers inside the Hacienda on April 10, 1919.

Although Constitutionalist soldiers displayed a badly shot-up body on the Cuatla plaza that they claimed to be Zapata, some witnesses believed otherwise. Rumors persisted for years that somewhere, Emiliano Zapata lived on; and that when the people needed him again, he would return.

see-sawed between revolutionary factions. Finally, Carranza, who controlled most of the country by 1917, got a convention together in Querétaro to formulate political and social goals. The resulting Constitution of 1917, while restating most ideas of the *reformistas'* 1857 constitution, additionally prescribed a single four-year presidential term, labor reform, and subordinated private ownership to public interest. Every village had a right to communal *ejido* land, and subsoil wealth could never be sold away to the highest bidder.

The Constitution of 1917 was a revolutionary expression of national aspirations, and, in retrospect, represented a social and political agenda for the entire 20th century. In modified form, it has lasted to the present day.

Obregón Stabilizes Mexico

On December 1, 1920, General Alvaro Obregón legally assumed the presidency of a Mexico still bleeding from 10 years of civil war. Although a seasoned revolutionary, Obregón was also a pragmatist who recognized peace was necessary to implement the goals of the revolution. In four years, his government pacified local uprisings, disarmed a swarm of warlords, executed hundreds of *bandidos*, obtained U.S. diplomatic recognition, assuaged the worst fears of the clergy and landowners, and began land reform.

All this set the stage for the work of **Plutarco Elías Calles,** Obregón's Minister of Gobernación (Interior) and handpicked successor, who won the 1924 election. Aided by peace, Mexico returned to a semblance of prosperity. Calles brought the army under civilian control, balanced the budget, and shifted Mexico's social revolution into high gear. New clinics vaccinated millions against smallpox, new dams irrigated thousands of previously dry acres, and campesinos received millions of acres of redistributed land.

By single-mindedly enforcing the pro-agrarian, pro-labor, and anti-clerical articles of the 1917 constitution, Calles made many influential enemies. Infuriated by the government's confiscation of church property, closing of monasteries, and deportation of hundreds of foreign priests and nuns, the clergy refused to perform marriages, baptisms, and last rites. As members of the Cristero movement, militant Catholics crying *"¡Viva Cristo Rey!"* armed themselves, torching public schools and government property and murdering hundreds of innocent bystanders.

Simultaneously, Calles threatened foreign oil companies, demanding they exchange their titles for 50-year leases. A moderate Mexican supreme court decision over the oil issue and the skillful arbitration of U.S. Ambassador Dwight Morrow smoothed over both the oil and church troubles by the end of Calles's term.

Calles, who started out brimming with revolutionary fervor and populist zeal, became increasingly conservative and dictatorial. Although he bowed out peaceably in favor of Obregón (the constitution had been amended to allow one six-year nonsuccessive term), Obregón was assassinated two weeks after his election in 1928. Calles continued to rule for six more years through three puppet-presidents: Emilio Portes Gil (1928–1930), Pascual Ortíz Rubio (1930–1932), and Abelardo Rodríguez (1932–1934).

For the 14 years since 1920, the revolution had first waxed, then waned. With a cash surplus in 1930, Mexico skidded into debt as the Great Depression deepened and Calles and his cronies lined their pockets. In blessing his minister of war, General Lázaro Cárdenas, for the 1934 presidential election, Calles expected more of the same.

Lázaro Cárdenas, President of the People

The 40-year-old former governor of Michoacán immediately set his own agenda, however. Cárdenas worked tirelessly to fulfill the social prescriptions of the revolution. As morning-coated diplomats and cabinet ministers fretted in his outer office, Cárdenas ushered in delegations of campesinos and factory workers and sympathetically listened to their problems.

In his six years of rule, Cárdenas moved public education and health forward on a broad front, supported strong labor unions, and redistributed 49 million acres of farmland, more than any president before or since.

Cárdenas's resolute enforcement of the constitution's Artículo 123 brought him the most renown. Under this pro-labor law, the government turned over a host of private companies to employee ownership and, on March 18, 1938, expropriated all foreign oil corporations.

The oil corporations, most of which were British, were not blameless. They had sorely neglected the wages, health, and welfare of their workers while ruthlessly taking the law into their own hands with private police forces. Although Standard Oil cried foul, U.S. President Franklin Roosevelt did not intervene. Through negotiation and due process, the U.S. companies eventually were compensated with $24 million plus 3 percent interest. In the wake of the expropriation, President Cárdenas created Petróleos Mexicanos (Pemex), the national oil corporation that continues to run all Mexican oil and gas operations.

Manuel Ávila Camacho

Manuel Ávila Camacho, elected in 1940, was the last general to be president of Mexico. His administration ushered in a gradual shift of Mexican politics, government, and foreign policy as Mexico allied itself with the U.S. cause during World War II. Foreign tourism, initially promoted by the Cárdenas administration, ballooned. Good feelings surged as Franklin Roosevelt became the first U.S. president to officially cross the Río Grande when he met with Camacho in Monterrey in April 1943.

In both word and deed, moderation and evolution guided President Camacho's policies. *"Soy creente"* ("I am a believer"), he declared to the Catholics of Mexico as he worked earnestly to bridge Mexico's serious church-state schism. Land-policy emphasis shifted from redistribution to utilization as new dams and canals irrigated hundreds of thousands of previously arid acres. On one hand, Camacho established IMSS (Instituto Mexicano de Seguro Social), and on the other trimmed the power of labor unions.

As World War II moved toward its 1945 conclusion, both the United States and Mexico were enjoying the benefits of four years of governmental and military cooperation and mutual trade in the form of a mountain of strategic minerals that had moved north in exchange for a similar mountain of U.S. factories that moved south.

CONTEMPORARY MEXICO
The Mature Revolution

During the decades after World War II, beginning with moderate President **Miguel Alemán** (1946–1952), Mexican politicians gradually honed their skills of consensus and compromise as their middle-aged revolution bubbled along under liberal presidents and sputtered haltingly under conservatives. Doctrine required of all politicians, regardless of stripe, that they be "revolutionary" enough to be included beneath the banner of the PRI (Partido Revolucionario Institucional—the Institutional Revolutionary Party), Mexico's dominant political party.

Mexico's revolution hasn't been very revolutionary about women's rights, however. The PRI didn't get around to giving Mexican women, millions of whom fought and died alongside their men during the revolution, the right to vote until 1953.

Adolfo Ruíz Cortínes, Alemán's secretary of the interior, was elected overwhelmingly in 1952. He fought the corruption that had crept into government under his predecessor, continued land reform, increased agricultural production, built new ports, eradicated malaria, and opened several automobile assembly plants.

Women, voting for the first time in a national election, kept the PRI in power by electing liberal **Adolfo López Mateos** in 1958. Resembling Lázaro Cárdenas in social policy, López Mateos redistributed 40 million acres of farmland, forced automakers to use 60 percent domestic components, built thousands of new schools, and distributed hundreds of millions of new textbooks. *"La electricidad es nuestra"* ("Electricity is ours"), Mateos declared as he nationalized foreign power companies in 1962.

Despite his left-leaning social agenda, unions were restive under López Mateos. Protesting inflation, workers struck; the government retaliated, arresting Demetrios Vallejo, the railway union head, and renowned muralist David Siqueiros, former communist party secretary.

Despite the troubles, López Mateos climaxed his presidency gracefully in 1964 as he opened the celebrated National Museum of Anthropology, appropriately located in Chapultepec Park, where the Aztecs had first settled 20 generations earlier.

In 1964, as several times before, the outgoing president's interior secretary succeeded his former chief. Dour, conservative **Gustavo Díaz Ordaz** immediately clashed with liberals, labor, and students. The pot boiled over just before the 1968 Mexico City Olympics. Reacting to a student rebellion, the army occupied the National University; shortly afterward, on Oct. 2, government forces opened fire with machine guns on a downtown protest, killing and wounding hundreds of demonstrators.

Maquiladoras

Despite its serious internal troubles, Mexico's relations with the United States were cordial. President Lyndon Johnson visited and unveiled a statue of Abraham Lincoln in Mexico City. Later, Díaz Ordaz met with President Richard Nixon in Puerto Vallarta.

Meanwhile, bilateral negotiations produced the **Border Industrialization Program.** Within a 12-mile strip south of the U.S.-Mexico border, foreign companies could assemble duty-free parts into finished goods and export them without any duties on either side. Within a dozen years, a swarm of such plants, called maquiladoras, were humming as hundreds of thousands of Mexican workers assembled and exported billions of dollars worth of shiny consumer goods—electronics, clothes, furniture, pharmaceuticals, and toys—worldwide.

Concurrently, in Mexico's interior, Díaz Ordaz pushed Mexico's industrialization ahead full steam. Foreign money financed hundreds of new plants and factories. Primary among these was the giant Las Truchas steel plant at the new industrial port and town of Lázaro Cárdenas at the Pacific mouth of the Río Balsas.

Discovery, in 1974, of gigantic new oil and gas reserves along Mexico's Gulf Coast added fuel to Mexico's already rapid industrial expansion. During the late 1970s and early 1980s billions in foreign investment, lured by Mexico's oil earnings, financed other major developments—factories, hotels, power plants, roads, airports—all over the country.

Economic Trouble of the 1980s

The negative side to these expensive projects was the huge dollar debt required to finance them. President **Luis Echeverría Alvarez** (1970–1976), diverted by his interest in international affairs, passed Mexico's burgeoning financial deficit to his successor, **José López Portillo.** As feared by some experts, a world petroleum glut during the early 1980s burst Mexico's ballooning oil bubble and plunged the country into financial crisis. When the 1982 interest came due on its foreign debt, Mexico's largest holding company couldn't pay the $2.3 billion owed. The peso plummeted more than fivefold, to 150 per U.S. dollar. At the same time, prices doubled every year.

But by the mid-1980s, President **Miguel de la Madrid** (1982–1988) was straining to get Mexico's economic house in order. He sliced government and raised taxes, asking rich and poor alike to tighten their belts. Despite getting foreign bankers to reschedule Mexico's debt, de la Madrid couldn't stop inflation. Prices skyrocketed as the peso deflated to 2,500 per U.S. dollar, becoming one of the world's most devalued currencies by 1988.

Salinas de Gortari and NAFTA

Public disgust with official corruption led to significant opposition during the 1988 presidential election. Billionaire National Action Party (Partido Acción Nacional, or PAN) candidate Michael Clothier and liberal Democratic Revolutionary Party (Partido Revolucionario Democratico, or PRD) candidate Cuauhtémoc Cárdenas ran against the PRI's Harvard-educated technocrat Carlos Salinas de Gortari. The vote was split so evenly that all three candidates claimed victory. Although Salinas eventually won the election, his showing, barely half of the vote, was the worst ever for a PRI president.

Salinas, however, seemed to be Mexico's "Coming Man" of the 1990s. His major achievement—despite significant national opposition—was the North American Free Trade Agreement (NAFTA), which he, U.S. President George Bush, and Canadian Prime Minister Brian Mulrooney negotiated in 1992.

Rebellion, Political Assassination, and Reconciliation

On the very day in early January 1994 that NAFTA took effect, rebellion broke out in the poor, remote state of Chiapas. A small but well-disciplined campesino force, calling itself Ejército Zapatista Liberación Nacional (Zapatista National Liberation Army—EZLN—or "Zapatistas") captured a number of provincial towns and held the former governor of Chiapas hostage.

To further complicate matters, Mexico's already tense 1994 drama veered toward tragedy. While Salinas de Gortari's chief negotiator, Manuel Camacho Solis, was attempting to iron out a settlement with the Zapatista rebels, PRI presidential candidate Luis Donaldo Colosio, Salinas's handpicked successor, was gunned down just months before the August balloting. However, instead of disintegrating, the nation united in grief; opposition candidates eulogized their fallen former opponent and later earnestly engaged his replacement, stolid technocrat **Ernesto Zedillo,** in Mexico's first presidential election debate.

In a closely watched election unmarred by irregularities, Zedillo piled up a solid plurality against his PAN and PRD opponents. By perpetuating the PRI's 65-year hold on the presidency, the electorate had again opted for the PRI's familiar although imperfect middle-aged revolution.

New Crisis, New Recovery

Zedillo, however, had little time to savor his victory. Right away he had to face the consequences of his predecessor's shabby fiscal policies. Less than a month after he took office, the peso crashed, losing a third of its value just before Christmas 1994. A month later, Mexican financial institutions, their dollar debt having nearly doubled in a month, were in danger of defaulting on their obligations to international investors. To stave off a worldwide financial panic, U.S. President Bill Clinton, in February 1995, secured an unprecedented multibillion-dollar loan package for Mexico, guaranteed by U.S. and international institutions.

Although disaster was temporarily averted, the cure for the country's ills was another painful round of inflation and belt-tightening for poor Mexicans. During 1995, inflation soared; more and more families became unable to purchase staple foods and basic medicines. Malnutrition, and a resurgence of Third World diseases such as cholera and dengue fever, menaced the countryside.

At the same time, Mexico's equally serious political ills seemed to defy cure. Raul Salinas de Gortari, an important PRI party official and the former president's brother, was arrested for money laundering and political assassination. As popular sentiment began to implicate Carlos Salinas de Gortari himself, the former president fled Mexico to an undisclosed location.

Mexican democracy got a much-needed boost when notorious Guerrero governor Ruben Figueroa, who had tried to cover up a bloody massacre of campesinos by police with a bogus videotape, was forced from office. At the same time, the Zedillo government gained momentum in addressing the Zapatistas' grievances in Chiapas, even as it decreased federal military presence, built new rural electrification networks, and refurbished health clinics. Moreover, Mexico's economy began to improve. By mid-1996, inflation had slowed to a 20 percent annual rate, investment dollars were flowing back into Mexico, the peso had stabilized at about 7.5 to the U.S. dollar, and Mexico had paid back half the borrowed U.S. bailout money.

Zedillo's Political Reforms

In the political arena, although the justice system generally left much to be desired, a pair of unprecedented events signaled an increasingly open political system. In the 1997 congressional elections, voters elected a host of opposition candidates, depriving the PRI of an absolute congressional majority for the first time since 1929. A year later, in early 1998, Mexicans were participating in their country's first primary elections—in which voters, instead of politicians, chose party candidates.

Although President Zedillo had had a rough ride, he entered the twilight of his 1994–2000 term able to take credit for an improved economy, some genuine political reforms, and relative peace in the countryside. The election of 2000 revealed, however, that the Mexican people were not satisfied.

End of an Era: Vicente Fox Unseats the PRI

During 1998 and 1999 the focal point of opposition to the PRI's three-generation rule had been shifting to relative newcomer Vicente Fox, former President of Coca-Cola Mexico and clean former PAN governor of Guanajuato.

Fox, who had announced his candidacy for president two years before the election, seemed an unlikely challenger. After all, the minority PAN had always been the party of wealthy businessmen and the conservative Catholic right. But blunt-talking, six-foot-five Fox, who sometimes campaigned in cowboy boots and a ten-gallon hat, preached populist themes of coalition building and "inclusion." He backed up his talk by carrying his campaign to hardscrabble city *barrios,* dirt-poor country villages and traditional outsider groups, such as Jews.

In a relatively orderly and fair July 2, 2000, election, Fox decisively defeated his PRI opponent Fernando Labastida, 42 percent to 38 percent, while PRD candidate Cárdenas polled a feeble 17 percent. Fox's win also swept a PAN plurality (223/209/57) into the 500-seat Chamber of Deputies lower house (although the Senate remained PRI-dominated).

Nevertheless, in pushing the PRI from the all-powerful presidency after 71 consecutive years of domination, Fox had ushered Mexico into a new, more democratic era.

Despite stinging criticism from his own ranks, **President Zedillo,** whom historians were already praising as the real hero behind Mexico's new democracy, made an unprecedented early appeal for all Mexicans to unite behind Fox.

On the eve of his December 1, 2000, inauguration, Mexicans awaited Fox's speech with hopeful anticipation. He did not disappoint them. Although acknowledging that he couldn't completely reverse 71 years of PRI entrenchment in his one six-year term, he vowed to ride the crest of reform, by revamping the tax system and reducing poverty by 30 percent, by creating a million new jobs a year through new private investment in electricity and oil production and forming a new common market with Latin America, the United States, and Canada.

Vicente Fox, President of Mexico

Wasting little time getting started, President Fox first headed to Chiapas to confer with indigenous community leaders. Along the way, he shut down Chiapas military bases and removed dozens of military roadblocks. Back in Mexico City, he sent the long-delayed **peace plan,** including the **indigenous bill of rights,** to Congress. Zapatista rebels responded by journeying en masse from Chiapas to Mexico City, where, in their black masks, they addressed Congress, arguing for indigenous rights. Although by mid-2001, Congress had passed a modified version of the negotiated

settlement, indigenous leaders condemned the legislation plan as unacceptable, while proponents claimed it was the best possible compromise between the Zapatistas' demands and the existing Mexican constitution.

On the positive side, by mid-2002, Vicente Fox could claim credit for cracking down on corruption and putting drug lords in jail, negotiating a key immigration agreement with the United States, clamping down on inflation, and attracting a record pile of foreign investment dollars.

Furthermore, Fox continued to pry open the door to democracy in Mexico. In May 2002, he signed Mexico's first **freedom of information act,** entitling citizens to timely copies of all public documents from federal agencies. Moreover, Fox's long-promised **"Transparency Commission"** was taking shape. In July 2002, federal attorneys were taking unprecedented action. They were questioning a list of 74 former government officials, including ex-President Luis Echeverría, about their roles in government transgressions, notably political murders and the University of Mexico massacres during the 1960s and 1970s.

But Mexico's economy, reflecting the U.S. economic slowdown, began to sour in 2001, losing half a million jobs and cutting annual growth to 2.5 percent, down from the 4.5 percent that the government had predicted.

In the July 7, 2003, congressional elections, voters took their frustrations out on the PAN and gave its plurality in the Chamber of Deputies to the PRI. When the dust settled, the PRI total had risen to 225 seats, while the PAN had slipped to 153. The biggest winner, however, was the PRD, which gained more than 40 seats, to a total of about 100.

Fortunately however, by 2004, the Mexican economy, reflecting that of the United States, was beginning to turn around. Exports to the United States soared to record levels in the spring of 2004.

Despite some modest gains, by 2005, with his term nearly spent, critics were increasingly claiming that Fox was a lame-duck president running out of time to accomplish what he promised. But Fox, despite a hostile congress that almost continuously blocked his legislative proposals, could claim some significant accomplishments. During his first four years, he had pushed through significant gains in indigenous rights, national reconciliation and government transparency, drug enforcement, U.S.-Mexico immigration policy, social security reform, housing, and education. Moreover, in addition to nurturing a recovering economy, Fox had kept the peso strong against the dollar and clamped the lid on inflation.

The Election of 2006

During the first half of 2006, as Vicente Fox was winding down his presidency, Mexicans were occupied by the campaign to elect his successor. Most headlines went to the PRD candidate, the mercurial leftist-populist Andres Manuel López Obrador, former mayor of Mexico City. Trying hard not to be upstaged was the steady, no-nonsense PAN candidate, Harvard-educated centrist-conservative Felipe Calderón, a leading light of President Fox's cabinet. Veteran politico Robert Madrazo carried the banner for what appeared to be a resurgent PRI. But after a half year of mudslinging and angry debates over the major election issues of drug-related mayhem, killings and kidnappings, police and judicial corruption and inefficiency, and lack of jobs for impoverished workers, Madrazo's initial popularity faded, narrowing the contest to a bitter neck-and-neck race between Calderón and Obrador.

On Sunday, July 2, 2006, 42 million Mexicans cast their ballots. In an intensely monitored election marred by very few irregularities, unofficial returns indicated that voters had awarded Calderón a paper-thin plurality. Four days later, after all returns were certified, the Federal Electoral Institute announced the official vote tally: only about 22 percent for Madrazo, with the remaining lion's share divided nearly evenly, with 38.7 percent going to Obrador and 39.3 percent for Calderón. This result, the Federal Electoral Institute ruled, was too close to declare a winner without a recount.

Besides the close Obrador-Calderón vote,

the election results revealed much more. Not only were the 32 electoral entitites (31 states and the Federal District) divided equally, with 16 going for Obrador, and 16 for Calderón, the vote reflected a nearly complete north-south political schism, with virtually all of the 16 PAN-majority states forming a solid northern bloc, while the 16 PRD-voting states did the same in the south. Furthermore, the election appeared to signal a collapse of PRI power, with no state (nor the Federal District) giving either a majority or a plurality to Madrazo.

A howl of protest came from Obrador and his PRD followers after the election results were announced. They claimed PAN had stolen the election. They jammed the Federal Electoral Institute with lawsuits, alleging a host of irregularities and ballot stuffing incidents, and demanding a complete recount of all 42 million ballots. They yelled, marched, blocked Mexico City's Paseo de la Reforma, and camped in the *zócalo* central plaza.

Election Aftermath

After weeks of hearing the PRD arguments for (and PAN counterarguments against) ballot fraud, the Federal Election Institute announced (in agreement with virtually all independent observers) that the election was nearly completely clean. The recount would be limited only to the questionable ballots. These amounted to about 9 percent of the total, all mostly in the Calderón-majority states.

For a month, the questionable ballots were gathered and examined exhaustively by the Supreme Election Tribunal, an impeccable panel of federal judges. They found that the recount shifted the margin by only a few thousand votes away from Calderón to Obrador. On Sept. 6, the Federal Electoral Institute declared Calderón the president-elect by a margin of about 240,000 votes, or a bit more than one-half of a percent of the total vote.

Obrador and his supporters screamed foul even louder and threatened to ignore Calderón and/or block his presidency. On Sept. 16, Mexican independence day, Obrador convened hundreds of thousands of his supporters in the Mexico City Zócalo that declared him the legitimate president. In the succeeding days, the PRD's obstructionist tactics reached an outrageous climax when a handful of PRD senators and deputies made such a ruckus during a joint session of the federal legislature that they prevented the President of Mexico, for the first time in history, from delivering his annual state of the union address. Mexican voters, watching the PRD's melodramatic tactics on television, began, in increasing numbers, to say enough was enough. National polls showed that more than two-thirds of Mexicans disapproved of the PRD's protest behavior. By October, many of the PRD's leaders agreed, further isolating Obrador and his rump government to a footnote in Mexican history. Mexico's new democracy, given a gentle shove forward ten years earlier by President Ernesto Zedillo and nurtured for six more years by Vicente Fox, seemed to have again surmounted a difficult crisis and emerged stronger.

An important result of the 2006 election—initially overshadowed by the intense struggle over the presidential vote, but potentially crucial—was the federal legislative vote, in which PAN emerged as the biggest winner by far. The final results showed that voters had given PAN candidates strong pluralities of 206/127/106 over the PRD and PRI, respectively, in the 500-seat federal Chamber of Deputies, and 52/29/33 in the 128-seat Senate, with the remainder of seats scattered among minor parties. This result may bode well for Mexican democracy. With some cooperation, Felipe Calderón may be able to use his party's pluralities to further the national political and economic reform agenda Vicente Fox promised six years earlier, but could only partially deliver.

As he prepared for his Dec. 1, 2006, inauguration, Felipe Calderón not only appeared to be both moving ahead with many of his predecessor's original proposals, but he also seemed to be reaching out to the PRI and the PRD with some new ideas. These, although containing much of PAN's pro-business pro-NAFTA ideas, also appeared to borrow considerably from the liberal-populist agenda of Obrador and the PRD and might produce much-needed cooperation that will allow their country to make progress toward a more just and prosperous motherland for all Mexicans.

Economy and Government

THE MEXICAN ECONOMY
Post-Revolutionary Gains

By many measures, Mexico's 20th-century revolution appears to have succeeded. Since 1910, illiteracy has plunged from 80 percent to 10 percent, life expectancy has risen from 30 years to nearly 70, infant mortality has dropped from a whopping 40 percent to about 2 percent, and, in terms of caloric intake, average Mexicans are eating about twice as much as their forebears at the turn of the 20th century.

Decades of near-continuous economic growth account for rising Mexican living standards. The Mexican economy has rebounded from its last two recessions because of plentiful natural resources, notably oil and metals;

diversified manufacturing, such as cars, steel, and petrochemicals; steadily increasing tourism; exports of fruits, vegetables, and cattle; and its large, low-wage workforce.

Recent Mexican governments, moreover, have skillfully exploited Mexico's economic strengths. The Border Industrialization Program that led to millions of jobs in thousands of border maquiladora factories has spread all over the country, especially to Monterrey, Mexico City, and Guadalajara. The increased manufacturing output has produced manifold economic benefits, including reduced dependency on oil exports and burgeoning foreign trade. Consequently, Mexico has become a net exporter of goods and services to the United States, its largest trading partner.

In 2001, however, the U.S. economic slowdown decreased demand for Mexican products; consequently, Mexico lost more than half a million jobs, forcing economic growth down to a weak 2.5 percent for 2001. Nevertheless, the slower growth resulted in neither significant inflation nor weakening of the peso, and by late 2004, the Mexican gross domestic product was again rising at a healthy annual rate of about 5 percent.

Long-Term Economic Challenges

Despite huge gains, Mexico's Revolution of 1910 is nevertheless incomplete. Improved public health, education, income, and opportunity have barely outdistanced Mexico's population, which has increased nearly sevenfold—from 15 million to 100 million—between 1910 and 2000. For example, although the illiteracy rate has decreased, the actual number of Mexican people who can't read, about 10 million, has remained about constant since 1910.

Moreover, the land reform program, once thought to be a Mexican cure-all, has long been a disappointment. The *ejidos* of which Emiliano Zapata dreamed have become mostly symbolic. The communal fields are typically small and unirrigated. *Ejido* land, formerly constitutionally prohibited from being sold, has not traditionally served as collateral for bank loans. Capital for irrigation networks, fertilizers, and harvesting machines is consequently lacking. Communal farms are typically inefficient; the average Mexican field produces about *one-quarter* as much corn per acre as a U.S. farm. Mexico must accordingly use its precious oil dollar surplus to import millions of tons of corn—which, remember, is indigenous to Mexico—annually.

The triple scourge of overpopulation, lack of arable land, and low farm income has driven millions of campesino families to seek better lives in Mexico's cities and in the United States. Since 1910, Mexico has evolved from a largely rural country, where 70 percent of the population lived on farms, to an urban nation where 70 percent of the population lives in cities. Fully one-fifth of Mexico's people now live in Mexico City.

People take many jobs to get by in Mexico, such as these street musicians in Acapulco.

Nevertheless, the future appears bright for many privately owned and managed Mexican farms, concentrated largely in the northern border states. Exceptionally productive, they typically work hundreds or thousands of irrigated acres of crops, such as tomatoes, lettuce, chiles, wheat, corn, tobacco, cotton, fruits, alfalfa, chickens, and cattle, just like their counterparts across the border in California, New Mexico, Arizona, and Texas.

Staples—wheat for bread, corn for tortillas, milk, and cooking oil—are all imported and consequently expensive for the typical working-class Mexican family, which must spend half or more of its income (typically $500 per month) for food. Recent inflation has compounded the problem, particularly for the millions of families on the bottom half of Mexico's economic ladder.

Although average gross domestic product figures for Mexico—about $12,000 per capita compared to about $40,000 for the United States—place it above nearly all other developing-world countries, averages, when applied to

Mexico, mean little. A primary socioeconomic reality of Mexican history remains: the richest one-fifth of Mexican families earns about 10 times the income of the poorest one-fifth. A relative handful of people own a large hunk of Mexico, and they don't seem inclined to share any of it with the less fortunate. As for the poor, the typical Mexican family in the bottom one-third income bracket often owns neither car nor refrigerator, and the children typically do not finish elementary school.

GOVERNMENT AND POLITICS
The Constitution of 1917

Mexico's governmental system is rooted in the Constitution of 1917, which incorporated many of the features of its reformist predecessor of 1857. The 1917 document, with amendments, remains in force. Although drafted at the behest of conservative revolutionary Venustiano Carranza by his handpicked Querétaro "Constitucionalista" congress, it was greatly influenced by Alvaro Obregón and generally ignored by Carranza during his subsequent three-year presidential term.

Although many articles resemble those of its United States model, the Constitution of 1917 contains provisions developed directly from Mexican experience. Article 27 addresses the question of land. Private property rights are qualified by societal need; subsoil rights are public property, and foreigners and corporations are severely restricted in land ownership. Although the 1917 constitution declared *ejido* (communal) land inviolate, 1994 amendments allow, under certain circumstances, the sale or use of communal land as loan security.

Article 23 severely restricts church powers. In declaring that "places of worship are the property of the nation," it stripped churches of all title to real estate, without compensation. Article 5 and Article 130 banned religious orders, expelled foreign clergy, and denied priests and ministers all political rights, including voting, holding office, and even criticizing the government.

Article 123 establishes the rights of labor: to organize, bargain collectively, strike, work a maximum eight-hour day, and receive a minimum wage. Women are to receive equal pay for equal work and be given a month's paid leave for childbearing. Article 123 also establishes social security plans for sickness, unemployment, pensions, and death.

On paper, Mexico's constitutional government structures appear much like their U.S. prototypes: a federal presidency, a two-house Congress, and a Supreme Court, with their counterparts in each of the 32 states. Political parties field candidates, and all citizens vote by secret ballot.

Mexico's presidents, however, have traditionally enjoyed greater powers than their U.S. counterparts. They need not seek legislative approval for many cabinet appointments, can suspend constitutional rights under a state of siege, can initiate legislation, veto all or parts of bills, refuse to execute laws, and replace state officers. The federal government, moreover, retains nearly all taxing authority, relegating the states to a role of merely administering federal programs.

Although ideally providing for separation of powers, the Constitution of 1917 subordinates both the legislative and judicial branches, with the courts being the weakest of all. The Supreme Court, for example, can only, with repeated deliberation, decide upon the constitutionality of legislation. Five separate individuals must file successful petitions for writs *amparo* (protection) on a single point of law in order to affect constitutional precedent.

Democratizing Mexican Politics

Reforms in Mexico's stable but top-heavy "Institutional Revolution" came only gradually. Characteristically, street protests were brutally put down at first, with officials only later working to address grievances. Generations of dominance by the PRI, the Institutional Revolutionary Party, led to widespread cynicism and citizen apathy. Regardless of who gets elected, the typical person on the street would tell you that the officeholder was bound to retire with his or her pockets full.

Nevertheless, by 1985, movement toward more justice and pluralism seemed be in store for Mexico. During the subsequent dozen years, minority parties increasingly elected candidates to state and federal office. Although none captured a majority of any state legislature, the strongest non-PRI parties, such as the conservative pro-Catholic Partido Acción Nacional (PAN) or National Action Party and the liberal-left Partido Revolucionario Democratico (PRD), elected governors. In 1986, minority parties were given federal legislative seats, up to a maximum of 20, for winning a minimum of 2.5 percent of the national presidential vote. In the 1994 election, minority parties received public campaign financing, depending upon their fraction of the vote.

After his 1994 inaugural address, in which he called loudly and clearly for more reforms, President Zedillo quickly began to produce results. He immediately appointed a respected member of the PAN opposition party as attorney general—the first non-PRI cabinet appointment in Mexican history. Other Zedillo firsts were federal Senate confirmation of both Supreme Court nominees and the attorney general, multiparty participation in the Chiapas peace negotiations, and congressional approval of the 1995 financial assistance package received from the United States. Zedillo, moreover, organized a series of precedent-setting meetings with opposition leaders that led to a written pact for political reform and the establishment of permanent working groups to discuss political and economic questions.

Perhaps most important was Zedillo's campaign and inaugural vow to separate both his government and himself from PRI decision-making. He kept his promise, becoming the first Mexican president in as long as anyone could remember who did not choose his successor.

A New Mexican Revolution

Finally, in 2000, like a Mexican Gorbachev, Ernesto Zedillo watched as PAN opposition reformer Vicente Fox swept Zedillo's PRI from the presidency after a 71-year rule. Moreover, despite severe criticism from his own party, Zedillo quickly called for the country to close ranks behind Fox. Millions of Mexicans, still dazed but buoyed by Zedillo's statesmanship

Locals display banners demanding justice in front of Templo y Ex-Convento de Santo Domingo in Oaxaca.

and Fox's epoch-making victory, eagerly awaited Fox's inauguration address on Dec. 1, 2000.

He promised nothing less than a new revolution for Mexico and backed it up with concrete proposals: reduce poverty by 30 percent, revitalize electricity and oil production, a Mexican Silicon Valley, and free trade throughout the Americas. He promised justice for all, through a reformed police, army, and the judiciary. With all of Mexico listening, Fox brought his speech to a hopeful conclusion: "If I had to summarize my message today in one sentence, I would say: Today Mexico has a future, but we have lost much time and wasted many resources. Mexico has a future, and we must build that future starting today."

It was truly a bold vision, and five years later, nearing the twilight of his six-year term, Fox could only claim partial success. He admitted that the path to democracy, which he believes cannot be reversed, would continue to be messy and difficult. His unfinished agenda therefore will remain a challenge to future Mexican presidents, especially his successor Felipe Calderón, who in his brief but emphatic inaugration speech on Dec. 1, 2006, vowed to continue Mexico's difficult but irreversable march toward a truly just, democratic, and prosperous homeland for all Mexican people.

People and Culture

Let a broad wooden chopping block represent Mexico; imagine hacking it with a sharp cleaver until it is grooved and pocked. That fractured surface resembles Mexico's central highlands, where most Mexicans, divided from each other by high mountains and yawning *barrancas,* have lived since before history.

The Mexicans' deep divisions, in large measure, led to their downfall at the hands of the Spanish conquistadores. The Aztec empire that Hernán Cortés conquered was a vast but fragmented collection of tribes. Speaking more than 100 mutually alien languages, those original Mexicans viewed each other suspiciously, as barely human barbarians from strange lands beyond the mountains. And even today the lines Mexicans draw between themselves—of caste, class, race, wealth—are the result, to a significant degree, of the realities of their mutual isolation.

POPULATION

The Spanish colonial government and the Roman Catholic religion provided the glue that through 400 years has welded Mexico's fragmented people into a burgeoning nation-state. Mexico's population, more than 100 million by the year 2000, increased during the '90s, but at a rate diminished to about half that of previous decades. Increased birth control and emigration largely account for the slowdown.

Mexico's population has not always been increasing. Historians estimate that European diseases, largely measles and smallpox, wiped out as many as 25 million—perhaps 95 percent—of the *indígena* population within a few generations after Cortés stepped ashore in 1519. The Mexican population dwindled from an estimated 20 million at the eve of the conquest to a mere one million inhabitants by 1600. It wasn't until 1950, more than four centuries after Cortés, that Mexico's population recovered to its preconquest level of 20 million.

Mestizos, *Indígenas*, Criollos, and African Mexicans

Although by 1950 Mexico's population had recovered, it was completely transformed. The mestizo, a Spanish-speaking person of mixed blood, had replaced the pure Native American, the *indígena* (een-DEE-hay-nah), as the typical Mexican.

Mexico's indigenous people travel far to sell their handicrafts. Here, a Trique woman from Oaxaca's uplands sells her weavings at Lake Chapala, near Guadalajara.

The trend continues. Perhaps three of four Mexicans would identify themselves as mestizo: that class whose part-European blood elevates them, in the Mexican mind, to the level of *gente de razón* (people of reason or right). And there's the rub. The *indígenas* (or, mistakenly but much more commonly, Indians), by the usual measurements of income, health, or education, squat at the bottom of the Mexican social ladder.

The typical *indígena* family lives in a small adobe house in a remote valley, subsisting on corn, beans, and vegetables from its small, unirrigated *milpa* (cornfield). They usually have chickens, a few pigs, and sometimes a cow, but no electricity; their few hundred dollars a year in cash income isn't enough to buy even a small refrigerator, much less a truck.

The usual mestizo family, on the other hand, enjoys most of the benefits of the 20th century. They typically own a modest concrete house in town. Their furnishings, simple by developed-world standards, will often include an electric refrigerator, washing machine, propane stove, television, and car or truck. The children go to school every day, and the eldest son sometimes looks forward to college.

Sizable *negro* communities, descendants of 18th-century African slaves, live in the Gulf states and along the Guerrero-Oaxaca Pacific coastline. Last to arrive, the *negros* experience discrimination at the hands of everyone else and are integrating very slowly into the mestizo mainstream.

Above the mestizos, a tiny criollo (Mexican-born white) minority, a few percent of the total population, inherits the privileges—wealth, education, and political power—of its colonial Spanish ancestors.

INDÍGENAS

Although anthropologists and census takers classify them according to language groups (such as Nahuatl, Mixtec, and Zapotec), *indígenas* generally identify themselves as residents of a particular locality rather than by language or ethnic grouping. And although, as a group, they are referred to as *indígenas* (native, or aboriginal), individuals are generally uncomfortable at being labeled as such.

Some people, mostly in Oaxaca and Guerrero, still wear the traditional indigenous dress: white cottons and a sombrero for men and a *huipil* for women.

While the mestizos are the emerging self-conscious majority class, the *indígenas,* as during colonial times, remain the invisible people of Mexico. They are politically conservative, socially traditional, and tied to the land. On market day, the typical *indígena* family might make the trip into town. They bag tomatoes, squash, or peppers, and tie up a few chickens or a pig. The rickety country bus will often be full and the mestizo driver may wave them away, giving preference to his friends, leaving them to trudge stoically along the road.

Their lot, nevertheless, has been slowly improving. *Indígena* families now almost always have access to a local school and a medical clinic. Improved health has led to a large increase in their population. Official census figures, however, are probably low. *Indígenas* are traditionally suspicious of government people, and census takers, however conscientious, seldom speak the local language.

Recent figures, however, indicate 8 percent of Mexicans are *indígenas*—that is, they speak one of Mexico's 50-odd native languages. Of these, a quarter speak no Spanish at all. These fractions are changing only slowly. Many *indígenas* prefer the old ways. If present trends continue, the year 2019, 500 years after the Spanish arrival, will mark the return of the Mexican indigenous population to the preconquest level of approximately 20 million.

Indígena Language Groups

The Maya speakers of Yucatán and the aggregate of the Nahuatl (Aztec language) speakers of the central plateau are Mexico's most numerous *indígena* groups, totaling roughly three million (one million Maya, two million Nahuatl).

Indigenous population centers, relatively scattered in the north of Pacific Mexico, concentrate in the southern states of Guerrero and Oaxaca. The groups are not evenly spread, however. The language map of Oaxaca, for ex-

INDIGENOUS POPULATIONS OF PACIFIC MEXICO

For the Pacific Mexico states (from north to south), the 2000 government census totals were:

STATE	INDIGENOUS POPULATION (OVER 5 YEARS OF AGE)	TOTAL POPULATION (OVER 5 YEARS OF AGE)	PERCENT OF TOTAL
Sinaloa	49,700	2,130,000	2.3
Nayarit	37,200	769,000	4.8
Jalisco	39,300	5,323,000	0.7
Colima	2,900	421,000	0.7
Michoacán	121,800	3,342,000	3.6
Guerrero	367,100	2,572,000	14.3
Oaxaca	1,120,300	2,924,000	38.3

The same government sources tabulate indigenous peoples by language groupings. Although such figures are probably low, the 2000 figures revealed significant populations in many local areas:

LANGUAGE GROUP	POPULATION	IMPORTANT CENTERS
Tepuan	17,000	Sinaloa-Durango
Cora	15,600	Nayarit (Acaponeta)
Huichol	27,900	Nayarit-Jalisco (Santiago Ixcuintla, Huejuqilla)
Nahua (north)	8,100	Jalisco (Ciudad Guzmán)
Tarasco	114,000	Michoacán (Pátzcuaro)
Nahua (south)	160,000	Guerrero (Taxco and Chilpancingo)

ample, looks like a crazy quilt, with important Zapotec, Mixtec, and other centers scattered along the coast and through the mountains surrounding Oaxaca city.

Dress

Maps and figures, however, cannot describe the color of a fiesta or market day. Many country people, especially in Oaxaca, still wear the traditional cottons that blend Spanish and native styles. Men usually wear the Spanish-origin straw sombrero (literally, shade-maker) on their heads, baggy white cotton shirt and pants, and leather huaraches on their feet. Women's dress is often more colorful. It can include a *huipil* (long, sleeveless dress), often embroidered in bright floral and animal motifs, and a handwoven *enredo* (wraparound skirt that identifies the wearer with a particular locality). A *faja* (waist sash) and, in the winter, a *quechquémitl* (shoulder cape) complete the ensemble.

LANGUAGE GROUP	POPULATION	IMPORTANT CENTERS
Mixtec	363,000	Western Oaxaca (Huajuapan, Tlaxiaco, and Santiago Jamíltepec)
Tlapanec	93,000	Eastern Guerrero (Tlapa de Comonfort)
Amusgo	40,000	Oaxaca-Guerrero (San Pedro Amusgos and ochistlahuaca)
Chinantec	107,000	Northern Oaxaca (Valle Nacional)
Chatino	40,000	Southern Oaxaca (Santos Reyes Nopala)
Zapotec	380,000	Central, Eastern, and Southern Oaxaca (Tlacolula, Ocotlán, Tehuantepec)
Chontal	5,000	Southeastern Oaxaca (Santiago Astata)
Trique	16,000	Western Oaxaca (Juxtlahuaca)
Chocho	1,000	Northwestern Oaxaca (Coixtlahuaca)
Cuicatec	12,000	Northern Oaxaca (Cuicatlán)
Huave	14,000	Southeastern Oaxaca (San Mateo del Mar)
Mazatec	175,000	Northern Oaxaca (Huatla de Jiménez)
Mixe	106,000	Northeastern Oaxaca (Ayutla)
Zoque	5,000	Southeastern Oaxaca (San Miguel Chimalapa)
Ixcatec	1,000	Northwestern Oaxaca (Ixcatlán)

RELIGION

"God and Gold" was the two-pronged mission of the conquistadores. Most of them concentrated on gold, while missionaries tried to shift the emphasis to God. They were famously successful; more than 90 percent of Mexicans profess to be Catholics.

Catholicism, spreading its doctrine of equality of all persons before God and incorporating native gods into the church rituals, eventually brought the *indígenas* into the fold. Within 100 years, nearly all native Mexicans had accepted the new religion, which raised the universal God of humankind over local tribal deities.

The Virgin of Guadalupe

Conversion of the *indígenas* was sparked by the vision of Juan Diego, a humble farmer. On the hill of Tepayac north of Mexico City in 1531, Juan Diego saw a brown-skinned version of the Virgin Mary enclosed in a dazzling aura of light. She told him to build

The Virgin of Guadalupe is celebrated yearly throughout Mexico on December 12.

a shrine in her memory on that spot, where the Aztecs had long worshipped their "earth mother," Tonantzín. Juan Diego's brown virgin told him to go to the cathedral and relay her instruction to Archbishop Zumárraga.

The archbishop, as expected, turned his nose up at Juan Diego's story. The vision returned, however, and this time Juan Diego's brown virgin realized that a miracle was necessary. She ordered him to pick some roses at the spot where she had first appeared to him (a true miracle, since roses had been previously unknown in the vicinity) and take them to the archbishop. Juan Diego wrapped the roses in his rude fiber cape, returned to the cathedral, and placed the wrapped roses at the archbishop's feet. When he opened the offering, Zumárraga gasped: imprinted on the cape was an image of the brown virgin herself—proof positive of a genuine miracle.

In the centuries since Juan Diego, the brown virgin—La Virgen Morena, or Nuestra Señora La Virgen de Guadalupe—has blended native and Catholic elements into something uniquely Mexican. In doing so, she has become the virtual patroness of Mexico, the beloved symbol of Mexico for *indígenas*, mestizos, *negros,* and criollos alike.

In the summer of 2002, Pope John Paul II journeyed to Mexico to perform a historically momentous gesture. Before millions of joyous faithful, on July 31, 2002, the frail aging pontiff elevated Juan Diego to sainthood, thus making him Latin America's first indigenous person to be so honored.

Every Mexican town and village celebrates the cherished memory of the Virgin of Guadalupe on Dec. 12. This celebration, however joyful, is but one of the many fiestas that Mexicans, especially the *indígenas,* live for. Each village holds its local fiesta in honor of its patron saint, who is often a thinly veiled sit-in for a local preconquest deity. Themes appear Spanish—Christian vs. Moors, devils vs. priests—but the native element is strong, sometimes dominant. During Semana Santa (Holy Week) at Pinotepa Nacional in coastal Oaxaca, for example, Mixtec people, costumed as Jews, shoot arrows skyward, simultaneously reciting traditional Mixtec prayers.

FESTIVALS AND EVENTS

Urban families watch the calendar for midweek national holidays that create a **puente** or "bridge" to the weekend and allow them to squeeze in a three- to five-day minivacation. Visitors should likewise watch the calendar. Such holidays (especially Christmas and Semana Santa, pre-Easter week, and Fiestas Patrias around Sept. 15) mean packed buses, roads, and hotels, especially around Pacific Mexico's beach resorts.

Country people, on the other hand, await their local saint's or holy day. The name of the locality often provides the clue. For example, in Santa Cruz del Miramar near San Blas, expect a celebration on May 3, El Día de la Santa Cruz (Day of the Holy Cross). People dress up in their traditional best, sell their wares and produce in a street fair, join a procession, get tipsy, and dance in the plaza.

Holiday and Festival Calendar

The following calendar lists national and notable Pacific Mexico holidays and festivals. Dates may vary. If you want to attend a specific local fiesta, first contact a local travel agent or tourism bureau for information. (But, if you happen to be where one of these is going on, get out of your car or bus and join in!)

- Jan. 1: ¡**Feliz Año Nuevo!** (New Year's Day; national holiday).

- Jan. 1–5: **Inauguration** of the Cora governor in Jesús María, Nayarit (Cora indigenous dances and ceremonies).

- Jan. 6: **Día de los Reyes** (Day of the Kings; traditional gift exchange).

- Jan. 12: **Día de Nuestra Señora de Guadalupe** in El Tuito, Jalisco, an hour's drive south of Puerto Vallarta (Festival of the Virgin of Guadalupe; parade, music, evening Mass, and carnival).

- Jan. 13–17: **Fiesta of the Sweet Name of Jesus** (Dulce Nombre de Jesús), in Santa Ana del Valle, Tlacolula, and Zimatlán, Oaxaca. Troupes perform many traditional dances, including the Dance of the Feathers.

- Jan. 20–21: **Fiesta de San Sebastián,** especially in San Sebastián del Oeste (near Puerto Vallarta), Jalisco, and Pedro y San Pablo Tequixtepec, Pinotepa Don Luis, and Jalapa de Díaz, Oaxaca.

- Jan. 23–Feb. 2: **Fiesta de la Virgen de la Salud** in Colima, Colima; processions, food, dancing, and fireworks.

- Feb. 1–3: **Festival of the Sea** in San Blas, Nayarit (dancing, horse races, and competitions).

- Feb. 2: **Día de Candelaria** (blessing of plants, seeds, and candles; procession; and bullfights).

- Feb. 7–23: **Fiesta de Villa Alvarez** (in Colima, Colima; bullfights, rodeos, and carnivals).

- February: During the four days before Ash Wednesday, usually in late February, many towns and villages (most famously Mazatlán), stage **Carnaval**—Mardi Gras—extravaganzas.

- Second Friday of Lent (nine days after Ash Wednesday): **Fiesta del Señor del Perdón** (Lord of Forgiveness); big pilgrimage festival in San Pedro and San Pablo Tequixtepec, Oaxaca.

- March 10–17: **Fiesta de San Patricio** (St. Patrick's Day festival); processions, boat regatta, dances, food, and carnival at San Patricio-Melaque (Barra de Navidad), Jalisco.

- March 11–19: Week before the **Day of St. Joseph** in Talpa, Jalisco (food, edible crafts made of colored *chicle,* or chewing gum, dancing, bands, and mariachi serenades to the Virgin of Talpa).

- Fourth Friday before Easter Sunday: **Fiesta of Jesus the Nazarene** in Huaxpaltepec,

Oaxaca; native Dance of the Conquest; big native country fair.

- March 18–April 4: **Grand ceramics and handicrafts fair,** in Tonalá (Guadalajara), Jalisco.

- March 19: **Día de San José** (Day of St. Joseph).

- March 21: **Birthday of Benito Juárez,** the "Hero of the Americas" (national holiday); especially in Benito Juárez's birthplace, Guelatao, Oaxaca, with a whirl of traditional dances.

- Late March or April (the Sunday preceding Easter Sunday): **Fiesta de Ramos** (Palm Sunday) in many towns and villages, but especially in Sayula, Jalisco (on Highway 54 south of Guadalajara; local area crafts fair, food, dancing, mariachis).

- April (Good Friday, two days before Easter Sunday): **Fiesta de la Santa Cruz de Huatulco** (Holy Cross of Huatulco) in Santa María Huatulco, Oaxaca.

- April: **Semana Santa** (pre-Easter Holy Week, culminating in Domingo Gloria, Easter Sunday national holiday).

- May 1: **Labor Day** (national holiday).

- May (first and third Wednesdays): **Fiesta of the Virgin of Ocotlán,** in Ocotlán, Jalisco (on Lake Chapala, religious processions, dancing, fireworks, regional food).

- May 3: **Día de la Santa Cruz** (Holy Cross) in many places, especially Salina Cruz and Tehuantepec, Oaxaca, and Mascota, Jalisco.

- May 3–15: **Fiesta of St. Isador the Farmer** in Tepic, Nayarit (blessing of seeds, animals, and water; agricultural displays, competitions, and dancing).

- May 5: **Cinco de Mayo** (defeat of the French at Puebla in 1862; national holiday).

- May 10: **Mothers' Day** (national holiday).

- May 10–12: **Fiesta of the Coronation of the Virgin of the Rosary** in Talpa, Jalisco (processions, fireworks, regional food, crafts, and dances).

- May 10–24: **Book fair** in Guadalajara (readings, concerts, and international book exposition).

- May 15–30: **Velas (Fiestas) de San Vicente Ferrer** (in Juchitán, Oaxaca; Chontal and Huave dances and fair).

- June 15–July 14: **National Ceramics Fair** in the Tlaquepaque district, Guadalajara (huge crafts fair; exhibits, competitions, and market of crafts from all over the country).

- June 24: **Día de San Juan Bautista** (Day of St. John the Baptist); fairs and religious festivals, playful dunking of people in water).

- June 28–29: **Regatta** in Mexcaltitán, Nayarit (friendly rivalry between boats carrying images of St. Peter and St. Paul to celebrate opening of the shrimp season).

- June 29: **Día de San Pablo y San Pedro** (Day of St. Peter and St. Paul).

- July 1–15: **Fiesta of the Precious Blood of Christ** in Teotitlán del Valle, Oaxaca, featuring the Danza de la Pluma (Dance of the Feather).

- July: **Lunes del Cerro** (in Oaxaca city; a two-week extravaganza of native dances, events and fairs, beginning on the first Monday after July 16; among Mexico's most colorful).

- July 20–30: **Fiesta de Santiago Apóstol** (St. James the Apostle) in many locations, but especially Santiago Laollaga, Suchilquitongo, Jamiltepec, Pinotepa Nacional, and Juxtlahuaca, Oaxaca.

- August: **Copper Fair** in Santa Clara del Cobre, Michoacán.

- Aug. 14: **Fiesta de la Virgen de la Asunción** (Virgin of the Assumption) in Tlaxiaco, Oaxaca; Aug. 15 in Nochixtlán,

About two or three weeks before September 15 and 16, the Mexican Independence Days, flags are sold on downtown street corners.

Oaxaca; and Aug. 13–16 in Huazolotitlán, Oaxaca.

- Sept. 14: **Charro Day** (Cowboy Day all over Mexico; rodeos).

- Sept. 15–16: **Independence Day** (national holiday; mayors everywhere reenact Father Hidalgo's 1810 Grito de Dolores from city hall balconies on the night of September 15).

- Sept. 27–29: **Fiesta de San Miguel** in San Miguel Tequixtepec and Teotitlán del Camino, Oaxaca; dance of the "Cristianos y Moros" (Christians and Moors).

- Oct. 1–2: **Fiesta de San Miguel Arcángel** in Puerto ángel, Oaxaca.

- Oct. 4: **Día de San Francisco** (Day of St. Francis); traditional dances, especially in Uruapan, Michoacán.

- Oct. 12: **Día de la Raza** (Columbus Day,

national holiday that commemorates the union of the races).

- Oct. 12: **Fiesta of the Virgin of Zapopan** in Guadalajara (procession carries the Virgin home to Zapopan from the Guadalajara downtown cathedral; regional food, crafts fair, mariachis, and dancing).

- October, second Sunday: **Fiesta del Santa Cristo de Tlacolula** (Holy Christ of Tlacolula) in Tlacolula, Oaxaca.

- October (last Sunday): **Día de Cristo Rey** in Ixtlán del Río, Nayarit (Day of Christ the King, with "Quetzal y Azteca" and "La Pluma" *indígena* dances, horse races, processions, and food).

- Nov. 1: **Día de Todos Santos** (All Souls' Day, in honor of the souls of children; the departed descend from heaven to eat sugar skeletons, skulls, and treats on family altars).

- Nov. 2: **Día de los Muertos** (Day of the Dead, in honor of ancestors; families visit cemeteries and decorate graves with flowers and favorite food of the deceased). Especially colorful in and around Morelia and Pátzcuaro, Michoacán, and in Oaxaca.

- Nov. 7–30: **Feria de la Nao de China** (in Acapulco; a fair celebrating the galleon trade which linked colonial Acapulco with Asia).

- Nov. 20: **Revolution Day** (anniversary of the revolution of 1910–1917; national holiday).

- Nov. 28–Dec. 5: **National Silver Fair** in Taxco, Guerrero. Mexico's most skilled silversmiths compete for prizes amid a whirl of concerts, dances, and fireworks.

- Late Nov.–Dec. 8: **Fiesta de la Virgen de Juquila,** Oaxaca's biggest fiesta; national pilgrimage in Santa Catarina Juquila.

- Dec. 1: **Inauguration Day** (National government changes hands every six years: 2000, 2006, 2012…).

- Dec. 8: **Día de la Purísima Concepción** (Day of the Immaculate Conception).

Children often participate as enthusiastically as the adults in local fiestas.

- Dec. 12: **Día de Nuestra Señora de Guadalupe** (Festival of the Virgin of Guadalupe, patroness of Mexico; processions, music, and dancing nationwide, especially in downtown Manzanillo and Puerto Vallarta).

- Dec. 16–18: **Fiesta de la Virgen de Soledad** in Oaxaca city.

- Dec. 16–24: **Christmas Week** (week of *posadas* and piñatas; midnight Mass on Christmas Eve).

- Dec. 23: **Fiesta de los Rábanos** (radish sculpture competition on the main plaza in Oaxaca city).

- Dec. 25: **¡Feliz Navidad!** (Christmas Day; Christmas trees and gift exchange; national holiday).

- Dec. 26: **Vela Tehuantepec** (in Tehuantepec, Oaxaca, everyone in town dances to the lovely melody of the *Sandunga*).

- Dec. 31: **New Year's Eve.**

Arts and Crafts

Mexico is so stuffed with lovely, reasonably priced handicrafts (*artesanías,* ar-tay-sah-NEE-ahs) that many crafts devotees, if given the option, might choose Mexico over heaven. A sizable fraction of Mexican families still depend upon homespun items—clothing, utensils, furniture, native herbal remedies, religious offerings, adornments, toys, musical instruments—which either they or their neighbors craft at home. Many such traditions reach back thousands of years, to the beginnings of Mexican civilization. The accumulated knowledge of manifold generations of artisans has, in many instances, resulted in finery so prized that whole villages devote themselves to the manufacture of a certain class of goods.

In Pacific Mexico, handicrafts shoppers who venture away from the coastal resorts to the source towns and villages will most likely ben-efit from lower prices, wider choices, and, most important, the privilege of encountering the artisans themselves. There, perhaps in a patio-shop on a dusty Tonalá side street or above a breezy Pátzcuaro lakeshore, you might meet the people and view the painstaking process by which they fashion humble materials—clay, wool, cotton, wood, metal, straw, leaves, palm fronds, bark, paper, leather—into irresistible works of art.

BASKETRY AND WOVEN CRAFTS

Weaving straw, leaves, palm fronds, and reeds is among the oldest of Mexican crafts traditions. Mat and basketweaving methods and designs 5,000 years old survive to the present day. All over Mexico, people weave *petates* (straw mats) upon which vacationers stretch out on the beach and which local folks use for everything, from keeping tortillas warm to shielding babies from the sun. Around Acapulco and along the Oaxaca coast, you might see a woman or child waiting for a bus or even walking down the street while weaving creamy white palm leaf strands into a coiled basket. Later, you may see a similar basket, embellished with a bright animal—parrot, burro, or even Snoopy—for sale in the market.

Like the origami paper-folders of Japan, folks who live around Lake Pátzcuaro have taken basketweaving to its ultimate form by crafting virtually everything—from toy turtles and Christmas bells to butterfly mobiles and serving spoons—from the reeds they gather along the lakeshore.

Hatmaking has likewise attained high refinement in Mexico. Workers in Sahuayo, Michoacán (near the southeast shore of Lake Chapala), craft especially fine sombreros. Due east across Mexico, in Becal, Campeche, workers craft Panama hats, *jipis* (HEE-pees), so fine, soft, and flexible that you can stuff one into your pants pocket without damage.

Although Huichol men in the states of Nayarit and Jalisco do not actually manufacture their headwear, they do decorate them. They take ordinary sombreros and embellish them into Mexico's most flamboyant hats, flowing with bright ribbons, feathers, and fringes of colorful wool balls.

CLOTHING AND EMBROIDERY

Although **traje** (ancestral tribal dress) has nearly vanished in urban Mexico, significant numbers of Mexican women, especially in remote districts of Michoacán, Guerrero, Oaxaca, Chiapas, and Yucatán, make and wear *traje*. Most common is the **huipil**, a full, square-shouldered, short- to midsleeved dress, often hand-embroidered with animal and floral designs. *Huipiles* from Oaxaca include designs from San Pedro de Amusgos (Amusgo tribe: white cotton, embroidered with abstract colored animal and floral motifs); San Andrés Chicahuaxtla (Trique tribe: white cotton, richly embroidered red stripes, interwoven

with green, blue, and yellow, and hung with colored ribbons); Yalalag (Zapotec tribe: white cotton, with bright flowers embroidered along two or four vertical seams and distinctive colored tassels hanging down the back). Beyond Oaxaca, Yucatán Maya *huipiles* are among the most prized. They are of white cotton, embellished with big, brilliant machine-embroidered flowers around the neck and shoulders.

Shoppers sometimes can buy other, less common types of *traje,* such as a **quechquémitl** (shoulder cape), often made of wool and worn as an overgarment in winter. The **enredo,** a full-length skirt, wraps around the waist and legs like a Hawaiian sarong. Mixtec women in Oaxaca's warm south coast region around Pinotepa Nacional commonly wear the *enredo,* known locally as the **pozahuanco** (poh-sah-oo-AHN-koh) below the waist, and when at home, go bare-breasted. When wearing their *pozahuancos* in public, they usually tie a **mandil,** a wide calico apron, around their front side. Women weave the best *pozahuancos,* using cotton thread dyed a light purple with secretions of tidepool-harvested snails, *Purpura patula pansa,* and silk dyed deep red with cochineal, extracted from the dried bodies of a locally cultivated scale insect, *Dactylopius coccus.* On a typical day, two or three women will be selling handmade *pozahuancos* at the Pinotepa Nacional market.

Colonial-era Spanish styles have blended with native *traje,* producing a wider class of dress, known generally as **ropa típica.** Lovely embroidered blouses *(blusas),* shawls *(rebozos),* and dresses *(vestidos)* fill boutique racks and market stalls all over Pacific Mexico. Among the most popular is the so-called **Oaxaca wedding dress,** made of cotton with a crochet-trimmed riot of diminutive flowers hand-stitched about the neck and yoke. Some of the finest examples are made in San Antonino Castillo, just north of Ocotlán in the Valley of Oaxaca.

In contrast to women, only a small fraction of Mexican men—members of remote groups, such as Huichol, Cora, and Tarahumara in the northwest, and Maya and Lacandón in the southeast—wear *traje.* Nevertheless, shops offer some fine men's *ropa típica,* such as wool jackets and serapes for northern or highland winter wear, and *guayaberas,* hip-length, pleated tropical dress shirts.

Fine embroidery *(bordado)* embellishes much traditional Mexican clothing, tablecloths *(manteles),* and napkins *(servilletas).* As everywhere, women define the art of embroidery. Although some still work by hand at home, cheaper machine-made factory lace and needlework is more commonly available in shops.

Leather

Pacific Mexico shops offer an abundance of leather goods, which, if not manufactured locally, are shipped from the renowned leather centers. These include Guadalajara (coats, purses, shoes, boots), Mazatlán, and Oaxaca (sandals and huaraches). For unique and custom-designed articles, you'll probably have to confine your shopping to the more expensive tourist resort shops. For the more usual though still attractive leather items such as purses, wallets, belts, coats, and boots, veteran shoppers go to local city markets. Most notable among these is Guadalajara's suburban Zapopan and Tlaquepaque villages and downtown Libertad Market, where an acre of stalls offer the broadest leather selection at reasonable prices (after bargaining) in Pacific Mexico.

FURNITURE

Although furniture is usually too bulky to carry back home with your airline luggage, low Mexican prices allow you to ship your purchases home and enjoy beautiful, unusual pieces for a fraction of what you would pay—if you could find them—at home.

A number of classes of furniture *(muebles,* moo-AY-blays) are crafted in villages near the sources of raw materials—wood, reeds, bamboo, or wrought iron.

Sometimes it seems as if every house in Mexico is furnished with wood **colonial-style furniture.** The basic design of much of it dates at least to the Middle Ages. Although variations exist, most colonial-style furniture

Equipal furniture, of leather or pigskin stretched over wooden frames, is made mostly in Tonalá and Tlaquepaque villages, near Guadalajara.

© BRUCE WHIPPERMAN

is heavily built. Table and chair legs are massive, often lathe-turned; chair backs are usually straight and vertical. Although usually varnished, colonial-style tables, chairs, and chests sometimes shine with inlaid wood or tile, or animal and flower designs. Family shops turn out good furniture, usually in the highlands, where suitable wood is available. Products from shops in Guadalajara's Tonalá and Tlaquepaque villages, Lake Pátzcuaro (especially Tzintzuntzán), Taxco, and Olinalá, Guerrero, are among the best known.

A second, very distinctive class of Mexican furniture is **equipal,** usually roundish tables, chairs, and sofas, made of brown pigskin or cowhide stretched over wooden frames. Factories are mostly in Guadalajara and nearby Tlaquepaque and Tonalá villages.

It is intriguing that **lacquered furniture,** in both process and design, has much in common with lacquerware produced half a world away in China. Moreover, Mexican lacquerware tradition both predated the conquest and was originally practiced only on the Pacific side, where legends persist of preconquest contact with Chinese traders. Consequently, a number of experts believe that the Mexicans learned the craft of lacquerware from Chinese artists, centuries before Columbus.

Today, artisan families in and around Pátzcuaro, Michoacán, and Olinalá, Guerrero, carry on the tradition. The process, which at its finest resembles cloisonné manufacture, involves carving and painting intricate floral and animal designs, followed by repeated layerings of lacquer, clay, and sometimes gold and silver to produce satiny, jewel-like surfaces.

A few villages produce furniture made of plant fiber, such as reeds, raffia, and bamboo. In some cases, entire communities, such as Ihuatzio (near Pátzcuaro) and Villa Victoria (in Mexico state, west of Toluca), have long harvested the bounty of local lakes and marshes as the basis for their products.

Wrought iron, produced and worked according to Spanish tradition, is used to produce tables, chairs, and benches. Ruggedly fashioned in a riot of baroque scrollwork, pieces often decorate garden, patio, and park settings. Many colonial cities, notably San Miguel de Allende, Toluca, Guanajuato, Guadalajara (Tlaquepaque and Tonalá), and Oaxaca are wrought-iron manufacturing centers.

GLASS AND STONEWORK

Glass manufacture, unknown in pre-Columbian times, was introduced by the Spanish. Today, factories scattered all over the country turn out mountains of **burbuja** (boor-BOO-hah)—bubbled glass tumblers, goblets, plates, and pitchers, usually in blue, green, or red. Finer glass is manufactured in Guadalajara; especially in suburban Tlaquepaque and Tonalá villages, you can watch artisans blow glass into a number of shapes, notably, paper-thin balls in red, green, or blue.

Artisans work stone, usually near sources of supply. Puebla, Mexico's main source of onyx (**onix,** OH-neeks), is the manufacturing center for the galaxy of mostly rough-hewn,

cream-colored items, from animal charms and chess pieces to beads and desk sets, which crowd curio shop shelves throughout the country. **Cantera,** a volcanic tufa stone occurring in pastel shades from pink to green, quarried locally, especially near Pátzcuaro and Oaxaca, is used similarly.

For a keepsake from a truly ancient Mexican tradition, don't forget the hollowed-out stone **metate** (may-TAH-tay), a corn-grinding basin, and the three-legged **molcajete** (mohl-kah-HAY-tay), a mortar for grinding *chiles.*

HUICHOL ART

Growing demand, especially around Puerto Vallarta, has greatly stimulated the supply of Huichol art. Best sources of Huichol handicrafts, besides many Puerto Vallarta shops, are the closer-to-the-source (and consequently more economical) shops in Tepic and the Huichol Cultural Center in Santiago Ixcuintla, north of San Blas.

Originally produced by shamans for ritual purposes, pieces such as **beaded masks, cuadras** (rectangular yarn paintings), **gourd rattles, arrows,** and yarn **cicuri** (God's eyes) have a ritual symbolism. Eerie beaded masks of wood often represent the Huichols' earth mother, Tatei Urianaka. The larger *cuadras,* of colored acrylic yarn painstakingly glued in intermeshing patterns to a plywood base, customarily depict the drama of life being played out between the main actors of the Huichol pantheon. For example, as Tayau (Father Sun) radiates over the land, alive with stylized cactus, flowers, peyote buds, snakes, and birds, antlered "Brother Deer" Kauyumari heroically battles the evil sorcerer Kieri, while nearby, Tatei Urianaka gives birth. (For Huichol art references, see *Suggested Reading* in the *Resources* chapter.)

JEWELRY

Gold and silver were once the basis for Mexico's wealth. Her Spanish conquerors plundered a mountain of gold—religious offerings, necklaces, pendants, rings, bracelets—masterfully crafted by a legion of native metalsmiths and jewelers. Unfortunately, much of that indigenous tradition was lost because the Spanish denied access to precious metals to the Mexicans for generations while they introduced Spanish methods. Nevertheless, a small gold-working tradition survived the dislocations of the 1810–1821 War of Independence and the 1910–1917 revolution. Silver-crafting, moribund during the 1800s, was revived in Taxco, Guerrero, principally through the joint efforts of architect-artist William Spratling and the local community.

Today, spurred by the tourist boom, jewelry-making is thriving in Mexico. Taxco, where guilds, families, and cooperatives produce sparkling silver and gold adornments, is the acknowledged center. Scores of Taxco shops display the results—shimmering ornamental butterflies, birds, jaguars, serpents, turtles, and fish from ancient native tradition. Pieces, mostly in silver, vary from humble but attractive trinkets to glittering necklaces, silver candelabras, and place settings for a dozen, sometimes embellished with precious stones.

Other subsidiary jewelry-crafting centers include Guadalajara (gold and opals), Oaxaca (preconquest replicas and gold and silver filigree), Pátzcuaro (silver filigree and earrings), Puebla (sand-cast gold and silver), and Guanajuato (gold and silver, especially earrings.)

WOODCARVING AND MUSICAL INSTRUMENTS
Masks

Spanish and native Mexican traditions have blended to produce a multitude of masks—some strange, some lovely, some scary, some endearing, all interesting. The tradition flourishes in the strongly indigenous southern Pacific Mexico states of Michoacán, Guerrero, and Oaxaca, where campesinos gear up all year for the village festivals—especially Semana Santa (Easter week), early December (Virgin of Guadalupe), and the festival of the local patron, whether it be San José, San Pedro, San Pablo, Santa María, Santa Barbara, or one of a host of others. Every local fair has its favored

© BRUCE WHIPPERMAN

Woodcrafts are made wherever wood is abundant in Pacific Mexico, such as in Tzintzuntzán in Michoacán.

dances, such as the Dance of the Conquest, the Christians and Moors, the Old Men, or the Tiger, in which masked villagers act out age-old allegories of fidelity, sacrifice, faith, struggle, sin, and redemption.

Although masks are made of many materials—from stone and ebony to coconut husks and paper—wood, where available, is the medium of choice. For the entire year, village master carvers cut, shave, sand, and paint to ensure that each participant will be properly disguised for the festival.

The popularity of masks has led to an entire made-for-tourist mask industry of mass-produced duplicates, many cleverly antiqued. Examine the goods carefully; if the price is high, don't buy unless you're convinced it's a real antique.

A number of stores in tourist centers, notably Puerto Vallarta, Taxco, and Oaxaca, have extensive for-sale mask inventories. Pacific Mexico's outstanding mask collection is on display in Acapulco, at the **Casa de la Máscara,** which, for lovers of masks, is alone worth the trip to visit it.

Alebrijes

Tourist demand has made zany wooden animals or *alebrijes* (ah-lay-BREE-hays), a Oaxaca growth industry. Virtually every family in certain Valley of Oaxaca villages—notably Arrazola and San Martin Tilcajete—runs a factory studio. There, piles of *copal* wood, which men carve and women finish and intricately paint, become whimsical giraffes, dogs, cats, iguanas, gargoyles, dragons, and most of the possible permutations in between. The farther from the source you get, the higher the *alebrije* price becomes; in Arrazola, what costs $5 will probably run about $10 in Pacific Mexico and $30 in the United States or Canada.

Others commonly available are the charming colorfully painted wooden fish carved mainly in the Pacific coastal state of Guerrero, and the burnished, dark hardwood animal and fish sculptures of desert ironwood from the state of Sonora.

Musical Instruments

The great majority of Mexico's guitars and other stringed instruments are made in Paracho, Michoacán (southeast of Lake Chapala, 50 miles north of Uruapan). There, scores of cottage factories turn out guitars, violins, mandolins, *viruelas*, ukuleles, and a dozen more variations every day. They vary widely in quality, so look carefully before you buy. Make sure that the wood is well cured and dry; damp, unripe wood instruments are more susceptible to warping and cracking.

METALWORK

Bright copper, brass, and tinware; sturdy ironwork; and razor-sharp knives and machetes are made in a number of regional centers. **Copperware,** from jugs, cups, and plates to candlesticks—and even the town lampposts and bandstand—all come from Santa Clara del Cobre, a few miles south of Pátzcuaro, Michoacán.

Although not the source of **brass** itself, Tonalá, in the Guadalajara eastern suburb, is the place where brass is most abundant and beautiful, appearing as menageries of brilliant, fetching birds and animals, sometimes embellished with shiny nickel highlights.

A number of Oaxaca family factories turn out fine **cutlery**—swords, knives, machetes—scrolled **cast-iron grillwork,** and a swarm of bright **tinware,** or *(hojalata;* oh-hah-LAH-tah), mirror frames, masks, and glittering Christmas decorations.

Be sure not to miss the miniature **milagros,** one of Mexico's most charming forms of metalwork. Usually of brass, they are of homely shapes—a horse, dog, or baby, or an arm, head, or foot—which, accompanied by a prayer, the faithful pin to the garment of their favorite saint whom they hope will intercede to cure an ailment or fulfill a wish.

PAPER AND PAPIER-MÂCHÉ

Papier-mâché has become a high art in Tonalá, Jalisco, where a swarm of birds, cats, frogs, giraffes, and other animal figurines are meticulously crafted by building up repeated layers of glued paper. The result—sanded, brilliantly varnished, and polished—resembles fine sculpture rather than the humble newspaper from which it was fashioned.

Other paper goods you shouldn't overlook include piñatas (durable, inexpensive, and as Mexican as you can get), available in every town market; colorful decorative cutout banners (string overhead at your home fiesta) from San Salvador Huixcolotla, Puebla; and *amate,* wild fig tree bark paintings in animal and flower motifs, from Xalitla and Ameyaltepec, Guerrero, and commonly sold in Acapulco, Taxco, and Oaxaca.

POTTERY AND CERAMICS

Although Mexican pottery tradition is as diverse as the country itself, some varieties stand out. Among the most prized is the so-called Talavera (or Majolica), the best of which is made by a few family-run shops in Puebla. The labels Talavera and Majolica

Day of the Dead is a popular theme in contemporary Mexican ceramics.

smooth, and cuddly as ceramic can be, the Tonalá animals—very commonly doves and ducks, but also cats and dogs and sometimes even armadillos, frogs, and snakes—each seems to embody the essence of its species.

Some of the most charming Mexican pottery, made from a ruddy low-fired clay and crafted following pre-Columbian traditions, comes from western Mexico, especially Colima. Charming figurines in timeless human poses—flute-playing musicians, dozing grandmothers, fidgeting babies, loving couples—and animals, especially Colima's famous playful dogs, decorate the shelves of a sprinkling of shops.

The southern state of Guerrero sustains a vibrant pottery tradition. Throughout Pacific Mexico, you'll find the humble but very attractive unglazed brightly painted animals—cats, ducks, fish, and many others—that folks bring to resort centers from their village family workshops.

Much more acclaimed are certain types of pottery from the valley surrounding the city of Oaxaca. The village of Atzompa is famous for its tan, green-glazed clay pots, dishes, and bowls. Nearby San Bártolo Coyotepec village has acquired equal renown for its black pottery, sold all over the world. Doña Rosa, now deceased, pioneered the crafting of big round pots without using a potter's wheel. Now made in many more shapes by Doña Rosa's descendants, the pottery's exquisite silvery black sheen is produced by the reduction (reduced air) method of firing, which removes oxygen from the clay's red (ferric) iron oxide, converting it to black ferrous oxide.

Although most latter-day Mexican potters have become aware of the health dangers of lead pigments, some for-sale pottery may still contain lead. The hazard comes from low-fired pottery in which the lead has not been firmly melted into the glaze. Acids in foods such as lemons, vinegar, and tomatoes dissolve the lead pigments, which, when ingested, eventually result in lead poisoning. In general, the hardest, shiniest pottery, which has been twice fired—such as the high-

derive from Talavera, the Spanish town from which the tradition migrated to Mexico; before that it originated on the Spanish Mediterranean island of Mayorca (thus Majolica), from a combination of still older Arabic, Chinese, and African ceramic styles. Shapes include plates, bowls, jugs, and pitchers, hand-painted and hard-fired in intricate bright yellow, orange, blue, and green floral designs. So few shops make true Talavera these days that other, cheaper, lookalike grades, made around Guanajuato, are more common, selling for as little as one-tenth of the price of the genuine article.

More practical and nearly as prized is hand-painted, high-fired stoneware from Tonalá in Guadalajara's eastern suburbs. Although made in many shapes and sizes, such stoneware is often sold as complete dinner place settings. Decorations are usually in abstract floral and animal designs, hand-painted over a reddish clay base.

From the same tradition come the famous *bruñido* pottery animals of Tonalá. Round,

© BRUCE WHIPPERMAN

Tapetes (wool hangings and carpets) are woven in the Valley of Oaxaca and are sold at all Pacific Mexico resorts.

quality Tonalá stoneware used for dishes—is the safest.

WOOL WEAVINGS

Mexico's finest wool weavings come from Teotitlán del Valle, in the Valley of Oaxaca, less than an hour's drive east of Oaxaca city. The weaving tradition, carried on by Teotitlán's Zapotec-speaking families, dates back at least 2,000 years. Many families still carry on the arduous process, making everything from scratch. They gather the dyes from wild plants and the bodies of insects and sea snails. They hand-wash, card, spin, and dye the wool and even travel to remote mountain springs to gather water. The results, they say, *valen la pena* (are worth the pain): intensely colored,

tightly woven carpets, rugs, and wall-hangings that retain their brilliance for generations.

Rougher, more loosely woven, blankets, jackets, and serapes come from other parts, notably mountain regions, especially around San Cristóbal de las Casas, in Chiapas, and Lake Pátzcuaro in Michoacán.

FINE ARTS

A number of Pacific Mexico resort towns and cities have acquired colonies of resident artists and galleries that display and sell their work. Fine sculptures and paintings, by a number of internationally recognized local artists are available for sale, especially in Mazatlán, Puerto Vallarta, Guadalajara, and Oaxaca galleries.

ESSENTIALS

Getting There

BY AIR
From the United States and Canada

The vast majority of travelers reach Pacific Mexico by air. Flights are frequent and reasonably priced. Competition sometimes shaves prices to as low as $250 or less for a Mazatlán or Puerto Vallarta round-trip from Los Angeles, Denver, or Dallas.

Air travelers can save lots of money by shopping around. Don't be bashful about asking for the cheapest price. Make it clear to the airline or travel agent that you're interested in a bargain. Ask the right questions: Are there special-incentive, advance-payment, night, midweek, tour package, or charter fares? Peruse the ads in the Sunday newspaper travel section for bargain-oriented travel agencies. Check airline and travel websites, such as www.orbitz.com, www.expedia.com, and www.travelocity.com.

Although some agents charge booking fees and don't like discounted tickets because their fee depends on a percentage of ticket price, many will nevertheless work hard to get you a bargain, especially if you book an entire air-hotel package with them.

Although few airlines fly directly to Pacific Mexico from the northern United States and Canada, many charters do. In locales near Van-

couver, Calgary, Ottawa, Toronto, Montreal, Minneapolis, Chicago, Detroit, Cleveland, and New York, consult a travel agent for charter flight options. Be aware that charter reservations, which often require fixed departure and return dates and provide minimal cancellation refunds, decrease your flexibility. If available charter choices are unsatisfactory, then you might choose to begin your vacation with a connecting flight to one of the Pacific Mexico gateways, such as San Francisco, Los Angeles, San Diego, Denver, Phoenix, Dallas, Houston, Atlanta, Chicago, San Jose, or Oakland.

From Europe, Latin America, and Australasia

A few airlines fly across the Atlantic directly to Mexico City. These include **Lufthansa,** which connects directly from Frankfurt; and **Aeroméxico,** which connects directly from Paris and Madrid. In Mexico City, connections to Pacific Mexico are available via Mexicana, Aeroméxico, Aerocalifornia and several other airlines.

From Latin America, **Aeroméxico** connects directly with Mexico City, from São Paulo, Brazil; Santiago, Chile; and Lima, Peru. A number of other Latin American flag carriers also fly directly to Mexico City.

Very few flights cross the Pacific directly to Mexico, except for **Japan Airlines,** which connects Tokyo to Mexico City, via Vancouver. More commonly, travelers from Australasia transfer at New York, Chicago, Dallas, San Francisco, or Los Angeles for Pacific Mexico.

Baggage, Insurance, "Bumping," and In-Flight Meals

Tropical Pacific Mexico makes it easy to pack light. (See the *Packing Checklist* chart in the *Tips for Travelers* section.) Veteran tropical travelers condense their luggage to carry-ons only. Airlines routinely allow a carry-on (not exceeding 45 inches in combined length, width, and girth), small book bag, and purse. Thus relieved of heavy burdens, your trip will become much simpler. You'll avoid possible luggage loss and long baggage-check-in

lines by being able to check in directly at the boarding gate.

Even if you can't avoid checking luggage, loss of it needn't ruin your vacation. Always carry your irreplaceable items in the cabin with you. These should include all money, credit cards, traveler's checks, keys, tickets, cameras, passport, prescription drugs, and eyeglasses.

Travelers packing lots of expensive baggage, or who (because of illness, for example) may have to cancel a nonrefundable flight or tour, might consider buying **travel insurance.** Travel agents and travel websites routinely sell packages that include baggage, trip cancellation, and default insurance. **Baggage insurance** covers you beyond the conventional domestic and international baggage liability limits (double-check with your carrier). **Trip cancellation insurance** pays if you must cancel your prepaid trip, while **default insurance** protects you if your carrier or tour agent does not perform as agreed. Travel insurance, however, can be expensive. **Travel Insurance Services** (toll-free U.S. tel. 800/937-1387, www.travelinsure.com), for example, offers $3,000 of baggage insurance per person for two weeks for about $65. Weigh your options and the cost against benefits carefully before putting your money down.

Alternatively, contact World Travel Center (tel. 402/343-3699 or 866/979-6753, www.worldtravelcenter.com) for similar travel insurance services.

It's wise to reconfirm both departure and return flight reservations, especially during the busy Christmas and Easter seasons. This is a useful strategy, as is prompt arrival at check-in, against getting "bumped" (losing your seat) by the tendency of airlines to overbook high-season vacationers. For further protection, always get your seat assignment and boarding pass included with your ticket.

Airlines generally try hard to accommodate travelers with **dietary or other special needs.** When booking your flight, inform your travel agent or carrier of the necessity of a low-sodium, low-cholesterol, vegetarian, or lactose-reduced meal, or other requirements.

AIRLINES

The air carriers with the greatest number of direct connections between Pacific Mexico and North American destinations are listed below in approximate descending order of activity. Destinations include Mazatlán (MZ), Puerto Vallarta (PV), Manzanillo-Barra de Navidad (MN), Guadalajara (GD), Ixtapa-Zihuatanejo (IX), Acapulco (AC), Mexico City (MX), Morelia-Pátzcuaro (MO), Huatulco (HU), Oaxaca (OA), Los Cabos (LC), and La Paz (LP). Other popular Pacific Mexico destinations, such as Puerto Escondido, are air-accessible via Mexico City.

AIRLINE	ORIGIN	DESTINATIONS
Mexicana	Los Angeles	MZ, GD, MX, LC, MO
tel. 800/531-7921	San Francisco	GD, MX, MO
www.mexicana.com	San Jose	GD, MX, MO
	Tijuana	GD, MX
	Denver	MX
	Chicago	GD, MX, MO
	Miami	MX
	San Antonio	MX
	Oakland	GD, MO, MX
	Toronto	MX
	Montreal	MX
	Las Vegas	GD, MX, LC
	New York	MX
	Portland	GD, MX
Aeroméxico	Los Angeles	GD, MX
tel. 800/237-6639	Tijuana	PV, MZ, GD, MO
www.aeromexico.com	New York	PV, MX
	Miami	MX
	Houston	MX
	Chicago	GD, MX
	San Diego	MX, LC
	Phoenix	GD, MX

(Seniors, travelers with disabilities, and parents traveling with children, see the *Tips for Travelers* section in this chapter.)

BY BUS

As air travel rules in the United States, bus travel rules in Mexico. Hundreds of sleek, first-class bus lines with names such as Elite, Turistar, Futura, Transportes Pacífico, and Estrella Blanca (White Star) depart the border daily, headed for Pacific Mexico.

Since North American bus lines ordinarily terminate just north of the Mexican border, you must usually disembark and continue on foot across the border to the Mexican immigration office *(migración)*. There, after having filled out the necessary but very simple paperwork, you can walk outside and bargain with one of the local taxis to drive you the few miles to the *camionera central* (central bus station).

First-class bus service in Mexico is much cheaper and more frequent than in the United States (you'll pay as little as around $50 for a 1,000-mile trip, compared to $100 in the United States).

In Mexico, you often have to take it as you find it. *Asientos reservados* (seat reservations), *boletos* (tickets), and information must gener-

AIRLINE	ORIGIN	DESTINATIONS
Aeroméxico	New York	MX
(cont.)	Ontario	GD
Alaska Airlines	Seattle	MZ, PV, IX, LC
tel. 800/426-0333	San Francisco	MZ, PV, MN, IX,
www.alaskaair.com	Los Angeles	MZ, PV, MN, IX, LC, GD, MX
	San Diego	LC
American Airlines	Dallas	PV, GD, AC, MX, LC
tel. 800/433-7300	Los Angeles	GD, LC
www.aa.com	Chicago	PV, AC, LC, MX
	Miami	MX
Delta	Los Angeles	PV, GD, MX
tel. 800/221-1212	Dallas	MX
www.delta.com	Atlanta	PV, GD, MX
	New York	MX
U.S. Airways	Phoenix	MZ, PV, GD, MN, IX, AC,
(formerly America West)		LC, MX
tel. 800/363-2597		
www.usairways.com		
Continental	Houston	MZ,PV,GD,MN,AC,LC,IX
tel. 800/231-0856		IX,HU,OA,MX
www.continental.com	Newark	MX
Air Canada	Toronto	PV,MX
tel. 888/247-2262		
www.aircanada.com		

ally be obtained in person at the bus station, and credit cards and traveler's checks are not often accepted. Reserved bus tickets typically are not refundable, so don't miss the bus. On the other hand, plenty of buses roll south almost continually.

Bus Routes to Pacific Mexico
From California and the western United States, cross the border to Tijuana, Mexicali, or Nogales, where you can ride one of several bus lines along the Pacific Coast route (National Highway 15) to points south: Estrella Blanca subsidiaries (Elite, Turistar, Transportes Norte de Sonora) or independent Transportes del Pacífico.

At Mazatlán or Tepic, depending on the line, you transfer or continue on the same bus, south to Puerto Vallarta and/or Manzanillo, or west to Guadalajara. Allow a full day and a bit more (about 30 hours), depending upon connections, for the trip. Carry liquids and food (which might be only minimally available en route) with you.

From the midwestern United States, cross the border from El Paso to Ciudad Juárez and ride independent line Omnibus de Mexico or Estrella Blanca subsidiaries (luxury-class

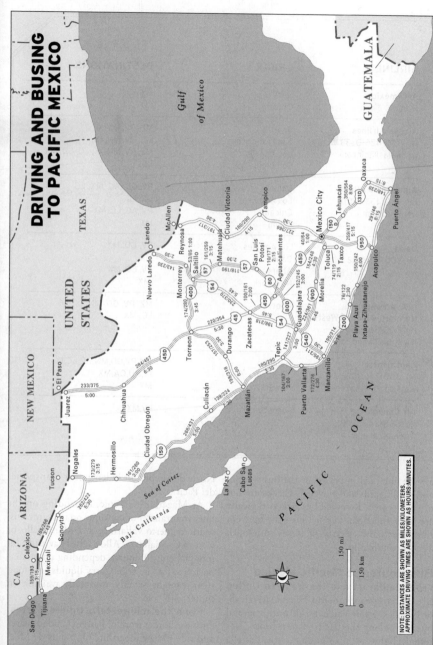

DRIVING AND BUSING
TO PACIFIC MEXICO

© AVALON TRAVEL PUBLISHING, INC.

NOTE: DISTANCES ARE SHOWN AS MILES/KILOMETERS.
APPROXIMATE DRIVING TIMES ARE SHOWN AS HOURS:MINUTES.

Turistar or Transportes Chihuahuenses) via Chihuahua and Durango. Both Transportes Chihuahuenses and Turistar may offer one or two daily departures direct to Mazatlán. Otherwise, transfer at Durango to a Mazatlán-bound bus, and continue as above.

From the southeastern and eastern United States, cross the border at Laredo to Nuevo Laredo and ride Estrella Blanca subsidiaries Transportes del Norte, Turistar, or Futura direct to Durango. At Durango, transfer to a Mazatlán bus, where you can continue south, as described above.

On the other hand, **from the central or eastern United States,** it may be more convenient to ride a bus from the border direct to Guadalajara, where you can easily transfer to one of many buses bound for Pacific Mexico western and southern destinations of Puerto Vallarta, Barra de Navidad, Manzanillo, and Michoacán. (For bus connections in Guadalajara, see *Getting There and Away* in the *Guadalajara* chapter.)

Travelers heading directly to Oaxaca city or the far southern coastal destinations of Acapulco, Ixtapa, Zihuatanejo, and the Oaxaca coast should ride from the border directly to Mexico City, Terminal Norte (North Terminal). At Terminal Norte, ride Autobúses del Oriente (ADO) or Cristóbal Colón directly to Oaxaca city. For the south coast from Terminal Norte, ride an Estrella Blanca subsidiary bus (Turistar or Futura) to Acapulco, where you can transfer to coast-route buses bound either northwest for Ixtapa and Zihuatanejo, or southeast for Puerto Escondido on the Oaxaca coast. If somehow the above connections are not available at Terminal Norte, share a taxi—don't try it by public transit—across town to either Terminal Tapo, the Mexico City east terminal, or Terminal Sur, the Mexico City south terminal. At Terminal Tapo, board a Oaxaca city–bound bus, probably Cristóbal Colón or ADO (Autobúses del Oriente)—via *corta*—the expressway "shortcut." At Terminal Sur, board an Acapulco-bound Estrella Blanca subsidiary (Turistar, or Futura) bus.

From the U.S. border east, allow two days' travel for Acapulco, Ixtapa, Zihuatanejo, or Oaxaca city, and three days for Puerto Escondido-Puerto Ángel. From midwestern or western border points, add another day.

BY CAR OR RV

If you're adventurous, like going to out-of-the-way places, but still want to have all the comforts of home, you may enjoy driving your car or RV to Pacific Mexico. On the other hand, consideration of cost, risk, wear on both you and your vehicle, and the congestion hassles in towns may change your mind.

Mexican Car Insurance

Mexico does not recognize foreign insurance. When you drive into Mexico, Mexican auto insurance is at least as important as your passport. At the busier crossings, you can get it at insurance "drive-ins" just north of the border. The many Mexican auto insurance companies are government-regulated; their numbers keep prices and services competitive.

Sanborn's Mexico Insurance (Sanborn's Mexico, P.O. Box 310, McAllen, TX 78502, toll-free 800/222-0158, tel. 956/686-3601, www.sanbornsinsurance.com), one of the best-known agencies, certainly seems to be trying hardest. It offers a number of books and services, including the *Recreational Guide to Mexico,* a good road map, "smile-by-mile" *Travelog* guide to "every highway in Mexico," hotel discounts, and more. Much of the above is available to members of Sanborn's Sombrero Club.

Alternatively, look into **Vagabundos del Mar** (tel. 800/474-2252, www.vagabundos .com), an RV-oriented Mexico travel club offering memberships that include a newsletter, caravaning opportunites, discounts, insurance, and much more.

Mexican car insurance runs from a bare-bones rate of about $6 a day for minimal $10,000/$50,000 (property damage/medical payments) coverage to a more typical $12 a day for more complete $20,000/$100,000 coverage. On the same scale, insurance for a $50,000 RV and equipment runs about $30 a day. These daily rates decrease sharply for six-month or one-year policies, which run from about $200 for the minimum to $400–1,600 for complete, high-end coverage.

If you get broken glass, personal effects, and legal expenses coverage with these rates, you're lucky. Mexican policies don't usually cover them.

You should get something for your money, however. The deductibles should be no more than $300–500, the public liability/medical payments should be about double the ($25,000/$50,000) legal minimum, and you should be able to get your car fixed in the United States and receive payment in U.S. dollars for losses. If not, shop around.

A Sinaloa Note of Caution

Although *bandidos* no longer menace Mexican roads (though loose burros, horses, and cattle still do), be cautious in the infamous marijuana- and opium-growing region of Sinaloa state north of Mazatlán. It's best not to stray from Highway 15 between Culiacán and Mazatlán or from Highway 40 between Mazatlán and Durango. Curious tourists have been assaulted in the hinterlands adjacent to these roads.

The Green Angels

The Green Angels have answered many motoring tourists' prayers in Mexico. Bilingual teams of two, trained in auto repair and first aid, help distressed tourists along main highways. They patrol fixed stretches of road twice daily by truck. To make sure they stop to help, pull completely off the highway and raise your hood. You may want to hail a passing trucker to call them for you (Mexico emergency number tel. 078 for the tourism hotline, or tel. 01-800/903-9200).

If, for some reason, you have to leave your vehicle on the roadside, don't leave it unattended. Hire a local teenager or adult to watch it for you. Unattended vehicles on Mexican highways are quickly stricken by a mysterious disease, the symptoms of which are rapid loss of vital parts.

In the Pacific Mexico back country, unleaded regular gasoline is sold by local shopkeepers and dispensed by hand.

Mexican Gasoline

Pemex, short for Petróleos Mexicanos, the government oil monopoly, markets diesel fuel and two grades of unleaded gasoline: 92-octane premium and 89-octane Magna. Magna (MAHG-nah) is good gas, yielding performance similar to that of U.S.-style regular or super unleaded gasoline. (My car, whose manufacturer recommends 91-octane, ran well on Magna.) It runs about $.65 per liter (or about $2.50 per gallon).

On main highways, Pemex makes sure that major stations (spaced typically about 25 miles apart) stock Magna.

Gas Station Thievery

Although the problem has abated considerably in recent years, boys who hang around gas stations to wash windows are notoriously light-fingered. When stopping at the *gasolinera,* make sure that your cameras, purses, and other movable items are out of reach. Also, make sure that your car has a lockable gas cap.

If not, insist on pumping the gas yourself, or be extra watchful as you pull up to the gas pump. Make certain that the pump reads zero before the attendant pumps the gas.

A Healthy Car

Preventive measures spell good health for both you and your car. Get that tune-up (or that long-delayed overhaul) *before,* rather than after, you leave.

Carry a stock of spare parts, which will be more difficult to get and more expensive in Mexico than at home: an extra tire or two, a few cans of motor oil and octane enhancer, oil and gas filters, fan belts, spark plugs, tune-up kit, points, and fuses. Be prepared with basic tools and supplies, such as screwdrivers, pliers including Vise-Grip, lug wrench, jack, adjustable wrenches, tire pump and patches, tire pressure gauge, steel wire, and electrical tape. For breakdowns and emergencies, carry a folding shovel, a husky rope or chain, a gasoline can, and flares.

Car Repairs in Mexico

The American big three—General Motors, Ford, and Chrysler—as well as Nissan and Volkswagen are represented by extensive dealer networks in Mexico. Latecomers Toyota and Honda are represented, although to a much lesser extent. Getting your car or truck serviced at such agencies is straightforward. While parts will probably be higher in price, shop rates run about half U.S. prices, so repairs will generally cost less than half of back-home prices.

Repair of other makes is more problematic. Mexico has few, if any, other Japanese car or truck dealers; and other than Mercedes-Benz, which has some truck agencies, it is difficult to find officially certified mechanics for other Japanese, British, and European vehicles. Parts, moreover, may not be locally available, and it may take as long as a week to have them shipped from the United States.

Many clever Mexican independent mechanics, however, can fix any car that comes their way. Their humble repair shops, or *talleres*

mecánicos (tah-YER-ays may-KAH-nee-kohs), dot town and village roadsides everywhere.

Although most mechanics are honest, beware of unscrupulous operators who try to collect double or triple their original estimate. If you don't speak Spanish, find someone who can assist you in negotiations. *Always* get at least a verbal (better if written) cost estimate, including needed parts and labor, even if you have to write it yourself. Make sure the mechanic understands, then ask him to sign it before he starts work. Although this may be a hassle, it might save you a much nastier hassle later. Shop labor at small, independent repair shops should run $10–20 per hour. For more information, and for entertaining anecdotes of car and RV travel in Mexico, consult Carl Franz's *The People's Guide to Mexico.*

Bribes (*Mordidas*)

The usual meeting ground of the visitor and Mexican police is in the visitor's car on a highway or downtown street. To the tourists, such an encounter may seem mild harassment by the police, accompanied by vague threats of going to the police station or impounding the car for such-and-such a violation. The tourist often goes on to say, "It was all right, though. We paid him $20 and he went away. Mexican cops sure are crooked, aren't they?"

And, I suppose, if people want to go bribing their way through Mexico, that's their business. But calling Mexican cops crooked isn't exactly fair. Police, like most everyone else in Mexico, have to scratch for a living, and they have found that many tourists are willing to slip them a $20 bill for nothing. Rather than crooked, I would call them hungry and opportunistic.

Instead of paying a bribe, do what I've done a dozen times: remain cool, and if you're really guilty of an infraction, calmly say, "Ticket, please." *("Boleto, por favor.")* After a minute or two of stalling, and no cash appearing, the officer most likely will not bother with a ticket but will wave you on with only a warning. If, on the other hand, the officer does write you a ticket, he will probably keep your driver's license, which you will be able to retrieve at the Presidencia Municipal (City Hall) the next day in exchange for paying your fine.

Crossing the Border

Squeezing through the border traffic bottlenecks during peak holidays and rush hours can easily take two or three hours. Avoid crossing 7–9 A.M. and 4:30–6:30 P.M. Moreover, with increased U.S. Homeland Security precautions, the return, northbound border crossing, under the best of conditions, generally takes at least an hour waiting in your car, along with a hundred or more other frustrated drivers.

Highway Routes from the United States

If you've decided to drive to northwestern Pacific Mexico, you have your choice of three general routes. At safe highway speeds, each of these routes requires a minimum of about 24 hours of driving time. Maximize comfort and safety by following the broad toll (cuota) expressways that often parallel the old narrow nontoll (libre) routes. Despite the increased cost (about $60 for a car, double or triple that for a motorhome) the cuota expressways will save you at least a day's driving time (including the extra food and hotel tariffs) and wear and tear on both your vehicle and your nerves. Most folks allow three full south-of-the-border driving days to Mazatlán–Guadalajara–Puerto Vallarta.

From the western and Pacific United States, follow National Highway 15 (called 15 D as the toll expressway) from the border at Nogales, Sonora, an hour's drive south of Tucson, Arizona. Highway 15 D continues southward smoothly, leading you through cactus-studded mountains and valleys, which turn into green, lush farmland and tropical coastal plain and forest by the time you arrive in Mazatlán. Watch for the peripheral bypasses (periféricos) and truck routes that guide you past the congested downtowns of Hermosillo, Guaymas, Ciudad Obregón, Los Mochis, and Culiacán.

Between these centers, you speed along via cuota (toll) expressway all the way to Mazatlán. If you prefer not to pay the high tolls, stick to the old libre (free) highway. Hazards, bumps, and slow going might force you to reconsider, however.

From Mazatlán, continue along the narrow (but soon to be replaced) two-lane route to Tepic, where Highways 15 and 15 D fork left (east) to Guadalajara and Highway 200 heads south to Puerto Vallarta and beyond.

If, however, you're driving to western Pacific Mexico from the central United States, cross the border at El Paso to Ciudad Juárez, Chihuahua. There, National Highway 45 D, the new cuota multilane expressway, leads you southward through high dry plains past the cities of Chihuahua and Jiménez, where you continue by expressway Highway 49 to Gómez Palacio–Torreón. There, proceed southwest toward Durango, via expressway Highway 40 D. At Durango, head west along the winding but spectacular two-lane trans-Sierra National Highway 40, which intersects National Highway 15 just south of Mazatlán. From there, continue south as described above.

Folks heading to western Pacific Mexico from the eastern and southeastern United States should cross the border from Laredo, Texas, to Nuevo Laredo. From there, you can follow either the National Highway 85 nontoll (libre) route or the new Highway 85 D toll (cuota) road, which continues, bypassing Monterrey, where you proceed via expressway Highway 40 D all the way to Saltillo. At Saltillo, keep going westward on Highway 40 or expressway 40 D through Torreón to Durango. Continue, via the two-lane Highway 40 over the Pacific crest, all the way to National Highway 15, just south of Mazatlán. Continue southward as described above.

Direct Routes to Pacific Mexico's Deep South

For folks heading from the United States directly for Pacific Mexico's southern destinations of Manzanillo, Acapulco, Ixtapa, Zihuatanejo, or Oaxaca, a few basic routes are available. From California or the west, the quickest way is to go via Nogales to Guadalajara, where you continue east toward Mexico City via cross-town expressway Av. Lázaro Cárdenas to toll expressway 15 D. If headed south for Manzanillo, fork right in Gaudalajara on to Av. Lopez Mateos sur (combined Highways 15, 80, and 54) and continue south, where you join with toll expressway 54 D, to Manzanillo and other points south.

If you're headed for Acapulco and the far southern coast, continue through Guadalajara on to toll expressway 15 D and continue to Toluca. There you should continue bypassing Mexico City, by turning south via toll expressway 55 toward Ixtapan del Sal, after which signs direct your connection with toll expressway 95 D south to Acapulco. If headed directly for Oaxaca city, ride expressway 90 D to Mexico City, where you must make your way east through the sprawling metropolis (see sidebar *Mexico City Driving Restrictions* in the *Acapulco and Taxco* chapter) and connect with east-side toll expressway 150 D through Puebla. Continue east to toll expressway 131 D, thence southeast, via Tehuacán to Oaxaca.

From the midwestern and eastern United States, cross the border from McAllen, Texas, to Reynosa. From there, head southward to Mexico City, where you continue across town either south, where you connect with toll expressway 95 D to Acapulco, or east, where you connect with toll expressway 150 D (through Puebla) to toll expressway 131 D via Tehuacán to Oaxaca.

BY FERRY

An alternative, but more complicated route to Puerto Vallarta is by ferry from the southern tip of Baja California. Bus travelers should cross the border at Tijuana or Mexicali and ride Autobuses Blanca Coordinados (ABC) (Tijuana local tel. 664/621-2424, www.abc .com.mx) through the long desert to La Paz (about 20 hours). Car travelers also can cross

at Tijuana or Mexicali and follow good, two-lane Mexico National Highway 1, a long 900 miles (1,500 km) south to La Paz.

At La Paz (a pleasant, midsized Mexican fishing port town during the winter, although usually very hot during the late spring and summer), you have your choice of two ferry crossings. **Baja Ferries** (at the La Paz ferry dock, from U.S. dial direct tel. 01152-612/125-6324, fax 01152-612/123-0504; or in Mex. toll-free tel. 01-800/122-2796, ventas.lapaz@bajaferries.com, www.bajaferries .com) ferries passengers and vehicles between La Paz and Topolobambo, near Los Mochis in northern Sinaloa (about $65 per adult, kids $32, cars and smaller four-wheel RVs about $200, motorhomes about double) and between La Paz and Mazatlán ($75, $35, and $230) in southern Sinaloa. Note: If you're planning on continuing south to Puerto Vallarta, you should probably opt for the Mazatlán crossing. Although it won't save you much time (since the bus or your vehicle travels much faster than the ferry), you might save the price of a hotel room and highway tolls (or bus fare).

The La Paz-Topolobampo run goes via the excellent Italian-built 1000-passenger *California Star*. At this writing, it leaves La Paz nightly at 11 P.M. and takes six hours. The La Paz–Mazatlán run, via the similarly fine but smaller 600-passenger **Sinaloa Star,** leaves La Paz Mon., Wed., and Fri. at 3 P.M. and takes 18 hours. Although seats are provided (comfortable bus-style in the **Sinaloa Star**), you may want to reserve one of their clean cabins with beds and private toilet (about $70 on the Topolobambo run, $40 on the Mazatlán run). Ferry facilities on both runs include bar, lounge, and restaurant, but pets are not allowed, and passengers are not allowed to stay in their vehicles during the crossing. MasterCard and Visa are accepted for payment.

Reservations are recommended at all times, and are a must during the super-crowded Christmas and Easter holidays. You can make reservations either through the website www .bajaferries.com or directly at the many reservations-ticket sales offices that the website lists. Of all of these, the most useful would probably be the U.S. agent, Native Trails, at 613 Queretaro, El Paso TX 79912-2210, tel. 915/833-3107, fax 915/585-7027, or the La Paz sales office, which has English-speaking agents, at the corner of Isabel la Catolica and Navarro, La Paz, Baja California del Sur, Mexico, toll-free Mex. tel. 01-800/122-1414, local tel. 612/125-7443, fax 612/125-7444.

Although greatly improved in recent years, Baja ferry service is subject to change. Be sure to check by phone or on the Internet for the newest ferry information before making the long desert trip south to La Paz. You can make reservations easily on the Internet, or with the Baja Ferries U.S. agent.

BY TOUR, CRUISE, AND SAILBOAT

For travelers on a tight time budget, prearranged tour packages can provide a hassle-free route for sampling the attractions of Pacific Mexico's coastal resorts and colonial cities. If, however, you prefer a self-paced vacation, or desire thrift over convenience, you should probably defer tour arrangements until after arrival. Many Pacific Mexico travel and tour agencies are as close as your hotel telephone or front lobby tour desk and can customize a tour for you. Options vary from city highlight tours and bay snorkeling adventures to inland colonial cities shopping-and-sightseeing overnights to boat adventures through wildlife-rich mangrove jungle hinterlands.

Travel agents will typically have a stack of cruise brochures that include Pacific Mexico ports such as Mazatlán, Puerto Vallarta, Ixtapa-Zihuatanejo, and Acapulco on their itineraries. People who enjoy being pampered with lots of food and ready-made entertainment (and who don't mind paying for it) can have great fun on cruises. Accommodations on a typical 10-day winter cruise (which would include several days in port) can run as little as $100 per day per person, double occupancy, to more than $1,000.

If, however, you want to get to know Mexico

and the local people, a cruise is not for you. Onboard food and entertainment is the main event of a cruise; shore sightseeing excursions, which generally cost extra, are a sideshow.

Sailboats, on the other hand, offer an entirely different kind of sea route to Pacific Mexico. Ocean Voyages, a California-based agency, arranges passage on a number of sail and motor vessels that regularly depart to Pacific Mexico ports such as San Diego, Los Angeles, San Francisco, Seattle, and Vancouver, British Columbia. It offers custom itineraries and flexible arrangements that can vary from complete round-trip voyages to weeklong coastal idylls between Pacific Mexico ports of call. Some captains allow passengers to save money by signing on as crew. For more information, contact Ocean Voyages, 1709 Bridgeway, Sausalito, CA 94965, tel. 415/332-4681 or 800/299-4444, fax 415/332-7460, sail@oceanvoyages.com, www.oceanvoyages.com.

SPECIAL TOURS AND STUDY OPTIONS

Some tour programs include in-depth activities centered around arts and crafts, language and culture, wildlife viewing, ecology, people-to-people work-study, and off-the-beaten-track adventuring.

Holistic Retreats

Mar de Jade (tel. 327/219-4060 or 327/219-4070, in Puerto Vallarta tel. 322/222-1171, toll-free U.S. tel. 800/257-0532, info@mardejade.com, www.mardejade.com), a holistic-style living center at Playa Chacala, about 50 miles (80 km) north of Puerto Vallarta, offers unique people-to-people work-study opportunities. These include Spanish-language study at Mar de Jade's rustic beach study-center and assisting at its health clinic in Las Varas town nearby. It also offers accommodations and macrobiotic meals for travelers who would want to do nothing more than stay a few days and soak in Mar de Jade's lovely tropical ambience. (For more details of the Mar de Jade area and accommodations and fees, see the *Road to San Blas* section in *The Nayarit Coast* chapter.)

Another similar, more deluxe (but simply spartan) holistic option is **Rancho Río Caliente Spa** (contact through North American agent, Spa Vacations, P.O. Box 897, Millbrae, CA 94030, tel. 650/615-9543, toll-free U.S. tel. 800/200-2927, fax 650/615-0601, riocal@aol.com, www.riocaliente.com), nestled in the sylvan pine-oak forest hinterland about 20 miles west of Guadalajara. Accommodations are in a tranquil cluster of brick cottages beside and above the steaming Río Caliente, which gushes, steaming hot, from a nearby cliffbottom. Inside, the approximately 50 comfortably austere accommodations, each with its own fireplace, are enclosed in attractively rustic brown brick walls, with shiny tile floors, comfortable beds, handmade wooden furniture, and immaculate shower baths.

Rates begin at about $160 per day per person, including taxes and all meals (macrobiotic, alcohol-free) and many activities, including sauna, hot pools, hiking, discussion groups, and wildlife viewing (but no exercise machines). Available spa treatments are extensive but extra.

Elderhostel

Elderhostel's rich offering includes several educational travel programs in a number of Pacific Mexico locations, such as the Copper Canyon, Mazatlán, Guadalajara, Pátzcuaro, Uruapan, Oaxaca, and more. Topics range widely, from art and history, to festivals, such as the Day of the Dead, and birdwatching and Spanish-language and cultural immersion. Offerings vary, but some past and presently scheduled programs offer interesting options. In Guadalajara, for example, the program "Art of Colonial Mexico" involves sketching and painting and exploration of Guadalajara's rich trove of art. A separate Guadalajara program, "Language and History of Mexico," provides Elderhostelers with opportunities to hone their language skills in practical encounters and appreciate history in context, while exploring the architectural, art, and craft treasures of Guadalajara and Zacatecas.

Elderhostel also offers festival programs, one of which centers around the November Day of the Dead in Michoacán. The 10-day tour (including four days in Pátzcuaro and its nearby island villages) includes ancient ruined cities, crafts villages, and folkloric dance performances, and climaxes with the Day of the Dead observances, which, although somber in most countries, are joyful and lively in Mexico.

Yet another pair of Elderhostel tours lead participants in explorations of Oaxaca's rich cultural and natural heritage. "Oaxaca: Spanish Language and Hispanic Culture" emphasizes practice in conversational Spanish, while "Exotic Mexican Birds and Their Habitat" centers on natural history in the countryside. Both programs include visits to archaeological sites of Monte Albán and Mitla and appreciation of indigenous tradition through visits to pottery, weaving, and woodcrafting villages, as well as evening excursions to enjoy Oaxacan food and folkloric music and dance. Accommodations options can include both hotel rooms and homestays with Mexican families. For more details and present schedules, write or phone for the international catalog: Elderhostel, 11 Ave. de Lafayette, Boston, MA 02111-1746, toll-free tel. 800/454-5768, www.elderhostel.org.

Eco-Adventuring and Wildlife-Viewing

A Puerto Vallarta ranch, **Rancho El Charro** (Francisco Villa 895, Fracc. Las Gaviotas, Puerto Vallarta, Jalisco 48300, tel. 322/224-0114, aguirre@pvnet.com.mx) organizes naturalist-led **horseback treks** in the mountains near Puerto Vallarta. The most extensive tours run several days to a week and include guided backcountry horseback riding, exploring antique colonial villages, camping out on the trail, swimming, hearty dinners, and cozy evenings at a rustic hacienda. Tariffs begin at about $1,000 per person. For more information, visit www.ranchoelcharro.com.

Naturalists should consider the excellent **Field Guides** birding tours, one customarily centered in wildlife-rich Jalisco and Colima backcountry, and the other in Oaxaca's central valley and tropical south coast. For more information, call toll-free tel. 800/728-4953, fax 512/263-0117, fieldguides@fieldguides.com, www.fieldguides.com.

The **National Audubon Society** also offers Mexico birding tours. Itineraries have included the Copper Canyon, Baja, and Oaxaca (which has included four days in the Valley of Oaxaca and four days in the lush south coastal mountain jungle near Puerto Escondido). Contact the National Audubon Society, 700 Broadway, New York, NY 10003-9562, toll-free tel. 800/967-7425, fax 212/979-8947, travel@audubon.org, www.audubon.org/market/no.

Grassroots Exploring

Adventurous travelers might check out **Manos de Oaxaca** (www.manos-de-oaxaca.com) of artisan guide and Oaxaca lover Eric Mindling. His bliss is leading like-minded folks in explorations of traditional clay and fiber arts of country artisans in communities in Oaxaca

Valley, the Mixteca, and the Coast. The approach is people to people, the accommodations sometimes rustic, the prices very reasonable, but the rewards potentially great. Eric customarily leads about four or five tours of 7–10 days per year.

Mar de Jade also provides people-to-people contact and volunteer work-study opportunities.

Spanish Language Instruction and Homestays

Other options exist for travelers interested in small-group Spanish-language instruction, including homestay options in several Pacific Mexico centers. Contact one of the experienced agencies, such as the **National Registration Center for Study Abroad** (P.O. Box 1393, Milwaukee, WI 53201, tel. 414/278-0631, fax 414/278-8884, study@nrcsa.com, www.nrcsa .com) or **Amerispan Unlimited** (117 S. 17th St., Philadelphia, PA 19103, tel. 215/751-1100 or 800/879-6640, fax 215/751-1986, info@ amerispan.com, www.amerispan.com).

Getting Around

BY AIR

Mexicana, Aeroméxico, Aviacsa, Aerocalifornia, other smaller carriers, and light-plane charters connect the main destinations of Pacific Mexico. In the north, a scheduled network connects Mazatlán, Puerto Vallarta, Guadalajara, Manzanillo–Barra de Navidad, Colima, Morelia, and other Mexico destinations. In the south, the same is true of Ixtapa, Zihuatanejo, Acapulco, Puerto Escondido, Puerto Ángel-Huatulco, and Oaxaca. Although much pricier than first-class bus tickets, domestic airfares are on a par with U.S. prices.

Travelers may book tickets by contacting agencies in the destination cities.

Local Flying Tips

If you're planning on lots of in-Mexico flying,

upon arrival get the airlines' handy (although rapidly changeable) *itinerarios de vuelo* (flight schedules) at the airport.

Mexican airlines have operating peculiarities that result from their tight budgets. Reconfirm your flight by telephone a few days ahead of time. Schedules sometimes change without notice. Don't miss a flight; you will likely lose half the ticket price. Adjusting your flight date may cost 25 percent of the ticket price. Get to the airport at least an hour ahead of time. Last-minute passengers are often "bumped" in favor of early-bird waiting-listers. Conversely, go to the airport and get in line if you must catch a flight that the airlines claim is full. You might get on anyway. Keep your luggage small so you can carry it on. Lost-luggage victims receive scant compensation in Mexico.

BY BUS

The bus is the king of the Mexican road. Dozens of lines connect virtually every town in Pacific Mexico. Three distinct levels of service—super-first-class (or luxury), first-class, and second-class—are generally available. **Luxury-class** (usually called something like "Primera Plus," depending upon the line) express coaches speed between major towns, seldom stopping en route. In exchange for relatively high fares (about $50 Puerto Vallarta–Guadalajara, or Oaxaca–Puerto Escondido, for example), passengers often enjoy rapid passage and airline-style amenities: plush reclining seats, air-conditioning, an on-board toilet, video, and aisle attendant.

Although less luxurious, but for about two-thirds the price, **first-class** service is frequent and always includes reserved seating. Passengers enjoy soft reclining seats and air-conditioning (if it is working). Besides their regular stops at or near most towns and villages en route, first-class bus drivers, if requested, will usually stop and let you off anywhere along the road.

Second-class bus seating is unreserved. In outlying parts of Pacific Mexico, there is even a class of bus beneath second-class, but given the condition of many second-class buses, it seems as if third-class buses wouldn't run at all. Such buses are the stuff of travelers' legends: the recycled old GMC, Ford, and Dodge schoolbuses that stop everywhere and carry everyone and everything to even the smallest villages tucked away in the far mountains. As long as there is any kind of a road, the bus will most likely go there.

Second-class buses are not for travelers with weak knees or stomachs. Often, you will initially have to stand, cramped in the aisle, in a crowd of campesinos. They are warm-hearted but poor people, so don't tempt them with open, dangling purses or wallets bulging in back pockets. Stow your money safely away. After a while, you will be able to sit down. Such privilege, however, comes with obligation, such as holding an old woman's bulging bag of carrots or a toddler on your lap. But if you accept your burden with humor and equanimity, who knows what favors and blessings may flow to you in return.

Tickets, Seating, and Baggage

Mexican bus lines do not usually publish schedules or fares. You have to ask someone who knows (such as your hotel desk clerk), or call the bus station. Few travel agents handle bus tickets. If you don't want to spend the time to get a reserved ticket yourself, hire someone trustworthy to do it for you. Another option is to get to the bus station early enough on your traveling day to ensure that you'll get a bus to your destination.

Although some lines accept credit cards and issue computer-printed tickets at their major stations, most reserved bus tickets are sold for cash and handwritten, with a specific seat number, *número de asiento,* on the back. If you miss the bus, you lose your money. Airline-style automated reservations systems have not yet arrived at many Mexican bus stations. Consequently, you can generally buy reserved tickets only at the local departure (*salida local*) station. (An agent in Puerto Vallarta, for example, cannot ordinarily reserve you a ticket on a bus that originates in Tepic, 100 miles up the road.)

Request a reserved seat, if possible, with numbers 1–25 in the front (*delante*) to middle (*medio*) of the bus. The rear seats are sometimes occupied by would-be smokers, drunks, and rowdies. At night, you will sleep better on the right side (*lado derecho*) away from the glare of oncoming traffic lights.

Baggage is generally secure on Mexican buses. Label it, however. Overhead racks are generally too cramped to accommodate airline-sized carry-ons. Carry a small bag with your money and irreplaceables on your person; pack clothes and less-essentials in your checked luggage. For peace of mind, watch the handler put your checked baggage on the bus and watch to make sure it is not mistakenly taken off the bus at intermediate stops.

If your baggage gets misplaced, remain calm. Bus employees are generally competent and conscientious. If you are patient,

DRIVING AND BUSING WITHIN PACIFIC MEXICO

NOTE: DISTANCES ARE SHOWN AS MILES/KILOMETERS. APPROXIMATE DRIVING TIMES ARE SHOWN AS HOURS:MINUTES.

© AVALON TRAVEL PUBLISHING, INC.

recovering your luggage will become a matter of honor for many of them. Baggage handlers are at the bottom of the pay scale; a tip for their mostly thankless job is very much appreciated.

On long trips, carry food, beverages, and toilet paper. Station food may be dubious, and the sanitary facilities may be ill-maintained.

If you are waiting for a first-class bus at an intermediate *salida de paso* (passing station), you have to trust to luck that there will be an empty seat. If not, your best option may be to ride a more frequent second-class bus.

BY CAR OR RV

Driving your own car in Mexico may or may not be for you. (See *By Car or RV* under the *Getting There* section before deciding.)

Rental Car

Car and jeep rentals are an increasingly popular transportation option for Pacific Mexico travelers. They offer mobility and independence for local sightseeing and beach excursions. In the resorts, the gang's all there: Alamo, Hertz, National, Dollar, Avis, Budget, Thrifty, and a host of local outfits.

They generally require drivers to have a valid driver's license, passport, and a major credit card, and may require a minimum age of 25. Some local companies do not accept credit cards, but offer lower rates in return.

Base prices of international agencies such as Hertz, National, and Avis are not cheap. With a 17 percent value-added tax and mandatory insurance, rentals run about double the United States tariffs. The cheapest possible rental car, usually a used, stick-shift VW Beetle or a Nissan subcompact, runs $35–50 per day or $200–400 per week, depending on location and season. Prices are highest during Christmas and pre-Easter weeks. Before departure, use the international agencies' toll-free numbers and websites to research availability, prices, and reservations. During nonpeak seasons, you may save lots of pesos by waiting until arrival and renting

ROAD SAFETY

Hundreds of thousands of visitors enjoy safe Mexican auto vacations every year. Their success is due in large part to their frame of mind: Drive defensively, anticipate and adjust to danger before it happens, and watch everything – side roads, shoulders, the car in front, and cars far down the road. The following tips will help ensure a safe and enjoyable trip:

Don't drive at night. Range animals, unmarked sand piles, pedestrians, one-lane bridges, cars without lights, and drunken drivers are doubly hazardous at night.

Although **speed limits** are rarely enforced, *don't break them.* Mexican country roads are often narrow and shoulderless. Poor markings and macho drivers who pass on curves are best faced at a speed of 40 mph (64 kph) rather than 75 (120).

Don't drive on sand. Even with four-wheel-drive, you'll eventually get stuck if you drive often or casually on beaches. When the tide comes in, who'll pull your car out?

Slow down at the *topes* (speed bumps) at the edges of towns and for **vados** (dips), which can be dangerously bumpy and full of water.

Extending the **courtesy of the road** goes hand-in-hand with safe driving. Both courtesy and machismo are more infectious in Mexico; on the highway, it's much safer to spread the former than the latter.

For maximum speed and safety, use Mexico's **cuota autopistas** (toll expressways) when convenient.

a car through a local agency. Shop around, starting with the agent in your hotel lobby or with the local Yellow Pages (under *Automoviles, renta de*).

Car insurance that covers property damage, public liability, and medical payments is an

DISASTER AND RESCUE ON A MEXICAN HIGHWAY

My litany of Mexican driving experiences came to a climax one night when, heading north from Tepic, I hit a cow at 50 mph head-on. The cow was knocked about 150 feet down the road, while my two friends and I endured a scary impromptu roller-coaster ride. When the dust settled, we, although in shock, were grateful that we hadn't suffered the fate of the poor cow, which had died instantly from the collision.

From that low point, our fortunes soon began to improve. Two buses stopped and about 40 men got out to move my severely wounded van to the shoulder. The cow's owner, a rancher, arrived to cart off the cow's remains in a jeep. Then the police – a husband and wife in a VW bug – pulled up. *"Pobrecita camioneta"* ("Poor little van"), the woman said, gazing at my vehicle, which now resembled an oversized, crumpled accordion. They gave us

a ride to Mazatlán, found us a hotel room, and generally made sure we were okay.

If I hadn't had Mexican auto insurance, I would have been in deep trouble. Mexican law – based on the Napoleonic Code – presumes guilt and does not bother with juries. It would have kept me in jail until all damages were settled. The insurance agent I saw in the morning took care of everything. He called the police station, where I was excused from paying damages when the cow's owner failed to show. He had my car towed to a repair shop, where the mechanics banged it into good enough shape that I could drive it home a week later. Forced to stay in one place, my friends and I enjoyed the most relaxed time of our entire three months in Mexico. The *pobrecita camioneta,* all fixed up a few months later, lasted 14 more years.

absolute must with your rental car. If you get into an accident without insurance, you will be in deep trouble, and could go to jail. Narrow, sometimes potholed roads and animals grazing at roadside make driving in Mexico more hazardous than back home.

BY TAXI, TOUR, AND HITCHHIKING
Taxis

The high prices of rental cars make taxis a useful option for local excursions. Cars are luxuries, not necessities, for most Mexican families. Travelers might profit from the Mexican money-saving practice of piling everyone in a taxi for a Sunday outing. You may find that an all-day taxi and driver—who, besides relieving you of driving, will become your impromptu guide—costs less than a rental car.

The magic word for saving money by taxi is *colectivo:* a taxi you share with other travelers. The first place you'll practice getting a taxi will be at the airport, where *colectivo* tickets are routinely sold from booths at the terminal door.

If, however, you want a private taxi, ask for a *taxi especial,* which will cost about three or four times the individual tariff for a *colectivo.*

Your airport experience will prepare you for in-town taxis, which rarely have meters. You must establish the price before getting in. Bargaining comes with the territory in Mexico, so don't shrink from it, even though it seems a hassle. If you get into a taxi without an agreed-upon price, you are letting yourself in for a more serious and potentially nasty hassle later. If your driver's price is too high, he'll probably come to his senses as soon as you hail another taxi.

After a few days, getting taxis around town will be a cinch. You'll find that you don't have to take the more expensive taxis lined up in your hotel driveway. If the price isn't right, walk toward the street and hail a regular taxi.

In town, if you can't find a taxi, it may be because they are waiting for riders at the local stand, called a taxi *sitio.* Ask someone to direct you to it: *"Disculpe. ¿Dónde está el sitio taxi, por favor?"* ("Excuse me. Where is the taxi stand, please?")

Local Tours and Guides

For many Pacific Mexico visitors, locally arranged tours offer a hassle-free alternative to rental car or taxi sightseeing. Hotels and travel agencies, many of whom maintain front-lobby travel and tour desks, offer a bounty of sightseeing, water sports, bay cruise, fishing, and wildlife-viewing tour opportunities.

Hitchhiking

Most everyone agrees hitchhiking is not the safest mode of transport. If you're unsure, don't do it. Hitchhiking doesn't make for a healthy steady travel diet, nor should you hitchhike at night.

The recipe for trouble-free hitchhiking requires equal measures of luck, savvy, and technique. The best places to catch rides are where people are arriving and leaving anyway, such as bus stops, highway intersections, gas stations, RV parks, and the highway out of town.

Male-female hitchhiking partnerships seem to net the most rides, although it is technically illegal for women to ride in commercial trucks. The more gear you and your partner have, the fewer rides you will get. Pickup and flatbed truck owners often pick up passengers for pay. Before hopping onto the truck bed, ask how much the ride will cost.

Visas and Officialdom

PASSPORTS

Your passport (or birth or naturalization certificate) is your positive proof of national identity; without it, your status in any foreign country is in doubt. Don't leave home without one. In fact, since January 2007, U.S. Immigration rules require that everyone, including U.S. citizens, must present have a valid passport in order to re-enter the United States. U.S. citizens may obtain passports (allow four to six weeks) at local post offices. For-fee private passport agencies can speed this process and get you a passport within a week, maybe less.

TOURIST CARDS AND ENTRY INTO MEXICO

For U.S. and Canadian citizens, entry by air into Mexico for a few weeks could hardly be easier. Airline attendants hand out tourist cards *(tarjetas turísticas)* en route, and officers make them official by glancing at passports and stamping the cards at the immigration gate. Business travel permits for 30 days or fewer are handled by the same simple procedures.

In addition to the entry fee, Mexican immigration officials require that all entering U.S. citizens 15 years old or over must present proper identification—either a valid U.S. passport, original (or notarized copy) of your birth certificate, military ID, or state driver's license, while naturalized citizens must show naturalization papers (or a laminated naturalization card) or valid U.S. passport.

Canadian citizens must show a valid passport or original birth certificate. Nationals of other countries (especially those such as Hong Kong, which issue more than one type of passport) may be subject to different or additional regulations. For advice, consult your regional Mexico Tourism Board Office or local Mexican consulate. Very complete and up-to-date Mexico visa and entry information for nationals of virtally all of the world's countries is available at the Toronto, Canada, Consulate website, www.consulmex.com.

For more complicated cases, get your tourist card early enough to allow you to consider the options. Tourist cards can be issued for multiple entries and a maximum validity of 180 days; photos are often required. If you don't request multiple entry or the maximum time, your card will probably be stamped single entry, valid for some shorter period, such

MEXICO TOURISM BOARD OFFICES

More than a dozen Mexico Tourism Board (Consejo de Promoción Turístico de Mexico) offices and scores of Mexican government consulates operate in the United States, Canada, Europe, South America, and Asia. Consulates generally handle questions of Mexican nationals abroad, while Mexico Tourism Boards serve travelers heading for Mexico.

For straightforward questions and Mexico regional information brochures, contact the Tourism Board (U.S./Can. tel. 800/44MEXICO or 800/446-3942, Europe tel. 00-800/111-2266, www.visitmexico.com). If you need more details and read a bit of Spanish, you might find visiting www.cptm.com helpful also. Otherwise, contact one of the North American, European, South American or Asian Mexico Tourism Boards directly for guidance.

IN NORTH AMERICA

From Alaska, Arizona, California, Colorado, Hawaii, Idaho, Montana, Nevada, Utah, Washington and Wyoming, contact the **Los Angeles** office (1880 Century Park East, Suite 511, Los Angeles, CA 90067, tel. 310/282-9112, fax 310/282-9116, losangeles@visitmexico.com).

From Alberta, British Columbia, Alberta, Saskatchewan, and the Yukon and Northwest Territories, contact the **Vancouver** office (999 W. Hastings St., Suite 1110, Vancouver, B.C. V6C 2W2, tel. 604/669-2845, fax 604/669-3498, mgto@telus .net).

From Arkansas, Colorado, Louisiana, New Mexico, Oklahoma, and Texas, contact the **Houston** office (4507 San Jacinto, Suite 308, Houston TX 77004, tel. 713/772-2581, fax 713/772-6058, houston@visitmexico.com).

From Alabama, Florida, Georgia, Mississippi, Tennessee, North Carolina, Puerto Rico and South Carolina, contact the **Miami** office (5975 Sunset Drive #305, Miami, FL 33143, tel. 786/621-2909, fax 786/621-2907, miami@visitmexico.com).

From Illinois, Indiana, Iowa, Kansas, Kentucky, Michigan, Minnesota, Missouri, Nebraska, North Dakota, Ohio, South Dakota, and Wisconsin, contact the **Chicago** office (225 North Michigan Ave., 18th Floor, Suite 1850, Chicago, IL 60601, tel. 312/228-0517, fax 312/228-0515, chicago@visitmexico.com).

From Connecticut, Delaware, Kentucky, Maine, Maryland, Massachusetts, New Hampshire, New Jersey, New York, Pennsylvania, Rhode Island, Vermont, Virginia, Washington D.C., and West Virginia, contact the **New York** office (400 Madison Ave., Suite 11C, New York, NY 10017; tel. 212/308-2110, fax 212/308-9060, newyork@visitmexico.com).

From Ontario, Manitoba, and the Nunavut Territory, contact the **Toronto** office

---

as 90 days. If you are not sure how long you'll stay in Mexico, request the maximum (180 days is the absolute maximum for a tourist card; long-term foreign residents routinely make semiannual "border runs" for new tourist cards).

Entry for Children

Children under 15 can be included on their parents' tourist cards, but complications occur if the children (by reason of illness, for example) cannot leave Mexico with both parents. Parents can avoid such red tape by getting a passport and a Mexican tourist card for each of their children.

Pacific Mexico travelers should hurdle all such possible delays far ahead of time in the cool calm of their local Mexican consulate rather than the hot, hurried atmosphere of a border or airport immigration station.

(2 Bloor St. West, Suite 1502, Toronto, Ontario M4W 3E2, tel. 416/925-0704, fax 416/925-6061, toronto@visitmexico .com).

From New Brunswick, Newfoundland, Nova Scotia, Prince Edward Island, and Quebec, contact the **Montreal** office (1 Place Ville Marie, Suite 1931, Montreal, Quebec H3B2C3, tel. 514/871-1052 or 514/871-1103, fax 514/871-3825, montreal@visitmexico .com).

IN EUROPE

In Europe, travelers may either contact the all-Europe Mexico tourism information (tel. 00-800/111-2266, www.visitmexico .com) or contact the local offices directly:

London: Wakefield House, 41 Trinity Square, London EC3N 4DJ, England, UK, tel. 207/488-9392, fax 207/265-0704, uk@ visitmexico.com.

Frankfurt: Taunusanlage 21, D-60325 Frankfurt-am-Main, Deutschland, tel. 697/103-3383, fax 697/103-3755, germany@visitmexico.com.

Paris: 4 Rue Notre-Dame des Victoires, 75002 Paris, France, tel. 1/428-69612, 1/428-69613, fax 1/428-60580, france@ visitmexico.com.

Madrid: Calle Velázquez 126, 28006 Madrid, España, tel. 91/561-3520, 91/561-1827, fax 91/411-0759, spain@visitmexico.com.

Rome: Via Barbarini 3-piso 7, 00187 Roma, Italia, tel. 06/487-4698, fax 06/487-3630, fax 06/420-4293, italy@visitmexico .com.

IN SOUTH AMERICA

Contact the Mexico Tourism Board in either Brazil, Argentina, or Chile:

São Paulo: Alameda Administrativo, Rocha Azevedo 882, Conjunto 31, Tercer Andador, São Paulo, Brazil, 01410-002, tel. 3088-2129, fax 3083-5005, brasil@visitmexico .com.

Buenos Aires: Avenida Santa Fe 920, 1054 Buenos Aires, Argentina, tel. 1/4393-7070, 1/4393-8235, fax 1/4393-6607, argentina@visitmexico.com.

Santiago: Felix de Amesti #128, primer piso, Los Condes, Santiago de Chile, tel. 562/583-8426, fax 562/583-8425, chile@visitmexico.com.

IN ASIA

Contact the Mexico Tourism Board in either Japan or China:

Tokyo: 2-15-1-3F, Nagata-Cho, 2-chome, Chiyoda-ku, Tokyo, Japan 100-0014, tel. 335/030-290, fax 335/030-643, japan@ visitmexico.com.

Beijing: San Li Dongwajie 5, Chaoyang 100600, Beijing, Peoples' Republic of China, tel./fax 106/532-1717 or 106/532-1744, jamezcua@visitmexico.com.

Entry for Pets

A pile of red tape may delay the entry of dogs, cats, and other pets into Mexico. Be prepared with veterinary-stamped health and rabies certificates for each animal. For more information, contact your regional Mexico Tourism Board, or your local Mexican Consulate.

If You Lose Your Tourist Card

If you lose your tourist card, be prepared with a copy of the original, which you should present to the nearest federal Migración (Immigration) office (on duty long hours at Pacific Mexico international airports) and ask for a duplicate tourist permit. Lacking this, you might present some alternate proof of your date of arrival in Mexico, such as a stamped passport or airline ticket. Savvy travelers carry copies of their tourist cards while leaving the original safe in their hotel rooms.

STUDENT AND BUSINESS VISAS

A visa is a notation stamped and signed on your passport showing the number of days and entries allowable for your trip. Apply for a student visa at the consulate nearest your home well in advance of your departure; the same is true if you require a business visa of longer than 30 days. One-year renewable student visas are available (sometimes with considerable red tape). An ordinary 180-day tourist card may be the easiest option, if you can manage it.

CAR PERMITS

If you drive to Mexico, you will need a permit for your car. Upon entry into Mexico, be ready with originals and copies of your proof-of-ownership or registration papers (state title certificate, registration, or notarized bill of sale), current license plates, and current driver's license. The auto permit fee runs about $30, payable only by non-Mexican bank Master-Card, Visa, or American Express credit cards. (The credit-card-only requirement discourages those who sell or abandon U.S.-registered cars in Mexico without paying customs duties.) Credit cards must bear the same name as the vehicle proof-of-ownership papers.

The resulting car permit becomes part of the owner's tourist card and receives the same length of validity. Vehicles registered in the name of an organization or person other than the driver must be accompanied by a notarized affidavit authorizing the driver to use the car in Mexico for a specific time.

Border officials generally allow you to carry or tow additional motorized vehicles (motorcycle, another car, large boat) into Mexico but will probably require separate documentation and fee for each vehicle. If a Mexican official desires to inspect your trailer or RV, go through it with him.

Accessories, such as a small trailer, boat shorter than six feet, CB radio, or outboard motor, may be noted on the car permit and must leave Mexico with the car.

For more details on motor vehicle entry and what you may bring in your baggage to Mexico, you might also consult the AAA (American Automobile Association) *Mexico TravelBook.* (See the *Unique Guide and Tip Books* section in *Suggested Reading* in the *Resources* chapter.)

Since Mexico does not recognize foreign automobile insurance, you must buy Mexican automobile insurance.

CROSSING THE BORDER AND RETURNING HOME

Squeezing through border bottlenecks during peak holidays and rush hours can be time-consuming. Avoid crossing 7–9 A.M. and 4:30–6:30 P.M.

Just before returning across the border with your car, park and have a customs *(aduana)* official *remove and cancel the holographic identity sticker that you received on entry.* If possible, get a receipt *(recibo)* or some kind of verification that it's been canceled *(cancelado).* Tourists have been fined hundreds of dollars for inadvertently carrying uncanceled car entry stickers on their windshields.

At the same time, return all other Mexican permits, such as tourist cards and hunting and fishing licenses. Also, be prepared for Mexico exit inspection, especially for cultural artifacts and works of art, which may require exit permits. Certain religious and pre-Columbian artifacts, legally the property of the Mexican government, cannot be taken from the country.

If you entered Mexico with your car, you cannot legally leave without it except by permission from local customs authorities, usually the Aduana (Customs House) or the Oficina Federal de Hacienda (Federal Treasury Office).

All returnees are subject to U.S. immigration and customs inspection. These inspections have become generally more time-consuming since Sept. 11, 2001. The worst bottlenecks are at busy border crossings, especially Tijuana and to a lesser extent Mexicali, Nogales, Ciudad Juárez, Nuevo Laredo, and Matamoros, all of which should be avoided during peak hours.

United States law allows a fixed value ($400

at present) of duty-free goods per returnee. This may include no more than one liter of alcoholic spirits, 200 cigarettes, and 100 cigars. A flat 10 percent duty will be applied to the first $1,000 (fair retail value, save your receipts) in excess of your $400 exemption. You may, however, mail packages (up to $100 value each) of gifts duty-free to friends and relatives in the United States. Make sure to clearly write "unsolicited gift" and a list of the value and contents on the outside of the package. Perfumes (over $5), alcoholic beverages, and tobacco may not be included in such packages.

Improve the security of such mailed packages by sending them by Mexpost class, similar to U.S. Express Mail service. Even better (but much more expensive), send them by Federal Express

or DHL international couriers, which maintain offices in Pacific Mexico resort centers.

GOVERNMENT CUSTOMS AND WILDLIFE INFORMATION

For more information on U.S. customs regulations important to travelers abroad, read or download the useful pamphlet *Know Before You Go,* by visiting the U.S. Customs and Border Patrol website, www.cpb.gov. Click on *Travel* at the bottom of the home page, then scroll down to *Know Before You Go.*

For more information on the importation of endangered wildlife products, contact the Fish and Wildlife Service, 1849 C. St. NW, Washington, DC 20240, toll-free tel. 800/344-WILD, www.fws.gov.

Sports and Recreation

BEACHES

It's easy to understand why many Pacific Mexico vacationers stay right at the beach. And not just at the famous crystalline stretches of Mazatlán, Puerto Vallarta, Manzanillo, Ixtapa, Acapulco, and Puerto Escondido. Many flee the big resorts and spread out along the whole coast—gathering at small beach hideaways such as San Blas, Rincón de Guayabitos, Cuyutlán, Playa Azul, Troncones, Pie de la Cuesta, and Puerto Ángel—while others set up camp and enjoy the solitude and rich wildlife of hundreds of miles of even more pristine strands. Shorelines vary from mangrove-edged lagoons and algae-decorated tidepools to shoals of pebbles and sand of dozens of colors and consistencies.

Sand makes the beach—and Pacific Mexico has plenty, from warm, black mica dust to cool, velvety white coral. Some beaches drop steeply to turbulent, close-in surf, fine for fishing. Others are level, with gentle, rolling breakers, made for surfing and swimming.

Beaches are fascinating for the surprises they yield. Pacific Mexico's beaches, especially the hidden strands near resorts and the hundreds of

miles of wilderness beaches and tidepools, yield troves of shells and treasures of flotsam and jetsam for those who enjoy looking for them. Beachcombing is more rewarding during the summer storm season, when big waves deposit acres of fresh shells, among them conch, scallop, clams, combs of Venus, whelks, limpets, olives, cowries, starfish, and sand dollars.

During the summer-fall rainy season, beaches near rivermouths are often fantastic outdoor galleries of wind- and water-sculpted snags and giant logs deposited by the downstream flood.

Viewing Wildlife

Wildlife-watchers should keep quiet and always be on the alert. Animal survival depends on their seeing you first. Occasional spectacular offshore sights, such as whales, porpoises, and manta rays, or an onshore giant constrictor, beached squid or octopus, crocodile, or even a jaguar looking for turtle eggs are the reward of those prepared to recognize them. Don't forget your binoculars and Steve Howell's *Bird-Finding Guide to Mexico* (see *Suggested Reading* in the *Resources* chapter).

WATER SPORTS

Swimming, surfing, sailboarding, snorkeling, scuba diving, kayaking, sailing, and personal watercraft riding are Pacific Mexico's water sports of choice.

Safety First

Viewed from Pacific Mexico beaches, the Pacific Ocean usually lives up to its name. Many protected inlets, safe for child's play, dot the coastline. Unsheltered shorelines, on the other hand, can be deceiving. Smooth water in the calm forenoon often changes to choppy in the afternoon; calm ripples that lap the shore in March can grow to hurricane-driven walls of water in November. Such storms can wash away sand, temporarily changing a wide, gently sloping beach into a steep one plagued by turbulent waves and treacherous currents.

Undertow, whirlpools, cross-currents, and occasional oversized waves can make ocean swimming a fast-lane adventure. Getting unexpectedly swept out to sea or hammered onto the beach bottom by a surprise breaker are potential hazards.

Never attempt serious swimming when tipsy or full of food; never swim alone where someone can't see you. Always swim beyond big breakers (which come in sets of several, climaxed by a huge one, which breaks highest and farthest from the beach). If you happen to get caught in the path of such a wave, avoid it by *diving directly toward and under it,* letting it roll harmlessly over you. If you are unavoidably swept up in a whirling, crashing breaker, try to roll and tumble with it, as football players tumble, to avoid injury.

Look out for other irritations and hazards. Now and then swimmers get a nettlelike (but usually harmless) jellyfish sting. Be careful around coral reefs and beds of sea urchins; corals can sting (like jellyfish) and you can get infections from coral cuts and sea-urchin spines. *Shuffle* along sandy bottoms to scare away stingrays before stepping on one. If you're unlucky, its venomous tail-spines may inflict a painful wound. (See *Health Problems* in the *Health and Safety* section for first-aid measures.)

Snorkeling and Scuba Diving

Many exciting clear-water sites, such as Puerto Vallarta's Islas Marietas, Manzanillo's Bahía Santiago, Zihuatanejo's Playa Las Gatas, Isla Roqueta at Acapulco, and Playa Estacahuite at Puerto ángel, await both beginner and expert scuba divers. Veteran Pacific Mexico divers usually arrive during the dry winter and early spring when river outflows are mere trickles, leaving offshore waters clear. In the major tourist centers, professional dive shops rent equipment, provide lessons and guides, and transport divers to choice sites.

While convenient, rented equipment is often less than satisfactory. Serious divers bring their own gear. This should probably include wetsuits in the winter, when many swimmers begin to feel cold after an unprotected half-hour in the water.

Surfing, Sailing, Sailboarding, and Kayaking

In addition to several well-known surfing beaches, such as Matanchén at San Blas, Puerto Vallarta's Punta Mita, and Barra de Nexpa south of Manzanillo, Pacific Mexico has the country's acknowledged best surfing beach—the Playa Zicatela "pipeline" at Puerto Escondido.

The surf everywhere is highest and best during the July–Nov. hurricane season, when big swells from storms far out at sea attract platoons of surfers to favored beaches (except at crowded Acapulco Bay, where surfing is off-limits).

Sailboarders, sailboaters, and kayakers—who, by contrast, require more tranquil waters—do best in the Pacific Mexico winter or early spring. Then they gather to enjoy the near-ideal conditions at many coves and inlets near the big resorts.

While beginners can have fun with the equipment available from rental shops, serious surfers, sailboarders, sailboaters, and kayakers should pack their own gear.

POWER SPORTS

Acapulco and other big resorts have long been centers for water-skiing, parasailing, and personal watercraft riding. In parasailing, a motorboat pulls while a parachute lifts you, like a soaring gull, high over the ocean. After 5 or 10 minutes it deposits you—usually gently—back on the sand.

Personal watercraft (such as Waverunners and Jet Skis) are like snowmobiles except that they operate on water, where, with a little practice, beginners can quickly learn to whiz over the waves.

Although the luxury resort hotels generally provide experienced crews and equipment, crowded conditions increase the hazard to both participants and swimmers. You, as the patron, are paying plenty for the privilege; you have a right to expect that your providers and crew are well-equipped, sober, and cautious.

Beach Buggies and ATVs

Some visitors enjoy racing along the beach and rolling over dunes in beach buggies and ATVs (all-terrain vehicles—*motos* in Mexico), balloon-

Although noisy, polluting ATVs (all terrain vehicles) are common on some beaches, some Pacific Mexico communities have banned them.

tired, four-wheeled motor scooters. While certain resort rental agencies cater to the growing use of such vehicles, limits are in order. Of all the proliferating high-horsepower beach pastimes, these are the most intrusive. Noise, exhaust, and gasoline pollution, injuries to operators and bystanders, and the scattering of wildlife and destruction of their habitats have led (and I hope will continue to lead) to the restriction of dune buggies and ATVs on beaches.

TENNIS AND GOLF

Most Mexicans are working too hard to be playing much tennis and golf. Although there are almost no public courses or courts, Pacific Mexico's resort centers enjoy excellent private facilities. If you are planning on a lot of golf and tennis, check into (or inquire about court rental at) one of the many hotels with these facilities. Use of hotel tennis courts is often, but not always, included in your hotel tariff. If not, fees will run about $10 per hour. Golf greens fees, which begin at about $50 for 18 holes, are always extra.

FISHING

Pacific Mexico is a world-class deep-sea and surf fishing ground. Sportspeople routinely bring in dozens of species from among the more than 600 that have been hooked in Pacific Mexico waters.

Surf Fishing

Most good fishing beaches away from the immediate resort areas will typically have only a few locals (mostly with nets) and fewer visitors. Mexicans typically do little sportfishing. Most either make their living from fishing, or they do none at all. Consequently, few shops sell sportfishing equipment in Mexico; plan to bring your own surf-fishing equipment, including hooks, lures, line, and weights.

Your best general information source before you leave home is a good local bait-and-tackle shop. Tell the folks there where you're going, and they'll often know the best lures and bait to use and what fish you can expect to catch with them.

FISH

A bounty of fish darts, swarms, jumps, and wriggles in Pacific Mexico's surf, reefs, lagoons, and offshore depths. While many make delicious dinners (albacore, red snapper, pompano), others are tough (sailfish), bony (bonefish), and even poisonous (puffers). Some grow to half-ton giants (marlin, grouper), while others are diminutive reef-grazers (parrot fish, damselfish, angelfish) whose bright colors delight snorkelers and divers. Here's a sampling of what you might find underwater or on your dinner plate.

albacore (*albacora, atún*): 2-4 feet in size; blue; found in deep waters; excellent taste
angelfish (*Ángel*): one foot; yellow, orange, blue; reef fish*
barracuda (*barracuda, picuda*): two feet; brown; deep waters; good taste
black marlin (*marlin negro*): six feet; blue-black; deep waters; good taste
blue marlin (*marlin azul*): eight feet; blue; deep waters; poor taste
bobo (*barbudo*): one foot; blue, yellow; found in surf; fair taste
bonefish (*macabi*): one foot; blue or silver; found inshore; poor taste
bonito (*bonito*): two feet; black; deep waters; good taste
butterfly fish (*muñeca*): six inches; black, yellow; reef fish*
chub (*chopa*): one foot; gray; reef fish; good taste
croaker (*corvina*): two feet; brownish; found along inshore bottoms; rare and protected
damselfish (*castañeta*): four inches; brown, blue, orange; reef fish*
dolphinfish, mahimahi (*dorado*): three feet; green, gold; deep waters; good taste
grouper (*garopa*): three feet; brown, rust; found offshore and in reefs; good taste
grunt (*burro*): eight inches; black, gray; found in rocks, reefs*
jack (*toro*): 1-2 feet; bluish-gray; offshore; good taste

mackerel (*sierra*): two feet; gray with gold spots; offshore; good taste
mullet (*lisa*): two feet; gray; found in sandy bays; good taste
needlefish (*agujón*): three feet; blue-black; deep waters; good taste
Pacific porgy (*pez de pluma*): 1-2 feet; tan; found along sandy shores; good taste
parrot fish (*perico, pez loro*): one foot; green, pink, blue, orange; reef fish*
pompano (*pómpano*): one foot; gray; inshore bottoms; excellent taste
puffer (*botete*): eight inches; brown; inshore; poisonous
red snapper (*huachinango, pargo*): 1-2 feet; reddish pink; deep waters; excellent taste
roosterfish (*pez gallo*): three feet; black, blue; deep waters; excellent taste
sailfish (*pez vela*): five feet; blue-black; deep waters; poor taste
sardine (*sardina*): eight inches; blue-black; offshore; good taste
sea bass (*cabrilla*): 1-2 feet; brown, ruddy; reef and rock crevices; good taste
shark (*tiburón*): 2-10 feet; black to blue; in- and offshore; good taste
snook (*robalo*): 2-3 feet; black-brown; found in brackish lagoons; excellent taste
spadefish (*chambo*): one foot; black-silver; found along sandy bottoms; reef fish*
swordfish (*pez espada*): five feet; black to blue; deep waters; good taste
triggerfish (*pez puerco*): 1-2 feet; blue, rust, brown, black; reef fish; excellent taste
wahoo (*peto, guahu*): 2-5 feet; green to blue; deep waters; excellent taste
yellowfin tuna (*atún amarilla*): 2-5 feet; blue, yellow; deep waters; excellent taste
yellowtail (*jurel*): 2-4 feet; blue, yellow; offshore; excellent taste

*generally too small to be considered edible

In any case, the cleaner the water, the more interesting your catch. On a good day, your reward might be *sierras, cabrillas,* porgies, or pompanos pulled from the Pacific Mexico surf.

You can't have everything, however. Foreigners cannot legally take Mexican abalone, coral, lobster, clams, rock bass, sea fans, shrimp, turtles, or seashells. Neither are they supposed to buy them directly from fishers.

Deep-Sea Fishing

Mazatlán and Manzanillo are renowned spots for the big prize marlin and sailfish, while Zihuatanejo and Acapulco run close behind.

A deep-sea boat charter generally includes the boat and crew for a full or half day, plus equipment and bait for 2–6 people, not including food or drinks. The full-day price depends upon the season. Around Christmas and New Year and before Easter (when reservations will be mandatory) a boat can run $400 and up at Mazatlán or Manzanillo. At lesser-known resorts, or even at the big resorts during low season, you might be able to bargain a captain down to as low as $200.

Renting an entire big boat is not the only choice. Winter business is sometimes so brisk at resorts that agencies can make reservations for individuals for about $60 per person per day.

Pangas, outboard launches seating 2–6 passengers, are available for as little as $50, depending on the season. Once in Barra de Navidad six of my friends hired a *panga* for $50, had a great time, and came back with a boatload of big tuna, jack, and mackerel. A restaurant cooked them as a banquet for a dozen of us in exchange for the extra fish, and I discovered for the first time how heavenly fresh *sierra veracruzana* can taste.

Bringing Your Own Boat

If you're going to do lots of fishing, your own boat may be your most flexible and economical option. One big advantage is you can go to the many excellent fishing grounds that the charter boats do not frequent. Keep your equipment simple, scout around, and keep your eyes peeled and ears open for local reg-

ulations and customs, plus tide, wind, and fish-edibility information.

Fishing Licenses and Boat Permits

Anyone 16 or older who is either fishing or riding in a fishing boat in Mexico is required to have a fishing license. Although Mexican fishing licenses are obtainable from certain travel and insurance agents or at government fishing offices everywhere along the coast, save yourself time and trouble by getting both your fishing licenses and boat permits by mail ahead of time from the Mexican Department of Fisheries (Oficina de Pesca). Call at least a month before departure (tel. 619/233-4324, fax 619/233-0344) and ask for applications and the fees (which are reasonable but depend upon the period of validity and the fluctuating exchange rate). On the application, fill in the names (exactly as they appear on passports) of the people requesting licenses. Include a cashier's check or a money order for the exact amount, along with a stamped, self-addressed envelope. Address the application to the Mexican Department of Fisheries (Oficina de Pesca), 2550 5th Ave., Suite 15, San Diego, CA 92103-6622.

BULLFIGHTING

It is said there are two occasions for which Mexicans arrive on time: funerals and bullfights.

Bullfighting is a recreation, not a sport. The bull is outnumbered seven to one and the outcome is never in doubt. Even if the matador (literally, killer) fails in his duty, his assistants will entice the bull away and slaughter it in private beneath the stands.

La Corrida de Toros

Moreover, Mexicans don't call it a "bullfight"; it's the *corrida de toros,* during which six bulls are customarily slaughtered, beginning at 5 P.M. (4 in the winter). After the beginning parade, featuring the matador and his helpers, the picadores and the banderilleros, the first bull rushes into the ring in a cloud of dust. Clockwork *tercios* (thirds) define the ritual: the first, the *puyazos,* or "stabs," requires that two picadores on horseback thrust lances into the bull's shoulders, weakening it. During the second *tercio,* the banderilleros dodge the bull's horns to stick three long, streamered darts into its shoulders.

Trumpets announce the third *tercio* and the appearance of the matador. The bull—weak, confused, and angry—is ready for the finish. The matador struts, holding the red cape, daring the bull to charge. Form now becomes everything. The expert matador takes complete control of the bull, which rushes at the cape,

past its ramrod-erect opponent. For charge after charge, the matador works the bull to exactly the right spot in the ring—in front of the judges, a lovely señorita, or perhaps the governor—where the matador mercifully delivers the precision *estocada* (killing sword thrust) deep into the drooping neck of the defeated bull.

Benito Juárez, as governor during the 1850s, outlawed bullfights in Oaxaca. In his honor, they remain so, making Oaxaca unique among Mexican states.

Accommodations

Pacific Mexico has thousands of lodgings to suit every style and pocketbook: world-class resorts, small beachside hotels, homey *casas de huéspedes* (guesthouses), palm-shaded trailer parks, and hundreds of miles of pristine beaches, ripe for camping. The high seasons, when hotel reservations are generally recommended, are mid-December through March, during pre-Easter week, and the month of August.

The hundreds of accommodations described in this book are positive recommendations—checked out in detail—good choices, from which you can pick according to your taste and purse.

Hotel Rates

The rates listed in this book are U.S. dollar equivalents of peso prices, taxes included, as quoted by the hotel management at the time of writing. Rates are usually listed in ascending order of price, and low- and high-season rates are quoted whenever possible. Although high and low seasons vary locally, Christmas-New Year's (Dec. 20–Jan. 6) and Semana Santa (Easter week) are high seasons everywhere. Winter is generally a high season in beach resorts, such as Mazatlán, Puerto Vallarta, Manzanillo, Ixtapa, and Zihuatanejo that are popular with American and Canadian vacationers. On the other hand, July–August is a high season in some resorts, such as Aca-

pulco, Taxco, and Pátzcuaro, popular with Mexican tourists.

Prices quoted in this book are intended as a general guide only. Since rates fluctuate sharply according to local demand, quoted figures will probably only approximate the asking rate when you arrive. Some readers, unfortunately, try to bargain by telling desk clerks that, for example, the rate should be $30 because they read it in this book. This is unwise, because it makes hotel managers and clerks reluctant to quote rates for fear readers might hold their hotel responsible for such quotes a few years later.

In Pacific Mexico, hotel rates depend strongly upon inflation and season. To cancel the effect of the relatively steep Mexican inflation, rates are reported in U.S. dollars. However, when settling your hotel bill, *you should always pay in pesos.*

Saving Money

The hotel prices quoted in this book are rack rates, the maximum tariff, exclusive of packages and promotions, that you would pay if you walked in and rented an unreserved room for one day. Savvy travelers seldom pay the maximum. Always inquire if there are any discounts or packages (*descuentos o paquetes*—des-koo-AYN-tohs OH pah-KAY-tays). At most times other than the super-high Christmas to New Year and Easter weeks, you can get at least one or two free days for a one-week stay. Promotional packages available during slack seasons may include free extras such as breakfast, a car rental, a boat tour, or a sports rental. A travel agent or travel website can be of great help in shopping around for such bargains.

You nearly always save additional money if you deal in pesos only. Insist on both booking your lodging for an agreed price in pesos and paying the resulting hotel bill in the same pesos, rather than dollars. The reason is that dollar rates quoted by hotels are often based on the hotel desk exchange rate, which is customarily about 5 percent, or even as much 15 percent, less than bank rates. For example, if the clerk tells you your hotel bill is $1,000, instead of handing over the dollars or having him mark $1,000 on your credit card slip, ask him how much it is in pesos. Using the desk conversion rate, he might say something like 9,000 pesos (considerably less than the 10,000 pesos that the bank might give for your $1,000). Pay the 9,000 pesos or have the clerk mark 9,000 pesos on your credit card slip, and save yourself $100.

For stays of more than two weeks, you'll most likely save money and add comfort with an apartment or condominium rental. Monthly rates range $500–1,500 (less than half the comparable hotel per diem rate) for comfortable one-bedroom furnished kitchenette units, often including resort amenities such as pool and sundeck, beach club, and private-view balcony.

Airlines regularly offer air/hotel packages, which, by combining your hotel and air fees, may save you lots of pesos. These deals customarily require that you depart for Pacific Mexico through certain gateway cities, which depend on the airline. Accommodations are usually, but not exclusively, in luxury resorts. If you live near one of these gateways, it may pay to contact the airlines for more information.

GUESTHOUSES, LOCAL HOTELS, AND BED-AND-BREAKFASTS

Most coastal resorts began with an old town, which then expanded to a new *zona hotelera*

(hotel strip) where big hostelries rise along a golden strand. In the old town, near the piquant smells, sights, and sounds of traditional Mexico, are the *casas de huéspedes* and smaller hotels where rooms are often arranged around a plant-decorated patio.

Such lodgings vary from scruffy to spic-and-span, and humble to luxurious. At minimum, you can expect a plain room, a shared toilet and hot-water shower, and plenty of atmosphere for your money. High-season rates, depending on the resort, average $20–50 for two, depending upon location and amenities. Discounts are often available for long-term stays. *Casas de huéspedes* will rarely be near the beach, unlike many local hotels.

Medium and Larger Older-Style Hotels

Locally owned and operated hotels make up most of the recommendations of this book. Many veteran travelers find it hard to understand why people come to Mexico and spend $250 a day for a hotel room when decent alternatives run $30–80, high season, depending upon the resort.

Many locally run hostelries are right on the beach, sharing the same velvety sand and golden sunsets as their much more expensive international-class neighbors. Local hotels, which depend as much on Mexican tourists as foreigners, generally have clean, large rooms, often with private-view balconies, ceiling fans, and toilet and hot-water bath or shower. What they often lack are the plush extras—air-conditioning, cable TV, phones, tennis courts, exercise gyms, and golf courses—of the luxury resort hotels.

Booking these hotels is straightforward. All can be dialed direct (from the United States, dial 011-52, then the local area code and number) for information and reservations; many can be booked via email, and like the big resorts, some even have U.S. and Canada toll-free information numbers. Always ask about money-saving packages (*paquetes*) and promotions (*promociones*) when reserving.

Bed-and-Breakfasts

Since the early 1990s bed-and-breakfast-type lodgings have been sprouting like mushrooms in certain Pacific Mexico resort towns, especially Puerto Vallarta, Guadalajara, Zihuatanejo, Pátzcuaro, and Oaxaca, popular with American and Canadian vacationers. Savvy North American expatriate owners are filling the need of many visitors, who are willing to pay a very substantial price for a room in a private home, provided it's comfortable enough, has a private bath and preferably air-conditioning, and comes with a hearty breakfast for two. Such lodgings, nearly all bookable by email, are just like their North American counterparts, often with plush amenities, such as a library or sitting room with soft couches, a flowery interior patio, maybe even a pool, and Internet access.

INTERNATIONAL-CLASS RESORTS

Pacific Mexico has many beautiful, well-managed international-class resort hotels. They spread along the pearly strands of Mazatlán, Puerto Vallarta, Manzanillo, Ixtapa, Acapulco, Bahías de Huatulco, and inland in Guadalajara, and Oaxaca. Their super-deluxe amenities, moreover, need not be overly expensive. During the right time of year you can vacation at many of the big-name spots—Barceló (formerly Sheraton), Westin, Hyatt, Best Western, Camino Real, Las Brisas, Fiesta Americana, NH Krystal—for surprisingly little. While high-season room tariffs ordinarily run $150–350, low-season (May–Nov., and to a lesser degree, Jan.–Feb.) packages and promotions can cut these prices to as low as $100. Shop around for savings via your Sunday newspaper travel section, travel agents, and by contacting the hotels directly through their toll-free 800 numbers or websites.

APARTMENTS, BUNGALOWS, CONDOMINIUMS, AND VILLAS

For longer stays, many visitors prefer the convenience and economy of an apartment or condominium or the luxurious comfort of a villa vacation rental. Choices vary, from spartan studios to deluxe beachfront suites and rambling, view homes big enough for entire extended families. Prices depend strongly upon season and amenities, from $500 per month for the cheapest to at least 10 times that for the most luxurious.

A Mexican variation on the apartment style of accommodation is called a bungalow, although, in contrast to English-language usage, it does not usually imply a detached dwelling. Common in Mazatlán and Manzanillo and in smaller beach resorts, such as Bucerías, Rincón de Guayabitos, Barra de Navidad, Zihuatanejo, and Puerto Escondido, a bungalow accommodation generally means a motel-type kitchenette-suite with less service, but with more space and beds. For families or for long stays by the beach, when you want to save money by cooking your own meals, such an accommodation might be ideal.

At the low end, you can expect a clean, furnished apartment within a block or two of the beach, with kitchen and regular maid service. More luxurious condos (which usually rent for $500 per week and up) are typically high-rise ocean-view suites with hotel-style desk services and resort amenities, such as a pool, hot tub, sundeck, and beach-level restaurant.

Higher up the scale, villas and houses vary from moderately luxurious homes to sky's-the-limit beach-view mansions, blooming with built-in designer luxuries, private pools and beaches, tennis courts, and gardeners, cooks, and maids.

Shopping Around

You'll generally find the most economical apartment, condo, and house rental deals through on-the-spot local contacts, such as the tourist newspaper want ad section, neighborhood "for rent" signs, or local listing agents.

If you prefer making rental arrangements before arrival, you can usually write, fax, email, or telephone managers—many of whom speak English—directly, using the numbers given in this book. Additional rentals are available through agents (such as those in Mazatlán, Puerto Vallarta, Bucerías, Barra de Navidad,

Manzanillo, Ixtapa, Zihuatanejo, Acapulco, and Puerto Escondido) who will make long-distance rental agreements.

Additionally, a number of U.S.- and Canada-based agencies list some of the more expensive Pacific Mexico vacation rentals through toll-free information and reservations numbers and websites. For example, try Villa de Oro Vacation Rentals (638 Scotland Dr., Santa Rosa, CA 95409, tel. 800/638-4552 www.villasdeoro .com); Villas of Mexico (P.O. Box 3906, Chico, CA 95927, tel. 800/456-3133, www.villasof mexico.com); and Condo and Villa World (6689 Orchard Lake Rd., Suite 332, West Bloomfield MI, 48322, U.S. tel. 800/521-2980 or Can. tel. 800/453-7556, www.villaworld.com).

Even more Pacific Mexico vacation rental homes and condos, many of them moderately priced, are accessible via websites. For starters, try the super www.vrbo.com and perhaps also www.choice1.com, and www.mexconnect .com. (For others, see *Internet Resources* in the *Resources* chapter.)

Yet another fertile vacation rental source is the Sunday travel section of a major metropolitan daily, such as the *Los Angeles Times* or the *San Francisco Chronicle,* which routinely list Pacific Mexico vacation rentals. Also, local real estate agents, such as Century 21, who specialize in nationwide and foreign contacts, sometimes list (or know someone who does) Pacific Mexico vacation rentals.

Home Exchange

You may also want to consider using the services of a home exchange agency or website whereby you swap homes with someone in Pacific Mexico for an agreed-upon time period. (See the *Internet Resources* section in the *Resources* chapter for home-exchange websites and toll-free numbers.)

CAMPING AND *PALAPAS*

Beach camping is popular among middle-class Mexican families, especially during the Christmas-New Year week and during Semana Santa, the week before Easter.

Other times, tenters and RV campers usually find beaches uncrowded. The best spots typically have a shady palm grove for camping and a *palapa* (palm-thatched) restaurant that serves drinks and fresh seafood. (Heads up for falling coconuts, especially in the wind.) Cost for parking and tenting is often minimal—typically only the price of food at the restaurant.

Days are often perfect for swimming, strolling, and fishing, and nights are balmy—too warm for a sleeping bag, but fine for a hammock (which allows the air circulation that a tent does not.) However, good tents keep out mosquitoes and other pesties, which may be further discouraged by a good bug repellent. Tents can get hot, requiring only a sheet or very light blanket for sleeping cover.

As for camping on isolated beaches, opinions vary, from dire warnings of *bandidos* to bland assurances that all is peaceful along the coast. The truth is somewhere in between. Trouble is most likely to occur in the vicinity of towns, where a few local thugs sometimes harass isolated campers.

When scouting out an isolated place to camp, a good rule is to arrive early enough in the day to get a feel for the place. Buy a soda at the *palapa* or store and take a stroll along the beach. Say *"Buenos días"* to the people along the way; ask if the fishing is good *("¿Pesca buena?")*. Above all, use your common sense and intuition. If the people seem friendly, ask if it's *seguro* (safe). If so, ask permission: *"¿Es bueno acampar acá?"* ("Is it okay to camp around here?"). You'll rarely be refused. For an informative and entertaining discussion of camping in Mexico, check out *The People's Guide to Mexico* (see *Suggested Reading* in the *Resources* chapter).

Some *palapas* (thatched beach houses) are still rented in small coastal resorts. Amenities typically include beds or hammocks, a shady thatched porch, cold running water, a kerosene stove, and shared toilets and showers. You usually walk right out your front door onto the sand, where surf, shells, and seabirds will be there to entertain you. *Palapa* rentals are available in Maruata and Barra de Nexpa (Michoacán Coast, not far north of Playa Azul), Playa

CAMPING AND TRAILER PARKS

Gulf of Mexico

Gulf of Tehuantepec

PACIFIC OCEAN

SEE "CAMPING AND TRAILER PARKS AROUND *PUERTO VALLARTA*" MAP

100 mi

100 km

© AVALON TRAVEL PUBLISHING, INC.

Durango
Mazatlan
Teacapan
Novillero
Acaponeta
Esquinapa
Tepic
San Blas
Rincon de Guayabitos
Puerto Vallarta
Jose Maria Morelos
Chamela
Perula
Barra de Navidad
Manzanillo
Colima
Tecoman
PLAYA LA BRISA
PLAYA TIZUPA
Faro de Bucerias
Maruata
Barra de Nexpa
CENTRO TURISTICO ANGAHUAN
Uruapan
Chapala
Guadalajara
Aguascalientes
Zacatecas
Fresnillo
Guanajuato
Morelia
Pátzcuaro
HOTEL CHUPICUARO
Playa Azul
Ciudad Altamirano
Ixtapa-Zihuatanejo
Troncones
Barra de Potosi
Pie de la Cuesta
Acapulco
Playa Ventura
Chilpancingo
Iguala
Taxco
Toluca
Mexico City
Cuernavaca
Puebla
Veracruz
Oaxaca
RIO ARENA
Pinotepa Nacional
LA ALEJANDRIA
Puerto Escondido
Zipolite
Puerto Angel
Huatulco
Tehuantepec

15 D
40
49
85
54
45 D
80
57 D
15 D
15 D
200
80
54 D
120
134
95 D
190
150 D
131
125
175
190
200

CAMPING AND TRAILER PARKS
AROUND PUERTO VALLARTA

To Mazatlán

15D

Acaponeta

Novillero

Laguna Agua Brava

Jesús María

Ruiz

Mexcaltitán

Santiago Ixcuintla

Playa Los Corchos

San Blas · TP

15

Bahía de Matanchén · TP · 76 · Tepic · 11

Santa Cruz · 200

Compostela · Chapalilla

68D · *Laguna Santa María* · TP

Bahía de Jaltemba

Chacala · Las Varas

La Peñita · TP

Rincón de Guayabitos · TP

Lo de Marcos · 15D

Sayulita · TP · 15

Punta Mita

Cruz de Huanacaxtle · Bucerías · San Sebastián · To Zacatecas

Bahía de Banderas · TP · 54

Puerto Vallarta · *Laguna Juanacatlán* · Guadalajara · TP

Playa Las Ánimas · Navidad · Villa Corona

Playa Quimixto · 200 · Mascota · Ameca · TP · 15

Cabo Corrientes · Yelapa · Talpa · Los Volcanes · Jocotepec · Ajijic

Tehualmixtle · El Tuito · *Lake Chapala*

Ipala · *Cajón de Peñas Reservoir* · Juchitlán · Ayutla · 54

P A C I F I C   O C E A N

Tomatlán · Autlán · Ciudad Guzmán

200 · 80 · 54D

Playa Chalacatepec · Perula · 110

TP · Chamela

TP · Colima

Playa Careyes · TP · 110

Playa Las Brisas · TP

Tenacatita · Melaque · Manzanillo · Tecomán

Boca de Iguana · TP · 200

Barra de Navidad · To Ixtapa-Zihuatanejo

Playa de Cocos

Playa de Oro · *Bahía Manzanillo* · Cuyutlán

0   25 mi

0   25 km

© AVALON TRAVEL PUBLISHING, INC.

Ventura (south of Acapulco), Puerto Escondido, and Zipolite, Mazunte, and La Ventanilla (near Puerto ángel).

TRAILER PARKS

Campers who prefer company to isolation usually stay in trailer parks. Dozens of them dot Pacific Mexico's beaches and inland cities, towns, and scenic mountain spots (especially along the coast of Nayarit, not far north of Puerto Vallarta). The most luxurious have electricity, water, sewer hookups, and many amenities, including restaurants, recreation rooms, and swimming pools; the humblest are simple palm-edged lots beside the beach. Virtually all of them have good swimming, fishing, and beachcombing. Prices run from a high of around $20 per night, including air-conditioning and power, to a few dollars for tent space only. Significant discounts are generally available for weekly and monthly rentals. Trailer parks are most numerous.

Food and Drink

© BRUCE WHIPPERMAN

Mexican food, truly a world-class cuisine, has its origin in the corn tortilla.

Some travel to Pacific Mexico for the food. True Mexican food is old-fashioned, home-style fare requiring many hours of loving preparation. Such food is short on meat and long on corn, beans, rice, tomatoes, onions, eggs, and cheese.

Mexican food is the unique product of thousands of years of native tradition. It is based on corn—*teocentli,* the Aztec "holy food"—called *maíz* (mah-EES) by present-day Mexicans. In the past, a Mexican woman spent much of her time grinding and preparing corn: soaking the grain in lime water, which swells the kernels and removes the tough seed-coat, and grinding the bloated seeds into meal on a stone metate. Finally, she patted the meal into tortillas and cooked them on a hot, baked mud griddle, a *comal* (KOH-mahl).

Sages (men, no doubt) wistfully imagined that gentle pat-pat-pat of women all over Mexico to be the heartbeat of Mexico, which they feared would cease when women stopped making tortillas.

Fewer women these days make tortillas by hand. The gentle pat-pat-pat has been replaced by the whir and rattle of the automatic tortilla-making machine in myriad *tortillerías,* where women and girls line up for their family's daily kilo-stack of tortillas.

Tortillas are to the Mexicans as rice is to the Chinese and bread to the French. Mexican food is invariably some mixture of sauce, meat, beans, cheese, and vegetables wrapped in a tortilla, which becomes the culinary be-all: the food, the dish, and the utensil wrapped into one.

If a Mexican man has nothing to wrap in his

A TROVE OF FRUITS AND NUTS

Besides carrying the usual temperate fruits, *jugerías* and especially markets are seasonal sources of a number of exotic (followed by an *) varieties:

The plum-like *ciruela* is as small and as sweet as a cherry, but is yellow instead of red.

avocado (*aguacate* – ah-wah-KAH-tay): Aztec aphrodisiac

banana (*platano*): many kinds – big and small, red and yellow

chirimoya* (*chirimoya*) : green scales, white pulp; sometimes called an anona

ciruela*: looks (but doesn't taste) like a small yellow-to-red plum

coconut (*coco*) : coconut "milk" is called *agua de coco*

grapes (*uvas*) : Aug.-Nov. season

guanábana*: looks, but doesn't taste, like a green mango

guava (*guava*) : delicious juice, widely available canned

lemon (*lima real* – LEE-mah ray-AHL): uncommon and expensive; use lime instead

lima* (LEE-mah): uncommon; like something between a California lemon and a Florida grapefruit

lime (*limón* – lee-MOHN): douse salads with it

mamey* (*mamey* – mah-MAY): yellow, juicy fruit; excellent for jellies and preserves

mango (*mango*): king of fruit, in a hundred varieties June-Nov.

orange (*naranja* – nah-RAHN-ha): greenish skin but sweet and juicy

papaya (*papaya*): said to aid digestion and healing

peach (*durazno* – doo-RAHS-noh): delicious and widely available as canned juice

peanut (*cacahuate* – kah-kah-WAH-tay): home roasted and cheap

pear (*pera*): fall season

pecan (*nuez*): for a treat, try freshly ground pecan butter

piña anona*: looks like a thin ear of corn without the husk; tastes like pineapple

pineapple (*piña*): huge, luscious, and cheap

strawberry (*fresa* – FRAY-sah): local favorite

tangerine (*mandarina*): common around Christmas

watermelon (*sandía* – sahn-DEE-ah): perfect on a hot day

yaca* (YAH-kah): Asian jackfruit relative, pebbly green skin, round, and as large as a football; yummy mild taste

zapote* (sah-POH-tay): yellow, fleshy fruit; said to induce sleep

zapote colorado*: brown skin, red, puckery fruit, like persimmon; incorrectly called *mamey*

---

lunchtime tortilla, he will content himself by rolling a thin filling of salsa (*chile* sauce) in it.

Spicy or Not?

Much of the food served in Mexico is not "Mexican." Eating habits, as most other customs, depend upon social class. Upwardly mobile Mexicans typically shun the corn-based *indígena* fare in favor of the European-style food of the Spanish colonial elite: chops, steaks, cutlets, fish, clams, omelettes, soups, pasta, rice, and potatoes.

Such fare is often as bland as Des Moines on a summer Sunday afternoon. *No picante*—not spicy—is how the Mexicans describe bland food. *Caliente*, the Spanish adjective for "hot" (as in hot water), does not, in contrast to English usage, imply spicy, or *picante*.

MEXICAN FOOD

On most Mexican-style menus, diners will find variations on a number of basic themes:

Chiles rellenos: Fresh roasted green *chiles*, stuffed usually with cheese but sometimes with fish or meat, coated with batter, and fried. They provide a piquant, tantalizing contrast to tortillas.

Enchiladas and **tostadas:** Variations on the filled-tortilla theme. Enchiladas are stuffed with meat, cheese, olives, or beans and covered with sauce and baked, while tostadas consist of toppings served on crisp, open-faced tortillas.

Guacamole: This luscious avocado, onion, tomato, lime, and salsa mixture remains the delight it must have seemed to its Aztec inventors centuries ago. In nontourist Mexico, it's served sparingly as a garnish, rather than in appetizer bowls as is common in the U.S. Southwest (and at Mexican resorts catering to North Americans). (Similarly, in nontourist Mexico, burritos and fajitas, both stateside inventions, seldom, if ever appear on menus.)

Carnes (meats): **Carne asada** is grilled beef, usually chewy and well-done. Something similar you might see on a menu is ce-

cina (say-SEE-nah), dried salted beef, grilled to a shoeleather-like consistency. Much more appetizing is **birria,** a Guadalajara specialty. Traditional *birrias* are of lamb or goat, often wrapped and pit-roasted in maguey leaves, with which it is served, for authenticity. In addition to *asada*, meat-cooking styles are manifold, including *guisado* (stewed), *al pastor* (spit barbecue), and *barbacoa* (grill barbecued). Cuts include *lomo* (loin), *chuleta* (chop), *milanesa* (cutlet), and *albóndigas* (meatballs).

Moles (MOH-lays): Uniquely Mexican sauces. Mole poblano, a spicy-sweet mixture of chocolate, *chiles*, and a dozen other ingredients, is cooked to a smooth sauce, then baked with chicken (or turkey, a combination called *mole de pavo*). So *típica* it's widely regarded as the national dish.

Quesadillas: Made from soft flour tortillas, rather than corn, quesadillas resemble tostadas and always contain melted cheese.

Sopas: Soups consist of vegetables in a savory chicken broth, and are an important part of both *comida* (afternoon) and *cena* (evening) Mexican meals. *Pozole,* a rich steaming stew of hominy, vegetables, and pork or chicken,

Vegetarian Fare

Strictly vegetarian cooking, although a growing trend, remains the exception in Mexico, as are macrobiotic restaurants, health-food stores, and organic produce. Meat is such a delicacy for most Mexicans that they can't understand why people would give it up voluntarily. If vegetable-lovers can manage with corn, beans, cheese, eggs, *legumbres* (vegetables), and fruit, and not be bothered by a bit of pork fat *(manteca de cerdo),* Mexican cooking will suit them fine. On the other hand, if pork fat bothers you, ask for your food *sin manteca* (without lard).

Much of Pacific Mexico basks in the tropics, where bugs of all kinds love to live. With common-sense precautions, it's nevertheless easy to eat healthy in Pacific Mexico. (For suggestions,

see *Safe Water and Food* and *Health Problems* in the *Health and Safety* section in this chapter.)

Seafood

Early chroniclers wrote that Aztec Emperor Moctezuma employed a platoon of runners to bring fresh fish 300 miles every day from the sea to his court. In Pacific Mexico, fresh seafood is fortunately much more available from thousands of shoreline establishments, varying from thatched beach *palapas* to five-star hotel restaurants.

Pacific Mexico seafood is literally there for the taking. When strolling certain beaches, I have often seen well-fed, middle-class local vacationers breaking and eating oysters and mussels right off the rocks. In the summer on some Pacific Mexico beaches, fish and squid have

often constitutes the prime evening offering of small side-street shops. *Sopa de taco*, an ever-popular country favorite, is a medium-spicy cheese-topped thick *chile* broth served with crisp corn tortillas.

Tacos or **taquitos:** Tortillas served open or wrapped around any ingredient.

Tamales: Known in the singular as one *tamal*, not a "tamale," they're as Mexican as apple pie is American. This savory mixture of meat and sauce imbedded in a shell of corn dough and baked in a wrapping of corn husks is rarely known by the singular, however. They're so yummy that one *tamal* invariably leads to more tamales.

Tortas: The Mexican sandwich, usually hot meat with fresh tomato and avocado, stuffed between two halves of a crisp *bolillo* (boh-LEE-yoh) or Mexican bun.

Tortillas y frijoles refritos: Cooked brown or black beans, mashed and fried in pork fat, and rolled into tortillas with a dash of vitamin-C-rich salsa to form a near-complete combination of carbohydrate, fat, and balanced protein.

BEYOND THE BASICS

Mexican food combinations seem endless. Mexican corn itself has more than 500 recognized culinary variations, all from indigenous tradition. This has led to a myriad of permutations on the taco, such as *sopes* (made with small, thick tortillas), *garnacho* (flat taco), *chilaquile* (shredded taco), and *chalupa* (like a tostada).

Taking a lesson from California nouveau cuisine, avant-garde Mexican chefs are returning to **traditional ingredients.** They're using more and more chiles – habanero, poblano, jalapeño, and more – prepared with many variations, such as *chipotle, ancho, piquín,* and *mulato.* Squash flowers *(flor de calabaza)* and cactus (nopal) leaves are finding their way into soups and salads.

More often, chefs are serving the **wild game** – *venado* (venison), *conejo* (rabbit), *guajalote* (turkey), *codorniz* (quail), armadillo, and iguana – that country Mexicans have always depended upon. As part of the same trend, *cuitlacoche* (corn mushroom fungus), *chapulines* (small fried grasshoppers), and *gusanos de maguey* (maguey worms) are being increasingly added as ingredients in fancy restaurants.

been known to swarm so thickly in the surf that tourists can pull them out by hand. Villagers up and down the coast use small nets (or bare hands) to retrieve a few fish for supper, while communal teams haul in big netfuls of silvery, wriggling fry for sale right on the beach.

Despite the plenty, Pacific Mexico seafood prices reflect high worldwide demand, even at the humblest seaside *palapa*. The freshness and variety, however, make even the typical dishes seem bargains at any price.

Fruits and Juices

Squeezed vegetable and fruit juices, *jugos* (HOO-gohs), are among the widely available delights of Pacific Mexico. Among the many establishments—restaurants, cafés, and *loncherías*—willing to supply you with your favorite *jugo*, the juice bars *(jugerías)* are often the most fun. Colorful fruit piles usually mark *jugerías*. If you don't immediately spot your favorite fruit, ask anyway; it might be hidden in the refrigerator.

Besides your choice of pure juice, *jugerías* will often serve *aguas* and *licuados. Aguas* are the Mexican equivalent of lemonade, fruit juice with water and sugar added, except they're made with a dazzling variety of fruits, from strawberry and watermelon, to mango and plum-like *ciruela.* Licuados by contrast are made with milk whipped into the mix, with your favorite fruit, and sugar to taste for a creamy afternoon pick-me-up or evening dessert. One big favorite is a cool banana-chocolate *licuado,* which comes out tasting like a milk shake minus the calories.

© BRUCE WHIPPERMAN

Try the the naturally nutritious juice of the coco (coconut).

Alcoholic Drinks

The Aztecs sacrificed anyone caught drinking alcohol without permission. The later, more lenient, Spanish attitude toward getting *borracho* (soused) has led to a thriving Mexican renaissance of native alcoholic beverages: tequila, mescal, Kahlúa, pulque, and *aguardiente*. Tequila and mescal, distilled from the fermented juice of the maguey, originated in Oaxaca, where the best are still made. Quality tequila (named after the Guadalajara-area distillery town) and mescal come 76 proof (38 percent alcohol) and up. A small white worm, endemic to the maguey, is customarily added to each bottle of factory mescal for authenticity.

Pulque, although also made from the sap of the maguey, is locally brewed to a small alcohol content between that of beer and wine. The brewing houses are sacrosanct preserves, circumscribed by traditions that exclude women and outsiders. The brew, said to be rich in nutrients, is sold to local *pulquerías* and drunk immediately. If you are ever invited into a *pulquería*, it is an honor you cannot refuse.

Aguardiente, by contrast, is the notorious fiery Mexican "white lightning," a locally distilled, dirt-cheap ticket to oblivion for poor Mexican men.

While pulque comes from age-old indigenous tradition, beer (introduced by 19th-century German brewers) is the beverage of modern mestizo Mexico. More full-bodied than "light" U.S. counterparts, Mexican beer enjoys an enviable reputation.

Those visitors who indulge usually know their favorite among the many brands, from light to dark: Superior, Corona, Pacífico, Tecate (served with lime), Carta Blanca, Modelo, Dos Equis, Bohemia, Tres Equis, and Negra Modelo. Nochebuena, a hearty dark brew, becomes available only around Christmas.

Mexicans have yet to develop much of a taste for *vino tinto* or *vino blanco* (red or white table wine), although some domestic wines (such as the Baja California labels Cetto and Domecq and the "boutique" Monte Xanic) are at least very drinkable and at best, excellent.

Bread and Pastries

Excellent locally baked bread is a delightful surprise to many first-time visitors to Pacific Mexico. Small bakeries everywhere put out trays of hot, crispy-crusted *bolillos* (rolls) and sweet *panes dulces* (pastries). The pastries vary from simple cakes, muffins, cookies, and doughnuts to fancy fruit-filled turnovers and puffs. Half the fun occurs before the eating: grab a tray and tongs, peruse the goodies, and pick out the most scrumptious. With your favorite dozen or so finally selected, you take your tray to the cashier, who deftly bags everything up and collects a few pesos (two or three dollars) for your entire mouthwatering selection.

Eating Out

A *restaurante* (rays-tah-oo-RAHN-tay) generally implies a fairly fancy joint, with prices to match. The food and atmosphere, however, may be more to your liking at other types of eateries (in approximate declining order of prices): *cafetería, comedor, lonchería, jugería, fonda, taquería.*

Shopping

What to Buy

Although bargains abound in Mexico, savvy shoppers are selective. Steep import and luxury taxes drive up the prices of foreign-made goods such as cameras, computers, sports equipment, and English-language books. Instead, concentrate your shopping on locally made items: leather, jewelry, cotton resort wear, Mexican-made designer clothes, and the galaxy of handicrafts for which Mexico is renowned.

Handicrafts

A number of Pacific Mexico regional centers are renowned sources of crafts. A multitude of family shops in Guadalajara and its suburban villages of Tlaquepaque and Tonalá, the Lake Pátzcuaro region, Taxco and its village hinterland, and the Valley of Oaxaca all nurture vibrant traditions with roots in the pre-Columbian past. This rich cornucopia spills over to the Pacific resort centers, where it merges with troves of local offerings to decorate sidewalks, stalls, and shops all over town. (For many more details, see the *Arts and Crafts* section of the *Background* chapter.)

Bargaining

Bargaining will stretch your money even further. It comes with the territory in Mexico and needn't be a hassle. On the contrary, if done with humor and moderation, bargaining can be an enjoyable way to meet Mexican people and gain their respect, even friendship.

The local crafts market is where bargaining is most intense. For starters, try offering half the asking price. From there on, it's all psychology: you have to content yourself with not having to have the item. Otherwise, you're sunk; the vendor will sense your need and stand fast. After a few minutes of good-humored bantering, ask for *el último precio* (the final price), in which, if it's close, may be just the bargain you've been looking for.

Buying Silver and Gold Jewelry

Silver and gold jewelry, the finest of which is crafted in Taxco, Guadalajara, and Guanajuato, fills a number of shops in Pacific Mexico. One hundred percent pure silver is rarely sold because it's too soft. Silver (sent from processing mills in the north of Mexico to be worked in Taxco shops) is nearly always alloyed with 7.5 percent copper to increase its durability. Such pieces, identical in composition to sterling silver, should have ".925," together with the initials of the manufacturer, stamped on their back sides.

GOING TO THE SOURCE

The fusion of Spanish and native tradition is attractively evident in the abundance of handicrafts that Pacific Mexico offers. The bounty overflows everywhere, in resort shops, public markets, and the thousands of family workshops in the towns where the handicrafts are made.

It's best to go to the sources for the widest selection and lowest prices. Guadalajara's villages of **Tlaquepaque** and **Tonalá** offers bright stoneware, glittering papier-mâché sculptures, gleaming brass, lustrous blown glass, supple leather, and unique *equipal* leather furniture. **Tepic** is known for the fascinatingly enigmatic Huichol ceremonial masks and yarn paintings. In **Colima,** find irresistible pre-Columbian ceramic figurine reproductions of people and animals, including Colima's famously appealing dogs. **Pátzcuaro** is the place for bright baskets, rich wool sweaters, festive masks, and rustic wood furniture. As Mexico's jewelry-making capital, **Taxco** dazzles with its silver finery and masks. **Oaxaca** overflows with irresistible pottery, fine wool carpets and hangings, glittering gold jewelry, bright tinware and holiday adornments, razor-sharp cutlery, *alebrijes* (fantastic wooden animals), and richly embroidered *huipiles* (native women's dress).

Other, less common grades, such as "800 fine" (80 percent silver), should also be stamped.

If silver is not stamped with the degree of purity, it probably contains no silver at all and is an alloy of copper, zinc, and nickel, known by the generic label "alpaca," or "German" silver. Once, after haggling over the purity and prices of his offerings, a street vendor handed me a shiny handful and said, "Go to a jeweler and have them tested. If they're not real, keep them." Calling his bluff, I took them to a jeweler, who applied a dab of hydrochloric acid (commonly available as "muriatic acid") to each piece. Tiny, tell-tale bubbles of hydrogen revealed the cheapness of the mer-

chandise, which I returned the next day to the vendor.

Some shops price sterling silver jewelry simply by weighing, which typically translates to about $1 per gram. If you want to find out if the price is fair, ask the shopkeeper to weigh it for you.

People prize pure gold partly because, unlike silver, it does not tarnish. Gold, nevertheless, is rarely sold pure (24 karat); for durability, it is alloyed with copper. Typical purities, such as 18 karat (75 percent) or 14 karat (58 percent), should be stamped on the pieces. If not, chances are they contain no gold at all.

Conduct and Customs

Safe Conduct

Mexico is an old-fashioned country where people value traditional ideals of honesty, fi-

delity, and piety. Crime rates are low; visitors are often safer in Mexico than in their home cities.

Mexican police, who are increasingly using squad cars, are generally very conscientious and helpful despite their rock-bottom pay rates.

© BRUCE WHIPPERMAN

MACHISMO

I once met an Acapulco man who wore five gold wristwatches and became angry when I quietly refused his repeated invitations to get drunk with him. Another time, on the beach near San Blas, two drunk campesinos nearly attacked me because I was helping my girlfriend cook a picnic dinner. Outside Taxco I once spent an endless hour in the seat behind a bus driver who insisted on speeding down the middle of the two-lane highway, honking aside oncoming automobiles.

Despite their ethnic and socioeconomic differences, all four men shared the common affliction of machismo, a sometimes-reckless obsession to prove one's masculinity, to show how macho you are. Men of many nationalities share the instinct to prove themselves. Japan's *bushido* samurai code is one example.

When confronted by a braggart, male visitors should remain careful and controlled. If your opponent is yelling, stay cool, speak softly, and withdraw as soon as possible. On the highway, be courteous and unprovoking – don't use your car to spar with a macho driver. Drinking often leads to problems. It's best to stay out of bars or cantinas unless you're prepared to deal with the macho consequences. Polite refusal of a drink may be taken as a challenge. If you visit a bar with Mexican friends or acquaintances, you may be heading for a no-win choice between a drunken all-night *borrachera* (binge) or an insult to the honor of your friends by refusing.

For women, machismo requires even more cautious behavior. In Mexico, women's liberation is long in coming. Although a handful of Mexican women have risen to positions of political or corporate power, they constitute a small minority.

Female visitors should keep a low profile and wear bathing suits and brief shorts only at the beach. They can follow the example of their Mexican sisters by making a habit of going out in the company of friends or acquaintances, especially at night. Many Mexican men believe an unaccompanied woman wants to be picked up. Ignore their offers; any response, even refusal, might be taken as an encouraging sign. If, on the other hand, there is a Mexican man whom you'd genuinely like to meet, the traditional way is an arranged introduction through family or friends.

As a source of protection and friendship, Mexican families should not be overlooked – especially on the beach or in the park, where, among the gaggle of kids, grandparents, aunts, and cousins, there's room for one more.

Even though four generations have elapsed since Pancho Villa raided the U.S. border, the image of a Mexico bristling with *bandidos* persists. And similarly for Mexicans: despite the century and a half since the *yanquis* invaded Mexico City and took half their country, the communal Mexican psyche still views gringos (and, by association, all white foreigners) with revulsion, jealousy, and wonder.

Fortunately, the Mexican love-hate affair with foreigners does not necessarily apply to individual visitors. Your friendly *"buenos dias"* or *"por favor,"* when appropriate, is always appreciated, whether in the market, the gas station, or the hotel. The shy smile you will most likely receive in return will be your small, but not insignificant, reward.

Women

For women traveling solo, it is important to realize that the double standard is alive and well in Mexico. Dress and behave modestly, and you are more likely to avoid trouble. Whenever possible, stay in the company of friends or acquaintances; find companions for beach, sightseeing, and shopping excursions. Ignore strange men's solicitations and overtures. A Mexican man on the prowl will invent the sappiest romantic overtures to snare a gringa. He will often interpret anything but a firm "no" as a "maybe," and a "maybe" as a "yes."

Men

For male visitors, alcohol often leads to trouble. Avoid bars and cantinas; and if, given Mexico's excellent beers, you can't abstain completely, at least maintain soft-spoken self-control in the face of challenges from macho drunks.

The Law and Police

While Mexican authorities are tolerant of alcohol, they are decidedly intolerant of other substances such as marijuana, psychedelics, cocaine, and heroin. Getting caught with such drugs in Mexico usually leads to swift and severe results.

Equally swift is the punishment for nude sunbathing, which is both illegal in public and offensive to Mexicans. Confine your nudist colony to very private locations.

Although with decreasing frequency lately, traffic police in Pacific Mexico's resorts sometimes seem to watch foreign cars with eagle eyes. Officers seem to inhabit busy intersections and one-way streets, waiting for confused tourists to make a wrong move. If they whistle you over, stop immediately or you will really get into hot water. If guilty, say *"Lo siento"* ("I'm sorry") and be cooperative. Although he probably won't mention it, the officer is usually hoping that you'll cough up a $20 *mordida* (bribe) for the privilege of driving away.

Don't do it. Although he may hint at confiscating your car, calmly ask for an official *boleto* (written traffic ticket, if you're guilty) in exchange for your driver's license (have a copy), which the officer will probably keep if he writes a ticket. If after a few minutes no money appears, the officer will most likely give you back your driver's license rather than go to the trouble of writing the ticket. If not, the worst that will usually happen is you will have to go to the Presidencia Municipal (City Hall) the next morning and pay the $20 to a clerk in exchange for your driver's license.

Pedestrian and Driving Hazards

Although Pacific Mexico's potholed pavements and "holey" sidewalks won't land you in jail, one of them might send you to the hospital if you don't watch your step, especially at night.

"Pedestrian beware" is especially good advice on Mexican streets, where it is rumored that some drivers speed up rather than slow down when they spot a tourist stepping off the curb. Falling coconuts, especially frequent on windy days, constitute an additional hazard to unwary campers and beachgoers.

Driving Mexican country roads, where slow trucks and carts block lanes, campesinos stroll the shoulders, and horses, burros, and cattle wander at will, is hazardous—doubly so at night.

Socially Responsible Travel and Ecotourism

Latter-day jet travel has brought droves of vacationing tourists to developing countries largely unprepared for the consequences. As the visitors' numbers swell, power grids black out, sewers overflow, and roads crack under the strain of accommodating more and larger hotels, restaurants, cars, buses, and airports.

Worse yet, armies of vacationers drive up local prices and begin to change native customs. While visions of tourists as sources of fast money replace traditions of hospitality, television wipes out folk entertainment, Coke and Pepsi substitute for fruit drinks, and prostitution and drugs flourish.

Some travelers have said enough is enough and are forming organizations to encourage visitors to travel with increased sensitivity to native people and customs. They have developed travelers' codes of ethics and guidelines that encourage visitors to stay at local-style accommodations, use local transportation, and seek alternative vacations and tours, such as language-study and cultural programs and people-to-people work projects.

A number of especially active socially responsible travel groups sponsor tours all over the world, including some in the Puerto Vallarta region. These include organizations such as **Green Tortoise** (www.greentortoise.com) and **Green Globe** (www.greenglobe.org), both of which run tours that visit Pacific Mexico. For more alternatives, visit the umbrella website, www.sociallyresponsible.org.

Tips for Travelers

TRAVELING WITH CHILDREN

Children are treasured like gifts from heaven in Mexico. Traveling with kids will ensure your welcome most everywhere. On the beach, take extra precautions to make sure they are protected from the sun.

A sick child is no fun for anyone. Fortunately, clinics and good doctors are available even in most small towns. When in need, ask a storekeeper or a pharmacist, *"¿Dónde hay un doctor, por favor?"* (*"¿DOHN-day eye oon doc-TOHR, por fah-VOHR?"*). In most cases, within five minutes you will be in the waiting room of the local physician or hospital.

Children who do not favor typical Mexican fare can easily be fed with always-available eggs, cheese, *hamburguesas,* milk, oatmeal, corn flakes, bananas, cakes, and cookies.

Your children will generally have more fun if they have a little previous knowledge of Mexico and a stake in the trip. For example, help them select some library picture books and magazines so they'll know where they're going and what to expect, or give them responsibility for packing and carrying their own small travel bag.

Be sure to mention your children's ages when making air reservations; child discounts of 50 percent or more are often available. Also, if you can arrange to go on an uncrowded flight, you can stretch out and rest on the empty seats.

For more details on traveling with children, check out *Adventuring with Children* by Nan Jeffries. (See *Suggested Reading* in the *Resources* chapter.)

TRAVEL FOR PEOPLE WITH DISABILITIES

Mexican airlines and hotels (especially the large ones) have become sensitive to the needs of travelers with disabilities. Open, street-level lobbies and large, wheelchair-accessible elevators and rooms are available in nearly all Pacific Mexico resort (and some smaller, especially boutique, hotels). Furthermore, most streetcorner curbs accommodate wheelchairs.

United States law forbids travel discrimination against otherwise qualified people with disabilities. As long as your disability is stable and not liable to deteriorate during passage, you can expect to be treated like any passenger with special needs.

Make reservations far ahead of departure and ask your agent to inform your airline of your needs, such as a boarding wheelchair or in-flight oxygen. Be early at the gate to take advantage of the preboarding call.

For many helpful details to smooth your trip, get a copy of *Survival Strategies for Going Abroad* by Laura Hershey, published in 2005 by **Mobility International USA** (132 E. Broadway, Suite 343, Eugene, OR 97401, tel. 541/343-1284 voice/TDD, fax 541/343-6812, www.miusa.org). Mobility International is a valuable resource for many disabled lovers of Mexico, for it encourages disabled travelers with a goldmine of information and literature and can provide them with valuable Mexico connections. They publish a regular newsletter and provide information and referrals for international exchanges and homestays.

Similarly, **Partners of the Americas** (1424 K St. NW, Suite 700, Washington, D.C. 20005, tel. 202/628-3300 or 800/322-7844, fax 202/628-3306, info@partners.net, www.partners.net) with chapters in 45 U.S. states, works to improve understanding of disabilities and facilities in Mexico and Latin America. It maintains communications with local organizations and individuals whom disabled travelers may contact at their destinations.

GAY AND LESBIAN TRAVEL

Although Puerto Vallarta is sometimes known as Mexico's gay travel capital, the gay male presence in Puerto Vallarta, compared to the total flow of Puerto Vallarta vactioners, is modest; and the lesbian presence is even more so. Nevertheless, gay and lesbian

PACKING CHECKLIST

Sure, everyone intends not to forget their passport and air tickets, but how many have experienced that sinking feeling when they arrive at the check-in desk without one of them? Prevent trouble ahead of time by going over the following checklist after you think you've finished your packing. You'll be surprised how many times you will discover that you forgot something important.

NECESSARY ITEMS

____ camera, film (expensive in Mexico)
____ clothes, hat
____ comb
____ guidebook, reading books
____ keys, tickets
____ mosquito repellent
____ passport
____ prescription eyeglasses
____ prescription medicines and drugs
____ purse, waist-belt carrying pouch
____ sunglasses
____ sunscreen
____ swimsuit
____ toothbrush, toothpaste
____ passport, tourist card, visa
____ credit and/or ATM cards,
        traveler's checks, money
____ watch, clock
____ windbreaker

USEFUL ITEMS

____ address book
____ birth control
____ checkbook
____ contact lenses
____ dental floss
____ earplugs
____ first-aid kit
____ flashlight, batteries
____ immersion heater
____ lightweight binoculars
____ portable music player
____ razor
____ travel booklight

____ umbrella
____ vaccination certificate

NECESSARY ITEMS FOR CAMPERS

____ collapsible gallon plastic bottle
____ dish soap
____ first-aid kit
____ insect repellent
____ lightweight hiking shoes
____ lightweight tent
____ matches in waterproof case
____ nylon cord
____ plastic bottle, quart
____ pot scrubber/sponge
____ sheet or light blanket
____ camp cup, fork, and spoon
____ single-burner stove with fuel
____ Swiss army knife
____ tarp
____ toilet paper
____ towel, soap
____ two nesting cooking pots
____ water-purifying tablets, iodine,
        or household chlorine bleach

USEFUL ITEMS FOR CAMPERS

____ magnetic compass
____ dishcloths
____ hot pad
____ coffee, tea, sugar, powdered milk
____ moleskin (Dr. Scholl's)
____ plastic plate
____ poncho
____ paraffin household candles
____ whistle

travelers generally enjoy a welcome from Puerto Vallarta people, especially at the many gay-friendly lodgings, restaurants, clubs, and bars, sprinkled largely around the south-of-Cuale Olas Altas (Zona Romántica) neighborhood. These venues are generally low-key and welcoming (to both men and women—homosexual or not), and quite tasteful.

A wealth of lodgings, restaurants, and services are available through gay and lesbian travel websites. Many of them advertise in the excellent *Gay Guide Vallarta* magazine (or online at www.gayguidevallarta.com). Furthermore, a good general gay travel website is San Francisco-based **www.purpleroofs .com.** Its many pages detail, for example, about two dozen gay-friendly Puerto Vallarta hotels, plus many more on the coast of Nayarit, north of Puerto Vallarta, in addition to Guadalajara, Manzanillo, Acapulco, and Oaxaca.

Also very helpful and specifically tuned to Puerto Vallarta is **www.discoveryvallarta .com/guide.html,** with many gay-oriented search headings, including hotels, vacation rentals, tours, galleries, shopping, transportation, and much more. It also includes a lesbian-oriented search heading that details a number of links in nearby communities of Bucerías, Yelapa, Sayulita, Paco's Paradise, and more. Other potentially useful gay and lesbian websites are **www.gayscape.com** and **www .gaytravel.com.**

If you're interested in travel agency advice and services, check out **Now Voyager** (4406 18th St., San Francisco, CA 94114, toll-free tel. 800/255-6951, www.nowvoyager .com), a reliable San Francisco–based travel agency that specializes in cruises. They offer a plethora of other services, from tours and air tickets, to travel insurance and hotel reservations.

TRAVEL FOR SENIOR CITIZENS

Age, according to Mark Twain, is a question of mind over matter: If you don't mind, it doesn't matter. Mexico is a country where whole extended families, from babies to great-grandparents, live together. Elderly travelers will benefit from the respect and understanding Mexicans accord to older people. Besides these encouragements, consider the number of retirees already in havens in Puerto Vallarta, Guadalajara, Manzanillo, Oaxaca, and other regional centers.

Several organizations support and sponsor senior travel. Leading the field is **Elderhostel** (11 Ave. de Lafayette, Boston, MA 02111-1746, toll-free tel. 800/454-5768, www .elderhostel.org), contact them for more information and/or one of their Elderhostel U.S. and international catalogs of special tours, study, homestays, and people-to-people travel programs.

A number of newsletters publicize senior vacation and retirement opportunities. Among the best is the *Mexico File* monthly newsletter that, besides featuring pithy stories by Mexico travelers and news updates, offers an opportunity-packed classified section of Mexico rentals, publications, services, and much more. Subscribe ($39/year) at Simmonds Publications, 5580 La Jolla Blvd. #306, La Jolla, CA 92037, tel./fax 858/456-4419 or 800/563-9345 (voice mail), mf@mexicofile.com (information), www .mexicofile.com.

Some books also feature senior travel opportunities. One of the pithiest is *Unbelievably Good Deals and Great Adventures You Can't Have Unless You're Over 50,* by Joan Rattner Heilman, published by McGraw-Hill (2003). Its 200 pages are packed with details of how to get bargains on cruises, tours, car rentals, lodgings, and much, much more.

The **Internet** is a gold mine of senior-oriented travel information. Look into **Transitions Abroad,** www.transitionsabroad .com, which offers a gold mine of a subsite (www.transitionsabroad.com/listings/ travel/senior) with a load of useful resources, centering around senior traveling and living abroad.

Health and Safety

STAYING HEALTHY

In Pacific Mexico, as everywhere, prevention is the best remedy for illness. For those visitors who confine their travel to the beaten path, a few basic common-sense precautions will ensure vacation enjoyment.

Resist the temptation to dive headlong into Mexico. It's no wonder that people get sick—broiling in the sun, gobbling peppery food, guzzling beer and margaritas, then discoing half the night—all in their first 24 hours. An alternative is to give your body time to adjust. Travelers often arrive tired and dehydrated from travel and heat. During the first few days, drink plenty of bottled water and juice, and take siestas.

Immunizations and Precautions

A good physician can recommend the proper preventatives for your Pacific Mexico trip. If you are going to stay pretty much in town, your doctor will probably suggest little more than updating your basic typhoid, diphtheria-tetanus, and polio shots.

For camping or trekking in remote tropical areas—below 4,000 feet or 1,200 meters—doctors often recommend a gamma-globulin shot against hepatitis A and a schedule of anti-malaria pills. While in backcountry areas, always use other measures to discourage mosquitoes—and fleas, flies, ticks, no-see-ums, "kissing bugs," and other tropical pesties—from biting you. Common precautions include sleeping under mosquito netting, burning *espirales mosquito* (mosquito coils), and rubbing on plenty of pure DEET (n,n dimethyl-meta-toluamide) "jungle juice," mixed in equal parts with rubbing (70 percent isopropyl) alcohol. Although supereffective, 100 percent DEET dries and irritates the skin.

Sunburn

For sunburn protection, use a good sunscreen with a sun protection factor (SPF) rated 15 or more, which will reduce burning rays to one-

Kids should wear suncreen, whether it's sunny or not.

fifteenth or less of direct sunlight. Better still, take a shady siesta-break from the sun during the most hazardous midday hours. If you do get burned, applying your sunburn lotion (or one of the "caine" creams) after the fact usually decreases the pain and speeds healing.

Safe Water and Food

Although municipalities have made great strides in sanitation, food and water are still major potential sources of germs in Pacific Mexico. Do not drink local tap water. Drink bottled water only. Hotels, whose success depends vitally on their customers' health, generally provide *agua purificada* (purified bottled water). If, for any reason, the water quality is doubtful, add a water purifier, such as "Potable Aqua" brand (get it at a camping goods stores before departure) or a few drops per quart of water of *blanqueador* (household chlorine bleach) or *yodo* (tincture of iodine) from the pharmacy.

Pure bottled water, soft drinks, beer, and fresh fruit juices are so widely available it is easy to avoid tap water, especially in restaurants. Ice and *paletas* (iced juice-on-a-stick) may be risky, especially in small towns.

Washing hands before eating in a restaurant is a time-honored Mexican ritual that visitors should religiously follow. The humblest Mexican eatery will generally provide a basin to *lavar las manos* (wash the hands). If it doesn't, don't eat there.

Hot, cooked food is generally safe, as are peeled fruits and vegetables. Milk and cheese these days in Mexico are generally processed under sanitary conditions and sold pasteurized (ask, *"¿Pasteurizado?"*) and are typically safe. Mexican ice cream used to be both bad-tasting and of dubious safety, but national brands available in supermarkets are so much improved that it's no longer necessary to resist ice cream while in town.

In recent years, much cleaner public water and increased hygiene awareness have made salads—once shunned by Mexico travelers—generally safe to eat in tourist-frequented Pacific Mexico cafés and restaurants. Nevertheless, lettuce and cabbage, particularly in country villages, is more likely to be contaminated than tomatoes, carrots, cucumbers, onions, and green peppers. In any case, whenever in doubt, douse your salad in vinegar *(vinagre)* or plenty of sliced lime *(limón)* juice, the acidity of which reduces bacteria.

First-Aid Kit

In the tropics, ordinary cuts and insect bites are more prone to infection and should receive immediate first aid. A first-aid kit (with aspirin, rubbing alcohol, hydrogen peroxide, water-purifying tablets, household chlorine bleach or iodine for water purifying, swabs, bandages, gauze, adhesive tape, Ace bandage, chamomile *(manzanilla)* tea bags for upset stomachs, Pepto-Bismol, acidophilus tablets, antibiotic ointment, hydrocortisone cream, mosquito repellent, knife, and good tweezers)

is a good precaution for any traveler and mandatory for campers.

HEALTH PROBLEMS
Traveler's Diarrhea

Traveler's diarrhea (known in Mexico as *turista* or "Montezuma's Revenge") sometimes persists, even among prudent vacationers. You can suffer turista for a week after simply traveling from California to Philadelphia or New York. Doctors say the familiar symptoms of runny bowels, nausea, and sour stomach result from normal local bacterial strains to which newcomers' systems need time to adjust. Unfortunately, the dehydration and fatigue from heat and travel reduce your body's natural defenses

MEDICAL TAGS AND AIR EVACUATION

Travelers with special medical problems should consider wearing a medical identification tag. For a reasonable fee, **Medic Alert** (P.O. Box 1009, Turlock, CA 95381; tel. 209/668-3333, toll-free tel. 888633-4398, www.medicalert.org) provides such tags, as well as an information hotline that will inform doctors of your vital medical background.

In life-threatening emergencies, highly recommended **Aeromedevac** (Gillespie Field Airport, 681 Kenney St., El Cajon, CA 92020, toll-free tel. 800/462-0911, from Mexico 24-hr. toll-free tel. 001-800/832-5087, www.aeromedevac.com) provides jet ambulance service from any Mexican locale to a U.S. hospital for roughly $20,000.

Alternatively, you might consider the similar services of **Med-Jet Assistance** (Birmingham, Alabama, Intl. Airport, 4900 69th St., Birmingham, AL, 35206, toll-free U.S. tel. 800/963-3538, www .medjetassistance.com; in emergencies, worldwide, call U.S. tel. 205/595-6626 collect).

and sometimes lead to a persistent cycle of sickness at a time when you least want it.

Time-tested protective measures can help your body either prevent or break this cycle. Many doctors and veteran travelers swear by Pepto-Bismol for soothing sore stomachs and stopping diarrhea. Acidophilus, the bacteria found in yogurt, is widely available in the United States in tablets and aids digestion. Warm *manzanilla* (chamomile) tea, used widely in Mexico (and by Peter Rabbit's mother), provides liquid and calms upset stomachs. Temporarily avoid coffee and alcohol, drink plenty of *manzanilla* tea, and eat bananas and rice for a few meals until your tummy can take regular food.

Although powerful antibiotics and antidiarrhea medications such as Lomotil and Imodium are readily available over *farmacia* counters, they may involve serious side effects and should not be taken in the absence of medical advice. If in doubt, consult a doctor.

Chagas' Disease and Dengue Fever

Chagas' disease, spread by the "kissing" (or, more appropriately, "assassin") bug, is a potential hazard in the Mexican tropics. Known locally as a *vinchuca,* the triangular-headed, three-quarter-inch (two-centimeter) brown insect, identifiable by its yellow-striped abdomen, often drops upon its sleeping victims from the thatched ceiling of a rural house at night. Its bite is followed by swelling, fever, and weakness and can lead to heart failure if left untreated. Treatment with drugs at an early stage can, however, clear the patient of the trypanosome parasites that infect the bloodstream and vital organs. See a doctor immediately if you believe you're infected.

Most of the precautions against malaria-bearing mosquitos also apply to dengue fever, which does occur (although uncommonly) in outlying tropical areas of Mexico. The culprit here is a virus carried by the mosquito species *Aedes aegypti.* Symptons are acute fever, with chills, sweating, and muscle aches. A red, diffuse rash frequently results, which may later

Dengue fever, which occurs in outlying areas of Pacific Mexico, has been largely minimized by vigorous public education programs at thousands of local health centers.

peel. Sypmtoms abate after about five days, but fatigue may persist. A particularly serious but fortunately rare form, called dengue hemorrhagic fever, afflicts children and can be fatal. Although no vaccines or preventatives, other than deterring mosquitos, exist, if you have symptoms you should nevertheless see a doctor immediately.

For more good tropical preventative information, get a copy of the excellent pamphlet distributed by the International Association of Medical Advice to Travelers (IAMAT).

Scorpions and Snakes

While camping or staying in a *palapa* or other rustic accommodation, watch for scorpions, especially in your shoes, which you should shake out every morning. Scorpion stings and snakebites are rarely fatal to an adult but are potentially very serious for a child. Get the victim to a doctor calmly but quickly.

Sea Creatures

While snorkeling or surfing, you may suffer a coral scratch or jellyfish sting. Experts advise you to wash the afflicted area with ocean water and pour alcohol (rubbing alcohol or tequila) over the wound, then apply hydrocortisone cream available from the *farmacia.*

Injuries from sea urchin spines and stingray barbs are painful and can be serious. Physicians recommend similar first aid for both: remove the spines or barbs by hand or with tweezers, then soak the injury in as-hot-as-possible fresh water to weaken the toxins and provide relief. Another method is to rinse the area with an antibacterial solution—rubbing alcohol, vinegar, wine, or ammonia diluted with water. If none are available, the same effect may be achieved with urine, either your own or someone else's in your party. Get medical help immediately.

Tattoos

All health hazards don't come from the wild. A number of Mexico travelers have complained of complications from black henna tattoos. When enhanced by the chemical dye PPD, results can include an itchy rash that can lead to scarring. It's best to play it safe. If you must have a vacation tattoo, get it at an established, professional shop.

MEDICAL CARE

For medical advice and treatment, let your hotel (or if you're camping, the closest *farmacia*) refer you to a good doctor, clinic, or hospital. Mexican doctors, especially in medium-sized and small towns, practice like private doctors in the United States and Canada once did before health insurance, liability, and group practice. They will come to you if you request it; they often keep their doors open even after regular hours and charge reasonable fees.

You will receive generally good treatment at the many local hospitals in Pacific Mexico's tourist centers. If you must have an English-speaking, American-trained doctor, the International Association for Medical Assistance to Travelers (IAMAT) publishes an updated booklet of qualified member physicians, several of whom practice in the Pacific Mexico centers of Mazatlán, Guadalajara, Puerto Vallarta, Ixtapa, Zihuatanejo, and Acapulco. IAMAT also distributes a very detailed *How to Protect Yourself Against Malaria* guide, together with worldwide malaria risk and communicable disease charts. Contact IAMAT, at 1623 Military Rd., #279, Niagra Falls, NY 14304, tel. 716/754-4883, or in Canada at 40 Regal Rd., Guelph, Ontario N1K 1B5, tel. 519/836-0102, or 1287 St. Clair Ave. W, Toronto, Ontario M6E 1B8, tel. 416/652-0137. You may also contact IAMAT at info@iamat.org or www.iamat.org.

For more useful information on health and safety in Mexico, consult Drs. Robert H. Paige and Curtis P. Page's *Mexico: Health and Safety Travel Guide* (Tempe AZ, Med to Go Books, 2004), or Dirk Schroeder's *Staying Healthy in Asia, Africa, and Latin America* (Emeryville, CA: Avalon Travel Publishing, 2000.)

Information and Services

MONEY
The Peso: Down and Up

At this writing, the peso trades at about 11 per U.S. dollar. Since the peso value sometimes changes rapidly, U.S. dollars have become a much more stable indicator of Mexican prices; for this reason they are used in this book to report prices. You should, nevertheless, always use pesos to pay for everything in Mexico. Incidentally, the dollar sign, "$," also marks Mexican pesos.

Overnight in early 1993, the Mexican government shifted its monetary decimal point three places and created the "new" peso (now known simply as the "peso"). Since the introduction of the new peso, the centavo (one-hundredth of a new peso) has reappeared, in coins of 10, 20, and 50 centavos. Peso coins (*monedas*) in denominations of 1, 2, 5, 10 and 20 pesos, and bills in denominations of 20, 50, 100, 200 and 500 pesos are common. Since banks like to exchange your traveler's checks for a few crisp large bills rather than the often-tattered smaller denominations, ask for some of your change in 50- and 100-peso notes. A 500-peso note, while common at the bank, may look awfully big to a small shopkeeper, who might be hard-pressed to change it.

Banks, ATMs, and Money-Exchange Offices

Mexican banks, like their North American counterparts, have lengthened their business hours. HSBC maintains the longest hours: as long as 8 A.M.–7 P.M. Mon.–Sat. Banamex (Banco Nacional de Mexico), generally the most popular with local people, usually posts the best in-town dollar exchange rate in its lobbies; for example: *Tipo de cambio: venta 10.799, compra 10.933,* which means it will sell pesos to you at the rate of 10.799 per dollar and buy them back for 10.933 per dollar.

ATMs (automated teller machines), or *Cajeros Automáticos* (kah-HAY-rohs ahoo-toh-MAH-tee-kohs), are rapidly becoming the money source of choice in Mexico. Virtually every bank has a 24-hour ATM, accessible (with proper PIN identification code) by a swarm of U.S. and Canadian credit and ATM cards. Note: Some Mexican bank ATMs will "eat" your ATM card if you don't retrieve it within about 15 seconds of completing your transaction. Retrieve your card *immediately* after getting your cash.

Although one-time bank charges, typically about $2 per $100, for ATM cash remain small, the money you can usually get from a single card is limited to about $300 or less per day.

Even without an ATM card, you don't have to wait in long bank service lines. Opt for a less-crowded bank, such as Bancomer, Banco Serfín, HSBC, or a private money-exchange office *(casa de cambio).* Often most convenient, such offices often offer long hours and faster service than the banks for a fee (as little as $.50 or as much as $3 per $100).

Keeping Your Money Safe

Traveler's checks, the traditional prescription for safe money abroad, are widely accepted in Pacific Mexico. Even if you plan to use your ATM card, buy some U.S. dollar traveler's checks (a well-known brand such as American Express or Visa) as an emergency reserve. Canadian traveler's checks and currency are not as widely accepted as U.S. traveler's checks, and European and Asian traveler's checks are even less so. Unless you like signing your name or paying lots of per-check commissions, buy denominations of $50 or more.

In Pacific Mexico, as everywhere, thieves circulate among the tourists. Keep valuables in your hotel *caja de seguridad* (security box). If you don't particularly trust the desk clerk, carry what you cannot afford to lose in a money belt. Pickpockets love crowded markets, buses, and airport terminals where they can slip a wallet out of a back pocket or dangling purse in a blink. Guard against this by carrying your wallet in your front pocket, and your purse, waist pouch, and daypack (which clever crooks can sometimes slit open) on your front side.

Don't attract thieves by displaying wads of money or flashy jewelry. Don't get sloppy drunk; if so, you may become a pushover for a determined thief.

Don't leave valuables unattended on the beach; share security duties with trustworthy-looking neighbors, or leave a bag with a shopkeeper nearby.

Tipping

Without their droves of visitors, Mexican people would be even poorer. Deflation of the peso, while it makes prices low for outsiders, makes it rough for Mexican families to get by. The help at your hotel typically get paid only a few dollars a day. They depend on tips to make the difference between dire and bearable poverty. Give the *camarista* (chambermaid) and floor attendant 20 pesos every day or two. And whenever uncertain of what to tip, it will probably mean a lot to someone—maybe a whole family—if you err on the generous side.

In restaurants and bars, Mexican tipping customs are similar to those in the United States: Tip waiters, waitresses, and bartenders about 15 percent for satisfactory service.

Credit Cards

Credit cards, such as Visa, MasterCard, and, to a lesser extent, American Express and Discover are widely honored in the hotels, restaurants, craft shops, and boutiques that cater to foreign tourists. You will generally get better bargains, however, in shops that depend on local trade and do not so readily accept credit cards. Such shops sometimes offer discounts for cash sales.

Whatever the circumstance, your travel money will usually go much further in Pacific Mexico than back home. Despite the national 17 percent ("value added" IVA) sales tax, local lodging, food, and transportation prices will often seem like bargains compared to the developed world. Outside of the pricey high-rise beachfront strips, pleasant, palmy hotel room rates often run $50 or less.

COMMUNICATIONS
Using Mexican Telephones

Although Mexican phone service has improved in the last decade, it's still sometimes hit-or-miss. If a number doesn't get through, you may have to redial it more than once. When someone answers (usually *"Bueno"*) be especially courteous. If your Spanish is rusty, say, *"¿Por favor, habla inglés?"* (¿POR fah-VOR, AH-blah een-GLAYS?). If you want to speak to a particular person (such as María), ask, *"¿María se encuentra?"* (mah-REE-ah SAY ayn-koo-AYN-trah).

Since November 2001, when telephone numbers were standardized, Mexican phones operate pretty much the same as in the United States and Canada. In Puerto Vallarta town, for example, a complete telephone number is generally written like this: 322/222-4709. As in the United States, the "322" denotes the telephone area code, or *(lada)* (LAH-dah), and the 222-4709 is the number that you dial locally. If you want to dial this number long distance *(larga distancia)*, **first dial "01" (like "1" in the United States),** then 322/222-4709. All Mexican telephone numbers, with only three exceptions, begin with a three-digit *lada*, followed by a seven-digit local number. (The exceptions are Monterrey, Guadalajara, and Mexico City, which have two-digit *ladas* and eight-digit local numbers. The Mexico City *lada* is 55; Guadalajara's is 33; Monterrey's is 81. (For example, a complete Guadalajara phone number would read 33/6897-2253.)

Although **Mexican cellular telephones** are as universally used as those in the United States and Canada, at this writing they operate a bit differently. Generally, in order to dial a cellular number locally, for example, the Puerto Vallarta number 322/222-4709, you must prefix it with "044." Thus, in Puerto Vallarta, enter 044-322/222-4709. However, outside of town, you enter a cellular number like a regular long-distance number. Thus, from Guadalajara, for example, simply enter 01-322/222-4709.

In Pacific Mexico towns and cities, direct long-distance dialing is the rule—from hotels, public phone booths, and efficient private computerized telephone offices. The cheapest, often most convenient, way to call is by buying and using a public telephone **Ladatel telephone card** *(tarjeta telefónica)*. Buy them in 30-, 50-, and 100-peso denominations at the many outlets—minimarkets, pharmacies, liquor stores—that display the blue and yellow Ladatel sign.

Calling Mexico and Calling Home

To call Mexico direct from the United States, first dial 011 (for international access), then 52 (for Mexico), followed by the Mexican area code and local number.

For station-to-station calls to the United States from Mexico, dial 001 plus the U.S. area code and the local number. For calls to other countries, ask your hotel desk clerk or see the easy-to-follow directions in the local Mexican telephone directory.

By far the cheapest way to call home (about $.50 per minute) is via one of the many public telephones with your Ladatel phone card.

Beware of certain private "To Call Long Distance to the U.S.A. Collect and Credit Card" telephones installed prominently in airports, tourist hotels, and shops. Tariffs on these phones often run as high as $10 per minute (with a three-minute minimum), for a total of $30, whether you talk three minutes or not. Always ask the operator for the rate, and if it's too high, buy a 30 peso ($3) Ladatel phone card.

In smaller towns, with no public street telephones, you must often do your long-distance phoning in the *larga distancia* (local phone office). Typically staffed by a young woman and often connected to a café, the *larga distancia* becomes an informal community social center as people pass the time waiting for their phone connections.

Post and Telegraph Offices and Internet Access

Mexican *correos* (post offices) operate similarly, but more slowly and less securely, than their counterparts all over the world. Mail services usually include *lista de correo* (general delivery, address letters *"a/c lista de correo"*), *servicios filatelicas* (philatelic services), *por avión* (airmail), *giros* (postal money orders), and Mexpost secure and fast delivery service, usually from separate Mexpost offices.

Mexican ordinary mail is sadly unreliable and pathetically slow. If, for mailings within Mexico, you must have security, use the efficient, reformed government Mexpost (like U.S. Express Mail) service. For international mailings, check the local Yellow Pages for widely available DHL, Federal Express, or UPS courier service.

Telégrafos (telegraph offices), usually near the post office, send and receive *telegramas* (telegrams) and *giros* (money orders). *Telecomunicaciones* (Telecom), the new high-tech telegraph offices, add telephone and public fax to the available services.

Internet service, including personal email access, has arrived in Pacific Mexico's cities and larger towns. Internet cafés are becoming increasingly common, especially in the resort centers. Online rates average about $2 per hour.

Electricity and Time

Mexican electric power is supplied at U.S.-standard 110 volts, 60 cycles. Plugs and sockets are generally two-pronged, nonpolar (like the pre-1970s U.S. ones). Bring adapters if you're going to use appliances with polar two-pronged or three-pronged plugs. A two-pronged polar plug has different-sized prongs, one of which is too large to plug into an old-fashioned nonpolar socket.

Pacific Mexico operates on central time except for the northwest states of Sinaloa and Nayarit, which operate on mountain time.

RESOURCES

Glossary

abarrotería grocery store

alcalde mayor or municipal judge

alfarería pottery

alfarero, alfarera potter

andando walkway or strolling path

antojitos native Mexican snacks, such as tamales, *chiles rellenos*, tacos, and enchiladas

artesanías handicrafts, as distinguished from **artesano, artesana** a person who makes handicrafts

audiencia one of the royal executive-judicial panels sent to rule Mexico during the 16th century

ayuntamiento either the town council or the building where it meets

bienes raices literally "good roots," but popularly, real estate

birria pit-barbequed goat, pork, or lamb, especially typical of Jalisco

boleto ticket, boarding pass

caballero literally, "horseman," but popularly, gentleman

cabercera head town of a municipal district, or headquarters in general

cabrón literally a cuckold, but more commonly, bastard, rat, or S.O.B.; sometimes used affectionately

cacique chief or boss

calandria early 1800s-style horse-drawn carriage, common in Guadalajara

camionera central central bus station

campesino country person; farm worker

canasta basket of woven reeds, with handle

casa de huéspedes guesthouse, often operated in a family home

caudillo dictator or political chief

charro, charra gentleman cowboy or cowgirl

chingar literally, "to rape," but is also the universal Spanish "f- word," the equivalent of "screw" in English

churrigueresque Spanish baroque architectural style incorporated into many Mexican colonial churches, named after José Churriguera (1665-1725)

científicos literally, scientists, but applied to President Porfirio Díaz's technocratic advisers

cofradía Catholic fraternal service association, either male or female, mainly in charge of financing and organizing religious festivals

colectivo a shared public taxi or minibus that picks up and deposits passengers along a designated route

colegio preparatory school or junior college

colonia suburban subdivision/satellite of a larger city

Conasupo government store that sells basic foods at subsidized prices

correo post office

criollo person of all-Spanish descent born in the New World

cuadra Huichol yarn painting, usually rectangular

Cuaresma Lent

curandero, curandera indigenous medicine man or woman

damas ladies, as in "ladies room"

Domingo de Ramos Palm Sunday

ejido a constitutional, government-sponsored form of community, with shared land ownership and cooperative decision making

encomienda colonial award of tribute from a designated indigenous district

estación ferrocarril railroad station

farmacia pharmacy or drugstore

finca farm

fonda food stall or small restaurant, often in a traditional market complex

fraccionamiento city sector or subdivision

fuero the former right of clergy to be tried in separate ecclesiastical courts

gachupín "one who wear spurs"; a derogatory term for a Spanish-born colonial

gasolinera gasoline station

gente de razón "people of reason"; whites and mestizos in colonial Mexico

gringo once-derogatory but now commonly used term for North American whites

grito impassioned cry, as in Hidalgo's *Grito de Dolores*

hacienda large landed estate; also the government treasury

hidalgo nobleman; called honorifically by "Don" or "Doña"

indígena indigenous or aboriginal inhabitant who speaks his or her native tongue; commonly, but incorrectly, an Indian *(indio)*

jardín literally garden, but often denoting a town's central plaza

jejenes "no-see-um" biting gnats, especially around San Blas, Nayarit

judiciales the federal or state "judicial," or investigative police, best known to motorists for their highway checkpoint inspections

jugería stall or small restaurant providing a large array of squeezed vegetable and fruit *jugos* (juices)

juzgado the "hoosegow," or jail

larga distancia long-distance telephone service, or the *caseta* (booth) where it's provided

licenciado academic degree (abbr. Lic.) approximately equivalent to a bachelor's degree

lonchería small lunch counter, usually serving juices, sandwiches, and *antojitos* (Mexican snacks)

machismo; macho exaggerated sense of maleness; person who holds such a sense of himself

mescal alcoholic beverage distilled from the fermented hearts of maguey (century plant)

mestizo person of mixed European/indigenous descent

milpa native farm plot, usually of corn, squash, and beans

mordida slang for bribe; literally, "little bite"

palapa thatched-roof structure, often open and shading a restaurant

panga outboard launch *(lancha)*

Pemex acronym for Petróleos Mexicanos, Mexico's national oil corporation

peninsulares the Spanish-born ruling colonial elite

peón a poor wage-earner, usually a country native

petate a mat, traditionally woven of palm leaf

plan political manifesto, usually by a leader or group consolidating or seeking power

Porfiriato the 34-year (1876–1910) ruling period of president-dictator Porfirio Díaz

pozole popular stew, of hominy in broth, usually topped by shredded pork, cabbage, and diced onion

presidencia municipal the headquarters, like a U.S. city or county hall, of a Mexican *municipio*, countylike local governmental unit

preventiva municipal police

pronunciamiento declaration of rebellion by an insurgent leader

pueblo town or people

puta derogatory term for women

quebracho slang for homosexual

quebrachón slang for gay man

quinta a villa or country house

quinto the royal "one-fifth" tax on treasure and precious metals

retorno cul-de-sac

rurales former federal country police force created to fight *bandidos*

Semana Santa pre-Easter Holy Week

Tapatío, Tapatía a label referring to anyone or anything from Guadalajara or Jalisco

taxi especial private taxi, as distinguished from *taxi colectivo*, or shared taxi

telégrafo telegraph office, lately converting to high-tech **telecomunicaciones,** or telecom, offering telegraph, telephone, and public fax services

tenate soft, pliable basket, without handle, woven of palm leaf

vaquero cowboy

vecinidad neighborhood
vinchuca "kissing" or "assassin" bug
yanqui Yankee
zócalo town plaza or central square

ABBREVIATIONS

Av. *avenida* (avenue)
Blv. *bulevar* (boulevard)

Calz. *calzada* (thoroughfare, main road)
Fco. Francisco (proper name, as in "Fco. Villa")
Fracc. *Fraccionamiento* (subdivision)
Nte. *norte* (north)
Ote. *oriente* (east)
Pte. *poniente* (west)
s/n *sin número* (no street number)

Spanish Phrasebook

Your Pacific Mexico adventure will be more fun if you use a little Spanish. Mexican folks, although they may smile at your funny accent, will appreciate your halting efforts to break the ice and transform yourself from a foreigner to a potential friend.

Spanish commonly uses 30 letters—the familiar English 26, plus four straightforward additions: ch, ll, ñ, and rr, which are explained in "Consonants," below.

PRONUNCIATION

Once you learn them, Spanish pronunciation rules—in contrast to English—don't change. Spanish vowels generally sound softer than in English. (Note: The capitalized syllables below receive stronger accents.)

Vowels

a like ah, as in "hah": *agua* AH-gooah (water), *pan* PAHN (bread), and *casa* CAH-sah (house)

e like ay, as in "may:" *mesa* MAY-sah (table), *tela* TAY-lah (cloth), and *de* DAY (of, from)

i like ee, as in "need": *diez* dee-AYZ (ten), *comida* ko-MEE-dah (meal), and *fin* FEEN (end)

o like oh, as in "go": *peso* PAY-soh (weight), *ocho* OH-choh (eight), and *poco* POH-koh (a bit)

u like oo, as in "cool": *uno* OO-noh (one), *cuarto* KOOAHR-toh (room), and *usted* oos-TAYD (you); when it follows a "q" the **u** is silent; when it follows an "h" or has an umlaut, it's pronounced like "w"

Consonants

b, d, f, k, l, m, n, p, q, s, t, v, w, x, y, z, and ch pronounced almost as in English; **h** occurs, but is silent–not pronounced at all.

c like k as in "keep": *cuarto* KOOAR-toh (room), Tepic tay-PEEK (capital of Nayarit state); when it precedes "e" or "i," pronounce **c** like s, as in "sit": *cerveza* sayr-VAY-sah (beer), *encima* ayn-SEE-mah (atop).

g like g as in "gift" when it precedes "a," "o," "u," or a consonant: *gato* GAH-toh (cat), *hago* AH-goh (I do, make); otherwise, pronounce **g** like h as in "hat": *giro* HEE-roh (money order), *gente* HAYN-tay (people)

j like h, as in "has": *Jueves* HOOAY-vays (Thursday), *mejor* may-HOR (better)

ll like y, as in "yes": *toalla* toh-AH-yah (towel), *ellos* AY-yohs (they, them)

ñ like ny, as in "canyon": *año* AH-nyo (year), *señor* SAY-nyor (Mr., sir)

r is lightly trilled, with tongue at the roof of your mouth like a very light English d, as in "ready": *pero* PAY-doh (but), *tres* TDAYS (three), *cuatro* KOOAH-tdoh (four).

rr like a Spanish r, but with much more emphasis and trill. Let your tongue flap. Practice with *burro* (donkey), *carretera* (highway), and Carrillo (proper name), then really let go with *ferrocarril* (railroad).

Note: The single small but common exception to all of the above is the pronunciation of Spanish **y** when it's being used as the Spanish word for "and," as in "Ron y Kathy." In such case, pronounce it like the English ee, as in "keep": Ron "ee" Kathy (Ron and Kathy).

Accent

The rule for accent, the relative stress given to syllables within a given word, is straightforward. If a word ends in a vowel, an n, or an s, accent the next-to-last syllable; if not, accent the last syllable.

Pronounce **gracias** GRAH-seeahs (thank you), **orden** OHR-dayn (order), and **carretera** kah-ray-TAY-rah (highway) with stress on the next-to-last syllable.

Otherwise, accent the last syllable: **venir** vay-NEER (to come), **ferrocarril** fay-roh-cah-REEL (railroad), and **edad** ay-DAHD (age).

Exceptions to the accent rule are always marked with an accent sign: (á, é, í, ó, or ú), such as **teléfono** tay-LAY-foh-noh (telephone), **jabón** hah-BON (soap), and **rápido** RAH-pee-doh (rapid).

BASIC AND COURTEOUS EXPRESSIONS

Most Spanish-speaking people consider formalities important. Whenever approaching anyone for information or some other reason, do not forget the appropriate salutation—good morning, good evening, etc. Standing alone, the greeting *hola* (hello) can sound brusque.

Hello. *Hola.*
Good morning. *Buenos días.*
Good afternoon. *Buenas tardes.*
Good evening. *Buenas noches.*
How are you? *¿Cómo está usted?*
Very well, thank you. *Muy bien, gracias.*
Okay; good. *Bien.*
Not okay; bad. *Mal or feo.*
So-so. *Más o menos.*
And you? *¿Y usted?*
Thank you. *Gracias.*
Thank you very much. *Muchas gracias.*
You're very kind. *Muy amable.*
You're welcome. *De nada.*
Goodbye. *Adios.*
See you later. *Hasta luego.*

please *por favor*
yes *sí*
no *no*
I don't know. *No sé.*
Just a moment, please. *Momentito, por favor.*
Excuse me, please (when you're trying to get attention). *Disculpe or Con permiso.*
Excuse me (when you've made a boo-boo). *Lo siento.*
Pleased to meet you. *Mucho gusto.*
How do you say . . . in Spanish? *¿Cómo se dice... en español?*
What is your name? *¿Cómo se llama usted?*
Do you speak English? *¿Habla usted inglés?*
Is English spoken here? (Does anyone here speak English?) *¿Se habla inglés?*
I don't speak Spanish well. *No hablo bien el español.*
I don't understand. *No entiendo.*
My name is... *Me llamo...*
Would you like... *¿Quisiera usted...*
Let's go to... *Vamos a...*

TERMS OF ADDRESS

When in doubt, use the formal *usted* (you) as a form of address.

I *yo*
you (formal) *usted*
you (familiar) *tu*
he/him *él*
she/her *ella*
we/us *nosotros*
you (plural) *ustedes*
they/them *ellos (all males or mixed gender); ellas (all females)*
Mr., sir *señor*
Mrs., madam *señora*
miss, young lady *señorita*
wife *esposa*
husband *esposo*
friend *amigo (male); amiga (female)*
sweetheart *novio (male); novia (female)*
son; daughter *hijo; hija*
brother; sister *hermano; hermana*
father; mother *padre; madre*
grandfather; grandmother *abuelo; abuela*

TRANSPORTATION
Where is... ? ¿Dónde está... ?
How far is it to... ? ¿A cuánto está... ?
from... to... de... a...
How many blocks? ¿Cuántas cuadras?
Where (Which) is the way to... ? ¿Dónde está el camino a... ?
the bus station la terminal de autobuses
the bus stop la parada de autobuses
Where is this bus going? ¿Adónde va este autobús?
the taxi stand la parada de taxis
the train station la estación de ferrocarril
the boat el barco
the airport el aeropuerto
I'd like a ticket to... Quisiera un boleto a...
first (second) class primera (segunda) clase
roundtrip ida y vuelta
reservation reservación
baggage equipaje
Stop here, please. Pare aquí, por favor.
the entrance la entrada
the exit la salida
the ticket office la oficina de boletos
(very) near; far (muy) cerca; lejos
to; toward a
by; through por
from de
the right la derecha
the left la izquierda
straight ahead derecho; directo
in front en frente
beside al lado
behind atrás
the corner la esquina
the stoplight la semáforo
a turn una vuelta
right here aquí
somewhere around here por acá
right there allí
somewhere around there por allá
street; boulevard calle; bulevar
highway carretera
bridge; toll puente; cuota
address dirección
north; south norte; sur
east; west oriente (este); poniente (oeste)

ACCOMMODATIONS
hotel hotel
Is there a room? ¿Hay cuarto?
May I (may we) see it? ¿Puedo (podemos) verlo?
What is the rate? ¿Cuál es el precio?
Is that your best rate? ¿Es su mejor precio?
Is there something cheaper? ¿Hay algo más económico?
a single room un cuarto sencillo
a double room un cuarto doble
double bed cama matrimonial
twin beds camas gemelas
with private bath con baño
hot water agua caliente
shower ducha
towels toallas
soap jabón
toilet paper papel higiénico
blanket frazada; manta
sheets sábanas
**air-conditioned–aire acondicionado
fan abanico; ventilador
key llave
manager gerente

FOOD
I'm hungry Tengo hambre.
I'm thirsty. Tengo sed.
menu lista; menú
order orden
glass vaso
fork tenedor
knife cuchillo
spoon cuchara
napkin servilleta
soft drink refresco
coffee café
tea té
drinking water agua pura; agua potable
bottled carbonated water agua mineral
bottled uncarbonated water agua sin gas
beer cerveza
wine vino
milk leche
juice jugo
cream crema
sugar azúcar

cheese *queso*
snack *antojo; botana*
breakfast *desayuno*
lunch *almuerzo*
daily lunch special *comida corrida (or el menú del día depending on region)*
dinner *comida (often eaten in late afternoon); cena (a late-night snack)*
the check *la cuenta*
eggs *huevos*
bread *pan*
salad *ensalada*
fruit *fruta*
mango *mango*
watermelon *sandía*
papaya *papaya*
banana *plátano*
apple *manzana*
orange *naranja*
lime *limón*
fish *pescado*
shellfish *mariscos*
shrimp *camarones*
meat (without) *(sin) carne*
chicken *pollo*
pork *puerco*
beef; steak *res; bistec*
bacon; ham *tocino; jamón*
fried *frito*
roasted *asada*
barbecue; barbecued *barbacoa; al carbón*

SHOPPING

money *dinero*
money-exchange bureau *casa de cambio*
I would like to exchange traveler's checks. *Quisiera cambiar cheques de viajero.*
What is the exchange rate? *¿Cuál es el tipo de cambio?*
How much is the commission? *¿Cuánto cuesta la comisión?*
Do you accept credit cards? *¿Aceptan tarjetas de crédito?*
money order *giro*
How much does it cost? *¿Cuánto cuesta?*
What is your final price? *¿Cuál es su último precio?*

expensive *caro*
cheap *barato; económico*
more *más*
less *menos*
a little *un poco*
too much *demasiado*

HEALTH

Help me please. *Ayúdeme por favor.*
I am ill. *Estoy enfermo.*
Call a doctor. *Llame un doctor.*
Take me to ... *Lléveme a ...*
hospital *hospital; sanatorio*
drugstore *farmacia*
pain *dolor*
fever *fiebre*
headache *dolor de cabeza*
stomach ache *dolor de estómago*
burn *quemadura*
cramp *calambre*
nausea *náusea*
vomiting *vomitar*
medicine *medicina*
antibiotic *antibiótico*
pill; tablet *pastilla*
aspirin *aspirina*
ointment; cream *pomada; crema*
bandage *venda*
cotton *algodón*
sanitary napkins *use brand name, e.g., Kotex*
birth control pills *pastillas anticonceptivas*
contraceptive foam *espuma anticonceptiva*
condoms *preservativos; condones*
toothbrush *cepillo dental*
dental floss *hilo dental*
toothpaste *crema dental*
dentist *dentista*
toothache *dolor de muelas*

POST OFFICE AND COMMUNICATIONS

long-distance telephone *teléfono larga distancia*
I would like to call ... *Quisiera llamar a ...*
collect *por cobrar*
station to station *a quien contesta*
person to person *persona a persona*
credit card *tarjeta de crédito*

post office *correo*
general delivery *lista de correo*
letter *carta*
stamp *estampilla, timbre*
postcard *tarjeta*
aerogram *aerograma*
air mail *correo aereo*
registered *registrado*
money order *giro*
package; box *paquete; caja*
string; tape *cuerda; cinta*

AT THE BORDER

border *frontera*
customs *aduana*
immigration *migración*
tourist card *tarjeta de turista*
inspection *inspección; revisión*
passport *pasaporte*
profession *profesión*
marital status *estado civil*
single *soltero*
married; divorced *casado; divorciado*
widowed *viudado*
insurance *seguros*
title *título*
driver's license *licencia de manejar*

AT THE GAS STATION

gas station *gasolinera*
gasoline *gasolina*
unleaded *sin plomo*
full, please *lleno, por favor*
tire *llanta*
tire repair shop *vulcanizadora*
air *aire*
water *agua*
oil (change) *aceite (cambio)*
grease *grasa*
My . . . doesn't work. *Mi . . . no sirve.*
battery *batería*
radiator *radiador*
alternator *alternador*
generator *generador*
tow truck *grúa*
repair shop *taller mecánico*
tune-up *afinación*
auto parts store *refaccionería*

VERBS

Verbs are the key to getting along in Spanish. They employ mostly predictable forms and come in three classes, which end in *ar*, *er*, and *ir*, respectively:

to buy *comprar*
I buy, you (he, she, it) buys *compro, compra*
we buy, you (they) buy *compramos, compran*
to eat *comer*
I eat, you (he, she, it) eats *como, come*
we eat, you (they) eat *comemos, comen*
to climb *subir*
I climb, you (he, she, it) climbs *subo, sube*
we climb, you (they) climb *subimos, suben*

Here are more (with irregularities indicated).

to do or make *hacer* (regular except for *hago*, I do or make)
to go *ir* (very irregular: *voy, va, vamos, van*)
to go (walk) *andar*
to love *amar*
to work *trabajar*
to want *desear, querer*
to need *necesitar*
to read *leer*
to write *escribir*
to repair *reparar*
to stop *parar*
to get off (the bus) *bajar*
to arrive *llegar*
to stay (remain) *quedar*
to stay (lodge) *hospedar*
to leave *salir* (regular except for *salgo*, I leave)
to look at *mirar*
to look for *buscar*
to give *dar* (regular except for *doy*, I give)
to carry *llevar*
to have *tener* (irregular but important: *tengo, tiene, tenemos, tienen*)
to come *venir* (similarly irregular: *vengo, viene, venimos, vienen*)

Spanish has two forms of "to be:"

to be *estar* (regular except for *estoy*, I am)
to be *ser* (very irregular: *soy, es somos, son*)

Use *estar* when speaking of location or a temporary state of being: "I am at home." *"Estoy en casa."* "I'm sick." *"Estoy enfermo."* Use *ser* for a permanent state of being: "I am a doctor." *"Soy doctora."*

NUMBERS

zero *cero*
one *uno*
two *dos*
three *tres*
four *cuatro*
five *cinco*
six *seis*
seven *siete*
eight *ocho*
nine *nueve*
10 *diez*
11 *once*
12 *doce*
13 *trece*
14 *catorce*
15 *quince*
16 *dieciseis*
17 *diecisiete*
18 *dieciocho*
19 *diecinueve*
20 *veinte*
21 *veinte y uno or veintiuno*
30 *treinta*
40 *cuarenta*
50 *cincuenta*
60 *sesenta*
70 *setenta*
80 *ochenta*
90 *noventa*
100 *ciento*
101 *ciento y uno or cientiuno*
200 *doscientos*
500 *quinientos*
1,000 *mil*
10,000 *diez mil*
100,000 *cien mil*

1,000,000 *millón*
one half *medio*
one third *un tercio*
one fourth *un cuarto*

TIME

What time is it? *¿Qué hora es?*
It's one o'clock. *Es la una.*
It's three in the afternoon. *Son las tres de la tarde.*
It's 4 A.M. *Son las cuatro de la mañana.*
six-thirty *seis y media*
a quarter till eleven *un cuarto para las once*
a quarter past five *las cinco y cuarto*
an hour *una hora*

DAYS AND MONTHS

Monday *lunes*
Tuesday *martes*
Wednesday *miércoles*
Thursday *jueves*
Friday *viernes*
Saturday *sábado*
Sunday *domingo*
today *hoy*
tomorrow *mañana*
yesterday *ayer*
January *enero*
February *febrero*
March *marzo*
April *abril*
May *mayo*
June *junio*
July *julio*
August *agosto*
September *septiembre*
October *octubre*
November *noviembre*
December *diciembre*
a week *una semana*
a month *un mes*
after *después*
before *antes*

Suggested Reading

Some of these books are informative, others are entertaining, and all of them will increase your understanding of Mexico. Virtually all of these will be easier to find at home than in Mexico. Although many of them are classics and out of print, Amazon.com, Barnesandnoble.com, Alibris.com, and libraries often have used copies. Take some along on your trip. If you find others that are especially noteworthy, let us know. Happy reading.

HISTORY AND ARCHAEOLOGY

Calderón de la Barca, Fanny. *Life in Mexico, with New Material from the Author's Journals.* New York: Doubleday, 1966. Edited by H. T. and M. H. Fisher. An update of the brilliant, humorous, and celebrated original 1913 book by the Scottish wife of the Spanish ambassador to Mexico.

Casasola, Gustavo. *Seis Siglos de Historia Gráfica de Mexico (Six Centuries of Mexican Graphic History).* Mexico City: Editorial Gustavo Casasola, 1978. Six fascinating volumes of Mexican history in pictures, from 1505 to the present.

Collis, Maurice. *Cortés and Montezuma.* New York: New Directions Publishing Corp., 1999. A reprint of a 1954 classic piece of well-researched storytelling. Collis traces Cortés's conquest of Mexico through the defeat of his chief opponent, Aztec emperor Montezuma. He uses contemporary eyewitnesses—notably Bernal Díaz de Castillo—to bring to life one of history's greatest dramas.

Cortés, Hernán. *Letters from Mexico.* Translated by Anthony Pagden. New Haven: Yale University Press, 1986. Cortés' five long letters to his king, in which he describes contemporary Mexico in fascinating detail, including, notably, the remarkably sophisticated life of the Aztecs at the time of the Conquest.

Davies, Nigel. *Ancient Kingdoms of Mexico.* London: Penguin Books, 1990. An authoritative history of the foundations of Mexican civilization. Clearly traces the evolution of Mexico's five successive worlds—Olmec, Teotihuacán, Toltec, Aztec, and finally Spanish—that set the stage for present-day Mexico.

Díaz del Castillo, Bernal. *The Discovery and Conquest of Mexico.* Translated by Albert Idell. London: Routledge (of Taylor and Francis Group), 2005. A soldier's still-fresh tale of the Conquest from the Spanish viewpoint.

Garfias, Luis. *The Mexican Revolution.* Mexico City: Panorama Editorial, 1985. A concise Mexican version of the 1910–1917 Mexican revolution, the crucible of present-day Mexico.

Gugliotta, Bobette. *Women of Mexico.* Encino CA: Floricanto Press, 1989. Lively legends, tales, and biographies of remarkable Mexican women, from Zapotec princesses to Independence heroines.

León-Portilla, Miguel. *The Broken Spears: The Aztec Account of the Conquest of Mexico.* New York: Beacon Press, 1962. Provides an interesting contrast to Díaz del Castillo's account.

Meyer, Michael, and William Sherman. *The Course of Mexican History.* New York: Oxford University Press, 1991. An insightful, 700-plus-page college textbook in paperback. A bargain, especially if you can get it used.

Novas, Himilce. *Everything You Need to Know About Latino History.* New York: Plume Books (Penguin Group), 1994. Chicanos, Latin rhythm, La Raza, the Treaty of Guadalupe Hidalgo, and much more, interpreted from an authoritative Latino point of view.

Reed, John. *Insurgent Mexico.* New York:

International Publisher's Co., 1994. Republication of 1914 original. Fast-moving, but not unbiased, description of the 1910 Mexican revolution by the journalist famed for his reporting of the subsequent 1917 Russian revolution. Reed, memorialized by the Soviets, was resurrected in the 1981 film biography *Reds*.

Ridley, Jasper. *Maximilian and Juárez*. New York: Ticknor and Fields, 1999. This authoritative historical biography breathes new life into one of Mexico's great ironic tragedies, a drama that pitted the native Zapotec "Lincoln of Mexico" against the dreamy, idealistic Archduke Maximilian of Austria-Hungary. Despite their common liberal ideas, they were drawn into a bloody no-quarter struggle that set the Old World against the New, ending in Maximilian's execution and the subsequent insanity of his wife, Carlota. The United States emerged as a power to be reckoned with in world affairs.

Ruíz, Ramon Eduardo. *Triumphs and Tragedy: A History of the Mexican People*. New York: W.W. Norton, Inc., 1992. A pithy, anecdote-filled history of Mexico from an authoritative Mexican-American perspective.

Simpson, Lesley Bird. *Many Mexicos*. Berkeley: The University of California Press, 1962. A much-reprinted, fascinating broad-brush version of Mexican history.

Townsend, Richard, et al. *Ancient West Mexico: Art and Archaeology of the Unknown Past*. New York: W.W. Norton, 1998. This magnificent coffee-table volume, with lovely photos and authoritatitive text, reveals the little-known culture being uncovered at Guachimontones and other sites, notably the "bottle tombs" in the Tequila valley west of Guadalajara. Dozens of fine images illuminate a high culture of scupltural and ceramic art, depicting everything from warriors, ball players, and acrobats, to loving couples, animals, and sacred ritals.

UNIQUE GUIDE AND TIP BOOKS

American Automobile Association. *Mexico TravelBook*. Heathrow, FL: 2003. Published by the American Automobile Association (1000 AAA Drive, Heathrow, FL 32746-5063). Short sweet summaries of major Mexican tourist destinations and sights. Also includes information on fiestas, accommodations, restaurants, and a wealth of information relevant to car travel in Mexico. Available in bookstores, or free to AAA members at affiliate offices.

Bayless, Rick. *Rick Bayless's Guide to Mexican Cooking*. New York: Scribner's, 1996. An award-winning author and cook explores the vibrant flavors of a world-class cuisine.

Burton, Tony. *Western Mexico, A Traveller's Treasury*. St. Augustine, FL: Perception Press, 2001. A well-researched and lovingly written and illustrated guide to dozens of fascinating places to visit, both well-known and out of the way, in Michoacán, Jalisco, and Nayarit.

Church, Mike and Terri Church. *Traveler's Guide to Mexican Camping*. Kirkland, WA: Rolling Homes Press (P.O. Box 2099, Kirkland, WA 98083-2099), 2005. This is an unusually thorough guide to trailer parks all over Mexico, with much coverage of the Pacific Coast in general and the Guadalajara region in particular. Detailed maps guide you accurately to each trailer park cited, and clear descriptions tell you what to expect. The book also provides very helpful information on car travel in Mexico, including details of insurance, border crossing, highway safety, car repairs, and much more.

Franz, Carl. *The People's Guide to Mexico*. Emeryville, CA: Avalon Travel Publishing, 12th edition, 2002. An entertaining and insightful A-to-Z general guide to the joys and pitfalls of independent economy travel in Mexico.

Graham, Scott. *Handle with Care*. Chicago: The Noble Press, 1991. Should you accept a meal from a family who lives in a grass house? This insightful guide answers this and hundreds of other tough questions for persons who want to travel responsibly in the Third World.

Guilford, Judith. *The Packing Book.* Berkeley: Ten Speed Press, third edition, 2006. The secrets of the carry-on traveler, or how to make everything you carry do double and triple duty. All for the sake of convenience, mobility, economy, and comfort.

Luboff, Ken. *Living Abroad in Mexico.* Emeryville, CA: Avalon Travel Publishing, 2005. A handy package of traveler's tools for living like a local in Mexico. Provides much general background and some specific details on settling (and perhaps making a living) in one of a number of Mexico's prime expatriate living areas, such as Mazatlán, Puerto Vallarta, Lake Chapala, Cuernavaca, and San Miguel de Allende.

Werner, David. *Where There Is No Doctor.* Palo Alto, CA: Hesperian Foundation (1919 Addison St., Berkeley, CA 94704, tel. 888/729-1796, www.hesperian.org). How to keep well in the tropical backcountry.

Whipperman, Bruce. *Moon Guadalajara.* Emeryville, CA: Avalon Travel Publishing, second edition, 2005. By far your most complete guide to culture-rich Guadalajara and its environs. *Moon Oaxaca* (fourth edition 2007), *Moon Puerto Vallarta* (seventh edition 2007), and *Moon Acapulco-Ixtapa-Zihuatanejo* (second edition 2006) offer similar expanded coverage for their respective regions.

SPECIALTY TRAVEL GUIDES

Annand, Douglas R. *The Wheelchair Traveler.* Self-published, ISBN 9990546738; order through Amazon.com. Step-by-step guide for planning a vacation. Accessible information on air travel, cruises, ground transportation, selecting the right hotel, what questions to ask, solutions to problems that may arise, and accessibility to many wonderful destinations in the United States and Mexico.

Jeffrey, Nan. *Adventuring with Children.* Emeryville, CA: Avalon House Publishing, 1995. This unusually detailed book starts where most travel-with-children books end. It contains, besides a wealth of information and practical strategies for general travel with children, specific chapters on how you can adventure—trek, kayak, river-raft, camp, bicycle, and much more—successfully with the kids in tow.

FICTION

Bowen, David, and Juan A. Ascencio. *Pyramids of Glass.* San Antonio: Corona Publishing Co., 1994. Two dozen–odd stories that lead the reader along a month-long journey through the bedrooms, the barracks, the cafés, and the streets of present-day Mexico.

Boyle, T.C. *The Tortilla Curtain.* New York: Penguin-Putnam 1996; paperback edition, Raincoast Books, 1996. A chance intersection of the lives of two couples, one affluent and liberal Southern Californians, the other poor, homeless illegal immigrants, forces all to come to grips with the real price of the American Dream.

Cisneros, Sandra. *Caramelo.* New York: Alfred A. Knopf, 2002. A celebrated author weaves a passionate, yet funny, multigenerational tale of a Mexican-American family and their migrations, which, beginning in Mexico City, propelled them north, all the way to Chicago and back.

Cohan, Tony. *Mexican Days* New York: Broadway Books, 2006. A captivating tale of surprise and adventure in a Mexico both old and new.

De la Cruz, Sor Juana Inez. *Poems, Protest, and a Dream.* New York: Penguin, 1997. Masterful translation of this collection of love and religious poems by the celebrated pioneer (1651–1695) Mexican feminist nun.

Doerr, Harriet. *Consider This, Señor.* New York: Harcourt Brace, 1993. Four expatriates tough it out in a Mexican small town, adapting to the excesses—blazing sun, driving rain, vast, untrammeled landscapes—meanwhile interacting with the local folks while the local folks observe them, with a mixture of fascination and tolerance.

Finn, María. *Mexico in Mind.* New York: Vintage Books, 2006. The wisdom and impressions of two centuries of renowned writers, from D.H. Lawrence and John Steinbeck, to John Reed and Richard Rodríguez, who were drawn to the timelessness and romance of Mexico.

Fuentes, Carlos. *Where the Air Is Clear.* New York: Farrar, Straus, and Giroux, 1971. The seminal work of Mexico's celebrated novelist.

Fuentes, Carlos. *The Years with Laura Díaz.* New York: Farrar, Straus, and Giroux, 2000. A panorama of Mexico from Independence to the 21st century, through the eyes of one woman, Laura Díaz, and her great-grandson, the author. One reviewer said that she "...as a Mexican woman, would like to celebrate Carlos Fuentes; it is worthy of applause that a man who has seen, observed, analyzed, and criticized the great occurrences of the century now has a woman, Laura Díaz, speak for him." Translated by Alfred MacAdam.

Jennings, Gary. *Aztec.* New York: Forge Books, 1997. Beautifully researched and written monumental tale of lust, compassion, love, and death in pre-Conquest Mexico.

Nickles, Sara, ed. *Escape to Mexico.* San Francisco: Chronicle Books, 2002. A carefully selected anthology of 20-odd stories of Mexico by renowned authors, from Steven Crane and W. Somerset Maugham to Anaïs Nin and David Lida, who all found inspiration, refuge, adventure, and much more, in Mexico.

Peters, Daniel. *The Luck of Huemac.* New York: Random House, 1981. An Aztec noble family's tale of war, famine, sorcery, heroism, treachery, love, and finally disaster and death in the Valley of Mexico.

Rulfo, Juan. *Pedro Paramo.* New York: Grove Press, 1994. Rulfo's acknowledged masterpiece, originally published in 1955, established his renown. The author, thinly disguised as the protagonist, Juan Preciado, fulfills his mother's dying request by returning to his shadowy Jalisco hometown, Comala, in search of this father. Although Preciado discovers that his father, Pedro Páramo (whose surname that implies "wasteland"), is long dead, Preciado's search resurrects his father's restless spirit, which recounts its horrific life tale of massacre, rape, and incest.

Traven, B. *The Treasure of the Sierra Madre.* New York: Hill and Wang, 1967. Campesinos, *federales,* gringos, and *indígenas* all figure in this modern morality tale set in Mexico's rugged outback. The most famous of the mysterious author's many novels of oppression and justice set in Mexico's jungles.

Villaseñor, Victor. *Rain of Gold.* New York: Delta Books (Bantam, Doubleday, and Dell), 1991. The moving, best-selling epic of the author's family's gritty travails. From humble rural beginnings in the Copper Canyon, they flee revolution and certain death, struggling through parched northern deserts to sprawling border refugee camps. From there they migrate to relative safety and an eventual modicum of happiness in Southern California.

PEOPLE AND CULTURE

Berrin, Kathleen. *The Art of the Huichol Indians.* Harry N. Abrams, New York, 1978. Lovely, large photographs and text by a symposium of experts provide a good interpretive introduction to Huichol art and culture.

Castillo, Ana. *Goddess of the Americas.* New York, Riverhead Books, 1996. Here, a noted author has selected from the works of seven interpreters of Mesoamerican female deities, whose visions range as far and wide as Sex Goddess, the Broken-Hearted, the Subversive, and the Warrior Queen.

Haden, Judith Cooper, and Matthew Jaffe. *Oaxaca, the Spirit of Mexico.* New York: Artisan, division of Workman Publishing, Inc., 2002. Simply the loveliest, most sensitively photographed and crafted coffee-table book of Mexico photography yet produced. Photos by Haden, text by Jaffe.

Medina, Sylvia López. *Cantora.* New York: Ballantine Books, 1992. Fascinated by the stories of her grandmother, aunt, and mother, the author seeks her own center by discovering a past that she thought she wanted to forget.

Meyerhoff, Barbara. *Peyote Hunt: The Sacred Journey of the Huichol Indians.* Ithaca: Cornell University Press, 1974. A description and interpretation of the Huichol's religious use of mind-bending natural hallucinogens.

Montes de Oca, Catalina. *Puerto Vallarta, My Memories.* Translated by Laura McCullough. Puerto Vallarta: University of Guadalajara, 2002. A longtime Puerto Vallartan breathes life into the early history and old times in Puerto Vallarta as she remembers them, from her arrival as a child in 1918, to the present.

Palmer, Colin A. *Slaves of the White God.* Cambridge: Harvard University Press. A scholarly study of why and how Spanish authorities imported African slaves into America and how they were used afterwards. Replete with poignant details, taken from Spanish and Mexican archives, describing how the Africans struggled from bondage to eventual freedom.

Riding, Alan. *Distant Neighbors: A Portrait of the Mexicans.* New York: Random House Vintage Books. Rare insights into Mexico and Mexicans.

Toor, Frances. *A Treasury of Mexican Folkways.* New York: Crown Books, 1947, reprinted by Bonanaza, 1985. An illustrated encyclopedia of vanishing Mexicana—costumes, religion, fiestas, burial practices, customs, legends—compiled during the celebrated author's 35-year residence in Mexico.

Wauchope, Robert, ed. *Handbook of Middle American Indians.* Vols. 7 and 8. Austin: University of Texas Press, 1969. Authoritative surveys of important Indian-speaking groups in northern and central (vol. 8) and southern (vol. 7) Mexico.

FLORA AND FAUNA

Goodson, Gar. *Fishes of the Pacific Coast.* Stanford, California: Stanford University Press, 1988. More than 500 beautifully detailed color drawings highlight this pocket version of all you ever wanted to know about the ocean's fishes (including common Spanish names) from Alaska to Peru.

Howell, Steve N.G. *Bird-Finding Guide to Mexico.* Ithaca, NY: Cornell University Press, 1999. A unique portable guide for folks who really want to see birds in Mexico. The author presents a unique and authoritative site guide, with dozens of clear maps and lists of birds seen at sites all over Mexico. Pacific sites include Mazatlán, San Blas, Puerto Vallarta, El Tuito, Manzanillo, Oaxaca, and many more. Use this book along with Howell and Webb's *A Guide to the Birds of Mexico and North America.*

Howell, Steve N.G., and Sophie Webb. *A Guide to the Birds of Mexico and Northern America.* Oxford: Oxford University Press, 1995. All the serious birder needs to know about Mexico's rich species treasury. Includes authoritative habitat maps and 70 excellent color plates that detail the male and females of around 1,500 species.

Leopold, Starker. *Wildlife of Mexico.* Berkeley: University of California Press, 1959. Classic, illustrated layperson's survey of common Mexican mammals and birds.

Mason Jr., Charles T., and Patricia B. Mason. *Handbook of Mexican Roadside Flora.* Tucson: University of Arizona Press, 1987. Authoritative identification guide, with line illustrations, of all the plants you're likely to see in Pacific Mexico.

Morris, Percy A. *A Field Guide to Pacific Coast Shells.* Boston: Houghton Mifflin. The compleat beachcomber's Pacific shell guide.

Pesman, M. Walter. *Meet Flora Mexicana.* Published in Arizona, in 1962, by D.S. King. Out of print, look online or at larger libraries. Delightful anecdotes and illustrations of hundreds of common Mexican plants.

Peterson, Roger Tory, and Edward L. Chalif. *Field Guide to Mexican Birds.* Boston: Houghton Mifflin, 1999. With hundreds of Peterson's crisp color drawings, this is a must for serious birders and vacationers interested in the life that teems on Pacific Mexico's beaches, jungles, lakes, and lagoons.

Wright, N. Pelham. *A Guide to Mexican Mammals and Reptiles.* Mexico City: Minutiae Mexicana, 1989. Pocket-edition lore, history, descriptions, and pictures of commonly seen Mexican animals.

ART, ARCHITECTURE, AND CRAFTS

Baird, Joseph. *The Churches of Mexico.* Berkeley: University of California Press. Mexican colonial architecture and art, illustrated and interpreted.

Cordrey, Donald, and Dorothy Cordrey. *Mexican Indian Costumes.* Austin: University of Texas Press, 1968. A lovingly photographed, written, and illustrated classic on Mexican Indians and their dress, emphasizing textiles.

Covarrubias, Miguel. *Indian Art of Mexico and Central America.* New York: Knopf, 1957. A timeless work by the renowned interpreter of *indígena* art and design.

Martínez Penaloza, Porfirio. *Popular Arts of Mexico.* Mexico City: Editorial Panorama, 1981. An excellent, authoritative, pocket-sized exposition of Mexican art.

Morrill, Penny C., and Carol A. Berk. *Mexican Silver.* Atglen, PA: Shiffer Publishing Co. (4880 Lower Valley Rd., Atglen, PA 19310). Lovingly written and photographed exposition of the Mexican silvercraft of Taxco, Guerrero, revitalized through the initiative of Frederick Davis and William Spratling in the 1920s and 1930s. Color photos of many beautiful, museum-quality pieces supplement the text, which describes the history and work of a score of silversmithing families who developed the Taxco craft under Spratling's leadership. Greatly adds to the traveler's appreciation of the beautiful Taxco silvercrafts. Widely available in many Puerto Vallarta and Guadalajara (Tlaquepaque) shops.

Mullen, Robert James. *Architecture and Its Sculpture in Viceregal Mexico.* Austin: University of Texas Press, 1997. The essential work of Mexican colonial-era cathedrals and churches. In this lovingly written and illustrated life work, Mullen breathes new vitality into New Spain's preciously glorious colonial architectural legacy.

Sayer, Chloë. *Arts and Crafts of Mexico.* San Francisco: Chronicle Books, 1990. All you ever wanted to know about your favorite Mexican crafts, from papier-mâché to pottery and toys and Taxco silver. Beautifully illustrated by traditional etchings and David Lavender's crisp black-and-white and color photographs.

Internet Resources

A number of websites may help you prepare for your Pacific Mexico trip:

Travel in General

www.travelocity.com
www.expedia.com
www.orbitz.com
Major sites for airline and hotel bookings

www.travelinsure.com
www.worldtravelcenter.com
Good for travel insurance and other services

www.sanbornsinsurance.com
Site of the longtime, very reliable Mexico auto insurance agency, with the only north-of-the-border adjustment procedure. Get your quote online, order many useful publications, and find out about other insurance you many have forgotten.

Specialty Travel

www.elderhostel.org
Site of Boston-based Elderhostel Inc., with a huge catalog of ongoing study tours, including three or four in the Guadalajara region.

www.miusa.org
Site of Mobility International, wonderfully organized and complete, with a flock of services for travelers with disabilities, including many people-to-people connections in Mexico.

www.purpleroofs.com
One of the best general gay travel websites is maintained by San Francisco travel agency Purple Roofs. It offers, for example, details of about gay-friendly Puerto Vallarta hotels, in addition to a wealth of gay-friendly travel-oriented links worldwide.

Home Exchange

www.homexchange.com
www.homeforexchange.com
Sites for temporarily trading your home with someone else in dozens of places in the world, including Guadalajara and Lake Chapala.

U.S. Government

www.state.gov/travelandbusiness
The U.S. State Department's very good information website. Lots of subheadings and links to a swarm of topics, including Mexican consular offices in the United States, U.S. consular offices in Mexico, travel advisories, and links to other government information, such as importation of food, plants, and animals, U.S. customs, health abroad, airlines, and exchange rates.

Mexico in General

www.visitmexico.com
The official website of the public-private Mexico Tourism Board; a good general site for official information, such as entry requirements. It has lots of summarily informative sub-headings, not unlike an abbreviated guidebook. If you can't find what you want here, call the toll-free information number 800/44-MEXICO (800/446-3942), or email contact@visitmexico.com.

www.mexonline.com
Very extensive, well-organized commercial site with many subheadings and links to Mexico's large and medium destinations, and even some in small destinations. For example, Guadalajara is typical, with manifold links, including many dozens of accommodations, from luxury hotels to modest bed-and-breakfasts. Excellent.

www.mexconnect.com

An extensive Mexico site, with dozens upon dozens of subheadings and links, especially helpful for folks thinking of traveling, working, living, or retiring in Mexico.

www.mexicodesconocido.com.mx

The site of the excellent magazine *Mexico Desconocido* (Undiscovered Mexico) that mostly features unusual and off-the-beaten-track destinations, many in the Puerto Vallarta region. Accesses a large library of past articles, which are not unlike a Mexican version of *National Geographic Traveler.* Click the small "English" button at the top to translate. Excellent, hard-to-find information, in good English translation.

www.planeta.com

Life project of Latin America's dean of ecotourism, Ron Mader, who furnishes a comprehensive clearinghouse of everything ecologically correct, from rescuing turtle eggs in Jalisco to preserving cloud forests in Peru. Contains dozens of subheadings competently linked for maximum speed. For example, check out the Mexico travel directory for ecojourneys, maps, information networks, parks, regional guides, and a mountain more.

www.vrbo.com
www.choice1.com

A pair of very useful sites for picking a vacation rental house, condo, or villa, with information and reservations links to individual owners. Prices vary from moderate to luxurious. Coverage extends to most of Pacific Mexico, including Mazatlán, Nayarit Coast, Guadalajara, Manzanillo, Ixtapa-Zihuatanejo, and Oaxaca.

www.tomzap.com

This project of Mexico lover Tom Penick is a very informative site, especially for downscale corners on the coasts of Jalisco, Colima, and Oaxaca. It's especially detailed about Puerto Escondido, Puerto Ángel, Zipolite, Mazunte, and the Bays of Huatulco. Information includes hotels, travel, history, surfing, scuba and snorkeling, and more, with much helpful advice on what to enjoy and what to avoid. Very good.

Mazatlán

www.mazinfo.com

No-frills site with lots of link-accessible information, arranged like a mini-guidebook: history, sights, hotels and vacation rentals, medical, Spanish lessons, and more. Very good.

www.pacificpearl.com

Website of the Mazatlán tourist newspaper *Pacific Pearl,* with broad, strictly commercial coverage of hotels, bed-and-breakfasts, trailer parks, restaurants, shopping, and fishing. Good.

www.mazatlan.com.mx

Commercial site in English with a good hotel section, with links to more than a dozen high-end hotels. Much of the other information, such as restaurants, for example, is limited to summaries or lists only. A fair site, overall.

The Nayarit Coast

www.turnay.gob.mx

Competent, compact site of the Nayarit Tourism Secretariat, with a well-translated English version. Details and links to an abundance of Nayarit hotels, destinations, tourist attractions, and services, such as car rentals, airlines, and travel agents.

www.sayulita.com

Rental and real estate-oriented site of Sayulita Properties, with lots of bungalows and villa rentals and houses for rent or sale, but also general information, such as beaches, surfing, and nightlife.

www.sanblasmexico.com

Compact but informative site, with details on

what to do and links to where to stay, eat, and more in San Blas.

Guadalajara

www.tlaquepaque.gob.mx
www.zapopan.gob.mx
Respective sites of Tlaquepaque and Zapopan municipal governments, with only rough English translations, however.

www.guadalajarareporter.com
Site of the English-language Guadalajara newspaper. Very extensive, even more extensive for subscribers. Non-subscribers, however, have access to the very useful classified section, especially for hotels, bed-and-breakfasts, and house and apartment rentals.

Puerto Vallarta

www.puertovallarta.net
Wow! All you need to prepare for your Puerto Vallarta vacation. Contains a wealth of details in dozens of competently linked subheadings, such as hotels—both humble and grand—car rentals, adventure tours, and on and on. Nearly every tourism service provider in Puerto Vallarta seems to be on board.

www.virtualvallarta.com
The website of *Vallarta Lifestyles* magazine. Like its parent magazine, it's strong in things upscale, such as boutiques, expensive restaurants, and condo sales and rentals.

www.pvmirror.com
Thoughtful and up-to-date Puerto Vallarta news magazine with lots of information on what's new in places to stay, eat, shop, invest, and much more.

www.gayguidevallarta
www.discoveryvallarta.com
A pair of good gay Puerto Vallarta websites, each with dozens of search categories, such as hotels, restaurants, bars, tours, art galleries, shopping, and vacation rentals, with many

links to associated websites. Furthermore, Discovery Vallarta has a good lesbian search category, containing information about lesbian-friendly hotels and services in the small beach communities, such as Sayulita, Yelapa, and Bucerías, near Puerto Vallarta.

The Jalisco Coast

www.tomzap.com/barra.html
Good, with lots of details, especially for the hidden beaches and resorts of the southern Jalisco Coast, including Tenacatita, Boca de Iguanas, La Manzanilla, Melaque, and Barra de Navidad.

Manzanillo and Colima

www.gomanzanillo.com
Good commercial site, by knowledgeable lover of Manzanillo and scuba instructor Susan Dearing, with lots of links to lodgings, shopping, virtual tours, useful websites, and much more.

www.tomzap.com/colima.html
Lots of details about hotels, restaurants, and services, especially for folks interested in going off the beaten track and paying moderate prices.

Pátzcuaro

www.mexonline.com/cityguide-patzcuaro.htm
Few websites include much about Pátzcuaro. This is one of the exceptions, with much about hotels, restaurants, sights, services, real estate, and more.

Troncones

www.troncones.com.mx
Good site, especially for hotels, with many links to Troncones's small beachfront hotels and bed-and-breakfasts. Also links to a number of restaurants, services, real estate, and much more.

Ixtapa and Zihuatanejo

www.zihuatanejo.com

A top-notch, very complete, and well-maintained commercial site, listing nearly everywhere to stay (with reservation and email links) and dine, everything to do, and much more in Zihuatanejo, Ixtapa, Troncones, and Barra de Potosí. In English or Spanish. Excellent.

www.zihua.net

Similar to but smaller than www.zihuatanejo .com, this site (along with its twin, www .ixtapa.net) nevertheless has lots of useful, mostly commercial information and links.

www.zihuatenejo-rentals.com

The site of savvy local resident Leigh Roth, who lists (with gorgeous photos) several high-end (and a few moderately priced) condo, apartment, and villa rental options, most near La Madera and La Ropa beaches. She also includes informative sections on restaurants, shopping, activities, personal anecdotes ("Who's Been to Huatla de Jiménez?"), and stories.

Acapulco

www.visitacapulco.com.mx

The website of the Acapulco Convention and Visitor's Bureau broadly covers the ground from sightseeing and shopping to hotels and transportation. Although potentially useful, the information is mostly neutral, without much detail and generally lacking links for booking hotel reservations.

www.acabtu.com.mx

Website of the web-only tourist newspaper *Acapulco Heat*. It provides useful links to many mid-scale hotels, rental condos, houses, apartments, real estate agencies, restaurants, community events and organizations, travel activities, and entertainments.

The Costa Chica

www.tomzap.com/oaxaca.html

This project of Mexico lover Tom Penick is a very informative site, especially for downscale corners of Oaxaca. It's unusually detailed about Puerto Escondido, Puerto Ángel, Zipolite, Mazunte, and the Bays of Huatulco. Information includes hotels, travel, history, surfing, scuba and snorkeling, and more, with much helpful advice on what to enjoy and what to avoid. Very good.

www.baysofhuatulco.com.mx

Here you'll find much on hotels (with prices), restaurants, events, tour operators, water sports, and land sports. It's a work in progress, however, but only in Spanish (though promised in English) at this writing. Good if you read Spanish.

www.puertoconnection.com

Website for Puerto Escondido Real Estate. Besides home sales, it lists and photo-illustrates many moderately priced and luxury hotels, vacation rental villas, condos, apartments, restaurants, and services. Very good.

www.zicatelaproperties.com

Site of Puerto Escondido's Zicatela Properties real estate company. It's especially good for moderately priced apartment, condo, and vacation homes.

Oaxaca City and Valley

www.aoaxaca.com

Very detailed website of the Oaxaca Secretary of Tourism. Good Tourist Guide section with archaeological sites, recipes, churches, museums, festivals, myths and legends, murals, handicrafts, and more. The site also provides extensive information (accessible by clicking on the home-page Oaxaca map) about off-the-tourist-track country villages. Much of the detailed information remains untranslated into English, however.

www.oaxaca.com

Commercial English-language community network guide to Oaxaca City with loads of noncommercial information. It has links to a long list of Mexico websites and much more.

www.oaxaca-travel.com

This excellent, very detailed site, besides covering Oaxaca City and Valley from A to Z, also has loads of hard-to-get information on indigenous communities. It would be very useful to someone planning an extended Oaxaca trip.

www.go-oaxaca.com
www.oaxacatimes.com

The websites of the two Oaxaca tourist newspapers, *Go Oaxaca* and the *Oaxaca Times*. They each host lots of travel-handy information (hotels, restaurants, galleries, handicrafts shops, services), and each includes a very useful list of Oaxaca City apartment, homestay opportunities, and bed-and-breakfast rentals.

Index

A

acacias: 682
Acapulco: 488-527; accommodations 501-510; entertainment 515-517; food 511-514; getting there and away 525-527; information 522-523; itinerary suggestions 24, 26-27, 30, 31; maps 490, 494-495, 496, 502-503; services 523-524; sights 493-501; shopping 520-522; sports and recreation 517-520
accommodations: 750-756; see also specific place
Adorito Central: 346
African Mexicans: 549, 556-557, 692, 708-709
Agua Dulce: 342
Agua Fria spring: 311, 342; itinerary suggestions 28
air evacuation: 769
airports: Guadalajara 183; Huatulco 623; Manzanillo 338; Mazatlán 76; Morelia 406; Oaxaca 659; Puerto Vallarta 251
air travel: 724-727, 736; see also specific place
alcoholic drinks: 760
alebrijes: 670-671, 673, 721
Amatitán: 173
amphibians: 686
Amusgo people: 561
Angahuan: 366, 424-427
Anson, George: 442
apartments: 752-753; see also specific place
Apiza: 362-363
Aquarium: 33, 46
Aquiles Serdán: 268-269
archaeology: Dainzu 664; Ihuatzio 390-391; itinerary suggestions 29-30; Ixcateopan 546-547; La Campana Archaeological Zone 346-347; Lambityeco 664; Michoacán 432; Mitla 666-670; Monte Albán 673-677; Palma Sola 497; Soledad de Maciel 479-480; Tampumachay 355; Tinganio 412; Tzintzuntzán 391-394; Xochicalco 543-546; Yagul 666; Zaachila 671-672
arid tropical scrub: 684
armadillos: 684
Arrazola: 673; itinerary suggestions 25

arts and crafts: 716-723, 761; Acapulco 521-522; Angahuan 426; Barra de Navidad-Melaque 306; Bays of Huatulco 621-622; Colima 350-351; Comala 354; Guadalajara 172, 175-176; Huazolotitlán 562; itinerary suggestions 24, 25, 30, 31; Ixtapa 472; Janitzio Island 389; Manzanillo 335-336; Mazatlán 69-71; Nayarit Coast 84; Oaxaca 653-655; Ocotlán de Morelos 671; Pátzcuaro 404-405; Puerto Ángel 602; Puerto Escondido 581-582; Puerto Vallarta 240-243, 248; San Bártolo Coyotepec 670; San Blas 106-107; San Martín Tilcajete 670-671; Santiago Jamiltepec 562; Santo Tomás Jalieza 671; Sayulita 147; Taxco 538; Teotitlán del Valle 665; Tepic 121-122; Tlaquepaque 176; Tócuaro 395; Tonalá 177-179; Tzintzuntzán 393-394; Uruapan 419-420; Zihuatanejo 470-472
Aticama: 110
ATMs: 772; see also specific place
Atotonilco Hot Springs: 587; itinerary suggestions 28
ATVs: 747
Aztecs: 688-689
Aztlán: 90

B

Bahía Cacaluta: 611-612; itinerary suggestions 27
Bahía Carrizalillo: 572
Bahía Chachacual: 612
Bahía Chahue: 609, 615
Bahía Conejos: 609, 617
Bahía de Bufadero: 375
Bahía de Coastecomate: 294
Bahía de Puerto Marquez: 500
Bahía el Maguey: 611; itinerary suggestions 27, 28
Bahía el Organo: 610-611; itinerary suggestions 27
Bahía San Agustín: 612; itinerary suggestions 29
Bahía Santa Cruz: 609-610
Bahía Tangolunda: 609, 615-617; itinerary suggestions 28
ballet: 350
banks: 772; see also specific place

bargaining: 761
Barra de Coyuca: 484
Barra de Navidad: 288-309; itinerary suggestions 24
Barra de Nexpa: 374-375; itinerary suggestions 26, 27, 29
Barra de Potosí: 437, 477-480
Barra Vieja: 500-501
bars: Acapulco 515; Barra de Navidad-Melaque 304; Bays of Huatulco 619; Guadalajara 171; Ixtapa 464-465; Manzanillo 330-331; Mazatlán 63; Oaxaca 651; Pátzcuaro 404; Puerto Ángel 600; Puerto Escondido 579-580; Puerto Vallarta 228-230, 231-233; San Blas 105; Taxco 536-537; Zihuatanejo 463, 464-465
baseball: 69
Basílica de Nuestra Señora de la Soledad: 640; itinerary suggestions 25
Basílica de Nuestra Señora de Zapopan: 160-161; itinerary suggestions 25, 29
Basílica María Inmaculada de la Salud: 388; itinerary suggestions 30
basketry: 716-717
Bay of Banderas: 253-262
Bay of Matanchén: 108-110; itinerary suggestions 26, 27
Bays of Huatulco: 604-625; itinerary suggestions 25, 27
beach buggies: 747
beaches: 745; Acapulco 497-501; Costera 499-500; Cuyutlán 358; itinerary suggestions 26-27; Ixtapa 448-449; Manzanillo 318-320; Mazatlán 47-49; nude beaches 591; Puerto Ángel 588-593; Puerto Escondido 569-573; Puerto Vallarta 201-205; Zihuatanejo Bay 447-448; see also specific beach
bed-and-breakfasts: 751, 752; see also specific place
beverages: 759-760
bicycling: Barra de Navidad 306, 307; Ixtapa 466; Puerto Vallarta 238; Zihuatanejo 466
"big corkscrew" sculpture: 158-159
birds: 685
bird-watching: 736; Barra de Navidad-Melaque 295; Bays of Huatulco 620; Boca de Pascuales and El Real 361-362; Isla Islote 129; itinerary suggestions 28; Laguna Coyuca 484; Laguna Manialtepec 567; Lagunas de Chacahua

National Park 563; Marismas Nacionales 685; Playa Anclote 260; Playa Azul 378; Playa Careyes 280; Playa Chacala 125; Playa el Tecuán 281; Playa la Ventanilla 593; Río Copalita 609; San Blas 100-101; Troncones 434, 435; Zihuatanejo 468
Blue Bay Club: 284
boat ramps: Acapulco 519; Barra de Navidad 305; Bays of Huatulco 621; Ixtapa 469; Manzanillo 334; Mazatlán 67; Pie de la Cuesta 483; Playa Guayabitos-La Peñita 130; Puerto Vallarta 236; Teacapán 82
boat trips: 749; Cajón de las Peñas Reservoir 271; Colimilla 293-294; El Paraíso 361; Isla Islote 129; Isla Roqueta 498-499; Laguna Coyuca 484; Laguna Manialtepec 567; Lagunas de Chacahua National Park 563-565; Mazatlán 33, 45-46; Novillero 87-88; Playa Anclote 260; Playa Chacala 125; Playa la Ventanilla 593; Puerto Escondido 573-574
Boca de Apiza: 362-363
Boca de Pascuales: 361-362
Boca de Tomatlán: 204
Bocanegra, Gertrudis: 386-387
booklist: 783-788
bookstores: Barra de Navidad-Melaque 306; Guadalajara 182; Mazatlán 72; Oaxaca 656; Puerto Escondido 583; Sayulita 147-148
border crossing: 732, 744-745; see also immigration
botaneras: 330; see also bars
bribes: 731-732, 764
Bucerías: 255-258
bullfights: 749-750; Acapulco 520; Barra de Navidad-Melaque 304; Guadalajara 173; Manzanillo 331; Mazatlán 69
Burton, Richard: 194, 200
business visas: 744
bus travel: 726-729, 737-739; see also specific place

C

cable tramway: Acapulco 532; Ixtapa 448; Taxco 489
Cabo Corrientes Country: 267-271
Cacahuatepec: 561
cactus: 682
Cajón de las Peñas Reservoir: 271
Calderón, Felipe: 703-704

calendar of events: 713-716
Caleta de Campos: 375-376
California gulf porpoise: 687
Calle de Muerte: 530
Calle de Oro: 43
Calles, Plutarco Elías: 697-698
Camacho, Manuel Ávila: 698-699
Campamento Tortuguero de Cuyutlán: 311, 358
camping: 753-756; Agua Fria 342; Angahuan 427; Apiza 363; Aquiles Serdán 269; Barra de Navidad-Melaque 301; Barra de Nexpa 375; Barra de Potosí 479; Bays of Huatulco 612, 617; Boca de Pascuales and El Real 361; Bucerías 255; Cajón de las Peñas Reservoir 271; Caleta de Campos 376; Chamela Bay 278; Cuyutlán 360; El Salto 341; El Terrero 342; itinerary suggestions 28-29; Laguna la María 354; Laguna Manialtepec 567; Lagunas de Chacahua National Park 564; La Saladita 433; Majahua 433; Manzanillo 326-327; Mazatlán 58; Oaxaca 646; Pátzcuaro 401; Pie de la Cuesta 486; Piedra Tlacoyunque 482; Pinotepa Nacional 559; Playa Azul 378; Playa Boca de Iguanas 285-286; Playa Careyes 280; Playa Chacahua 565; Playa Chalacatepec 271; Playa la Brisa 371; Playa Lo de Marcos 139-140; Playa Maruata 373; Playa Mora 283; Playa Porto Bello 377; Playa Punta Raza 137-138; Playas San Agustinillo and Mazunte 592; Playa Tenacatita 281; Playa Tizupa 373-374; Playa Ventura 552; Puerto Ángel 598-599; Puerto Escondido 577-578; Puerto Vallarta 221; San Blas 104; Sayulita 146; Tampumachay 355; Taretan 423; Teacapán 82; Tepic 119-120; Troncones 433; Zihuatanejo 459
candelilla: 683
Capilla del Señor de Tlacolula: 666
Cárdenas, Lázaro: 698
Carnaval: 713; Mazatlán 43, 64; Pinotepa Don Luis 560; Puerto Escondido 580; Puerto Vallarta 234; Taxco 537
car permits: 744
car rentals: 739-740; see also specific place
car travel: 728, 729-733, 738, 739-740, 744; see also specific place

Casa Borda: 530
Casa de Cortés: 638; itinerary suggestions 30
Casa de Cultura (Taxco): 530
Casa de Cultura (Uruapan): 415, 419
Casa de Juan Escuita: 116
Casa de Juárez museum: 639; itinerary suggestions 30
Casa de la Máscara: 489, 497, 720-721; itinerary suggestions 24, 30, 31
Casa de Once Patios: 366, 388; itinerary suggestions 25
Casa Humboldt: 531; itinerary suggestions 30
Casa Kimberley: 200; itinerary suggestions 31
Casa Machado: 43; itinerary suggestions 30
Cascada de Golgota waterfall: 416
Catamaran rides: 520
Catedral Basílica de la Purísima Concepción: 37; itinerary suggestions 30
Catedral de Guadalajara: 150, 155; itinerary suggestions 29
Catedral de Oaxaca: 627, 637-638; itinerary suggestions 30
Catedral de San Felipe de Jesús: 345
cathedral (Tepic): 113-114
Catholicism: 712-713
cave exploring: Grutas de Cacahuamilpa 541-543; Grutas de San Miguel 546-547; itinerary suggestions 28; Majahua 435
Caverna del Diablo: 47
cellular phones: 773-774
Central Market (Mazatlán): 69-70
Centro Cultural Cuale: 197
Centro Cultural de Santo Domingo: 627, 638-639
Centro Cultural Huichol: 91-93
Centro Cultural Vallartense: 197, 248-249
Centro Internacional de Convivencia Infantil (CICI): 520
Centro Mexicano de la Tortuga: 549, 592-593; itinerary suggestions 25
Centro Turístico Angahuan: 427
ceramics: 721-723
Cerro Creston: 45, 49; itinerary suggestions 27, 31
Cerro Cruz: 315, 320; itinerary suggestions 27
Cerro de la Santa Cruz: 130

Cerro de las Peñas: 480
Cerro de San Basilio: 84, 95-97, 101
Cerro Nevería: 46
Cerro San Francisco: 289
Cerro Vigía: 33, 45, 97; itinerary suggestions 30-31
Cerro Vigía Chico: 311, 315, 320
Chagas' disease: 770
Chamela Bay: 273-279
charreada: 174; Barra de Navidad-Melaque 304; Guadalajara 173; Mazatlán 69
Chico's Paradise: 266-267
children, traveling with: 765; Best Beaches itinerary suggestions 26-27; Centro Internacional de Convivencia Infantil (CICI) 520; Mágico Mundo water park 498; Mazatlán 64; tourist cards 742
Chivos island: 46
Christmas celebrations: 715; Oaxaca 652
Chupícuaro: 397
Church of San Juan de Dios: 640
Cinco de Mayo: 714
cinema: Mazatlán 63; Pátzcuaro 404; Puerto Escondido 580; Puerto Vallarta 234
Citlaltépetl: 679-680
Civil War: 694
cliff diving show: 31, 47
climate: 680
clothing, traditional: 711, 717-718
cloud forest: 684
coatis: 684
Cochoapa: 556
cocodrilario: 109
coconut: 681
Colima: 343-356; itinerary suggestions 24, 27, 29
Colima palm: 682
Colimilla: 264, 293-294
Colonial history: 691-692
Comala: 353-355
Community Museum (Zapotec): 665
concerts: Colima 350; Guadalajara 171; Manzanillo 331; Oaxaca 650; Puerto Vallarta 234
Concordia: 78-79
condominiums: 752-753; *see also specific place*
conduct: :762-764
Constitution of 1917: 696-697, 706
consulates: Acapulco 524; Guadalajara 181; Mazatlán 74-75; Oaxaca 657; Puerto Vallarta 248

Continuidad de la Vida sculpture: 47
Copala: 79
Corral de Riscos: 259-260
corrida de toros: 749-750; Acapulco 520; Barra de Navidad-Melaque 304; Guadalajara 173; Manzanillo 331; Mazatlán 69
Cortés, Hernán: 689-690, 691
Costa Chica: 548-625; itinerary suggestions 27
Costa Grande: 476-487; itinerary suggestions 26
Coyotepec: 670
Crater Lake Santa María de Oro: 84, 117-118; itinerary suggestions 28, 29
credit cards: 773
crime: 583-584, 730-731
Criollos: 692, 708-709
Cristo del Monte: 532-533
crocodiles/crocodile farms: 686; Bay of Matanchén 109; Chacahua 564; Laguna de Ixtapa 449; Playa la Manzanilla 286
Crucecita: 607-609, 612-614
cruises: 734; Acapulco 519-520; Bays of Huatulco 619-620; Puerto Vallarta 190, 205; Zihuatanejo 463-464
Cruz de Huanacaxtle: 258
Cruz de Loreto: 270
Cuajinicuilapa: 556
Cuauhtémoc Mural: 531
cuisine: 756-760
currency: 772-773; devaluation 700
customs: 745; Acapulco 524; Bays of Huatulco 623; Mazatlán 74; Puerto Vallarta 248
customs, social: 762-764
Cuyutlán: 356-363; itinerary suggestions 28
cypress trees: 663

D

Dainzu Archaeological Site: 664
Dampier, William: 442
dancing: *see* discos, folkloric dancing
December 12: 234
deep-sea fishing: 749; *see* fishing
Dengue Fever: 770
departure tax: 76
Día de los Muertos: 715; Colima 350; Oaxaca 652; Pátzcuaro 404
Día de Nuestra Señora de Guadalupe: 713, 716
Día de Santiago Apostól: 419

diarrhea: 769-770
Diego, Juan: 712
disabled travelers: 765
discos: Acapulco 515; Barra de Navidad-Melaque 304; Bays of Huatulco 619; Guadalajara 172; Ixtapa 465; Manzanillo 331; Mazatlán 63; Oaxaca 651; Puerto Ángel 600; Puerto Escondido 579; Puerto Vallarta 230-233; Rincón de Guayabitos 135-136; San Blas 105
diving: 746; Acapulco 517-518; Barra de Navidad-Melaque 304-305, 307; Bays of Huatulco 609, 611, 620-621; Faro de Bucerías 372; Isla Ixtapa 450; Ixtapa 467-468; Manzanillo 333; Mazatlán 66-67; Playa Boca de Iguanas 285; Playa Escondida 481; Playa Guayabitos-La Peñita 129; Playa las Gatas 448; Playa Manzanillo (Puerto Escondido) 572; Playa Tizupa 373-374; Puerto Ángel 601; Puerto Escondido 581; Puerto Vallarta 236; San Blas 106; Tehualmixtle 270; Zihuatanejo 467-468
dolphin-watching: 129
Donaji: 630
Doña Marina: 689
driving: 728, 729-733, 738, 739-740, 744; restrictions in Mexico city 527; *see also specific place*

E
economy: 700, 702, 704-706
ecotours: 735-736; Barra de Navidad-Melaque 307; Bays of Huatulco 620; Laguna Manialtepec 567; Manzanillo 333-334; Mazatlán 68; Puerto Escondido 583, 587; San Blas 101; Singayta 101-102
Ecuador: 432
Ejido de la Palma crocodile farm: 109
El Arte del Cobre: 409
El Careyes Beach Resort: 264, 279-280
El Cora waterfall: 111, itinerary suggestions 28
Elderhostel: 735, 767
elections: 703-704
electricity: 774
El Faro lighthouse: 45, 49, 97, 318
El Grito de Dolores: 692-693
El Paraíso: 361; itinerary suggestions 28
El Playon: 612
El Rebalsito: 283
El Sacrificio: 612

El Salto waterfall: 311, 341; itinerary suggestions 28
El Super: 273, 275
El Tamarindo: 287-288
El Terrero: 341-342
el tigre: 685
El Tuito: 267-268
El Tule: 627, 663
embroidery: 717-718
emergency services: Acapulco 524; Barra de Navidad-Melaque 307-308; Bays of Huatulco 623; Chamela Bay 279; Colima 352; Cuyutlán 360; Guadalajara 181; Ixtapa 474; Manzanillo 337-338; Mazatlán 73-74; Oaxaca 657; Pátzcuaro 406; Puerto Ángel 602-603; Puerto Escondido 584; Puerto Vallarta 247-248; Rincón de Guayabitos-La Peñita 136; San Blas 107; San Francisco 143; Taxco 540; Tepic 122; Uruapan 421; Zihuatanejo 474
environmental concerns: 764
Erongarícuaro: 396-397
escorpión: 686
Esquinapa: 82
Estero San Cristóbal: 101
Etla: 677
events: *see* fiestas
Ex-Colegio Jesuito: 387-388
Ex-Colegio San Nicolás: 366, 386-387; itinerary suggestions 25, 30
Ex-Convento de Santa Catalina: 638; itinerary suggestions 30
exercise gyms: Guadalajara 174-175; Puerto Escondido 580; Puerto Vallarta 239
Ex-Templo San Agustín: 366, 388; itinerary suggestions 25, 30

F
Fábrica Ecología de Cosméticos Naturales de Mazunte: 593
factory tours: 420
family travel: 765; Centro Internacional de Convivencia Infantil (CICI) 520; itinerary suggestions 26-27; Mágico Mundo water park 498; Mazatlán 64; tourist cards for children 742
fan palm: 681
farming: 705
Faro de Bucerías: 372-373; itinerary suggestions 29
fauna: 684-687

Feria Todos Santos: 350
ferry travel: 733-734; *see also specific place*
Festival of October: 172
Festival of Santa Prisca: 537
Festival of the Radishes: 652
Festival of the Sea: 713
Festival of the Virgin of Zapopan: 172-173
festivals: *see* fiestas
Fideicomiso Cuitzmala: 280
Fiesta Charrotaurina: 345, 350
Fiesta Costeño: 580
Fiesta de Coros y Danzas: 419
Fiesta de la Inmaculada: 64
Fiesta de la Virgen de Guadalupe: Manzanillo 331; Mazatlán 64; Pie de la Cuesta 487; Puerto Vallarta 234; Taxco 537
Fiesta de la Virgen de la Asunción: 562
Fiesta de la Virgen de la Salud: 713; Colima 350; Pátzcuaro 404
Fiesta de la Virgen de Soledad: 580
Fiesta de los Jumiles: 537
Fiesta de Mayo: Manzanillo 331; Puerto Vallarta 234
Fiesta de San José: 350
Fiesta de San Patricio: 713
Fiesta de Santa María Magdalena: 419
Fiesta de San Miguel Arcangel: 600
Fiesta Mexicana: Mazatlán 64; Puerto Vallarta 233
Fiesta of Santiago: 425
Fiesta of the Señora de la Asunción: 397
fiestas: 713-716; Erongarícuaro 397; Guadalajara 172-173; Huazolotitlán 562; Ixcateopan 547; Manzanillo 331; Mazatlán 64; Oaxaca 651-652; Pie de la Cuesta 487; Pinotepa Don Luis 560; Pinotepa Nacional 558; Puerto Ángel 600; Puerto Escondido 580; San Pedro Amusgos 561; Santiago Jamiltepec 562; Taxco 537-538
fine arts: 723; *see also* galleries
fire department: *see* emergency services
first aid: 769
fish: 686-687, 748
Fish and Wildlife Service: 745
fishing: 747-749; Acapulco 518-519; Aquiles Serdán 269; Barra de Navidad-Melaque 305, 307; Bays of Huatulco 611, 621; Cajón de las Peñas Reservoir 271; Chamela Bay 273; Cuyutlán 358; Isla Ixtapa 450; Ixtapa 468-469;

Janitzio Island 388-389; Manzanillo 334; Mazatlán 47-48, 67-68; Parque Nacional Lic. Eduardo Ruiz 416; Piedra Tlacoyunque 482; Playa Anclote 260; Playa Careyes 280; Playa Chacahua 565; Playa Chacala 125; Playa Escondida 481; Playa Guayabitos-La Peñita 129-130; Playa Larga 500-501; Playa Linda 449; Playa Lo de Marcos 138-139; Playa Pie de la Cuesta 483; Playa Principal 569; Playas San Agustinillo and Mazunte 592; Playa Tenacatita 282; Playa Ventura 552; Puerto Ángel 601; Puerto Escondido 581; Puerto Vallarta 202, 204, 236-237; Punta Chalacatepec 271-272; San Blas 106; Sayulita 147; Tehualmixtle 270; Troncones 435; Zihuatanejo 468-469
flora: 681-684
Flower Games: 652
folkloric dance shows: 650; Pátzcuaro Viejecitos dance 403-404
food and drink: 756-760; Oaxacan specialties 647
Fox, Vicente: 701-703, 707
Franciscan monastery and church: 393
French Intervention: 694
frigate birds: 685
Frisa de los Fundadores: 158
Frissell Museum: 668
fruit: 757, 759
Fuente de Janintzizic: 416
Fuerte de San Diego: 489, 493; itinerary suggestions 24, 30, 31
Fuerte 31 de Marzo: 47
furniture: 718-719

G

Galería de Arte y Diseña: 409
galleries: Oaxaca 655; Santa Clara de Cobre 409
gardens: Jardín Morelos 415; Museo Regional de las Culturas de Oaxaca ethnobotanical garden 639
gasoline: 730
gay and lesbian travel: 765-767; Playa del Amor 591; Puerto Vallarta 217-221, 228, 231-233, 244-245
geography: 679-680
getting around: 736-741; *see also specific place*
getting there: 724-736; *see also specific place*

ghosts: 410
Gila monsters: 686
glass art: 719
glossary: 775-777
golf: 747; Acapulco 517; Barra de Navidad-Melaque 305; Bays of Huatulco 620; Guadalajara 175; Ixtapa 465-466; Manzanillo 333; Mazatlán 68-69; Puerto Vallarta 238; Taxco 537
gourd tree: 681
government: 706-708; see also history
Green Angels: 730
Green Wave: 357-358
Gringo Gulch: 190, 197-200; itinerary suggestions 31
Grupo Ecológico de la Costa Verde: 141
Grutas de Cacahuamilpa: 489, 541-543; itinerary suggestions 25, 28
Grutas de San Miguel: 546-547
Guadalajara: 149-188; accommodations 163-167; entertainment and events 171-174; food 168-170; getting around 182-183; getting there and away 183-188; information and services 180-182; itinerary suggestions 25, 29; maps 152-153, 156-157; shopping 175-179; sights 154-162; sports and recreation 174-175
Guelaguetza: 651-652
guitars: 721
Guzmán, Nuño de: 35, 90, 112-113, 115

H
Hacienda Noguera: 311, 353; itinerary suggestions 29
handicapped travelers: 765
handicrafts: see arts and crafts
health: 768-771
Hidalgo, Miguel: 692-693
Hierve el Agua Mineral Springs: 669-670
high coniferous forest: 683
highlights: Acapulco and Taxco 489; Costa Chica 549; Guadalajara 150; Ixtapa, Zihuatanejo, and the Costa Grande 437; Jalisco Coast 264; Manzanillo and Colima 311; Mazatlán and Southern Sinaloa 33; Michoacán Coast and Pátzcuaro 366; Nayarit Coast 84; Oaxaca 627; Puerto Vallarta 190
hiking: itinerary suggestions 27; Barra de Navidad-Melaque 294-295; Bay of Matanchén 110-111; Bays of Huatulco 620; Isla Roqueta 499; La Tzararacua waterfall 422-423; Manzanillo 320;

Mazatlán 49; Oaxaca 646; Playa el Tecuán 281; Puerto Escondido 573, 580; Puerto Vallarta 204-205; San Blas 101; Sayulita 147; Tepic 117
history: 688-704; historical sites itinerary suggestions 29; Acapulco 491-492; Barra de Navidad 288-289; Bays of Huatulco 604-605; Colima 343; Guadalajara 151-154; Ixtapa and Zihuatanejo 440-443; Manzanillo 313; Mazatlán 35-36; Michoacán Coast 368-370; Oaxaca 630, 631-633; Pátzcuaro 382-383; Puerto Vallarta 193-195; San Blas 94-95; Taxco 527-529; Tepic 112-113; Uruapan 412-414
hitchhiking: 741
holistic retreats: 734-735
home exchange: 753
horseback riding: Bays of Huatulco 620; Laguna Tres Palos 501; La Tzararacua waterfall 422-423; Mazatlán 66; Playa Chacala 125; Playa Linda 449; Puerto Ángel 600-601; Puerto Vallarta 238, 245, 735; Sayulita 147; Taxco 537
Hospicio Cabañas: 150, 159; itinerary suggestions 25
hospitals: Acapulco 524; Colima 352; Cuajinicuilapa 556; Guadalajara 181; Guerrero 474; Lázaro Cárdenas 430; Manzanillo 337; Mazatlán 73-74; Oaxaca 657; Pátzcuaro 406; Puerto Escondido 584; Puerto Vallarta 247-248; San Blas 107; San Francisco 136, 143; Taxco 540; Uruapan 421
hot springs: Atotonilco 587; Hierve el Agua 669-670; itinerary suggestions 28; Tlalpuyeque 264, 268
Hotel Playa Hermosa: 97
hotels: 750-752; see also specific place
Huatápera: 415-416
Huazolotitlán: 562
Huichol art: 719
Huichol people: 92, 97, 111
Huston, John: 194, 197

I
Iglesia de Santa María de la Asunción: 546
Iglesia Santa Fe de la Laguna: 397-398
Ihuatzio: 366, 390-391; itinerary suggestions 30
immigration: Acapulco 524; Bays of Huatulco 623; Manzanillo 338; Mazatlán 74; Oaxaca 658; Puerto Vallarta 248; Zihuatanejo 474

immunizations: 768
Imolación de Quetzalcoatl: 158-159
Independence: 692-694
Indígenas: 692, 708-711
inflation: 705
Instituto Cultural Cabañas: 159, 171
Instituto de Artes Gráficos de Oaxaca: 639
Instituto Nacional de Arqueología y Historia (INAH) museum: 89; itinerary suggestions 29
insurance, automobile: 729-730
Internet access: 774; Acapulco 524; Barra de Navidad-Melaque 307; Bays of Huatulco 622-623; Colima 351; Cuyutlán 360-361; Guadalajara 181; Ixtapa 473-474; Lázaro Cárdenas 430; Manzanillo 337; Mazatlán 73; Oaxaca 657; Pátzcuaro 406; Pinotepa Nacional 560; Puerto Ángel 602; Puerto Escondido 584; Puerto Vallarta 247; San Blas 107; Sayulita 147; Taxco 540; Uruapan 421; Zihuatanejo 473
Internet resources: 789-793
Ipala: 270
Isla de las Abandondas: 260
Isla del Mono: 260
Isla del Rey: 100-101
Isla Isabel: 99-100; itinerary suggestions 28
Isla Islote: 129
Isla Ixtapa: 437, 450-451; itinerary suggestions 28
Isla Montosa: 437
Isla Navidad: 293, 294
Isla Presidio: 437
Isla Río Cuale: 190, 196-197; itinerary suggestions 31
Isla Roqueta: 489, 498-499, 517-518; itinerary suggestions 24, 27, 28
itinerary suggestions: 24-31; Best Beaches 26-27; Cultural, Historical, and Archaeological Treasures 29-30; One-Day tours 30-31; Outdoor Adventures 27-29; The 28-Day Best of Pacific Mexico 24-25
Iturbide, Agustín de: 693
Ixcateopan: 546-547; itinerary suggestions 30
Ixtapa: 440-476; itinerary suggestions 26

J
jaguars: 685
jai alai: 520

Jalieza: 670-671
Jalisco Coast: 263-309; itinerary suggestions 26
Jalisco State Band: 171
Janitzio Island: 366, 388-389, itinerary suggestions 25
Jarácuaro: 395-396
jejenes: 283
jellyfish: 771
Jet Skis: see personal watercraft
jewelry: 719-720, 761-762; Taxco silver 538-539
jogging: Acapulco 517; Chamela Bay 274-275; Guadalajara 174; Mazatlán 66; Oaxaca 652-653; Playa Azul 380; Playa Boca de Iguanas 285; Playa el Tecuán 281; Playa Larga 501; Playa Pie de la Cuesta 483; Puerto Ángel 600-601; Puerto Escondido 580; Puerto Vallarta 237; San Blas 106; Zihuatanejo 465
Juárez, Benito: 694
Juluapan Peninsula: 318
jungle canopy rides: itinerary suggestions 28; Las Juntas 267; Puerto Vallarta 239
jungle river trips: 84, 99; itinerary suggestions 28
jungle tours: 147

KL
kayaking: 746; Bays of Huatulco 609, 610, 611; Cajón de las Peñas Reservoir 271; Isla Ixtapa 450; itinerary suggestions 28; Ixtapa 468; Laguna de Potosí 478; Laguna Manialtepec 567; Lagunas de Chacahua National Park 564; Manzanillo 332-333; Mazatlán 66; Playa Careyes 280; Playa Escondida 481; Playa la Brisa 371; Río Arena 559; Zihuatanejo 468
kid-friendly attractions: Best Beaches itinerary suggestions 26-27; Centro Internacional de Convivencia Infantil (CICI) 520; Mágico Mundo water park 498, 520; Mazatlán 64
La Boquita: 319-320
La Campana Archaeological Zone: 311, 346-347; itinerary suggestions 29
Laguna Agua Grande: 81
Laguna Coyuca: 437, 482-484, 518
Laguna de Ixtapa: 449
Laguna de Juluapan: 320
Laguna de Navidad: 264, 289-293
Laguna de Potosí: 478

Laguna Iguanero: 80
Laguna Manialtepec: 549, 566-567, itinerary suggestions 25, 28
Laguna Pichi: 378
Laguna Santa María: 84, 117-118; itinerary suggestions 28, 29
Lagunas de Chacahua National Park: 563-566; itinerary suggestions 28
Laguna Tres Palos: 501; itinerary suggestions 28
Lake Pátzcuaro: 394-398
Lake Zirahuén: 410-412; itinerary suggestions 25
Lambityeco Archaeological Site: 664
land: 679-680
language courses: see Spanish-language courses
language groups: 710-711
La Parroquia de Nuestra Señora de Guadalupe: 200
La Peñita: 127-137
La Placita: 372
La Quebrada: 489, 497; itinerary suggestions 24, 31
La Saladita: 431-433
Las Alamandas: 272-273
Las Ánimas: 204
Las Islitas: 108-109
Las Juntas village: 267; itinerary suggestions 28
La Tovara Jungle River Trip: 84, 99; itinerary suggestions 28
La Tzararacua waterfall: 422
laws: 764
Lázaro Cárdenas: 428-431
leather: 718
leatherback turtles: 358
libraries: Acapulco 522-523; Mazatlán 66, 72; Oaxaca 656; Taxco 539-540; Zihuatanejo 473
licenses, fishing: 749
lighthouses: El Faro 45, 49, 97
Llano Grande: 268
long-distance calling: 773-774; see also specific place
Longfellow, Henry Wadsworth: 98
Los Angeles Locos: 284-285
Los Arcos: 190; itinerary suggestions 24, 31
Los Conejos: 268
Los Venados baseball: 69
Lunes del Cerro festival: 651-652, 714
Lunes del Tule festival: 652

M

machismo: 763
Mágico Mundo water park: 498
maguey: 683
mail: 774; see also specific place
Majahua: 433
mala mujer tree: 683
malecón (Puerto Vallarta): 200-201
male travelers: 763-764
Malinche: 689
Manantlán Biosphere: 342
mangrove jungle boat trips: 361
manta rays: 687
Manzanillo: 310-342; accommodations 321-327; entertainment and events 330-331; excursions from Manzanillo 341-342; food 327-330; getting there and away 338-340; information and services 336-338; itinerary suggestions 26, 27; maps 312, 316-317; shopping 335-336; sights 314-320; sports and recreation 332-334
Manzanillo Bay: 318
maquiladoras: 699-700
mariachi music: 173; Guadalajara 159-160, 171
marinas: Acapulco 519; Ixtapa 469; Manzanillo 334; Puerto Vallarta 236
marinelife: 686-687
Marismas Nacionales: 685
Maruata 2000: 373
masks: 562, 720-721
Matanchén: 108-109; itinerary suggestions 26, 27
Maximilian: 694
Mazagua water park: 64
Maza, Margarita: 634-635
Mazatlán: 32-77; accommodations 49-58; beaches 47-49; entertainment and events 62-64; food 59-62; getting there and away 75-77; information 72; itinerary suggestions 26, 27 29, 30; maps 35, 38-39, 40-41, 42; services 73-75; sights 36-47; shopping 69-72; sports and recreation 65-69
medical services: 769, 771; Acapulco 524; Barra de Navidad-Melaque 307; Bays of Huatulco 623; Colima 352; Cuajinicuilapa 556; Cuyutlán 360; Guadalajara 181; La Peñita 136; Lázaro Cárdenas 430; Manzanillo 337; Oaxaca 657; Pátzcuaro 406; Pie de la Cuesta 487; Pinotepa Nacional 560; Playa

Azul 380-381; Puerto Ángel 602-603; Puerto Escondido 584; Puerto Vallarta 247-248; Rincón de Guayabitos 136; San Blas 107; San Marcos 556; Sayulita 148; Taxco 540; Tecomán 363; Tepic 122; Uruapan 421; Zihuatanejo 474
Melaque: 288-309; itinerary suggestions 24
Mendoza, Don Antonio de: 691
Mercado (Manzanillo): 315-318, 335
Mercado Central (Mazatlán): 37; itinerary suggestions 30
Mercado Libertad (Guadalajara): 159; itinerary suggestions 25
mescal liquor: 666, 683
mesquite grassland: 683
Mestizos: 692, 708-709
metalwork: 721
Mexcaltitán: 84, 89-91; itinerary suggestions 29
Michoacán Coast: 365-381; itinerary suggestions 26, 27
Minatitlán: 341-342
mineral springs: Atotonilco 587; Hierve el Agua 669-670; itinerary suggestions 28; Tlalpuyeque 264, 268
Misión de Nuestra Señora del Rosario: 79-80
Mismaloya: 190, 202-203, 270
missionaries: 690
missions: 116-117
Mitla: 627, 666-670; itinerary suggestions 30
Mixtec people: 553, 557
Moctezuma: 690
money: 772-773
money exchange: 772; Acapulco 523; Barra de Navidad-Melaque 307; Bays of Huatulco 622; Colima 351; Guadalajara 180-181; Ixtapa 473; Lázaro Cárdenas 430; Manzanillo 336-337; Mazatlán 72; Oaxaca 657; Pátzcuaro 405-406; Pinotepa Nacional 559; Puerto Ángel 602; Puerto Escondido 584; Puerto Vallarta 247; Rincón de Guayabitos-La Peñita 136; Sayulita 147; Taxco 540; Tecomán 363; Uruapan 421; Zihuatanejo 473
monkeys: 684
Monte Albán: 627, 673-677; itinerary suggestions 25, 30
Montezuma pine: 683
Monumento al Pescador: 47

Monumento Mujer Mazalteca: 46
mordidas: 731-732, 764
Morelos, José Maria: 693
morning glory tree: 682
mosquitoes: 283, 768
mountain climbing: itinerary suggestions 27; Pico de Tancítaro 427-428
mountains: 679-680; *see also specific mountain*
movies: *see cinema*
murals: 160
Museo Alejandro Rangel Hidalgo: 353
Museo Amado Nervo: 114; itinerary suggestions 29
Museo Arqueología (Mazatlán): 33, 43-44; itinerary suggestions 29, 30
Museo Arqueología de la Costa Grande: 437, 447
Museo Arte Prehispánico de Rufino Tamayo: 640; itinerary suggestions 25
Museo de Arte: 44; itinerary suggestions 29, 30
Museo de Arte Contemporaneo de Oaxaca: 638
Museo de Arte Popular: 387
Museo de Culturas del Occidente: 311, 346; itinerary suggestions 24, 29
Museo de Culturas Populares: 346; itinerary suggestions 24, 29
Museo de Historia: 345
Museo de la Soledad: 640
Museo de la Virgen: 161
Museo de las Culturas Afromestizos: 549, 556-557
Museo de los Cuatro Pueblos: 116
Museo de Sal: 311, 357
Museo del Cobre: 409
Museo Guillermo Spratling: 489, 530-531; itinerary suggestions 25, 30
Museo Huichol Wirrarica: 161; itinerary suggestions 25, 29
Museo José Clemente Orozco: 159; itinerary suggestions 25, 29
Museo Lola Beltrán: 80
Museo Platería: 531; itinerary suggestions 25
Museo Regional de Antropología y Historia de Tepic: 114-116; itinerary suggestions 29
Museo Regional de Cerámica y Arte Popular: 176
Museo Regional de Guadalajara: 158; itinerary suggestions 29

Museo Regional de las Culturas de Oaxaca: 638–639; itinerary suggestions 25, 30
Museo Regional Tonallán: 178
Museo Río Cuale: 196
Museo Universitario de Arqueología: 311, 318
Museum of the Mexicans: 89; itinerary suggestions 29
musical instruments: 721

N

NAFTA: 700
National Audubon Society: 736
National Ceramics Fair: 172, 714
National Silver Fair: 537, 715
Nayarit Coast: 83–148; itinerary suggestions 26
Nevado de Colima: 347; itinerary suggestions 27
newspapers: see publications
nightlife: Acapulco 515–517; Barra de Navidad-Melaque 304; Bays of Huatulco 619; Guadalajara 171–172; Ixtapa 464–465; Manzanillo 330–331; Mazatlán 63; Oaxaca 650–651; Pátzcuaro 404; Pie de la Cuesta 487; Puerto Ángel 600; Puerto Escondido 579–580; Puerto Vallarta 227–234; Rincón de Guayabitos 135–136; San Blas 105; Taxco 536–537; Zihuatanejo 464–465
Night of the Iguana, The: 194, 203
Nochebuena: 652
Novillero: 87–88
Nuestra Señora del Rosario church: 97; itinerary suggestions 29
Nuevo Vallarta: 253–255

O

oak trees: 683
Oaxaca: 626–662; accommodations 640–646; entertainment and events 650–652; food 647–650; getting there and away 659–662; information 656; itinerary suggestions 25, 30; maps 628–629, 636–637; services 657–659; shopping 653–656; sights 634–640; sports and recreation 652–653
Oaxaca Valley: 662–678; itinerary suggestions 25
Oaxaca wedding dress: 717
Obrador, Andres Manuel López: 703–704
Obregón, Alvaro: 695, 697–698
Ocotlán de Morelos: 671

Olas Altas: 44–45, 47–48
olive ridley turtles: 358
Ometepec: 556
Opongio: 397
Orizaba: 679–680
Orozco mural: 160
Our Lady of Solitude cathedral: 493

P

Pacific green turtles: 358
packing: 23; checklist 766; first-aid kit 769
Pájaros island: 46
Palace of Columns: 668
Palace of Six Patios: 666
Palacio de Gobierno (Colima): 345
Palacio de Gobierno (Guadalajara): 160
Palacio de Gobierno (Oaxaca): 634, 635
Palacio de Gobierno (Tepic): 116–117
Palacio Municipal (Mazatlán): 37
palapas: 753–756; see also specific place
Palma Sola Archaeological Site: 497; itinerary suggestions 24, 30, 31
Papanoa: 480–481
papier-mâché: 721
parasailing: 746–747; Acapulco 518; Mazatlán 67; Playa del Palmar 449, 467; Puerto Vallarta 236
Paricutín: 424–427; itinerary suggestions 27
Parque Agua Azul: 160
Parque Nacional Lic. Eduardo Ruiz: 366, 416
Parque Nacional Pico de Tancítaro: 427–428
Parroquia Nuestra Señora de Guadalupe: 315
Partido Acción Nacional (PAN): 700, 701–702, 707
Partido Revolucionario Democratico (PRD): 700, 707
Partido Revolucionario Institucional (PRI): 700, 701, 706–707
passports: 741
Pátzcuaro: 382–409; itinerary suggestions 25, 30
Península de las Playas: 498, 504–506, 513–514
Peña Colorada: 341
Peñitas: 270
people: 708–713
Peralta, Ángela: 36, 44
permits, boat: 749
personal watercraft: 746–474; Acapulco

518; Mazatlán 67; Playa del Palmar 449; Playa Pie de la Cuesta 483; Puerto Vallarta 236

pets: 743

peyote: 92

pharmacies: Acapulco 524; Barra de Navidad-Melaque 307; Bays of Huatulco 623; Colima 352; Cuajinicuilapa 556; Cuyutlán 360; Guadalajara 181; Ixtapa 474; Lázaro Cárdenas 430; Mazatlán 73-74; Oaxaca 657; Pie de la Cuesta 487; Pinotepa Nacional 560; Playa Azul 381; Puerto Ángel 602; Puerto Escondido 584; Puerto Vallarta 248; San Blas 107; San Marcos 556; Sayulita 148; Taxco 540; Tecomán 363; Zihuatanejo 474

photography supplies: Acapulco 522; Bays of Huatulco 622; Colima 351; Guadalajara 182; Ixtapa and Zihuatanejo 472; Manzanillo 336; Mazatlán 71-72; Oaxaca 655-656; Pátzcuaro 405; Pinotepa Nacional 559; Puerto Ángel 602; Puerto Escondido 582-583; Puerto Vallarta 243; San Blas 106; Taxco 539; Uruapan 420

Pichilinguillo: 374

Pico de Tancítaro: itinerary suggestions 27

Pie de la Cuesta: 482-487

Piedra Tlacoyunque: 482

pine trees: 683

Pinocoteca Universitaria: 345-346

Pinos cove: 47

Pinotepa Don Luis: 560

Pinotepa Market: 549, 558

Pinotepa Nacional: 557-560

piñatas: 721

pirates: 442

Planetarium: 653

planning: 22-23; Acapulco and Taxco 491; Costa Chica 551; Guadalajara 149-151; Ixtapa, Zihuatanejo, and the Costa Grande 438-439; Jalisco Coast 265; Manzanillo and Colima 313; Mazatlán 34; Michoacán Coast and Pátzcuaro 367-368; Nayarit Coast 86-87; Oaxaca 630-631; Puerto Vallarta 192-193

plants: 681-684

Playa Anclote: 190, 260

Playa Angosta: 499

Playa Arena Blanca: 374

Playa Atracadero: 431-432

Playa Audiencia: 311, 319; itinerary suggestions 26

Playa Azul (Manzanillo): 318, 321-322, 328-330

Playa Azul (Michoacán Coast): 377-381

Playa Bachoco: 572

Playa Barra de Colotepec: 573

Playa Barra de Navidad: 289

Playa Blanca: 477

Playa Boca de Iguanas: 285-286; itinerary suggestions 29

Playa Boca de Tomatlán: 204; itinerary suggestions 26

Playa Borrego: 97

Playa Brujas: 48-49

Playa Caleta: 498; itinerary suggestions 26

Playa Caletilla: 498

Playa Camarón: 48

Playa Camarones: 204

Playa Carecitos: 374

Playa Carey: 450-451

Playa Careyes: 280

Playa Carrizalillo: 572; itinerary suggestions 27

Playa Cayaquitos: 481

Playa Cerritos: 33, 49; itinerary suggestions 26

Playa Cerro Hermosa: 564

Playa Chacahua: 564-565

Playa Chacala: 123-127; itinerary suggestions 26

Playa Chalacatepec: 271-272

Playa Chamela: 273

Playa Coastecomate: 294

Playa Conchas Chinas: 202

Playa Coral: 450; itinerary suggestions 26

Playa Cuachalatate: 450; itinerary suggestions 27

Playa Cuata: 451

Playa de Cocos: 301-302

Playa del Amor: 591

Playa del Beso: 137

Playa del Palmar: 448-449, 465

Playa de Navidad: 294

Playa de Oro: 204; itinerary suggestions 26

Playa Destiladeras: 259

Playa el Almacén: 447

Playa el Gato: 202

Playa el Tecuán: 264, 280-281

Playa el Tunel: 374

Playa el Venado: 140

Playa Entrega: 609-610; itinerary suggestions 27, 28
Playa Escolleros: 449
Playa Escondida: 481-482
Playa Estacahuite: 549, 589-591; itinerary suggestions 27
Playa Fortuna: 274
Playa Garza Blanca: 202
Playa Gaviotas: 48; itinerary suggestions 26
Playa Gemelas: 202
Playa Guayabitos-La Peñita: 129; itinerary suggestions 26
Playa Hermosa: 448
Playa Hornitos: 499-500
Playa Hornos: 497
Playa la Boca: 283
Playa la Brisa: 371-372; itinerary suggestions 29
Playa la Caleta: 125
Playa La Manzanilla: 286-287
Playa Larga: 500-501
Playa la Ropa: 447; itinerary suggestions 24, 26
Playa las Brisas: 318, 321-322, 328-330
Playa Las Cabañas: 376
Playa Las Cuevas: 125
Playa las Gatas: 437, 447-448; itinerary suggestions 24, 26, 27
Playa Las Glorias: 204
Playa Las Miñitas: 140
Playa la Soledad: 376-377
Playa las Pozas: 477; itinerary suggestions 26
Playa la Ticla: 372; itinerary suggestions 26, 27
Playa la Ventanilla: 593
Playa Linda: 437, 449
Playa Lo de Marcos: 138-140
Playa los Ayala: 137
Playa Los Carrizos: 202
Playa los Muertos (Nayarit): 130
Playa los Muertos (Puerto Vallarta): 201-202; itinerary suggestions 26
Playa los Tules: 204
Playa los Venados: 202
Playa Madera: 447
Playa Maito: 264, 269; itinerary suggestions 26
Playa Manzanillo (Puerto Escondido): 549, 572
Playa Manzanillo (Puerto Vallarta): 258
Playa Marinero: 569

Playa Maruata: 373
Playa Matanchén: 108-109; itinerary suggestions 26, 27
Playa Mazunte: 592, 598
Playa Melaque: 294; itinerary suggestions 26
Playa Miramar: 319
Playa Mora: 283; itinerary suggestions 27
Playa Morro: 499-500
Playa Municipal: 447
Playa Norte: 47
Playa Ojo de Agua: 481
Playa Olas Altas (Manzanillo): 319
Playa Olas Altas (Mazatlán): 47
Playa Panteón: 589, 595; itinerary suggestions 25
Playa Papagayo: 499-500
Playa Perula: 274; itinerary suggestions 26
Playa Pie de la Cuesta: 483; itinerary suggestions 26-27
Playa Piedra Blanca: 258-259
Playa Porto Bello: 377
Playa Principal (Puerto Ángel): 589
Playa Principal (Puerto Escondido): 569; itinerary suggestions 27
Playa Punta Negra: 202
Playa Punta Raza: 137-138; itinerary suggestions 26
Playa Quieta: 451
Playa Revolcadero: 500
Playa Rosada: 273
Playa Sábalo: 33, 48; itinerary suggestions 26
Playa Salagua: 318
Playa San Agustinillo: 592, 597-598
Playa San Francisco: 140-143; itinerary suggestions 26
Playa San Pedrito: 318
Playa Santa Cruz: 609
Playa Santiago: 319
Playa Secreta: 481
Playa Tenacatita: 264, 281-284; itinerary suggestions 29
Playa Teopa: 280
Playa Tizupa: 373-374
Playa Tlacopanocha: 498
Playa Varadero: 450
Playa Ventura: 552-553; itinerary suggestions 29
Playa Viejo: 320
Playa Zicatela: 549, 569-572, 573; itinerary suggestions 27
Playa Zipolite: 591-592, 595-597; itinerary suggestions 25, 27

Plaza de Armas: 190, 200-201; itinerary suggestions 31
Plaza de los Mariachis: 159-160, 171
Plaza Liberación: 158
Plaza Tapatía: 150, 158-159
Plaza Zaragoza: 65
Plazuela Machado: 33, 37-43, 66; itinerary suggestions 30
Pochutla: 589
police: 731-732, 764; see emergency services
political parties: 700, 701-702, 706-708
population: 690, 708-711
Porfirio Díaz, Don: 694-695
porpoises: 687
Portales de Cannobio: 43
post offices: 774; see also specific place
pottery: 721-723; itinerary suggestions 25
pozahuancos: 558
publications: 767; Acapulco 522; Bays of Huatulco 623; Colima 351; Guadalajara 181-182; Manzanillo 336; Mazatlán 72; Oaxaca 656; Puerto Escondido 583; Puerto Vallarta 244-246; Uruapan 420-421
Puerto Ángel: 588-604; itinerary suggestions 25
Puerto Escondido: 568-586
Puerto Vallarta: 189-253; accommodations 205-221; beaches 201-205; entertainment and events 226-234; food 221-226; gay and lesbian 217-220, 231-233, 244-245; getting around 249-250; getting there and away 250-253; information 244-246; itinerary suggestions 24, 26, 31; maps 191, 196, 198-199; services 247-249; shopping 239-243; sights 195-201; sports and recreation 235-239
Puerto Vicente Guerrero: 481-482
Pulido, Dionisio: 426
pulmonías: 37
Punta Camarón: 46, 47-48
Punta de Clavadistas: 47
Punta del Burro: 259
Punta Hermanos: 281
Punta Mita: 259-262
Punta Veneros: 259
Pyramid of Quetzalcoatl: 544

QR

Quémaro: 273
Quetzalcoatl: 688
Quimixto: 204

Quiroga, Vasco de: 382-383
raicilla: 268
rays: 687, 771
real estate: 324
Reconstruction: 694-695
recreation: 745-750; see also specific activity
red mangrove: 681
regatta: 714
regional overview: 16-21
religion: 712-713
reptiles: 686
resorts: 752; see also specific place
restaurants: 760; see also specific place
Revolution: 695-697
Rincón de Guayabitos: 127-137
Río Arena: 559
Río Balsas Dam: 431
Río Copalita: 609; itinerary suggestions 25, 28
Río Cuale: 196
Río Cupatitzio: 414
Río Grande: 565-566
Río Tovara: 99, 101
river rafting: itinerary suggestions 25, 28; Río Copalita 25, 609
rodeos: 174; Barra de Navidad-Melaque 304; Guadalajara 173; Mazatlán 69
Rodilla del Diablo: 416
Rosario: 79-80
Rotonda de los Hombres Ilustres: 155
running: see jogging
RVing: 728, 729-733, 738, 739-740, 753-756; Angahuan 427; Apiza 363; Barra de Navidad-Melaque 301; Barra de Potosí 479; Bays of Huatulco 617; Boca de Pascuales and El Real 361; Cajón de las Peñas Reservoir 271; Chamela Bay 275-277; Cuyutlán 360; Guadalajara 167; itinerary suggestions 28-29; Laguna Manialtepec 567; La Peñita 133-134; Mazatlán 57-58; Oaxaca 646; Pátzcuaro 401; Pie de la Cuesta 486; Piedra Tlacoyunque 482; Playa Azul 380; Playa Boca de Iguanas 285-286; Playa Chalacatepec 272; Playa la Brisa 371; Playa Lo de Marcos 139-140; Playa los Cocos 110; Playa Maruata 373; Playa Porto Bello 377; Playa Tenacatita 282-283; Playa Tizupa 373-374; Playa Ventura 552; Puerto Ángel 598-599; Puerto Escondido 577-578; Puerto Vallarta 221; Rincón de Guayabitos

133; San Blas 103-104; Sayulita 146; Tampumachay 355; Taretan 423; Teacapán 82; Tepic 119-120; Zihuatanejo 459

S

safety: 762, 768-771; driving 730, 739, 764; money 772-773; pedestrians 764; Puerto Escondido 583-584; water sports 746

sailboarding: 746; Acapulco 518; Bays of Huatulco 609, 610; Chamela Bay 274; Costera beaches 500; Ixtapa 468; Manzanillo 332-333; Mazatlán 66; Melaque 304; Playa Boca de Iguanas 285; Playa Careyes 280; Playa la Brisa 371; Playa Revolcadero 500; Puerto Ángel 601; Puerto Vallarta 235-236; Teacapán 81; Zihuatanejo 468

sailing: 734, 746; Acapulco 518; Bays of Huatulco 609, 610, 611; Costera beaches 500; Ixtapa 468; Laguna Manialtepec 567; Manzanillo 332; Mazatlán 66; Melaque 304; Playa Revolcadero 500; Puerto Ángel 601; Puerto Vallarta 235-236, 245; Zihuatanejo 468

San Andres Huaxpáltepec: 561-562

San Bártolo Coyotepec: 670

San Blas: 93-108; itinerary suggestions 28, 29

sand box tree: 681

San Francisco: 140-143

San Francisco Day (October 4): 419

sangre de dragón: 683

San Juan Colorado: 561

San Juan de Alima: 371

San Marcos: 553-556

San Martín Tilcajete: 670-671

San Patricio: 293

San Pedro Amusgos: 561

Santa Anna, Antonio López de: 693-694

Santa Clara de Cobre: 366, 409-410; itinerary suggestions 25

Santa Cruz: 607-609, 614-615

Santa Cruz de Huatulco: 638

Santa Fe de la Laguna: 397-398

Santa Prisca church: 489, 529-530; itinerary suggestions 25, 30

Santiago Bay: 319-320, 325-326

Santiago Ixcuintla: 91-93

Santiago Jamiltepec: 562

Santiago Peninsula: 318, 323-325

Santo Tomás Jalieza: 670-671

savanna: 681

Sayulita: 84, 143-148

scorpions: 770

scuba diving: see diving

seafood: 758-759

sea lions: 687

seals: 687

seasons, travel: 22

Semana Santa: Cacahuatepec 561; Pinotepa Don Luis 560-561; Pinotepa Nacional 558; Puerto Vallarta 234

senior citizens: 767

Señora de Misericordias: 397

September 15: 234

Serra, Junípero: 116-117

sharks: 687

shopping: 761-762; see also arts and crafts, specific place

Sierra Lagunillas: 267

silver: 538-539

Sinaloa: 77-82; itinerary suggestions 26

Sinaloa Fiesta de los Artes: 64

Singayta: 101-102

snakes: 686, 770

snorkeling: 746; Acapulco 517-518; Aquiles Serdán 269; Barra de Navidad-Melaque 304-305, 307; Bays of Huatulco 609, 610, 611, 620-621; Faro de Bucerías 372; Isla Ixtapa 450; Isla Roqueta 499; itinerary suggestions 26, 27; Ixtapa 467-468; Los Arcos 203-204; Manzanillo 333; Mazatlán 66-67; Playa Anclote 260; Playa Careyes 280; Playa Chacahua 565; Playa Chacala 125; Playa Escondida 481; Playa Guayabitos-La Peñita 129, 130; Playa Hermosa 448; Playa las Gatas 448; Playa Madera 447; Playa Manzanillo (Puerto Escondido) 572; Playa Maruata 373; Playa Mora 283; Playa Principal 569; Playas Caleta and Caletilla 498; Playa Tizupa 373-374; Puerto Ángel 601; Puerto Escondido 581; Puerto Vallarta 202, 203-204, 236; San Blas 106; Sayulita 147; Tehualmixtle 270; Zihuatanejo 467-468

Soledad de Maciel Archaeological Zone: 479-480

Spanish-language courses: 734, 736; Acapulco 523; Guadalajara 182; Mazatlán 75; Oaxaca 658-659; Playa Chacala 125-126; Puerto Escondido 583; Puerto Vallarta 245, 246; Sayulita 148

Spanish phrasebook: 777-782

spider monkeys: 684
sportfishing: see fishing
sports: 745-750; see also
    specific activity
Spratling, William: 530-531
stingray: 687
stoneware: 721-723
stonework: 719
strangler fig: 682
student visas: 744
subway: 183
suggested reading: 783-788
sun protection: 768
surf fishing: 747-749; itinerary
    suggestions 26-27; see fishing
surfing: 746; Acapulco 517; Aquiles Serdán
    269; Barra de Navidad 304; Barra de
    Nexpa 374-375; Bay of Matanchén
    108-109; Bays of Huatulco 609;
    Boca de Pascuales and El Real 362;
    Bucerías 255; Cuyutlán 358; itinerary
    suggestions 26, 27; Ixtapa 466-467;
    La Saladita 432-433; Manzanillo 332;
    Mazatlán 47-49, 66; Piedra Tlacoyunque
    482; Playa Anclote 260; Playa Azul
    377; Playa Carecitos 374; Playa
    Chacahua 565; Playa Chacala 125; Playa
    Chalacatepec 271; Playa el Tecuán 281;
    Playa Escolleros 449; Playa Escondida
    481-482; Playa Guayabitos-La Peñita
    129-130; Playa la Ticla 372; Playa Linda
    449; Playa Marinero 569; Playa Maruata
    373; Playa Porto Bello 377; Playa Tizupa
    373-374; Playa Ventura 552; Playa
    Zicatela 569-572; Playa Zipolite 591;
    Puerto Ángel 601; Puerto Escondido
    580-581; Puerto Vallarta 235; Punta el
    Burro 259; San Blas 105-106; San Juan
    de Alima 371; Sayulita 147; Teacapán 81;
    Troncones 435; Zihuatanejo 466
swimming: 746; Acapulco 517; Agua Fria
    342; Aquiles Serdán 269; Bays of
    Huatulco 609, 610, 611, 620-621; Boca
    de Pascuales and El Real 362; Faro de
    Bucerías 372; Guadalajara 174-175;
    Isla Roqueta 499; Ixtapa 466-467;
    Manzanillo 332; Melaque 66; Melaque
    304; Oaxaca 653; Playa Chacala 125;
    Playa Guayabitos-La Peñita 129; Playa
    la Brisa 371; Playa la Ticla 372; Playa
    Madera 447; Playa Manzanillo (Puerto
    Escondido) 572; Playa Maruata 373;
    Puerto Ángel 601; Puerto Vallarta 201,

235; Río Grande 566; Sayulita 143-144;
    Zihuatanejo 466

T
Tampumachay: 355-356
tapirs: 684
Taretan: 423-424
tattoos: 771
Taxco: 527-541; itinerary suggestions
    25, 30
Taxco Hieroglyph: 532
taxis: 740
Taylor, Elizabeth: 194, 200
Teacapán: 80-82
Teatro Alcalá: 638; itinerary
    suggestions 30
Teatro Ángela Peralta: 43; itinerary
    suggestions 29, 30
Teatro Degollado: 150, 158, 171; itinerary
    suggestions 29
Tecomán: 363-364
Tecuanillo: 362
Tecuitata waterfall: 110; itinerary
    suggestions 28
Tehualmixtle: 264, 269-270; itinerary
    suggestions 26
Telares Uruapan: 420
telegraph offices: 774; see also
    specific place
telephones: 773-774; see also
    specific place
Temple of the Steles: 545
Templo y Ex-Convento de la Cruz de
    Zacate: 117; itinerary suggestions 29
Templo y Ex-Convento de Santo Domingo:
    638-639; itinerary suggestions 25
tennis: 747; Acapulco 517; Barra de
    Navidad 305; Bays of Huatulco 620;
    Guadalajara 175; Ixtapa 465-466;
    Manzanillo 333; Mazatlán 68-69;
    Oaxaca 653; Puerto Escondido 580;
    Puerto Vallarta 237-238
Teotihuacán: 688
Teotitlán del Valle: 627, 664-665
Tepic: 111-123; itinerary suggestions 29
Tequila Express: 173-174
Terra Noble: 201
textiles: 562
theater: Guadalajara 171; Mazatlán 63
"The Bells of San Blas": 98
thorn forest: 682
Three Sister Virgins: 162
Tilcajete: 670-671

timeshare properties: 324
time zones: 774
Tinganio Archaeological Zone: 412
tipping: 773
Tlacolula: 627, 666
Tlalpuyeque: 264, 268; itinerary suggestions 28
Tlaquepaque: 161-162, 165-166, 170; itinerary suggestions 25
tlatchtli: 545
Tócuaro: 395-396
Tonalá: 161-162, 166, 170
tourism board offices/tourist information: 742-743; *see also specific place*
tourist cards: 741-743
tourist shows: Bays of Huatulco 619-620; Ixtapa 464; Manzanillo 331; Mazatlán 64; Puerto Vallarta 233-234
Tourneo de Pez Vela: 469
tours: 734, 735-736, 741; Bays of Huatulco 620; Mazatlán hiking 49; Oaxaca 658; Pátzcuaro by trolley 383-386; Puerto Vallarta 200, 238-239; Rincón de Guayabitos-La Peñita 136; Southern Sinaloa 78; *see also* ecotours
trailer parks: 756; *see also* RVing, *specific place*
transportation: 724-741; *see also specific place*
trees: 681-684
Troncones: 433-435
tropical deciduous forest: 682-683
trusts, real estate: 324
turtles: 138, 141, 279, 358, 374, 592-593, 686
Tzintzuntzán: 366, 391-394; itinerary suggestions 30

UV

Uruapan: 412-422
vegetarian fare: 758
vegetation zones: 681-684
Venados island: 46
Viejecitos dance: 403-404
Viernes Santa: 404
Villa, Francisco "Pancho": 695-696
villas: 752-753; *see also specific place*
Villa Temazcalli meditation and massage center: 584
Virgin of Guadalupe: 712-713
Virgin of Guadalupe Fiesta: *see* Fiesta de la Virgen de Guadalupe
Virgin of Guadalupe mural: 607

Virgin of Innocence: 155
Virgin of Solitude: 652
Virgin of Zapopan: 155
Volcán de Fuego: 347
volcano tours: 333-334
Volcán Paricutín: 366, 424; itinerary suggestions 27
volunteer opportunities: 246

W

walking: Acapulco 517; Guadalajara 174; Mazatlán 66; Oaxaca 652-653; Playa Azul 380; Playa el Tecuán 281; Playa Larga 501; Puerto Escondido 573; Puerto Vallarta 237; San Blas 106; Zihuatanejo 465
water, drinking: 768-769
waterfalls: Bay of Matanchén hikes 110-111; itinerary suggestions 28; San Blas hikes 101; *see also specific waterfalls*
water parks: Centro Internacional de Convivencia Infantil (CICI) 520; Mágico Mundo 498; Mazagua 664
waterskiing: 746-747; Acapulco 518; Isla Ixtapa 450; Laguna Coyuca 500; Playa del Palmar 449; Playa Pie de la Cuesta 483; Puerto Vallarta 236
Waverunners: *see* personal watercraft
weather: 680
weaving: 665, 716-717
websites: 789-793
whales: 687
whale-watching: Isla Islote 129; Playa Escondida 481-482; Puerto Vallarta 245; San Blas 100
whitewater rafting: *see* river rafting
wildlife: 684-687
wildlife-viewing: 735-736, 745; Barra de Navidad-Melaque 295; Bays of Huatulco 620; Cuyutlán 358; itinerary suggestions 28; Laguna Tres Palos 501; Playa el Tecuán 281; Playa la Brisa 371; Playa Tenacatita 283; Río Copalita 609; San Blas 99-100; Troncones 434, 435
windsurfing: *see* sailboarding
women travelers: 763
woodcarving: 720-721
woolen goods: 723

XYZ

Xochicalco: 489, 543-546; itinerary suggestions 25, 30
Xochistlahuaca: 556

Yagul Archaeological Zone: 666; itinerary suggestions 30
Yelapa: 204; itinerary suggestions 24
Yuñuen Island: 389-390; itinerary suggestions 25
Zaachila: 627, 671-672; itinerary suggestions 30
Zapata, Emiliano: 695-697
Zapopan: 150, 160-161, 170; itinerary suggestions 25
Zapotalito: 563-564
Zedillo, Ernesto: 700-701, 707
Zempoateptl mountain range: 669-670
Zihuatanejo: 440-476; itinerary suggestions 24, 26
Ziracua: 423
Zócalo (Acapulco): 489, 493, 515
Zona Dorada: 48, 70-71

Acknowledgments

I thank the dozens of kind, unnamed Mexican people, such as the boy who stood on the road warning trucks away as I changed a tire, the men who pulled my car from the edge of a cliff one night atop a mountain in Oaxaca, and the staff who patiently answered my endless queries at many *turismo* offices. They all deserve credit for this book.

In many of my Pacific Mexico destinations I benefit from the help, knowledge, and hospitality of a treasury of friends. Near the beginning of my southward journey, at San Blas, I owe a debt of gratitude to Josefina Vásquez and her family for their kindness and hospitality. I owe the same to my friend Jorge Castuera in Rincón de Guayabitos, and Estela and Arturo Magaña in Guadalajara, and Sandra Richards in Punta Mita.

In Puerto Vallarta, I give many thanks to Victoria Pratt, for her persistent efforts in finding me accommodations in some of the excellent Mexico boutique hotels. Similar thanks are due to María Elena Zermeño of Casa María Elena, and Janice Chatterton of Hacienda San Ángel for their kind hospitality.

Similarly, I give thanks to Susan Dearing and Carlos Cuellar of Underworld Scuba, for the friendly welcome that they extend to me every time I arrive in Manzanillo.

No thanks can match the generosity of Adolfo Santiago, owner of the lovely Hotel los Flamingos, my home away from home in Acapulco.

Farther south in Puerto Escondido, my special thanks go to eco-ornithologist Michael Malone for helping me appreciate Pacific Mexico's wildlife treasury and to Gina Machorro for sharing her vast local knowledge with me.

In Oaxaca, I give many thanks to Henry Wangemann, owner of the excellent Librería Amate bookstore, for his constant support. I owe a similar debt to María Díaz, owner of the superb Casa María, for her kind hospitality.

Back in my hometown, my thanks go out to all the kind workers, especially Ricardo, Ernesto, Bertha, Jorge, and Octavio, at my office-away-from-home, the café Espresso Roma, whose luscious lattes became essential to the writing of this book.

Thanks also to Bill Dalton, Moon Handbooks' founder and former publisher, for undertaking this project with me, and to Avalon Travel publisher Bill Newlin for continuing it to the present. I also owe a debt of gratitude to my first editor, Mark Morris, who coined the name "Pacific Mexico." Furthermore, I give many thanks to the present staff at Avalon Travel Publishing for their super-fine editing, graphics, and layout work, and especially to editor Erin Raber, who saw the whole project through to completion.

I also owe a debt of thanks to my friends Akemi Nagafuji and Anne Shapiro, who opened my eyes to the world.

A heap of credit is also due to my friend and business partner Halcea Valdés, to whom I am grateful for managing without me while I was on the road for nine months in Pacific Mexico.

Finally, my biggest thanks go to my loving life partner, Gundi Ley de Gamboa, who took care of me during critical times, and later traveled and worked right beside me during happy times in Pacific Mexico as we updated this book.

www.moon.com

For helpful advice on planning a trip, visit www.moon.com for the **TRAVEL PLANNER** and get access to useful travel strategies and valuable information about great places to visit. When you travel with Moon, expect an experience that is uncommon and truly unique.

MAP SYMBOLS

▬▬▬	Expressway	◖	Highlight	✗	Airfield	♪	Golf Course
▬▬	Primary Road	○	City/Town	✈	Airport	🅿	Parking Area
▬▬	Secondary Road	◉	State Capital	▲	Mountain	⬗	Archaeological Site
▪ ▪ ▪ ▪	Unpaved Road	⊛	National Capital	✚	Unique Natural Feature	⬤	Church
------	Trail	★	Point of Interest			⬛	Gas Station
··········	Ferry	•	Accommodation	🗢	Waterfall		Glacier
⊢+⊢+	Railroad	▼	Restaurant/Bar	⬥	Park		Mangrove
▬▬	Pedestrian Walkway	▪	Other Location	🚩	Trailhead		Reef
⊞⊞⊞	Stairs	Λ	Campground	⛷	Skiing Area		Swamp

CONVERSION TABLES

°C = (°F – 32) / 1.8
°F = (°C x 1.8) + 32
1 inch = 2.54 centimeters (cm)
1 foot = 0.304 meters (m)
1 yard = 0.914 meters
1 mile = 1.6093 kilometers (km)
1 km = 0.6214 miles
1 fathom = 1.8288 m
1 chain = 20.1168 m
1 furlong = 201.168 m
1 acre = 0.4047 hectares
1 sq km = 100 hectares
1 sq mile = 2.59 square km
1 ounce = 28.35 grams
1 pound = 0.4536 kilograms
1 short ton = 0.90718 metric ton
1 short ton = 2,000 pounds
1 long ton = 1.016 metric tons
1 long ton = 2,240 pounds
1 metric ton = 1,000 kilograms
1 quart = 0.94635 liters
1 US gallon = 3.7854 liters
1 Imperial gallon = 4.5459 liters
1 nautical mile = 1.852 km

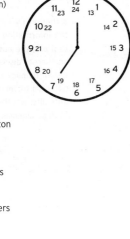

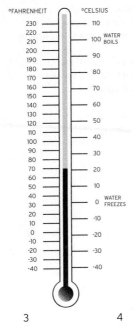

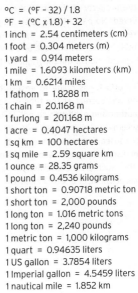

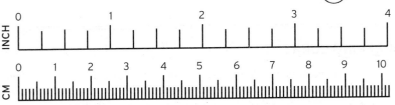

MOON PACIFIC MEXICO

Avalon Travel Publishing
a member of the Perseus Books Group
1400 65th Street, Suite 250
Emeryville, CA 94608, USA
www.moon.com

Editor: Erin Raber
Series Manager: Kathryn Ettinger
Copy Editor: Emily McManus
Graphics and Production Coordinator:
   Nicole Schultz
Cover Designer: Nicole Schultz
Map Editor: Kevin Anglin
Cartographers: Chris Markiewicz, Kat Bennett,
   Suzanne Service, Amy Tam, Kansai Uchida,
   Mike Morgenfeld
Proofreader: Deana Shields
Indexer: Valerie Sellers Blanton

ISBN-10: 1-56691-848-0
ISBN-13: 978-1-56691-848-0
ISSN: 1533-418X

Printing History
1st Edition – 1993
8th Edition – October 2007
5 4 3 2 1

KEEPING CURRENT

If you have a favorite gem you'd like to see included in the next edition, or see anything
that needs updating, clarification, or correction, please drop us a line. Send your
comments via email to feedback@moon.com, or use the address above.